HANDBOOK OF EDUCATIONAL IDEAS AND PRACTICES

HANDBOOK OF EDUCATIONAL IDEAS AND PRACTICES

GENERAL EDITOR

NOEL ENTWISTLE

Associate Editors
Ruth Jonathan
Kenneth King
Gordon Kirk
Alan Paisey
Keith Percy
Margaret Sutherland
Brian Wilcox
Phillip Williams

ROUTLEDGE
LONDON AND NEW YORK

First published 1990
by Routledge
11 New Fetter Lane, London EC4P 4EE
Simultaneously published in the USA and Canada
by Routledge
a division of Routledge, Chapman and Hall, Inc.
29 West 35th Street, New York, NY 10001

Typeset in 10/12½ Ehrhardt, Linotron 300 by
Input Typesetting Ltd, London
Printed in Great Britain by
Richard Clay Ltd, Bungay

British Library Cataloguing in Publication Data

Handbook of educational ideas and practices.
  I. Entwistle, N. J. (Noel James, 1936–)
  370

  ISBN 0–415–02061–1

Library of Congress Cataloging-in-Publication Data

Handbook of educational ideas and practices/general editor, Noel
  Entwistle, associate editors, Ruth Jonathan . . . [et al.].
    p.   cm.
  Bibliography: p.
  Includes index.
  ISBN 0–415–02061–1
    1. Education—Handbooks, manuals, etc.   2. Education—Aims and
objectives—Handbooks, manuals, etc.   I. Entwistle, Noel James.
LB17.H267   1989
370—dc20   89–10482
                                                 CIP

ISBN 0–415–02061–1

CONTENTS

B   THE MANAGEMENT AND CONTENT OF EDUCATION

CONTRIBUTORS

SANDRA ACKER
Lecturer in Education, University of Bristol

PATRICIA ASHTON
Senior Lecturer, University of Leicester School of Education

CHARLES BAILEY
Ex Senior Tutor and Head of Education Studies, Homerton College, Cambridge

ROBIN BARROW
Professor of Philosophy of Education and Director of Graduate Programs, Simon Fraser University, Canada

NEVILLE BENNETT
Professor of Primary Education, University of Exeter

JOHN BIGGS
Professor of Education, University of Hong Kong

DEREK BIRLEY
Vice-Chancellor, University of Ulster

MARION BLYTHMAN
Head of Professional and Curriculum Support Studies, Moray House College of Education, Edinburgh

JOHN BRENNAN
Registrar for Information Services, Council for National Academic Awards

PATRICIA BROADFOOT
Lecturer, University of Bristol School of Education

SALLY BROWN
Director, Scottish Council for Research in Education

TOM BRYCE
Head of Education and Psychology, Jordanhill College of Education, Glasgow

LEONARD CANTOR
Schofield Professor of Education, Loughborough University of Technology

WILFRED CARR
Senior Lecturer in Education, University of Sheffield

ELIZABETH K. CHAPMAN
European Chairman, International Council for Education of the Visually
Handicapped

MAURICE CHAZAN
Emeritus Professor of Education, University College of Swansea

CHENG KAI MING
Lecturer in Education, University of Hong Kong

CLYDE CHITTY
Lecturer in Curriculum Studies, Institute of Education, University of London

RICHARD CLARK
Chief Executive, Devon County Council (formerly County Education Officer,
Hampshire)

GERALD COLLIER
Former Principal, Bede College, University of Durham, and Honorary
Research Fellow, University of East Anglia

HELEN COWIE
Senior Research Fellow, Division of Education, University of Sheffield

CRISTIÁN COX
Research Fellow, Centro de Investigación y Desarrollo de la Educación, Santiago, Chile

BERNARD CRICK
Emeritus Professor of Politics, Birkbeck College, University of London

BRUCE CURTIS
Associate Professor, Wilfrid Laurier University, Waterloo, Canada

JOHN DARLING
Lecturer in Education, University of Aberdeen

CHARLES DESFORGES
Professor of Education, University of Exeter

ROSALIND DRIVER
Reader in Science Education, University of Leeds

MARY JANE DRUMMOND
Tutor in Education 3–13, Cambridge Institute of Education

CHRIS DUKE
Professor and Chairman of Continuing Education, University of Warwick

JOHN EGGLESTON
Professor and Chairman of Education, University of Warwick

NOEL ENTWISTLE
Professor of Education, University of Edinburgh

MICHAEL ERAUT
Professor of Education, University of Sussex

BERTIE EVERARD
Visiting Fellow, University of London Institute of Education

INGEMAR FÄGERLIND
Professor of Education, University of Stockholm

PETER FARRELL
Honorary Lecturer in Education, University of Manchester

DAVID FONTANA
Reader in Educational Psychology, University College of Wales of Cardiff

HAZEL FRANCIS
Professor of Educational Psychology, Institute of Education, University of London

JOAN FREEMAN
President, European Council for High Ability, and Honorary Tutor, University of Manchester

DESMOND FURNEAUX
Professor Emeritus, Faculty of Education and Design, Brunel University

HOWARD GARDNER
Professor of Education and Co-Director, Harvard Project Zero, Harvard University

W. A. GATHERER
Formerly Chief Adviser, Lothian

FRANK GLENDENNING
Honorary Senior Research Fellow, Centre for Social Gerontology, University of Keele

MICHAEL GOLBY
Senior Lecturer in Education, University of Exeter

ROBERT GRIEVE
Professor of Psychology, University of Edinburgh

IAN HAFFENDEN
Staff Tutor (Youth and Further Education), University of Surrey

MARY HAMILTON
Senior Research Fellow, Institute for Research and Development in Post-Compulsory Education, University of Lancaster

DAVID HART
General Secretary, The National Association of Head Teachers

ANTHONY HARTNETT
Senior Lecturer, Department of Education, University of Liverpool

SEAMUS HEGARTY
Deputy Director, National Foundation for Educational Research in England and Wales

LEO B. HENDRY
Head of Department of Education, University of Aberdeen

LESLIE HILLS
Producer, Consultant, and Writer

BRIAN HOLMES
Emeritus Professor of Comparative Education, University of London

MAURICE HOLT
Director, American Academy, Larnaca, Cyprus

MEREDYDD HUGHES
Emeritus Professor of Education, University of Birmingham

CAROLYN HUTCHINSON
Research Associate, Godfrey Thomson Unit, University of Edinburgh

FRED INGLIS
Reader in Education, University of Bristol

RUTH JONATHAN
Senior Lecturer, Department of Education, University of Edinburgh

PETER KALLAWAY
Associate Professor of Education, University of Cape Town

JOHN KAY
Consultant Architect, formerly Chief Architect, Department of Education and Science

A. V. KELLY
Dean of the Faculty of Education, Goldsmiths' College, London

KENNETH KING
Chairman of the Centre of African Studies and Reader in Education, University of Edinburgh

GORDON KIRK
Principal, Moray House College of Education, Edinburgh

JAMES KULIK
Research Scientist, University of Michigan

KRISHNA KUMAR
Professor of Education, Delhi University

DAVID LAYTON
Professor of Education (Science), University of Leeds

DEREK LEGGE
Retired Head, Department of Adult Education, University of Manchester

GEOFF LINDSAY
Senior Educational Psychologist, Sheffield LEA, and Associate Tutor, Division of Education, University of Sheffield

JIM MCCALL
Vice-Principal, Jordanhill College, Glasgow

ERIC MACFARLANE
Principal, Queen Mary's College, Basingstoke

DONNIE MACLEOD
Senior Lecturer, Professional and Curriculum Studies, Moray House, College of Education, Edinburgh

KEITH MCWILLIAMS
Chief Executive, Book Trust, formerly Chief Executive, School Curriculum Development Committee

JACK MANSELL
Formerly Director, Further Education Unit

GAYE MANWARING
Co-ordinator of Tertiary Education, Northern College of Education

C. G. N. MASCIE-TAYLOR
Acting Head, Department of Biological Anthropology, University of Cambridge

MORRY VAN MENTS
Director, Centre for Extension Studies, Loughborough University of Technology

DAVID MITCHELL
Associate Professor of Education, University of Waikato, Hamilton, New Zealand

PETER MITTLER
Professor of Special Education, University of Manchester

BOB MOON
Professor of Education and Director of the Centre for Curriculum and Teaching Studies, The Open University

GEOFFREY MORRIS
Chief Education Officer, Cambridgeshire Education Department

HENA MUKHERJEE
Associate Professor, Department of Social Foundations, Faculty of Education, University of Malaysia

FRANK B. MURRAY
Dean and H. Rodney Sharp Professor, College of Education, University of Delaware

MICHAEL NAISH
Senior Lecturer in Education, University of Liverpool

DONALD NAISMITH
Director of Education for Wandsworth

JON NIXON
Lecturer, Division of Education, University of Sheffield

ALAN PAISEY
Freelance Consultant in Education Management

AUDREY PAISEY
Freelance Consultant in Education Management

KEITH PERCY
Organizing Tutor for Extra-Mural Studies, University of Lancaster

GLYNN PHILLIPS
Senior Lecturer, Westminster College, Oxford

ALISTAIR POLLITT
Assistant Director, Godfrey Thomson Unit, University of Edinburgh

CYRIL POSTER
Education Management Consultant, lately Deputy Director, National Development Centre for School Management Training

JOHN RAE
Director of the Laura Ashley Foundation, formerly Headmaster of Westminster School

REA REASON
Senior Educational Psychologist, Oldham GER, and Honorary Lecturer in Education, University of Manchester

LAUREN RESNICK
Learning Research and Development Centre, University of Pittsburgh

COLIN ROGERS
Lecturer in Education, University of Lancaster

JEAN RUDDUCK
Professor of Education, University of Sheffield

ALEX SHARP
Lecturer in Education, Leeds Polytechnic

DEREK SHARPLES
Dean of Education, Worcester College of Higher Education

TERESA SMITH
Lecturer in Applied Social Sciences, University of Oxford

ROGER STRAUGHAN
Reader in Education, University of Reading

MARGARET SUTHERLAND
Professor Emeritus of Education, University of Leeds

WILLIAM TAYLOR
Vice-Chancellor, University of Hull

PHILIP WALKLING
Professor and Dean of Education, Birmingham Polytechnic

KEVIN WARD
Pioneer Work Co-ordinator, Department of External Studies, University of Leeds

JOHN WHITE
Reader in Education, Institute of Education, University of London

BRIAN WILCOX
Chief Adviser, Sheffield LEA

PHILLIP WILLIAMS
Emeritus Professor of Education, University College of North Wales, Bangor

WELLFORD WILMS
Associate Professor, Graduate School of Education, UCLA

MAUREEN WOODHALL
Senior Lecturer, Institute of Education, University of London

CREAM WRIGHT
Director, CREST Research Centre, Sierra Leone

NICOLA YUILL
Lecturer in Psychology, School of Cognitive and Computing Sciences, University of Sussex

PREFACE BY THE GENERAL EDITOR

BACKGROUND AND PURPOSE

This *Handbook of Educational Ideas and Practices* is addressed to practitioners and students in the field of education and related services. It has been compiled by authors who, with the exception of the contributors to a section on comparative education, are mainly working in Britain. The topics have, however, been treated in a way intended to appeal to educationists of whatever nationality. Although there are major differences in educational systems, the issues that have to be faced in developing effective practices, and in reaching high standards of attainment, have considerable commonality. In the research literature there is a common language being used to describe organizations, teaching and learning, which has developed through an interplay between the contributory disciplines and practitioners. This language is increasingly international and so it makes sense for the contributors to this *Handbook* to draw on ideas from the whole international community, and to address their conclusions to an equally wide audience. Inevitably, readers will find illustrations drawn predominantly from Britain, but the principles and practices described have wide currency.

Faced with a book of this size, the reader may wonder what can justify such a large set of chapters – 101 to be precise. Education in Britain and across the world is again facing a period of reappraisal. There are discussions about both its purposes and its effectiveness. Yet the debates on such important issues often fail to take account of the most recent ideas and practices. It is extremely difficult for politicians, administrators, school management teams, teachers, and students to discover what is currently being said and done in education: its scope is too vast and the literature is extensive, diverse and scattered. At school level, increasingly, teachers are being involved in working groups to consider the implementation of new approaches to management, to the curriculum, to teaching methods, and to ways of encouraging more meaningful learning among the students. This *Handbook* is intended to make available for practitioners, summaries of the most recent thinking, research findings, and innovatory practices in the belief that crucial decisions about the future of education should be informed by the most up-to-date knowledge in the field. Providing an adequate survey of the main educational ideas and practices necessitated the large number of chapters included, and even then there are gaps created by limitations of space.

The term 'handbook' was chosen to differentiate it from 'encyclopaedia'. A handbook does not claim to cover all possible topics, rather it samples a restricted number of important topics and deals with them in more depth than will be found in an encyclopaedia. In this *Handbook* each topic has been discussed by an acknowledged expert, writing in sufficient detail to avoid trivialization. To reach the audience we had in mind, it was essential to use a minimum of jargon, but technical terms could not, of course, be avoided when describing research findings or current theories. Some of the chapters will inevitably prove demanding to readers without any background in the subject, but it is envisaged that the information will be accessible to most people prepared to engage the ideas with interest and concern.

STRUCTURE AND RATIONALE

There could be no consensus of what should be included in a survey of educational ideas and practices, even with 101 chapters to work on. The first problem was to provide a mapping of the whole area which would make it relatively easy for the reader to locate areas of particular interest. Of course, with a handbook of this size, the Index provides the most obvious starting point, but it was hoped that readers would also browse through chapters. It was thus decided to group the chapters within sections which had sufficient coherence to form readable entities in their own right.

It was also necessary to create an overall structure which would justify the order in which the sections were introduced. The framework selected allows the *Handbook* to start from a broad view of education, as a product of historical development through the interplay of economic, political, and social forces over time, and also influenced by characteristically different philosophical views about the nature and function of education (Section 1). The historical element is not at the forefront of these early chapters: the main focus is on the social, political, and economic forces at work in recent times. Particularly revealing aspects of the resulting educational systems are used to illustrate this process within several contrasting societies (Section 2).

Although the *Handbook* does cover most forms of education, it was decided to pay most attention to formal education over the period of compulsory schooling. However, to ensure that a complete picture was presented, a separate section has been included which discusses education beyond school – pre-school level, post-secondary, and the burgeoning area of adult and continuing education (Section 3). There are also individual chapters in other sections dealing with aspects of organization, curriculum, and teaching in various forms of tertiary education.

From the initial broad view of educational systems and sectors, the *Handbook* then progressively narrows its focus to look next at the organization and management of institutions, first in general terms and then in relation to particular types of educational institution (Section 4). Restrictions on the overall size of the book have prevented there being any extensive treatment of developments in the curriculum or teaching within each individual school subject. More general discussions are provided, together with some illustrative examples of teaching and learning in certain subjects and at different age-levels. Narrowing the focus again we are led to a series of important curriculum issues facing administrators and teachers which are discussed in Section 5. From the curriculum we move into the classroom itself, with the results of recent research and development work relating to learning and teaching being introduced in Section 6, first in general terms and then in relation to a selection of specific subject areas. Teaching methods designed to improve the quality of learning using various innovatory techniques are then described and evaluated (Section 7).

The final stage in narrowing the focus, or in the level of analysis, is reached in the remaining two sections. By now we have reached the individual learner. Section 8 draws on recent research to describe important facets of variations among learners in their capabilities and development. In the final section, the ways in which education can help to satisfy the special needs of children with specific forms of handicap or disadvantage are discussed (Section 9).

WRITING AND EDITING

Given the wide range of topics reflected in this *Handbook*, it was essential to leave specialist Associate Editors with the task of defining the individual sections and inviting appropriate authors to contribute to them. The editing process then involved extensive discussions with the individual authors, first to define the scope of the topic, and then through successive drafts to produce a typescript which fitted the particular requirements of this *Handbook*. This procedure proved to be very time-consuming but it has significantly improved the consistency of writing, and the coherence of each section.

Each section contains an introduction written by the editor responsible, which presents an overview of the area showing how the individual chapters contribute to thinking about education at that particular level of analysis. The introductions seek to demonstrate the rationale for the choice of topics within the section, and to draw together the different aspects represented in the contributory chapters. Given the range of topics even within each section, the task of providing coherent overviews was challenging, but it is hoped that readers will appreciate the guidance provided.

The editors as a whole are particularly grateful for the time and effort put into the writing of the individual chapters, and for the toleration and patience with which individual authors met our comments and requests for modifications. The value of the *Handbook* as a whole depends, inevitably, on the quality of these contributions. We believe that readers will be impressed by what has been achieved.

INDEXING AND REFERENCING

A detailed index has been prepared to enable readers to identify topics of special interest. The index was derived from a 'conceptual index' provided by the authors in the form of sets of keywords describing their chapters, supplemented by additional detailed references identified by the publishers. The authors were also asked to provide either references or further reading, within a limit of about twelve. The references chosen are intended to be a guide into the literature, rather than to provide detailed evidence in support of the arguments being developed in the chapters. Many of the references will thus point to influential books which, in turn, will lead on to specific articles for those with sufficient interest in the topic.

Finally, there must be a word of thanks to the editorial staff at Routledge. Jonathan Price set the whole endeavour in train and nurtured the idea through its various stages. In the end, the editorial staff were faced with a daunting pile of typescript, much of which contained extensive hand-written additions or deletions as a result of the negotiations between authors and editors. The final production reflects their efforts, and in particular those of the desk editor, Alison Barr.

Noel Entwistle
Edinburgh, April, 1989

ABBREVIATIONS

ABC	*A Basis for Choice*
ABE	adult basic education
ACACE	Advisory Council for Adult and Continuing Education
ACC	Association of County Councils
ACE	Advisory Centre for Education
ACSET	Advisory Council on the Supply and Education of Teachers
AEI	Adult Education Institutes
AFE	advanced further education
AIDS	acquired immune deficiency syndrome
AIT	Access to Information Technology
ALBSU	Adult Literacy and Basic Skills Unit
A level	Advanced level
AMA	Association of Metropolitan Authorities
AMMA	Assistant Masters and Mistresses Association
AO level	Alternative Ordinary level
AS level A/S level	Additional Supplementary level
ASSB	'A Study of School Building'
ATS	Adult Training Strategy
BA	Bachelor of Arts
BBC	British Broadcasting Corporation
BEd	Bachelor of Education
BIM	British Institute of Management
BSc	Bachelor of Science
BTEC B/TEC	Business and Technician Education Council
CA	chronological age
C and G	City and Guilds
CARE	Centre for Applied Research in Education
CASE	Campaign for the Advancement of State Education
CATs	Colleges of Advanced Technology
CATE	Council for the Accreditation of Teacher-Educators

CBI	Confederation of British Industry
CD	Christian Democrat
CEE	Certificate of Extended Education
CGLI	City and Guilds of London Institute
CIPFA	Chartered Institute of Public Finance and Accountancy
CLEA	Council for Local Education Authorities
CNAA	Council for National Academic Awards
CNE	Christian National Education
COTU	Coventry Open Tech Unit
CPVE	Certificate of Pre-Vocational Education
CR	criterion referenced
CSE	Certificate of Secondary Education
CVCP	Committee of Vice-Chancellors and Principals
DEA	Data Envelopment Analysis
DES	Department of Education and Science
DETA	Department of Employment Training Agency (previously Manpower Services Commission)
DHSS	Department of Health and Social Security
Dip Tech	Diploma in Technology
DISTAR	Direct Instructional System for Teaching and Remediation
DIY	do it yourself
DTI	Department of Trade and Industry
EBD	emotional and behavioural difficulties
EDY	Education of the Developmentally Young
EEC	European Economic Community
EITB	Engineering Industry Training Board
EOC	Equal Opportunities Commission
EPQ	Eysenck Personality Questionnaire
ESG	education support grant
ESL	English as a second language
ESN	educationally sub-normal
FE	further education
FEMIS	Further Education Management Information System
FESC	Further Education Staff College
FEU	Further Education Unit (previously Further Education Curriculum Review and Development Unit)
FHE F/HE	further and/or higher education

FP	Fundamental Pedagogics
g	general factor in intelligence
GCE	General Certificate of Education
GCSE	General Certificate of Secondary Education
GNP	gross national product
GRC	Grade Related Criteria
GRE	grant-related expenditure
GRIDS	Guidelines for Review and Internal Development in Schools
GRIST	grant-related in-service training
GSA	Girls' Schools Association
HCP	Humanities Curriculum Project
HE	higher education
H level	Higher level of the Scottish Certificate of Education
HMC	Headmasters' Conference
HMI	Her Majesty's Inspector/Inspectorate
HMSO	Her Majesty's Stationery Office
HRD	human resource development
IAPS	Incorporated Association of Preparatory Schools
IBE	International Bureau of Education
IBIS	Inspectors based in schools
ICI	Imperial Chemical Industries
ILEA	Inner London Education Authority
INSET	(teachers') in-service education and training
IQ	intelligence quotient
ISIS	Independent Schools Information Service
IT	information technology
ITBS	Industrial Training Boards
k:m	spatial-mechanical factor in intelligence
LAPP	Lower Achieving Pupils Project
LCPs	Local Collaborative Projects
LEA	local education authority
LEN	local employer network
LFM	local financial management
MA	Master of Arts
MBA	Master of Business Administration

MBD	management by objectives
MI	Multiple Intelligences
MSC	Manpower Services Commission (renamed Department of Employment Training Agency in 1988)
NAB	National Advisory Board
NAFE	non-advanced further education
NAGM	National Association of Governors and Managers
NAHT	National Association of Head Teachers
NAS/UWT	National Association of Schoolmasters and Union of Women Teachers
NATO	North Atlantic Treaty Organization
NCERT	National Council of Educational Research and Training
NCPTA	National Confederation of Parent-Teacher Associations
NCTA	National Council for Technological Awards
NCVQ	National Council for Vocational Qualifications
NDC	National Development Centre for School Management Training
NECC	National Education Crisis Committee
NEDC	National Economic Development Council
NEDO	National Economic Development Organization
NIACE	National Institute of Adult Continuing Education
NR	norm referenced
NUT	National Union of Teachers
NVQ	National Vocational Qualification
OD	organizational development
OECD	Organization for Economic Co-operation and Development
OL	open learning
O level	Ordinary level
OPEC	Organization of Oil Producing and Exporting Countries
ORACLE	Observational Research and Classroom Learning Evaluation
OTTO	one-term training opportunities
OU	Open University
PAT	Professional Association of Teachers
PE	physical education
PEL	paid educational leave
PESC	Public Expenditure White Paper
PEVE	Post Experience Vocational Education
PGCE	Postgraduate Certificate of Education
PICKUP	Professional, Industrial and Commercial Updating

PMA	primary mental abilities
PPA	Pre-School Playgroups Association
PSME	Personal, Social, and Moral Education
PU	Popular Unity
three Rs	reading, writing and arithmetic (i.e. basic education)
RAPAL	Research and Practice in Adult Literacy
RDD RD and D }	research, development, and diffusion
RE	religious education
RNIB	Royal National Institute for the Blind
ROSBA	Review of School Based Assessment
RSA	Royal Society of Arts
RSG	rate support grant
RVQ	Review of Vocational Qualifications
SAIRR	South African Institute of Race Relations
SBCD	school-based curriculum development
SCALA	Society of Chief Architects of Local Authorities
SCDC	School Curriculum Development Committee
SCISP	Schools Council Integrated Science Project
SCOPE	Scottish Committee on Primary Education
SCOTVEC	Scottish Vocational Education Council
SEC	School Examinations Council
SHA	Secondary Heads Association
SLD	specific learning disability
SMP	School Mathematics Project
SNAP	Special Needs Action Programme
STC	Schools Year Twelve and Tertiary Entrance Certificate
STOPP	Society of Teachers Opposed to Physical Punishment
TAPS	training access points
TEC	Training and Enterprise Council
TOPS	Training Opportunities Scheme
TOSIPAR	tuning in; objectives; success criteria; information and ideas; plan; action; review
TUC	Trades Union Congress
TVE	Technical and Vocational Education
TVEI	Technical Vocational Education Initiative
UBI	Understanding British Industry
UCLA	University of California at Los Angeles

UDACE	Unit for the Development of Adult and Continuing Education
UGC	University Grants Council
UN	United Nations
UNESCO	United Nations Educational Scientific and Cultural Organization
UVP	Unified Vocational Preparation
VCP	Values Clarification Programme
v:ed	verbal-educational factor in intelligence
VET	vocational education and training
WEA	Workers Educational Association
WJEC	Welsh Joint Education Committee
WRNAFE	work-related non-advanced further education
YMCA	Young Men's Christian Association (hostel)
YOP	Youth Opportunities Programme
YTS	Youth Training Scheme

A. THE NATURE AND FUNCTION OF EDUCATION

1. RECURRENT ISSUES

I.0

INTRODUCTION: A PERSPECTIVE ON RECURRING CONTROVERSIES

RUTH JONATHAN

This first section of the *Handbook of Educational Ideas and Practices* addresses a range of issues which are the subject of contemporary debate in education. The agenda of the debate surrounding education in any complex society is influenced by economic and socio-political circumstance, and by the findings and fashions of educational theory. Some questions, however, cannot, by their nature, be definitively settled, and recur with changing emphasis as society continues to reappraise the fundamental questions of what constitutes the good life for individuals, and what social arrangements and institutions may most justly promote the well-being of the community now and in the future. Since these questions are necessarily matters of dispute, and since all educational policy and practice embodies implicit commitments in respect of them, it is inevitable that in any open society the formal influences on the development of the young which are offered through the provision of education will remain the focus of controversy. This series of articles sets out to map the nature and interrelationships of those issues which are and which remain at the centre of educational debate.

Accordingly, Hartnett and Naish open the discussion with an exploration of the complex relationship which exists between a system of formal education and the society it serves both to reproduce and to modify. They emphasize the reciprocity of this relation, with social change modifying the demands made on education, and consequent provision opening up some possibilities for society in the future whilst foreclosing others. They draw attention, therefore, to the moral and political nature of our decisions in this area, since these are basic to formation of the social future. There will thus be struggle for control of the system, and conflicts concerning its content, process, and management, which will reflect the dominant values of society and divergences of interests within it. After mapping the manner in which current values and interests are reflected in the educational preoccupations of the Western capitalist democracies, and arguing that they are neither adequate nor inevitable, these writers propose an alternative view. The conception of education they propose implies a wider notion of social identity than that of worker and consumer, and requires a schooling system which should not be thought of as principally a service industry to the economy. Certain conditions are required, however, they argue, for a general education to provide an effective preparation for adult life as a fully autonomous citizen, and these conditions require changes in social ethos and arrangements which lie beyond the school.

In the contribution which follows, White approaches the primary question of what should be the aims of education by declaring this to be a fundamentally evaluative matter, though not thereby arbitrary. On the grounds that in such matters we can only seek to persuade properly by the offering of good reasons, he deploys arguments to justify the claim that in a complex industrialized society we must aim to promote personal autonomy of a certain sort. This would involve the assimilation and understanding of the beliefs, values, and practices of society, together with the ability to evaluate and possibly modify them. As an overarching aim for the education of all the young, this, he argues, is compatible both with personal well-being and with the flourishing of the social group. A later entry in this section addresses the question of moral education as *one* proposed task for schooling: White argues here that the fundamental aim of education is to promote the capacity for a certain style and quality of life.

In today's climate of opinion such a perspective is eclipsed by the perceived need for schooling to attend to the urgent task of fitting the young for existing society and its likely employment conditions, since it is undeniable that a certain level of group prosperity is required to fund the universal provision of a general education. Chitty thus focuses on that recurrent strand of controversy concerning the proper purpose of schooling, which has dominated debate over the past decade, by examining the tension between the demands of education and the need for training. He reviews the recent resurgence of the vocational impetus, locating this in an economic and social context, and seeks to sift reality from rhetoric in assessing its impact on practice. Chitty highlights the dilemma implicit in overtly vocationalist policies which, if pursued for all, would be incompatible with an open future for society as a whole, or, if pursued only for some, would militate against the presumption of equality embodied in the comprehensive ideal.

The next two entries make further contributions to discussion of the legitimate requirement on education that it simultaneously serve the interests of society as a whole whilst disadvantaging none of its members, but rather promoting their optimum development. Darling explores the nature of the progressive movement, which stressed individual development, and which characterized much educational change in the post-war period of economic expansion and social optimism. He describes the social and intellectual background to this shift in goals and pedagogy, and the view both of the nature of the child and of the role of the teacher which it implies. Darling indicates that progressivism's relaxed view of each child as a unique individual with a potentially open future, with the teacher's role being that of guide and resource, was facilitated by the expectation of growing prosperity and of concomitant increases in social equality. The concurrent weakening of traditional authority structures within society and the popular acceptance of the part played by upbringing and environment on personal development combined to produce an ethos in which child-centred notions were welcomed in theory, if less than comprehensively pursued in practice. Though a salutory reaction to much preceding practice, progressivism, Darling notes, embodies countervailing weaknesses of its own which should be carefully distinguished from the insights it offers.

Bailey then reconsiders the notion of liberal education which, he argues, has acquired connotations of academicism and irrelevance that place it currently at a discount. He suggests that both the popular political complaint, that liberal education is a luxury we cannot afford, and the standard Marxist critique, that it is an instrument for preserving the power and values of the dominant class, must be seriously addressed in any attempt to reassert the value and redefine the content of an education aimed at personal emancipation and rational autonomy. He argues, however, that in reasserting these aims we are committed neither to static content nor to stultifying pedagogy, for if the social context both of the learner and of what is to be learned is taken seriously, then what constitutes a liberal education cannot be historically static, although some conceptions of education are clearly illiberal in assumptions and effects. Bailey sketches accordingly some substantive proposals for the type of educational content and process which would be required to liberate the young from the constraints of the here and now, of the perceived concerns of today, and which would thereby permit them to flourish as individuals whilst contributing to the continuous evolution of society in general.

The debates explored to this point in the section are general, and underlie our broad conceptions of the nature and function of education. Others are more specific and more obviously matters of immediate controversy. The next four entries in this section of the *Handbook* therefore address topics which are of current and enduring overt concern. Phillips examines the complex area of personal, social, and moral education, differentiating the three areas, but showing their interrelationships and their shared grounding in moral values. He looks at the basis of arguments for and against the school's involvement in principle in the ethical development of the young, and at the form that that involvement might take, concluding that much empirical and conceptual work needs to be done if confusion is to be minimized in an area which gives rise to more muddled thinking than most. Phillips emphasizes here that our doubts and uncertainties over the content and propriety of personal, social, and moral education are an inescapable concomitant both of the nature of ethical theory and of our collective commitment to a form of life in which the expectations of individuals are not fixed, nor their social roles predetermined.

Crick then turns to the sensitive issue of what part the school should play in the political education of the young. He reviews the extent and type of teaching which takes places in schools in order to prepare the young for the political and economic life of their society, setting the developments of recent decades in their historical context. This includes debate concerning the relative priority and propriety of differing facets of political education: transmitting knowledge, developing attitudes, and fostering action skills, against a background of certain procedural values – tolerance, fairness, respect for truth and reason – without which political teaching would scarcely be termed educative. He notes wide variation in both styles of political education and in commitment to it, with serious study most evident, as ever, in preparation for relevant public examinations. Given the widespread agreement on the necessity for schools to prepare for political literacy – shared by teachers' professional bodies, the TUC, the CBI and parent organizations – he notes the remarkable absence of such provision from the proposed national curriculum, presumably on grounds of politically expressed fears of indoctrination and bias. On this issue, Crick points out the naivety, both of supposing that established subjects such as history or geography are free of political content or implications, and further, of expecting that the effects of political education on knowledge and attitudes would be either pervasive or dramatic, whether for good or ill. For political learning, like other learning, seems to be far more strongly influenced by the home, the media, by the ethos of society at large, and by the institutional practices of schooling, than it is by the efforts of teachers or by any formal curricular offerings.

In the entry on multicultural education, Walkling charts education's response to the cultural diversity produced by post-war immigration to Britain, from earlier remedial and assimilationist goals to later practices which celebrate pluralism. He suggests that though commitment to multiculturalism varies widely, it is now seen to imply a perspective which treats knowledge as the common property of diverse cultures, and which promotes sensitivity to the valued ways of life of other people. In rejecting both radical relativist and ethnocentric notions of what is educationally worthwhile, Walkling builds up a case for the feasibility, as well as the desirability, of a multicultural approach to schooling process and content. This is seen as part of a broader reforming tendency which aims at an increase in social equality through educational change.

That, too, is the perspective from which Acker reviews the growing awareness that schooling practices reflect and reproduce the gender stereotypes and sex-linked divisions of labour of society, such that if these outcomes are considered neither inevitable nor desirable, schooling change will be indicated. She reports sex-linked differences in access to education, in experiences within the system, and in consequent educational, economic and social outcomes. In each of these areas, Acker documents the extent and pervasiveness of sex-linked differences, exploring their sources and cumulative effects. These latter in turn act as powerful obstacles to subsequent reform, since each age cohort provides, through its choices and destinations, its successes and failures, potent role models for those who follow. Though outcomes are attributed to a complex of social and school-based factors, it is argued that education has a primary role to play in counteracting gender-related inequalities.

The final group of recurrent issues addressed in this section return to more general matters which are less obviously controversial than questions of explicit moral and political education, or of schooling's influence on relations between the sexes and differing races. Carr examines the relation of theory to practice in education, revealing that these apparently separate spheres of activity are in fact mutually interdependent. A brief historical survey illustrates how theory and practice mirror and institutionalize the dominant priorities and perspectives of a given era. Differing approaches to educational theorizing reflect, Carr shows, changes in our way of thinking about educational practice, and thus are no more free from value commitments and from the effects of evolving social circumstance than is practice itself. Once theory is itself considered from a historical perspective, it becomes evident that a popular natural science analogy of cumulative progress is inappropriate, for each succeeding style of theorizing is a response to changing social conditions and to a changing agenda of practical concerns. Carr thus goes on to explicate the new 'critical' paradigm of educational theory, which, by taking account of the social, political and economic context of education, aims to rescue both theory and practice from ideological constraints by making explicit those values they embody and reflect.

The value-laden nature of apparently aseptic theory is then explored by Barrow, who looks particularly at curriculum theory. He shows that in this expanding area of research and writing there is controversy first about how inquiry into the curriculum should be pursued, and also about what range of educational concerns it should cover. Barrow suggests a range of questions which curriculum theory might properly seek to answer, concerned with the selection, development, presentation and evaluation of intended learning content. Given these parameters, this area gives rise to different types of questions – philosophical, sociological, psychological – none of which are free from value commitments. Barrow argues that although such commitments are more pervasive than is immediately obvious, they need be neither arbitrary nor subjective, but must be consistent with a clearly and coherently argued conception of education. Only when such a conception is made explicit can theory which echoes and sustains it be rationally evaluated.

Inglis's consideration of culture and curriculum change extends this perspective, showing how our educational practices and preoccupations are far from immune to the backwash of national economic and geopolitical events. At a time when old political and epistemological certainties are crumbling, the curriculum becomes disputed ground, with competing interest groups attempting to influence the directions of change. Inglis sees current policy making in education – as elsewhere – as dominated by managerialism, which implies not just a particular approach to organization but more importantly the espousal of technicist and instrumental values in the content and process of education itself. He notes that the political and economic realities to which education is asked to respond, though real, are not inevitable, being the outcome of prior social choices which are open to rational judgements. Similarly, a technicist ethos presents means as all important, obscuring their dependence on the acceptance of ends which should be the proper subject of reasoned evaluation and open debate. Inglis explicates the curriculum as a story which society tells the rising generation about what was important in the past and what should be pursued in the future. He advances a view of education and culture which rejects both totalitarian and technocratic perspectives, and in which the criterion of curricular priority is ethical significance, since to debate curriculum questions is to ask what kind of life we wish the next generation to lead.

The final entry in this section is appropriately concerned with the plurality of functions which education is expected to fulfil. Since there is a necessary tension between many of these competing functions, and since public education should be pursued in the interests of all, it is therefore of crucial importance, Golby argues, that the widest possible representation of interests should be sought in the control of education. Though not undervaluing the private pursuit of education, the focus of this contribution is on education as a public service, which is expected to deliver both individual and societal benefits. Some accommodation between these types of outcome must be secured as part of the common arrangements which society makes for its future. In making or remaking these arrangements we must remain aware that change takes place against a background of existing practice which is difficult to reform and of which respectful account must be taken if changes are to be effective. To accept this is not to endorse tradition for its own sake, but to emphasize the need for sophistication in any analysis of the existing educational situation, and for subtlety in proposing and implementing new policy and practice. Such a view is antipathetic to the managerial model of educational change which was also rejected in the preceding entry, for it is opposed to the assertion of technology over art in teaching and to the dominance of means over ends as the questions of central concern. Having presented the case that educational institutions should serve the interests of all and must inevitably be in continuous evolution, Golby examines what would be required for education to represent more adequately this plurality of interests. These implications range from teacher-training procedures to education's institutional frameworks and to the mechanisms for its political control. Throughout this entry, as in all those which comprise this section, the contentious nature of these issues is stressed, as is their basis in moral and political theory.

Just as this section of the *Handbook of Educational Ideas and Practices* attempts to address significant recurrent issues in education, so it is clear that certain themes recur within the issues themselves. Several entries refer to the apparent conflict between individual and social outcomes, for in recessionary periods these are dichotomized, with emphasis shifted to the latter. At such times it seems apparent that to propose the development of rational autonomy as a primary purpose for education is to promote a luxury which few seek and which collectively we can ill afford. Throughout the section, attention is drawn to the contentious assumptions which support this shift in emphasis and to the policy directions to which they give rise. It would seem that the values of the market, which constitute powerful influences on both general social ethos and on educational policy, give rise to a narrow conception of social well-being based on economic aggregates, and to a short-term vision of the social future for which education must of course prepare. These perspectives give plausibility to an apparent conflict between the development of individual potential and the flourishing of the group. In social conditions where the demands of the immediate future, seen largely in collective economic terms, appear to require priority of consideration, that apparent dichotomy is resolved in favour of promoting collective economic welfare in the short term, by emphasizing the social outcomes of education. Many entries in this section argue that the dichotomy is more illusory than real, and that its currently preferred resolution has consequences which are not only damaging for education – implying attrition of the more liberal educational aims which accompanied the social optimism of the preceding period – but which are ultimately damaging for the society which education reproduces.

Though today's approach is presented as an appropriate response to reality, the entries of this section emphasize that such realities are *social*, such that our collective response to them is the outcome of moral and political choices made against a background of objective constraints. Our *educational* response to social conditions, however, must be considered with the greatest circumspection, for through education we have the possibility, in the longer term, of either reinforcing, mitigating, or modifying those objective constraints which serve as parameters for our actions and choices today. It is this necessary feature of universal general education, that it simultaneously reflects the past, sustains the present, and produces the future, which makes the nature of educational provision the perennial subject of controversy.

I.I

SCHOOLING AND SOCIETY

ANTHONY HARTNETT AND MICHAEL NAISH

EDUCATION, POLITICS, AND SOCIAL REPRODUCTION

Although the continued existence of any society has a biological basis, no society can continue unless those born into it acquire a social identity, that is to say, become persons or social beings. In the absence of such an identity, no new generation will be able to take over from the preceding one those roles (for example, of citizen, worker, parent, or whatever), and their associated institutions, of which social life and society are constituted. This social identity, however, is not a gift of nature, acquired by maturation or biological development. It is, rather, a distinctively human achievement which is acquired by one generation learning it from another, and adapting and developing it as circumstances require. It is with the transmission of social identity and with the cognate notions of intergenerational continuity and of social reproduction that education, taken most generally, is concerned. As such, it has a central role in shaping a society, and it is, in its turn, shaped by the society of which it is a constituent and which it helps to shape.

The general problem, then, to which the enterprise of education is addressed is 'What preparation is to be given to the young so as to enable a society to sustain itself?' This problem has at least two important features. The first is that it is a political problem in the sense that any answer to it involves some view about the nature, organization, quality, and direction of society. This is because, other than in the most exceptional circumstances, a society will be concerned not simply to sustain itself, but to sustain itself in some favoured form. Answers to questions about what best form a society might take and about how it might be best ordered presuppose a political theory, and any such political theory will, in its turn, contain an educational theory, since it will require that the preparation of the young be of such a kind as to sustain the society in the form it favours (Hollis 1971). In addition, issues about the nature of the justly ordered society and of an educational system appropriate to it involve questions about what constitutes the good life for members of a society, that is to say, a life that is satisfying and morally acceptable. Answers to these questions involve judgements about the interests of members of a society, for a central element in the justification of any view of the nature of a justly ordered society will be that it best serves its members' interests and maximizes the opportunities for each of them to live a good life. The ability to live a good life, to make something of a life, and, hence, of oneself, depends to a large extent on those modes of living and on those roles a society permits and enables its members to prepare for, and on access to them (access which may well be affected by differences in class, status, power, and wealth).

A second important feature of this general educational problem is that it is an enduring one. Enduring problems are recurrent and often continuous problems to which there is no permanent solution. Solutions to them consist in developing strategies and responses that enable those who face them to make the best of the predicaments they pose. The preparation that is to be given to a society's young will alter as a society changes from, say, an agriculturally-based to an industrially- or post-industrially-based one, as a society becomes more or less culturally diverse, as its political institutions change, and as it sustains more or less unemployment.

If all this is true, then education is not an enterprise that can have one specific definitive form. It is, rather, variously interpretable. These differences in interpretation will arise from differences about how the notion of preparing the next generation for sustaining a society is to be interpreted. To say this is to say that education is an enterprise that admits of different conceptions. Embodied in these different conceptions are different views about how best the general educational problem identified above it to be solved. These conceptions will differ in part because different people and groups will hold different political and moral views about the good society, the good life, their interests, and so on – views that will be affected by their own cultural background, religious, and other beliefs. They will differ, too, because no conception can afford to be static. It will be subject to revision, as changing circumstances render its view of a suitable preparation for the young outmoded or inappropriate (Naish 1984).

SCHOOLS AS ARENAS OF POLITICAL AND EDUCATIONAL STRUGGLE

Schooling is what goes on in schools, but the connection between schooling and one or other conception of education is a contingent one. Institutions may or may not be informed by the ideals, or pursue the goals, which give them their formal purposes and identity. Even so, schools are conventionally taken to be among those institutions which are bearers of conceptions of education.

If this is the case, then schools are likely at various times to be the focus of political struggle, at least in societies where political debate has not been extinguished. There may be, for example, a group in a society which does not believe that a widely institutionalized conception of education acknowledges its interests or views of the good life, and which, accordingly, rejects judgements about such matters made by others on its behalf. The conception will lack legitimacy for it. It will require that its own conception and its own views of interests and of the good life embodied in it are not only put on the public agenda but are given the *institutional* weight they merit. In another case, when a favoured conception is institutionalized but access to it is restricted, members of an excluded group may press for access on the grounds that their exclusion is unjust, is against their interests, and severely restricts their opportunities to live satisfying lives. Examples would be, in the first case, the desire amongst some Muslims in the UK for their own schools, and, in the second, women's wish for greater access to science and to technology (Hartnett and Naish 1986a).

The political struggle will focus on issues about the control of schools and of their curricula (Apple 1986). It will be about what is to be taught and why, about what must be compulsory and what need not be, about what is to be left to other agencies, about what is and what is not to be left to home and family, and about what is not to be passed on at all. It will be about who is to decide all of this, and will involve related issues about the scope of teachers' autonomy and hence about their education and their professional role, and about how they are to be appointed and controlled. In at least part of the nineteenth century in the UK, the struggle to 'capture' schools and their curricula was, according to Williams (1965, Part 2, Chapter 1), between 'the public educators, the industrial trainers, and the old humanists'. These elements in the argument can still be seen, he suggests, in our own time. Evidence from the USA, and attempts in the UK in the 1980s to make the whole educational system responsive to what are described as the 'needs of industry', suggest that, in political terms at least, the industrial trainers or their modern counterparts have recently won much of the argument.

There will also be a struggle over who should get access to what curricula. Should there be a common curriculum for all? Should it be differentiated, and, if so, on what principles? It is worth noting that the idea that different conceptions of education and hence different curricula are suitable for different kinds of children (on one or other classification) has a long history. It is seen, for example, in Plato's *Republic* where the Guardians receive a quite different education from the rest of the society. In the UK, it is seen in The Taunton Commission of 1867 with its three grades of secondary school which corresponded roughly, as the Report put it, to 'the gradations of society'; in the post-war tripartite system where there was curricular and institutional differentiation on the basis of 'age, aptitude, and ability'; and in the 1980s where a particular form of vocationalism and an associated national curriculum are to be imposed on state schools while the private sector, to which the rich alone largely have access, is left to its own devices. The struggle for control over access is likely to be particularly strong where differentiated curricula act as sorting devices for access not merely to more education but to better life chances, better paid or higher status work, or even to no work at all.

SCHOOLING, SOCIETY, AND DOMINANT MODES OF POLITICAL AND ECONOMIC ORGANIZATION

The general issue

If there is an inextricable connection between politics, on the one hand, and schooling and conceptions of education, on the other, then particular political values and their associated conceptions of education are likely to be reflected in the policies and practices of schooling proportionately to the degree of political power they can summon in their support.

In general in Western democracies, the dominant modes of economic organization are corporate capitalist. Since economic power brings with it political power, modes of political organization, kinds of democracy that have been developed, and views of the good and justly ordered society, of the good life, and of interests, are likely to be strongly influenced by the values of capitalism. Among them are the overriding importance of maximum material production and consumption and of the growth of technological knowledge, of competition, and of that kind of division of labour which is required for the facilities of processing and consumption to operate at maximum capacity (Feinberg 1975:196).

There is evidence to suggest that, in such societies, many schools are strongly influenced by values of corporate capitalism, although there is disagreement as to exactly how and to exactly what extent (Hussain 1976). Bowles and Gintis (1976), for example, in their well-known and widely cited study, claim that in the United States, at any rate, the form and substance of schooling is so bound up with capitalist values that its major role is to produce 'a work-force able and willing to staff occupational positions in the capitalist system' (p.265) and, in so doing, it helps to sustain and to reinforce the economic and other related inequalities prevalent in the wider society. Wood (1984) in a discussion of this claim notes that some find it too deterministic (cf. Willis 1977). Bourdieu (1977) for one, Wood notes, argues that the knowledge and culture seen in school curricula reflect the values of the dominant class or classes and legitimate their interests, all at the cost of the values and interests of subordinate classes. This means (Wood 1984:223) that social and cultural structures as

15

well as economic ones 'influence and control the logic of schooling'. Other accounts (Apple 1982) give the state a mediating role. They suggest ways in which the state is related to a capitalist economic order and then how the state is related to schooling. On this view, the state needs to harmonize both the conflicting demands of different groups within the dominant capitalist class itself (whose members may not all share the same view about what form of schooling best furthers capitalist production) as well as those of other groups in society. This harmonization is required for 'the accumulation of capital *in the long run*' (Shapiro 1985:58).

As Feinberg (1983:152) points out, whatever technical criticisms have been brought against the work of Bowles and Gintis (1976), 'little significant criticism has been directed against [its] overall message'. All of this suggests that in societies in which corporate capitalism has a central place, conceptions of education institutionalized in schools are likely to reflect its values; that schooling's most important role is to support its political economy; that schooling will help to serve and maintain the differences in power, status, and material reward that such an economy sanctions; and that schooling will be particularly concerned to prepare children, in terms of both knowledge and skill as well as of attitudes, for those adult roles that production requires, and will only encourage in children such values as independence, individuality, creativity, autonomy, and the ability to make sense of and evaluate the political, social, and economic structures they inherit, to the extent that this does not conflict with preparing them for employment.

Embodied in the justification of this mode of political and economic organization and the schooling it engenders is the view that the interests of labour and capital are the same. Whether this is the case is contentious. And as Feinberg (1975:190) points out, in a relevant discussion, where schooling is linked to the maximization of the growth of technological knowledge, there may be a 'direct connection between technological growth and the rewarding of talent' but 'the link between the rewarding of talent and the widest possible distribution of rewards is much more tenuous'.

School organization

Dominant modes of political and economic organization are likely to affect not merely curricular goals and content but the style in which schools are run. Wood (1984:224–5) suggests that in the USA schools limit 'student and teacher participation in school decision making, glorifying a hierarchical, rule-governed administrative organization'. This together with other features of schools and of their curricula, he argues, reflects the limited vision of democracy prevalent in the wider society, where the only choices are those 'between competing élites, not between competing social visions'. Shapiro's comments

(1985:69) reinforce this view. He notes that although there is no simple one-to-one correspondence between the practices of schools and those found in industry or in work places generally, current recommendations in the USA about the behaviour of adolescents in school parallel those required for adult workers. The case is similar for teachers, where there are demands for weakened job security, merit pay, evaluation, scrutiny of performance. Above all, the split between the conception and execution of a task that is increasingly being imposed on teachers' work and the depoliticized and narrow view of professionalism that goes with this reflect the style of the relationships of production in capitalism, and are likely to reinforce the alienation that they bring. All of this reflects, Shapiro suggests, 'the accelerating obsession with output, performance, and productivity' which is 'part of the encompassing *Zeitgeist* of our time'. All of this, too, is seen increasingly in the UK, not merely in its schools, but in its institutions of further and higher education (Hartnett and Naish 1986a and 1986b).

On this view, then, schools and schooling are conceived not (to take one alternative view) as places where the young are given space to begin to make something of their human inheritance, detached from their 'immediate local world' and 'its current concerns and the directions it gives' to their attention (Oakeshott 1971:49). Schools and schooling are related to society much as factories are. Their task is to make human products (people with employable skills) out of the raw material given them (children) in response to the wishes of employers (significantly, though not unexpectedly, redefined here as the consumers of education).

Teaching and pedagogy

Dominant political and economic values are likely, in addition, to affect the *aspect* under which curriculum content is passed on. Subjects will be taught, and knowledge and skills passed on, primarily for their *exchange* value – that is, their role in making their possessors more marketable. Science provides an example. It is, in many educational circles, as elsewhere, conflated with technology. Science is likely to be taught less as a practice involving the exercise of distinctive human excellences and virtues (MacIntyre 1981, Chapter 14), and for its contribution to the understanding of fundamental problems about the human condition, human life, and its purposes, than for its value in the market place and its role in the growth of technological and, therefore, of financially exploitable knowledge. In Oakeshott's words (1967:309), what is learned is likely to be 'how to use those products of scientific thought which contribute to our current manner of living . . . The skill acquired is the skill of using the information, not of speaking the "language" ' (cf. Gordon 1984). And where schools are concerned primarily with what is taken to be relevant useful knowledge, there is likely to be little room for the political and moral issues that are inseparable from the ends in terms of which utility and relevance are determined. In addition, the aspect under which things are taught is likely to affect the manner in which they are taught. When knowledge is seen as useful information, its worth and nature are likely to be rendered uncontentious, and teaching is likely to be regarded as predominantly instruction. Wood (1984:225) again comments on how in the USA 'a steady stream of objective facts is given students who are never encouraged to see knowledge as a contested terrain', and on how 'the curriculum has become "teacher-proofed" and thus reflects a world where all the important issues are resolved'.

Selection

If the kind of social reproduction and the kinds of conceptions of education with which schools are concerned are overridingly work-related, then at some stage in the educational process systems of selection are required and, with them, differentiated curricula. This differentiation need not be at the level of schooling, but it is commonly so and has been so for a good time in the UK. There are a number of reasons why such differentiation is needed, above all in a society whose overriding concern is to maximize the growth of technological knowledge. One reason is that there will be a need to identify and select the talent required for technological growth, and the system must be such that it enables selections to be made that claim to match the number of occupational roles available at various levels in the wider society. Such a process of selection, involving not educating people above the work role to which their talents, as these are identified by this very process, destine them, will be justified in two linked ways. In the first, it will be justified by an appeal to the need for efficiency in producing technological growth, and, in the second, by an appeal to the need for social control and the maintenance of stability in society without which technological and capital growth are impossible. As one DES official in the UK put it, 'There may be social unrest but we can cope with the Toxteths. But if we have a highly educated and idle population, we may possibly anticipate more serious social conflict. People must be educated once more to know their place' (quoted in Simon 1985:223). A similar view about the role of education and about the dangers of 'over-education' is seen in Hayek (1960, Chapter 24).

Any system of selection has, however, to be justified and legitimated. Differences in social class, for example, no longer provide, at least overtly, acceptable criteria by which different kinds of children are to be matched to different kinds of curricula. The rise of IQ testing and other 'objective' tests can be understood, in part, as an attempt to replace no longer acceptable modes of determining differences in educational provision. The ostensible purpose of

IQ and related testing was to ensure that a child received an education related to his or her abilities. There are grounds, however, for thinking that such a system of testing could only have a substantial place in a system of schooling overridingly concerned with technological growth and with fitting children for the various roles the current divisions of labour in a society require (Bowles and Gintis 1976, Chapter 4; Feinberg 1983, Chapters 2, 3, 5). Moreover, such a selection system has the added advantage, in a capitalist society, of tightening the competitive aspects of schooling, and, in so doing, brings its ethos more in line with that of the free market.

EDUCATION, SCHOOLING, AND SOCIETY: AN ALTERNATIVE VIEW

On the conception of education discussed so far, schooling is primarily intended to produce people who participate in the process of production and in the market. The social identities which it is concerned to impart are those of worker and consumer. The views of interests and the good life underpinning its practices are market-based. Schooling is, in effect, a service industry to the economy and an investment, like any other, whose worth is judged solely by the economic return it brings. It gives little weight to imparting any social identity relating to a political role that a society's citizens might play in its affairs.

This privileging of the role of worker and consumer over that of citizen is not, of course, the mark of schooling in capitalist societies only. It is, at first sight, however, surprising to see it in capitalist *democracies*, where it is commonly claimed that democracy and its liberties, on the one hand, and capitalism and economic prosperity, on the other, sustain each other. But such a system of schooling and the political economy it serves is at best compatible only with an 'equilibrium' or 'pluralist élite' conception of democracy (Macpherson 1977, Chapter 4). Here democracy is conceived on 'an entrepreneurial market analogy'. It takes its tone, form, and view of human nature (men and women as naturally acquisitive and competitive) from the political economy of capitalism itself. The role of citizens in such a democracy is not to decide political issues but to choose between competing élites who will decide them for them. Citizens are seen as political consumers, choosing between the political 'goods' the élites variously offer them. There are grounds for thinking that this conception of democracy is a limited one (ibid.). In the first place, for it to deliver whatever degree of political, economic, and social stability it can (a central merit claimed for it) seems to require a politically apathetic citizenry; in the second, it is a democracy where political power and influence are likely to be proportional to wealth, and hence it is likely to sustain or increase inequalities.

Other conceptions of democracy are possible, however, in which citizens have a more active role in the political life of their society and its institutions. For the sake of brevity these can be called 'conceptions of participatory democracy' (Macpherson 1977, Chapter 5). Any such conception of democracy makes economic demands in that it is incompatible with those inequalities of wealth generated by the political and economic system discussed earlier. Such a conception would require there to be institutionalized in the schooling system a conception of education that, whatever place it contained for preparation for adult work roles, would be primarily concerned to further in each student 'social participation as a member of the public through the development of interpretive understanding and normative skills' (Feinberg 1983:228). This would be 'a general education' that 'prepares students for a common life, regardless of the nature of their vocation' (ibid.). The social identity that schooling is here concerned to impart is that of 'free persons . . . who are . . . capable of making unmanipulated judgements on the basis of reason and theoretical understanding, but who also find solidarity with their fellow human beings' (Feinberg 1983:229). So here curricular aims, content, and distribution; modes of teaching, of learning, of school organization (White 1981); aspects under which things are taught; and the style of teacher education and professionalization (Scheffler 1968–9) are all chosen with a view to reasoned public participation in the political life of society (Gutmann 1987).

As Feinberg's work (1983:234) suggests, at least three important conditions are required for this public participation to be effective, and for the general education associated with it to be a substantive, and not token or merely formal, preparation for adult life. The first is a political condition that the distribution of power is such that no group can impose its will on another group 'independently of an understanding' of that group's perspective; the second is an economic condition that, with allowances made for individual incentive, wealth is distributed in a way 'that is consistent with the development of unmanipulated judgement'; and the third is a knowledge condition that the relevant forms of knowledge 'be developed and exercised in the context of interpretive and normative understanding'.

These conditions cannot be brought about by changes in schooling alone, if at all. They require, for a start, changes in the prevalent distribution of political and economic power in capitalist democracies, as well as in the views of interests and of the good life underpinning it. The difficulties of getting an alternative view of society, of democracy, and of education and the role of schooling onto the public agenda and then institutionalized are severe (Edgley 1980:13–15). But only a democracy with substantial elements of public participation is compatible with a fully open society. And only in such a society is there any chance of there being a free and equal debate, with unmanipulated opinion and an unmanipulated agenda, about political and other communal problems, and of the proposed or actual solutions to these problems being assessed on their merits by the public use of reason rather than being imposed, irrespective of the weight of argument in their favour, by and in the interests of one or other dominant group. It is only in such a society that political traditions of communal problem-solving and the educational traditions associated with them can be sustained in good order, and a central role of schooling in this society is to do what it can to ensure that they are so sustained.

REFERENCES

Apple, M. W. (1982) *Education and Power*, London: Routledge & Kegan Paul.
    (1986) 'Curriculum conflict in the United States', in A. Hartnett and M. Naish, (Eds.) (1986):161–70.
Bourdieu, P. (1977) *Outline of Theory and Practice*, Cambridge: Cambridge University Press.
Bowles, S. and Gintis, H. (1976) *Schooling in Capitalist America: Educational Reform and the Contradictions of Economic Life*, London: Routledge & Kegan Paul.
Edgley, R. (1980) 'Education, work, and politics', *Journal of Philosophy of Education* 14,1:3–16.
Feinberg, W. (1975) 'Educational equality under two conflicting models of educational development', *Theory and Society* 2,2:183–210.
    (1983) *Understanding Education: Toward a Reconstruction of Educational Inquiry*, Cambridge: Cambridge University Press.
Gordon, D. (1984) 'The image of science, technological consciousness, and the hidden curriculum', *Curriculum Inquiry* 14,4:367–400.
Gutmann, A. (1987) *Democratic Education*, Princeton, N.J.: Princeton University Press.
Hartnett, A. and Naish, M. (Eds.) (1986) *Education and Society Today*, London: Falmer Press.
    (1986a) 'Introductory essay: conceptions of education and social change in a democratic society', in A. Hartnett and M. Naish (Eds.): 1–17.
    (1986b) ' "The values of a free society" and the politics of educational studies' in A. Hartnett and M. Naish (Eds.): 183–204.
Hayek, F. A. (1960) *The Constitution of Liberty*, London: Routledge & Kegan Paul.
Hollis, M. (1971) 'The pen and the purse', *Proceedings of the Philosophy of Education Society of Great Britain* 5,2:153–69.
Hussain, A. (1976) 'The economy and the educational system in capitalist societies', *Economy and Society* 5,4:413–34.
MacIntyre, A. (1981) *After Virtue: A Study in Moral Theory*, London: Duckworth.
Macpherson, C. A. (1977) *The Life and Times of Liberal Democracy*, Oxford: Oxford University Press.
Naish, M. (1984) 'Education and essential contestability revisited', *Journal of Philosophy of Education* 18,2:141–53.
Oakeshott, M. (1967) 'The study of politics in a university' in M. Oakeshott, *Rationalism in Politics and Other Essays*, London: Methuen: 300–33.
    (1971) 'Education: the engagement and its frustration', *Proceedings of the Philosophy of Education Society of Great Britain* 5,1:43–76.

Scheffler, I. (1968–9) 'University scholarship and the education of teachers', *The Record* 70:1–12.

Shapiro, H. S. (1985) 'Capitalism at risk: the political economy of the educational reports of 1983', *Educational Theory* 35,1:57–72.

Simon, B. (1985) *Does Education Matter?* London: Lawrence and Wishart.

White, P. (1981) 'Political education and school organisation' in B. Simon and W. Taylor (Eds.) *Education in the Eighties: the Central Issues*, London: Batsford Academic and Educational Ltd.:176–88.

Williams, R. (1965) *The Long Revolution*, Harmondsworth: Penguin Books.

Willis, P. (1977) *Learning to Labour: How Working Class Kids Get Working Class Jobs*, London: Saxon House.

Wood, G. A. (1984) 'Schooling in a democracy: transformation or reproduction?' *Educational Theory* 34,3:219–39.

THE AIMS OF EDUCATION

JOHN WHITE

What the aims of education should be cannot be definitively laid down. We are in the territory of visions of the good life, and these will differ. In this essay I am articulating a personal vision of education. This cannot be seen as a handbook article in any more authoritative sense.

But personal visions need not be freewheeling. Behind this one there are reasons. I hope that these are good reasons and that others will share them and the account which rests on them. Something, but not everything, of these reasons will emerge as I proceed.

The aim of education should be to promote the well-being of those being educated. Personal well-being is not self-contained: it has a large altruistic dimension to it. This is not a definitional point. Individuals can flourish with little or no concern for others. There are no impregnable arguments to show that such people mistake their own good. What educators should do, however, is to bring people up to see their own good as containing altruism.

This is in opposition to the view that part of education promotes people's good, while another part, 'moral education', is to make them attentive to that of others. This privatizes personal well-being from the start, and there is no good reason for doing so.

Other agencies than education aim at promoting well-being. Education's role is via the formation of dispositions and the enlargement of understanding. There are two parts of education, an earlier part and a later part.

EARLY EDUCATION

The first task is to shape the tendencies and propensities with which children are born into settled dispositions of certain sorts. We can think of this as bringing their actions and reactions under the sway of certain values. Another way of putting this is to say that children are brought up in conformity with certain reasons for action. And *this* is to say that they are encouraged to come to have certain desires rather than others.

These values, reasons, or desires do not divide neatly into the prudential and the moral. We can forget these labels, since they only get in the way. The values include the following:

1. Physical pleasures, such as eating, drinking, physical vitality, being in a comfortable temperature, sexual enjoyment (in its due season). Children are to be brought up to want to enjoy specific forms of such pleasures, dependent not least on their culture.
2. The avoidance of harm to themselves, in the shape of pain, physical injury, disease, incapacitating mental states.
3. Close personal relations, with family, friends (including pets), lovers (in due season).
4. Protecting the well-being of people universally. This means learning not to harm them, learning to tell them the truth, being considerate, keeping one's word, leaving them free to lead their own lives. It also means acquiring favourable dispositions towards those engaged in such protection in a professional sense, for example towards government, the police, conservation agencies, insurance companies, the law, the media (in so far as these institutions are acting for the benefit of all and not just some).
5. Promoting the well-being of people universally. This includes being friendly and well-disposed, as well as helping people to acquire the necessary conditions of well-being, for example food, clothing, shelter, necessary liberties, health, education, income, company, and social recognition. Children should come to look favourably on those involved in associated vocations, to do with the production of food and material goods, politics, medicine, teaching, social work, and other things.
6. The values of activities in which one engages which are pursued at least for their own sake, but perhaps along with extrinsic goals. The values can include some determinate goal (like winning a game), the activity itself (like playing a piano for fun), or being with those who engage in an activity with one, and enjoying the mutual recognition of each person's contribution.
7. Higher-order values arising from the regulation of conflicts between lower-order values. An example is temperance: children must learn to regulate their desires for, say, food and drink (under item 1) so that they do not lead to harm (under 2) or hinder their pursuit of other values in the other categories. Courage, likewise, regulates feelings of fear and confidence. Children need, above all, to begin to acquire the practical wisdom by which they can establish orders of priorities on their burgeoning desires.

This list may not be complete. Its items, too, are not discrete. Activities under 6, for instance, may be pursued with friends (see 2). Children can engage in activities falling under 5 – for example some kind of service to others in the community, organized in school – which exhibit the values falling under 6.

I do not think the idea that these kinds of dispositions should be fostered is likely to be controversial. In so far as the list is acceptable, it is noteworthy that it is impossible to divide it into prudential reasons and moral reasons. I am never too sure what people mean when they talk about the latter. If altruism, in the sense of some kind of sensitiveness to and concern for others' well-being, is all that is intended, then 3 is obviously altruistic. So are 4 and 5. So for the most part is 6. In most of the activities in which one engages under this heading the values will be shared with fellow participants, whether one is with them face-to-face, as in playing hockey, or not, as in enjoying poetry. In promoting these values, one will be forwarding not one's own good alone, but others' good also. None of this is to exclude from 6 activities without shared ends, but examples without this feature are going to be hard to find. (Going for solitary walks? But this is a social practice in which many of us share. Idiosyncratic private practices like collecting and classifying one's nail-clippings? But even this shares features with other forms of collecting and classifying.) Finally 1, 2, and 7 cannot be classified as self-regarding rather than other-regarding. Physical pleasures are typically pursued as parts of social practices; my being free of pain or other harm may benefit not only me but you as well, and this is true also of my regulation of my desires.

Many would build more into morality than altruism alone. Concern for friends and family, they might say, is not in itself a moral reason. Morality involves impartiality. Acting partially towards one's friends is acting immorally. Impartiality leads one to universality: not having any good reason for favouring oneself over others, or the smaller group over the larger, the person who lives a moral life acts impartially for the good of all.

From this point of view, only 4 and 5 seem to count as moral reasons. But there are still problems over universality. I do not write this in in any wholly global sense. To promote or protect the well-being of people *universally* is to do this for *all* those concerned in some context, and this context is not always humanity (or sentient life) taken as a whole. A matron of a hospital attends impartially to the well-being of all the patients in her hospital, not to that of the whole human race. On some views of morality, therefore, the universal altruism I am advocating in 4 and 5 is not universal enough.

The first stage of education is an initiation into values 1 to 7. Each of these embraces a host of more determinate values. To come back to 5, the universal promotion of well-being can be found at different levels and in different kinds of social groups. Think of: parents of large families; members of a work group, a school, or other institution; local community groups; local communities themselves; religious groups; ethnic minority communities; national communities; international institutions; the world community of those now living; the world community of those now living and yet to live.

Values can conflict, both across categories and within categories (in so far as these distinctions can be usefully made). Within 4 and 5, attending to the needs or rights of one group may conflict with attending to those of another. Within 6 one's commitment to one activity may compete, in resources or time, with one's commitment to another. Some activities under 6 may involve one in the risk of personal injury (see 2). Telling the truth (see 4) may get a friend into trouble (see 3).

Even with very young children a start should be made not only on building up dispositions governed by different kinds of value, but also on helping them to cope with conflicts between these values. The latter aim takes us to the values under 7, as we have seen.

The first stage of education, from birth through to early adolescence, should be devoted to these tasks. To some of those who look at education against the background of schooling as we know it, this approach may look incomplete. What place in all this has language, mathematics, science, and other types of knowledge?

Education is centrally to do with the growth and organization of desires. But this operates against a certain background. Every child is born into a specific society, which has its own language, its own space, its own traditions and ways of doing things. Behind these things lie values like those we have been discussing. One way, and not the least important, by which children come to acquire these values, is by learning their mother tongue and, partly thereby, coming to know the world in which they live. By 'the world' I do not mean the scientist's world of invisible physical forces. I mean the life-world which envelops children: their home, their local streets, their town, the mores and traditions of the smaller and larger communities to which they belong; it includes, too, the natural world – of gardens, parks, earth, trees, clouds, day and night, seasons, sun, and stars – which both belongs to their social worlds and sets frameworks for them.

Part of early education is to initiate children into this life-world and the language which defines it. It is against this taken-for-granted background that upbringing in values takes place. So there should be no fear that language will be neglected. As for other forms of knowledge found in schools today, some of our conventional priorities may need readjusting. Mathematical and scientific activities have their place in modern life-worlds, but more attention should be paid to just what this place is and how important it is against the larger background. It will then be seen, I think, that counting is of ubiquitous importance, and aspects of astronomy, evolutionary biology, meteorology, and other sciences help us to make sense of our life-world; whereas other parts

26

of physical science, together with more advanced types of mathematics, are important largely for more specific reasons, largely to do with welfare-promoting activities falling under 5. To understand the life-world in general, other forms of knowledge are of great relevance: local or environmental studies, aspects of human geography, the historical understanding of contemporary values and ways of doing things, elementary sociology, and politics. But not only knowledge can help. Poetry and other forms of literature reinforce our attachments to our social world and the natural world which frames it; so, too, do music, dance, painting and other arts.

LATER EDUCATION

The aim of education in a complex industrialized society like our own should be the cultivation of personal autonomy of a certain sort. Personal well-being does not, in the abstract, entail personal autonomy. People can flourish in a highly traditional society where there is no question of their determining their own route through life. They, too, are initiated in their childhood into different values and the pursuit of different goals. How these are integrated into a personal pattern of living is determined not by individuals themselves, but by the customs of their society. If a life of well-being is one in which one's major goals – the desires towards the top of one's hierarchy of desires – are by and large achieved, then such non-autonomous individuals can achieve personal well-being to a greater or lesser extent.

In modern society one's goals and the priorities between them are not laid down for one. There is no alternative, except for those of us who live in traditional communities within the larger society, to our making our own way. Promoting well-being in *modern* society must involve preparing young people for the autonomous life. Whether the aim should be any different for those brought up in the traditional communities among us – ethnic minority or religious communities, for instance – is a further question. Its answer depends partly on whether there are good reasons for keeping to a minimum the contact which individuals have with the larger society.

Preparation for autonomy rests on the gradual formation of the dispositions already described under *Early education*. For the most part young children have no choice about these dispositions: value judgements on their behalf are made by their parents and other educators, and their character is formed accordingly. So far there are superficial similarities with upbringing within traditional societies. But the underlying spirit is different. Children are being prepared throughout for self-determination, not for unquestioning social conformity.

Already at this early stage the higher-order dispositions acquired under 7 are accustoming children to resolve value conflicts, although not in a self-conscious or comprehensive way. Children are acquiring virtues, among them

27

the master virtue of practical reasoning. This enables them better to reflect, not only on what means are most suitable for different goals, but also on which goals are more important to them than others.

As they grow older – not for any reason to do with biological development, but because their progress in practical rationality now allows this – children will gradually take over the task of shaping their own characters, which their early educators have begun. They will come not only to resolve conflicts but also to appreciate more clearly the different values at stake and so be able more sensitively to weigh them against each other. This self-awareness will be found not only at the level of particular value conflicts but also more globally, in making sense of one's life as a whole. Dispositions which have been built up in partial isolation from each other must be brought into self-conscious relationships with others.

As part of this progress towards self-understanding, young people will come to have more determinate ideas about the kind of life they wish to lead. They will have become acquainted with a range of possible paid occupations, seen from the perspective of the benefit they bring to people; they will have come to see their possible roles as friends and lovers, parents, more or less active members of democratic institutions and communities at different levels; they will have been introduced to a host of activities pursuable for their own sake. Now they will select from these possibilities, exercising their imagination to form and reform pictures of personal ways of life. Again this is a matter of weighing different values: for some people work will be more salient in their ideal pictures, for other personal relations, for others commitment to some form of creative activity or to politics.

Much of this imaginative activity will remain at the level of the wish, unfettered by practical constraints. It is important that it should, since priorities among values will change in the course of one's lifetime and so may one's circumstances. But the life one fashions for oneself must ultimately be anchored in such realities as the income one might expect to earn, one's bents and talents, the opportunities open to one, competition for more attractive jobs, conditions of work which go with different occupations, and other things. This anchoring brings with it its own new sets of weightings and trade-offs, and once again we should bear in mind that to form realistic plans for one's future is not to map out a blueprint that will last throughout one's life. People will differ in the extent to which they wish to plan out their lives: here, too, weighting will vary.

What might all this imply for the objectives of secondary schooling? It means, I think, that work often done now under the heading of 'personal and social education' becomes centrally important, with elements in the 'academic' curriculum finding their rationale, if at all, in relation to these central concerns.

The work described under *Early education* will broadly continue. Subdivisions of value within categories 1 to 6 will be further explored and assimilated not least by imaginative involvement in possible roles and situations. The integrative dispositions of category 7 will become especially important.

Subserving this will be knowledge and understanding of all kinds. The broad contours of their life-world will already be familiar to students. Now they will need to know more of the details, especially, but not only, in areas covered by their pictures of their possible futures. They will need to know something about: what different careers and other pursuits involve; the socio-economic structure of their own society, its political arrangements and values, and the alterability of all these things; the means of attaining possible goals and the obstacles in their way. Their horizons will be widened beyond their own society to world needs and world politics. At the same time the expansion of their interests, wishes and knowledge on every front must not deracinate them from their life-world. Literature and the other arts will now acquire a new significance for them. For a younger child, if not disadvantaged, the life-world is secure, taken for granted. As so many new worlds open up on every side, however, retaining one's primordial attachments, one's sense of being in the world, has to become a conscious intention. The arts can invoke and reinvoke in us this intention and remind us of its necessity if we are to keep the different sides of our nature in some sort of harmony.

It is a too familiar fact that the technological, economic and political pressures which have produced the world of large-scale, complex, bureaucratic firms and other institutions in which we live make such harmony difficult to achieve. Students need to be acquainted with this as well as with the positive role this complex economy plays, or can play, in promoting universal well-being. This entails knowledge of the scientific and technological bases of their economy; and this in turn entails a good grounding in mathematics.

By the time students leave school they will ideally have already begun to see something of the rationale for their own education and be in a position to direct their own future self-education. Some people will have got further along these roads than others. After school comes the time for specialist learning of different sorts. This is not at odds with education, but reflects further weightings within it. Counterbalancing this comes deeper immersion in the whole value world, with self-understanding becoming more and more important as one becomes more reflectively aware of one's priorities. Balances must be struck between such reflectiveness and engagement in first-order activities, between the inner and the outer. There will be differences here between different individuals and for the same individual at different times. All this requires that before they finish their compulsory schooling students are pointed in these directions. Practical wisdom cannot be an option to be taken up or shed as they may take up or cast off gardening or bridge. It is an indispensable element in their well-being and they must come to know this. In a decently ordered society there will be educational safety nets to protect those of us – all of us? – who find it difficult to keep our priorities in order in a non-educational open environment. Or rather, perhaps, steps will be taken to make the open environment educational: workplaces and the media, for instance, will be reshaped so as to reinforce and not contradict values earlier acquired.

CONCLUSION

This concludes my vision of the aims of education. It will have its competitors. Some will not like its universalism and will advocate different aims for an élite from those for the masses. I do not know how such discrimination could be justified. On my scheme not everyone will reach the same point along the road at the same time. This does not matter as long as we are all moving in the same broad direction. An education which seeks autonomy for some while debarring others is ethically indefensible.

Other objectors will dislike my emphasis on forming children's characters, on building up in them certain dispositions and value-attachments. The objections may be biological-developmentalist or more straightforwardly libertarian. The first school holds that left to themselves in a suitably stimulating environment children will develop naturally towards their full potential. I reject this on the grounds that the notion of mental, as distinct from physical, development is incoherent. Libertarians need not be developmentalists. They may object that my scheme imposes unjustifiable restrictions on children's liberty. I would answer that the principle of liberty applies only to people who are already autonomous, at least in part: non-interference with one's plan of life is a condition of its realizability. A somewhat separate objection from the same side might be that my 'autonomous' persons are not really autonomous, because they do not freely choose their own way of life, but merely add their own marginally significant weightings to structures of values that have been indelibly built into them: they have been made over, in the broad, into conforming creatures of their society. To this I would say that the ideal of radical autonomy, whereby individuals choose their own values and life-plans from their own resources alone, is unintelligible. What could they choose that belonged to no actual social practice? More fundamentally, how can one conceive this choosing self without its being a social creature? The mere fact that it operates with concepts in using language is enough to claim it as a social entity. As we have seen, conceptual distinctions reflect values, values not chosen, but assimilated, by those who acquire them. Radical choosers, again, are generally pictured in such objections as people at least on the way to maturity. But how did they become radical choosers? What sort of upbringing did they have? What account could one give of this without including some kind of building-in of dis-positions?

A final objection might come from those who reject my rejection of the prudential/moral divide. They may need to hold on to this as it fits in with their larger, perhaps metaphysical, pictures of human life. This is true for many Christians, Kantians, utilitarians, socialists, and others. As far as the aims of education go, some may want to bring children up with an overriding attachment to morality, making personal interest subordinate to this. Others will see moral and prudential reasons in uneasier relationships, still separate but neither overriding the other. Yet others will reduce moral demands to a minimum so as to enlarge the space for personal fulfilment.

Each of these outlooks can produce unattractive results. They all see human beings as radically divided. In learning to cope with this division some students may turn out stiffly puritanical, or even fanatical, ready to blame themselves and others for any deviation from the way of duty. Others may find such a path too strenuous, living instead for self as conceived within the dichotomous framework, because this is the only way of life now open to them. A third and a fourth group may pay only lip-service to morality, or may minimize its demands, while in each case giving 'the self' full rein. All these character types are common in our society and one or more of them may be mirrored in ourselves. The intransigence, cynicism, hypocrisy, and lack of fellow-feeling to which they severally give rise are found, too, in larger social and political attitudes. Confrontations between opposing viewpoints are too easily rep-resented in terms of clashes between principle and self-interest, or principle and principle, or interest and interest. We have come to live with polarization and have no clear views about how to overcome it.

But all this comes from the initial dichotomy between morality and self-interest. What I am suggesting is that we do not have to work with this dichotomy. We can start with a more generous, altruistically inclined concep-tion of personal well-being.

FURTHER READING

Cooper, D. E. (Ed.) (1986) *Education, Values and Mind*, London: Routledge & Kegan Paul.

Dearden, R. F., Hirst, P. H., and Peters, R. S. (Eds.) (1972) *Education and the Development of Reason*, London: Routledge & Kegan Paul.

Griffin, J. (1986) *Well-being*, Oxford: Clarendon Press.

Hargreaves, D. H. (1982) *The Challenge for the Comprehensive School*, London: Routledge & Kegan Paul.

Kleinig, J. (1982) *Philosophical Issues in Education*, London: Croom Helm.

Lindley, R. (1986) *Autonomy*, London: Macmillan.

Nagel, T. (1979) 'The fragmentation of value', in *Mortal Questions*, Cambridge: Cambridge University Press.

O'Hear, A. (1981) *Education, Society and Human Nature*, London: Routledge & Kegan Paul.

White, J. (1982) *The Aims of Education Restated*, London: Routledge & Kegan Paul.

Williams, B. (1985) *Ethics and the Limits of Philosophy*, London: Fontana.

1.3

EDUCATION AND TRAINING

CLYDE CHITTY

The debate about education and training has assumed a special significance in the past ten years, associated as it is with questions related to the purposes of schooling, the relationship of education to the world of work, and the practical implications of the New Vocationalism. Indeed, it has been common practice to view the actual starting-point of the debate as James Callaghan's Ruskin College Speech of October 1976.[1] There are still good reasons for treating 1976 as the crucial year when curriculum questions were diverted from the issue of how best to develop a curriculum suited to the philosophy of comprehensive education and became instead a matter of finding ways of training pupils to occupy specific roles in modern capitalist society. Yet it is also important to take account of Reeder's argument[2] that recent complaints emanating from employers and politicians about the contribution being made by schooling (at all levels) to industrial development and the quality and attitudes of the labour force represent only 'the most recent phase of a long-standing controversy about the role of schooling in a modern industrial society'.

THE LEGACY OF RUSKIN

In the Ruskin Speech James Callaghan argued that schools were failing in that youngsters were not being trained in the skills necessary to find employment in industry and commerce:

> I am concerned on my journeys to find complaints from industry that new recruits from the schools sometimes do not have the basic tools to do the job that is required. . . . The goals of our education, from nursery school through to adult education, are clear enough. They are to equip children to the best of their ability for a lively, constructive place in society and also to fit them to do a job of work. Not one or the other; but both. . . . There is no virtue in producing socially well-adjusted members of society who are unemployed because they do not have the skills.

33

The same emphasis on the reluctance of schools to train pupils to meet the needs of wealth-producing industry is evident in the subsequent Green Paper published by the Department of Education and Science in July 1977. Here reference is made to the criticisms voiced at the regional conferences which followed the Ruskin Speech.

> It was said that the school system is geared to promote the importance of academic learning and careers with the result that pupils, especially the more able, are prejudiced against work in productive industry and trade; that teachers lack experience, knowledge and understanding of trade and industry; that curricula are not related to the realities of most pupils' work after leaving school; and that pupils leave school with little or no understanding of the workings, or importance, of the wealth-producing sector of our economy.[3]

The Department of Employment White Paper *A new training initiative: a programme for action*, published in December 1981, reaffirmed, without reservation, a strictly utilitarian view of education and training:

> To get a better trained and more flexible workforce, we need to start with better preparation for working life in schools and better opportunities for continuing education and personal development in the early years at work ... The last two years of compulsory education are particularly important in forming an approach to the world of work. Every pupil needs to be helped to reach his or her full potential, not only for personal development, but to prepare for the whole range of demands which employment will make.[4]

This was, of course, one of the key documents leading to the launching of the Youth Training Scheme (YTS) in September 1983.

The 1981 White Paper can be said to contain three key paragraphs which reveal two implicit models of the nature and causes of unemployment and of the role of education and training in a modern competitive economy:

> The skill shortages which have held back our economic progress in the past could reappear when the economy recovers. They cannot be met solely by training the new intake of young people, but will require considerable readaptation of the existing labour force. Skill needs will continue to change and require updating. Wider opportunities for training and retraining of people in their 20s, 30s and later in life are bound to be required in the future. (paragraph 48)

> For the immediate future, the Government sees an increase of public expenditure ... as the only way of plugging the gap in the training provision required if we are to be ready to meet the skill needs of the economy as trading conditions improve and to offer adequate opportunities to the current generation of young people. It is applying these extra resources to help secure longer term reforms in the quality of training and bring about a change in the attitudes of young people to the value of training and acceptance of relatively lower wages for trainees. (paragraph 58)

> For many years now, our system of training has failed to produce the numbers

of skilled people required by a modern competitive economy. This paper sets out a framework within which employers, employees, unions, educationists and Government can more clearly see what they need to do for the system to work. (paragraph 61)

As Wellington has pointed out,[5] these paragraphs are interesting because they tacitly rely on *two* distinct models of unemployment. All three paragraphs make use of the 'skills-deficit' model (previously adopted by Callaghan) which argues that one of the key factors in the rise of unemployment is the shortage of relevant skills. Schools and teachers can then be blamed for failing to teach those skills (whatever they may be) which would make their students more employable. The second model of unemployment, which Wellington calls the 'cyclical model', suggests that an upturn in the economy is to be expected in the very near future and that unemployment will decrease as 'trading conditions improve' and the economy recovers. The role of the teacher is, then, to train pupils to be ready to respond to the skill needs of a revived economy. But there are many who would argue that unemployment patterns are not fundamentally altered by skills shortages or by cyclical changes in trading conditions.

The Technical and Vocational Education Initiative (TVEI), launched by Prime Minister Margaret Thatcher in a Commons written statement in November 1982, was designed, in the words of the accompanying Department of Employment press release, 'to stimulate technical and vocational education for 14- to 18-year-olds as part of a drive to improve our performance in the development of new skills and technology'. It was also seen as a follow-up to the 1981 White Paper in acknowledging 'the importance of the last two years of compulsory education and the need for more vocationally-orientated courses for those continuing full-time education past 16'. In a letter to all LEA Directors of Education in England and Wales in January 1983, David (now Lord) Young, the then Chairman of the Manpower Services Commission (MSC), stated that the first objective of the TVEI was:

> to widen and enrich the curriculum in a way that will help young people to prepare for the world of work, and to develop skills and interests, including creative abilities, that will help them to lead a fuller life and to be able to contribute more to the life of the community.

It has been obvious throughout the 1980s that vocational preparation is to be an important part of the school curriculum from at least the age of 14, leading on to a continuing programme of adult training and retraining. And perhaps nowhere is a strictly instrumental view of education and training more clearly articulated than in the DES document *Better Schools* published in March 1985.

> It is vital that schools should always remember that preparation for working life

is one of their principal functions. The economic stresses of our time and the pressures of international competition make it more necessary than ever before that Britain's work-force should possess the skills and attitudes, and display the understanding, the enterprise and adaptability that the pervasive impact of technological advance will increasingly demand. This applies equally to those who will be employed by others and to the many who may expect, for part or all of their working lives, to be self-employed. The balance within the curriculum – and the emphasis in teaching it – now needs to alter accordingly.[6]

DEFINITIONS

So far, we have used the terms 'education' and 'training' without attempting to define them. Indeed, as Lawton has pointed out,[7] there has been a tendency in recent years to indulge in discussions about education and training without being clear or consistent about their meaning: 'sometimes contrasting the two words, sometimes blurring the distinction between them, sometimes treating them as completely synonymous'.

The 1985 document *Better Schools* actually makes no attempt to define the terms, but treats them merely as twin concepts with clear vocational objectives:

> Education and training cannot always be distinguished, but they are comple-
> mentary. They need to be brought into closer relation in a variety of ways, given
> the fact that compulsory education ends at age 16, the wide range of pupils'
> attainments, aptitudes and aspirations at that age, and the diversity of facilities
> for post-16 education and training. The Government believes that the linking
> of education and training, whatever form it takes, should have preparation for
> employment as one of its principal functions.

Over twenty years ago, Peters sought to clarify the issue in an influential work *Ethics and Education*, published in 1966. According to Peters:

> We do not call a person 'educated' who has simply mastered a skill, even though
> the skill may be very highly prized such as pottery. For a man to be 'educated',
> it is insufficient that he should possess a mere know-how or knack. He must
> have also some body of knowledge and some kind of a conceptual scheme to
> raise this above the level of a collection of disjointed facts. . . . 'Education' implies
> that a man's outlook is transformed by what he knows (whereas) 'training'
> suggests the acquisition of appropriate appraisals and habits of response in
> limited conventional situations (and) lacks the wider cognitive implications of
> 'education'.[8]

More recently, it has become fashionable to argue that there should be a 'breaking down' or 'moderation' of the harsh distinction between education and training. This is part of the justification for the Technical and Vocational Education Initiative put forward by the TVEI project director for Birmingham, in an article in *Forum* in 1984:

What we are striving to develop within TVEI is a loosening of the subject-bound curricular strait-jacket; a moderation of the harsh distinction between education and training; and an approach to the presentation of the curriculum that more readily generates the motivation and builds the confidence of many young people from the age of fourteen to eighteen.[9]

Lord Young has certainly not found it easy to sustain a consistent stance on this subject. In an article for the journal of the Institute of Directors published in October 1982, he argued that 'training should not be confused with education. Training is about work-related skills and is intimately connected with employment'.[10] Yet by the time he was interviewed on the BBC Radio Four *Brainwaves* programme in September 1986, he appeared to have changed his mind quite radically: 'Of course, the difference between education and training is very slight. . . . Training is merely the practical application of education.'

For Holt, the issue is simple and clear-cut:

A fundamental decision we have to make about education is whether it should transform the mind so as to equip us for independent judgement and rational action, or whether it should be directed towards practical skills for particular ends. This is the distinction between liberal education – education for freedom, for tackling problems as yet unknown – and schooling as training, for instrumental tasks as they are currently perceived.[11]

This is an important perspective on the present situation, but, couched in these terms, it is also a view which can, perhaps, be interpreted rather too easily as an assertion that *all* education is good and *all* training is bad. It is probably sensible to opt for definitions that are fair to both concepts. Education can then be seen as an open-ended process with the aim of transforming a student's view of the world; and training as the correct term for tasks where there are clearly pre-specifiable objectives with identifiable criteria for right and wrong. A trained doctor or a trained pilot can be defined as a person who has mastered certain specific skills, which does not mean she or he is necessarily an educated person in the wider sense.

If these definitions have any validity, it follows that education and training are different but not mutually exclusive. It can also be argued that many worthwhile activities and experiences in schools may be a mixture of both education and training – particularly if training at school level is seen as the process of instruction in specific skills thought to be useful acquisitions for *all* potential citizens. What would seem to have no place in a worthwhile 11–16 curriculum is a popular concept of training which is narrowly vocational in the sense of being simply preparation for work. It has been all too easy to see training as a low-level activity, as an alternative to experiences that are genuinely 'educational'. What we have become accustomed to is a system divided along lines of class: according to Green, all the government employment and

37

training initiatives of recent years have been based on the idea that you educate the middle class . . . and train the working class.[12]

NEW VOCATIONALISM OR NEW EDUCATION?

The government's training strategy is part of the whole philosophy of what has been called the New Vocationalism. But here again we have a difficult problem of terminology. What do such terms as vocationalism, the New Vocationalism, and a vocationalized curriculum actually mean?

When politicians and employers talk glibly about the need for courses of a *vocational* nature for specified groups of young people, they are clearly using a term which is capable of many different interpretations. For one thing, it is not to be confused with the noun from which it comes. *The Collins English Dictionary*, for example, defines 'vocation' as both a specified occupation, profession, or trade, and as a special urge, inclination, or predisposition to a particular calling or career, especially a religious one. Deriving from the Latin words *vocatio* (a calling) or *vocare* (to call), it is this second nobler, perhaps even bourgeois, meaning which is in use when one talks of someone having a vocation to become a priest or nurse or teacher. It has nothing to do with the cruder notion of simply preparing someone for 'the world of work'. Indeed, it can be argued that both original definitions have been lost since current training strategies are explicitly concerned with training for work in general and not preparation for a particular job. Then again, there are clearly 'vocational' aspects to traditional 'academic' education which are rarely acknowledged when the concepts 'vocational' and 'academic' are treated as being mutually exclusive. And it is also clear that vocational *education* is not the same as vocational *training*. In its wider sense of learning about, rather than preparing for, the world of employment, there is certainly a place for vocational *education* in the secondary curriculum. But this is not the sense in which *vocational* courses are currently being advocated.

In January 1976, an article by Arnold Weinstock, managing director of the General Electric Company, was published in The *Times Educational Supplement*. Entitled 'I blame the teachers', it alleged that the shortage of skilled workers, especially in engineering, could be attributed to the 'anti-industry' attitudes of many teachers. Since such teachers usually lacked any direct experience of industry, it was deplorable that they were able to propagate views based on their hostility *and* inexperience. Their freedom to influence the young, without any external control over their teaching and without any accountability to society at large, was, for Weinstock, the key to the current malaise. The situation could be remedied only when schools saw it as their chief function to be concerned with the deliberate and selective preparation of the future labour force.

Ten years later, these views were being echoed by Parry Rogers, Chairman of the Institute of Directors and newly-appointed Chairman of BTEC, in an article in *Manpower Policy and Practice*:

> We have gone astray . . . in what we expect of our educational system. It has been allowed to live in a private world of its own and to become an end in itself. In this information age, it must be redirected to being an integral part of our economic system; its job is to supply to the world of employment the human skills that are – and will be – needed. . . . The pursuit of knowledge for its own sake is a commendable goal and so is the fulfilment of an individual's educational desires, but these are examples of wealth consumption which can be afforded only when the wealth-creating task has been accomplished.[13]

This, then, is the basic premiss of the New Vocationalism: that schools have been allowed to fail in their responsibility to the nation's economy. For too long, according to this view, the emphasis in schools has been on education rather than training leading to the inevitable consequences of an inefficient workforce and youth unemployment on a massive scale. To remedy the situation, schools must abandon whole areas of the traditional curriculum and equip pupils with the necessary basic skills and attitudes to enter work. This is the view being promulgated by employers and industrialists in a wide range of articles and speeches and by DES and MSC officials in a whole series of White Papers and policy documents. Yet it can be argued that their programme for redefining the content and purposes of education is as one-sided as the one they seek to replace: a narrow emphasis upon practical and vocational learning simply replaces what, in their view, was a narrow emphasis upon cognitive skills and academic achievement. The New Vocationalism may avail itself of the rhetoric of curriculum relevance and personal development but is actually intended to meet the interests of the owners of capital.

According to Ranson, Taylor and Brighouse in their introduction to *The Revolution in Education and Training*, published in 1986, the New Vocationalism is only one of two mainstream philosophies associated with the current revolution in the education and training of 14–19-year-olds. We are, in their view, experiencing a Janus-headed revolution. The emphasis upon practical and vocational learning can be seen as an essentially retrograde step encouraging selection and a narrow utilitarian experience. But there *is* an alternative perspective with many positive aspects. This can be called 'the new education', and it rejects selection either of student or of curriculum content while, at the same time, seeking to design learning experiences which meet the needs of each young person or adult.

> The new education argues that traditional schooling has been straight-jacketed by an unduly limited conception of academic achievement. Passing exams may not adequately test cognitive skills, let alone assess other aspects of personal development. By celebrating practical, creative and social skills, the new pedagogy

seeks to acknowledge and to reinforce the diversity of human capacity. There is an important attempt here to redefine what counts as achievement. The new education pursues a policy of whole curriculum planning for whole people and seeks to weaken the boundaries between areas of experience so as to integrate the curriculum.[14]

Ranson, Taylor, and Brighouse argue rightly that the current framework of 16–19 education and training in no way reflects the high ideals of the 'new education'. What we have at tertiary level is a rigid differentiation of routes for young people, with advanced level courses constituting a grammar stream, TVEI and BTEC (Business and Technician Education Council) programmes representing a technical track, and the YTS (Youth Training Scheme) and CPVE (Certificate of Pre-Vocational Education) providing a further extension of vocationalism in the tertiary modern curriculum. Where the authors are sadly misinformed is in suggesting that differentiation 'has almost been eliminated from secondary education'. If anything, the situation at secondary level is moving steadily towards less coherence and even greater differentiation.

The 1985 Document *Better Schools* acknowledged that the new GCSE (General Certificate of Secondary Education) with its first candidates in 1988 would be only one of a number of examinations competing for the custom of aspiring sixteen-year-olds.

> Some schools prepare for pre-vocational examinations other than O level and CSE (e.g.: those of the City and Guilds of London Institute, the Royal Society of Arts, and the Business and Technician Education Council) during the years of compulsory schooling. Such courses will continue to be available to complement GCSE examinations as well, in the service of a curriculum which is broad, balanced, relevant, and differentiated in accordance with pupils' abilities. (paragraph 99)

The Joint Board for Pre-Vocational Education, set up in May 1983 to administer the new CPVE, was soon preparing its own plans for the 14–18 age range. A press release was issued in January 1984 to announce that:

> BTEC and CGLI see their decision to adopt a joint approach to pre-vocational education as a major contribution to helping schools and colleges provide young people with a more effective transition from school to work. The two bodies want to create a new curriculum pathway for that majority of those between the ages of 14 and 18 for whom the traditional academic curriculum is unsuitable.

This was followed by a further statement in September 1985 announcing that:

> the Councils of BTEC and City and Guilds have agreed jointly to develop and operate a new pre-vocational provision for students aged 14–16 which will offer a national alternative to traditional subject-based school courses.

And these resulted in the publication of *The framework description of BTEC – City and Guilds pre-vocational programmes for pupils aged 14–16* in May 1986.

Not that the age of 14 is necessarily thought to be early enough to begin the process of differentiation in schools. Lord Young and the Education Secretary, Kenneth Baker, were quoted in June 1986 as agreeing that 'greater emphasis must be placed in schools on vocational training from the age of 11 – at least for less bright pupils – to give them a better chance of finding work'. This would mean that 'academic school work would be afforded a lower priority for the less bright and that more "training for work" classes would be encouraged'.[15] And in a *Weekend World* television interview at the beginning of December 1986, the Education Secretary argued that education for 'the bottom 40 per cent' should be more 'vocational' from the age of 11 or 12. It remains to be seen to what extent plans for 'new curriculum pathways' will be effectively blocked by the implementation of a subject-based national curriculum.

CONCLUSION: THE AIMS OF EDUCATION AND TRAINING

At a European Conference in May 1985 on 'Education and training for young people aged 16 to 19: problems and prospects', a resolution adopted by the delegates argued that 'education and training should aim to encourage a creative and versatile attitude to active life and especially a willingness and ability to learn and to adjust to change throughout life'.[16] Simon would wish to go further than this and stress the role of education and training in enabling youngsters not merely to *adjust* to change but to play an active part in *facilitating* and *promoting* it:

> Schools have the function of deliberately promoting not only the skills of numeracy and literacy, but, through a progressively deepening grasp of knowledge and culture, the autonomy of the student able to function effectively within society, and to use his or her abilities to change that society according to developing aspirations.[17]

There has been an ideological conflict between those concerned with transforming the social order and those concerned with improving its effectiveness for at least the last hundred years. In America, just after the turn of the century, it took the form of a debate between the educationist John Dewey and those who argued for educational reform in the interests of social control. In the words of Dewey:

> The kind of education in which I am interested is not one which will adapt workers to the existing industrial regime; I am not sufficiently in love with the regime for that. It seems to me that the business of all those who would not be educational time-servers is to resist every move in this direction, and to strive for a kind of vocational education which will first alter the existing industrial system, and ultimately transform it.[18]

41

This could not be said to represent a popular view among members of the present government but it remains a respectable and humane vision of the true purpose of education and training.

NOTES

1. See for example, Maurice Holt, 'Vocationalism: the new threat to universal education', *Forum* 25,3 (Summer 1983): 84–6; Denis Lawton, 'Education and training: issues for further enquiry', *Report on proceedings*, Liaison seminar no. 1 (10 May 1985), Post Sixteen Education Centre, University of London Institute of Education: 3–10; Clyde Chitty, 'TVEI: the MSC's trojan horse', in Caroline Benn and John Fairley (Eds.) (1986) *Challenging the MSC; on jobs, education and training*, London: Pluto Press: 76–98; Jerry Wellington, 'Skills for the future?: Vocational education and new technology', in Maurice Holt (Ed.) (1987) *Skills and Vocationalism: The Easy Answer*, Milton Keynes: Open University Press: 21–42.
2. David Reeder, 'A recurring debate: education and industry' in Gerald Bernbaum (Ed.) (1979) *Schooling in Decline*, London: Macmillan: 115–48.
3. Department of Education and Science (DES) (July 1977) *Education in schools: a consultative document* (Green Paper) Cmnd. 6869, London: HMSO: 34.
4. Department of Employment (D of E) (December 1981) *A new training initiative: a programme for action*, Cmnd. 8455, London: HMSO: 5.
5. Jerry Wellington, 'Skills for the future?: Vocational education and new technology' in Maurice Holt (Ed.) (1987): 23.
6. Department of Education and Science (DES), (March 1985) *Better Schools*, Cmnd. 9469, London: HMSO: 15.
7. Denis Lawton, op. cit. p.3.
8. R. S. Peters (1966) *Ethics and education*, London: George Allen & Unwin: 30, 31, 33.
9. C. J. Lea, 'Vocational focus', *Forum* 26,2 (Spring 1984): 47–8.
10. David Young, 'Worried about Unemployment? How you can help. . . .', *The Director* (October 1982): 34–5.
11. Maurice Holt, op. cit. pp.84–6.
12. Andy Green, 'Education and training: under new masters' in Ann Marie Wolpe and James Donald (Eds.) (1983) *Is There Anyone Here from Education?*, London: Pluto Press: 61.
13. Parry Rogers, 'Vocational education: first define the task', *Manpower policy and practice: the IMS review* 2,3 (Spring 1987): 17–18.
14. Stewart Ranson, Barry Taylor, and Tim Brighouse (Eds.) (1986) *The Revolution in Education and Training*, Harlow: Longman: 3–4.
15. 'Wet-dry axis on education', The *Sunday Telegraph*, 15 June 1986.
16. Council of Europe (1986) *Education and training for young people aged 16 to 19: problems and prospects*, Report on the 14th session of the Standing Conference of European Ministers of Education (Brussels, 7–9 May 1985): 20.
17. Brian Simon, 'Education and the right offensive', *Marxism Today*, February 1980: 7–13.
18. John Dewey, *The New Republic*, 5 May 1915.

PROGRESSIVISM AND INDIVIDUAL NEEDS

JOHN DARLING

In education, 'progressivism' is a term equivalent to the British notion of 'child-centred' education, or the American idea of 'open' education. While many of the ideas associated with these terms may be applicable to educational practice in a variety of contexts, a preliminary indication of what is involved in progressivism can probably best be given by examining the way in which education currently proceeds in many primary schools.

Suppose that a modern primary school is visited by someone whose only previous experience of primary education has been as a pupil in the 1950s or earlier. The first surprise that will register with such a visitor will be the sound emerging from the school. Primary education used to be conducted in silence: all that could be heard was teachers' voices. Today there are audible sounds of activity and discussion. Entering a classroom, today's visitor sees that children are sitting round tables or have their desks pushed together in a way that facilitates conversation. Partly this shows the teacher's recognition that social intercourse is natural: prohibition is inappropriate and seems, at least for much of the time, unnecessary. Partly the teacher may view pupil interaction as an educationally profitable enterprise – 'working together', a skill which more traditional forms of schooling have tended to neglect except on the games field.

There is a second way in which communication has become easier. Teachers are now less likely to be held in awe by their pupils than they used to be. This reduction of the psychological barrier between teacher and taught means that children are less reluctant to ask for help with difficulties and at the same time can make decisions and take initiatives on their own without fear of repercussions. Permission need not be sought for moving from one's seat for legitimate purposes like the consultation of books. More generally, the absence of fear means that it is easier for the teacher to build good personal relationships with the pupils.

These new patterns of classroom life reflect a more fundamental change in the way education is conceived: they are the practical tip of the iceberg of progressive educational theory. This theory is not a new one. The earliest influential version was expounded by Jean-Jacques Rousseau in *Emile* in 1762 in which Rousseau declared:

> Nature provides for the child's growth in her own fashion, and this should never be thwarted.

This approach to thinking about children and their education was taken forward by such writers as Pestalozzi and Froebel, John Dewey, and William Kilpatrick. Each of these writers knew of the work of his predecessors, and developed or revised, sometimes quite critically, what had already been said. In Britain, the influence of these thinkers, beyond the world of ideas, was for a long time very limited. From the 1920s, however, increasing numbers of people working in the school system were becoming interested, until in the 1960s progressivism was publicly endorsed by official reports of which the best known are *Primary Education in Scotland* (the 'Primary Memorandum', 1965) and *Children and their Primary Schools* (the 'Plowden Report', 1967).

If this body of educational theory was available for a couple of centuries, why did it have to wait till the 1960s before it had a really significant influence on classroom practice? There are several features of this period which either facilitated or positively encouraged this development.

One important enabling condition was that at this time the UK enjoyed widespread prosperity. Unemployment was low and parents had every reason to assume that when their children left school they would be able to get jobs without much difficulty. Where there is anxiety about employment there tends to be pressure on schools to pursue narrow vocational ends. Where the reverse holds, parents are prepared to entertain broader goals for their children's development and they become less apprehensive about innovative approaches.

What gave positive encouragement to the introduction of progressive education in this period was a new climate of ideas described by its critics as 'permissive'. First, there was an increased emphasis on individuals and their right to self-determination – to choose, to think, to decide for themselves. The converse of this was a heady truculence towards authority figures and an enthusiasm for exposing their pretensions. The police, and even the royal family, were openly criticized, and politicians *en bloc* were derided and ridiculed. The exercise of authority became a fraught and uncomfortable business since respect could no longer be taken for granted. In this new social climate a move away from authoritarian styles of teaching became inevitable.

More pertinent, perhaps, to our treatment of children was the increased acceptance of Freudian strictures on repressiveness. While the general public knew as little as ever about Freud, there was a broad acceptance of the idea that

44

harsh discipline or undue restraint imposed on the young was not conducive to healthy emotional development but was likely to have undesirable repercussions. Adults themselves felt a new entitlement to the good things in life, including sexual gratification – a goal which required the overthrowing of old taboos and personal inhibitions. School was seen as having been instrumental in fostering a mindless acceptance of traditional morality. For their children, people now expected something better and more positive.

These, then, were optimal conditions for the advance of educational progressivism in schools. In attempting now to characterize this set of ideas, it will be helpful to bear in mind that progressive educational theory has to be understood as stemming from radical dissatisfaction with traditional practice. A necessary preliminary, therefore, to producing an intelligible outline of progressivism, is to bring to mind the nature of the traditional, subject-centred, teacher-directed approach to education – or at least the nature of this approach as it is portrayed, fairly or otherwise, by progressives themselves.

In terms of curriculum content this is taken to involve first the systematic imparting of basic skills in language and numerical calculation, followed by instruction in a range (usually broad at first and narrow later) of established school subjects. Mastery of factual information is emphasized. In pedagogical terms, the traditional approach involves the teacher expounding the subject, and instructing the whole class at once. Pupil motivation depends on compliance and competition: there is no resort to devices which might convert tedium into fun. Gritty application and memory work are regarded as unavoidable and perhaps as constituting beneficial preparation for adult life. Support for progressivism depends in large measure on the view that this traditional approach has had very limited success.

Progressive reactions to the traditional approach have been by no means uniform. What follows therefore is not, and could not be, a definitive summary of progressivism: rather, it identifies some central, recurring themes in the alternative tradition.

As a starting point, progressives see themselves as having taught us an appreciation of children as individuals. Their focus is less on what each might become and more on what each already is. This does not, however, entail a static conception of education. Indeed, quite the reverse: progressive writing exudes an awareness of children's growth and development. In progressive education, however, children's educational development is not understood in terms of things that should be known, rules that must be followed, or adult characteristics that ought to be adopted. Children's development is seen as a gradual and 'natural' progression which is best aided by adults who have an appreciation of and a respect for the ways of children. Childhood, it is insisted, is not a defective version of adulthood: if it were, all schooling would have to be thought of as one long remedial course. Sometimes progressivism's positive

45

valuing of the state of childhood has been coupled with a relative devaluing of adulthood; and perhaps it does no harm for educators to be reminded of some of the demerits of adult character and adult society. In *Democracy and Education*, Dewey observes:

> With respect to sympathetic curiosity, unbiased responsiveness, and openness of mind, we may say that the adult should be growing in childlikeness.

Further, progressives emphasize that it is in the nature of the child to be active. Traditionalists are seen either as being unaware of this central characteristic, or as seeing it as something regrettable, or as preferring not to take it into account in their approach to education. This neglect can be seen in simple form in the insistence that children remain seated at their desks for most of the school day. More serious, perhaps, is the treatment of children as *mentally* inactive, as the passive (and often reluctant) recipients of knowledge provided by teachers.

The progressive view is that education should be designed to reflect the nature of the child. Importance is therefore attached to the study of children. The findings of educational psychology as well as common observation are seen as showing that, contrary to the assumptions implicit in traditional practice, children are intellectually curious, keen to find things out, and actively engaged in making sense of the world they live in. This picture explains why progressives prefer to think of education in terms of 'natural' development: the nature of the child, it seems, is geared towards learning.

Another side of this claim about children is that they are natural doers, makers, and creators. Schools should cater for this by providing opportunities and materials for a range of physical activity and creative work. This has been much taken to heart in primary schools in one very obvious way: the provision for art work. The displays of paintings in classrooms and corridors show the positive value attached to children's work. Progressive teachers expect such painting to be 'spontaneous' rather than created by the conscious application of taught technique. This reflects their positive estimation of each child's inherent talents, and their regard for the way the personality of each is expressed. Progressivism is not just a respecter of childhood, but a respecter of individual children and their differences. Diversity is welcomed as something that makes life richer: hence there is in progressivism a built-in suspicion of the kind of schooling which puts pressure on children to conform. The Plowden Report speaks of the model primary school as a place which allows children 'to be themselves'.

Where does this leave the teacher? If all this developing, discovering, and creating is going to take place anyway, are teachers still necessary? There are, at the very least, implications for the teacher's role which point to the need for a change in style. The job can no longer be one of imparting a fixed body of valuable knowledge. If education is to be essentially a response to the enquiring mind of the child, the teacher's role would be better understood as one of research consultant or manager of resources. In American terminology, the teacher becomes primarily a 'facilitator'. As with any kind of investigative learning, this approach requires that children be given considerable freedom and independence. Learning cannot be interpreted as 'finding out for oneself' if the learner is always to be confined to a desk or even to a classroom. Progressive teachers must be able to accommodate this enlarged freedom and monitor the use that is made of it – no small task if a teacher has responsibility for twenty or thirty children. On the other hand, if it is true that children are naturally eager to learn, there is *prima facie* reason to be optimistic about the feasibility of this approach. Teachers would theoretically be relieved of the burden of having to coax and nag children into intellectual activity. The exercise of authority would be little required except for sorting out the kind of inter-personal difficulties that arise from time to time within any institutional group.

It is about this point in progressive educational theory that some teachers begin to feel that the pedagogical implications fail to match reality as they experience it. Many children in classrooms do not display eagerness to learn, nor do they respond positively to the opportunities which teachers organize for them. Teachers often feel compelled to resort to incentives and disincentives, to a system of sticks and carrots: their experience convinces them that abandoning these strategies for a liberal non-authoritarian regime would produce a classroom situation where little of educational value occurred. Recognizing the substance of the sceptic's reaffirmation of the reality of life in so many classrooms, progressives offer two different diagnoses of what they see as a pathological situation. Both explanations attempt to reconcile the progressive claim that children have a natural intellectual curiosity with the feeling that in school children are often minimally motivated.

The first claim is that children *become* reluctant learners because of their experience of schooling. Progressive pedagogy cannot readily be introduced with a class of children who have previously been exposed to traditional teaching. Even without actually experiencing authoritarian and didactic approaches, children come to school with the expectation that they will receive instruction and will not be able to do as they see fit: parents tell them this, and the whole image of school in our culture transmits this message. Once children see education as something that other people do to them, so it is argued, they lose the ability to take any initiative or responsibility for their own learning.

The second explanation is given in curricular rather than in pedagogical terms. There is said to be a mismatch between what children want to find out and what teachers think they ought to learn. In particular the kinds of enquiry

47

that children naturally pursue are not reflected in the way traditional schooling categorizes knowledge into different 'subjects'. It is this lack of correspondence which accounts for children's low motivation. In fact, primary schools have now moved some distance away from a subject-based curriculum at least in the sense that few have timetabled periods with bells ringing every forty minutes. The primary curriculum has become much more fluid and flexible, with the non-disciplinary 'project' a significant vehicle for enquiry-based learning in many classrooms. But if subject boundaries are to be collapsed or ignored, is there a new guiding principle for shaping the curriculum?

The progressive answer is that if the school is to be made to fit the child rather than the other way round, the curriculum should be determined by the child's needs and interests. This dictum, however, is not unproblematic, as consideration of 'interests' and 'needs' will show.

An interest-based curriculum could be understood to mean a number of different things. At its most radical it might mean allowing children to do whatever they want to do: given a free choice, children will opt for whatever interests them most. Few schools have moved very far down this particular road. Such a policy is at odds with the entrenched idea that a curriculum consists of certain kinds of knowledge and activities which are prescribed for children by society or by tradition or by teachers, but which are certainly not selected by children themselves.

Alternatively, interest might be accorded a more modest, if still crucial, place. An interest-based curriculum might be interpreted as one which starts from and uses children's existing interests. Many boys are interested in their local football club, its activities and its league record: it is not hard to see how this could be exploited to extend their awareness of the country's geography and history. Skilful teachers may employ the strategy of linking what they want children to learn to their existing interests, hoping that by association children will become interested in whatever subject matter is being introduced. Some see this as a recipe for manipulation and deviousness in teachers; others accept it as an important part of a teacher's professional expertise.

It appears reasonable to claim that to take no account of a child's existing interests is to show scant respect for the person that the child already is. On the other hand, there seems no good reason to accept a child's established interests as limiting the range of his or her school activities. No individual's interests are innate or immutable: they are socially learned – sometimes from parents, sometimes from peers, sometimes from television or the culture at large. It would seem unwise to exclude that well-educated person, the teacher, from this group of influential contacts. In fact, one thing that we might reasonably expect schooling to do for pupils is to *extend* their interests: the hope is that they will *acquire* an interest in things deemed valuable by the teacher or by society. One of the highest commendations for a teacher is to

48

be recognized as someone who can 'get pupils interested'. A belief which is often associated with this kind of talk is that children learn best when they are interested: the converse of this is that where coercion or bribery is relied on to motivate pupils, real learning is unlikely to take place (though the plausibility of such a view may depend on how 'real learning' is defined).

A similar thought sometimes underlies the desire to tailor the curriculum to children's needs. Neglect of these can be seen as offering an explanation for a particular curriculum failing to produce satisfactory results. Thus, the Schools Council Working Paper No. 11 observed:

> ... a frequent cause of failure seems to be that the course is often based on the traditional belief that there is a body of content for each separate subject which every school-leaver should know. In the least successful courses this body of knowledge is written into the curriculum without any real consideration of the needs of the boys and girls. ...

While this kind of argument has a degree of plausibility, it would be unduly optimistic to suppose that a curriculum which was carefully geared to meeting pupils' needs would eliminate problems of pupil motivation. The relationship between need and motivation is not a sufficiently direct one. Even though I know that I *need* dental treatment, I may feel strongly tempted to cancel my appointment with the dentist if I have an aversion to that kind of experience. To get from existing needs to appropriate action can require strength of will and an ability to overrule disinclination in favour of long-term benefits. Clearly, however, young children cannot be expected to be motivated by very distant gains.

A further difficulty in basing a curriculum on children's needs is the problem of knowing who should define what a child's educational needs are. At the beginning of *Primary Education in Scotland* we are told:

> The suggestions now being made are based on what is known of the growth and development of the child, and emphasis is laid on the importance of fashioning the curriculum according to his needs at the various stages of his development.

This suggests that for the identification of needs progressivism is likely to turn to developmental psychology. It is worth remembering here that the identification of a need does not always require an expert. We all know that if a man is starving he needs food. But it is true that we often expect scientists, including psychologists and doctors, to tell us what we need. Suppose a scientist insists that we all need fresh air, exercise, and vitamin X. The natural question to ask is, what do we need these things *for*? If the answer is, to prevent premature senility and disintegration of the knees, we shall readily agree that fresh air, exercise, and vitamin X are among our needs. Just as it is better to have some food than to starve to death, it is obviously very undesirable to have knees or minds that refuse to function.

In education, however, there is likely to be disagreement about what it is to enjoy educational health or to be educationally well-nourished. Another way of putting the same point is to say that there appears to be no consensus about the kind of person we want education to produce: some people, for example, will demand that schools foster the acceptance of conventional social norms; others will emphasize encouraging pupils to develop independence of mind. Thus, identification of educational needs cannot proceed independently of a consideration of educational aims and values. What, after all, is the difference between claiming (as the Primary Memorandum does) that children have a need for understanding, and asserting (as the Primary Memorandum also does) that in education the promotion of understanding is a fundamental aim? Disagreements about aims, however, reflect differences over values: consequently this is not an area where we can appeal to psychologists for a scientific judgement.

This has led to one further charge being levelled at the use of the concept of 'need': needs-talk is ultimately vacuous because it offers no basis for judging one kind of curriculum to be preferable to another. Where a vocationally-oriented curriculum is favoured, it can be said that such a curriculum is desirable because of the pupil's need to be financially self-supporting. If one advocates a curriculum which gives priority to the promotion of spiritual development, then one is claiming that spiritual development is the child's overriding need. If any curriculum can be construed or defended as a needs-based curriculum, it might indeed seem that the injunction to base the curriculum on the needs of the child offers no positive guidance.

There are two possible ways this charge might be met. It might be argued that 'need' points to something fairly basic, and that many things that are educationally valuable are not in this category. What, it might be asked, is a knowledge of Shakespeare necessary *for*? The assumption in such an argument is that a needs-based curriculum should be understood to mean providing learners with essential skills – a kind of personal survival kit. While this is at least meaningful in the sense that it excludes a range of learning that makes no useful contribution to such an end, it is not the kind of curriculum that appeals to many progressives who, as we have seen, are likely to stress the importance of schools catering for the child's need for self-expression and independent discovery.

The other possible response to the charge of vacuousness is to shift the emphasis from the *needs* of the child to the needs of the *child*, and to stress that children's needs must be given priority over the needs of industry (or of the state, the party, the church or whatever). In a convenient world, of course, there might be no conflict between these different aims. However, one has to allow for the possibility (and surely it is more than a possibility) that sometimes one of these aims will have to be given priority over the others. The progressive view is that the needs of the individual child must come first.

Partly this position is seen as stemming from a moral commitment to the children for whom the educator is responsible. A pupil ought to be respected as a person, not for his or her potential as a future contributor to the national economy. But further, the insistence on attending to the child's needs involves a reaffirmation of the importance of making education 'harmonize' with the nature of the child: for where there is a mismatch between the nature of schooling and the nature of children, it is believed that education will make little headway. As has already been noted, guidance on the nature of the child has customarily been sought from psychologists. Progressivism has thus been seen as having a dual basis in ethics and scientific psychology – a combination which may appear irresistible or suspect according to taste!

In fact, however, psychologists seldom see themselves as making pronouncements about the nature of the child. And where such views appear in psychological writing, rival accounts have tended to emerge. Further, thinkers with a non-scientific bent have their own different perspectives on the nature of the child: whether children are seen as intelligent machines or immortal souls will make an important difference to how their needs are understood. This chapter has outlined the picture of children favoured by progressives: for many educators this portrayal has been a persuasive one. But it should be clear that progressivism, like any other set of educational prescriptions, is not a scientific theory but an ideology.

FURTHER READING

Barth, R. S. (1975) 'Open education: assumptions about children', in M. Golby, J. Greenwald and R. West (Eds.) *Curriculum Design*, London: Croom Helm.

Central Advisory Council for Education (English) (1967) *Children and their Primary Schools* (The Plowden Report), London: HMSO.

Darling, J. (1986) 'Child-centred, gender-centred: a criticism of progressive curriculum theory from Rousseau to Plowden', *Oxford Review of Education* 12,1.

Dearden, R. F. (1968) *The Philosophy of Primary Education*, London: Routledge & Kegan Paul.

Entwistle, H. (1970) *Child-Centred Education*, London: Methuen.

Galton, M. (1987) 'Change and continuity in the primary school', *Oxford Review of Education*, 13,1.

Kogan, M. (1987) 'The Plowden Report twenty years on', *Oxford Review of Education*, 13,1.

Scottish Education Department (1965) *Primary Education in Scotland* (The Primary Memorandum), Edinburgh: HMSO.

Wilson, P. S. (1971) *Interest and Discipline in Education*, London: Routledge & Kegan Paul.

I.5

LIBERAL EDUCATION RECONSIDERED

CHARLES BAILEY

It is timely to reconsider the notion of liberal education for a number of reasons. Perhaps the most important of these is the currency of the debate, in many countries, about the content, methodology, and purpose of an education which is intended to be at once compulsory, universally available, and comprehensively equitable in terms of some principle of justice. One group in this debate sees education as instrumentally serving alleged social needs of an economic kind. The other sees education in some wider sense as less directly instrumental, more intrinsically worthwhile, more to do with liberation than with preformation and predetermination, and more to do with the development of critically autonomous persons than with the production of socially convenient conformists, however technically sophisticated these may be.

Debates, however, are one thing and power struggles are another. A potent reason for an urgent refurbishing of the notion of liberal education is that liberal educators, caught without any clear formulation of their intuitively held view, and burdened with many negative signals from the expression 'liberal education', are losing the power struggle for education. At least this seems clearly the case in Britain. Some traditional images of liberal education are seen by many influential people in government, industry, and commerce, and even in trade unions and the labour movement, not as ideals to be pursued, riches to be equally available to all, but hindrances and encumbrances to the proper preparation of people trained and disposed to form a virile and technically competitive nation. Such hindrances therefore, say the powerful, are to be swept away and replaced by an education which emphasizes training, industrial and commercial needs, capability, and vocational motivation and orientation. In Britain there has been a steady push in this direction which most commentators agree dates from the speech by James Callaghan, the then Labour Prime Minister, at Ruskin College, Oxford, in 1976. If the push to instrumentalize general education is to be reversed, a clear formulation and justification of liberal education in modern terms is necessary, if not entirely sufficient, as a condition of that achievement.

There is a further reason for a serious reappraisal at the present time. I refer to a debate, less topical than the debate over vocationalism, more difficult to discuss in brief compass, but nevertheless of great importance. Many Marxist writers on education (for example Althusser 1971; Harris 1979) deride the notion of liberal education, at least in any genuinely liberating sense, because they believe that in any capitalist society, however ostensibly liberal and demo- cratic, the educational system can never do more than service, as it were, the dominant capitalist ideology and reproduce the human productive require- ments of such a society. What the Marxist critics would have educators do is not very clear. What a modern theory of liberal education must do, however, is clear enough: it must take the Marxist critique seriously whilst showing the power of a truly liberal education to liberate from dominant ideologies as well as from other restrictions and constraints of the human mind. (See Bailey 1984: 205–28.)

Liberal political philosophers have become increasingly aware in recent years of the significance of the place and characterization of liberal education in their theories. John Stuart Mill, of course, was well aware that the kind of knowledge passed on to the young, the way in which it was passed on, and the control and direction of education were all issues of importance to him as a liberal philosopher. I have more in mind, however, contemporary political and moral philosophers like John Rawls (1971), Alan Gewirth (1978), and Bruce Ackerman (1980). Their interest in education derives from the idea that if a person is to be considered as having some right to pursue his or her own purposes and maintain self esteem in a framework of liberty only con- strained by equal liberties for all others, then certain conditions must obtain. These conditions, necessary to operate as a free agent and to esteem oneself as such, would include freedom, knowledge, education, wealth, and income in at least some minimum sense. Education is significant here because of the unique way in which it is both a prerequisite and an implication of the other conditions. Thus these philosophers have found it necessary to give increasing consideration to education's place and significance in the liberal state.

This is most clearly exemplified in the work of Bruce Ackerman, who finds it impossible to give an adequate account of the liberal state without devoting a considerable part of his book to the appropriate treatment of children in the family and in the school.

We should not be surprised to see this concern with education on the part of writers dealing mainly with the philosophy of morals and politics. Such writers are not simply polemicists for democracy or whatever. Rather they are trying to work out and justify the principles which should govern a society in which persons are to be respected as, in some sense, autonomous moral agents.

In order to do this they must respect and use reason in two ways. First, by its use in making their arguments as cogent, as coherent, and as consistent as possible. Second, by building into the principles they seek to justify the idea that morality, justice, and the good society themselves involve the reasonable treatment of persons by persons, and that this in turn involves the proposal of institutional arrangements for developing, maintaining, and protecting the personal use of reason. Among other things this implies an educational system that will help all young persons to become rational, autonomous agents to whatever extent is practically possible given the constraints of economic circumstance and individual difference.

This has not always been the rationale within which the characterization of education as 'liberal' was located. Aristotle, whilst considered by many as fathering the notion of liberal education, clearly saw it as an education only appropriate for those already free, and therefore not for women or for those who by virtue of slavery did 'mechanical' work (Aristotle 1984: 2113–29). Similarly the conception has suffered from its association with the idea of an education suitable for 'the English gentleman' or those aspiring to such status (Rothblatt 1976: *passim*). History has therefore shackled the idea of liberal education with associations which militate against the valuing of the idea in an age charged with both democratic and technological assumptions. Liberal education is seen as elitist, non-practical, basically useless, and connected with perverse ambitions of social mobility via socially divisive grammar, gymnasia, lycée-type schools of a selective kind. How could such an idea have currency in a society paying at least lip-service to the idea of equality, and believing especially in equal education for all?

Present-day advocates of liberal education, however, *do* see such education as helping all children and young people to achieve more rather than less freedom of choice of action and belief as they approach adulthood. The implications of this aspiration of political theorists like those already mentioned, in terms of curriculum content, arrangements for the grouping of pupils, and teaching styles and methods, are usually only vaguely adumbrated, at best only sketched. Others, as we shall see, have tried to put flesh on the skeleton.

The approach starts either from some idea of children's rights, or from what is perhaps (though I do not think so) only the other side of the coin, namely, the moral duty of adults towards children and young persons in the state. What is held here is that adults, parents, teachers, or other citizens, have no right to mould children within a framework of their own beliefs, customs, or social convenience and perceived need. The adult moral duty is clearly to help youngsters towards moral, intellectual, and actual autonomy. Ackerman, for example, whilst most clearly affirming the need for young children to have the security of early childhood in a family with a determinate cultural homogeneity and pattern, goes on to note the limits of rightful parental influence and the need for this to give way to the more impartial influence of the school. The cultural coherence which the child should find in the family is necessary in order for the child to develop 'an awesome series of cognitive, linguistic, and behavioral skills' which are the prerequisites of participation in the liberal dialogue Ackerman believes to be the ultimate rationale of the liberal state (Ackerman: 140–1).

This cultural homogeneity of the family is for Ackerman a necessary start to liberal education. It is not, however, a formula for its continuance. The *control* of the parents, appropriate to the maintenance of cultural coherence, must give way to the *guidance* necessary to start the development of autonomous powers; and this in turn must give way to the young person's own autonomy. Parents must not, under these liberal education assumptions, use 'their powers of guidance to mask their illegitimate desires for control' (Ackerman: 150).

The agency for the transfer from parental control and guidance, from a necessary cultural coherence, to the wider requirements of liberty in a liberal state, is the liberally educating school. The parents, says Ackerman, must acknowledge the right and the duty of others to 'provide the child with cultural materials with which she may forge the beginnings of an identity that deviates from parental norms'. These others are to be the secondary liberal educators, the teachers in the schools. Their aim is not to be a mere extension of the child's primary culture, but 'to provide the child with access to the wide range of cultural materials that he might find useful in developing his own moral ideas and patterns of life' (Ackerman: 153–6). The early days of such schooling must be handled with respect and sensitivity to the family primary culture from which the child is emerging, but should not be totally constrained by parental wishes and desires. Even if all parents saw the scenario as Ackerman does – an unlikely event – this would nevertheless be a time of tension, which he acknowledges. Four principles, or strategies, are suggested, which might ameliorate this somewhat, whilst also serving to characterize the liberal educator's task.

First, liberal educators should seek to teach things opening out prospects of belief and action at first not too far removed from the existing familiarities of the child. Second, liberal educators should avoid confident predictions of what the child's social needs are likely to be. The child should be equipped with such skills, and presumably with such knowledge and understanding, as will have wide and varied applications. More important even than the development of these generalizable skills will be the development of the child's autonomous moral judgement based upon an awareness of moral insights, other than those of the child's family, held by other groups in a liberal society. Third, there should be a proper focus of diagnosis which would have little to do with competitive comparison, success, failure, or promotion and demotion, but much to do with ensuring a steady, continuous, and widespread involvement in and knowledge of the 'dimensions of a liberal culture'. Over-confident prediction of cultural and social needs, and too much diagnosis of what the child is good or bad at, encourages a narrowing of focus and runs the danger of a number of significant areas of liberal knowledge, understanding, and practice becoming unavailable to the child, thereby diminishing the chances of a proper autonomy. Fourth, and implied by all of the foregoing, is the idea that eventually the pupil should become responsible for his own curriculum choices as he 'gains increasing familiarity with the range of cultural models open to him in a liberal society'. The teacher, like the parent at an earlier stage of liberal development, must also move from control to guidance. Both teachers and parents, as it were, work themselves out of business. They must become, if a relationship is to be maintained, adult companions, who may or may not have intellectual and moral advice to give, which may or may not be taken (Ackerman: 154–60).

Although the issues are not always put as clearly as in Ackerman, nor indeed argued as clearly, there is some measure of consensus, among avowed advocates of liberal education at least, that an education will be considered liberal to the extent that it helps pupils to become informed and rational free choosers of what to believe and what to do. There also appears to be consensus on the view that an education could not be considered liberal unless it was available in some real sense to all the children in the state. The consensus lessens perhaps as to the extent to which such an education necessitates a common curriculum for all, and still more as to whether and why it should be compulsory for all over a given number of years. Some writers have a notion of liberty, autonomy, and authenticity which makes it impossible almost by definition to embrace the idea of compulsion. (See for example Bonnett 1978 and Wilson 1971; for an interesting attempt to justify compulsion from a libertarian point of view see White 1973.) There has been considerable debate about the curriculum content of a liberal education, and to some extent about teaching styles and methods appropriate to liberal education, especially in connection with the nature and danger of indoctrination. On content there has been a plethora of prescription but rather fewer attempts at justification and argument. I shall consider two that do seek to argue.

Here the work of Paul Hirst is agreed by all to be seminal (Hirst 1974). Hirst's arguments gain their force and significance from a rigorous drive towards what is most fundamental. Hence his starting point is the value of reason itself, which is to be necessarily presupposed in the meaningful asking of justificatory questions. In other words, to ask questions like, 'Why should we educate people?' 'What should the curriculum of a liberal education contain?' is already to suppose the value of having reasons and reasoning on which the issues would be decided. The questions only have point on such a presupposition or assumption. If this is the case, then the most general and fundamental

education, and the one needing least justification of any particular or specialized kind, would be one which was itself the most free development of rational
minds. This would have two senses for Hirst in terms of justification. First,
he points to the oddity of seeking justification for the development of rationality, the presupposition of *all* justification; and, second, he argues that the
development of the rational mind 'in whatever form it freely takes' is the
necessary and most fundamental basis of any proper knowledge and understanding that can be acquired.

To have a rational mind, for Hirst, is not to possess a body of free-floating
skills which can, as it were, be turned on to anything. It is rather to have a
mind structured in a number of discriminately different ways which human
beings have evolved to make sense of their world as experienced. These
different ways of making sense of the world Hirst refers to as 'forms of
knowledge', a phrase that has become very well known among philosophers
of education and some teachers. There are two main characteristics which
make each form distinctive from each and every other form. Each form is held
to have unique and constituent central concepts, and each form is supposed
to have distinctive ways of testing its propositions for truth or falsity. There
could thus be confusion and error by using a central concept from one form
as though proper to another, or by applying tests of truth only appropriate in
one form to another. Claims that the conduct of persons is totally explainable
in terms of physical causation, or that religious notions of life after death can
be shown to be biologically impossible, would be examples of the confusion
and error that is to be avoided if Hirst is correct.

Liberal educators, on this account, would involve all pupils in each and
every form of knowledge that can properly be ascertained, or that (it seems)
is seriously claimed to be such by enough people (Bailey 1984: 75–6). How
this would all work out in terms of timetable arrangements and teaching
methods is not considered by Hirst, not simply by omission, but because he
believes that many considerations other than philosophical ones about the
nature of knowledge must enter into these decisions. It is clear, however, that
he is not saying that there must be in any sense an exact match between forms
of knowledge and subject divisions: 'It is simply false to imagine that an area
of study, teaching or research must direct itself to knowledge of one fundamental kind.' (Hirst 1974:136)

It is doubtful whether one can press the requirements of fundamentality
further than Hirst has done, and this remains the attraction and significance
of his account. Unfortunately a number of critics have come to believe that
the tight logic of the argument does not hold in a number of respects and
that, therefore, the case cannot be pushed even as far as Hirst believes. A
good deal of the difficulty arises from the attempt to characterize a number
of forms of knowledge in ways that actually do satisfy Hirst's own criteria of

discrimination. Hirst only gets near to doing this in some areas, religion and art, for example, by describing them in terms so propositional as to make them barely recognizable to those who find value in them. This has been seen as impoverishment of the liberal curriculum by some (Martin 1981), and as unnecessarily restrictive distortion by others (Bailey 1984:75–82). Even Hirst himself finds it necessary to assume that certain other components, of physical and moral education for example, would have to be added to a strictly interpreted liberal education in order to constitute a satisfactory general education. This seems to defeat the purpose of the original justification.

An attempt to develop a complete theory of liberal education which avoids some of these difficulties has been made by Bailey (1984). This work attempts a characterization of liberal education, a justification of it as the main part of a universal and compulsory education, an account of the appropriate curriculum content and teaching methods, and an examination of contemporary threats and challenges to the idea of a liberal education.

On justification Bailey sees Hirst's presupposition argument as an important but insufficient part of the justification and adds to this an ethical argument. This sees liberal education as a necessary part of a proper moral respect for young persons, in somewhat the same way as in the liberal political philosophers already mentioned. A third important justification for Bailey is the very generalizable utility that derives from a liberal education in ways far less restrictive and changeable than with the short-term specifics of vocational education (Bailey Chapter 4).

A liberal education thus justified would be characterized in the following way:

1. by its capacity to liberate a person from the restrictions of the present and the particular;
2. by its involvement of pupils in what is most fundamental and general;
3. by its involvement of pupils in intrinsically worthwhile ends and not only instrumental means; and
4. by its involvement of pupils in reason and the development of the rational mind. (Bailey: 29)

In describing an appropriate content for such an education Bailey subjects Hirst's account to a detailed critique and reluctantly rejects it. The only logical distinction to be made is that between inquiries into all those 'goings-on' that are only understandable as activities or practices of persons or minds, and inquiries into all those other 'goings-on' that are only properly understandable as *not* products of minds. Examples of the former would be (as objects of inquiry) politics, art, and literature; examples of the latter (as objects of inquiry) would be rock formations, wave motions, and the composition of water. Since this distinction, which derives from Michael Oakeshott (1975), and is of course most important if correct, cannot of itself provide a curriculum structure, Bailey builds his liberal curriculum on three main elements. First, a number of serving competencies, so called because they are competencies essential to pursuing any kind of intelligent inquiry whatsoever. Some of these would be familiar necessities like language, elementary mathematics, and perhaps keyboard skills, whilst others would be dispositional characteristics to be acquired, such as attending, concentrating, imagining, organizing, and reasoning. Second, a group of studies which might be called the humanities proper, i.e. developing knowledge and understanding of what it is to be a person in a world of persons, probably through certain aspects of literature, history, morality, and religion. Third, and most extensively, there would be an involvement of pupils in the nature of those inquiries falling under Oakeshott's twofold division that appear to be the most pervasive and significant in human societies. Here, since such a list cannot be decided by any further logical division, there is room for judgement and argument. Bailey makes proposals for such a list and orders of priority within it, moving from the areas with the strongest claim for compulsory inclusion to those where compulsion might be more debatable (Bailey, Chapter 7).

To this account of content Bailey adds arguments for appropriate teaching styles and methods to serve the aim of developing pupils' autonomy. Here the emphasis is on the importance of evidential teaching and getting pupils to care about reason and about persons. Bailey's work ends with a substantial discussion of what he sees as threats and challenges to such a conception of liberal education. These are seen as coming first from the overt and fashionable drive in Britain and other countries towards a vocational and instrumental conception of education, supported by government policies and by policy-directing selective injections of finance, and second from the rather more academic critiques of liberal education coming from various schools of Marxist thought.

There are, of course, other formulations of a liberal curriculum precluded from discussion here by limitation of space. (See especially Phenix 1964; Devlin and Warnock 1977; White 1982; and O'Hear 1981.) Nor has there been space to more than mention the more radically child-centred approaches to a liberating education exampled by Wilson and Bonnett.

One returns with some sadness, however, to the point that however convincing the arguments may be in clarifying and supporting liberal educators' own intuitions, their power and influence is overshadowed at this historical time, in Britain at least, by a powerful and widely present orthodoxy which sees education almost solely as an instrument of individual and national economic competitiveness. As some have noted, resistance to this destructive view must, perhaps, take the form of exercises in politics, as well as the exercises in philosophy of education we have been describing here.

REFERENCES

Ackerman, B. (1980) *Social Justice in the Liberal State*, New Haven and London: Yale University Press.

Althusser, L. (1971) 'Ideology and ideological state apparatuses', in *Lenin and Philosophy*, London: New Left Books.

Aristotle (1984) *Politics*, Book VII, 13–17 and Book VIII, in J. Barnes (Ed.) *The Complete Works of Aristotle*, Princeton and Guildford: Princeton University Press.

Bailey, C. (1984) *Beyond the Present and the Particular: A Theory of Liberal Education*, London: Routledge & Kegan Paul.

Bonnett, M. (1978) 'Authenticity and education', in *Journal of Philosophy of Education* 12:51–61.

Devlin, T. and Warnock, M. (1977) *What Must We Teach*, London: Temple Smith.

Gewirth, A. (1978) *Reason and Morality*, Chicago and London: University of Chicago Press.

Harris, K. (1979) *Education and Knowledge*, London: Routledge & Kegan Paul.

Hirst, P. H. (1974) *Knowledge and the Curriculum*, London: Routledge & Kegan Paul.

Martin, J. R. (1981) 'Needed, a new paradigm for liberal education', in J. F. Soltis (Ed.) *Philosophy and Education*, 80th Year Book, NSSE, Chicago: University of Chicago Press.

Oakeshott, M. (1975) *On Human Conduct*, Part I, Oxford: Clarendon Press.

O'Hear, A. (1981) *Education and Human Nature*, London: Routledge & Kegan Paul.

Phenix, P. (1964) *Realms of Meaning*, New York and London: McGraw Hill.

Rawls, J. (1971) *A Theory of Justice*, Oxford: Clarendon Press.

Rothblatt, S. (1976) *Tradition and Change in English Liberal Education*, London: Faber and Faber.

White, J. P. (1973) *Towards a Compulsory Curriculum*, London: Routledge & Kegan Paul.

(1982) *The Aims of Education Restated*, London: Routledge & Kegan Paul.

Wilson, P. S. (1971) *Interest, Discipline and Education*, London: Routledge & Kegan Paul.

1.6

PERSONAL, SOCIAL, AND MORAL EDUCATION

GLYNN PHILLIPS

INTRODUCTION

Public discussion about education has in recent years emphasized the importance of personal, social, and moral education (P.S.M.E.) for the full age range
in compulsory education.[1] Indeed, this is an expanding area of the curriculum
and appears to encompass health education (which has its own 'branches' such
as sex education, drugs education – with further divisions such as alcohol
education, education about smoking); environmental education (clearly, this
overlaps with aspects of health education); political education (a broad umbrella
covering such inquiries as certain aspects of history, economics, political science, and political thought); careers education and vocational guidance; moral
and religious education. Schools are also beginning to leave this area far less
to chance, assigning responsibility for it to specific departments or teachers or
to the pastoral system.

Is there a unity to P.S.M.E.? How do its three elements interrelate? One
writer has remarked that it is a conceptually messy area.[2] A start can be made
by drawing a distinction between those inquiries which are either empirical or
logical or both, and those which involve practical action. Certain types of
knowledge depend upon reasoning which is conducted by deductive inference:
mathematics and logic are obvious examples. Other types of knowledge depend
upon a combination of deductive reasoning and empirical judgement. In the
natural sciences, theoretical explanations of the behaviour of matter lead to
the construction of laws, which, in conjunction with statements describing
certain conditions, lead to predictions of the behaviour of matter. Such predictions are then rigorously tested, and in the light of the results obtained, the
theories and laws either survive, are amended, or are abandoned. Clearly, this
activity requires practical activity but it is in the course of experimentation. By
contrast, there is a domain of human activity in which the prime questions are
not 'Is this true or false?' but (typically) 'What ought to be done?' 'What is the

right thing to do?' 'What sort of person do I want to be?' 'What kind of life do I want to lead?' One of the features of such questions is that they, too, seek for some generalization, some broader view, which acts as a guideline, enabling people to take action. This 'broader view', whether it be held in a deliberately worked-out framework of beliefs, or as a set of emotional or habitual responses to situations, indicates that the holder places some importance on the beliefs, feelings, habits etc. which form it.

I shall call this area of our life 'the ethical dimension' and turn to the task of differentiating the elements of 'the social', 'the personal', and 'the moral' within it, in that order, making points about education as I go along.

THE SOCIAL

The 'social aspects of life' is a phrase carrying a number of differing meanings. First, we can regard it as referring to the set of social institutions and associated practices which constitute the framework of a society – its judicial system, its law-making system, its economic system and so on. There is clearly much here which can be learned about. Such learning need not be confined to one's own society, nor need such learning be of the Gradgrind kind, for it is quite possible to learn about social institutions in a variety of ways, some of which may enable students to engage in practical activity. Closely associated with such social institutions are the *issues* which divide people over such questions as how social institutions are to be managed, what their nature should be, perhaps even whether they should exist. Clearly, there is much to learn about here as well, and such knowledge is pertinent to the above 'ethical' questions.

Second, 'social aspects of life' can refer to the process of socialization, in which new members are inducted into a social group's norms, i.e. its values, habits, rules; the normative order of the group. The experience of being inducted is one we all share or have shared as members of the rising generation. Teachers new to a school experience it. Again, the socialization process, either in a general or more specific context, may be studied, and so could be an object of learning in schools. There is, though, one aspect of socialization which is especially worth singling out. Schools are both institutions in their own right and institutions within a societal framework. They have their own socialization processes, and they reflect the wider processes of the society in which they exist. In both respects, there will be rules, habits, values, which will be required of the individuals who make up the school. Indeed, unless such a normative order existed, any institution would find it very hard to function. So, a school in its socialization processes will reinforce all sorts of patterns of behaviour, and there is here a close affinity with moral training. Though some such devices are normatively necessary, there is also a clear danger which educationalists would do well to note. It could be that certain types of socialization are at the expense of the development of critical abilities in the young. For example, an over-emphasis upon such traits as loyalty or conformity may stifle the ability to criticize social life.

Third, we may note that social living involves the ability to know something about others. Indeed some such knowledge is a necessary condition of having a relationship with others, though clearly it is not sufficient. There are understandings and skills here which most of us possess to some minimal extent, though there are some individuals who do not possess these and so can make virtually nothing of the company of others. There are degrees of awkwardness, from the person who is totally isolated, to the person who is shy in company: it may even be that some who are the life and soul of the party share some of this underlying awkwardness. For the extreme cases, probably educationalists are well advised to obtain other professional help in trying to make such students sociable in this sense. Very young children have to start at the ground level, by coming to recognize others as persons. The sort of understanding which is required can become ever richer, nor is it always gained by social contact. Our understandings of others can be enhanced by, for example, history and literature.

THE PERSONAL

The first section picks out some ways in which the individual can develop as a person. Personal development also lies in forming a moral point of view, but before turning to that, a few brief remarks are in order about 'the personal'. Young people are at a stage of their lives where the questions 'what sort of person am I/should I be?' hover around them. It is the sort of query which lies behind the choice of an occupation, behind one's evolving life-style; it is connected closely with how one relates to other people. It goes beyond the wishes of the present, seeking more deeply rooted desires, nor should this be taken to mean that this sort of quest is empty of thought. On the contrary, all sorts of thoughts are apt to crowd in on a person, often in a rather chaotic, ill-assembled way. Can a person's educational experiences offer assistance in these quests? There would seem to be opportunities for at least clarifying one's thoughts and for beginning the task of sorting our priorities. It is an interesting question as to *how* this can be done. No doubt direct discussion of these matters has its place, but it seems equally plausible to suggest that a person's thinking will occur as a spontaneous reaction to some other educational experience, such as reading a poem. Indeed, the example of others may be influential – perhaps a yet further indication that the so-called hidden curriculum is not entirely heinous. It also ought to be asked whether this kind of personal development should be encouraged, and not just because of the pressing claims

63

of other educational activities. The issue here is that of whether it is a correct view of man to see him as capable of a profound self-awareness.[3]

THE MORAL

Morality

Turning now to morality and moral education, one is immediately faced with a rather crude characterization of this, caught in the term 'moralizing', conjuring up a list of dos and don'ts which reflect a stern puritanism where pleasure is outlawed and duty is all-important. We may distinguish, however, between particular moral codes or regimes and what 'morality' is, rather in the same way that Socrates was never satisfied with particular examples of some virtue, such as justice, but wanted to know what united them. 'Morality' has been thought notoriously difficult to define,[4] but it at least stands in sharp contrast to the ethic of the entirely selfish, or the entirely self-centred person; morality thus can be said to describe that type of thinking (whether in a judgement, emotional response, or habit of mind) in which the individual is concerned not (or not just) about him or herself but about others too, such that the individual acts in an other-regarding way. This point having been made in connection with selfishness or self-centredness, it is an interesting question – and a suggestive one so far as children are concerned – as to whether we are to rule out as 'moral' those who act partly for selfish and partly for other-regarding reasons. There is undoubtedly a range of types here, for example there are those who do good things, recognizing what is the moral thing to do, but still predominantly swayed by personal motives (and the balance of moral and nonmoral motives could shift); there are those who weigh their own concerns impartially with the interests of others; there are those who subjugate their own concerns, approaching 'pure' altruism.

It is worth dwelling on selfishness/self-centredness a little longer, partly because it should be unsurprising that children have these traits – they are part of the raw material with which moral educators have to work, and partly because the question 'Why ought I to be moral?' has a particular force for the young. It is not infrequently a question which is genuinely asked. It is sometimes held that we are basically selfish: if this is true, it would suggest there is a monumentally difficult task for moral educators ahead, for we are presumably to take 'basically' as telling us that selfishness is deeply rooted in us, perhaps part of our animal natures, and thus either very difficult or impossible to change. This view may be one source of an unease about whether moral education is worth attempting. Indeed, if it is true, the nature of such education as would be attempted would be quite altered. If self interest were the overriding principle of action, the most that could be squeezed out for moral education would be such virtues as those of caution and enlightened prudence. If X's acts produce such hostile reaction from Y that X's own interests were thereby put at risk, X would need to modify his demands to take account of such reaction. In this sense others' interests would be taken into account, as they also would be if X realized that his, X's, interests might be advanced if X co-operates with Y.

Does the thesis of psychological egoism have to be accepted (for on this question rests the very possibility of moral education)? Against it, it can be urged that even if it is true, this in itself does not show that we ought to continue like this, unless a further premiss is inserted and shown to be true – that nothing can be done to alter such a human condition. Nor is the suggested supplementary premiss without its difficulties. Aside from possibilities such as genetically engineering a benevolence gene,[5] it can be observed that we live as social beings and this forces us to take some regard of others if for no other reason than that our lives could be made miserable if we did not. This does not establish that we are moral creatures but it helps to disestablish that we pay no regard to others. Further there is plenty of evidence that people do act in others' interests in a way which makes the 'basically selfish' thesis implausible; we are at least owed an account of how this is possible. Further, it may be urged that we have other basic i.e., natural, character traits, of an other-regarding kind.[6] An objection may anyway be placed against the lurking fatalism in the egoist's position.

Should Schools be Involved in Moral Issues?

In so far as these arguments are successful, we may proceed to the question of whether schools should be concerned with the moral education of the young. This question is not really satisfied by it being pointed out that moral issues are constantly arising in schools, just by virtue of the fact that people interact with each other. Recall the points about the socialization of the young. Dealing with others is consistent with giving orders, getting others to obey rules, giving them rebukes. Moral *educational* development does not automatically arise. There are really two questions here. Ought schools to be engaged in the moral educational development of students, as well as their moral socialization, and, ought schools to be involved in the forming of moral attitudes at all? It may be that there has to be acceptance of certain rules in order that social life may proceed, but this is a prudential reason and hardly touches this last question which is about forming the *moral* beliefs of the young. Now this is not simply an unease about the school, as opposed to parents, doing such work. The unease can be traced to metaphysical and epistemological problems, and it has exercised an influence over such moral education programmes as the Humanities Curriculum Project, and the Values Clarification Programme.

The HCP is well known for its reluctance to allow teachers to voice their opinions, especially over issues of controversy involving values, preferring teachers to act as neutral chairmen. The VCP has regarded its main task as that of getting students to grasp what their values are on specific issues, leaving alone any further probing of such values as are brought to light.[7]

The epistemological problem can be expressed in the remarks 'there are no moral truths' (nor, presumably, moral falsehoods) or 'we cannot *know* what is right or wrong, good or bad'. The metaphysical problem can be expressed by the remark 'there is no existent realm of values, awaiting discovery by whatever methods are appropriate'. On the first of these, it is certainly true that in ordinary language, we do sometimes say things like A) 'you know you should not have done that', or B) 'torture is a truly monstrous thing to do', or C) 'it is true that X is wrong'. C) uses 'true' in a different way from the way 'truly' is used in B) (one could not substitute 'truly' in the latter sentence), but 'truly' still has some epistemic significance. On the other hand, we also say D) 'you ought not to have done that', or E) 'torture should never be allowed'. Do the latter pair of examples, D) and E), mean the same as their respective 'partner' in the former pair, A) and B)? Ordinary language seems not decisive here. We should ask rather what is at stake in the problem. The general view about knowledge has been that it is 'justified true belief' though dispute now rages over whether this is so, because cases can be produced in which X's true belief is justified by reliance on statements which turn out to be false. This has left the account of 'knowledge' in some disarray.[8]

It seems that we are driven by such arguments to be restrictive rather than liberal in what we allow as knowledge. This leads to the metaphysical issue. If we have a statement of knowledge, necessarily we have a true statement. 'X knows that p' entails the truth of 'p'. This raises the question – what makes a statement true? In the statement 'snow is white', the state of affairs of snow being white is what makes the statement a true one. Generalizing, we can say that true statements are those which refer to or describe some possible state of affairs which obtains. If no such state of affairs obtains, any statement which claims that it does obtain is in some way false. It is necessary to use the phrase 'in some way' because there are interestingly different ways in which some statements are false. Thus, if snow is not white, the above statement is straightforwardly false. Other statements, however, in so far as they claim to refer to states of affairs which cannot possibly obtain, are neither true nor false (on one view) or indirectly false (on another view).

Armed with these points, we are in a position to see the source of the doubts, noted above, over forming moral attitudes and beliefs. For these doubts are about the grounds of such attitudes and beliefs. The position may be expressed as follows. Even if some statements are regardable as statements of knowledge, this cannot be extended to moral statements because the standards of justification, which apply in the former type of statement, cannot be extended to moral statements. Further, even if some statements are regardable as true statements, no out-there world of moral values exists which has a status akin to the physical states of affairs of snow being white (nor a status which is derived from some sort of existent object). It is worth noticing that it would be consistent with this view to agree that a person's moral beliefs could be true to (say) the beliefs of his group or society, for what this means is that X's belief is the same as Y's belief. The issue would then return to asking whether this belief, i.e. the one which X and Y have in common, is a true belief.

These are formidable problems for anyone who wishes to hold the view that we can have moral knowledge (being knowledge, it could be taught and learned). Plato would without doubt have argued that these difficulties are more apparent than real. Impressed by the power of deductive reasoning to produce indubitable conclusions, but mindful that such reasoning rests on hypothetical principles, he would have argued that there are moral truths, graspable in acts of intuition by a prepared mind. Such axiomatic, moral, true statements would provide the basic principles from which more specific moral beliefs would be derived. This position has been taken up in the twentieth century by the intuitionists, and may reflect a more widely-held view that some things just are wrong, others just are right. But this appealing line of thinking faces its own difficulties. Suppose these are rival sets of beliefs, each with its own fundamental principle. How does one decide between them? What is one to do if faced with different intuitions of what is right and wrong, for intuitionism evidently leaves us with no apparatus to reach a decision. Why should we accept the view that moral argument has to be structured deductively? There are, indeed, alternative accounts such as that of Rawls,[9] which allow of a sort of empirical process whereby general moral principles are constructed by a process of trial and error in which there are two-way passages between potential principles and particular judgements.

A common reaction to these difficulties is to embrace moral scepticism but it should not be thought that this position escapes criticism. Perhaps one of the most trenchant difficulties lies in trying to formulate a sceptical position. If moral knowledge is not possible, we may believe what we like, for there are no grounds by which to sift better beliefs from not-so-good beliefs. It follows that if two people have differing moral beliefs, one person has no grounds for trying to alter the other person's belief. It follows that if this were to be attempted, one would have to say that the attempt should not be made. It follows that the moral sceptic holds a moral belief. Further difficulties can be uncovered. If moral scepticism is a scepticism about moral knowledge as opposed to other sorts of knowledge which are allowed, it will be telling us that knowledge has to be grounded in a particular way – as 'snow is white' is grounded in snow's being white. We are entitled to ask whether the sceptic's statement about the impossibility of moral knowledge is similarly grounded.

There are good reasons for rejecting moral scepticism. Are there good reasons for accepting moral beliefs as rationally defensible? Suppose two people were arguing about whether one soccer team was better than another. No such discussion could hope to make any progress unless some standards of excellence in soccer were established in the light of which particular performances could then be assessed. We think that lying is wrong, that it is right to keep to agreements, that harming individuals is wrong, that helping those who are in distress is right. These are standards by which we judge the behaviour of others. No society can avoid having such standards. We may dispute their applications to particular cases, we may be unsure over what qualifications it is reasonable to place upon such standards. But this does not mean that they have to be abandoned.

Moral Education

What features might be expected in a moral education programme? Because it is moral *education*, one may, with reason, expect to see the capacity for reasoning being developed. How deeply is reason embedded in the moral life? One might be tempted to think that it is not all-embracing. Is not *feeling* just as much a part of the moral life? One could readily agree to this but reply that our feelings are certainly not devoid of thoughts and beliefs, and this provides material for reasoning to occur. Or, again, is not at least some of morality concerned just with giving commands? It will be instructive to probe this a little deeper. People give orders because they want certain things to be done, and they see the actions which are supposed to follow from the orders as conducive to the sought-for objectives. Thus, even here, reasons lie behind such examples of moral behaviour. Further, prescriptions ('you ought to . . .') invite the question 'why?' and quickly take us into reasoning. Take 'you ought to be more punctual'; (say) the office will run more smoothly and this is important because customers' needs can be better attended to . . . and this is important because we should generally act so as to respect the wishes of people. Out of 'oughts' comes an edifice of reasons with some movement towards generality.

Moral *theory* proceeds on the assumption that this is a correct view of reason in morality. Utilitarianism, for example, tells us that there is a fundamental principle which determines the moral life, this being that one ought to do that which produces the greatest satisfaction of preferences. Rawls argues for two principles and a lexical ordering of them which will guide the construction of our social institutions and policies from the viewpoint of justice. Rawls offers his theory as an improvement on utilitarianism. It is not being suggested that the examination of moral (and political) issues proceed at this level of debate in schools, though it is not being denied either that something of this order may be possible with some students.[10] The general point is that at least a part of moral education should consist in the giving and examining of reasons with regard to particular issues. One aspect of reason-giving will be to explore how a reason given with regard to one issue affects what one may think about other issues, for example, if a reason for criticizing (say) certain treatments of animals is that this reduces the life that such animals can live to a level below any activity appropriate to animals of that kind, how does some such reason operate when we are considering the use of animals in scientific experiments which may result in medical benefits?

It should also be added that an important aspect of moral reasoning will be the paying of due regard to the empirical evidence upon which much moral debate depends.

It may be thought that if moral education is conceived of entirely in terms of reasoning, an important aspect has been omitted. Indeed, does this not simply assume that people have a disposition for being moral? Does not the willingness to engage in puzzling out moral problems depend upon people seeing life in moral terms and being prepared to act morally? What good has been done if a person has been intellectually equipped to discuss the meanings and applications of the principle(s) of justice, but has no disposition to behave justly? Thus at least part of moral education must consist of efforts to develop dispositions to behave in a certain way; they are habits, though this does not mean that they are empty of thought or of the wish to so behave.[11] We can, however, contrast the person who acts virtuously with the person who acts in the same way out of fear. The Greeks held that man's nature is in part constituted by passions and appetites. The virtues then hold such anti-moral tendencies in check.

One problem in developing 'virtuous education' is to decide which virtues to promote. There are some which come in, as it were, by the demands of reason – the intellectual virtues such as perseverence in one's studies, curiosity, a respect for evidence, a caring that one gets at the truth. Others may be associated with the basic nature of morality, for example, a concern or a compassion for the plight of others, being honest, being trustworthy. Others are less easily argued for. Thus being temperate, being modest, or having humility, may well be tied to particular cultural milieus, not applicable to everyone, or perhaps even survivors of a bygone age. There is much detailed work still to be done in this area of moral education both of a conceptual and empirical kind. To take but one example, emphasis today is laid in schools on the importance of young people becoming 'responsible' as a way of preparing them to be autonomous individuals. Some care is needed with how this is to be taken. It might mean that the young are to learn to do things, such as looking after their possessions, or that they are to take charge of activities and assume a managerial role ('taking on' responsibilities), or behave in ways which respect the rights and interests of others (as opposed to being 'irresponsible' in the sense of reckless). Such concepts need to be worked through and then, equally carefully, activities should be planned which may lead to the development of such characteristics, after also having worked out why such virtues are important to develop.

CONCLUSION

Perhaps there was a time when people were simply not exercised by wondering about what sort of person they should be. They had their roles and allotted stations in life, and they just got on with it. We no longer think that the young should be brought up just like that, but with what do we replace such a traditional upbringing? That is the central problem for personal, social and moral education. This problem is intimately connected with some central philosophical issues.

NOTES

1. See particularly DES (1980) *Aspects of Secondary Education*, Chapter 9; DES (1981) *Personal and Social Development*; K. David (1982) *Personal and Social Education in Secondary Schools* (Longmans for Schools Council); DES (1984) *The Curriculum from 5 to 16*.
2. See R. Pring (1982) 'Personal and social developments; some principles for curriculum planning' *Cambridge Journal of Education* 12,1.
3. An interesting discussion of this issue is by C. Hamm (1985) 'Moral education and the distinction between social and personal morality' *Westminster Studies in Education* 8.
4. Moore, G. E. (1903) *Principia Ethica*, Cambridge: Cambridge University Press.
5. Glover, J. (1984) *What Sort of People should there Be?* Harmondsworth: Penguin Books.
6. Singer, P. (1982) 'Ethics and sociobiology' *Philosophy and Public Affairs* II,1.
7. There is a considerable literature on the problems of values clarification. See J. Harrison (1976) 'Values clarification: an appraisal, *Journal of Moral Education* 6,1; B. Wakeman (1984) *Personal, Social and Moral Education*, Chapter 3; R. Elliot (1986) 'Making children moral' *Educational Theory* 36,3.
8. Kirkham, R. L. (1984) 'Does the Gettier problem rest on a mistake?' *Mind* XCIII.
9. Rawls, J. (1971) *A Theory of Justice*, Cambridge, Mass.: Harvard University Press.
10. Ward, P. (1983) 'In defence of philosophy in schools', *British Journal of Educational Studies* XXXI,3.
11. Foot, P. (1978) *Virtues and Vices*, Chapter 1, Oxford: Basil Blackwell.

FURTHER READING

Bond, R. E. (1983) *Reason and Value*, Cambridge: Cambridge University Press.
Cambridge Journal of Education 12,1 (1982). A special edition on personal and social education.
Educational Analysis 5,1. (1983). A special edition on personal, social and moral education.

Elliot, J. and Pring, R. (Eds.) (1975) *Social Education and Social Understanding*, University of London.

Foot, P. (1978) *Virtues and Vices*, Oxford: Basil Blackwell.

Hare, R. M. (1981) *Moral Thinking: Its Levels, Method and Point*, Oxford: Clarendon Press.

Mayo, B. (1986) *The Philosophy of Right and Wrong*, London: Routledge & Kegan Paul.

Peters, R. S. (1974) *Psychology and Ethical Development*, London: Allen & Unwin.

Pring, R. (1984) *Personal and Social Education in the Curriculum*, Hodder & Stoughton.

Straughan, R. (1982) *Can We Teach Children to be Good?*, London: Allen & Unwin.

Warnock, G. (1971) *The Object of Morality*, London: Methuen.

Wilson, J. (1973) *The Assessment of Morality*, Windsor: NFER-Nelson.

POLITICAL EDUCATION
AND THE SCHOOL

BERNARD CRICK

A recent survey showed that political education, by whatever name, in some reasonably coherent form or other, is on the timetable in just over half the secondary schools in England and Wales. The same is probably true in Northern Ireland. And in Scotland it is present in all local authority schools, at least as a popular option, as a major constituent of modern studies. But unlike in the United States and in most European countries, political education is not required by public law. Until the last twenty years most people in Britain have felt that our parliamentary and local representative institutions worked so well that the example somehow permeated down into schools without the need for it to be taught. Whether to teach politics at all, and if so how, became controversial.

ORIGINS

The history of political education in British education is obscure and, as yet, unwritten. But a history would show discontinuities more than continuities. Political education seemed to grow quite rapidly in the 1970s from very little; but after the first Education Acts Cassells in 1885 could claim '260th thousand' on the cover of *The Citizen Reader* in their Modern School Series. And in the introduction, H. O. Arnold-Foster (whose cousin, W. E. Foster MP, had been Gladstone's vice president of the Board of Education, wrote the Preface) noted that there had been three Scottish editions and that the Education Department had placed 'civic duty' on the syllabus of the Evening Continuation Schools. However, Arnold-Foster's reading of 'civic duty' was neither uncritical nor without Gladstonian resonance:

> I said that I hoped you were all proud of your country, but I trust you did not think that I wished you to be proud of it only because it was big. That would be a great mistake. It would be just as sensible to say that a man was a good

man simply because he was a big one, as to say that a country was to be admired because it covered a great many square miles.

What happened between then and the 1970s is unclear, but either civics became discredited for such flagrant Liberal anti-imperialist bias, or it was crowded out as the curriculum in the 1900s and 1920s became dominated by demands of the university examination boards. An Association for Education in Citizenship in the 1930s had top-drawer support, but apparently little or no influence in ordinary schools, and faded away after the war. In the more liberal post-war educational atmosphere, surviving elements of civics in England and Wales became subsumed into social studies or history, and in Scotland, preserved to rise again in the plaid dress of modern studies.

The Politics Association was founded in 1969 and the Modern Studies Association in Scotland a little earlier. The Politics Association arose basically from the desire for comfort and support of individual teachers, usually teaching in isolation with no colleagues in the subject, and sometimes working in an almost clandestine manner in odd holes and corners of the timetable. These teachers were predominantly historians doing a little 'politics', 'civics', 'current affairs' or 'British Constitution' on the side. The teachers wanted a professional association, like the Historical Association, to help raise standards and provide materials, meetings, and short courses etc. About half the original membership were FE teachers, those who taught some politics under the then broad 'liberal studies' remit. The particular academics who helped them begin a remarkably influential campaign, both for more professionalism and more provision in more schools, while all interested in the academic standing of the subject and reform of examination syllabuses, were predominantly interested in the Politics Association as a potential to promote civic education throughout the schools.

The prolonged debate over what to call the new body was revealing. 'Association for Civic Education' was rejected. It suggested the old condescending 'top-down' movements for good citizenship, some of which had seemed less interested in encouraging active citizens than in creating law-abiding subjects. Oddly the word 'citizen' unqualified has a republican ring to it, whereas 'good citizen' sounds no trouble to anyone. And yet 'Association for Political Studies' was thought too academic by many who wanted to sound more 'civic', if the term's meaning had not become debased. 'Association for Political Education' might have passed but for, at that time, an unfortunate verbal association with the Youth propaganda activities of the Communist Party. So 'Politics Association' was adopted as the least objectionable name, some favouring it as the most usual name in Britain for university and polytechnic departments. Besides this, it was the traditional name (from translations of Aristotle) of the discipline. Furthermore, the name was supported more positively by some to stress that the subject must be realistic, deal with the public issues of political debate, and escape from the then GCE tradition of teaching 'British Constitution' in a purely institutional and legalistic way. It was said that the British Constitution only existed in school textbooks.

Some teachers remained worried, however, that public authorities and the press would confuse 'Politics' with politics, the study with the activity – as if the Criminological Society had called itself the Criminal Society. But others insisted that since the misunderstanding was both common and crucial, it had to be faced. The subject was not worth having if they could not get across to objectors the simple points that political issues can be studied in a reasonably balanced way and in the context of a liberal education, and that politics has some vocational relevance in preparing young people for adult life.

Six events can be singled out as establishing politics as a common part of the curriculum in Great Britain:

1. The founding of the Politics Association, since professional bodies rightly exercise considerable influence in curricular thinking and the promotion and retention of subjects.
2. The publication of Derek Heater's pioneering and influential anthology of 1969, *The Teaching of Politics*.
3. The issuing of a 'discussion document' by two HMIs authorized by the DES, John Slater and R. H. S. Hennessey, shrewdly titled *Political competence* (22 February, 1977), a concept which implied some practical outcome; indeed successive Secretaries of State have all made passing references to the importance of political education, often saying 'political and economic', even though (as we will see) it is not to be part of the new national curriculum.
4. The publication in 1978 as *Political education and political literacy* of the report of the working party of the Hansard Society's programme for political education.
5. The change in 1976 of the University of London A level from a highly traditional 'British Constitution' to a more innovative syllabus, much influenced by the Hansard thinking, which then had an influence on nearly all the other Examinations Boards.
6. The steady growth of modern studies in Scotland, so that it is now part of what is virtually a national curriculum in a system in which a single Scottish Examination Board is closely connected with the Scottish Education Department.

AIMS AND METHODS

Slater and Hennessey began their semi-official discussion paper:

> Although the idea of political education is suspect to many people, there are
> nevertheless compelling reasons for asserting its importance in the official cur-
> riculum. It is, of course, already present in many subjects of the curriculum: in
> History, Geography, Economics, even English and Religious Education
> classes. . . . So political education does not necessarily mean the addition of a
> new subject to the curriculum. But its importance to society requires a clearer
> definition of its objectives, and of the knowledge and skills and attitudes which
> are necessary to support it.

The Hansard Report tried to specify the kinds of knowledge, skills, and
attitudes which are necessary for the growth of what it called 'political literacy'.
The concept tried to bridge the very dilemma the new Politics Association
had faced in choosing their name: academic versus practical purposes. Political
education cannot be purely a matter of knowledge, but neither (as some radical
sociologists of education sometimes advocated – to others) a matter purely of
experience and activity.

Institutions can themselves become contentious – whether they are rightly
used, or whether they need reform. But the subject matter of political education
cannot simply be facts about institutional and constitutional arrangements. For
politics is about issues and how they are expressed or contained in institutional
frameworks. We have rules because we want to play a game. We only read
the rules to learn to play new and invented games; we learn all the big and
popular games by actually playing them; and the rule book is only then
consulted if there are disputes. The change from an institutional to an issue-
based approach was fundamental.

So the Hansard Report began with issues and asked how a hypothetical
politically literate person approaches them: he or she requires to have *relevant
knowledge*, perceptions of *self-interest and social responsibility*, and to gain *action
skills*.

The first kind of *knowledge* one needs is knowledge of who promotes what
policies, of the institutional context for conflicts, and of different ways and
means of influence in our present society. One would then go on to develop
scepticism about factual claims, some knowledge of alternative sources (on the
simplest level, to look at rival tabloid newspapers), and lastly knowledge of
alternative viewpoints and ways of settling disputes in different societies. The
consideration of alternative ways of organizing society has great educational
value in terms both of developing knowledge and imagination; but the Hansard
Report argued against the so-called critical or alternative sociology school
(usually a polite euphemism for Western Marxists) that such considerations
are a bad beginning for teaching: we have to work outwards from the familiar,

75

and have a moral duty to help pupils understand what the main range of conventional views in their society are, and prepare them for what difficulties and opportunities they will encounter in society. Only after this is speculation about alternatives educationally sensible (and likely to be comprehensible).

First of all, students should be encouraged to try to see simultaneously the likely effect of different policies both on themselves and on others. Next they should try to enhance and assess their abilities both to express their own interests and values, and to perceive the values and principles of others. Finally, at however simple a level, justifications have to be offered, not just correct perceptions of one's own interests and values, as well as an ability to understand and reproduce the justifications and reasons of others.

The first political *action skills* that can and should be encouraged in an educational context are the ability to perceive and express conflicts of values and interests in the home, everyday life, and school, together with some gradual experience in having to make real choices in school work, use of independent study time, etc. Then experiences of participation can be increased by means of debates, games, simulations, and projects etc., indeed the very experience of interactive learning rather than the image of 'the well-taught pupil'. (Traditionalists who imagine good education as a teacher talking and silent pupils writing it down are rarely aware, rarely remember, how much discussion goes on in a truly well-taught class – or if they do remember, think that this is only for sixth formers.) The experience of public debate and discussion is fundamental to free politics. It begins in the home or the classroom, preferably in both, but sometimes sadly in neither.

The Hansard 'action skills' stopped far short of what some radical theorists were demanding. But they were realistic, and certainly went beyond what some still mistakenly regard as proper for schools, as one can have 'good citizenship' without the unpredictable troubles that come from having citizens. The philosopher Karl Popper has pointed out that one property of free actions is that they are unpredictable. The Hansard Report formally professed to say that the probable consequences of ever having a politically literate population were not their concern and were, in any case, unpredictable. But critics pointed out that the assumption of a balanced and empathetic approach to the identification and discussion of issues was inherently liberal. Nobody thought, indeed, that a politically literate population would either want to return to autocratic government or aspire to the permanent salvation of revolutionary hopes. But the Report did indeed see a necessary link between what it called 'procedural values' and the whole idea of a liberal education in a liberal society.

The idea of 'procedural values' was to formulate the truth conditions of a genuine political education, values which if not held, exemplified, and encouraged, at least minimally, would render political education, as distinct say from political indoctrination or agitation, incapable of proceeding at all. These were put forward as *freedom, toleration, fairness, and respect for truth and for reasoning.* These are also fundamental values in the whole idea of liberal education. People can be trained, like conscript soldiers, to do something without understanding either why or how it works. Most factories work that way, as do many offices. But education involves knowing the reasons and learning to reason. It must presume that teachers teach what they hold to be true, not what they are (as in so many countries) told to teach, and that what they hold to be true can in some minimal sense be tested by knowledge of other theories or beliefs, or at least an open-mindedness to new viewpoints, or old ones revived – which involves tolerance and fairness, and indeed freedom to be criticized and to criticize, or at least to question and be questioned.

Although the Report argued that political literacy is best gained by learning about policies and discussing issues, it suggested, that as well as the underlying procedural values, 'a politically literate person would possess, among other things, a knowledge of those concepts minimally necessary to construct simple conceptual and analytical frameworks'. The report suggested a minimal simple vocabulary, drawn from the tradition of political thought, which people need to use, however vaguely and unconsciously, to comprehend and act in the political world. Politics was presented as a kind of dialectic between the demands and needs of *government* and the demands and needs of *people*. These are mediated by *relationships*, that is, all the procedures, processes, and institutions of political life. Under 'Government' it was suggested that the concepts of *power, force, authority,* and *order* need distinguishing, and together cover all cases (if their negations are also allowed, for example 'revolution' can be treated as a 'negation' of 'order', and similarly 'war' can be treated both as a negation of order and, at times, as a kind of order). The fundamental kinds of different relationship between government and people were seen as *law, justice, representation,* and *pressure.* And 'people' are conceptualized in terms of needs or demands for *natural rights, individuality, freedom,* and *welfare.*

'War' and 'peace' did not figure. Presumably 'war' could be treated as an attribute of both 'power' and 'force', and 'peace' derived from 'welfare' and 'natural rights'. But that would seem somewhat strained and esoteric, likely to be missed by many. It was either a political evasion of an already contentious issue or just a massive oversight by a committee. But it is fair to surmise that most of the authors of the Hansard Report would have had a fairly clear view of the current controversy over 'peace studies': a) that consideration of these issues in schools is important and perfectly proper if properly taught; and b) that it is educationally unsound to pick out one problem area from the whole of politics as if it could constitute a subject on its own: issues of war and peace need approaching as part of the kind of general framework of political education as advocated by the Hansard Society or found in the general 'guidelines' for political education actually embodied in the public law of the West German *Länder* or state governments.

PROVISION

Politics as an examination subject is now established in British schools, and while not a large subject, is not small either; rather a medium-sized one. In 1984 nearly 9,000 candidates entered for A level politics, almost half for the London Board. In the previous year, 12,577 candidates took O levels, and for CSE, while politics is not separately categorized, nearly all the syllabuses contain some modules of politics, and in all had 91,591 entries in 1984. But for non-examination provision there are no hard figures. A survey by Dr Robert Stradling and Martin Nocter in 1981 of a ten per cent sample of schools in England and Wales showed some definite provision, either exclusive courses or modules in other courses, in about half their sample, and either no provision at all or claims to provide it indirectly in the other half, often through history, geography, and social studies, or less plausibly, as some replied, 'through the whole life and character of the school, we like to think'.

The publications of the Politics Association and of the Association for the Teachers of the Social Sciences often report interesting and imaginative courses or projects for the 11–14 age group: 'desert island' survival games, for instance, in which some children choose strong leaders and others set up democratic decision-making procedures and, what is more, both can often give good justifications of their different choices or strategies. But it is difficult to know how much of this goes on. Stradling and Nocter's figures suggested a doubling of exclusive or modular provision between 1977 and 1981, but it is extremely unlikely that that rate of increase survived into the hard times of the 1980s, and was in any case a leap, stimulated by the campaigning of the early 1970s, from a very low initial base. Some authors have shown that political concept formation begins in primary school, and that some teaching and projects even at that early age can create a modest if appreciable political understanding. There is some evidence that use of concepts like 'fairness' (which modern philosophers like John Rawls and W. G. Runciman have treated as a near synonym of 'justice' itself) occurs more spontaneously among the last years in primary than among the middle years in secondary education (something gets lost or is educated or socialized out – as art and moral education teachers often believe).

The argument has often been, of course, that in British schools a subject carries no prestige and would have no advocates without public examinations. Perhaps. But it certainly does not follow that because politics is strong in the sixth and even fifth forms that it spontaneously and benignly percolates down the long ladder. Far from it. Common sense and personal observation suggest that many GCE teachers understandably spend much energy preventing their own timetable being flooded and polluted with teaching lower down the school. And while the subject associations mean well and say the right things, it is clear that most of their members' practical interests determine that most of their efforts go into providing materials relevant to examination success. The catalogues of educational publishers for subjects like history and geography reveal a clear and mercenary provision of books and teaching materials for every age group throughout the school. There is little or no equivalent for political education, though the situation is better, of course, if one thinks that political education should form part of a broader social studies, as has happened so sensibly with the concept of modern studies in Scotland. But while relevant knowledge of political issues and processes often forms part of social studies, what may be missed are the quite specifically political skills and attitudes needed for effective citizenship, or for a politically literate electorate.

PROBLEMS

There are continuing problems of the place of the subject in the curriculum, arising from educational dilemmas, and also problems arising from politically expressed fears of indoctrination and bias.

To achieve any sensible objectives, political education has to be seen as a commitment for a school rather than the public-spirited activity of particular teachers. Opinions vary as to whether 'political literacy' is best infused directly and given its own timetable hours by whatever name; or whether diffused indirectly through other subjects where political issues arise naturally or can easily be induced – for example land use and environmental inquiries and disputes in geography, different doctrinal interpretations of contemporary history, themes of freedom and justice in English (as in *The Lord of the Flies* and *Animal Farm* – neither compulsory but each well-nigh universal). Opinions differ, and so do circumstances; so assessments differ with equal confidence, and the school that wishes to promote political literacy obviously has itself to be political, tactical, or opportunistic in the best sense, and to adjust its aims to local opinions and resources. Either can work well. In some schools both strategies are pursued at different levels, and in others neither.

When the idea of a national curriculum was first floated in the formal public debates that followed the Labour Government's Green Paper of July 1977, *Education in schools*, a diversity of bodies testified for some form of political education in the curriculum, notably the NUT and the National Association of Teachers in Further Education, but also the CBI: 'schools can . . . ensure that (i) pupils are much better prepared for the change from school to adult and working life'; the TUC: 'if there is a core curriculum . . . young people must be helped to become politically and economically literate'; the Headmasters' Association 'included in this should be an awareness of the major social, political and moral issues that our society faces'; the National Consumer Council asked 'how far schools are able to encourage the development of a critical and analytical approach . . . to social issues . . . and to achieve the necessary high standard of what is coming to be known as "politeracy"; the Church of England Board of Education demanded rhetorically, 'How far is the educational system not only "fitting" children for life in our society, but enabling them constructively to criticize and reshape it?'; and the National Association of Head Teachers pontificated 'due attention should be paid to the study of aesthetic and cultural values no less than those which provide the knowledge and skills necessary for the pupil's future life as a political and economic member of the community'.

The proposed national curriculum must have disappointed the Head Teachers by containing neither the aesthetic nor the political. The complete absence of political education, as well as social studies, seems to mirror political and industrial prejudices rather than any serious thinking about the aims of *education* or even useful *training* as it should surely apply to preparation for citizenship. The absence was particularly poignant because the Secretary of State who introduced the national curriculum, mainly to curtail the powers of numerous LEAs in England and Wales, Mr Kenneth Baker, had himself been the chairman of the Hansard Society when its working party on political education reported, and presented it in person with enthusiastic understanding and advocacy to the then Secretary of State, Mrs Shirley Williams.

The political prejudices against political education are not entirely limited to the Conservative Party; some Labour LEAs were resistant to such innovations as openly teaching controversial issues in 'their schools', or anyone else other than old councillors presuming to know anything about 'how politics really works'. One Labour authority denounced the emphasis of the Hansard programme on balance, open-mindedness, and empathy. Among Conservative ranks there was at first much support for the programme, and many Conservative LEAs appreciated the need for clear guidelines and assessment objectives. But opponents of political education gained ground and publicity in Mrs Thatcher's second and third governments. A strong lobby of Conservative intellectuals has argued that the subject has no place in schools and that the teaching of it is inherently biased. Oddly they seemed to regard history teaching as untroubled by bias, although they did begin to distinguish between political history (good) and social history (bad). Some even professed to fear the influence of political education, mirroring some of the less cautious and sillier hopes expressed for its speedy efficacy in totally democratizing British society.

The truth is likely to prove depressing to both camps: that schools have far less effect on pupils' basic values than is often supposed by both the fearful and the over hopeful. Some degree of bias is inevitable in all teachers and teaching, but is rarely harmful if empathy and professional competence are cultivated. Numerous 'socialization' studies reach the banal result that 'the home' and/or 'society at large' have the predominant effect on values. What schools can influence are skills and knowledge. The fear of indoctrination is misplaced, for to induce whole doctrines on large numbers of resistant or apathetic people seems to require an almost total control of an entire timetable, and propaganda and censorship in the larger non-school world. Even when this is attempted, as in Eastern Europe since the Second World War, it is unlikely to succeed, creating cynicism and foot-dragging far more often than enthusiasm. The conditions for indoctrination do not exist in British schools, although it could be argued that a national curriculum could be a step in that direction – it is certainly proving a Greek gift to those over-rationalizing educationalists who have argued for it for so long.

It should be an inference from the concept of a free society that much local diversity, inefficiency, and even folly has to be tolerated because centralized general remedies are worse. Any political education must begin by considering that politics itself arises, as Aristotle first taught, from the natural diversity of values and interests which exists in any free society – a proposition basic to Western culture. So while we need precise and professional schemes, like Wittgenstein's ladder they must each be knocked down once we have climbed the wall.

REFERENCES

Crick B. and Porter A. (Eds.) (1978) *Political Education and Political Literacy*, London: Longman.

Harber, C. (Ed.) (1987) *Political Education in Britain*, Brighton: Falmer Press.

Heater, D. and Gillespie, J. (Eds.) (1981) *Political Education in Flux*, Sage.

Lister, I. (1984) *Teaching and Learning About Human Rights*, Strasbourg: Council of Europe.

Porter, A. (1983) *Teaching Political Literacy*, University of London, Institute of Education.

(Ed.) (1985) *The Principles of Political Literacy*, University of London, Institute of Education. (This is a digest of Crick and Porter, *op. cit.* now out of print.)

Short Life Working Group [sic] (1987) *Report on Modern Studies* . . . Scottish Examination Board.

Stradling, R., Noctor, M., and Baines, R., (1984) *Teaching Controversial Issues*, London: Arnold.

I.8

MULTICULTURAL EDUCATION

PHILIP WALKLING

This is the name of a reforming tendency in educational practice, too broad and too diverse in aims to be called a movement, to respond to the cultural diversity produced by postwar immigration to Britain. It is part of a widespread international interest in the representation of ethnically diverse populations in education, but not all educational responses to plurality are multicultural. Separate education for different linguistic, cultural, or racial groups is not multicultural education, which is a part of a wider interest in equality of opportunity. It is also known as 'multiracial education', 'multiethnic education' (particularly in the USA), and 'intercultural education' (particularly in a European context).

Under the name of multicultural education are found educational recommendations ranging from attempted ameliorations of disadvantages with the aim of equality of educational outcomes for individuals, to radical reconstructions of the curriculum and of the relationships between schools and their communities. This range is influenced by notions of the cultural determinations of self-image and of the proper content of education, including the nature of knowledge. Dissatisfaction with the pace of change has led some educators to reject multicultural education as ineffective and hypocritical and to move towards an analysis of the under-achievement in school of Black children in terms of racism. The resulting 'antiracist education' movement is often hostile to the measures recommended by 'multiculturalists', and in some of its forms regards educational measures as useless, preferring to work for radical reconstructions of society to eliminate racism in schools, and in other forms to press for individual teachers, as one alleged source of racism, to engage in 'racism awareness' programmes to reorient their perceptions.

DEVELOPMENT

What are the issues which led to the development of multicultural education? The first step was the perceived educational difficulty of children whose mother tongue is not English or whose expectations of education were thought not to prepare them to benefit from British schooling. These children, the 'coloured immigrants' of the 1950s and 1960s, were offered remedial programmes, particularly in language, in order that they should become assimilated into British society. The assumption was that they would wish to merge into the fabric of British life and that the fabric itself – a 'free society' – would assimilate them without itself significantly changing.

During this period, the roles of language, particularly of class-related codes, and of sub-cultures in educational attainment, were coming under scrutiny as explanations were sought for the failure of 'equal opportunity' policies to correct the educational under-achievement of the poorer sections of the indigenous population. In the early 1970s multicultural education began to emerge more clearly as a recognition that language-related remediation and assimilationist social goals were insufficient. Race relations ('community relations') became an explicitly political issue. Multiculturalists argued for a more open curriculum, so that the school should become more friendly towards children from non-indigenous cultures. The obvious points of difference – dress, diet, religion, language, the arts – were seen by some as resources through which traditional educational goals could be achieved. At its worst, this has been seen as hypocritical lip-service to equality of opportunity, and stigmatized as the 'saris, samosas, and steel bands' approach: superficial, trivializing and a harmful influence in community relations because of its emphasis on differences and the bizarre. At its best it has continued to cause a reappraisal of the curriculum in terms of its relevance to the needs of children and communities, and has played a part in the development of high-status parts of the curriculum like science, maths, history, literature, and languages.

Reconsideration of the place of culture in education had its first influence among children of Asian origin. Afro-Caribbean communities were held to be culturally British and their language a debased form of English. Research into the alleged linguistic and subcultural causes of the under-achievement of working-class children reinforced the view that Afro-Caribbean children suffered because their language and way of life were educationally poverty-stricken. They were thought to have values inimical to the achievement of educational goals and a language which inhibited the manipulation of abstract ideas. Remedial treatment was the answer to this, with its implicit invitation to adopt White evaluations of themselves and their way of life. The drift of Afro-Caribbean children to the bottom of the education system, and their

83

massive over representation in remedial classes and ESN schools, mirrored the standing of their parents in political, social, and economic life. The realization that racism is a cause, not a consequence, of this existence on the margin was a long time coming.

With the development, in the late 1960s and early 1970s, of pluralist rather than assimilationist policies in education, multicultural education as usually understood came into its own. This development was not rapid and was, as is common with such changes, introduced piecemeal under the influence of active professionals and agencies such as the National Council for Educational Research and the Schools Council. Urban LEAs were much quicker than central government to fund developments which sought to celebrate cultural diversity rather than to regard it as a problem. From the developing recognition that cultural diversity is here to stay, and that racism springs from fear and ignorance rather than malice, the multicultural education tendency has moved from remediation to celebration.

For Black children themselves, the teaching of and through mother tongues, Black Studies programmes, the genuine enrichment of the curriculum referred to previously, and positive attempts to recruit Black teachers and involve parents in the school, have all been aimed at removing those barriers to educational success which spring from a poor self-image. This approach reaches its culmination in the attempts of minority communities to establish their own mainstream or supplementary schools. Of greater general educational significance was the development at the same time of measures aimed not solely at Black children but at all children. The benefits to education generally of using the variety of cultural resources a plural society makes available were beginning to be appreciated. Multicultural education is most commonly defended now as an absolute of the curriculum and educational practice generally, rather than as a reform which aims at improving the education of Black children. It involves an orientation which treats knowledge as the common property of all peoples, and which encourages sensitivity to the valued ways of life of other people. Its political roots lie in liberal democratic pluralism.

It would be a mistake to regard the evidence of historical development in the *ideas* of multicultural education as showing a uniformity of adoption or practice. It is still common to find teachers and schools who regard multicultural education as an ameliorative approach needed only in schools with Black pupils. The greatest progress has been in urban centres, and even there resistance to multicultural approaches can easily be found. Future progress will depend upon the Black communities continuing to use their political voice and becoming properly represented in the educational professions. The influence of the broadcast media and educational publishers will also continue to be crucial. Here the general movement towards making materials more relevant to the ordinary lives of pupils has helped, as has the scrutiny of materials for racist assumptions.

CONCEPTUAL ISSUES

The fact of cultural diversity in Britain has forced a reassessment of the relationship between education and culture. In a monocultural society this relationship can easily be kept inexplicit, and there have been many attempts to produce philosophical arguments to 'prove' that a particular arrangement of knowledge or set of educational values is required by some taken-for-granted concept of 'education' which accords with the modern European (also often called the 'classical') tradition. This tradition stresses the schooling of individual intellects in ways of understanding which are taken to be transcultural in their conceptual range and objective in their dependence upon rational principles for discovering truth. This intellectual training is taken, in the tradition, to have moral benefits in terms of respect for truth, for individual responsibility, and for the rights of others.

The presence in schools of children from non-indigenous cultures has meant that this tradition can no longer be taken for granted. This has become apparent especially in matters to do with faith and values, such as religious, moral, and social education. Its effects are felt in the arts and humanities, especially history, and spill over into the physical sciences. Special considerations arise in practical subjects like physical education and home economics. Two general areas of speculation will illustrate the range of reappraisal opened up and the complexity of the issues. These are first, whether education should serve the needs of communities or of individuals, and second, whether knowledge (and, by implication, rational belief and the principles of intellectual and moral judgement) is the same for all cultures or relative to particular ways of life.

Community and individual rights

The classical tradition conceives of the development of the individual intellect as the chief purpose of education. In freeing the intellect from the ties of ignorance and prejudice it serves the social purpose of promoting freedom and responsibility. Critics have often attacked this as rhetoric hiding an ideology and educational practice which condemn many children to poor life chances whilst convincing them that their failure is their own responsibility. It thus aids the replication of a stratified society. But this individualistic professional ethic has also been used to promote much educational reform, such as experiential methods in learning. The fact that as rhetoric it can support competitive and alienating practices does not deny its libertarian effect when taken seriously. A problem for those whose impulse towards multicultural educational reform arises from their libertarian values has therefore been how to react to demands from ethnic minority communities which are themselves anti-libertarian and conformist.

In some cases, these demands are not significant in any educational sense. For example, what girls wear for physical education is unimportant in terms of the purposes of the activity, and the sensibilities of, say, Muslim parents can be satisfied. Similar solutions can be found to modify school uniforms to permit modest dress, turbans for Sikh men, and so on. More serious problems arise over demands for single-sex schools for adolescents, or for a kind of religious education which confirms faith rather than encouraging speculation. The problem reaches its strongest expression in demands by young people themselves that they shall not be subject to the educational expectations of their community elders.

In many ways, this issue is not special to educational responses to cultural diversity. Mass education has always had to address the problem of balancing legitimate parental and community involvement against fostering the independence of the child. There are many people who have education to thank for providing a route out of stifling conformity. But, in making that point, it must be remembered that this escape may result in personal insecurity and rootlessness. When we make it possible for ethnic minority parents to pass on to their children their traditions and beliefs, we are assisting the development in the children of confidence and a sense of personal worth. These are essential for individual educational success. Logic shows us that speculation, with its valuing of scepticism and the pursuit of rational belief, is dependent upon notions of truth and commitment. In order for anyone to doubt anything in a way which can lead to the increase of knowledge, it is necessary for that person to know what belief is like. The ideas that children are born speculative philosophers or that it is harmful to introduce general beliefs too early are absurdities. Children are not deficient in beliefs, and education is not, or should not be, a process of increasing the stock of putative facts to which they are committed. The world view of a child is complete. What matters is the range of experience it covers. And one of the benefits of education can be to learn that it is an intellectual vice to come too easily to conclusions and that our knowledge is all hypothetical. There is thus an irresolvable, but creative, tension between the need for security in belief and the equal need for speculation and enquiry.

This is not a matter special to ethnic diversity, but it has been made more public by the variety of beliefs and other cultural norms which children bring to school. It can create explicit and damaging conflicts when libertarian educational policies run counter to conformist religious or moral values held by parents.

Cultural relativism

It will be noted from the previous section that the argument tends to the view that education has its duty primarily to the needs of the individual child, and the rights of parents and communities are subordinate to those rights. This leaves a role for the culture of the child's community, but it can seem merely therapeutic or motivational: it gives roots and confidence but may seem worthwhile solely in terms of its instrumental value to that child's education. The question of the absolute worthwhileness of any way of life seems to be left out of account. Critics might argue with some justice that if this is so, then multicultural education is merely rhetoric because the traditional school curriculum embodies Western European culture and ways of understanding of which the worthwhileness remains unquestioned. The key practical and theoretical questions then become, to what degree should the curriculum be changed and by what principles should the change be controlled?

A fair amount of absurdity occurs in discussions on either side of these issues. There are those who espouse a complete relativism of knowledge and value, and who argue that they are solely to be understood as the products of particular times and places. This has the implication that any practice genuinely rooted in a discrete culture is as good, as true, as any other. At its worst this implies a cultural solipsism which, as an explanation of the world, cannot even account for how persons are mutually intelligible across cultures. On the other hand, as was noted above, there are those who claim that the particular conception of what is educationally worthwhile which is embodied in Western European education is somehow eternally valid because it can be 'deduced' from *the* 'concept of education'. While just as solipsistic as is complete relativism, this error is perhaps even more pernicious because it implies a cultural superiority which happens to be backed by the inertia, if not the power, of White institutions. It even involves a denial that the English have a culture at all. An interesting example of how matters to do with ethnicity can be assumed not to apply to English society is the increasing use by the press of 'ethnic' to mean 'ethnic minority'. The assumption is that the majority has no ethnicity: it is simply and eternally right.

The more sensible interpretations of the issues around the questions will pay attention to the following:

1. truth can be difficult to find, but all explanations in all cultures are attempts to discover it;
2. the means for that search will have taken different routes in different places, but the circumstances in which beliefs arise are not the same as the beliefs themselves;
3. since beliefs have this independent reference to the truth, they are sharable across cultures.

The first point means that humility combined with a recognition of the hypothetical nature of all beliefs will make us more ready to learn from others. The second will make us indifferent to the origins of beliefs. The third will rid us of any quasi-mystical notions that certain persons have unique access to or are confined by special ways of life and thought because of who they are or where they come from. (This latter is close to Nazi ideology: relativist arguments are also found among proponents of Apartheid.)

Thus we can see that, with reference to those curriculum areas to do with knowledge and belief, so long as education is pursuing systematic, critical approaches to the truth no one culture's methods will be more intrinsically worthwhile than another's. Some will be more fruitful than others, but multiculturalism is premissed upon the mutual intelligibility of ways of thought and upon allowing a genuine competition of ideas. In curriculum areas to do with aesthetic and practical matters, there seem to be no arguments which stand in the way of the genuine celebration of diversity, and music, art, literature, drama are all at the forefront in the best schools of genuinely multicultural approaches.

Careful analysis of the epistemology of cultures will show that multicultural education implies a thoroughgoing overhaul of curriculum so that it genuinely provides education with the resources of all humanity, but that this resource will not be a mere rag-bag. It will be structured and selected using principles which rule out the isolationism of the relativist and the cultural supremacist but which permit a competition of ideas in which winners and losers are possible for reasons unrelated to relative social power.

Religious education can be the source of a special problem if its aim is taken to be the establishment and maintenance of faith. In practice, the great religions are good examples of cross-cultural competitors, and RE has been a very fruitful ground for multicultural education. Some writers have doubted whether confessional schools can ever be truly multicultural in orientation. It is certainly true that religious fundamentalism is anathema to pluralism, but that is a function of its hostility to education in general.

ANTIRACIST EDUCATION

Multicultural education has always been motivated in part by the evidence of racial hostility and xenophobia in society. It is an educational response to poor race relations which works to raise the consciousness of both aggressor and victim. However, its concentration on curricular change, or even on wider changes in the context and processes of schooling, has never satisfied those who accept the analysis of the school as an irreformable agent of social reproduction. Children and teachers may, wittingly or not, have racist preconceptions, expectations, attitudes, and it may be held that no amount of 'multiculturalism' woven cleverly into the fabric of the curriculum will work changes in their hearts and minds quickly enough to change the miserable lot of those who are victims of racism in their daily lives at school or in the streets. There are those who see the need, therefore, to add to a multicultural curriculum and the modification of contexts and practices some direct interventions which shock or persuade the recipients out of their ingrained racism. This direct action – in the form of training experiences which confront the individual with his or her own racism and its consequences – is only dubiously educational. Some critics emphasize that it is a training, and therefore has outcomes which do not permit a variety of alternative beliefs or dispositions. This puts it sharply in contrast with educational outcomes in the same area of social or moral development. On the other hand, if schools are to be effective as agencies for social change rather than merely social replicators, then complete freedom of outcomes can never be permitted. One might indeed argue that racism is never a permissible outcome of education. If it does result, then education has failed. And teachers, surely, cannot be permitted to be racists, for racism implies that an individual's worth is determined by matters inaccessible to education. Moreover, teachers need to be sensitized to spot and correct the implicit and explicit racism in such matters as teaching materials, teaching and organizational styles, school and classroom structures, social relations, and so on. A wide variety of methods has been used in this style of antiracist training, including 'racism awareness' experience. These tend to stress that Whites can never fully understand racism because they can never experience it.

Whilst this kind of antiracist activity is on the margins of education as justified by the values usual in multicultural approaches, there are other antiracist stances adopted by some educational professionals which are directly opposed to those values. These see multicultural education as a hypocrisy used by White society to prevent any substantial change. White versions of Black folk culture are tacked onto White curricula in a patronizing exercise in palliation. Nothing in schools really changes, and will not until power relations in society change. Teachers, in such a case, must directly confront racism in schools and engage in political activity to reconstruct society. Here we leave the realm of education altogether, and therefore the scope of this chapter.

SUMMARY

Multicultural education is concerned with the response education should make to cultural pluralism. It is neither morally nor politically neutral, but is part of a wider reforming tendency which aims at promoting equality through educational change. Its particular characteristic lies in addressing diversity as a resource and strength for education rather than as a problem. This involves a rejection of those derivations of the curriculum which see 'real' knowledge as rooted in some taken-for-granted concept of 'education' which is in fact the result of a particular, European, cultural tradition. The problem for the multiculturalist lies in developing a transcultural conceptual scheme in education the expression of which in educational practice demonstrates that knowledge is the common property of all peoples. To neglect either part of this problem results in, on the one hand, a relativism which denies the very possibility of intercultural understanding, or, on the other hand, a superficiality which emphasizes folklore and the bizarre. Either results in effects contrary to those the multiculturalist desires.

Although a living educational tendency for about thirty years, the adoption of genuine multicultural approaches in education has been patchy in Britain, and many see them as irrelevant in areas with no ethnic minority children. This reminds us that the origin of the tendency lies in a remedial approach. The slow pace of change has led some to see a direct assault upon the racism of schools, teachers, and society as the only way forward. This 'antiracist' movement is not always educational in style.

FURTHER READING

1. For a useful collection of readings ranging over critical perspectives, language, attainment, curriculum, pupils and teachers, see A. James and R. Jeffcoate, (Eds.) (1981) *The School in The Multicultural Society: A Reader*, London: Harper & Row and the Open University.

2. The principles to be attended to in addressing the question of how curriculum changes in a multicultural direction might occur is further explored in a paper of the author's: P. H. Walkling (1980) 'The idea of a multicultural curriculum', *Journal of Philosophy of Education* 14,1.

3. A wide-ranging survey, including a useful version of the history of multicultural education, is J. Lynch (1986) *Multicultural Education: Principles and Practice*, London: Routledge & Kegan Paul.

4. For opposing views of antiracist approaches see the contributions by Chris Mullard and Robert Jeffcoate in M. Arnot (1985) *Race and Gender: Equal Opportunities Policies in Education: A Reader*, Oxford: Pergamon Press and the Open University.

5. Two splendid surveys of the research into the education of children of Afro-Caribbean and South Asian origin were prepared for the Rampton and Swann Committee of Inquiry into the Education of Children from Ethnic Minority Groups: Taylor, M. J. (1981) *Caught Between: A Review of Research into the Education of Pupils of West Indian Origin*, Windsor: NFER-Nelson.Taylor, M. J. and Hegarty, S. (1985) *The Best of Both Worlds . . . ? A Review of Research into the Education of Pupils of South Asian Origin*, Windsor: NFER-Nelson.

6. The Swann Report is currently the most important statement of Government in Britain: Committee of Inquiry into the Education of Children from Ethnic Minority Groups (1985) *Education for All*, London: HMSO (Cmnd. 9453).

I.9

GENDER ISSUES IN SCHOOLING

SANDRA ACKER

It is perhaps a little trite to start a chapter by defining its key terms, but even if we take 'schooling' as reasonably self-evident for our purposes, some amplification is needed for 'gender' and 'gender issues'. Increasingly sociologists distinguish between 'sex' and 'gender', the former referring to biological characteristics of males and females, the latter to culturally specific assignments of traits and roles to each sex. As with heredity and environment, it is terribly difficult to separate the two. When a 'sex difference' (that is, a difference between a group of males and one of females) in some educational outcome such as an average test score is reported, we are usually speaking simultaneously of a 'gender difference', one due at least in part to differentiated learning experiences provided by the culture. The matter is further complicated by international and disciplinary variations in conventional usage. Readers of educational literature cannot yet expect much consistency.

The nature, and even existence, of 'gender issues' is a matter of dispute. For some, the only issue is why people with such concerns should enjoy access to public forums or financial resources of the state or local government. Others, whilst not wishing to deny campaigners the right to join the battlefield of public policy, nevertheless hold that gender divisions are a matter of biological necessity and/or a requirement of social order. Others still subsume gender issues into universalistic concerns such as the pursuit of human rights, or the creation of conditions whereby individuals can more effectively develop their talents or serve society's economic needs. Gender issues may be considered subordinate or even antagonistic to an alternative commitment such as antiracism or class struggle.

This chapter draws upon the arguments of those who believe gender issues in education are a priority area for research and reform. Such work could broadly be labelled feminist. There are different feminist perspectives. Most often three categories are identified: liberal feminism, socialist feminism, and radical feminism. These categories are convenient but any rigid adherence introduces some distortion. Each feminist tendency produces distinctive interpretations of educational issues. Liberal or equal rights feminists try to remove barriers that prevent girls reaching their full potential, whether in the mind, the family, school, or workplace. They concentrate on providing information, changing attitudes, and using antidiscrimination legislation. Socialist feminists hope in the long run to end oppression under capitalism. In the short run most of the analysis asks how education produces or reproduces a sexual division of labour whereby women are locked into low paid, dead end jobs and heavy domestic responsibilities. Radical feminists aim to eliminate male dominance and put girls and women at the centre of concern. Two clear areas of interest in the quite considerable educational literature are patriarchal ('man-made') knowledge and the everyday sexual politics of educational institutions. Borrowing from all the various perspectives, it seems much of the work in what is now a voluminous literature can be summed up as the '3 Rs' of gender issues in schooling: routes; regimes; and relationships.

ROUTES

We can compare the typical pathways (routes) taken by the sexes through the education system and into employment. Issues of access and representation fit most neatly into liberal feminism although others will see it as important, if not as an end in itself. Questions of access are most often raised about the last years of secondary school and about tertiary education. In Scotland, girls are more likely than boys to leave school with four or more H grades. But in England and Wales, the proportion of girls leaving school at 17 with three A levels is still slightly lower than the corresponding proportion of boys (8.6 per cent of girls and 10.5 per cent of boys). On the other hand, girls are less likely than boys to leave school with no examination qualifications and are more likely to enter full-time further education. Women students are still a minority in polytechnics, where they were 38.7 per cent of students on advanced courses in 1984. Women's share of undergraduate places in British universities has risen dramatically since 1965–6, when it was 27.6 per cent, to 41.5 per cent in 1984/5. (Figures from DES 1986a:36, 39; EOC 1986: 16, 17.)

Interest in access extends to adult women (for example Hughes and Kennedy 1985). Recommendations have been made for flexible courses and outreach strategies to draw in women who would otherwise not come into contact with higher or further education. The present system is often criticized for operating on a model of the male life cycle, for example in its assumption that tertiary education follows soon after secondary and in the lack of part-time provision or childcare facilities.

The most striking differences between the sexes in educational profile are in subjects studied rather than level reached. The Equal Opportunities

Commission (1986:9) provides tables which suggest boys predominate in technical drawing and physics at CSE, O and A levels, mathematics and computer science at A level and computer studies at O level; girls predominate in domestic subjects or cookery at all levels, office practice at CSE, French at CSE and A level, sociology at O and A level and English at A level. Metalwork and woodwork (currently being absorbed into craft, design and technology) are also studied almost entirely by boys to examination level (EOC 1985).

Unemployment among school leavers has increased dramatically in the past decade. Manpower Services Commission schemes have attempted to fill the gap for school leavers (Youth Training Scheme) and also to introduce more vocational training into the upper years of secondary education (Technical and Vocational Education Initiative). The MSC has made a commitment to equal opportunities and breaking down vocational sex stereotyping on its schemes but so far its success seemed limited.

Gender differentiation is also strong in the further education sector, where there are close links with the labour market. The Women's National Commission (1984:44) describes parts of non-advanced further education (NAFE) as 'huge "bastions" of male dominated disciplines ... nearly one quarter of all students in NAFE were males in engineering'. There are also female worlds within further education such as secretarial or 'caring' courses. In universities, too, subject differentiation is marked. For example, women undergraduates are in the majority in French, English, and sociology but are a very small proportion of students in physics. In Great Britain in 1984–5 there were 31,093 male full-time undergraduates studying engineering and technology, compared with 3,504 females (EOC 1986:18).

The statistics can only describe general trends. Recent work tries to avoid the tendency to generalize about 'all girls' and 'all boys' and find ways of taking into account other facets of identity such as social class, ethnicity, rural/urban residence, and so forth to construct a better model of the distribution of educational life chances. Theorists are also attempting to grasp the complex ways in which individual choice and school-based or societal constraints interact in producing these patterns.

Something of a sideline here is the question of *teacher* career routes. Women are the majority of full-time teachers in the nursery/primary sector (78 per cent) but not in the secondary sector (46 per cent) in England and Wales (DES 1986b). UK figures for 1984–5 show women are 24.7 per cent of academic staff in further education and 12.9 per cent in the universities (DES 1986a:11). In all sectors except the nursery and infant age range, women are concentrated in the bottom grades, becoming almost invisible in the upper echelons of further and higher education. DES figures (1986b) for full-time teachers in maintained schools in England and Wales show that in secondary schools 69.2 per cent of women (and 42.7 per cent of men) were on Scales 1 and 2; in primary schools corresponding figures are 76.4 per cent and 36.1 per cent.

Most (83.8 per cent) secondary school headships are held by men. In the primary sector, women hold nearly all (97.6 per cent) the headships of separate infant schools. But men take over in junior-with-infant schools, where they hold 69.4 per cent of the headships, in separate junior schools (79.6 per cent), and in middle schools (80.9 per cent). Although Scales 1 and 2 are to be amalgamated as of October 1987 and higher scale posts replaced by a system of incentive allowances, the sex differentials are unlikely to diminish. These figures may have an importance beyond their impact on teachers' careers; it is possible that they convey messages to pupils and students about roles of men and women. Such messages are part of what can be termed a 'gender regime', the subject of the next section.

REGIMES

'Gender regimes' is a phrase coined by some Australian researchers (Kessler, Ashenden, Connell, and Dowsett 1985) to describe 'the pattern of practices that constructs various kinds of masculinity and femininity among staff and students, orders them in terms of prestige and power, and constructs a sexual division of labor within the institution' (p.42). The equivalent 'gender code' is more often found in British literature (MacDonald 1980). The intent is to convey the pervasiveness of the structuring of school life by gender. The models of masculinity and femininity are not unchanging, nor need they be consciously pursued. They are embedded in taken-for-granted aspects of everyday school life. Different schools will have different gender regimes. In one Australian upper class boys' private school, for example, boys who were good at debating, academic work, and non-violent games were scorned while football was elevated into a cult which 'celebrates toughness and endurance, relentlessly promotes competitiveness and fear of losing, and connects a sense of maleness with a taste for violence and confrontation' (Kessler et al. 1985:39). In an English study of four primary schools, Clarricoates (1980) shows distinct differences in types of masculinity/femininity expected and rewarded, linked to social class and urban/rural location.

The curriculum has been of particular interest to those studying gender regimes. Stereotypes in stories, textbooks, and examination materials are frequently singled out. Buswell (1981), for example, looks at a humanities course in a secondary school in the north of England and finds

> in 326 pages ... 'he', 'him' or 'man' was used to refer to people 252 times. These pages also contained 169 drawings of men compared with 21 pictures of women. ... The emphasis of the units on Kings, armies, explorers etc. helps to

explain how 102 individual men – past or present – received a mention compared with 14 women (p.197).

Radical feminists such as Spender (1982) see such examples as part of a long tradition of treating knowledge created by men and based on their experiences as *universal* knowledge.

At least since the HMI survey on curricular differentiation for the sexes carried out in 1973 (DES 1975), schools have come under feminist criticism for creating or exaggerating divisions between girls and boys by their administrative arrangements for timetabling and option choice. Since the Sex Discrimination Act and greater public consciousness, sex segregation is no longer so rigid. Nevertheless, each year the Equal Opportunities Commission receives parental complaints about criteria schools use for allocation to craft subjects. It has proved difficult to get pupils to opt for nontraditional subjects even when some of the obvious barriers have been removed. One reason may be that children are unwilling to be 'pioneers' unless a number of same-sex friends join them. Some commentators argue that it is the practice of choosing options itself that is at fault. Option choice in comprehensive schools is thought to have become a kind of hidden streaming, guided by the school and reinforcing class and gender divisions in the process. For each choice, something else is foregone; thus, girls who want to do childcare must give up something in return (Grafton, Miller, Smith, Vegoda, and Whitfield 1983).

It also appears that, in less formal ways, children are classified as 'girls' or 'boys' repeatedly in school, from nurseries on up, as when teachers routinely divide the sexes within a mixed class for competitions, seating, registration, or queueing. Buswell (1981:196) remarks that 'one of the most important messages that the pupils receive is that they are a boy or girl foremost'.

Concern about deleterious effects on girls of gender regimes in mixed-sex schools has meant that the question of 'single-sex versus mixed schools', long thought to be dormant in educational debate as comprehensive reorganization increasingly produced coeducation (almost as a byproduct), has resurfaced as a feminist issue. Some writers believe that girls' achievements, especially in science, are enhanced by single-sex schooling. It is difficult to make systematic comparisons between single-sex and mixed schools, even if one confines attention to the state system, for other factors make them not strictly comparable, for example the single-sex schools may have different (grammar school) traditions, or parents who send their children to single-sex schools may have reasons for doing so which set them apart from others. A comprehensive survey of relevant research by and large did not support the case that academic advantages are caused by girls' schools themselves rather than their intake (Bone 1983:85). Another argument for girls' schools is the greater career possibilities they give women teachers and the effect on girls of seeing role models who are powerful and competent. However, the most common feminist argument is that the general well-being of girls is best served by separating them from boys for at least part of their studies. Some attention has been given in mixed schools to experiments comparing mixed and single-sex sets, especially for mathematics. One such study lasting five years found a learning advantage for the single-sex girls' sets only clearly evident in the first two years of secondary school. Nevertheless girls' mathematical achievements improved for the school as a whole (although remaining below boys') probably because of the generally raised consciousness about the issues involved (Smith 1986).

RELATIONSHIPS

Another interesting area is teacher-pupil and pupil-pupil relationships in school. Research suggests teachers often hold stereotyped beliefs about capacities and characteristics of the sexes; ascribe girls' accomplishments to rule-following or hard work rather than creativity or flair; know little about girls' real career and educational aspirations (for example Buswell 1984). The most frequently reported finding is that boys receive a disproportionate share of teacher attention in mixed classrooms (Kelly 1986). But this state of affairs is not *inevitable*: a few studies find that teachers prefer girls over boys; not all studies report preferences; there is evidence that 'equity training' reduces teacher bias (Kelly 1986). Feminist researchers are now seeking to gain a more precise understanding of the classroom dynamics of gender, asking what form the interactions take under what circumstances and why (for example Kelly 1985). Teachers' attention can be disciplinary or negative, and it can be a response to children's behaviour, which may itself be a response to previous experiences.

Looking at interaction among pupils, there is a growing concern, particularly associated with radical feminism, with what might be called the sexual politics of everyday school life. Jones (1985) and Mahony (1985) paint a horrifying picture of what school can be like for girls when their classroom contributions are met with systematic ridicule from boys and when their existence outside classrooms is filled with verbal and nonverbal sexual abuse, even assault. Jones (1985:30) writes that 'male violence – visual, verbal, and physical sexual harassment – was part of daily school life' in a London secondary school. It is unlikely that all mixed schools are like this – but if some are, we need to discover when and where and how the phenomenon can be tackled. A perhaps less alarmist but fascinating picture of teenage girls' lives comes from Sue Lees's recent book *Losing Out* (1986), which shows sixteen-year-old girls caught in a sexual double standard reminiscent of the 1950s. Girls walk a tightrope where all aspects of their lives are shaped by fear of being labelled as sexually immoral, the labels being imposed by both sexes and having remarkably little to do with actual sexual behaviour. There is a strong and developing interest among socialist feminists as well as radical feminists in understanding the cultural responses of adolescents and their part in perpetuating or resisting gender divisions in and out of school.

TOWARDS A FOURTH 'R'

If we add a fourth 'R' there is a good case for 'reform'. We could look at the extent to which central government, local authorities, schools, and teachers are responding to the points raised by feminist research (see Acker 1986). There has been little in the way of a lead from the top. Equal opportunities discourse is acceptable there, as is some alteration of the school curriculum to ensure girls as well as boys receive scientific and technological training. The introduction of a national curriculum may avoid some of the gender differentiation of option choice. There is also some governmental support for encouraging mature women students into higher education and mention of equal treatment of boys and girls as desirable in several government publications. But there is nothing like a consistent policy nor any indication that gender equality is of special interest. There is no equivalent to the Swann Report on education of ethnic minorities, and gender inequality has not been included in the lists of national priority areas for inservice teacher training. Local education authority policies vary enormously (see Whyte, Deem, Kant, and Cruickshank (Eds.) 1985). Some, like the Inner London Education Authority, have put money and publicity into antisexist initiatives and the appointment of equal opportunities advisers; others avoid taking such measures, believing they might be attacked by press and politicians as 'loony left'; in others the issues seem hardly to have been aired.

Resources for teachers wishing to develop antisexist curricula or strategies are increasingly being developed but are still rather difficult to obtain, especially outside London. A recent publication based on research sponsored by the School Curriculum Development Committee, called *Genderwatch*, is available for teachers to use in identifying and tackling areas for reform within their schools (Myers 1987). Clearly there are individual teachers and schools at various points on the liberal-to-radical feminist spectrum working hard to change school practices. On the other hand teachers as a group have not yet taken on gender equality as a high priority goal. There are a number of possible reasons for this. Some teachers are likely to be suspicious of outsiders, feminists, and social scientists, and understandably reluctant to accept what may seem criticism of their fundamental skills. There is also evidence that teachers believe schools should be neutral on socio-political issues (Pratt, Bloomfield, and Seale 1984) and that many do not define gender divisions as an *educational* problem (Whyte 1986). It is also indisputable that teachers are working under a great deal of stress with rapidly expanding demands on their time and good will. In these circumstances, demands to prioritize gender equality may be seen as just another outside pressure.

On the optimistic side, as Kelly (1985) points out, public consciousness of gender issues is much higher than it was a decade ago. Teachers-in-training are more likely to encounter the relevant debates. Education journals, newspaper supplements, and books on gender and education regularly appear. Research on gender issues is extending into so-far underdeveloped areas such as sexual harassment in schools, the impact of gender on educational policy, and the reproduction of masculinity. It is becoming more sophisticated in its attempts to take account of the interactions with gender of class, ethnic group membership, and other attributes in producing distinctive educational experiences and outcomes, and in its understanding of classroom complexities. Change is much slower than the feminists of the early seventies hoped but neither is it wholly absent: gender issues in schooling both recur and endure.

REFERENCES

Acker, S. (1986) What feminists want from education, in A. Hartnett and M. Naish (Eds.) *Education and Society Today*, Lewes: Falmer Press: 63–75.

Bone, A. (1983) *Girls and Girls-only Schools: A Review of the Evidence*, Manchester: Equal Opportunities Commission.

Buswell, C. (1981) 'Sexism in school routines and classroom practices', *Durham and Newcastle Research Review* 9, 46:195–200.

(1984) 'Sponsoring and stereotyping in a working-class English secondary school', in S. Acker, J. Megarry, S. Nisbet, and E. Hoyle (Eds.) *World Yearbook of Education 1984: Women and Education*, London: Kogan Page: 100–9.

Clarricoates, K. (1980) 'The importance of being Ernest . . . Emma . . . Tom . . . Jane. The perception and categorization of gender conformity and gender deviation in primary schools', in R. Deem (Ed.), *Schooling for Women's Work*, London: Routledge & Kegan Paul: 26–41.

Department of Education and Science (1975) *Curricular Differences Between the Sexes*, London: HMSO.

(1986a) *Education Statistics for the United Kingdom 1986 edition*, London: HMSO.

(1986b) *Statistics of Education: Teachers in Service England and Wales 1985*, London: HMSO.

Equal Opportunities Commission (1985) *Equal Opportunities and the School Governor*, Manchester: EOC.

(1986) *Women and Men in Britain: A Statistical Profile*, London: HMSO.

Grafton, T., Miller, H., Smith, L., Vegoda, M., and Whitfield, R. (1983) 'Gender and curriculum choice: a case study', in M. Hammersley and A. Hargreaves (Eds.) *Curriculum Practice: Some Sociological Case Studies*, Lewes: Falmer Press: 151–69.

Hughes, M. and Kennedy, M. (1985) *New Futures: Changing Women's Education*, London: Routledge & Kegan Paul.

Jones, C. (1985) 'Sexual tyranny: male violence in a mixed secondary school', in G. Weiner (Ed.) *Just a Bunch of Girls*, Milton Keynes: Open University Press: 26–39.

Kelly, A. (1985) 'The construction of masculine science', *British Journal of Sociology of Education* 6, 2:133–54.

(1986) 'Gender differences in teacher-pupil interaction: a meta-analytic review'. Paper presented at the British Educational Research Association Annual Conference, Bristol.

Kessler, S., Ashenden, D., Connell, R. W., and Dowsett, G. W. (1985) 'Gender relations in secondary schooling', *Sociology of Education* 58, 1: 34–48.

Lees, S. (1986) *Losing Out*, London: Hutchinson.

MacDonald, M. (1980) 'Socio-cultural reproduction and women's education', in R. Deem (Ed.) *Schooling for Women's Work*, London: Routledge & Kegan Paul: 13–25.

Mahony, P. (1985) *Schools for the Boys? Co-education Reassessed*, London: Hutchinson.

Myers, K. (1987) *Genderwatch*, London: School Curriculum Development Committee.

Pratt, J., Bloomfield, J., and Seale, C. (1984) *Option Choice: A Question of Equal Opportunity*, Windsor: NFER-Nelson.

Smith, S. (1986) *Separate Tables? An Investigation into Single-sex Setting in Mathematics*, London: HMSO.

Spender, D. (1982) *Invisible Women: The Schooling Scandal*, London: Writers and Readers.

Whyte, J. (1986) *Girls into Science and Technology: The Story of a Project*, London: Routledge & Kegan Paul.

Whyte, J., Deem, R., Kant, L., and Cruickshank, M. (Eds.) (1985) *Girl Friendly Schooling*, London: Methuen.

Women's National Commission (1984) *The Other Half of Our Future*, London: Cabinet Office.

EDUCATIONAL THEORY AND ITS RELATION TO EDUCATIONAL PRACTICE

WILFRED CARR

I

Whatever subtle nuances of meaning it may have for educational theorists, for educational practitioners 'theory' is something to be regarded with suspicion and mistrust. 'Theory' is opposed to 'practice' and that very opposition is usually enough to arouse expectations of irrelevant jargon which has nothing to do with everyday practical problems and concerns. Over the years, educational theorists have made strenuous efforts to overcome this kind of antagonism, but all the signs suggest that they are making little progress. Despite our best intentions, the gap between theory and practice stubbornly remains.

As somebody who works at the 'theory' end of the education business, I naturally find this situation hard to accept. At the same time, though, I also believe that it is based on a misunderstanding which has impeded the development of a proper relationship between theorists and practitioners for a long time: the twin illusion that some people 'theorize' about education without any concern for how it is practised, while others 'practise' education without any concern for how it is theoretically to be studied or understood. This is an illusory understanding of the theory-practice relationship because there is not one set of concerns about how to engage in educational theorizing and another separate set of concerns about how to engage in educational practice. To hold a view about educational theory is also to hold a view about educational practice. It follows from this that questions about educational practice and questions about educational theory are always closely related. It also follows that contentious arguments about the nature and role of educational 'theory' are, at one and the same time, contentious arguments about the nature and role of educational practice.

In this chapter I want to substantiate this general claim by providing a highly compressed historical outline of the evolution of educational theory in the twentieth century.[1] I do this to show how the different versions of educational theory now available to us are not just the product of a series of abstract methodological arguments about the nature of 'theory'; they also reflect changes in our way of thinking about educational practice as well. My hope is that this kind of historical understanding of different forms of educational theorizing will make it easier to reveal the different conceptions of educational practice each incorporates.

II

Throughout much of the nineteenth century, teachers acquired their training in a demonstration school under the supervision of a Master or Mistress of Method. Towards the end of the century, as the provision of elementary education expanded, it was felt that this 'apprenticeship' method of teacher training was no longer adequate and that, as well as learning practical teaching skills, prospective teachers should also acquire some knowledge of 'theory'. One influential educationalist, writing in 1884, put the point like this:

> What English Schoolmasters now stand in need of is *theory*; and, further, that the Universities have special advantages for meeting this need.[2]

As this opinion carried the day and teacher education moved into universities, so courses in 'Educational theory' began to proliferate. These courses reflected a conventional assumption of the times: that educational theory was essentially a form of philosophical enquiry concerned to raise fundamental questions about the nature of education and its relationship to society through a philosophical study of knowledge, human nature, and the good for man. In practice, however, the kind of educational theory courses that actually appeared did not so much raise fundamental questions as give potted accounts of the answers provided by various historically influential philosophers. Writing in 1928 John Adams, a Professor of Education at London University, gives a telling explanation of why educational theory took this somewhat uncritical form:

> When education as such began to be recognized ... as a subject in University curricula, it was only natural that lecturers in education should look out through world literature for great names wherewith to adorn their list of prescribed readings. Quite naturally, Socrates, Plato and Aristotle were seized on at the very start and a good deal of ingenuity was shown in bringing out educational principles from their work ... Even at the present day, the best way for a young lecturer in education to establish his claim as an educationalist is to select some well known writer and publish a book under the title 'so and so as Educator'.[3]

Needless to say, this kind of 'Great educators' approach to educational theory was immediately perceived to be inadequate to the actual needs of teachers and schools – needs that were then being shaped by the expansion in state education resulting from the Forster Education Act of 1876 and the Balfour Education Act of 1902. Although it was always intended that this expansion would give expression to a variety of educational aspirations and ideals, it was also firmly linked to an overriding pragmatic concern: the need to create a highly differentiated labour force equipped to fill the range of occupational roles appropriate to the advancement of a modern industrial society. This, in turn, meant that education had to be institutionalized to an unprecedented degree, not only to ensure that educational provision and the flow of qualified teachers could be regulated and controlled, but also to make sure that the policies of schools, the content of their curriculum, and their methods of assessment were more securely harnessed to the economic needs of society.

One of the major effects of this new level of institutionalization was gradually to transform the way in which education itself was understood. It now became increasingly attractive to see education as a 'system' which had to be efficiently organized, managed, and administered. Moreover, a necessary prerequisite for the effective management and administration of this 'system' was the creation of a greater consensus about the goals of education. And the need to make education more responsive to economic demands made it imperative that this consensus took it as self-evident that a primary goal of education was to prepare pupils for the kind of occupational positions available in modern society.

In this climate of increasingly institutionalized educational provision, educational theory had to develop new forms. The most pressing problems were not now philosophical problems about the purpose of education, but instrumental problems about how education was to achieve those social and economic purposes prescribed in modern society. What was needed was a form of educational theorizing which could suggest better ways of achieving accepted and established educational goals rather than simply provoking a seemingly endless dialogue about what these goals should be. The form of educational theory which emerged to fill this need was one which construed educational theory as an 'applied science' – a form of theorizing designed to produce a body of sophisticated scientific principles and techniques which could be used to improve the functioning of the educational system.

One of the earliest and clearest examples of the link between this 'applied science' approach to educational theory and the demands being made of educational practice is the emergence of psychometry in the 1920s. Under the powerful leadership of Sir Cyril Birt, a 'scientific' theory of human intelligence was invoked in order to legitimize procedures for measuring the 'educability' of pupils – procedures that were urgently required if schools were effectively to segregate pupils in line with the demand for a hierarchical and stratified division of labour. The interconnections that obtained throughout the inter-war period between educational theorizing of a predominantly psychometric kind and the rise of mass education have often been discussed by educational historians. Brian Simon, for example, has made it clear that any explanation of why psychometry dominated educational theory throughout this period,

> ... needs to be sought not only in the history of ideas but also in the actual circumstances of the time which called insistently for theories which legitimised the hierarchical system brought into being from 1902 ... There appears to be a clear relationship between the economic and social conditions ... in the inter-war period ... and the dominant theory legitimising and lubricating this system[4]

In the period immediately following the second world war, educational theories of an applied science form proliferated and affected all areas of educational practice. Behaviourist theories of teaching and learning, bureaucratic approaches to educational organization, and administration and technical models of curriculum development appeared – all purporting to improve education by applying scientific principles and knowledge. By the early 1950s educational theory had become fully accommodated to the scientific and technological spirit of the age. Fundamental philosophical questions about the purpose of education and its relationship to society could no longer find adequate theoretical expression, and educational theory surrendered its traditional claims to offer moral guidance and support. As educational practice was transformed into a neutral instrument for pursuing given social objectives, so educational theory was transformed into a neutral instrument for overcoming the technical problems to which the pursuit of these objectives gave rise.

By the 1960s other academic disciplines had joined psychology in making claims to have important applications to educational practice. Sociology had become an established empirical science, providing research findings critical of existing selection procedures and supportive of egalitarian proposals to extend equality of opportunity through comprehensive reorganization. Educational philosophy resurfaced with a new name – 'the philosophy of education' – but in a truncated and much reduced form. Drawing inspiration from the 'linguistic revolution' that had already transformed mainstream academic philosophy, the new 'philosophy of education' was no longer defined by the enduring nature of the questions it addressed but by the particular method it employed – a method of 'conceptual analysis' by means of which the 'logic' of the concepts used in everyday educational discourse could be 'clarified'. By embracing this method the philosophy of education could claim that it was no longer contaminated by rival 'educational ideologies', but had now followed other forms of educational theory in becoming a respectable value-neutral academic pursuit.[5]

Throughout the 1960s, as educational theory became increasingly dependent on the 'parent' disciplines of philosophy, psychology, and sociology, so it was increasingly seen to rest on 'foundations' that were outside the field of education itself. It is hardly surprising, therefore, that the officially sanctioned view that dominated this period defined educational theory as a stock of 'practical principles' that were entirely justified by appeals to knowledge provided by the 'foundation' disciplines. At a theoretical level, this 'inter-disciplinary' view of educational theory derived its main impetus from the collection of papers in J. W. Tibble's *The Study of Education*.[6] At an organizational level, the philosophy, psychology and sociology 'of education' had, by the end of the 1960s, managed to carve up the domain of educational theory amongst themselves. Educational departments were reorganized, courses in educational studies were restructured, professional identities were changed, and new journals and academic societies were established, all displaying total allegiance to the view that educational theory was nothing other than the application to education of these 'foundation' disciplines.[7] By 1970, educational theory as an autonomous field of practical knowledge had ceased to exist.

Almost immediately, however, the initial enthusiasm for this kind of educational theory was tempered by a growing realization that the 'educational disciplines' did not easily relate to educational practice. Practical educational problems were not accessible from the narrow confines of the academic disciplines, and the interdisciplinary co-operation between philosophers, psychologists, and sociologists which this approach envisaged never actually got off the ground. As it became clear that 'academic respectability' had only been achieved at the price of 'practical relevance', so complaints about 'the disciplines approach' intensified. As a result, the past decade has been marked by attempts to forge a new 'paradigm' which would bridge the 'gaps' between educational theory and the educational practice to which it is supposedly addressed.

One of the most influential of these new paradigms has emerged in the field of curriculum theory, where reactions against the increasing use of scientific and technical language have been particularly strong. This overreliance of curriculum theory on academic and scientific theories was explicitly recognized and attacked by Joseph Schwab in his seminal paper, *The practical: a language for the curriculum*.[8] In this, Schwab mounts a critique which is equally telling against both the 'applied science' and the 'disciplines' view of educational theory. Briefly, what he argues is that: these approaches fragment the curriculum as an object of study; distort education as a mode of autonomous practice; fail to equip teachers to make informed practical judgements; lead to contradiction and confusion, and foreclose discussion about the moral aspects of education and its role in modern society. Schwab thus proposes a view of curriculum theorizing as a 'practical' discipline. He makes it clear, however, that

By the 'practical' I do *not* mean the curbstone practicality of the mediocre administrator and the man on the street for whom the practical means the easily achieved familiar goals which can be reached by familiar means. I refer rather to a complex discipline relatively unfamiliar to the academic and differing radically from the disciplines of the theoretic. It is the discipline concerned with choice and action, in contrast with the theoretic, which is concerned with knowledge. Its methods lead to defensible decisions where the methods of the theoretic lead to warranted conclusions.[9]

When Schwab's 'practical' approach erupted onto the American scene, it quickly attracted adherents from the ranks of those curriculum theorists who were disaffected by the dominant technical and theoretical perspectives. In Britain, the main focus for this kind of unrest was provided by Lawrence Stenhouse's influential vision of curriculum theorizing as a form of creative and critical inquiry through which teachers could explicitly explore their own implicit educational 'theories' by researching their own educational practice.[10] This gave rise to a radically new understanding of 'educational theory' – one which asserted the indivisibility of theory and practice and which gave the notion of 'teacher-as-researcher' a central place.

As developed by Schwab, Stenhouse, and others, 'practical' approaches to educational theorizing have now emerged which reinstate the image of the teacher as a professional educator whose deliberations about what to teach and how to teach it are once again informed by philosophical beliefs and ethical concerns. At the same time, however, it is apparent that the progressive institutionalization of education has severely curtailed the extent to which teachers are still able to construe their work as an ethical activity based on morally informed deliberation and choice. As a result, many educational theorists are becoming more conscious of the need to expose the ways in which the institutionalized mechanisms that now regulate the work of schools may be frustrating teachers in their attempts to express their professional aspirations and pursue genuine educational values and goals.

The anti-educational effect of the institutionalization of schooling was itself made a major topic of debate by the de-schooling polemic of the 1970s. Ivan Illich, the chief architect and principal exponent of de-schooling[11] argued that because schools had, in effect, become *social* institutions serving the economic needs of modern technological society, they could no longer operate as viable *educational* communities serving the learning and developmental needs of their individual pupils. This argument not only challenged the cherished belief that more schooling equals more education; it also challenged educational theorists to develop a form of educational theorizing which did not simply solve the technical problems arising *within* the institutionalized educational system, but raised critical questions about how the process of institutionalization had itself become a major obstacle to genuine educational development and reform.

This challenge is now being met by the development of a new 'paradigm' of educational theory – a 'critical' paradigm – which, like philosophical and practical forms of educational theorizing, incorporates a central concern with fundamental questions about the nature of education and its role in society. What makes it distinctive is that it is also concerned to explore the social, political and economic structures within which educational provision and practice are now embedded. It is thus a form of theorizing specifically designed to raise critical questions about the tensions and contradictions that occur between prevailing social values and educational values. In particular it seeks to reveal how the process of institutionalization may distort educational values and constrain opportunities for their practical realization.

III

Once it is considered from a historical perspective, it is clear that the evolution of educational theory is not one of progressive development towards a unified interpretation of its meaning and use. On the contrary, the history of educational theory is the history of an ever-increasing range of different interpretations each of which has emerged in response to a changing political climate and a changing agenda of practical concerns. What this suggests is that any quest for a unitary view of 'educational theory' is illusory. What it also suggests is that the diverse range of approaches to educational theory that has emerged during the last hundred years or so is not simply the product of an on-going 'philosophical' debate about the kind of 'theory' appropriate for education to adopt. It is also the product of an on-going political debate about educational policy and practice. This connection between interpretations of educational theory and interpretations of educational practice is usually left implicit and undisclosed. In order to make it more explicit and visible, it may now be useful to summarize the major forms of educational theorizing that have emerged in the twentieth century in a way that draws attention to the rival views of educational practice each incorporates.

The common-sense approach

This approach is favoured by many members of the teaching profession and the HMI. As the name indicates, it refers to those approaches which base educational theory on a common-sense understanding of practice.[12] Thus, with this approach educational theory is always 'practice-focused'; educational theorizing is simply a matter of codifying ideas, concepts and principles embedded in practice and then using this 'theory' to test practical competence and identify deficiencies in practical performance. With this kind of theory, fundamental value-laden questions about educational practice are regarded as uncontentious and largely ignored. Practice determines theory rather than theory determining practice. Educational practice is, on this view, simply a matter of acting within a given tradition.

The philosophical approach

Within this approach 'common sense' is regarded as too unreflective and uncritical to provide an adequate basis for educational theory. It therefore offers a form of theorizing designed to enable practitioners to extend and enrich their common-sense thinking by relating it to a philosophical understanding of the true meaning and purpose of education. Educational practice, therefore, is not interpreted simply as a form of common-sense action but as a form of reflective practice based on educational ideals which can be articulated and justified in the light of some coherent 'philosophy'.[13]

The 'applied science' approach

This is the approach adopted by those educational psychologists, educational researchers, and curriculum evaluators who insist that any defensible view of educational theory must conform to standards laid down by science.[14] On this view, educational theory is a form of 'applied science', using value-free empirical knowledge as a basis for resolving educational problems and improving educational practice. Because, in this approach, questions about the 'ends' of education involve value judgements which cannot be settled scientifically, they cannot therefore be a legitimate concern of educational theory. The only genuinely scientific questions that educational theory can resolve are instrumental questions about the most effective means of achieving those educational ends that have been deemed desirable. Because it incorporates this view of education as a means to a given end, the applied science approach always interprets educational practice as a technical activity: a neutral instrument for bringing about some 'given' educational goals.

The 'practical' approach

This is the approach underpinning 'illuminative' and 'naturalistic' approaches to curriculum evaluation and research and 'process' models of curriculum development.[15] With this approach, the aim of educational theory is not to provide solutions to technical problems but to help practitioners to make morally defensible judgements. It seeks to do this by rehabilitating the practical art of 'deliberation' as a basis for acting educationally in particular practical situations. Thus, from this perspective, educational practice is morally informed action: it is an essentially ethical activity guided by educational values rather than any narrow utilitarian concerns. 'Practice' is thus not seen as an instrumental means to some fixed educational ends but as a fluid and flexible activity in which the choice of both means and ends is guided by values immanent in the educational process itself.

The critical approach

Although this approach has yet to penetrate fully the field of education, it is now the subject of considerable discussion and debate.[16] Like the 'practical' approach, this approach rejects the view of educational theory as an 'applied science' and sees it instead as a form of 'moral science' in which the importance of educational aims and values is given full recognition. Where it differs from the 'practical' view is in its explicit recognition of how practitioners' own understandings of their educational aims may become distorted by various non-educational social forces and of how the practical realization of their values may be impeded by institutional structures and political constraints. Educational practice is thus interpreted not simply as a moral practice but also as a social practice which is historically located, culturally embedded, and hence always shaped by ideology.

In education today, these rival views of theory and practice compete with one another for the allegiance of theorists, researchers, policy makers, and teachers. Those who view educational practice as a form of activity based on inherited tradition and common sense will favour the approach to educational theory which endorses this view. Those who see educational practice as an essentially instrumental activity – as a means to some uncontentious fixed ends – want a form of theorizing which can produce solutions to the technical problems to which attempts to achieve those ends give rise. Others, because they see educational practice as primarily a moral activity, are attracted to a form of theorizing in which the ethical quality of the professional judgements of practitioners is given a central place. Yet others, for whom the ethical dimension of educational practice is being gradually subverted by the modern institutionalization of education, support a form of educational theorizing that can expose the contradictions between educational values and institutionally imposed values, bring them under critical scrutiny, and make them more open to rational dialogue and debate.

Normally, the interdependence of these competing views of theory and practice is either unacknowledged or undisclosed. Indeed, it is common for both educational theorists and practitioners to regard methodological debates about the nature and purpose of educational theory as quite separate from political debates about the nature and purpose of educational practice. What I have tried to show in this paper is that they are not. In education, theory is an indispensable dimension of practice.

NOTES

1. For a more detailed philosophical argument in support of this claim see W. Carr (1986) 'Theories of theory and practice', *Journal of Philosophy of Education* 20, 2:177–86. The brief historical reconstruction of educational theory in this paper owes much to the work of my close colleague, Stephen Kemmis. Of particular significance is S. Kemmis (1986) *Curriculum Theorizing: Beyond Reproduction Theory*, Victoria: Deakin University Press, especially Chapter 2, 'The rise of modern educational theory under the influence of mass education'.
2. R. H. Quick, 'Proceedings of the International Conference on Education', IV 1884 p. 76. Quoted in J. W. Tibble (Ed.) (1966) *The Study of Education*, London: Routledge & Kegan Paul: 4.
3. J. Adams (1928) *Educational Theories*, London: Ernest Benn: 32.
4. B. Simons (1983) 'The history of education' in P. H. Hirst (Ed.) *Educational Theory and Its Foundation Disciplines*, London: Routledge & Kegan Paul: 78–9.
5. The most influential exponent of this view of the philosophy of education was of course R. S. Peters. See in particular the first chapter of R. S. Peters (1966) *Ethics and Education*, London: Allen & Unwin, and, R. S. Peters 'The philosophy of education' in J. W. Tibble op. cit. pp.59–89.
6. See, in particular, P. H. Hirst, 'Educational theory' in J. W. Tibble op. cit. pp.29–58.
7. For a good example of how the 'disciplines' approach to educational theory became a ruling orthodoxy see R. D. Woods (Ed.) (1972) *Education and its Disciplines*, London: University of London Press.
8. Schwab, J. J. (1969) 'The practical: a language for curriculum', *School Review* 8:1–24.
9. Ibid.: 1–2.
10. Stenhouse, L. (1975) *An Introduction to Curriculum Research and Development*, London: Heinemann Education.
11. Illich, I. (1970) *Deschooling Society*, Harmondsworth: Penguin Books.
12. For a recent attempt to link educational theory to common-sense thinking see P. H. Hirst (1983) 'Educational theory' in P. H. Hirst (Ed.) *Educational Theory and Its Foundation Disciplines*.
13. See for example, L. A. Reid (1962) *Philosophy and Education*, London: Heinemann.
14. The clearest and most influential presentation of the case for this approach remains D. J. O'Connor (1957) *An Introduction to the Philosophy of Education*, London: Routledge & Kegan Paul.
15. The most eloquent account of the 'practical' approach remains J. J. Schwab (1969). See also W. H. Reid (1978) *Thinking about the Curriculum*, London: Routledge & Kegan Paul, and M. Holt (1987) *Judgement, Planning and Educational Change*, London: Harper & Row.
16. For a more detailed exposition of this critical approach to educational theory see W. Carr and S. Kemmis (1986) *Becoming Critical: Education, Knowledge and Action Research*, Brighton: Falmer Press. For an example of critical curriculum theorizing see F. Inglis (1985) *The Management of Ignorance: A Political Theory of the Curriculum*, Oxford: Blackwell.

I.II

CURRICULUM THEORY AND VALUES

ROBIN BARROW

The themes of this chapter are that certain questions about values are crucial to curriculum theory and that to some extent they are none the less ignored by curriculum theorists.

Curriculum theorists engage in a great deal of meta-theory. That is to say, they theorize about the most appropriate way in which to conduct their theorizing about curriculum, because they are by no means agreed on the precise nature and boundaries of their domain. Some, for example, suggest that curriculum inquiry may constitute a discipline – a well-organized body of knowledge revolving round its own unique concepts and involving its own distinctive methodology or form of inquiry, in the manner of the natural sciences or mathematics. Others regard it as a subject matter or area of study that needs to draw on a variety of other established disciplines, such as philosophy and psychology, as is the case with peace studies or the study of education generally. Some feel that the focus of attention should be child psychology and principles of teaching, while others argue that the key to understanding curriculum lies in an exploration of the way in which social forces influence or even govern our behaviour and understanding. Disagreement extends to, and to some extent arises from, different conceptions of what a curriculum is, ranging from the view that it should be defined in terms of the content provided, by way of the view that it is best characterized in terms of proposed learner engagements, to the suggestion that it should be seen as the actual experiences of students. Furthermore, even those who agree on a definition of the curriculum may then disagree with each other as to what precisely the content, engagements or experiences provided should be.

While few would dispute the importance of finding out and taking note of what students actually get out of a curriculum, and seeking to ensure that what they get out of it matches our intentions, there is a case for saying that to define the curriculum in terms of students' actual experiences rather than in terms of what we provide or intend to provide is to be resisted. A conception in terms of learner experiences is unmanageable in that it covers too much (for who is to say what the limits of possible experiences may be?) and cannot be anticipated or even, in some cases, discerned after the event. For such reasons it seems preferable to adopt the view that a curriculum is essentially a programme of intent, which is to say the programme of study or activity that we intend students to engage in. Such a definition is tolerably clear, and broadly in accord with common usage and the etymology of the word (the dictionary defines 'curriculum' as 'a series of studies required' and the origin of the word is the Latin word meaning 'a course to be pursued'). It is also manageable, in that we can recognize, plan, and raise various questions about curriculum in this sense without difficulty, and yet it is sufficiently broad (as befits a generic term such as curriculum) not to pre-empt the important questions of what the content of the programme should specifically be and what form or forms it should take. (Should the programme, for example, be conceived in terms of subject matter, development of skills, opportunities to undergo certain experiences, or in some combination of these or other elements?)

Theorizing in any area is concerned with trying to establish general and necessary principles. Scientific theory is not interested in the particular and local history of a particular chemical, but in the principles that necessarily govern the behaviour of any such chemical. Psychological theory does not explore the particularities of one person's responses to a particular situation, but seeks to establish the principles that govern human psychological responses. By the same token curriculum theory is concerned with establishing the general principles that necessarily govern the various aspects of curriculum. Conventionally, the aspects of curriculum theory to be distinguished are curriculum design, development, implementation, and evaluation (although it is not always clear how development is to be distinguished from either design or implementation, and there are in any case obvious and important interrelationships between the aspects).

Given some such definitions of curriculum and the nature of theory, and in line with the conventional distinctions, it may be said that curriculum theory consists in trying to answer such questions as:

1. In what should the programme formally consist? (for example subjects, skills, or activities?)
2. In what should the programme substantively consist? (for example what subjects or what skills?)
3. How should any such programme be presented? (i.e. what general principles can be said to govern any well designed curriculum?)
4. What are the best ways of ensuring the successful adoption of a new curriculum? (i.e. what general principles govern effective implementation?)

III

5. What are the best ways to ensure that curricula are modified and improved, rather than left as moribund relics? (i.e. what general principles govern curriculum development?)

6. What sociological factors may affect the chances of the student's actual experience matching our intentions? (i.e. what general sociological principles govern teacher-learner interaction?)

7. What are the best ways to evaluate curricula? (i.e. what general principles govern evaluation or particular types of evaluation?)

When we think of curriculum theory as being concerned with such questions, it becomes clear:

(a) that questions to do with particular situations, such as whether resources are available to support a proposed curriculum at a given time and place, though obviously extremely important in themselves, are not of concern to theorists, whose job is rather to determine necessary and generalizable truths;

(b) that curriculum theory cannot sensibly be seen as a discipline in its own right. Rather it involves a variety of questions that are different in kind and will accordingly have to be approached in different ways, some being philosophical, some sociological, some empirical, and so on;

(c) that value questions arise throughout curriculum theory. It is not only that some questions such as 'In what should the programme consist?' are straightforwardly questions of value, but also that questions such as 'How should a curriculum be presented?' or 'What are the best ways to implement or evaluate curricula?' are partially evaluative and not simply technical. For the question is not 'What principles will ensure the adoption of a curriculum?' but 'What will ensure the *successful* adoption of a *desirable* curriculum?' Similarly, we are not interested in rules for designing a curriculum, but in rules that are good for ensuring a *worthwhile* curriculum design.

Since our concern is with school curricula (as opposed to, say, the curriculum in a reform centre, a curriculum for trainee nurses, or a curriculum for those studying for the priesthood) the first question in both logic and importance for a curriculum theorist must be, in what would a successful schooling consist? What are the aims that we hope to achieve by means of schooling? Since most people would respond to that question with reference at least to education, socialization, and moral and emotional maturity, the question rapidly becomes, what is it to be successfully educated, socialized and morally and emotionally mature?

We come here to one of the great paradoxes of curriculum theory. The question 'what are our aims?' is clearly crucial. Without a clear answer to it we cannot begin to answer questions about the content of the curriculum;

without a clear notion of a worthwhile curriculum content we cannot seek to arrive at principles of design, since the nature of what is being designed (i.e. an educationally worthwhile curriculum) must have a bearing on what constitutes good design; if we have not sorted out our educational values, how can we talk of successful implementation, for success here implies not only reference to willing adoption, but also adoption that does not do damage to our educational goals. We cannot meaningfully argue about the desirability or otherwise of such specific suggestions as that objectives should be framed in behavioural terms, if we do not know what our aims are and hence what kinds of objective we are dealing with. Yet, while the importance of questions about aims or ends is formally recognized by curriculum theorists, for the most part they are not willing to engage with them directly. Thus some hive it off as a question for philosophers to deal with. Some maintain that society at large should dictate the ends, leaving the curriculum theorist to worry about means. Others adopt some formal principle for determining content which allegedly bypasses the need to determine aims, such as the principle that the curriculum should be based upon children's needs. It would be rash and out of place to speculate on the reasons that lie behind this reluctance to grapple with the question, but two points do seem fairly clear: there is a widespread view that judgements of value are essentially subjective and arbitrary, and a common tendency to regard curriculum theory as a species of applied science, and, as such, not concerned with debatable issues of value. Both of these assumptions are highly questionable.

VALUE JUDGEMENTS

It is certainly true that different people, in different places and times, do hold different values, that value disputes cannot finally be settled by empirical research, and that at the present time, even within a particular culture, we have total agreement neither on our values nor on a means to resolve our differences. It is possibly also true that there is no way of ultimately resolving conflicts of value such as those between people who prize freedom above equality and vice versa, or those who dispute the relative merits of a life devoted to contemplation and a life devoted to some form of practical activity. However, on the other side of the argument, it must be said that at least some of the apparent diversity arises from the fact that different particular circumstances lead to different particular value judgements made in the light of the same general principles. (For example, it is not clear that principles such as those of impartiality, beneficence, the value of an educated mind, and the value of truth have ever been formally denied. Differences centre on how to interpret them.) It is also not the case, as is sometimes implicitly assumed, that what cannot be empirically established is necessarily subjective or arbitrary, if those somewhat obscure concepts are taken to indicate that the question of truth or falsity does not arise. (For example whether God exists is not a question that it is possible to resolve empirically. None the less God either does or does not exist.) Third, and most important, even if it is true that we are not in a position to resolve conflicts of ultimate value or conflicts about the value of different kinds of activity, it does not follow and it is not the case that we cannot distinguish between reasonable or informed value judgements and unreasonable or ill-informed ones within a particular sphere.

Any activity, be it morality, art, education or soccer, is understood as being of a certain sort. That is to say, it is defined in certain terms. It has its particular nature and its organizing principles. Those principles constitute criteria which set limits on what it makes sense to say in respect of value judgements in that sphere. It is not, for instance, even coherent, let alone reasonable or plausible, to maintain that someone who kicks people, cannot run, and cannot control a soccer ball, is a good soccer player. Conversely people who perform in such a way as to contribute to the winning of games within the bounds of what are taken to be the constitutive rules of soccer are by definition good players. It is true that one might wish to argue about the accepted view of what truly constitutes soccer (and such disputes are more common and more real in areas such as morality), and that there will still remain difficulties in establishing that one particular player is superior to all others. None the less, soccer being what it is, some judgements about the quality of individual players are clearly, and in some sense objectively, false, and others equally clearly reasonable.

So far as curriculum goes, since we are concerned to provide a programme that will serve our various educational aims, it is evident that views as to what constitutes a good curriculum are not simply arbitrary. A curriculum cannot be a good one if it does not serve our aims. As to what those aims should be, that too is not simply a matter of personal whim or predilection. Our choice of aims must be directed and governed by consideration of what it is to be educated, to be socialized, and so forth. It may of course be pointed out that there is a certain amount of dispute as to what it is to be educated (more so than in the case of, say, soccer). As to that, one may question how plausible some of the dispute is: surely, for example, no one would seriously dispute that education is at least partially about the development of mind, the acquisition of understanding. And, if that is agreed, there are similarly limits on what may plausibly be maintained about the nature of understanding or the developed mind. In other words some suggestions, such as that an educated person is one who dresses well, can be dismissed as absurd, and, consequently, some curriculum aims can likewise be rejected without being arbitrary. In any case, whatever the degree of agreement that might be gained, it remains clear that the view that one can hold any view one chooses will not do: the aims to which one commits oneself, and consequently the criteria whereby one assesses the worth of a curriculum, must at least be consistent with one's conception of education, and, if one does not have a clearly and coherently articulated conception of education, then one is not in a position to make informed value judgements in this area.

The notion that aims and values can be determined by some such formula as 'based on children's needs' is not necessarily false, so much as misleading. No doubt a curriculum should meet children's needs. But the question is how one determines people's needs. The concept of need is itself value-loaded: the judgement that somebody needs something is partly empirical (the observation that the person lacks something which is a means to some end), but partly evaluative (the judgement that a particular end matters). Furthermore, in the case of curriculum, it is not simply needs that have to be met, but educational needs. (There is also the question of whether schools should not also be concerned about certain of society's needs as well as children's needs.) In other words, if we are to base the curriculum on needs, we shall still have to work out and be guided by our conception of what it is to be educated. Needs assessment procedures typically do not assess what we want to know: they combine to produce a picture of what various people think children need, and seldom concentrate even then on what specifically educational needs people think children have.

The point that it scarcely makes sense to separate the question of our aims from our theorizing and research about means is less readily recognized than the point that value judgements within the sphere of education must be constrained and guided by an understanding of what education is. This would be so, even if it is accepted that there will continue to be disagreement about aims, for the claim that a particular means or principle of procedure is a good one only makes sense if it is understood in the light of some particular aim or aims. If curriculum theorists do not themselves discuss or reveal their aims, how are we to judge the value of the means they propose? A textbook on curriculum design may, for example, claim that a curriculum should be set out in terms of stated objectives couched in behavioural terms. But any argument for such a claim would have to relate to its tendency to serve our educational aims. If the author is not inclined to discuss his aims, we do not even know what ends the means are alleged to serve, let alone whether we are satisfied that they are truly educational ends.

This point is related to a serious deficiency in some of the empirical research conducted by and relied upon by curriculum theorists. For research into such things as principles of effective teaching and principles of good organization of curriculum content to be meaningful, it is obviously necessary that it should be conducted in the light of a clear conception of educational success. Some would doubt that this is very often the case. It is not uncommon, for example, for research into teaching to draw its conclusions on the basis of a perceived relationship between a certain manner of teaching and student success in terms of performance of particular skills or on particular achievement tests. What is not done is to make any attempt to relate such performances to a conception of educational success. It is implicit that the ability, for the sake of example, to perform well on a simple comprehension multiple choice exam, to produce an allegedly creative poem, and to solve certain arithmetic problems, is one and the same thing as being successfully educated. But that, to say the least, is a highly questionable assumption. It is not, of course, an assumption that could not be argued for and defended. The important thing to recognize is that the research is being conducted on certain value assumptions that are not being explicitly highlighted and justified. The situation becomes particularly serious when the research itself is not directly before us, but its conclusions are quoted and built upon by the curriculum theorist, for at that stage we do not even have any clues before us as to what the concept of educational success involved actually was. Thus a curriculum textbook may abjure us, on the basis of research, to use multiple choice examinations, involving four possible answers for each question. But did the researchers who concluded that four was the optimum number and that multiple choice was the ideal form of examination conduct their inquiry in the light of anything that we would regard as an adequate conception of what as teachers we are trying to achieve in our various different areas?

It is arguable that at the present time curriculum theory and the research on which it relies is in a somewhat confused and parlous state, essentially because the value questions are not directly faced, and the interrelationship between them and other questions is not sufficiently recognized. The suggestion made here is that the value questions are central to the enterprise and that, while there may be no definitive way of resolving them, they can be addressed in a rational manner, such that some value claims may be regarded as more reasonable than others. In any case, it is necessary for each individual to relate their curriculum theorizing to a clearly articulated set of educational values, in order to make sense of their work. It may be added that a clear conception of the nature of the educational enterprise will itself to some extent furnish direct guidance in respect of questions of appropriate means to achieve ends – questions that are usually regarded as necessarily requiring empirical research.

It is crucial to base one's detailed curriculum specifications on one's understanding of the aims of schooling and education. It is in turn necessary to base one's research on the observation of an educationally worthwhile curriculum being taught with a view to achieving one's educational aims. Curriculum theory must then draw on such research and seek to evolve principles that govern design, implementation, development, and evaluation in terms of being contributory towards achieving our aims. If the centrality of values is not recognized, we are doomed to the bizarre situation in which theorists assert the efficacy of principles in a vacuum – as if there were proper ways to design a curriculum, regardless of who it is for and what particular purposes it is supposed to achieve.

REFERENCES

Apple, M. W. (1979) *Ideology and Curriculum*, London: Routledge & Kegan Paul.
Bantock, G. H. (1965) *Education and Values*, London: Faber.
Barrow, R. (1981) *The Philosophy of Schooling*, Brighton: Wheatsheaf.
  (1984) *Giving Teaching back to Teachers*, Brighton: Wheatsheaf.
Dearden, R. F. (1972) 'Needs in Education' in R. F. Dearden et al. (Eds.) *Education and the Development of Reason*, London: Routledge & Kegan Paul.
Egan, K. (1978) 'Some presuppositions that determine curriculum decisions', *Curriculum Studies* 10,2.
Gress, J. R. (Ed.) (1978) *Curriculum: An Introduction to the Field*, Berkeley, California: McCutchan.
Lawton, D. (1975) *Class, Culture and the Curriculum*, London: Routledge & Kegan Paul.
Peters, R. S. (1966) *Ethics and Education*, London: Allen & Unwin.
Sockett, H. (1976) *Designing the Curriculum*, London: Open Books.
Stenhouse, L. (1975) *An Introduction to Curriculum Research and Development*, London: Heinemann.
Warnock, G. (1976) *The Object of Morality*, London: Methuen.
White, J. P. (1982) *The Aims of Education Restated*, London: Routledge & Kegan Paul.
Wilson, J. (1979) *Fantasy and Common Sense in Education*, Oxford: Martin Robertson.

I.12

CULTURE, COMMON SENSE, AND CURRICULUM CHANGE

FRED INGLIS

I

Curriculum theory, as the huge weight and protean contents of this collection indicate, reaches after many different practices in a society. Its educational origins, low in the hierarchy of intellectual inquiry, render it naturally obedient to other disciplines with more power, wealth, and prestige. Thus, it is in the present moment of political reaction a creature to some of the rougher methods of the policy sciences which seek to bend it into the crude sequences of managerial objectives-planning.[1] It has also been subject to the hardly less crude but decidedly less influential analyses of radical critics on the political left, whose joyous shouts of hunt-the-hegemony and spot-the-ideology led them to find the old enemy, the bourgeoisie, assiduously at work with their ruling-class preferences in some very small corners of the progressive junior school.[2] More typically, the planning of curricula follows the reach-me-down methods of the negotiation culture, in which a simple recipe book of social and psychological theories is kept on the table while the representatives of different interest groups ensure that their paragraphs in the working papers are still sufficiently visible in the final exam syllabus.[3] It is, of course, entirely to the credit of the ideology-spotters that this messy procedure must be seen as none the less ideological, for all its messiness. What it embodies, in its common-sensible way, is an acknowledgement that some subjects carry greater weight than others in the big world, that outside the working party are the durable, invisible structures of society, making up the endless traffic of parents, employers, local authorities, and Government Inspectors which later turns out so surprisingly to be the march of history through classrooms and curricula.

Of course, it *cannot* be a surprise that the practical administration of the curriculum gives rise to more or less bloody disagreement. For the longish period of the epoch, which opened at Bretton Woods in 1946, with the agreement of the NATO allies and their client states that the marvellous reconstruction of Europe would be their common task, and would become the arena for the truly unprecedented splendours of consumer capital, is now ending. The enormous, arctic fixities of the Cold War which have been the public boundaries and carriageways of a world whose personal source of energy has been so literally the automobile, ignited by our common enjoyment of what Raymond Williams calls 'mobile privatization',[4] are just beginning to dissolve. Economic innovation has shifted for a new season to the Pacific Basin. Nuclear weaponry has become uncontrollable. Radical Islam and Latin Catholicism are sweeping unpredictably across forgotten subcontinents.

These are very large animals to wheel into any intellectual circus ring. To come on cracking the whip of curriculum theorist at them is to risk being simply swallowed up, and the essay left empty for the monstrous forces of destiny to gaze at, vaguely licking their lips. And yet these *are* the monsters whose force we feel through the most trivial decision of the curriculum. It is in tune to their savage rhythms that in Britain since 1979 the curriculum has been blamed for political and economic displacements whose consequence is that we simply cannot revive the safe old factions of 1959, nor follow without crass irresponsibility the antique drums of national glory and uninhibited personal affluence. When the yellow press utters its maledictions over reading standards, or when Cabinet Ministers insist on industrial skills and vocational training, or merely when parents complain about the unintelligibility to them of the new maths and their preference for the multiplication tables, they are all paying tribute money to an educational world in which the old stories about the way things are and the way they ought to be have split and crumbled, and the various authoritarians of the times – parents and populists and Lord knows what – either conjure them severely to work harder, or calmly adjure their audience to believe a new revision of the future magicked out of old fragments for the occasion.

Curriculum theory is by these tokens the most practical of appliances, and everybody has one. Like all theories, however, theories about what you need to know if you are to be educated, what it is to have acquired your culture, and what of the many things in the world you want to know about are relevant (and does it matter if they aren't?) are becoming the domain of certain kinds of government adviser and educational expert, bossed about by the authoritarians who know what is going to be good for us and will ensure that we have it. The curriculum policy combination which emerges from this deadly collusion is the work, as Saul Bellow immortally put it, of high-IQ morons, whose irrational rationalizations do little more than reassert the power of the managers over the managed.

Putting things this way is another reminder that the curriculum is much disputed ground, and even allowing for the obliging stability and settled peacefulness of educational orders in the anglophone polities, the disputes become the more fiercely contested as the governments of the nation states in question use their power to push the contradictions of the political economy out of that irreconcilable area into the province of ideology dominated by the culture industries. The primary state institution in those industries is, of course, education, producer and circulator of the prime resource of meaning.[5]

In so describing the key displacement by modern governments as being out of the political economy into ideology, I ascribe no particular volition or intentions to the agents of those governments. Rather, with Michel Foucault, I invoke the symphonic notion of the 'discourse of power' to cover the *structural* drive for domination of modern intellectual-bureaucratic fields of analysis.[6] Foucault's thesis, documented across histories of the prison, the clinic, the asylum, and the self itself (especially as a sexual entity), was that power is successful in so far as it inscribes its lexicon and categories upon the body and soul of society, and that the depth and pervasiveness of this process in the modern surveillant society are irresistible and ubiquitous.

The historical formation of the process makes Foucault's argument much more than ideology-spotting; the process is, indeed, severely determinist, radically immune to radical opposition. However, with Charles Taylor,[7] I intend to suggest voluntarist remedies to Foucault's grim picture of our helplessness, to identify oppressive *intentions* in the grip of modern managerialism, and to put debate about the curriculum back where it belongs. In that imaginary forum of the polity, we discuss on occasions the human significance and meaning of our busy productivity, the reasonableness of our arrangements as to who shall work, and who shall not, and what either group will be paid for doing something or nothing, and whether what they make – weapons plutonium, say, or hair gel – is what we want and need.

II

There is always a pious shiver to be gained from appeals of this kind to democratic debate. We had better remind ourselves that the present vein of *populist authoritarianism*[8] which has so stained the structure of general feeling in many countries at the present time does not bode particularly well either for old progressivism or even older forms of more communitarian freedoms. My proposal is only half political; the other half, so to speak, cognitive-anthropological.

As to politics, it is surely true that Western societies are in some sort of 'legitimation crisis', as Habermas puts it.[9] That is to say, they cannot reconcile the collision of the welfare state values, those of mutuality and generosity, with the values of *consumer individualism*, in which the self is encouraged in terms of a more or less sanctified egoism to find its own fulfilments, often in satisfying desires for material acquisition and physical pleasure purely (*sic*) for their own sake. If this analysis is correct, our societies are driven by both lines of force, and the two are constantly and bitterly at odds. Given that an absolute value of the culture, now under serious strain from exactly these political-economic pressures whose reality is denied by the governments which cannot control them, is tolerant negotiation, the attempt to suppress debate by turning thinking and making into skills and techniques is extremely dangerous.

Such, however, is the project of power, and power today characteristically masquerades as management. Such is also the barbarous movement of a whole civilization. It needs to be said again and again that the successes of technique and technology over things and objects have led people to suppose that they can gain the same successes over human beings and subjects.

Thus, once you have a problem, you can devise techniques to overcome it. Techniques generate skills. Cognition and morality are displaced to the ivory tower. Thought and wisdom disappear; expertise substitutes itself. The expert sets up the aims and objectives. The research team describes the skills and techniques which will ensure they are achieved. The implementation team come in to show people how to reach these goals. Sometimes the team listen to criticisms in order to indicate why they are irrelevant. This is called feed-back. Then everyone in the scheme goes away to do as they've been told.

Such and such are the sequences of the planners and the plan. Management turns out to mean persuading others to assent with a more or less good grace to ends which are systemic and unavailable to question.

These ends are what are commonly called political realities. They are real enough. But they are not inevitable, except inasmuch as those with power, duly and democratically come by, have decided that this is what will happen. The managers are then hired to persuade people that what is real and nasty has its own necessary momentum, and is not just an act of coercion. The manners of power are now to pussyfoot about in the hope that people will never catch power in the act. Either they will learn to be managed into assent, or they will not see power in action at all, only the old transparency, reality, as it assembles those easily recognized hardnesses, the facts.

Naturally, not everybody will oblige by seeing things the realistic way. After all, the very words should ring like a warning bell. To be managed is to be persuaded of something against your better judgement. The huge tendency of industrial society is to devise ways of organizing agreement to its prior and determinate ends, and to find space for all its members within which they may be sufficiently quiescent not to challenge those ends but to leave the system to go on producing whatever it pleases, including its own destruction. Regulative practices exfoliate from the larger motion of this machine. Counselling is largely a process reserved in state bureaucracies for those who in one way or another have been chewed up and spat out by the system, and its administrations are intended to console or otherwise sedate its victim for his or her anti-social disappointment when life hasn't quite matched up to desires. The grander motions of *scientific administration* ensure everyone else's complicity in the ends of a system too vast and inaccessible for question.

These are the ways to control a world in which morality and politics are set in opposition as respectively the realms of subjectivity and of reality. Your morality is defined by your deepest feelings, and is therefore yours and immune to reason. Politics is defined by the hard facts of reality and is immune to individual action. 'You can't do anything about it.' Either way, there is room neither for rational dissent, nor for the living out of moral judgement, nor for decisions about significant action.

This is why managerial techniques make such a business of the shady speculations of social psychology about role-play and the variegated self. The very notion of graspable moral realities is excluded from their framework. Such words as admiration or disgust, virtue or wickedness, even courage or cowardice, truth or falsehood, must be kept out of a conversation of the culture whose structures institutionalize hypocrisy and justify lying. The idea of speaking so unscientifically at a seminar of scientific administrators is enough to make the cat laugh. Hence the psychologizing of all action. Nobody is simply late for a meeting. They are timing their intervention. No one takes someone's arm out of affection. They are confirming an alliance by body-contact.

The trouble about speaking so harshly is that so many of the managers and their theorists are nice, goofy men and women who would fervently disclaim such manipulative intentions and declare themselves only on the side of such uncontested political concepts as niceness, co-operativeness, a modest dose of efficiency, and a quiet life. Alas, they are in the sick state of those who believe their own propaganda. It is their whole occupation to achieve effectiveness by influencing the motives of subordinates, and to ensure that those subordinates argue from premises which will produce agreement with their own prior conclusions. All heads of department will recognize that process. If they try to sidestep the facts and the realities in the usual arguments about resources, they are brought firmly back into the received frame of mind. (What they then do, of course, is spend a lot of time dodging round the back of those same premises, trying to get what they really want by stealth.)

The defects of managerialism are severe and threefold: in its rationality, its ethics, and its politics. In the first case, managerialism is unexaminedly utilitarian, and like all utilitarian systems, irrational and superstitious. In the second case, the historical ambiguities of its origins in the alliance of utilitarianism and liberalism mean that managerialism structurally produces in its practitioners a tendency to hypocrisy and lying. In the last case, it is impelled by its theory of power to deny resistance and establish dominance; it is cruelly oppressive, and the enemy of freedom.

I have defended these brusqueries in detail elsewhere.[10] But I have made them a strong theme in this chapter because it is no good teachers supposing on the one hand that these processes are the helpful, non-exploitative techniques propaganda would have them be, nor on the other spinelessly accepting power by the Foucauldian talisman, and acquiescing in its ends 'because there's nothing you can do'.

Indeed, my political point may be said to entail my cognitive one. Anthony Giddens remarks that 'the fulfilment of technical imperatives becomes the main legitimating ethos of politics',[11] and this is of a piece with the view argued for already that management simply *is* the present-day embodiment of effective power. Its effectiveness, however, is strictly ideological; that is, it claims causal efficacy only when the desired ends are achieved, and denies it when they are not. In the curriculum, as hardly less often in the economy, I shall say baldly that we scarcely ever have a causally accurate theory of prediction. We do not know for sure, and certainly can never guarantee, what forms or contents of teaching will bring about desired ends. This being so, debate about the curriculum can only rationally take place over human purposes and meanings, and hardly at all over techniques or controls.

Curriculum theory, as Plato implies in *The Republic*, is therefore a main issue in the grand theory of politics. But we cannot simply join hands with Plato across three thousand years and pretend that the divisions of intellectual labour, let alone those of class and nation, have never happened. And here I put in my cognitive-anthropological claims. For science makes a distinction between public and local knowledge, and takes for granted that public knowledge is the only reliable kind. *Public knowledge*, as Popper has famously codified it,[12] has its objective and international protocols: the criteria of evidence and authority, the methods of self-repudiation (falsification), the careful checks on permission to proceed, the recognition of accident, the control on idiosyncracy.

These are the public features of science as we have come to revere it. But the local knowledge by which all men and women including scientists really conduct their business has a rather different view of it. The contrary pulls between local and public knowledge may be read in the standard science textbooks for final year secondary school students. Take an international best-seller like M.B.V. Roberts's *Biology: A Functional Approach* (Nelson, 1971). Its scientific report is of the formal or public kind; it is this which A level students or twelfth graders are expected to copy out faithfully. But alongside it goes a quite different narrative, one in which the giants of the subject – Krebs at Oxford, Pauling at the California Institute of Technology, Sanger at Cambridge – work in intense but friendly rivalry, racing towards cognate discoveries in these glamorous places, turning up all over the globe to congratulate or be disappointed by those who are successful elsewhere.

The two most dashing heroes of the subject were, and remain, Francis Crick and James Watson, and their victory in theorizing the structure of deoxyribonucleic acid (DNA) as a double helix qualifies them exceptionally for the unfailing designation of newspaper and novellette, 'brilliant', and brilliance indeed breaks out from their tale of passion, overwork, intrigue, and blinding intuition in the grave corridors of the Cavendish Laboratory.

The local tale of science wins over the public one. It is a thrilling *novel*, in which as Clive James memorably put it of science as done in television history, one man with a black beard is misunderstood and ostracized by a lot of other men in white beards, but in the end is proved right to the benefit of us all. The classical *novel* of the struggle between the generations, the supersession of the elders by the young, transpires in the narrative of science as the forward march of reason and human improvement by the universal application of the rules of scientific method.

The standard form of local knowledge is a narrative. Let us turn this into a *curricular axiom*. Every subject tells a story. The story is of course partial. Every subject assures us that *its* methods will ensure intellectual, or emotional, or vocational redemption for its students. That is what ideology means: the powerfully *interested* and partisan nature of claims to truthful and original and useful ideas.

At the same time, the story is told and made intelligible by its closeness to the universal forms (and wholly specific contents) of common sense, the local knowledge whose authority is by definition unquestioned. And the harmlessly trite conclusion of this essay is that curriculum theory must be cast in the idiom of *popular aesthetics*. Only then will we get the shared and open public debate which I began by asserting is so urgently needed, as the world turns, and what we know and what we teach children to expect must take account of its new shadows and broken promises.

Casting an argument in the idiom of common sense does not at all mean failing to criticize it. Common sense, the idiom we all speak 'naturally' (as we say), is none the less there to criticize like any grander modality of thought, only when we know what it's like. I have said that it typically tells us a *tale*, long or short or tall. Clifford Geertz also tells us that it is 'natural, thin, practical, immethodical, accessible,'[13] and that it has these qualities wherever it is spoken, even though common sense over there looks decidedly common-senseless over here.

'Naturalness' is easy: it is how things are, *of course* ('Of course, science is expensive; it's difficult and creative'). 'Practicalness' is moreover as natural to the philistine as breathing: to reject the theoretic and the intellectual is sensible to most of us most of the time. (It's no easy task to show the practical man what a lot of theory he has.) 'Thinness' might translate as 'straightforwardness': it is the principle of the self-explanatory description – 'he's a stupid child', 'what do you expect of the fourth year?' are explanations too down-the-line to need any more discussion. They will do exactly as they are. 'Immethodicality' is the shamelessly contradictory quality of common sense ('All Principals are two-faced except her'; 'The exception proves the rule'). And lastly, 'accessible-ness' means what it says: it is, in Geertz's words, that central plainness of common sense such that 'any person with faculties reasonably intact can grasp common sense conclusions, and indeed, once they are unequivocally enough stated, will not only grasp but embrace them' (p.91).

II

It is clear from my abrupt summary of Geertz's paper that there is plenty of room for irony at the expense of common sense, if less for the sort of desperate tearing-of-the-hair-at-human-fatheadedness which understandably charac-terizes the Gramscian revolutionary's view of *hegemony*. Its strength is precisely its commonness, and so is its weakness. I suggested the designation '*popular aesthetics*' by way of catching the unmistakable strain in such a phrase: on the one hand, its everyday, customary quality; on the other, its edificatory and academic touch.

Let it be said that '*popular aesthetics*' intends no sentimental indulgence of the intuitive rightness of either the masses or the *Volk*. It merely connects pedagogy with the typical form of local knowledge, which is the story. This gives rise to an axiom. The characteristic movement of mind is narrative, and by narrative I mean only what that notion usually connotes in everyday usage: a story with a plot[14] and a form capable of turning mere eventuality into experience which makes sense.

This is the point of stories: that they make sense of eventuality, transforming it into history, theory, and biography. This in turn is the mode of reflexivity: a story gives us back ourselves – our human *interestedness* – as a variously distorted mirror which we can ponder over (even a real mirror notoriously turns us back-to-front, halves the width of our faces, and so forth). According to whether the multiple reflections of the culture are capable of showing us truthful and admirable forms of life, so we are the more or the less able to live well or badly.

There is a lesson from liberalism here for all those whose view of education or culture is either totalitarian or technocratic. The lesson is that there just are many different human values in play in the world – a value on this definition being an intensification of life in action – and that these in virtue of their meanings are bound at times to clash with each other. To find that different values from our own have deep and creative significance in the life of others is not necessarily to have caught those others out in a mistake or an impoverishment. Others may indeed be wrong or impoverished, or even wicked, as we may be ourselves, but not simply because we disagree with them.

I counterpose these genteel pieties to an educational momentum in many countries which seeks to bind all values to the cost-effective wheels of efficient production. The relevance of *popular aesthetics* to the lesson of liberalism is that, if I am right in asserting the canonical form of the faculty of imagination as being the story, the news of the world necessarily presents itself to us all in *stories*. Sorting amongst those stories for the innumerable versions of the good life is itself one such life. It both teaches and embodies the facts of the larger life, that the deepest significance of things is their human variety. There are plenty of bad lives around, but a good life cannot be lived which denies the rational possibility of altruism, another word for tolerance.

'Tell me a *story*': every subject (or curricular area) tells a story. As I have said, we then use our many stories to interpret the world and guide our actions in it. But this domestic-sounding adjuration actually squares very ill with what educated knowledge conventionally does to *customary experience*. An example from junior schools either side of the Atlantic brings this out. Most such schools start by teaching aesthetics (art) to their small members as a practical, making activity (*poesis*). This matches happily with my claims about the uses and gratifications of literacy in stories. Our customary (or popular) habit is to make critical use of stories. That is to say, we use them for thought, taking an imaginary part in them to see what the consequences might be. In this process, the art-object and the experience are given equal standing; the expressive capacity of the representation of the object is equal to the object (life) itself. We naturally ask ten-year-olds 'What do you think is going on in the tale?' and we love it when they love it.

But then we try to teach them formalism, and pull them right away from this practical, contextual, meaning-making (*praxis*). Form is set before function as a student progresses upward through the hierarchies of learning. Intention is privileged over use. Aesthetic accuracy, as measured by examination and degree, aspires to a pure perception of the work of art, untainted by merely personal associations. In this, obviously enough, it aspires also to join the cartesian project of pure inquiry, disinterested, objective, pure, detached, atemporal, of which the ideal form is science.

My preferred picture of *aesthetics*, and therefore of curricular discussion, starts from what is useful and informative and beautiful. Within such an *aesthetic*, the things of art and the affairs of life are equivalent, and it will be the ethical significance of either which decides which is to come first in any dispute. This argument aligns *aesthetics* with the narrative-making faculty of mind. Hence aesthetics is the foundation of education, as Collingwood instructed.[15] This is a truth well acknowledged in English junior schools at least, and its ethical weight is very great. For it sets *aesthetics* as the realm and fount of both personal and social (or class) assurance and self-understanding. Your *aesthetics* define you. And so wherever there is a struggle over art there is struggle over the art of living.

All this is not to say that the plain blunt man has it over the magus, only that in debating what kind of curriculum we want – which is to ask 'What kind of life do we want our children to lead?' – we meet bluntness with bluntness, we adopt its plainspoken ways and thereby prevent the discourse of power having things all its other way. Common sense says, 'Don't bite the hand that feeds you'; and common sense replies, 'What if I could then be better fed?' If education is to be rescued for old humanism from the dire hands of managers and trainers, it needs a curriculum of 'really useful knowledge', in the phrase; one which reminds people of what they do know, and teaches them to be at home in thinking about it.

NOTES

1. I am rehearsing a case put at length in my *The Management of Ignorance: A Political Theory of the Curriculum*, Basil Blackwell, 1985.
2. See for example Rachel Sharp, *Knowledge, Ideology and the Politics of Schooling*, Routledge & Kegan Paul, 1980.
3. See for example almost any new syllabus in Communication Studies, or the discussions on Media Studies in *Screen*, passim.
4. Raymond Williams, 'An Epoch's End', *New Left Review*, 140, 1983.
5. This contention borrows from Claus Offe, *Disorganized Capitalism*, John Keane (Ed.), Polity Press, 1985.
6. The most accessible of Foucault's work in this vein is his *Discipline and Punish: The Birth of the Prison*, Penguin, 1979. See also *The History of Sexuality*, Vol. 1, Penguin, 1979.
7. Charles Taylor, 'Foucault on freedom and truth', in his *Philosophy and the Human Sciences*, Cambridge University Press, 1985 (*Philosophical Papers*, Vol. 2).
8. The phrase is Stuart Hall's in his *The Politics of Thatcherism*, co-edited with Martin Jacques, Pluto Press, 1981.
9. Jurgen Habermas, *Legitimation Crisis*, Heinemann Educational Books, 1975. See also Taylor, as cited, Chapter 10.
10. I develop these criticisms in my *Popular Culture and Political Power*, Harvester Press, 1988.
11. Anthony Giddens, *Central Problems in Social Theory*, Macmillan, 1979, p.69.
12. Karl Popper, *The Logic of Scientific Discovery*, Hutchinson, 1959.
13. Clifford Geertz, *Local Knowledge: Further Essays in Interpretive Anthropology*, Basic Books, 1983, especially Chapter 4.
14. On this no-nonsense view of narratives, see Paul Ricoeur 'The narrative function', in his *Hermeneutics and the Human Sciences*, John Thompson (Ed.), Cambridge University Press, 1981.
15. R.G. Collingwood, *Speculum Mentis, or The Map of Knowledge*, Clarendon Press, 1924.

I.13

THE MULTIPLE FUNCTIONS OF EDUCATION

MICHAEL GOLBY

Because education serves multiple functions it is undesirable that its control should fall into the hands of any single predominant interest. For the same reason it is undesirable that the practice of education should be unduly influenced by the values of sectional interests. In a democratic society the widest possible representation of interests in the control of education should be sought. More than this, the practice of education should be open to influence from as wide a variety of sources as possible. Education, it will be argued in this chapter, is in a profound sense *for all*, and formulations of its purpose in terms of sectional interests are inevitably faulty and usually partisan. The implications of this understanding of education will be examined in the light of some recent proposals for the reform of education. Tentative suggestions for an alternative agenda responsive to the view of education proposed will be put forward.

The context for the ensuing discussion is provided by proposals to make the education service more responsive to the demands of those thought of as 'consumers'. Education, it is said, should be 'consumer-' not 'producer-'led. The consumers are variously described as parents and employers, seldom as the professions or the universities, practically never as the pupils and students themselves. The detail of such ideas is less important than the issues raised, and it is the purpose here to consider whether there are any principles available which may help in sorting out challenges to the *status quo* without assuming the rightness of the present arrangements.

That there are fundamental questions arising from such proposals is clear. For whom is education provided? On what principles is education to be distributed? How are the activities of teachers and other professionals to be monitored and brought into relationship with the social goals represented in the answers to these questions?

We are here considering education as a public service, not a private pursuit. Certainly there are important senses in which education consists in states of mind, inner satisfactions, and accomplishments valued and exercised only for their own sakes. These are perhaps aspects of education of paramount importance and arguably 'what school is for'.[1] The evidence of *Schools Council Enquiry 1* was that teachers, by contrast with other parties to their work, emphasized intrinsic values like personal development more than extrinsic values like employability.[2] Here are two broadly different functions for education. There is obviously much to be understood about the relationships between and within such broadly conceived ideas as 'intrinsic' and 'extrinsic' educational values. The history of the post-war period can itself be seen as an articulation between the idea of education as an undefined good in itself, safe in the hands of the teachers, and education as a public service delivering societal benefits.[3] Today's situation is one in which the latter holds sway.

Because today's emphasis is so very heavily upon the accountability of the education service in a value-for-money climate, we are primarily concerned here with the public context within which education is provided. Though the public provision of education may facilitate private satisfactions of an intrinsically worthwhile nature and of no public significance, and though this will be the aim of many teachers, our interest here is in understanding the accommodation which must necessarily be reached when a conflicting variety of values meet in a debate about the provision of education through public institutions across large and diverse populations as part of the common arrangements made by a society for its future.

Education in modern societies is not a purely personal transaction between individuals but is conducted within institutions. The standard case of education is not the private music lesson nor the child 'educated otherwise' at home, but the boy or girl going to school or the student to college. Such cases incidentally remind us that education is overwhelmingly something offered to the young, though again there are important developments in continuing and adult education. Thus, though there is private tuition and adult education, and there are significant moves to break down important parts of the established system, some of which moves will be noticed in this chapter, it remains the case that the established institutions are in place and have given meaning to standard educational practice. Included in such institutions are schools, colleges, and universities, together with the infrastructure of local education authorities (LEAs), the Department of Education and Science (DES) and all their associated divisions and subdivisions.

The education system is of course a bureaucracy, or set of bureaucracies, and despite its internal conflicts it can be regarded as an educational establishment inimical to fundamental reform. Asked to name any one educational expert who supported the proposal in the 1987 Conservative Party Manifesto to allow maintained state schools to opt out of LEA control, the Secretary of State could only reply that all such experts were by definition part of the professional establishment, all thinking alike in defence of sectional professional interests. Similarly, the entry of the Manpower Services Commission (MSC) into school education in 1982 with its Technical and Vocational Education Initiative (TVEI) was a spectacular, highly funded entry into territory which until then had been uncontestedly the teachers' and the LEAs'. TVEI is a curriculum initiative emanating from a Department of State outside the educational establishment precisely because of the Prime Minister's impatience with the normal channels for educational change. Yet, despite the high energy behind the TVEI, both its cost and its impact remain small by comparison with the expenditures channelled through the DES and LEAs and the great body of existing practice in the daily activities of nearly half a million teachers.

The establishment is both hard to reform and impossible to disinvent. This is not to say that educational practice is set in concrete nor that the currently fashionable methods of centralized initiatives backed by financial coercion cannot make significant changes. It is obvious that schools and colleges have changed considerably over the past ten years and dramatically over the past forty years. It is also true that what evaluations have been forthcoming do report powerful effects within TVEI classrooms, commonly a more relaxed pedagogy related to what is taken to be good primary school practice. Much less is heard about the impact of the technical and vocational curriculum as such.[4] This indicates that, given the wherewithal, teachers will teach well and by their own lights. The TVEI is strong on means but excessively weak on ends, especially if you look for outcomes such as the employability of its graduates or, still harder to discern, its effects on industrial and commercial regeneration. On aims, no less than any other form of education, TVEI is very much a matter of casting your bread upon the waters. Even the most vigorously promoted initiative is grist to the mill of practice.

Practice is practice is practice. The existing system and all the activities going on inside it define the starting points for subsequent change. The existing system is as it is as a result of successive accommodations to a great variety of interests and pressures. It will certainly go on changing, but those who seek change, particularly radical change (and this includes most people at least some of the time), will do well to recognize that the fundamental assumptions of practice, the 'common sense' of its practitioners, is profoundly contra-suggestible and resistant to sudden and radical change. Even coercion will be ineffective once the main force is relaxed. Though frustrating for activists, there is something deeply humbling about this fundamental feature of social change, of which educational change is a part, that it cannot be wished into being by even the most powerful forces in the social order without the practical consent of those subject to it. The tendency of old wine to fill new bottles, which can be observed in studies of innovative comprehensive schools such as Countesthorpe and Madeley Court, and of innovation to occur without change, is the result of the absolute supremacy of practice over theory.[5]

In social affairs things have a tendency to remain much as they are, changing in any important way only in so far as a practical consensus allows. Theoretical discourse and research play their parts in the creation of such consensus but should not be overrated, for their credibility is a function of factors outside themselves. Research gets a hearing to the degree that it addresses the concerns of the day. In doing so it may not necessarily confirm conventional beliefs; the point here is only that it counts at all only by responding to the *Zeitgeist*. An example of this would be the work of Bennett which in the early seventies addressed preoccupations about 'progressive methods' in primary schools.[6] At the time the work was supposed to confirm the idea that 'informal methods' reduced standards. (Later reanalysis of the data yielded no such conclusion.) Theorists and researchers need to pay much closer attention to the ideological contexts into which their work flows; the direction from which it springs is going to be increasingly stringently controlled financially with a closer audit of university activities and the already severely constrained Research Councils.

These observations are not put forward as a reason for complacency or glorifying reactionary tendencies, nor for militancy from the research community. Rather they point to the complexity of the processes of educational change and the need for sophistication in the analysis of the existing educational situation. In particular, what is called for is an examination of the traditions within which practice is conceived. The traditions need to be examined for their adequacy to modern life, for there is no other starting point for any reform that is to last.[7]

This view of things contrasts starkly with received views about curriculum planning in the most influential official quarters. Bodies such as the Further Education Unit (FEU) of the DES, the Business and Technician Education Council (BTEC), and MSC adopt various versions of rational curriculum planning.[8] All of these stress the use of objectives as starting points for planning and as the basis for a contractual relationship between teachers, employers, and learners. Objectives, it is assumed, derive from an analysis of the behaviours and skills needed for the future. Thus the model of planning is future-oriented; curriculum planning is a matter of predicting the future and preparing people, especially in the form of manpower, for the future. This is planning in a vacuum conducted in conscious ignorance of the nature of actual practice, which is regarded as unquestionably redundant. It is an assertion of technology over art in teaching. The defects in such an approach are manifold and cannot be detailed here. Perhaps it is the arrogance of those who think they can not only predict the future but also bend the present to it that is most striking. Consider Toffler:

> As for curriculum, the Councils of the Future, instead of assuming that every subject taught today is taught for a reason, should begin from the reverse premise: nothing should be included in a required curriculum unless it can be strongly justified in terms of the future. If this means scrapping a substantial part of the formal curriculum, so be it ...
>
> Anyone who thinks the present curriculum makes sense is invited to explain to an intelligent fourteen year old why algebra or French or any other subject is essential for him. Adult answers are almost always evasive. The reason is simple: the present curriculum is a mindless holdover from the past.[9]

There is much more in the same vein but no coherent alternative to the basic fabric of present curriculum is suggested, only a multitude of possibilities (probability, logic, computer programming, philosophy, aesthetics, mass communications, the stages of the human life cycle, contemporary social problems, significant technologies, all on one page alone). This incoherence derives from the fact that, while not perfect, the present curriculum is the state of the art. It is, for all its considerable flaws and many contradictions, where we are and where we have to start from. The arrogance in the belief that the slate can be wiped clean in favour of an analysis of the future is manifest in a book of such influence, written in 1970, whose substantial index has no entry on oil, feminism, or women, but half a column on technology. *Future Shock* tells us a lot about the late sixties but, self-contradictorily, nothing about what has happened since. Like history, futurology is about stories a generation tells itself. Unlike history, (and by definition) nothing in futurology is verifiable in time for it to be of use. And very little of it turns out to be true.

Of course education must make its assumptions about the future. But these need to be modest, provisional, and not the vehicle for special interests, such as those of the technocrats. Education has an important conservative function in helping to preserve and develop the culture, and this function is paradoxically the more important at those very times when neophilia and change are most celebrated.

It is assumed therefore that schools, colleges, polytechnics, universities, and the rest will continue to be the major providers of education within a service administered by governmental institutions. There will be no at-a-stroke revolution in either teaching or its administration and government. This is because of the impermeability of practice to immediate change. Those who seek change will need to educate practice rather than attempt to direct it. Changes there will be, and they will only be intelligible as responses to discontents with the pre-existing arrangements. Changes are mediated through channels of control, influence, and persuasion on practitioners. Given the proposition that there are multiple functions for education and a wide variety of legitimate interests in its conduct, it is likely that change will be less swift and effective than any individual interest would like. This is not only inevitable but, provided that the widest, most equitable and effective representation of interests is fostered, it is also desirable.

This is not to say that the present forms of representation are themselves ideal. From a post-war period when teachers' assumptions permeated the 'secret garden of the curriculum' to today when the industrial trainers are having a new heyday, there has been too sudden a transition. What is needed is a cooler look at the forms of government of schools, clearer understanding of how legitimate influence can be brought to bear upon practice, and above all a shared vision that 'our schools' are precisely that. In response to these three needs, there have indeed been successive formulations of the responsibilities of school governing bodies ever since the Taylor Report of 1977.[10] But there have been no parallel (and logically entailed) attempts to clarify how such responsibilities are to fit in with those of parents, the LEAs, and central government. Indeed, parental choice is pursued as a goal on the one hand and a national curriculum on the other, with no attention to the ways in which the one may diminish the other! In regard to influence upon practice, there are few studies of the springs of change in the practice of education, but many of curriculum innovations of the expansionary period which largely failed.[11]

It is to the concept that the schools are 'ours' and not the exclusive territory of any particular groups that the following discussion is addressed. The first sense in which this is important is geographical. Schools do not belong to local communities but in fact to the LEAs. Still less do they belong to the parents of the day, parents of those children who happen to be attending them at a particular time. Both these groups have important interests, but that does not amount to a right of control. Schools are social institutions whose rationale must be subsumed under a theory of social benefit. Children are educated not only for their parents' and not only for their own sakes but for a common good. How this good is to be understood is exactly what is at issue. For the present let us notice that as social institutions schools are part of the wider social fabric and ought to respond not only to their immediate clientele but also to the collective social need.

In fact, of course, ever since the beginning of compulsory education this has been well recognized to be the case. The Elementary Schools that followed the Act of 1870 came into existence from a variety of motives. There is a citizenship motive in making the newly enfranchised literate; there is a religious motive in making them godly; there is an economic motive in making them employable; there is a philanthropic motive in making children unavailable for damaging and exploitative employment. The list could be extended and interpreted in many ways, and it is arguable that without some such broad spectrum of impulses no far-reaching legislation will stick. The institutions that came into being stood, and still stand, in specific localities up and down the country. They have undergone many internal changes but they have always, in whatever guise, represented the interests of the wider society in the future of the children of the locality. They are the people's schools but not exclusively the schools of the local people.

In this respect schools resemble churches, and of course there are many historical connections between the two as local outposts of a larger authority. Even when secularized, schools maintain this cosmopolitan status. Just as churches vary in the degree to which individual officers and congregations go their own way, so there is a central issue today how far and on what basis schools in the maintained sector should be liberated from the forms of control, particularly LEA control, under which they now relate together as institutions of the same kind. It should be noted, however, that there is no proposal that schools should be independent of all authority and the assumption is that the central authority will take power where the LEAs are compelled to relinquish it. It is also worth noting that schools in the independent sector are also local outposts of larger authorities, though they are administratively autonomous. Public schools derive their legitimacy from their connections with the outside world, principally the great universities and the academic traditions they instantiate.

This very general feature of schools may be looked upon in a number of ways. The elementary school may be looked upon as a civilizing mission or a means of social control, the grammar school as the spreading of sweetness and light among those capable of apprehending it and/or a more or less equitable rationing of the common wealth dispersed in the form of white-collar jobs.[12] In its turn the comprehensive school can be seen as a more efficient machine to such ends or a new chance to create a more equal society through a common curriculum offered to all young people.[13] The independent school can be viewed as a bastion of the ruling élites or, as in the Assisted Places Scheme, centres of excellence offering a distinctive new choice to parents. In any case, the individual institution is one of a network taking its identity and deriving its curriculum and practice from its wider affiliations. Importantly, also, these connections are not only contemporary but also historic.

An institution is such a thing precisely because it is one of a kind, set up on a social basis to contribute to overall social goals. If this is so, two central facts confront reformers. First, social institutions are bound together under a system of government which has some responsibility for their activities. We must look at what these responsibilities might be. Second, these institutions are individually and collectively inheritors of educational traditions which, as has already been remarked, must be taken into account by reformers, for they cannot be disregarded with impunity.

Institutionalized education is both inevitable and desirable. This is not to say that all privately contracted education is undesirable, nor that the current state of development of public educational institutions is satisfactory. Dissatisfaction with existing educational practice is not a reason for dismantling the system that exists in England and Wales, which is the result of historic, but flawed, attempts to represent a range of legitimate interests in the conduct of education. Even if there were good cause, it has already been argued that the prevailing traditions will always limit the effectiveness of radical reform. Instead of attempting the impossible by way of imposing on education a model of control and accountability derived from market economics, a proper appreciation of the multiple functions of education demands the development of existing institutions, not their replacement. In particular, the LEAs must continue to play a central part, since they are the best available approximation to a democratic and cohesive form of government and an appropriate administrative apparatus.[14]

What are the implications of this view that educational institutions are for all and inevitably in continuous evolution? How can the great democracy of practice be supported so that it more adequately represents the multiplicity of interests it serves?

There are two sorts of answers to these questions. At the level of educational ideology, the professionals themselves need to reconsider the beliefs that underlie received practice. Only sustained study can achieve this, and it has to be study of the appropriate practice-related kind. The truncation of teachers' opportunities for high level study in favour of centrally identified 'system-needs', and the predominant vogue for technological and skills-based teacher education, threaten a proper consideration of aims in education. There is no ready-made educational ideology that resolves the profoundest conflicts of interest in education; progressives value the child's interests but give no account of the form of social life presumed or entailed by their individualistic view.[15] Classical humanists identify the value of scholarship but offer no suggestions how excellence can be matched to equality. Teacher education is then a priority.

At the level of the institutional framework, more openness is called for. But openness is itself dependent upon structure, for successful *carte-blanche* openness would simply swamp the schools with over-participation. The representative apparatus of school governing bodies as reformed in the 1986 Act needs to be closely monitored and developed. But the abutting responsibilities of headteachers and LEAs need clarifying. It is likely that this clarification will come about more by case law and perhaps litigation than by legalistic enactment at local or national level. Principles should include both the balance of legitimate interests and the protection of minority interests.

Probably of greatest urgency is a clarification of the proper balance of interest between local and central government. Here the debate is caught up in ideological currents deeper than those provided by education alone and beyond the scope of this chapter. It is indeed most surprising that so little has been heard of the implications for local democracy in general provided by the attack on local expenditure of the Conservative governments since 1979. So far as education is concerned, the responsibility of central government for national manpower planning can be recognized but certainly this general responsibility has been well exceeded in the central authority's prescriptions for a national curriculum. This debate needs to be vigorously promoted and the coming power struggle between central government and the LEAs attended by considerations from democratic theory. Educationalists, as major local level spenders of public funds, should be preparing their position and rallying support in terms of participatory principles. To do this in good faith they should be giving impetus to those very many school, governing body, and LEA measures which are encouraging citizen participation in schools.

NOTES

1. Eloquent statements of this function of education are to be found in H. Entwistle, *Child-centred Education* (Methuen, Worcester and London, 1979) and G. Chanan and L. Gilchrist, *What School is For* (London: Methuen, 1974). The best philosophical account is in P. S. Wilson, *Interest and Discipline in Education* (London: Routledge & Kegan Paul, 1971).
2. Schools Council (1968) *Young School Leavers, Enquiry I*, London: HMSO.
3. Centre for Contemporary Cultural Studies (1978) *Unpopular Education*, London: Hutchinson.
4. See, for example, University of Exeter (1986) *TVEI in Exeter: The First Three Years, (May 1983–May 1986)*, Exeter: University of Exeter School of Education. TVEI Evaluations are catalogued in the TVEI Unit's Evaluation Bulletin (1987), London: MSC.
5. J. Watts (Ed.) (1977) *The Countesthorpe Experience: The First Five Years*, London: Allen & Unwin, and P. Toogood (1984) *The Head's Tale*, Dialogue Publications, are both vivid accounts of secondary school experiments that went awry.
6. Bennett, S. N. (1976) *Teaching Styles and Pupil Progress*, London: Open Books.
7. Schwab, J. J. (1969) 'The practical: a language for curriculum', *School Review*, 78, pp.1–24. A collection of Schwab's papers is in I. Westbury and N. J. Wilkof, *Science, Curriculum and Liberal Education*, (1978) Chicago: University of Chicago Press. The British popularizer of Schwab is Reid. See W. A. Reid (1978) *Thinking about the Curriculum*, London: Routledge & Kegan Paul. See also M. Holt (1987) *Judgment, Planning and Educational Change*, London: Harper and Row.
8. For a discussion of rational curriculum planning see L. A. Stenhouse (1975) *Introduction to Curriculum Research and Development*, London: Heinemann, Chapters 5–6.
9. A. Toffler (1971) *Future Shock*, New York: Bantam, pp. 409–10.
10. Taylor Committee (1977) *A New Partnership for Our Schools*, DES, London: HMSO.
11. Shipman, M., Bolam, D., and Jenkins, D. (1974) *Inside a Curriculum Project*, London: Methuen, and S. Humble and H. Simons, (1978) *From Council to Classroom: The Evaluation of the Humanities Curriculum Project Diffusion*, London: Macmillan Education, are both examples.
12. S. Hall, 'Education and the crisis of the urban school' in J. Raynor and E. Harris (Eds.) (1977) *Schooling in the City*, London: Ward Lock.

13. HMI advocate a common curriculum in many of their publications from *Curriculum 11–16*, (London: HMSO, 1977) onwards.
14. Hainsworth, G. (1989) 'A future for the LEAs?' in *Ten Years of Curriculum Change*, Exeter: Exeter Society for Curriculum Studies.
15. See K. Jones (1983) *Beyond Progressive Education*, London: Macmillan.

2. EDUCATION IN CONTRASTING SOCIETIES

2.0

INTRODUCTION: EDUCATION IN CONTRASTING SOCIETIES

KENNETH KING

The following set of chapters is principally concerned with the tension between continuity and change in educational systems. The mix of countries represented here is particularly suited to examining the process of formation and change in educational traditions. One or two (for example China) have had a national identity for thousands of years; others have been politically independent for a century or two (for example Chile and USA); others again, such as India and Sierra Leone, experienced long periods of colonial rule before gaining their independence along with the majority of colonial territories between the end of the Second World War and the early 1960s. And one country, South Africa, is still under a system of minority white rule in the late 1980s.

One series of transitions likely to affect the character of schooling might seem to be the moves from precolonial autonomy, to colonial rule, and finally to independence. In reality the transition to political independence may not involve crucial changes in the popular understanding of education, since this is likely to have been very powerfully shaped by the formation of state systems of education earlier in the colonial period. The negotiations and conflicts that took place in these formative years are well illustrated here by Canada, and the point is made that what to later generations may seem like the ordinary and obvious shape of schooling was often an arena of intense conflict.

One advantage of studying the recently independent countries, such as Malaysia and others in Africa, is that these formative years lie only a little way back. Already, however, particular missionary or colonial arrangements for education, especially in the sphere of examinations, language policy, and local financing have tended to become incorporated into the popular conception of schooling. The greater state control of schooling at independence may therefore merely reinforce these already hardening traditions of education. Africa offers peculiarly important insights into these formative processes, for unlike the development of state systems of education in North America and Europe, the aspirations to control, centralize, and expand educational opportunities frequently surpass the capacity of the new states to deliver them. As a result, there has been a tendency to rely on the older traditions of private, community, and local initiative to deliver what are meant to be national systems.

Another comparative advantage of examining the formation of traditions of education in newer and older nations is that what is now the hidden curriculum of some of the longer-established school systems is still quite open in societies where the education system is expected directly and explicitly to address attitudes and behaviours. Malaysia, for instance, has recently introduced a moral education curriculum with a whole series of character traits to be adopted. Meanwhile, in parts of Anglophone Africa, enormous quantities of 'developmental knowledge' about agriculture, health, nutrition, and behaviour are being introduced into primary school texts.

This explicit approach to the promotion of appropriate skills and behaviours is part of a wider political assumption about the use of schools for forms of social engineering. In many of the societies represented in these chapters schools are one of the most obvious sites for the attempted resolution of interracial and inter-community competition. Communities, such as the Creoles of Sierra Leone, which have early profited from schools, later find schools being expected to deliver schemes of positive discrimination in favour of the majority who came later to a realization of the pivotal role of schools in access to paid employment. Malaysia demonstrates even more vividly the belief that schools can be expected to undo the very damage in educational disparities that they have been partly responsible for.

There is no doubt that the state can apparently very powerfully intervene in the shaping of the educational system, and some of the most telling illustrations of this correspondence between the political culture and the school can be seen here in Chile. On the other hand, some of the more fundamental educational relations and assumptions about knowledge seem almost impervious to the changes in government. Amongst these most crucial determinants of the character of schooling are popular attitudes towards human potential and towards the role of the teacher. In China and several other countries of East Asia, the widespread view that a rather significant standard of educational achievement is within almost everyone's reach, and that diligence can compensate for initial differences, has a potent influence on the whole scheme of educational relations. It directly affects the role and expectations of the teacher, the insistence on a uniform curriculum, and the attitude towards examinations.

Similarly in India, the precolonial tradition of respect for teaching and learning was overlaid by a bureaucracy in which the teacher became one of the lowest and least respected state functionaries. The resulting mix of traditional authority and almost total lack of status in the modern civil service has helped to produce a teaching and learning style that political independence has done little to alter.

The deep and often obscure roots of modern educational practice pose particular problems for school reform, whether of teaching styles or of administrative arrangements. In the following section some of the most dramatic attempts to dismantle educational principles of a hundred years' standing can be seen in Chile, with its policy of reducing the role of the state in education and exposing the whole system to market forces. In the USA a very different tension exists between the agenda of reform and prevailing practice; for almost fifty years there has been available a coherent critique of traditional schooling, associated with Dewey and others. And yet today there is apparently an almost complete absence of the practical implications of Dewey's philosophy to be found in American classrooms.

This extraordinary resistance to change within state educational systems that have been politically independent for anywhere between three decades and several hundred years is of particular importance in thinking about the situation of the one state in our sample that is still under a system of minority white rule. Naturally a great deal of planning is currently going on about the form and content of new post-liberation people's education. It is argued here that although the crudely racist definition of education would be dismantled overnight, as has happened in several other African states, the more fundamental shaping of mass education in South Africa has been going on for several decades. The character of this schooling must be understood by all those committed to radical educational change.

A good deal remains to be researched in the processes of forming state systems of education. It is hoped that the chapters in this section will both prove useful to practitioners seeking to understand the forces that have shaped the systems in which they work, and also be suggestive to researchers of areas within the culture of schooling that need much more attention.

THE NORMALIZATION OF EDUCATIONAL RELATIONS IN ONTARIO, CANADA

BRUCE CURTIS

By the middle of the nineteenth century, a broad consensus existed among governing and middle classes in Europe and America over the necessity of some form of education for the masses. Disagreements raged, to be sure, over precisely how this education should be administered. In many countries, debates over church involvement retarded the organization of public education. In others, serious conflicts over the precise nature of educational organization – whether it should be centrally or locally controlled, for instance – had a similar effect. Still, a vibrant educational press and a rich international educational literature contributed to the generalization and widespread acceptance amongst the dominant classes in various countries of the necessity of popular education.

A set of educational innovations in the areas of curriculum, pedagogy, teacher-training, and administrative practice became generally known. By the 1840s, if not earlier, experiments by educational reformers in various countries were being regularly scrutinized, both by large numbers of those active in the promotion of educational plans, and by other interested tourists. A well-travelled educational circuit linked Pestalozzi's school at Yverdon, de Fellenberg's school for the industrial classes at Hofwyl, several Prussian schools, schools in Amsterdam and Rotterdam, the schools of Paris, Edinburgh Sessional, Glasgow Normal, London's Borough Road, and the Dublin Normal and Model Schools. Interested visitors also made side-trips to Robert Owen's co-operative community at New Lanark. The schools run by the Boston school committee attracted a considerable amount of attention at a somewhat later date, and after 1850, the Normal and Model Schools of Toronto were also included in this educational circuit.

Pestalozzi's 'lessons on familiar objects' became a keystone of international practice in curriculum and were adapted to the practices of collective instruction. His concern to develop the understanding and the general perceptual capacities of the learner was also broadly shared.[1] In educational administration, the practice of inspection became universal, although the models of inspectoral practice adopted in Holland and Prussia appealed differently to different reformers. The system of teacher training developed by the Commissioners of National Education in Ireland, and the production and central regulation of schoolbooks practised by that body, were also replicated in other cases.[2]

But while the first half of the nineteenth century saw the emergence of a broad consensus over general educational practices and objectives among educational reformers and members of the governing classes in most European and American countries, the translation of this consensus into a set of effective educational practices aimed at local (and especially working-class) populations was a continually problematic matter. The translation of educational theory and philosophical propositions into effective practices necessitated first, the creation of a set of educational relations and rituals, and also the transformation of these things into *taken-for-granted features of the educational landscape*. The organization of public educational systems typically involved the creation of new authority relations – between states and local populations, between teachers, students, and the community, between teachers and educational administrators. Public educational systems tended to define school knowledge in novel ways, insisting upon the acquisition of certain kinds of knowledge and skill, and marginalizing or stigmatizing others. And as systems of public administration, public educational systems commonly involved the creation of new institutions of political governance. Public educational systems were successfully created only where these kinds of social relationships were established and institutionalized. However, state educational reformers frequently encountered opposition and resistance from students, local school supporters, and other groups and classes in society.[3] These points can be illustrated in the formation of the public educational system of the Canadian province of Ontario (known as Upper Canada from 1791 to 1840 and as Canada West from 1841 until the confederation of the Canadian provinces in 1867).

ORIGINS OF PUBLIC EDUCATION IN ONTARIO

The foundations of the educational system of Ontario were laid in the turbulent decade of the 1840s. During this period, where a network of locally supported voluntary schools had already produced a generally literate population, educational organization figured centrally in political conflicts over the issue of colonial self-government. The British colonies of Upper Canada (Ontario) and Lower Canada (Quebec) were rocked by violent rebellions in 1837–8. Insurrectionists in Upper Canada were easily defeated by local militias, while two lengthy armed revolts by Lower Canadian *patriotes* were put down by British regulars. Incursions by armed groups based in the United States continued along the Canadian frontier until 1841. Many members of the governing classes in both Britain and the Canadas attributed the rebellions to the absence of organs of representative government in the colony, and to the failure of educational institutions to provide an adequate political socialization in loyalty to the Crown and the colonial connection.

Until 1846, however, attempts to introduce a centralized system of 'public instruction' to Canada West were defeated by a colonial Reform Party which was interested in 'responsible' (or autonomous ministerial) government for the colony. While both the imperial state and colonial Tories urged the centralization of educational organization as a means of undercutting the local educational autonomy seen as responsible for the rebellions, Reformers opposed the concentration of power in the hands of an executive government not 'responsible' to Parliament. A Reform-sponsored School Act of 1843 bolstered a system of local educational management in which elected school trustees exerted most powers of educational direction. Under this legislation, elementary education was co-ordinated by an Assistant Superintendent of Education who distributed educational monies and compiled educational reports. District Councils taxed ratepayers to raise an amount at least equal to a central school grant, and appointed District Superintendents of Schools who were to visit schools annually, to distribute school monies and examine teachers, and to present annual reports both to the District Councils and to the Assistant Superintendent. Practical educational management rested with locally elected trustees, who controlled and maintained the schoolhouse, hired and fired teachers licensed by District Superintendents, exempted indigent residents from school taxes and, most important, controlled curriculum and pedagogy. Under this legislation, school expenditure and attendance increased markedly. Several District Model Schools for teacher training were established, and in several instances experiments at local systematization were undertaken.

However, an initiative by the Colonial Office against the movement for colonial political autonomy produced a centralized elementary educational system. Reformers resigned from office in 1843 over a conflict with the Governor General, Lord Metcalfe, about the distribution of colonial patronage. For nine months Parliament did not meet, but in October 1844 the Ministry assembled by the Governor won a small majority, largely through the propagation of a colonial 'loyalty scare'. The Methodist minister Egerton Ryerson, an active opponent of colonial autonomy, was appointed Assistant Superintendent of Education and charged with reconstructing the educational system. Ryerson embarked on a European educational tour in which he visited most of the best-known educational institutions. His *Report on a system of public elementary instruction for Upper Canada* (1847) outlined a programme of educational reconstruction which was put in place over the next three decades.

The School Act of 1846 produced a radical educational centralization. A newly-created Chief Superintendent of Education for Canada West was empowered to formulate rules and regulations for school management and could withhold state grants from any school district not complying with them. An appointed General Board of Education now specified approved textbooks for all colonial schools. District Councils still appointed District Super-intendents, who licensed teachers, but these officials were now subject to instructions from the central authority. The taxation powers of locally elected trustees were extended, while their powers over curriculum and pedagogy were sharply restricted in principle. In addition, a Normal School for the training of teachers was created and opened in 1848. A School Act of 1847 centralized elementary educational organization in towns and cities under the management of a common Board of Education with unlimited powers of taxation.

This educational centralization was the source of considerable political conflict in Canada West, both in and out of the colonial Parliament. Reformers opposed the centralization of educational authority in the hands of an 'irrespon-sible' (i.e. appointed) official. Local school supporters found themselves increasingly cut off from management of and participation in local educational practice. For instance, it was common in Canada West in the 1830s and 1840s for all school matters to be decided by the vote of locally convened school meetings. The School Act of 1846 and the administrative practice sponsored by the central authority severely limited the occasions on which school meetings could be called and the matters which could be decided in them. The Act specified that all school meetings were to be presided over by the senior magistrate of the district and gave other members of local élites – judges, clergy, district wardens – the power to assemble at will for any educational purpose and to license teachers. An amendment of 1853 imposed fines upon any person found guilty of 'disturbing a school'.

The Reform Party moved against centralized education after the coming of colonial political autonomy in 1848. While the Chief Superintendent acted to modify the Act of 1846 to respond to mounting criticism and in keeping with a reorganization of local government, a leading member of the left wing of the Reform Party produced and secured passage of an entirely different School Act of 1849. This Act removed the privileges granted to local élites in school matters, and decentralized control over school books and pedagogical practices by vesting these in elected County Councils. The Chief Superintendent was subordinated to the General Board of Education, and District Superintendents were required to give advance notice of all school visits.

But while the Act of 1849 was passed by Parliament and declared, the

Reform Ministry suspended it in December 1849 and called upon the Chief Superintendent to draft replacement legislation. The repeal of the Navigation Acts and the coming of Free Trade provoked a commercial depression in the Canadas and adversely affected that large section of the capitalist class interested in the canal system and the trade in staples. Colonial Tories were disaffected politically by the perception that the colonial Parliament had fallen into the hands of the 'French rebels', and the Irish famine migration of 1847 placed the first substantial proletariat in the Canadian towns. News of the revolutions in France and Germany, the Irish revolt, and the rise of English Chartism contributed to the political unease of the governing classes in the Canadas. All of these events encouraged a resurgence of the popular agrarian radicalism which had issued in the rebellions of 1837–8.

When the Governor General, Lord Elgin, gave the royal assent in May 1849 to a piece of legislation called the Rebellion Losses Bill (which sought to compensate property owners for damages incurred by British troops in suppressing the rebellion) a Tory-inspired mob stormed the Parliament buildings in Montreal. Elgin's carriage was attacked, the Parliament sacked and burned, and the mob attacked the houses of leading Reformers. Mob violence, encouraged by the Tory press, rocked cities and towns in many parts of the colony throughout the summer and fall of 1849. The Reform Party split under the impact. The left of the party broke away to form a new party of agrarian radicalism, the Clear Grits, whose platform drew heavily upon the English People's Charter. The remaining moderate Reformers rapidly lost whatever opposition to centralized education they had possessed and moved to sustain a modified system of public instruction.

The School Act of 1850 remained in force until a major consolidation of the Ontario educational system took place in 1871. Under it, an appointed Chief Superintendent of Education continued to exert broad powers for the formulation of rules and regulations for school management. In connection with an appointed Council of Public Instruction, this official also managed the Normal School for teacher training. After 1853, the Chief Superintendent could grant certificates to teachers valid throughout the Province. The Council of Public Instruction specified school books and school rules. In keeping with the Municipal Corporations Act of 1849, educational inspection was decentralized. Township Councils appointed Township School Superintendents, who inspected schools at least four times a year and prepared detailed school reports using categories determined by the central authority. County Boards of Public Instruction, composed of the trustees of County Grammar Schools and Township Superintendents, conducted teachers' examinations and licensed successful candidates. From 1858 the central authority began to specify the minimum qualifications for different classes of teachers. (Teachers, it is remarkable, are the only occupational group in Canada whose moral character and comportment is specified by statute. This dates from 1846.)[4]

Parliamentary debate over education in the rest of the nineteenth century centred upon the existence of clauses allowing for the separate schooling of Roman Catholics (and of 'coloured people' – Ontario's last 'coloured school' was closed by ministerial order in 1971). Bitterly fought battles in the 1850s and 1860s provided funding for Catholic separate schools under denominational control, and these provisions were included in the British North America Act of 1867, through which the colonies became the Dominion of Canada. Until 1985, Ontario provided tax support for Catholic separate schools to grade 10, although at a lower rate than that granted to public non-denominational schools. In 1985, full funding for Catholic separate schools to the end of secondary school (grade 13) was enacted by the provincial legislature.

Apart from serious political divisions over the universality of the educational system, educational organization in the period after 1850 was consolidated. The elementary and secondary schools were integrated under an Act of 1871, which also demanded professional qualifications of school inspectors, who henceforth operated at the County level. County Boards of Public Instruction were replaced by much smaller County Boards of Examiners, in which centrally-trained inspectors played the leading role. The central authority specified standards of teacher examination. After 1877, County Boards lost their certification powers over all but the lowest class of teachers, and these could only be granted certificates for a maximum of three years. From 1907, this power attached to the central authority. Centrally-set high school entrance examinations administered to primary school leavers, and central definition of school books, sharply limited the ability of teachers to innovate in the schoolroom, and salaries remained low. The Act of 1871 also introduced a compulsory attendance requirement of four months for students between the ages of 7 and 14, but in the countryside the majority of students continued to attend for less than one hundred days per year. Elementary school teaching came to be a predominantly female occupation, while secondary school teaching and educational administration remained a male preserve. No woman was principal of a mixed school before the 1880s at least. During this period as well, the range of subjects taught in the elementary school curriculum increased, although many of these remained optional for local school managers.

In the last quarter of the nineteenth century, the range of teacher training facilities increased markedly, with the opening of additional Normal Schools and with the creation of a School of Pedagogy in Hamilton. These institutions provided teacher training until the 1960s, when university faculties of education were created in the province.

While substantial powers rested with the central authority, day-to-day management of the elementary schools of the nineteenth century rested with locally elected trustees. Until a major educational consolidation took place in the 1960s, elementary education was directed by several thousand relatively autonomous local school boards. Especially in the countryside, board officials could limit or undercut central policy in a variety of ways. In the nineteenth century particularly, they could refuse or neglect to follow central policy in school construction, design and maintenance. They could refuse to tax for the provision of school supplies, and they could (and frequently did) hire only teachers with third class qualifications (and hence lower salary expectations). Trustees' powers over teachers could be exerted practically to a certain degree to limit what was taught in local schools and to regulate pedagogical practices. Teachers, in particular, found themselves in a contradictory position in this system. On the one hand, they were charged by statute and administrative regulation to follow certain kinds of pedagogical practices and to teach a set curriculum. Their execution of central regulations was subject to centrally-regulated inspection, and inspectors could suspend teachers' certificates. At the same time, a teacher's continuing employment was entirely dependent upon her or his pleasing local school managers. The central authority worked to limit the autonomy of local managers, but, until the 1960s, they retained considerable influence.[5]

THE NORMALIZATION OF EDUCATIONAL RELATIONS

From its inception the school system of Ontario was intended as a system of political discipline and socialization for the mass of the population. The establishment of a system of *state* schools necessitated the elimination or marginalization of a pre-existing educational organization. School reformers in Canada West in the 1840s encountered a network of locally-controlled common schools and a largely literate population. State educational organization subordinated these schools to the central authority and attempted to reorganize both the acquisition and the exercise of the skills of literacy in the colony.

Schooling was (and remains) a way of remaking popular character and culture. Educational practice in Canada West sought to produce a loyal, rational, intelligent, and morally upright populace which would reject political violence and which would accept established relations of authority. The regulation of society was increasingly seen by governing classes here to centre upon the regulation of persons through the formation of *reliable habits*. Punctuality, neatness, co-operation, respect for property and authority relations, temperance, piety, modesty, chastity – as these were interpreted by middle-class school reformers – were virtues in which the population was to be schooled. Educational practice, or exercise in the schoolroom, was intended to transform these desirable middle-class habits into elements of popular character. Schooling is a moral politics.

The successful institutionalization of this politics involved the creation, stabilization, and normalization of a structure of educational persons and relations. These elements of schooling have come to constitute what many writers have called 'the hidden curriculum' of schooling. The hidden curriculum refers to those elements in the structure of the educational process which are formative and educative, but which do not figure explicitly in the public programme of schooling. In the formative period of the school system of Ontario, however, what later generations have come to take for granted as normal elements of the educational landscape stand forth as a novel set of practices and initiatives. The transformation of these things into *obvious* elements of schooling was a conflict-laden process. Two examples will suffice, one from the structure of educational relations, one from the nature of school knowledge.

The logic of educational relations posited students as 'school children', as incomplete social subjects in need of discipline and training. For the public educational system effectively to claim the practical habituation of the population, students had to be so defined. At the same time, habituation demanded the regular attendance of students. School children could be effectively transformed into good citizens and moral individuals only if they were regularly exercized in desirable activities at school.

Both of these requisites of state schooling conflicted with the social reality lived by many, if not most, young people in nineteenth-century Ontario. On the one hand, before the organization of public education and throughout its formative period, young people were not 'children'. In the countryside, both boys and girls were active participants in agricultural labour as soon as they were physically able, and certainly by the age of nine in most cases. In the towns, young people from a very early age made an active contribution to the domestic economy through such things as street trading, scavenging, running errands, child care and so forth. At the same time, participation in the agricultural and domestic economies made regular and punctual school attendance undesirable for many young people (and for their parents and friends).[6]

Educational administrators attempted to devise and put in place mechanisms and practices which would secure the definition of students as children. Attendance and report cards, the awarding of prizes for regular attendance, home visitations by school inspectors, the formation of a corps of truant officers, the demanding of written notes from parents and guardians, fines for parents of 'habitual truants', and later, punitive legislation leading to the incarceration of those absent from school, combined with a related campaign against child labour to solidify the 'infantilization' of students.

In the domain of curriculum in Canada West/Ontario, the process of normalization took a rather different course. Here one sees a shift in the presentation of school knowledge away from direct moral didacticism towards more implicit forms of instruction. For instance, the Irish Readers, a series of schoolbooks produced by the Commissioners of National Education in Ireland, were adopted in Canada West in 1846 and remained in use until 1866, when they were replaced by the domestically-produced 'Red Readers'. The Irish texts were very widely used in nineteenth-century Britain and America, and were also translated into several European languages.

The predominant curricular tactic in the Irish Readers was a direct address to the audience which enumerated desirable behaviour and enjoined acceptance of it. Especially in the books designed for those above the age of ten, students were addressed directly as rational readers in lessons which extolled the virtues and advantages of the existing political and economic order. Alternative ways of organizing society were explicitly rejected, and heavy doses of scientific information were (particularly, although not solely) intended to increase the economic usefulness of the population.

In the series of readers which replaced the Irish books in Canada West in 1866, direct didacticism and the rational form of address had largely disappeared. (This transformation in curricular form was replicated in England and Scotland in the same period.) Here students were exposed instead to exciting and diverting narratives, tales of warfare, adventure, and heroism in both prose and poetry.[7]

The same shift can be seen in the area of agricultural instruction, an important matter in a primarily agricultural country. The Irish Commissioners produced an *Agricultural Class Book*, subtitled *How best to cultivate a small farm and garden: together with hints on domestic economy* (1850). Here a wise and experienced local Irish resident recounted his meeting with a smallholder intending to emigrate to America. The smallholder claimed he could not make a living on his farm. The narrator of this tract took the prospective emigrant in hand, reorganized his domestic life so that cleanliness, economy, and comfort prevailed, ensured that he paid his rent, and made his social situation tolerable and respectable, if clearly limited. This account was interspersed with questions about soil composition, and lessons on the history of agriculture drawn from the Bible.

This book was replaced in Ontario by *First Lessons on Agriculture; for Canadian Farmers and their Families* (1871), a work produced by the Chief Superintendent of Education. *First Lessons* provided factual information about soil chemistry and natural scientific information with agricultural applications. Very little space was devoted to the morality of domestic economy; discussions of the subject centred upon such things as techniques of bread making and milking.

In both of these instances – educational relations and curricular forms –

what one witnesses is a restructuring of the politics of education such that political relations become *implicit* rather than *explicit*. The institutionalization of educational practices and procedures which assumed that students were children effectively transformed the reality of studenthood. An alternative vision of students has become difficult to entertain. Direct didacticism and lessons on moral economy prevail in educational systems only where the routines and rituals of instruction have not yet successfully incorporated certain moral habits and certain political assumptions into the structure of schooling. For instance, that students should come to school 'with hands washed and faces clean' became an effective demand only after schools practically established the right to inspect students in these matters, and to restrict access or to administer punishment to deviants. The establishment of an inspectoral regime with respect to cleanliness tends over time to eliminate the necessity of such inspections, as students and others come to take it for granted that certain kinds of behaviour will be enforced. Injunctions to follow such behaviours tend at the same time to recede from school curricula.

The study of the formative period of state educational systems is particularly instructive for its revelation of the processes of educational normalization. In practice, the successful normalization of relations of power in educational systems means that they disappear from view. They become submerged in an obviousness which tends to be accepted unquestioningly. Historical study calls into question the taken-for-granted nature of contemporary educational relations and structures. By examining the conditions under which educational systems were organized, and by detailing the kinds of changes in social relationships which these systems provoked and continue to sustain, we may better understand the basis of the existing social order.

NOTES

1. Pestalozzi, J. H. (1801) *How Gertrude Teaches Her Children*, London. For the English influence of Pestalozzi's work see for instance Elizabeth Mayo (1840) *Lessons on Objects*, London.
2. See D. H. Akenson (1971) *The Irish Education Experiment*, Toronto: University of Toronto Press.
3. In this regard see Phil Gardner (1983) *Lost Elementary Schools of Victorian England*, London: Croom Helm.
4. For the early history of elementary education in Ontario, and for the period to 1871, see Bruce Curtis (1987) *Building the Educational State: Canada West, 1836–1871*, London: Falmer; also 'Capitalist development and educational reform: comparative material from England, Ireland and Upper Canada to 1850', *Theory and Society*, 14, January 1984; Robert Gidney, 'Elementary education in Upper Canada: a reassessment', in M. B. Katz and P. H. Mattingly (Eds.) (1975) *Education and Social Change: Themes from Ontario's Past*, New York: New York University Press; N. McDonald and A. Chaiton (Eds.) (1978) *Egerton Ryerson and His Times*, Toronto: Macmillan; Alison Prentice (1977) *The School Promoters: Education and Social Class in Mid-Nineteenth Century Ontario*, Toronto: McLelland & Stewart.
5. For the period after 1876 the only general work is Robert M. Stamp (1982) *The Schools of Ontario, 1876–1976*, Toronto: University of Toronto Press. See also Philip Corrigan, Robert

Lanning and Bruce Curtis, 'The Political Space of Schooling' in T. Wotherspoon (Ed.) (1987) *The Political Economy of Canadian Schooling*, Toronto: Methuen.
6. See for instance, John Bullen, 'Hidden workers: child labour and the family economy in late nineteenth-century urban Ontario', *Labour/Le Travail*, 18, Fall 1986; R. L. Jones (1946) *History of Agriculture in Ontario*, Toronto: University of Toronto Press.
7. See J. L. Goldstrom (1972) *The Social Content of Education*, Shannon, and Bruce Curtis, 'Curricular change and the Red Readers: history and theory', in G. Milburn, (Ed.) (forthcoming) *Quality in the Curriculum*, London, Ontario.

THE MEEK DICTATOR: THE INDIAN TEACHER IN HISTORICAL PERSPECTIVE

KRISHNA KUMAR

Although ancient and medieval Indian societies recognized teaching as a specialized activity, it was something rather different from what is regarded as a profession today. Education on a mass scale, and the teaching of a large number of students personally unknown to the teacher, are modern phenomena. The commonly held view is that these phenomena date from the early nineteenth century when colonial policies in education began to take shape. This view may be somewhat erroneous if we consider that in many parts of pre-colonial India, villages had teachers who taught groups of children.[1] However, these village schools cannot properly be regarded as comparable to the schools that came into being from the early nineteenth century onwards. For one reason alone we may distinguish the new schools from this earlier tradition, namely that at the new schools the teacher had no control over what was to be taught.

THE TEACHER AND THE STATE

The key to this distinction lies in the imposition of state control over education. Once a colonial trading organization had turned into a colonial state, and the colonial state had taken education under its control, the identity of the teacher and that of his functions moved into a new era. It was a total break with the past. By the turn of this century, the break was complete. Before the break, the teacher had followed his own ideas and judgement to determine what to teach. He was guided by tradition and by the needs of the village community. What he taught had mostly to do with the basic skills. His freedom lay mainly in the fact that he could pace his pedagogy to suit individual children. The ordinary village teacher shared this freedom with the teachers of specialized arts such as music and dance, and of specialized areas of higher knowledge, for example in literature, philosophy, and religion.

After the early nineteenth century break, the teacher lost all freedom. He could no longer decide what to teach or how to teach. Tradition lost its hold too when syllabuses and prescribed textbooks came into being. The syllabus and textbooks set down not only what had to be taught, but also the time within which it had to be completed. It meant that the teacher could no longer pace his pedagogy to suit his pupils. Yet another aspect of the change was the concept of impersonal examinations. The satisfaction of the teacher was no longer the criterion for termination of studentship; the new criterion was the student's performance at a test designed by someone other than the teacher.

This brief sketch could, however, mislead us if we do not place it in a historical and geographical perspective. It could mislead us into thinking that pre-colonial pedagogy was 'progressive' in the sense this adjective is used now to characterize child-centred methods of teaching. This may not be an accurate impression, for the milieu we are talking about permitted little space for individuality in either the child or the teacher. It was a tradition-bound milieu in which the teacher performed the role expected of him without conscious preparation or training. The tradition itself, in teaching and learning, was not in a flourishing phase as far as we know. There was, for sure, an enormous amount of geographical variation in these matters. Present-day Bengal, Tamilnadu, and Kerala are among the areas that had numerous village schools supported by the community. In several parts of central and northern India, on the other hand, the tradition of the teaching of literacy and numeracy most probably did not exist on any wide scale.

With these qualifications, we can move further along in our understanding of the break that occurred in the nineteenth century in the traditional function and status of the teacher. Whereas earlier the teacher was supported by the community, he now became a functionary of the state, working for a salary. He became part of the evolving structure of government service. Although the teacher was never officially described as a civil servant, this is what he in effect became, but with low status. Right from the start of the colonial education system, the teacher's job carried with it the possibility of being assigned several functions unrelated to teaching. He could be used as postmaster, census surveyor, distributor of textbooks, and so on. To this day, this range of possible duties of a school teacher remains, with new additions like the responsibility of manning a polling booth during elections. The varied functions tightened the teacher's relationship with the state but did not offer him higher status or more power, for two reasons.

One reason was that the teacher was a powerless subordinate within his own profession.[2] Above him stood the rank and file of a bureaucracy, starting with a sub-deputy inspector who had the power to examine students on a brief tour of the school and to make remarks on a teacher's performance. At the top of the bureaucracy sat the Director of Public Instruction. His office not only framed the rules of recruitment, promotion, and dismissal, but also had the power to transfer the teacher from place to place. The teacher was the most junior subordinate in the hierarchy of the education department. His job was to teach what he was asked to, to fulfil all the routine duties he was assigned, and to keep the visiting inspector satisfied with his hospitality and good behaviour. In keeping with his low position in the hierarchy, his salary was kept low. At the beginning of this century a primary school teacher's salary was at least five times lower than that of a sub-deputy inspector and ten times lower than that of a deputy inspector.

The other reason explaining the teacher's low status was the poor image of school teaching as a profession in comparison with the other professions that emerged along with the expansion of colonial education.[3] Low salary was of course one major source of this poor image. Someone earning about ten rupees per month could not possibly compete for status with engineers, doctors, and lawyers. The other source of the poor image was that in comparison with these professions, teaching projected a rather unspecialized image. Professional training was never applied as a mandatory requirement for a teaching job. Training institutions were too few to cope with the number of teachers required. Since the government did not insist on training as a pre-condition, the number of teachers who remained untrained grew at a rapid pace. This was true of schools run at state expense, but even more true of privately run schools.

What training there was consisted largely of classroom management and the craft of lesson planning. It did not require much intellectual exertion, and in any case the qualifications required for a teaching job were low, in keeping with the low salary. Poor-quality training and poor salary together resulted in a weak professional identity which made teachers indistinct from office clerks. After all, an important part of the teacher's daily routine was to maintain school records pertaining to children and to expenses. Any lapse or deviation from the given format in this task could lead to a damaging remark in the teacher's service book by an inspector. Indeed, in matters of expenditure, the teacher was always open to suspicion even though the amount of money available to him for running the school was extremely small. The loss of a single book, even after repeated use, could lead to punishment. Poor examination results would have meant the same.

Under these conditions, only those young men[4] who could find nothing else to do opted for teaching in a school, and whenever they got a chance to go into something else – an office job for instance – they did so. Although more than a century has passed since these conditions were formalized, and although India is no longer a colonial state, the image of school teaching has not changed much to this day. Over recent years, there has been some improvement in the salary of teachers, but the primary school teacher's salary still remains very meagre. The status value of the increase in teachers' salaries has in general been offset by the far higher rise in the earnings of other professions and by the rise of new professions. The choices available to young job-seekers now include careers in industry, management, and accountancy, apart from the traditional professions and the civil service. School teaching does not figure in this list. The teacher's powerlessness in the face of the bureaucracy has not changed much despite the rise of teachers' unions which resist extreme forms of victimization and which struggle for higher salaries. Officers may now be less capable of openly intimidating or oppressing a teacher, but they still have enough influence to produce obsequious hospitality or servile gestures at many interactions with teachers.

THE TEACHER AND THE CURRICULUM

In India all decisions regarding what is to be taught in schools are taken by bureaucratic authorities. This is now a mature tradition, the only new element in it being the role that quasi-bureaucratic experts now play in determining the curriculum. For the last twenty-five years, this role has been played by the National Council of Educational Research and Training (NCERT), which has affiliated structures in all parts of the country. Along with the state-level bureaucrats in charge of education, the NCERT's experts determine what is taught in most schools in the country. Teachers have virtually no role to play in this decision, except as token participants in committees and evaluative studies. It is not just the individual teacher who is deprived of the right to shape his daily curriculum; collectively too, teachers' organizations have had no say, or interest, in the curriculum. The assumption under which the school teaching profession works is that curriculum planning is not a part of the teacher's job. It is expected that every teacher will be given a syllabus to cover and textbooks to teach.

Although the distinction between the syllabus and the textbook is officially maintained, in practice the textbook serves as the *de facto* syllabus. Each child is required to have his own textbooks. The syllabus, on the other hand, is not easily accessible even to the headmaster or principal. So for most teachers, the textbooks represent the syllabus. Official policy insists that textbooks are only a means of fulfilling curriculum objectives, but in actual practice this insistence carries little meaning, for two reasons. One is that textbooks are 'prescribed', not recommended. Second, resources other than the textbook are not available in the majority of schools. For instance, fewer than one third of all primary schools have any sort of library. The availability of other resources, such as play material and science equipment, is even more uncertain.[5] The textbook is the only resource available in most classrooms since children are required to purchase it themselves. Assessment of students by means of tests or end-of-year examinations is based on their mastery of the content of the textbook.

By the beginning of this century the prescribed textbook and the examination system had become the two key factors influencing classroom teaching. The English administrators saw and used textbooks as instruments for the maintenance of norms and standards. The textbook was a convenient yardstick enabling an inspector to judge a teacher's coverage and his students' progress. From the teacher's perspective, the textbook was a symbol of the same authority structure which had the power to appoint, promote, penalize, and transfer teachers. The best means for the teacher to protect himself against this power structure was to stick to the textbook.

Traditions of mechanical reading of texts and rote learning already existed when the colonial system of education was established. The tradition found in the newly introduced textbooks a suitable agency for self-perpetuation. The content of the new textbooks, often reflecting an alien view of knowledge and foreign images, aided this process. For instance, the texts used for the teaching of English – a prized school subject since English was the medium of post-elementary education and the means of upward mobility – consisted of literary pieces rooted in the English landscape and the domestic world of the Victorian bourgeoisie. Such pieces could not be read for meaning, for the world they represented was altogether alien to the Indian teacher and student. The texts could only be memorized, along with interpretations given by authoritative literary critics.

Bureaucratic control and alien content left little room for the teacher to infuse local relevance into teaching. The possibility was excluded altogether by the dominant role that the examination system acquired in shaping student expectations. Since the colonial administration could not trust the teacher to examine his own students impartially, it developed a centralized system of examination which worked in an aura of secrecy and bureaucratic ritual. The symbolic value of such a system was no less than its functional value. It enhanced the faith of the rising middle class in the fairness of the colonial order. It also acted as an agency of social control since it permitted just about any extent of student failure. Fear of failure led both teachers and students to concentrate on the specific demands of the examination. The teacher's job was reduced to preparing the student with the right kind of answers. The rational way to do this was to restrict teaching to the content of the textbook.

Patterns of teaching, once established, do not give way easily. Colonial pedagogy outlasted colonial rule. Sitting in a classroom today one can still notice distinct features of teaching that are related to the colonial legacy. The fixed nature of the content permits the teacher to switch off any ability or resources he might possess for making fresh associations or for drawing upon new examples. The tacit belief is that he *need* not do these things even if during his training he has learnt that they improve teaching. The fear of being perceived as departing from the prescribed text, and of running out of time to finish the required content, serves as the background against which the 'decision' to stick to the text is taken.

Freed from the urgency to reorganize knowledge in interesting ways, the teacher persists with the task of maintaining order in the classroom to facilitate safe and speedy delivery of the prescribed content. This is how classroom management, by sundry pedagogical techniques, becomes his supreme concern. Voice control, blackboard work, questioning, and recapitulation – all means are directed towards helping children focus on the prescribed content. The ultimate purpose is to help them learn it by heart so well that they can reproduce it months later at the examination.

Ironically, thus, the lack of any role in curriculum planning and in the choice of materials – one of the sources of the teacher's meek professional status – contributes to his acting as a dictator in the classroom. The prescribed curriculum and textbook serve as the backdrop against which the drama of dictatorial power over docile children is played out. The syllabus and the textbook conceal the teacher's lack of professional power; they are the 'givens' of the situation. The children do not know that their teacher is a feeble servant of the authorities who frame syllabuses and prescribe textbooks; nor do they perceive him as a mere delivery man. For them the teacher is the man on the spot with all the power in the world to force them to do what he wants. They do not know that what he is forcing them to do is not what *he* wants but what he is required to do to make them learn. The teacher hides his powerlessness behind the mask of being all powerful.

TEACHERS AND STUDENTS

The colonial interlude, thus, had a paradoxical effect on the teacher's job. In terms of status he stood at the lower end of the hierarchy of the new professions, losing a great deal of his revered – although monetarily poor – status in the traditional society. Within his own government department too, he was powerless. But in the classroom he could maintain an aura of power and total command. There he was under no one's visible control. He retained his link with pre-colonial values and traditions in the context of the teacher-pupil relationship. Colonization and modern life could not greatly influence the core of this relationship, although one can now see some surface cracks.

The traditional view of the teacher-pupil relationship is based on the notion that the teacher is supreme. He possesses knowledge, and he knows how to impart it. The pupil's job is to be modest, obedient, and receptive. Several ancient texts describe the supremacy of the teacher and the modesty of the ideal disciple. The descriptions are rooted in an epoch when the teacher had a handful of disciples, each of whom got his fair share of individual attention. The teacher-pupil pair later on became a metaphor of worship, and many medieval poets used it to construct anti-sectarian, secular images of devotion. In the popular mind, the teacher (*guru* as he is called) shares his symbolic supremacy with God. The pupil must submit to him in order to learn.

The cracks one sees on the surface of this age-old belief also favour the teacher. People talk of the decadence that has set in among students, of how unruly and disrespectful they have become to teachers. The blame is sometimes placed at the door of modernism or its symbols, such as movies, money, and the cigarette. But the teacher escapes criticism. There are however other contexts in which he receives public criticism. For instance, he is criticized for making money from private tuition, for being a negligent or corrupt examiner, and for being irregular in his classes. However, none of this negative behaviour is regarded as sufficient to justify disrespectful treatment of a teacher by his students. The expectation is that, despite his deficiencies, a given teacher must receive the respect due to *any* teacher.

His supremacy *vis-à-vis* the students receives substantial support from the cultural norms that govern family relationships and the wider social organization. It has been recognized[6] that authority often takes the form of a nurturing autocrat in Indian families and in other social institutions. Independent decision making, questioning, and criticism are not encouraged among children and young people. Fantasizing and role-play among children are often confined to the imitation of adults in the family, especially the parents. This is not due to the lack of toy figures, but rather the absence of encouragement of the child's urge to imagine himself in a variety of roles. On the other hand, there is usually no lack of encouragement for modelling oneself on an ideal, invariably an adult figure similar to one's father or mother in the possession of supreme and nurturing power.

The teacher standing in the classroom assumes the only role that the hierarchical social organization permits him to assume. His age, knowledge, and the power to control – all these contribute to the unlikelihood of any fraternal or friendly relationship emerging between him and the children. Teacher training, under Western influence, makes a feeble attempt to lure him towards the virtue of friendliness towards his wards. The attempt is far too weak to break the hold of the traditionally expected behaviour, and in any case, much of what is learnt during training is widely regarded as inapplicable to actual teaching. The lone teacher who tries to practise friendliness towards his students often becomes the subject of unfriendly gossip in the staff room. Even in colleges and universities, where students are close to adulthood, a teacher's attempt to treat them as equals is regarded as a cheap strategy to gain popularity. Such a teacher is perceived as a threat to the collective status of the staff, and is therefore treated as an outcast. It is not unusual to see this sad fate befalling the teacher in charge of such activities as physical education, drama, or dance. Such activities seldom count towards the student's academic performance, nor does the teaching involved in them usually count as serious work. To some extent, at least, this could be due to the close intimacy these activities force upon the teacher and the student.

The 'proper' teacher, of a 'proper' school subject, is expected to maintain a distance from students. This is consciously held to be the right means to uphold one's position of command. In several schools and colleges, this position is physically expressed by the wooden or cement platform upon which the teacher's desk and chair are placed. Secondary school teachers are told during training never to leave the vicinity of their desk. The trainee who walks around the classroom and readily reaches out to children is penalized. The blackboard too is in the zone invested with symbolic power. Trainees are told never to stand with their face turned towards the blackboard, even while writing on it. The idea is that the teacher must never turn his face away from the students. They must always feel and actually find him looking at them.

Questioning by students is a rare phenomenon in Indian classrooms. Teachers are expected to encourage students to ask questions, and trainees are even required to write down the questions they expect their students to ask. Once training is over, few teachers find it possible or necessary to leave time for student questioning. It is true that students are rarely eager to ask questions, since their upbringing does not encourage questioning. But even the teacher who has managed to remain concerned about student questioning usually encourages questions in order to ensure that nothing in the lesson is left unclear. Like everyone else, he treats questioning as a means of seeking clarification or further information, never as a means of independent inquiry. Typically, he ends his lesson by asking 'Anything you want me to repeat? Anything not clear?' The message is that a question indicates lack of understanding. There is no scope for a question that opens up a possibility of fresh inquiry. If by chance such a question is ever asked, its freshness is likely to be ignored. Worse still, it may be regarded as inconvenient if the teacher has difficulty responding to it. 'Good' students are supposed to regard the teacher's discomfiture in such a situation as unfortunate. The teacher is not supposed to say 'I don't know'. It may take years of classroom visits for one to hear a sentence like 'I'll look it up' or 'Why don't you check it?'

It can be argued that this is a global phenomenon, that genuine inquiry among students is not encouraged anywhere. Whatever the truth of such a general statement, it will still leave Indian classroom reality a somewhat special phenomenon. What we see in Indian classrooms is not just reluctance on the part of students or apathy on the part of the teacher, but a conscious pursuit of unquestionable knowledge. As I have explained above, school knowledge is regarded in India as fixed. It is literally *enshrined* in the syllabus and the textbook. The teacher's job is to deliver this fixed knowledge, and the student's duty is to ingest it. There is no room in this process for genuine inquiry, for it is assumed that all necessary inquiry has already been made, and that the results of the inquiry have been packaged in the syllabus and the textbook. Questions can only be asked to clarify one's understanding of this packaged knowledge. This perception of knowledge[7] may be common among some other colonized countries, but it is not a global phenomenon.

NOTES

1. One of the best-known descriptions of vernacular education in India during the early nineteenth century can be found in *The Adam Reports*, although they may not be totally reliable for the statistics they provide. For a new edition of these reports, see *One Teacher, One School*, edited by Joseph Dibona (New Delhi: Biblia Impex, 1983). Also see Poromesh Acharya (1978) 'Indigenous vernacular education in pre-British era, traditions and problems', *Economic and Political Weekly*, 13, 48:1981–8.
2. For graphic descriptions of this relationship, see Arthur Mayhew (1926) *The Education of India*, London: Faber & Gwyer.
3. See Anil Seal (1968) *The Emergence of Indian Nationalism*, Cambridge: Cambridge University Press.
4. Throughout this paper I stick to the male pronoun because the teaching profession in India continues to be male-dominated. Even at the primary level, where the proportion of female teachers is now increasing, male teachers were more than a million out of the total of 1.4 million reported in 1982–3 (Ministry of Education, *Selected Educational Statistics*, 1984).
5. According to the Fourth All India Educational Survey (New Delhi: NCERT, 1982), only 29 per cent of all primary schools in the country had libraries, 47 per cent had a play space, and 60 per cent had blackboards.
6. See Sudhir Kakar (1978) *The Inner World*, New Delhi: Oxford University Press, and D. Narain (1964) 'Growing up in India', *Family Process*, 3, 1:127–54.
7. See Krishna Kumar (1987) 'Curriculum, psychology and society', *Economic and Political Weekly*, 22, 12:507–12.

2.3

THE CULTURE OF SCHOOLING IN EAST ASIA

CHENG KAI MING

This chapter attempts to discuss something that seems to be of prime importance to educational development, and yet has received little serious attention. It pertains to educational thought and practice in five settings in East Asia: Mainland China, Taiwan, Hong Kong, South Korea, and Japan. It also discusses Singapore as a sixth, somewhat marginal case. The discussions are mainly generated from examples in Mainland China and Hong Kong, of which the writer has first-hand knowledge, but which are closely related to other communities in the neighbourhood.

COMPULSORY ACHIEVEMENT

China launched its compulsory education programme in 1985. This is intended to phase in nine years of education for all.

Even before 1985, however, universalization of primary education had started. In fact, in the school year 1986–7, the net enrolment ratio was already 95.95 per cent (Cheng 1987b). This is an extremely high figure by the standards of developing countries, and even developed countries do not always achieve such a high ratio. Although there are international organizations which doubt the validity of the figure, there is little evidence to contradict it. In a vast country with a population of ten billion and great disparity in economic development, spreading education to almost every child aged six to eleven has been quite an amazing achievement.

The net enrolment ratio, however, tells only part of the story. The meaning of universal primary education in China can be specified by four ratios of which enrolment ratio is only one. The other three ratios are: retention ratio, universalization ratio, and achievement ratio. In practical terms, a county is regarded as having universalized primary education if it has achieved certain high values in the four ratios. There is in fact a special mechanism to verify that the county has done so.

Retention ratio is the proportion of pupils who enrol at the beginning of the school year and remain in school at the end of the same school year. Universalization ratio is the proportion of 12–15-year-olds who have completed primary education. These two ratios are just to ensure continuous universal attendance over time.

The fourth ratio, achievement ratio, is, however, far beyond a requirement for attendance. The achievement ratio is the percentage of primary 6 leavers who pass the graduation examination. That is, universal primary education entails not only high attendance; children are also expected to attain a certain standard.

The children, country-wide, follow the same curriculum, the same syllabuses and uniform textbooks. The examinations are uniform, conducted at prefecture level, sometimes at county level, and monitored by the provincial authority. That is, the graduation examination is in reality a public examination which runs across a candidate population of the order of hundreds of thousands. If one looks at the graduation examination papers and the way they are marked, one will agree that they are by no means casual tests.

The national achievement ratio for the year 1986–7 was 94.3 per cent (Cheng 1987b) for primary schools. The target for the whole nation is to maintain 95 per cent each year up to the year 2000. A similar ratio, 85 per cent, is set for junior secondary graduation (of the 15- or 16-year-olds).

One has to be further reminded that repetition is in many places insignificant. Some provinces allow for an annual repetition ratio of five per cent, but schools seldom use up their permitted quota.

In brief, the whole picture is that children are not only required to attend schools; they are also required to achieve an overall minimum standard and yet do so in the same time period. It is not only a case of compulsory attendance, but it is also a situation of 'compulsory achievement', although the latter is less a matter of legal obligation than one of common expectation.

MANAGEMENT BY OBJECTIVES

It would be much easier for foreigners to understand the situation if 'compulsory achievement' was simply a ritual, or a matter of unpopular coercion. The facts seem to indicate the opposite.

Teachers in China tend to believe that with due effort, a child should always be able to achieve the expected standard. They believe that genetic factors are always secondary, so long as the pupils are trying hard. The motto 'diligence compensates for stupidity' is seldom challenged.

Recently, there have been attempts to revise the junior secondary curriculum, because the current curriculum has proved difficult for the vast population. However, even after revision there will still be a unified curriculum.

As a corollary to this assumption, teachers believe that student performance is attributable to teacher performance. It is because of this belief, rather than any pressure from the administration, that teachers work extremely hard in order that their pupils should achieve better.

In an important way, the notion of 'ability' in its Western sense does not prevail in China. The term 'ability' comes into play mostly on two occasions. First, educators talk about 'cultivation of ability'. They believe that ability is something that can be developed and improved, and that that is the job of teaching. There are numerous writings, both academic and lay, which discuss the various components of ability and how it can be enriched or upgraded. Second, the old Confucian motto 'teaching according to ability' is still prevalent. This usually means that students with different abilities should be taught with different methods. This is not to be confused with the Western way of satisfying individual needs. In the Western version, pupils follow different curricula and achieve different levels in the end. In China, pupils follow the same curriculum and in the end are expected to achieve the same level.

In this context, one should not be astonished to see a school in a small village practising 'management by objectives' (MBO). The class teachers put up a small plate on the classroom door, with the following goals:

Management by objectives:
pass ratio = 40%
credit ratio = 40%
distinction ratio = 20%[1]

That is, by the end of the school year, the class is expected to achieve the respective ratios. This is a kind of productivity target for both the pupils and the teachers. Teachers will make every effort to achieve this target and, moreover, the target is made public.

The term MBO is not very widespread among Chinese teachers, but the notion of targets and productivity prevails. Teachers work towards some desired target of student achievement.

It is noticeable that such targets are usually fixed by the teachers on a voluntary basis. It is regarded as a sign of professionalism, as a matter of accountability to the society rather than to the superior.

UNIFORM CURRICULUM

The notion that ability can be 'taught' is not always shared by educators internationally, but it is by no means restricted to Mainland China. The same assumption is also prevalent in other Chinese communities, such as Taiwan and Hong Kong, and in some non-Chinese communities, such as South Korea and Japan.

If we take these five settings together, we shall find their education systems notable for very similar characteristics. The five systems all have a unified school system at least up to junior secondary level. (The system is unified in the sense that all the five systems have a single-stream primary school system of six years and a single-stream junior secondary school system of three years.)

This is very markedly different from the school system in some Western European countries. In Holland, for example, students go through one common core year for orientation after primary school and then divide into different school types – *LAVO, MAVO, HAVO,* and *VWO.* In West Germany, apart from the *Länder* with comprehensive schools, the tripartite system of *Hauptschule, Realschule,* and *Gymnasium* still starts immediately after primary education, at the early age of nine, although the first two years are mainly orientational in nature. In France, pupils are divided after a two-year 'observation' period at the age of thirteen. In the United Kingdom and the United States, schools are not streamed, but pupils are divided by their choice of subject.

In Japan, South Korea, and Hong Kong, the uniformity even reaches senior secondary level. The enrolment ratio in these three situations is around or above 90 per cent (Ministry of Education 1986; Thomas and Postlethwaite 1983; Education Commission 1985). There is some streaming within the unified curriculum – students are given some choice, for example, between science, arts and commercial subjects – but the choices do not differ enough to cater for different abilities, and most of the time, the different streams are hierarchical (for example the science stream is always more prestigious). Hong Kong, Japan, and South Korea all offer fairly comprehensive and sophisticated systems of technical education and vocational training, but the populations in these sectors remain small.

In Mainland China and Taiwan, there has been in recent years some diversification at senior secondary level. Both places are incidentally moving towards a fifty-fifty ratio between general and technical/vocational senior secondary education. However, general (academic) senior secondary schools are still regarded as the mainstream and technical/vocational schools are paid rather less respect. The curricula at junior secondary level and below are still totally uniform and compulsory.

The uniformity in curricula reflects the above-mentioned notion that although students are born different, they should be able to achieve the same. This goes along with the basic philosophy that it is the individuals who should adapt themselves as far as possible to the system. It is almost directly opposite to the Western philosophy that the community should cater as far as possible for individual needs.

The basic assumption about the relationship between individuals and the

166

education system has implications for the practice of education. The following are just a few examples.

DILIGENCE OR ABILITY

When a child is not doing very well in England, the parents tend to think that his or her ability is low. When a child is doing poorly in Hong Kong, his or her parents will say that he or she has not worked hard enough.

This helps to explain the process of selecting pupils for different streams. In England, although schools are not streamed as they used to be, streaming within schools is common. Pupils at Form 4 equivalent (and earlier) are allocated into different streams. This happens very often even in comprehensive schools. The allocation is very much based on the school's judgement and the parents trust the school in its judgement. The same happens in the Netherlands when pupils after the orientation year are allocated to MAVO, HAVO, or VWO. It is not only that parents have confidence in teachers' professional judgement, but parents also believe that ability matters.

In Hong Kong, by contrast, parents always want their children to be put into the best stream, regardless of their performance. They believe that their children should be put under greater pressure and that that is the way to success. Hence, one has to resort to 'objective' and 'scientific' methods of allocation. This has given birth to Hong Kong's fairly sophisticated systems of allocating students, not only to different streams, but also to different schools. The method employs sophisticated mathematical modelling and claims to take care of student performance, and parental preference, as well as geographic distribution.

In the end, although there is over-provision in Hong Kong of well-equipped technical/vocational institutions, parents of 'under-achieving' children still opt for private schools with much poorer facilities, simply because such schools operate classes in the 'academic' stream.

This mentality also explains the examination pressures that are prevalent in the Eastern Asian region. People respect uniform examinations; they respect competition. It is a competition on a uniform course for an overall champion, rather than a competition amongst different talents, separately developed.

INDIVIDUAL DEVELOPMENT AND SOCIALIZATION

Pre-school educators in Mainland China, Taiwan and Hong Kong have faced similar dilemmas in early childhood education.

On the one hand, most of the trained pre-school educators have received their own education in the Western tradition which emphasizes the importance of individual needs and individual development. Hence, there is a tendency to minimize elements of conformity and an attempt to avoid disciplinary measures as far as possible.

On the other hand, there is the strong Chinese tradition that children should be socialized as early as possible and conform to social norms. There is a strong pressure from parents who opt for conformity. Children are traditionally taught at a very early age to behave and act according to social expectations. Even the educators, themselves obviously influenced by the culture, are not totally convinced that conformity is unnecessary. Often, they find themselves pulled in two different directions.

As an example, parents believe that kindergartens, and sometimes even nurseries, are part of regular schooling. Children should, according to this view, be taught to write Chinese characters from the very first day of kindergarten. Educators realize that early writing is inappropriate and try to postpone the practice. This has caused many disputes in one way or another. Some kindergartens have refused to introduce early writing and parents have withdrawn their children. Others have submitted to parents' wishes and surrendered their principles. Only the best kindergarten can brave the tide and survive.

As a further example, children are taught at a very early age to hold chopsticks, and even pens and pencils, in a uniform, 'proper' way. This is not always thought to be necessary by Westerners. Just recently, the Japanese have even invented a small rubber device that can be put on the pencil and thus help very young children to hold the pencil in a 'proper' way. The device soon flourished in the Hong Kong and Taiwan markets. The Mainland Chinese have more recently produced their own model and have extended the device to calligraphy brushes and ball-pens.

The adoption of the *activity approach* in kindergarten and primary classes offers another example. Educators sincerely believe that learning should be lively and interesting. With some reluctance, teachers in Hong Kong have moved towards an *activity approach* which divides the class into groups; student activities have become a central concern. However, this does not entail the Western type of *activity approach* where different groups may progress at different speeds and the main idea is to cater for individual needs. By contrast, in Hong Kong, the *activity approach* is simply regarded as a better way of motivating all pupils to achieve.

SPECIAL EDUCATION

The notion that ability can always be upgraded to a desired level encounters a particular challenge in the realm of special education. This issue is currently very significant amongst Mainland Chinese for whom the Western notion of 'special needs' was foreign until recently.

With the introduction of compulsory education, children with special needs have become a new focus of attention. On the one hand, there is a consensus that children with special needs should be included in the compulsory education programme. On the other hand, it is admittedly impossible for some children to achieve the 'normal' standard. The expectation of a high 'achievement ratio' can easily break down.

Special classes and special schools are rare in China but are increasing at a rapid rate. There is evidently a paradox here. Children with an IQ of 69 and below receive special care, following a different curriculum and going through a different period of schooling. Those with an IQ of 70 are thought to be normal and are expected to achieve the normal graduation standard. The difference of one point in the quotients simply does not justify the large gap between the two levels of expectation. It is a case which challenges the deep-rooted belief that 'hard work compensates for stupidity'.

However, this dilemma has underlined two important issues. On the one hand, it reveals the reality of individual needs and it stresses the impossibility of putting the entire population of school children into one identical system. On the other hand, it also reveals that many of the teachers in ordinary schools are *de facto* offering some service of special education. There are numerous reports and newspaper stories about how teachers sacrifice their own leisure time to help 'backward' students to achieve the desired target. They may well in one process have solved many of the mental health problems which these 'backward' students suffer.

The situation in Hong Kong is different, though with similar underlying assumptions. There is a rather comprehensive system of special education, but it is always a problem to persuade parents to send their children to make use of the service. Apart from the understandable fear of 'special' identity, many parents think their children should and could overcome their handicap by striving harder. Parents simply do not accept the notion that there are children who are not suitable for certain types of competition.

JOB SATISFACTION OR JOB SATISFACTORINESS

Career counsellors usually provide students with two types of information: personality information and job-market information. The best career education should provide both, in the hope that the students can hit a balance when they face career selection.

In Western communities, there used to be an emphasis on the students' self-realization of personality data. One cannot have a satisfactory career if one does not know enough of one's own personality and does not try to match it with the desired career. This can be called job satisfactoriness (Fan 1985).

Career counselling in the five settings seldom relies on students' interest tests, personality measures or aptitude tests. In Hong Kong, institutions of higher education offered personality test facilities some fifteen years ago, but had to stop offering them simply because they proved so unpopular. Students took job prospects as the most important criterion for job selection. Personal suitability came very low in their priorities. In other words, they look for job satisfaction rather than job satisfactoriness (Cheng 1987a).

The case in Mainland China is of course markedly different. It is still very much a planned economy and education is still very much designed to serve the nation's manpower needs. There used to be an expectation that individuals should sacrifice themselves for community needs. Recently, the view has been that a satisfactory career is one which merges individual needs with community needs. Even more recent developments allow for self-employment and job-seeking. This has created a kind of entrepreneurship which urges young people to pay high attention to job-market signals. Although these ideologies seem to contradict one another, the underlying philosophy is still the submission of individual personalities to external requirements.

DOES CULTURE MATTER?

After reviewing these different issues, what seems to be central in all the five settings under consideration is the notion that individuals are supposed to adapt themselves to the system.

This is a strong tradition and is reflected in plenty of ancient Chinese stories where scholars strove extremely hard, followed the uniform syllabus (The Four Books and the Five Classics), and eventually became national champions in the contest of the civil examinations.

It is remarkable that the five settings in East Asia have very little in common in their political and economic arrangements. They belong to very different categories of development, economy, and political structure. Mainland China and Taiwan, for example, are rivals in political ideology. Mainland China is still very much a centrally-planned system whereas Hong Kong is almost completely *laissez faire*. Japan has extremely high economic status, while Mainland China is still very low. Yet they share more or less the same educational assumptions and have more or less similar educational systems which are distinctively different from those of other parts of the world.

What is this element that seems to override all the economic, political and ideological differences? Although the five areas are all inhabited by yellow-skinned peoples, race certainly does not seem to be an acceptable explanation.

One possible explanation is that there is a cultural factor that exists and exerts its influence independently of the economic, political, and ideological factors. It remains to be discovered what precisely this cultural factor is. But these five East Asian settings certainly offer a fertile ground for developing research on cultural elements in educational achievement.

One thing is certain, and that is that the five places have all been influenced by Confucius. Much has been written about Confucius and his philosophy, but how exactly Confucius has influenced modern lives and modern thought in the sphere of education is still an area of research to be fully developed.

Nevertheless, what the Chinese sociologist Fei Shiaotung remarked forty years ago is still valid (Fei 1947). In Fei's view, members of most Western societies participate as individuals in an association, whereas members of Chinese societies participate as elements in a hierarchy. In the former, people interact according to a kind of social contract; in the latter, people act according to social expectations.

How this is related to Confucius is yet to be explored. A point of regret is that the 'Confucian culture', if it does continue to influence modern societies, has not received a systematic analysis that is acceptable to the established framework of social sciences. This is similar to the case of traditional Chinese medical science which works without a theory that can fit readily into any Western framework. Therefore, it is not easy even for people within the culture to compare and contrast with other cultures. It is something that is sensed but not understood.

This lack of self-understanding of the culture in the East Asian countries has created varying degrees of confusion in different places.

In Mainland China, where the 'open-door policy' is only recent, educators find Western educational thought not easily acceptable. There is still a strong tendency to 'go the Chinese way', although Western ideas are well respected. In Taiwan, there has long been a literature introducing Western educational theories, but such theories seldom infiltrate into educational practice and research. Some Japanese educators have cried out for a rethink of 'imported educational theories'. The case of Hong Kong is more confusing. Educators seem to accept both traditional values and Western ideas without much hesitation; they are now in the process of trying to combine the two into a coherent system.

THE CASE OF SINGAPORE

Those who are familiar with the Asian scene may readily suggest the inclusion of Singapore in the same category as the other five.

The Singaporean education system differs significantly from the five systems mentioned in that it streams pupils right after Primary 3, at the age of nine, and yet again after primary school. The streaming is based on language abilities and results in different curricula and different durations of schooling in different streams (Goh 1978; Seow et al. 1982).

However, apart from the recognition of student abilities and a different system, Singapore shares almost exactly the same philosophy which underlies the five systems discussed above.

Pupils of lower language ability are still made to finish their primary schooling in eight years, two years more than their counterparts in other streams. This goes along with the belief that more effort may compensate for poor ability. The construction of the system is based on the nation's development needs and not on individual needs. The structure of the education system very much matches the manpower structure required for economic development. The streams are structured according to fixed quotas which are predetermined by state policies. It is a highly competitive system where the state acts as judge.

It is not possible to go into detail of the Singaporean system in this short account, but it is safe to say that the Singaporean system does share the same cultural characteristics of the Eastern Asian model, although it differs significantly in form.

EDUCATION, SOCIALIZATION AND UNEMPLOYMENT

The discussion above would be less interesting if it explained nothing more than differences in education. In Western European countries, there have recently been all kinds of training programmes, 'breeding centres', and schemes to develop the 'enterprise culture' and to encourage young entrepreneurs (see Cheng 1986). The idea is to increase the adaptability of young graduates so as to reduce the pressure of structural unemployment.

Two points can be developed from here. First, the idea of training for adaptability is a significant move away from the Western emphasis on individual needs. Adaptability, in the sense of catering for employment needs, can be viewed as the adjustment of one's personal characteristics and interests to suit community needs. This can be seen as a step towards the East Asian model.

Second, the lack of adaptability among young people in the West may be partly attributable to the education system which emphasizes individual development. There are already places in the Western world which refrain from using interest tests or aptitude tests, from a fear that these might further encourage diffidence in self-adjustment for job-seeking.

The argument can be carried further to make some more speculative comments. If the lack of individual adaptability contributes to structural unemployment in the narrow sense, the lack of collective adaptability may have reduced the international competitive power of some of the Western nations. That might be one of the explanations for the Western European unemployment crisis which is nowhere found on a comparable scale in the East Asian countries we have been discussing.

Put in another way, the East Asian model incurs social cost in the form of competitive pressures and individual sacrifices; the social cost in the Western model may be unemployment.

NOTES

1. This happens in the Zhaozhangzi primary school in a poor county, Lingyuan, in the province of Liaoning (see Cheng 1987b).

REFERENCES

Cheng, K. M. (1986) 'Traditional values and Western ideas: Hong Kong's dilemma in education', *Asian Journal of Public Administration*, December 1986.

Cheng, K. M. (1987a) 'Where are the trainees? – Trainers' plans versus students' aspirations', in E. D. Fortuijn, W. Hoppers, M. Morgan (Eds.) *Paving pathways to work*. The Hague: CESO, 59–64.

(1987b) *Planning basic education in China: two case studies in the province of Liaoning*, August, 1987. UNICEF document, forthcoming.

Education Commission, Report No. 1, Hong Kong: Government Secretariat, 1985.

Fan, P. H. (1985) 'Appreciating economic and psychological signals in planning careers education for Hong Kong'. Paper prepared for the WGOO/CESO conference on 'Youth programmes and the transition from school to work', held in Wageningen, The Netherlands, December 16–21 1985.

Fei, S. T. (1947) *Earth-bound China*, Hong Kong: Joint Publishers. (Reprinted 1985, in Chinese.)

Goh, K. S. and the Education Study Team (1978) *Report on the Ministry of Education, 1978*, Singapore National Printers.

Hiroshi Kida, Rentaro Ohno, Toshio Kanaya, Koji Kato and Ryo Watanabe (1983) 'Japan', in R. M. Thomas and T. N. Postlethwaite *Schooling in East Asia: Forces of Change*, Oxford: Pergamon Press.

Ministry of Education, Republic of China (1987) *Educational statistics of the Republic of China*.

Ministry of Education, Republic of Korea (1986) *Education in Korea, 1985–86*, Seoul.

Planning and Finance Department, State Education Commission (1986) *Achievements in Education: Educational Statistics 1980–1985*, Beijing: People's Educational Press.

Seow, C. H., Foo, L. H. and Hsu, D. (1982) 'Education and examination system in Singapore'. Country Report delivered at a seminar on 'Innovative approaches to classroom testing and measurement in secondary science and mathematics'.

Tokyo Metropolitan Government (1979) *Education in Tokyo*.

THE STRUCTURING OF SCHOOLING IN DIFFERENT POLITICAL CONTEXTS: THE CASE OF CHILE

CRISTIÁN COX

INTRODUCTION

In the last two decades Chile has seen three comprehensive and markedly differing attempts at changing its economic base and the principles of its national ethos. Between 1964 and 1970 a Christian Democrat government applied a programme of reforms oriented towards both economic development and a more egalitarian and participatory social and political order. An alliance of the Left led by Marxist political parties was then elected to government in 1970 and attempted to create the basis of a transition to socialism. Finally, in 1973, amid conditions of economic crisis and widespread social and political conflict, the military staged a violent coup against the leftwing Popular Unity government, inaugurating a period of political repression and *laissez-faire* economics which had in 1988 not yet come to a close. All three periods saw major attempts at changing the structures and practices of institutionalized education. The result has been a complex historical pattern of changes and continuities in the equitable distribution, institutional organization, and transmission of the knowledge and values with which the school system is concerned.

In these last twenty years, the country has seen the emergence of groups and ideologies which, apart from their specific references to Chile do illustrate to an important extent the basic political alternatives open to developing societies. This chapter examines how the dynamic relationship between a society and its school system reflects a historical context, powerfully influenced by the contrasting nature of the groups and ideologies in government. First we shall see how the different institutional domains, actors, and ideologies have defined, very generally, the school system's position and key functions in society. In the second section we shall discuss the main continuities and changes in the way the school system has been organized, and its resources distributed.

STRUCTURAL CONTINUITIES

Independent Chile's public education was organized in the mid nineteenth century. Its initial inspiration owed more to political interests than to the needs of industry. Its designers were an intellectual and political élite who offered education to the people from above and viewed it as a crucial pre-condition for citizenship and for the realization of republican ideals. Thus, public education was originally justified by processes of socio-political democratization and participation rather than by the demands of business and industry, and the values associated with these. This essentially political rationale for state education has remained until now the crucial determinant of the main features of education.[1]

The foundations of the public educational system were, therefore, laid by an élite of intellectuals and politicians connected with the universities, public administration, and the professions, rather than to the world of material production. They represented secularism, equality, and responsible reformism rather than the *laissez-faire* side of the liberal world-view. They pinned their hopes for social and economic progress to the state's capacity for transforming society.

The educational system which this élite organized was developed in a situation where mass illiteracy was the basic cultural condition. It consisted of a highly centralized set of institutions modelled after the French Napoleonic system and it was underwritten by the concept of *estado docente* (the notion that the state should have a monopoly of education). *Estado docente* was literally a 'teaching state', responsible for the education of all its citizens. *Estado docente* involved rigid central control and national uniformity in all aspects of instruction: curriculum, syllabuses, school texts and evaluation. The state regulations included, after decades of conflict in the second half of the nineteenth century, the schools of the Catholic Church, which at the time were attended mainly by the landed upper class.[2]

From the 1920s until the radical break imposed by the military in 1973, the dilemmas about state education invariably revolved round 1) the absence from it of the dominant groups, 2) the control of education by middle class and at times working class groups, and 3) the unquestioning acceptance by all forces of the *estado docente*. Within the parameters represented by the latter, the fundamental aims of both centre and leftwing policies for education were the following: expansion of access and educational opportunities in general; moves towards institutional unification and cultural uniformity across different educational settings; and finally the need to strengthen the relationships between educational outcomes and the productive needs of the country. Underlying these overarching aims was the belief in education as a strategic resource for redressing social inequalities and providing the means for a more participatory and democratic political life, as well as for a modern economic basis.

While both the Christian Democrat (CD) and the Popular Unity (PU) governments shaped their educational policies within these general parameters, the political rationales of their specific projects, as well as their respective results, varied considerably. The CD government, for example, sought to implement a very significant and comprehensive educational reform. The PU government's education policy was different, however, in that it was not merely reformist but also revolutionary in conception; the education bill also suffered political defeat (prior to the military coup) before any of its proposals could be implemented. We shall turn now to look in more detail at the period 1964–1973, before the coup. The analysis will concentrate on three principal policy areas: the changes in educational opportunity, the organization of schooling, and its relations with production.

Educational opportunity

For both governments in this period the expansion of educational opportunities at all levels of the educational system was a top priority. Primary education enrolments rose from 1.5 million students in 1964 (85 per cent of the age group) to 2.3 million in 1973, reaching the 100 per cent enrolment rate first defined as a national objective back in 1920. Secondary education enrolments rose, also, in the same period, from 142,154 to 445,862, or from a school enrolment rate of one in six of secondary school age children to one of almost one in two. At the university level, student numbers grew by over 130 per cent during the Christian Democrat period and by almost 90 per cent in the three years of the socialist government (PU).[3]

Institutional organization

Neither the CD reform of 1965 and following years, nor the policies and projected changes of President Allende's PU government questioned the organizational principles of the 'teaching state'. Within the traditional framework of the educational system, the measures implemented during the CD period emphasized moves towards institutional unification and increasing uniformity amongst the system's different modalities. The boundaries between the academic and technical-vocational modes of secondary education, for example, became less rigid. The reformers decreed that both types of education qualified for continuation of studies in higher education (until then a possibility restricted exclusively to the academic track). Furthermore, modifications in the curriculum were aimed at reducing the differences between the teaching/ learning styles of the two modes. None of these measures was altered during the government of the leftist alliance which followed.

Relations with production

For the CD government the accelerated growth of technical-vocational schools was one response to the need to make education more directly relevant to development. It is worth re-emphasizing, though, that despite the expansion and improvement of technical education, the actual changes in the relations between technical and academic education as well as in curricular restructuring were aimed not towards the world of production and specialized skills, but rather towards higher, and not necessarily technical, education.

The main plank of the abortive educational project of the Popular Unity government was going to be a radical opening of the boundaries of schools to incorporate elements from the world of work. The actual processes of schooling, particularly at the secondary level, were to be directly linked to productive activities in the nationalized sector of the economy. However, the rationale for this proposal was not so much the need to produce skilled workers or technicians, but rather the belief that a weakening of the manual/intellectual divide was a necessary condition for the emergence of a new, profoundly less class-conscious society.[4]

Hence, the intentions behind the policies of both the CD and the PU governments were not so much concerned to respond to societal production needs or to demands for specialized skills (demands which, interestingly enough, the leaders of industry never voiced); the real priorities of the two administrations were, respectively, to promote educational mobility and to create a new, less class-based consciousness. From our viewpoint these policies can be seen as very much in line with the forces influencing the development of education, not only in the 1960s and 1970s, but more generally, from the beginning of this century. As mentioned at the outset, throughout this century, the functions of education, as defined by national politics and by parental demands, have underlined the importance of social mobility and political participation rather than the modernization of production. In fact, in Chile, as in many other Latin American societies, the growth of education and the increasing complexity of educational institutions have been processes which have taken place ahead of developments and restructuring in the economy. Education was able to achieve this pre-eminence through the very close links between the state and the social and political forces supporting educational developments.[5] The present military government, however, has attempted to dismantle the basis of this divergence between social-institutional growth and economic stagnation.

THE AUTHORITARIAN AND NEO-CONSERVATIVE REVOLUTION

The violent resolution of the crisis of 1973 put an end not only to the socialist government of Salvador Allende but also to an order whose pillars had been, for five decades, the broadening of the welfare state, the sanctity of democratic politics, and the development of a national industrial base. The military take-over was a revolution aimed at reversing the historical relations between the state and the whole area of private and local initiatives. The aim was to reduce dramatically the role of the state, and of politics in general, while strengthening the whole fabric of private and communal institutions.

Since the cost of this process has been the suffocation of politics, however, there is a question of whether there really has been a strengthening of private and local initiative. Within the ensuing order, and despite the intention of reducing the role of the state, it has emerged with a vastly-increased capacity to use its monopoly of the means of violence against any manifestation of opposition in society as a whole.

The worlds of the military and the leaders of industry and commerce (in the beginning supported by a wider social spectrum) have come together in a historic task, based on two sets of key assumptions. On the one hand there are the views and values of those inspired by the 'Doctrine of National Security', who conceive of society as under permanent risk of disintegration from the subversive action of Marxism; they see the armed forces as guarantors of the threatened national unity, and the state as free to stifle all national opposition. On the other hand there are the ideas of an extreme economic liberalism, whose key assumptions are the freedom of the individual, a notion of the state with functions limited to only those domains such as defence and foreign relations, which cannot be regulated by private enterprise, and the celebration of the market as the primary mechanism for the integration and regulation of society.[6] These two 'voices' have combined in the educational sphere to produce the most important changes in direction this century.

In the first years after the coup, the military applied force in education, as in the rest of society. The educational system came directly under the control of military personnel from the national to the local level. Institutions and courses judged to be Marxist or too political were simply purged. Thousands of school teachers and a quarter of the university staff were expelled for political reasons; subject matters considered 'contaminated' were eliminated from the syllabuses, and university libraries were searched and books banned and burned. The regime's direct intervention controlled discussion, either by actual violence or by the threat of violence, and it restored principles of curriculum organization that had been weakened during the 1960s.

The military government did not, however, attempt changes in the structures of the educational system until 1980. Deeper changes started to unfold at this point. A technical task force, close to the groups ruling the economy and strongly doctrinaire in its adoption of the new conservatism, took control of the educational sector. Thus, for the first time since its organization at the beginning of the republic, the educational system came directly under the influence of industrial and commercial interests, and its functions began to be defined by the political principles of the Right.

Despite its unprecedented power and the apparent certainty of its purpose, the military regime has imposed changes upon the educational system which are not unequivocal in their meaning. Between the armed forces' need for control and the neo-conservative technocracy's need to deregulate, there is evidently a clear conflict of interest. The policies we now outline have combined these opposing principles in ways which make their results less radical than the architects would have us believe.

Educational opportunity

In marked contrast with every previous government of the century, the military regime did not define the expansion of enrolments as a goal, and, in fact, it reduced the previous growth rates. Indeed, in absolute terms, fewer resources were allocated to education in 1984 than in 1972, the year before the coup. In relation to the population, if the expenditure in education per inhabitant was 100.0 in 1970, in 1983 it was 89.1. Although in absolute terms enrolments increased slightly from 2.99 million in 1973 to 3.12 million in 1985, proportionately for the same period, they dropped from 54.5 per cent to 50.6 per cent for the 0–24-year-old group.[7] Education is no longer viewed as a priority; 'more of it' is no longer seen as 'better'. Further, and again in marked contrast with the past, the present government does not conceive of education as a strategic means of social transformation. This role is reserved for industry and production.

Institutional organization

The strategic hub of the regime's initiatives in education has been the attempt to change the institutional basis of the *estado docente*. The attempt has included a policy of decentralization, which has stripped the Ministry of Education of much of its power over the schools, and a policy of privatization. However, the results of these policies have not meant, in our view, the end or even an amelioration of the role of the state in education, but rather its redefinition. We shall try to delineate the direction of this redefinition.

Decentralization

The present authorities have sought to decentralize the system, making the schools dependent on local bureaucracies and in principle more accountable to the community, through a process of transfer of the administration of state schools from the Ministry of Education to district and town councils. The rationale for the changes has been to improve the quality of education through greater efficiency in the allocation and use of resources as well as through a closer school-community relationship intended to enhance parents' participation in the educational process. This pro-local community measure, originating in neo-conservative assumptions about the need to pass responsibilities from the state to individuals and local groups, actually collapsed because of the military's dread of practically any form of social organization or participation. The transfer of schools from the Ministry of Education to the local councils has taken place in a context where no local official is elected and participation is tightly controlled. Hence, the decentralization process has meant a certain continuity with historical patterns of centralized control over teachers and the day-to-day running of schools. The difference is now that this control is openly political, as the schools and teachers no longer depend on the specialized, relatively autonomous, and distant bureaucracy of the Ministry of Education, but rather on political officials such as mayors, directly appointed by the Executive and dependent upon the Ministry of the Interior. The process of decentralization, as it stands today, has meant a strategic by-passing of the Ministry of Education by political authorities which perceive it and the teaching corps as basically suspect. It is not the 'voice' of the local community which is now heard in the schools, but that of the Ministry of the Interior. The decentralization process has also added new inequalities to the educational system through the differences in resources which rich and poor councils can allocate to their schools (to supplement the centrally-defined per capita payments).

Privatization

The privatization of as much as possible of the public education system has been a constant, strategic goal for the neo-conservative groups in the regime. Their efforts have been tempered, though, by the more centralizing views of the armed forces and by the open opposition of much of the educational community (the teachers, the bureaucracy, and the experts).

In 1981, out of the total school enrolment (excluding higher education), 78 per cent corresponded to the state system, 15 per cent to the privately-owned but state-subsidized system, and 7 per cent to the completely private fee-paying system. In 1985, the proportions varied significantly in favour of the private (subsidized) sector: state enrolments now represented only 65 per cent of the total; the private state-supported sector 29 per cent, and the private fee-paying, 6 per cent.[8]

The process of privatization has produced a number of changes in the education system. First of all, it has meant the emergence of entrepreneurs and market principles in a domain where they had rarely functioned and where they were seen as socially not quite legitimate. Second, through the fostering of competition between subsidized private and public education in the poorer areas, a type of educational distinction which previously did not have an institutional basis has been favoured. Finally, it has produced new conditions of employment for teachers, more often than not tantamount to exploitation.

It is important to note that, except for the small proportion of fee-paying schools (6 per cent of enrolments in 1985), the 'private' system is entirely financed by the state, which pays a certain amount per student. What has been taking place then is not the end of the 'teaching state' but rather the emergence of a *mixed* system where the 'public' and the 'private' spheres are linked and in control of different aspects of education within domains which are still public in their resources.

Relations with production

It is interesting to emphasize here that the authoritarian regime, representing in so many ways the views of commerce and industry, has not given any particular priority to the development of technical education in the school system. On the contrary, its major undertaking has been to halve the time allocated to technical subjects, thus making this stream much closer to its academic counterpart than in the past. Additionally, in a bid to make them more relevant to production, the government has transferred the best secondary technical schools (1.4 per cent of the enrolment of secondary education) from the Ministry of Education to associations of employers. At the post-secondary level the government has created 'Centres for Technical Training', but these are not state-supported, and serve only the small fraction of school leavers able to afford them.

In our view these measures relate to a drastic change in development strategy, from one based in industry, government intervention, and the growth of the internal market, to one based in the export of primary products and private enterprise. The new strategy is labour-saving and demands from education only a small fraction of highly skilled workers and technicians. The latter would attend the schools run by the associations of employers although no hard evidence on the quality or relevance of their educational programmes is yet available.

Central control of curriculum and syllabuses

Ever since the 1840s, when the founders of public education sought to control school norms and content completely, lest 'religious obscurantism' should influence them, right up to the remarkably specific definition of every single 'unit of learning' by the reformers of the 1960s, central control of the curriculum and the syllabuses has always been comprehensive and thorough. This long line of continuity has been altered by measures of the military regime. These have allowed some opportunity for local variation at the level of the individual teacher or school. The post-1980 reforms, with their anti-state and pro-individual principles, have relaxed the central control of the syllabuses, thus opening some space for teacher control of the curriculum. At the same time, head teachers of state primary schools have been authorized to alter elements of the still centrally-determined curriculum; they may redefine time allocation per subject and suspend or drop some subjects according to the resource characteristics of the schools and needs of the locality.

We want to mention two aspects in relation to these changes. First, this less comprehensive and less specific central definition of what should be communicated in the classroom runs parallel to a strengthened ideological control of teachers by the municipal authorities. Thus, the new freedom available to teachers is confined within fairly explicit ideological boundaries. These latter, however, operate more by underlining what cannot be discussed in the classroom rather than by setting out anything like a programme of political indoctrination. Second, the new freedom which head teachers now have to decide what subjects to offer (out of a centrally-set list) implies the official acceptance and legitimation of a type of state educational provision whose character will vary according to differences in material and cultural resources between urban and rural groups, as well as between the poorer and better-off groups within the urban areas. The available evidence about primary education in the rural areas (20 per cent of enrolments at this level) indicates that 'adaptation' of the official curriculum is already synonymous with its 'reduction'.[9] Chilean education has always been scarred by grim class inequalities but it was also a historical constant that state policies were aimed against these. The present government's 'realism' about the poorer groups' chances of cultural and social mobility makes it difficult to argue that state policies still maintain a similar orientation.

REFERENCES AND NOTES

1. Brunner, J. J. (1981) *La cultura autoritaria en Chile*, Santiago: FLACSO.
2. Silvert, K. H. and Riessman, L. (1976) *Education, Class and Nation. The Experiences of Chile and Venezuela*, New York: Elsevier Publications.
3. Echeverría, R. (1982) *Evolución de la Matrícula en Chile, 1935–1981*, Santiago: PIIE.
4. Cox, C. (1984) 'Continuity, conflict and change in Chilean education: the pedagogical projects of the Christian Democrat and the Popular Unity governments'. Ph.D Thesis, University of London, in *Collected Original Resources in Education*, 10,2, 1986, Oxford.
5. Rama, G. and Tedesco, J. C. (1979) 'Education and development in Latin America (1950–1975)', *International Review of Education*, XXV, 2–3.
6. Tironi, E. (1986) *El liberalismo real*, Santiago: Sur Ediciones.
7. Cox, C. (1986) *Chilean Education in 1985: Institutional Profile*, Santiago: CIDE.
8. Ministerio de Educación Pública (1986) *Estadísticas nacionales 1985*, Santiago. The completely private fee-paying schools have been of less interest to the state than the private subsidized schooling (non-fee paying).
9. Gajardo, M. and de Andraca A. M. (1987) *Estructura y funcionamiento de la escuela en las zonas rurales*, Santiago: FLACSO.

CULTURAL AND POLITICAL INFLUENCES ON THE DEVELOPMENT OF EDUCATION IN SIERRA LEONE

CREAM WRIGHT

INTRODUCTION

There can be little doubt that cultural and political factors are key elements in any attempt to understand the history and development of a society. This is particularly significant for most African societies, since their very existence and destiny as nation states are inextricably linked with the political domination and cultural penetration of the colonial era. As the African political scientist, Ali Mazrui, expresses it:

> Colonialism was not simply a political experience for Africa; it was even more fundamentally a *cultural* experience. The values of the African world were profoundly disturbed by what would otherwise have been a brief episode in African history.

Within this context, it can be argued that education was one of the principal vehicles used in the cultural penetration of Africa. It is much more difficult, however, to try to unravel the positive and negative effects of education in this regard. On the one hand, education is often blamed for fostering a kind of cultural enslavement, which has resulted in the demise of African culture and values in preference to those of the colonial powers. Yet, on the other hand, education is also regarded as the key to modernization and development in most African countries. This type of dilemma richly illustrates the principle that education can act equally as a force for domination or as a force for liberation. In a quite fascinating sense therefore, the history of educational development can be regarded as a reflection of the complex history of cultural and political interactions within and between societies. Thus to understand the development of education in an African society, we need to examine the interactions within that society as well as between that society and its former colonial power.

In this chapter, I propose to explore some of the complex cultural and political interactions which have influenced the development of education in the West African state of Sierra Leone. The case of Sierra Leone offers a particularly interesting study for several reasons. First, in terms of the early introduction and subsequent development of Western-style education in Africa south of the Sahara, Sierra Leone undoubtedly played a crucial role and exerted an influence out of all proportion to its population, geographical size, political power, or economic strength. Second, the existence in colonial Sierra Leone of a group of liberated Africans having unprecedented affinity with British culture provided a platform for cultural penetration, but also acted as a catalyst for the destabilization and rejection of colonial domination. Third, the case of Sierra Leone typifies a strong reciprocal link between education and political power, which was exploited by various groups during the colonial era and beyond. Finally, the peculiarities of educational development in Sierra Leone during and after the colonial era have culminated in the entrenchment of certain attitudes and values, which continue to have a profound effect on the national development process.

EMANCIPATION AND EDUCATION

The circumstances in which Western-style education was first introduced to Sierra Leone were deeply imbued with the spirit and ideals of emancipation. This more than anything else engendered an attitude of profound respect for education, with an inordinate value being attached to its acquisition. In this regard however, education was valued more for instrumental reasons to do with social power and status, than for utilitarian reasons connected with knowledge and skills development, or intrinsic reasons to do with human enlightenment. Much that is wrong with education in Sierra Leone today can justifiably be traced to the entrenchment of such attitudes and values in the national psyche.

Initially, the colony of Sierra Leone, which had been founded in 1787 for the settlement of liberated slaves from Britain and other places, was confined to a peninsula area within the present capital of Freetown. Although the introduction of Western-style education to Sierra Leone came about with the founding of this settlement, it is important to appreciate that pre-colonial Sierra Leone had its own rich history of forms of education and patterns of government (Abraham, 1978). The development of education in Sierra Leone is therefore not simply a linear progression starting with the colonial settlement.

Rather, it should be seen as a complex process of interaction and evolution,

involving existing socio-cultural values and patterns of education, which under-
went profound changes in response to the introduction of Western-style
education and values. In this evolutionary process of interaction and change,
one of the earliest and most enduring features of educational development in
Sierra Leone has been the establishment of a strong link between education
and emancipation at the individual, community, and national levels.

The roots of emancipation through education

For the Creoles (descendants of liberated slaves) in particular, the principle
of emancipation through education was extremely important in the light of the
traumatic experiences of slavery and their determination to rebuild their lives
in the 'province of freedom', as Freetown came to be known. The Creoles
also never lost sight of the fact that the battle against slavery was championed
by learned men of the educated and enlightened classes in Britain, or that the
eventual abolition of slavery in 1772 was premised on high moral principles
and religious convictions and secured through democratic legislation. Against
this background, it is hardly surprising that the Creoles of the early colonial
period manifested an extremely profound and somewhat naive respect for
Western education, and Christian religious values and morality, as well as the
democratic process and the rule of law. Importantly also, because of their
unprecedented affinity with British culture during the period of slavery, the
early Creoles had an intimate insight into, and first-hand experience of the
British class system. An important aspect of this class system for the Creoles
was that the most menial and degrading tasks in society were ultimately
relegated to the least educated classes. Hence the Creoles came to understand
and value strongly the link between education and social status.

Consequently the activities pursued most intensively by the Creoles in the
early colonial period included the establishment of schools and churches.
Although these activities were pursued mainly in conjunction with missionary
efforts and/or as part of the colonial administration's policies, there were many
excellent examples of schools and churches established independently by the
Creoles, which survive to the present day. As education developed in colonial
Sierra Leone, Freetown became not only the place where it all started, but
also the main locus of educational opportunity. The Creoles, being enthusiastic
participants and purveyors of Western education, naturally had extreme advantages in terms of educational enrolment, and so completely dominated the
early education scene both as pupils and teachers. Because of this early
domination, certain attitudes, values, and perceptions emanating from Creole
culture took root in the education system. These proved to be so enduring
that successive educational policies, plans, and strategies have failed to erode
them completely from Sierra Leone's education system.

For instance, as descendants of liberated slaves, the Creoles understandably had a built-in antipathy towards menial tasks and most forms of manual labour. Education therefore quickly came to be seen as an escape route from these kinds of activities since, even in those early days, being educated meant having access to such 'respectable' occupations as teaching, religious ministry, and the civil service. Very often, being educated meant little more than being literate and numerate, but these were very highly valued skills in the civil service, the Church and schools. Those who could not readily find employment in these areas or preferred not to seek such employment became merchants and engaged in extensive trade with local communities outside Freetown, as well as importing goods from outside Sierra Leone. Others who were failures of the education system resorted to becoming artisans and craftsmen through being apprenticed to established Creole craftsmen. Thus in one form or the other, participation in education led to an escape from the drudgery of menial tasks and unpleasant manual labour. This perception of education is still prevalent in Sierra Leone, amongst pupils and parents alike.

Education developed fairly rapidly in colonial Sierra Leone, culminating in the establishment of Fourah Bay College (University of Sierra Leone) in 1827. The Creoles agitated for and took full advantage of this rapid development, as well as making increasing use of educational opportunities outside Sierra Leone, to enhance their status within the colonial hierarchy. At the official level many Creoles benefited from missionary sponsorship as well as the support of a colonial administration which was very much in need of trained Sierra Leonean manpower. Outside official circles, successful merchants and others were able to sponsor their children for further studies abroad (inevitably Britain). These trends resulted in fairly remarkable higher education successes for the Creoles and probably gave rise to a marked preference amongst educated Creoles for the so-called 'learned professions' of medicine and law. These professions were regarded not only as providing the highest possible status for the Creoles, but also as guaranteeing them an independent career outside the colonial bureaucracy, as an insurance against discrimination. Medicine and law are still by far the most popular career aspirations of secondary school pupils in Sierra Leone.

Another facet of Creole culture which became entrenched in the education system was the tendency to aspire to what was best in Western culture, as an essential hallmark of being educated. Thus a high premium was placed on proficiency in the English language, substantial familiarity with Western music, religion, art and literature (including their antecedents in Greek and Latin), as well as a somewhat exaggerated aping of Western cultural appendages such as dress and etiquette. All of this was an integral part of a two-pronged strategy designed to enhance and secure the status of Creoles in the hierarchy of colonial Sierra Leone. On the one hand, the Creoles believed that by being educated in the best Western tradition and manifesting key elements of British culture in their way of life, they could effectively challenge the colonial claim to cultural superiority and display a close proximity to the colonial ruling class. On the other hand, by attaining Western education and adopting British cultural values and practices, the Creoles sought to distance and distinguish themselves from the rest of the local population whom they regarded as being lower down the colonial hierarchy. Ironically, degree of Westernization (often via Creolization) is still regarded as an important hallmark of being educated.

In general then the Creoles as individuals and as a community benefited greatly from the principle of emancipation through education. Indeed it would be difficult to exaggerate the importance of this principle in the survival and development of the Creoles as a high-status community in the colonial era as well as in post-independence Sierra Leone. From the humble beginnings of 300 liberated slaves originally settled in the colony of Freetown, the Creoles grew to dominate and exert an overwhelming influence on all aspects of Sierra Leone's development into a modern nation state. The privilege of early access to and *de facto* control of education undoubtedly played a major role in the phenomenal rise of Creole society. In turn the perceptions, attitudes, and values of Creole culture played a major role in shaping educational development in Sierra Leone. It goes without saying that the Creoles did not achieve such a phenomenal rise on their own. They benefited from substantial support and a 'favoured status' accorded them by the colonial administration, often at the expense of the rest of the local population. This is not to say that colonial support was purely benevolent, or that the relationship was mainly harmonious. The Creoles became indispensable instruments to the missionaries and the colonial administration, in their efforts to spread the gospel and Western civilization. Indeed the role of Creoles as teachers, administrators, religious workers, and colonial functionaries, was not confined to Sierra Leone, but extended throughout the then British West Africa and even into parts of Central Africa. Understandably the Creoles exploited this instrumental role to enhance their own status within the colonial hierarchy. In the process the Creoles must undoubtedly have exploited many other local communities, so that the ascendance of Creole society is not without its shady side. It is particularly noteworthy that the survival and development of the initially fragile colony of Freetown owed much to the accommodation of the Temnes of Koya Kingdom (Landlords of the Colony), and especially to the benevolence of their Chief Naimbana (Adelaye Ijagbemi 1976).

The lure of emancipation

Colonial rule in Sierra Leone, as elsewhere, thrived on the twin weapons of political domination and cultural penetration. It is almost impossible to separate these in accounting for the phenomenon of colonialism, since in some stages cultural penetration laid the ground for political domination, whilst at other points political domination (with its attendant military superiority) created fertile conditions for cultural penetration. In the case of Sierra Leone, although British colonial rule was strongly opposed at several points and in several places (resulting in some major armed uprisings), it can be argued that the success of colonial rule owes much more to cultural penetration than to military-backed political domination. In this process of cultural penetration, education and religion played a most crucial role, and it could be argued that the local population was attracted to this twin vehicle of colonialism by what can best be described as the 'lure of emancipation'.

The Creoles had already had a taste of Western education and culture, and therefore soon developed an insatiable appetite for both as the cornerstone of their newly liberated society. In contrast, the rest of the local population in Sierra Leone did not need such input since they already had their own religion, political entities, governmental structures, and traditional forms of education as an integral part of their respective cultures. The introduction and spread of Western education and culture in these local communities was therefore in its truest sense a form of cultural invasion. Much has been made of the dedication, bravery, and perseverance of colonial missionaries in accounting for the successful introduction and spread of Western education, religion, and culture in Africa. Evidently this aspect cannot be ignored, just as one must not lose sight of the role the Creoles played in facilitating this form of cultural penetration in Sierra Leone. However it is equally important, and perhaps much more interesting, to view these developments from the perspective of the recipients, and try to understand the rationale and motivations underlying *acceptance* of Western education and religion. It is quite remarkable for instance that the Mendes, with their rich culture of traditional education and religion, and highly developed forms of government and administration, were amongst the most enthusiastic and devout converts to Christianity. This in turn meant that next to the Creoles, the Mendes gained the greatest benefits in terms of access to Western education. In contrast the Temnes, who offered the greatest resistance to Christianity (partly due to an earlier Islamic influence), were the most disadvantaged in terms of access to Western education. This sharp contrast between the two largest and most powerful tribal groups in Sierra Leone richly illustrates the workings of the package deal (religion and education) offered by the missionaries.

Much scholarly work remains to be done in unravelling the complexity of indigenous responses to Western education and religion. One can therefore only advance tentative speculations concerning the rationale and motivation underlying the acceptance of Christianity and Western education by the indigenous population. First, there was undoubtedly some attraction towards the material artefacts which formed part of the Western cultural baggage that accompanied colonial adventurism. Even before the colony of Freetown was established, indigenous traders along the Sierra Leone coast (especially the Temnes of Koya Kingdom) had become accustomed to possessing such European goods as rum, looking-glasses, knives, tobacco, trinkets, pipes, and clothing. This type of materialist emancipation undoubtedly created a new appetite for participation in other facets of European life and culture.

Second, the indigenous population found that some amount of literacy and numeracy, as well as fluency in the English language, was advantageous in the conduct of trade and other business with Europeans. In the absence of such rudiments of education, indigenous rulers had to resort to hiring outsiders as interpreters and secretaries. This state of affairs must have provided a strong incentive for the indigenous population to acquire some Western education.

Third, the 'civilizing virtues' of Christianity and Western education were a major weapon in the colonial diplomatic arsenal, and these were used extensively and repeatedly as a manifestation of the goodwill the British had towards the indigenous population. Offering these civilizing virtues free of charge was portrayed as a great gift of emancipation and enlightenment. The lure of this type of emancipation appeared to have taken strong hold amongst the Sherbros and Mendes of the Southern Province, and to some extent amongst the Mendes of the Eastern Province. Importantly also, this lure of emancipation was a major factor in winning concessions from the Temnes of Koya, for the colony settlement of Freetown. King Naimbana of the Temnes was told that:

> It is the hope of the people of England that the black settlers would be able to assist in spreading civilization among the peoples of this country, and of the adjoining territories. (Ijagbemi 1976)

In turn Naimbana expressed happiness about such pronouncements, and he is said to have shown continuous benevolence towards the colony because of his strong desire to use the colonists for spreading 'civilization' among his people. Undoubtedly, the lure of emancipation was based at least partly on a genuine respect for and admiration of British culture and way of life as perceived by the indigenous populations. Education was therefore a major liberating force through which people could break out of the restrictions of a traditional life style into a much admired way of life.

A fourth rationale for acceptance of Western education and religion could well be that the indigenous population came to value good social relations with the British, and the new spiritual experiences resulting from Christianity.

Finally, although the indigenous population already had their own forms of government and administration, it must have become evident, as colonial rule took hold, that a new order of things and a changing social hierarchy were in the making. Familiarity with and proximity to the new ways and life style of the colonial authorities were now the key to success, and education was the principal means of achieving this. Further significance must have been given to this point by the eagerness of missionaries and the colonial authorities to grant free education and other special privileges to the heirs of traditional rulers. This tendency reached its height with the creation of a secondary boarding school in the Southern Province, which was modelled along the lines of English public schools, and intended exclusively for the sons of chiefs and other traditional rulers.

Whatever the rationale and motivation for accepting Western education and religion, social demand for education soon became a major factor of considerable political significance in Sierra Leone. The demand for education rapidly outstripped the rather ambivalent provision of educational opportunities. Initially, the colonial administration had a *laissez-faire* attitude towards providing educational facilities, and left this mainly to the various missionary bodies. Such facilities as were provided tended initially to be concentrated in Freetown, partly due to the enthusiasm, agitation, and active involvement of the Creoles. Missionary attempts to spread education into the interior of the country were hampered by various conflicts and uprisings which did not make for stable and secure conditions. It did not appear either that the colonial administration was keen to support the rapid spread of education throughout the country. The ascendance of the Creoles, and their increasing tendency to challenge their former benefactors or question various aspects of colonial rule, were already making it disturbingly clear that education was very much a double-edged sword. Its spread therefore needed to be controlled and calculated, to ensure that it served the best interest of the colonial power. The question of finance was another obstacle, since funding from Britain for the colonies tended to be minimal, and intended mainly to facilitate a more efficient extraction of wealth from the colonies. As such it was difficult for the colonial administration to provide any substantial funding for education without some form of local taxation, and although the missionary bodies were quite philanthropic, their financial resources were not limitless. In the face of this ambivalence, the missionary societies achieved some remarkable successes in establishing primary and secondary schools in Freetown and the provinces. Rivalry between different missionary bodies played an important part in the proliferation of schools, and prior to intervention by the colonial authorities the number of schools in an area was determined largely by the number of missionary bodies operating in the area. Indeed such was the proliferation of primary schools which had been established in Freetown since 1806, that when the colonial authorities eventually entered into educational partnership with the missionaries (in 1928), one of the main outcomes was a reduction in the number of schools.

In general, then, educational opportunities were over-concentrated in Freetown, and the schools themselves tended to be overwhelmingly religious in their orientation. These characteristics of the early education system in Sierra Leone had two important consequences which have become entrenched as problematic aspects of education in modern Sierra Leone.

First, Freetown became a very powerful magnet in terms of educational opportunities, and this was one of the factors accounting for large-scale migration from other areas into Freetown. Apart from the Southern Province where the United Methodist Church had substantial success in establishing schools, educational opportunities were few and far between outside Freetown. In any case the best primary and secondary schools were located in Freetown, and everyone wanted a share of the best. Furthermore, seeking education in Freetown was inevitable for many who migrated to the city for reasons other than education. As the headquarters of the colonial administration, and later the seat of government, as well as the location of the country's port, and centre of most commercial activities, Freetown attracted substantial migration from other areas. Most of these migrants also had the added incentive of educational opportunities for their children. Even those who could not or did not wish to migrate made extensive use of educational opportunities in Freetown by sending their children to live with relatives in the city, or giving them as wards to Creole families. All of this created even greater pressure for educational expansion and development to be concentrated in Freetown. The intensity of this distorted pattern of educational development was such that by the early years of independence it was estimated that 88 per cent of primary-age children in the Western Area (Freetown) were enrolled in primary schools, whereas at the other extreme the figure for the Northern Province was only 16 per cent (1964–5 statistics). Much has been done to redress this balance and create a more democratic availability of educational opportunities. Such redress has resulted largely from intensified social demand for education and the vote-seeking responsiveness of successive independent governments whose power base has been outside Freetown. Despite these achievements it is still the case that the Western Area (Freetown) has the highest educational enrolment figures, even though its population is the lowest of the country's four regions. Moreover the tendency to migrate to Freetown for education (and other services) still persists, and might well be intensifying again in the current economic climate when schools outside Freetown are experiencing the worst aspect of a general decline in quality of education.

An important consequence of the religious orientation in Sierra Leone's early education system is that learning was imbued with what has been described as a prudish other-worldliness. This was characterized by such tenets as 'learning is better than silver and gold'; 'obey first and complain later'; 'selfless sacrifice in this world for spiritual reward and glory in the next world'; 'accepting one's place in the world and trusting in God's purpose' etc. In these circumstances, pupils tended towards memorizing and reciting religious doctrines rather than developing a critical understanding and appreciation of them. The same became true *ipso facto* of non-religious subject matter, and the resulting problem of rote learning has continued to plague the country's education system.

EDUCATION AND DOMINATION

If the lure of emancipation was a major factor in the development of education in Sierra Leone, then the other side of the coin is that the advantages inherent in education can equally lead to exploitation and domination of others. This is most evident first in the relationship between the colonizers and the colonized, which was pervaded by the portrayal of an inherent cultural superiority on the part of the colonizers. At all times and in all places the British made much of this alleged cultural superiority as a rationale for dominating their colonial subjects. Education and religion were held out as possible means whereby these subject peoples might in due course come to share in the progressive achievements and civilizing virtues of British culture. Naturally enough, that other important facet of civilized achievement, military prowess, was always at hand to reinforce the claim to cultural superiority where necessary.

Colonial domination

In the case of education, although it was offered as a force for emancipation, it also contained, both by design and default, a potent formula for colonial domination, i.e. ideological control. On the one hand the colonial administration favoured a rather circumscribed education which would make its subjects useful to the administrative bureaucracy. The missionaries on the other hand favoured a kind of education which would lead to moral uprightness, loyalty, and devotion to Christianity. Both types of education emphasized subservience as a virtue, with 'civility and servitude' being the key requirements of the colonial administration, while pious religiosity and selfless sacrifice were the essentials for the missionaries. Beyond certain levels of competence in literacy, numeracy, and related skills, the colonial administration demanded most of all efficiency, loyalty, and an unquestioning adherence to the rules and procedures laid down. In the case of the missionaries, their demands were much more damaging to the local cultures. Participating in missionary education often meant renouncing one's culture, even to the extent of changing one's tribal name to a Christian one. The missionaries condemned most traditional practices (which they hardly understood) as primitive and evil manifestations to be stamped out and replaced by the light of Christianity. Furthermore the pious religiosity and moral uprightness emphasized in missionary education encouraged a situation in which educated locals naively acquiesced in the material exploitation of their country.

It would be wrong to infer from all of this that nothing good came out of colonial education. Certainly many valuable skills were acquired, and much excellent work was done by dedicated, sincere, and well-meaning missionaries, as well as colonial administrators. In any case, education itself is as much about what learners wish to take from the process as it is about what the system puts on offer. Once a certain threshold of literacy and numeracy had been achieved, education in fact proved to contain the seeds whereby colonial domination was eventually challenged and rejected. The important point for the present education system is that the values and attitudes engendered during the colonial period have persisted with detrimental consequences. For instance, although there is much rhetoric about education for leadership, the reality is that Sierra Leone's education system is still best at turning out good followers. Education is still too readily equated with social conformity, moral uprightness, and a merely bookish brilliance. Deviations from such entrenched values are quickly interpreted as indicative of falling standards in education. At the very least, these entrenched values now need to be counterbalanced by a new emphasis on initiative, constructive criticism, inventiveness, pragmatic morality, and a down-to-earth brilliance in practical problem solving. Several reform proposals and curriculum initiatives have embraced such a new emphasis, but in the main they continue to be haunted by the spectre of values from another era.

Creole domination

The Creoles sought to use their early advantage in education in three major ways to dominate other groups. First there was much propaganda aimed at getting other groups to acknowledge the cultural superiority of the Creoles by virtue of their proximity to the ruling British culture. In the worst form of such propaganda, die-hard Creoles in the colonial era argued that there was a natural order of things in the country, in which the corresponding hierarchy was God, the White man, the Creoles, and the rest. This type of arrogance naturally attracted resentment and hostility from other groups, and detracted greatly from the substantial benefits which the Creoles undoubtedly brought about through their role in spreading education. In more subtle versions of propaganda, the Creoles point not just to education (schooling), but to a whole way of life which has evolved over several generations, as a basis for their claim to cultural superiority. There tends to be an undercurrent of this type of propaganda amongst the older generation of present-day Creoles, since they realize that the Creoles no longer have any kind of monopoly of education at any level. The propaganda essentially is that, as other groups become educated and strive to portray themselves as part of modern civilization, they invariably find that they need to adopt various cultural manifestations which are already an integral part of Creole culture. For instance, adopting Western dress and etiquette, to which several generations of Creoles have become accustomed in every fine detail; or operating a rational-bureaucratic form of administration, which the Creoles have mastered through service in the colonial era. Most important, progressing from any of the tribal languages to English often entails going through Krio (the language of the Creoles), which has effectively become the lingua franca of Sierra Leone. Whilst there may be some simple truths in some of these claims, their significance is grossly exaggerated in this type of propaganda. The really important point is that in Sierra Leone, as in most African countries, modernization is still too closely equated with Westernization. The Creoles undoubtedly have an advantage where Westernization is concerned, but this should not be confused with modernization efforts in Africa. As Mazrui expresses it, modernization is here to stay, and the task for Africans is to decolonize it. The Creoles should not make a virtue out of being an obstacle to the decolonization of modernization in Sierra Leone. The younger generation of Creoles seem to recognize this and are strongly involved in the drive for cultural relevance in the education system.

The second major way in which the Creoles used their advantage in education to dominate other groups was by exploiting these groups as a price for access to education, over which they had strong *de facto* control. Because of the concentration of educational opportunities in Freetown during the colonial era, many families from the provinces sent their children as wards to Creole families so that they could be educated. This was not necessarily a matter of finance, as was the case with the Creole's own internal system, whereby poor relations sent their children to rich relatives for schooling. Rather, families from the provinces hoped that by giving their children as wards to Creole families, the children would acquire not only the benefits of formal schooling, but the whole cultural baggage and life style necessary for success in the colonial hierarchy. In some cases generous presents of money and goods were regularly sent to the Creole families in return for this arrangement. On the positive side this type of arrangement ensured access to education (often even up to post-secondary level) for children from the provinces. Many leadership figures and prominent citizens owe their education to this system, and indeed the country's current and immediate past Presidents often refer to their experiences with the Creoles under this arrangement. On the negative side this type of arrangement was sometimes misused by the Creoles, who exploited their wards as household labour beyond any reasonable degree. This exploitation often carried with it an implication that these wards were somehow inferior to the Creole children with whom they were growing up. Not surprisingly many who went through this system have mixed feelings of gratitude and bitterness about their experiences with the Creoles. In extreme cases such feelings can lead to vindictive discrimination against Creoles, and this is hardly constructive in a country which needs to make maximum use of its educated and trained manpower.

The third and most significant way in which the Creoles used their educational advantage to dominate other groups, was by monopolizing all the key positions in the country, short of *de jure* political power. This was no doubt due to the fact that initially at least they were the only qualified Sierra Leoneans who could effectively hold these posts. Subsequently some conspiracy of privilege and favouritism must have been at work in keeping other groups from reaching these top positions. Such was the stranglehold that the Creoles had on key posts that, at the time of independence in 1961, there was hardly a government ministry, department, institution, or organization in which the administrative head, professional head, and top echelon were not all Creoles. For a minority group numbering around two per cent of the total population, this was indeed a precarious and highly untenable situation in the long term. It says a lot for the maturity and restraint of Sierra Leoneans that this overwhelming Creole domination was not ended in fairly explosive circumstances, as was the case with the Americo-Liberians (descendants of liberated slaves from America) in the neighbouring state of Liberia. An important factor is that unlike the Americo-Liberians, the Creoles stopped short of holding *de jure* political power and this safety valve provided a mechanism for other groups to erode Creole domination over time. However, entrenched privilege does take a long time to erode, so that is was not until the latter part of the 1970s that Sierra Leone had its first non-Creole as head of the civil service, and not until the 1980s that non-Creoles held such posts as Chief Justice, Chief Education Officer, Principal of Fourah Bay College, etc. The country still awaits the appointment of the first non-Creole as Chief Medical Officer.

As entrenched domination by any privileged group is eroded by other groups, a fair amount of so-called positive discrimination is likely to come into play to accelerate the process. However it does get to a point where such positive discrimination becomes victimization of the formerly privileged group. Many Creoles currently believe that this point has been reached, and are convinced that whether it is scholarship awards, job appointments, career promotions, or whatever, the Creoles are at a disadvantage simply because they are Creoles. Whether or not this is a correct reading of the current situation, there is already in progress a trend in which the Creoles are once again directing their children towards areas of study which would guarantee them a career independent of the government bureaucracy. Once again Creole families are making inordinate sacrifices to sponsor their children for higher education overseas, with law and medicine again the favourite fields, followed by such 'newly-discovered' areas as accountancy and engineering. There are also signs that the Creoles are again returning to the field of commerce, which they once dominated, but abandoned in favour of more prestigious occupations in the government bureaucracy. Ironically, these leads which are apparently based on Creole frustrations are inevitably being followed by other groups, as a declining economy and saturated bureaucracy make public-sector jobs scarce for all groups, positive discrimination notwithstanding.

REFERENCES

Abraham, A. (1978) *Mende Government and Politics Under Colonial Rule*, Freetown; Sierra Leone University Press.

Brown, G. N. and Hiskett M. (Eds.) (1975) *Conflict and Harmony in Education in Tropical Africa*, London: George Allen & Unwin Limited.

Fyfe, C. (1962) *A History of Sierra Leone*, London: Oxford University Press.

Hawes, H. and Coombe T., with Coombe, C. and Lillis, K. (1984) *Education Priorities and Aid Responses in Sub-Saharan Africa*, London: Overseas Development Administration, University of London Institute of Education.

Ijagbemi, A. (1976) *Naimbana of Sierra Leone*, Malta: St. Paul's Press Limited.

Mazrui, A. (1978) *Political Values and the Educated Class in Africa*, London: Heinemann.

Porter, A. T. (1963) *Creoledom*, London: Oxford University Press.

Sumner, D. L. (1963) *Education in Sierra Leone*, Freetown: The Government of Sierra Leone.

Thomas, A. C. (1983) *The Population of Sierra Leone*, Freetown: The Demographic Research and Training Unit, Fourah Bay College.

THE STRUGGLE TOWARDS COMPREHENSIVE EDUCATION IN SWEDEN: AN HISTORICAL ANALYSIS

INGEMAR FÄGERLIND

When the decision was taken in 1527 by the Swedish parliament that the Lutheran rite should become the official state religion, a fundamental educational idea was also introduced. The new religion had as one of its goals that all people should be able to read and understand the Gospel. Formerly only a small élite had learnt how to read and write, and usually in Latin, which was the language of the learned. Very few books had been available in the Swedish language, but with the Lutheran reformation the national language achieved official status. The New Testament had already been translated into Swedish in 1526, and in 1541 the entire Bible was available in the Swedish language, while the Finnish-speaking minority got their translation of the New Testament in 1548. The Bible was too expensive for most families, and, as a result, the hymn book and the Catechism of Luther had more importance for the ordinary people.

At the time of the Reformation there were schools in almost every major town in Sweden. Luther had suggested that schools should be started up in every village and that all children should attend them. This did not happen initially, and, instead, many schools that had earlier been funded and run by the church were actually closed down. The University of Uppsala, which had been founded in 1477, was also closed. The struggle between comprehensive and élite ideas during the early Reformation resulted, despite the new Lutheran policies, in a weak formal education system and cultural isolation at the same time as a national literature appeared which was easy to read and which later on played an important role in the education of the masses.

ÉLITE EDUCATION

At the beginning of the seventeenth century Sweden was strengthening its economic and political power in Northern Europe. Trade was flourishing and exports were increasing. Sweden furnished 70 to 80 per cent of the world's supply of copper, and iron and steel production was significant. As the country was also growing geographically with more and more control over land all around the Baltic Sea it was considered important by those in power to develop and centralize the administration. Civil Servants for the growing central and local administration began to be educated through a new formal school system.

During a period of thirty years beginning in the 1620s substantial funds were made available by the state to strengthen the formal school system. During this time, thirteen upper secondary schools – *gymnasia* – were established in different parts of the country. The University of Uppsala, which had been reopened in 1566, received a donation of 350 farms from the state, and new universities were opened in Turku (Åbo), Finland, and in Estonia. The established aristocracy did not send their children to the new schools. Their children usually had private tutors with whom they were sent abroad to foreign universities after the age of 12. The upper secondary schools and the universities were attended by middle-class and farmers' children as well as a few gifted children of the very poor. The schools made it possible for these children to climb the social ladder. Most became ministers in the state church or Civil Servants at the local level. If they became Civil Servants at the central level and reached a high position, they were commonly ennobled. The seventeenth-century educational reform to strengthen élite education was in fact successful in many respects. Thanks to huge allocations of state land or money for educational purposes a stable educational system was established. This system gave rise to some social mobility and to a stable administrative system of civil servants from other social strata than the old feudal land-owning nobility. The system established in the seventeenth century continued to function for 250 years with very few changes in the administrative framework. The curriculum was well defined and decided upon centrally. A teacher/student ratio of one to 20–25 was kept through the centuries. In spite of this, frequent complaints about poor teaching were made by educational commissions. The new élite used its power to oppress other groups, both financially and intellectually. At the end of the century a new educational reform for the masses was decided upon by the leading élite.

LITERACY – THE FIRST COMPREHENSIVE REFORM

After the time of the Reformation the Lutheran Church was the ideological apparatus of the Swedish state. Religious and civic education of the masses was carried out by the ministers of the church. Attendance once a week at religious services was compulsory in most parts of the country, and if people did not attend, various types of punishment were used. The goal was to make the population more orthodox in its Lutheran beliefs and practices; but ministers and bishops complained that most people did not follow in practice what was preached by the church. In this situation the church in a law of 1686 initiated a reform with the goal of making the population literate. The law stated that every head of household was responsible for the teaching of reading to all his family and servants. Children, farm-hands and maidservants should 'learn to read and see with their own eyes, what God bids and commands in His Holy Scripture'.[1] If the head of the household could not read himself, he had to find somebody who could do so to teach the household. The first book to be used was the Catechism of Luther, published in a more modern version in 1689. For more than 100 years this book was used in most Swedish homes. A very important part of the Catechism was a collection of texts from the Scriptures, which set out the rules of the social order in society.

In all parishes of the country annual examinations were held of all parish members. They were held in small groups where a few households, usually neighbours, gathered. The results of the oral examinations were recorded in special registers, and the social pressure not to fail in this public event was great. At the beginning of the reform, reading was recorded as '*cannot* read', 'has *begun* to read', 'can read *a little*', 'can read *acceptably*', and '*knows* how to read'. Later on a five-point scale was used.[2] As most of the examination registers are still available, it has been possible to study the development of reading ability in Sweden. It was found that the reading campaign was a success, but it took about sixty years for the majority of the population to become literate. Over and above the examinations, other social pressures and controls were used. Young people who wanted to marry but had not learned how to read had to postpone their marriage until they could prove they were able to do so. Later on only people who were able to read were admitted to Holy Communion. The goal of making every adult literate was accomplished in most communities except Stockholm, where the social control was not as thorough as in smaller towns and villages.

The church and the state took a risk in teaching everybody how to read. People started reading books and pamphlets that were banned, as well as reading such material to others. In 1726 a new law was passed stating that it was forbidden for laymen to read religious books to others than their own family. The clergyman was the only one who had the right to read and to preach to people outside his own family. The aim of this law was to preserve the purity of the Lutheran Orthodox religion and to see to it that only the religious and civic ideology of the state church was transmitted. In spite of severe penalties for breaking the law, people gathered to read religious books, and laymen continued to read and preach. The ideological message transmitted by most of the forbidden literature was that the individual was responsible for his own salvation, and man was made to feel free in relation to the church as an institution. The Pietistic movement was perceived as a great threat to the established order. The state tried to control the printing and importation of books, but nothing helped. Books were brought in illegally and translated into the Swedish language. At the beginning the people who read to others were found in the upper classes, but as the ability to read spread to lower social strata, they also began to break the law.

At the beginning of the nineteenth century a rapid population growth, combined with a land reform, produced a landless proletariat. This group began to challenge the authoritarian structure of the society as transmitted by the state church. The members of the new proletariat *were literate*, and were also likely to be more receptive to new ideas. The growing proletariat was a problem, and at parliamentary sessions in the 1830s possible solutions to the problem of the poor were discussed. A liberal opposition to the very conservative government was formed. The liberals consisted of a new class of merchants, industrial owners, and a few noblemen who had employed waged workers on their farms. They suggested the establishment of elementary schools for the children of the masses. The debate concerning this suggestion lasted for more than a decade. During this time the new evangelical movement of Pietistic origin had spread rapidly. These people were called 'readers', since they read and discussed the Bible and other books together. This was still against the law, and they were seen as in opposition to the State, which consequently tried to punish them. In his novel, *The Emigrants*, the Swedish writer Wilhelm Moberg describes how groups of this kind, when punished, sold their belongings and left for the United States. In some areas of Sweden many thousands left for this reason at the same time, since they and many of their relatives were opposed to the regime. After long discussions at the parliamentary sessions of 1840 and 1841 a bill was enacted in 1842 that within five years every parish should establish at least one school, that every school should have a qualified teacher, and that the head of the school board should be the parish minister.[3] The clergy split into two groups: the conservatives, against the new schools that could compete with the Church, and the liberals, who saw the schools as a way for the church to strengthen its power.

THE ELEMENTARY SCHOOLS

As the teaching of reading had for centuries been the task of the family it was assumed that children would know how to read when entering school. It was now important that the students were reading the right things. Catechism, with its civic education, became the most important subject. Writing, which had not been taught in the informal system, became compulsory. Boys had to learn some mathematics, but girls could also do so if they wanted to.

The primary schools were administered by the church. The school boards were dominated by the rich, who decided for the poor. However, it very soon became clear that the teachers to a greater extent supported the people against the conservative state. The schoolmaster enjoyed high prestige in the local community, and was often active and a leader of democratic organizations, such as the Evangelical Free Churches that could no longer be stopped, the teetotal movements, and liberal-thinking political parties. The schoolmasters had little to do with the wealthy in society as their children usually had their own tutor or went to private schools leading directly to élite institutions. Conflicts frequently arose between the schoolmaster and the religious and political leadership. Such conflicts were not as common with the secondary school teachers as the latter felt that they belonged to the establishment. When greater democracy was introduced in the 1860s both at local and central level, the primary school teachers were often elected to the governing bodies, but this was not so common for the secondary school teachers. When the ideas of social democracy appeared in the country, many elementary school teachers were interested. In 1880 these elementary school teachers also started their own Union, where improvements in the elementary schools were discussed. In 1883 one of the young Union activists, Fridtjuv Berg, proposed a comprehensive school where children from all strata of society should have their education. At the beginning this idea was looked upon as too radical, and it took almost 30 years for it to become the programme of the elementary school teachers' Union, and 70 to 80 years for the idea to become acceptable in the parliament. During this period Fridtjuv Berg had, at one point, been Minister of Church and Education, and the elementary school teachers had become well represented in the parliament.

ECONOMIC, POLITICAL, AND IDEOLOGICAL BACKGROUND TO THE COMPREHENSIVE SCHOOL REFORM

In 1870 Sweden was a comparatively poor European country, while a century later it was among the richest in the Western world. Industrialization had gone very slowly until the end of the nineteenth century when 25 per cent of the labour force were employed in industry. When the world-wide depression hit Sweden in the early 1930s, 35 per cent of the workforce were found in industry. After World War II Swedish industry was able to expand, and by 1950 43 per cent were employed in industrial work. While more than 70 per cent were occupied in agriculture in 1870, only 14 per cent remained on the farms in 1960, a figure which is down to less than five per cent in the late 1980s.[4] As Sweden was transformed from an impoverished agrarian to an industrial community, the political structure also gradually shifted. In 1866 a new bicameral parliament replaced a *Riksdag* of four estates. Suffrage remained highly restricted until after World War I, when male and female suffrage was adopted for both chambers. It was the Social Democratic Party and the Liberals who were winning the struggle against the Conservatives after the War, and during the depression the Social Democrats took power, in 1932, and were able to stay in government as the leading party until 1976. Founded in 1889, the Social Democratic Party very soon moderated its original Marxist views and worked for pragmatic rather than doctrinaire ends in economic development. During the whole period of Social Democratic government there were no great changes in ownership of industry, of which approximately 95 per cent is still in private hands.

A COMPREHENSIVE SYSTEM BECOMES REALITY

During the first four decades of this century the German school system influenced the Swedish at both the elementary and secondary levels. The system was highly selective and the selection took place at the age of nine or ten. Approximately five per cent of an age group had access to secondary education. Repetition was common in the elementary as well as the secondary system. The secondary system had a high drop-out rate. After World War II most interest groups in the Swedish society agreed that changes in the educational system were called for. In several cities the compulsory six-year elementary school had already been prolonged to seven or eight years with elementary school teachers responsible. A new school system was needed, and as many as possible of the authoritarian ideas had to be abolished. The country needed a school system that could produce democratic individuals. A blueprint for the development of the future Swedish school system was submitted in 1948 by the School Commission, a committee established in 1946. Its first chairman was the Minister of Education, Tage Erlander, son of an elementary school teacher, who from October 1946 was Prime Minister of the country for a period of 23 years. A compulsory nine-year comprehensive school was to replace all schools catering to students from seven to sixteen years of age. The elementary school teachers favoured the new proposal, as did the workers' union and the white-collar federation. The industrial owners also saw the proposed new system as something positive. Only the Conservative Party and the Secondary School Teachers' Organization were opposed to the unstreamed secondary school system. In 1950 a ten-year programme of experimentation was enacted by parliament.[5] During the first year of the experiment fourteen communities took part, and ten years later the number increased to 367. Every participating school should be an 'experimental' school, and every teacher should try his or her own ways to improve pedagogical methods.

Considerable educational research accompanied the experimental programme. As many teachers and researchers at the universities had joined the opposition of the secondary school teachers, new units for educational research were created at the new schools of education where all teachers for the comprehensive system were educated. In 1962, just before parliament voted for a nine-year comprehensive school system for the whole country, a study[6] was able to show that students who were in unstreamed classes in the new experimental system achieved the same levels as students who were in the selective secondary school. The study had taken advantage of a unique situation, where the city of Stockholm was divided into two sectors, one with a comprehensive and one with the older dual system. Social background and initial ability, measured by tests and school marks, had been controlled in the five-year follow-up. The final decision by parliament was however a political one, which might have been the same even if the study had shown a different result. New curricula were suggested for the new schools, and they were built onto studies surveying the knowledge and skills required of the individual in Swedish and mathematics, both as the follower of an occupation and as a citizen. Such studies were also conducted for physics, chemistry and civic education.[7] All school books for the comprehensive system had to be rewritten. The books had to follow the central curriculum decided by parliament and the explanations given by the National Board of Education. Several private publishing houses competed to produce the best textbooks. One state-owned publishing company also produced textbooks.

When the ten-year experimental programme was decided upon there was a considerable inequality between regions in the quality of schools. Even within cities some schools could be much better equipped than others. With the experimental programme, favourable State loans were made available for school buildings and equipment, the only condition being that state norms were followed. In this way new, modern schools were built all over the country. Communities were competing with each other, to see which one had the best schools. There was also a tendency that communities with a higher percentage of voters for the Social Democratic Party were more eager to change to the new system, while more conservative communities were hesitant. The conservative communities already had good schools and in this way the goal of equalization was achieved. The massive teacher-training and up-dating programme helped to equalize what was going on inside the classroom. In 1973, when science education was evaluated in nineteen countries, it was found that Sweden had the lowest inter-school variation in achievement, which meant that schools in the north or the south, in the cities or the countryside, had very similar achievements.[8] In this way the political goal of equalizing education had been achieved. The same study also showed that when the top one, five, and nine per cent of the total age group at upper secondary school level were compared amongst countries with selective and comprehensive systems, their results were similar. But when Swedish results were compared with results from the very selective system in the Federal Republic of Germany, Sweden's top students had much better results. Through early selection the German system had lost many of the gifted students from a working-class background.

The comprehensivization of the Swedish school system did not stop with the nine-year compulsory school. Traditionally, the *gymnasium* had been a school leading to university studies and civil service jobs. For centuries only a small percentage of an age group passed through this kind of school. By 1945, eight per cent of the relevant group attended such schools. There were also great differences between regions, with much higher percentages in the cities than in the more sparsely populated areas. Technical and vocational schools were not included in this figure. From the late 1950s to the early 1970s the demand for non-compulsory secondary education increased rapidly. Starting in 1971 all schools for the age range 16 to 19 were combined. The new schools inherited the traditional name *gymnasium/gymnasieskola* but were no longer selective. At the end of the 1980s about 95 per cent of all 16-year-olds stay on to such schools. Some twenty timetables are divided up between a vocational and an academic bias. But students on the vocational and academic sides can have up to 12 hours a week together. Some of the vocational programmes have become more prestigious than the academic ones, and for this reason it is more difficult to get enrolled on them. It is possible, however, for students from all disciplines (sometimes after supplementary studies in Swedish and English), to be eligible for university admission. At the same time, since 1972, adults of 25 years of age, with at least four years of work experience, can enter institutions of higher learning. There is a tendency today for adults to specialize in courses useful for future occupations.[9] A reform of tertiary education enacted in 1977 can be seen as a continuation of the intentions of the reforms at lower educational levels. Education is looked upon as a means of social improvement for both the individual and the society as a whole. Several goals of the reform at tertiary level have been achieved; 25 per cent of the relevant age group now enter higher education. Substantially higher proportions of students with working-class backgrounds are now recruited. Although more girls enter higher education today than previously, traditional ideas about male- and female-dominated subjects and occupations have been difficult to change. For this reason extensive programmes have been tried for changing traditional sex roles through education. In an evaluation of science achievement over time it was found that girls had better results in physics and chemistry in the 1980s compared to the 1970s. More girls also study technology in the 1980s compared with ten years ago.

From the mid-1950s to the present day, Sweden has made its whole formal education system comprehensive. Few countries have been able to change their school system in such a systematic and planned way. Most of the changes were made during economically prosperous times where the political climate was stable. However, the Literacy Reforms of the seventeenth century, which made Sweden and Finland the first countries in the world with a literate population as early as the 1750s, played a very important role in the establishment of the popular movements, such as the 'free churches', the teetotal organizations, the workers' unions, and the producers' and consumers' co-operatives. The Social Democratic Party in turn was supported by these popular movements in its endeavour to make good quality formal education available to everybody in Swedish society.

REFERENCES

1. Johansson, E. (1977) *The History of Literacy in Sweden in Comparison With Some Other Countries*, Umeå: Department of Education, 11.
2. Ibid.: 26,47.
3. Isling, Å. (1980) *Kampen för och mot en demokratisk skola (The Struggle For and Against a Democratic School)*, Stockholm: Sober.
4. Lindbeck, A. (1974) *Swedish Economic Policy*, Berkeley: University of California Press.
5. Marklund, S. (1980) *The Democratization of Education in Sweden*, Stockholm: Institute of International Education.
6. Svensson, N. E. (1962) *Ability Grouping and Scholastic Achievement*, Stockholm: Almqvist & Wiksell.
7. Husen, T. (1978) 'Educational research and educational reform. A case study of Sweden', in P. Suppes (Ed.) *Impact of Research on Education: Some Case Studies*, Washington, D.C: National Academy of Education.
8. Comber, L. C. and Keeves, J. P. (1973) *Science Education in Nineteen Countries*, Stockholm: Almqvist & Wiksell.
9. Marklund, S. and Bergendal, G. (1979) *Trends in Swedish Educational Policies*, Stockholm: The Swedish Institute.

THE CHARACTER OF SCHOOLING IN SUB-SAHARAN AFRICA

KENNETH KING

INTRODUCTION

By 1990 the majority of the 41 states of sub-Saharan Africa will have experienced in the twentieth century some 60 years of colonial rule and some 30 years of independence. Of the total number of countries, two (Liberia and Ethiopia) largely retained their independence, and in the late 1980s two others (South Africa and Namibia) were still under systems of minority white rule. During this century the images of Africa in Europe and America have shifted significantly, depending on the extent of political and personal involvement by the different industrialized countries. Awareness of Africa's schools has obviously also shifted during this time. Thus, when African schooling was principally a responsibility of the missionary societies from North America and Europe, strong ties were built up between particular schools, along with their mission stations in parts of Africa, and the network of congregations in the mother country from which the bulk of their funds and teaching personnel were derived. In Scotland, for example, this mechanism meant that certain schools and mission stations, such as Kikuyu and Tumutumu in Kenya, Blantyre and Livingstonia in Malawi, and Lovedale in South Africa, were household names to thousands of church-going people of the Free Church and Church of Scotland.

Immediately after the independence of most African states in the early 1960s, this missionary factor was significantly reduced as the state shouldered the major responsibilities for education. However, detailed knowledge of African schools – especially at the secondary level – was maintained through the outflow of thousands of graduate volunteer teachers from Europe and North America to help staff and expand the hitherto very restricted secondary school systems of most African countries. By the early 1970s the numbers of such expatriate teachers were being rapidly reduced, particularly in anglophone Africa, and by the late 1980s the numbers have become really insignificant except in parts of francophone Africa and also Botswana. As for the massively expanded primary school systems of Africa, there has been virtually no expatriate teaching presence there for 30 years. Personal experience of education in Africa has been dramatically reduced for populations in the industrialized world over the last two decades, and correspondingly, although for different reasons, the images of Africa have moved to those of bloodshed, refugees, and of starving children. The household names are now Ethiopia, Sudan, and Uganda, but there are no longer any more localized contact points. The particularity of the mission stations with their schools well-known to thousands in Canada, USA, Germany, or Britain has gone, and Africa is now to many outsiders a generalization of the images of drought and starvation, to which there has been more recently added the scourge of AIDS.

There are, however, still significant links between the school systems of Africa and the industrialized nations of the West, but these are now principally mediated by aid, whether bilateral aid from individual countries, or multilateral aid from the World Bank and the United Nations. The character of these aid transactions is fundamentally different from the earlier missionary relationships which had stressed the endeavours of particular people in named localities. By contrast, these new educational relations are the result of agreements between governments. They may be concerned with the improvement of primary schooling, but they do not involve the transfer of hundreds of personnel from Europe or America to live and work in the schools. Expatriates are now principally found in advisory positions, or in new institutions at a post-secondary level. The main item now transferred via aid is funds not people.

This basic change in the nature of aid from the missionary era to the present day is important for our current discussion of the character of schooling in sub-Saharan Africa. Missionary 'aid' was essentially delivered to a particular context, location, and language group, via particular schools, clinics, and churches. Much modern aid, by contrast, is almost 'decontextualized', suggesting general policies for all countries where the agency is operating. This tendency is most evident with multilateral agencies such as the World Bank. In its policy work, there are strong pressures to lay out educational options for all of sub-Saharan Africa, even though the variety present in the 40-odd constituent countries may be admitted. The result can well be a set of policy options for primary, secondary, or higher education that appear to be generalizable across the whole of Africa. For instance, in the 1988 policy document, *Education policies for sub-Saharan Africa*, there are just seven major recommendations (World Bank 1988).

Despite disclaimers to the contrary, this current World Bank policy paper will indeed be widely used in the next several years to understand the character and problems of African education. Almost inevitably, the analysis in this and other similar documents is concerned with aspects of schooling that seem not to be context-specific, with school investments that have a proven track record, and with outcomes of schooling that are attested to by major cross-national research studies. The specificity of national and subregional traditions of schooling cannot be captured in such overviews. Nor can the interplay of the state, the voluntary agencies, and the local communities in the formation and maintenance of schools be taken account of.

Accordingly in this brief chapter, an attempt will be made to indicate something of the complexity of the educational map that is being missed in these general accounts of schooling. In the process it will become clear that there is a dearth of literature that looks at schooling in Africa from a cultural, social, and historical perspective. So powerful has been the concern with current policy and evaluation studies, and so critical the shortage of research funds in some countries, that insufficient attention has been paid to the analysis of the recent history of education, and particularly in post-independence Africa. We shall suggest that for much of Africa we not only lack coherent accounts of the formation of state systems of education, but also, at the micro-level, there are very few accounts of the quality of classroom life or of institutional innovation. By contrast, in the 1920s and 1930s there was a well-trodden circuit of good practice that beckoned to educational enthusiasts in places as far apart as the Gold Coast, South Africa, Nyasaland, Uganda, Tanganyika, Northern and Southern Rhodesia. And doubtless there was a comparable trail of good practice amongst the francophone territories (Jones 1922; Jones 1925).

THE TRANSITION TO STATE SYSTEMS

The process whereby the missionary networks penetrated different cultures in East, West and South Africa has been relatively well documented (Ajayi 1965; Oliver 1952). The crucial role played by the mission schools in providing both for the needs of the church and for the jobs in the lower reaches of the colonial economy was acknowledged in most countries, as was the fact that indigenous societies responded to missions and schools in rather different ways. This was not just a question of the distinction between agricultural and pastoral societies, with many of the latter continuing even in the 1980s some of their earlier patterns of school resistance. Nor was it simply a question of the most 'education-oriented' missions giving an educational headstart to the peoples amongst whom they worked. There was a more fundamental level at which the precolonial attitudes to trade, towards initiative by the young, and towards authority meshed in with the new opportunities brought by the missionary societies. The chemistry of these early interactions between what could be called local knowledge systems and the imported systems of the missions and colonial governments had a good deal to do with new cultures of schooling which emerged (Marris and Somerset 1971; Levine 1988).

In many parts, especially of anglophone Africa, there was for many years a crucial distinction between the central school and the village, elementary or 'bush' school of just three or four grades, staffed by local teachers, and dealing primarily with religious knowledge and a little of the three Rs. Success in the village school allowed a transition to the central school, which was in effect an upper primary school, normally a boarding institution, where children encountered European staff, and where it was often obligatory to speak only in English. One of the most insightful analysts of education in British colonial Africa, Victor Murray, put the rationale for these boarding schools in the following way:

> In other words . . . the boarding school represents a new world – an association of people to whom the subjects of 'education' are not 'subjects' but part of life itself. This, for instance . . . is the reason for the compulsory use of English during the working day. To get hold of the ideas that lie behind the course . . . it is necessary not to study them as 'subjects' but to live them, to make them part of your everyday thought, so that when you think of them you will always think of them in a certain way. (Murray 1967: 231–2)

This issue of boarding schools is mentioned because it illustrates the character of schooling experienced by the very small numbers who made the transition from lower primary to upper primary (or central school) in the colonial period in anglophone Africa. With the exception of the earliest centres of colonization in West and South Africa, the small groups of young people who reached these higher primary schools were the first generations in their families to do so. The very small numbers who went on even further to the handful of true secondary schools also found them exclusively boarding institutions. In due course these graduates of the 1930s, 1940s and early 1950s became the architects of the massive expansion plans for secondary education at the time of independence. For this level of schooling, the only 'tradition' that was available to them was of boarding institutions where there had been intimate contact with native speakers of English. And this was accordingly the tradition they drew upon as they negotiated school expansion.

By this time, around 1960, the distinction between lower and upper primary was being removed, as parents and politicians argued against the severe selection examination in the early primary years. Progressively, as full primary education became ordinary and available, it was offered in day schools, and it became uncommon ever to be taught by a native speaker of English at this level. However, in many parts of Africa today, where the mid-primary selection is now a thing of the past, there is still retained very strongly the view that children should make the transition to full English-medium teaching at Standard IV, in their fourth year of school. In other words, the provision that had once been available only to a tiny selected élite who acquired their English in primary boarding schools directly from native English speakers now became the rule for all children, in ordinary day schools, taught by local teachers, many of whom were not only not native speakers but were actually untrained.

Murray had argued that the primary boarding school with its English medium was 'an attempt to provide for the African that general world of ideas in which the English child lives by the mere fact of being in a country where literature, the newspapers, and ordinary conversation assume those ideas' (Murray 1967:232). By the 1970s and 1980s, this larger environment of English was unobtainable in ordinary primary schools, but the 'tradition' of the switch to English was now deeply entrenched. Interestingly enough, this older pattern of the divided primary school can still be seen in some of the poorer regions of Africa where some communities still only have lower primary schools, and more obviously in Namibia where there are lower primary schools lasting just three years before an examination, and where the colonial vocabulary of 'sub-standard A' and 'sub-standard B' is still retained.

Even though it was commonplace for the new African governments to remove from missionary societies at independence their direct control of primary and secondary schools, an important legacy of missionary practice was kept in the building and equipping of schools. From very early on in the process of evangelization, it became clear that the new skills and knowledge associated with primary schools were sufficiently attractive to local communities that they would be prepared to build and equip simple classrooms and even collect money through fees that would help to cover the cost of the teacher-catechist.

This tradition of community provision of school buildings, land, and some partial support to maintenance through fees, was originally dictated by the sheer inability of missionary societies to meet the demands for schooling. But it was a mechanism that was to prove extremely valuable at the point when the new state was obliged dramatically to expand opportunities for both primary and secondary education at the time of independence. In 1960 the gross primary enrolment ratio was 40 per cent in anglophone Africa; but parents had been encouraged to believe that independence would mark the end of the era of educational restriction associated with the colonial governments and the missionary societies. The only feasible route to meet these popular expectations for education was to elevate to a national principle the local-level negotiations of the missionary societies, and to declare that educational expansion would involve self-help, self-reliance, or *harambee* (pull together), as the new political slogan was termed in Kenya. Not all African countries built this earlier mechanism of community provision into their new politics of mass education. Those who did so found that communities were prepared to dedicate enormous energies to providing facilities that would allow their young people a headstart in competing for further education and for the many new jobs opening up with the Africanization of the public sector.

Of course, one of the problems of incorporating this principle of self-help into a national system for school expansion was that it contained significant elements of very local competition. Missionary competition to offer their adherents the best educational opportunities within their 'sphere of influence' had encouraged a very localized form of negotiation about schooling. Much of this survived within the supposedly national systems of education. District or local education committees might be set up, but for many communities the crucial unit of negotiation remained the parents of the local school or prospective school. School committees with funds available from cash crops would build and improve primary schools, provide houses for teachers, and would be ready to tax themselves to build a secondary school. But what was extremely difficult to arrange was for local communities to be taxed so that funds could be dispersed equitably amongst a whole group of village or district schools.

Clearly the patterns whereby the very localized mission networks were built into national systems of education differed markedly from country to country. In most cases the state has desired some form of central control over schools, especially as good schools determined access to higher education and the best-paid jobs in the very small modern sector of the economy. On the other hand, the revenue base of the majority of states prevented their being able to take over full financial responsibility for education. Accordingly, a variety of compromises have been worked out between central control and the provision of teachers on the one hand and local sources ready to provide and maintain school buildings on the other. Although in recent years the study of school mapping has become commonplace in national units for educational planning, in reality the map of what schools are actually built is determined by an intensely local set of decisions about school fund-raising.

The continuation from the colonial period of very localized nuclei of support for schools has been little studied, but this mission legacy has had both positive and negative effects on educational development, depending on the strength or weakness of the state structures. In conditions such as in Uganda, where during the war the state had effectively retreated from the provision of services to rural areas, the buoyancy of this local resource base had been vital to the maintenance of schooling at the village level.

In other situations, the national legitimation of this intensely local type of development strategy has probably accentuated the regional disparities in provision of schooling that were inherited from the colonial period. However, even with strong states deeply committed to a more equitable pattern of educational development, it has proved extremely difficult over the longer term to arrange for one educationally-advantaged group to mark time whilst others were allowed to catch up. Tanzania, aided by the socialist philosophy of its first President, Nyerere, was one of those most committed to this path. But, now, some 20 years after the policies designed to achieve a more egalitarian pattern of educational development were first implemented, it could be argued that the most educationally advanced areas at independence have even increased their lead. In the late 1980s it would seem that the long-standing attempt to limit and make more equitable the provision of secondary education is being quietly abandoned.

Even though the Tanzanian state was able to restrict rather severely the number of government secondary schools, it proved to be politically quite impossible to prevent specific communities from sponsoring and opening private secondary schools. And, again, the reasons lie back in the colonial period. One of the themes that runs through the educational history of several countries is that colonial education (whether government- or mission-sponsored) could not expand at the rate that parents desired. One result was the setting up of what were termed independent schools. These were essentially low-cost community schools, but in the colonial period they were also identified as an early indication of political opposition to some of the cruder restrictions on schooling. One important legacy of this colonial connection between independent schooling and early nationalist politics was a reluctance by the new African governments to move against any form of self-help schooling. The colonial image of government persecuting independent education initiatives was translated into a post-colonial refusal to police private schooling.

CONTINUITIES AT THE LEVEL OF THE CLASSROOM

Thus far we have illustrated a number of ways in which the character of post-colonial schooling continues to be affected by some rather fundamental values which came to be taken for granted in the colonial period. Often the particular origin of what may now be thought of as the 'Kenya tradition of schooling' has been lost, and people will regard self-help, local fund-raising, or boarding as simply the way schooling is organized. But in addition to these features that affect the structure and organization of the whole school, there are other elements which characterize the life of the individual classroom. And again it would seem that the determinants of classroom quality are a good deal more complicated than they appear in the evaluations associated with the donor agencies. There often seem to be important historical continuities with earlier practice, now forgotten.

One of the more striking features of the primary schools in many African countries is how much 'developmental knowledge' is now being introduced into the curriculum. By this is meant subject matter related to health, nutrition, agricultural practice, and local technologies. The pattern is by no means uniform, but now, 20 years after independence, such subjects are being strongly promoted by local politicians and national education commissions. In fact in many of the upper primary schools of the colonial period, subjects such as arts and crafts and manual training were prominent. And, given the highly selective nature of these senior primary institutions, it was possible to provide specialist teachers and arrange for both the practical and theoretical examination of such practical subjects. The government and missionary rationale for the explicit teaching of health, nutrition, mothercraft, manual training, and domestic science was related to ideas about improved family life, the role of women, the value of manual labour for character formation, and the importance of agricultural knowledge in a continent that was 90 per cent agricultural in its pattern of employment.

It is interesting to note that at independence a good number of African countries dropped all the practical and agricultural instruction from primary schools. This was partly for logistical reasons – shortage of trained teachers – but perhaps primarily because these subjects seemed somehow part of a colonial prescription for Africa. Twenty years later, however, these subjects are fast making their reappearance at the primary level, possibly influenced by the continuation of major health and early childhood problems, by the continuing precariousness of African agriculture, and by the realization that most primary school leavers will not find work outside the rural sector. Hence the textbooks are filling up with enormous amounts of very explicit teaching about health, contraception, fertilizers, and discussion of appropriate rural technologies.

A second continuity with colonial education is the pervasiveness of the examination. The colonial era frequently had examinations which effectively prevented the majority of children from proceeding beyond the fourth standard (fourth year) of schooling. This selection device did mean that the fortunate few who completed primary school were virtually certain of securing a paid job in the modern sector of the economy. The inevitable removal of this early selection device at independence ensured that a large part of the primary cohort reached the end of primary. But as the jobs available in the modern sector of the economy had not expanded on anything like the scale of the schools, these new waves of full primary leavers had not much greater opportunities of getting a good job than their predecessors who had been selected out at Standard III or IV. For the colonial student, failure at this level implied virtually no chance of work in the civil service or modern firms; in the independence period failure to reach the highly selective secondary schools meant the same thing. The democratization of primary schooling had little counterpart in the opportunity structures of employment. Hence the priority agenda of both colonial and independence school systems has been examinations. The organization of teaching and of learning is deeply affected by the importance of selection. A good deal of the renowned order and discipline in African classrooms is probably directly attributable to this.

There are still very few studies of classroom life in Africa, but what exists suggests that primary schools exhibit few features associated with progressive primary education. For one thing there is an absolute shortage of learning materials. This means that millions of children are coping with full immersion in a non-home language (French, English, or Portuguese) with very few pupil texts or supplementary materials. The oral culture outside the school is too often the dominant mode in school, as children chant in chorus after their teachers definitions and axioms not fully understood. Doubtless the use of a foreign language for all subjects from age nine and sometimes age five or six does not make pupil-centred learning an easy proposition. And the sheer size of the classes makes other forms of group work highly unlikely. Much of the developmental knowledge we have talked of earlier is merely packaged in preparation for examinations, and very little is taught through projects or practical experience.

What we have now in many parts of Africa is a form of survival or subsistence schooling. The ravages of the fiscal crisis make it unlikely that the character of schooling can be readily changed. The use of foreign languages as the media of instruction certainly encourages the accumulation of inert ideas. But the alternatives in states that sometimes have one to two hundred local languages are not much more promising. And, equally, any attempt to prevent the bulk of the population's children from having an opportunity to compete in English or French for further education, and perhaps eventually well-paid work, would founder on political grounds. Especially in anglophone Africa, parents fought to be educated in English because the colonial governments sought to restrict it. Today, removing the right to be schooled in a foreign language would be seen as a blow against the achievements of independence. Thus in a very complex way English and French act as symbols of quality education, as inspirations to educational achievement, and yet also as substantial causes of the poor quality of African primary education. Unlike the colonial period where English medium was really only available to those few selected into upper primary schools, now the hum of English can be heard rising from almost all the primary schools of anglophone Africa, from high- and low-achieving pupils. And yet it remains true that only those successfully selected to the next level of schooling will have their English or French confirmed. For the rest – the great majority – the language will slip away quite quickly, unsupported by any regular use of the medium in any village situation.

CONCLUSION

We began this short account by arguing that the image of the African school in the West was for obvious reasons much less sharp now than during the era of intimate missionary contact with particular localities. Even within African states, since independence, the principal image of primary schools has been of a facility to expand. Only more recently in a number of states has there been a realization of the 'developmental potential' of mass primary education, and a consequent interest in providing 'development information' to primary school children. This information about agriculture, skill, health, and disease is aimed at the majority of young people who will proceed no further than primary. But the vehicle through which this locally relevant knowledge is offered is a foreign language, and the context of the offer is that knowledge must be processed for examinations which will crucially determine whether children are paid wages and salaries, or work the land.

Very little is known about the effects of exam success and failure upon the utilization of such knowledge. But what is clear is that primary education remains extraordinarily popular in Africa. Within the living memory of every village with a school, some child has risen from peasant boy or girl to the dizzy heights of government or commerce apparently through success in school. Class inequities are doubtless growing fast in Africa, but at the level of popular wisdom, 'the race is to the swift'. The expectation also that it will be possible, somehow, to reach secondary and higher education is still very widely held. Scarcely anywhere in Africa has there developed a disenchantment with the common school.

We would argue that much in this African pursuit of schooling is not understood. A good deal of these very ordinary features of primary schooling can be illuminated from the history of primary education in Africa, and from an untangling of the threads that led to the formation of state systems. Much can also be understood – unlike in the West – from the weakening of the state in a number of countries, and from the re-assertion of the elements that were responsible for education in an earlier, colonial period. For external bodies that seek to intervene in the current situation, whether as aid agencies or as non-governmental organizations, it should be clear that individual African countries already possess rather powerful traditions of education, forged by colonial scarcities, by intensely local systems of self-reliance, and by the continuation of two very different labour markets. There may well appear to be something contradictory about an education system so powerfully shaped by the aspirations for paid work that so few will succeed in reaching. On the other hand, the consequences of parents deciding that schools are very unlikely instruments for the improvement of their families' fortunes have not been explored, but they could well be more serious than the present imbalance between school expectations and paid employment.

REFERENCES AND FURTHER READING

Abernethy, D. B. (1969) *The Political Dilemma of Popular Education: An African Case*, Stanford, California: Macmillan.

Ajayi, J. F. A. (1965) *Christian Missions in Nigeria 1841–1891: The Making of a New Elite*, London: Longmans.

Anderson, J. (1970) *The Struggle for the School*, London: Longmans.

Crehan, K. (1985) 'Bishimi and social studies: the production of knowledge in a Zambian village', *African Affairs*, 84, 334:89–110.

Jones, T. J. (1922) *Education in Africa*, New York: Phelps-Stokes Fund.

(1925) *Education in East Africa*, New York: Phelps-Stokes Fund.

King, K. J. (1971) *PanAfricanism and Education*, Oxford.

Levine, R. A. *et al.* (1989) *Children of Africa: Infants and Parents in an African Community*, Cambridge.

Marris, P., and Somerset, A. (1971) *African Businessmen*, London: Routledge & Kegan Paul.

Murray, A. V. (1967) *The School in the Bush*, London: Cass.

Oliver, R. (1952) *The Missionary Factor in East Africa*, London: Longman.

World Bank (1988) *Education Policies for Sub-Saharan Africa*, Washington: World Bank.

EDUCATION AND NATIONAL DEVELOPMENT IN MALAYSIA

HENA MUKHERJEE

INTRODUCTION

The growth of formal education in Malaysia is intricately linked with the history of her economic, social, and political development as a nation, and this is reflected in her educational objectives and structures. From the late eighteenth century, apart from the period of the Japanese occupation (1942–1945) during the Second World War, the Malay States, then known as Malaya, were subject to British rule as her Crown Colonies and Protectorates until the granting of independence in 1957. In 1963 the Federation of Malaysia was formed: today it comprises two geographical regions, West Malaysia on the Malay Peninsula, and East Malaysia, consisting of the territories of Sabah and Sarawak, on the island of Borneo.

During the British colonial period before the Second World War, the economic, social, and political requirements of the colonial rulers brought into being a modern bureaucratic government that needed the services of clerical and low-grade administrative officers trained in Western-style schools. At the same time, the rapid expansion of the tin and rubber industries attracted a significant flow of labour from China and the Indian subcontinent bringing in its wake new sets of cultural and social needs. The influx of ethnic groups different in religion, language, and culture, both from the indigenous, Islamic Malay community, and from each other, transformed the country irrevocably from a monolingual, fairly homogenous society to a plural society with nearly half the population comprising Chinese and Indians. Consequently independent Malaya inherited an education system which reflected the efforts of the British government, missionaries, and immigrant communities to fashion a system of schooling that responded to each group's social, economic, and political needs.

The formation of Malaysia in 1963 served to deepen the existing complexities. Today 85 per cent of Malaysia's multi-ethnic population of approximately 15 million live on the Malay peninsula. Malay and other indigenous groups (officially termed *Bumiputeras*, meaning 'sons of the soil') make up about 55 percent of the population; Chinese 33 per cent; and Indians about 10 per cent of the remaining 12 per cent. Islam is the official state religion and this is also the religion of the Malay community. Buddhists make up 17 per cent of the population, Christians and Hindus 7 per cent each, and there are significant smaller religious groups such as Confucianists, Sikhs, and Bahai, including those who practise ancestor worship and animism. Apart from Malay, the national language and the mother tongue of the Malays, spoken languages include English, which is the language of commerce; Mandarin and several Chinese dialects; Tamil and several Indian regional languages; and the languages and dialects of the indigenous population of Sabah and Sarawak. Malaysia, a federation of thirteen states, is governed on the pattern of western-style parliamentary democracy, and the bureaucracy (predominantly Malay) that manages the administration is fashioned on the British model.

This chapter attempts to present briefly the growth of Malaysia's formal educational system in relation to the key social, economic, and political issues that have shaped its course. Weaving through the presentation are two ideas that have dominated educational policy and implementation: first, the attempt to build a unified nation with which Malaysia's various ethnic communities can identify; and, second, the effort to distribute the benefits of development equitably among all Malaysians.

THE GROWTH OF FORMAL EDUCATION

By the middle of the nineteenth century, a multi-stranded educational landscape had emerged that has been perceived by historians and political commentators as the major source of issues that have dominated educational policy and planning in the post-independence period.[1] The colonial government had not formulated a recognizable educational policy that had an impact on all communities, preferring to follow an *ad hoc* course.[2] In response to the increasing demand for recruits to serve the British administration and rapidly growing trading and commercial interests, English education developed, catering primarily to the Malay élite and urban Indian and Chinese. The rest depended on traditional vernacular systems. Among the Malays, residential Koranic or religious schools for boys were well-established. They generally lived with a renowned religious teacher, learning to recite the Koran mechanically, and practising good manners in speech and conduct. Between lessons, pupils assisted their master in chores in the house and on his farm. These Koranic schools later became the basis for primary-level Malay vernacular schools which were provided for by the British administration as part of their paternalistic sense of obligation towards the Malays.

Throughout the nineteenth and the first two decades of the twentieth century, the British administration did not consider itself obliged to provide education for what was perceived as a temporary, alien population – the Chinese and the Indians. Chinese communities financed their own schools which looked towards China for their traditional curriculum with its emphasis on the learning of the classics. By the beginning of the twentieth century, however, many progressive Chinese schools, led by reformists, were characterized by a combination of Confucianist teaching using teachers and textbooks imported from China, and western science. Both ethos and knowledge bases were divorced from the Malayan cultural and political environment initially and the schools later came to be known for their revolutionary, anti-colonial thinking. In order to defuse the growing anti-British political stance of Chinese school graduates, some control was attempted through a financial grants system and the compulsory registration of schools and teachers. Similarly outward-looking were the primary-level Tamil schools, whose curriculum content was centred on India and Ceylon. These schools, located largely on rubber estates, were normally the results of private effort, until 1902, when the growing demand for a cheap and stable labour force induced the administration to introduce a Labour Code. Under this code, estates with ten children of school-going age were required to provide staff and a school. But these schools did not prove to stimulate mobility: the primary level vernacular education socialized pupils to remain on the estates and provide cheap labour for the management.

The provision of limited education in English has been interpreted by many apologists of colonial rule as a benign, paternalistic policy aimed at promoting the well-being of the indigenous Malay, resulting in the promotion of education in the vernacular. The amiable intention of making sons of fishermen and farmers more intelligent fishermen and farmers was perceived by many nationalist critics as a consequence of the unhappy British experience in India where local English-educated malcontents emerged as a political force to be reckoned with. It became increasingly clear, however, that the English-educated had access to modern sector employment opportunities at the junior levels of government service in Malaya, while religious and vernacular education responded to cultural needs with their graduates remaining in the traditional sectors.

POST-WAR RECONSTRUCTION

The period after the Second World War manifested conscious expressions of the crucial role of education in nation building, and all the major communities set about evaluating existing educational provision.[3] The fragmented school system was seen as a fundamental source of disunity among ethnic communities while it forged intra-group class distinctions, with the urban English-educated Malays, Chinese, and Indians forming the élite. Having fought to defend the country against the Japanese, Chinese and Indians no longer saw their life in Malaya as a temporary sojourn. They demanded a system of education that would recognize them as equals while allowing them to maintain their own cultures and languages. As independence from the British became imminent, education was seen as an instrument indispensable to national development, both in terms of economic progress and socio-political cohesion. The national education policy formulated at independence in 1957, and subsequent national development plans, had the overriding objective of forging national unity which was to be operationalized through a national language, common school system, a common, centrally-planned and administered school curriculum that would foster a common Malaysian outlook, followed by common public examinations. The remodelled system was planned to bring about:

> a national system of education acceptable to the people of the Federation [of Malaya] as a whole which will satisfy their needs and promote their cultural, social, economic and political development as a nation, having regard to the intention of making Malay the national language of the country whilst preserving and sustaining the growth of the language and culture of other communities living in the country.[4]

Until the traumatic race riots of 1969 after which the implementation of education was subjected to fresh scrutiny, English-medium schools ran alongside Malay-medium and Chinese-medium primary and secondary schools and Tamil-medium primary schools. In 1961, in an effort to move closer to the national education policy, Chinese-medium schools were directed either to be self-supporting or to change to Malay medium. Chinese and Tamil vernacular education at the primary level were to remain intact with the Malay language taught as a single subject. Any attempt to change their medium of instruction to Malay brought and still brings forth vociferous and emotional protests from the two communities who point to the policy which committed the government to 'preserving and sustaining the growth of the language and culture of other communities'.

EDUCATION AND SOCIAL RESTRUCTURING

The 1969 communal riots drew the attention of the Malays to educational, occupational, and income disparities between them and the Chinese and Indian communities (especially the former), leading them to see themselves as the dispossessed in their own country, unable to enjoy the benefits of moderniz-ation and development. Radical socio-economic policies of redress were put forward culminating in the formulation of the New Economic Policy (NEP) in 1970. The basis of the NEP was the argument that national unity and integration could not be achieved where one or more groups felt disadvantaged in relation to other social groups. The NEP had two major prongs: the eradication of poverty in the country as a whole and the restructuring of society to reduce and eventually to eliminate the identification of race with function.[5]

In terms of implementation, the second facet of the NEP may be said to have received more attention, and is often interpreted to mean that high income and prestige occupations must reflect existing ethnic proportions in the population. Identified as one of the NEP's primary agents, education seemed to be peculiarly suited to the role it was called upon to play. Education has always been seen in Malaysia as society's major and most valid instrument of upward social and occupational mobility. The successful participation of the élite English-educated groups in the prestigious modern economic sector served to strengthen this perception. Besides, the educational process carried with it the notion of open competition connoting objectivity and fair play. Within the span of one decade (1970–1980) the outcomes of social redress policies became evident. While the target of proportional representation in all occupational sectors had not been achieved, imbalances were less glaring, with increasing proportions of Malays moving into high status occupations. Before 1970, Malays were predominant in the rural, agricultural sector, among the country's lowest earners and occupying a large segment of the low-status occupations in the labour force. But by 1980, aggressive policies and their implementation had rendered the identification of ethnic group with occu-pational category a thing of the past.

HIGHER EDUCATION FOR ECONOMIC AND SOCIAL DEVELOPMENT

The democratization of education was a logical aim in post-independence Malaysia. Since the sixties the school system had expanded phenomenally especially at primary level. Primary schooling was made free in 1960 with automatic movement through the grades guaranteeing a child six years of elementary education. The social demand for education had always been high so that it had never been found necessary to make schooling compulsory.

Numbers were further improved when, in 1965, with the abolition of the secondary school entrance examination, every child was guaranteed nine years of schooling. Today primary school enrolment includes approximately 97 per cent of the relevant age cohort. Figures decrease as one climbs the educational ladder but retention rates improve yearly. At tertiary level, Malaysia's selective university system can only cater for an extremely small fraction of the age cohort. This results in higher education becoming a major issue, with economic and political implications, as it represents the key to élite positions in society. As the educational system expands at primary and secondary levels, pressure constantly grows for increased tertiary level provision.

The New Economic Policy provided a launching pad for national development policies which suggested rapid economic and social development geared to the redistribution of goods and facilities in order to provide a bigger proportion for the *Bumiputera* population. In the case of higher education it meant expanding and orienting the system to meet the new human resource needs of the country, particularly in the industrial and manufacturing sectors, which were expected to provide the greatest impetus for economic growth.[6] At the same time, the higher education system was the means by which young people from low socio-economic backgrounds were to be channelled into the upper echelons of the occupational structure, and consequently into the upper political and social strata.[7] The policy of promoting the educational mobility of the Malays, largely through government sponsorship, aimed at moving a large proportion of them from low-status traditional occupations into high-income, high-status jobs in the prestigious modern sector. As a result of insufficient local capacity to meet the demand for higher education, large numbers of both Malays and non-Malays seek admissions overseas in Commonwealth countries and the United States, and to a lesser extent India (especially for medical education), Taiwan (usually Chinese students), and more recently Japan. Recently two problems have emerged that have prompted the government to review their policy on overseas students. Apart from increasing fees and disadvantageous foreign exchange rates, policy makers are becoming wary of growing fundamentalist Islamic influence on Malay students as a consequence of their interacting with fundamentalist groups from other countries. Mindful of the destabilizing influences such thinking may have on the local religio-political scene, changing policies project a dramatic decrease in the numbers of government-sponsored Malay students studying abroad in the future. But over the last one-and-a-half decades, government intervention in admission and sponsorship policies designed to ensure *Bumiputera* representation at tertiary level at home and abroad has indeed borne fruit. While different types of higher education programmes offer different opportunities for employment, nevertheless the overall picture of tertiary education indicates that an equitable distribution among the races has been achieved in educational opportunities at the tertiary level.

ISLAMIC REVIVALISM AND DEVELOPMENT POLICIES

The success of Malaysia's socio-economic policies of positive discrimination in favour of Muslim *Bumiputeras* in the seventies became a source of concern among fundamentalist members in the community. During this period, the country saw the proliferation of several Islamic missionary groups (known as *dakwah*) who disputed western, capitalist approaches to the accumulation of material wealth. The rapid creation of a visible *nouveau riche* class against a background of wide disparities in income led a substantial proportion of Muslims to question government developmental strategies.[8] To appease critics, the government assumed a leadership role in Islamic religious matters and supported a range of missionary activities in the country. These include the increase of resources for the teaching of *agama* (Islamic religious studies) in schools, and a revitalized teacher-training programme for religious teachers. A course on Islamic civilization (*Tamadun Islam*) has been made compulsory in all undergraduate programmes for non-Muslim students, a move that has given rise to fears of an active campaign in the proselytizing of Islam among other religious communities. The establishment of the English-medium International Islamic University, funded by Islamic nations, chiefly Saudi Arabia, seemed to observers to strike the high note in Malaysia's support of Islamic thought and education. Its aims include the need to spread Islamic teachings while encouraging the progress of scientific research, and to prove that a religious education is not at odds with the aims of modernization.

RELIGIOUS EDUCATION AND MORAL EDUCATION

The teaching of religious education and moral values has always received a great deal of attention in independent Malaysia. Malay vernacular schools had evolved from Koranic schools, and a large proportion of the English-medium schools from schools run by Christian missionaries, chiefly Roman Catholic and Anglican. In both cases, unlike the Chinese and Tamil schools, the commitment to religious values was very strong. With the establishment of Islam as the official religion of the country, Islamic religious studies were set to play a more prominent role in formal education. Prior to the formulation of the common curriculum, Christian mission schools taught religious studies based on their own faiths. In some cases, this was compulsory for all pupils, and in others it was optional for non-Christians, in which case they attended classes on 'ethics' or 'morals'. These were usually watered-down versions of religious studies. In the post-1957 curriculum, however, only *agama* could be taught in schools; the teaching and learning of any other religion could only be done out of school hours. That the state undertook responsibility for Islamic religious studies and not for the other religions practised in the country was perceived as anomalous by non-Muslims but not by the Government: Islam being designated as the official religion was seen as sufficient justification. Non-Muslims, many of whom were granted Malaysian citizenship in the late fifties and early sixties, after independence, were not concerned at this time about religious or moral education in schools, seeing this primarily as a responsibility of the family and the religious community. Besides, their major preoccupation then was upward economic and social movement, making good in the country of their adoption.

Directly on the heels of the race riots, in the early seventies, attempts were made to address worsening relations among the various communities. At school level, civics was introduced as a compulsory subject, but by 1974, as the only non-examinable subject in a heavily examination-oriented system, programme evaluation indicated that it was not being effectively handled. At about the same time, the wave of student unrest in the west, widespread drug abuse, and growing street violence caught up with Malaysia. Expressions of concern were voiced in the press and other public fora, culminating in a parliamentary discussion which concluded that schools should be responsible for some form of moral guidance for all pupils; that formal learning in school should be continuous with the world outside the school; and that the school had the responsibility for developing not only marketable knowledge and skills but also those skills and values that assist in the growth of morally mature and responsible members of society. The mandate given by the Cabinet Committee on Education to the Curriculum Development Centre resulted in the formulation of a moral education programme for non-Muslim pupils, to be taught during the periods Muslim pupils were to attend *agama* classes.

As in many other developing societies, life styles in Malaysia are moving from the rural agrarian to the modern urban. Due to the rapidity of socio-economic changes, various influences compete and conflict with the traditional norms and values of any one social group. The complexity of the situation is compounded by the existence of several distinctive social groups, and the moral education curriculum, with its goal of strengthening the moral fibre of the 'nation', in order to provide 'the basis for political, economic, and social stability as well as unity within the context of a plural . . . democratic society'[9] has set itself a most difficult task. Based on a core of universal moral values and using problem-solving approaches to the making of moral judgements, the curriculum was arrived at through a system of negotiations by a committee comprising representatives of various religious, educational, and voluntary welfare and social groups. The outcome was perceived by some as simplistic, unable to grapple with the subtle interplay among the varied norms in Malaysian life. Others feared that it was potentially iniquitous. Even if it were possible to develop a sense of unity through classroom lessons with school pupils aware of pervasive economic and social tensions outside, the segregation of Muslim children from non-Muslims during the teaching of values was perceived as a divisive strategy. Religious groups took exception to the rationale that universal ethical principles should form the judgemental basis of moral thinking rather than revealed religion, and that as long as the fostering of cultures other than Islam was enshrined in the constitution, schools should include the teaching of other religions. In addition, a fundamental contradiction existed between the non-religious framework of the curriculum and the national ideology's first tenet – 'Belief in God'.[10] Government support none the less may be explained in terms of the desire to defuse religious fervour among non-Islamic groups while providing an opportunity for developing what is perceived as a set of socially desirable attitudes and values.

THE ROLE OF WOMEN IN DEVELOPMENT

Malaysian women make up approximately a quarter of the labour force, with the majority in difficult, low-paid, manual occupations chiefly in the agricultural sector, followed by jobs in the production and transport industries. Of the small proportion in professional occupations, most are concentrated in the traditional 'feminine' and lower status professions such as teaching and nursing. Very few reach top level management positions. One may conclude that women tend to be in jobs that have minimal possibilities for career development and advancement, and this may be attributed to their traditionally established roles in production and home maintenance as well as their lower educational levels. More than a quarter of women in the labour force have had no formal education at all, but the situation is changing.[11]

Access to education for girls is not a limiting factor in Malaysia today. By the seventies, previous imbalances between enrolments of girls and boys had been almost completely eliminated, a situation which can be attributed to the policy of free, universal primary education and the practice of automatic promotion for the first six, then later nine years of schooling. But at upper secondary level enrolment of girls decreases sharply with rural girls faring much worse than those in urban areas. Many factors contribute to lower enrolment for girls. The end of automatic promotion after the ninth year pushes many girls and boys out of the system. Despite widespread positive attitudes towards the value of education, traditionally many Muslim parents prefer to send their daughters to single-sex schools and, since many secondary schools are co-educational, girls may be kept at home or sent to Islamic religious schools where they are segregated from boys, and are little exposed to modern ideas. Where parental educational levels are low, all communities perceive schooling as an interim activity before early marriage, and consequently would support the notion that sons rather than daughters should continue with schooling. In the low income groups, both boys and girls may be taken out of school to help their parents at work, or, for older girls, to care for younger siblings while parents are at work, although this is tending to change. In the traditional Chinese Confucian home and the Tamil (South Indian) Hindu family, women are expected to adjust to the families they marry into, and the ideal wife is portrayed as one who obeys and respects her husband, with the pattern of husband-wife relationship typified in male dominance and female dependence.

These traditional perceptions may be held responsible in many cases for retarding the progress of women, especially among rural women and the urban poor. Activists among Malaysian women are calling for concerted efforts in order to raise female literacy and general educational levels without which women become marginal to the process of national development. Interestingly, at tertiary level, enrolment figures reveal that women students comprise about forty per cent of the total student population. But choice of specialization shows preferences for typical 'female-oriented' programmes such as arts, social sciences, and education, with fewer in engineering, accountancy, and architecture. Practitioners attribute this profile of course options to the channelling of girls at school level away from mathematics, science, and technically-based programmes, leading to generally poor performance, thereby reinforcing the assumptions that girls are less able in these areas. It is evident that the offer of equal opportunity and access to education at all levels does not guarantee uptake and utilization: positive discrimination strategies need to be planned to increase and optimize women's potential contribution to the development process in Malaysia. It is also clear that forms of gender discrimination cut across all groups in Malaysia, even though Malay women – and especially the élite – have benefited from the terms of the New Economic Policy.

LOOKING AHEAD

Three decades after independence, Malaysia's formal education system shows that far-reaching modifications have been made to inherited structures in efforts to serve national developmental goals better. In order to bring about unity and the sense of a common Malaysian identity among the various ethnic communities, a common curriculum was introduced using the national language as the main medium of instruction from primary to tertiary levels. This policy can be said to have met with success to the extent that a generation of young people can communicate with each other in the national language at work and play. And yet national unity continues to be more evident in the political rhetoric than in the reality of Malaysian life. The perceived contraction of educational and economic opportunities appears to have had a more lasting effect on behaviour and attitudes than have changes in curriculum and language policies.

Complex restructuring of educational and economic institutions was undertaken after independence in order to correct inherited inequities. While considerable advances have been made in the redistribution of resources, the same strategies have been responsible for effecting new imbalances, especially marked in recent years in the face of reduced opportunities resulting from an unforeseen down-turn in the economy. Outstanding among these is the fact that the greatest educational and occupational advantages resulting from the New Economic Policy have gone to the privileged among the *Bumiputeras*, although this is not to deny that some benefits have been derived by all groups among them. Similarly, among the other ethnic communities, particularly the Indians, educational and occupational privileges are becoming increasingly out of reach for lower- and middle-class social groups. The picture emerging is one in which intra-group divisions have become apparent where inter-group divides were predominant.

The third decade after independence showed a new focus in the continuing concern for national unity, a concern that was qualitatively different from more tangible policies such as the development of a common curriculum and the restructuring of educational and economic institutions. The emphasis on a more subtle domain of knowledge – that of values – emerged as an important centre in educational and political arenas. National initiatives were taken by the central government who assumed a dominant leadership role in the teaching of Islamic religion and civilization as well as in the orchestration of a national moral values curriculum for non-Muslims. These new strategies may be indicative of policy makers' perceptions that quantitative measures by themselves have been unable to achieve the larger goals of national development, i.e. a common identity and sense of unity among all Malaysians. A new style in educational policy making may have been signalled by the new approach. At birth, the young nation launched eagerly into sweeping reforms, many of which have not been able to achieve planned goals. A more mature nation may have learnt to move with greater caution, aware that blueprints on a drawing board rarely anticipate obstacles such as race riots and global economic recessions. Policy makers may have learnt too that subtle interplays between quantitative and non-quantitative factors must be heeded in order to lead the country towards development goals that can be shared by all.

NOTES

1. Philip Loh Fook Seng (1975) *Seeds of Separation: Educational Policy in Malaysia*, Kuala Lumpur: Oxford University Press.
2. Francis Wong Hoy Kee and Ee Tiang Hong (1971) *Education in Malaysia*, Kuala Lumpur: Heinemann Educational Books: 7–16.
3. Ibid. Chapter 6.
4. This extract from the *Report of the Education Committee* 1956 is quoted by Hena Mukherjee and Jasbir Sarjit Singh in 'Education and social policy: the Malaysian case', *Prospects*, XV, 2 (1985): 292.
5. Mukherjee and Singh: 290–1.
6. Amnuay Tapingkae (Ed.) (1976) *Higher Education and Economic Growth in Southeast Asia*, Singapore: Regional Institute of Higher Education.
7. Ozay Mehmet and Yip Yat Hoong (1985) 'An empirical evaluation of Government scholarship policy in Malaysia', *Higher Education*, 14:197–210.
8. Ratnam, K. J. (1969) 'Religion and politics in Malaya', in R. O. Tilman (Ed.), *Man, State and Society in Contemporary Southeast Asia*, New York: Praeger Publications.
9. Hena Mukherjee (1983) 'Moral Education in a Plural Society: Malaysia', *Journal of Moral Education*, 12, 2:125–30.
10. The *Rukenegara* (or the 'Pillars of the Nation') constitutes the national ideology with which the school curriculum is not expected to conflict. These are Belief in God, Loyalty to King and Country, Upholding the Constitution, Good Behaviour, and Morality. See R. S. Milne, 'National ideology and nation building in Malaysia', *Asian Survey* (July 1980): 563–73.
11. For commentaries on various aspects of women, education, and development in Malaysia, see Hing Ai Yuen, Nik Safiah Karim and Rokiah Talib (Eds.) (1984) *Women in Malaysia*, Kuala Lumpur: Pelanduk Publications.

2.9

FROM BANTU EDUCATION TO PEOPLE'S EDUCATION IN SOUTH AFRICA

PETER KALLAWAY

In making a contribution on South African education to this *Handbook* in 1988 – forty years after the National Party came to power in South Africa – it is sobering to realize that apartheid has effectively cut this country off from the international educational community in the second half of the twentieth century. Thus many of the assumptions, continuities, and enduring characteristics of the 'culture' of the international educational community have evolved remote from the day-to-day realities of schooling systems, educational administrations, and educational research in South Africa. Cut off from outside influences through lack of interaction with the United Nations Development Programme, UNESCO, OECD, and the World Bank, and from the free international exchange of educationalists so characteristic of the rest of Africa during the post-colonial era, educational development in South Africa has been uniquely isolated from the mainstream of international educational thought.

Within South Africa a second set of circumstances has worked to promote a distinctive form of educational policy development. These relate to the emergence of an alternative educational discourse in the form of Christian National Education (CNE) – or Fundamental Pedagogics (FP) as it has been known in more recent years. This is the framework of analysis favoured by the National Party and therefore by the country's educational bureaucracy. The vast majority of educationalists and teachers trained from the fifties were required to master the labyrinthine functionalist discourse and convoluted terminology of FP whether they were white or black, and whether they studied at Colleges of Education, the Afrikaans universities, or the black universities (the so-called 'bush colleges' for the African, coloured, and Indian students, created by the Nationalists in the 1960s).[1]

Only at the four English-language universities, and latterly at the University of Bophuthatswana and the University of the Western Cape, has there been any attempt to continue earlier traditions of international contact. Yet the faculties of education of even these few universities on the whole represent notably conservative enclaves within the overall conservative ethos of the liberal universities. The latter condemn the racism of apartheid and the lack of academic freedom that is a consequence of ever-increasing state control of education, but only very small numbers of the predominantly white faculty have ever committed themselves to anything other than the upholding of basic liberal conservative values. Few have identified themselves whole-heartedly with the struggles of black South Africans.

In short, the so-called 'English Universities' which were the only institutions capable of providing a challenge to apartheid education within South Africa, failed to establish a sufficiently powerful alternative ethos. They failed to give student teachers or those following professional degrees in education a sufficiently critical perspective on their profession and failed to produce a radical challenge to apartheid education through research. That lack of research is in part to be explained by the narrow teacher training ethos of most university education departments, and partly by the difficulty of carrying out such research – the unco-operative stance of the educational authorities and their unwillingness to allow research to be carried out in state educational institutions.

In an environment where few English speakers or blacks saw much hope of advancement within the ranks of the educational bureaucracy beyond the rank of head teacher, there was little incentive to further one's academic qualifications to master or doctoral level. The field was therefore left to the practitioners of Fundamental Pedagogics, who in consequence have come to control educational research and administration. They used this position to entrench and give legitimacy to the practices of apartheid education.

What critical documentation of apartheid education took place, did so under the aegis of the only independent research initiative to emerge in this field – the research branch of the South African Institute of Race Relations (SAIRR) under the guidance of Muriel Horrell (Horrell 1968). This invaluable work will remain our basic source on the subject for many years to come.

The challenge of radical black politics since 1976 has thrown the whole arena of educational theory and practice into the melting pot. The assumptions embodied in 'Bantu Education'[2] have been more fundamentally challenged. Most important, the issue of educational change has been placed high on the agenda of political programmes for democratic rights in a strident form that overshadows the resistance to Bantu Education in the fifties. Educational reform and transformation are now key aspects of the agenda of change for radical students, parents, nationalists, populists, socialists, and trade unionists.

A monumental task of educational reconstruction lies ahead. The form to be taken by that new dispensation is of immense importance to the shaping of the new society now emerging.

UNDERSTANDING BANTU EDUCATION

In this situation it is important to ask whether the goals, the experience, and the ethos of Bantu Education are indeed *different in kind* from the experience of mass education elsewhere, or whether Bantu Education is simply *different in degree*. If we hold the former view we need to be consistent and question the value of comparative perspectives on this topic, since the implication is that *race* provides a *sui generis* analytical category that is self-explanatory. The politics of racism, it follows, is irrational by definition, and therefore not open to explanation in other terms.

This racial view of Bantu Education is based on a specific type of analysis which emphasizes the unique political character of South African history in general, and apartheid in particular. Apartheid, or the ideology and practice of Afrikaner Nationalism since 1948, are on this view to be understood in terms of assumptions about:

- the psychological make-up of the Afrikaner and his allegedly unique propensity for racial prejudice
- the unique historical experience of the Afrikaner nation (the background of Calvinism, the experience of the frontier, and the fact that Afrikaners are somehow trapped in the world views of the nineteenth century and cannot come to terms with the modern world)
- the fundamental opposition between liberal capitalist values and the spirit of Afrikaner nationalism. (Popular common sense among South Africans of a liberal persuasion – black and white – holds that apartheid must inevitably crumble in the face of economic growth and modernization because it is outmoded, irrational, and not compatible with modern free market values.)

The conclusion arrived at on the basis of this perspective is that the South Africa situation is unique and to be understood entirely in its own terms – that it is the result of historical forces specific to South Africa.

David Yudelman, however, has recently made some trenchant criticisms of this perspective of South African history. He deserves quotation at some length:

> Contemporary South Africa is almost inevitably seen as a deviant, even bizarre, case among modern industrial states ... It is portrayed internationally as a combination of seventeenth century fanaticism ... and twentieth century technology ... The heavy overemphasis on the unique aspects of South African society, such as the highly institutionalised and rigid system of race discrimination, has tended to blind observers to the way South Africa fits into an

international comparative perspective . . . *the problem arises in the tendency to believe that what is unique is necessarily salient.*

The image is, of course, convenient for those anxious to distance themselves from, and to avoid obvious comparisons with the dark sides of their own societies, past and present. For South Africa represents in almost caricatured form the ugly side of most developing industrial states: the concentration of a disproportionate amount of growing wealth in the hands of a minority, the decline of civil and human rights, the centralization of power, and the systematic exploitation of the powerless. It is far more comfortable to relegate such a creature to a lunatic asylum than to conceive of living with it as a blood relative. . . .

The Afrikaner, in general, has been credited with a far larger role in the evolution of contemporary South Africa than he deserves. This is partly the result of Afrikaner nationalist mythology . . . but it is equally the fault of Anglophones, who have portrayed the Afrikaner as the villain, the fanatic who created or at least perfected institutionalised racial discrimination in the name of apartheid.

(Yudelman 1983: 5, 13–14)

As early as 1972 both liberal and Marxist writers pointed out the limitations of modernization theory when confronted by the realities of South African history in the period since 1945. Adam (1971) and Johnstone (1970: 69) both argued quite conclusively that capitalism had thrived under apartheid and that it was misguided to argue for a contradiction between apartheid and capitalism. All the evidence was to the contrary. Apartheid was shown to have a positive or organic relationship with the growth of capitalism in the post-war era – or to put it another way – South Africa had flourished in the sixties during the international 'long boom' precisely because apartheid had provided the preconditions for growth. Apartheid legislation and the state's bureaucratic machinery had enabled it to harness and exploit a key factor of production (black labour) at a crucial moment of expansion. If there was no fundamental conflict between the state (in the hands of the National Party) and big business, that meant that dominant assumptions about the agenda of the Nationalists themselves had to be re-examined. Such insights into the relations between capitalism and apartheid were of great assistance to those who set about examining the significance of state reform initiatives in the 1970s (see Saul and Gelb 1981; Nolutshungu 1983).

Bantu Education has been a key focus for those who want to emphasize the deviant nature of the South African State – whether they were liberals, Africanists or Marxists. Bantu Education, above all the other institutions of apartheid, has been singled out for special treatment by critics as epitomizing 'the lunatic creature to be set outside of civilized society' – to continue with Yudelman's metaphor. Bantu Education has been universally criticized – it has become a byword for 'education for barbarism' (Tabata 1959) in the post-war world. It is universally recognized as a unique and bizarre form of human domination.

In addition to the moral outrage expressed about this form of schooling, those with an eye to the link between morality and profitability have also pointed out that, not only is Bantu Education immoral, but it is also unprofitable. These arrangements are stressed as being contrary to the 'rational' economic interests of the modern industrial, capitalist state as they constitute a brake on the growth of the free market economy by limiting the supply of skilled manpower in the marketplace, and therefore once again reveal the backward-looking nature or anti-modernization stance of Afrikaner Nationalism.

What then is the nature of the argument that backs up this extraordinary phenomenon, and what is the nature of the condemnation?

The statements of President Verwoerd in the early 1950s are cited *ad nauseam* as proof of the evil intent of the policy. The evidence is based almost exclusively upon *stated intentions* as put forward by various National Party ideologues, usually based on speeches given in parliament, and designed to impress a specific audience. What did these statements amount to in terms of policy intention?

Bantu Education policy centred around the following issues:

– the need to promote a specific 'culture' that was said to be the unique inheritance of 'the Bantu';
– the need to ensure that the educational experience of 'the Bantu' did not alienate them from 'their own culture' and make them aspire to social and political rights on a par with whites;
– the need to adapt schooling and make it relevant to employment and work in the context of South Africa's labour market, segmented by the colour bar;
– the need to ensure that the nature of the school curriculum was compatible with the above goals;
– the need to promote mother-tongue education in order to satisfy the above aims;
– the need for centralized state control of schooling in the interests of efficiency and in order to bring educational policy in line with general apartheid policy;
– the need to settle the question of the financing of education for South Africa's indigenous peoples.

(based on Shingler 1973: 284)

By contrast, the criticisms of the National Party agenda for Bantu Education can be located broadly within the following categories:

1. An *ethical claim* which asserts that Bantu Education negates individual human rights and sets itself against the mainstream goals of mass education which are to increase equality in society; it thus restricts the enlargement of the general *political good*.

2. A *rationality claim* which asserts that Bantu Education is 'irrational' in terms of neo-classical economics and counter-productive to the manpower needs of a modernizing, industrial state. That is to say, it inhibits the stock of skills in society and thus puts a brake on productivity or growth – therefore restricting the national good in the economic sphere.

3. An *indoctrination charge* which holds that Bantu Education is aimed at intentionally restricting the intellectual development and critical abilities of the young by deliberately distorting school knowledge and promoting elements of State propaganda rather than the regular school curriculum.

4. A rather vague claim that state control of schooling, and in particular, the state's take-over of the mission schools in the 1950s, was a negative or sinister step. This argument was often linked to the claim that educational policy should be left partly in the hands of professional educators, voluntary agencies, or community groups, which is out of step with 1, 2 and 3 above.

MASS EDUCATION IN INDUSTRIAL, CAPITALIST SOCIETY AND BANTU EDUCATION

The central question to be posed in the light of the debates outlined above is whether Bantu Education is simply a local variation of mass schooling under capitalism or whether Bantu Education is a unique form of schooling, perhaps to be compared with the extreme form of ideological manipulation and indoctrination that was characteristic of Nazi schooling. To put it bluntly, 'Is Bantu Education the bizarre phenomenon that it is usually made out to be, or is it just that "what is unique (namely the racist nature of the schooling) comes to be seen as what is necessarily salient"?' (Yudelman 1983: 13).

The fact that Bantu Education had the declared aim of maintaining black South Africans in a permanent state of political and economic subordination is often cited by liberal and radical commentators as sufficient grounds for its condemnation. The breach of the injunction (codified in the United Nations Declaration of Human Rights) to treat all individuals equally when making provision for schooling, and to refuse to accept arguments designed to treat racially different pupils differentially all underwrote the outrage at the policy of Bantu Education in the fifties and sixties.

What was missed by most commentators was the fact that Bantu Education, far from being a unique form of schooling, was simply a locally specific form of mass schooling under capitalism, that had the eccentric feature of identifying working-class children by the colour of their skin, or latterly by the nature of their culture. The intentions behind the extension of educational provision to the mass of the population were essentially similar to those noted elsewhere by a large number of researchers in this field. The parallel between the evolution of mass schooling in Britain, Europe, and the USA in the late nineteenth century, and the evolution of mass education (Bantu Education) during the course of South Africa's second industrial revolution in the post World War II era, are too obvious to be denied.

Education, in the context of liberal ideology, is held to be free from politics or ideology – characterized by the induction of children into 'worthwhile' forms of thought – and as such to be distinguished from indoctrination, which exhibits features of prejudice and bias. In this sense Bantu Education was said to exhibit marked features of indoctrination rather than education – it was indeed, like Nazi education, 'education for barbarism', as it set out with the intention of inducting children into beliefs derived from Christian National Education and Afrikaner nationalism. But what has been universally missed in this regard is that mass education in capitalist societies is far from free of an ideological component. The rationale for both was the need for the state to gain greater political, social, and ideological control over the mass of citizens and workers who had recently been drawn into the orbit of the modern industrial state as *citizens* or *workers* or *urban dwellers*. They were to be inducted to a common national ideology, and provided with a minimum set of basic skills (the three Rs) which would ensure that they were loyal citizens and efficient and productive workers.

Mass educational strategies were distinctively about the need for ideological uniformity and the induction of working-class children into the ideology of nineteenth-century liberalism and the norms of capitalist or nationalist society, rather than any goal to ensure that working-class youth acquired the habits of critical thought.

In addition, a universal feature of mass education for working-class children has been that it was financially disadvantaged when compared to that provided for the middle class, even within the context of western democracies. Although there was much discussion of the need for the provision of specific work – or employment-related forms of education for working-class children, in the event the state did very little to encourage such developments. Both of these characteristics apply alike to mass education and Bantu Education.

What has been widely neglected by commentators is that Bantu Education was as much about inducting black South Africans into the ideology of capitalism as it was about putting forward its declared intention of promoting Afrikaner nationalism and the ideals of Christian National Education. Although Bantu Education was dismally unsuccessful in achieving the latter aim, I would argue that it has been remarkably successful – through its hidden curriculum as much as its overt content – in ensuring the commitment of black South Africans to capitalist society and ideology, something which is of profound importance for the future of education in South Africa.

In short, Bantu Education, far from being a unique kind of schooling system, characterized by racism, is more accurately to be seen as an example of mass education under capitalism, with the unique feature that race distinction has coincided with the class divisions to be found in many other contexts. Bantu Education is, therefore, not simply to be seen as a unique and deviant form of schooling, but is fundamentally similar in kind to other forms of mass education under capitalism. The criticisms of mass education elsewhere are therefore relevant to our understanding of the South African context. The implications of these observations for an understanding of reform strategies need, however, to be related to contemporary debates on what is termed People's Education in South Africa.

It would, therefore, appear that the international experience of educational reform in industrial and post-colonial societies does potentially have applicability to South Africa. It is also important to recognize that the South African experience might hold some important insights for others.

PEOPLE'S EDUCATION: THE IMPLICATIONS

The last decade has graphically demonstrated the significance of education as a site of struggle in South Africa. The SOWETO uprising was only the beginning of a long and bitter struggle between radical students and community leaders, and the state. Even in small country towns, black communities have been radicalized as never before, and demands for adequate schooling have been at the top of the agenda for change. The repressive arm of the state has been used repeatedly and often with great brutality in an attempt to check this political challenge – mass detentions (30,000 in 1986–7), the prolonged imprisonment of children, the closing of schools, the transfer or dismissal of radical teachers, the refusal of educational authorities to readmit radical students, the fencing off of educational institutions, the presence of the police and army in schools, have all been everyday features of the educational scene in the townships of South Africa in recent years.

Students, parents, and local communities have repeatedly responded with school boycotts, school strikes, and attempts to establish alternative education initiatives. These have always been linked to broader demands for political rights, more adequate housing, medical care, and an end to influx control, the reservation of specific categories of jobs for whites, and the Group Areas Act (which forces people of designated 'racial' groups to live in specific areas). The government has been forced to give way in some limited areas, only to reassert control more tightly in others. The basic structures of power remain.

In this context the National Education Crisis Committee (NECC) has been formed to attempt to find some solutions to the schools' crisis, and plan a way forward. At a recent mass conference on black education the central problem of education for the future was posed: 'We are all agreed that we don't want

Bantu Education but now we must be clear about what we want to take its place'. (NECC 1986: 24)

How can we make use of the above perspective on the fundamental similarity between Bantu Education and mass education under capitalism to define the necessary conditions for People's Education? How do we ensure that People's Education is a true force for liberation, democracy, and equality?

Before attempting to answer that question it might be analytically useful to distinguish between the needs of an educational strategy which is part of the struggle for liberation, and the necessary characteristics of an *educational system in post-apartheid society* that is to be an expression of the politics of 'People's Power'.

It is not possible or desirable to distinguish too clearly between the requirements of *an educational strategy to achieve liberation*, and an *educational system to be implemented in post-apartheid society*. Yet this distinction might be useful for the purposes of this present account which wishes to consider the necessary conditions for a post-liberation educational dispensation that will of necessity be a central aspect of state policy rather than something based on Freire's ideas of an education that challenged the dominant ideology of the society.

The essential features of People's Education, as outlined during various NECC congresses during 1985–6 are as follows:

> The broad *goals* of People's Education are the setting up of a 'free, compulsory, unitary, non-racial and democratic system of education' relevant to the establishment of a unitary, non-racial government 'for all sections of our people', and so organised that it allows students, parents, teachers, and workers 'to participate actively in the initiation and management of people's education in all its forms'. The *values* to be promoted in People's Education would be 'democracy, non-racialism, collective work and active participation'. The educational objectives, to be reached through the stimulation of critical and creative thinking, analysis and working methods, are
>
> * the elimination of illiteracy, ignorance, capitalist norms of competition, individualism, stunted intellectual development and exploitation;
> * to enable 'the oppressed to understand the evils of the apartheid system' and to prepare them 'for participation in a non-racial, democratic South Africa';
> * to equip and train 'all sectors of our people to participate actively and creatively in the struggle to attain people's power in order to establish a non-racial, democratic South Africa'.
>
> (Hartshorne 1986)

In sum, 'People's Education means education at the service of the people as a whole, education that liberates, education that puts people in command of their lives'. (NECC 1986: 24) 'People's Education has become the struggle of the whole community.' (NECC 1986: 20)

Clearly in the discussion so far regarding the nature of People's Education a great deal depends upon what is meant by the term 'People', or 'Community', or 'National'.

What is taken for granted in the current discourse about People's Education is that the call for a national liberation struggle automatically implies that power is to be placed in the hands of the people. Such an assumption does little to contribute to our debate about the nature of a future educational strategy beyond asserting that there is a need for an end to colonial education or the schooling of apartheid. The claim being made amounts to an appeal for individual rights, for an end to racism in education, and for equality of opportunity in education. It amounts to an appeal for mass education in the familiar form in which it is found in the northern industrialized world – in the tradition of calls for educational reform throughout the last century. In these terms the call for People's Education is simply another way of expressing the original liberal call for schooling based on the tenets of the UN Declaration of Human Rights. In South Africa it often looks like a simple demand for an extension to all citizens of the present system enjoyed by whites.

In short, such a call ignores the massive evidence available that mass education strategies in capitalist society do not necessarily empower the people, nor do they dramatically increase equality, nor do they work to increase the chances for working-class children in the employment market. On the contrary, much of the evidence suggests that mass education under capitalism acts as a mechanism of political and ideological control, and does not materially alter the dominance of liberal capitalist values and middle-class interests.

If People's Education is to ensure that education is not only to put an end to the politics of racism in education, but is to be instrumental also in creating a more just society by eliminating injustices based on class, this will entail moving beyond the common formula for mass education to an understanding of how reform in education is related to a fundamental redistribution of power, wealth, and privilege in society. It will be necessary also to explore how power is to be effectively devolved to local levels, how 'people's knowledge' is to come to inform the curriculum, and how critical thinking can be advanced in the school context. It is difficult to conceive how such fundamental changes could be achieved within the framework of current common sense assumptions about educational reform.

An education system which aims to encourage maximum freedom and to be 'an expression of the will of the people' will remain a rhetorical ideal unless it forms part of a broader programme of popular liberation, and places the politics of people's schooling within the context of the perpetuation of capitalist hegemony in politics, economics, and ideology.

If we are indeed seeking educational policies 'which will advance the broad mass of students not just the select few' (NECC 1986: 25), we will need to look beyond the classic formulas for mass schooling in capitalist society or the conventions of educational aid and planning embodied in such documents as the World Bank Education Sector Policy Paper (1981). These kinds of recipes still remain unthought out, behind the radical rhetoric of 'People's Education'. But if we are completely to abandon Bantu Education in favour of People's Education, we urgently need to explore an agenda of debate, research, and experimentation that takes us beyond these classic formulas of liberal educational provision in capitalist society to some form of socialist alternative. At present there is little sign of such an initiative, which may mean that post-colonial education in South Africa will lose its present 'colour coding' but not many of the other features that connect it to mass education in other capitalist societies.

NOTES

1. The use of these terms merely follows popular usage in South Africa, and should not be taken to assume that the author agrees with this state-imposed racial categorization of the population.
2. Bantu Education formally legislated that educational provision be differentiated in a variety of ways along racial lines.

REFERENCES

Education

Atkinson, N. (1978) *Teaching South Africans: A History of Educational Policy in South Africa*, Salisbury: University of Zimbabwe: Faculty of Education.

Beard, P. N. G. and Morrow, W. E. (1981) *Problems of Pedagogics*, Durban: Butterworths.

Brooks, A. and Brickhill, J. (1980) *Whirlwind Before the Storm: The Origins and Development of the Uprising in SOWETO and the rest of South Africa from June to December 1976*, London: International Defence Aid.

Buckland, P. (1983) *Education Policy and Reform in South Africa*, Cape Town: University of Cape Town.

Christie, P. (1985) *The Right to Learn*, Johannesburg: Ravan Press.

Dean, E. *et al.* (1983) *History in Black and White – an Analysis of South African School History Textbooks*, Paris: UNESCO.

Hirson, B. (1979) *Year of Fire, Year of Ash: The SOWETO Revolt* 2nd edn, London.

Horrell, M. (1968) *Bantu Education to 1968*, Johannesburg: SAIRR.

Kallaway, P. (Ed.) (1984) *Apartheid and Education*, Johannesburg: Ravan Press.

Kallaway, P. *et al.* (1986) *A Bibliography of Education for Black South Africans*, University of Cape Town School of Education, Education Policy Unit.

Malherbe, E. G. (1924) *Education in South Africa*, PhD Thesis, Teachers College, Columbia, New York.

Mbere, A. M. (1979) 'An analysis of the association between Bantu Education and Christian Nationalism: A study of the role of ideology in education', Ed. D. Harvard (Ann Arbor, UMI).

NECC (1986) 'People's Education for People's Power'. Address by Zwelake Sesulu to the Second Consultative Conference of the National Education Crisis Committee, Durban.

Rose, B. and Tumner, R. (1975) *Documents in South African Education*, Johannesburg: A. D. Donker.

Shingler, J. D. (1973) 'Education and the political order in South Africa 1902–1981', Ph.D. Yale, Ann Arbor, UMI.

Tabata, I. D. (1959) *Education for Barbarism*, Durban: United Movement of South Africa.

Troupe, F. (1976–7) *Forbidden Pastures: Education under Apartheid*, London: International Defence Aid.

General

Adam, H. (1971) *Modernising Racial Domination*.

Hartshorne, K. (1986) 'Post-apartheid education', unpublished paper, University of Cape Town.

Johnstone, R. (1970) 'White prosperity and white supremacy in South Africa today', *African Affairs*: 69.

Lodge, T. (1984) *African Politics in South Africa since 1945*, Johannesburg: Ravan Press.

Nolutshungu, S. (1983) *Changing South Africa*, Cape Town: David Philip.

Saul, J. and Gelb, S. (1981) 'The crisis in South Africa: class defence, class revolution', *Monthly Review* 33, 3, July-August.

Yudelman, D. (1983) *The Emergence of Modern South Africa*, Cape Town: David Philip.

2.10

EDUCATIONAL TRANSITION AND REFORM: THE STATUS OF DEWEY IN CONTEMPORARY SCHOOLS

WELLFORD WILMS

Integrating practical experience with classroom studies has long been regarded by some educators as a panacea for a host of educational problems such as increasing student interest in school, and stemming dropouts, while providing a stimulus for learning. Advocates maintain that by combining theory with practice, students see connections between their studies and the larger community, and develop abstract principles from practical application. Thus, according to this view, students find new meaning in their classwork, developing internal control and motivation, and developing the ability to make reasoned, independent judgements. This view took hold in the twentieth century, when a leading American educator, John Dewey, vigorously promoted 'experience-based education', an idea that laid the philosophical foundations for both the progressive education and the vocational education movements.

However, despite its pedagogical promise, integrating theory and practice seems to be largely absent from most American schools. Instead, education in elementary and secondary schools appears to place a high priority on ensuring that students master large bodies of factual material, most of which is quite remote from students' own lives and interests. To test this hypothesis, 30 UCLA students who were studying to become teachers, and I, investigated 25 Los Angeles high schools to see if John Dewey's philosophical imprint could be found in modern classrooms. This chapter elaborates on the theory behind Dewey's ideas, and reports the findings. The chapter concludes with a discussion of the implications of these findings for improving educational policy and teaching.

DEVELOPMENT OF THE IDEA

Experience is a living part of society and culture, which makes it difficult to grasp and fit into the structure of organized schooling. Because it goes beyond the boundaries of most schools' concerns, integrating experience with education necessarily means broadening the focus of education itself, which has generated debate for centuries. For example, Socrates' approach to education (now known as the 'Socratic method') held that learning begins with the self, not with external knowledge. Within this concept of the self as the initiator of the learning process lies a basic tenet of experiential learning. Questions are both raised and answered through experience in a give-and-take between the individual and his or her environment. In contrast to Aristotelians, who believed that education should be based on fact and logic external to the student, this early Greek approach to learning was student-centred. Knowledge, or facts, were secondary, and useful only in so far as they aided the student's inquiry.

Experience played a major educational role as Europe moved out of medieval time and into the modern world. Houle (1976) argues that key forms of advanced learning were mostly experiential. These included apprenticeship training carried out by the craft guilds; the chivalric system of education, where important skills, knowledge, and attitudes were gained in the courtyard, the tourney-ground, the forest, and the battlefield; and finally, the self-directed study of priests, kings, and scholars carried out in monasteries, courts, and private libraries.

The core of these activities was learning by doing – some with more supervision than others; and today the apprenticeship concept is still used as a means to teach occupational skills. Combining on-the-job training with supervision from a knowledgeable craftsman was sound educational methodology and the forerunner to individual instruction.

It was John Amos Comenius who in the seventeenth century observed that knowledge should grow from the roots up; that it must be based on childrens' own opinions and own examination; that less should be learned from books and more from experience (Drake 1967). Educators who subscribed to this point of view came to be called 'Realists'. They believed that sense perception should be at the core of learning. Accordingly, activities that emphasized sensation were part of the active process of learning. Later, Rousseau argued that formal schooling corrupted the natural goodness inherent in man. In his major work, *Emile*, Rousseau outlined the beginning of a more humanistic and progressive educational philosophy that emphasized experience with nature, and which followed the natural tendencies of the child (Drake 1967). *Emile* captured the joy and excitement that is apparent in learning through discovery and generated debate on the process of education and the role experience should play in it. Thus, the seventeenth and eighteenth centuries laid the foundation for many of today's educational beliefs.

In the early nineteenth century, Friedrich Froebel, who had been heavily influenced by the earlier 'Realists', developed a set of educational principles that can be easily seen in contemporary progressive education programmes. According to Froebel, students' self-activity promoted development; unbroken continuity helped ensure the acquisition of correct knowledge; creativeness ensured the assimilation of knowledge and fostered the growth of power and skill acquisition. Well-organized physical activity would develop the body (Bowen 1893:180-1).

It was only a matter of time before these new educational ideas found their way to the United States. Here they profoundly influenced Francis Parker (considered by many to be the true father of progressive education), William James, William Kilpatrick, Alfred Whitehead, and John Dewey, as they grappled with the way in which experience should be integrated with classroom instruction. Whitehead and Dewey added new dimensions in grasping the elusive teaching power of experience. Whitehead, in the *Aims of education* (1929) conceived of experience as a way of keeping knowledge alive, thus preventing it from becoming inert. This, according to Whitehead, is *the* central problem of all education. Above all, Dewey and Whitehead each felt that education was synonymous with self-discovery.

But there is little doubt that while Whitehead was an important figure in education, John Dewey was probably the most influential writer on the role of experience in learning. In *Experience and Education* (1938), Dewey asked:

What is the proper relationship between subject matter and experience?
How can freedom be used to foster learning?
How many students lose the impulse to continue learning because of negative experiences in school?
Why should students acquire information if they are unable to extract meaning from future experience?

Trying to answer these and other questions led Dewey to define an educational experience as one that has at least three characteristics. First, an educational experience should promote personal growth and move students toward new experiences. Second, an educative experience should cause the learner constantly to examine, evaluate, and modify his or her inner beliefs as a result of conflicts presented by external events. Third, despite its often provocative nature, experience should be enjoyable so that learners continue learning and are not discouraged.

In Dewey's analysis, the problem lay not so much in the fact that most students lacked experience, but rather the experiences they had were miseducative. By 'miseducative' Dewey meant experiences that arrested or distorted students' growth, or inhibited their willingness to continue learning.

Although Whitehead's and Dewey's themes were never fully embraced by most educational practitioners, they were nevertheless profoundly important. Today, their lasting influence can be seen in the work of more modern developmentalists including Kohlberg and Mayer (1972), Schaefer-Simmern (1949), Erikson (1968), and others.

CAN DEWEY BE FOUND IN THE CLASSROOM?

It was with this background in mind that I recently taught a class in UCLA's Teacher Education Laboratory called 'Can You Find Dewey in the Classroom?' to see if we could find evidence of John Dewey's educational philosophy in a systematic study of Los Angeles junior and senior high schools. The investigators were 30 bright student-teachers who were enrolled in UCLA's Graduate School of Education where they were working for their teaching credential. Most were recent UCLA graduates, with bachelors' degrees in English, mathematics, the sciences, or humanities. In their teacher education programme, students spent three academic terms combining half-days of observation and teaching with classroom studies. They were assigned to hand-picked Los Angeles schools that were selected to give students experience with superior master-teachers in a variety of socioeconomic and racial settings. By most accounts, these schools represented some of the best educational practice available in greater Los Angeles.

In the first few weeks of class we read and discussed Whitehead's *Aims of Education*, and Dewey's *Experience and Education*, though for the sake of efficiency, we focused most attention on Dewey. Early in the discussions, it became clear that some of the student-teachers held the view that teaching was little more than transmitting organized material to students to develop their academic 'skills'. However, Dewey's ideas seemed to resonate with most students, though many remained sceptical about the feasibility of implementing them in modern classrooms. Through group discussion, students culled Dewey's guiding principles from *Experience and Education*, and 'operationalized' them, by defining them in ways that would allow their observation in the classroom. Three chief principles emerged.

First, some educationally purposeful activities drawn from outside the classroom should be present in day-to-day classroom instruction, and students should be actively involved in them. Second, evidence of continuity and progression of the subject under study should be apparent. For example, does the master-teacher draw on past lessons or experiences that hold interest for students to help them see connections between one lesson and another? Does the organization of the course and students' involvement in it lead them naturally from one issue to another? Are students engaged in issues from the larger community in ways that help them understand abstract principles? Third, evidence of interaction between students' inner thoughts and beliefs and external events should be observable. Are students fully engaged in the lesson and participating actively in their learning? Do they appear to reflect on their experiences and draw connections between them and the subject matter? Can they transfer classroom learning to their own lives?

These and other questions were formed into a set of questionnaires to capture classroom behaviour that would indicate the presence or absence of Dewey's educational philosophy. The 30 student-teachers systematically observed their master-teachers during one class period in each of the 25 host high schools. Student-teachers were familiar with their master-teachers' classrooms, and were thus able to confirm the generalizability of their observations to other periods and days. Additionally, they randomly chose five students from each class, for a total of 150 student respondents, to complete an abbreviated version of the questionnaire. Student-teachers were asked to reflect on their observations and write a paper on their findings and conclusions. Results from the questionnaires were entered in the UCLA computer, analysed using simple cross-tabulations, and were presented to the student-teachers for discussion the following week.

A LITTLE DEWEY SLIPS IN THE BACK DOOR

The schools' profile conformed to the larger universe of public schools in Los Angeles. The average sampled school enrolled nearly 2,000 students, and classes included social studies, science, maths, music, and English. About half of the schools were in urban Los Angeles, while the other half were located in suburbs. Nearly two thirds of the schools were 'receiver schools', meaning that students were bused to them to achieve racial balance. On average, class size ranged from 25 to 30 students. Six in ten classes offered the 'standard' academic fare, whereas nearly three in ten were 'advanced', indicating those students who were most likely college-bound. Thirteen per cent of the classes observed were 'remedial', populated by students who did not do well in the standard programme.

Master-teachers' years of teaching experience ranged from a low of five years to a high of forty. On average, master-teachers had close to twenty years of teaching experience.

Most student-teachers rated their master-teachers favourably. Nearly half (49 per cent) said their master-teachers were 'very effective' as mentors, and 80 per cent characterized their relationships with their master-teachers in positive terms.

Student-teachers observed whether or not their master-teachers provided some form of purposeful activity in their lessons, and whether or not such activity appeared to help integrate other subject matter with the classroom studies. Surprisingly, in only nine per cent of the classrooms, student-teachers reported their master-teachers 'frequently' integrated their lessons with such activity. Slightly more than half (53 per cent) reported the occurrence 'rarely or never'. In a few cases, classroom activities included truly creative projects like writing poetry that drew on imagery, mythology, literature, and students' own experience. But more often, activities were of a mundane variety like filling out workbook assignments or practising with musical instruments for a presentation. One student-teacher observed:

> After the master-teacher had demonstrated how to work a few problems, students were given a ditto on which they were to work out a set of problems, just like those the master-teacher had just done. There was absolutely no self-discovery or thought involved. Students were just passive learners.

Student-teachers noted that most master-teachers also failed to integrate theory and practice, or issues of the larger community with the classroom lesson. Student-teachers also observed the degree to which class activity was student-directed, and reported that in most cases activities were directed by the teacher. Though the vast majority of the student-teachers reported that students appeared to understand the purpose of the activity (83 per cent) when it was present, most observers agreed this key element of Dewey's philosophy was not a regular part of classroom instruction. One student-teacher summed up others' views as she wrote:

> Dewey's principles seem alien to the everyday operation of this class. Students' interests are just not engaged. Class is a drudgery for both the teacher and student.

Student-teachers also investigated the extent to which the master-teachers ensured continuity between lessons, and if they made efforts to connect issues raised in class to students' interests and daily lives. While more than half (54 per cent) of the master-teachers provided continuity between classes, only 27 per cent of the master-teachers were observed taking steps to relate class issues to students' daily lives. One student-teacher in music said:

> The true purpose of instrumental music should be to provide students with an expressive experience. But, playing the right notes becomes the main purpose for my master-teacher. Music can and should be related to other fields, but I have never observed connections being made in my master-teacher's classroom. He honestly isn't aware that there are other aspects to music than pushing down the keys and playing the right notes.

Student observers said that the apparent lack of connectedness between classroom studies and students' lives probably accounts for many students' lack of interest in their studies and the resulting 'pandemonium', 'inattention', and 'mischief', leading to the need for the imposition of teacher control. As one student noted:

> ... all students have interests. The failure of education is its failure to engage them. This failure, rather than any evil in the nature of children, leads to the lack of control among students. Is it any wonder that the teacher is grim and unenthusiastic?

Responses from the 150 sampled students confirmed the finding that Dewey's educational philosophy appeared to be honoured more in the breach than observed in practice. According to these students, classroom learning appears to stand alone, having little relationship to their lives, other studies, or the larger community. More than a quarter of the students (29 per cent) said they were 'not at all interested' in their class, and a further 59 per cent answered that they were only 'somewhat' interested. Students' lack of interest no doubt stemmed in part from their inability to relate classroom studies to their own lives. Eighty-two per cent said they found no connections between their lessons and their lives or the larger community. None reported being able to transfer learning from one class to another. In the face of soaring student dropout rates, it came as little surprise that nearly two thirds of the students reported that their classes failed to interest them to continue their education.

In describing his master-teacher's classroom, one student-teacher captured the dynamics that characterize many American classrooms:

> After the tardy bell rings, the master-teacher gives the students a vocabulary test to settle them down. He does this every morning without fail. He says that it's important to begin the class with a quiet activity to get the students under control. After the students finish, the lecture for the day begins. Sometimes he uses prerecorded lectures that run the entire period. He often ignores raised hands, leaving students confused and frustrated. After the lecture, students do workbook exercises. 'It's good to have them busy right up to when the bell rings,' the master-teacher explained.
>
> Dewey would cringe. There was no discovery, no stimulation, no exploration. The zest to learn, participate, discover and explore are clearly absent in room F-116. Dewey is not there, but that doesn't mean that some learning doesn't take place. It is possible that on occasion, a little Dewey slips in the back door, and when he does, the students are relieved of the endless routine that they have been trained to endure.

WHAT HAPPENED TO DEWEY?

The virtual absence of the stream of educational philosophy from Socrates to Dewey in these classrooms raises important questions about its failure to endure. Because the Deweyan concept has been so influential, and because its educational promise has been so widely recognized, it is important to explore plausible reasons that may account for its absence in these American schools.

In discussing their findings, the UCLA student-teachers reasoned that classroom education frequently becomes detached from students' interests and the larger community because of a self-reinforcing cycle of circumstances that seems to characterize American education. First, curricula are developed to ensure that students acquire specified information. Typically, curricula are imposed from the top down, and are increasingly driven by tests as the USA grapples with educational reform – particularly in academically-oriented classrooms. Consequently, teachers become responsible for ensuring that students get through large amounts of abstract information on which they are routinely tested. It is little wonder that students lose interest. One student-teacher reported that his master-teacher admonished him for attempting to engage students' interests. 'I looked at my class and saw boredom.' 'Just give them information,' his master-teacher said, 'You're not in the entertainment business.'

Second, most student-teachers said they felt that teachers were paid too little and worked too hard, with few opportunities for professional advancement. 'A teacher's chief job is to get through the subject matter. Beyond that, everything else is extra,' observed one student-teacher. 'There are plenty of barriers to being creative in the classroom, and few incentives.' Another student-teacher noted:

> To give students the right kind of educational experience takes more effort than most teachers are willing to give. Mr Brown's plans are already drawn up. He has stacks of his 30-page syllabus just waiting.

It comes as no surprise that students quickly lose interest in classroom learning that has little or no value for them. The need to impose classroom order is a natural consequence, taking the place of order that would otherwise come from students who are truly interested and engaged in their studies. One student-teacher wrote:

> The school isn't a group or community, held together by participation in common, meaningful activities. Their absence invites direct intervention by the teacher, who keeps order – literally.

Many student-teachers described their classrooms as 'prisons', 'dictatorships', and 'police states'.

It is within these realities of abstract curricula, designed to advance some students to higher education while weeding out the less academically-inclined with standardized tests, that uninterested students learn to play the game of school. And, as one student-teacher observed, the results are negative:

> Academically advanced classes faithfully mirror society. We may produce good test-takers, but we do not produce good learners; we produce people who work for a specific reward. Most students want that which is easiest and familiar; they have learned how to work within the system.

In the end, according to the UCLA student-teachers' analysis, both students and teachers lose. One young woman said:

> On the one hand, most teachers are afraid to let students have any control. On the other, most students fear having to take responsibility and be in control.

What is left is an educational system in which authority for educational decisions is increasingly centralized to maintain classroom order with the effect of alienating both teachers and students. As a result of this impersonal control, education has witnessed a slow death of ideas in teaching – it is little wonder that education is rarely broadened to accommodate practical experience. Too often, by the time teachers get to the classroom, the creative thinking has been done for them. Salaries, working conditions, and class size have been negotiated elsewhere; curricula have been established by school boards; content has been specified by subject-matter experts; disciplinary procedures have been prescribed by the courts.

Anyone who has had the good fortune to encounter a truly remarkable teacher would probably agree that the teacher found creative ways to engage students' interests and made connections between their studies and the community around them. Yet increasingly large numbers of teachers are leaving the profession because of the lack of opportunity to breathe life into the deadening classroom routine. According to the US Census Bureau, about nine per cent of the national teaching force leaves each year. Most studies agree that within the first few years of teaching, 40 to 50 per cent of all new teachers leave. A recent study done for the Montgomery County School District (Commission 1987), which is regarded as one of the finest public school districts in the nation, revealed that 40 per cent of its new teachers left within the first three years, and that many of them left the profession entirely. The report pointed to 'top-down bureaucratic control' as a chief cause of teachers failing to enter the career, or leaving in mid-career. One discouraged teacher was reported to say, 'I'm just a drone in the system'. The report observes:

> Decisions that are made far removed from the classroom can also result in unrealistic expectations, as well as frustration and cynicism, for both administrators and teachers. Teachers feel some curricula are paced too fast for many

students. They feel they must push kids from objective to objective, regardless
of retention, to meet the standards that have been set.

(Commission 1987: 46)

In its chief recommendation, the Commission echoed Whitehead, who half
a century earlier warned that unless education helped students see the woods
by means of the trees, and unless school reform worked from the schoolhouse
level up, education would lurch from one 'dung-hill of inert ideas to another'
(Whitehead 1929: 25). The Commission recommended that teachers must
become managers of learning, and not drones or assembly-line workers. It
called for giving teachers 'breathing room' to do their jobs, noting:

> This will require recognition that children are not educated by directives from
> above, comforting as the belicf might be. We must trust our teachers, and
> restructure the schools and the way we deal with the schools, to enhance, not
> frustrate their efforts.

(Commission 1987: 47)

While it is impossible to generalize to all American schools on the basis
of the observations from 25 Los Angeles high schools, the evidence dces,
nevertheless, fit into an emerging pattern. In his epic study of American
schooling, Goodlad (1984) revealed how little things had changed over the
past century. As in the nineteenth century when students merely recited
lessons, students in many modern American schools endure years of schooling
that may touch their real interests only marginally. Sirotnik (1981) also found
the same behaviour as did the UCLA student-teachers – that teachers spent
about half of the class time talking to students, but less than one per cent of
the time was devoted to asking open questions that would demand more than
a simple recall of information.

It should be noted that this pattern is found in other industrialized nations
as well. For example, Watts and his colleagues in Great Britain (1983) show
that few educational programmes rooted in experiences outside the conventional classroom survive and prosper. While Watts lays some of the blame at
the feet of immature students and uninterested employers (who provide work
experience), he mainly blames teachers and school administrators who allow
little deviation from formal instruction. According to Watts, while most educators fail to embrace experience as a legitimate part of education, most
students like it. Though his data are limited, some students are motivated by
their experiences to work harder in school. Others think they learned more
outside school than in it. One student is quoted as saying, 'To be quite honest
I think I learned more in those two weeks of work experience than in the three
years at school' (Watts 1983: 88). Other studies noted by Watts reveal that
nearly two thirds of students in work experience programmes became keener
to leave school, perhaps because they felt a sense of power over their own

lives as they assumed, at least temporarily, adult roles. Said one student, 'You feel how big you are, then you've got to shrink back doon (*sic*) into school size' (Watts 1983: 91).

What seems clear is that it is the cultural expectations of formal schooling in the US, as well as in most other industrialized nations, that account for its rigid nature. In this conception, traditional schools pass along the dominant culture. Dewey and others nearly a century ago saw how traditional schools were rationally organized to achieve their purposes – transmitting subject matter, rules, or moral conduct, and skills that were defined by earlier generations. This purpose explains why schools are set off from the larger community and organized systematically to move students through predetermined bodies of information. Classwork is made up of highly structured information, and students' progress is measured in clock-hour credits and examination scores. Most often, structured classwork is taught as a finished product, thus requiring little original thinking, but rather rewarding students' abilities to absorb, store, and recall it. To absorb and store structured information effectively, students naturally develop learning styles that are characterized by passivity and docility.

Subject matter in American public schools is taught by teachers who have themselves been trained and qualified in the same way. Subject areas are formalized in lesson plans that break down subject matter into units with statements of objectives of what is to be learned and how. Traditional schools, which were heavily influenced by the corporate model, place a high value on efficiency. To achieve necessary efficiencies in transmitting the culture, its skills, and moral codes to students, traditional schools must exert control over students and their learning. Classrooms of Dewey's era, as well as those of today, are characterized by students sitting facing the teacher to receive information. As I have already noted, the purpose of such learning is determined by authorities, distant from the schoolhouse and from the students' own interests.

Thus, it is also not surprising to find education that is rooted in students' own experience failing to achieve its full educational potential in traditional schools. Studies of the failures of the American alternative schools of the 1960s and early 1970s help describe why traditional schools may be inhospitable hosts for education that is oriented to students' experience (Deal 1975). Deal pointed out how traditional schools were unable to cope with new organizational problems produced by new authority patterns and by the alternative educational processes that were messy and hard to control. For example, alternative school programmes, like educational programmes based on experience, encompass a much larger group in the learning and teaching process. Unlike teaching in the traditional school, teachers are no longer the only ones in control. Rather, supervisors and off-campus mentors become equally important teachers, which not only dilutes teachers' control but requires added work in co-ordinating the selection and training of supervisors and off-campus mentors.

Programmes that integrate practical experience with classroom studies dramatically change the substance of what is learned. In these programmes, students' education is no longer limited to concepts that can be reflected in textbooks and reduced to units that can be tallied up in lesson plans and converted to clock-hour credits. Instead, students' learning becomes highly individualistic, dependent on discovery. Also, such individualistic education eludes easy measurement and evaluation, which are the chief requirements for allocating resources in an efficient system.

Programmes rooted in experience change the reasons for learning. Students' own intrinsic motives take priority, and shifting the locus of motivation for learning from school authorities to students upsets the sequence in which learning takes place. Instead of teachers 'delivering' predigested information to students, students learn more from their own experiences – a process in which teachers act more as guides and mentors than as authorities. Learning becomes redefined as a process of development that works from the inside out, rather than from the top down.

In conclusion, I think a primary reason that traditional schools appear to have such difficulty in truly embracing experience is because their purposes are culturally defined according to an unchanging conception of education. Traditional schools, by and large, treat education as a systematic process of inculcating students in externally defined bodies of information that demand the imposition of coercive order. In contrast, programmes that are based on students' experience treat education as a developmental process in which the students' own experience becomes a primary locus of motivation and learning. So long as the traditional school's purpose remains simply to transmit the culture, and not to rediscover and renew its meaning with each generation, efficiency and external control will probably continue to characterize its educational approach.

Though policy makers and educational authorities of the 1960s assumed that changing schools' organizational incentives through federal grants for experiments would clear the way for progressive change, successes have been modest at best, as the structure of schools has proved remarkably resistant to change. More important, there appears to have been no broad-based social mandate for substantially changing the traditional school model. To the extent that there is any social mandate for educational change today, it appears to be one of tightening up the control on the information students receive and enforcing the social and moral order. It seems likely that for the foreseeable future the social mandate for education will be to continue to transmit the culture, morals, and skills from the top down.

Thus, Dewey's position of nearly half a century ago, that the full potential of learning through experience can be brought forward only with a well thought-out theory of experience, still holds true. But, without a social consensus about the purposes and process of education, any such movement will remain abstract and only theoretical. It seems most likely that until such a change is mandated by society, most schools will probably continue to respond to the predominant social mandate to serve their educational purposes in the same way.

REFERENCES

Bowen, H. C. (1893) *Froebel*, New York: Charles Scribner.

Commission on Excellence in Teaching (1987) *Attracting, Keeping, and Enabling Excellent Teachers*, Rockville: Montgomery County Board of Education.

Deal, Terrence (1975) 'An organizational explanation of the failure of alternative secondary schools', *Educational Research*, 4,4:10–16.

Dewey, John (1938) *Experience and Education*, New York: Collier Books.

Drake, W. (1967) *Intellectual Foundations of Modern Education*, Columbus: Merrill Books.

Erikson, E. (1968) *Identity, Youth and Crisis*, New York: W. W. Norton Co.

Goodlad, John (1984) *A Place Called School*, New York: McGraw Hill.

Houle, C. (1976) 'Deep traditions of experiential learning', in M. Keeton (Ed.) *Experiential Learning*, San Francisco: Jossey-Bass.

Kohlberg, L. and Mayer, R. (1972) 'Development as the aim of education', *Harvard Educational Review*, 42,4.

Schaefer-Simmern, Henry (1949) *The Unfolding of Artistic Activity*, Berkeley: University of California Press.

Watts, A. G. (Ed.) (1983) *Work Experience and Schools*, London: Heinemann.

Whitehead, A. (1929) *The Aims of Education*, New York: Macmillan Company.

3. EDUCATION BEYOND SCHOOL

3.0

INTRODUCTION: EDUCATION BEYOND SCHOOL

KEITH PERCY

The ten chapters of this section are linked pragmatically. They all deal with topics or themes from outside the period of compulsory full-time education required for all children and young people by the law of the land. In Great Britain this period of initial education applies to the ages five to sixteen years. Thus, there is no compulsion to attend pre-school education before the age of five, and its provision (and the nature of that provision) varies across the country. It is increasingly the case, but by no means universal, nor yet compulsory, for young people between the ages of 16 and 19 who have left school to continue with different forms of education, often vocationally relevant. As the chapter by Haffenden suggests, this phenomenon is not unrelated to the level of youth unemployment. Participation by young adults (aged about 18–21) in higher education has significantly increased in the last twenty years and, as Brennan demonstrates in his chapter, the growth has been particularly marked in the non-university sector of polytechnics and colleges. But it remains only a relatively small proportion of this age group who enter higher education, and, despite the steady increase in enrolments of older, mature, students, it is unusual for an older adult to become a degree student. As for the broader and more varied expanses of what is variously called adult, continuing, community, recurrent, or lifelong education in Great Britain, adults participate in a great range of often ill-resourced and discontinuous provision. Such participation is always a minority interest and takes place in varying proportions according to such social indicators as age, sex, social class, race, and domicile. In chapter 3.4, Percy indicates that much systematic adult learning can be found outside the classes and courses of formal providers of adult education such as colleges and local education authorities but, in arguing this, he extends the scope of this section of the *Handbook* to, and perhaps beyond, the discernible educational horizon.

Formally, the ten chapters which follow are divided thus: one, by Smith, on pre-school education; two, by Brennan and Woodhall, on higher education; the remainder, seven in total, on adult and continuing education. Such formal divisions are too absolute, however. The discussion by Smith of parent education is echoed – from a very different perspective – in the chapter by Legge. When Brennan indicates the future of higher education to be with the development of part-time, modular, discontinuous units of study 'tailor-made to meet the needs and interests of the individual student at different points in his or her life', the overlap between these sentiments and the trends and philosophies identified in most of the chapters on adult and continuing education which follow is complete. When Duke and Ward illustrate that the debate on what constitutes education, and what training, and how each should be resourced, is alive and active in adult and continuing education, they cover ground which is being simultaneously turned over in British higher education.

Of course, the ten chapters of this section of the *Handbook* are not comprehensive; they do not cover the field, raise all the relevant issues, stake out all the necessary territory. They are examples, tasters, indicators of some of the relevant areas of study and debate in educational ideas and practices beyond school. One article cannot do justice to the full complement of research and practice in pre-school education, and the article by Smith attempts to delineate only one important aspect. The section could logically have included chapters on learning and teaching in higher education, on the development of the higher education curriculum, and on priorities in access. There are only glancing references (for example, in the chapters by Brennan and Duke) to the large and diverse sector of post-school education known in Great Britain as further education. Colleges of Further Education, in their best forms, touch both higher education on the one hand, and the more general forms of adult education on the other. Their prospectuses contain technical, vocational, and general courses of all kinds; their courses are full and part-time, day and evening; their students of all ages from 16 to what Glendenning calls 'the third age'. Similarly, in the chapters on adult and continuing education, there is little discussion of so-called 'mainstream' non-vocational education for adults, an area which has traditionally been a major concern of many local authority, voluntary, and university providers.

It is impossible to read the chapters which follow without being struck by their references – despite the disparate nature of their content and concerns – to the same external influences, causes, and pressures. It is quite clear that if this *Handbook* had been published fifteen years ago, in the mid-1970s, the chapters on 'education beyond school' would have been startlingly different. There have been marked changes in policy and practice in all sectors, and few of them have anything to do with advances in systematic knowledge. Demography looms large over each chapter. In the 1990s, there will be fewer children, fewer 18–21-year-olds available for higher education, and more elderly people, particularly 'older' elderly people. Thus, educational institutions perceive themselves as threatened or challenged; resources seem likely variously to be more available, more stretched, or more likely to be diverted from or to areas of interest or benefit. Self-evidently, the performance of the British economy and the size of the Gross National Product provide a backcloth for every chapter in this section. Equally important are the perceptions of the economy which the government of the day has and its perceptions of the roles of education and training (of different kinds) in strengthening and supporting that economy. The interventionist and centralist tendencies of the policies of British governments since 1975 are a marked theme of all the chapters concerned with post-compulsory education which follow. The paymaster's opinions of different aspects of further, adult, and higher education have become crucially important; government departments have become radical and confident interventionists eager to re-shape and re-structure where they see fit. Well-resourced central initiatives have come to dominate the field – the Adult Training Strategy of the MSC (Manpower Services Commission – renamed the Department of Employment Training Agency in Autumn 1988) and the DES's REPLAN and PICKUP initiatives are among those in adult and continuing education mentioned in the chapters following; the many directives and decisions of the University Grants Committee and the National Advisory Body have similarly changed the shape of higher education. It is too early yet adequately to evaluate all of this rapid change. One test, however, must be the extent to which it has stemmed from knowledge rather than prejudice.

In the first chapter, on pre-school education, Smith concludes that 'the debate has moved on' – there has been some systematic enquiry and conceptualization in the last decade and 'we can no longer ask large simplistic questions'. Compare this with the final chapter in the section, by Glendenning, who laments the lack of research and the absence of 'scientific data' in British educational gerontology. 'A clearer ground-plan' has yet to emerge, he says. These comments apply to all of the articles on adult and continuing education in the section. Hamilton writes of adult basic education as 'under-researched'; Duke reflects that the extent and effects of vocational education and training for adults are just not known; both Haffenden and Ward describe government sponsored developments in adult education practice and policy which surge ahead without being properly monitored. In British higher education – and this theme lies behind the chapters by both Brennan and Woodhall – the hunt for students, resources, cost-cuttings, and performance indicators and appraisals has concentrated the minds of academics and institutions wonderfully. However, these concerns are not quite the same as the broader and more leisurely interest of the 1960s and 1970s in reflecting upon, and researching into, student satisfaction, alternative curricula, and the nature of higher education. As Brennan implies, the notion that there is anything justifiably special or separate about education in a university is no longer part of public policy. If the orientation of Woodhall's chapter is correct, then students (and their parents) in Great Britain in the 1990s will come to bear a much higher proportion of the cost of their higher education experience; the phenomenon of living away from home (in the university or polytechnic residential 'community') will be much less common.

Such developments may, or may not, be an advance. If resources are released through shifts in allocation or through more efficient management then the issue is what use will be made of them – for example, to improve access for disadvantaged students, to promote curriculum reform, or to enhance student performance through student-centred learning and teaching methods. It is interesting that many of the articles in this section contain a rhetorical undertow of approval for non-didactic, non-pedagogical (i.e. more 'androgogical'), and more 'open' methods of teaching and learning. The received opinion is that adults learn best in different ways, and under different conditions, from children. Their experience, interests, and diversity should be respected, their confidence built or rebuilt, and curricula and teaching methods individualized and negotiated. It may well be so – although there is more advocacy here than proof. There are others who assert that 'good' teaching is the same whatever the age of the learner. What is interesting is that some of the authors in this section imply, through their advocacy, that good teaching is sometimes not present in educational situations beyond school.

This assembly of chapters in one section of the *Handbook* to deal with pre-school and post-school education is fortuitous in one important respect. It emphasizes that learning is not synonymous with children sitting in school classrooms. Learning, both formal and non-formal, is part of all stages of life: it is lifelong. It is not a life sentence, it is a life opportunity. At least, that is the ideal, but in Great Britain it is an ideal recognized neither in public policy nor in the public mind. Several of the authors in this section deplore what they perceive as a 'creeping vocationalism' in British post-compulsory education. They may be right, but it is not evident what is to bar its way. It is not clear that British educators have put together a coherent vision of what they can achieve in education beyond school. As Legge points out, work (whether paid or not) is one of the major status and life-style defining roles in adult life, and educators must relate to it. Indeed, what we must all feel towards in the 1990s is an over-arching concept of lifelong education which transcends divisions of education and training, which convinces the guardians of the public purse, and which enthuses fellow citizens with the belief that education beyond school is different from, perhaps better than, education within school, and is equally important.

3.1

PARENTS AND PRE-SCHOOL EDUCATION

TERESA SMITH

INTRODUCTION

This chapter sets out to review recent trends in research and policy on parents and pre-school education. What do we mean by parental involvement? Starting with the well-documented links between educational performance and potential in working class and middle class children, and parents' interest in their children's progress and aspirations for their future education and employment (for example Douglas 1964), the Plowden Committee's emphasis was on 'good practice' in home-school links as two-way information and communication between parents and teachers (Central Advisory Council for Education 1967; DES 1968; Young and McGeeney 1968). Contemporary interests focus more on 'parents as educators' and children as 'active learners' (Bruner 1980), and a more careful analysis of the definition – ranging from parents simply 'being there' at one end of the scale to a home-school 'partnership' based on 'reciprocity' at the other (Pugh and De'Ath 1987; Pugh et al. 1987; Wolfendale 1983).

However, any review of parental participation must be set in a wider context. What are the major issues of the 1980s in the pre-school field? Pessimism was widespread throughout the 1970s about the effectiveness of pre-school provision in breaking the 'cycle of disadvantage' and boosting children's educational progress. Both British and American early intervention programmes, after initial gains, seemed to result in 'wash out', dashing the hopes that pre-school attendance would narrow the gap in educational performance between the advantaged and the disadvantaged (Tizard 1974). However, others (for example Smith and James 1975; Woodhead 1985) have argued for more detailed examination of the different forms of pre-school experience and their effects; and the 1980s have seen both growing evidence as to long-term results, and also sharper questioning as to precisely what factors make such experience effective.

Lazar and Darlington's (1982) re-analysis and follow-up of twelve American programmes of the 1960s is widely accepted as the most robust evidence for long-term effectiveness. Children who had attended pre-school programmes were more likely to meet the basic requirements of schooling, and both they and their families were more likely to feel good about their progress and to have high hopes for the future. However, this evidence derives from 'special programmes' – carefully structured and implemented, although very varied. Can similar effects be achieved by 'ordinary' provision? New evidence from Britain (Osborn, Butler, and Morris 1984; Osborn and Milbank 1987) suggests that attendance at ordinary pre-school provision shows up in ten-year-olds' school performance; but the strongest effects were found for the least disadvantaged children who had attended small home playgroups, and the weakest for the most disadvantaged in local authority day nurseries, and the study has been criticized for failing to take adequate account of the influence of the home on children's performance. It is increasingly clear that different types of programme do have different effects. Both British and American research shows that different pre-school curriculum models produce different patterns of later behaviour: in one study, reception class children with different pre-school experiences had different expectations of work and play, different patterns of concentration, activity, and independence; in the American High/Scope follow-up studies, adolescents had different approaches to school and to social life, although apparently no significantly different long-term IQ or school achievement scores.

What is it, then, that makes provision effective? Although the quest for a 'magic ingredient' is attractive (whether 'curriculum' or 'parent involvement'), arguments of the 'either-or' variety are probably too simplistic. Following the general experience of 'wash out', initial explanations for changes later on in school drew on the notion of the 'sleeper effect'; but the recent research proposes a different model. Lazar and Darlington suggest a cycle of 'positive reinforcement', and connect this with the notion of 'active learning':

> Although we have little information at present on family processes and outcomes, it seems possible that mutual reinforcement processes occurred between the early education participants and their parents. Perhaps the children's participation in a program raised the mothers' hopes and expectations for their children . . . Perhaps children interpreted these parental attitudes as a belief in and support of their efforts, and it served to spur them on . . . the early education experience may change children from passive to active learners who begin to take the initiative in seeking information, help, and interaction with others. When this increased motivation to learn is met by a positive response at home and at school, long-term gains on outcome measures of cognitive development can result . . . Once set in motion, success tended to breed success . . .'
>
> (Lazar and Darlington 1982:63–4)

The interactional or transactional model is more fully developed by the

High/Scope research team (Berrueta-Clement *et al.* 1984). We have here the notion of positive interactions between child and family, between home and school/pre-school experience – a 'positive cycle' rather than the 'negative cycle' of disadvantage – a model which takes into account both motivation and cognitive development, and focuses on process as well as outcome.

As Woodhead (1985) comments, the transactional model takes us straight into the territory of the family, and

> the social processes which transform some children into motivated achievers, while others become disillusioned under-achievers. The implication is that in order to explain the effectiveness of pre-school education we may need to look not only at the characteristics of the programme and the population to whom it was applied, but also at the social context of family and school processes both during the period of intervention and during the later stages of education ...
>
> (Woodhead 1985:141)

Thus the major issue – the effectiveness of pre-school provision for children's educational achievement – requires us to examine the context of the family and the home for the pre-school child. This chapter charts the shifting definition of that relationship.

FROM 'GOOD PRACTICE' TO 'PARENTS AS PARTNERS'

The Plowden Committee was deeply interested in the close association between 'home and social circumstances and academic achievement'. Its conclusion from the national survey of parents to discover 'how much parents influence children's achievement at school and how their influence operates', was that more information for parents and better contact between home and school could provide the key to changing parents' attitudes towards their children's education. The post-Plowden orthodoxy has prompted a number of surveys of 'good practice', with questions such as, how are parents involved in the work of the school or pre-school? – what do they do? – what sort of contact is there between teachers and parents? – what sort of information is made available? In Cyster, Clift, and Battle's survey (1980) of parental involvement in primary schools in the mid 1970s, over three quarters of the schools surveyed had parents helping with school visits and outings; 65 per cent had parents providing practical help such as mending school equipment; the list goes on to include helping with craft, cookery, reading, etc. 'under supervision of the teacher', after school clubs, bringing in 'specialist knowledge' to 'give talks' to the children. Parents' formal contacts with the school were less encouraging: only about one third of the primary schools had a PTA, and a further quarter an informal 'Friends of the School' association, although parents' evenings and open days were the norm.

Since the mid 1970s there has been a tremendous increase in activity. A new survey brings the picture up to date for the mid 1980s, and preliminary information has been gathered from all local education authorities on home-school policy and practice. Many authorities are developing 'outreach' work with home-link volunteers or home-school liaison teachers, or setting up home-school reading schemes, as well as inviting parents to help in school. The outline has still to be filled in, but it seems that 'good practice' approaches are more likely to include encouragement for parents to work with their own children and to be involved in the school curriculum than was the case ten years ago. The obstacles to involvement appear to lie in teachers' apprehensiveness about working with parents and parents' apprehensiveness about schools, rather than lack of interest on the parents' part.

Surveys provide useful information about trends. Yet 'good practice' is not the whole story. More important are the assumptions about parents' and teachers' roles concealed in the data. Cyster and his colleagues (1980) found considerable discrepancy between head teachers' claims that parental involvement had increased and that parental attitudes had 'changed markedly as a result', and parents' unease about 'interfering'. Just under two thirds of the head teachers thought that parents found it easier to visit the school to talk to teachers or the head, that parents and teachers understood each other more easily, and that parents had more understanding of the difficulties with which teachers had to contend and of the school's educational objectives, and derived personal benefit from their involvement with school activities. Parents, on the other hand, 'consistently claimed that if there was anything they wanted to know, anything they were unsure about, they could always visit the school and discuss it with the head or class teacher', yet relatively few took advantage of this – for three reasons:

> First, certain parents felt that their queries did not come into 'proper' areas of concern; that they were not 'legitimate' questions which they could expect teachers to answer, rather inarticulate feelings of unease and bafflement . . . Secondly, parents were often perplexed as to which questions to ask when they were unsure what they were asking about . . . Thirdly . . . was the inadequacy many parents may feel when faced with a situation in which they themselves experienced failure. One mother claimed a real interest in her son's progress at school, but confessed her own illiteracy made her feel completely inadequate to enquire about her son's reading and writing at parents' evenings . . .
>
> (Cyster et al. 1980:123)

This mismatch is echoed in other reports. For instance, Tizard et al. (1981) give a vivid example of the gap between teachers' and parents' understanding of nursery education:

> The most misunderstood piece of equipment was the home corner or wendy house. The teachers' aim in providing these miniature homes was to stimulate group imaginative play. Between 30 and 50% of parents in all the schools except

(one) thought that they were intended either to provide early domestic science training 'it's to teach them to set the table' or 'it's to make it easier for them at school by reminding them what home is like'...

(Tizard *et al.* 1981:65)

The rather bland assumption behind the concept of 'good practice' that the problem is one of lack of information on the part of parents does not fit with what we know about the very different views and expectations parents and teachers have about education. For instance, in one study of 'the first transition' for the child moving from home to pre-school, parents were more likely than the teachers to think of pre-school for their children as 'a preparation for later school life', and less likely to attach importance to its value in helping them to understand their children or helping their children to learn through play. An inner London study of teachers' and parents' attitudes to preparing children for the infant school found that parents placed more emphasis on teaching their children reading, writing, and number than did the teachers, whereas the teachers stressed the importance of language development – reading to the children, telling stories, encouraging language, and questions. Theories also differed on 'educational success': parents were more likely to stress the importance of the school and the teachers to the child's development; teachers placed more stress on the home and the family. Will more information for parents, or for teachers, necessarily lead to a change in attitudes or practice?

But a wider definition of 'partnership' between parents and professionals is growing. The National Children's Bureau's study (Pugh and De'Ath 1987; Pugh *et al.* 1987) of 130 or so schemes and centres (including nursery classes and schools, day nurseries, family centres, adult and community education centres, clinics and community health projects, under fives networks, family support schemes, playgroups, and mother and toddler groups) outlines a useful framework for defining home-school relationships. The framework begins with non-participation: either deliberate, because parents work or want time away from their children; or 'passive' – parents would like to participate but are unable to because they are too tired or depressed, lack confidence or cannot speak the language, or have younger children. Second, there is 'outside' support, with practical help like fund-raising or donating materials, and attending events. Third comes participation in the centre under staff supervision, either as helpers – servicing the group, working with the children on a rota basis, helping run the toy library; or as learners – parents working with their own child, or taking part in open evenings, workshops, assemblies, or adult education activities. Fourth comes partnership, defined as 'a shared sense of purpose, mutual respect and the willingness to negotiate'. This is the most complex category, and includes parents as co-workers with equal access to information, sharing decisions about their own child or in management, running groups, counselling other parents, and visiting homes. Finally there is control, when it is the parents who ultimately are responsible for management – planning, setting objectives, appointing staff, selecting children, budgeting.

Parental control, the final category in the framework, takes us straight into the political arena – a topical debate with the requirements of the Education Act (No 2) 1986 for stronger representation by parents on schools' governing bodies and for more information provided for parents by governors, and with forthcoming legislation intended to give parents more choice in their children's schooling and greater powers to define and shape the education they think should be provided. There are two important questions to ask here. First, it is not yet clear how far parents will avail themselves of greater power and responsibility; studies of governing bodies suggest that the relationship between governors and professionals is a complex one. Second, reforming the education system must have as its aim the creation of more effective schools; but we are far from understanding the link between parents' control of their children's educational experience, and their children's academic achievement.

'PARENTS AS EDUCATORS' 1 – READING SCHEMES

The Plowden orthodoxy of simply increasing information to parents about schools' aims and objectives, and increasing resources in general available to schools working with parents, does not fit with the evidence that one of the crucial ingredients for effectiveness is parents' involvement with their own child. The British Child Health and Education Study (Osborn and Milbank 1987) showed that ten-year-olds did better at school if their parents were interested enough in their education to make contact with the school, and if their mothers had helped in their pre-school group. Programmes which involve parents in working with their own children can clearly result in changed behaviour and educational performance on the part of the children. Radin's (1972) classic comparative 'before and after' study in the United States compared three groups of four-year-olds: all had a good pre-school programme for nine months and home visits from the classroom teacher, but in addition one group had small-group discussion with useful hints about 'how to handle your child', and another of the three groups home visits aimed at working with the child but not the mother. Radin found that the children who gained most were those whose mothers had been most closely involved with their own children, and concluded that the programme worked by 'enhanc[ing] the mothers' perceptions of themselves as educators of their children and of their children as individuals capable of independent thought'. Studies of parent programmes in this country indicate similar results. The target, quite specifically, is the child and the parent together – whether in school or at home.

There have been two major growth areas in the 'parents as educators' theme in the 1980s. The first is reading schemes with older children; the second is parent and community education.

The debate about parents as educators and children learning to read provides the best opportunity so far for comparative evaluation of different types of involvement (Topping and Wolfendale 1985). Does parental involvement have to be 'taught', or is it rather a matter of 'anything goes'? Is there an 'optimum amount'? There is little agreement on this. Different techniques, from 'lightweight intervention', such as parents listening to their children at home, to more behavioural 'paired reading', all seem to 'work'. But which approach is more effective, for which age group, or for particular difficulties? The Newsons' Nottingham studies (1977) showed four fifths of the parents in their sample helping their pre-school children with reading without any prompting from school. We might suppose that parents listening to their children reading at home would be effective for most children needing a bit of encouragement: parents here do not have to be 'taught', merely encouraged, or 'given permission', perhaps, to try out their own ideas. Common sense tells us that parents may have to learn more focused techniques for children with more severe reading problems.

The 'Haringey' reading project (Tizard, Schofield, and Hewison 1982; Hewison 1985) is most often cited as evidence that 'intervention works'. This was a large-scale experiment in six primary schools, comparing the performance of children who took books home to read to their parents with groups who were given extra reading tuition at school. At the end of the study, children from the 'experimental' classes were reading at a considerably higher level than the control groups, and in particular the proportion of very weak readers was greatly reduced – and this was still the case at the close of their junior school career. These findings provide evidence for a link between parents hearing their children read and their children's reading attainment; and this seemed to be the case without any special training in reading techniques, and for parents who could not read English (or indeed read at all).

A rush of schemes followed – Hackney's Pitfield Project, which developed at the same time and grew enthusiastically into PACT; the Belfield Reading Project (Hannon, Jackson and Page 1985); 'paired reading'; 'shared reading'; behavioural approaches; and so on. But the Haringey research provided no answers to questions about the mechanisms underlying changes in children's reading: are changes due to children's increased motivation, or parents' increased motivation, or extra practice and increased skill? At bottom, most of these schemes appear simple – 'just send school reading books home with children and encourage and support parents to "hear" their own children read'; others require more detailed instruction in techniques for parents – something that looks more like a programme. How different are these different schemes? At first sight, 'parent listening' seems far removed from 'pause, prompt and praise' strategies or even 'token economies', with their carefully graded cue-and-appropriate-response systems; and clearly different approaches seem more appropriate in different contexts. Topping and Wolfendale's conclusion to their overview (1985) of different types of programme is that 'lightweight' low cost interventions like 'parent listening' schemes produce lower gains than the more carefully structured programmes, but are easier to implement and absorb into schools' ordinary routine; whereas the more structured approaches are more effective for severe reading problems (where parents are 'remedial teachers').

But we have little evidence so far on the essential ingredient – is it 'curriculum' and parent training, or motivation on the part of the child or parent? Are there different ingredients in different programmes? The most recent hypothesis is that what seems to be happening is a form of skill-acquisition plus motivation, where the key is 'extra practice in a motivating context': 'when parents hear their children read, they are providing them with a very special and very potent combination of benefits' (Hewison 1985).

However, there is still the fundamental question as to whether parent involvement reading schemes *do* work. Findings from the Belfield Reading Project do not indicate significant gains: children in the project scored no higher than children who had been through the school earlier. Why should there be such significant differences between apparently similar schemes? Possible explanations suggest that the home visiting by the researchers in the Haringey scheme was a key ingredient previously overlooked; that the level of involvement prior to a new scheme must be taken into account; that new attempts at involvement may be particularly powerful for ethnic minority families. Another study, of infant schools in inner London, suggests that a careful look at the process and practice of involvement is required. Schools' policies varied considerably – some sent reading books home with all the children at least three nights a week throughout the infant school; others did so for some part of the children's infant career; others did not follow this practice at all – but the average reading scores came out about the same, perhaps because parents gave their children similar help, irrespective of the school's policy. Small differences were found in the amount of support given by parents, but the children receiving the most support had overall reading scores similar to the group receiving the least help, although slightly fewer poor readers had frequent help compared with the above average readers. One possible explanation is that parental help is most effective if it coincides with a planned approach by the school: it is no good if the school sends home the same book every night, or if the teachers cut down on school reading time. It is clear that children's progress is not linear, and that parental involvement is a complex set of activities rather than a unitary concept: an initial 'spurt' in involvement may be followed by latent support.

Reading schemes are one area where evidence on the impact of parent involvement is slowly building up. But we need to look most carefully at what is going on if we are to untangle the complex processes, and establish what is successful and why.

'PARENTS AS EDUCATORS' 2 – PARENT EDUCATION AND COMMUNITY EDUCATION

Reading schemes focus on how children learn. Yet the other side of the coin is the question of how adults learn. New schemes clearly give parents new ideas. As one mother said in an Oxfordshire study (Smith 1980), 'I would never have thought of giving a two-year-old a jigsaw . . . It's widened my ideas about young children.' Mothers in the Lothian home visiting schemes (McCail 1981) talked about discovering 'how interesting their children were . . . They began to believe that it was more possible to influence the sort of person their child would become.'

Home visiting schemes which set out to develop skills and knowledge for child development, and to boost parents' enthusiasm, confidence, motivation, and sense of competence clearly do affect parents. This change is not simply a matter of 'what sort of toys are good for children'; it is a fairly fundamental shift in views about the nature of education and the parents' role. This is well demonstrated in a follow-up study of a home visiting scheme (Armstrong and Brown 1979). After three years in school, although there were minimal differences in performance between the 'home visited' children and a second group which had not been visited, there were substantial differences in their parents' views on education and child development. Mothers in the 'visited' group were more likely to have prepared the child for school; they talked about 'playing and learning in preparation for work', while those in the comparison group were more concerned with formal educational skills like 'learning to read and write'. Mothers in the visited group were far more likely to say that they tried to help with their child's education; and they put this in terms of 'answering questions and explaining things' to the child. Mothers in the home visiting programme thus came to hold a much wider view of education and early learning, and their role as parents. What is going on here? A clue comes from Clarke-Stewart's classic studies of mother-child interaction (1973). She isolates a pattern of 'optimum maternal care' or 'general maternal competence' – a pattern of warm, accepting, stimulating interaction, responsive to the child's behaviour, adaptive as the child grows older, related to the mother's willingness to experiment and be imaginative and to her language skills and knowledge about child rearing and development – with the mother acting as mediator between the child and the environment. The mother's style is closely related to her child's development. Tizard and Hughes's study (1984) of four-year-olds vividly illustrates the strength of the home as a learning environment, through the intensive relationship and shared contexts of meaning and motivation between parent and child.

There is a didactic ring to the notion of parent education, however, which seems 'to convey three messages to parents: first, they probably do not have the competence for child-rearing; second, knowledge and techniques for dealing with child-rearing are available; third, if they wish, they can acquire these skills. A fourth message is implicit but unavoidable – if parents are not successful, it is their own fault'. Community education programmes which emphasize self-help and learning from the shared experience of others in the community, rather than teaching by professionals, may provide the answer to Hess's criticism. Studies of isolated and depressed young mothers by Shinman (1981) and others show that stress and depression on the part of the mother clearly have detrimental effects on mother-child interaction. Projects such as SCOPE in Southampton, Home Link in Liverpool, and Home Start in Leicester and elsewhere adopt a community education approach to their work with families under considerable stress – often living in poor housing, in areas of high unemployment and poor services, suffering from ill-health and depression, and frequently failing to make use of what facilities there are. How can we evaluate work of this kind? Home visiting schemes may have clear objectives to do with boosting children's development through changes in parents' child-rearing skills and knowledge; but for projects such as Home Link, which vividly illustrates the shift from 'parent programme to community education', the goals are more diverse, and changes are consequently harder to measure. That change does occur is certain – new provision; a different approach on the part of service-providers to the needs and views of local neighbourhoods; new confidence amongst local people to tackle problems, get a job, or use education for themselves; fresh understanding that their difficulties are not unique. The best evidence about the change as experienced by parents comes from the consumers themselves: 'It's made me a lot more confident – I got the job'; 'I went on from Home Link to do the English in the school; I wouldn't have thought about it myself'; 'we have ideas of what we'd like to see up in Netherley – if you start fighting for something, you know, if you see something at the end of it, well it's been worth it'; 'I can come up against an apparent brick wall, and . . . if I put my head together with someone else in the community, we'll solve it together. Once I was too frightened to ask, now I have the confidence.'

But we still know relatively little about the impact on children's development of community-based programmes with their wider goals. What is the connection between a mother's sense of being in control of her own life, and her child's development? Studies of projects such as Home Start are rich in comments from mothers growing in confidence and learning about their children, but do not measure change in the children. From the growing evidence of the 'parents as educators' programmes, where effects for the children are probably mediated through the parent, it would be reasonable to expect a relationship; however, research which has considered programme effects separately for children and their parents indicates that we must study the process with care. Parental support programmes are important in their own right; the effects on children are probably indirect, through an interactional or transactional model. The issue of effectiveness is not a simple one: to ask 'whether self-help groups are more or less "effective" than individually based intervention' is too simplistic: we must ask what interventions work in which circumstances and for whom.

NEW STYLES OF SERVICE DELIVERY – AN EXAMPLE: FAMILY CENTRES AND THE PARENT-PROFESSIONAL PARTNERSHIP

New forms of community-based services for parents and pre-school children – toy libraries, drop-in centres, resource centres, family groups – have proliferated in the last few years, often combining centre-based work with 'outreach' work in the community or children's own homes, and combining different approaches from education, social services, health, adult education, and the voluntary sector. What can these developments add to the discussion on parental involvement? Let us take family centres as an example.

Family centres (Smith 1987) have grown out of three debates – the educational debate on the home-school partnership; the relationship between statutory services and the informal networks of care and support of family, friends, and neighbours; and questions about preventive or crisis work with families and children at risk. The major starting points have been 'nursery education plus' – nursery schools or classes which have shifted focus from 'education for the under-fives' to include work with parents, and 'day nursery plus' – again where attention has shifted from 'day care for priority children' to families as a unit. Their interest for this chapter lies in the illustration they provide of the dilemmas in some of the approaches already discussed – is the focus on the child or the parent? Is the learning model child-centred, parent education, or community education?

Most centres claim to serve both parent and child, but this needs careful scrutiny. Centres with a care or therapeutic orientation focus largely on family functioning – that is, whether the parents can cope, how parents and children get on together; they tend to operate with parent education models, although they may run services such as toy libraries and drop-ins; and they pay more attention to children's social than cognitive development. Centres with an education focus tend to be child-centred and view parents as 'educators' rather than 'learners' and 'consumers' in their own right, although they may also run adult education activities and information services such as welfare rights. So the models do not fit particularly neatly.

How effective are these new developments in developing or working with notions of parent involvement? Many mothers using family centres grow in confidence and in understanding of their children much as mothers in other community projects, and develop stronger friendships and social networks. But it is clear there are two real dilemmas here for the development of parent involvement. The first is the uneasy relationship between the notions of self-help and individual counselling – between an 'open door' approach on the one hand, with its emphasis on people learning through shared experience, and reciprocity between helpers and helped; and 'referrals only' on the other, with individual casework by professionals, carefully negotiated contract work, and controlled environments. Can these two approaches usefully co-exist? They appear to spring from different analyses of adult learning, but it remains to be seen which approach is more appropriate for which type of problem.

The second dilemma is that of power – who ultimately has the right to make decisions? At one level, this is not difficult: simply put, management (whether a parent committee or the local authority) makes decisions. But at another level, matters become more complicated. When parents are encouraged to develop their confidence, take decisions about their own lives, think about how they relate to their children, it is not surprising if they begin to make suggestions about the toys in the toy library, the programme in the centre, or the school curriculum. And at a political level, this is the stuff of democracy. As Shinman points out, there are different lessons here. One is the easy danger of generalization – 'parents want this', 'professionals want that'. A second lesson is the importance of clear roles and boundaries between parents and professionals: as the Newsons pointed out, the similarity in roles obscures deep differences between the parent, who must be flexible, inconsistent, and partial to meet the needs of the individual child, and the professional who must by contrast be impartial, consistent, and structured (Newson and Newson 1977). These issues are crucial to the development of a parent-professional partnership, and they are clearly visible in family centre work.

CONCLUSION

So what should we conclude from this review of parental involvement in the 1980s?

First, a comparison with earlier reviews reveals how the debate has moved on. We can no longer ask large, simplistic questions like 'Does parental involvement work?' or 'Which is more effective at helping the under fives – parental involvement or curriculum?' Our questions must be more precisely targeted to uncover what sort of interventions or combinations of interventions are most useful for different age groups and different objectives.

Second, the evidence for outcomes, although still thin, is mounting. However, we need to be far more precise about the effects of different sorts of strategies, and the processes that link these effects both to the intervention and to other factors in families and their neighbourhoods. Parental involvement is a complex and multi-faceted notion, far from uniform, and may operate differentially at different ages and stages.

Third, we must consider different roles. Tizard and Hughes's study (1984) of four-year-old girls talking with their mothers at home and their teachers at school shows how parents share with their children a highly individualized and emotionally charged context of past and present, and intense expectations on both sides – a context that 'outsiders' do not share.

Finally, although we still cannot claim certain proof for the transactional model, reading schemes involving parents provide the clearest evidence so far for virtuous circles of 'mutual reinforcement'. We need further study to lay bare the process of skill-plus-motivation at work between parent and child.

REFERENCES

Armstrong, G. and Brown, F. (1979) *Five Years On: A Follow-up Study of the Long Term Effects on Parents and Children of an Early Learning Programme in the Home*, Oxford: Social Evaluation Unit, Department of Social and Administrative Studies.

Berrueta-Clement, J., Schweinhart, L. J., Barnett, W. S., Epstein, A. S., and Weikart, D. P. (1984) *Changed Lives: The Effects of the Perry Preschool Program on Youths Through Age 19*, Monographs of the High/Scope Educational Research Foundation No. 8, Ypsilanti, Michigan: High/Scope Press.

Bruner, J. S. (1980) *Under Five in Britain*, London: Grant McIntyre.

Central Advisory Council for Education (England) (Plowden Committee) (1967) *Children and Their Primary Schools*, London: HMSO.

Clarke-Stewart, K. A. (1973) *Interactions Between Mothers and Their Young Children: Characteristics and Consequences*, Monographs of the Society for Research in Child Development, No. 153.

Cyster, R., Clift, P. S., and Battle, S. (1980) *Parental Involvement in Primary Schools*, Slough: National Foundation for Educational Research.

Department of Education and Science (1968) *Parent/Teacher Relations in Primary Schools*, London: HMSO.

Douglas, J. W. B. (1964) *The Home and the School*, London: MacGibbon and Kee.

Hannon, P., Jackson, A., and Page, B. (1985) 'Implementation and take-up of a project to involve parents in the teaching of reading', in Topping and Wolfendale.

Hewison, J. (1985) 'Parental involvement and reading attainment: implications of research in Dagenham and Haringey', in Topping and Wolfendale.

Lazar, I. and Darlington, R. (1982) *Lasting Effects of Early Education: A Report from the Consortium for Longitudinal Studies*, Monographs of the Society for Research in Child Development, 195.

McCail, G. (1981) *Mother Start*, Edinburgh: Scottish Council for Educational Research.

Newson, J. and Newson, E. (1977) *Perspectives on School at Seven Years Old*, London: Allen & Unwin.

Osborn, A. F., Butler, N. R., and Morris, A. C. (1981) *The Social Life of Britain's Five Year Olds*, A Report of the Child Health and Education Study, London: Routledge & Kegan Paul.

Osborn, A. F. and Milbank, J. E. (1987) *The Effects of Early Education: A Report from the Child Health and Education Study*, Oxford: Clarendon Press.

Pugh, G., et al. (1987) *Partnership in Action: Working with Parents in Preschool Centres* Vols 1 and 2, London: National Children's Bureau.

Pugh, G. and De'Ath, E. (1987) *Parents and Professionals as Partners: Rhetoric or Reality?* London: National Children's Bureau.

Radin, N. (1972) 'Three degrees of maternal involvement in a preschool program: impact on mothers and children', *Child Development*, 43, 1355–64.

Shinman, S. M. (1981) *A Chance for Every Child? Access and Response to Preschool Provision*, London: Tavistock.

Smith, G. and James, T. (1975) 'The effects of preschool education: some American and British evidence', *Oxford Review of Education*, 1(3) 223–40.

Smith, T. (1980) *Parents and Preschool*, London: Grant McIntyre.

Smith, T. (1987) 'Family centres: prevention, partnership or community alternative?' in J. A. Macfarlane (Ed.) *Progress in Child Health*, 3, London: Churchill Livingstone.

Tizard, B. (1974) *Early Childhood Education: A Review and Discussion of Research in Britain*, Slough: Social Science Research Council/National Federation for Educational Research.

Tizard, B. and Hughes, M. (1984) *Young Children Learning: Talking and Thinking at Home and at School*, London: Fontana.

Tizard, B., Mortimore, J., and Birchall, B. (1981) *Involving Parents in Nursery and Infant Schools: A Source Book for Teachers*, London: Grant McIntyre.

Topping, K. and Wolfendale, S. (Eds.) (1985) *Parental Involvement in Children's Reading*, London: Croom Helm.

Wolfendale, S. (1983) *Parental Participation in Children's Development and Education*, Special Aspects of Education, New York and London: Gordon & Breach, Science Publishers.

Woodhead, M. (1985) 'Preschool education has long term effects: but can they be generalised?' *Oxford Review of Education*, 11(2):133–55.

Young, M. and McGeeney, P. (1968) *Learning Begins at Home: A Study of a Junior School and its Parents*, London: Routledge & Kegan Paul.

3.2

THE CHANGING NATURE AND FUNCTIONS OF HIGHER EDUCATION

JOHN BRENNAN

GROWTH AND DIVERSITY

Looking ahead to the development of higher education into the 1990s, the British government, in a White Paper published in May 1987, was able to find continuity with the aims and purposes enunciated by the Robbins Committee report on higher education published in 1963. These were summarized in the 1987 White Paper as

> instruction in skills, the production of general powers of the mind, the advancement of learning, and the transmission of a common culture and common standards of citizenship. (HMSO 1987:1)

Yet the shape and character of British higher education had been transformed in the quarter century since the Robbins Committee reported. In considering the contours of these changes, we shall find reflected in them distinct shifts in emphasis given to the various aims and purposes of higher education.

A higher education in the 1960s was a university education. It was almost certainly taken immediately after leaving secondary school. It entailed full-time study. Most students followed three year degree courses which built on subjects studied for the advanced level examinations of the General Certificate of Education (GCE). However, of the new entrants to British higher education in 1984, only 34 per cent were attending universities. The numbers taking first degree courses accounted for little more than half (54 per cent) and a sizeable minority of them was enrolled on four year sandwich degrees. Twenty-three per cent of new entrants to full-time and sandwich courses were mature students, i.e. aged 21 or over at the time of enrolment. In addition, mature students comprised almost all the students on part-time courses, and these accounted for 37 per cent of the total student population.

The twenty years following the publication of the Robbins report have witnessed major increases in student enrolments, the establishment of new institutions, changes in the function of others, developments of new curricula, new kinds of relationships between degree qualifications and employment, and changing expectations among students and their teachers. These are trends common to most other industrialized societies, although there remain some distinctive British contours.

Table 1 shows the distribution of all home students on full-time, sandwich and part-time courses between 1970 and 1983. Fifty-five per cent were enrolled on polytechnic or college courses (the public sector) in 1983. Thirty-seven per cent were on part-time courses. Twenty-one per cent were on advanced courses below the level of a first degree. By far the greatest increase in enrolments was on part-time degree courses, 221 per cent between 1970

Table 1 Higher Education: all home students on full-time, sandwich and part-time courses

	Thousands				Percentage Change
	1970	1975	1980	1983	1970–1983
Universities					
Full-time:					
Postgraduate	31.3	32.6	31.1	30.6	−2
First degrees	NA	196.0	232.7	227.5	NA
Other advanced	NA	1.5	1.6	1.4	NA
All full-time	210.1	230.1	265.4	259.5	+24
Part-time:					
Postgraduate	17.6	21.5	27.4	29.0	+64
Undergraduates	4.9	3.5	4.5	5.6	+15
Open University	19.6	56.0	67.8	76.1	+288
All part-time	42.1	81.0	99.7	110.7	+163
University Total	252.2	311.1	365.1	370.3	+47
Public Sector					
Full-time:					
Postgraduate	NA	NA	12.1	10.8	NA
First degrees	36.3	65.1	121.4	164.6	+354
Other advanced	NA	NA	69.2	84.4	NA
All full-time	211.6	226.1	202.7	259.8	+23
Part-time:					
Postgraduate	7.5	8.2	12.3	14.0	+86
First degrees	5.3	6.8	16.8	20.0	+275
Other advanced	106.8	119.1	159.4	166.8	+56
All part-time	119.6	134.1	188.5	200.8	+68
Public Sector Total	331.2	360.2	391.2	460.7	+39
All students	583.5	671.3	756.3	830.8	+40

Based on tables 6 and 9 of DES Statistical Bulletin 9/85 (1985): Student Numbers in Higher Education – Great Britain = 1970–83

(NA = Not available)

and 1983, much of it accounted for by the expansion of the Open University.

Opportunities to obtain higher education in Britain do not compare unfavourably with those which exist in other European countries. Age participation rates are higher in the Netherlands and France but lower in Germany and Italy. However, where Britain is distinctive is in the smaller share which the universities have of the total. Although many countries have developed non-university institutions of higher education (for example, the German Fachhochschulen or the French Instituts Universitaires de Technologie and the Grandes Écoles), these developments have not been on the same scale as the growth of the polytechnic and college sector in Britain. Opportunities to enter higher education are comparable with those in other countries, but British students are much less likely to go to a university.

Looking at the first year enrolments on full-time and sandwich courses in 1984, there were 70,000 entering university first degrees, 57,000 entering polytechnic and college first degrees, and 51,000 entering other advanced courses in the polytechnic and college sector. Part-time enrolments in the public sector reveal a predominance of non-degree advanced work, 83 per cent of the total part-time provision in 1983. Students on non-degree courses study for qualifications such as the higher national certificates and diplomas of the Business and Technician Education Council (BTEC), or professional qualifications linked to entry to a specific occupation.

The diversity of higher education provision is matched by the wide range of jobs which students enter after completing their courses. The degree and diploma holders of the 1980s are to be found in virtually all sectors of the labour market. Many jobs which had previously demanded only secondary school qualifications today require the possession of a degree. Thus, the accountancy profession is rapidly becoming all-graduate, and increasing numbers of graduates are entering the hotel and catering industry, the retail trade, and administration and management in organizations of all kinds. Many of them will have taken new kinds of vocational courses geared explicitly to preparation for their chosen careers. One of the largest growth areas in the polytechnics and colleges has been undergraduate business studies. Other new areas of degree study include hotel and catering, nursing, sport and recreation, and tourism. What we have seen is a 'qualifications spiral' whereby jobs formerly done by people without degrees come to be taken by people with degrees.

In summary, British higher education in the 1980s comprises some 831,000 students who will be destined for very different futures when they enter or re-enter the labour market. While they are within higher education, full-time or part-time, they will be studying for a variety of qualifications in different kinds of institutions.

FUNCTIONS

Modern industrial society has often been characterized as a 'knowledge society' as more and more areas of social and economic life become dependent upon the application of bodies of systematic knowledge for their effective functioning. The possession of knowledge in its systematic forms gives power and control. Greater emphasis comes to be placed upon its certification through educational credentials.

The American sociologist Alvin Gouldner has described the products of the expanded systems of higher education as a 'new class' whose capital is based on educational qualifications. He distinguishes between the 'intellectuals' and the 'technical intelligentsia' and notes the tendency of universities to 'both reproduce and subvert the larger society' (Gouldner 1979:45).

The German writer Ulrich Teichler has drawn attention to the effects which expansionist educational policies have on the opportunity structures of society. By creating the appearance of greater opportunities, they raise aspirations which cannot be met by the existing system of social rewards. He notes the emergence of hierarchies of prestige in higher education and the segregation of students in terms of ability and occupational or professional objectives. Such segregation provides the means of getting students to adjust their status aspirations. Teichler concludes

> it is not enough to possess a degree – the prestige of the university and the type of course followed are of equal or more importance in gaining access to the highest socio-economic occupations. (Teichler *et al.* 1982:135)

The French sociologist, Pierre Bourdieu, distinguishes between students who are 'professional apprentices' and those who are 'apprentice professionals'. Like Gouldner, he sees in educational qualifications a form of 'cultural capital', but capital which can only be 'cashed in' if a person possesses other capital grounded in social status and economic power (Bourdieu 1977).

A major study of British graduates published in 1972 bore the sub-title 'the sociology of an élite' (Kelsall *et al.* 1972). A similar study produced in the 1980s would certainly not be so described. Writing about the British binary division between universities on the one hand and polytechnics and colleges on the other, the American writer, Martin Trow, saw

> the distinction between the academic education for gentlemen provided in the universities and the vocational education for 'other ranks' offered by the institutions for further education. (Trow 1973:245)

Like the other writers we have mentioned, Trow saw in the differentiation of institutional forms of higher education a differentiation of function. His fellow Americans, Samuel Bowles and Herbert Gintis, described the 'non-élite' institutions of higher education as processing large numbers of students to attain that particular combination of technical competence and social acquiescence required in the skilled but power-less upper-middle positions in the occupational hierarchy of the corporate capital-ist economy. (Bowles and Gintis 1976:212)

Governments too have emphasized differentiation of institutional function although not quite in the terms used by Bowles and Gintis. However, some-times they have come close. A Green Paper on higher education published by the British government in 1985 saw little place in the polytechnics and colleges for the study of the humanities and 'non-vocational' social sciences.

Whatever its formal attachment to pluralist statements of aims and purposes, the priorities of the British government for higher education are clear. In the preface to the 1987 White Paper on higher education, it was emphasized that

> above all there is an urgent need, in the interests of the nation as a whole, and therefore of universities, polytechnics and colleges themselves, for higher education to take increasing account of the economic requirements of the coun-try. (HMSO 1987:1–2)

Bowles and Gintis describe it as a shift from 'ivory tower' to 'service station for the economy'. What all the writers we have referred to would endorse is the differentiated nature of modern higher education systems. Different kinds of student receive different kinds of educational experience in different kinds of institution. The separate parts of the higher education system serve different parts of society.

CLIENTS

Despite these differences, it remains possible for a recent writer to describe British higher education convincingly as the 'middle class university' (Rustin 1986). Examination of the social backgrounds of full-time students would seem to justify such a description. Table 2 shows the social class distribution of full-time students in 1977 and compares it with 1961. It is clear from this table that modest increases in participation among young people from working class backgrounds did nothing to alter the social class balance of the universities during the 15 years after the Robbins report signalled the major expansion of higher education. Moreover, the social origins of students in the polytechnic and college sector show a similar pattern to that found in the universities.

However, these figures do not reveal the institutional differences which exist in the social class composition of higher education. To take just one example from a study by Boys and Kirkland, the social class composition of an Oxbridge engineering degree course was 70.6 per cent fathers in senior professional jobs to 5.9 per cent fathers in manual jobs, whereas the composition of

Table 2 Age participation rates for full-time students by social class, 1961-2 and
1977

| | c. 1961 (A) | c. 1977 (B) | *Percentage distributions assumed in (B)* | | |
| | | | Universities | Advanced further education | 18-yr-olds |
Class					
I	45	42.6	20.9	13.3	5.3
II	19	25.4	41.2	36.7	19.6
IIIN	10	21.2	14.7	18.9	9.7
Middle	19.5	26.9	76.8	68.9	34.7
IIIM	4	5.6	16.6	20.0	40.2
IV		4.7	5.2	8.9	17.8
V	2	2.8	1.2	2.2	7.3
Working	3.2	5.0	23.0	31.1	65.3
All	7.5	12.7	99.8	100	100
		N=	65340	39460	831000

Source:
(A) *Higher Education* (1963) App 1:39–40, based on survey of 20–21-year-olds.
(B) UCCA *Statistical Supplements*, 1978–9, Table E5 for universities in 1977. Advanced further education estimated from Table 2.17(7), (9), (10) (above). 18-year-olds: *Census 1971. Household Composition* Table 46, aged 10–14. Oliver Fulton (Ed.) (1981) *Access to Higher Education*, Table 2.18.

(Williamson 1986: 72, Table 1)

Key to social class categories
I   Professional occupations
II   Intermediate occupations   } middle
IIIN Skilled occupations: non-manual
IIIM Skilled occupations: manual
IV   Partly skilled occupations   } working
V   Unskilled occupations

polytechnic social science courses was 9.4 per cent in senior professional jobs to 47.2 per cent in manual jobs (Boys and Kirkland, 1988). The overwhelming middle and upper class composition of the full-time student body as a whole should not disguise the large differences which exist between institutions and courses.

We have described a differentiated system of institutions, courses, and modes of study. If the appellation 'middle class university' has some degree of force as a description of full-time higher education, it does less than justice to part-time provision.

Part-time higher education needs to be seen in two halves. There is the Open University which alone accounts for 24 per cent of all part-time students. Higher education courses provided by the Open University are mainly part of first degree programmes and therefore, whatever the innovations in pedagogy and form, are modelled on university conventions concerning the nature of an honours degree. However, the largest single type of part-time provision is the advanced non-degree work of the polytechnics and colleges sector. In 1983 this accounted for 54 per cent of the whole. It is a form of higher education which gets little public prominence. Unlike full-time higher education, it

279

receives comparatively little by way of financial aid and grant support. It shades into a much larger system of non-advanced post-school education which provides an alternative route to qualifications for those who have left full-time education at the age of sixteen.

In a study which compares this route to the university route (plus a third largely disappeared route in the colleges of education which is not considered here), Halsey, Heath, and Ridge reveal the very different profiles of the student bodies.

Table 3 Social composition of students attending post-secondary institutions

Father's social class	P/T further education	University
I, II	14.1	52.4
III, IV, V	34.1	27.9
VI, VII, VIII	51.8	19.7
	100	100
N	(3620)	(412)

Source: Halsey, Heath, and Ridge (1980), abbreviated version of p.183 Table 10.

For large sections of society, the part-time further education route has been the main source of access to post-school education. But this alternative route has led traditionally to very different places from the 'middle class university'. The part-time further education route has provided practical training and opportunity to learn a trade, to prepare for a profession. Moreover, the links between the two routes have been minimal.

However, as full-time higher education has expanded, has developed its own part-time variants, and has acquired more of the vocational emphasis of part-time further education, the distinctions between the two routes have become more blurred. As full-time higher education itself becomes more differentiated, so its boundaries with other forms of post-school education become less clear-cut. So too with the students. Graduates no longer form the distinct and élite group in society described in the Kelsall study of the late sixties.

Where do the graduates of the 1980s end up? Two recent studies of graduate employment have shown how graduates are permeating more and more parts of the labour market. A study of polytechnic and college graduates found that, three years after their graduation in 1982, only 25 per cent regarded themselves as in 'traditional graduate level jobs', only 34 per cent had needed to possess a degree to obtain their current jobs, and only 39 per cent regarded their current jobs as inherently requiring graduate level skills or abilities (Brennan and McGeevor 1988). A second study has demonstrated the enormous 'institutional effect' upon postgraduate employment prospects of attending the ancient universities of Oxford and Cambridge (Boys and Kirkland 1988). The latter conclusion finds support in the messages that have come out of studies of employers (for example Roizen and Jepson 1985) which have revealed graduate recruitment preferences which reflect traditional hierarchies of social and academic prestige among higher education institutions.

Any discussion of British higher education must refer, if only briefly, to the dominant position of the universities of Oxford and Cambridge in so many areas of British social life: politics, the civil service, the media, law, the top positions in leading companies. As Rustin has recently commented

> Their social prestige, superior endowment, and privileged access to subsequent élite positions have allowed them to retain a position at the apex of the English system of educational stratification. . . . (Rustin 1986:25)

If boundaries between different institutions and forms of higher education are beginning to break down, these should not disguise the continued existence of a strong élite core to the system, recruiting predominantly from élite groups in society and supplying the future membership of those groups. As one travels from the élite core towards the edges of the system, through the rest of the universities, the polytechnics and colleges, the part-time non-degree work in the further education colleges, one finds institutions catering for different social groups and supplying different parts of the social and economic structure of society.

POLITICS AND CONTROL

Although government continues to acknowledge the multiple functions of higher education, it is increasingly clear that not all functions are intended to apply equally to all parts of the system. The importance of research is recognized, but should be concentrated in a limited number of 'centres of excellence'. The humanities are seen to be important, but not really the sorts of subjects to be encouraged in the polytechnics and colleges. Since the arrival of the Conservative Government in 1979, the subject balance of higher education has shifted firmly to the advantage of the sciences. Enrolments in science subjects showed a 24 per cent increase between 1979 and 1984 (64 per cent in mathematical sciences) compared with a 2 per cent increase in the humanities (DES 1986).

For most of higher education, it is economic functions which must become increasingly dominant. Plans announced in the 1987 White Paper aim to encourage greater responsiveness to economic needs – particularly in the polytechnic and college sector – through new funding arrangements and new planning bodies for both sectors of higher education. It is the 'needs of the economy' which are to steer the number and subject balance of the graduates to be produced in the 1990s. The membership of the new Universities Funding

Council is to include 'a strong element of people from outside the academic world'. Two of the three statements of aims and purposes for higher education in the White Paper are to 'serve the economy more effectively' and to 'have closer links with industry and commerce, and promote enterprise'. Foreshadowing another major thrust of the White Paper, the Committee of Vice Chancellors and Principals has announced a figure of 25 per cent as the average amount of non-governmental funding secured by the universities.

A major study of the responsiveness of higher education only recently published describes how curricula, organizational processes, and values within institutions have already changed – albeit at the margins – in directions which indicate the growing importance that is being attached to economic requirements (Boys *et al.* 1988). Opportunities to develop new courses were often dependent on finding external sponsors who would endow a university chair, lectureship, or research fellowship. Thus, new courses tended to have vocational purposes reflecting the sponsors' needs. In the technologies in particular, research activity has been shaped increasingly by the need to obtain commercial funding. As staff research interests change, so too do the contents of the courses they teach. The study found lecturers in almost all subjects keeping an increasingly watchful eye on the first employment destinations of their graduates. In some institutions, wholesale restructuring of the curriculum had occurred in an attempt to increase the relevance of courses to employment.

FUTURES

Government priorities for higher education are thus clear and institutions have begun to respond to them. In operational terms, the system is moving from a situation where student demand shaped development to one where employer needs are intended to assume priority. What then of student needs and preferences?

In a recent study of polytechnic and college graduates, graduates were asked three years after they had left higher education what they felt ought to be the main functions of higher education (Brennan and McGeevor 1987). The results are shown in Table 4. Although there are differences in emphasis between graduates from the various subject fields, the overall picture is clear. Like government, the graduates see a multiplicity of functions for higher education but, unlike government, they do not accord absolute priority to employment. In some ways, the graduates appeared to want the best of all worlds, some optimum combination of subject interest, broad education, and employment relevance.

These values are shared by at least some lecturers, particularly in the more vocational fields of study. In another study, the phrase 'a liberal vocationalism' has been used to describe the coming together of separate traditions of higher

Table 4 Polytechnic and college graduates' perceptions of the social functions of higher education

Subject Field	'Training for industry'	'Personal growth'	'Helping disadvantaged'	'Perpetuate élite'	'Critical intellectuals'	'Culture transmission'	'Produce knowledge'
Arts and humanities	3.13	3.45	2.76	1.41	2.48	2.56	3.3
Social sciences	2.93	3.19	2.65	1.42	2.26	2.22	3.2
Business and management	3.1	2.8	2.0	1.39	2.17	1.91	3.0
Science (1)	3.12	3.0	2.3	1.36	2.28	2.05	3.2
Science (2)	3.23	3.23	2.53	1.47	2.46	2.25	3.4
Built environment	3.1	3.0	2.17	1.29	2.28	2.10	3.1
Engineering	3.25	2.87	2.02	1.37	2.1	1.94	3.2
Art and design	3.14	3.22	2.53	1.35	2.17	2.49	3.1
Interfaculty	2.93	3.34	2.59	1.42	2.29	2.37	3.4
All	3.09	3.15	2.45	1.39	2.29	2.23	3.2
Gradmodel							
Generalist	2.92	3.34	2.71	1.42	2.36	2.31	3.3
Generalist plus	3.12	3.12	2.42	1.35	2.31	2.17	3.2
Occupational generalist	3.13	3.16	2.29	1.36	2.26	2.22	3.2
Occupational specialist	3.19	3.0	2.34	1.41	2.82	2.18	3.2

Source: Brennan and McGeevor (1987) Table 10.1

Note
Two years after graduation, graduates were asked the following questions:

The following have all been claimed as functions of higher education in our society. Please mark each item in terms of the importance you think should be attached to it –

a) The training of highly qualified specialists for industry and commerce.
b) Personal growth and the development of the individual.
c) A means of improving the social position of disadvantaged groups.
d) A contribution to the perpetuation and justification of a social élite.
e) The production of critical intellectuals.
f) The preservation and transmission of the society's culture.
g) Engagement in research in order to produce new knowledge which can lead to social progress.

The table indicates the mean scores on a 4-point scale where 1 = none 2 = a little 3 = a lot 4 = a great deal.

education into a new integrated form (Silver and Brennan 1988). Thus, degrees in areas such as business studies seek to combine an education in several social science disciplines and the functional areas of business activity (marketing, finance, etc.) with skills training and work experience. Traditional forms of academic work are combined with the traditions of the day-release apprentice.

It is this coming together of traditions, of easier movement between them at all stages of adult life, which points the way to a possible direction for future developments of higher education in Britain. Arrangements whereby individual units of higher education can be studied at different times and places for different purposes are becoming more widespread. They can involve the accumulation of credits – including credits for work experience – to form a programme of study of the individual's own design. This is a higher education that is part-time and tailor-made to meet the needs and interests of the individual student at different points in his or her life. The Open University forms an important part of this provision although its curriculum continues to be shaped by the English liberal tradition of higher education. Polytechnics and colleges have in some cases joined together in regional consortia to provide credit transfer facilities between a diverse range of courses at different levels. Formal education and the training provided by employers are being linked in some of these schemes. A national system for co-ordinating these developments is emerging through the Credit Accumulation and Transfer Scheme of the Council for National Academic Awards.

This extension of higher education reflects partly the growing need for training and re-training throughout adult life, partly the anticipated decline in the numbers of eighteen-year-olds available for full-time degree courses. What is not clear is whether these developments – while fully supported by government – will receive sufficient funding ever to challenge the dominance and prestige of the traditional élite forms of higher education in British social life.

REFERENCES

Bourdieu, P. (1977) 'Cultural reproduction and social reproduction' in J. Karabel and A. H. Halsey (Eds.) *Power and Ideology in Education*, Oxford: Oxford University Press.

Bowles, S. and Gintis, H. (1976) *Schooling in Capitalist America*, London: Routledge & Kegan Paul (1985).

Boys, C., Brennan, J., Henkel, M., Kirkland, J., Kogan, M., and Youll, P. (1988) *The Responsiveness of Higher Education to the Labour Market*, London: Jessica Kingsley Publishers.

Boys, C. J. and Kirkland, J. K. (1988) *Degrees of Success: Career Aspirations and Destinations of a Cohort of College, University and Polytechnic Graduates, 1982–5*, London: Jessica Kingsley Publishers.

Brennan, J. L. and McGeevor, P. M. (1988) *Graduates at Work: Degree Courses and the Labour Market*, London: Jessica Kingsley Publishers.

Finch, J. and Rustin, M. (1986) *A Degree of Choice? Education after Eighteen*, Harmondsworth: Penguin Books.

Gouldner, A. V. (1979) *The Future of the Intellectuals and the Rise of the New Class*, London: Macmillan.

Halsey, A. H., Heath, A. F., and Ridge, J. M. (1980) *Origins and Destinations: Family, Class and Education in Modern Britain*, Oxford: Clarendon Press.

HMSO (1985) *The Development of Higher Education into the 1990s*, London: HMSO, Cmnd 9524.

HMSO (1987) *Higher Education: Meeting the Challenge*, London: HMSO, Cmnd 114.

Kelsall, R. K., Poole, A., and Kuhn, A. (1972) *Graduates: The Sociology of an Elite*, London: Tavistock/Methuen.

Robbins Report (1963) *Committee on Higher Education*, London: HMSO, Cmnd 2154.

Roizen, J. and Jepson, M. (1985) *Degrees for Jobs: Employer Expectations of Higher Education*, Guildford: Society for Research into Higher Education.

Rustin, M. (1986) 'The idea of the popular university' in Finch and Rustin.

Silver, H. and Brennan, J. L. (1988) *A Liberal Vocationalism*, London: Methuen.

Teichler, U., Harting, D., and Nuthmann, R. (1980) *Higher Education and the Needs of Society*, Windsor: NFER-NELSON.

Trow, M. (1973) 'Binary dilemmas – an American view', in R. Bell, G. Fowler, and K. Little (Eds.) *Education in Great Britain and Ireland*, London: Routledge & Kegan Paul.

Williamson, W. (1986) 'Who has access?', in Finch and Rustin.

3·3

PRIORITIES IN POST-SCHOOL EDUCATION: WHO BENEFITS AND WHO PAYS?

MAUREEN WOODHALL

INTRODUCTION

Some years ago the Carnegie Commission on Higher Education in the USA published a book entitled *'Higher Education: Who Benefits? Who Pays? Who Should Pay?'* This title neatly encapsulates the fundamental questions that need to be answered about how the costs of post-school education should be shared. Education is now recognized to be an investment in human capital that generates benefits both for the individual – in the form of better employment prospects and higher lifetime earnings – and for society at large – by increasing the skills and productivity of the labour force. How should that investment be financed?

This raises issues both of efficiency and equity. Since education benefits society as a whole, then some form of public subsidy is justified on efficiency grounds, to prevent under-investment and provide the skilled manpower necessary for economic growth and prosperity. In the case of post-compulsory education, however, the decision to continue in school or enter further or higher education yields *private* as well as *social* benefits. Workers with additional education can expect higher earnings and less likelihood of unemployment than those who left school at the minimum age, with no qualifications. Thus on efficiency grounds this is a case for the costs to be shared between public and private sources. It can be argued that, since post-compulsory education is a profitable private investment, then individual students, or their parents, should bear some of the costs, either by paying fees or by accepting the opportunity cost of earnings forgone. For if post-school education is completely subsidized – with no fees and with grants to cover living expenses – then students will be enabled to reap private benefits at public expense.

On the other hand, if students are required to pay fees or finance their own living expenses, then this is likely to deter those from working class families who cannot afford to meet the direct or indirect costs of post-compulsory education. So some form of subsidy is necessary and justified on equity grounds also to prevent inequalities of opportunity. And many would argue that the recent decline in the real value of student grants has seriously reduced equality of access to higher education in Britain.

On the other hand, some economists have argued that present patterns of financing post-school education are inequitable, not because the level of subsidy is too low but, on the contrary, because the present fee and grant structure offers too great a subsidy to those who could afford to pay more towards the costs of higher or further education. This effectively transfers resources from the average taxpayer to those who will enjoy higher-than-average lifetime incomes as a result of their education – a transfer of income from the poor to the rich.

Others would argue that employers should contribute more towards the cost of producing skilled manpower, since it is they who will benefit from higher levels of output and productivity, and the Government's attempts to persuade industry to finance City Technology Colleges can be seen as one attempt to shift some of the financial burden of even compulsory education from public to private sources.

The question of how the costs of education should be shared between the individuals and their families who will benefit directly from their education, employers who may enjoy higher levels of output and profits as a result of employing more skilled manpower, and the taxpayer who can expect long-term benefits to the economy and to society at large, as a result of improved levels of skills and knowledge is complex. Indeed, the questions 'Who benefits?' and 'Who pays?' are far from easy to answer, quite apart from the question 'Who should pay?'

This chapter therefore examines the evidence on the social and private benefits of post-school education in the UK as well as the distribution of financial burdens, in order to throw light on the question of priorities for public spending on post-school education and possible changes in methods of finance. The chapter ends by suggesting that the present system of finance is unsatisfactory on both efficiency and equity grounds.

INVESTMENT IN HUMAN CAPITAL

The idea that education represents investment in human capital, which will bring benefits in the form of increased earning power for the individual, in the same way as the purchase of a machine represents investment in physical capital, was first explored in the eighteenth century by Adam Smith:

> When any expensive machine is erected, the extraordinary work to be performed by it before it is worn out, it must be expected, will replace the capital laid out upon it, with at least the ordinary profits. A man educated at the expense of much labour and time to any of those employments which require extraordinary dexterity and skill, may be compared to one of those expensive machines. The work which he learns to perform, it must be expected, over and above the usual wages of common labour, will replace to him the whole expense of his education, with at least the ordinary profits of an equally valuable capital. It must do this too in a reasonable time, regard being had to the very uncertain duration of human life, in the same manner as to the more certain duration of the machine. The difference between the wages of skilled labour and those of common labour is founded upon this principle. (Smith 1775: Book 1, Chapter 10)

Concerned as he was with the power of the market, and with the way in which the forces of demand and supply interact to produce and maintain equilibrium in the marketplace, Adam Smith saw education primarily as a *private* investment. But a hundred years later Alfred Marshall emphasized that education was a public as well as a private investment: 'The wisdom of expending public and private funds on education is not to be measured by its direct fruits alone. It will be profitable as a mere investment, to give the masses of the people much greater opportunities than they can generally avail themselves of. . . . There are few practical problems in which the economist has a more direct interest than those relating to the principles on which the expense of the education of children should be divided between the State and the parents' (Marshall 1890).

Despite these early references to the notion that there are parallels between investment in human and physical capital, and that the profitability of both types of investment can be measured using the same tools of cost – benefit or rate of return analysis – there was in fact very little economic analysis of how the costs of education should be shared between public and private sources until the 1960s, when American economists such as Schultz, Dennison, Mincer, and Becker seized upon the concept of investment in human capital and made it a central theme of a newly emerging branch of economic theory: the economics of education and vocational training.

Dennison (1962) was primarily interested in education as a *social* investment and tried to measure the contribution of education to economic growth by comparing the relative rates of growth of national income, physical capital, formation, labour force participation, and the educational level of the labour force in the USA. The results suggested that at least a quarter of the observed growth of GNP in the USA between 1910 and 1960 could be explained by increases in the educational qualifications of American workers.

Becker (1964) and Mincer (1962) on the other hand, were equally interested in education and on-the-job training as a private investment, and emphasized that the question of who reaps the benefits of the investment is crucial for determining who should pay for the investment. Initially, their analysis was concerned with on-the-job training, rather than formal education, and it is instructive to take this as a starting point, since the issues about who benefits from education and training can be posed particularly starkly when we consider on-the-job training. In fact, many of the arguments are equally applicable to all forms of post-school education.

INVESTMENT IN VOCATIONAL TRAINING

We start, therefore, by looking at the question of who benefits from investment in vocational training. Becker and Mincer drew a distinction between 'general' training, which can be expected to increase a worker's productivity in a wide range of jobs, and 'specific' training, which increases productivity in only one type of job, and is therefore of particular benefit to a single employer. Whereas employers can be expected to finance specific training, in the hope of higher levels of worker productivity and output in the future, there will be little or no incentive for them to finance general training, since there is no guarantee that the employer paying for the training will enjoy the benefits. Instead the skilled workers may be 'poached' by competitors who will offer higher wages in order to reap the benefits of highly skilled workers without incurring the costs of training. In the case of general training, therefore, the employer will pass on the costs of training to the individual worker, in the form of lower wages while he or she is receiving on-the-job training. At the same time, the worker will be willing to accept low wages in the expectation of higher earnings in the future, when the training is complete.

This argument assumes that decisions about training can safely be left to employers and employees, since they will be well informed about the benefits of training, and since market forces can be relied upon to generate the right 'signals' in the form of relative prices or wages for different types of skills. However, since there are imperfections in the labour market and since employers or employees lack perfect information about the costs and benefits of training, and find it impossible to forecast what the benefits will be in the future, then there is a case for public intervention to prevent under-investment in vocational education or training. What form should this intervention take?

It may take the form of exhortation to employers to invest more in training, on the grounds that they will benefit in the future. The Manpower Services Commission and the National Economic Development Office have tried that particular solution. In a series of publications with titles like *Competence and competition* and *Challenge to complacency*, the MSC and NEDO have urged

employers to devote more resources to vocational training. Yet there is mounting evidence that many employers continue to disregard these 'exhortations'
about the benefits of training (MSC).

An alternative policy is to force employers to contribute to the costs of
training either by means of a special training tax, as has been tried in France,
or through a compulsory levy-grant system, as was tried in the UK in the
1960s and 1970s, under the Industrial Training Act. The Industrial Training
Boards, with their powers to impose compulsory levies, were abolished, however, in the belief that employers could be relied upon to assess their own
training needs. Yet recent reports from the MSC question this assumption,
and in fact the whole thrust of publications like 'Challenge to Complacency'
is that employers do not perceive the benefits of training, and therefore there
is under-investment.

A third solution, therefore, is for the government to subsidize the costs of
vocational training either by giving grants to employers or individual trainees,
or by providing grants or other financial incentives to Local Education Authorities to spend more on vocational training. The last few years have seen a
major shift in this direction, with the growth of MSC expenditure on training.

Part of this can of course be explained by rising unemployment. The rapid
increase in expenditure on the Youth Training Scheme (YTS) and programmes for adult unemployed has meant a considerable increase in public
expenditure on training. But other trends, notably specific funding for the
Technical and Vocational Education Initiative (TVEI) and the transfer of
funding for work-related non-advanced further education (NAFE) have also
had important implications for the level of public expenditure on vocational
training.

Yet not of these shifts has been subjected to rigorous analysis including
analysis of the costs and benefits of training. The benefits of training are too
often assumed to be self-evident, although, at the same time, employers are
criticized for failing to recognize these benefits and for investing too little in
training. There have been few attempts to measure the costs and benefits of
vocational training in Britain. Let us turn, therefore, to general post-school
education, where there have been several attempts to measure social and
private costs and benefits.

SOCIAL AND PRIVATE COSTS AND BENEFITS OF EDUCATION

The first attempt to measure the rate of return to investment in education in
this country was by Blaug (1967) who also examined the assumptions underlying this form of cost-benefit analysis.

The crucial assumption behind the use of earnings differentials to measure the *social*, as opposed to the *private* benefits of education is that the higher earnings of educated workers reflect their higher productivity. The extra life-time earnings of a graduate, compared with a school leaver who entered employment at 16 or 18, are therefore regarded as a measure of the higher levels of output achieved by more educated workers. This assumption has been frequently challenged, notably by those who argue that education does not increase productivity, but simply acts as a convenient 'screening device' which enables employers to identify those who they believe will be more productive by virtue of superior ability, motivation, or simply a more privileged social background.

Few economists would now argue that the social rate of return, obtained by comparing the present value of the total social costs of education with the present value of expected lifetime benefits in the form of increased earning capacity, is a wholly satisfactory measure of the profitability of investing public resources in post-school education. Quite apart from the fact that relative earnings clearly do not perfectly reflect differences in productivity, there is the fact that no-one has yet succeeded in measuring the external or 'spill-over' benefits to society of having a well-educated population.

However, estimates of the private rate of return do show that education can be very profitable for the individual, and the difference between the social and the private rate of return therefore provides a measure of the extent of public subsidy of education, which can be used as a starting point for an analysis of 'Who benefits?' and 'Who pays?'

Table 1 Estimates of social and private rates of return to first degrees in UK, 1979–84

Subject	Social rate of return (Including costs of research) Assuming		Private rate of return (Including value of maintenance award) 'education factor'	
	1.0	0.67	1.0	0.67
Arts	negative		10	9
Engineering	6	4	32	25
Science	5	3	22	19
Social Science	11	8	27	23

Source: Clark and Tarsh (1987)

The most recent attempt to measure social and private costs and benefits of education in the UK (Clark and Tarsh 1987) concludes that for the individual, university education can be very profitable indeed, and that the private rate of return is well in excess of the social rate. Table 1 shows alternative estimates of the private and social rate of return to a first degree in 1979–84. The different values represent different assumptions about how much of the extra earnings of graduates are actually the result of their education, as opposed to differences in ability or social background. If the whole of the extra earnings can be attributed to higher education, then the rate of return will be higher than if we assume that only two thirds of the earnings differential is due to education (an 'education factor' of 0.67) and that one third is due to differences in ability or social background.

This is simply one reason why attempts to measure social and private rates of return are subject to uncertainty and error. Alternative assumptions can also be made about the likely growth of earnings in the future and about how much of the cost of university education should be attributed to research, rather than teaching. Much more fundamental, there is considerable disagreement among economists about the extent to which earnings differentials actually measure productivity.

Nevertheless, despite all these uncertainties the fact that there is such a marked difference between the social and private rates of return, shown in Table 1, raises some serious issues about the size of public subsidy for higher education in Britain. The difference between the social and the private costs reflects the fact that not only do British students pay none of the costs of university tuition, which amounted on average to £23,000 per graduate in 1984, but also many receive a full maintenance award, which covers most, if not all, living expenses. The difference between the social and the private benefits in this calculation simply measures the effects of income tax; private benefits are measured after tax, whereas social benefits include the extra tax paid by graduates. What Table 1 tells us, therefore, is that the extra taxes paid by the average graduate are less than the total subsidy received, and therefore the private rate of return is considerably higher than the social rate.

As we argued above, some public subsidy is justified, because the social benefits, including the 'spill-over benefits' that cannot be measured, are believed to be greater than the direct benefits to the individual. The question is whether such a large subsidy is justified, on efficiency grounds. Even if we believe that there are substantial indirect benefits to society from having highly-educated manpower, and even when we recognize that earnings are not necessarily a good measure of productivity, the difference between private rates of return for social science and engineering of 27 per cent and 32 per cent and the social rates of 11 per cent and 6 per cent is so substantial that it raises grave doubts about whether such a large subsidy is necessary on efficiency grounds. In the case of an arts degree the fact that the social rate of return appears to be negative, while the private rate of return is about 10 per cent, raises even graver doubts. But perhaps the subsidy can be justified on equity grounds.

THE EQUITY IMPLICATIONS OF PUBLIC SUBSIDIES FOR EDUCATION

In Britain, as in most countries, 'It has been repeatedly shown that, for young people of equal ability, the likelihood of continuing in full-time education after the minimum school-leaving age diminishes the lower the social class of their parents' (Fulton 1981). This means that it is the children of high income, upper social class families who are most likely to benefit from the subsidies for higher education. The present system of mandatory awards for full-time degree level students also ensures that those who are most likely to benefit from grants for higher education are full-time students entering degree level courses straight after school. Those who wish to study part-time, or to take non-degree level courses, those wishing to study for a second qualification, and mature students, are much less likely to receive financial support, since they are reliant on discretionary rather than mandatory awards.

This is why the present pattern of subsidies for higher and further education has often been criticized as inequitable, since it discriminates against certain categories of student, such as part-time students doing vocational courses, in favour of full-time university students who are most likely to come from privileged social backgrounds (Woodhall 1982), or as Blaug argued: 'Without splitting hairs it is fair to say that almost half of the grants system simply gives to those who already have. There is nothing wrong with this if we really believe in supporting an educational élite. But to defend grants in higher education on grounds of social equality is a monstrous perversion of the truth' (Blaug 1976:296).

The alternative is to provide financial aid for students in post-school education through a mixture of grants and loans, which would be both more equitable and more efficient than the present pattern of grants. Such combined systems of grants and loans exist in many other countries, including Canada and the USA, as well as several European countries (Woodhall 1982).

CONCLUSION: TOWARDS A NEW SYSTEM OF STUDENT SUPPORT

A recent comparison of the pattern of cost sharing in higher education in Britain, West Germany, France, Sweden, and the USA (Johnstone 1986) concluded that in the UK the individual student bears less of the costs of higher education and the taxpayer bears a greater proportion of the costs than in the USA or any of the European countries:

The students' share is by far the lowest among these five nations in the UK, which not only has no governmentally sponsored loan programmes (and the students and the opposition clearly intend to keep it that way), but also actively discourages students from working part-time. (Johnstone 1986)

A shift towards some form of student loans for higher education, combined with grants or scholarships for particular groups of students, including those from the lowest income families, could help to share the costs of higher education more equitably, and at the same time encourage greater participation from those who, like part-time students, are the least likely to benefit from current arrangements.

The development of a new system of student support needs to ensure that the distribution of costs and benefits are taken into account. While this chapter has done no more than sketch an outline of such a shift, it has attempted to show how an analysis of who benefits from post-school education could help to throw light on the fundamental question of how the costs of investment in human capital should be shared among all those who benefit, including the individual, employers, and society as a whole.

REFERENCES

Becker, G. S. (1964) *Human Capital. A Theoretical and Empirical Analysis, With Special Reference to Education*, Princeton University Press.

Blaug, M. (1967) 'The private and the social returns on investment in education: some results for Great Britain', *Journal of Human Resources*, Summer 1967.

Clark, A. and Tarsh, J. (1987) 'How much is a degree worth?' in A. Harrison and J. Gretton (Eds.) (1987) *Education and Training UK 1987* Policy Journals.

Dennison, E. F. (1962) *The Sources of Economic Growth in the United States and the Alternatives Before Us*, New York: Committee for Economic Development.

Fulton, O. (Ed.) (1981) *Access to Higher Education*, Guildford: Society for Research into Higher Education.

Johnstone, D. B. (1986) *Sharing the Costs of Higher Education*, New York: College Examination Board.

Manpower Services Commission *Competence and Competition: Challenge to Complacency*, London: MSC.

Marshall, A. (1890) *Principles of Economics* (Various editions).

Mincer, J. (1962) 'On-the-job training: costs, returns and some implications.' *Journal of Polit. Econ. Rev.*, December 1962.

Schultz, T. W. (1963) *The Economic Value of Education*, Columbia University Press.

Smith, A. (1776) *The Wealth of Nations* (Various editions).

Woodhall, M. (1982) 'Financial support for students' in A. Morris and J. Sizer (Eds.) (1982) *Resources and Higher Education*, Guildford: SRHE.

3.4

ADULT ACCESS TO LEARNING OPPORTUNITIES

KEITH PERCY

CONTEXT

In international discussions, it is conventional to subdivide the topic of adult and continuing education into three categories: formal, non-formal and informal adult and continuing education.[1] Thereafter, the definitions tend to differ in important ways. A useful formulation gives the following content to the categories:

> *Formal* What is provided by the education and training system set up or sponsored by the state for the specific purpose of educating and training adults.
> *Non-formal* The learning and educational opportunities available to adults outside the formal system in agencies and contexts with primary objectives to which education and training are subordinate.
> *Informal* The lifelong process by which every person acquires and accumulates knowledge, skills, and attitudes and insights from daily experience and exposure to the environment – at home, at work, and in leisure.

It is on this formulation that the following paper is based.

Policy concerns and discussions of practice in the United Kingdom, however, largely confine themselves to formal adult and continuing education. There is an occasional nod towards, for example, the educational activities of some, easily recognized, non-formal agencies, and an unspoken presumption that informal adult learning is too unsystematic and too unstructured to be grasped. That is not to say that there is coherence in policy and practice in formal adult and continuing education in the United Kingdom. In fact, there is an absence of a clear and connected rationale for what goes on in the formal sector, and only unco-ordinated and isolated attempts to accumulate and to bring together the systematic knowledge from which such a rationale could be constructed.

Nevertheless, since the mid 1970s, there has been a consistent intervention-ist trend in government actions in relation to adult education and training. No longer are the latter permitted to exist as a provision at the fringes of public expenditure – harmless, perhaps even worthy, but marginal. Specifically funded government programmes (aimed, for example, at adult literacy, education for unemployed adults, vocational training and re-training for workers, up-dating in colleges and universities for professionals and others) have stemmed from related sources. Such programmes, generally conceived, are part of the armoury of politicians in their search for solutions to other and more immediate problems (in their terms) than mere educational problems. Moreover, the direction and required conditions of such programmes enable civil servants to call for the thrustfulness, cost-effectiveness, and clarity about objectives which some of them regard as normally absent from adult and continuing education practice.

Specific, targeted, funding can, of course, distort provision. It is not neces-sarily so, but it can concentrate time, effort, innovation, and concern onto certain areas and topics to the neglect of others; it can encourage the cutting of corners, the taking of action on the basis of immediacy, slogan, and rhetoric. Bad practice can be stimulated alongside good practice and neither evaluated.

Since the mid-1970s, all of this has happened in the United Kingdom at one level, the real level, of adult and continuing education. But it is not the whole story. At another level, worthy and important things have been said, written, and sometimes done. In 1973, the Russell Committee delivered its major, and broadly balanced, report on adult education. The Report concerned itself mainly with the formal sector, took the positive view that 'the explicit and latent demands for all kinds of adult education have increased and will continue to increase. Adults in their own right have claims for the provision of a comprehensive service which can satisfy these demands in appropriately adult ways', and called on the government to establish a 'Development Council for Adult Education' with a brief for expansion.[2] A few years later, in 1976, the Open University published its own report on continuing education (the so-called 'Venables Report'), which went beyond its own internal concerns to consider national issues. It, too, recommended a national Development Council which, by implication, would signal the channelling of additional resources to the expansion of learning opportunities for adults. In 1977, the government of the day set up a national body – significantly not a 'development' but an 'advisory' council – the Advisory Council for Adult and Continuing Education (ACACE). It was granted an initial three-year period of existence, renewed for a second three-year period, and then discontinued in 1983. The Advisory Council commissioned and published a large number of research and develop-ment studies, most of them useful, and some of them important. It published a sequence of policy documents. But it did not, of its own, institute change or break the mould in the development of adult access to learning opportunities. Interestingly, in its swansong Report[3] in 1982 it recognized a great array of provision outside the formal sector and noted that 'it is impossible to make any accurate assessment of the scale of educational activities undertaken ... The main difficulty is to distinguish between directly educational and indirectly educative provision'; it called for 'the creation of a comprehensive system of continuing education' and for 'a coherent national policy for the promotion of continuing education (to be) ... drawn up and put into practice without delay'. Fastidiously diplomatic to the end, the Council did not comment upon its own demise, nor did it identify a need for a national Development Council to draw up such a plan.

Nevertheless, in 1984, the Department of Education and Science (DES) announced that the now defunct ACACE would have a successor, but it would be of a different shape. There would be no drawing up of national blueprints. The Unit for the Development of Adult and Continuing Education (again established on the basis of renewable three-year cycles) would have objectives closer to the 'field', concerned with the development of practice. The Unit would work short term on 'development topics' agreed with the Department of Education and Science. The normal *modus operandi* would include practitioner steering groups, initial consultative paper, short-term research and development studies (with emphasis upon innovation and good practice among practitioners), final reports, and recommendations checked with, and ultimately disseminated to the 'field'. Agreement of the DES would be necessary at all important stages. The first three development topics of UDACE were educational guidance, education of older adults, and, significantly, relationships between voluntary and statutory providers. These choices of topic were probably the outcome of a process of mediation between the climate of opinion as interpreted by the Department of Education and Science's civil servants and active lobbying by interested parties. Other themes subsequently added were 'new technology' and, importantly, 'access to learning opportunities'.

UDACE, then, is one of the modes through which the centralized steer of adult and continuing education in the United Kingdom in the 1980s had manifested itself. So far it is clear that UDACE has done some very good work. However, to subdivide practice and policy into 'topics', of course, may throw up barriers as well as cast them down. It is a matter of definition of what is included for analysis and development, and what is excluded. For example, the major thrusts of UDACE's development work on 'access' are specific and indicate a particular orientation. Much of the resource available has been put into the testing of the American Student Potential Programme with British adults, and into an encouragement of the development nationwide of accreditation models of Open Colleges (of which more below).

In fact, concern about 'access' for adults to educational opportunities is one of the watchwords of British adult and continuing education in the mid to late 1980s. Professional and quasi-professional associations have been formed to promote 'access'; journals founded, conferences held, courses established. Yet, a Pandora's box of aims, aspirations, concepts, and values are mixed together in talk of 'access'. Some of those who use the term are referring to access to higher education courses and to higher education qualifications for adults; others mean access by adults to all formal learning opportunities of any kind; many are thinking particularly of access by 'disadvantaged' adults who might be black people, disabled, working-class, women, or from several other categories. The original, specially funded, so-called 'Access Courses' of the late 1970s were set up to recruit black adults and to prepare them for professional courses leading, chiefly, to qualifications in teaching and social work.

The usual conceptual model which underlies current observations and analysis on 'access' is that of 'barriers'. On the one hand are adults, on the other are formal learning opportunities of all kinds. Only a minority of adults participate in these opportunities – usually they are adults who are advantaged on most social indicators. Therefore, the model runs, there are barriers, external and internal, which prevent adults from participating in formal learning opportunities. External barriers usually cited include physical (geographical; travel time; type of accommodation), financial (tuition fees; cost of books and equipment), structural (availability of appropriate courses and learning opportunities; availability of appropriate tuition; entry requirements; use of appropriate publicity; availability of guidance services). Barriers internal to the adult usually cited include motivation, attitudes, educational preparedness, self-image and concept and perceptions of educators and of the value of learning. For example, UDACE's initial short discussion paper on access urged that 'an accessible system would be perceived by its users (individuals, groups and employers) to be:

- *appropriate* to their needs as they see them;
- *attractive* in form, approach, timing, and location, and able to compete on equal terms with other users of the time and money;
- *possible* – designed for 'people like me' (which will need to reflect many kinds of perception);
- *of high quality* – competently delivered and capable of meeting its stated objectives;
- *comprehensible* – with aims, objectives, and interrelationships between the parts clearly stated;
- *responsive* – capable of changing in the light of new, or newly expressed, needs'.

Of course, talk of a 'system' and of 'users' and the setting of an agenda emphasizing 'design', 'delivery', and 'quality' immediately focuses attention upon formal learning opportunities and upon the practices of providers. This paper goes on to consider, however, the full range of learning opportunities to which adults potentially have access and in which they may participate.

PARTICIPATION

Formal learning

The most recent comprehensive national survey of adult participation in learning was undertaken by ACACE in 1980.[4] In a doorstep survey it asked a representative sample of almost two and a half thousand of the adult (17 years and over) population in England and Wales if they had 'done any kind of study, learning, or practising part-time or full-time at work or elsewhere' since leaving full-time education. The question appears to have been unlikely to pick up non-formal or informal learning and likely to have emphasized work-related formal training.

The survey concluded that ten per cent of the adult population were (on self report) engaged in 'some form of continuing education or training' at the time of the survey. A further ten per cent said that they had been engaged in some form of education or training in the preceding three years. A further 27 per cent said that they had done so at some other time. Thus a total of 47 per cent of the adult population had at some time since completing full-time education participated in continuing education or training. On self report 53 per cent said that they had never done so.

Analysis of the survey showed 'current' (i.e. 'now' or in the past three years) participation in continuing education and training to be strongest among young (i.e. under 25) men and women; this age group was most likely to be engaged in study related to current work and future prospects. Similarly, said the report on the survey, 'the C_1 group, which shows a high current participation for both sexes, is a group of people in jobs requiring at least some education but in which people may well have aspirations to make further progress'. Rate of participation fell with increasing age, particularly for men. Participation by pensioners was markedly low.

Table 1 summarizes some of the findings of the survey. Percentages quoted are of the relevant sample interviewed; 'current' includes 'past three years'.

Another survey,[5] wholly confined to institutionally-provided 'substantial' courses, shows the profile of adults participating in courses which lead to qualifications (and are often, therefore, job-related) to be markedly different from that of adults on 'non-qualifying courses'. Over 50 per cent of those on 'qualifying courses' were aged 30 or under, and 80 per cent were aged 40 or under. In contrast, fewer than 50 per cent of adults on non-qualifying courses were 40 or under and 20 per cent were over 60. Women made up almost 80

Table 1 Current participants in continuing education by age group, social class and sex*[4]

Age	Men %	Women %	Class	Men %	Women %
17–24	21	22	A B	10	23
25–44	14	13	C_1	18	21
45–64	5	10	C_2	7	11
65–75	4	9	D/E	6	5
All	11	13	All	11	13

* includes 2% currently in full-time initial education

per cent of those on non-qualifying courses but less than 50 per cent on qualifying courses. Working-class adults, particularly women, were 'massively' under-represented on qualifying and non-qualifying courses. By contrast, 'service' class adults (particularly lower-grade professionals, administrators, and managers), both men and women, were well represented in qualifying courses. Nine out of ten adults on qualifying courses had previous qualifications (the level varying according to the course); in the non-qualifying courses more than one fifth of the adult students had no qualifications (but one third had qualifications of around degree level).

The value of these surveys is the reminder they give of the complexity underlying questions of adult access to learning opportunities. While it is possible to generalize about participation in the formal sector, such generalizations have only limited significance. It is necessary to delineate which learning opportunities (qualifying, job-related, advanced, etc.) and which adult groups (age, sex, social class, ethnic origin, etc.) are at issue before discussion of access can be fleshed out into meaningful research questions and worthwhile matters of policy. It is most likely that the external and internal 'barriers to access' between, say, on the one hand, a black working-class male shift worker, aged 25 years, and participation in a non-vocational part-time humanities course, and, on the other hand, a white middle-class woman of pensionable age and participation in a full-time university science degree course are, in both instances, very great, but require analysis and remedies on dimensions which (except in the remoter regions of social science) do not overlap.

We are left with the stark statistic from the ACACE survey that 53 per cent of the adult population reported that they had never participated in continuing education and training – a statistic which it is reasonable to associate with the formal sector. A rather different investigation[6] in the north-west of England in the late 1970s/early 1980s (also under the auspices of ACACE) suggested, by contrast, that more than 20 per cent of the adult population were involved in education and training currently (meaning in the current session). This survey had stretched beyond formal learning into non-formal learning. It attempted to investigate not only all types of private and commercial adult education, but also the variety and range of activities and learning experiences which might be associated with voluntary and community organizations. In this way, it deduced that more than one in five of the adult population were participating in 'systematic learning' in which a 'provider' was involved. It laid the groundwork for a further study in the north-west of England described in the next section of this chapter.

Non-formal learning

As long ago as 1963, a large survey of adult students in the United States[7] found that (even setting adult independent learning on one side) more than half of the educational activities in which adults were involved took place outside the classroom setting. This finding excited little interest in the United Kingdom and, over the next twenty years, there were almost no comparable studies. However, as a result of more recent research,[8] we now know more about the broader horizons of adult learning in this country.

Over ten per cent of the adult population at any one time may be involved in the activities of voluntary organizations – organizations, which, broadly, may be defined as under the control of unpaid voluntary members, outside the statutory sector and not operating for commercial profit. The recent study[8] proposed a framework for the categorization of voluntary organizations which allocated them according to their 'orientation' (the cluster of objectives, motivations, and tendencies which brought organizations into existence and caused members to enrol). Six 'orientations' constituted the framework; these were typified as:

Interest	pursuit of an interest, hobby or topic
Service	service of others
Advocacy	promotion of a cause
Social	meeting others
Vocational	job- or unemployment-related
Community	concern for community or locality

The study found significant levels of 'learning activity' among adults in voluntary organizations (and these organizations varied in scope and size from national organizations to little local clubs and societies). But the findings were complex. Adults may not be intending to learn, or realize that they are involved in 'learning activity'; indeed, they may reject the notion, whatever their behaviour suggests. There are variations between the types and frequency of 'learning activity' to be found in voluntary organizations with different orientations and combinations of orientation. There were hints in the study that working-class people find voluntary organizations more accessible than evening classes; certainly elderly people are prominent in the voluntary sector.

Perhaps, more importantly, the study reported data which challenge some of the sacred cows and shibboleths of the formal sector of adult and continuing education. It constructed an empirically-derived taxonomy of the 'learning activities' to be found among adults in voluntary organizations, of which the main constituents were:

Formal learning activities	*Informal learning activities*
teaching	practice learning
organized discussion	apprenticeship learning
training	learning from experience
assessment and certification	learning through social interaction

Voluntary organizations, it appears from the study, have more of a propensity towards being 'learning democracies'. The teacher role, where it exists, is demystified and deprofessionalized. In certain circumstances, learners will become teachers. Experienced and senior members will train and assess less experienced and junior members. Yet it is just as frequent an occurrence for the less experienced to learn in less formal ways, even without the teacher-learner relationship being apparent through conventions or words. In the study, junior members sat by, helped, queried, and were assisted by, senior members. They tried, failed, and tried again. They did, performed, acted, and their peers commented, drew on their experience, advised. It seemed likely also that members learned by carrying out the tasks and roles which the organization's continued existence required: they took responsibility, spoke, sat on committees, organized, became officers. Further, through the structure of roles and relationships which the life of the organization made available to them, it seemed possible to say that members had the opportunity for self-development. 'They learned about other people', some claimed – and this, being interpreted, means that they learned about themselves.

In crude quantitative terms, the numerical participation of adults in learning opportunities is significantly enhanced if one takes into account the extent of non-formal learning which is implied by the extrapolation of these findings. However, the study also appeared to lead to qualitative, perhaps philosophical, conclusions. Almost exclusively, adults – in both the formal and non-formal sectors – are volunteers, not conscripts, for learning. By definition, then, learning has not only to be attractive and to seem worthwhile to them, it also has to reach out to them, both physically (time, place, cost, convenience) and mentally. The latter may mean, from the evidence of the voluntary organizations' study, in situations which are not hierarchical, are de-professionalized, and in which doing and experience are promoted, as ways of learning, over theorizing and verbalizing.

Adult independent learning

Since the late 1960s, the research of the Canadian, Tough, and his associates, into adult independent learning[9] has been replicated throughout the developed world, but has not occasioned much interest in the United Kingdom. There have been a number of small-scale studies but none that have been carried through to implications for practice.

In brief, it has been shown by Tough and his followers to be the case that self-directed, or independent, learning among adults is a major phenomenon, involving most of the adult population. Indeed, it may be taken that it is almost a definition of an adult existence in Western society that self-directed learning continues throughout most of life. Such a view parallels the formulation by the humanistic psychologists for whom the human condition implies curiosity about the changing world around one, and the inner drive to learn the skills and knowledge necessary to adapt to shifting roles and circumstances.

Tough concluded that adults engage in many 'learning projects' throughout life. The definition of a 'learning project' has nothing, necessarily, to do with attendance at a class or involvement in a group, in either the formal or non-formal sectors. Stemming from curiosity or the need for superior performance, learning projects are pieces of planned and intended learning defined by time duration. A learning project lasts for at least seven hours, but is made up of discontinuous 'learning episodes'. A 'learning episode' may last for anything from ten minutes to four hours, and is marked by 'relatively uninterrupted' primary intention to learn, to learn about, to learn how. The object of learning is not part of the definition; the learning might be of advanced egyptology, how to mend a fuse, how to improve at a sport, or anything else.

Tough's methodology is based chiefly upon lengthy face-to-face interviews in which the subject is led to reconstruct, through dialogue with the interviewee, past learning episodes and learning projects. The methodology has been questioned, especially for its small sample sizes and for doubts about its relevance to, and success with, blue-collar workers. Nevertheless, Tough's findings are striking. Ninety per cent of adults engage in learning projects, he claims. The 'median person' conducts five distinct learning projects per year, and spends an average of one hundred hours on each learning project. In one study, Tough found that 73 per cent of learning projects were self-planned and only 17 per cent were planned by or with 'professionals', either in a group or one-to-one situation. However, it was also the case that in two thirds of the instances recalled, adults turned to 'outside assistance' during a project. 'Acquaintances' were called upon to assist much more often than 'experts' were.

If one leaves aside the questions about Tough's methodology and the generalizability of his findings to the United Kingdom, some significant issues, nevertheless, remain. The debate about liberal education needs to be matched up with his findings. Are all objects of study of equal worth? Do some provide more cognitive perspective than others, do some feed curiosity, challenge, lead on to further stages of enquiry more easily than others do? Lying further back are yet more fundamental questions. What are the springs of human curiosity? What makes an adult liable to be 'interested' in one thing rather than another, and thus to undertake a learning project? Adult educators have only partial and unproven answers to this latter question. They talk variously about the major change points in the life cycle, or about the experience of initial schooling, or about sub-cultural socialization, etc. Putting the two knotty problems together – if we were able satisfactorily to argue that some objects of study are intrinsically more worthwhile, then we would then wish to examine empirically which adults, and in what circumstances, are more likely to pursue them as self-directed learners, and why, and with what success.

An easier, or more immediate, course of debate and enquiry relates to the facilitation of adult independent learning. Do adults in self-directed learning projects take false steps, deviate into learning *culs-de-sac*, make mistakes, learn unsuccessfully? It appears to be important that, if Tough is right, adults are more likely to turn to friends, acquaintances, or peers for assistance than to experts and professionals (teachers, librarians). Yet significant resources are bound up in the formal and non-formal sectors, some of which could, perhaps, be extended, modified, or redirected towards supporting independent learners – perhaps through the provision of learning guides, learning resources, and learning centres accessible in the home or in the community. Thus, the phenomenon of independent learning touches upon the notion of open learning (to be discussed later).

DEVELOPMENTS

This chapter began by discussing the absence of a clear and connected rationale for what takes place in British continuing education and training, and by outlining the emergence of a central 'steer' based less on the evaluation of practice and the accumulation of systematic knowledge, and more on 'developments', 'topics', and 'directions'. These latter are derived from the collective wisdom of practitioners and from the beliefs and prejudices underlying 'government' (more appropriately, in this context, 'civil servant') policy towards continuing education and training.

Some of these 'developments' are outlined below. All of them merit much more detailed discussion. In relation to this chapter, however, what is important is to consider the assumptions about access and the models of adult participation in learning which lie behind the developments.

Educational guidance

The lobby for widespread availability of educational guidance for adults has been gathering strength since the mid-1970s. Several sponsors have acted as midwife to it; the Open University was probably the first and, more recently, UDACE and the Manpower Services Commission the most effective.[10] The work of UDACE's development group has given high prominence to the topic and the DES agreed in 1987 to fund a national unit for educational guidance.

The notions inherent in the call for availability of educational guidance for adults on-course, in college and centre settings, and in local, independent, inter-agency, networked guidance units are that there is a maze of educational opportunities, and an adult normally has poor knowledge and understanding of them. He or she, therefore, probably needs information and advice, may need counselling and assessing, and sometimes needs support and advocacy in contacts with educational agencies. An educational guidance unit can also provide a service to employers and to educational agencies by keeping them informed of the kinds of needs which adults have. New technology obviously has a role in supporting educational guidance with easily up-datable and interactive information systems.

Of course, an adult has to know that educational guidance is available, and under what conditions, before it becomes useful. An adult has to make the first approach, has to be aware of a need, has to be interested in learning opportunities before educational guidance units can be held to make a contribution to access. Although, in theory, guidance units should be able to make available information and advice about learning opportunities in private and commercial adult education and in organizations in the non-formal sector, it is not likely that they will have such information comprehensively and systematically available.

Open learning

'Open learning' is certainly one of the powerful watchwords of the climate of opinion of British adult and continuing education in the 1980s.[11] In the late 1970s, the Council for Educational Technology sought to popularize the term in order to encourage formal (and often traditional) institutions of further and adult education to become more liberal and to minimize the barriers which they placed between aspirant adult learners and themselves. Open learning might involve no more than improving marketing, running courses outside the institution or during the vacation, or putting some of the teaching into writing for out-of-class use. Or it might involve the sophisticated use of educational technology. Thus location, timing, pace, and convenience of learning for adults could be made more accessible by use of distance learning materials, flexible learning packages, learning resource centres, telephone conferencing, and – as technology has developed in the 1980s – computer-based training, interactive video, and other systems. In the early 1980s, an amazing largesse of money, literally millions of pounds, was poured by the government's Department of Employment and the Manpower Services Commission into what turned out to be a relatively restricted concept of open learning. The 'Open Tech' programme concentrated upon the production of written materials, local 'delivery' systems, and local resource centres for the upgrading and retraining of working adults at technician and sub-professional level. After mixed success, the Manpower Services Commission transmuted the 'Open Tech' programme into its more broadly conceived 'Open Learning' programme. Alongside it, the so-called Open College (of the Air) began in 1987 with the intention of providing vocational training for employers and their employees through radio, television, and learning packages.

The success (for the adult learner) of these technology-based learning-packages, schemes, and systems of open learning depends crucially upon the quality of the materials. Some, hypothetically, can do more harm than good in terms of motivation and effective learning. Large set-up costs are involved in the writing of media-based learning packages; problems of inflexibility and difficulty of updating arise. There remain unanswered questions about the styles of learning and the attitudes to knowledge which learning packages can evoke in the adult learner – learning must be more than the uncritical acquisition of pre-digested information.

Clearly, though, notions of open learning relate significantly to the phenomenon of independent learning among adults discussed above, and to possibilities of access to learning outside the classroom and without obvious contact with an educational institution. Access to learning in the home, in the local community, whenever interest is fired, and whenever convenience allows, is bound to be crucially enhanced by the successful implementation of open learning concepts. It would, however, require immense resource and a fundamental re-orientation of the attitudes and experience of educators of adults to allow for that successful implementation.

Accreditation of prior learning

The acceptance into the received wisdom of adult and continuing education in the United Kingdom in the mid-1980s of the importance of the accreditation of prior adult learning, especially of prior experiential learning, is instructive. It has primarily been achieved through the writing and activities of one man (Norman Evans[12]) and of the agencies in which he has worked (Policy Studies Institute) and created (Learning from Experience Trust). The models and inspirations which he has used all derive from North American experience. In this country acceptance has been largely at the theoretical and 'policy' level; there are so far only a few examples of good practice on which to build.

Yet the contribution which ideas of the accreditation of adult prior experiential learning have to make to issues of access in the formal sector is potentially great. The simple thesis is that adults, during their lives both at work, and in the community and at home, have made significant learning gains in knowledge and skills through doing and experiencing. Adults learn through experience as well as from courses of study. The links with the findings of the report on learning activity in voluntary organizations discussed above are evident. In formal courses of study adults may be asked to learn skills and knowledge which they have already gained from life experience; it is, therefore, logical to find ways of giving them credit for learning achieved through experience prior to the course. Thus, courses of study would be shortened and participation made a more attractive proposition.

The problem is to devise systematic and comprehensive systems of giving credit for experience which are both credible and cost-effective, and which students, educational institutions, and employers will find manageable and meaningful. Thus, 'making-experience-count' courses have been devised, through which adults have been helped to put together portfolios of the experiential learning gains which they have made throughout life, and which they could, if they wish, produce as evidence to convince admissions officers and employers. A significant spin-off has been the gains in self-confidence and in the construction of a positive self-image which such a process can begin.

These ideas are far from being fully proven and far from being embedded in the formal sector of adult learning. But they fit well with other notions of the value of giving to adults 'credit' for their learning.

Credit transfer; credit accumulation; modularization

Courses of higher and further education in the United Kingdom have historically been relatively closed and confined to a continuous and prescribed period of study (in higher education, normally full-time) in one location. Limited schemes of credit transfer between educational institutions (aimed at students who for personal reasons had to drop out of courses) began to appear in the 1970s. In the 1980s, there has been a flurry of credit transfer and credit accumulation schemes, agreements, and agencies – the most important of them funded nationally – to assist adults to put together connected courses of study and to move towards qualification despite job mobility, child bearing and rearing, changes in motivation and orientation, and other factors. Such developments are assisted by beliefs that, in the 1990s, there will be more need to attract adults to formal courses of higher and further education because of a decline in the birth rate.

National and regional moves towards systems of credit transfer and accumulation necessarily mean moves towards standardization, and towards redefinition of courses into self-contained units of study (or 'modules') which can be slotted into an exchange system to the benefit of the mobile student. There is much talk of, and several initiatives towards, the 'modularization' of curricula as means to enhance adult access to certain kinds of learning opportunity.

Open College schemes

It would seem probable that interest in 'giving credit' to adults, credit transfer, and credit accumulation would be confined to vocational and 'qualifying' courses in the formal sector. The development of Open College schemes since the mid-1970s appears to show that this is not the case. These schemes are consortial regional arrangements designed to promote access specifically or primarily for adults to the range of formal educational opportunities, both vocational and non-vocational.

The first Open College Federation was created in the north-west of England in 1976 as an agreement between a university, a polytechnic, and one of the nearby further education colleges. It consisted of part-time courses devised and taught in the colleges but validated and (at the higher levels) examined by the university and the polytechnic. The twin objectives of the scheme were to prepare adults for entry to higher education and to provide liberal academic courses at an intermediate level 'for interest only'. The Open College Federation of the North West grew steadily over the next decade or so until, in 1988, it included sixteen colleges and 7,000 adult student enrolments.

In 1981, partly stimulated by the example of the North West Federation, but also by American models of accreditation, the Manchester Open College Federation was established. Through structures bringing together the further and higher education institutions of the major conurbation of Manchester, the Federation constituted a model of an Open College very different from that in the North West. Pre-existing courses of all kinds in the colleges and centres of the conurbation were recognized for credit at one of four levels, the amount of credit being related to the hours spent by the student in study on, or related to, the course. The Federation offered students the facility of a 'study passport', on which all accredited courses completed would be recorded and accumulated over time. By 1987, several thousand 'study passports' had been issued. The scheme was devised with adults mainly in mind, but was easily extendable to young people both in the later stages of school and in youth training and education courses. In a limited manner, it was also extending to learning activity in voluntary organizations and, in theory, could take on board the accreditation of adult prior experiential learning.

By 1988, there were at least seven Open College Federations in existence in the United Kingdom, and several in prospect. Most were based on the accreditation model devised in Manchester. The spread, and significant success of this model, brings into prominence the question of the motivational power for adults of credit earning as a means of attracting them to, or retaining them in, learning opportunities. It appears to be the case that for many adults in otherwise non-certificated vocational, quasi-vocational, and even non-vocational courses, the prospect of credit from the Manchester Federation is a potent lure or a welcome bonus. In many courses, such as those in adult basic education, it is a badge of success to show an employer and a reward for endeavour. However, the evidence is not yet collected which will show the extent to which the 'study passport' really is a significant factor in motivating adults to re-enrol in new courses and to make progression from one level of study to another.

The Manchester Federation is not confined to adults. However, the Open College of the North West makes great play, in its promotional and marketing activities, of being 'specially for adults', 'relating to adults' life experience', and using teaching and learning methods appropriate for adults. Whatever the truth of these claims (the truth is mixed), the evidence exists that the image is a potent one and that adults are attracted to return to study, and to re-enter the formal classroom setting, because of it. If learning opportunities for adults are not presented as 'going back to school', and do not necessarily imply sitting alongside young people – at least not during the first few faltering steps of the return – then it appears that, for some adults, the opportunities for access are more real.

CONCLUDING REMARKS

Four things, at least, should be apparent from this paper:

1. that current 'developments' in promoting access to learning opportunities for adults in the United Kingdom (as exemplified in the preceding section) are somewhat discontinuous, and based on semi-conceptualized models of access and incomplete theories of adult participation in learning;
2. that these 'developments', and most thinking about adult access to learning, relate to the formal learning sector;
3. that 'developments' and policy are planned in the absence of systematic research into most matters which are relevant to access and participation;
4. that certain sectors of society (for example working class, black) do not have, or do not use, access to most areas of formal learning. Other sectors

(for example women, the elderly) do not have, or do not use, access to certain areas of formal learning. As far as we can tell, participation in learning activity in voluntary organizations and adult independent learning is more widespread, but there is much which needs confirming by research.

In what has been described in this paper, there are indicators of a model of adult access to, and participation in, learning opportunities which might be relevant to more (if not most) of the adult population. The key is the concept of learning. Learning is not something which is confined to classrooms and available only at the hands of expert educators. It takes place informally; it is often self-directed; it is a necessary adjunct of survival in complex civilized society; it is deprofessionalized and democratized in voluntary organizations; it is brought to the individual, the home, the community, by the concepts and technologies of 'open-learning' systems; it can be derived from life experience, and there are techniques for helping adults to systematize their learning from experience and, in so doing, to value it.

What follows, then, for professional adult educators and for institutions of further, adult, and higher education? They remain, and will remain, important gatekeepers of skills, resources, knowledge, buildings, equipment and, above all, of a commitment. The commitment is to a belief that learning is integral to a balanced and happy quality of life. In the United Kingdom, the commitment is often overlaid by enrolment numbers, reorganizations, salary grades, and careers but without it the whole complex superstructure is meaningless. To serve only ten per cent of the adult population (and usually those already advantaged) at any one time, and only 50 per cent of the adult population ever, is a poor realization of that commitment. The broader notions of participation in learning, and the wide opportunities for access to it, with which this paper has been concerned, suggest lines of development which professional adult education in the United Kingdom could face with confidence, and which they would not exhaust until well into the next century.

REFERENCES

1. Organization for Economic Co-operation and Development (1977) *Learning Opportunities for Adults*, Volume 1, General Report, Paris: OECD.
2. HMSO (1973) *Adult Education: A Plan for Development. Report by a Committee of Inquiry . . . under . . . Sir Lionel Russell*, London: HMSO.
3. Advisory Council for Adult and Continuing Education (1982) *Continuing Education: From Policies to Practice*, Leicester: ACACE.
4. Advisory Council for Adult and Continuing Education (1982) *Adults: Their Educational Experience and Needs*, Leicester: ACACE.
5. Woodley, A., Wagner, L., Slowey, M., Hamilton, M., and Fulton, ·O. (1987) *Choosing to Learn: Adults in Education*, Milton Keynes: Society for Research into Higher Education and the Open University Press.
6. Percy, K., Butters, S., Powell, J., and Willett, I. (1983) *Post-Initial Education in the North West of England: A Survey of Provision*, Leicester: ACACE.

7. Johnstone, J. W. C. and Rivera, R. J. (1965) *Volunteers for Learning*, Chicago: University of Chicago Press.
8. Percy, K. (1988) *Learning in Voluntary Organisations*, Leicester: Unit for the Development of Adult and Continuing Education.
9. Tough, A. (1978) 'Major learning efforts: recent research and future directions' in *The Adult Learner: Current Issues in Higher Education*, Washington D.C.: American Association for Higher Education.
10. Butler, L. (1985) (Ed.) *Educational Guidance: A New Service for Adult Learners*, Milton Keynes: The Open University.
11. Hodgson, V. E., Mann, S., and Snell, R. (Eds.) (1987) *Beyond Distance Learning Towards Open Learning*, Milton Keynes: Society for Research into Higher Education and Open University Press.
12. Evans, N. (1987) *Assessing Experiential Learning: A Review of Progress and Practice*, York: Longmans Resources Unit.

3·5

ADULT BASIC EDUCATION

MARY HAMILTON

THE DEVELOPMENT OF ADULT BASIC EDUCATION IN BRITAIN

Background

Adult basic education is one of the most challenging and innovative areas of educational provision in Britain today. It covers basic literacy and numeracy for all adults, including those for whom English is a second language. It also covers the related communication and coping skills which are an essential foundation for other learning or for autonomy in everyday life. It is based on principles of open access and learners' rights to define their own learning needs and to take part fully in the decisions that affect their learning. There is a commitment to learner-centred methods including the right to individual tuition and to exploring new methods of learning which do not simply repeat or continue traditional schooling.

Beginning with a national adult literacy campaign in the early 1970s, adult basic education in Britain has developed from almost nothing to a complex and dynamic area of activity. This has been achieved within a period of general contraction of funding for education and for adult education in particular. Who needs adult basic education? Each year, two thirds of 16 year olds leave full-time schooling, many of them without the basic skills needed to return to academic or vocational study. Only one in five of 16 year old leavers has any GCE qualifications. Fifteen per cent have no qualifications at all. Older adults have even fewer qualifications.

Figures from the National Child Development Study have revealed that 13 per cent of 23-year-olds considered themselves to have difficulties with reading, writing or number work in their everyday lives. This gives an estimate of over five million people in the adult population at large and is now the accepted figure within Britain.[1] We also know that there is a great variety of needs within this group and that the cut-off point for adequate basic skills is arbitrary and changes with time and context.

Literacy and numeracy are difficult concepts to define and measure. UNESCO has adopted several different definitions over the years.[2] Different countries use different criteria for compiling their statistics, such as grade levels reached, or number of years in school, or even the number of people enrolled in school. Some studies have devised functional competency tests of literacy and numeracy by asking a sample of adults to carry out everyday tasks like filling in forms. These have typically produced much higher estimates of need.

Whichever measure we adopt, however, that there is a need for adult basic education (ABE) in Britain is not in question. Ever since help with basic skills has been on offer, demand has always outstripped supply, with waiting lists of potential students. And, despite the success of the last decade or so, and the large numbers of people in need, government expenditure on ABE is still very small compared with other areas of the education budget.

Problems of adult literacy and numeracy are structural – that is, they are built into our educational and social system – despite the fact that they are often 'discovered' with disbelief and treated as an isolated disease that can be eradicated from individuals. Such problems have always existed in Britain, despite universal compulsory schooling, and there are similar concerns in other western industrialized societies.[3]

It has always been accepted that school will fail many children. Schooling has been seen as a competition geared toward academic success for a minority, rather than a means for meeting the basic right of every child to adequate, useful competence in literacy and numeracy. Basic skills are of concern at the present because of changes in the economy and rising unemployment. These highlight the underachievement of many school leavers and the lack of post-school opportunities for adults to return to education or training at whatever level they need and especially for those with no formal qualifications.

Adult literacy and basic education in the industrialized countries of Europe and north America is a late-comer to the field of ABE. UNESCO has developed a large body of experience in third world countries since the early 1950s[4] and many other countries have initiated their own programmes of adult basic education, sometimes involving spectacular national mobilization as part of broader changes in the power structure of their society as in the Soviet Union, Tanzania, China, Cuba, and Nicaragua.[5] These activities form a body of experience and theoretical perspectives from which lessons can be drawn by those involved in ABE in industrialized countries.[6] Much of this work emphasizes the necessary links of adult education with community development and access to power and resources for disenfranchised groups.

The situation in industrialized, schooled societies might seem to have different roots from those in third world countries where there is no universal education. Differences among countries – in geography, language situation, social and political structures – make comparison difficult. However, despite the differences, links can be made, for example applications of Freire's work in the USA, the development of critiques of culture and schooling which help us understand how schools reinforce dominant and unjust cultural patterns and social structures. Such patterns make access to information and control of basic skills a very real problem for linguistic and cultural minorities and other non-dominant groups, working-class people, and women[7] in our societies, and their situation has direct parallels with populations in developing countries.

Links are also being made through anthropological and historical work[8] that is increasing our understanding of the roles of literacy in society. This work helps to uncouple literacy from schooling so that we can see it in its broader context as a means of communication and access to information.

The adult literacy campaign in Britain

The adult literacy campaign in Britain was launched in 1973 as a result of pressure from community workers and educators. A Labour Government released one million pounds in 1974 for the first year of the campaign. This money, combined with an enormous amount of volunteer effort and the involvement of the BBC in a novel media campaign, quickly established adult literacy provision. It became part of adult education in every local education authority, supported by a central agency, now known as the Adult Literacy and Basic Skills Unit (ALBSU). Adult basic education has now taken its place among the range of continuing education opportunities for adults in Britain.[9]

In 1973 it was estimated that only 5,000 adults in England and Wales were getting help with reading and writing. Tuition was provided by fewer than half of local authorities and mainly in classes of 12 or more students. By 1980 this number had risen to 85,000. ALBSU has supported this expansion through staff training, publishing resource materials for tutors and learners and through short-term funding for innovative 'special development' projects.

Apart from some work within the United States, Britain was the first of the industrialized countries to pay national attention to adult literacy. Other countries still look to the British experience for materials and ideas as they develop their own provision. Nevertheless, Britain still has a long way to go in certain respects. For example, adult literacy emerged in Britain as a single issue and has only gradually broadened its scope to make connections with the wider educational context – with other types of continuing education for adults and with issues about basic skills in schools. We have still not secured adequate funding or the statutory right of adults to basic education within a coherent policy of continuing education.

One of the major strengths of ABE in Britain is that it takes place within a wide variety of settings, some more educationally defined and others related to community-based projects or to organizations geared to the needs of specific groups of people, for example unemployed people, the homeless, the elderly, or disabled groups. In addition to voluntary organizations and local authority provision, the Manpower Services Commission, the armed forces, the prison service, trade unions, health authorities and social services have all been involved with adult basic education. Each setting shapes ABE in its own way and cross-fertilizes it with ideas from its own aims and ways of working. Such variety gives scope for innovation and flexibility. Just as voluntary groups were largely responsible for lobbying for the literacy campaign at the beginning, they continue to play an important role in pushing forward innovations in ABE. The National Federation of Voluntary Literacy Schemes (NFVLS) provides a voice for many of these organizations. Increasingly, ABE takes place in colleges of further education, offering learners contact with and the possibility of moving into the more formal world of further education courses.

The involvement of volunteers in ABE has enabled people from diverse backgrounds to become involved and to achieve a great deal with minimal funding. However, the use of volunteers has a double edge: it can be seen as 'education on the cheap', working against a properly resourced and managed service. Conditions and training for paid staff (who are largely part-time and female) are gradually improving. The increasing professionalization of ABE is an issue for the 1980s along with the need to attract a greater range of staff, closer to the cultural and class background of learners.

KEY ISSUES AND ACHIEVEMENTS IN ABE IN BRITAIN

Literacy for what? Defining aims and making links

What are the purposes of literacy and numeracy teaching with adults and how do these purposes shape the content and methods of different programmes? Different types of organizations involved in ABE may see their aims very differently. The most obvious example of this is the rise of an instrumental, functional approach to literacy and numeracy which focuses around training and employment. This approach is embodied in Britain by the Manpower Services Commission and has parallels in other countries. That basic skills up-grading should be seen as a chance to repeat the curriculum offered at school and enable people to step back onto the academic ladder is a well-entrenched view in North America. This view leads to an ABE that is defined by standardized testing and accreditation. In contrast, where ABE emerges from community activities and concerns its main focus is on social change and empowerment for the participants, with literacy and numeracy seen as tools among others for achieving these ends. This has been the main focus of basic education work in Scotland.

The implications of these different approaches are important for methods and materials, the roles of learners and teachers, and overall institutional arrangements. ALBSU has always taken an eclectic view, assuming there is no necessary conflict between the different approaches – all add to the options for students. However, theories about literacy[10] point out that there is potential conflict between them and the prevailing ideology within a society will favour some developments over others. Being aware of and articulating these different approaches to adult basic education is important for the future in order better to understand the implications of changes in funding and to press for forms of provision that are appropriate to learners' needs.

Whatever model of ABE is chosen, it is accepted that literacy and numeracy learning with adults must be closely tied to their uses in peoples' day-to-day lives. How best to make ABE relevant to everyday life and integrate literacy and numeracy with the activities in which they will be used has been a central dilemma for UNESCO over the last 30 years.[11] Failure to achieve this integration is one criticism levelled at educational institutions in Britain, both in schools and colleges. One way is to approach literacy and numeracy through other courses of study or other activities, rather than focus directly and exclusively on basic skills as the central aim: for example, teaching literacy and numeracy as part of a wood-working course or photography course, linking it to cookery or welfare rights, or home maintenance. The idea is similar to teaching reading or study skills across the curriculum, rather than as a special subject in its own right. Almost any adult course, especially in craft and technical areas, has elements of literacy or numeracy that can be developed within the wider framework of the course and there are some interesting examples of how this has been done. Those working in community-based groups have obvious ways of linking basic skills to other activities. Single parent groups, playschools and parent/toddler groups, unemployment and advice centres can all deal with basic skill needs as they arise as part of the concerns of their group.

Student participation in learning decisions

Student participation in learning and management of programmes has always been a prominent part of the rhetoric of ABE in Britain, especially within community-based groups. This approach fits in with models of adult learning and androgogy and with practice in parallel adult education courses such as Second Chance to Learn and many women's courses.[12] It is particularly important that people whose needs have not been met by traditional schooling should be given a voice to define learning in ways that suit them, reflecting their own experiences and concerns and ways of expressing themselves.

In practice real participation is often difficult to achieve. A truly participative learning programme presents a challenge to those with existing power and voice, and runs counter to the past educational experience of both tutors and learners. However, there have been some important developments in this respect, which provide pointers for the future.

Student participation in learning in adult basic education is encouraged through negotiated assessment and evaluation of programmes. Small-group work, in which learners use each other as resources and work co-operatively, help to break down traditional roles of tutors and learners. There are student associations which give learners opportunities to exchange experiences and articulate their point of view to teachers and policy makers. The National Association of Students in adult basic education (NSA) has a network across the country and holds conferences and other activities. A few schemes have emphasized learner participation in managing schemes, through management committees, experience in chairing groups and taking minutes, all of which becomes an integral part of the learning that goes on. A collective of students is setting up a residential centre for adult basic education.

The emergence of student writing and publishing has been one of the most interesting developments of adult basic education in Britain and is another way in which commitment to learner participation has been taken beyond words to practice. The production of material written by learners for the use of others in literacy schemes grew initially from a lack of teaching materials suitable for adults. Production has been supported by local community publishing in Britain, through organizations such as The Gatehouse Project and Centreprise publishing project, part of the Federation of Worker Writers and Community Publishers. This writing movement is better developed than in any other industrialized country, but is carried out with little financial support. Many collections have now been produced by students for use in local schemes. For several years ALBSU supported a national newspaper run by a collective of students and tutors; there have been residential writing weekends, development of regular writing groups and resource packs on writing.

Student writing not only helps creatively solve the problem of what adult learners can be offered as reading matter, it also fits in with the idea of participation and validating the experience of learners themselves. The very process of producing such writing, translating spoken words into written form, editing, and laying out for publication has proved to be an extremely powerful way of learning about literacy.

The idea of open learning in adult basic education

Learners in ABE have as diverse backgrounds and needs as any other adult group – all ages, men and women, employed and unemployed, people with responsibilities for children, people from many different cultural and language groups. The principle that ABE should be available to anyone who asks for it has led to teachers and organizers trying to devise flexible learning opportunities to cater for people with differing needs. This involves listening carefully and learning from students themselves about what are appropriate content, aims, and settings for learning. This approach, plus the fact that there are no entry qualifications for ABE, makes it an interesting model of open learning in the widest sense of 'access for all'. In terms of the kind of opportunities available there is probably more variety than in other types of adult education – one-to-one tutoring, small groups of various sorts – writing groups, book clubs, drop-in centres, distance learning (for example numeracy), independent learning initiatives, and residential weekend courses. This variety reflects the fact that not everyone is looking for a traditional course spread over a defined number of weeks, but that many people will drop in and out of tuition irregularly according to need.

Mainstream ABE has in the past not been particularly sensitive to the needs of different cultural and language groups and is only recently addressing these issues directly. For a long time, for example, teaching English as a Second Language was a very separate tradition from literacy work. However, ESL literacy work has a great deal to say about cultural and language issues that affect all literacy work, as does work within womens' groups and with people with disabilities. Some of these issues are being dealt with in projects such as the Central Manchester Caribbean English Project sponsored by the European Community, which discuss ideas of language and power, and how different varieties of English are valued and used. There are useful reports of work with hearing- and sight-impaired people and those with other special learning needs. But there is a great deal more to do, especially in terms of the training and support of tutors from minority groups, and changing the ethos of organizations involved in adult basic education to the point where it is understood that such issues affect everyone.

We have already seen that the adult literacy campaign emerged in Britain as a single issue problem, and the idea of a coherent policy and opportunities for adults to return to study at whatever level they need to has grown only sporadically since then. The lack of a proper continuing education framework has meant that there are no clear and natural pathways for adults who start back into ABE to find their way into mainstream courses of education and training. A number of initiatives are beginning to set up such pathways: first, post-basic bridging courses to get people to O level or the craft and technical qualification stage; second, accreditation of ABE experience for people who want to go on to further study, as in the work of the Manchester Open College Federation; third, non-traditional access routes for those without formal qualifications, especially geared to adult learners; fourth, recognition of the need for better advice, guidance, and counselling services for adults to help them find their way around existing courses.

Finally, the biggest constraint on open learning in ABE is funding. A typical learner gets two or three hours tuition per week. Opportunities are limited to part-time study because there is no right to student grants or to paid educational leave for basic education. Even the limited full-time opportunities provided by the MSC a few years ago have now disappeared. There are no supporting services such as childcare, for students either, although we know that many potential learners, especially young women, have dependent children. For ABE to be truly 'open' such opportunities and services should be made available to all adults who need them.

Research and evaluation

Adult basic education in Britain and in other countries is underfunded and under-researched. Although the initial development of the adult literacy campaign was well-documented,[13] the results of nearly 15 years of experience and innovation are largely unwritten or described only in locally distributed reports. Practice has moved ahead of reflection and comparison. Until very recently, ALBSU has not been involved in sponsoring research, but it has now formulated research priorities for the immediate future. These include methods of assessment and evaluation, a comparison of part-time tuition with more intensive courses, and the needs of bilingual learners.

Because of the general approach of ABE, which is learner centred and committed to the participation of adults in the programmes, certain types of research and evaluation, consistent with this approach, are more appropriate than others. These are models which emphasize co-operation among all those involved in research, which reduce the distance between the 'researcher' and the 'researched', and which treat the learner's experience as central to any enquiry. One such model is research-in-practice, similar to the idea of teacher-researchers developed in schools, but taken further to involve adult learners themselves.

The development of this type of research and evaluation is linked into training and development opportunities for workers within ABE enabling them to reflect on their own practice and circulate their knowledge to others. Since research in ABE is a new field in Britain we have the chance to develop models and arrangements for funding which avoid the pitfalls of much traditional educational research and continue to innovate within ABE.

In 1985 the Research and Practice in Adult Literacy group (RAPAL) began with the aims of improving communication between researchers and practitioners, and to support and promote new models of research along these lines. RAPAL has identified a number of areas as important for research. These include: identifying barriers to effective participation in groups; writing in basic education; how basic skills get transferred and used from one situation to another; comparative descriptions of adult basic education work and better understanding of the social context of literacy and numeracy, their uses in everyday life. It also urges the need to integrate research on adult learning generally and apply it to ABE.

CONCLUSIONS

As in other countries ABE is a growing and increasingly well-established aspect of adult education in Britain. With the new emphasis on opportunities for unemployed people and on life-long education, this trend is likely to continue. However, despite the increase in learning opportunities over the last decade or more, adult basic education still only reaches a small number of those estimated to be in need of help, and the funding is minimal when compared with any other sector of the education system. The widespread use of volunteers has meant that conditions of work for staff are poor, and recognition of adult basic education as a demanding and valuable field of teaching is long overdue. ABE has drawn a new group of adults into adult education, and cuts across traditional divisions of vocational/non-vocational courses, both in its aims and ways it is funded. ABE in Britain is committed to exploring new methods of learning which do not simply repeat or continue traditional schooling: this has been one of the strengths of the British model. In these, and in other respects, practice in ABE in Britain has been very innovative. Its achievements should be taken seriously by other sectors of education which could learn from it: it has implications, for example for earlier education in the areas of literacy and numeracy, and for wider developments in open learning. Other industrialized countries, particularly within Europe, look toward the British adult literacy campaign of the 1970s as they develop models for provision of their own. In the immediate future the issues confronting ABE concern its maturing into a permanent feature of the continuing education scene, articulating a more conscious critique of traditional schooling and the alternatives available, and lobbying for more funding, especially to support full-time students to make ABE truly open.

NOTES AND REFERENCES

1. Hamilton, M. (1987) *Literacy, Numeracy and Adults. Evidence from the National Child Development Study*, London: ALBSU.
2. Hamadache, A. and Martin, D. (1986) *Theory and Practice of Literacy Work: Policies, Strategies and Examples*, UNESCO/Canadian Organization for Development through Education.
3. Giere, U. (1987) *Functional Illiteracy in Industrialised Countries: An Analytical Bibliography*, Hamburg: UNESCO Institute for Education.
4. UNESCO (1976) *The Experimental World Literacy Programme: A Critical Assessment*, Paris: UNESCO.
5. Hamadache and Martin (1986) op.cit.
6. Freire, P. (1985) *The Politics of Education: Culture, Power and Liberation*, London: MacMillan.
7. World-wide, illiteracy is experienced by more women than men. In Britain, however, access to numeracy and 'technological literacy' is particularly a problem for women. Participation rates for women in basic education generally are much lower than for men.
8. Barton, D. and Hamilton, M. (1988) 'Social and cognitive factors in the development of writing', in A. Lock and C. Peters (Eds.) *Handbook of Human Symbolic Evolution*, London: Sage; De Castell, S., Luke, A., and Egan, K. (1986) *Literacy, Society, and Schooling. A Reader*, London: Cambridge University Press; Graff, H. (Ed.) (1981) *Literacy and Social Development in the West*, London: Cambridge University Press; Levine, K. (1986) *The Social Context of Literacy*, London: Routledge & Kegan Paul; Street, B. (1984) *Literacy in Theory and Practice*, London: Cambridge University Press.
9. Jones, H. and Charnley, A. (1978) *Adult Literacy: A Study of its Impact*, Leicester: National Institute of Adult Education.
10. Freire (1985) op. cit.; Street (1984) op. cit.
11. UNESCO (1976) op. cit.
12. Thompson, J. (1983) *Learning Liberation: Women's Response to Men's Education*, Radical Forum on Adult Education, London: Croom Helm.
13. Jones and Charnley (1978) op. cit.; Charnley, A. and Jones, H. (1981) *The Concept of Success in Adult Literacy*, London: ALBSU.

FURTHER READING

Adult Literacy and Basic Skills Unit (1981) *Adult Literacy in Industrialised Countries: An International Seminar*, October 1981.
  (1983) *Credit Where It's Due: Special Development Report on the Manchester Open College Federation*.
  (1985) *Adult Literacy: The First Decade*.
  (1985) 'Literacy and second language speakers of English', *Viewpoints* Issue No. 3.
  (1985) *Special Needs Viewpoints* No. 2.
Bhola, H. (1984) *Campaigning for Literacy*, UNESCO.
Brookfield, S. (1983) *Adult Learners, Adult Education and the Community*, Oxford: Oxford University Press.
Charnley, A, and Jones, H. (1981) *The Concept of Success in Adult Literacy*, ALBSU.
Craven J. and Jackson F. (1986) 'Whose language: A teaching approach for Caribbean Heritage Students'. *Central Manchester Caribbean English Project*, Manchester Education Committee.
Edwards, J. (1986) 'Working class adult education in Liverpool: A radical approach', *Manchester Monographs*, University of Manchester.
Frost, G. *et al.* (1986) *Opening Time*, Gatehouse Project.
Fuchs-Bruninghoff, E. and Kreft, W. (1986) *Literacy in the Federal Republic of Germany*, Pedagogische Arbeitsstelle, Deutscher Volkshochschulverband.
Gardener, S. (1986) *Conversations with Strangers*, ALBSU.
Giroux, H. A. (1983) *Theory and Resistance in Education. A Pedagogy for the Opposition*, Mass.: Bergin & Garvoy.
Good, M. and Holmes, J. (1978) 'How's it going?', London: Adult Literacy Unit.
Gray, W. (1956) *The Teaching of Reading and Writing: An International Survey*, Paris: UNESCO.
Hamilton, M. and Barton, D. (1985) *Research and Practice in Adult Literacy*, Association for Recurrent Education.
Harmon, D. and Hunter, C. St. John (1979) *Adult Illiteracy in the US*, McGraw Hill.
Heath, S. (1983) *Ways with Words: Language, Life and Work in Communities and Classrooms*, Cambridge: Cambridge University Press.
Howatt, A. (1979) *Making Progress. A Functional Approach to Assessing Progress in Adult Literacy*, SCALA.
Hughes, M. and Kennedy, M. (1985) *New Futures: Changing Women's Education*, London: Routledge & Kegan Paul.
Kirkwood, C. and Griffiths, S. (Eds.) (1984) *Adult Education and the Unemployed*, WEA.
Knowles, M. (1980) *The Modern Practice of Adult Education: From Pedagogy to Androgogy*, Chicago: Follett Pub. Co.
Lawrence, J. (1985) *It Used to be Cheating: Working Together in Literacy Groups*, Cambridge: National Extension College.
Limoges, L. (1986) 'Adult literacy policy in industrialised countries', *Comparative Education Review* 30 (1):50–72.
Mace, J. and Yarnitt, M. (1987) *Time Off to Learn*, Methuen.
MORI Poll (1987) (Market and Opinion Research International Ltd) World in Action: Rochdale Literacy, February 1987.
Norris, M. (1985) *Wood, Words and Numbers*, London: Lee Centre, Goldsmiths College.

Rockhill, K. (1987) 'Gender, language and the politics of literacy', *British Journal of Sociology of Education*, 8(2):153–67.

Rogers, B. (1984) 'The trend of reading standards re-assessed', *Educational Research*, 26:153–66.

Ruddock, J. and Hopkins, D. (1985) (Eds.) *Research as a Basis for Teaching: Readings from the Work of Lawrence Stenhouse*, Heinemann Educational.

Schwab, I. and Stone, J. (1987) 'Language, writing and publishing', *Afro-Caribbean Language and Literacy Project*, Inner London Education Authority.

Scribner, S. and Cole, M. (1980) *The Psychology of Literacy*, Harvard University Press.

Shor, I. (1987) *Freire in the Classroom*, Boynton and Cook/Heinemann.

Simon, B. (1985) *Does Education Matter?*, London: Lawrence & Wishart.

Thomas, A. (1983) 'Adult illiteracy in Canada – a challenge', Canadian Commission for Unesco, *Occasional Paper 42*.

Thompson, J. (1980) (Ed.) *Adult Education for a Change*, Hutchinson.

3.6

THE EDUCATION OF
16–19-YEAR-OLDS

IAN HAFFENDEN

In this chapter we shall consider the education of young adults between the ages of 16 and 19 years; the years that mark the end of adolescence and the beginning of the final transition to adulthood. The chapter is structured under the following four headings: the developmental characteristics and educational needs of young adults; the effects of the wider national context in England and Wales; the characteristics of the current educational provision for 16–19-year-olds in England and Wales; and some conclusions and the way ahead.

THE DEVELOPMENTAL CHARACTERISTICS AND EDUCATIONAL NEEDS OF YOUNG ADULTS

As a sub-population of the lifelong process 16–19-year-olds can be distinguished by their developmental characteristics. They are in their final stages of bodily growth and are involved in an increased and accelerated acquisition of adult roles, status and responsibility. In Great Britain, they acquire the right to vote and the legal right to self-determination. 16–19-year-olds are in a period of rapid physical and mental growth, and as such, they experience a strong urge to experiment with alternative identities and to find a self-image. There is a search for 'self' (Wall 1977), that, for some young adults, can lead to periods of identity crisis (Erikson 1968) and/or 'anti-social behaviour'. Thus, as stated by Darkenwald and Knox there is a need for adults to

> be sensitive to the fact that late adolescents are going through a period of internal turmoil as they negotiate the difficult passage to full adult status. 'Immature' attitudes and behaviour are symptomatic manifestations of the struggle for identity and independence. (Darkenwald and Knox 1984:104)

Furthermore, Merriam (in the USA) in attempting to combine the research findings on young adults has suggested that their general characteristic growth can be considered under two related headings: psychological concerns

marked by diminishing preoccupations with self, peer status, and sexual development (Brocknek 1980). Attention turns to finding one's place in the larger world,
a task that requires the youth to grapple with the issues of independence, identity
and intimacy. (Merriam 1984:39)

and sociocultural tasks, where young adults are developing appropriate cultural
norms associated with occupational choice, the family, and the community.

However, of these developmental concerns and tasks it is those connected
with career selection and preparation that, it is suggested, provide the greatest
challenge for the young adults (see Chickering and Havighurst 1981). Moreover, it is their need to seek an identity linked to the need for occupational
direction and choice that makes appropriate educational provision for 16–19-
year-olds problematic and difficult to achieve. However, the education of
young adults should at least enable them to: a) learn through satisfactory
personal relationships; b) perceive the material learned as relevant to them
personally; and c) see how all learning fits together (King *et al.* 1975:183) –
recommendations that fit the developmental characteristics identified above.
In short, the education of 16–19-year-olds should be relevant, integrated, and
articulated to their developmental needs. We shall return to these points later.

THE EFFECTS OF THE WIDER NATIONAL CONTEXT IN ENGLAND AND WALES

This section moves on to consider the socio-political and economic environment in which the characteristics and needs of young people are realized. This
environment, it will be shown, plays a significant role in structuring educational
provision for 16–19-year-olds, because it provides the rationale for what is
considered as relevant programme content. As argued elsewhere:

Across the world, the central role of governments in the initiation and support
of youth education and training makes their definition of 'needs' a major factor
for consideration. However, programmes for young adults are usually initiated
as a means of developing the skills required for manpower planning (skills that
relate to national development). As such, political and economic expediency
often become the foremost consideration in the design of programmes from the
government perspective. (Haffenden 1987:156)

Furthermore, Slater (1985) has identified two primary groups in Britain
(England and Wales) with the power to change, modify and control the educational provision for the 16–19-year-olds.

The first group, termed by Slater the 'education sub-government', is comprised of the Department of Education and Science (DES), the local education
authorities (LEAs), and the local government system in which these agencies
operate. The second group, termed the 'training sub-government', is comprised of the Department of Employment (and historically its predecessor the

Ministry of Labour), and its 'sibling' the Manpower Services Commission (MSC). Together these two 'sub-governments' provide the educational environment and infrastructure for 16–19-year-olds.

The two 'sub-governments' differ markedly however in their perspectives on 'general education'. The 'education sub-government' having compulsory schooling as its basic responsibility – with this being chronologically prior to the 16–19 age-range – usually equates 'general education' to academic excellence. On the other hand, the 'training sub-government' with responsibility for employment stretching (chronologically) beyond the 16–19 age-range has always viewed 'general education' more in terms of vocational preparation. However, during the early 1980s the relative influence of these two 'sub-governments' (particularly on the educational provision of the 16–19-year-olds) has shifted strongly in favour of the 'training sub-government' and its particular educational perspective.

The reason for this is quite simple. A continuing decline in the British economy brought about by outdated technology and the aftermath of problems from the early 1970s (rising prices following the oil crisis, and lost Commonwealth subsidies following entry into the European Economic Community) was perceived by government, in the early 1980s, as requiring an immediate training response. Only the 'training sub-government' was able to respond rapidly enough to the pressing needs of government, and to attempt to reduce its (then) record levels of unemployment and re-train the work force in the knowledge and skills perceived to be required by modern industry. The 'education sub-government' was not able to make such a rapid response because of its decentralized administration and slow-moving financial structure. Thus, through a series of short-term grants, administered by the MSC, the government was able to initiate a wide range of alternative programmes in the attempt to alleviate its problems.

The early success of the MSC subsequently led to the extension of its influence beyond the further education sector (where between 1986 and 1987 it came to administer some 25 per cent of the work-related non-advanced further education budget) to include the compulsory education sector, via the Technical and Vocational Education Initiative (see next section), and then eventually on to the university sector of higher education.

THE CHARACTERISTICS OF THE CURRENT EDUCATIONAL PROVISION FOR 16–19-YEAR-OLDS IN ENGLAND AND WALES

As a result of the national context considered in the last section, during the early 1980s, there was a proliferation of courses for young adults, set up in an attempt to reduce the number of young unemployed and to satisfy the needs of the rapidly changing labour market. In fact, the increase in the provision resulted in some 43 per cent of 16-year-olds in 1983–84 (in comparison to 35 per cent in 1977) remaining in full-time education with 13 per cent of these in further education. Further, of the remaining 57 per cent, only 28 per cent were receiving no form of continuing education, and a quarter of them were on courses involving either work placements (22 per cent) or employment with further education (7 per cent) (DES 1984).

Figure 1 Educational courses for 16–19-year-olds

Vocationally oriented courses	Pre-vocationally oriented courses	Academically oriented courses
Youth Training Scheme	Technical and Vocational Education Initiative	General Certificate of Secondary Education
National Certificates	Certificate of Pre-Vocational Education	General Certificate of Education A Levels
Higher National Diplomas		
plus a range of other courses offered by the Royal Society of Art (RSA), City and Guilds of London Institute (CGLI) ...		

The range of courses offered to 16–19-year-olds can be differentiated under the following three headings (see Figure 1): vocationally oriented courses for those young adults who have chosen a vocational area in which to pursue a career; pre-vocationally oriented courses that provide either a general preparation for a range of vocations or a means of helping the undecided choose a course of action; and academically oriented courses designed for those hoping to enter higher education.

However, due to the uncontrolled expansion of courses, during the early 1980s, particularly in the vocational and pre-vocational areas it became necessary by the middle of the decade for the government to undertake a review of vocational qualifications and make recommendations for a rationalization of the education system. As a result of that review a new body, the National Council for Vocational Qualifications (NCVQ), was set up. The purpose of the NCVQ was to develop a national framework for vocational courses, with bridges and ladders to allow for progression and/or change.

The National Council's first set of recommendations were reported in 1986 and led to the publication of 'The National Vocational Qualification

Framework' the following year. In this document the Council set out and defined five levels of occupational competence. These competences were to become the new 'yardstick' for the standardization of all vocational courses. The five levels of competence were: Level 1 – Basic; Level 2 – Standard; Level 3 – Advanced; Level 4 – Higher; and Above Level 4 – Professional. The descriptors used to define the levels of competence ranged from: competence in performing a range of tasks under supervision (at Level 1); through performing a wider and more demanding range of tasks with less supervision; to the occupational competence required for a satisfactory and responsible performance in a defined occupation on a range of jobs; to greater responsibility for the work of others (at Level 4). The span of courses appropriate to these levels corresponded to YTS (Youth Training Schemes) at Level 1 and Higher National Diplomas at Level 4.

It should be noted, however, that at each level, competence was defined and accredited in terms of workplace learning and/or application of skills and knowledge. This in turn was expected to encourage far greater involvement of employers than before in the education and training of young people. In addition, at least according to the rhetoric, the vocationalization of all education and training in the 16–19 age-range was further to lead to a widening recognition of the need to apply for young adults more 'flexible' approaches to the teaching and learning process. Thus, greater enterprise, independence, and self-direction were to be encouraged in the new courses through major, but complementary, changes in the curriculum process (see Further Education Unit/PICKUP 1987 for example). These changes were to include, for example: changes away from 'teacher-centred' towards more 'student-centred' approaches; from knowledge-based content to skill- and work-related competence-based content; from examination-dominated and norm-referencing towards the use of formative- and summative-criteria-referencing of skills, knowledge, and attitudes; and finally from class-based group learning to the use of individualized, open, distance, work-based, activity-centred, and simulated learning environments (Thorpe and Grugeon 1987).

Before concluding this section, some brief reference needs to be made to the provision made for 16–19-year-olds by institutions in the non-formal educational sector. In particular, the outreach provision of Adult Education Institutes (AEI); The Open College (a new government-sponsored mixed media initiative designed for 16–44-year-olds); and the statutory and voluntary youth and community services (the YMCAs and Duke of Edinburgh Scheme, for example) have all been active in providing a range of vocational, social, and/or leisure activities and opportunities for 16–19-year-olds. The universities' extramural provision also has a role to play.

Thus in summary, the formal provision of educational opportunities for 16–19-year-olds, in England and Wales (prior to university entrance), comprises of a complex array of alternatives that can be differentiated into three basic strands: academically oriented courses, pre-vocational oriented courses, and a range of vocationally oriented courses all of which hold in common a propensity to competence-based vocationalism and the utilization of a range of flexible learning strategies. In addition to these, a range of vocational, social, and leisure courses have also been offered by institutions in the non-formal educational sector.

SOME CONCLUSIONS AND THE WAY AHEAD

In the first section of this chapter the review of the developmental and educational needs of the 16–19-year-olds identified that for this group: a) all learning should have regard to satisfactory personal relationships; b) that the content should be relevant and integrated 'horizontally' in a meaningful way; and c) that the provision should be related 'vertically' into an understandable set of choices that enable personal (and professional) progression to further continuing development. We shall now consider these briefly in relation to the characteristics of the current educational provision identified above.

Taking points a) and b) together, it would appear that a more holistic approach to the education of young adults is required, where the relevant content is made meaningful by its application to a wide range of situations and problems: personal/developmental, local/neighbourhood, national, and international, for example. Issues relating to the environment and the economy need to be addressed, such as unemployment and the changing economic base, or social issues such as drugs, AIDS, homelessness, mass media, special education, handicap, and child abuse. What is required is an education that involves the youth in and with the local institutions, with voluntary organizations and their personnel, and with commerce and industry: an education where visits and visitors are commonplace and fully integrated into the curriculum; an education whose pedagogy enables the young adults to become independent learners who are able to relate theory to practice and see their productive and creative capacity as educational.

Yet, although the new competence-based approaches and the emphasis on enterprise can be viewed as a move in these directions (FEU/PICKUP 1987), the range of skills and practice in their applications (through the wider use of role play and simulations, for example), still need to be developed further if the 16–19 curriculum is to become a platform on which young adults are to acquire the skills for life. In particular, the further development of political and social skills, as identified by the Advisory Council for Adult and Continuing Education, needs to be addressed:

> The public education service offers relatively little in the way of coherent practical programmes of parent or health education; and forms of education designed to

enable people to understand complex political questions and the political process, to act as informed citizens in a democratic society, to fulfil important civic roles at work and in the community, are all far less well developed than in many other advanced countries. (ACACE 1983:175)

Finally, moving on to vertical articulation or progression, it is here where the most important progress has been made in recent years. In particular, the setting up of the National Council for Vocational Qualifications, and the greater involvement of employers in the provision and financing of both initial and on-going education and training, has enabled substantial bridging between the education and employment sectors. However, there is still room for development. Most young adults are aware that over the next twenty years the future of Britain (and other industrial countries for that matter) will be shaped by

the increasingly rapid application of recently developed technologies: bringing higher productivity and the need for a more skilled and adaptable labour force. (ACACE 1985:7)

Nevertheless, few are probably aware that it has been reported in the USA that – between 1978 and 1990 – of the twenty fastest growing occupations only six are associated with high technology, with this representing only 7 per cent of new jobs (Levin 1974).

Clearly, the links that have been developed between the education and the employment sectors should be reviewed and strengthened. For example, full use should be made of the opportunity presented by the falling population of 18-year-olds, over the next decade (between 1985 and 1995 there will be a 30 per cent drop in the number of 18-year-olds), to improve and finely adjust the current provision of education for the 16–19-year olds. However, this is only possible so long as there is not a drastic reduction in the levels of funding – as was the case with falling rolls in schools. On the contrary, plans should be made to compensate for the falling number of school leavers by a further unification of adult, professional, and continuing education with the upper end of the compulsory education sector – producing a more unified and articulated system. This could then lead, for example, to the development of new colleges of lifelong learning; a plea in the direction of which has been made elsewhere:

It is also necessary, and long overdue, for the discussion and experimentation around continuing and lifelong education to cease to be the preserve of those in the adult education tradition and to be taken fully on board for those 'in the mainstream' where continuing education must surely appear ... (Duke 1986:269)

This would not only lead to more effective use of capital and investment, but also allow adults and young adults of varying ages to mix in the formal learning process. This would then provide a wider context of experience and adult contact in which the younger adults could develop and form their self-image.

What is crucial is that the education of 16–19-year-olds, although usually seen in the context of vocational preparation and selection, should at its best also provide the skills and knowledge necessary for young adults to make informed choices and to establish and maintain an adequate self-image in a rapidly changing society.

REFERENCES

Advisory Council for Adult and Continuing Education (1983) *Continuing Education: From Policies to Practice*, Leicester: National Institute of Adult and Continuing Education.

Chickering, A. and Havinghurst, R. (1981) in A. Chickering and Associates, (Eds.) *The Modern American College: Responding to the New Realities of Diverse Students and Changing Society*, San Francisco, California: Jossey Bass Inc.

Darkenwald, G. and Knox, A. (1984) 'Themes and issues in programming for young adults', in G. Darkenwald and A. Knox (Eds.) *Meeting the Educational Needs of Young Adults*, San Francisco, California: Jossey Bass Inc.

Department of Education and Science (1984) *The Youth Training Scheme in Further Education 1983–4: An HMI Survey*, Stanmore, Middlesex: Department of Education and Science.

Duke, C. (1986) 'Continuing education trends and policy implications', *Journal of Education Policy*, 1 (3):253–70.

Erikson, E. (1968) *Towards Contemporary Issues: Youth Identity: Youth and Crisis*, New York: Norton.

Further Education Unit/PICKUP (1987) *Competency-Based Vocational Education*, London: FEU

Haffenden, I. (1987) 'Youth education and training in the context of lifelong learning and continuing education', *International Journal of Lifelong Learning*, 6 (2):153–66

Levin, H. (1974) *Education and Training for a Technological World*, Information Series Number 267, National Center for Research in Vocational Education, Columbus: Ohio State University.

King, E., Moor, C. and Mundy, J. (1975) *Post Compulsory Education, Vol 2*, London: Sage Publications.

Merriam, S. (1984) 'Development issues and tasks of young adulthood', in Darkenwald and Knox.

Slater, D. (1985) 'Sixteen to nineteen: towards a coherent policy?' in M. Hughes, P. Ribbins, and H. Thomas, (Eds.) *Managing Education*, Eastbourne, Sussex: Holt, Rinehart and Winston.

Thorpe, M. and Grugeon, D. (1987) *Open Learning for Adults*, Harlow, Essex: Longman Open Learning.

Wall, W. (1977), *Constructive Education for Adolescence*, Harrap: Unesco.

3·7

EDUCATING AND TRAINING THE WORKFORCE

CHRIS DUKE

INTRODUCTION

The scope of this chapter is large; its subject matter a source of potential ambiguity. The distinction between education and training in Great Britain is periodically, and of late more frequently, pronounced obsolete, yet it persists with an energy that suggests strong ideological and political value. It seems to have relevance both for people of different persuasion about what education should be and for those with an interest in the way education and training resources are allocated.

As to the 'workforce' – there are certainly ambiguities. We might focus on the relative participation rates of women and men, economy-wide and by sectors, and on the decline of primary and manufacturing sectors in favour of the service sectors and information technology. But today the unemployed are an unavoidable factor in almost any calculation to do with education and training as an investment. Does 'workforce training' include the training and retraining of the several million unemployed adults officially thus registered? Does it include the unknown considerable number with the capacity but no longer the expectation of taking paid employment? Confusion and political controversy surround official unemployment, job, and workforce figures. For instance, the inclusion or exclusion of the self-employed, the obscured shifts between full-time and fractional employment, the shadowy questions about the hidden or 'black' economy necessitate complex answers to apparently simple questions.

Approaching contemporary issues historically in Britain is doubly hazardous. Not only do institutions (and attitudes and values associated with them) power-fully influence what can be done or contemplated today, but Britain is also a deeply conservative society. Lack of respect for traditional ways of doing things is prone to engender stiff opposition to proposals for change. Nevertheless, it is difficult to escape the view that the arrangements and practices for workforce education and training appear seriously inadequate to meet the needs. Moreover, there persist major differences as to the fact and nature of such a need: for instance, we do not know clearly the reach of new information and other advanced technologies and their implications for the size and nature of the workforce. Conflict over these matters (crudely between 'optimists', 'pessimists', and agnostics) must affect decisions about provision of workforce education and training.[1]

These issues help to set the framework and means of discourse for this chapter. There is another set of issues, a little more focused, of which we might now take note. They are naturally interrelated, so that ordering is somewhat arbitrary. Not all will be fully addressed, much less resolved, but there is need to set them out. They are presented in summary form.

What is the system? Does it make sense to talk about a system of workforce education and training? The term VET (vocational education and training) in Great Britain is gaining acceptance but the provision, and the policy behind it, is by no means coherently agreed and presented. Widely differing claims are made as to the amount of VET that takes place. Its financing and provision are divided among different parties in differing proportions from sector to sector, and change over time. Despite the divisions of status, age, and subject matter, it is reasonable to speak of an education system for the compulsory and initial post-compulsory years but a 'VET system' is aspiration rather than fact.

Whose responsibility? There is fundamental disagreement, stemming from conflicting political and social ideologies, over who should assume responsibility and pay for VET, as between the government, representing the interests of society at large, the employers, and the individuals who receive VET. Those favouring a planned economy lean to the former; free market advocates prefer a mix of the second and third. Different funding arrangements must be seen in this context: the present government of Great Britain, for example, exhorts employers to carry the responsibility and is inclined to reduce levies on employers to pay for training. Nevertheless, it makes available 'pump-priming' grants which are meant to get VET (especially updating courses) started, with a view to employers and employees then paying for continued provision.

Who provides and controls? Three parties were mentioned above: government, employers, and employees. Another stake holder, sometimes having control and perhaps also making provision of VET, is the trade or professional association. Associations may regulate entry and even the continuing right to practise, by means of VET, both initial and continuing. Some provide VET themselves, others work with educational institutions in partnership while the association provides or assesses examinations. Employees have little influence over VET other than through such associations, in which capacity they may be quite powerful.

Alongside the government (central and local) and employer (or 'industry') interests, there are the educational institutions and various private VET agencies and consultancy groups. There are important questions to be asked about the relative advantages and implications of employer (or in-house) and educational off-site (public or private sector) provision, but the evidence is not available to answer them. Central government is exercising increasing control over education and training for employment. The role of the Manpower Services Commission (MSC), and reduction of educational or academic autonomy, are common concerns in British further and higher education.

What is the need? VET is approaching 'motherhood' status. Few publicly suggest that it is unnecessary although there is little direct evidence to prove that it enhances productivity and profitability. Despite high unemployment figures, one reads in the same areas (such as the West Midlands) of skills shortages and of concern that economic recovery will be stifled by skills shortages and bottlenecks. There is controversial talk about 'training for stock' of the unemployed: trying, that is, to keep the unemployed skilled and motivated to be ready for employment should jobs become available. Equally controversial is the issue of which occupational groups most need VET investment and in what proportion (an issue which excited controversy in Canada in recent times).[2] An allied broader dispute concerns equity and economic recovery; should enhanced welfare benefits wait upon economic recovery providing a capacity to pay? Should VET be concentrated on those with least skills and greatest economic needs, or used to raise further the competence of the highly skilled, and already advantaged, whose managerial and technical skills in information and other high technology and 'sunrise' industries may be the key to national prosperity?

Attitudes and rigidities. Traditional attitudes and rigidities in the UK can make it exceedingly hard to secure appropriate educational provision for the workforce – even assuming that there is agreement as to what is needed. Educational institutions still tend to consider the young to be the proper clientele for schools, colleges, and universities and, more insidiously, to consider vocationally-oriented work demeaning, even anti-educational. On the other hand, although many further and higher education institutions have changed their clienteles and modes of provision dramatically in recent years, traditional attitudes and stereotypes still prevail, so that they are charged with failing to adapt even as they adapt. Employers in Britain, noting the small proportion of the population taking higher education, and small proportion of these going into industry, have tended not to look to further and higher education for practical training and assistance. Industry thus attracts charges of anti-intellectualism and complacency for the low level of interest and investment shown in upgrading the workforce. Many employers seem to have difficulty in coming to terms with Britain's current economic situation and the success of its competitors; and in seeing any link between this and the generally low level of investment in human resources via training and retraining.[3]

Is there life after school? Or rather, is there work after school and how does school relate to and prepare for it? Recurrent education, a philosophy and strategy propounded particularly by the Organization for Economic Co-operation and Development (OECD),[4] looks to greater integration of educational, social, and economic policy, with education and training available on a recurrent basis throughout life. Implications of recurrent education for schooling include 'education of the workforce', at least to the extent of fostering favourable attitudes, providing work experience, and securing a base of knowledge, skills, and attitudes conducive to continuing learning and periodic study throughout working life. Consideration of workforce VET should, therefore, take note of what happens in the period of full-time schooling, as well as the continuing education and training of adults which more commonly comes to mind.

VET strategies and methodologies. At the heart of the subject is the individual in or seeking to enter or re-enter employment, who needs to learn something. Whereas adult learning has generated little new research of practical application in recent years, there is wider awareness of the need for learners to be involved in and committed to what they are studying, to find it of practical relevance in the case of VET. This goes hand in hand with a tendency to make educational delivery more flexible, diverse, and 'learner-centred'. Self-directed and self-paced learning as approaches to the continuing education of adults have produced various forms of correspondence, computer-based and assisted learning, and other variations of pace and place of study which go under the umbrella of 'open learning'. The utility of 'open learning' for different categories of VET and different learner groups is an important and complicated matter. Other questions concern institutions' capacity to 'deliver learning' more flexibly, for example, via modularization of courses, and credit recognition, accumulation and transfer.

Credentialling and mandation. Recognizing and certifying VET attainment is closely associated with provision and control. Where one party provides the VET and another assesses and validates it, sensitive partnerships are involved. Making continuing education and training obligatory, or mandatory, is another sensitive matter. In the United States this trend was heralded as a 'bonanza' for higher education; more recently, there has been a slowing down, with scepticism about the connection between it and competence on the job. Employers tend to prefer VET to be conducted in-house and without the certification which may enhance employee mobility and increase turnover problems and the problem of investing in employees to a competitor's advantage. Employees, on the other hand, tend to seek qualifications from their further study and so to look to related matters such as recognition of workplace experience by educational institutions and credit accumulation.

The 'British Way' – and the influence of other models. Britain is reputedly pragmatic and practical, more concerned with practical results than grand theory. Such a stereotype may appear fanciful but it can influence and even control attitudes and behaviours. The term 'complacency' has appeared in various reports about Britain's industrial performance, and specifically about employers' often indifferent attitudes to VET, or human resource investment. A tradition for 'making do' and appearing to get away with it – although Britain's economic supremacy may have derived from quite other factors than excellence of management or the workforce – may be a uniquely British obstacle to workforce VET. The present British government, free market and individualistic, seeks to build on the characteristic of pragmatism as a strength but also risks indulging *laissez-faire* individualism where highly directive policies for VET investment may be required. Some who are searching for better forms of workforce education and training, for example for managers in industry, seek to exploit this British tradition and way of doing things so that innovation, perhaps industry-led and government supported, will appear attractive to those of traditional, and pragmatic, bent.

One way of trying to goad or shame people into improving their performance is to suggest how much better it is done elsewhere. The 'global village' nature of the world today makes it easier to draw comparisons with what is done abroad – particularly in the leading industrialized OECD nations, the Federal Republic of Germany, Japan, and the USA. Several recent reports have done just this, and the OECD provides a constant source of comparative data and reports on economic performance and on effort in such fields as VET. It is not clear that international comparing, challenging, and attempted shaming, has significant effect. So long as there is in fact a sense of complacency, and superiority, what 'the foreigner' does is unlikely to provide a successful lever.

THE NATIONAL PICTURE

The difficulty with taking a snapshot of VET is getting the focus right and the exposure brief. Any simple presentation of the plethora of brokers, providers, and provision over-simplifies, and arrangements change so rapidly that a blur of movement is created by more than a precise snapshot – which in turn becomes somewhat arbitrary. Referring just to one sector of provision, Cantor and Roberts write, apropos of changes in 1983–5, of 'the bewildering and exponential character of the many changes'. 'Indeed, the problem of coping with the 'management of change' is probably greater for further education than any other sector of our educational systems'.[5] Different attempts to summarize VET recently make reference to the following: the Manpower Services Commission (MSC – now renamed the Department of Employment Training Agency); further education or further and higher education (FE, F/HE); the Department of Education and Science (DES), together with bodies like the Further Education Unit (FEU) and the Further Education Staff College (FESC); the Industrial Training Boards (ITBS), sometimes presented as close to the MSC and sometimes as totally separate; employers as providers of VET; private or independent vocational training agencies; trade unions (or the Trades Union Congress – TUC); and professional and other associations which stimulate VET or themselves make direct provision. Other funding and policy-making bodies also play a role: the local authorities through the local education authority powers (LEAs); and central bodies such as the Department of Trade and Industry (DTI), the National Advisory Board (NAB) and the University Grants Committee (UGC). There is an ever-changing kaleidoscope of special purpose programmes, most of them known by their acronyms. The MSC has its overarching Adult Training Strategy (ATS). Its programmes include the Youth Training Scheme (YTS) and the Technical and Vocational Education Initiative (TVEI) at pre-experience level. The DES supports, *inter alia*, REPLAN for the adult unemployed, and Professional, Industrial, and Commercial Updating (PICKUP). These national bodies serve as catalysts which attempt to shift some of the effort of the schools, colleges, polytechnics, and universities towards more directly 'relevant' education and training.

The MSC, set up in 1974, is the pre-eminent governmental agency for fostering workforce VET. 'One of the chief attractions to a government in a hurry must be the MSC's apparent ability to effect change much more rapidly than the education service.'[6] The Commission launched its major initiative in adult training with a discussion paper in 1983, which noted the priority thus far accorded the young in work-related training. The document emphasized specific economic objectives (training for those in or about to start a job rather than 'purely speculative training or training for stock'). The Commission would 'indirectly support and helpfully influence initiatives by those in industry and elsewhere. The MSC can also act in a broker role to help secure changes, e.g. of attitude. We would want to work with and through other organizations . . .'.[7]

The main impact of the MSC has been on education for those aged 16–19 years. In 1986, the YTS was extended to span two years rather than one year of post-school experience. A combination of work experience, education, and training geared to employment should become available in the school-to-adult transition years 16–19. The MSC's first attention was to the work-related learning needs of unemployed and potentially unemployed youth and also to the school curriculum, to prepare the young with skills and attitudes suited to employment; hence the Technical and Vocational Education Initiative in secondary education. Commission initiatives for young school-leavers have continued to diversify. Like some of the initiatives for adults, they periodically attract the criticism that they are designed more to reduce unemployment figures than to achieve a real long-term fall in unemployment.

Following the 1983 adult training initiative, the Commission created an Adult Training Strategy Branch. MSC programmes include the Training Opportunities Scheme (TOPS) for the unemployed and Work Preparation schemes: TOPS gave way in 1985–6 to the Job Training Programme, comprising Job Training Schemes and Training for Enterprise Schemes. Training for Enterprise includes Self-Employment and Small Business Programmes. In 1984–5, the MSC started an Access to Information Technology (AIT) Scheme of up to thirty hours' training and introduced Local Collaborative Projects (LCPs) fostering industry-education partnerships in identification and satisfaction of training needs. The Wide Opportunities Training Programme also started in 1985 embracing the old TOPS work preparation activities and including full and part-time Wider Opportunities for Women's Courses. The MSC also supports the Industrial Language Training Service for ethnic minorities at the workplace. Skill centres, under the Commission's Skill-centre Training Agency, were reduced in number from 87 to 60 more intensively used centres in 1985–6. At the same time, the Mobile Training Scheme, started in 1985, was extended countrywide. In 1982, the MSC launched the Open Tech, with an initial five-year remit to April 1987, its original and major commitment to 'open learning'. Diverse and rapid change 'will place increased emphasis on the need for new approaches in education and training . . . local authority further and higher education institutions will increasingly find themselves attracted to the advantages of implementing open learning, particularly in continuing education'.[8] 1987 saw the launch of the media and distance learning based Open College, which requires a major commitment from employers and relates to the training needs of industry.

The number of adults trained by various MSC schemes shows an increase from 1984–5 to 1985–6 of over 80 per cent from some 136,000 to 247,000, with an MSC budget of £209.9 million and £349.9 million respectively.[9] This increase is partly an artefact of the transfer of part of the funding for work-related Non-Advanced Further Education – NAFE – from local education authorities to the MSC.

The MSC is the predominant public influence in shaping VET but provision is by many parties, especially further and higher education and employers.

The MSC currently controls 25 per cent of the funds for work-related non-advanced further education (NAFE) and its influence over the VET of polytechnics and universities is also increasing. Does investment in VET, or more narrowly in training, yield an adequate return? It is commonly described as an act of faith. What kind of VET is worth supporting? There is a choice between more general education for suitable awareness, attitudes and knowledge, and specific skills; choice of subject matter and over levels of investment in different sectors of the workforce; and a choice between providing VET within the company and making use of outside educational providers. And there is the question of who pays.

One can distinguish between education which prepares people for the workforce by way of general understanding of, for example, a technical field, and the specific updating in skills as new equipment is installed and other innovations occur. In theory, the first falls within education and is a responsibility of society and the education system, while the latter rests with the employer and can often best be done on site and with the actual equipment of the employing organization. There is a tendency for employers to feel sceptical about the quality and especially the relevance of what educational institutions have to offer. Yet further and higher education is becoming more open and adaptive *as a system* to the training needs of employers; 'market-led' is the common expression. Contraction of familiar sources of government funding leads institutions to create 'cost centres' with income targets. This in turn leads them to seek closer partnerships with employers and new forms of partnerships. Colleges' teaching staff go out to work in companies more freely. For some, work in close partnership with industry is planned into the normal work of the institution.

Some employers may have spent money on VET uncritically and be reshaping what they support; others include training and staff development in strategic planning for the whole enterprise. Many companies use private training firms and consultants and also further and higher education expertise, buying these resources into the company rather than making the work over to an educational institution as an institution. As if this was not complicated enough, there is uncertainty as to the total level of expenditure by employers on training, although a common view, shared by the government, is that it is too low, relatively and absolutely. VET expenditure is confusing because of the plethora of government schemes and funding sources, European Community as well as national. Advising industry on its training needs and on the different sources of funds has become a thriving business. Meanwhile, some companies have built up fine training facilities, particularly in recent years, open learning centres. These tend to be highly focused on specific company needs though not to the exclusion of all choice of subject matter, or of expertise, on or off site, drawn from further and higher education.

The Industrial Training Boards, originally 23 statutory bodies, now reduced to seven, also support VET from a levy from the relevant sector of industry for training. Companies may secure exemption by demonstrating investment in training themselves. There are ideological and practical differences about the utility of the levy and training board scheme. The present government prefers voluntary effort by employers yet castigates them for failure adequately to invest in workforce training. The direct provision of ITBs is quite small but their work, often in partnership with other providers, is seen as setting standards and fostering good practice.

The Department of Education and Science also seeks to foster good practice, new partnerships, and other forms of innovation, with its Professional, Industrial, and Commercial Updating (PICKUP) funds of a start-up, or pump-priming, kind. PICKUP grants have been used to employ PICKUP officers in educational institutions whose job is to identify and create a response to the training needs of local industry. Some have fuelled the proliferation of local consortia of educational institutions. The DES through PICKUP also works with the MSC to 'pump-prime' local collaborative projects between industry and educational institutions. The PICKUP initiative is widely acclaimed. Ministers responsible call for a five-fold increase in this kind of educational provision. Finally, the Further Education Unit, a semi-autonomous agency linked with DES and PICKUP, plays a research and development role in fostering change in FE. It has produced many practical reports to foster the dissemination of innovation in FE, especially more and better work-related education and training.

This by no means exhausts the actors on the national scene or the issues which might be addressed. The National Institute of Adult Continuing Education (NIACE) has increasingly moved towards VET, complementing a mainly non-vocational interest. In trade union education, there are issues of content, purpose, and control as well as small quantity of education, which reflect the difficulties of the union movement in the late 1980s more generally. Paid educational leave (PEL) is not as live a prospect as it appeared in the early 1970s despite heightened awareness of the deficiencies of VET and also of the persisting high level of unemployment: nationally many millions of 'wasted person hours' might, in principle, be shared more equitably for purposes of VET. The level of VET by professional and business associations from Chambers of Commerce to medical specialisms, and also their indirect influence, is matter for surmise. Much of the information required comprehensively to describe VET provision does not at present exist.[10] Other than in a special sociological sense, we cannot, indeed, speak of a VET *system*.

A LOCAL VIEW

How does education and training of the workforce appear from the perspective of the Coventry Consortium, a consortium of five further and higher education institutions in the West Midlands city of Coventry, set up with PICKUP pump-priming support in 1983 and the first of its kind in the country?

The substantial post-experience programmes of the largest member, the University of Warwick, are mostly handled by the departments concerned direct with different employers. The other higher education institution in Coventry, the Coventry (Lanchester) Polytechnic, has chosen to put virtually all its special VET provision through the Coventry Consortium. The Consortium's PICKUP work comprises a spectrum. There are open, or 'mail-shot', short courses of one or two days of a general orientation kind (identifying training needs, aids to industry) or, more commonly, on a specific technique, skill, or area of innovation – which might be in legislation as well as technological. More of the work is of a closed, in-house, or tailor-made kind. Here the Central Unit identifies resources in one or more of the Consortium members and acts as broker or match-maker with a particular firm, meanwhile offering a guarantee of quality. Further along the spectrum there are consultancy and research and development relationships of a continuing kind. While the Consortium provides a single access point to further and higher education in the city, much of the VET of the three colleges is of a direct, bilateral kind, reflecting long-standing direct relationships which have flowed over into the newer VET containers. The Consortium plays the role of catalyst, identifying and creating new markets; and it seeks to enhance employers' awareness of their need for VET to survive and thrive in new economic and technological circumstances and to show them ways of meeting this need.

Much time is spent understanding new initiatives and chasing new opportunities. The Consortium co-ordinates proposals for funds for VET from the European Community and bids in response to central government (DES/MSC) initiatives such as for language export centres and new technology centres. It is involved with the MSC-initiated local employer network (LEN) for Coventry and one of the country's first TAPS (Training access points, data bases for training opportunities, also MSC-led). It works locally with the Engineering Industry Training Board (EITB), and with the city through its economic development group as well as the education authority, and with the local Chamber of Commerce. It has initiated or been involved with a number of Local Collaborative Projects (LCPs). The Colleges' increasingly ambitious 'income targets' have to be met in part by increasing their short-course VET provision, and there is competition for business. Apart from DES PICKUP funds to the Consortium itself, the Polytechnic and the University have been awarded substantial PICKUP grants from national sources. Open

Tech supported a large open learning development in the form of the Coventry Open Tech Unit (COTU) to develop open learning materials being subsumed into local involvement with Open College, increasingly built into the open learning arrangements of the colleges themselves. The Consortium, though strictly a Coventry affair, naturally attracts participants from further afield, so relations and area of provision in the West and East Midlands must be taken into consideration; contact with the regional representatives of MSC, DES (PICKUP), and DTI are necessarily close.

The local snapshot suggests something of the variety and energy of VET locally. The economic collapse of the Coventry area from prosperity to high unemployment indicates an acute need. Coventry presents a compact area to provide training for economic recovery. But there is naturally preoccupation with short term survival, especially among small to medium enterprises; sometimes traditional, nostalgic, if not complacent attitudes; and great confusion and turbulence as to who needs what VET, and how it is best paid for, organized, and delivered. Coventry, the first Consortium cab off the ranks, experiences high levels of ambiguity, rapid evolution and change in its work. Undoubtedly, other educational providers and partnerships still more recently gaining experience find the work equally volatile and confusing.

CONCLUDING OBSERVATIONS

The nature of 'educating and training the workforce' in the late 1980s precludes any kind of 'conclusion'. The shifting diversity of arrangements eludes the scope of any single account. Any such account would be out of date before the results could be printed. This chapter concludes, therefore, simply by underlining some of the major issues and trends of particular importance.

A recent overview of VET summarized as follows:

– Just over 10 per cent of the workforce received off-the-job work-related training provided or sponsored by employers in 1984–5 (over two million adults), 43 per cent of them in higher education;

– The MSC trained over 247,000 adults, most unemployed, in 1986, and spent some £350 million on this work in 1985–6;

– At the same time MSC-supported work in FE was reduced proportionately (55 per cent to 39 per cent) while increasing absolutely, compared with the previous year.[11]

The MSC has been a powerful influence in VET. It has proved directive and, for Britain, very fast moving. This has been a source of severe criticism by those in some sense competitors, recipients, or 'victims', and of albeit grudging admiration. A recent official report also criticized it for high levels of spending without any real idea of the skills required by industry (a charge which could be levelled against almost any area of education and training, where 'acts of faith' are so commonly required).[12] It remains impossible to measure the education and training needs of the workforce, though international comparisons suggest that these far exceed current provision. Creation and articulation of needs logically precede needs-meeting and there are signs of wider acceptance that there is a gross deficiency and that this deficiency is one of the reasons for Britain's limited economic performance.

Various forms of partnership and collaboration are seen to be important if stereotypes are to be broken down, different kinds of resources effectively mobilized, and need for VET better met. LCPs and PICKUP Consortia are among the manifestations of this. It is also realized that information systems must be greatly improved. Various data bases are being developed; the MSC's TAPS initiative is the most recent attempt to provide local information together with national networking of VET provision. Open learning has won quite startling support in recent times. Colleges and companies vie with one another in creating open learning units and centres, while the Open College, assuming it can win the financial support of the private sector on which it is predicated, is intended to build upon the success of the MSC's Open Tech.

In Great Britain this is a time of experimentation, rapid change, much trial and error; a time when rhetoric often runs ahead of actual provision. Rhetoric is important, however: at the heart of the problem of inadequate training and retraining lie the cultural traditions and attitudes referred to at the beginning of this chapter; without a change of hearts and minds, VET will fall short of what demographic as well as economic and technological changes suggest is necessary. The extension of the Youth Training Scheme (YTS) which lies outside the main scope of this chapter, illustrates this problem of attitude and perception. Those teaching the new two-year YTS in colleges are already encountering the problems of alienation – the 'holding bay' phenomenon familiar to teachers of reluctant detainees in the last years of compulsory secondary education. If YTS becomes a form of extended compulsory education, holding young people out of the workforce and thus reducing unemployment figures, then we appear to come back full circle to the alienation from schooling which was a main source for the concept and strategy of recurrent education in the late 1960s and early 1970s. Recurrent education means reducing initial full-time and pre-experience education (this could apply equally to high prestige university courses such as law and medicine) and shifting to a lifelong pattern of recurrent vocational and other education and training, as need and motivation dictate. Two year YTS, like other elements of the MSC's work, and especially its whole Adult Training Strategy, is conceived, for all the scepticism and indeed cynicism which it attracts, as making education and training meaningful and relevant, and shifting attitudes to employment especially in industry. There is a danger, however, that education and training for the workforce could be pulled back from the vision of recurrence which it, at its best, perceives, to the nightmare of periodic imprisonment in the global classroom. The balance of definition and perception is a fine one.

REFERENCES

1. Nora, S. and Minc, A. (1978) *The Computerisation of Society*: Report to the President of the French Republic, Paris: Government of France.
2. Ministry of Labour (Canada) (1983) *Learning a Living in Canada*, Ottawa: Government of Canada.
3. Mangham, I. L. and Silver, M. S. (1986) *Management Training: Context and Practice*, University of Bath School of Management.
4. OECD (1973) *Recurrent Education: A Strategy for Lifelong Learning*, Paris: OECD/CERI.
5. Cantor, L. M. and Roberts, I. F. (1986) *Further Education Today* (3rd edn.), London: Routledge & Kegan Paul.
6. ibid.
7. Manpower Services Commission (1983) *Towards an Adult Training Strategy – A Discussion Paper*, London: Manpower Services Commission.
8. Further Education Unit and Open Tech (1986) *Implementing Open Learning in Local Authority Institutions*, London: FEU and MSC.
9. Keys, W. (1988) unpublished draft paper on '*Provision and participation in adult education and training*', summarized in published Further Education Unit *Bulletin*, London: FEU.
10. Woodhall, M. (1980) *The Scope and Costs of the Education and Training of Adults in Britain*, Leicester: Advisory Council for Adult and Continuing Education; Percy, K. *et al.* (1983) *Post-Initial Education in the North West of England – A Survey of Provision*, Leicester: Advisory Council for Adult and Continuing Education.
11. Keys, op. cit.
12. National Audit Office (1987) *Department of Employment and Manpower Services Commission: Adult Training Strategy*, London: HMSO.

3.8

BEYOND THE TRAINING MODEL: EDUCATION WITH UNEMPLOYED ADULTS

KEVIN WARD

INTRODUCTION

According to government figures, in the United Kingdom 3,343,000 people (14 per cent of the workforce) were unemployed in September 1982 – the highest figure ever recorded at that time. Since that time numerous changes have been made in calculating the number of officially registered unemployed. In spite of these changes which have reduced considerably the official levels, the Department of Employment announced in January 1986 that a new all-time record total of 3,407,729 unemployed had been reached.

It is not possible in this chapter, which focuses on educational responses to unemployment, to examine in detail socio-economic questions about the extent and nature of unemployment, but it is worth indicating that there has been in the UK a great deal of debate about the problem of youth unemployment; in 1982 school leavers and young adults took up more than half of the total number of places available on the special measures schemes which were funded through the Manpower Services Commission (MSC) – the Government quango responsible for temporary employment schemes and training initiatives. Since 1982 there have been further initiatives focused on youth unemployment (for example in 1986 the introduction of the two-year Youth Training Scheme), but there have also been, additionally, initiatives for the adult unemployed which are generally part of the MSC's Adult Training Strategy, concerned with training, re-training and temporary employment.

The impact of unemployment, and the responses outlined above, have had both specific and general effects on educational institutions and traditional adult educators. At a general level, unemployment and the responses to it, together with other broad socio-economic developments such as demographic and technological changes, have led to a questioning of the priorities, strategies and in a limited manner, of the aims and objectives of educational institutions.

This questioning, however, has been heavily influenced, if not determined in many instances, by government economic policies and ideological interests which reflect particular views about the need for an exclusive emphasis on 'employability' or training for jobs. More specifically, in the United Kingdom, further education colleges have utilized MSC finance to provide a wide range of training courses, and responded to increased demands for basic academic qualifications. In the higher education sector, there has been increasing interest in the notion of 'continuing education' which has become the most recent fashionable term in educational debate within higher education institutions – and is often taken primarily to indicate vocationally-related education of adults.

The traditional providers of adult education – the local education authorities' adult education services, and the responsible bodies (the Workers' Educational Association and the university adult education departments) – as well as being affected by the priorities and developments outlined above, have also responded in other ways to long-term structural unemployment. Since 1982, there has been a proliferation of specifically educational (as distinct from training or 'employability') schemes, courses, and activities for unemployed people, organized sometimes by the traditional providers but also by a range of other organizations and voluntary bodies. Fee remissions have been extended in order to facilitate easier access to mainstream educational courses for unemployed people, but in addition, special projects and courses, specifically for unemployed people, have been initiated in many parts of the UK.

Some have argued that these developments viewed nationally are patchy, piecemeal, and *ad hoc*.[1] Certainly they are dependent in many cases on short-term projects or part-time temporary staff, and the effects of these programmes, numerically at least, on unemployed people overall must be marginal. But, notwithstanding these limitations, the experiences gained have raised a number of critical questions for educational providers and institutions generally. Before examining these it is necessary to outline the broad categories of developments and to comment briefly on them.

EDUCATIONAL DEVELOPMENTS FOR UNEMPLOYED PEOPLE

'Second chance education'

Since the early 1970s, in the UK at least, adult educators have organized a wide range of courses under such titles as 'Second chance', 'Access courses', 'Return to learn', and 'New horizons'. These were intended to make special provision for adults who for a variety of reasons (social, economic, or personal) had not realized their full educational potential and who wished to return to study as mature students. A number of them were specifically designed for women. As is the case with other developments, these courses were well developed before unemployment became a major concern, but the 'unemployment crisis' has given an added impetus.[2]

It is interesting that higher education institutions have recently shown more interest in access courses. Given the inequalities in the higher education sectors in particular (for example, the extremely low participation rate of working-class students in universities has hardly changed in spite of dramatically increased student numbers since the 1950s), this interest is welcome and long overdue, even though it may have been forced onto institutions through demographic changes.

Access courses are often based on an implicit acceptance of the vertical educational progression model. This assumes that for personal, social, and economic reasons, individual access onto formal qualification-based courses is highly desirable. Unfortunately, in the medium term at least, even improved access courses will ultimately attract only a minority of unwaged people. Many (in spite of improved marketing of provision) will still be deterred from institutions, and others may simply not want educational qualifications gained through formal study.

A common element of many second-chance courses, however, is the stress on personal, vocational, and educational counselling. Through this process individuals may, instead of progressing onto qualification-based courses, be more interested in developing their own interests and hobbies. In many cases this may be through traditional recreation or leisure-oriented courses.

Recreational/leisure courses

It has often been assumed that the bulk of traditional adult education provision for unemployed people has fallen within this category – although it should be noted that there is no up-to-date research evidence on this point. It could certainly be hypothesized that much daytime provision of this sort is utilized by unwaged people, and it is the case that many specific initiatives about unemployment include substantial elements of this type of adult education. In many unemployed centres and community centres, for example, there are numerous courses on keep fit, craft, photography, art, etc.

Clearly it can be argued that a range of accessible recreation and leisure opportunities need to be widely available, particularly for unwaged people. The underlying aims and objectives of this type of provision however, are rarely analysed critically. Are these courses narrowly therapeutic – easing the process of adjustment and, thereby, acceptance of unemployment? Is there an implicit acceptance of a social control model – ensuring that unemployed people do not drift into alienation, and thereby ensuring that potentially disruptive elements in society are neutralized? A vivid illustration of this latter point is the critical comment made by an unemployed woman who was discussing activities at an unemployed centre in West Yorkshire early in 1987. Referring to staff who had organized arts, crafts, and particularly French polishing, she stated indignantly: 'They're just trying to keep us quiet by these things. . . . It's a bloody insult.'

If these types of courses are all that is offered for unwaged people, then they are inherently conservative in that they underpin the prevailing consensus about the nature and causes of unemployment; they foreclose discussion on any alternative analyses, and they integrate and undermine potentially 'deviant' political stances among unemployed people.

Coping and survival courses

Some of the courses in this category obviously overlap with recreational and leisure provision, but there is no doubt that unemployment has led to adult educators organizing activities or courses which are intended to provide practical and/or emotional support for unwaged people. Thus there are many courses on 'Know your rights', 'Welfare rights', 'Eating healthy on the dole' (unemployment benefit), as well as counselling provision, general discussion groups, and explicitly practical DIY-type courses designed particularly for unwaged people.

Again, such provision should be part of a range of opportunities, but at a practical level it has been discovered that the same courses may lead to very different responses from unwaged people. In one project, for example, 'Eating healthy on the dole' was successful with one group, but another group reacted critically to what they interpreted as a patronizing attitude by a middle-class tutor telling them how to manage on a low income. These differing responses raise general critical questions about the role of professional adult educators as they respond to problems such as unemployment which are encountered predominantly by working-class groups.

A variety of models may underlie this type of provision. These include a *broad* therapeutic model which assumes that personal and practical support is an essential prerequisite for further personal development and purposeful activity, but the *narrow* therapeutic – the social control model referred to in the previous category – may also be relevant here.

In recent years, there has been pressure on adult educators to 'do something for the unemployed'. Thus, 'moral panic' responses[3] have led to a wide range of activities which sometimes imply, albeit inadvertently, an acceptance of a social control model. It is not that the activities *per se* are crudely 'controlling' (they may in fact be highly desirable and welcomed by some unwaged people), but rather that participants in some activities, such as DIY, may not be given opportunities or support for wider questioning or involvement in other types of activity.

Social purpose and community action courses

This category refers to courses which resource unwaged people *collectively*. These may be courses at unemployed centres such as 'Unemployment issues' or 'Alternatives to unemployment' or 'User group' courses; or they may be courses organized with a range of groups in the community, such as tenants' groups, residents associations, etc. The number of courses in this category is probably considerably lower than the other types of provision. (Given the lack of up-to-date research in this area it is not possible to be more precise but material which is available suggests or implies that this is likely to be the case.)

Some examples from current practice may illustrate this category.

a) *Courses for users from a network of unemployed centres* Regular residential courses and dayschools are organized with users who wish to analyse how their centre operates, its aims and objectives in practice, and issues of control and the involvement of unwaged people. These courses are 'socially purposeful' in that they provide an educational support and resource for groups who wish to explore organizational and political issues related to their roles as users in unemployed centres.

b) *Courses with tenants' groups* Over a five-year period, community-based courses have been organized with tenants' associations living on working-class council estates. These include housing, 'how community groups work', and 'know the system'; starting from concerns expressed by tenants in detailed pre-course negotiations, these courses provide an educational response for the collective concerns of community-based groups.

The commitment to collective social purpose adult education has existed as a continuous albeit minority strand at the radical end of the 'liberal tradition' in adult education.[4] In the current political climate in the UK, funding for such provision is problematic and this is obviously one reason why it is not so widespread; it is sometimes labelled as too 'political', as if other types of education, and indeed training, are not underpinned by political and ideological considerations.

ISSUES AND LESSONS FROM EXPERIENCE

Reference was made earlier to the relative proliferation of educational schemes, courses, and activities for unwaged people which have developed since 1982 in the UK. This can be examined critically through two phases: 1981 to 1985, and 1985 onwards. From 1981 to 1985, there was a move in adult education with unwaged people from marginality to relative expansion; from 1985 onwards questions can be raised about whether there is a move from expansion to encapsulation.

From marginality to expansion

Although the developments in the first phase (1981 to 1985) were *ad hoc*, unco-ordinated and piecemeal, initiatives over this period were taken both by educational bodies and by non-educational organizations and institutions. Initially the responsible bodies made pioneering appointments in this area of work (for example the northern district of the Workers' Educational Association, as in the 1930s, appointed a tutor organizer for work with the unemployed, as did the university adult education departments of both Leeds and Surrey). More significantly, however, a number of local authorities, who had already developed significant provision for disadvantaged adults, gradually extended this to include work with unemployed people.

There were also significant developments through non-educational organizations (although this often involved links with educational providers). The Trades Union Congress (TUC) for example, set up (with MSC finance initially) a network of centres for the unemployed. From 1981 to 1985 210 such centres were established throughout the country. The majority of these provided various types of educational opportunities, often in conjunction with educational providers.

Voluntary organizations have played a significant role in recent developments. In many areas they have initiated a wide variety of schemes for unemployed people, sometimes in partnership with local authorities. These include skills workshops, drop-in centres, community enterprises, co-operatives and skills and learning exchanges.

During this phase then, from 1981–5, there is evidence of increased activity, and reports were produced which contributed to an emerging debate about the educational needs of unwaged adults. There was increasing concern also in education generally about the financial and ideological predominance of the MSC. Allied to a generalized concern about unemployment, it was probably a combination of these factors which led to the Department of Education and Science (DES) developing its own initiative.

In 1984 the DES set up a three-year programme to improve educational opportunities for unemployed adults. The main elements in this programme (subsequently entitled REPLAN) were (1) the appointment of a team of eight regional field officers and a national co-ordinator based at the National Institute for Adult and Continuing Education (NIACE); (2) a programme of local development projects – by 1987, 84 such projects have been established. A complementary programme of curriculum development projects is run by the London-based research and guidance organization, the Further Education Unit (FEU); (3) regional staff development programmes organized through the Regional Advisory Councils for Further Education. In 1985–6 approximately 3,000 people took part in these; (4) Education Support Grants: these aim to 'promote the development of co-ordinated local strategies for meeting the needs of the unemployed'. Forty-seven two-year projects from local authorities were approved in 1985–6 and a further twenty-nine for 1986–7.[5]

Detailed evaluative comments about REPLAN cannot be made since no significant overall research has been commissioned. (It should be noted, however, that the FEU/REPLAN Projects have recently been evaluated.)[6] Initial suggestions about the need for an overall evaluative programme were rejected by the government. Belatedly, various elements (such as the Education Support Grants, and some of the local development projects) are being evaluated, but the lack of an overall and systematic research programme from the outset is a major weakness. From involvement in several local development projects and the Regional Staff Development programmes however it is possible to highlight a number of general issues.

The current annual cost to the DES for the REPLAN programme is approximately £3.5 million. Given the major crisis of unemployment, a national temporary[7] education initiative on this financial scale can hardly be regarded as a major significant long-term response.

It is interesting to compare REPLAN with other Government programmes which focus on training. The DES's PICKUP (Professional Industrial and Commercial Updating) programme aims to forge links between industry and local colleges, universities, and polytechnics in order to increase and improve training for adult employees. In 1987–8 this will cost the DES £12.4 million. In 1986–7, the MSC spent £270 million on its adult training programmes.

These figures help put the REPLAN initiative into context, but its announcement in 1984 was a reflection of long overdue concern that 'something must be done' *educationally* for unemployed adults over and above the MSC's short-term work schemes and training initiatives. Although REPLAN reflects increasing centralization in the form of definitions of priorities by a central funding agency, it has none the less helped to legitimate a range of educational initiatives either as an alternative, or complementary to the exclusive vocational approach to adult unemployment which is exemplified in the statements and programmes of the MSC.

What, then, are the major issues and lessons in educational work with unemployed adults in this phase 'marginality to relative expansion' (1981–5)? Apart from the major general issue of providing an alternative to the exclusive vocational responses, there are a number of lessons which it is important to highlight.

Unemployment has provided a new constituency for educational institutions and traditional providers of adult education. Although there have always been large numbers of adults who have been effectively excluded from post-school educational opportunities (even in times of so called 'full employment') the recent unemployment crisis has highlighted this issue of the 'missing millions'.

In order to contact these people, the majority of the educational initiatives described so far were not institution- but community-based. Courses and activities took place in community centres, nurseries, church halls and unemployed centres rather than in educational institutions. For these community-based programmes to succeed, effective outreach and pre-course negotiations are of paramount importance. Outreach has been defined as 'a process whereby people who would not normally use adult education are contacted in non-institutional settings and become involved in attending and eventually in jointly planning and controlling activities, schemes, and courses relevant to their circumstances and needs'.[8] According to this definition, outreach is much more than simply additional or new types of publicity for pre-existing educational packages. Without effective outreach, however, the new constituency of unemployed adults will not become involved significantly in education.

Successful projects have also adopted specific targeting approaches and emphasized inter-agency co-ordination. Thus, courses have been organized with groups of older adults, Asian women, tenants, and community groups etc. There is certainly evidence of increased inter-agency collaboration in recent years. This has helped avoid overlap and duplication, and maximized scarce resources; in addition, it has in some areas led to a more comprehensive range of opportunities for unwaged adults. In some unemployed centres or community centres for example there are daytime opportunities ranging from practical courses and recreational/leisure activities through to social purpose courses. Various parts of these programmes are financed by different providers; and voluntary organizations have become involved increasingly in discussion about the priorities, roles, and approaches both of educational institutions and of adult educators.

One result of these varied initiatives from 1981–1985 has been the development of networks of adult educators and voluntary organizations in a number of local authority areas or regions. More recently this has been supported by the ESG REPLAN appointments and/or the REPLAN regional field officers. Although these are at a relatively early stage, and need to overcome many organizational and practical problems, they can provide forums for co-ordination, support, and a critical examination of policy (or, rather, the lack of it) for unwaged adults.

Given this and other developments outlined so far in this chapter, it seems that educational approaches with unemployed adults have not, as was sometimes predicted earlier in the 1980s, become 'ghetto' initiatives focusing narrowly on those who are formally registered as unemployed. In the main, they have adopted broad definitions of unemployment to include unwaged people generally and have been able to link up and utilize both new and existing (albeit in modified form) types of provision.

In spite of the fact that these developments overall have been piecemeal and uneven – some would argue tokenistic – they have raised fundamental questions for educational institutions and adult educators. Some of these critical questions for adult educators arising out of the first phase are outlined above: the need for outreach, the adoption of broader community-based roles for adult educators, the need for more effective inter-agency collaboration, etc. More recently, however, questions have been raised about educational institutions.

From expansion to encapsulation?

Throughout 1986 and 1987 educational activities with unemployed adults seem to have levelled out. Some REPLAN projects have finished, but a limited number of new ones started; the number of TUC centres has dropped from a peak of 210 in 1985 to 200, but an increasing number are now supported by local authorities, instead of by the MSC. In many local authorities, there is increasing awareness that the long-term nature of structural unemployment requires long-term, rather than piecemeal and *ad-hoc* responses.

The major question is what precisely will the nature of these responses be. In local authorities, adult education, or at least community adult education, is marginal in resource terms compared with the educational institutions. Reference was made earlier to increasing emphasis in colleges on low-level skill-based courses financed by the MSC. Colleges, then, are in danger of becoming centrally-controlled training agencies. As a result of demographic changes, financial problems, and the imposition of political priorities, they have accepted in many cases a purely instrumental vocational approach – the concept of training as preparation for work. In higher education, institutions, (for similar demographic reasons and the need to exploit new sources of funding) have enthusiastically, albeit belatedly, accepted another form of the training model. In this case, it is continuing education which mainly means the provision of Post Experience Vocational courses (PEVE) for updating, although there has also been increasing interest in access courses and provision for mature students.

The continuing ideological and financial dominance of the training model in educational institutions may mean that the *educational* responses to unemployment outlined in this chapter may remain marginalized or become encapsulated. Encapsulation occurs when a particular development (in this case educational work with unwaged people), organization, or social movement is modified or taken over by more dominant forces.[9]

There has recently, for example, been political pressure on REPLAN to become more involved in training or 'employability' provision rather than community-based educational work. REPLAN, and indeed other educational responses to unemployment, could potentially, then, become weighted towards the training model. A number of colleges are currently developing some outreach *strategies* (although rarely an outreach philosophy as identified in the definition provided earlier) – the aim being to develop new forms of publicity in order to reach the new constituency of unemployed people – but these may still be predicated on a narrow training model. In these cases, the aims, objectives, and priorities of the institutions have not changed.

There is, then, in this more recent phase, the danger of encapsulation. This may be avoided, however, if the educational responses to unemployment which expanded in the earlier phase can combine with developments within some educational institutions and local authorities which are not necessarily dominated by a narrow training model. This includes emphasis on access and the emergence of tertiary and open colleges. Access, however, would have to be defined broadly in order to avoid an exclusive emphasis on individual vertical progression. It must include both (1) preparation for entry into higher education for mature students, and (2) the innovative use of institutions' resources to devise relevant educational activities *with* working-class communities which may not be directly related to qualification-based courses.

It is this latter point which poses the greatest challenge to institutions. The educational responses to unemployment, supported only marginally by some institutions in the first phase, allied to factors mentioned earlier, such as demographic changes and an increasing realization of the long-term nature of unemployment, have raised fundamental questions. These include issues about priorities, resources, pedagogy, and curriculum. It is not possible to explore these issues in detail here, but clearly major reorientations and radical shifts of emphasis are necessary on the part of institutions, if they are to move beyond pious expressions of concern about the educational needs of their local communities. There is evidence, for example, that unwaged people in working-class communities want education to service their *collective* as well as their individual needs. They want relevant education which relates to their concerns and problems, as much as, if not more than, individual acquisition of new knowledge and skills. In practice, this means institutions developing a dialogue with targeted groups in the community, such as tenants and community groups, centres against unemployment, and a wide range of voluntary organizations.

If these issues are taken seriously by educational institutions, there is the possibility of counterbalancing the dominance of the training model. Based on a critical dialogue between 'providers' and 'users', *educational* strategies about long-term unemployment can be developed at local and regional levels, and this in turn can become part of corporate strategies about unemployment generally. These could eventually contribute to a reshaping of social attitudes and public policies. If such developments do not take place, then educational initiatives will remain either marginalized or encapsulated as minor adjuncts within an expanded centralized training strategy for unwaged adults.

NOTES AND REFERENCES

1. McGivney, V. and Sims, D. (1986) *Adult Education and the Challenge of Unemployment*, Oxford: Oxford University Press; Ward, K. and Taylor, R. (1986) 'Responses to unemployment', Chapter 2 in *Adult Education and the Working-Class, Education for the Missing Millions*, London: Croom Helm.
2. It is not possible to examine definitions of unemployment here, but in practice most of the educational developments referred to in this chapter have adopted a broad definition of unemployment, which includes large numbers of unwaged people, particularly women, who according to government definition are not formally counted as registered unemployed. See J. McDonald (1984) *Education for Unemployed Adults*, London: HMSO: p.21.
3. A moral panic response can be defined as a situation in which politicians, policy makers, administrators, and professional staff all agree that a rapid response must be made to a pressing problem.
4. Taylor, R., Rockhill, R., and Fieldhouse, R. (1985) *University Adult Education in England and the USA*, London: Croom Helm.
5. Watts, A. and Knasel, E. (1985) *Adult Unemployment and the Curriculum*, London: Further Education Unit.
6. Percy, K. A. (1988) *Evaluation of FEU/REPLAN Projects – Report to FEU*, London: Further Education Unit.
7. The programme was originally established for three years, extended for a further year, and after much uncertainty it was announced in 1987 that it would be extended until the end of 1989.
8. Ward, K. (1986) 'In search of the missing millions', *REPLAN Review No. 1*, London: Department of Education and Science.
9. Etzioni, A. (1967) *Studies in Social Change*, New York: Holt, Rinehart and Winston.

3·9

ADULT ROLE EDUCATION

DEREK LEGGE

INTRODUCTION: DEFINITIONS AND AIMS

Role had been defined as 'one's function, what one is appointed or expected or has undertaken to do'. In this sense adults have many types of role and these may change as they progress through life. Some roles are very personal, for example those of husband or wife, while others are associated with work, such as those of a manager or trade unionist, or today with non-work in a world of increasing numbers of unemployed or retired people. All play some role in the community in which they live as citizens. For some this may be a largely passive role, but others may be more active as politicians, magistrates, school governors, participants in voluntary civic work etc. Obviously some roles are self-defined or self-imposed, but many people do not have much choice and are given roles defined by others, perhaps expressed in job descriptions or in codes or regulations. In this complex situation the task of role education is seen as that of helping people to undertake their various roles with greater efficiency, and perhaps more personal fulfilment.

SOME ISSUES AND EXAMPLES

Roles, of course, may conflict or be given different significance, obvious examples being the choice between a person's role as an employee and his or her role as the parent of a sick child, or when the community insists on a role an individual does not want. A major issue in role education is the choice of the exact basis for the provision. Is the emphasis to be on the needs of an individual, or on those of a family, an employer, or perhaps the whole community? Attempts to answer the question 'For whose benefit?' lead at present to very mixed answers and to some distortions. An example of the latter is the attempt of some people to equate role education with work-related, or vocational, education alone on the grounds that the needs of the community come first and that productive efficiency is paramount. This, however, it can be argued, is a limited and misleading perception: work roles are closely intertwined with personal roles, each influencing the other, and it is essential to think of the whole person. All roles are overlaid by powerful emotional dimensions and are much conditioned by the values, attitudes and relationships associated with them. Self respect, respect for other people, the willingness to adapt to change, may be the key issues, as is evident when people become redundant through the collapse of the industry in which they work, or when family life changes as children grow up or perhaps a spouse dies.

The timing of role education is also a crucial issue. On the whole it seems to be more acceptable and effective when people acquire new responsibilities in personal life or in their work (as for example when they have their first child, or take up a new post, or retire). There are, however, emotional problems which may obstruct the provision. Thus the pre-retirement courses arranged by some industrial firms and local authorities in recent years can be seen as being not only too short – a day or even a half day is common – but as being offered too near to actual retirement. Courses in mid life would probably be more effective, but these are often resisted by employees for whom retirement is regarded as a distant and not very agreeable prospect.[1] A few examples will perhaps bring these issues more clearly into focus.

Education for a management role depends very much on the type of management envisaged, on the beliefs and attitudes currently associated with management, and on whether it is regarded as being for the personal development of the individual, or for the benefit of the company employing him or her, or to meet some external demand imposed by the state. The role of the manager can be portrayed at one extreme as that of a dictator carrying out his task by coercion, or at the other as being that of a gentle leader working through understanding and co-operation. Courses of various lengths – from a weekend to over a year in length – have been provided for managers by some of the larger industries, by some local authority colleges and polytechnics, and by the Business Schools as in London and Manchester. The objectives are clearly to provide both knowledge and understanding, but attitudes are slow to change and the results seem often to rest on the perception individuals have of their jobs, on the views of higher management, and on the general ethos of the company in which they work. Pre-existing stereotypes sometimes seem to be more potent than the course content.

Similarly *education for the role of citizen* depends on the answer to the question 'what is a good citizen?' There are obvious differences in the roles expected of citizens in a democracy and in those expected in an authoritarian dictatorship. Are citizens to be taught only to give unquestioning obedience to those in power, or are they to learn how to participate actively in the affairs of the community and exercise responsibility? Is this kind of role education a form of education for emancipation, or for the preservation of the status quo, or for an active share in constructing more effective democratic control over the process of economic and social change?[2]

In Britain many agencies have attempted to make a contribution to citizenship education. In particular the Workers' Educational Association (WEA) with a declared 'social purpose' objective, has provided, often in association with university extramural departments, one-night-per-week non-vocational courses, as well as weekend meetings, on government, current affairs, and a whole range of political, social, and economic issues. Some residential colleges have also provided short courses, some recent examples being entitled 'Building Britain's future' and 'Behind the scenes in Parliament'. This type of provision was particularly successful in the decade after the Second World War, but has tended to decline since then.[3] Other subjects have become more popular, especially those concerned with individual hobby interests, and the promoters have tended to turn their attention elsewhere to special groups such as trade union officials or magistrates, or to professional up-dating courses which may well become a source of funds. Voluntary organization officials have not unnaturally looked to the provision for which there is easier recruitment. Even so, some courses continue, and there are several television programmes which are now designed to raise interest and the sort of questioning which can stimulate more effective citizenship. Channel 4 television, for example, offers 'The world this week' as well as the long-running 'What the papers say'.

The evidence shows, however, that all this provision has reached only a minority of the population, and that that minority is probably the section of the population already most active as citizens. It is also clear that the mere provision of information, even with discussion, is not enough. People may know much about the workings of government and the complexities of national or international problems and rivalries, and yet remain quite inactive as citizens. Feelings of helplessness may also militate against attendance at courses linked to citizenship: the temptation is to leave affairs to others. Some would say, too, that there is an inbuilt potential for conflict in this type of role education: if the product is to be active democratic citizens, they may arrive at conclusions not felt to be desirable by the sponsors. Most local education authorities in fact have tended to leave citizenship education to others on the grounds that it is 'too controversial' or 'too party-political'. Similar suspicions surrounded, for example, the provision of the wartime army discussions based on the eighteen booklets of the 'British way and purpose' scheme. The regular series of meetings led to a large extent by civilian tutors on army sites were felt by some to be dangerously subversive.

Some argue that, instead of courses, good democratic citizenship is better achieved by a process of 'learning by doing'. It is said for example that citizenship education in the WEA has been best achieved by members sharing in the running of each branch, becoming not only committee members but chairmen, secretaries, and treasurers. In this way active interest is stimulated and powers of self expression developed, a view supported by the great multitude of voluntary societies run on democratic lines. The women's organizations in Britain, especially the Women's Institutes and the Townswomen's Guilds, have given much attention to this. Members are actively encouraged to participate in the organization and meetings; short courses on committee work, chairmanship, etc. are offered especially by the district federations; and handbooks of guidance are issued by the central headquarters. Stimulus to responsible democratic action can also be seen in the non-formal activities provided by some churches and political parties. A major difficulty, however, is that the active members tend to remain but few, sometimes only a handful dominating the rest. Many people would therefore argue that if Britain is to develop as a democracy, much greater attention must be given to citizenship education for everyone. As the famous 1919 Report declared, 'An uneducated democracy cannot be other than a failure'.

Much the same can perhaps be said about *parent education*. Many parents feel uncertainty about their roles and need help if they are to cope with the requirements of the modern world. At present most rely a good deal upon what they learn about parental roles when growing up, developing attitudes and competencies partly in response to the contributions of previous generations, but also partly from incidental advice and information obtained from peer groups, neighbours, broadcasting, and magazines or newspapers. As adults they may be much influenced by the portrayal of parental roles in stories and soap operas. All these sources, however, are likely to be often inconsistent and quite inadequate in a changing world in which the small 'nuclear' family has largely replaced the extended family in Britain, in which the single parent family has become more common and in which more women combine a career with motherhood.

To meet the general need for parent education, some provision of a more formal kind is made – as when people join classes in child psychology, or regularly attend courses in welfare clinics. Most people, however, do not join organized classes of this kind, and a less formal approach seems more successful. Health visitors, for example, assist parents with specific problems, perhaps through home visits. Help, especially for women, has also been given by the build-up of supportive networks, through which adults and children come together in a learning situation. Much informal group work, for example, takes place in 'Mother-and-toddler groups' and in 'Family workshops'. These are often regular meetings of an hour or two in length, organized by health or community workers, and similar groups have been established by the Pre-School Playgroups Association (PPA) and other voluntary organizations. Often the groups are the result of much patient 'outreach' work and inter-agency co-operation, and in general they suffer from a lack of resources. In an attempt to help, the Community Education Sector of the Open University, in association with the Health Education Council, the PPA, and other bodies, has produced a series of study packs which can be used by individuals as well as groups. These are carefully devised in the form of printed material or video-cassettes on family education, and seek to provide stimulus, information, and understanding.

Many people, however, find such material both too expensive and difficult to use without some training in the appropriate skills. There are also problems of ensuring that, like the rest of this type of role education, it is available in all areas and to both sexes. At present the geographical distribution is patchy and male parents are relatively neglected. Almost any part of the provision of education for adults, of course, can contribute to parent education, especially when concerned with the development of confidence, and much greater co-operation among all providers would enhance the results. The role of parent-hood seems now to be more demanding and more perplexing in a society in which values are under constant challenge, and a combined effort is vital.

In the past few decades, greater attention has been paid to the *role of women* both in the family and in society in general. Particular emphasis has been given to the development of education for roles outside the home, and since the late 1960s more and more courses have been provided under the broad title of 'Women's Studies'. These courses are sometimes as short as one day, but may range through those of a few weeks in duration up to those of a year or more. They are organized by polytechnics and universities, by local education authority colleges, and by a multitude of voluntary organizations, including the WEA. Some are concerned with the role of women in trade unions, as for example the 'Trade Union and Basic Education' project in Manchester, while others have been linked more to re-entry to paid employment after a period of home duties and child care. The most famous of these were the 'Fresh horizons' courses at the City Literary Adult Education Institute in London, but there is now more widespread provision. Such courses tend to emphasize the development of confidence and self esteem as well as of personal and intellectual skills. In almost all the formal provision, the role women have been expected to play in a male-dominated society is called into question and alternatives are offered. This is also true of the less formal contribution of the various branches of the women's liberation movement. The sharing of interests in regular meetings, with the emphasis on informality, mutual support and informed dialogue, tends to promote greater awareness of possible changes in role.[4]

CONCLUSION

From these examples it will be seen that adult role education is very complex, taking many forms and using a great variety of methods. The importance of adult role education, especially in terms of parental and citizen roles, is so great that there is an obvious need to give it priority and to make it the basis for a comprehensive provision of education for adults.[5] The general objective is greater competence, which in turn influences the ability to cope in all other aspects of life. At present, however, role education is beset by many problems. A clear policy has been lacking, and little attempt has been made to resolve the possible conflicts of role facing the individual. Perhaps conditioned when young to believe in the acceptability of certain roles, a person may be faced by inner conflict when these beliefs are challenged by experience, or an external conflict if the state requires him or her to change role. Examples include the roles of men and women in the family, or roles at work, or roles in the community. When modification is obviously needed, too rapid a change from fixed concepts or stereotyped behaviour may cause confusion and instability, unless help is given.

Role education suffers also from a crisis in funding which has weakened the already inadequate provision made by local education authorities, universities, and voluntary agencies. Despite all the efforts indicated above, role education suffers from neglect, and resources must be provided if it is to make an impact. Perhaps there is a particular need for support to be given to non-formal provision where the injection of even a small amount of finance would greatly increase the results. Some increase in full-time staff is also required, although the major need is for more adequate training of everyone concerned. Support is also needed for the educational guidance and advice services. Development of the general provision of role education is now a major and urgent requirement. Without it people are likely to be unable to cope in a satisfactory way with a world which changes with ever-increasing rapidity.

REFERENCES

1. Phillipson, C. and Strang, P. (1983) *The Impact of Pre-Retirement Education: A Longitudinal Evaluation*, Keele: University of Keele.
2. Legge, D. (1982) *The Education of Adults in Britain*, Milton Keynes: Open University Press.
3. Kelly, T. (1962) *A History of Adult Education in Great Britain from the Middle Ages to the Present Day*, Liverpool: Liverpool University Press, (2nd revised edn) 1972.

4. Thompson, J. (1983) 'Women and adult education', in M. Tight *Education for Adults, Volume 2*, Milton Keynes: Open University Press.
5. Department of Education and Science (1973) *Adult Education: A Plan for Development – Report of a Committee of Enquiry . . . under . . . Sir Lionel Russell*, London: HMSO.

3.10

EDUCATION FOR OLDER ADULTS

FRANK GLENDENNING

Education for Older Adults is a new concept in educational philosophy and in educational provision. It is still rare for those in Britain who write about the theory and practice of adult education, and indeed the nature of lifelong learning, to include any appraisal of educational gerontology. By 'educational gerontology' we mean that field of study and practice which has recently developed at the interface of adult education and social gerontology (Peterson 1976). Social gerontology is the study of ageing and its significance for society, the social problems resulting from an ageing population, and the response of society in terms of service delivery. Such studies in the United States began during the 1940s, based upon sociology, psychology, and education. Social gerontology in Britain has taken much longer to emerge as a discipline, but, in the late 1980s, it is now developing fairly rapidly and the first textbooks are beginning to be published. It was not until the early 1980s that the British movement concerned with education for older adults began to be effective (Glendenning 1985: 100–41).

THE IMPACT OF DEMOGRAPHIC FACTORS

A growing awareness of the changing demographic factors led many adult educators to believe that the projected world growth of the older adult population was likely to have an impact on the educational system of the country concerned (UNESCO 1979).

Britain

Certainly in Britain, this has not so far occurred. Abrams believes that the principal reason is to be found in the number of pupils attending secondary school. There were no more than 45,000 in the 1930s (Abrams 1982). In 1987 the government funded an action research project which had the stated

364

aim of establishing guidelines which would enable local education authorities to change their existing policy and establish education for the older age groups as part of mainstream provision. (The report was published in 1988.) Such statutory provision has only occurred fortuitously in ordinary all-age classes in further education. Lifelong education in Britain is governed by sections 7, 41 and 42 of the 1944 Education Act, which apply to the 'spiritual, moral, mental, and physical development of the community'. Traditionally, local authorities and government have paid little heed to this interpretation. The result has been the growth of the self-help education movement for older adults. We shall return to this development later.

United States of America

A similar situation exists in the United States. The 1976 Mondale Bill on lifelong learning enacted for the first time legislation which was concerned with older people's 'continuing development as human beings'. The full effect of such legislation has not yet been felt, dependent as it must be on the support of the academic community and the necessary appropriations to make it a reality. Nevertheless, the emergence and growth of the Elderhostel movement and other nationally organized programmes, such as the Senior Center Humanities Program, are good examples of the way in which the older population has begun to respond. 'Elderhostel' by 1985 had enrolled 100,000 elders on 800 campuses and the Humanities Program had 75,000 members.

France

Again, in France, the *Universités du Troisième Age* sprang up after the 1968 revolution. The French universities had never been involved in adult education before. Now legislation stated that they must be open to all, committed to lifelong education (or *éducation permanente*) in collaboration with all interested parties. Legislation in 1971 decreed that all firms with more than ten employees should pay one per cent of their salaries bill towards the lifelong programme in the university, industrial, and voluntary sectors. From 1973 onwards an increasing number of universities opened up their facilities to retired people, especially in the summer vacations, and so the universities of the third age were born. (The term 'third age' is used because the four ages of human life are childhood and adolescence; occupational and wage-earning activity; retirement from the world of work; and dependency on others.) U3As now exist in numerous European countries, Canada, Latin America, and Japan.

CHANGING CONCEPTS OF RETIREMENT

Certainly when all these movements began, mainly in the 1970s, the emphasis was on the needs of retired people, those who became economically inactive at the end of a working life, usually around the age of 60 to 70. During the last decade, the concept of 'retirement' has changed. The economic recession, coupled with the arrival of high technology, has created a situation where some are finding that they will not work again after their mid-forties. This in itself has transformed the contemporary approach to pre-retirement education, which is increasingly interpreted by the pre-retirement Association of Great Britain and Northern Ireland as involving strategies to prepare people for retirement from mid-life onwards, rather than a short information-giving course arranged immediately before the retirement date. Early retirement, redundancy, and long-term unemployment have changed the post-second world war picture of society.

The Pre-Retirement Association is currently funded partly from government sources in order to develop training and interactive models which are relevant to a variety of situations. The numbers who participate in any kind of pre-retirement programme are unlikely to be more than 20 per cent of the retiring workforce at any one time, and currently in Britain about 9,000,000 (18 per cent) are now of state pensionable age. It is with this group especially that we are concerned here. Many will have nearly one third of their life ahead and it is reasonably well accepted that the quality of life of those who 'disengage' after retirement is likely to be less satisfactory than for those who keep their bodies and minds active. Statistics indicate that a higher percentage of men and women die in the 65 to 70 age range than in the older age groups.

LOW TAKE-UP OF COURSES

To a greater or lesser degree, this large cohort is involved in learning how to adapt to new social settings as ageing progresses. Only a small proportion of them will feel at ease when taking part in educational programmes. Both in Britain and the United States, only two per cent of the over-60s participate in such organized activities. (However, in London, the Inner London Education Authority claims that eight per cent of pensioners were enrolled in their classes for 1984–5.) In Denmark, the figure is ten per cent; in Argentina (where 50 per cent of the population is over 60) it is one per cent; in Israel (depending upon educational background for those over 50) the figure stretches from 21 to 34 per cent; in Japan, where there are no comparable figures, the Chu-kyoshin survey of 1980 claimed that 50.2 per cent of those over 56 expressed a wish to enrich their lives by learning activities (Glendenning 1987).

A variety of reasons have been produced to explain this generally low take-up of courses by students who have passed the age of 60. Education in Britain has an unfavourable image, especially among those who attended school before the 1940s, calling to mind learning by rote, corporal punishment, and a regimented atmosphere. There are more practical reasons also: cost, time, transport, unsuitable buildings, poor sight, hearing impairment, or other physical disabilities, and lack of awareness. Not surprisingly then, the main thrust in the movement of education for older adults has come from the adult educators themselves, and although a large body of research indicates the ability of older people to learn, there are probably incorrect assumptions being made about motivation, incentives, and the conditions and circumstances of learning.

Nevertheless, the 1982 survey of the educational experience and needs of adults in England and Wales revealed that 34 per cent of men and 30 per cent of women, aged 45 to 64, expressed interest in taking courses after they retired, and ten per cent of both sexes wished to study a foreign language after retirement (ACACE 1982). But learning is not confined to 'courses'. There is an increasing awareness that learning can be facilitated through activity, and libraries also have begun to reassess their role.

LEARNING ABILITY

In the early part of the century research appeared to demonstrate that learning ability peaked in youth and then declined steadily. This assisted the building up of the stereotype of increasing age meaning inevitable decline. Later, these studies were seen to have been biased, when it was realized that the older test subjects had fewer years of education compared with their younger counterparts. In addition, the speed of response had been measured rather than the quality of response. Recent research at the Open University has indicated that students aged 60–64 are among the most successful in degree examinations.

It has been suggested that there are three common approaches to life-span changes in learning performance. (1) Little can be done to arrest irreversible decrement; (2) life-span development is fundamentally stable and differences in performance are due to environment, education, or even health, not to ageing; (3) any small decline in performance can be modified by intervention. The latter suggests a major role for educators and trainers in developing learning skills in the later years.

One of the singular difficulties of the British situation is that there are hardly any psychologists researching and publishing in the area of the psychology of ageing. Bromley published his standard text in 1966. In more recent years, none, with the exception of Allman (who is American by birth), Jones, and Shea have paid any attention to learning aptitude in later life, in relation to educational provision. Rabbitt however has asserted that the rate of learning is determined by the IQ level in precisely the same way as that of young adults, and of course this counters the myth of inevitable mental decline. It has been shown that people in their seventies and eighties can absorb new ideas and learn new skills. Schaie wrote in 1975:

> Our studies strongly suggest that in the areas of intellectual abilities and skills old people in general, if they are reasonably healthy, have not declined, but rather become obsolete. This conclusion might be viewed as a rather negative value judgement. That is not true at all because obsolescence can be remedied by training, while deterioration is irreversible. (Schaie 1975)

Both longitudinal and cross-sequential studies are expensive and time consuming. Yet until they have been designed in Britain (and in European countries) rather than in America, where there have already been several, and necessarily followed through and appraised, we shall be unable to be completely confident about the relationship between ageing and intelligence. Nevertheless, 'it seems reasonable to predict that persons well exercising their abilities will retain them into their fifties, sixties or even their seventies'. There is also need for more evidence (than, for example, the Open University study produces) to show whether and in what situations older adults might perform better or worse than younger adults 'in real-life situations'. What is empirically clear is that older adults can and do learn and develop new skills. The effect of environmental and situational factors however needs to be recognized and minimized. This is a task for adult educators.

THE PROCESS OF LEARNING

The process of learning for older adults is to be found in the writings of Belbin and Belbin (1972), Peterson (1983), and others. Belbin and Belbin stress the role of the tutor in helping the student to overcome his or her feelings of insecurity, 'supporting the efforts of students rather than attempting to set an example that they feel they cannot achieve', as Peterson writes. Older people are not all alike. It is impossible to generalize about the needs of a homogeneous group; the age-range is too large. But their life experience, their accumulated knowledge, their practised skills and their established or still-changing attitudes are the basis for their educational experience in later life. Frequently this will take the form of finding solutions to problems that confront them. These may consist of the need for new social skills, the need for empowerment in the face of welfare or legal needs, their ability to use computers, their desire for the extension of their existing knowledge in literature, the arts, local history, or the natural environment. Their motivation is caused by an interest or a specific need, and learning becomes an active process through which their search is facilitated by the tutor. Many will argue that this is the basis for all adult education: what Knowles has called the androgogical model. It is a sound basis for work with older adults because it is student-centred and rooted in interaction and the search mode, enabling the student to be self-pacing. Botwinick (1978) and others have advocated pacing and self-pacing to reduce the psychological pressure of increasing learning speed. This is true even in the most unpropitious situations. Work in geriatric and psychiatric hospitals, and in residential homes has shown how a variety of classes, whether in current affairs, foreign languages, painting, sculpture, art, exercise, and other group activities can raise confidence and morale, improve physical condition (even incontinence), and renew the patient's search for a quality of life (Glendenning 1980).

GOOD PRACTICE

All of this must be accompanied by good practice on the part of both the tutor and the organizer. Five principal points have been suggested. (1.) Classes must be accessible. This implies that the organizer must ensure that the premises are suitable and that meetings take place in a ground floor room. Fees should be waived where possible or charged at not more than 20 pence a week. The Inner London Education Authority offers an unlimited number of courses to pensioners qualified by residence at £1.00 per head. (2.) Classes should be organized through the appropriate educational institution and not through non-educational agencies. Overall educational standards must be maintained and any offer of second-rate education should be rejected. (3.) Students should be offered a choice between attending a 'segregated' class designed to meet the needs of older people, and more general all-age classes which have traditionally been the norm. Older students frequently feel that they have been away from 'education' for so long that they welcome starting again within the supportive atmosphere provided by members of their own generation. (4.) There should be a careful monitoring from the outset of both courses and students to ensure that the course is meeting the needs of the individuals for which it was designed. (5.) It must be recognized (as we have noted above) that the over-60s are not a homogeneous group. For example, in educational terms, the majority left school at 14 and have been cut off from educational opportunities ever since. Some can afford fees; others cannot. Some have access to transport; some have not.

Working with those who left school early, 50 or 60 years after they left school, is labour intensive and therefore costly. It is still unusual for outreach work of this type to be facilitated apart from experimental grant-supported work (for example, Leeds University's 'Pioneer work programme' in Bradford from 1983–6). This has tended to be unco-ordinated and short-lived, operating in various parts of Britain from time to time, over the last 25 years. There is little evidence so far that it has been built into existing statutory provision, and the current research project of the Unit for the Development of Adult Continuing Education (see above) is attempting to counteract this continuing situation.

OUTREACH WORK

The term 'outreach work' which was used in the previous paragraph has been used in recent years to describe the provision of education outside the traditional institutional framework. Groombridge (1987) has defined 'outreach' as 'a way of attempting to provide educative experiences for natural deschoolers. . . . If the educational opportunities are provided by an educational body, that educational body needs to keep a very low profile. . . . The work has to be done in idioms that are acceptable to people who have rejected the rituals and symbols of education.'

EXISTING PROVISION AND OPPORTUNITIES

A great deal of 'education for older adults' is therefore not outreach at all. It is subsumed within the statutory provision of what, in Britain, is called 'further' or 'higher' education. Special concern for older adults is not the norm. In Britain, further education is the responsibility of the colleges of further education, the adult education departments of universities and the Workers' Educational Association. Higher education is the responsibility of the universities and the polytechnics. There are no reliable figures extant upon which to place a considered judgement in relation to degree-level work for persons over 60. There is however a general impression that more universities are now opening their doors to older students. There is little evidence to demonstrate that this is based on a growing interest on the part of university staff in the relevance of the androgogical model. The reasons behind a more open access are likely to be economic. The numbers of older undergraduates continue to be small. The Open University claims 90 per cent (3,000 in 1982) of all students over 60 years of age who are studying at degree level.

Five university adult education and extra-mural departments and as many polytechnics have during the last decade specialized in making special provision for the over-60s. The Polytechnic of North London, for example, has held a 'Learning in later life' programme every year since 1981. Keele University has arranged courses for over-60s since 1975. Many colleges of further education have included courses for older people within their programmes. Braintree College in Essex is a conspicuous example. Stafford College of Further Education has specialized in relaxation and exercise courses for over-60s for a number of years. The Workers' Educational Association has pioneered outreach work in London hospitals for long-stay geriatric patients. Newton-le-

Willows College of Further Education, Merseyside, has been involved in work with both geriatric and elderly psychiatric patients since 1973. Numbers of adult educators in recent years have considered the possibility of tutors for the elderly housebound. This has now been achieved by the Inner London Education Authority in its home tutor scheme. Educational work in residential homes for the elderly is now organized in a number of areas. There is insufficient space here to describe in detail these projects, many of which have been described elsewhere (for example Glendenning 1980; Groombridge 1987).

THE SELF-HELP MOVEMENT

On the other side of the coin, we find the significant self-help movement which began substantially in the late 1970s (although Friends in Retirement – FIRcone – Birmingham, with over 3,000 members has been in existence since the mid-1960s). This was a reaction to existing statutory provision, on the grounds of cost, timing of courses, physical, practical, and geographical unsuitability. The most recent estimate has put the figure of older people's self-help education groups at over 200 networks and over 35,000 regular participants. The Forum on the Rights of Elderly People to Education (FREE) came into existence in 1980 and has acted as a clearing house for news and as a political pressure group. Its regular bulletin contains much day-to-day information about the self-help movement.

The British University of the Third Age (U3A) is part of this movement. Its own unique approach has been expounded by Midwinter and others (Midwinter 1984). Its largest branch, of nearly 1,000 members, is in Huddersfield. Bearing in mind the university orientation of the U3A in France, it is noticeable that the British model 'cocks a perky snook at the conventional university'. There are still unanswered questions about its academic standards and the 'quality control' of its subject groups, but these questions apply to the other self-help groups also. Like the U3A, they have come into existence because of the failure of the British educational system to accommodate the needs of older people. Recognizing and even applauding these developments in principle, some would, nevertheless, welcome a more rigorous pursuit of academic standards which can be openly discussed throughout the whole movement. Assessment is currently difficult to achieve, as there is an absence of evidence. There is however a strong impression that some, at any rate, of the 'education' offered by the self-help movement is not of a standard that would be accepted by professionals who are engaged in the education of younger age groups.

LACK OF RESEARCH

In spite of all this activity, the lack of interest in all fields of research in relation to the needs of older adults is profoundly clear. In the fields of psychology and educational methodology the number of researchers and original thinkers is minimal (Norton 1987). The number of books published in Britain in the 1980s which deal with education and older adults can be counted exactly on the fingers of one hand (Glendenning 1980, 1985; Midwinter 1982, 1984; Johnston and Phillipson 1983). There is only one book (which has been available for the last 20 years) on the psychology of ageing (Bromley 1966) and there is no text at all on educational methodology. The British are more or less totally reliant on American psychologists and educators. The single attempt to break the mould is the British *Journal of Educational Geronotology*, which was launched in 1986.

A NEW FIELD OF STUDY

We have attempted to sketch the outline of a new field of study in Britain: educational gerontology. We have described briefly the type of activities that are taking place within the context of older people's learning. Learning has been defined as an inference based upon changed behaviour. Within this tapestry of experience woven from the multitude of different activities listed above, it is evident from observation that the quality of life of those who have participated has been enhanced, that 'behaviour' or response has been changed. But there are no scientific data to justify this statement. Educational gerontologists in America repeat the same point. 'Society as a whole benefits from the increased education of older people' (Peterson 1983). This assertion, this conviction, is based merely upon subjective observation and as such it presents an obstacle to recognition and funding by the state. Although, at the end of the day, the hypothesis is probably correct, it remains difficult to prove. Here is a gap in our knowledge that urgently requires to be filled.

Attention has been drawn to our need for more texts both in methodology and psychology. There are a few brief articles on teaching method, but no extended text. Similarly, there are only a few essays by British writers on learning aptitude in later life. Does it take longer to learn something when you are older? Does fatigue play any part in learning and memory use? If new knowledge is in conflict with present knowledge, what is the implication for teaching? How can teaching be matched to learning styles? How do we respond to Laslett's view that the British over-60s are the worst instructed people, not only in our own population, but also among the advanced western countries as a whole (Laslett 1984)? Or how do we respond to the view expressed by the Rapaports that 'People with cultivated interests have been found to have a greater repertoire with which to face retirement than those who have lower educational attainments'?

We have mentioned the wide range of disciplines which contribute to the development of this new field of study. Related to social gerontology, educational gerontology requires constant evaluation research. It requires close contact with and understanding of life-span developmental psychology. It requires the best that adult educators can give in establishing viable learning models. It is a multi-disciplinary field of study and as such, in Britain, deserves far more attention than it has hitherto received. Unless a clearer ground-plan has emerged within the next decade, a major academic blunder will have been made in a society where one adult in four is of state pensionable age.

REFERENCES

Abrams, M. (1982) *Education and Elderly People*, Mitcham: Age Concern Research Unit.

Advisory Council for Adult Continuing Education (1982) *Adults: Their Educational Experience and Needs*, London: ACACE.

Belbin, E. and Belbin, R. M. (1972) *Problems in Adult Re-Training*, London: Heinemann.

Botwinick, J. (1978) *Ageing and Behaviour*, New York: Springer.

Bromley, D. B. (1966) *The Psychology of Ageing*, Harmondsworth: Penguin Books.

Glendenning, F. (1980) *Outreach Education and the Elders: Theory and Practice*, Stoke-on-Trent: Beth Johnson Foundation and Department of Adult Education, University of Keele.

(Ed.) (1985) *Educational Gerontology: International Perspectives*, London: Croom Helm.

(1987) 'Educational gerontology in the future – unanswered questions', in S. de Gregorio (Ed.) *Social Gerontology: New Directions*, London: Croom Helm.

Groombridge, B. (1987) 'Older students: perceptions of educational providers in Great Britain', *Journal of Educational Gerontology*, 2 (1).

Johnston, S. and Phillipson, C. (Eds.) (1983) *Older Learners: The Challenge to Adult Education*, London: Bedford Square Press.

Laslett, P. (1986) 'The education of the elderly in Britain', in Midwinter (1984).

Midwinter, E. (1982) *Age is Opportunity: Education and Older People*, London: Centre for Policy on Ageing.

(Ed.) (1984) *Mutual Aid Universities*, London: Croom Helm.

Norton, D. (1987) *Education and Older People: Select Bibliographies on Ageing – No. 2*, London: Centre for Policy on Ageing.

Peterson, D. A. (1983) *Facilitating Education for Older Learners*, San Francisco/London: Jossey Bass.

Schaie, K. W. (1975) 'Age changes in adult intelligence', in D. S. Woodruff and J. E. Birren (Eds.) *Ageing: Scientific Perspectives and Social Issues*, New York: Van Nostrand Reinhold.

UNESCO (n.d. 1979?) *Educational Questions Concerning the Elderly*, Paris: UNESCO.

B. THE MANAGEMENT AND CONTENT OF EDUCATION

4. ORGANIZATION AND MANAGEMENT

4.0

INTRODUCTION: ORGANIZATION AND MANAGEMENT

ALAN PAISEY

The two key words which provide the title for this section stand for inseparable concepts. 'Organization' is the people involved in an enterprise – their numbers, their characteristics, and their capabilities. 'Management' is the human process among such people by which objectives are established and developed, work is accomplished and desired, and results are actually achieved.

It is unlikely that a separate section on organization and management would have appeared in a volume entitled *Handbook of Educational Ideas and Practices* if it had been published in any decade prior to the 1980s. The reason is not that organization and management in education have only recently been 'invented', although it may be the case that organization and management in education have only recently been 'discovered'. They have always existed in education: indeed, it is impossible to do without them. They have always been present in terms of ideas and practices variably appropriate to the conditions and needs of the education system and its institutions.

The factor which has made all the difference and led to the inclusion of organization and management in this book is the new scale of awareness and emphasis which they have received in society at large as well as in education itself. Once they were implicit in educational activity, now they are explicit; once they were incidental, now they are regarded as instrumental; once they were low-profile considerations, now they are high profile; once they were left to the practitioner, now they are matters of public concern and overt national policy.

The previous absence of significance attached to organization and management in education was reflected in the virtually complete indifference of the intellectual and academic estate to it as a serious, worthwhile and justified field of study. The study of organization and management was reserved almost exclusively for manufacturing and commercial activity. Only gradually were other types of enterprise included. Education began to receive attention in the learned journals, such as *Administrative Science Quarterly*, by way of studies of universities and the schools administrative system. This neglect of education, it might be said, came to an end with Bidwell's timely contribution 'The school as a formal Organization' as Chapter 23 in J G March (Ed.) *Handbook of Organizations* (Chicago: Rand McNally, 1964).

Meanwhile, higher degree and funded research studies in the United States were in full spate in the 1960s and particularly the 1970s. They focused openly on topics classifiable as organization and management relating to universities, colleges, schools, and the wider administrative system at local and State levels. In the United Kingdom developments of a similar nature took place but on a comparatively small scale and with a time lag. The founding achievements of the Institute of Education, University of London, in the late 1960s and early 1970s were supplemented by other institutions throughout the United Kingdom during the rest of the 1970s. At this time the British Educational Management and Administration Society was established and quickly developed. Textbooks, specialized journals and other publications on both sides of the Atlantic appeared, giving organization and management in education its own literature base. By the early 1980s in the United Kingdom, national funds were being made available for in-service training and education in organization and management. Thus, within two decades or so, organization and management in education assumed an identity, rose from obscurity, and became a recognized discipline and widespread academic and professional field of study based on its own research and experimental practice. During this period, the two words which best sum up the dominant trends in organization and management ideas and practices in education are 'consumerism' and 'privatization', affecting both the United Kingdom and the United States.

In the United Kingdom, growing concern about the volume of expenditure on education and the cost-effectiveness of it appeared during the 1970s, culminating in the speech by Prime Minister James Callaghan in 1976 at Ruskin College, Oxford on the issue. Since then, falling rolls and financial contraction have become a reality, quality output has been demanded, and the close scrutiny or involvement of many new or previously acquiescent parties to the educational contract has become a standard feature – together with the more active intervention of national government.

In the 1980s, amid the substantial privatization of state-owned industries, proposals have been emerging for reconceiving the standing and funding of maintained sector educational institutions – polytechnics, colleges and schools – at the expense of local government's prerogatives and powers. These proposals have included greater or complete financial self-management, freedom over admissions, and, at the extreme, the advocacy of institutional autonomy on the basis of direct national funding.

379

It is in the context of the ideas and practices associated with and fuelled by the twin themes of consumerism and privatization that the following contributions on organization and management have been made. The contributors are all experienced and accomplished authors in either their own professional or subject fields in organization and management or both. They hold or have recently held positions in the education system, or from their positions they engage or have recently engaged in voluntary additional commitments in the system, which serve as the bases for their contributions.

The first six chapters are concerned with system-wide organization and management. Chapter 1 draws attention to the existence and influence of the European Community and discusses the extent of its actual and potential effects on education in the United Kingdom. Chapters 2, 3, 4, and 5 are variously concerned with the distribution of powers and resources. Chapter 2 analyses the relations between national and local government, Chapter 3 the mechanics for obtaining and disbursing resources, Chapter 4 the provision, maintenance, and modification of buildings and capital properties and Chapter 5 the supply and development of staff as a key resource in the labour intensive education system. Chapter 6 completes the first section by focusing on a relatively new phenomenon – the intense and widespread political and professional activities of organized groups seeking to influence the content, course, and conduct of the education system.

The second group of six chapters respectively present the organization and management of the different types of particular institutions which make up the education system – namely, primary schools (Chapter 7), secondary schools (Chapter 8), independent schools (Chapter 9), sixth form and tertiary colleges (Chapter 10), further education colleges (Chapter 11), and higher education institutions – universities, polytechnics, and colleges or institutes of higher education – (Chapter 12).

Finally, three chapters address specific central features of the landscape of organization ideas and practices. Chapter 13 is on the ideas and practices of organization development, Chapter 14 on those of institutional effectiveness and evaluation, and Chapter 15 on those of management education and training.

Part I. System Organization and Management

NATIONAL GOVERNMENT AND EDUCATION IN THE EUROPEAN CONTEXT

BRIAN HOLMES

HISTORIC BACKGROUND

In spite of the fact that modern European systems of education share common traditions whose origins can be found in the theories of man, society, and knowledge formulated by Greek, Roman and Jewish philosophers, education was not mentioned in the 1957 Treaty of Rome which created the European Economic Community (EEC). Indeed for many years no mention was made of education in discussions designed to harmonize policies in a community of sovereign states. The free movement of workers made it necessary to pay attention to the provision of vocational training and the mutual recognition of academic qualifications to permit professional people to move from one country to another. Early interpretations of clauses in the Treaty of Rome began to change in the 1970s.

The Janne Report presented to the European Commission in 1973 recognized that a) there was an educational dimension to the affairs of the Community and that b) in 1971 the Ministers of Education from the (then) member states had agreed that educational policies, in addition to those dealing with vocational training and qualifications, should be considered under the Treaty of Rome. A formal decision along these lines was taken by the Commissioners in 1973 and the stage was set for co-operation in the field of education, if not for the harmonization of educational policies throughout the Community and the adoption of specific EEC educational policies which would be binding on all members.

Before 1939, systems of administration in Europe owed much to the French. In most countries bureaucrats in national Ministries of Education were at the heart of the policy formulation and adoption processes. They were able to lay down in regulations the national curricula and to determine how teachers were trained, appointed, paid, and promoted. They engaged in party political debates about the retention or abolition of differentiated second-level schooling. Teachers in publicly maintained schools were, and still are, civil servants, and their salaries fall on generous civil service scales.

Variations on the highly centralized French system of administration are found. Each of the eleven *Länder* in the Federal Republic of Germany is responsible for its own system of education. The administration of each system is, however, based on a host of detailed regulations. Members of the Federal Committee of Ministers have relatively little power. Politics enter into policy processes in the various *Länder*. In Belgium there are two Ministries of Education in recognition of the fact that both linguistic groups – the French and the Flemish – want to run their own schools. Administratively, Switzerland has many systems. Each of the 28 Cantons is responsible for its own system of education. Thus, while the size of the administrative units varies, the principles of administration laid down in the *code Napoléon* inform most of them.

Cut off from the continent by more than the Channel, the British never developed a national system of administration which, within limits, ensured equality of provision. Officials in the old Board of Education and in the present Department of Education and Science have possessed little power but until recently had a monopoly on what power could be exercised from the centre. HMIs (His/Her Majesty's Inspectors) have always been advisers. Only recently have they become involved in national curriculum development. Even so they cannot easily insist that a national curriculum is introduced at any of the levels of education.

Teachers in individual schools, under pressure in academic secondary schools from the examination system, are still free within fairly broad limits to decide what is taught, how it is taught and, within a school, to whom it is taught. In 1939 university regulations laid down that a range of subjects must be studied, and successfully taken in examinations, if a student was to matriculate and thus meet minimum university entrance requirements. After 1945 political party pressure reduced examinations at the end of compulsory schooling to passes in individual subjects. University academics reduced the number and range of subjects needed to gain admission to a university. A small number of closely related subjects – in either the humanities or the sciences – became the norm. Only recently (mid-1980s on) has the strait-jacket placed on school curricula by university academics been eased.

Nevertheless, in spite of British government pressure to broaden sixth form curricula, the situation is vastly different from that which exists in most continental systems of education. British leaders may have received a liberal education in the Greek sense of the term but, compared with their counterparts in the rest of Europe, few of them have received a broadly based general education.

COMMON EDUCATIONAL PROBLEMS IN EUROPE SINCE 1945

The many common features in the educational systems of Europe make it surprising that little attempt has been made to harmonize policies throughout the EEC or to establish for the EEC a pattern of policies. Diversity explains why any such attempt would have been doomed to failure. Curricular differences guarantee differences of outlook. The absence of well-developed systems of vocational and technical schools sets Britain off from the rest of Europe. The absence in Britain of one powerful Ministry of Education makes it impossible for the Secretary of State in discussion with other Ministers of Education to guarantee that agreed policies will be implemented. England and Wales, Scotland, and Northern Ireland each have their own system of education. Local education authorities are legally responsible for the provision of education in their areas. Perhaps only in the Federal Republic of Germany can regional policies be found which differ from each other. Elsewhere national governments have a good deal of responsibility for the formulation, adoption, and implementation of educational policy. Which of the two tendencies will prevail in the European Community (EC) remains to be seen.

Will member states, through their appointed Ministers, be prepared, as some people believe, to allow the Commission of the EC to determine such matters as the structure of the school system, the content of education, and the way schools are administered? It seems likely that for many years to come governments throughout the EC will be no more prepared to hand over to the Commission the task of formulating educational policies than they will be to abandon their national sovereignty.

At an international level there exist difficulties similar to those in most federal nations, such as the USA, where there is constant tension between the rights of individual states to decide for themselves, and the federal government, which wants to participate actively in many aspects of policy. The Constitution in the USA guarantees that individual states cannot pass legislation which runs contrary to clauses in the Constitution. The Treaty of Rome laid down an institutional framework which included a Commission, a Council of Ministers, a European Assembly, and a Court of Justice. A structure exists within which it would be possible for the Community to pass legislation which is binding on all its members. It is just possible that EC policies for the Community as a whole might be developed in those areas of activity which do not touch on the spirit of national systems with long histories.

In spite of appearances to the contrary, curriculum reform in Europe is the responsibility of educationalists. In the so-called centralized systems they are involved at the national, regional, and local levels in the formulation of reform policies. Their allies, and opponents, in Ministries of Education and the universities have been, or still are, teachers. Inspectors are usually recruited from among the body of teachers. Industrialists and parents, whatever their concern about the appropriateness of the content of education, have few opportunities to participate in curriculum debates. Much less are they able to participate actively in the formulation and adoption of policy. Party politicians, except on crucial issues such as the place of religious instruction in school curricula, hesitate to challenge the authority of the educational establishment as regards general education.

The content of technical education is subjected to different political pressures. In most European countries curricula in schools which prepare pupils for the world of work rather than the universities are administered by national agencies other than the Ministry of Education, and industrialists are able to influence, in accordance with their wishes, the content of technical courses. The creation in England of the Manpower Services Commission went some way to meeting this requirement. A National Council for Vocational Qualifications has been set up to monitor training courses for industry and commerce. It will have very little power to insist that nationally prescribed syllabuses are followed in any of the many trades which constitute the industrial enterprise.

In the final analysis however, what goes on in the classroom or workshop lies in the hands of the teacher. Examination syllabuses and question papers are more likely than anything else to determine what they do. Textbooks too have a profound influence on the actual content of education. There is very little Ministry of Education officials can do to ensure that individual teachers carry through effectively the intentions of those who draw up syllabuses. At one time inspectors, selected from among the best teachers, were expected to fulfil these tasks. Present-day climates of opinion tend to support the view that inspectors should be advisers rather than policemen whose task it is to make sure teachers obey the pedagogical laws. However, at local level the inspectorial function has been increasing in some education authorities.

A further issue, which has been debated in member states without an input from the EC, has been the relationships between national, regional, and local governments. Since administrative arrangements are central to notions of sovereignty it is inconceivable that an EC directive should *require* the French government to devolve some of its authority or require the Department of Education and Science in the United Kingdom to reduce the power of local education authorities. The distinction made between centralized and decentralized systems of educational administration is useful but too simplistic.

In short, the complexity of the processes involved in the formulation, adoption, and implementation of policy, and the range of people taking part, are too great to justify an assertion that a national Ministry of Education anywhere is responsible for all educational decisions, or that in decentralized systems all policies are formulated, adopted, and implemented at the local and school levels.

The difficulties of introducing structural innovations in education are illustrated by the situation in the Netherlands where the rights of parents to establish schools in accordance with their wishes are fundamental to the administration of education. A small number of parents who wish to set up a primary school can do so with the full financial backing of the government. A larger number of parents must petition to set up a secondary school. Catholic, Protestant, and secular schools receive substantial support. A great many smaller organizations also run schools. To introduce comprehensive schools on a national basis has been difficult and taken a long time. At the same time in spite of the great variety of primary and general secondary schools throughout the country, curricula at the various levels of education are the same everywhere.

Generally speaking it might be said that in those countries where historically the power of the central government has been considerable, attempts to devolve power are now being made. In countries where the authority and power of the national government have been weak, proposals are under consideration to increase the role of the national government in policy making and its implementation. It is unlikely that an EC policy on administrative arrangements could be formulated in a way which would satisfy all the conflicting opinions throughout the Community.

THE POTENTIAL FOR CONCERTED ACTION

None of the problems facing educationalists in Europe since 1945 has been solved to the satisfaction of all the protagonists. Debates have certainly become more party politicized in ways that make compromise difficult. Educational establishments are divided into conservatives who wish to retain all that they consider valuable in the European tradition, and radicals who fundamentally seek to increase equality of opportunity and provision so that the rights of all children can be promoted. Within each of the member states of the EC some progress has been made to remedy perceived weaknesses in pre-1945 systems of education. Debates continue.

Meanwhile new problems to which no great attention was previously paid have arisen; the movement of large numbers of foreign workers into Britain, the Federal Republic of Germany, the Netherlands, and France has created problems of accommodation which have an educational dimension. Increases in the number and proportion of unemployed school-leavers is a common phenomenon. Given the assertion that everyone has the right to work this raises fundamental problems of policy to which educational panaceas have been offered as solutions. Adult unemployment and changes in industry have raised questions about the re-education and training of industrial workers through some form of recurrent education.

The free movement of labour within the EC in accordance with the Treaty of Rome implies that technical and professional qualifications should be recognized as valid throughout the Community. Advances in the medical sciences and the treatment of patients have meant that many children who previously would not have survived now live well beyond the age of compulsory school attendance. The identification and education of children with special needs have received more and more attention in recent years. The more extensive employment of mothers has created the need for pre-school facilities.

The explosion of knowledge induced by wartime scientific developments, the development of mass media of communication, improvements in printing techniques, and so on, have given rise to mountains of documents and data banks. The dissemination of this knowledge suggests that there should be increased co-operation and interchange between personnel in the universities and institutions of higher education throughout Europe, and that documents should be collected and the information therein disseminated as widely as possible. The collection and dissemination of information undoubtedly has a European dimension in addition to its world-wide dimension.

Substantially, if the EC is to operate as an entity in the world of superpowers, its role in the pattern of international relations has to be examined and explained. This is a task for educational systems which until 1945 were far more interested in the analysis of national affairs and colonial relationships than in Europe as a whole and its position in the world. Clearly a Community initiative is desirable if national parochialism is to be avoided.

The unity and diversity which find expression in the educational systems of Europe give rise to fascinating possibilities. Notions of sovereignty and concepts of national identity will inhibit the formulation and adoption of Community-wide educational policies. The international pressures on Europe to unite will promote the formulation of policy solutions to common problems as the result of negotiations between representatives of national governments. In education these will be the appointed or elected Ministers of Education. A Minister who cannot speak with authority for his government and nation will be at a disadvantage. Expediency is likely within the Community to strengthen the hand of individual Ministers of Education. In far more respects than in the past education will become a national government responsibility with all the reservations about over-simplifying this notion that have already been referred to in this analysis.

Recognition of the difficulties which would be associated with attempts to persuade Europeans to abandon their national traditions, and sovereign governments to abandon their right to educate citizens as they think fit, helps to explain the caution built into the 1976 Resolution to establish co-operation between member states of the EC. In the Resolution of the Council of Ministers a distinction was made between actions which could be carried out at the level of the Community and those which were reserved to individual member states.

Further distinctions are needed and an analysis of the role agencies of the EC can play and are likely in future to play. For example, it is necessary to locate the levels at which policy can be formulated, adopted, and implemented. A simple suggestion would be that the Council of Ministers and the Commission formulate policy which is adopted by the governments of member states and put into practice, depending on the action needed, by local administrators and teachers. The processes are not so simple. Moreover the politics of policy making are influenced by what aspect is under consideration – aims, administration, finance, structure of the system, curricula, or teacher education. To long-standing problems national governments have proposed national solutions. Novel problems might require solutions which are formulated at the Community level in the interests of all its members.

Implicitly the EC has drawn a distinction between problems with which national governments were wrestling before 1957 and those which emerged after the Treaty of Rome. Between 1945 and 1957 expansionist policies were adopted to meet demographically created demands for education. Plans to increase equality of education were debated, and in some countries put into practice, by reducing selectivity and differentiation by school type at the second level of education. On these issues as they relate to compulsory periods of education, the Council and Commission have had very little to say. They restrict their initiatives to those levels of education which have been neglected. They have also taken up new problems of policy.

In terms of the processes identified over a wide range of economic, social, and now educational policy, members of the EC are in a position to lay down general objectives and on the basis of commissioned research suggest specific policies. Some of the policies recommended can be adopted within the EC itself without reference to member states. In a few cases Community policy can be implemented without reference to member governments. In general, however, action can take place only when member government representatives are prepared to adopt Commission policies and to persuade those responsible for implementing them at home to do so.

Naturally, aims and objectives, if stated in very general terms – and the Community is wont to do this – can be more readily accepted than specific policies which have a direct bearing on the provision of education in member states. Policy has to be put into practice by administrators and teachers. They need to behave as Europeans rather than nationals, in practice. Their deeply-held beliefs influence their actions more than the higher valuations they are prepared publicly to accept. Agreement on general aims and objectives may be achieved without consensus on how to realize them in practice.

The agencies within the Community take account of these differences. The Council of Ministers is made up of representatives from the member countries. It has legislative and executive authority. The Commission of the European Communities has somewhat similar powers in that it formulates policies legitimized by the Treaties or referred to it by the Council of Ministers.

Since, as stated, education does not figure in the original Treaties, while the Council and the Commission may formulate policies and have them agreed by the various Ministers of Education, each government is free to interpret and implement policies in the light of its own self interest. The unusual character of education is reflected in the establishment of a permanent Education Committee. Members of this committee, nominated by Ministers of Education from the member states, formulate policy for submission to the Ministers for approval. Once adopted, Community educational policies are monitored by the Education Committee. In administrative terms therefore Community procedures acknowledge the difficulties of arriving at a pattern of policies without the prior approval of national governments. They are reflected in the establishment and operation of the Community Education Action Programme.

In the case of the one aspect of this programme which reflects concerns which pre-date the creation of the EEC, namely equality of educational opportunity, the Ministers agreed that it is an essential aim of education. A glance at the stated aims of education submitted by Ministries of Education to the International Bureau of Education (IBE) in Geneva, and summarized in its *International Guide to Educational Systems* published in 1979 and subsequently revised, confirms that child-, society-, and, to a limited extent, knowledge-centred aims inform the educational systems in all Community countries.

In terms of general aims, emphases vary, but in all cases the provision of free and compulsory education is regarded as a major aim. Belgium mentions free primary and secondary education without discrimination. In the Federal Republic of Germany every *Land* guarantees everyone the right to education without distinction according to his or her talents. In Italy the rights of ethnic minorities are protected. Luxembourg makes specific mention of the equal rights of all residents to free and compulsory education regardless of race, religion, sex, and social class. The right of parents to bring up children in accordance with their own convictions is stressed in the stated aims of the Netherlands and the Republic of Ireland. France regards an essential free education which prepares all citizens for life-long learning as the aim of education. The aim of Danish education is to provide compulsory comprehensive education to ensure the same educational opportunity for all young people.

The overriding aim of education in England and Wales is to provide for the well-being and progress of individual pupils, and the aim of education in Northern Ireland is not significantly different.

Thus a child-centred aim finds its most positive expression in the stated aims of the United Kingdom, Belgium, and the Federal Republic of Germany. Parents' rights are emphasized in the Netherlands, the Republic of Ireland, and Denmark. As for society-centred aims, France expects education to prepare all pupils for modern society and changes in it. Italy aims to produce citizens who are capable of participating fully in a democratic society and who have been introduced to the world of work. Education in Greece is to create self-sufficient and responsible citizens, and the second stated aim of education in the Netherlands is to satisfy manpower demands. In no case is knowledge for its own sake regarded in modern Europe as a major educational aim – though once it might have been. Indeed, knowledge is hardly mentioned in any of the IBE submissions. By implication the provision of knowledge is seen as instrumental – as a way of achieving child- or society-centred aims.

There is implicit and even explicit agreement that the all-round potential – intellectual, spiritual (moral), aesthetic, and physical potential of all children should be developed. There are enough statements to confirm that the kind of society to which education should contribute is, in Western Europe, democratic. The desired economic life or world of work is not stated. It may be inferred from the aims laid down by the founders of UNESCO that education should contribute to raised standards of living and to the maintenance of peace.

These shared general aims are sufficiently comprehensive to gain widespread acceptance among European educationalists. At the same time they are so general as to allow for many national interpretations. In the Community Education Action Programme, EC interpretations are given to aspects of provision which are somewhat novel and have present-day significance. In the case of equal opportunity activities, the Community restricts itself to a consideration of policies relating to freedom of access to various levels of education and to aspects of education which prior to 1957 received rather little attention. The provision of pre-primary school education is therefore receiving attention. The access of girls to types of education which will equalize their general and vocational educational chances, employment opportunities, and career prospects is also on the Community's programme. One Community Report – the Byrne Report – advocated the introduction of co-education at all levels of education. A policy which has been criticized is the failure to provide the full range of opportunities for girls offered in single-sex schools.

Finally, on other relatively neglected aspects of education, namely the education of adults who have left the formal system of education, Community seminars have been held under the auspices of the Commission. The need for adults to have another chance to re-enter educational programmes, whether they are designed to fill the gaps in their general education, or to retrain them for jobs in agriculture, industry, commerce, or the professions, is recognized by the Community at the level of general policy as worthy of a great deal of attention.

Action research by the Community has focused on what kind of education and training school-leavers need if they are to get jobs; on the development of guidance services; on the need for compensatory provision for certain groups of school-leavers who are at risk; and on the initial and in-service training of teachers.

Again, central to Community policy is the belief that as much as possible should be known about various forms of disability and the kinds of provision which should be made during the period of compulsory education and as disabled youngsters prepare for work. Proposals to integrate the education of children with special needs into regular schools, to provide educational and psychological guidance services, to involve parents and industrialists, to improve the training of teachers so that they are all aware and can cope with disadvantaged children in regular classrooms, are again very general and could well be agreed at the ministerial level by all members of the Education Committee.

Co-operation in higher education, teaching about Europe, pupil exchanges, and the teaching of foreign languages so that all people within the Community will have the opportunity of learning at least one other Community language appear rather technical in character. It is apparent, however, that traditional attitudes to foreign language learning and the pragmatic advantages of learning one rather than another language will influence the willingness of teachers and students to learn a foreign language.

In conclusion, it may be said that education in the European context can best be analysed by recognizing its common features and the diversity which exists as a result of historical developments. European culture is envied, despised, copied, and rejected by people all over the world. Colonialism introduced European education to people everywhere. At the same time colonialism has made European ideas suspect. European standards of living are envied except perhaps in the USA, Japan, and some of the English-speaking former British Dominions. Post-1945 pressures have drawn the peoples of Europe together. The seeds of co-operation were sown in the Treaty of Rome. It seems unlikely, however, that in the foreseeable future the differences which exist between European systems of education will be eliminated by fiat. Some of them may be eroded with the passage of time.

FURTHER READING

Archer, M. S. (1979) *Social Origins of Educational Systems*, London: Sage.

Burgess, T. (Ed.) (1986) *Education for Capability*, Windsor: NFER-Nelson.

Clark, B. R. (Ed.) (1985) *The School and the University*, London: University of California.

Fenwick, K. and McBride, P. (1981) *The Government of Education in Britain*, Oxford: Martin Robertson.

Harling, P. (1984) (Ed.) *New Directions in Educational Leadership*, London: Falmer.

Holmes, B. (1983) 'Educational development trends', *International Yearbook of Education* Volume XXV – 1983, Paris, Unesco/IBE.

(Ed.) (1983) *International Handbook of Educational Systems, Vol. 1, Europe and Canada*, Chichester: John Wiley.

(Ed.) (1985) *Equality and Freedom in Education*, London: George Allen & Unwin.

Husen, T. (1986) *The Learning Society Revisited*, Oxford: Pergamon Press.

Lauglo, J. and McLean, M. (Eds.) (1985) *The Control of Education*, London: Heinemann Educational.

Mallinson, V. (1980) *The Western European Idea in Education*, Oxford: Pergamon Press.

Neave, G. (1984) *The EEC and Education*, Stoke-on-Trent: Trentham Books.

OECD (1983) *Compulsory Schooling in a Changing World*, Paris: OECD.

(1985) *Education in Modern Society*, Paris: OECD.

Russell, B. (1946) *A History of Western Philosophy*, London: George Allen & Unwin.

UNESCO/IBE (1979) *International Guide to Education Systems* (prepared by Brian Holmes), Paris: UNESCO.

LOCAL GOVERNMENT AS PROVIDER OF INSTITUTIONS AND EMPLOYER OF STAFF

RICHARD CLARK

HISTORIC FORMULA

'It is a basic feature of the public service of Education in England and Wales that, while it is a national service, it is locally administered. Except at University level, it is in the words of Selby-Bigge, a decentralized service "conducted by representative local bodies, which are not the agents of the central authority". Unlike the Ministries of Education in, say, France or Italy, the central department itself takes virtually no part in the running of educational institutions. It maintains no schools or colleges; it employs no teachers; it does not control the curriculum.' Thus Sir William Pile, a former Permanent Secretary at the Department of Education and Science, epitomized the relationship between central and local government in the English and Welsh educational system, for since 1902 it has been the role of the local education authority (LEA) to be the prime provider of the service.

THE DEVELOPMENT OF THE LOCAL EDUCATION AUTHORITY

1870 Act

The establishment of public elementary education by the 1870 Education Act demanded a body which could ensure that schools were established, financed, and run. The School Boards, formed by the Act, fulfilled that function and first demonstrated the power of a local body as the practical provider of schooling within a framework of central legislation. They had remarkable success. By 1902 there were 2,500 School Boards in existence. Given the task of establishing schools to supplement those provided by the church and by voluntary Trusts, they had built 5,694 schools, but even more significantly had begun to develop higher grade schools to meet the needs of young people to go beyond the narrow confines of elementary studies. Their developing initiatives were cut short by the High Court of Justice in the case of *Rex* v. Cockerton in which the Court ruled that the powers of School Boards were limited to providing education which was strictly at the elementary level. This strait-jacketing of the powers of the Boards led parliament to introduce the 1902 Education Act which established the first formal local education authorities and set out their powers.

1902 Act

The 1902 Education Act established 332 local education authorities. Whereas the School Boards had been single-purpose elected bodies with a power to raise a rate, the new Act gave education powers to the new County Councils (established in 1888) and the County Boroughs. Boroughs with more than 10,000 population, and Urban Districts with more than 20,000, were given powers as 'Part III authorities' for elementary education only, powers which they largely lost in 1944.

The 1902 Act therefore marks the point at which local government was entrusted with education powers. The scope of local provision was extended beyond the primary level and the principle of democratic local accountability through the Education Committee of the Council was established.

1944 Act

The next stage in the evolution of the local education authorities came with the 1944 Education Act which reduced the number of LEAs to 146 by taking away elementary education from the Boroughs and Districts. This move, strongly resisted by the losers, recognized the need for a local authority to have adequate size and resources if it were to provide the whole range of educational services, a theme taken up again when local government reform was undertaken in 1974 with a subsequent further reduction in the number of local education authorities to 104.

But it is the 1944 Act which established the functions of the local education authority largely as we know it today, and for the first time also created the post of Minister of Education. It set out the respective functions of the Minister, the local authorities, and the voluntary providers. Its strength, demonstrated by its long survival as the basis of control of the service, derives from three factors.

First, it sought a balance of power between the church and the local education authority, and between them and the Secretary of State. Second, it enshrined the notion of a partnership between local government and central government in which the former was given broad duties and powers and responsibilities, within a legal framework, whilst the Minister held the power to ensure they discharged those responsibilities effectively. Third, it recognized three stages of education, Primary, Secondary and Further Education.

GENERAL POWERS

The most important statement of the duties of local education authorities is set out in Section 7 of the 1944 Act:

it shall be the duty of the local education authority for every area, so far as its powers extend, to contribute towards the spiritual, moral, mental and physical development of the community by securing that efficient education throughout those stages (primary, secondary and further) shall be available to meet the needs of the population of their area.

The Act goes on to be specific about the responsibilities of the local education authority as a provider of schools:

and the schools available for an area shall not be deemed to be sufficient unless they are sufficient in number, character, and equipment to afford for all pupils opportunities for education offering such variety of instruction and training as may be desirable in view of their different ages, abilities, and aptitudes ...

It is interesting to note that the local education authority is given the duty and the power to 'provide' – but that the choice of how and when and where to do so is left to local initiatives.

PROVISION OF SCHOOLS

When the need for a school is established, the local education authority will publish Notices of its intention. Where there is significant objection, the Secretary of State makes the final decision. So far as the nature of the school is concerned, the local education authority may propose the detail of its age range, its size, and its educational character. The Secretary of State may approve or reject their proposals to establish or change, but importantly he has no power to amend or to propose himself. Therein lies one source of recurring government dissatisfaction. Whilst the Secretary of State can frustrate local wishes by his exercise of the power to refuse proposals, he cannot initiate. Labour governments have wished to promote the development of comprehensive schools and have found the need to introduce legislation to compel local education authorities to submit plans for change. The Conservative Government of 1979 repealed these measures, leaving some frustration with local education authorities whose plans to change the character of grammar schools were then sometimes refused.

In the early post-war years, after 1945, when the need to build new schools was at its peak, government used its powers to determine detailed constraints on the building of schools. First, all building programmes were subject to stringent control. Projects were included in a building programme by government after close scrutiny of proposed lists. Government examined control of loan sanction to regulate the size of programmes. Second, regulations tightly constrained such features as the minimum teaching area to be attained, levels of lighting, hard paved play areas, and numbers of washbasins. Third, costs per pupil place were centrally determined. Whilst government still determines the total amount a Council may borrow for capital expenditure purposes, many of the detailed constraints no longer apply.

The pressures to build for rapidly increasing numbers have passed, and the skills of local authority architects have been well established. The control of finance, however, remains to frustrate the local authority. Successive governments have found the need to control the totality of public borrowing, and the controls devised have limited the powers of local education authorities to provide schools, replace, or extend them as they would wish. More recently, government has found it necessary to limit the ability of the local education authority to use in full money raised from the sale of assets to meet their aspirations.

TEACHERS

Legislation makes no direct reference to the number of teachers a local education authority should employ or a school should have. In practice, it is the Secretary of State who exercises a power to determine the number of teachers who shall be trained, the qualifications required for entry to teacher training, and the process of certification. However, it is the local education authority (or the governors in the case of aided schools) who employs teachers, determines how many to engage, pays and deploys them. The local education authority is responsible for their management and further training.

The pay of teachers has until 1987 been determined by the Burnham Committee, and its recent history again illustrates the changing nature of the balance of interests between central and local government. The Burnham Committee consisted of two parties, the teachers' side, reflecting the relative strengths of the teacher unions, and the management side. The latter embraced the employers, the local education authorities, represented through their associations, the Association of Metropolitan Authorities (AMA), the Association of County Councils (ACC) and the Welsh Joint Education Committee

(WJEC) and the Department of Education and Science (DES), who enjoyed a weighted vote in negotiations but had no majority. However, the Secretary of State, since the late 1950s, carried, in the normal event, a right of veto within the Committee on matters directly affecting the size of the award and also the right to set aside an arbitral award subject only to Parliament's concurrence. The seeds of tension therefore lay in a) teachers' frustration that a settlement negotiated with their employers could be set aside by government; b) local education authorities' frustration that such agreements could be blocked by their government partners on the management side; and c) the government's inability to enter debate about the conditions of service of teachers whose pay they substantially contributed to through the grant system.

Conditions of service for teachers were separately negotiated by the Council of Local Education Authorities (CLEA) acting on behalf of all local education authorities with the teacher associations. Prolonged attempts by the local education authorities to bring pay negotiations into the same arena as conditions of service matters and to consider a pay settlement in return for a new teacher's contract foundered in 1987 after prolonged negotiations, giving the Secretary of State the opportunity to introduce legislation bringing the Burnham Committee to an end, and giving him the direct power to settle the dispute by himself determining levels of pay and the terms of new contractual conditions of service.

As employers, it is the local education authorities who individually decide how many teachers to employ. No legislation governs the size of classes, as in some other countries. In practice, the limits are set on the one hand by the supply of teachers, and on the other by controls on local authority finance. More than half of a local education authority's expenditure is accounted for by the pay of teachers, and in a county, some two thirds of all the expenditure of the Council will be attributable to the education service, so that teacher numbers are of necessity affected by any control on grant received or on limits placed on overall spending. The political will to reduce class size in practice has been governed by levels of rate support grant or penalties introduced in the 1980s through 'capping' the levels of permitted spending.

At the local level, prior to the 1988 Education Reform Act, the local education authority determined the establishment of the individual school or college and then in practice delegated the appointment process to school governing bodies. The local education authority retained the right under the 1944 Act to confirm or refuse the appointment, and of the dismissal of teachers. It enjoyed, under the Burnham Reports, substantial discretion in deciding the level and number of promoted posts to be made available to the school for its management.

It is the local education authority which has the responsibility for the teacher's in-service educational training (INSET), as opposed to initial training. It will take responsibility for the induction of probationary teachers, provide advisory support, operate teachers' centres, and fund the courses to which teachers are released. By managing the in-service training budget, the local education authority has been able to determine its priorities for the curriculum and the development of staff skills. However, since 1986 the government has introduced new measures to control the level of INSET through a new grant system, and to set national priorities for the programme.

All matters relating to the conditions of service of teachers have been the concern of the local authorities. Teachers' conditions have been negotiated in the School Teachers' Committee of the Council of Local Education Authorities. The DES are not party to these negotiations, and neither do they participate in matters such as the appointment, deployment, redeployment, discipline, and dismissal of staff. With well over 400,000 teachers in the profession in well over 20,000 schools the control of individual staffing matters has been seen essentially as a matter for local decision. Dealings with teacher associations, both collectively and on behalf of individual members, rest at local authority level, with the governors of the school and with the LEA.

STEPS TO REFORM

It is a justifiable generalization to say that from 1944 to the present, the local education authorities were the providers of the service, its buildings, its staff, its resources, and its curriculum, the latter in partnership with the schools. However, the continuance of that position came under challenge. It has been a feature of the annual conferences of the Council of Local Education Authorities that the central local partnership has been increasingly under strain. The authorities point to the development of the Manpower Services Commission (MSC) in funding and specifying curriculum changes, and to growing centralism seen, for example, in the introduction of education support grants, grant-related in-service training (GRIST) schemes and the proposed direct establishment by the DES of city technology colleges. The division of responsibility created by the 1944 Act was broken in that some staff salaries are now directly funded by the MSC or by Education Support Grants.

The reasons for this shift are many. First, a concern about the impact and fairness of the rating system has prompted firm measures to limit the powers of local government to spend, through reductions in grant and rate capping. There is now an intention by government to 'abolish the rates', and in pursuit of that objective measures such as the removal to the Exchequer of teachers' salaries were suggested in the debate which preceded the introduction of the community charge.

Second, a perception by government that local education authorities have not always exercised their powers wisely. Fears of the use of the curriculum for political ends led, in the autumn of 1987, to proposals for a national curriculum, the dilution of local education authority participation in governing bodies, and the transfer of increased powers over finance and staffing to the governors.

Third, the strong belief in the place of market forces and parental choice as agents which can bring quality to the system led to proposals for 'open enrolments' and for 'opting out'.

Fourth, major higher education institutions were taken from the control of the LEA in 1989 and held accountable to a National Polytechnic and Colleges Funding Council which will fund them and commission their courses. Changes in the constitution of further education governing bodies will increase the power of local employers at the expense of the LEA in the management of non-advanced further education. These measures, consolidated in the 1988 Education Reform Act, will substantially change the relationship in several ways.

Under the 'open enrolment' provisions, local authorities have largely lost the power to determine the capacity of schools and fix admission limits. The ability of local education authorities to manage the availability of places as school rolls rise and fall has sharply diminished.

Now that measures to permit 'opting out', and seeking Grant Maintained Status have been enacted, it will no longer be the case that the local education authority is the unchallenged local provider, as grant maintained schools and city technology colleges will be established with the Secretary of State's approval and directly grant-aided by him.

The provisions for financial delegation to schools involve the loss by the local education authority of its part in the appointment of the head teacher, and schools will have the power to vire expenditure to the extent that the local education authority will no longer be the sole body to determine staffing levels. Similar measures apply to colleges.

From their inception, the Board of Education, the Ministry of Education, and the DES have maintained no schools or colleges, employed no teachers, and have not controlled the curriculum. The traditional balance now seems set for a substantial tilt to the centre as the Education Reform Act (1988) removes many of the local education authorities' powers to appoint and deploy staff, to determine the size and capacity of schools, and to provide higher education. Other powers are destined to flow to governing bodies and the schools themselves, whilst governing bodies have been reconstituted to emphasize the parental and industrial voice and diminish the power of LEA appointees. Local education authorities remain charged with duties to ensure that 'efficient education throughout those stages (primary, secondary and further) shall be available to meet the needs of the population of their area', but are left without the direct powers to initiate the provision and control of establishments, to appoint and control staff, and to share major responsibility for what is taught. The indications are that the partnership is giving way to increased central powers on the one hand and to greater devolution of power to individual school governing bodies on the other.

The expected Education Act of 1988 will be seen as a historic watershed, in that it marks the consolidation of measures which have as their effect the removal of local education authorities as prime providers of the service.

FURTHER READING

Alexander, W. P. and Taylor, G. (1977) *County and Voluntary Schools*, London: Councils and Education Press.

Brooksbank, K. (Ed.) (1980) *Educational Administration*, London: Councils and Education Press.

Casson, W. A. and Whiteley, G. C. (1903) *The Education Act 1902*, London: Knight & Co.

Cooke, G. and Gosden, P. (1986) *Education Committees*, London: Councils and Education Press.

Dent, H. C. (1952) *The Education Act 1944* (4th edition), London: University of London Press.

  (1961) *The Educational System of England and Wales*, London: University of London Press.

Eagleston, E. J. R. (1956) *From School Board to Local Authority*, London: Routledge & Kegan Paul.

Fowler, G. (1974) *The Local Government of Education*, Milton Keynes: Open University Press.

Great Britain, Her Majesty's Government (1988) *Education Reform Act 1988*, London: HMSO.

Liell, P. and Saunders, J. B. (1987) *The Law of Education* (9th edition), London: Butterworth.

4·3

RESOURCE PROCUREMENT AND ALLOCATION

GEOFFREY MORRIS

THE LOCAL EDUCATION AUTHORITY

Wide variations exist throughout the world in the balance between central and local resourcing of public education. These of course reflect the variety of approaches to the control of education: some countries have a highly centralized model, others a devolved one, but all public education systems have in common the raising of public finance through various forms of taxation whether national or local. The purpose of this chapter is to describe the methods of resource procurement and allocation in a system which has a balance between national and local responsibilities – England and Wales – but which is in the process of rapid change. A brief examination of this system may reveal points of general principle which could also be of interest elsewhere.

The responsibility for providing education in England and Wales is placed on local education authorities (LEAs) by the 1944 Education Act. However, LEAs have no money of their own and funds are provided from three sources: the rates (a local property-based tax), central government grants (thus ultimately from nationally levied taxes), and direct fees and charges, but this latter category is so small that it will not be discussed within the scope of this short account. The proportions of local government funding provided by central government and the rates respectively have fluctuated considerably and often quite rapidly over the years, but at present stand at approximately 40 per cent central government grant and 55 per cent rates. The rates system itself is being replaced by the Community Charge in April 1990.

GOVERNMENT GRANT – GENERAL

Each year central government calculates how much local government as a whole needs to spend (relevant expenditure), and then how much of that expenditure it is going to support financially. This government support is known as rate support grant (RSG) and consists of a number of elements of which block grant is by far the biggest and is therefore worth examining in a little detail. At one time education, and the other local government services, received grant in a way that enabled the individual amounts to be clearly identified. This is no longer possible. In 1980 a system of block grant was introduced which covers all services so that an individual local authority does not know precisely how much is intended for each individual service. The purpose of block grant is to supplement the income a local authority derives from the rates. Central government analyses in some detail the features peculiar to individual authorities and then calculates how much it would cost to provide these. The result is a figure known as grant-related expenditure (GRE) which is unique to each authority. The kinds of factors which are taken into account in calculating each GRE figure include the client groups (for example numbers of children of different ages), the sparseness of the school population, pupils with additional needs (for example those in large families or in one-parent families), and other special needs. The authority will then receive its block grant based on these factors. Recent governments have set a limit above GRE beyond which grant will be deducted for each percentage increase in the rates, and have devised other penalties for restricting the level of rates.

The way in which government decides each year what level of expenditure it will accept for RSG purposes is through discussions which include a degree of negotiation with representatives of local government. The starting point is the expenditure steering group for each service, consisting of the senior officials of the relevant government department and of the local authorities. Their main function is to prepare forecasts of demographic change and other needs together with resulting expenditure requirements and policy recommendations based on these forecasts. These steering groups will also have before them the Public Expenditure White Paper (PESC) which is published each March and describes the government's expenditure plans. These plans will already have had a local government input, but will also reflect the success or otherwise of individual government Ministers in persuading Cabinet colleagues, and in particular the Treasury, of the needs of their particular service areas. The process, then, is essentially one of marrying together technical information and the forecasting of need and political priorities in which the restraining hand of the Treasury will have been in contention with the spending aspirations of service Ministers and local authorities.

GOVERNMENT GRANT – SPECIFIC

A new and growing approach towards resourcing education is the development of direct grants for specific purposes. It has always been a source of frustration for Secretaries of State for Education and Science that they have fought with the Treasury for the inclusion of a particular piece of expenditure within block grant, but cannot guarantee that it will be spent for that particular purpose by all LEAs. In 1984, therefore, the Education (Grants and Awards) Act was passed. Its purpose was to give the Secretary of State power to make grants to LEAs (to be known as education support grants – ESGs) which are earmarked for particular projects or activities which seem to him to be important. This was a revolutionary step. Secretaries of State had previously had no power to disburse funds: block grant is administered through the Department of the Environment to local government as a whole, not by individual service Ministers. LEAs would not have been too concerned about this had ESGs been funded as additional to basic local authority expenditure, but the money was to be found by government deducting one per cent from RSG for the purpose. Moreover, if a LEA was successful in its bid for an ESG it would only receive 70 per cent of the cost of the particular project – the other 30 per cent had to be found out of the rest of the LEA's income. Small wonder, then, that there were vigorous protests about the practice as well as the principle. ESGs are available for such things as teaching science and technology in primary schools, improving the curriculum in rural primary schools, pilot schemes for ethnic minority education, and similar curriculum development projects. Notwithstanding objections in principle on the part of many, most authorities have in practice made bids in accordance with their local needs and priorities.

Other ESG programmes have followed since 1984–5 and have become an important element in educational developments in schools and colleges. The principle has been extended to include such things as midday supervision and, importantly, in-service education and training for teachers and others, the funding of which was radically changed along ESG lines in 1987 through a system known as grant-related in-service training (GRIST). There can be no doubt that the earmarked grant funding mechanism represents an important element in the strong and rapid thrust towards a more centrally controlled education service which has been a feature of the 1980s, and which will undoubtedly continue.

MANPOWER SERVICES COMMISSION (MSC)
RENAMED DEPARTMENT OF EMPLOYMENT TRAINING
AGENCY IN 1988

A parallel but earlier development in the funding of the public education service in England and Wales has been the huge growth in the power and influence of the MSC and its ability to fund very much larger educational activities than has so far been possible through ESGs. The MSC came into being in 1974 as a government agency responsible to the Department of Employment, not the Department of Education and Science (DES). Its training brief was initially in the field of special programmes for the young unemployed, but this has grown to cover a substantial part of the government-funded element of LEA expenditure. Its initial growth was encouraged by the inability of the DES to fund the education service directly. The MSC with its huge resources was seen as filling the gap in the powers of the Secretary of State for Education and Science, but even since the coming of ESGs the MSC has continued to use its substantial budget to fund and influence the education service to a considerable degree.

The two most significant developments, in addition to the various youth training schemes referred to above, have been the Technical Vocational Education Initiative (TVEI) and the work-related Non-Advanced Further Education (NAFE) programme. TVEI was introduced as a pilot scheme in 1983 as a curriculum initiative for 14–18-year-olds with the object of encouraging more vocationally biased courses in secondary schools. Generous funding encouraged LEAs to apply to the MSC and to satisfy it on a number of criteria. The scheme is now being extended widely throughout the country and is an important example of the growing dependence of LEAs on earmarked central funding.

The work-related NAFE scheme was introduced in 1985–6 when Government decided to reduce block grant by 25 per cent of the cost of providing these courses and transfer the money to the MSC. Each LEA had then to submit a three-year development plan to the MSC, which funded the relevant courses if the plan satisfied various criteria. In order to determine whether or not to fund the 25 per cent of courses for which it has the money the MSC has, reasonably, to view the whole of the LEA's proposed programme: thus 25 per cent financial control actually delivered direct influence on 100 per cent of the NAFE programme to the MSC.

It has therefore become a key feature of resource procurement to require LEAs to apply for finance to central government or its agencies and in doing so to satisfy stringent criteria. This reflects not only the growing power and interest of central government in educational matters and a consequent decline in the standing of LEAs, but also an instrumental utilitarian view of education.

CAPITAL EXPENDITURE

The provision and improvement of educational buildings is made in the same way that individuals procure their own homes: by means of loans. Governments have always maintained stringent controls over local authority capital spending. At one time loan sanction was required for individual projects; now a block allocation ('allocation' in this context is not a distribution of money by central government, simply permission to spend money raised by the authority itself) is given to each authority, which can then determine its own priorities within general policy guidelines. The determination by government of an LEA's allocation takes into account basic need in relation to pupil numbers, sub-standard accommodation which needs to be replaced, and surplus places which may exist in the area because of falling school rolls. Capital expenditure for voluntary schools is the responsibility of the governors rather than the LEA. Voluntary school buildings attract a grant of 85 per cent from government and there is a voluntary sector programme which controls capital expenditure in that area.

RESOURCE DISTRIBUTION BY LEAs

Having raised the finance to provide the education service the LEA must decide how best to use it. The fundamental responsibility of the LEA is to secure that efficient education is provided to meet the needs of the population of their area. Therefore the majority of mechanisms for distributing resources at local level are geared to pupil and student numbers and to the geographical areas where the population is concentrated. Thus the three basic resources required to run the service, staff, materials, and buildings are allocated broadly according to the number of pupils in the case of the first two, and to be as near as possible to pupils' homes in the case of buildings.

The provision of staff is far and away the most costly item in resourcing education, and within that heading teaching staff form much the higher proportion. The starting point for the distribution of teaching staff will always be pupil numbers. In drawing up its schools' budget, the LEA will be working on a particular ratio of pupils to teachers, which might typically be 22:1 in primary schools and 16:1 in secondary schools. Having thus calculated the total number of teachers to be employed, the authority's education officers will then distribute these to schools in accordance with other formulae and criteria which take into account not only the number of pupils but also the particular circumstances of each school. In a very small rural primary school, for example, the head might be expected to be responsible for a class of pupils; in a very large secondary school where the job of head is largely managerial only a very small teaching programme would be possible. Another school might be on a split site and need extra staffing for that; another might have a high incidence of pupils whose mother tongue is not English, and need additional language and other help. So the distribution of teaching staff is made by using formulae which are based on pupil numbers together with other needs indicators and professional judgement, and the result is likely to be as many different pupil-teacher ratios as there are schools in the authority. Many LEAs are now moving away from this traditional approach and attempting to gauge needs more accurately through 'curriculum-led' or 'activity-led' staffing formulae. Nevertheless, the basic approach remains of the LEA specifying the establishment of teaching staff to which individual schools are entitled on the basis of perceived need. Similarly, support staff are generally allocated in accordance with formulae designed to indicate need, the main factor again being pupil numbers.

The other main area of resourcing is that of teaching materials: books, equipment, stationery, and other consumable supplies required for the teaching and learning process. These items are invariably financed on a per capita basis (and the money allocated to schools for this purpose is therefore known as 'capitation'). Heads of schools are usually given freedom in the way this money is spent and allowed to manage the whole sum in the way that best meets the school's needs. Considerable differences exist between LEAs about the range of items included within capitation. Books, equipment, and basic teaching materials are invariably included, but by no means all authorities will include administrative items such as office requisites, telephone charges, and cleaning materials, and fewer still include entry fees for public examinations.

The remaining resources needed to run the school are provided direct by the authority: premises-related costs such as heating, lighting, caretaking, and cleaning and grounds maintenance, the provision of school meals and of transport, and the centrally-provided professional support groups: advisers and inspectors, education welfare officers, careers advisory officers, and paramedical staff. Colleges of Further Education are resourced either on the basis of their proposed programme of courses or, in some LEAs, by an average student-cost method of financing.

NEW DEVELOPMENTS

However, this traditional model of the LEA not only providing resources but being quite specific about how they are used is being challenged by a number of authorities which are adopting or experimenting with the block-grant approach to resourcing schools. This system, commonly called local financial management (LFM), was pioneered by a small number of LEAs during the early 1980s, later followed by others, and then taken up with some enthusiasm by central government. It is an important feature of the Education Reform Act 1988, affecting the future of schools throughout the country.

The essence of a fully developed scheme of LFM is that the LEA distributes resources to the schools in a block sum without specifying how it is to be spent except within the most general of frameworks. The school is then free to construct and manage its own budget, the main constraint being the cash limit rather than any limits on, for example, the number of staff to be employed. The scheme follows the basic management principle of delegating responsibility to the lowest level compatible with efficiency, and its purposes are value for money and freedom for the school to determine its own priorities within the cash limit. In these respects it resembles closely the way in which government distributes resources to the LEA – and shares most of the problems of that system too. Among the major difficulties is the question of how to divide the central budget among schools: the early pilot schemes were based on working out the 'historic' budget for each school and requiring them to work within that, but once a pilot scheme becomes generalized to all schools the sheer scale of the operation and the need to respond to countless arguments about the make-up of individual budgets have led LEAs to seek suitable formulae to simplify the task. However, although a formula approach is relatively simple, its results can, at best, be 'rough justice' unless the formula becomes so complicated and detailed that there is little point in moving away from the historic budget approach. The secret is to steer a middle course between a formula so complex that no-one can understand it, and one so simple that its application has a crude and unfair impact on schools. At the time of writing the state of the art has not shown the way to formula budgeting which is generally acceptable by schools and LEAs – notwithstanding Government's confident assertion that a formula system will be introduced nationally.

By mid-1987 the education service in Britain stood on the brink of sweeping change in resource procurement and distribution in the education service. The government is likely to succeed in further blurring the edges between the public and private sectors in a number of areas of social provision including education: certainly there seems little commitment on the part of government to the kind of balanced partnership between central and local government and the institutions with their governing bodies which has underpinned the service since 1944. The intended action plan has the twin approach of increasing central government control and influence (over the curriculum, over direct grant funding, over the direct funding of institutions such as the city technical colleges) while at the same time giving more freedom to the schools (through LFM, through inviting schools to 'opt out' of LEA control, through increasing governor and parent power). The role of the LEA in the resourcing, provision, and control of education will consequently be diminished. The rating system is being replaced by a local tax based not on property but levied on residents whose names appear on the electoral register. It is not the purpose of this chapter to comment on the wisdom (or otherwise) of these proposals, but the profundity of the changes in resourcing (and thus controlling) the education service needs to be emphasized.

FURTHER READING

Association of County Councils (1985) *Understanding Block Grant*, (pamphlet), London: A.C.C.

Bennett, R. (1982) *Central Grants to Local Government*, Cambridge: Cambridge University Press.

Chartered Institute of Public Finance & Accountancy, *C.I.P.F.A. Financial Information Service – Education*, available from C.I.P.F.A. 2/3 Robert Street, London WC2 N6BL.

Cooke, G. and Gosden, P. (1986) *Education Committees*, London Councils & Education Press.

Henney, A. (1984) *Inside Local Government*, London: Sinclair Browne.

Humphrey, C. (1985) 'Giving schools the money', *Education*, 10th May 1985.

Morris, G. H. (1986) 'The County L.E.A.' in S. Ranson and J. Tomlinson (Eds.) *The Changing Government of Education*, London: Allen & Unwin.

Travers, T. (1986) 'Finance of education' in S. Ranson and J. Tomlinson (Eds.) *The Changing Government of Education*, London: Allen & Unwin.

4.4

EDUCATIONAL BUILDINGS: DESIGN AND MAINTENANCE

JOHN KAY

This review of current ideas and practices in the design and maintenance of buildings for education is based chiefly on recent experience in England. Sources of further information are suggested. The history of educational building in this country since 1945 has been covered comprehensively in two recent books by Maclure (1984) and Saint (1987). The OECD Programme for Educational Building (1987) helps to promote good practice in its member countries.

THE AIMS OF EDUCATIONAL BUILDING DESIGN

A well-designed educational building is one that both meets the present educational and social needs of its occupants effectively and can be adapted readily to future changes. It provides a comfortable working environment for a range of modes of use in a variety of weather conditions, and it is energy efficient. It meets statutory regulations and other agreed health and safety requirements. It provides adequate security against unauthorized access. It can be cleaned easily and maintained economically. The initial cost of the building is within the agreed budget and subsequent running costs are reasonable. It makes a positive contribution to the amenities of its neighbourhood.

THE AIMS OF PROPERTY MANAGEMENT IN PUBLICLY-FINANCED EDUCATION

In local education authorities (LEAs) in England and Wales the officers chiefly responsible for the provision and management of the authority's estate are usually architects and other building professionals, working with administrators and advisers in the education department. The authority's estate will probably consist of buildings from most periods of the history of public education over the past century. Resources for building will be budgeted annually. The aims of property management in these circumstances can be summarized as:

1. to match the quantity of accommodation as closely as possible to the number of pupils or students;
2. to bring all schools and buildings for further and higher education as far as possible up to the standards of a well-designed new building;
3. to put the day-to-day upkeep (repairs, maintenance, and cleaning) of the buildings, engineering services, furniture, and grounds on a cost-effective basis;
4. to establish, in the face of limited resources, a system of priorities for tackling the problems that exist.

The most pressing problems overall are that, first, in most parts of the country there is a surplus of accommodation, which ties up capital resources and leads to unnecessary running costs (these are estimated to average £150 each year for each surplus place). Second, many of the buildings that are still required have had too little spent on them in recent years to keep them abreast of changes in educational needs and constructional requirements. And last, although expenditure on repairs and maintenance has been rising significantly in recent years, it has not grown rapidly enough to deal with the maintenance needs of the large volume of new accommodation built in the period of rapid growth from 1950 to 1975.

THE STATE OF THE STOCK

The best current source of information on the stock of school buildings in England and Wales is 'A study of school building' (ASSB), published by the Department of Education and Science (DES) in 1977. It was based on a survey made in 1975 of a random ten per cent sample of all maintained primary and secondary schools (special schools were excluded).

In 1975 in England and Wales there were some 23,000 primary schools (for children in the five to eleven age range) and 5,000 secondary schools (for 11 to 18). At that time 12 per cent of the teaching spaces had been built before 1903, 30 per cent before 1945 and nine per cent were in temporary buildings. The study recorded the degree of overcrowding or under-occupancy found, and compared existing schools with the standards to be expected of a well-designed new school. In 1975 one fifth of all primary schools and one quarter of all secondary schools were more than ten per cent overcrowded. However, the study noted that the number of pupils in the country as a whole had been falling since 1964, and that by 1986 there would be about two million surplus places if nothing were done to dispose of them. In the ten years following the publication of ASSB, programmes were mounted to reduce this surplus, either by closure or by finding alternative uses for the spare space. About one million surplus places have been removed but much remains to be done. The number of young children entering school is now growing overall, but in most areas the existing surplus accommodation will be sufficient for them. In some parts of the south and south-east, and in certain inner-city areas, new schools may be needed to cope with rising rolls, but there is a need at the same time to review the existing stock to make sure the fullest possible use is made of it, and to seize opportunities for improvement.

The 1975 survey found that:

- much of the temporary accommodation was of poor quality (there were then over 900,000 temporary places in use, some of them a generation old);
- staff space in some three quarters of the schools was inadequate;
- about one quarter of the schools still had outside lavatories;
- most secondary schools were deficient in practical accommodation (for example for science and crafts);
- about one fifth of primary schools were in poor surroundings or had grossly inadequate sites.

Since 1975 progress has been made in remedying these deficiencies, and some of the worst old buildings will have been closed in the course of rationalization; nevertheless, the task of upgrading the existing school stock is undoubtedly still a substantial one. A more recent survey, based on a smaller sample, was carried out in 1986 and published by the DES in 1987 as 'Survey of school buildings'. It contains information on the nature and scale of improvement work LEAs consider they would need to undertake to bring buildings up to a defined standard for 1991 pupil numbers. The government has made additional allocations for school improvements in the three years from 1987.

Expenditure on the repair and maintenance of local authority educational buildings is monitored annually by the Society of Chief Architects of Local Authorities (SCALA). From the analysis of the returns in 1987 the view of SCALA was that maintenance was seriously under-funded. On average, expenditure in real terms had remained constant since 1984, and this had not enabled any appreciable reduction to be made in the backlog of outstanding work.

RESPONSIBILITIES FOR EDUCATIONAL BUILDING

One aim of the public education system in the UK is to provide a broadly comparable service throughout the country, including the standard of accommodation. Responsibility for this is shared between central government, local authorities, and the institutions themselves.

Schools

For central government the DES establishes the broad national policy for school building and makes known the government's priorities – in the 1980s, for example, these have been to reduce the surplus accommodation left by falling rolls, and to make maintenance systems more efficient and cost-effective. The DES co-ordinates government policy that has a bearing on educational building with other central departments such as the Department of the Environment and the Department of Energy.

The DES lays down, through regulations (DES 1981), minimum standards for certain key aspects of school buildings, for example minimum teaching areas, environmental and human comfort needs, and health and safety requirements. Constructional standards are also mandatory (DES 1985a). LEAs are not required to submit plans or details of construction of new building projects to the DES for approval but must certify that the scheme meets the statutory requirements.

Design advice is available from the DES through publications (DES 1986) and through consultation with territorial architects, each of whom is responsible for a group of LEAs. This design advice is based on current good practice by LEAs and on development work carried out by the DES architects and building branch. This development work includes 'live' building projects and acts as a bridge between, on the one hand, policy and technical developments in education and building and, on the other, the architects producing designs for schools (Kay 1983).

Beyond the design stage the LEAs are responsible for obtaining tenders for the construction of the school and then supervising the building contract. In the case of voluntary aided and special agreement schools, which amount to about 16 per cent of all schools in England and Wales, the school governors are responsible for obtaining professional services for the design of the building work and for supervision of the building contract.

Typical major capital projects are: new schools or extensions where there are insufficient school places in an area; building work to facilitate the disposal of surplus places; the replacement of grossly sub-standard old schools; and substantial projects for the renewal of outworn parts of the building, for example roofs or heating installations. The greater part of repair and maintenance work is funded from current expenditure.

Financial resources for capital projects, including professional fees and the purchase of land, are provided by the LEAs who own the school premises. These resources are obtained by borrowing and from other sources, including capital receipts from the sale of surplus land and buildings. Each year LEAs submit their plans for the following year's capital building programme. The DES then notifies each LEA, in the light of these proposals and the available national resources, of the limit upon its capital expenditure. In the case of voluntary aided and special agreement schools, DES approval is required. Once this has been given, grant aid on the approved cost of the project (currently at the rate of 85 per cent) is available from the DES.

Further and higher education (FE and HE)

There are no mandatory building standards for LEA colleges and polytechnics, which provide further and higher education, other than the national building regulations covering health and safety and other constructional requirements. However, the DES provides design advice for FE and HE building in the same way as for schools. The method of funding is also similar. University buildings too are subject to national building regulations. The University Funding Committee (UFC) (formerly University Grants Committee – UGC) provides design advice and the central government input to university building projects.

GOOD PRACTICE IN DESIGN AND MAINTENANCE

Briefing

The production of a well-designed educational building has to start with a clear understanding by the architect and other members of the design team of the use to which the building will be put. Many LEAs provide a brief which explains the educational objectives and the range of uses to which the building is likely to be put. Advisory committees draw on practical experience from other similar buildings run by the authority.

In 1979 the DES published a report, 'The briefing process in school design', A & B Paper No 5 (DES 1979), which reviews what is desirable in the relationship between the client and the designer, and includes a check-list covering all stages of the design process. Similar considerations apply to the briefing stage of buildings for further and higher education.

Number of teaching places required

Before the design of individual buildings can be started, an essential first step is to assess the capacity of the schools in the neighbourhood being considered, and to compare this with projections of pupil or student numbers in the catchment area. This will show the extent of the shortfall – or the surplus – of places in the area under review. Techniques for undertaking area reviews of this type have been developed over the past decade, and the outcome of a joint study by English local authorities and the DES A & B Branch was published in 1987 as 'Guidelines for school building reviews', A & B Paper No 11 (DES 1987). It describes the close co-operation that is desirable, in many cases involving the diocesan authorities and other voluntary bodies. The paper offers a framework for the review process and emphasizes the importance of establishing clear objectives at the start for the educational, social, and economic aspects, and then considering and comparing all feasible options which meet the objectives.

Meeting educational needs

The design of an educational building has of course to meet the needs of the first users and their specific educational requirements. In the course of its life, however, the building will have many users with varying curricula, course structures, and methods of teaching. The purpose of the institution may change quite radically. Care over the range of room sizes provided, their layout in the building, and the design of its engineering services and equipment can increase the day-to-day flexibility of the building and the ease with which it can be adapted to changes in use. Appropriate design techniques are described in publications by the DES, the Scottish Education Department and the former UGC. These include a series of DES Design Notes giving area guidelines for secondary schools (No 34), sixth-form, tertiary and non-advanced further education colleges (No 33), and advanced further education institutions (No 44). Design Notes 37 and 45 (for further and higher education respectively) offer methods of assessing the capacity of existing buildings. The special problems of designing for adaptability in teaching and research laboratories are dealt with in studies published by the Laboratories Investigation Unit.

Statutory requirements

The statutory requirements for schools maintained by LEAs are given in the Education (School Premises) Regulations 1981 (DES 1981) and in DES Administrative Memorandum 2/85 (DES 1985a). The former includes minimum standards for such items as sites and playing fields, teaching area, staff accommodation, and sanitary provision. The latter covers constructional standards, including health and safety requirements, access for the disabled, and energy efficiency. The buildings of all new schools operated by LEAs and voluntary (usually religious) bodies have to comply with these standards, and the aim is that as resources become available, existing schools should be brought into line.

The regulations are reviewed from time to time. In 1981, for example, the minimum teaching area required for pupils aged nine to eleven was increased so as to permit the provision of a wider range of facilities, including those for practical work. DES publications are available which support the regulations, for example Building Bulletin 7: Fire and the Design of Schools; Design Note 17: Guidelines for Environmental Design and Fuel Conservation in Educational Buildings; and Design Note 18: Access for the Physically Disabled to Educational Buildings.

School and community

A school and, in different ways, a college or a polytechnic, can play an important part in the local community, relating to parents, employers, and local residents generally. The siting and design of its premises can make a positive contribution to this. There are now many examples of purpose-built new schools or adaptations to existing ones which provide for both educational and social activities, to mutual advantage. In Crewe the district authority providing leisure and recreation facilities pooled its capital resources with the LEA so that in the new Victoria Centre both the school and the community have access on a cost-effective basis to a much wider range of facilities than if each authority had gone it alone on separate sites (see DES Building Bulletin 59 and A & B Paper No 8).

Where falling rolls produce surplus accommodation it may be possible to find for the spare space non-educational users who can make a positive contribution to the life of the school and relate it more closely to the community as a whole. In the mining town of Ollerton in Nottinghamshire nearly one third of the accommodation in the secondary school, left empty by falling rolls, was adapted economically to provide for a wide range of community activities. The Dukeries Complex now includes a public library, a club for senior citizens, a mini town hall, and a sports and recreation centre (see DES Design Note 42). A carefully formulated management structure is an important part of such joint institutions.

Repairs and maintenance

Good practice in maintenance calls for a systematic approach to assessing needs and determining priorities, based on accurate and up-to-date property records. DES Design Note 40 (DES 1985b) recommends a 'rolling programme' approach in which planned maintenance should form about two thirds of the budget, and is protected against last-minute cuts, with day-to-day work forming about one third. Figure 1 shows what this process involves.

Figure 1 Decisions and Influences on the Functional Curriculum

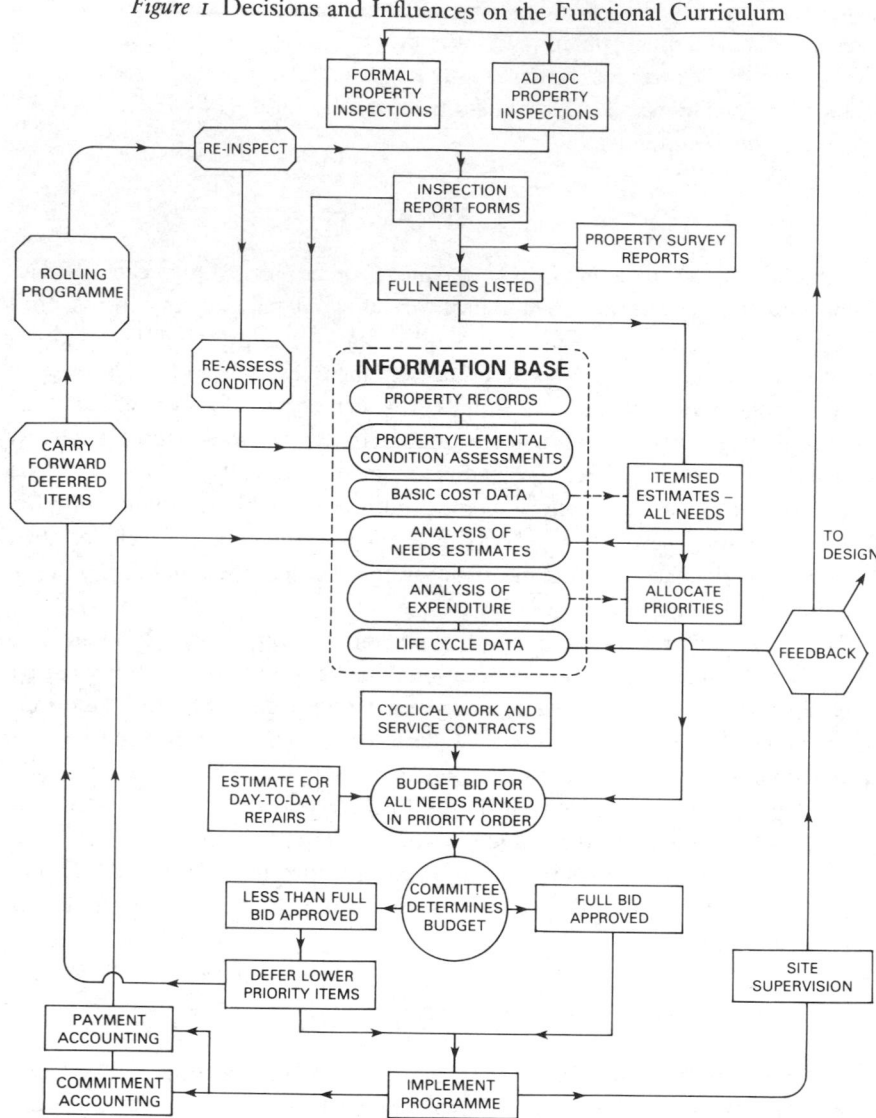

Value for money

Resources for education are always under pressure. For this reason, local education authorities, voluntary bodies, and central government share a concern that, in addition to meeting priority educational needs, both capital and recurrent expenditure on buildings should be employed as cost-effectively as possible. The good practice referred to above, and elaborated in recent reports

416

by the Audit Commission, includes cost-effectiveness in maintenance programmes, in energy efficiency, in making investment appraisals of options, and in rationalization and improvement schemes. The educational performance and life cost of a building are no less important than its initial cost. The right balance between them is what constitutes value for money.

FURTHER READING

Department of Education and Science (1977) *A Study of School Building*, London: HMSO.

(1979) *The Briefing Process in School Design*, A & B Paper No 5, London: DES.

(1981) *The Education (School Premises) Regulations 1981*, London:HMSO.

(1985a) *Administrative Memorandum 2/85: Constructional Standards for Maintained Educational Building in England*, London: DES.

(1985b) *Design Note 40: Maintenance and Renewal in Educational Buildings*, London: DES.

(1986) *Architects and Building Branch Publications*, London: DES.

(1987) *Guidelines for School Building Reviews*, A & B Paper No 11, London: DES.

Kay, J. (1983) *Development Work – A Bridge Between Research and Production*, Stockholm: Proceedings of CIB.

Maclure, S. (1984) *Educational Development and School Building 1945–73*, London: Longman.

Organization for Economic Co-operation and Development (1987) *Programme for Educational Building*, Paris: OECD.

Saint, A. (1987) *Towards a Social Architecture – The Role of School Building in Post-War England*, New Haven, Ct. and London: Yale University Press.

Society of Chief Architects of Local Authorities (1987) *Maintenance Expenditure 1987*, Luton: SCALA.

4.5

STAFF SUPPLY AND DEVELOPMENT

WILLIAM TAYLOR

ORGANIZING THE SUPPLY

The complexity of many of the tasks that have to be performed if modern societies are to be politically stable and economically successful, the current speed and scale of knowledge growth, and the ability to generate surpluses that support 'non-productive' labour, all extend the proportion of people's lives devoted to formal learning. A high proportion of citizens now spend at least thirteen years in full-time education and training. Many remain in full-time education until their early twenties. Increasing numbers engage in full- or part-time learning activities for longer and shorter stages throughout their working lives and after retirement.

All this means that teaching and learning, at various levels of formality and institutionalization, are among the most distinctive and important activities of modern society. The numbers of men and women employed in the occupations that contribute to such learning are now very large. Just to take England and Wales alone, there were in 1985 (the last year for which at time of writing there are national figures available) some 480,000 men and women teaching in maintained nursery, primary, and secondary schools, another 80,000 or so in maintained adult and further education, and 37,000 more in universities. To these numbers need to be added teachers in independent schools, the members of Her Majesty's and Local Authority Inspectorates, and instructors and teachers employed by industry, commerce, and the Armed Services. Thus those employed to teach within educational institutions in England and Wales number well in excess of 600,000, a sizeable group within the total employed population.

The supply, training and development of teachers has from earliest days been a matter of concern to those responsible for the provision of education – initially the churches and private foundations and to an increasing extent from the mid-nineteenth century, the State. Commonsense and experience indicated that learning could be undertaken in ways that, on the one hand, were ineffectual, wasteful of time and energy, and personally disagreeable, or on the other, in a manner that made efficient use of available resources, had enduring effects, and whilst requiring considerable effort on the part of the learner, could be personally rewarding and satisfying. Whether the norm was one or the other was seen to depend in large measure on the quality of teaching and instruction offered.

Institutional provision for teacher education has developed through several stages. To meet the need for teachers competent to teach young children in elementary schools, in societies where secondary education was available only to an élite minority, 'normal schools' and training colleges were set up which required of their entrants no more than completion of elementary and, as time went on, the first stages of secondary, schooling.

As educational opportunities became more freely available, so these colleges and normal schools became post-secondary institutions, although still recruiting mainly from the ranks of students unqualified to enter universities and other forms of advanced post-secondary education. The expansion of post-secondary provision led some teachers' colleges to become degree-granting institutions and to diversify their work to achieve self-standing university status. Such developments took place in Canada and the United States during the first half of this century, much more recently in Germany and the United Kingdom.

FOUR STRUCTURES

On the basis of these developments, four main versions of what is now the college or university model of teacher education can be identified.

In the United States, most parts of Canada, and in some other countries, the term university embraces institutions which vary greatly in size, quality of programme, status, and scholarly output, and offer courses of preparation for many vocations and professions. Teacher education is provided within such universities by departments, colleges, schools, and faculties subject to overall governance by appropriate internal and external bodies, and by staff employed by the university and paid on its normal scales. This can be called the *integrated university model* of teacher education.

In countries which have *binary* systems of education, where degree-level work is offered in both university and non-university institutions (examples are England and Australia), initial teacher education is provided by institutions on both sides of the binary line, although there is a general tendency for most primary teachers to be prepared outside the university, and for most advanced studies and research to be a university responsibility. This can usefully be called the *binary model*.

In many parts of Europe, particularly in countries where there are significant historical distinctions in the status and the rewards of secondary and primary teachers, the pre-service education and training of the latter is undertaken in specialist non-university institutions, with status and funding equivalent to or in some cases superior to that of universities, while preparation for secondary teaching is a university task. This may be called the *European model*.

There are still a few countries in which all initial teacher preparation, for both primary and secondary teachers, is undertaken by self-standing colleges that are not part of universities, although they may be associated with them through validation and other academic arrangements. In such systems, advanced studies and research are the responsibility of university departments, faculties, or schools of education. Scotland and New Zealand offer examples of such arrangements. This can be called the *self-standing model*.

STRENGTHS AND WEAKNESSES

Each of these models – university, binary, European, and self-standing – has its strengths and weaknesses. Within some systems there is still debate about which best serves the needs of schools and society.

An essential prerequisite for the success of the integrated university model is a sufficient flow of candidates who can satisfy minimum entrance requirements for degree level study. There must also be an adequate supply of staff in the professional subjects of the teacher education curriculum. Where preparation for subject teaching in schools is provided within a faculty, school, or college of education, rather than in the Faculties of Arts and Science, appropriately qualified staff are needed in the subjects of the school curriculum.

By requiring that all entrants to teacher training possess minimum qualifications for university study, the integrated university model tends to raise the status of primary teachers, facilitates closer integration of school-based work and experience with advanced study and research, encourages interest and involvement by university staff other than in education in the preparation of teachers, and avoids the potential loss of status from institutional separation characteristic of some other models. In practice, however, the status of schools, colleges, and faculties of education in universities varies greatly. High status is not necessarily associated with either size or research focus, although the burden of much recent argument has been that initial teacher training benefits from being conducted in institutions which also have a strong research orientation.

One motive for governmental advocacy of *binary* models was to meet an increasing demand for higher education without creating large numbers of new universities which would compete for scarce resources of money and high level manpower to support their claims to be research institutions. In England and in Australia, polytechnics, colleges, and institutes of higher and advanced education offer work at degree level and undertake a certain amount of research, but have hitherto enjoyed less freedom than universities in determining their curriculum and standards, and received lower levels of per capita funding. In both countries, however, there have been recent moves to fund similar levels of teaching on a common basis, irrespective of its location in one type of institution or another.

Non-university institutions are still distinguished from their university counterparts by lack of authority to issue their own degrees. The validation of awards has been the responsibility of bodies such as the Council for National Academic Awards in the United Kingdom, and State Validating Authorities in Australia. The growing maturity of some non-university institutions has encouraged moves to grant greater academic autonomy and to modify central oversight of course design, provision, and assessment.

Non-university institutions in binary systems have been increasing the amount of work they do for post-experience advanced diplomas and degrees and their involvement in research (although in practice rather few grants for educational research are made to polytechnics and colleges of advanced education). The existence within such institutions of such advanced work encourages recruitment of well-qualified staff, narrows the gap in status and scholarly output between different kinds of institution, gives teachers *local* opportunities for study, and takes advantage of the presence within many polytechnics and colleges of specialist staff originally recruited to the former colleges of education.

Teacher-training arrangements that conform with the *European* model tend to reflect sharper distinctions in salary, status, and prestige (and often in professional organization) between primary and secondary teachers. The staff of the *lycées*, *Gymnasia*, and equivalent secondary institutions operate within an academic tradition akin to that of the university rather than the elementary school, and one that has little in common with the separate primary, technical, and teacher-training sectors. In Burton Clark's (1985) terms, teacher training on this model is 'upwardly coupled'.

Where teachers have been trained in specialist institutions separate from the university, a strong pedagogical tradition has been encouraged which sometimes attracts better qualified school leavers than do the so-called 'open faculties' of the universities. Such institutions aim to foster high levels of professional commitment to teaching, especially that of young children, and maintain closer contact with the work of the schools to which their alumni proceed than is often expected of the multi-faculty university.

A long-standing problem in European teacher education has been lack of primary school experience among the predominantly *lycée-/Gymnasia-/*university-trained lecturing staff. The creation of departments explicitly devoted to pedagogy within such colleges, staffed by ex-primary or elementary teachers, has tended to create significant rifts of value and orientation.

The distinctive feature of the *self-standing* model is that both primary *and* secondary teachers are trained in specialized colleges outside the university. This holds even when a consecutive pattern of professional preparation exists, whereby most students, especially those going into secondary schools, have pursued degree level courses in universities prior to embarking upon professional training. The advantages of such arrangements include a clear professional mission for the colleges, and more freedom for universities to concentrate upon advanced work and research in education without having to devote time and energy to the minutiae of arrangements for, for example, school experience and meeting demands for 'relevance'. Such separation is not however all gain. University staff in education, without pre-service students to supervise, have more difficulty than their college counterparts in maintaining direct contact with teachers and schools. There is also a danger that advanced work and research in such conditions may become 'etherealized', and university staff may have greater difficulty in maintaining professional credibility among classroom teachers.

EIGHT ELEMENTS IN TEACHER DEVELOPMENT

Whatever the structural arrangements, it can be said that teacher development involves eight organizationally distinguishable but related elements.

First, trainees have to be *recruited*, usually today from the ranks of those who have completed a full secondary education and are qualified to pursue degree-level studies, but sometimes still from among those who have pursued other careers and who only later turn to teaching.

At one time recruitment to teaching depended heavily upon groups for whom other educational and employment opportunities were restricted, particularly women and rural youth. This is no longer the case. Teaching must compete in a more open market place of courses and jobs in which relative salaries and conditions of service play an important part in adjusting demand and supply.

Ups and downs in the birth rate also cause difficulties. At times when the numbers of primary age children needing to be taught are rising, the numbers of university-age students are falling. By the mid-1990s, for example, teaching will need to attract a much higher proportion of the available eighteen-year-olds and graduates than in the mid-1980s.

A second stage is that of *selection*, whereby training institutions pick out those applicants who seem likely to respond well to training and to make good teachers. Given the complexity of the variables involved, it is unsurprising that fifty years of research effort have failed to yield clear indicators of promise and performance that can be used to pick winners. In any case, lengthy periods of teacher shortage in some countries have precluded rigorous selection. Relying upon such research findings as are available, and on their own and colleagues' accumulated experience, selectors (who increasingly include serving teachers and heads) look for a good academic record, evidence of interest in children and young people, and, in the words of the official circular that lays down standards for the accreditation of courses, a 'sense of responsibility, a robust and balanced outlook, awareness, sensitivity, enthusiasm, and facility in communication'.

Pre-service education and training constitutes the third stage. Most programmes now take the form of four years' work for a Bachelor of Education (BEd) degree (the route followed by most primary teachers) in which subject and professional studies are pursued concurrently, or a one-year Post Graduate Certificate in Education (PGCE) course consecutive upon success in obtaining a degree in arts or science (the route for most secondary and an increasing proportion of primary teachers).

The relative merits of the BEd and the PGCE route have been vigorously argued. The average 'A' level performance of BEd candidates is less good than that of their PGCE counterparts. Subject studies in a degree and PGCE programme are pursued to greater depth than in the BEd but with less relevance to the classroom. PGCE courses, especially those for primary teachers, are often seen as too short for a properly phased introduction to the teacher's task. For the foreseeable future, it seems likely that both routes into teaching will continue to be available, although by mid-1987, the four-year concurrent courses offered by universities in England and Wales were all redesignated BA or BSc rather than BEd.

A debate has been going on since the earliest days of systematic teacher education about the time that should be allocated to subject studies and professional studies respectively (Borrowman 1952). It continues today, focused in England, Wales, and Northern Ireland around the official accreditation requirement that students should devote the equivalent of two years of their course to subject studies. It is complicated by a history of sometimes uncomfortable relations between subject and Education departments within colleges and polytechnics. The new accreditation requirements being implemented by the Council for the Accreditation of Teacher Education are regarded by its critics as running counter to important elements in the progressive, child-centred primary tradition that during the 1970s was beginning to be embodied in BEd courses and aimed at a closer integration of subject and professional studies.

Practical work in schools has always been an important feature of pre-service education and training – often valued more highly by students than any other part of the programme – and today constitutes about one-sixth of a

BEd and 40 per cent of a PGCE course. In recent years a variety of fresh approaches to organizing such experience and linking it more closely to the remainder of the pre-service programme have emerged, including group practice and school-based professional studies.

A fourth element in teacher education comprises the process of *certification*, whereby a teacher is recognized as qualified by the appropriate authority – such as the Secretary of State in England and Wales, and Provincial or State governments in North America. Such certification usually turns on the successful completion of a properly accredited course. Sometimes it is limited to work in a particular type of school or with a particular age group. In England, the certificate is endorsed with details of the course that has been followed, although without formal restriction on the kind of teaching for which the holder may be employed.

Although the case has often been made for term certification, which would be renewed only after appropriate post-experience training and continuing service, certification is usually permanent, revoked only when an individual is found guilty of some specific offence relevant to work in schools.

A fifth element in teacher development is *induction*, for which the medical analogy of 'internship' is sometimes used. Over the years considerable effort has been expended in persuading employing authorities and schools to ensure that beginning teachers have a lighter timetable than their more experienced colleagues, that advice and help are freely available, and that adequate opportunities exist to reflect upon experience in the light of pre-service preparation. Such arrangements have become increasingly common, although some beginners are still thrown in at the deep end and judged by their ability to handle students and situations that cause difficulty for experienced practitioners.

Sixth comes *in-service training and refreshment* (INSET), designed to improve the way in which the teacher performs his or her role. Recognition of the importance of the serving teacher as an agent of educational change and improvement has resulted in much more systematic attention being given to INSET in recent years. The requirement to participate in such training has in some systems been written into conditions of service. Methods of delivery have become more sophisticated; school-based and school-focused approaches are now part of in-service orthodoxy. Local authority inspectors and advisers are active in the provision of courses and consultancies.

A seventh element in teacher development which features strongly in current government policies for the schools but is still by no means universal is *appraisal and evaluation*. This element is seen by its advocates as offering the opportunity for teachers to discover how performance is perceived by management, to share professional problems and seek solutions with experienced help, to plan ahead and consider individual career development needs, including those for training or wider experience, and to help the school or college improve standards by setting goals to which staff are committed and prepared to define their own contribution.

An eighth stage, often seen as an element of INSET, but distinguishable from it in purpose and mode of organization, is the provision of *longer courses of post-experience training for specialized roles*, such as educational psychologist, counsellor, audio-visual specialist or head teacher, and programmes of study designed to 'convert' teachers of one age group or specialism to work with others.

Most of these longer courses have been provided by universities, polytechnics, and colleges. Teachers either attend part-time or take a year or more of paid secondment. Success has often been marked by the award of a certificate, diploma, or master's degree. The new basis of funding in-service education introduced in 1987 (grant-related in-service training, or GRIST), which channels a larger proportion of available funds through employing authorities, seems likely to reduce the number of full-time secondments in favour of shorter, possibly modular courses, more closely related to school and system requirements than to the career needs of individual practitioners.

Training for headship, management, and school leadership has been an area of particular growth, reflected in the establishment – with Department of Education and Science support – of the National Development Centre for School Management Training (NDC) at Bristol University. There has also been renewed interest in an old idea – that of setting up an education staff college which would exercise similar functions for the education service to those of the long-established military and professional staff colleges.

Efforts have been made at various times to tie these eight elements more closely together – for example in the recommendations of the Committee on Teacher Education and Training of 1972, the James Report – but at present they remain only very loosely articulated in the careers of individual teachers.

STAFF DEVELOPMENT IN TERTIARY EDUCATION

The only teachers who require formal professional certification as a condition of employment are those who work in primary and secondary schools. Teachers and lecturers in further education (FE) colleges, polytechnics, colleges and institutes of higher education, universities and in adult education need no such qualifications. In practice, a high proportion of FE staff, and increasing numbers in other higher education colleges and polytechnics, do possess formal teacher credentials. Over the last twenty years there has been increasing emphasis on their value and importance. The requirements of the Council for National Academic Awards in validating advanced further education qualifications and degrees has encouraged public sector colleges to attend to many aspects of staff development. In this they were ahead of the universities, which have only recently begun to give serious attention to the improvement of teaching.

In 1987 the Committee of Vice Chancellors and Principals (CVCP) issued a Code of Practice on Academic Staff Training which requires each university to have in place arrangements for the induction of new staff, for the provision of training in lecturing, the conduct of seminars and tutorials, research supervision, and the management of research and academic units.

Nor has interest in leadership training been restricted to the schools. The CVCP has a Staff Development Policy Committee which sponsors and encourages participation in short courses aimed at university 'top management'.

ISSUES AND PROSPECTS

Political and policy perspectives tend to be shorter than those needed to put the planning of staff supply and development on a proper basis. There is concern in several countries about recruitment in the mid-1990s, when the supply of graduates will be at its lowest point and the numbers of school-age children will be increasing. Action has already had to be taken to remedy specific shortages in science and mathematics, and supply considerations are likely to loom larger as overall demand increases.

Government initiatives such as the introduction of a national curriculum and regular progress testing will also have important consequences for the organization and content of both pre-service and in-service training, as will the redistribution of administrative responsibilities that follows any large-scale 'opting out' from local authority control.

Debate is likely to continue about the optimal design and content of initial teacher education programmes, with particular reference to the balance and treatment of 'subject studies', the closer involvement of schools and practising teachers in professional and curriculum courses, and renewed attempts to secure better integration of pre-service and post-experience education.

Systematic training opportunities for those educators who have not hitherto required professional qualifications, especially in post-secondary institutions, and for those involved in evaluation and administration, seem set to expand, albeit with closer attention than in the past to what constitutes value for money and is directly relevant to enhanced performance.

The ideals and practices that characterize the supply and development of educators have less to do with the application of a technology than with the continual adjustment of political, economic, and social interests. It is thus unlikely that coming decades will see spectacular 'breakthroughs'. It will be enough if the structural and administrative arrangements within which the interplay of ideas and practices takes place are of a kind that protect individual democratic freedoms, encourage rationality and objectivity, enhance flexibility, and promote greater effectiveness in achieving worthwhile competence and understanding. It is within such a framework that significant new ideas and practices for staff supply and development are most likely to emerge, to be tested, and to play their part in educational improvement.

FURTHER READING

Alexander, R. J., Craft M., and Lynch J. (Eds.) (1984) *Change in Teacher Education*, London: Holt, Rinehart & Winston.

Borrowman, M. L. (1952) *The Liberal and Technical in Teacher Education: A Historical Survey of American Thought*, New York: Bureau of Publications, Teachers' College, Columbia University.

Bok, D. (1986) *Higher Learning*, Cambridge, Mass. and London: Harvard University Press.

Clark, B. R. (Ed.) (1985) *The School and the University: An International Perspective*, Berkeley: University of California Press.

Department of Education and Science (1987) *Quality in Schools: the Initial Training of Teachers. An HMI Survey*, London: HMSO.

Soltis, J. A. (Ed.) (1987) 'Reforming teacher education: A symposium on the Holmes Group Report', *Teachers College Record*, 88 (3) Spring.

Taylor, W. (1969) *Society and the Education of Teachers*, London: Faber.

(1978) *Research and Reform in Teacher Education*, Windsor: National Foundation for Educational Research Publishing Company.

4.6

PROFESSIONAL BODIES AND PRESSURE GROUPS

DAVID HART

HISTORICAL BACKGROUND

In the lead-up to the Education Act 1944, the history of the teaching profession could be summed up as a struggle for status. It took until 1920 for the elementary teachers to succeed in achieving an increase in their status, whereas secondary teachers had gained in status at a much earlier stage, and indeed were regarded by many as superior to elementary teachers. It was not until the 1944 Education Act, which unified elementary and secondary education, that it could truly be said that a united profession was in place. Perhaps one of the significant results of that Act was the diminution in status of the secondary grammar school teacher. As will be seen later, many of the reasons for the formation of various teachers' organizations, let alone the changes in their composition, can be traced back to the pre-1944 period.

There can be no doubt that the union which was largely in the forefront of the great campaign for raising the status of elementary teachers was the National Union of Teachers (NUT). They recognized that their members were poorly regarded, in terms of both status and intellectual ability. This led to very considerable bitterness between the NUT and the government of the day, not least at the turn of the century in the run-up to the passing of the Education Act of 1902, and the subsequent expulsion from office of Sir Robert Morant, the then Permanent Secretary of the Education Department.

At the same time as the NUT was growing in size, the secondary teachers were looking to their organizations to look after their interests. Their sector was looked after by four separate associations of Headmasters, Headmistresses, Assistant Masters, and Assistant Mistresses.

In the post-1902 period all these professional bodies found it necessary to campaign vigorously, not only in terms of raising the status of teachers, but also on the salaries front. In the post-First World War situation, the salary grievances of teachers were reinforced by a serious shortage of entrants and by the profession's inability to attract sufficient applicants from amongst the middle classes. The history of the period between the two World Wars is almost a mirror image of the last 20 years – action to improve the salary levels of teachers interspersed with inaction. In 1919 the Burnham Committee was set up with the purpose of negotiating teachers' salaries at national level, but that did not prevent the Exchequer attempting to hold down teachers' salary and pension improvements in the interest of the national economy.

By 1944 it could be argued that the teaching profession had undergone a revolution: first, in terms of status; second, by means of an improvement in academic qualifications; third, as a consequence of salary and conditions of service improvements; and fourth, by the very importance given to education in the passing of the 1944 Act.

THE STATUS OF EDUCATION TODAY

Just as the 1944 Education Act brought home to the general public the importance of education, so recent developments have conspired to bring education to the forefront. After a relatively quiet period after the 1944 Act, concerns about the quality of education began to surface, particularly in the late 1960s and early 1970s. The 'black' papers appeared bewailing the rapid departure of selective education and questioning the standards achieved by comprehensive schools. However, it was not until the then Prime Minister, James Callaghan, added his weight to these concerns in a speech made at Ruskin College in 1976 that politicians finally grasped the importance of the 'education vote'.

Every general election since 1979 has seen an increase in the commitment by political parties to education reform with the manifestos for the 1987 election pre-eminent. Concern about standards has been fuelled by high unemployment, by the significant change in the educational requirements of employers underpinned by the switch from manufacturing to service industries, by the long-running teachers' pay dispute with its lengthy period of industrial action, and by the production of a whole range of statistics which purport to show that school leavers in the UK, and indeed educational standards in general in the UK, compare unfavourably with the standards achieved by competitive countries, particularly France, Japan, the United States, and West Germany. The country is now faced with an Education Act as radical in as many ways as the 1944 Act, containing concepts such as a national curriculum, national testing, the devolvement of more power and responsibility to the governors and heads, an expansion of the quasi-independent sector through grant maintained schools and city technology colleges, and a considerable expansion of parental choice, thereby sharpening up competition between educational institutions. This presents a particularly severe challenge for all those professional bodies and pressure groups involved in education.

THE DEVELOPMENT OF ORGANIZED OPINION AND ACTION

As already noted, in the early part of the century teachers' organizations could basically be divided into the National Union of Teachers, which looked after the elementary school interests, and the four separate associations in the secondary sector, commonly known as the 'Joint Four'. It is worth looking at the development of all the current teachers' organizations, including the above, because this in many ways demonstrates how opinion within the teaching profession has changed dramatically in terms of its approach to issues which go way beyond the traditional bargaining role of trade unions in the salaries and conditions of service sphere.

National Union of Teachers

Although the NUT was for many years the dominant union, it has suffered a decline in membership which means it no longer represents the majority of the teaching profession. It rapidly expanded throughout much of the twentieth century and took into its ranks teachers from all types of schools. Notwithstanding that fact, a significant majority of its membership remains in the primary sector. Its position as the main 'spokesman' for the profession lasted until the late 1970s, but the combination of a Conservative Government and the rapid increase in membership of other teachers' organizations has undermined that position significantly. Its own membership loss can be put down to a combination of a reduction in the number of teachers in the profession and the pursuit of policies regarded with disfavour by sections of its membership, not least in the field of industrial action. Nevertheless, the NUT remains a powerful force with a well-respected input on education policy making backed by good quality research.

National Association of School Masters and Union of Women Teachers (NAS/UWT)

The NAS/UWT was formed out of an amalgamation of the NAS and the UWT. It was founded in 1922 when some 2,000 teachers in the NUT disagreed with its policy of equal pay for women teachers. Accordingly, in the years leading up to its amalgamation with the UWT, the NAS had the image of support for positive discrimination against women teachers in salary terms. The introduction of equal pay for teachers, irrespective of sex, combined with the Sex Discrimination Act of 1975, made a change of emphasis inevitable, hence the merger with the UWT.

The NAS/UWT has strong policies on salaries, on discipline, and on teachers' conditions of service. It still calls itself the 'career teachers' organization', which tends to continue to give it, fairly or unfairly, a male-dominated image. Its membership increased rapidly during the 1960s and it became the second biggest teachers' organization. Its growth, however, has slowed down significantly, largely because of its periodic militant stance, and it is now rivalled in membership terms by the Assistant Masters and Mistresses Association.

Assistant Masters and Mistresses Association (AMMA)

The AMMA was created out of a merger of the Assistant Masters Association and the Assistant Mistresses Association, which were both members of the Joint Four. While they were separate members of the Joint Four, it could be fairly said that until latterly they largely represented the interests of grammar school teachers. However, the development of comprehensive education changed all this. But even at the time of their merger, which was largely influenced by the Sex Discrimination Act of 1975, the AMMA was predominantly a secondary teachers' body. Since the amalgamation it has campaigned vigorously for membership in the primary sector and its strong stance, largely short of industrial action, appeals to both primary teachers and to its secondary membership. It represents all teachers below the level of headship and therefore has a distinctive image. It has a long track record of making a significant contribution to educational policy making, particularly in the secondary sector, and this is especially evident in the field of secondary examinations.

Professional Association of Teachers (PAT)

PAT was founded on a simple but nevertheless vital issue, namely that of teachers going on strike. PAT is fundamentally against strike action and it has rapidly recruited a large number of members to whom strike action by teachers is abhorrent. Its future, in terms of membership, will no doubt depend upon whether there is continuing militancy within the teaching profession, and whether it can develop coherent policies on educational as well as salary and conditions of service issues.

National Association of Head Teachers (NAHT)

The NAHT, which was founded shortly before the turn of the century, represented the interests of heads only until 1985 when it admitted deputy heads for the first time. For many years it was the case that a number of its members had dual membership, with the NUT, NAS/UWT, or the Secondary Heads Association. The amount of dual membership has decreased significantly so that only a very small proportion of NAHT members now belong to another organization. It currently represents over three quarters of all the country's heads and has recently linked with the IAPS (Incorporated Association of Preparatory Schools) so that all preparatory school heads belong to both organizations, thereby bringing the independent and maintained sectors of education closer together. The NAHT represents heads and deputies of all types of schools, and has in recent years significantly increased its educational policy input as well as maintaining its output on salaries, pensions, and legal and professional advice issues.

Secondary Heads Association (SHA)

SHA was formed out of the merger of the Headmasters' Association and the Headmistresses' Association, which were also components of the Joint Four. Its development from an organization whose sum parts were largely seen as looking after grammar school interests very much mirrors the change in the AMMA. SHA also has links with the independent sector through the Headmasters' Conference and the Girls Schools' Association, who represent boys' and girls' independent schools respectively. The admission of deputy heads has significantly increased SHA's membership. As its title implies, it does not admit heads or deputies from any sphere other than secondary schools and colleges.

PROMINENT PRESSURE GROUPS

It would be quite wrong to give the impression that the only organized opinion from within the education service is confined to teachers' organizations. There are many pressure groups – of which the following are some of the most currently active – other than professional teacher bodies.

Society of Teachers Opposed to Physical Punishment (STOPP)

In many ways STOPP has been one of the most successful pressure groups of all. Its long-running campaign against corporal punishment, underpinned by decisions reached by the European Court of Human Rights, was in many ways largely responsible for the ultimate decision to abolish corporal punishment in all maintained schools and in independent schools in receipt of public money with effect from August 1987.

Campaign for the Advancement of State Education (CASE)

CASE has been an influential body during the years of development of comprehensive education. It has provided a valuable forum whereby parents and teachers can lobby local and national politicians. CASE, like other pressure groups, will be tested to the full by the current Government's educational policy making. Its attitude towards vital issues, such as parental choice, might well demonstrate how representative it is in terms of parental views.

National Confederation of Parent-Teacher Associations (NCPTA)

The NCPTA has grown rapidly in terms of its public profile during the past few years. It claims to represent several million parents although, like CASE, its ability to represent the views of parents will be subject to rigorous examination when it comes to campaigning on key issues. There are some who argue that the NCPTA would do better to drop its reference to teachers and that it should confine itself to representing parents only, but the link between parents and teachers is crucial. It may have been placed under strain during the recent years of industrial action, but from a point of view of effective pressure-group work, it would be a significant step to cut that link.

National Association of Governors and Managers (NAGM)

NAGM has come to the fore of late because of the continuing trend to devolve more and more power to governing bodies. It has long campaigned for an effective voice for governors in the education system, and it is particularly active in the field of training governors, both new and experienced, to meet the challenges of the decades to come.

Subject associations

There are very many subject associations. For instance, the Association for Science Education is particularly well-known. The subject associations are professional associations which make a significant educational input in their specialist spheres. The detailed implementation of the national curriculum and testing will see these associations coming into their own as significant contributors to policy making at national level.

METHODS OF EXERCISING INFLUENCE

All pressure groups and, in particular, the teachers' organizations, have had significantly to rethink their position, not least during the years of Conservative government since 1979. The NUT and NAS/UWT are both affiliated to the Trades Union Congress, but the influence exercised by that body has diminished significantly during the 1980s. It is quite true that it can be argued that the teachers would not have received their significant pay increase in 1987 if it had not been for their willingness to undertake a long campaign of industrial action at a time when public sympathy was with them, at least until the latter stages. But militancy will not always achieve its ends by any stretch of the imagination. If the teaching profession eventually moves towards a review body on salaries, as opposed to negotiating machinery, it will find its room for industrial action even more limited.

If industrial action has a part to play in salaries and conditions of service negotiations, it is highly unlikely to achieve much when it comes to educational policy making. A Conservative government with a substantial majority, committed to radical reform, needs to be persuaded to amend those policies which have been ill thought through, and the same goes for back benchers, who must be convinced that policies, or aspects of policies, really are unworkable or damaging before they are likely to change their minds.

The Education Reform Act of 1988 shifts power and responsibility from local education authorities to governors and heads. Teachers' organizations will now have to think long and hard about their role, not least in the conditions of service arena. Will they be able to operate as effectively across some 28,000 individual institutions as opposed to 104 local education authorities?

The tide in favour of educational change is flowing fast, prompted by concern about educational standards, and urged on by a few examples of policy making on the part of a small number of local education authorities. For the pressure groups who wish to change the Government's educational policy making or support the Government's reforms it is a question of ensuring that they are indeed in touch with and are truly reflecting the views of their constituents, not least the parents and the communities served by the schools. For the professional bodies, the problem goes a great deal deeper. They must not only seek to make common cause with those who truly reflect the views of parents and governors, but they must look also at the whole future image of the teaching profession. Above all, they must give significant emphasis to underlining the true professionalism of the overwhelming majority of their members by endorsing concepts such as a General Teaching Council. The lack of such a council, or similar body, which could put teachers on a par with professionals such as doctors, lawyers, and dentists, has been one of the significant factors behind the ability of the Government to put forward and gain support for a number of reforms with relative ease.

FURTHER READING

Baron, G. (Ed.) (1981) *The Politics of School Government*, Oxford: Pergamon Press.

Croner Publications (1989) *The Head's Legal Guide*, Kingston upon Thames: Croner.

Reese, W. J. (1986) *Power and the Promise of School Reform*, London: Routledge & Kegan Paul.

Roy, W. (1983) *Teaching Under Attack*, Beckenham: Croom Helm.

Tropp, A. (1957) *The School Teachers*, London: Heinemann.

Part II. Organization and Management of Institutions

4.7

PRIMARY SCHOOLS

AUDREY PAISEY

THE DEVELOPMENT OF PRIMARY EDUCATION

The concept of primary education originated with the Hadow Report in 1926. This report recommended that education for children up to eleven years of age should be regarded as a distinct phase of education preceding a secondary or junior technical phase. Within a few years, two consultative committees under the chairmanship of Sir Henry Hadow produced reports on primary schools (1931) and nursery schools (1933) which outlined the content and structure of primary education.

The Education Act 1944 required local education authorities (LEAs) to provide a three-tier system of primary, secondary, and further education. The Act made the division at age eleven legal: all-age schools were forced to disappear. Currently the maintained school system of education consists of two stages – primary from five to eleven years, and secondary from eleven to sixteen years. Nursery education, increasingly considered to be of great importance, lies outside the compulsory school age range. Nursery places are provided by a number of LEAs in separate nursery schools or nursery departments, or in classes attached to primary schools. Attendance is voluntary and may be on a full-time or part-time basis.

Two categories of publicly maintained primary schools exist. These are county schools, established and run by LEAs, and voluntary schools, which are financially maintained by LEAs – either wholly or to a large part – but established and supported financially by other bodies, almost exclusively the Church of England or the Roman Catholic Church.

The main classification 'primary school' applies to infants' schools (for children aged five to seven) and junior schools (for children aged seven to eleven) as well as to the single school which caters for children aged from five to eleven. In some areas the system consists of first schools (for children aged five to eight or nine) and middle schools, deemed primary (for children aged eight to twelve). Where schools exist for the entire age range, five to twelve,

437

they are called combined schools. All of the above schools are within the primary sector, but middle schools for children aged nine to thirteen are deemed secondary. For the purposes of this chapter the focus is on the generally found primary school age range of five to eleven.

In 1985 some 95 per cent of the five to eleven school population in the UK were in maintained primary schools. Over 4,500,000 children were working with approximately 205,000 teachers in almost 25,000 schools. Nearly 70 per cent of these primary schools catered for 100–299 pupils. A further five per cent were schools with under 100 pupils on roll. Since 1985 more schools have fallen into the 100–199 pupil category, many having between 150 and 190 pupils. Staff numbers for these schools range from five to eight teachers according to size. About 25 per cent of primary school teachers are graduates, but this percentage increases annually as each successive cohort of all-graduate probationary teachers enters the schools.

Growth in the number of secondary comprehensive schools in the 1970s freed many primary schools from the constraints of the eleven plus selection examination process for grammar school places. Inspired by the Plowden Report (1967), and released from the external examination pressures, a significant number of schools showed a willingness to experiment and provide a broader curriculum than ever before. The child-centred philosophy of the Plowden Report, written at a time when optimism about the education service was widespread, echoed the main themes of the Hadow Report. It concurred with the Hadow Report (1931) that the curriculum should be thought of in terms of activity and experience rather than knowledge to be acquired and facts to be stored. At the same time, however, a reaction to the permissive society of the 1960s was in evidence. This took the form of concern about national levels of attainment. That same concern exists today, but in the climate of the late 1980s the national government's social and economic intentions are more clearly articulated.

Primary education is the foundation upon which the rest of the education system is built. Experiences and treatment received at the primary stage can have a profound effect on a child's future attitudes and achievements. In many respects the essence of good primary school education still reflects the spirit of the Hadow Report – not least in its concern for the well-being and development of children.

In other respects new dimensions have been added. Primary schools, with secondary schools, are called upon to examine their objectives and their results in a way never demanded before. Every primary school is confronted with the following issues: the school's accountability, including the performance of teachers and children; the need for curriculum planning, monitoring, and evaluation within the new national curriculum framework; the responsibility for local financial management; the higher profile and involvement of the governing body; a more active partnership with parents; and the integration of handicapped pupils.

VALUES AND OBJECTIVES

The organization and management of the primary school centres round its values and the way in which these are interpreted through the climate and curriculum provided for the pupils. The central concern is to develop each individual child to his or her full potential. The school's values govern the quality and quantity of the objectives pursued and so the outcomes for the children. Clarifying, selecting, and prioritizing objectives require time and effort on the part of the head and staff, and form a significant portion of all staff discourse. Governors are increasingly involved in this process.

The Plowden Report observed that primary school objectives in the 1960s were implicit rather than explicit, but the Government's Circular 6/81 required schools to produce written statements of their aims and objectives. The publicity given to them, the extent to which the making and understanding of them is shared with governors and parents, and the determination and success with which they are pursued in daily practice now give the primary school its public image and standing.

STRUCTURE

The head is responsible through the governing body for the internal organization, discipline, and curriculum of the school. The overall leadership of the head is of paramount importance to the primary school. The majority of heads are men, while four fifths of primary school teachers are women. In 1986 the average teaching staff number was seven with a school roll average of less than 200 pupils. Schools with over seventy-six pupils are entitled to appoint a deputy head.

As the school's general manager, the head's task is to have and maintain an overall view of the school. The deputy head and other class teachers usually have additional specific responsibilities. Most heads encourage the teaching staff, particularly the deputy head, to take as wide a view of the school as possible and to engage in corporate activity to guarantee its continual development.

A deputy head with high motivation and job satisfaction is a very considerable asset to a primary school. The Inner London Education Authority's study of junior schools in 1986 pointed out the key role which the deputy head plays in a successful school. Given managerial responsibilities and the opportunity to work in partnership with the head, a deputy head helps to achieve the

439

smooth running and development of the school and is thereby enabled to prepare himself or herself for headship.

Almost all primary school teachers, including deputy heads – and in very small schools, heads – have specific management responsibilities for a class of children. Class registration groups consisting of a single age cohort or vertical two-year span usually number twenty-five to thirty children – sometimes more. As class teachers, the majority of primary school teaching staff cope with most areas of the curriculum but may need specialist support in certain fields.

A variety of teaching styles including didactic and exploratory approaches are employed, some teachers leaning more heavily towards one or the other. Primary schools generally try to expose children to a variety of learning styles in whole class, group, and individualized activities. A safe, supportive, but challenging environment within the school is sought, giving enough flexibility and stimulation to provide for a very diverse range of children.

The essential job of the primary school teacher is to have pastoral responsibility for a whole class and academic responsibility for all or most of the work they engage in. But beyond this, the majority of heads expect and encourage teachers to take on a particular responsibility which has a wider impact on the school as a whole. Typically this will be to manage a complete year group or other sub-section of the school, or to manage a subject or group of subjects in the curriculum. In some schools the latter practice is limited to particular subject areas such as language, science, and mathematics, but many schools assign a curriculum area to every member of staff. In a school of eight or more teachers the whole range of curriculum areas can be covered, each being given leadership by one member of staff. Difficulties arise in the pursuit of this policy when staff interests and specialisms overlap leaving some areas uncovered, and when the number of staff is too small to make it workable.

Such management tasks beyond class teaching can be formal appointments carrying titles, or they may be undertaken on a voluntary and informal basis and seen by the member of staff concerned as a useful step and experience for promotion. To adjust the structure is a key task of the head who must bear in mind the claims of staff management and development as well as those of the curriculum. In recent times when promotion opportunities have been limited heads have become more interested in such devices as job rotation, action research, and whole-school project management to interest and motivate the more energetic and able staff.

A dominant theme in the primary school is teamsmanship. It has characterized small groups of staff working officially together as in a staff year team in the larger schools. But it has become adopted by the staff as a whole, particularly in smaller schools. Pastoral or curricular leadership and co-ordination require the preparation and discussion of papers with colleagues and the development of business skills and the ability to handle meetings. In many schools the team is overtly extended to non-teaching staff, symbolized by the use of a shared staff room.

Whilst formal appraisal is not yet widespread in primary schools, many schools have for some time favoured staff appraisal at an informal level or with some degree of formality. In schools where voluntary appraisal schemes are already in place, most teachers are positive and appreciative in attitude. Discussing achievements, sharing problems, talking about aspirations, and setting personal objectives are for such teachers a profitable professional experience. Primary heads and staff members are likely to have regular interchanges during the working day which establish relationships and provide a data base for the formally allocated appraisal time. Heads are commonly able to see teaching staff in action in the course of the normal day so the need to set aside special observation time may not be necessary, thus avoiding artificial circumstances.

Staff performance to date in the primary school has been concerned with class teaching and any wider responsibilities which a teacher may have for the school as a whole. In future a new dimension may well emerge. On 10 August 1987 a circular from the Secretary of State for Education charged LEAs to begin the process of devolving financial management to schools as a result of the Education Act No 2 1986. The delegation of financial management, as opposed to financial administration, to primary school governors and heads is intended to enable them to make the most effective use of resources.

Consequently, primary school heads and possibly deputy heads will need to have a complete grasp of the school's finances in a different way and for a different purpose than before. Accountability will follow the exercise of discretionary expenditure. In future, financial management is likely to be prominent in the thinking and practice of heads and most if not all primary school teachers. Individual teachers with organizational responsibilities will become budget-conscious and strictly accountable.

The performance of children as well as staff is a critical concern of management in the primary school. It requires careful monitoring and documentation. Better development of pupil profiles by all primary schools is envisaged. Standards of performance for the primary school pupil derive from the school's objectives. Work output in terms of both quantity and quality is subject to inspection and review internally by the head.

Standards are maintained nationally by Her Majesty's Inspectorate (HMI), which has access to all primary schools and has an advisory function. The major task of the HMI is to report to the Secretary of State on the education being provided and to offer advice on corrective measures which may be needed. Since 1985 HMI reports on schools have been made public. This is regarded by many as an important step towards the improvement of standards.

Currently there is a prevalent belief that children need to be challenged and pressed to work more than they already are. The Department of Education and Science (DES) has pointed out in this context that performance indicators need to include the assessment of social behaviour as well as academic achievements. Primary school children's achievements vary according to personal attributes and abilities, home circumstances, and the quality of management in the school. Academic attainment testing is part of achievement, but other elements of achievement which the primary school keeps to the fore are the capacity to apply knowledge, the production of creative work, the acquisition of personal and social skills, and positive attitudes concerning commitment, perseverance, motivation, and coping with difficult tasks. Either subjective or objective means to measure progress in these areas can be and are being used.

For some years now the Assessment Performance Unit established by the DES has been working on the feasibility of formulating standards of performance in various subject fields applicable at different ages. With the advent of the 1988 legislation to test academic performance at ages seven, eleven, and fourteen, heads are obliged to ensure that pupil performance standards are in the forefront of their thinking. Adequate information systems are needed to make it possible to take early corrective action in the case of underperformance. Closing the gap between a child's potential and his or her actual achievement under this system will be a central management task with more emphasis than perhaps has been the case – at least in some areas of the curriculum.

The curriculum as the productive process of the primary school will continue to be centre-stage for the ideas and practices of the head and teaching staff. Its management will continue to be primarily concerned with matching what is intended in terms of stated objectives with what is actually provided. Its formulation and implementation will continue to be the subject of discussions and negotiations between the head and the governors and the head and the teaching staff. The new dimension to these deliberations in future, however, will be the terms and requirements of the intended national guidelines for the curriculum, and discretionary powers at school level already established by the Education Act No 2 1986 and codified in the Education Reform Act 1988.

EXTERNAL RELATIONS

With public relations to the fore and accountability a main feature of education, primary schools have been introduced to a sphere of activity which, if not entirely new, is certainly of a scope and scale previously unknown. A prudent head now builds a complete network of external contacts to serve the interests of the school. The most important of these is the partnership fostered with parents. Parental involvement has substantially increased in recent years, both as regards taking an interest in the school, and in one way or another making direct contributions such as giving auxiliary help. The majority of heads welcome and encourage this development. In a sample of forty schools inspected by HMI in the first half of 1984 it was found that most schools made commend-able efforts to forge links with parents and the local community and keep them informed of events in the school and the progress of the children.

The Education Act of 1980 enabled parents to have a greater say in the running of the primary school through the election of parent governors. Aimed at raising standards by improving the management of schools and promoting teaching quality, the Education Act No 2 1986 provided that the governing body should comprise equal numbers of parents and LEA-appointed gover-nors. Given a stronger voice on governing bodies, parent power is a force which will in future play a larger part in the primary school. The 1986 Act requires that all parents receive an annual report from the governing body and have the opportunity to discuss it at an annual meeting.

Other external links are commonly forged with industry and commerce, social and welfare services, the police, fire, and other public bodies. Relations with other educational institutions can also be extensive. Notably, there ought to be close, constructive and continuous interaction with secondary schools to which children from the primary school move at age eleven. In practice there remains much to be done to achieve the kind of thoroughly professional liaison which is required.

Overall, the community now looks to education to produce hard-working, resource-conscious and socially-committed citizens who can cope with techno-logical advances and live at ease in ethnically mixed neighbourhoods, and alongside those who may be handicapped. The primary school is aware of its task, as recent adaptations of organization and management have shown. There seems to be no shortage of ideas and practices by which future adaptations will be accomplished.

FURTHER READING

Blyth, W. (1984) *Development, Experience and Curriculum in Primary Education*, Becken-ham: Croom Helm.

Coulson, A. (1985) 'The managerial behaviour of primary school heads', *Collected Original Resources in Education*, 9, 1.

Craig, I. (Ed.) (1987) *Primary School Management in Action*, Harlow: Longman.

Croner Publications (1989) *The Head's Legal Guide*, Kingston upon Thames: Croner.

Day, C., Johnston, D., and Whitaker, P. (1986) *Managing Primary Schools: A Professional Development Context*, London: Harper & Row.

Department of Education and Science (1984) *Education Observed*. A review of the first six months of published reports by HM Inspectors, London: DES.

—— (1984) *Education Observed 2*. A review of published reports by HM Inspectors on primary schools and comprehensive schools, London: DES.

—— (1985) *Better Schools*, London: DES and Welsh Office.

—— (1985) *Education Observed 3. Good Teachers*, London: DES.

—— (1986) *Education Statistics for the United Kingdom* (1986 Edition), London: DES.

Great Britain, House of Commons, Education Science and Arts Committee (1986) *Achievement in Primary Schools*, Vol 1, London: HMSO.

Harling, P. (Ed.) (1984) *New Directions in Educational Leadership*, Lewes: The Falmer Press.

Inner London Education Authority (1986) *The Junior School Project*, London: ILEA Research and Statistics Branch.

Paisey, A. (1984) *School Management – A Case Approach*, London: Paul Chapman Publishing.

Paisey, A. and Paisey, A. (1987) *Effective Management in Primary Schools*, Oxford: Blackwell.

4.8

SECONDARY SCHOOLS

CYRIL POSTER

THE EMERGENCE OF SECONDARY SCHOOLS

The Hadow Report (1926) advocated the reorganization of education in England and Wales into primary (5–11) and secondary (11–15 and beyond). It was, for its time, a radical document:

> The advance contemplated is not on a narrow and selective front, but the whole line is to move forward.

There was to be parity of class size, accommodation, and staff qualification for all children over the age of eleven. Yet the report's practical impact was so slight that, for a further two decades, the designation 'secondary' continued to be applied only to public and grammar schools, and the parities remained wholly chimerical.

It was not until the Spens Report (1938) that the concept of secondary education for all was revived, gained support across the political spectrum, and was enshrined in the Education Act of 1944. This Act made provision for the education of each child according to age, aptitude, and ability. It is needful to recall that in 1947, as the act began to be implemented, more than a million children – 22 per cent of all those in full-time education – were in neither primary nor secondary schools, but in all-age schools; and a decade was to pass before that number was even halved and the percentage reduced to single figures. Rural areas were particularly badly served. In 1952, of 5,000 all-age schools, 3,000 were to be found in the country, two-thirds with an annual intake of ten pupils or fewer.

In urban areas, the demand for equality of educational opportunity was more clearly and speedily articulated and funding more readily available for massive school building programmes to replace or improve the former elementary schools. Although these new secondary modern schools were in the main larger than the schools they succeeded, they were rarely of a size or complexity to give rise to problems of management. With parity of esteem in mind, they

445

consciously or unconsciously modelled themselves on the secondary grammar schools. Their headteachers frequently invested themselves with ritualistic authority, maintaining formal relationships with staff and pupils and practising 'social distancing' with parents. Student achievement was recognized by the presentation of symbolic insignia, and conformity was fostered through competition for group and individual awards.

In the early postwar years there was little difference between secondary grammar and modern schools, except in the crucial area of academic performance. Even here the criterion for admission to a grammar school was the availability of places, and there was therefore no national standard, but great regional variations, ranging from seven per cent to 40 per cent of the related age group. It is not surprising, therefore, that their management structures were essentially similar: hierarchical and pyramidal. There was no need for a formal middle management structure. The senior master or mistress was the headteacher's factotum and channel of communication with the staff. The more experienced and long-serving members of staff were expected to take responsibility, as a matter of course, for materials and equipment within their subject areas, and for the standard of teaching performance and class control of junior members of staff. For such duties there might be some financial reward, but until 1956, when the teaching unions negotiated through the Burnham Committee a complex set of stratified grades, the amounts were insignificant, largely at the headteacher's discretion and from a pool calculated by the local education authority (LEA).

Yet alongside the tripartite system – the third element of which was the comparatively rare secondary technical school – the 1944 Act had permitted the establishment of 'multilateral' schools, soon to be widely known as 'comprehensive'. The effect of this innovation on secondary school organization and management was to be profound.

MANAGEMENT STRUCTURES

A number of features of these new schools rapidly made the traditional school management structure inappropriate. The early comprehensives were, by English though not by North American standards, very large: from 1,500 to over 2,000 pupils. The case for a school of this size now seems curiously at odds with the vision of parity of educational opportunity for all and concern about the fallibility of the selection procedure for grammar school entry: an annual intake of 300–400 pupils was necessary to ensure two to three streams of 'grammar' ability and, eventually, a viable sixth form.

A school of this size demanded a good deal of delegation of function to what now would be called senior management staff – responsible to the headteacher for complex organizational matters like the timetable, accommodation, and finance, or for horizontal or vertical divisions of the school to reduce for pupils and parents the impersonality of the large school – and to middle management staff – mainly with responsibility as heads of subject department.

Even though the success of comprehensive reorganization in Anglesey and the Isle of Man – where geographical considerations made comprehensive schools of about 750 the norm – demonstrated that the urban schools were unnecessarily large, the management demands on this new generation of schools did not diminish. Indeed with the need for an alternative external certification for the increasing numbers of pupils staying voluntarily to sixteen and beyond, and the consequent introduction of the Certificate of Secondary Education (CSE) in the mid-1960s, the raising of the school leaving age in the early 1970s, and the spate of curricular innovation in the same period, the management of all secondary schools became increasingly more complex.

It has become evident, however, certainly in the last decade, that the pyramidal concept of management structure no longer meets the needs of the secondary school. Lines of communication become unduly extended and the co-ordination of the work of the school's departments and subsystems is no longer under control from the top. Furthermore, the school is increasingly encountering day-to-day situations which require organic organization, with the ability to respond rapidly to change, rather than mechanistic organization, which is unable to do so.

Mintzberg (1979) extended the traditional bureaucracy theory and suggested five configurations, of which one, the professional bureaucracy, is appropriate to schools. He further identified in all organizations five parts, related in a characteristic way. Secondary school management increasingly identifies with this model. The senior management team constitutes the strategic apex. Curricular and pastoral heads form the middle line providing the link with the teaching force, the operating core – of which they are themselves also a part. The remaining elements are of particular importance, as schools increasingly recognize that they are 'joined to the mainland of life', as the Plowden Report felicitously puts it. This is the technostructure of professional support made up from Her Majesty's Inspectorate (HMI), LEA advisers and officers, higher education providers, and the statutory and voluntary support agencies, together with the support staff of school bursars and secretaries, technicians, caretakers and cleaners, and so on.

Though this core model may address the central issues of day-to-day school management, it does not well meet the growing demands made upon secondary schools by the introduction of innovatory practices.

In the early stages of an innovation – before it has been effectively welded into the management structure – schools are more and more turning to matrix management, to the setting up on a relatively short-term basis of what industry

447

calls task teams, which schools – still rather reluctant to empower them – call working parties. The merit of matrix management is that it cuts across hierarchies and promotes job satisfaction at a time when contraction makes promotion difficult to obtain.

ACCOUNTABILITY

One word more than any other sums up the prevailing climate in secondary education: *accountability*. Schools are both being given far more responsibility and power and at the same time – rightly, it can be argued – being made more accountable for their actions and responses. Increasingly secondary schools are faced with the problem of teasing out the various levels of accountability. For the delivery of the curriculum, for example, the headteacher is primarily accountable to the pupils and their parents. Under the Education Act No 2 1986 the governors are required to decide what the curricular aims of the school shall be, and this they must do in the light of the LEA's published policy for the curriculum of all its maintained schools. However, both the governors and the headteacher must take account of any views expressed by 'persons in the community', including the chief of police. The Education Reform Act of 1988 extended further the role of governors, giving them almost complete freedom over the appointment and dismissal of staff, among other matters. This radical shift in accountability must be implemented alongside the requirements of examination boards and the introduction of a national curriculum.

The Education Reform Act of 1988 also gave the Secretary of State powers to phase in Local Financial Management to all secondary schools. While this innovation has given some headteachers concern, there are many who welcome the innovation – always provided they can be given the necessary ancillary support staff to enable them to be managers of the budget and not highly overpaid bursars. There have been pilot schemes in a number of LEAs for some years, particularly those with community schools and colleges. Provided that a reasonable degree of virement is permitted, including the carry-over of unspent balances to the next financial year, schools have usually been willing to undertake the additional accountancy involved. The ability to make direct payment through an imprest account often enables the school to get better value for money. There is, however, an important corollary: if the school is now fully informed by the LEA of its total financial resources, then there is no excuse for the secrecy with which some headteachers have shrouded the disbursement of funds. Even though the fine tuning of proposed expenditure may need to be done by senior management, the full involvement of middle-line management is essential for school-based budgetary control.

Since the reorganization of in-service funding in June 1986, LEAs have had control – with certain constraints – of the way in which large sums of in-service education and training (INSET) money are to be spent. They are required by the Department of Education and Science (DES) to share their decision making with their schools, and a growing number of LEAs are, in a variety of ways, allocating funds directly to schools. Just as the LEAs are accountable to the DES, so are the schools accountable to the LEA for the sensible disposition of these funds. The change of emphasis from 'response to opportunity' to 'response to need' has made schools aware of the increasing importance of the identification of further training and developmental needs of their staff. Even in its early days the effect on secondary schools in particular of these innovatory procedures has been considerable. They are becoming, through the computer analysis of in-service needs questionnaires and through staff discussions, far more aware of the merits of school-based and school-focused INSET. Workshops, quality circles, action learning, and consultancies are becoming part of the vocabulary of school improvement. The fact that the school must now take ownership of both process – since it will decide what is most appropriate to its present situation and future needs – and product, has considerable significance for school management.

Arguably the most significant new accountability for schools of the present decade is the introduction of an appraisal scheme. Whether the summative appraisal which will become part of the serving teacher's continuing record of service will prove to be of great value is open to question; it is difficult, for instance, to envisage it superseding the written reference and the extensive interview in the appointment to seniority. On the other hand, a formal system of formative appraisal is already proving its worth in those schools, mainly secondary, which have already embarked upon it voluntarily, within pilot projects or of their own initiative.

The most valuable feature of appraisal is the identification of objectives, for the teacher as an individual, for the group or department within which he or she works, and for the school as an entity. The very complexity of the interweave of responsibility within the professional bureaucracy of the secondary school – where a teacher charged with the management of a large department may also be a subordinate within a pastoral structure – has led in the past to schools being much clearer about their aims than about their objectives. The identification of what industrial managers call 'key result areas', and the annual negotiation between appraiser and appraisee of the activities which will realize them, is the first step towards the clarification of objectives. The rate of change in secondary schools now demands of senior and middle management decision-making and evaluation procedures of a very different order from those that formerly appeared effective.

449

CURRICULUM DEVELOPMENT

During the late 1960s and early 1970s secondary schools were having laid before them a menu of curriculum projects: Nuffield Science, the Schools Council Integrated Science Project (SCISP), the Integrated Humanities Project, the Schools Council Moral Education 13–16 Project, and a host of others. Schools were able to involve themselves or not as they chose. Because extensive support funding was available, many schools did so choose, but not necessarily for sound educational reasons.

There was a general euphoria about innovation: because it was new, it must be good. There was little forward planning or costing in terms of staffing, staff training, or equipment and materials. Little consideration was given to the effect on other areas of the curriculum of radical changes in the methodology of subjects engaging in the various projects. Little attempt was made to visualize the impact on a school of the eventual adoption throughout five or even seven years of curriculum development in the area of innovation. Worst of all, perhaps, at a time when educationalists in the United States were evaluating for 'instant results', and pulling up the plant to see if the roots had taken, schools in the United Kingdom were innovating without any serious evaluation procedures at all.

Today major curriculum developments are of a different order. The most important is undoubtedly the Technical and Vocational Education Initiative (TVEI) and its current extension, funded by the Manpower Services Commission (MSC), and intended to make a powerful but controlled impact on the entire framework of secondary and further education. Schools are involved in – and sometimes feel submerged by – extensive evaluation and accountability procedures. Those in the pilot schemes initially, and now increasingly those entering the dissemination and development phase, have found themselves responsible to co-ordinators, advisers, and officers not only within their LEAs, but also within the MSC bureaucracy. Further, there has grown up a previously little regarded need for cross-phase (secondary/further) and inter-school collaboration.

Closely locked into this major innovation has been a change in the form of certification for 16+ pupils: the introduction of the General Certificate of Secondary Education (GCSE); the emergence and increasing use of the Business and Technical Education Certificate (BTEC) and the Certificate of Personal and Vocational Education (CPVE). All these are making heavy demands upon the time and resources of the secondary teaching force, both for training in new procedures, and for the effective discharge of the responsibilities involved in new methods of assessment and recording.

These innovations originate from central government, even though the LEA may be largely charged with their implementation. Other developments, the

450

implementation of which is more directly the responsibility of the LEA, derive from recent Acts of Parliament. The Education Act, 1981, which gave effect to many of the recommendations of the Warnock Report on Special Educational Needs, has given LEAs the task of radically reorganizing their provision for the education of physically, mentally, and emotionally handicapped children. The Education No 2 Act of 1986 requires of all LEAs a curriculum statement on sex education 'within the context of moral values and family life' even though the governors are empowered to make the final decision about whether sex education should be provided and, if so, in what form. For many LEAs the requirements of Equal Opportunities legislation have led to statements on multiracial education, women's, and minority rights to all of which the school must pay heed. Plainly, secondary schools are being required to make judgements in areas of the overt and hidden curriculum and the general ethos of the school as never before in their history.

ISSUES AND PROBLEMS

For secondary school pupils, and therefore for their teachers, the crucial educational issue is the extent to which they will be able to make use of their educational achievements, whether in terms of examination success, or in the less measurable but no less important area of self-development. Although there are marked regional variations, most of these young people are faced everywhere with very limited job opportunities. The Youth Training Scheme (YTS) is now the means whereby those over the statutory school age who do not continue in full-time traditional education have an alternative to unemployment. At eighteen, however, many will be unemployed. This prospect undermines the morale of even young secondary pupils, and teachers find it hard to motivate them, whatever their educational potential.

Teachers too are encountering situations that sap morale. The government's introduction of City Technology Colleges, the opportunity for parents to seek Grant Maintained status for schools, and talk of the introduction of 'magnet schools' are all widely regarded as assaults on the comprehensive system of secondary schooling, in the development of which many teachers have spent their entire career. Even without these radical changes, throughout the United Kingdom falling rolls are threatening most secondary schools with contraction, some with closure. LEAs seeking, in most cases, to reorganize with the least dislocation to the education service are faced in their decision-making with the dual constraints of the possibility that parents and governors of a school under threat may seek to 'opt out', and the further complication that the Education Reform Act has introduced new admission limits which often negate the LEAs' attempt to balance school intakes. Furthermore, the 'all-through' (11–18) comprehensive school is in many areas being replaced with 11–16 schools and sixth form and tertiary colleges, a policy based not on proven good practice but on expediency. With the virtual elimination of middle schools – whether 'middle deemed primary' (8–12) or 'middle deemed secondary' (9–13) – a number of secondary schools are facing alterations to their intakes at both ends. These changes, though they may sometimes save a school from closure, are disruptive to its sense of purpose and plunge it into yet another unlooked for and unwanted cycle of innovation.

Nevertheless, there are good grounds for believing that secondary schools will come out of this slough of despond with credit. Teachers, both those who are newly qualifying, and those in service, are probably better trained than at any time in the past. There has been a considerable movement towards corporate management, so that teachers at all levels of seniority may feel a greater sense of ownership of the decision-making process. The earlier maturation of secondary pupils is often matched by more cordial interpersonal relationships between teachers and young people. Parents and the community are more involved in the day-to-day affairs of the schools. Industry, thanks to organizations like Understanding British Industry (UBI) and schemes like Young Enterprise, has a closer understanding of and a better working relationship with a growing number of schools. This perception – that education is not solely a matter for the professional – has widened horizons and gives hope for the future.

FURTHER READING

Buckley, J. (1985) *The Training of Secondary School Heads in Western Europe*, Windsor: NFER-Nelson.

Dennison, W. F. and Shenton, K. (1987) *Challenges in Educational Management: Principles into Practice*, Beckenham: Croom Helm.

Drucker, P. F. (1974) *Management Tasks, Responsibilities, Practices*, London: Heinemann.

Handy, C. B. (1985) *Understanding Organisations*, Harmondsworth: Penguin Books.

Mintzberg, H. (1979) *The Structuring of Organisations*, Englewood Cliffs, New Jersey: Prentice-Hall.

Poster, C. (1976) *School Decision Making: Educational Management in Secondary Schools*, London: Heinemann.

Wilkinson, C. and Cave, E. (1987) *Teaching and Managing: Inseparable Activities in Schools*, Beckenham: Croom Helm.

4.9

INDEPENDENT SCHOOLS

JOHN RAE

IDENTITY AND GOVERNANCE

For the purpose of this chapter an independent school is defined as a school that is independent of the local education authority and in membership of one of the associations reporting to the Independent Schools Information Service (ISIS).

There are some 1,360 independent schools in the United Kingdom that annually submit statistics to ISIS, which was established in 1972 as an information centre for the schools. The most important of the associations reporting to ISIS are the Headmasters' Conference (HMC), the Girls' Schools Association (GSA) and the Incorporated Association of Preparatory Schools (IAPS). In 1987 these schools catered for about seven per cent of the children and young people at school in the UK.

HMC includes all the leading 'public schools' and has a total membership of 225. Although some of the schools are co-educational and others admit girls to sixth form courses, HMC is essentially an association of boys' schools. Only 13 per cent of the pupils in HMC schools are girls. The criterion for membership is academic performance, though in recent years schools whose performance has fallen below the declared standard have continued in membership.

GSA represents 245 girls' independent schools. IAPS represents 560 preparatory schools, that is, schools which prepare boys and girls for entry to an independent secondary school at eleven or thirteen. Preparatory schools for girls are rare but an increasing number of boys' preparatory schools admit girls: 26 per cent of pupils in IAPS schools are girls.

There are independent schools outside the umbrella of ISIS. In a few cases this is because they chart an eccentric course and have no wish to be associated with the mainstream of independent education. A school such as Summerhill would be in this category. In other cases, the schools are transitory institutions whose standards and stability are questionable.

The great majority (77 per cent) of independent schools as defined here are educational charities. The remainder are limited companies or proprietary schools.

The constitution of the leading boys' independent secondary schools – the so-called Clarendon schools, including Eton, Winchester, and Westminster – is laid down in statutes and regulations, the key statute being the Public Schools Act of 1868. Other independent schools have their own trust deeds. Whatever the legal instrument under which the schools operate, there are broad similarities in the organization and management of independent schools.

The governing body is the ultimate authority in an independent school. Neither the Secretary of State nor the local education authority has power to dictate matters of school policy, *except* in relation to pupils under the Assisted Places Scheme whose fees are paid from public funds. The issue of corporal punishment illustrates the relationship between an independent school and the central government. The government can ban the use of corporal punishment in schools maintained by the local authority, but in independent schools that ban only applies to Assisted Place pupils. Whether it is banned for fee-paying pupils is entirely a matter for the governing body and the head. Independent schools are however subject to non-educational statutes such as those regulating health and safety at work.

The constitution of the governing body is also a matter for the school concerned. The central government cannot, for example, prescribe the extent of parental representation. Membership of the governing body of most independent schools is self-perpetuating, though in some of the older schools there is an ex-officio element. At Westminster almost half the total complement of governors is ex-officio. Typically ex-officio governors will represent the Universities of Oxford and Cambridge, the church to which the school is affiliated, and learned institutions such as the Royal Society. The other, elected, governors are chosen because they have a particular expertise (though seldom in education), because they are former pupils, or because their names 'look good on the notepaper'.

The full governing body meets three or four times a year, its executive committee approximately once a month during term. The closest liaison between the governing body and the officers of the school is between the head and the chairman of the governing body, and between the school's finance officer, the bursar, and the chairman of the executive committee.

The governors of an independent school are non-executive directors. They appoint the head but do not have a role in other appointments with the possible exception of the bursar or deputy head. Their delegation of all other appointments to the head reflects their underlying philosophy that it is the head's responsibility to run the school. The head is the chief executive. The governing body controls the finances (in most schools the bursar reports directly to the governing body), and the chief executive is responsible for educational policy, for the hiring and firing of teachers, and for the admission and, if necessary, the expulsion of pupils.

How well the governors are informed about the school's educational policy will depend on the attitude of the chairman and the head. It is not uncommon for governors to have little or no idea about the content of the curriculum or the academic structure of the schools. But they are sensitive to shifts in the school's reputation and in its academic performance as recorded in public examinations.

While the governing body may be more inclined to leave the running of the school to the head than is the case in the maintained sector, they can and will dismiss the head if they are not satisfied with his or her performance. The greater freedom enjoyed by the head of an independent school carries with it a greater risk. Most heads are on one year's notice. On the other hand it would be unusual for them to have fixed-term contracts (such contracts are officially opposed by HMC), and this is one reason why despite the risk independent school heads remain in office longer than their counterparts in maintained schools.

THE HEAD AS CHIEF EXECUTIVE

It would be unusual for the head of an independent school to be given a job description. In so far as his or her responsibilities are defined, they are expressed in broad terms in the trust deed. In a typical case they are expressed as 'the internal management and discipline of the school'. In practice the head of an independent school has, with the exception of financial control, the sort of absolute power that is associated with the monarch of the *ancien régime*. Not only does the head hire and fire staff: he may also, by his patronage, advance or retard staff careers. The head decides which pupils enter the school and which subjects appear on the timetable. However much he or she consults with colleagues, it is recognized that the final decision is always the head's. What limits the head's power is not any constitutional check but public opinion in the staff room, among the parents, and among the pupils. Teachers and parents (though seldom pupils) can appeal to the governing body if they believe that the head is abusing his or her power.

There has been increasing emphasis on management skills for heads in the independent sector, with short courses for new heads run by their more experienced colleagues. The idea of a staff college for senior management in independent schools has been discussed but not implemented. In their style, independent heads have become less autocratic, more consultative. The change is reflected in the internal management structure, which is more formalized than in the past; the head will now have regular meetings with key senior colleagues, such as the director of studies and the chaplain, as well as with the principal committees of heads of academic departments and of housemasters. Formal consultation modifies but does not remove the head's power of final decision. Most heads do not call for a vote at committee meetings, preferring to 'take the sense of the meeting' before deciding on a particular policy or course of action. However much heads may wish to be seen as a first among equals, they cannot altogether escape the shadow of the absolute monarch.

The one area in which the head of an independent school does not exercise absolute power is finance. An absolute monarch such as Louis XIV could and did tell his Controller General of Finance how the royal revenue should be spent. The head of an independent school cannot dictate in a similar way to the bursar. The relationship, both constitutional and personal, between the head and the bursar, is *the* key factor in the internal management of an independent school and it is important that this is understood.

The theoretical relationship between the two fields of responsibility would typically be expressed as follows. While the head is responsible for 'the internal management and discipline of the school', the bursar is responsible *'to the Governing Body* for the conduct of the financial affairs and business management of the School'. This theoretical relationship raises two problems in practice. First, the distinction between 'internal management' and 'business management' is not always easy to make. Second, the fact that the bursar is responsible directly to the governing body introduces an ambiguity into his role. Is he the head's lieutenant or the governing body's watchdog? No doubt most heads and bursars work out an acceptable *modus operandi* but the potential for conflict is always there.

If every disagreement between the head and the bursar had to be resolved by the governing body the authority of both would be undermined and important decisions postponed. Though governors are aware of the potential conflict between the head and the bursar, they are unwilling to change the constitutional relationship because they are not prepared to trust the head, who has no financial expertise, with the financial control of the school's operation.

It is often said that a significant difference between the role of the head in the maintained and independent sectors is that in the latter the head has control over the school's budget. That is an incorrect interpretation of what happens in practice. What the head of an independent school does have is direct access to the governing body, the ultimate authority for deciding priorities in expenditure. In other words, the head's chances of influencing the decisions are probably greater than those of a head in the maintained sector.

For example, the head of a maintained school may have to accept a directive from the local education authority to 'lose' a number of teachers. The governing body of an independent school would be very reluctant to impose such a decision on its head without his or her agreement. It is not the case that this situation never arises, just because an independent school can raise its fees. Independent schools have to operate in the market place. The tension that occurs is between two different marketing arguments: a diversity of subjects attracts more customers *and* a diversity of subjects cannot be economically justified. It is in this debate that the head and the bursar engage (not always on different sides). When the debate goes to the governing body, the head, unlike his or her counterpart in the maintained school, may well be the only expert on the educational issues involved. There is no chief education officer to weigh the head's arguments or scrutinize staffing levels. Few governors of independent schools would know what the school's staff-pupil ratio was or how it compared with other schools.

It is worth noting at this point that the policy of the current Conservative Government is to give greater budgetary control to the heads of maintained schools. It is believed that this will make the role of maintained school heads comparable to that of heads of independent schools. But unless the former have efficient bursars, they will soon become enmeshed in financial calculations for which they are not trained. If such heads do have bursars, this may, as we have seen, lead to a different sort of problem in the conflict of interest between bursars and heads. The real distinction between the head's role in the independent and maintained sectors lies in the control of the appointment of teaching staff and of the admission of pupils. In the appointment of staff, the head of an independent school will involve and consult academic colleagues, but the idea that any non-professional should have a say in selection is anathema. Heads choose their own team. The selection of pupils is also in the hands of the head, though in practice the objective criteria of entrance examinations and the active involvement of colleagues means that the head's effective area of decision is limited to borderline cases. It would be unwise and uncommon for a head to refuse entry to a candidate who had reached the published pass mark, but one may exercise a prerogative in favour of a candidate who has narrowly failed. In the selection of scholars, that is those whose performance in a competitive examination wins a partial or total reduction of fees, the head has a more personal influence, but even here the marks leave little room for idiosyncratic choice. The increasing emphasis on academic performance as the sole criterion for entry to the more successful independent schools has effectively reduced the head's power to decide who enters the school except in terms of broad policy.

The appointment of staff and the admission of pupils are not day-to-day occurrences. For the routine exercise of internal management and discipline the head will normally set up regular face-to-face contact with key individuals and groups, heads of academic departments, housemasters, the bursar, the director of studies, the prefects, and so on. Once again the model of Louis XIV comes to mind, because even in the larger independent schools, particularly boarding schools, the head's leadership style is personal. The school bears his or her stamp. He or she will chair the heads of department and housemasters' committees.

The head of an independent school knows that he or she will be judged by the quality of the school's academic performance and by the quality of the discipline. Academic and pastoral matters will therefore absorb much time and attention. In academic matters, the head's role is to decide strategy (for example, 'all pupils in the first year will have a broad curriculum with no subject choices'); few take direct responsibility for drawing up the timetable. But by close liaison with the director of studies the head can monitor the way strategy is being implemented, and where necessary referee the disputes that arise between academic departments.

The head's concern for pastoral and disciplinary matters will probably be an even more central preoccupation than the successful carrying out of academic policy. Though some heads delegate 'discipline' to a deputy, no-one involved with independent schools has any doubt that it is the head who is responsible and who should be blamed if discipline is bad. This situation is reflected in the fact that in most independent schools, the head will meet with the housemasters, who have responsibility for the discipline and pastoral care of a group of pupils, more regularly than with the academic heads of department. The responsibility of the housemaster or housemistress (or in a day school of the form master or mistress) has increased as the traditional role of the senior pupil in matters of discipline has been eroded. Many independent schools still have a structure of pupil prefects or monitors (the experiments with elected school councils that characterized the 1960s have mostly been abandoned), but these boys and girls now see their role as one of liaison between the head and the pupil body, and are generally reluctant to impose any but the most routine discipline. Every head of an independent school will be familiar with the tension between the prefects' concept of their role as 'spokesperson' for their peers, and the head's concept of their role as 'friendly neighbourhood policemen'. The role of senior pupils in the internal management and discipline of an independent school is an issue that has not been successfully resolved.

The internal management of an independent school has, therefore, certain distinctive features. The most important of these are the role of the bursar and the head's control of educational policy as well as of staff appointments and the admission of pupils. Freed from the need to deal with teachers' unions and local education offices, the heads of independent schools probably have more time and more inclination to adopt a personal style of leadership. But their freedom to decide priorities for expenditure is not as wide as is often thought. Though the extent of their power has echoes of enlightened despot-

458

ism, there is no divine right of heads, and they hold their office only as long as they continue to enjoy the support of the governing body.

Whatever differences there are between their role and that of their counterparts in the maintained sector, they share with all heads the same fundamental challenge – to develop the management and organization style that will bring out the best in both teachers and pupils.

FURTHER READING

Fox, I. (1985) *Private Schools and Public Issues: The Parents' View*, London: Macmillan.

Griggs, C. (1985) *Private Education in Britain*, London: Falmer Press.

Independent Schools Information Service (1987) *Annual Census Statistical Survey*, London.

Kalton, G. (1966) *The Public Schools: A Factual Survey*, London: Longman.

Percival, A. (1969) *The Origins of the Headmasters' Conference*, London: John Murray.

Rae, J. (1981) *The Public School Revolution, Britain's Independent Schools 1964–1979*, London: Faber.

Salter, B. and Tapper, T. (1985) *Power and Policy in Education. The Case of Independent Schooling*, London: Falmer Press.

Wakeford, J. (1969) *The Cloistered Elite: A Sociological Analysis of the English Public Boarding School*, London: Macmillan.

Walford, G. (Ed.) (1984) *British Public Schools: Policy and Practice*, London: Falmer Press.

(1986) *Life in Public Schools*, London: Methuen.

4.10

SIXTH-FORM AND TERTIARY COLLEGES

ERIC MACFARLANE

EDUCATION FOR THE 16–19 AGE GROUP

A major challenge recognized by most local education authorities (LEAs) since the 1960s has been the growing need to rationalize the educational provision for the 16–19 age group. The key factors contributing to this situation have been:

1. the development of comprehensive sixth forms that require a diversified curriculum;
2. the strain this has imposed upon the resources of most schools, particularly those with sixth forms of fewer than 100 students;
3. the widespread dissatisfaction with the very large school community that is usually required for a comprehensive school to produce a viable sixth form;
4. the desire of older teenage students for an adult, college-style environment.

Sixth-form and tertiary colleges are alternative ways of responding to the need to re-organize the 16–19 provision. The first sixth-form colleges opened in the late 1960s, followed by several tertiary colleges in the early 1970s. By 1989 there were 174 sixth-form and tertiary colleges in England and Wales. Others are planned or under serious consideration.

SIXTH-FORM COLLEGES

In 1989 there were 115 sixth-form colleges, accommodating 70,000 students and ranging in size from 250 to 1,300 students. The majority of these colleges have a student population near the average of 600. There are 50 LEAs with at least one college, but a quarter are concentrated in three large authorities: Hampshire (ten), Cleveland (nine) and Surrey (seven).

Sixth-form colleges are run under schools regulations. Most evolved from grammar schools at the time of the change-over from a selective to a comprehensive secondary school system. Some LEAs that originally established 11–18 comprehensive schools have subsequently changed to a system of 11–16 schools linked with one or more colleges. Staff are paid on the schoolteachers' salary scale and must have a teaching qualification. With very few exceptions students are all aged 16–19 and attend full time. The pattern of the academic year and length of the working day are similar to those for schools.

The central curriculum of the sixth-form college is academic, its characteristic feature being a wide range of General Certificate of Education (GCE) and General Certificate of Secondary Education (GCSE) work. The advanced level (A level) programme is of particular importance, catering for many minority as well as popular interests. It provides a choice between traditional and modern syllabuses, between pure and applied approaches to science and mathematics, between different aspects of complex subjects (periods of history, literary, and linguistic emphases to English etc.), and between familiar courses and new subjects such as communication studies and computer science. Academic excellence is a major objective and the colleges have maintained and often improved upon the examination and higher education entrance successes of the grammar schools from which they evolved.

The sixth-form college has the student numbers, timetabling flexibility, and range of staff expertise and experience in curriculum development to respond readily to new initiatives and changing circumstances. Thus an extensive programme of 'mature' GCSE syllabuses has replaced the previous range of GCE ordinary level (O level), alternative O level (AO level) and Certificate of Secondary Education/Certificate of Extended Education (CSE/CEE) courses. The colleges are also taking a lead in the introduction of the newly-devised additional supplementary level (AS-level) courses aimed at broadening A level students' examination work.

All but a handful of sixth-form colleges are open-access, admitting students of all abilities and backgrounds, including, in some instances, those with special needs such as the physically handicapped and young people with moderate learning difficulties. In response to the diverse needs of a comprehensive intake, the curriculum has been widened from its academic base to include a range of practical, pre-vocational, and even vocational courses. Commonly-found options are the commercial courses leading to the examinations of the Royal Society of Arts (RSA), Pitman Institute, and London Chamber of Commerce, and the Certificate of Pre-Vocational Education (CPVE) introduced in 1985 by the newly-formed Joint Board for Pre-Vocational Education. Most of these courses represent an incursion into further-education-style package options that are very different from the standard sixth-form college 'choice curriculum' from which students compile their own individual programmes of study.

So far the full range of vocational courses has been denied sixth-form colleges by examination board and validating body regulations and local agreements confining certain courses to existing further education (FE) colleges. Many such courses also require very expensive facilities that sixth-form colleges neither possess nor have the capacity to use cost-effectively. There is, in addition, a hesitancy on the part of the colleges themselves to proceed too far down the vocational path: whilst pre-vocational education, such as that embodied in the CPVE framework, fits quite well into their curricular philosophy, full-time training options, such as catering and hairdressing, do not.

The training function comes into sharp conflict with one of the most distinctive features of sixth-form colleges: their continuing commitment to the school role of providing a broadly-based general education. Thus, although students narrow the range of their specialist work in order to devote more time to the subject areas which they most enjoy, which they are most successful in, and which they require for their chosen careers, they are given many opportunities to combine subjects from across the curriculum, to devote time to non-examined courses of general interest, and to participate in the busy extra-curricular life offered by the colleges.

A prominent manifestation of this interest in providing students with a broad educational experience is to be found in the colleges' imaginative programmes of non-examination work, bearing designations such as 'liberal', 'humane', and 'personal development' studies, that owe much to Renaissance-style ideals of educating the whole person. In some institutions this work is raised to the status of 'main', 'core', 'foundation', or 'basic' studies, a deliberate inversion of the concept of general studies as an insignificant part of the sixth-form curriculum.

On these courses particular emphasis is often given to practical and creative activities and to participatory learning situations, offsetting what is seen as a more narrowly academic approach and passive student role in examination courses. The pioneering work that has gone into the creation of these general studies programmes has created an expertise in course design, material preparation, and innovatory teaching that is generally recognized to have had benefits for the management of the whole curriculum.

Students enter sixth-form colleges at 16 and for most of their course remain under 18. It is thus assumed that staff will retain at least a modified version of the schoolteacher's *in loco parentis* role. Nearly all full-time members of staff are likely to be 'personal' or 'group' tutors, working within a structured system of student care and guidance, under the leadership of a vice principal or several 'senior tutors'. The senior members of staff in charge of the care system usually combine this role with responsibility for liaising with the college's designated contributory schools, working closely with year and house heads and careers staff in the schools to inform and advise pupils on their college courses and to guide them through the admissions procedures. This exercise is recognized to be of great importance in enabling pupils to make a smooth transition from school to college.

Personal or group tutors have a dual responsibility for the progress and welfare of each individual student in their care and for developing a group identity which gives its members a sense of belonging, in what for some can be an intimidatingly large and complex institution. The tutor is the students' mentor, helping them meet the demands of their studies and college routines, and counselling in times of stress and difficulty. The advisory services of the school system provide specialist help if referral becomes necessary.

Control of students is less directive than in a school. The fact that everyone in a sixth-form college has chosen to be there removes the need for elaborate lists of rules and regulations. Attendance and work are seen to have a contractual basis: an understanding is reached between student and staff over what is a desirable level of study and an acceptable pattern of behaviour in a community of near-adults. Students are encouraged to assume responsibility for choosing, or at least negotiating, their own programme of study, for pacing their work, for making sensible use of private study time, and for playing a major part in organizing clubs, societies, and social events. At the same time staff are expected to monitor progress closely and to assume a strong advisory and supportive role in relation to extra-curricular activities and consultative councils, committees, and working parties. The role of the home is still felt to be important, and school-type parents' consultation evenings and reporting procedures are normal.

Much of the routine pastoral and advisory responsibility that members of staff take on has no contractual foundation. Their time is given on the basis of a long tradition of altruism within the schoolteaching profession which, until the protracted and often bitter industrial dispute of the mid-1980s, was accepted by teachers and largely taken for granted by parents and the general public. The introduction of more specific contracts for the schoolteaching profession has had implications for sixth-form colleges, but has not altered their fundamental commitment to the provision of a strongly supportive system for students making the transition from childhood to adulthood.

Where staff undertake major pastoral and advisory responsibilities, particularly those involving leadership roles, they receive incentive allowances in accordance with the 1987 schoolteachers' pay provisions. Most of these allowances, however, are reserved for the holders of head of department posts. Just like schools, colleges retain a multiplicity of such posts, although there are attempts to rationalize the structures for managing the curriculum in larger colleges by the establishment of faculties or integrated 'subject areas'. LEA secondary school subject advisers/inspectors provide a support service for departmental heads and their staff.

Sixth-form college governing bodies are constituted in the same way as those for schools, with equal representation for parents and LEA nominations. Co-opted members are likely to be drawn from industry, commerce, and institutions of higher education. Governors have ultimate responsibility for all aspects of a college's work and management.

Sixth-form colleges, like secondary schools, have been largely dependent upon centralized LEA administrative systems for their financial management. The 1988 Education Reform Act, however, required LEAs to transfer direct control of their annual budgets to the colleges and schools themselves, a process likely to be completed by the early 1990s. An important factor in allocating funds to colleges is the LEA's assessment of staffing needs in accordance with student numbers, as revealed by a January return to the Department of Education and Science (Form 7 Schools). The colleges are currently staffed on a staff-student ratio of between 1:11 and 1:14, according to the LEA.

TERTIARY COLLEGES

Tertiary colleges bring sixth-form and further education provision under one roof rather than presenting them as competing alternatives in separate institutions. The original concept was for a single college to be the sole provider of 16+ education in an area, thereby providing the ultimate in a cost-effective, fully comprehensive 'tertiary' system. In some large towns and cities, however, tertiary colleges have been developed as part of a more complex mixed system of 16–19 provision.

In 1989 there were 59 tertiary colleges, accommodating 60,000 full-time students. With an average of over 1,000 full-time students each, tertiary colleges are larger institutions than sixth-form colleges, although the average size is somewhat distorted by some very large colleges of nearly 2,500 students. Although the majority of students are in the 16–19 age group, others are older and classes may combine teenage and mature students. There are also well over 100,000 part-time students attending day and evening classes. The tertiary colleges are distributed among 29 LEAs with four accounting for over half of them – Sheffield (six), Lancashire (five), Hampshire (four), and Somerset (four).

Tertiary colleges are run under further education regulations. They have usually resulted from the absorbing of existing school sixth forms by colleges of further education, but some sixth-form colleges have become tertiary by expansion or merger with existing FE colleges. Staff are paid on the FE salary scale. Although the majority have a teaching qualification this is not a requirement, and a considerable number of staff have industrial or commercial experience. As well as running a three-session day, the colleges are open for most of the year.

Tertiary colleges offer the same academic courses as sixth-form colleges, but a considerably wider range of vocational options, including a variety of courses for part-time students. The opportunity exists to follow 'mixed economy' courses, combining elements that would have previously only been available in isolation, and colleges would like to see more of their students prepared to adopt this approach. Business and Technician Education Council (BTEC) and City and Guilds (C and G) courses provide full-time training opportunities for those wishing to work in the caring professions, in engineering and construction, and in the service industries, such as hairdressing, catering, and tourism. Individual colleges generate specialist courses which reflect local occupations and interests, such as agriculture or high technology, so that one college's provision may differ considerably from another's. The full-time academic and vocational courses for the 16–19 age group exist alongside provision for trainees on day or block release from employment, those following evening recreational and vocational courses, and school pupils on Technical and Vocational Education (TVE) link schemes. An important growth area has been created by the Manpower Services Commission (MSC) and its Youth Training Schemes (YTS).

The colleges appreciate the need to respond flexibly to such externally-initiated projects, not least because the latter provide a generous source of income. In addition to funding specific courses to meet their training needs, employers give assistance in the form of staff expertise, surplus equipment, and work experience opportunities. Consultation with employers is often a prerequisite for mounting vocational courses, and college departments frequently formalize this procedure by setting up advisory boards with strong employer representation. The tertiary colleges' service role in relation to industry and commerce means that, alongside their GCE A level and GCSE work, they are heavily committed to the development of an extensive utilitarian curriculum and a teaching programme that emphasizes employable skills. Non-examined general studies often receive less emphasis than in a sixth-form college; games are usually optional.

The staffing of a tertiary college is based on a November DES statistical return completed in accordance with an elaborate 'unit total' system of calculating students' participation hours, varying according to the status of students and the courses they are following. The number of short-term FE courses and a need for numerous small inputs of specialist work mean that part-time and temporary lecturers are an important part of the staffing arrangements. Full-time staff also have to be prepared to adjust to shifting emphases and changing demands throughout the year. High enrolment and close monitoring of student attendance are important to maintain course viability. Energetic marketing methods are employed as colleges seek to increase the staying-on rate of their contributory schools and departments compete for students.

The kind of staff contract towards which the schoolteaching profession is moving has long been a feature of FE regulations. Student contact hours are specific, varying according to a lecturer's salary grade. Overtime payments, or time off in lieu, are provided for additional commitments that take a member of staff over the prescribed maximum. Conditions of service and contractual rights and obligations have always been clearly laid down, and are still more precise than the newly-formulated teachers' contract. Union-management negotiating procedures are well-established, and staff have a strong voice on the academic board, an advisory and consultative body on which management and students are also represented. The academic board is particularly concerned with the development of the curriculum, but has wider responsibilities in some colleges. Governing bodies are often larger than those of sixth-form colleges, with stronger representation of industry and unions. The governors are expected to delegate substantial responsibility to the principal, and the detail of this delegation is clearly laid down.

The industrial model extends to staff-student relationships. All tertiary colleges have student unions, many of which are funded by LEA grants. Elected student officers represent the student body to the principal and senior management, and run a range of clubs, societies, and other social activities. A staff liaison officer is normally appointed to advise the student officers on financial and other administrative procedures, and to help maintain harmonious relationships between staff and students.

With the existence of an academic board, and active staff and students' unions, principals and senior management in a tertiary college have more closely-defined consultative and decision-making procedures to adhere to than their opposite numbers in a sixth-form college. Conversely, the control exerted by the LEA has been significantly less: from the outset, tertiary colleges have been responsible for their own administration and have had considerable discretion over how they spent their funds. This situation creates a need for a large administrative staff headed by a registrar. Tertiary colleges have a bigger budget than sixth-form colleges: they are larger, more complex organizations; many of their practical and technical courses incur a higher level of expenditure than academic subjects do; extra sources of funding are available, for example from industry and the MSC. In addition, extensive evening use of the premises by the local adult community justifies the provision of more sophisticated and wide-ranging facilities and resources.

The tertiary colleges have a large and growing investment in 16–19 education and are keen to ensure that their younger students receive appropriate care and attention. There is, as a consequence, a deliberate humanizing of the more formalized and politicized relationships and structures of the adult FE community. Staff from school backgrounds have often introduced a more supportive and protective attitude towards teenage students, which has helped

466

those unused to this age group to recognize their needs. The development of courses for the less able and those with special needs has contributed to this process.

Significantly, a growing number of colleges have introduced a matrix system of management to replace the traditional federal FE system in which students are admitted to a departmental course and function almost exclusively within its sub-culture. The matrix system allows for a college approach to admissions, publicity, timetabling, and guidance. Heads of department become 'directors' with college-wide management roles, or 'deans of study' overseeing broad groupings of allied subjects from which they assemble students' programmes of study in consultation with specialist teams of staff led by 'heads' of 'subject schools', 'divisions', or 'sections'. As well as being more appropriate for students seeking a broadly-based programme of studies, this system encourages both staff and students to identify with the whole college, which is part of the tertiary philosophy. The centralized admissions system is normally linked with a sixth-form college style of student care and guidance. Colleges usually appoint, in addition, a professionally-trained 'casualty' counsellor. A close relationship is sought with each of the designated contributory schools. All these attitudes and structures have been fostered and developed to create an environment responsive to the needs of students who in the past would have been sixth-formers in schools. They distinguish tertiary colleges from traditional FE establishments, although some of the latter are also moving in the same direction.

Sixth-form and tertiary colleges belong unmistakably to quite different traditions. Each type of institution is, however, consciously diverging from its origins: the sixth-form college dispensing with many school practices in favour of approaches more appropriate to an adult community, the tertiary college recognizing the need for more structured systems of care and guidance for its younger full-time students.

These converging paths lead many educationalists to hope that the two types of college will eventually be resourced and run under a single, newly-devised set of regulations that will remove existing anomalies and divisions, whilst allowing sufficient flexibility for the two types of college to retain their distinctive characters. In the meantime, sixth-form and tertiary colleges are still adapting to their roles, constantly changing and responding to the new demands being made of them. They are, as a consequence, frequently dynamic institutions characterized by lively educational debate and interesting curriculum development.

The steady development of sixth-form and tertiary colleges during the seventies and eighties has led to speculation that they would lead to the eventual demise of school-based sixth-forms. However, the declining influence of LEAs, brought about by the 1988 Education Reform Act, will make the reorganization of groups of schools to form two-tier secondary school systems much more difficult in the future.

FURTHER READING

Cantor, L. M. and Roberts, I. F. (1986) *Further Education Today: A Critical Review*, London: Routledge & Kegan Paul.

Cotterill, A. B. and Heley, E. W. (1981) *Tertiary, a Radical Approach to Post-Compulsory Education*, Bath: Stanley Thomas.

Council for Local Education Authorities (1985) *Conditions of Service for Schoolteachers in England and Wales*, London: CLEA.

Dean, J., Bradley, K., Choppin, B., and Vincent, D. (1979) *The Sixth-Form and its Alternatives*, Windsor: NFER.

Department of Education and Science (1988) *Education Reform Act*, London: HMSO.

Department of Education and Science and Associations of Local Education Authorities (1980) *Education for 16–19 Year Olds*, London: HMSO.

Further Education Unit (1985) *Signposts '85: A Review of 16–19 Education*, London: Longman.

Holt, M., Pring, R., and Whitfield, R. (1980) *The Tertiary Sector*, Sevenoaks: Hodder & Stoughton.

James, F., Kershaw, N., Austin, M., and Miles, J. (1985) *Going Tertiary: A Commentary on Secondary-Tertiary Reorganisation*, London: The Tertiary Colleges' Association.

King, R. Wearing (1968) *The English Sixth-Form College*, Bletchley: Pergamon Press.

Macfarlane, E. J. (1978) *Sixth-Form Colleges*, London: Heinemann.

National Joint Council for Teachers in Further Education in England and Wales (1981) *Conditions of Service for FE Teachers in England and Wales*, London: Local Authorities' Conditions of Service Advisory Board.

Standing Conference of Tertiary and Sixth-Form College Principals (1988) *Compendium of Sixth-Form and Tertiary Colleges*, London: SCOTVIC.

Watkins, P. (1982) *The Sixth-Form College in Practice*, London: Edward Arnold.

4.11

FURTHER EDUCATION COLLEGES

LEONARD CANTOR

THE CONCEPT AND DIMENSIONS OF FURTHER EDUCATION

The further education sector in England and Wales has, until recently, been commonly defined as comprising all forms of post-school education except the universities. It has normally been sub-divided into advanced further education (AFE) and non-advanced further education (NAFE), the former consisting of all courses leading to a final qualification above GCE A level or its vocational equivalent, and the latter consisting of courses leading to a final qualification up to and including GCE A level or its vocational equivalent. AFE, or public sector higher education as it has been commonly called, is mainly concentrated in two types of institution – polytechnics and colleges or institutes of higher education – which are dealt with in another chapter of this book. However, since the working out of the 1988 Education Reform Act, the polytechnics and major colleges of higher education have been transferred out of local education authority control and defined as higher education. As a consequence, further education now covers all other provision for those who have left school, which is virtually synonymous with what was formerly called non-advanced further education, and it is on the institutions which come into this category that this chapter will concentrate.

These are widely called colleges of further education or technical colleges and offer a broad range of programmes including those which are vocational in purpose, those which cater for general education, and a wide range of leisure and cultural activities. In addition, there is a limited number of specialist institutions like Colleges of Art and Colleges of Agriculture which offer courses covering a restricted vocational range. The general colleges of further education, or technical colleges, number about 600 in England and Wales, and a further 30 in Scotland, and cater principally for the sixteen-to-nineteen age group. In all, they annually provide for over three million students, the great

469

majority of whom are attending on a part-time basis. They are maintained by their respective local education authorities and are scattered throughout the country. In an increasing number of authorities, tertiary colleges – institutions which combine further education colleges and secondary school sixth forms – are being established as a result of demographic changes which are bringing about a declining sixteen-to-nineteen age group; however, for all practical purposes they are very similar to colleges of further education but are dealt with in a separate chapter. Finally, there is also a private sector of further education, made up of approximately 565 institutions, comparable in provision to maintained colleges of further education, and catering for over 450,000 students.

This chapter of the book will be concerned with examining the organization and management of a typical college of further education, maintained by a local authority. A medium-sized establishment of this kind will have perhaps 800 full-time and 3,000 part-time students, some 150 full-time and 200 part-time teaching staff, approximately 100 non-teaching staff, and a gross annual budget in excess of four million pounds. It will be one of the largest employers in the district and will handle a flow of people, including both students and public, greater than many other educational institutions of a comparable size.

The college's organizational structure is, to some extent, determined by its size, but traditionally the wide variety of subjects it offers and students it caters for have been reflected in a departmental structure. This has been reinforced by the fact that, until relatively recently, college curricula have been subject-based and vertically stratified, and because other educational institutions like schools and universities have also commonly been organized on a departmental basis. However, as subject areas in further education colleges are more broadly based than those in schools, collective forms of college departments have evolved, such as engineering, catering, general education, and business studies. A typical department will employ between 20 and 50 full-time staff, and probably a similar number of part-time staff, many of whom will only be employed for a few hours a week. Thus, in a college of this kind, the senior management team has consisted of a principal, a vice-principal, and perhaps six heads of departments, assisted by a senior administrative officer such as a registrar. This type of administrative organization has dominated the colleges in the post-war period since 1945 and, to a large extent, still does.

The key figure is, of course, the principal, who traditionally has tended to be 'all-powerful' within the college, though, as will be seen, in recent years his or her role has changed considerably. Principals have to work through and with their boards of governors who are charged with general responsibility for the direction of the college and its educational provision, and academic boards which advise on academic matters. In recent years, however, the colleges of further education have had to adjust to a rapidly changing environment and, as a consequence, many of them are evolving new management structures. To understand why this has become necessary, an examination of the ways in which the college environment has changed is needed.

THE CHANGING COLLEGE ENVIRONMENT

Further education colleges have always seen as their prime function the training of skilled personnel to meet the needs of the national economy. Consequently, the traumatic changes which have taken place in the last decade in the British economy have necessarily had a profound impact upon the colleges. The decline in manufacturing production and in heavy industries such as steel making and coal mining has resulted in the virtual collapse of the traditional apprenticeship system: for example, the number of apprenticeships in manufacturing has declined from a peak of 236,000 in 1968 to under 100,000 today. The effect on the traditionally important college departments such as engineering and science has been equally profound. In addition, existing apprenticeship schemes are being reformed and, as examples, the engineering and construction industries have developed skill-testing systems as integral parts of their programmes.

On the other hand, there has been a greatly increased demand for trained personnel in business and office skills, especially from the public sector, and as a result the business studies departments in many colleges have expanded greatly and are flourishing. Leisure and service industries have also grown apace, with a consequently increased demand for trained personnel, and courses in such areas as tourism and catering have, in many colleges, substantially increased. Last, but not least, the introduction of new technologies into industry and business, notably in the areas of automation, robotics, and the use of computers, micro-processors, and word processors has greatly increased the demand for staff with these specialist skills.

Another major area of change affecting the organization of the colleges of further education has been concerned with financial management. Until fairly recently, the colleges have derived the great bulk of their finance from their local education authorities who, on the whole, have allowed them a reasonable degree of room for manoeuvre in developing programmes and in accounting for expenditure. However, in recent years, policy has been increasingly directed in certain areas of public-sector further education by financial means, so that finance is only available to local education authorities if they pursue priorities consistent with those of central government. This development is perhaps best illustrated by changes in the funding of what is termed Work-Related Non-Advanced Further Education (WRNAFE), namely all the bread-and-butter technical and vocational courses in the colleges. Since the fiscal year 1985–6, 25 per cent of WRNAFE has been financed through the Manpower Services

Commission (MSC), renamed the Department of Employment Training Agency in 1988, and local authority rate support grants have been reduced by a corresponding amount. As a result, local authorities have had to produce both detailed 'development plans' covering three academic years, and also one-year 'programmes of courses' of WRNAFE, which are then submitted to the MSC for approval and are monitored by them. In the case of individual colleges, they have had to devote a great deal of time and effort to the preparation of individual development plans. In the words of one local authority to its further education colleges, '... MSC are holding some £2 m. of ours yearly. To get it back we have to provide a quite detailed justification for what we are doing. This justification will require the involvement of colleagues at all levels' (Nottinghamshire County Council, undated). In addition to its funding of one-quarter of WRNAFE, the Training Agency also funds other college-based programmes, notably those which form part of the Youth Training Scheme (YTS). As a result, in some colleges, as much as 40 per cent of their funds now come from the Training Agency, with all the bureaucratic procedures, including detailed monitoring, that are involved.

In real terms, the funds made available by local authorities to their colleges have decreased in recent years and, as a consequence, colleges have become increasingly entrepreneurial in seeking out industrial and business customers for their courses. Industry increasingly requires tailor-made courses, usually of relatively short duration, to meet specific needs, and colleges have not been slow to respond to this demand. As part of the college structure, each department in the college is likely to have its own advisory committee, made up of a majority of members from local industry and business, and a minority from the college itself. As the colleges have developed closer links with their immediate commercial and industrial environments, so the role of the advisory committees has become more important.

As a result of these various developments, the accountability of the colleges, both in terms of expenditures and also in the range and quality of provision, has grown considerably. Nowadays colleges find themselves increasingly accountable to a growing variety of outside bodies – their local authorities, the Training Agency, local industry, and a wide variety of clients – and with this increase in accountability has gone a greatly increased level of reporting, monitoring, and evaluation. In 1985, the Audit Commission of the Department of the Environment published its report on the way in which resources are utilized in the colleges, 'Obtaining better value from further education', and this, too, has resulted in initiatives to assess the efficiency of the colleges, including the establishment of a joint Department of Education and Science (DES)-local authority study group on the subject, and the adoption by some colleges and their local authorities of the further education management information system (FEMIS), a computer-assisted system designed by the Further Education Staff College to monitor the cost effectiveness of the colleges.

Another major development that has had a considerable impact upon the colleges in recent years has been the dramatic change in the nature of the student population. Once it consisted largely of 16–19-year-olds, attending specifically vocational courses on a part-time day release basis, usually well-motivated towards their studies, whose successful completion was an integral part of the apprenticeship system. Nowadays the colleges have to cater for a much wider ability range, including youngsters on such programmes as the YTS, some of whom have few, if any, academic qualifications, have been alienated from education, and are poorly motivated towards their college courses. In addition, there is a growing proportion of full-time students and of adults on retraining courses of one sort or another. Finally, the needs of students from ethnic majorities and of those with special needs have also to be catered for. The magnitude of these changing demands on college staff is such as to make the provision of programmes of in-service training and staff development a priority, and many colleges have developed their own programmes, sometimes in collaboration with local authority officers and advisers.

Finally, in some ways, the greatest changes in the organization of further education colleges have been brought about by curriculum developments. In the words of a Further Education Unit publication (Miller et al. 1986), 'The increase in the rate of curriculum innovation experienced by colleges in recent years can hardly be overstated.' This innovation has taken many forms: more than a decade ago, the introduction of the new Technician Education Council courses, replacing the former National Certificate/Diploma and City and Guilds technician level courses, had a marked effect on the colleges by involving in various forms of curriculum development many members of the teaching staff who had little or no previous experience of it.

More recently, other forms of curriculum innovation have taken place in the colleges, including programmes of vocational preparation such as YTS and the Certificate of Pre-Vocational Education (CPVE), courses of adult retraining, and new approaches to teaching and learning involving distance and open learning, the integration of on- and off-the-job learning, the development of core curricula, the adoption of modular structures, and the adoption of profile records of achievement. The development and introduction of such curricula have had profound implications for college structures and practices, which are increasingly being measured against the extent to which they support curricular provision. Many of the new curriculum developments cut across the traditional college departmental structure: for example, the adoption of the MSC's 'Occupational training families' as part of its YTS programmes, and the introduction of the CPVE, which introduces students to a wide range of broad occupational areas, both transcend departmental boundaries, and the same is true of the Technical and Vocational Educational Initiative (TVEI) which is beginning to have an increasing impact upon the colleges. These initiatives have accelerated the adoption of modular course structures with their implications for college organization.

Finally, recent government legislation and initiatives have also begun to effect substantial changes in the ways in which colleges are managed. The 1988 Education Act has required local education authorities to delegate financial and other powers to their further education colleges and to reform the size and composition of college governing bodies. Just how these changes will work out in practice still remains to be seen but there seems little doubt that the governing bodies of colleges will be much more responsible for managing their own budgets, including the appointment of staff (Kedney and Parkes, 1988). Their composition is also changing to ensure that at least half of their members will be representatives of industry and business. As a result of proposals included in the government White Paper of December 1988, 'Employment for the 1990s', there is a nationwide network of some one hundred Training and Enterprise Councils (TEC) being set up. Their membership will be dominated by representatives from business and industry and their prime function is to ensure that local training priorities are geared to their needs. As they are established, they will take over responsibility for programmes presently run by the Training Agency, such as YTS and the adult Employment Training Programme. During the next few years, one of the major responsibilities of senior college managers will be to establish close relationships with their local TECs, in order to ensure that colleges are fully contracted to provide training programmes.

To sum up, the high level of change and turbulence to which the further education colleges have been increasingly subject has caused them to examine their existing structures to see how far they can cope with such radical developments. The character of the institutional reorganization resulting from this is now examined.

THE INSTITUTIONAL REORGANIZATION OF FURTHER EDUCATION COLLEGES

As already stated, the most powerful and authoritative person in the further education colleges has been, and still largely remains, the principal. However, his or her role has, for a variety of reasons, changed considerably in recent years so that, in Richmond's words, 'The days of the entrepreneurial, autocratic principal, single-handedly directing a complex institution with inadequate lines of communication and management structure, have long since disappeared and neither will, nor should, re-emerge' (Richmond 1983). In the late 1960s, the DES sought to influence the colleges to adopt more democratic structures, and of particular significance was DES Circular 7/70 which recommended that members of the college teaching staff be represented on governing bodies and that, more importantly, academic boards be set up to advise the principal on 'the planning, co-ordination and development of the academic work of the college as a whole'. In practice, the extent to which academic boards play a significant role in making academic policy depends in large part on the attitude of the principal: some principals continue to exert authority much as they have always done, with the tacit consent of the academic board, while others delegate to the board much of their responsibility for the academic work of the college.

A more powerful force in diffusing the authority of the principal has been the growing complexity of the managerial task facing him or her. Colleges have grown in size and in variety of provision, as has the money spent on them. At the same time, successive governments have sought reductions in public expenditure, while placing greater emphasis on efficiency and productivity. This process has called for greatly increased managerial skills on the part of principals and, indeed, on the part of heads of department, to whom executive responsibility for their areas of responsibility has increasingly been delegated in recent years. As a consequence, the principal has in many cases become what Twyman (1985) calls 'the general manager', who sees himself or herself as the leader of a senior management team rather than as the sole manager.

As we have seen, a significant part of the growing complexity of the further education colleges has been due to the introduction of new programmes, such as YTS and CPVE, which cut across the traditional college boundaries. As they have come into the colleges, so it has become necessary to appoint co-ordinators whose task it is to ensure that all the departments concerned contribute to the courses, and who have therefore to negotiate for teaching and resources with the appropriate heads of department. At the same time, the facilities required by college teaching staff, such as computers, micro-processors, and audio-visual aids, have become more varied and more expensive. In order to ensure that these resources are used economically and efficiently, many colleges have created senior posts whose holders are responsible for the use of such facilities throughout the college. The much greater variety of students, of all ages, who now attend the colleges, has led to similar appointments with responsibility for student affairs and records.

In addition, the growing importance of staff development, to equip staff at various levels with the complex skills they increasingly require in areas such as curriculum development and financial management, has persuaded many colleges of the need to appoint a senior member with specific responsibility for promoting in-service training. And as the colleges have necessarily had to become more entrepreneurial and seek out customers in industry and business, so they have appointed persons with responsibility for marketing their courses.

Last but not least, the growth in the volume and variety of financial management with which the colleges have had to involve themselves has resulted in the appointment of persons with major co-ordinating roles in this area of administration, including the particularly complex matter of staff remuneration and conditions of service.

Although the tensions between the traditional departmental structure of the colleges and the introduction of college-wide structures are relatively long-standing, they have inevitably grown in recent years, with the result that, as Ferguson (1980) has put it, 'During the last few years there has been a relatively small but nonetheless significant move in further education to find alternatives to the traditional hierarchical structure based on departments', a move which has undoubtedly grown since he wrote those words. This has found extreme expression in a few colleges which have adopted the 'matrix', or 'functional director matrix', as it is sometimes called, form of college organization. A typical form of matrix structure consists of two branches: the first is made up of cognate subject areas, commonly called faculties or divisions, with responsibility for courses, time-tabling, the deployment of staff, and the care of students; and the second combines administrative groupings, often called 'schools', which are responsible for the utilization of resources such as equipment, the allocation of rooms, and the deployment of technicians. Thus, a two-way system is created, with one arm of the matrix being essentially academic and the other essentially administrative. The supporters of this system contend that it facilitates horizontal as well as vertical flow of information and work, that it is more flexible than the traditional departmental structure, and that it is more adaptable to the complex demands which are being placed upon the colleges.

But if the matrix system has its advantages, it also has corresponding disadvantages: among them are the accompanying network of time-consuming committees it seems to require, and the uncertainty and stress it places upon many members of the college teaching staff who lose the feeling of identity and security that comes from being a member of a department, and who are uncertain to whom they should turn to obtain a decision. As a result, few colleges have adopted the matrix system in its extreme form, and an increasing number are adopting a compromise between it and the departmental structure in the hope of combining the best features of each. For example, a typical college of further education in the Midlands is proposing to replace its present structure, which consists of seven departments, by one with three divisions, each representing a spectrum of subject areas and with subject sub-divisions within them. This would release four heads of department for major co-ordinating roles in such areas as student services, resources, marketing, and finance. In practice, the precise form of new organizational structures, as with the existing ones, will vary from college to college, according to what Harding

476

and Scott (1982) call 'strategic choice', namely the particular decisions made by principals and senior management teams in response to the specific circumstances of their colleges.

In conclusion, it is clear that the further education colleges are going through a period of complexity, confusion, competition and change, a situation which is likely to continue into the foreseeable future. Indeed, the greatest challenge facing the colleges is the management of change itself. If this is to be accomplished successfully, it will require a positive and flexible response from college staff, and in particular from senior management teams. To this end, the identification of management training needs and the provision of appropriate programmes of training are crucial to their future success.

FURTHER READING

Advisory Council on the Supply and Education of Teachers, Further Education Teachers Sub-Committee (1984) *Report of the Education Management Working Group*, London: Department of Education and Science.

Alsop, M. (1986) 'Non-advanced further education', *Physics Education*, 21:328–32.

Cantor, L. and Roberts, I. (1986) *Further Education Today: A Critical Review*, London: Routledge & Kegan Paul.

Ferguson, C. (1980) *Alternative Structures in Higher and Further Education*, Blagdon, Bristol: Further Education Staff College.

Harding, P. and Scott, G. (1982) 'Management structures in colleges of further education', *Educational Management and Administration*, 10:50–3.

Hollyhock, R. (1982) 'The college in its environment', *The Changing Face of FE*, December, pp. 27–30, London: Further Education Unit.

Kedney, B. and Parkes, D. (Eds.) (1988) *Planning the FE Curriculum: Implications of the 1988 Education Reform Act, Perspectives from Administrators and Managers*, London: Further Education Unit.

Miller, J., Turner, C., and Inniss, S. (1986) *Preparing for Change: The Management of Curriculum-Led Institutional Development*, London: Further Education Unit.

Nottinghamshire County Council (undated) *Work Related NAFE, MSC – And You*, Nottingham: Advisory and Inspection Service.

Richmond, A. (1983) Foreword to 'The role of the college principal', *Coombe Lodge Reports*, 15 (10): 387.

Theodosin, E. (1986) *Management Restructuring in an FE College*, Blagdon, Bristol: Further Education Staff College.

Twyman, P. (1985) 'Management and leadership in further education', in Meredydd Hughes, Peter Ribbins, and Hywel Thomas (Eds.) *Managing Education: The System and the Institution*, Eastbourne: Holt Saunders.

Waitt, I. (Ed.) (1980) *College Administration: A Handbook*, London: National Association of Teachers in Further and Higher Education.

Williams, G. and Woodhall, M. (1979) *Independent Further Education*, London: Policy Studies Institute.

4.12

HIGHER EDUCATION INSTITUTIONS

DEREK BIRLEY

THE TWO SECTORS OF HIGHER EDUCATION

The Education Reform Act 1988 marks a further stage in the United Kingdom's slow and somewhat erratic progress towards a unified system of higher education. The underlying causes of the prevailing differences and divisions are social and historical. About half the full-time students are in fifty-three universities, collectively known as the private sector despite generous public funding from the University Grants Committee (UGC), the rest in some 500 institutions – thirty polytechnics, fourteen Scottish central institutions, forty-three direct grant or voluntary colleges and over 400 other colleges – known as the public sector. Of these, mostly funded through local education authorities or directly by central government, only about eighty are mainly concerned with advanced work. The dominant interest of almost all is vocational education and training, a concept with which universities are relatively unfamiliar. Similarly most of the part-time courses, for people already working, wanting to get on in their present posts, re-train, or find a new job after unemployment, are in public sector institutions. In the private sector the main contribution has been made by the Open University, which opened in 1970–1, and one or two individualistic institutions.

Since the Robbins Report – of which more later – expansion of the public sector has proceeded apace despite (i) the creation of new universities and the conferment of university status on a significant number of large colleges, and (ii) a drop of some 98,000 in number of teacher training students between 1973–4 and 1983–4. The pattern of development was as follows:

Students in higher education (figures in '000s)

UNIVERSITY	65/66	70/71	75/76	80/81	85/86	86/87
Full-time	173	235	269	307	310	316
Part-time*	13	23	26	33	42	45
NON-UNIVERSITY						
Full-time	133	222	247	228	290	297
Part-time	110	121	137	192	217	234

* excluding Open University (20,000 in 1970–71; 80,000 in 1986–7)

The traditions of governance in the universities, reflecting their creation by Royal Charter or Act of Parliament, are based on the authority of their senates – committees drawn from the academic staff – loosely responsible to *ad hoc* councils or courts led by prominent lay people. Universities' decision-making is collegial and their senior officers, though latterly thrust into managerial postures, still tend to set great store by academic and amateur values. The English universities' highest office, Chancellor, is unpaid: it is held by a distinguished person who presides on ceremonial occasions and formally exercises power to award degrees, but whose other duties are optional and undefined. Hence the customary title of the chief academic and administrative officer in English universities is not President as in the USA, Rector, as in Europe, or Principal, as in Scotland, but Vice-Chancellor. Historically the preferred leadership style of Vice-Chancellors has been that of primus inter pares, a concept nowadays sometimes at odds with the realities of managerial responsibility. Similarly the traditional tendency of university professors, powerful in committees and in the protection of academic values and freedoms, to regard managerial posts such as Dean of Faculty or Head of Department as unworthy of full-time attention, even if they hold them, is increasingly being put to the test.

This contrasts with the traditions of the public sector. Characteristically the colleges created by local education authorities or by technical or professional initiative are controlled by management committees set up by the parent body. These committees in turn delegate power to internal academic boards, which, unlike university senates are not free to award their own degrees but must seek external validation or accreditation. The official collective name for heads of colleges is still the old-established 'principal', but as the colleges concerned with advanced work have themselves taken on grander or more specialized titles so have their leaders. Thus the heads of polytechnics, created in the 1960s as local authority counterparts to the universities, were known generally as directors, expressing the current emphasis on organization, logistics and control. Many of them, however, coming from universities, preferred more traditional academic titles such as 'Rector', 'Provost' or even 'President'. The managerial structure of most colleges initially reflected the chain of command of local government, and though they have since made changes, some of which – like the appointment of professors – were once thought radical, the limitations of national salary scales, negotiated separately from universities, and applicable to a very wide range of institutions, have tended to emphasize managerial rather than academic values.

Local government control, which had social as well as operational connotations for higher education, was a central factor in the formal articulation of the binary system propounded by the Labour government's Secretary of State for Education in 1967. It was not something new, he declared, but the embodiment of two distinct traditions which had 'been developing steadily since the turn of the century'. The subsequent governmental preference for 'steady development' instead of stated, thought-out policy has only recently been set aside and then only partially. The extent of this continuing bipartisan political support for a hierarchical and by now artificially divided system illustrates how much deeper than the turn of the present century are the roots of the binary divide.

THE PRIVATE SECTOR LEGACY

The name and social status of the private sector stem from times when universities were not dependent on public funding. Oxford and Cambridge predate by some six hundred years the first government grants to universities in 1889. In the past their private wealth was not always well directed and the quality of their scholarship and their prestige not always matched by open-mindedness or innovation. The first Scottish Universities – St. Andrews, Glasgow, Aberdeen, and the late sixteenth century Edinburgh – were slightly more enterprising but much less influential. Britain's failure to take advantage of her early lead in industrial development through technological education reflected the preference of Oxford and Cambridge for humane studies.

It was not until the nineteenth century that the university circle was widened, and then only fitfully. The new ventures had mixed parentage: London began as a joint stock enterprise; St David's Lampeter was a college for training Welsh clergy; and Durham was founded by a Cathedral Chapter to ward off attacks on their wealth. The 'redbrick' urban colleges which aspired towards university status later in the century were founded by civic enterprise and local philanthropy. This encouraged a climate of opinion in which locally-relevant specialized studies, scientific, technological, industry-oriented, could be developed, and Manchester in particular was greatly and beneficially influenced by the methods and achievements of German institutions (Green, 1969). An equally important factor, however, in most 'redbricks' – as in London and Durham – was the development of medical schools, a major source of students and eventually of social esteem. The professions were the chief destination of university graduates.

The new institutions were to a large extent moulded by the old. London University's decision in 1858 to cease to require attendance at its constituent colleges for the award of a degree turned it into first a metropolitan and then a national examining body: students in colleges that had no charter of their own took London external examinations. The abiding influence, though, was that of Oxford and Cambridge, overtly through the extension lecture movement, but principally through the diffusion of their values and methods of teaching by the professors they supplied for the new creations and for London staff.

In 1900 the university population was some 20,000. Charters were granted more freely in late Victorian and Edwardian times but with no great expansion of numbers: Wales (1893) struggled for many years and Belfast (1908) was scornfully described by a local newspaper as the smallest in the United Kingdom. In England Birmingham (1900) and Bristol (1909) developed from local colleges; Liverpool (1903), Leeds (1904), and Sheffield (1905) were breakaways from the Manchester-led Victoria university federation. The new universities did not yet compete much for students, most of whom lived locally – halls of residence were a rarity – but they soon began to compete for government funding, such as it was. It had begun reluctantly and modestly and was still only £25,000 a year in 1900. The calls of socialists like Sidney Webb for state aid on twenty times that scale were out of step with the laissez-faire notions of the time, as was the inclusion of the 'higher technical colleges' in his proposals.

The First World War was a turning point in popular education. However, the pattern of institutional provision was slow to change. The universities benefited greatly from an increase in scholarships from both central and local government, and from the channelling of government funds for scientific and industrial research through Research Councils. The UGC, excluded from the domain of the Board of Education to prevent political interference, was set up in 1919 with £1 million to disburse. Oxford and Cambridge, which had earlier remained aloof, came into the fold, retaining their pre-eminence through continued superior private endowment, but increasingly impelled to innovation, as in the provision of degrees of doctor of philosophy which the provincial universities had started to offer, at government behest, in face of German and American competition.

Recession soon cast its shadow. Only one university college, Reading, gained a charter (1926) in the inter-war years, though two new ones, Leicester and Hull, were founded by local enterprise. Conversely the potential of public sector technical education, not well served by the 1918 Education Act, began to be looked at more seriously in the years of recession. Committees and co-ordination of local voluntary effort rather than public investment were the main immediate results, but the Board of Education initiated, in association with professional bodies, a system of national certificates and diplomas, advanced qualifications that were relevant to industry and which also gave a greater share in planning and greater discretion in teaching to the technical institutes. But the gap between the two sectors was wide. The university degree retained its pre-eminence, and for the small number of full-time and day-release as well as the bigger number of evening students in technical colleges, the London external degree was the pinnacle. Industry for its part was still a small and relatively unconsidered employer of full-time university graduates compared with the professions.

ERA OF EXPANSION AND CONTRACTION

In the post-war welfare state after 1945, the context, for nearly thirty years, was of assumed economic growth which allowed expanded higher education facilities without reference to specific industrial or commercial relevance. A second batch of civic universities, Nottingham (1948), Southampton (1952), Hull (1954), Exeter (1955), and Leicester (1957), received charters, as did Keele (1949), which deliberately set out to counter modern trends towards specialization.

Meanwhile, however, the public sector began to develop its own, more utilitarian measures of excellence. In 1955 a National Council for Technological Awards (NCTA) was set up as a mechanism for approving selected courses leading to a Diploma in Technology (DipTech). This seemed to have great possibilities and to be likely to suit industry. In 1957 in pursuit of a newly-declared government policy of concentrating resources, a number of institutions were designated Colleges of Advanced Technology (CATs), and became funded directly by central government, thus removing the caste-mark of local government control. Other caste-marks remained, however. The capacity to award degrees was still the exclusive prerogative of the universities, which therefore retained social and educational cachet. The DipTech attracted much less attention than the government's plans for new 'whitebrick' universities, county foundations mostly remote from large centres of population, set up on the lines of Keele, with an eye to innovative curricular variations rather than industrial, commercial, or vocational relevance. Sussex (1961) was followed by York and East Anglia (1963), Essex and Lancaster (1964), Kent and Warwick (1965), Stirling (1966), and the New University of Ulster, Coleraine (1967).

Local government aspirations strongly influenced the emerging new pattern of advanced further education in the public sector. The influence was largely political; but it was also a matter of administrative convenience. The Ministry of Education, without adequate machinery or tradition, had not found it easy to administer the CATs. When in 1961 the National Council for Art and Design was set up on the model of the NCTA, with its own National Diploma qualification, local education authorities retained control of the colleges chosen to offer it. And in 1962 the introduction of a 75 per cent Ministry grant for advanced further education courses stimulated rapid expansion in the new group of colleges that the LEAs cherished as the pinnacle of their educational services.

However, for many young people and their parents the status of the institution mattered more than the subject of study. As the universities expanded, pre-war class and income divisions were modified to accommodate an emergent meritocracy with an assumed entitlement to a degree. Following the Anderson Report of 1961 maintenance grants according to parental income were given to all qualified students who gained a place on a degree course, regardless of subject. This greatly enhanced the prospects of the new 'white-brick' universities. In 1963 the Robbins Report spelled out the hitherto implicit policy of social demand as the criterion for higher education provision and further emphasized the priority given to full-time study for 18-year-old school-leavers.

Between 1961–2 and 1967–8 the full-time student population in Britain went up from 193,000 to 379,000. Not surprisingly most of the increase was in universities – from 110,000 to 200,000, compared with a rise from 38,000 to 66,000 in further education colleges. The figures were distorted by the elevation of the CATs and their Scottish counterparts to university status after the Robbins Report – Aston, Bath, Bradford, Brunel, City, Heriot-Watt, Loughborough, Salford, Surrey, and Strathclyde. But the statistical shift emphasized the social nature of the change, underlined by the decision of the new 'technological universities' to offset the qualifying adjective by not only forsaking the DipTech in favour of degrees, but also abandoning their other industrially-oriented certificate and diploma work to the public sector.

Industrial recession and political realism later sharply challenged the Robbins principle of entitlement to higher education regardless of economic and vocational relevance. At the time, however, critics were more concerned with the quantitative implications of the Report's call for an even greater expansion of the universities. Traditionalists vociferously argued that more must inevitably mean worse, both of teachers and taught. They looked down on technology and askance at the burgeoning social sciences. Reformers wanted wider access to educational opportunity and saw social science as a key to unlock many doors.

The reforms of the Labour Government of 1964, which came in on a narrow majority after 13 years in opposition, were tempered by pragmatism, modifying Robbins but leaving its principle and its values intact. The chief effect of their changes was to emphasize public sector development within the existing local authority framework. They called a halt to university expansion beyond what was in the pipeline – the elevation of the CATs and the launching of the 'whitebricks'. Instead of giving university charters to the fifteen local authority higher technical colleges who were next on the list, the government devised a new and somewhat larger category of polytechnics. These were to be formed by the amalgamation of existing technical, commercial, and art colleges to provide not only degree but sub-degree courses, part-time as well as full-time, and they were to work closely with industry, business and the professions. They would remain under local authority control and their qualifications would be nationally validated. At sub-degree level this meant chiefly scrutiny by the evolving Business and Technician Education Councils (since amalgamated) (BTEC) and at degree-equivalent by a myriad of professional bodies. For degrees, the new Council for National Academic Awards (CNAA) proposed by Robbins would operate a sort of collective charter. There were complementary arrangements in Scotland – where monotechnics, headed by fourteen with 'central institution' status, were still preferred – and in Northern Ireland, which set up a college that was intended to do advanced but not degree work.

The Labour Government also rejected the Robbins recommendation that the teacher training colleges, administered by local education authorities or by voluntary agencies, should become part of the university sector. These institutions, to be known as colleges of education, had from humble beginnings attained higher social, if not academic status than most technical colleges. They had also more than doubled their size – to over 100,000 students – to meet the demands of a substantial increase in the birthrate, and by 1967 represented some two thirds of the full-time students in the public sector.

This gave rise to new administrative and political expedients in the 1970s. The preponderance of teacher-training students in the public sector continued to the middle of the decade despite the increased range of opportunity offered by the CNAA. But as the tidal wave of increased population spent itself the demand for teachers decreased. The colleges of education were given the new challenge of converting teaching to an all-graduate profession with longer courses of study. Yet there remained the embarrassing prospect of possible closures. To avert this they were encouraged to diversify – either alone, by absorption into universities or polytechnics, or by amalgamation with other colleges of education or colleges of further education – offering degrees not only in teacher education but in whatever subjects they could, to be validated either by the CNAA or by local universities.

The new ventures, introduced in 1976, known as institutes or colleges of higher education, aroused much anxiety in the polytechnics, who saw them as a threat to their own supremacy within the public sector. Precedence was now doubly important since the special funding arrangements for advanced further education had been transmuted into more restrictive pooling arrangements, and money – for everything – was tight, as the recession and inflation took firm hold. The polytechnics also looked askance at events which, under the guise of teacher-training re-organization, expanded liberal arts courses at the very time when the Prime Minister, James Callaghan, was launching a 'Great Debate' about the drift away from science and technology.

The universities' chief concern in the later 1970s was the government's introduction of cash limits which reduced the value of their quinquennial UGC funds by some four per cent. The Vice-Chancellor of Cambridge warned that university departments might be forced to close – an early wolf cry that showed how ill-prepared anyone was for the realities to come. Some argued for the expansion of education as an antidote to recession, but this begged the question of how much of higher education was relevant to such purposes. In fact the earlier projections of students were being steadily reduced: in 1970, 835,000 full-time students by 1981; in 1974, 650,000; in 1976, 600,000; in 1977, 560,000. (The actual total achieved was 550,000.) Numbers, on both sides of the argument, seemed to be all that mattered. A 1978 discussion paper produced by Gordon Oakes, the Minister for Higher Education, whilst purporting to offer alternative plans for the future, was in fact preoccupied with numbers and was submerged in a welter of debate about demography and participation rates. Its most popular option foresaw continued expansion through taking more working-class, mature and part-time students. The general preference for this amongst academics seemed to be clutching at straws, in view of the built-in bias of the existing system against such developments.

1979 AND AFTER

The pace of calls for change, if not for change itself, increased rapidly with the advent in 1979 of a Conservative Government, headed by a former Secretary of State for Education, Margaret Thatcher. Her determination to eliminate inflation and reduce inefficiency required everyone to stop and be counted, and the experience for higher education was salutary. The government's relations with the universities became particularly strained, largely because it attempted to introduce new policies and economies simultaneously, and to do so through machinery which had hitherto dealt with nothing but varying levels of expansion. Now there came, in succession, a freeze on expansion; a policy of 'level funding' with no compensation for the misguided decision to charge full-cost fees to overseas students; actual cuts which showed the UGC to be effective neither as cushion nor axeman; and an expensive premature retirement scheme which failed to achieve planned reductions in staff or indeed to evoke any serious interest in planning for contraction.

485

The public sector, though it enjoyed no golden age, was better able to respond, because more attuned, to calls for greater productivity. The new colleges and institutes of higher education, furthermore, had made the most of their opportunities, illustrating that institutional initiative counts for more in the British system than do doctrinaire policies. A 1987 White Paper announced that, after some decline in the late 1970s, the polytechnics and colleges had accounted for nearly all the 84,000 increase in full-time students and three quarters of the 72,000 increase in part-time students, despite a reduction of some 15 per cent in unit costs compared with five per cent in the universities. Nor was this uncontrolled expansion. In 1983 the government had set up a National Advisory Board (NAB) to co-ordinate policies and allocate resources in public sector higher education. NAB had no responsibility for validation, but its appearance was a corrective to the drift of the CNAA towards the role of spokesman for the public sector. It also favoured programme planning rather than individual course approval, in which Her Majesty's Inspectorate (HMI) shared responsibility with the validation bodies. Above all, though the Board had a local authority majority, it much reduced the power of the local authorities both individually and collectively, and paved the way for greater institutional autonomy.

By now the private sector's days were numbered. The Government's 1985 Green Paper went further than ever before in the direction of intervention in higher education. In particular it looked to universities to foster science and technology in support of entrepreneurism, to eschew snobbery about business, and to contribute more to the flagging economy. It specifically challenged the Robbins principle, indicating that arts subjects, which could only be afforded if the country were prosperous, ought to achieve high excellence and be ultra-selective if they sought public funding. Outside funding was commended for both teaching and research, in which selectivity was to be the watchword.

The Chairman of the UGC, Sir Peter Swinnerton-Dyer, had the unenviable task of straddling the divide between the universities and the Government. His attempt to restore credibility and introduce openness to the universities' funding and planning was courageous and constructive. But realities are unpalatable and unfortunately his chosen methods, relying heavily on mathematical formulae, were open to the charge of over-sophistication whilst failing to address fundamentals. Essentially UGC's new policies of selectivity in research seemed likely to strengthen existing hierarchical assumptions, allowing little scope for innovation.

By this time, of course, the ambiguity of the UGC's role was in the spotlight. It manifested itself in the various exhortations to better management and planning and to improving quality that began to emanate from the uneasy alliance between the UGC and the Committee of Vice-Chancellors and Principals. It was not clear whether these were likely to achieve results or merely put up a smoke-screen. The government took no chances, but instituted a high-level review of the UGC itself, a committee chaired by Lord Croham, a former Head of the Civil Service, and announced within a month of publication that they were able to accept the 'broad thrust' of its recommendations, notably in agreeing that the UGC should be led in future by someone from outside the university world, and should have a stronger industrial element in its membership.

The White Paper that announced this decision departed significantly from Croham's recommendations. In other ways, however, the Government had already rejected as 'impractical' the notion of an 'over-arching body' to co-ordinate the public and private sectors, and it now rejected Croham's insidiously milder version – a United Kingdom Education Commission: it was sceptical of the value of purely advisory bodies, and considered that the DES could do what was needed i.e. service the Government's decision-making process. Furthermore it proposed that the UGC be replaced by a University Funding Council with a more interventionist role based on 'contracting with' the universities for approved programmes of work.

While retaining the binary division the government – belatedly rejecting the term 'private sector' as 'unhelpful' and 'misleading' – proposed a parallel Polytechnics and Colleges Funding Council with similar powers, to 'contract with' the 29 polytechnics, 28 local education authority colleges of higher education and some 25 voluntary or other institutions in England with a large proportion of advanced work. Wales would retain its existing Advisory Board, and Scottish proposals for a separate transbinary body would be modified. Northern Ireland's innovation in 1984, ending the binary system and serving the Province by two universities, was recorded with apparent approval but no discussion. Local authorities would lose their political control and administrative and financial involvement, which the Government deemed to be restrictive. The NAB would be dissolved.

That these proposals have been translated into Parliamentary action with remarkably little fuss and are at the time of writing on the brink of implementation illustrates how out-moded the existing system had become. Early discussion of the implications of 'contracting' as a method of financing educational discussions, has given way to concern about the practical and financial readiness of the new PCFC colleges, hampered as they have sometimes been by the LEAs from whom they have been severed, to face the demands of independent status. Instances are regularly reported of attempts by groups of institutions to band together for strength in order to contend with the new arrangements. So far these mainly involve institutions in the old 'public sector'. Social attitudes and consequent local and personal antipathies have so far prevented much trans-binary re-grouping.

Optimists profess to see the presently emergent arrangements as the prelude to a truly unified higher education system. Realists, hoping for the best, point out that if this is to come about then the initiative lies with the institutions. If universities in particular want to protect their proper independence and yet respond to social imperatives it is up to them to take the lead in dismantling artificial barriers and make common cause with the colleges not only against the perceived immediate enemy (bureaucratic and political interference) but against the real one – ignorance and elitism.

FURTHER READING

Carter, C. (1980) *Higher Education for the Future*, Oxford: Basil Blackwell.

Crowther-Hunt, Lord (1983) 'Policy-making and accountability in higher education', in Shattuck, M. (Ed.) *The Structure and Governance of Higher Education*, London: Society for Research into Higher Education.

Great Britain, Department of Education and Science (1965) *Higher Education in Northern Ireland* (The Lockwood Report), London: HMSO.

(1978) *Higher Education into the 1990s*, London: HMSO.

(1982) *Higher Education in Northern Ireland – the Future Structure*, London: HMSO.

(1982) *The Future of Higher Education in Northern Ireland* (The Chilver Report), London: HMSO.

(1987) *Higher Education : Meeting the Challenge*, London: HMSO.

(1987) *Review of the University Grants Committee*, London: HMSO.

Green, V. H. H. (1969) *The Universities*, Harmondsworth: Penguin Books.

Kogan, M. and Kogan, D. (1983) *The Attack on Higher Education*, London: Kogan Page.

Law, H. D. (1976) *Polytechnics: The Reality*, paper presented to the British Association for the Advancement of Science, London, September.

Robbins, Lord (1980) *Higher Education Revisited*, London: Macmillan.

Robinson, E. (1968) *The New Polytechnics: A Radical Policy for Higher Education*, London: Cornmarket.

4.13

ORGANIZATION DEVELOPMENT IN EDUCATIONAL INSTITUTIONS

BERTIE EVERARD

THE CONCEPT OF ORGANIZATION DEVELOPMENT

Organization development (OD) played a significant part in getting a man on the moon. TRW Systems, which built the lunar module, used OD to ensure effective co-operation between its engineering teams. Imperial Chemical Industries (ICI) practised OD over a period of 20 years to improve its effectiveness; so have other complex organizations, both commercial and public service. Despite the obviously growing complexity of the education service and its institutions, however, the use of OD in education is still in its infancy in the UK. The time is ripe to adopt an OD approach here, too, as many educational institutions in North America and Scandinavia have done.

OD is not an easy concept to describe. It is best seen as a complex cluster of ideas, philosophy, a way of life, values, skills, approaches, and techniques, underpinned by theory but essentially pragmatic. It is principally concerned with:

1. the people in the organization and how they work together;
2. what the organization and the community expect of people and how they respond;
3. the philosophy of management and how it affects the way people work;
4. the organization as a whole in its wider setting.

If there is one simple aim of OD, it is to improve organizational *effectiveness*, by systematically identifying and changing whatever is inhibiting effectiveness. Hence OD provides a 'technology' for improving organizations and the quality and purposefulness of working life within them. A characteristic of OD is that subsystems like institutions and faculties are always viewed in the context of the total system. So it deals with environments, markets, society, and political pressures, as well as with the motivations of individuals within the system. Everything along the 'organizational dimension' is potentially included: individual behaviour, classroom behaviour, departmental performance, school ethos, local education authority (LEA) systems, Department of Education and Science regulations, and the government's attitude to the allocation of resources. All of these interact in a complex way. An institution cannot be isolated from its setting; therefore *open* systems theory applies. In practical terms, this means that a manager of an institution may often find himself or herself working *outside* its boundaries, in order to modify conditions in the external environment in the interests of the institution.

Another characteristic is that OD tries to address itself to what *actually* happens. It is grounded in accurate observation of organizational phenomena, viewed as objectively as human frailty allows. Not only are cause-and-effect relationships examined, as in the physical sciences, but also purpose-and-outcome relationships. Indeed, outcomes and results, both desired and actual, are brought sharply into focus; inputs and activities are always assessed in relation to them. There is no other way in which effectiveness can be measured. So training for OD includes objective-setting skills, which many academics and teachers find difficult.

The word *problem*, and the process of *problem solving*, are central concepts in OD. A problem exists when the situation we are now in differs from the situation we would rather be in. Problem solving is about how we get from one to the other. In an organization run on OD lines, effort is regularly applied to uncovering and articulating what organizational problems seem to exist, and analysing what they really are (i.e. trying to pinpoint possible causes rather than just describing symptoms). Analysis is then followed by creative synthesis of a solution. A *systematic approach* is used (explained below).

A difference between OD and a purely rational approach is that it is associated with certain values: the liberal ones of humanistic psychology, the personal growth movement, democratic management, the primacy of individuals, the tolerance of differences, and 'doing one's own thing'. Quality of life, job satisfaction, and personal development are all seen as prime targets for improvement.

These are indeed desiderata in building healthy organizations. However, organizational as well as individual requirements have to be met. These become more salient in conditions of contraction rather than growth. OD has to deal constructively with hard issues like strategy, resource allocation, value for money, and the realities of power in organizational life. It has to help bureaucracies and hierarchies to work better. True, there may be more desirable forms of organization, such as one in which everyone has an equal share of power; but OD practitioners who want to subvert existing forms and replace them with others tread on dangerous ground. Idealism and reality have to co-exist. Successful OD is essentially pragmatic and functional rather than ideological; its exponents see individuals and organizations as interdependent. Problem solving is likely to consist of seeking trade-offs between the two, so that both benefit.

OD has other associations too. A snapshot of OD taken in the late 1950s, when the term originated, would have in the background applied behavioural science, group therapy, T-group or sensitivity training, managerial grids, group dynamics, process consultancy, and organizational climate inventories. In the 1960s, theories of motivation, job enrichment, team-building, organizational renewal, and socio-technical systems came into view. In the 1970s, open-systems planning, management of change, action learning, assessment centres, development training, and the use of psychometric tests emerged. By the 1980s, the concepts of quality and competence came to the fore, and there were signs that the very title 'OD' might give way to 'HRD' – human resource development. In the context of educational institutions, OD may arrive in the guise of curriculum development or with the advent of an Education Reform Act. Not only is OD a complex cluster of related ideas, but the pattern and saliency of the ideas has been changing over time. OD means different things to different people; there is a gap between how full-time practitioners conceive it and what non-practising academics write about it.

In these circumstances, it can be misleading to offer a definition, though definitions abound. In 1969 Bennis defined OD as 'a response to change, a complex educational strategy, intended to change the beliefs, attitudes, values and structures of organisations'; and Beckhard (1969) wrote: 'OD is an effort, (1) planned, (2) organisation-wide and (3) managed from the top, to (4) increase organisational effectiveness and health through (5) planned interventions in the organisational processes, using behavioural science knowledge'.

However, this is too tidy; OD in real life can be haphazard, be managed from anywhere, and thrive in pockets of the organization without the rest of it knowing what is going on. Thus one of the best-researched books on OD in action, Pettigrew's *The Awakening Giant: Continuity and Change in ICI* (1985), runs to 540 pages, yet most of the action passed some senior directors by.

A corollary of the difficulty of conceptualizing OD is that there is plenty of scope for making untrue statements about it, such as

'We have always practised OD in this school.'
'No OD goes on in this LEA.'
'OD is bound to undermine management; it will lead to anarchy.'
'OD may work in industry, but not in educational institutions; they are different.'
'OD is a "con"; it achieves nothing.'
'OD is nothing but common sense.'

The wise manager needs to approach OD with an open mind and work hard to grasp its significance and utility for the improvement of effectiveness in his or her institution.

A RATIONALE FOR OD

The *first* proposition is that there is always a better (i.e. more effective) way of doing something. Perfection may elude us, but it is there. This applies to educating people, organizing an educational institution, managing its staff, running a staff meeting, influencing an LEA, and indeed dealing with every aspect of organizational life.

Second, the way people behave is influenced by organizational arrangements, processes, and ethos, and by other people collectively, as well as by individuals. An understanding of and ability to diagnose organizational behaviour are therefore needed in order to uncover and characterize problems.

Third, a body of knowledge based on scientific enquiry and a repertoire of skills and techniques based on accumulated practical experience exist, which facilitate the *diagnosis* of organizational problems; the same is true of problem-*solving*.

Fourth, it is more probable that the systematic application of the received wisdom, knowledge, skills, and techniques will lead to a better way than if intuitive processes alone are used, or if improvement is left to chance.

Fifth, the quest for a better way is a professional duty – a moral obligation to do with stewardship. This applies both to those who see themselves primarily as teachers or lecturers and those who consider themselves managers.

There is an alternative to this rationale. It is possible to assume that institutions are inherently 'good' or 'bad', and only the fittest should survive. The rest can go to the wall. Likewise, principals and teachers are inherently either competent or incompetent. Rather than waste time trying to get them to learn, it is better to replace them. The process of natural selection is hard on those that do not survive. A process of adaptation, whereby the institution and its members take responsibility for systematically *learning* to survive and thrive in a changing and sometimes hostile environment, is fundamental to OD.

HOW OD OPERATES IN PRACTICE

Organizations seldom pick themselves up by their own bootstraps; either someone new arrives, such as a new head or principal, an adviser or consultant, or else a member of the organization will be trained as a 'change agent'. TVEI co-ordinators are an example. The Technical and Vocational Education Initiative, which came from outside the education system, was a means of bringing about curriculum development and pedagogical change within British schools. A process of school review, imposed by an LEA, can also catalyse OD. The first thrust is often a response to what is perceived as an impending crisis. In this case it was a crisis of confidence in public education. In ICI it was the threat of international competition.

The role of the 'new broom' in initiating change is crucial. Recent research on secondary school headship has demonstrated that organizational change is much more prevalent in the early years of headship than thereafter.

An external consultant works through organizational members. He does not usurp the role of management; instead, he 'facilitates' the process by which members identify organizational problems and set about solving them. He avoids prescribing what should be done, for that is a management decision. (See Gray's *Management Consultancy in Schools* (1988) for further reading.)

While OD ultimately operates at the strategic planning level, a typical organizational process on which to start work is the conduct of a regular meeting. The aim is to improve its effectiveness, for example by deepening communication, by dealing with more items in a given time, by getting more tangible results, or by having fewer, more, or different people attend. A consultant would observe what goes on. At the close of business he would conduct a review, in which members would take part. He might explore what was achieved, how people felt, what they thought was good about the meeting, and what needed improvement. He might provide data on the frequency and nature of each member's contributions (for example, seeking information, suggesting, disagreeing, summarizing) and invite comments. He might choose a particular episode to analyse what happened and why. After getting participants to articulate and reflect upon their experience of the meeting, and to draw conclusions concerning its effectiveness (and theirs), he would encourage them to plan the conduct of their next meeting so as to capitalize on their successes in this one and to overcome their difficulties. He would 'coach' them to improve.

The outward and visible signs of working on the process during a series of such meetings might be:

1. the agenda would state not just the topics to be discussed, but also what was intended to be achieved by discussing them;
2. the items would be prioritized at the beginning of the meeting;
3. a flipchart would be used to focus attention and record decisions;
4. if actions were agreed, it would always be clear who would do what by when;
5. there would be more constructive comments about the process of the meeting;
6. other members than the chairperson might at times lead the discussion;

7. prolix members would become more succinct and quiet members would say more;
8. members would listen to one another more carefully, so that one contribution would build on the previous one;
9. there would be more pauses for reflection;
10. a process review would always conclude the meeting.

A concrete example is of a college, one of whose deputy principals attended a management course, and who, on his return persuaded the principal to agree to the appointment of an external consultant to undertake an organizational diagnosis. The consultant paid five visits to the college, interviewing staff and students, attending meetings, and studying documents such as prospectuses. He analysed the results and fed them back to the management team. The team used these results to deal with the problems the college had. The decision to adopt an OD approach in no way implied that the college had a poor reputation or that the management was incompetent: quite the contrary. The object was to help a good institution become even better.

In an LEA faced with school reorganization, falling rolls, and contracting resources, an adviser and an industrial chaplain arranged for some heads to meet some local industrial managers from a firm that had had to manage substantial contraction. They had successfully used an OD approach for this. Some of the LEA's problems had already been faced by the firm, which had used techniques judged to be transferable into education. The LEA recruited one of the firm's consultants to operate from a teachers' centre and provide training and consultancy for the schools affected. The LEA adviser was subsequently appointed a trainer of other advisers in the region; in this way the OD approach became widely disseminated.

In a survey the author conducted of the management problems in a sample of British schools, the following were found to lend themselves to OD approaches:

- integrating handicapped children into mainstream schools;
- introducing computer technology into school administration and teaching;
- collaborating with the local rural community in promoting information technology;
- introducing staff performance appraisal;
- building the school staff into a more effective team;
- curriculum development (especially changing the knowledge/skills balance);
- becoming a community school;
- multicultural education;
- better collaboration with the youth service;
- upgrading discipline, demeanour, and morale.

In the United States OD in schools began to flourish in 1967 when Schmuck and Runkel started a major programme at the University of Oregon. This was subsequently replicated elsewhere. It involved a sustained experiential training programme to increase teachers' capacity for problem solving, clear communication, establishing clear objectives, uncovering and working with conflict, conducting effective meetings, and making decisions. By the early 1980s there were over 300 OD consultants at work in American schools in some 76 districts.

SOME USEFUL OD TECHNIQUES

The *Encyclopaedia of Organisational Change Methods* (Huczynski 1987) lists some 300 OD techniques. Some of those most relevant to educational institutions are described in *Effective School Management* (Everard and Morris, 1985). Only two types are exemplified here.

Diagnostic techniques

One of the best known diagnostic instruments is a questionnaire designed by Likert (1967) which leads to a profile of organizational characteristics:

leadership processes;
motivational forces;
communication processes;
interaction-influence processes;
decision-making processes;
goal-setting and priority-ordering processes;
control processes.

Peters and Waterman, whose best seller, *In Search of Excellence* (1982), provided effectiveness criteria that have been applied to school organizations by Handy (1984), propounded a diagnostic framework of seven Ss: superordinate goals, style, systems, staff, skills, strategy, and structure.

Some diagnostic instruments have been developed specifically for use in schools, for example ILEA's *Keeping the School under Review* and GRIDS (Guidelines for Review and Internal Development in Schools). These are all useful tools, but they have to be used properly. It is no use going through the motions of organizational diagnosis unless there is a clear commitment to tackle the problems revealed.

Problem-solving techniques

One key technique is a systematic approach. This is used in various forms, but one that is catching on in schools goes by the acronym TOSIPAR:

T tuning in to the problem: appreciation of the situation; reconnaissance

O objectives: specifying what has to be achieved to solve the problem

S success criteria: how shall we know that the problem has been solved?

I information and ideas: what we need to know to solve the problem; generating alternative ideas for solving it and deciding which to adopt

P plan: specifying what must be done by whom and by when in order to solve the problem

A action: implementing the plan

R review: monitoring and evaluating to check plan is working; identifying both causes of success (to consolidate) and difficulties (to overcome).

Skill in using this approach does not come naturally, especially to intuitive people: it requires about a week's training, followed by practice on real problems. But when teams find that it works, it enhances their intuitive approach and gives them confidence in tackling long-standing organizational problems.

FURTHER READING

Beckhard, R. (1969) *Organization Development: Strategies and Models*, Reading, Mass.: Addison-Wesley.

Bennis, W. G. (1969) *Organization Development: Its Nature, Origins and Prospect*, Reading, Mass.: Addison-Wesley.

Everard, K.B., and Morris, G. (1985) *Effective School Management*, London: Paul Chapman Publishing.

Fullan, M. (1982) *The Meaning of Educational Change*, New York: Teachers College Press and Ontario Institute for Studies in Education.

Gray, H. L. (Ed.) (1988) *Management Consultancy in Schools*, London: Cassell.

(Ed.) (1982) *The Management of Educational Institutions*, Lewes: Falmer Press.

(1985) *Organisation Development (O.D.) in Education*, Stoke-on-Trent: Deanhouse.

Handy, C. B. (1984) *Taken for Granted: Looking at Schools as Organisations*, Harlow: Longman.

Huczynski, A. (1987) *Encyclopaedia of Organisational Change Methods*, Aldershot: Gower.

Likert, R. (1967) *The Human Organization*, New York: McGraw Hill.

Peters, T. J. and Waterman, R. H. (1982) *In Search of Excellence*, New York: Harper & Row.

Pettigrew, A. M. (1985) *The Awakening Giant: Continuity and Change in ICI*, Oxford: Basil Blackwell.

Schmuck, R., Runkel, P., Arends, J. and Arends, R. (1977) *The Second Handbook of Organizational Development in Schools*, Palo Alto: Mayfield.

4.14

EFFECTIVENESS AND EVALUATION IN EDUCATIONAL INSTITUTIONS

DONALD NAISMITH

THE TASK OF EDUCATION

For the foreseeable future the education systems of the developed and developing countries will be dominated by the need to produce a higher proportion of better educated and trained young people than in the past. This is in the face of increasing international competition and relatively declining resources.

> What was unimaginable a generation ago has begun to occur – others are matching and surpassing our educational attainments. . . . The world is indeed one global village. We live among determined, well-educated, and strongly motivated competitors. We compete with them for international standing and markets, not only with products but also with the ideas of our laboratories and neighbourhood workshops. America's position in the world may once have been reasonably secure with only a few exceptionally well-trained men and women. It is no longer.

These words are taken from The Report by the Commission on Excellence in Education in the United States of America, *A Nation at Risk* (1983). The title speaks volumes and reflects the position of most countries – what applies to General Motors certainly applies to the rest of the world. Effectiveness, however, with which *A Nation at Risk* is largely concerned, is, like patriotism, not enough. Efficiency must go hand-in-hand with effectiveness.

According to Benjamin Franklin two things are certain, death and taxation. To this, as far as educationalists are concerned, must be added the inescapable fact that we are never going to have either enough money or sufficient resources to do all the things we would like to do. Resources will constantly be outstripped by the increasing expectations laid on the education service by society at large as well as by individuals, parents, students, and employers. In any case

497

it is doubtful if throwing money at the problem is the answer. The government's White Paper *Better Schools* (1984) pointed out that expenditure on education in England and Wales doubled in real terms over the preceding years, whilst numbers increased by only 11 per cent, without, it implied, an improvement in standards. And international comparisons made by the National Institute of Economic and Social Research between attainment levels suggest that West Germany and Japan are able to reach higher standards of achievement than we do using less of their gross domestic product.

For these reasons, *management* will become increasingly important in education as a means of narrowing the gap between resources and expectations, and *evaluation* in turn will become increasingly important, as without it the better management called for simply cannot take place.

DEFINITIONS AND DIFFERENT APPROACHES

Evaluation of any educational activity is particularly delicate for obvious reasons, and it is important that terms are used precisely. The Department of Education and Science's (DES) publication *Quality in Schools: Evaluation and Appraisal* (1985) has provided the following helpful definitions.

evaluation: a general term used to describe any activity by the institution or the local education authority where the quality of provision is a subject of systematic study;

review: a retrospective activity implying the collection and examination of evidence and information;

appraisal: the forming of qualitative judgements about an activity, or person, or organization;

assessment: the use of management and/or grading, based on known criteria.

No definitions were attempted of 'effectiveness' or 'efficiency', perhaps because neither is considered to be the concern of government, or because the difference is taken as self-evident, or is already sufficiently widely understood. It is important, however, that the distinction is clearly recognized from the outset. 'Effectiveness' means the degree of success with which targets are met. 'Efficiency' means the degree of success with which targets are met in relation to the resources used. An effective school or organization may be inefficient and vice versa.

It is hardly surprising that, in these circumstances, attempts to measure educational effectiveness and efficiency have become a major academic and political activity. A good up-to-date *tour d'horizon* is given in the Spring 1987 edition of *Educational Management and Administration* (Glatter 1987).

All examinations into institutional effectiveness or efficiency fall, more or less, into one of two broad categories. First, there are self-evaluative exercises such as the Schools Council's GRIDS system (Guidelines for Review and Internal Development in Schools), which is one of the most respected methods widely in use. It aims to bring about 'change in the teaching and learning process or in the management and organization of the school, which is intended to help the school accomplish its goals more effectively'. Second, there are those which seek to identify and relate objective factors and characteristics in the make-up of a good school, which can be used as the basis of comparisons.

The trouble with the first method is that, by its own admission, there is plenty of evidence that it is hard to bring about real changes. 'Too often school self-review and development stop short at the review stage: recommendations are produced, but no action results' (The Schools Council 1984). Another difficulty is that however helpful such exercises are to the institutions and people immediately involved – and there is real evidence of the genuine value to them in identifying in-service needs, for example – they command little respect among those who want hard evidence of the effectiveness or efficiency of schools and of other educational institutions, either within their own terms or in comparison with others.

The difficulty with the second set of exercises is that it is almost impossible to identify criteria of sufficient objectivity and general application from which useful managerial lessons can be drawn, and that when they are identified schools are inevitably ranked in hurtful and unfair league tables.

The answer to the question 'What makes a good teacher or a good school?' (or a good education service, for that matter), has all too often, and properly, little to do with measurable qualities. But if they are to be improved, as they must, the more difficult question of relating resources to expectations will need to be tackled. This is in spite of the justifiable worry that in seeking to do so, education is put in danger of being regarded and treated in terms of production, of 'input' and 'output', with all the disagreeable and inappropriate associations these terms have with manufacture. This could mean that education would be drawn and narrowed into measurable activities to the exclusion of those intangible considerations which all of us agree are central to anything we would recognize as belonging to a good education. In the words of W. H. Auden, 'Culture is what you cannot aim at'.

The Chartered Institute of Public Finance and Accountancy (CIPFA) (1986) has made a valuable contribution to the identification of performance indicators, and its definitions of those off-putting terms 'input' and 'output' are worth mentioning.

> 'Input' is what we work with, the staff, the money, schools, the equipment, the children and young people themselves. 'Inputs' are determined by policy making, and performance indicators can play a part in that policy making.
>
> 'Output' is what has happened by the end of the educational process. It includes practical, social and intellectual skills, attitudes to work, readiness to be

active as a citizen, examination courses completed . . . the whole profile. In sum, it is the effect of the Education Service on individuals and on their life chances.

'Input', and 'process', and 'output', all have qualitative aspects and some interdependence. For instance, indicators of 'input' alone are not appropriate as indicators of quality, but they contribute towards an overall view of the service, not least to a judgement about 'effectiveness' and 'efficiency'.

'Output' in what is learned and taken away is the factor which matters most. Assessing it quantitatively and qualitatively, and its relation to the objectives and the qualities which people brought into the process, are the ultimate goals of work in performance indicators; we are now at only the very first stages of a very long process.

Performance indicators recommended by CIPFA, some which may of course be used interchangeably as 'inputs' or 'outputs', are given in the Appendix to this chapter.

All attempts to measure educational efficiency, whether at school, local, national, or international level, should share the following essential characteristics:

1. the establishment of a relationship, if possible beyond merely a statistical correlation, between one or more inputs and outcomes, in ways capable of expression through the use of as far as possible objective performance indicators, capable of enabling comparisons between institutions and systems to be made, because it is in such comparisons that much of the value of the exercise lies;
2. a recognition that the performance of the pupil is the most important element in the measurement of the efficiency of the school, the system as a whole, and the teacher. Evaluating pupil performance will broadly take two forms: profiles covering those areas of activity and aptitude which do not lend themselves to quantifiable results and depend largely on the subjective view of the teacher; and scores achieved in attainment tests where these are available. This approach is greatly helped by the growing acceptance of clearly defined criteria whether related to age, ability, or a specific task as a means of raising standards throughout the ability range. The reappearance of general standards is probably the most significant educational development for many years marking the end of the 'Plowden era';
3. comparisons of unit costs, pupil teacher ratios, capitation allowances, class sizes, and so on, such as produced by the Audit Commission in their profiles of the expenditure of each local education authority (LEA), are in themselves, whatever their value in other directions, useless as indicators of education efficiency, unless they relate to the demonstrable achievement of pupils;
4. a recognition that the measurements of the efficiency of schools, the system

as a whole, and teachers, are interdependent and that each should not be undertaken separately: in the same way as the appraisal of teachers cannot be detached from the performance of their pupils, neither can be examined without regard to the way schools and the system to which they belong are managed, and the appropriateness of the resources available to them;

5. acceptance that the introduction of performance measurement within and across the local education system will mean changes in management practice, processes, and structures, particularly ones which will achieve a closer and more direct operational link between 'resource input' and 'educational output', through, for example, better targeted expenditure. The days of budgetary allocations based on open-ended indiscriminate 'formula' entitlements are over;

6. recognition that in any system of efficiency measurement, in spite of the importance of objectivity, there must be room for subjective opinion and for participants to negotiate their own terms to some extent.

DATA ENVELOPMENT ANALYSIS

It is the capacity of a technique known as Data Envelopment Analysis (DEA) to accommodate the latter characteristic in efficiency measurement without compromising its reliance on objective data which has prompted its introduction into one English education authority, Croydon, on an experimental basis.

In addition, in the words of the management consultants responsible for the project, Spicer and Peglar Associates,

DEA differs from other methods of performance measurement in the following major respects:

– all performance measures generated as a result of the analysis are relative; the maximum to which they are compared is the efficiency attained by the relatively most efficient unit(s) of the system;

– the weightings used to determine the relative efficiencies are computed from the data in such a way as to view each unit in the best possible light;

– the technique allows the use of multiple non-commensurate inputs and outputs simultaneously;

– the effect of 'uncontrollable' variables on the relative efficiency measures may be clearly perceived.

Many people have suspected that in a large number of cases the 'downtown school' does a far better job with what it has got and has to cope with than the apparently more successful selective schools adept at avoiding and weeding out the problems. DEA provides a means whereby schools are seen in the best possible circumstances according to their own lights, and whereby they can form a view of the degree of success with which they are turning their assets into measurable achievement, and what steps they need to take to effect improvement.

One of the best descriptions of DEA was given in the following extract from a paper by John Trundle (1986):

> DEA is a technique to help compare the performance of a group of decision-making units which have more than one input and more than one output. Efficiency, however, is usually measured as output divided by input, and this is only an unambiguous measure for a relatively well understood production process with only one input and output.
>
> Some performance measures attempt to cope with the problem by assigning weights e.g. representing some monetary measure of the cost of inputs or the value of outputs. Inevitably, these weights are arbitrary. The key feature of DEA is that it does not prejudge the appropriate weights to be put on inputs or outputs.
>
> The concept can be illustrated using a simple model with two inputs and two outputs, as in the figure shown. In the top diagram, all three schools have the same inputs but they have different outputs. A obtains better exam results but worse job-placing than B and vice versa. A can argue that producing well-qualified pupils is the most important aspect of teaching and weight it more heavily than jobs. B can do the reverse and both may be reasonable options. But C is producing less of both outputs with the same inputs as A. It is relatively less efficient than A even though it could claim to be doing better than B if exam results were weighted heavily enough.
>
> Similarly, the bottom diagram compares the performance of schools which have the same outputs but different inputs. D has a higher teacher-pupil ratio but less able pupils than E, so it is not easy to distinguish D and E on this basis. F, however, has as high an input of teachers but has the benefit of more able pupils than D, yet it does not do any better than D. It seems to be relatively less efficient than D.
>
> This example is based on only two inputs and outputs in order to explain the idea graphically. The sample of schools is small so the technique is not very good at discriminating between schools. The idea can be generalized to many dimensions. In principle it can cope with any number of inputs and outputs. Nevertheless, it is best that the number of variables be rather less than the number of units under comparison.
>
> Clearly there needs to be some consensus as to the range of relevant inputs and outputs (this is discussed below). Once agreed, a school can claim to be efficient relative to others if it is not 'dominated' by another school. That is, there is no other school that produces more of at least one output (without producing less of another output), using no more of any input. Similarly there must be no school that uses less of one input (and no more of any other input) and produces at least as much of every output. This is the notion of relative efficiency.
>
> The technique is equivalent to asking whether there is *any* set of weights on which this school would not be dominated by another school. It shows the school in the best possible light. For example if any school has the maximum of any output or the minimum of any input in the authority, it can automatically be

SIMPLE DATA ENVELOPMENT ANALYSIS MODEL

I) 3 schools A, B and C
with identical inputs

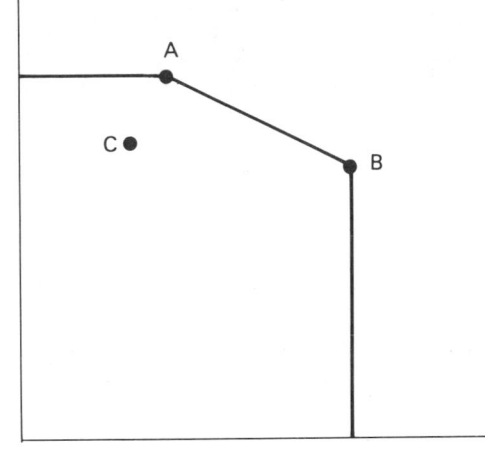

Output 1
(exam results)

Output 2 (job-placement)

II) 3 schools D, E and F
with identical outputs

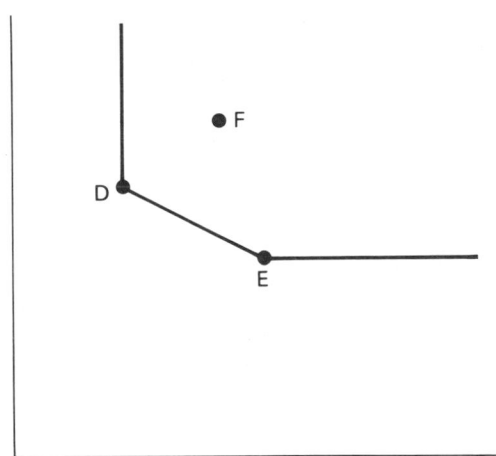

Input 1
(teachers)

Input 2 (able pupils)

considered relatively efficienct by giving a 100% weight to that factor and zero to the others. Many or indeed all schools may be deemed relatively efficient, particularly with a small sample of schools or a large number of variables.

With agreement on the relevant inputs and outputs the notion of relative efficiency should be uncontroversial. But it may seem a weak measure. It can be argued, however, that the fact that it does not automatically produce a league table is a strength not a weakness. The technique is very positive in that all schools can learn from the analysis, all schools can improve and all schools can be classed as 'relatively efficient'.

The technique produces a relevant set of schools for a fair comparison. A school that is not relatively efficient can gain from examining the organization and the teaching skills of the members of a peer group of schools produced by the analysis. It is important to note that DEA is only the *beginning* of the analysis. It is an effective way of making comparisons between schools which become obvious when stated in words, but are not always apparent from the mass of uncoordinated data. The technique is an effective sieve of data. It draws attention to anomalies in performance but it does *not* attempt to explain them. It is therefore a device for asking relevant questions.

Schools which are relatively efficient can also learn much from the analysis. It can tell them how sensitive their position of relative efficiency would be to changes in the weights. It can also give an idea of the areas where the school performs less well than others and in which of these it may be easiest to make progress. This can help establish priorities. For schools which are not efficient relative to others, the extent to which particular outputs would have to rise or inputs fall can be calculated.

The technique is not revolutionary. It simply tries to allow for reasonable differences of emphasis and experience between schools. It also allows for differences in uncontrollable inputs such as the social environment. Indeed, the ILEA already attempts an input-output analysis of its schools, but without the assistance of DEA software. Its justification is much the same as that for Croydon's use of the relative exam performance of particular groups of pupils in different subjects in the same school. This is used as the start of discussions between subject teachers and LEA inspectors about their performance and effectiveness. DEA, likewise, is only the beginning and cannot be used without professional judgement.

Comparisons, however valuable, are, of course, nowhere more odious than in education, where the importance rightly attached to individual and personal qualities conspires with the complexity of the processes of learning and teaching to confound attempts to draw broad managerial conclusions about the way we do things of sufficient usefulness to be worth the effort. It is, however, self-evident that some schools and some education systems perform better than others, and it is no longer sufficient to claim immunity for the education service from the kind of scrutiny described in this chapter. 'A national education system, costing over £15bn, having as its central purpose the education of the people of England and Wales, that was not subject to review, evaluation and assessment, is unthinkable' (Eric Bolton, Senior Chief Inspector, Her Majesty's Inspectorate). Clearly, unless we attach importance to managerial efficiency in education the ultimate loser will be the pupil and the society to which he or she belongs.

APPENDIX
CIPFA RECOMMENDED PERFORMANCE INDICATORS

Our view is that these indicators

- are valid, relevant, and helpful at the LEA level
- can be applied to schools in the 11 years of compulsory education
- can be used to tackle issues of quality.

We see 1–6 in the next paragraph as the indicators of the LEA's performance, and 7 as indicators of the social and economic context of the LEA.

Indicators of the LEA's performance:

1. Client satisfaction

- the number of appeals arising from admissions policies, and appeals per '000 pupils transferring
- the percentage attendance by pupils (at Form 7)
- the percentage of out-county pupils in the LEA's schools
- the percentage of the LEA pupil population going to out-county schools
- whether or not the LEA takes periodic or occasional surveys of opinion, with samples of parents, employers, or pupils.

2. The paths taken by 16-year-olds
   The percentage of 16-year-olds entering

- post-compulsory-age schooling
- further education (full-time)
- employment within six months of leaving school
- the Youth Training Scheme.

3. The pupils with examination achievements
   The percentage of those aged 15 in the appropriate earlier year for

- 1 or more A levels and their equivalents
- 5 or more higher grade passes at O level/CSE and their equivalents
- 1 or more higher grade passes at O level/CSE and their equivalents
- no graded O level/CSE result

Supported by:

- the percentage of pupils with higher grade passes at O level/CSE
   in English
   in mathematics

505

- the percentage of pupils with passes in examinations at 16+ other than O Level and CSE
- whether or not the LEA has a policy of 'pupil profiling'. We take this to include extra-curricular activities, with or without awards and distinctions gained, as well as the range of work done and experiences had. At this time, a relevant indicator would be the proportion of school-leavers for whom a profile was available.

4. The quality of teaching

- the percentage of graduate teachers

Supported by:

- the pupil-teacher-ratio provided in the budget (as in the Code of Practice)
- the average class size
- the average number and range of teaching hours per week, in primary and secondary schools separately
- the teachers on secondment, as a percentage of the teaching-force (and the ratio of INSET costs to salary costs)
- the ratio of advisers/inspectors to primary and secondary teachers
- the percentage of teachers teaching in curriculum-areas *only*, for which they have course-qualifications or at least 3 years experience
- the fact of whether or not the LEA has a policy of teacher appraisal that includes goal-setting, a review of achievement, and staff development (and the proportion of schools operating the policy)

5. The costs per pupil
   The gross cost per pupil (as in the Code of Practice):
   Supported by the cost per pupil for:

- teaching staff,
- non-teaching staff,
- books, supplies, and services,
- home-to-school transport.

6. The use of school premises

- numbers-on-roll as a percentage of the places reckoned to be available by the D.E.S. standards

Supported by:

- the percentage of places in temporary accommodation
- the costs per pupil on planned and unplanned maintenance of premises (separately, and the ratio between them)

7. Indicators of the social and economic context of the LEA
The socio-economic variables used as 'additional education needs':

- children born outside the UK or belonging to non-white ethnic groups
- children living in households whose head is a semi-skilled or unskilled manual worker or farm worker
- children living in households lacking exclusive use of one or more of the standard amenities, or living in a household at a density occupation greater than 1.5 persons per room
- children in one-parent families
- children in families with 4 or more children.

FURTHER READING

The Chartered Institute of Public Finance and Accountancy (CIPFA) (1986) *Performance Indicators of Public Finance and Accountancy*, London: CIPFA.

Department of Education and Science (1985) *Quality in Schools: Evaluation and Appraisal: An HMI Study*, London: DES.

(1985) *Better Schools: Evaluation and Appraisal*, Conference Proceedings, London: DES.

Glatter, R. (1987) 'Towards an agenda for educational management', *Educational Management and Administration*, 1(1) Spring.

Great Britain (1984) *Better Schools*, White Paper Cmnd. 9469, London: HMSO.

Prais, S. J. (1985) 'Educating for productivity: comparisons of Japanese and English schooling and vocational preparation, National Institute Economic Review, May 1985.

Prais, S. J. and Wagner, K. (1987) 'Schooling standards in England and Germany: some summary comparisons bearing on economic performance', *National Institute Economic Review*, February 1987.

The Schools Council (1984) *Guidelines for Review and Internal Developments in Schools* (GRIDS), London: The Schools Council.

Trundle, J. (1986) 'Performance measurement in the public sector', unpublished paper, London: London Business School.

United States, Department of Education (1983) *A Nation at Risk: Report of the National Commission on Excellence in Education*, Washington D.C.: Department of Education.

4.15

EDUCATION AND TRAINING FOR MANAGING EDUCATIONAL INSTITUTIONS

MEREDYDD HUGHES

Over the last two decades attitudes to management education and training for the education service in Britain have undergone remarkable change and are still changing. Not so long ago it was unusual and controversial to suggest that the heads and senior staff of educational institutions, like other managers, would benefit from initial preparation and further management development (Glatter 1972; Hughes 1970). The case for such provision is now widely accepted, and it is an essential requirement, as preceding chapters have made evident, both in promoting organizational development, and in achieving institutional effectiveness. This chapter will indicate that the revolution in attitudes and ways of thinking has still some way to go.

CONTRASTING APPROACHES

The terms 'management education' and 'management training', when used separately, may imply a significant difference of emphasis. Management education is the wider concept implying a broad concern with the understanding of relationships and issues, while management training is more specifically the learning of skills and techniques to be used in a particular context.

The two emphases are sometimes posed as alternatives, just as the ancient Greeks differentiated between the abstract branches of knowledge considered appropriate for free men, namely the liberal arts, and illiberal pursuits, i.e. the useful skills learnt for economic purposes by slaves and other inferior persons. Social values may today be reversed, so that the practical is often more highly prized than the theoretical, but the 'either/or' mentality, the tendency to differentiate sharply between conceptual understanding and practitioner skill, is perhaps one of the less helpful residual legacies of classical antiquity.

A similar duality of approach has been evident in the development of educational administration as a field of study in the United States. Proponents of the so-called Theory Movement of the 1950s and 1960s had little time for traditional practice-oriented courses which they criticized for their 'naked empiricism'. By the 1970s, while the assumptions of the Theory Movement were being questioned by academics (Greenfield 1975), competency-based or performance-based administrator education programmes were becoming the standard type of provision for practitioners in many states. The emphasis was thus again, but in a more sophisticated manner than previously, on the acquisition and appraisal of specific management skills (Lipham 1975).

In discussing educational management in the United Kingdom, Harry Gray (1987) observes that there is some confusion concerning the terms 'education' and 'training', and suggests that 'on the whole management "education" can be considered the generic term while management "training" refers to specific elements and programmes' (p. 37). In similar vein the national Development Centre for School Management which initially restricted its interest to management *training*, is nowadays concerned more broadly with management *development*. Training in specific skills is now seen as an essential part of management education, not an alternative concept.

Another way to avoid polarization is to regard education and training as complementary concepts, each being necessary for the other, just as good theory and good practice are inextricably intertwined. It is in this sense presumably that the Department of Education and Science (DES) almost invariably uses the two-term phrase 'education and training' in referring to provision for the 16–19-year-old age group. A similar approach is adopted in the title of this chapter.

MANAGEMENT EDUCATION AND TRAINING PROVISION

Inspired by a number of experimental initiatives, a variety of courses and other forms of professional development provision became available in the 1970s, notable influences in this development being the relevant Open University courses and the establishment and growth of what became the British Educational Management and Administration Society. During 1980 a DES-supported project based at Birmingham University carried out a comprehensive, but non-evaluative, survey of course provision in England and Wales (Hughes, Carter, and Fidler 1981). Eighty-six award-bearing courses at diploma or degree level were identified as involving some study of educational management/administration, nearly a third of them being specialized courses. Nearly half of the 58 higher education institutions involved were universities, the others being polytechnics and colleges of higher education in about equal proportions. Of the 1,600 students who completed their course in 1980, one in five were full-time students, the rest dividing about equally between day-release and evening courses. Demand was well in excess of provision, and the project noted that 'those involved in the courses, whether as tutors or students, were highly motivated and very positive in their attitudes' (p. 213). Comments by students led to the conclusion that 'courses adopting very different approaches are achieving a high degree of credibility and usefulness' (p. 213).

The overall position concerning short-course provision was less reassuring, though the total number of participants involved was substantial. In 1979–80 about 20,000 heads and senior school staff attended management-related short courses of varying kinds and duration. Some were arranged by universities, colleges, and other agencies, but over two thirds were organized by local education authorities (LEAs) for their own personnel. Provision across the country was found to be patchy, uneven, and fortuitous, often dependent on the enthusiasm or otherwise of strategically placed individuals. The Birmingham study therefore recommended the mounting of a national initiative to improve and co-ordinate management education and training for heads of schools and senior staff.

The proposal was well received, similar recommendations being made by the professional associations of teachers and headteachers. In 1983 the Secretary of State announced a three-phase programme. A National Development Centre for School Management Training was thus established at Bristol University in conjunction with Bristol Polytechnic; funds were provided for basic short courses on a regional basis and also for 'one-term training opportunities' (soon described as OTTO courses) for experienced heads and senior staff.

In further education, management training needs had long been recognized through the establishment in 1962, under collective LEA aegis, of a Further Education Staff College at Coombe Lodge. This imaginative initiative was not universally matched, as envisaged, by supportive activity within individual LEAs. A recent report by the Advisory Committee on the Supply and Education of Teachers (ACSET) has called for more effective general provision, and expresses a particular concern that decisions on priorities should be institution-based:

> We are convinced that a fundamental prerequisite for improved education man-agement training is a coherent and systematic approach to management development at institutional level which enables an institution-based review clearly to bring out management training needs. (ACSET 1985:6)

SOME UNDERLYING ISSUES

The relationship to mainstream management studies

In his seminal report on educational management development, Glatter (1972: 9) observed that 'it is scarcely possible to conceive of administrative training without substantial borrowing from studies of management in other contexts – particularly the industrial'. He was able to report the 'broadening experiences' available on the newly established educational management courses at the University of London Institute of Education, through first-hand examination of the operation of modern management methods in industry. Another pioneering course, at Cardiff University College, included the substantial involvement of the college's Department of Industrial Relations and Management Studies (Thomason 1970), while a similar indebtedness has been evident in the Open University educational management texts and in the writings of John Davies, Harry Gray, and Alan Paisey, to name but a few.

Recently the importance of the relationship has been re-affirmed, notably through the activities of Understanding British Industry and the Industrial Society, and through the programme of work of the National Development Centre, which since 1988 has been operating on a self-funding basis. The interest in education of mainstream management specialists such as Handy (Handy and Aitken 1986) and Everard (1986) has also been helpful.

A difficulty in building bridges between education and general management is the outmoded view of management theory which is still widely held, and not only by educationalists. As Everard has observed, 'it is false to assume that there is one model of management, a model that bears a distinct resemblance to Taylorism; in fact the most effective models have gone far beyond this' (1986:190). Much developmental work still needs to be done, however, if educational managemental is to benefit from the multiple-model approach advocated by Everard, which has a close affinity with recent thinking in educational management (Hughes, Ribbins, and Thomas 1985).

How different is educational management?

Research by Jenkins (1985) identified a number of similarities and some significant differences in the ways in which managers in manufacturing industry and in schools perceive their job. Some educationists appear to be deeply suspicious of management ideas, claiming – as a deputy head (Fielding 1984: 13) put it – that 'there is much about commercial management practice that is not only inappropriate but hostile to the kind of considerations which are crucial for headteachers and those responsible for running educational institutions'. Others are simply unwilling to take it for granted, as White (1984:

37) observed in the same volume, 'that those whose whole lives are spent grappling with the problems of industrial management or writing about them, will have valuable knowledge to pass on to heads and other senior teachers'.

A widely-held view is that work done in an industrial context 'must be re-interpreted for its relevance to education' (Glatter 1972). Such re-interpretation has to take account of the special characteristics of the field. Often cited are the long-term nature of the educational experience and the peculiar difficulty which is involved both in defining educational objectives and in devising evaluative procedures which yield useful information without unacceptable distortion of educational processes. Such problems, however, are hardly unique to education or even to the public services. It must also be recognized that under the market economy conditions of the late 1980s managers in education, as elsewhere, are under pressure to be clear as to what their enterprise is trying to achieve and with what order of priorities, and to make judgements concerning task achievement, based on such quantitative and qualitative procedures as are available.

It can still be argued that one special characteristic of educational management is that educational organizations are staffed by persons who need to exercise a significant degree of professional discretion in order to carry out their work effectively. This is also a characteristic of health and social services management, and there is a substantial and helpful literature on the management and leadership of professionally staffed organizations. In education the key role of heads and senior staff as simultaneously professionals and managers has been much discussed, and is clearly of relevance in management education and training for educational leaders.

The growth of non-traditional learning methods

The Birmingham survey found that many education management courses in 1980 relied substantially on the 'lecture followed by discussion' format, but also reported instances of imaginative opportunities for action learning through active group work on both short and award-bearing courses. Typically these involved in-tray and other simulation exercises of varying complexity, role playing situations with background briefing and detailed guidance for participants, and case studies, sometimes issued in successive stages with corresponding opportunities for analysis and discussion. Such occasions were generally highly valued as opportunities for testing models and concepts in a practical context, but required a clear understanding by all concerned of the purpose of the exercise.

Participants on OTTO courses in the mid 1980s found carefully planned outside visits helpful. These can be to other educational institutions, whether similar or significantly different from one's own, or they can be to industrial or commercial firms to learn how particular activities, such as staff appointment and appraisal, are carried out in those undertakings. A less usual type of learning experience is a period of attachment in order to work with an experienced manager, institutionalized in the United States as the 'internship system'.

Experiential learning also takes other forms. It may involve, individually or in groups, the systematic study of an area of concern or a specific problem, either across institutions or within a single institution, which may be one's own school or college. The outcome may be a project report of dissertation, or simply a verbal or written report to the peer group. Effective learning can also occur as a triad of heads meets regularly in each other's schools collectively to analyse problems of practice and monitor their progression. It can similarly happen as a school staff work with the head and/or an external consultant to establish a scheme of organizational development and school appraisal. All such activities have at least one thing in common: they require careful planning within an agreed framework if they are to contribute meaningfully to management education and training (Gray 1988).

Implementing the 1988 Education Reform Act

It may fairly be claimed, irrespective of political viewpoint, that the 1988 legislation constitutes the most far-reaching restructuring of the educational system of England and Wales since the 1944 Education Act. The new emphasis is on the exercise of consumer choice in a market economy monitored and regulated in the main not by LEAs but by multifarious ministerial powers. It thus involves a radical redefinition of the constituencies of educational decision making. In order to be more responsive and accountable to consumers, schools and colleges are granted greater autonomy, albeit with strengthened governing bodies. The impact of the changes on the management and government of educational institutions, and particularly on the crucial roles of principals and headteachers, will clearly be substantial.

The relevant implications for the education and training of educational managers have been recognized to some extent. Thus a report by external consultants in relation to the delegation of financial control, which was commissioned by the Department of Education and Science, makes the cogent point that technical training in accounting and related skills is unlikely to be the first priority:

> The changes require a new culture and philosophy of the organization of education at school level. They are more than purely financial; they need a general shift in management. (Coopers and Lybrand 1988:5)

Similarly the texts which have become available to assist practitioners in undertaking new responsibilities give careful attention to the analysis of context and cases before proceeding to provide practical guidance (Caldwell and Spinks 1988; Thomas *et al.* 1989).

The fact that changes in management and government are accompanied by profound changes in relation to school curriculum and examinations and the appraisal, employment conditions, and pay structure of teachers, cumulatively provides a massive challenge to the national system of in-service training (INSET). As Bolam (1988) has observed in discussing the future role of the NDC, 'the problem of managing multiple innovations simultaneously is likely to be a generic one which will only be solved if politicians, administrators, and professionals recognize this and act accordingly'.

Free market conditions have resulted in a considerable variety of courses being on offer. New governmental financial arrangements for INSET, which came into operation in 1987, provided LEAs with specific allocations for designated national priority areas which include the organization and management of schools in the context of the responsibilities of headteachers and senior teachers, and of further education in the context of the responsibilities of further education teachers (DES Circular 6/86). Initially these arrangements have tended to favour in-house training opportunities and short courses rather than the more expensive longer courses leading to academic awards. The previously cited Birmingham study (Hughes, Carter and Fidler 1981), on the basis of observation and structured interviews with participants and tutors, had concluded that, in large measure, the two types of provision should be regarded as complementary rather than as alternatives. Short courses can focus on proficiency in specific skills, and are best for achieving a quick response to perceived needs as they arise. It may still be argued that flexibly structured award-bearing courses are essential to provide basic preparation for those with major responsibilities for the management of change in education.

The long-term resource implications of adequate professional development opportunities for the senior managers of educational institutions are considerable, but have yet to receive public attention. It may therefore be salutory to end this chapter with two comparisons: first with recent developments in educational administration in the United States, and second with the planned expansion of general management training in the United Kingdom.

COMPARISONS

Educational administration in the United States

Throughout 1986 a widely representative National Commission on Excellence in Educational Administration, under the chairmanship of Daniel E. Griffiths of New York University, conducted a major study of the field, involving 'almost 1,300 people who participated in meetings, wrote papers, critiqued drafts of reports, and gave advice' (National Commission on Excellence in Educational Administration 1987:XI). The final report, entitled *Leaders for America's Schools*, offers a 'vision of what schools must become, how schools will be led, and what policy-makers should contribute to preparing and supporting school leadership' (p. xvi).

The vision of what schools will become is not unfamiliar. Schools will operate.

> so that teachers will play significant roles in helping to formulate and implement educational policies affecting the instructional program, teachers will have more discretion over classroom decisions, and individual schools will have more control over curricula, personnel, and budget matter within district-wide policy. (p.9)

What is unfamiliar in the UK context is the assumption that the management of such institutions is a professional activity which requires substantial training and expertise.

The report proposes modification in the system of state licensure of school principals and superintendents in order to raise standards. Licensing requires initial preparation by means of a university degree programme, full licensing being granted later after successful administrative performance for three years. Under the new proposals licences are for a specified time period, renewal being dependent on performance and continuing professional development.

The Commission recommends the concentration of initial preparation in fewer universities in the interest of quality, and calls for programmes to be modelled on those in other professional schools 'which emphasise theoretical and clinical knowledge, applied research, and supervised practice' (p.20). It is also critical of the continuing professional development which States make available:

> A few States have attempted to keep education leaders up to date, but the Commission generally is unimpressed with the quality and scope of these programs. Moreover these programs often are disassociated from professional control and preservice preparation; they lack sequence and continuity.' (p.27)

The Commission warns that 'high quality programs of professional development will be costly but they are a needed investment' (p.28).

General management education and training in the UK

Two recent authoritative reports, one for the British Institute of Management (BIM) and the Confederation of British Industry (CBI) (Constable and McCormack 1987), and the other for the National Economic Development Council (NEDC) (Handy 1987) both call for radical reform and expansion of management education and training in the UK. They recommend particularly a strengthening of award-bearing courses with a better mix of academic and work-based study and increased recruitment.

As well as calling for an expansion of full-time courses, the BIM report recommends the establishing of a new Diploma in Business Administration on a part-time basis for those in the first few years of business life. It favours an expansion of mid-career courses such as the MBA, diversified to include modular and part-time provision and some work-based study. As in the American report, streamlining and amalgamation across teaching institutions is recommended, in order to produce larger and more effective management schools.

Handy's report for the NEDC examines management development in other countries, and concludes that Britain should find the additional resources necessary to develop its own pattern of initial and continuing management education. Initial award-bearing courses in business education should be followed, he suggests, by a combination of study and managerial apprenticeship, akin to the concept of 'internship' mentioned earlier in this chapter. This would be part of a systematic programme intended to assist managers throughout their careers.

The two reports were warmly welcomed by the UK Secretaries of State for Employment and for Education and Science (*Times Higher Education Supplement* 1 May 1987).

CONCLUSION

It has been shown that management education and training for senior staff in schools and colleges is widely recognized as an area of great interest and potential development. A brief glance at developments elsewhere heightens awareness of some of the issues that urgently need to be resolved.

It may be encouraging finally to note that many of the providing institutions, the universities and colleges on which the study and teaching of educational management depends, are responding to the challenge of GRIST by modularizing courses, by providing greater flexibility within their part-time course arrangements, and by co-operating with LEAs and schools in developing and supervising relevant school-based activities. These developments, very much in the spirit of the new ideas in comparable areas which have been cited, deserve the support of professional associations, local education authorities, and national government.

FURTHER READING

ACSET (Advisory Committee on the Supply and Education of Teachers) (1985) *The Preparation of Further Education Teachers for Education Management*, London: Department of Education and Science.

Bolam, R. (1988) 'Role of a national agency and the United Kingdom context', Symposium on Leadership Development for School Improvement, New Orleans: American Educational Research Association Annual Meeting.

Caldwell, B. J. and Spinks, J. M. (1988) *The Self-Managing School*, Lewes: Falmer Press.

Constable, J. and McCormack, R. (1987) *The Making of the British Manager – A Report for the BIM and CBI*, London: BIM.

Coopers and Lybrand Associates (1988) *Local Management of Schools*, London: HMSO.

Department of Education and Science (1986) Circular 6/86 *Local Education Authority Training Grants Scheme: Financial Year 1987–8*, London: DES.

Everard, K. B. (1986) *Developing Management in Schools*, Oxford: Blackwell.

Fielding, M. (1984) 'Asking different questions and pursuing different means: a critique of the New Management Movement', in J. Maw *et al.* (Eds.) *Education plc?*, London: Heinemann for London University Institute of Education.

Glatter, R (1972) *Management Development for the Education Profession*, London: Harrap for London University Institute of Education.

Gray, H. L. (Ed.) (1988) *Management Consultancy in Schools*, London: Cassell.

Gray, H. L. (1987) 'Problems in helping head teachers to learn about management', *Educational Management and Administration*, 15: 35–42.

Greenfield, T. B. (1975) 'Theory about organisation: a new perspective and its implications for schools', in M. Hughes (Ed.) *Administering Education: International Challenge*, London: Athlone.

National Commission on Excellence in Educational Administration (1987) *Leaders for America's Schools*, Temple, Arizona: University Council for Educational Administration.

Handy, C. (1987) *The Making of Managers – A Report on Management Education, Training and Development in the USA, West Germany, France, Japan and the UK*, London: National Economic Development Council.

Handy, C. and Aitken, R. (1986) *Understanding Schools as Organisations*, Harmondsworth: Penguin Books.

Hughes, M. G. (Ed.) (1970) *Secondary School Administration: A Management Approach*, Oxford: Pergamon Press.

Hughes, M. G., Carter, J., and Fidler, B. (1981) *Professional Development Provision for Senior Staff in Schools and Colleges*, Birmingham: University of Birmingham Department of Social and Administrative Studies in Education.

Hughes, M., Ribbins, P., and Thomas, H. (Eds.) (1985) *Managing Education: the System and the Institution*, Eastbourne: Holt Saunders.

Jenkins, H. O. (1985) 'Job perceptions of senior managers in schools and manufacturing industry', *Educational Management and Administration*, 13: 1–11.

Lipham, J. M. (1975) 'Competency/Performance-based administrator education (C/PBAE): recent developments in the United States', in M. Hughes (Ed.) *Administering Education: International Challenge*, London: Athlone.

Thomas, H. with Kirkpatrick, G. and Nicholson, E. (1989) *Local Management of Schools in Action*, London: Cassell.

Thomason, G. F. (1970) 'Organisation and management', in M. Hughes (Ed.) *Secondary School Administration: A Management Approach*, Oxford: Pergamon Press.

Times Higher Education Supplement, 1 May 1987.

White, J. (1984) 'Managing heads', in J. Maw *et al.* (Eds). *op cit.*

5. DESIGNING AND EVALUATING THE CURRICULUM

INTRODUCTION: DESIGNING AND EVALUATING THE CURRICULUM

BRIAN WILCOX

In recent years the curriculum has come increasingly to occupy a central position on the educational agenda. At the same time the curriculum is the focus of much of the enhanced attention being paid to education by the government. The debate about the nature of the school curriculum has been growing apace particularly since the middle of the 1970s, when the educational consensus really began to fall apart. When Prime Minister Callaghan delivered his now famous speech at Ruskin College in October 1976, inaugurating what became known as the 'Great Debate', he gave expression to the mounting disquiet felt since the late 1960s by some in government and elsewhere about the state of the public education system. The year 1976 represented a watershed (a metaphor used several times in the contributions which follow) when the hitherto educationally unquestioned and unthinkable became increasingly the reality. Although the debate which followed the Ruskin speech had its fits and starts it resulted, as the years unfolded, in a truly remarkable profusion of curriculum documents from the DES and HMI. More such documents have been produced in the last dozen years than in the rest of the history of the public education service put together.

Looking back over the last few years events can now clearly be seen as an inevitable movement towards the control and direction of the curriculum by the government. Thus if October 1976 represents one watershed then July 1987 represents another. For at this time the government issued a major statement on the curriculum as one in a series of consultation documents which eventually led to a new Education Act becoming law on 29 July 1988. The Act gives a special place to the establishment of a national curriculum. As with 1976, 1987 represented the culmination of significant events in the immediately preceding years. Future historians of education may come to argue that the true watershed was 1984. This was the year when Sir Keith Joseph, the former Secretary of State for Education, outlined at the North of England Conference in Sheffield the Government's intentions for reaching greater agreement on the school curriculum and raising pupil achievements.

It is worth pausing to ask the question why it is that there is such enormous interest in the curriculum. Why is it that much of the contemporary educational debate is conducted so passionately around the issue of the curriculum? Superficially it reflects a concern for educational standards – thought to be inadequate for the demands of the time – and the need to ensure that the education service contributes, through the preparation it gives to a future work force, to the economic competitiveness of the nation.

However, concerns such as these, important though they be, are second-order ones. The interest in the curriculum is evidence of the more fundamental concern, seldom explicitly articulated, that in a secular world the curriculum carries the increasing burden of being a major means for socializing the young. In providing young people with a basic understanding of their society and its values the curriculum plays a vital part in maintaining the coherence of society and its continued existence. In the past the exercise of this implicit requirement was fairly unproblematic and was subtly reinforced by institutions other than the school – the family, the community, and the temporal and spiritual structures of the state. Such a situation can no longer be assumed.

There are two principal reasons for this. First, the sheer complexity of the modern world has made it impossible even for the most talented polymath to begin to understand it in its entirety. New knowledge – especially in the natural and social sciences – has added enormously to the potential curriculum load on all educational institutions. Second, the effects of science and technology have had a much more profound influence than ever before on the values and beliefs of society. It is starkly apparent that there has been no expansion of our understanding of moral and ethical matters anywhere near commensurate with the phenomenal growth of scientific and technological knowledge. Indeed moral and ethical values have been more and more determined by the theories of science and the imperatives of technological advance.

It has become increasingly difficult to talk meaningfully of a common value system. Without such a system it seems unlikely that a society can survive. It is therefore the recognition of the extreme vulnerability of our society that accounts for the current obsession with the curriculum. In brief then, the curriculum is important because it is perceived as a major means for society's continued survival.

The practical consequence of this insight is that education (and thereby the curriculum) is considered by the state as being needful of systematic development. Thus the ways in which the curriculum has been regarded over the last three decades include such notions as: *design, implementation*, and *evaluation*. The aim is to make the curriculum an ever more effective agent of social engineering.

The contributions to this section of the *Handbook* fall into two broad groups. There are those which are concerned with the development of the curriculum in specific sectors of the education service (Drummond, Ashton, McWilliams, Mansell). The aim of these is to deal with the curriculum from early childhood to the post-16 stage. Other contributions deal with developments and aspects which are not sector-specific (Eggleston, Eraut, Moon, Holt, Wilcox, Nixon, and Broadfoot).

The section is introduced by John Eggleston, who sets the context for the contributions which follow. He offers a succinct framework for making sense of much of the curriculum debate and the developments which it has spawned. His framework identifies six dichotomous factors and the compromises currently adopted between them. The factors are concerned with aspects of the curriculum which are: child-centred or society-centred; vocational or non-vocational; subject-centred or integrated; normative or criterion-based; differentiated (by class, gender, or race) or non-differentiated; locally or centrally controlled. The last of these factors is particularly significant given the imminent introduction of a national curriculum.

At the heart of the new approach to the curriculum which emerged towards the end of the 1950s and at the beginning of the 1960s was the idea that the curriculum should be consciously designed with the needs of the learner and the subject clearly in mind. Surprisingly though there is little in the literature which looks analytically at what the curriculum designer does. Michael Eraut's chapter goes a good way to redressing this situation. He distinguishes between what people are doing when they are said to be engaged in curriculum design (i.e. involved in political, bureaucratic, marketing, or public relations exercises) and what the literature says they should be doing (i.e. adopting scientific, knowledge-structure, engineering, artistic, and problem-solving approaches). The implications of the final category – the one which he favours himself – is outlined in some detail.

Mary Jane Drummond provides the first contribution amongst those concerned with the curriculum for particular age ranges. She casts a critical eye over the curriculum of the early years – so often seen as the jewel in the English curriculum crown. Starting from a brief historical review of approaches to educating young children she questions several of the assumptions that are deeply embedded in professional practice, such as the role of language within the home, the use of physical play. She concludes with the disturbing observation that there is an 'intellectual hole at the centre of the early-years universe'.

Pat Ashton continues with a review of the primary curriculum, reminding us that it is 'easy to take for granted a consensus of ideas and a similarity of practice far greater than may actually exist'. Like some other contributors she is cautious about the value of formulating aims. Whilst she regards these as important as criteria for judging the value of children's everyday experience, she stresses that if they are to be effective within a school they need to be discussed by staff again and again. She argues that curriculum plans frequently assume a single child as their object – or a body of children behaving as one. Furthermore, some of the differentiated response to curriculum plans is inevitably unpredictable. She suggests a need for a shift away from the temporal sequence of aims – plans worked out – plans put into operation.

Keith McWilliams considers the much vexed question of the nature of the secondary curriculum. The 30 years following the 1944 Education Act were ones in which the context of education was the dominant theme. Since the mid 1970s the spotlight has been increasingly sharply focused on the curriculum of secondary schools rather than upon their organization. The publication of *Better Schools* in 1985 is identified as a significant watershed. In recent years GCSE, TVEI and possibly modularization have been factors impelling the system inexorably towards a common curriculum. McWilliams concludes by commenting that 'There is good reason to anticipate that after decades of indecision we are on the threshold of providing a coherent framework for the content, process, and context of the school curriculum as a whole.'

Few can be better placed than Jack Mansell (former head of the FEU) to make sense of the events which have led up to the emergence of the curriculum for the age range 14–19. The origins of the 14–19 curriculum lie essentially in the post-16 culture. This was clearly underlined when the Government accepted the recommendations of *A Basis for Choice* over those of the *Keohane Report*. Mansell argues the case for basing a common core for the 14–19 curriculum on the generic needs of adolescence. The divide between the 14–16 curriculum – subject-based and DES-inspired – and the 14–19 curriculum – biased towards integrated courses and frameworks – continues to persist. Modularization may help to bridge the gap. However for the moment it must be recognized that the 14–19 curriculum is in an evolutionary state and lacking a unified concept.

Bob Moon provides an economical review of the developments over three decades concerned with the systematic implementation of curriculum change. Although much of the inspiration of the curriculum reform movement comes from the academic and research communities, Moon reminds us of other sources outside of this mainstream. Important amongst the latter were the small number of innovative schools of the 1960s and 1970s. This tradition of innovating schools continues into the 1980s particularly through involvement in TVEI. Attempts have been made towards synthesising the accumulated knowledge of curriculum change. However that is far from being satisfactorily realized at the present time. As a result, as Moon suggests, 'however rational the planning process, curriculum implementation is inevitably an unpredictable affair'.

One of the major agencies established in this country for the implementation of planned educational change was the Schools Council. Maurice Holt suggests that the Council for most of its life was committed to a research, development and diffusion (RDD) approach to curriculum change. Eventually criticism of the model gave place to a social interaction model through involvement with local centres. In its last phase of existence, and before its liquidation in 1984, the Council was espousing more of a problem-solving model. Holt suggests that the perceived failure of rational curriculum-planning models has been attributed to the fault of the schools rather than to the models themselves. The continuing appeal of the rational model to government is all too apparent. Holt sees the current situation as one in which the problem-solving approach has been 'diverted and reinterpreted as the task of persuading the school to solve not its own problems but the problems of the bureaus'. In other words the task of the schools, in the government's view, is to implement change rather than originate it.

Perhaps one of the most striking aspects of the luxuriant flowering of curriculum theory in recent times has been the emergence of curriculum evaluation as a distinctive discipline and professional task. The lively debate about the conduct of evaluation, carried on over the years, is part of a more general one concerning the nature of educational research. Jon Nixon interprets the debate in terms of three main paradigm shifts involving movements from measurement to description; summative evaluation to formative evaluation; and 'outsider' evaluator to participant evaluator. He sees the emergence of a new paradigm where the emphasis is on policy making and decisions that affect the broad structures of schooling. Working within this paradigm the evaluator acts as a major influence in shaping the *Zeitgeist*. Nixon is sensitive to the danger of the evaluator thereby being seen 'as co-operating in the interests of ideologically imposed power'. To avoid that he urges the need for evaluation to have strict procedures for the negotiation and release of data, confidentiality, and negotiation of an agreed code of conduct.

Schools have been constantly exhorted in recent years to review the curriculum − presumably with a view to identifying its deficiencies and providing a sound basis for its improvement. Like many of the terms used in educational parlance, *curriculum review* turns out to be a somewhat diffuse and generally unworked-out notion. Brian Wilcox's contribution attempts to pin down this slippery concept by locating it within related fields such as evaluation, self-evaluation, and curriculum analysis. Wilcox is concerned to develop the outline of a provisional model for curriculum review which provides practical guidance to those in schools who would wish to initiate a review of the curriculum. The model proposed starts with a consideration of the curriculum as a whole which then allows a progressive focusing onto individual aspects of the curriculum.

The final chapter is provided by Trish Broadfoot. She is concerned that assessment should be integral not only to the curriculum itself but also to the practice of teachers. There are some promising signs of a growing recognition amongst teachers of the potential for assessment as a teaching tool. Developments such as the growth of profiles involve the assessment of pupils by themselves. As a result Broadfoot sees the criteria for assessment being more democratically determined. She urges the end of the curriculum assessment divide; a state of affairs which she whimsically terms *curssessment*! Teachers however still have little experience of integrating heavy assessment demands into their teaching. For this to happen curriculum and assessment procedures need to be planned as a package from the outset. Modularization provides a major example of how that can be achieved. One of the problems which Broadfoot sees is that new ideas about assessment are being imposed upon teaching methods and curriculum content which are as yet little changed. In her view 'a major struggle is currently being waged between "separated" and "connected" approaches to assessment'.

The authors of this section of the *Handbook* have attempted a broad sweep of the development of the curriculum for 5-to-19-year-olds as it has progressively developed over the last thirty or so years. During that time curriculum theory has grown into a major educational discipline and has subtly and significantly transformed the way in which a generation of teachers and other educationalists have regarded the task of teaching. Its initial origins lie, as several contributors have suggested, in a rational, managerialist conception of change. As the years have unfolded the adequacy of that viewpoint has been increasingly questioned.

Alternative approaches have been developed which recognize the centrality of the teacher's role in the process of change, the importance of the context within which change occurs, and – not least – the limits of predictability which are possible in any human enterprise. The latter insights however do not seem to have significantly influenced the government who remain in thrall to a 'top-down', essentially bureaucratic model of implementing change according to a predetermined agenda. In recent years this has been particularly apparent in the government's discovery of the *categorical funding* mechanism. This involves grants being awarded to LEAs to develop initiatives under particular priority headings within a contractually determined framework. In a situation in which resources to education have been severely constrained, categorical funding – the method *par excellence* of the MSC and increasingly the DES itself – has represented offers which no LEA could refuse. Thus the bureaucratization of the change process has been massively advanced. It is nowhere more apparent than in the new arrangements for the funding and organization of in-service education (Grant Related In-Service Training – GRIST).

The latest government initiative in the curriculum field – the intention to implement a national curriculum – was announced in a consultation document (July 1987) some time after the majority of the contributions to this section had been submitted. The consultation document initially met with widespread dismay. Its proposals seemed to hark back to a rigid subject-based curriculum reminiscent of the 1904 Regulations, and seemed totally out of keeping with the flexible and imaginative integrated curriculum approaches pioneered by primary schools and, increasingly, by secondary schools. To some extent these early anxieties have been dispelled, as it has become clear that the Act specifies neither the time to be spent on subjects, nor the way in which they should be taught. Furthermore, the recommendations of the science and mathematics working parties, established by the Secretary of State, specifying attainment targets and programmes of study, have been well received by teachers and others.

However as long as it is believed that a broad consensus about the nature and purpose of the curriculum already exists there is little chance that the curriculum experience of pupils will be significantly enhanced. The simple fact is that we have not yet achieved such a consensus. Beneath the banal superficialities associated with generalized statements of aims there lurk the unresolved conceptual and value issues referred to at the beginning of this Introduction. These issues need to be confronted seriously. There are no neat managerial short cuts to working them through systematically with teachers and others. It will take time. In so far as these issues relate to ultimate questions about the nature of persons and their relationship to their society there can be no final answers. As a result the curriculum itself must be regularly reviewed and renewed. The curriculum – its design, development, and evaluation – must be a continually evolving entity. Any initiatives which seek to ossify the curriculum and its structures in order to achieve a premature and bogus consensus are to be deplored.

EDITOR'S NOTES

1. The chapters of this section were written in 1987 and before the sequence of events which eventually culminated in the Education Reform Act. Some limited revision of chapters was however possible to include reference to the effects of the National Curriculum where appropriate.
2. Since the time of writing the Manpower Services Commission has been retitled as the Training Agency. The former designation however is used throughout this section. It should also be noted that the national extension of TVEI is now well established under the Training Agency's auspices.
3. The General Certificate of Secondary Education (GCSE) has moved from being an event in the future to an implemented reality.

5.1

THE CURRICULUM, CONTEMPORARY ISSUES, PERSPECTIVES, AND IDEOLOGIES

JOHN EGGLESTON

Until recently the curriculum was not a major area of study for educationalists. There was keen interest in history, psychology, sociology, and philosophy, and much emphasis on the methodology of teaching specific subjects or age groups. But the curriculum itself was usually seen as given, not made; received rather than created by the decisions and actions of educators. Yet in the past two decades the curriculum has become a central focus of debate in schools, LEAs, and training institutions. Moreover Callaghan's famous speech at Ruskin College in 1976 has made it into a highly political issue at local and national level. A string of DES and HMI reports, and a veritable flood of books, journals, and articles have fuelled the debate.

In the 1988 Education Act the process was taken even further with the legal establishment of a *National Curriculum*. This is a wholly new creation consisting of three *core subjects* – mathematics, English, and science and other *foundation subjects* – history, geography, design and technology, music, art, and physical education. These subjects will be followed by all children in state schools from the age of 5. Additionally children from the age of 12 will follow a modern foreign language. In each subject area a *working group* has or will produce a detailed set of *attainment targets*, and *programmes of study* for each of the *Key stages* (age groups) to be tested at ages 7, 11, 14 and 16. The working groups' recommendations, when approved by the new *National Curriculum Council* and the Secretary of State for Education become *Statutory Orders* which become law when passed by Parliament. At no previous time in Britain has there been so extensive and explicit an endeavour to determine and implement a uniform curriculum.

As a background to identifying the current issues, perceptions, and ideologies it is necessary to consider how the change has come about. In the primary schools the pivotal point probably occurred in the 1950s when the emphases on child-centred education deriving from the earlier twentieth-century work of Dewey and his contemporaries developed from an emphasis on the child to a parallel emphasis on the curriculum needed by the child. The effects were to be seen clearly in the work of many primary schools, most notably those of Leicestershire, which became famous throughout the world for their innovations in curriculum matters. In the secondary sector the new concept of *planned curriculum change* was the trigger. This was the attempt to impose a rational order on a previously spasmodic and often unordered process of updating knowledge. Centuries of predominantly unplanned change were followed by 'a new certainty that all aspects of curriculum were susceptible to planning'.[1] Many reasons have been advanced for this dramatic change of emphasis. A widespread belief in the desirability of a planned social system that could alleviate, if not eliminate, the handicaps and hardships of social and economic inequality, arose in most Western societies in the late 1950s. It involved, in particular, a belief that suitable changes in our educational arrangements could be used to bring about desired social changes: many arguments implied that a redistribution of educational opportunity could in itself change the class structure, unaided by other instruments. Curricular change, not only in content but also in methodology, came to be seen as an important component of social engineering through education.

In Britain the most notable pioneering work was undertaken by the Nuffield Foundation in the science subjects. Largely based upon the work of the Science Masters Association (later with the Association of Women Science Teachers, forming the Association for Science Education), this opened up a wave of rational curriculum development. In these new Nuffield approaches the *objectives* of the curriculum were diagnosed and formulated, the *methodologies* that would best implement them were designed, and the ensuing learning *achievements* were identified. Somewhat later, the concept of *evaluation* was added, whereby the achievement was compared to the original objectives in a feedback loop, and allowed appropriate modifications to the original analysis to be set in train. Kerr (1967) was able to write:

> The Nuffield model for curriculum construction is becoming a standard pattern. Teams of school teachers, college lecturers and university consultants backed by advisory committees draft new programmes which are tried out in selected schools. As a result of feedback from the pupils and teachers, the courses are modified and put to more extensive trial before publication. A wide range of course material is produced, including guides for teachers, texts for pupils, reference books, laboratory notes and background readers; newly designed apparatus and equipment; films, charts and models; and test instruments designed to measure specific outcomes of the course . . . If the objectives of a course have

been identified and described in concise operational terms, it is logically a simple exercise to identify those aspects of a course which it is desirable to evaluate and then to choose an appropriate instrument or technique for each.[2]

Early models of curriculum development may have suffered because they were largely formulated for use in the science areas of the curriculum. In consequence their development had a 'scientific' orientation which led developers to identify characteristics such as 'measurable behavioural activities'. Such an *objectives model* was seen to be inappropriate for many of the more expressive areas of the curriculum; thus *process models* came to be established that focused more sharply on the experience of learning rather than on its end results. Associated with process models came the concept, developed from anthropological models, of *illuminative evaluation*. Parlett and Hamilton wrote:

> Illuminative evaluation is introduced as belonging to a contrasting 'anthropological' research paradigm. Attempted measurement of 'educational products' is abandoned for intensive study of the programme as a whole; its rationale and evolution, its operations, achievements and difficulties. The innovation is not examined in isolation, but in the school context or 'learning milieu' . . . Observation, interviews with participants (students, instructors, administrators and others), questionnaires, and analysis of documents and background information are all combined to help 'illuminate' problems, issues, and significant programme features.[3]

The growth of curriculum development since the late 1950s through objective and process models and the associated evaluation techniques has been one of the great growth areas of the 'education industry'. The development of curriculum projects has now covered almost all areas of the curriculum of all schools for all age groups, and has spread to universities, colleges, and most other educational institutions. An army of curriculum developers has been recruited: increasingly sophisticated techniques have been developed, and libraries of books have been written. New specialist institutions for the promotion of curriculum development have burgeoned on both sides of the Atlantic.

How has this new consciousness of curriculum been interpreted? This chapter attempts to consider the main contemporary issues by identifying a series of dichotomous positions and the compromises currently being formulated between them. These are:

1. Child-centred or 'society'-centred curriculum
2. Vocational or non-vocational curriculum
3. Subject-centred or integrated curriculum
4. Normative or criterion-based curriculum assessment
5. Class-, gender-, and race-differentiated or non-differentiated curriculum
6. Locally or centrally controlled curriculum

CHILD-CENTRED OR 'SOCIETY'-CENTRED CURRICULUM

The pressure on teachers to respond to the curriculum needs of their pupils has, properly, been a key thrust of curriculum development. Teachers aware of the changing emotional, intellectual, social, and psychological needs of their children seek to deliver a curriculum that responds to them fully. A complex series of decisions are required of the teachers, who have to interpret regularly what is appropriate for the various children in the classroom at the various stages in the school day.

Set against these 'reflexive' strategies are the longer-standing 'standards' that have been traditionally imposed by teachers acting for 'society'. Dyson puts the matter fluently:

> In place of rich and tried styles of human and social living we have a restless quest for novelty as an end in itself. Great ideas, great schools and institutions are recklessly bulldozed, before there in anything clear or coherent to put in their place. Or worse they are replaced by structures attuned to their individual creators or to the guessed needs of the moment ('social relevance'), and made wholly subservient to fashion and whim. The most basic insight of all civilisation is violated – that freedom, happiness, fulfilment exist only in a framework of law and structure, and in continuing and fruitful tension between present and past. By the same token structure is the essence of all reputable and efficient institutions which cannot be always and restlessly in change. A school exists to pass on numeracy and literacy, civilised manners and morals, skills and achievements; how can it do this if its purpose is challenged or lost?[4]

The quotation illuminates a major aspect of the traditional role of the curriculum: to act as an instrument of social control, transmitting approved standards and values, and reproducing society. Sociologists such as Young[5] have argued that such a curriculum is also used to allocate or reaffirm class status and power positions. In its contemporary form the debate recognizes that all curriculum experiences act in this way but that the child-centred curriculum offers a more open set of opportunities for the individual's capabilities and motivations to determine adult roles. Much of the public debate is concerned with ensuring that young people do not 'waste their opportunities'. Much of it is reminiscent of Rousseau's advocacy of 'forcing people to be free'. Certainly the enthusiasm of significant sectors of the population to buy traditional curricula for their children indicates that the debate is still active. Many, but by no means all, aspects of the National Curriculum support a renaissance of traditional curriculum orientations; the emphasis on established, discrete subjects, basic skills and 'mainstream' values is to be seen in many working group recommendations and ministerial statements.

VOCATIONAL AND NON-VOCATIONAL CURRICULUM

The origins of most curricula are unashamedly vocational: Latin and Greek for the doctors and priests, the three Rs and deference for the labourers. But the curriculum developments for the past quarter of a century have moved away from what has been seen as the narrow and restricting vocationalism of training for specific jobs which was so clearly expressed by Durkheim at the turn of the century:

> It can be said that there are as many different kinds of education as there are different milieux in a given society. Is such a society formed of castes? Education varies from one caste to another; that of the patricians was not that of the plebeians; that of the Brahman was not that of the Sudra. Similarly in the Middle Ages, what a difference between the culture that the young page received, instructed in all the arts of chivalry, and that of the villein, who learned in his parish school a smattering of arithmetic, song and grammar! Even today do we not see education vary with social class or even with locality? That of the city is not that of the country, that of the middle class is not that of the worker . . . each occupation indeed constitutes a milieu *sui generis* which requires particular aptitudes and specialised knowledge, in which certain ideas, certain practices, certain modes of viewing things, prevail; and as the child must be prepared for the function that he will be called upon to fulfil, education, beyond a certain age, can no longer remain the same for all those to whom it applies.[6]

Teachers and administrators have sought to challenge this 'railroading' for a variety of reasons – that it diminishes the open range of life chances that can be offered by the curriculum, and that it fails to allow for rapid changes in contemporary occupational and social structures, and thereby denies young people the adaptability and flexibility they need to respond to change. Instead, it is argued, the emphasis should be on qualities of initiative, adaptability, and creativity that will be of enduring use. Allied to this is the powerful Marxist critique, most clearly articulated by Bowles and Gintis, which argues that the curriculum is but a device to provide capitalist society with 'factory fodder' ready to perform the basic tasks needed by industrialists uncontaminated by alternative capabilities or aspirations.[7]

In recent years there has been a backlash to the predominantly liberal non-vocational education which has dominated the 1970s. The changing conditions of the labour market in virtually all Western societies, notably the incidence of widespread youth unemployment, have substantially increased the power of employers *vis à vis* potential employees, particularly the young. Employers have publicly articulated critiques of the curriculum, complaining of low standards, inappropriate content, and unawareness of the world of work and its requirements. A major government-funded response has been the Manpower Services Commission's (MSC – now renamed the Training Commission) activities, notably the Youth Training Scheme, which is available to all school leavers,

531

who are able to receive a two-year course of vocational preparation which has become, for many, virtually the sole route to employment. In addition the MSC has set up the Technical and Vocational Educational Initiative (TVEI) in which 14–18-year-old pupils can receive a part of their regular schooling devoted to specifically technical- and vocationally-oriented education. This occurs in a range of areas, such as Business Studies, Computer Studies, Applied Science, and Technology. The scheme is now being extended to all schools and most are accepting it, though often with some misgiving.

But in addition to responding to the technical and vocational initiative of the Manpower Services Commission, many schools are now introducing work as a 'new subject' in the curriculum in which components such as work experience, shadowing, simulated production, and work ethics are packaged together as a course, often examined by newly developed City and Guilds schemes or by the new Certificate of Pre-Vocational Education. The development is reviewed in Eggleston.[8]

Yet though TVEI and 'work' are being accommodated by many schools, the accommodation is uneasy and the debate continues unresolved.

SUBJECT-CENTRED OR INTEGRATED CURRICULUM

The traditional curriculum has always been subject-centred, yet in the world outside the school adult roles are almost invariably integrated. The incongruity was first challenged in the primary schools as teachers introduced curricula in which knowledge and understanding were not only related to the perceived needs of the child, but also integrated and applied to a variety of real-life situations. The 1970s saw an extension of this movement to the secondary schools, as a range of integrated sciences, humanities, contemporary studies, and community projects were set in train.

Yet the move to integrated curricula never attracted universal support. It became very clear in secondary schooling that many of the integrated studies approaches, notably those being introduced by the Schools Council, were focused on the needs of the lower-ability children. Eggleston wrote:

> . . . in parts of its work the Schools Council has tended to embrace traditional dichotomies of 'academic' and 'non-academic' children. The major focus of much of the early development work of the Council was to anticipate the problems that secondary schools would experience after the raising of the school-leaving age when they would be faced with substantial numbers of children who were not committed to the examination programmes that had, up to that time, been the main or even the only offering of the schools for their older pupils. Using various descriptions of such children, ROSLA, Newsom, non-academic or average, the Council sponsored a number of projects that focused on the needs of these pupils and not on the more able, academic children.[9]

It is certainly the case that, virtually unchanged, the high-status subjects continued to dominate the academic curriculum and that most able pupils have remained wedded to them. The preferences of employers and university and polytechnic admission tutors strongly reinforce this tendency. Qualifications in the pure sciences, the arts, and languages are still seen as the most attractive if not the only valid credentials. More recently a 'retreat to subject teaching' has been emphasized by the document *Teaching Quality*[10] which places strong emphasis on the need for identifiable subjects on content (though not necessarily specialist subject teaching) in the primary schools as well as secondary schools. The teacher-training institutions are now experiencing considerable pressure from the Council for the Accreditation of Teacher Education to ensure that the role of subject studies in initial training courses is both strong and unambiguous. In this way many teachers and teacher-training students find themselves at the focal point of the debate as they endeavour to apply specific subject content in schools that may still be organized on predominantly integrated curricula patterns. However the strong subject emphasis of the National Curriculum even in the early years of schooling suggests the ascendancy of subject orientation.

NORMATIVE OR CRITERION-BASED CURRICULUM ASSESSMENT

Assessment is properly the subject of other chapters in this volume. However the debate over normative and criterion-referenced assessment must be listed as one that is at the heart of much contemporary curriculum discussion. For many years virtually all curriculum assessment has been normative – pupils have been labelled as distinction candidates, failures, top ten per cent, winners, and losers with little reference to the specific achievements that have led them to acquire these labels. Moreover they have often been determined, at least in part, as a consequence of the restrictive or open examination entry patterns of schools and education authorities. This normative approach has, for some years, forced an uneasy compromise on the school curriculum; many teachers have split curriculum activities into two often completely unrelated parts – what children should know, and what they need to do in order to pass the examinations.

The alternative, criterion-based assessment, involves the identification of criteria of achievement for the various components of the curriculum; assessment is a record of the extent to which individual pupils can achieve these and at what level. As the criteria cover all levels of curriculum activity all children have at least some recordable achievements within their grasp. Much of the detailed technical work needed to make criterion referencing available for widespread use has been undertaken by and for the Assessment of Performance Unit of the Department of Education and Science. The work of the Unit has also probably made the major contribution to the professional acceptability of criterion-referenced testing by demonstrating not only its feasibility but also its capability to enhance curricular experience.

Yet, although there is general professional support for criterion-referenced assessment, there is much debate about its implications, and notably about its implementation through the new General Certificate of Secondary Education being held nationally for the first time in summer 1988. And beyond the profession there are fundamental uncertainties about the new system from parents and, in particular, from employers. Employers used to 'hiring the best they can get for the money available' find it difficult to adapt to a system in which they can match their job criteria to a candidate's achievement profile, especially if this indicates an appropriate appointment at less than the highest examination grades available. As one employer put it 'we can consider all those with grades A, B and C and forget the rest'.[11]

CLASS-, GENDER-, AND RACE-DIFFERENTIATED OR NON-DIFFERENTIATED CURRICULUM

The differential experiences of the curriculum brought about by social class, gender, and ethnic membership are well known. They have been recorded in detail since Floud, Halsey, and Martin wrote their classic text *Social Class and Educational Opportunity* in 1956[12] through to contemporary volumes such as Eggleston, Dunn, and Anjali *Education for Some: The Educational and Vocational Experiences of 14–18 Year Old Pupils of Minority Ethnic Groups*.[13] There is now little debate about the need to diminish, if not to eradicate, these differences in access to the curriculum, and in the opportunities to achieve in it and through it. But the debate on how this may be achieved remains largely unresolved. Many teachers believe that the curriculum should not be adapted to increase the advantage of disadvantaged groups; instead the changes must be made by the disadvantaged themselves. In this way working-class children must become 'more motivated', girls must become 'more scientific', and black children must become 'more acculturated', and also 'solve' their language problems. The necessary assimilation, if it is to be facilitated by the school at all, involves the removal from the mainstream curriculum of disadvantaged young people into special remedial sessions or classes. Usually these are based on language difficulties, and a full return to the mainstream curriculum is only permitted when appropriate remediation has occurred. In this way full participation in the curriculum is commonly delayed and thereby differential achievement, far from being diminished, may be reinforced.

A compromise solution is to offer alternative curricula: practical subjects for working-class children, 'girls' subjects' for the girls, or 'ethnic subjects' (community languages, Asian music, African crafts) for the ethnic minority pupils. This usually amounts to no more than an exchange of high achievement in non-negotiable accreditation for non-achievement in highly negotiable accreditation. The relative advantage of the advantaged and the relative disadvantage of the disadvantaged remains untouched.

The true alternative to 'client change' is 'school change', so that the negative aspects of schooling and its curriculum are eliminated and replaced by positive ones. The experience of universities and polytechnics in working with overseas students with relatively limited English suggests that the initial weakness in English is not a necessary impediment to successful degree study; most students learn English successfully 'on the job'. This is in direct contrast to many schools where difficulties in language have to be largely remedied before entry is permitted to academic courses. But many of the impediments are less visible. Wright[14] has drawn attention to the covert differences in access to examination streams whereby able black children may be allocated to lower streams than their ability indicates because of expectations of difficult behaviour; expectations which have a tragically self-fulfilling capability. Whyte, looking at science and technology teachers, noted a range of discriminatory attitudes to girls. She reports:

> Teachers' attempts to be friendly and create rapport often involve calling attention to gender, even when it is clearly irrelevant to the task in hand:
> Teacher helping girls in the workshop says jokingly,
> 'I don't often get the chance to put my arms round a pretty girl.' The girl blushes.
> While rebuking the girls, the metalwork teacher adopts a softer more pleading tone of voice 'go and do what you're told' with a rising inflection at the end of the sentence. This contrasts with the monotone exclamation 'Stop it, lad!' directed towards boys, in a more abrupt and aggressive tone.
> When girl asks why she has to wear safety goggles, teacher replies, 'You want to stay beautiful, don't you?'
> These well-meant asides make children more conscious of gender, and incidentally, of the associated differential expectations that the teacher has for boys and girls: boys must be dealt with firmly, even aggressively: girls can be flirted with, to 'encourage' them along. Boys will be messy and careless, girls are 'neat writers'. The expectations quickly become self-fulfilling prophecies.[15]

It is the prevalence of such attitudes in the schools (albeit often unintentionally expressed and even unconsciously held) that leads many teachers and parents who are deeply concerned about the markedly inferior curriculum achievement of black young people to advocate strong anti-racist policies. Predictably, the reaction to such policies is often equally strong, and the two positions have come to dominate much of the contemporary debate on curriculum achievement. There is considerable concern that the age related testing of the National Curriculum will, through an emphasis on 'mainstream' cultural

535

values, disadvantage black people. However a counter view suggests that the subjective patterns of assessment characteristic of much recent curricular development make it difficult for black children to have a clear self image of success and achievement and that the more precise and negotiable diagnoses of age related testing may help them and their parents to ensure a better recognition of their capabilities.

LOCALLY- OR CENTRALLY-CONTROLLED CURRICULUM

The debate between local or central control of the curriculum encapsulates most of the dichotomous positions that have been listed so far. The growth of central government initiatives on the curriculum, including public examinations, core curriculum, subject teaching, regular testing, and in-service training, is extensive. Alongside this have been a range of HMI papers, for example *Better Schools: Evaluation and Appraisal*[16] which have considered a range of aspects from the primary curriculum to teacher education. There has also been extensive work by the Assessment of Performance Unit, the Further Education Unit and, of course, the work of the MSC with its influential TVEI.

The centralizing role of government was epitomized by the former Secretary of State for Education, Sir Keith Joseph. Speaking at a History Association Conference on 10th February 1984 he noted:

> The Government has embarked on a programme to improve standards within schools, including proposals set out at the North of England Education Conference last month. Central to these aims is the attempt to reach widespread agreement on the objectives of the school curriculum, of each phase, and of each of its main subjects.
>
> We have begun the process of moving towards such agreement in consultation with our partners in the education service.
>
> It is no part of the responsibilities of the holder of my office to put forward a single model curriculum for all our schools. But I am quite clear that we must arrive at a broadly agreed view of what should be offered to all pupils, and what should additionally be available to some.

Sir Keith Joseph's successor, Mr Kenneth Baker, speaking to the Society of Education Officers on 20th January 1987, strongly reiterated these approaches:

> We now need quickly to establish a curriculum which effectively develops pupils' potential at all levels of ability or aptitude and which leads to worthwhile qualifications for a proportion as close to 100 per cent as we can achieve. There are so many common purposes of learning, and there is so much that all need to learn, that a 5–16 curriculum which is broad and balanced is essential for all pupils. Raising standards through a better curriculum and a better examination system, is not just for the more able pupils, but across the ability range. We were far 'too ready to write off children as dull, or slow or difficult and then to prove

a point by offering them too little, stimulating them too little and challenging them too little,' said Mr Baker.

'For too many of our children it seems that our system sets out to discover what they cannot do and then tests and fails them on that basis. All children can achieve something. The job of education is to discover what they can achieve and to help them to achieve it.'

Six months after, however, Mr Baker had introduced a consultative document on a national curriculum which, as we have noted, became established in law in the Education Act 1988.

Such centralizing initiatives are, not surprisingly, strongly resisted by many LEAs, schools, and their teachers, who see them as an erosion of the individual initiatives and responsibility which have led to much of the dynamism of British education practice in the curriculum in recent years. Linked with central government initiatives on teachers' pay and conditions of work, they are seen as a threat to the very nature of education.

Yet, as in all the conflicts listed in this chapter, there are middle positions that are drawn with a sharp eye to what is feasible, achievable, and acceptable in contemporary conditions. One such is by Murphy, who in a paper entitled *Assessing a National Curriculum* writes:

> In order to support rather than subvert the move towards a national curriculum, assessment methods, which encourage the recording of the disparate achievements of pupils, at whatever age these are reached, need to be promoted. Assessment needs to be largely formative and school-based so that it can be integrated into classroom practice to provide motivation, guidance and feedback to pupils and teachers as they work together towards optimising progress through the full breadth of the national curriculum. Teachers certainly need to be given support to develop such assessment methods, so that they can use them to support their own teaching, and to recognise and affirm the disparate, but worthwhile, pupil achievements that emerge from it.[17]

Approaches such as these are essential if the new era of public and professional debate over the curriculum is to be creative and fruitful. However, the alternative outcome – destructive and negative conflict – is an ever-present risk. To achieve the gain and to avoid the loss requires a new political sensitivity that educators must achieve with maximum speed.

REFERENCES

1. Mackenzie, G.N. (1964) 'Curricular change', in M.B. Miles (Ed.) *Innovation in Education*, New York: Teachers College, Columbia.
2. Kerr, J.F. (1967) *The Problem of Curriculum Reform*, Leicester: Leicester University Press.
3. Parlett, M. and Hamilton, D. (1972) *Evaluation as Illumination: A New Approach to the Study of Innovating Programmes*, Edinburgh: Centre for Research in the Educational Sciences, mimeo.
4. Dyson, A.E. (1972) 'The structures we need', in R. Boyson (Ed.) *Education: Threatened Standards*, Enfield: Churchill: 126–7.

5. Young, M.F.D. (Ed.) (1971) *Knowledge and Control*, London: Collier-Macmillan.
6. Durkheim, E., trans. Fox, S.D. (1956) *Education and Sociology*, Chicago: Free Press.
7. Bowles, S. and Gintis, H. (1976) *Schooling in Capitalist America*, London: Routledge & Kegan Paul.
8. Eggleston, J. (1978) *Work Experience in Secondary Schools*, London: Routledge & Kegan Paul.
9. Eggleston, J. (1977) *The Sociology of the School Curriculum*, London: Routledge & Kegan Paul.
10. Department of Education and Science (1986) *Teaching Quality*, London: HMSO.
11. *Times Educational Supplement*, 8 May 1987 p.1.
12. Floud, J. and Halsey, A.H. (1955) *Social Class and Educational Opportunity*, London: Hutchinson.
13. Eggleston, J., Dunn, D. and Anjali, M. (1986) *Education for Some: The Educational and Vocational Experiences of 15–18 year-old Members of Minority Ethnic Groups*, Stoke on Trent: Trentham Books.
14. Wright, C. (1986) in Eggleston, Dunn and Anjali.
15. Whyte, J. (1986) *Girls into Science and Technology*, London: Routledge & Kegan Paul.
16. Her Majesty's Inspectorate (1986) *Better Schools, Evaluation and Appraisal*, London: HMSO.
17. Murphy, R. (1987) 'Assessing a national curriculum', unpublished paper given at Warwick University, 2 May 1987.

5.2

APPROACHES TO CURRICULUM DESIGN

MICHAEL ERAUT

Curriculum Design can be defined as one of the four main tasks of curriculum development: analysis of needs and context, design, implementation, and evaluation.[1] The chapters in this section partly reflect this fourfold division, with phase-oriented chapters concentrating on needs, context, and general curriculum shape, and other chapters focusing either on implementation or on evaluation. However, it must be remembered that the distinction is primarily one of logical convenience, and is only sometimes observed in practice. Curriculum development does not always begin with analysis of needs, because needs are often taken for granted. Nevertheless it is right to argue that needs should be properly reconsidered at the appropriate stage in the process. In the most organic form of curriculum development, the various tasks interpenetrate and recycle; but the distinction still provides a useful form of analysis, as well as reminding those concerned that ignoring any of the tasks is likely to lead to failure.

This chapter focuses in turn on the purposes and scope of curriculum design, the situational factors which affect it, and the range of opinion about what it is that curriculum designers do or, more usually, should do. But first it is important to clarify what a curriculum is and where it comes from.[2] In many countries the answer to this question is apparently unproblematic: the curriculum is a document specifying what is to be taught and which has been officially approved by national, provincial, or local government. But then one finds that the documents cover more than course content, and that a number of their prescriptions are being ignored in practice. Hence the need, in my view, to distinguish between the *official curriculum* and the *functional curriculum*. The former comprises all curriculum decisions given formal policy status either by government or by the institution itself. The latter comprises the full framework of assumptions which underpins the daily preparation of teaching.

Such a distinction is equally useful in the UK where the relationship between the official curriculum and the functional curriculum has often been somewhat obscure. Before the recent demand for documentation it was common to find primary schools with no written curriculum policy. Yet one could not easily regard them as not having a curriculum, when much of what they were doing was similar both from year to year and often from school to school. Indeed the main effect of being asked to provide curriculum guidelines was an attempt to express an already existing 'functional curriculum' in an acceptable written format. This process did not necessarily lead to either more accurate or more comprehensible accounts of what primary schools were doing.

In contrast, at secondary level we had in examination syllabuses official documents which were not called 'curricula' but nevertheless had substantial influence on what was taught and how. Moreover it was often the examination papers even more than the syllabuses which transmitted messages about what was required.

The example of the British primary school illustrates the enormous importance of curriculum traditions. These permeate the various teacher cultures and sub-cultures of the teaching profession with normative assumptions about what should be taught and how. New teachers acquire these norms by professional socialization, partly into the phase community, for example infant teachers or sixth-form teachers, and partly into specialized subject communities, for example teachers of mathematics or accountancy. Then even within these communities there are distinctive traditions, such as Leavisite English teachers, new geographers, practitioners of the integrated day. These traditions pervade the whole teaching process and affect that rarely explained set of assumptions which teachers call their 'philosophy'. Thus teachers bring to both curriculum design and curriculum implementation values and assumptions which influence their thinking, often only at semi-conscious level. Nor are these influences confined to professionals. The views of parents usually owe more to what they themselves were taught in school than to any analysis of children's needs in the early twenty-first century.

Other important elements in curriculum specification are textbooks, materials, and curriculum projects. It could be argued that best-selling textbooks provide more information about the curriculum than either the education literature or even government reports. Often they encapsulate the curriculum tradition of the ordinary class teacher, while educators choose to talk about the work of more innovatory teachers who constitute only a small minority. Indeed before the fancier, more complex packages of the last decade, Southgate described the primary purpose of a reading scheme as defining the curriculum.

The significance of curriculum projects lies partly in their production of materials with some official backing and partly in their commitment to disseminating their ideas. Though they were always 'temporary systems', they usually sought not only to produce materials but also to revive, redirect, or even initiate curriculum traditions. The historical link with the notion of 'curriculum development' is also important; for before the days of the Schools Council and Nuffield Foundation projects the term was rarely used. Hence for many people 'curriculum development' became identified for a while with the work of such projects, and much conceptual confusion ensued.

Figure 1 attempts to unravel some of this confusion by mapping the range of decisions and influences which give rise to the *functional curriculum* in a particular institution. The term *official curriculum* here refers to decisions made outside the school or college, and published either in national or local policy documents or in the requirements of recognized examining bodies. Relevant *institutional decisions* are of many different kinds, but could include any of the following:

- the timetable and the shape of the whole curriculum
- the decision to follow a particular external qualification or to submit an internally designed course proposal for external approval
- guidelines, syllabuses or schemes of work for particular subjects and age groups
- equipment, facilities, and staffing
- selection and purchase of curriculum materials
- the decision to use external INSET or to organize school-based INSET in a particular area of the curriculum.

Other influences come from curriculum traditions or projects, and from the use of particular curriculum materials. Curriculum traditions are often the most pervasive influence but nevertheless, one which is difficult to characterize.

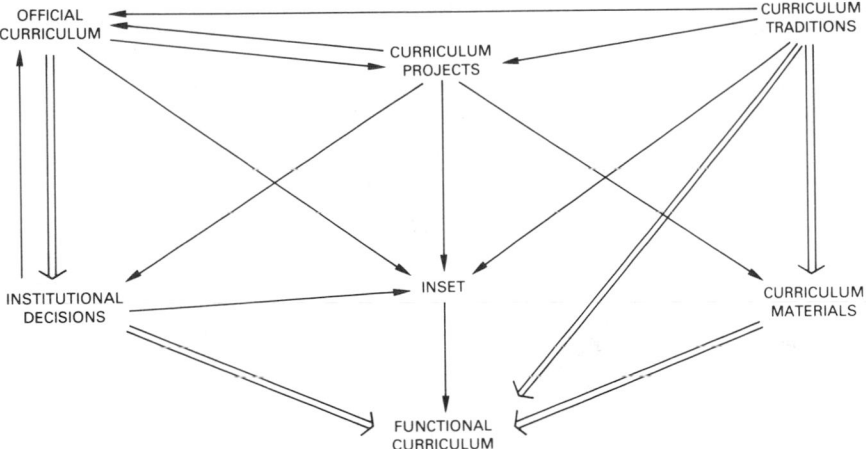

Figure 1 Decisions and Influences on the Functional Curriculum

Usually there are at least four aspects: the traditions of teaching associated with particular subject or phase communities, parental and community assumptions about what is normally taught in school, the curriculum history of particular institutions, and the professional biographies of individual teachers.

PURPOSES

We are now ready to consider the range of purposes for which people engage in curriculum design. These clearly depend on where they are in the system and where their product is destined to go. Let us begin at institutional level, where the range is probably greatest, remembering that designers often have to serve several different purposes at once. One such purpose is gaining external approval. Many teachers in higher education are used to submitting course proposals for approval by external agencies such as CNAA, BTEC or CATE, sometimes within specified guidelines, always within recognizable curriculum traditions. Schools had a similar task with Mode 3 CSE and now with CPVE. Colleges of further education have moved rapidly over the last decade from external prescription to external approval within specified curriculum frameworks. A second institutional purpose of growing importance is that of explaining current practice to external audiences – practitioners, LEA advisers, governors and parents. This has been the primary purpose of many primary school curriculum documents. Third, and of much longer ancestry, comes the use of a syllabus or scheme of work to indicate aims and map subject territory for internal coherence and continuity. This has traditionally been performed by a primary head, a secondary head of department, or a principal lecturer, with varying degrees of consultation. Now it is commonly more of a collegial activity. However, when people talk of school or college-based curriculum development they usually imply more detailed work than that pursued for the purposes outlined above. Such work moves beyond syllabuses and schemes of work to some joint planning and preparation of teaching. Attention is then given to how things are taught and to the selection and/or design of materials to support that teaching.

This level of detail can also be found in curriculum projects, sponsored by national agencies or LEAs: but not all projects take on this kind of role. Some are more concerned with establishing a framework of curriculum principles and setting up organizational structures to assist institutions to apply those principles in ways most appropriate for local circumstances. More recently, national projects like the Secondary School Science Review have sought to set up networks of essentially local curriculum projects, raising questions about the national responsibilities of local projects supported in this kind of way.

Other agencies concentrate mainly on materials development. Though curriculum frameworks have to be taken into account, they are seen more as situational factors than decisions to be made. Success is seen primarily in market terms, by the purchase and use of their material products. Most activity of this kind is financed by publishers, but significant public money is also involved in materials development, especially where new technology is concerned. The national Microelectronics Project sponsored the development of computer-based learning resources; and the Manpower Services Commission has supported several courseware development projects.

Both curriculum projects and materials development projects share certain features: (1) they are expected to be innovative – their purpose is to add to the existing repertoire of curriculum practice; (2) the uptake of their products is voluntary, though not free from external influences at national and local level; (3) even though the relationship has changed over time, and some designers may be practising teachers, there is still a separation of roles between designers and implementers, with all the concomitant advantages and disadvantages.

The design of official curricula or guidelines tends to have a very different character. The process is more one of political decision making than developmental problem solving. The need for political compromise often reinforces a tendency towards vagueness and ambiguity. There is a reluctance to get involved in too much detail, except perhaps in the further education sector, where it is part of the historical tradition. So official documents, at least in the UK, have focused primarily on general aims, content priorities, and broad advice on teaching methods and objectives. It is only when public examinations have been involved that prescriptions have been much more specific. However, the prominence of attainment targets in the statutory proposals for the new national curriculum suggests that the level of specificity hitherto associated only with examinations will henceforth characterize the official curriculum throughout the 5–16 age range.

THE SCOPE OF A CURRICULUM DESIGN

The scope of any particular curriculum design depends on several factors: course duration; the extent to which existing practice or other known curriculum traditions are to be modified or changed; the amount of explanation or justification that is needed; the curriculum elements to be specified; and the degree of detail expected for each aspect. Many of these factors are logically related. For example, one might expect more explanation when the design is novel, and greater detail where there is an important external examination. But in practice these considerations are often outweighed by situational factors such as time available and the personal preferences of the designers.

The curriculum studies literature concentrates mainly on definitional and ideological issues, which appear to offer little guidance to practitioners. But curriculum design is an activity where important assumptions frequently remain undetected, and to neglect such questions is to deny one's professional responsibilities. Moreover, models derived from the literature allow us to examine designs and to discuss the factors which affect their scope. Figure 2 is not dissimilar to many models in the literature, though its details represent the particular preferences of this author. Its purpose is to reveal the key decisions and assumptions embedded in any curriculum design and to depict some of their interrelationships. Thus it is a descriptive, analytic model of the curriculum, and should not be confused with prescriptive models of the curriculum development process like that originally proposed by Ralph Tyler.

Figure 2 A Model of the Curriculum, showing five curriculum elements in interrelationship

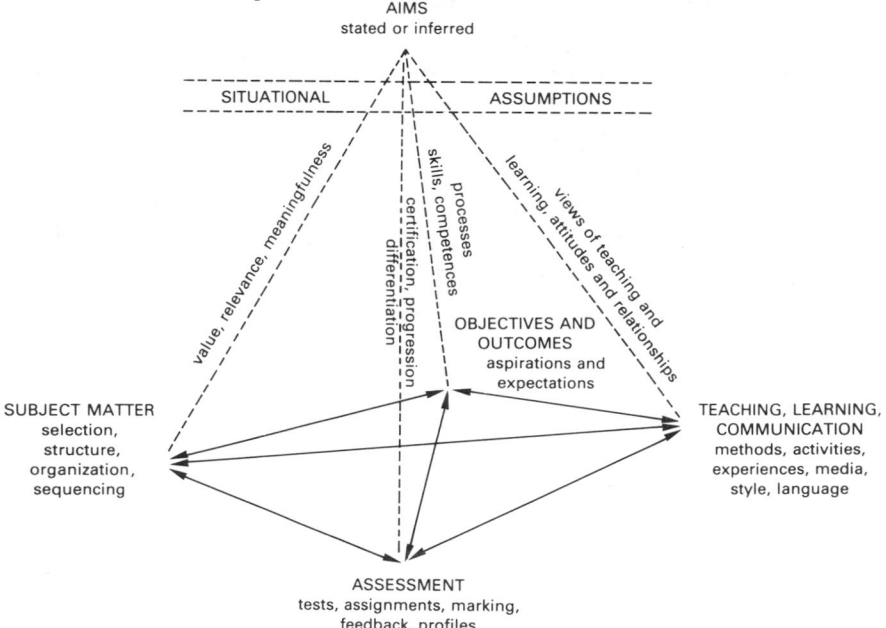

Each of the four elements forming the base of the pyramid incorporates decisions of the indicated type, or leaves them open to be decided later. *Subject matter* decisions, for example, cover selection, structure, organization, and sequencing; and *assessment decisions* concern such matters as tests, assignments, profiles, marking, and feedback. Decisions about *objectives* and *outcomes* often have a rather ambiguous status, whether they depict aspirations or expectations being unclear, or possibly even varying from one pupil to another. The *teaching, learning, and communication* element covers strategic decisions made (or assumed as normal practice) when planning the teaching of a course or topic, not tactical decisions made within individual lessons.[3]

At the peak of the pyramid *aims* may be either stated or inferred from the way curriculum decisions are explained. The logical relationship between *aims* and the other four elements is indicated by the dashed arrows. But the full explanation also incorporates a set of *situational assumptions* about particular pupils, teachers, resources, and other practical factors. The *aims* themselves constitute the main justification for the curriculum, but tend to be stated at such a general level that they are not very frequently challenged. More often the debate is about their interpretation and about their respective priority.

By drawing attention to key curriculum decisions the model helps us to establish which decisions are made at each stage in the design process. For example the Certificate of Prevocational Education (CPVE) is based on a framework decided by the Joint Board of CGLI and BTEC; and this framework, summarized in Figure 3, provides the starting brief for school- or college-based design teams. These teams then submit institutionally specific proposals for approval (sometimes involving co-operative arrangements), which then become the starting brief for preparing the teaching of individual course components. The design for GCSE courses has evolved in a somewhat different way: from national criteria to examination board syllabuses to institutional teams to individual teachers. Yet another sequence of stages is involved when a primary school selects a mathematics scheme. For in choosing a scheme the school effectively adopts a package of curriculum decisions. These are then

Figure 3 A Model of the CPVE Programme

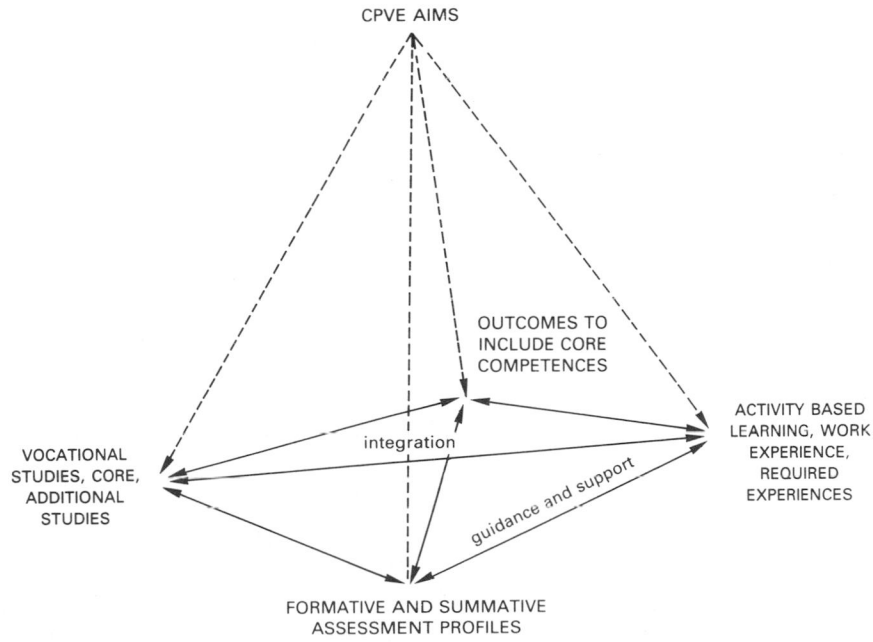

amplified and in some cases modified by further decisions about how the scheme is to be used. The model in Figure 2 is particularly useful for characterizing the interface between each stage in the process and for establishing a brief for each design team.

Another use of the model is for considering questions of priority, coherence, and consistency. Not only does one have to identify curriculum decisions, but also to justify them and to examine their compatibility. In practice certain decisions take priority over others, either because they were made at an earlier stage in the design process or because the conditions of implementation led to them being given prior attention. Most people are familiar with curricula where decisions about subject matter (such as an overstuffed syllabus) or assessment (such as an examination demanding rote memory) dominate all other considerations. In the Youth Training Scheme we have a curriculum dominated by the decision to spend the majority of time in the ordinary workplace, with consequent variation in quality according to the extent to which particular work environments do or do not support learning. My own university's school-based system of initial teacher training provides another example of an experience-dominated curriculum. So also is the integrated-day approach to the primary school curriculum. The first courses approved by the Technicians Education Council were dominated by objectives and the phase-test mode of assessment.

It is not always an easy task for a curriculum analyst to distinguish the critical decisions from the rhetoric; and designers can easily delude themselves as well. It is increasingly common for high-sounding aims and principles to be used for infilling curriculum documents, containing decisions which effectively prevent the realization of such aspirations.

APPROACHES TO CURRICULUM DESIGN

Surprisingly, one of the most difficult questions to answer is 'What do curriculum designers do?' Prescriptions abound; but case studies of the design process in action are relatively rare and largely focused on curriculum projects. However, from reading and listening to people discussing curriculum design it is possible to discern several different styles and approaches. They vary according to circumstance, preference, and people's awareness of the choice. Though I shall describe them as distinctive 'types' in order to point out their salient characteristics, it is usually some mixture of these types that is found in practice.

The *political approach* usually dominates where the product is an official curriculum. The focus is on aims, prescribed content, and general statements about objectives and assessment. But these are not built into a coherent plan or design, rather presented as a list of requirements. The process is primarily one of negotiation, both about what is to be included and what omitted, and about the detailed wording of particular sentences. The language may be rather vague, because getting agreement is often more important than clarification: indeed the two may be incompatible. There is a natural tendency towards syllabus inflation because it is easier to negotiate additions than subtractions. It is not unusual for course designs within institutions to take a similar form, especially when several departments are involved, like feudal barons, in competing for course territory.

Political considerations are also important when external approval is being sought for institutional course proposals. This encourages a *bureaucratic approach* in which the documentation reigns supreme. Close attention is paid to all regulations and to administrative issues; official documents are searched for clues about what will be acceptable; and the appropriate language of presentation is carefully chosen. Skill in writing such documents is highly valued and often confers considerable power on those who possess it. However, such preoccupation with documents and presentation may inhibit genuine course design for internal purposes and encourage centralized rather than devolved decision making. As a result the consequences of a design take second place to the dominant concern for getting it approved.

In areas of further education, such as skills updating courses, the external agency is the customer, so a *marketing approach* is needed. Once more the presentation is important, but this may involve visits and negotiation as well as the dissemination of documents. The key issues for customers are whether the course meets their needs and whether it offers value for money. Needs analysis takes the leading role in the course design, and costings are also important. In-service courses for teachers are also becoming market driven, with the added complication of having three sets of customers – the LEA, the schools, and the teachers themselves. Often there are difficult judgements to be made about the extent to which more theoretical and generalizable knowledge should be introduced in order to meet medium and long-term needs; and whether this can be achieved without destroying the practical ethos of a course.

Where external groups are neither customers nor official agencies, the approach may become one of *public relations*. For example, many curriculum guidelines in primary schools are written for presentation to governors and parents, avoiding the task of curriculum design either by describing current practice in new documentary form or by using such general language that almost any practice is covered. The latter is particularly true of many LEA curriculum documents. However, given the lack of public relations awareness in education, documents do not always meet the information needs of their readers. Instead they present the headteacher's image of his or her school, or the officers and/or inspectors' preferred view of their LEA.

It could be argued that none of the above approaches necessarily involves genuine curriculum design, though sometimes they are combined with other approaches that do. But that is not the point. What they do offer are four plausible interpretations of what is going on when people are said to be doing curriculum design. For contrast, let us turn to some of the literature on curriculum design, which tends to argue more about what curriculum designers should be doing than about what they actually do.

One section of the literature is based on psychology and defines itself as making a *scientific approach* to 'instructional design' (their term). The best-known theorists in this tradition are probably Gagné and Briggs, though others have adopted and developed their work in a number of ways.[4] The primary focus of this approach is on the identification and analysis of learning tasks, and Merrill's performance – content matrix (shown in Figure 4) illustrates it well. Merrill's theory classifies learning tasks according to content (four types) and performance (three types); then discusses how each of the ten possible types of task should be taught. Like much writing in instructional design attention is confined to the micro-level; and is therefore relevant to planning a single topic or lesson, or to the design of instructional materials. My main criticisms of this approach are (1) that it is based on an oversimplified and somewhat reductionist view of knowledge and (2) that it ignores the wider learning context and its influence on meaningfulness and motivation. Its strengths are a more detailed examination of learning tasks than is customary even on curriculum projects, and the close attention it gives to matching these tasks to what the learner already knows.

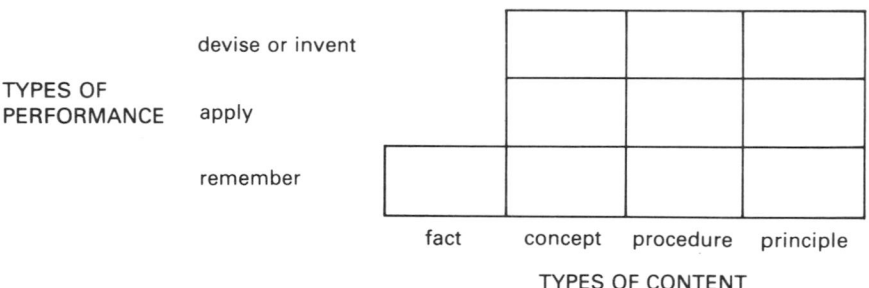

Figure 4 Merrill's Performance–Content Matrix (adapted by the author)

Another growing section of literature is primarily concerned with the structuring and sequencing of content. This *knowledge-structure* approach takes several different forms. General ideas are put forward by cognitive psychologists such as Ausubel (advance organizers), Bruner (the spiral curriculum), Norman (web learning) and Reigeluth (elaboration theory), who pick appropriate areas of subject matter – usually mathematics, science, or social science

– to illustrate their theories.[4] The literature on the teaching of specific subjects also presents maps of subject knowledge which may incorporate some of these psychologists' ideas or the results of research on children's acquisition of that knowledge. The range of possible approaches to sequencing is covered in a useful review article by Posner and Strike[5] who distinguish between five main sequencing principles: world-related, i.e. organized according to spatial or temporal properties or physical attributes; concept-related, as in theoretical approaches to school subjects; inquiry-related, according to the logic or empirics of inquiry; learning-related, using criteria like prior knowledge, familiarity, difficulty, interest, development, and internalization; and utilization-related, in personal, social, and vocational contexts.

An *engineering approach* is also strongly advocated in a section of the curriculum development literature.[6] This argues that the way to get a design to work is to define one's goals, prepare a prototype design, and then test and modify it until it is effective. Hence there is a need to define goals in terms of behavioural objectives, which can provide criteria for the assessment of effectiveness. The strength of this approach lies in its emphasis on piloting prototype designs several times if necessary, before there is any large-scale implementation, unlike most curriculum projects whose trials are more public, and timetables determined by financial and publication restrictions. New solutions to difficult curriculum problems may require much more experiment before being written into trial materials. The weaknesses of the engineering approach derive partly from the straitjacket imposed by behavioural objectives, and partly from its lack of attention to the design process itself, i.e. the preparation of the prototype. Testing can suggest how to improve ideas by modification, but it cannot indicate whether other ideas might not provide better starting points. Combining the scientific and engineering approaches sounds like the road to efficiency, but there is a danger that they will only produce designs which are effective for those who want to achieve, but so dull and unimaginative that they deaden curiosity and lose the interest of ordinary students.

This is perhaps the time to comment further on the use of objectives in curriculum design, a topic I have reviewed at greater length elsewhere.[7] Objectives are very convenient for those designing official curricula who want to convey a general sense of direction and to emphasize skills and processes in addition to mere recall and comprehension of content. They provide a useful language for expressing intentions about learning rather than teaching, and are easily compiled into lists of requirements. However, they raise many problems for the recipient because they cannot be translated into course designs as easily as the literature suggests. Some objectives are specific and short-term: they can be taught within a single topic and mastered. Others are developmental and long-term: they may need to be borne in mind throughout a year's course of teaching, if not over several years. Progression will need to be considered, together with problems of individual differences. When one puts several such objectives together, then the complexity of the design process becomes greater than most teachers can handle. In practice objectives are more useful as criteria for evaluating and modifying an existing course than as starting points for some new curriculum design. Only in very limited areas of the curriculum can they acquire the precision and lack of ambiguity which their advocates in the literature suggest are essential.

The *artistic approach* to curriculum design provides a total contrast, for its criteria are not mastery and effectiveness, but attention, engagement, and impact. Apart from the work of Eisner, it has received little coverage in the curriculum design literature. However, one finds it implicit in much talk about educational practice in general, whether discussing the stimulus of children's television, the quality of experience on a school visit, or the response to a poem or piece of music. When applied to curriculum design, the emphasis is on including experiences which inspire by their quality and excite children's interest, on the assumption that learning will follow from involvement and reflection.

Often the reason for adopting a particular approach to curriculum design is simply expediency. Designing courses is not seen as a problem that deserves much attention. Hence the scientific, knowledge-structure, and engineering approaches are far too cumbersome. The negotiating style of the political approach is unnecessary, and the artistic approach is seen as too risky. External considerations may cause the adoption of a bureaucratic, marketing, or public-relations approach. Otherwise, expediency wins the day. The *expedient course design* can be either dictatorial or totally delegated, anything to reduce the time and hassle of consultation. Its aim is to get a short document produced which provides the minimum planning necessary for adequate co-ordination. Thus it concentrates mainly on dividing up the content between teachers or year-groups, with occasional embellishments on aims and teaching style that are usually ignored.

Finally we come to the *problem-solving approach*. This requires two preconditions; first, that the curriculum design is recognized as a task for which time and effort are needed; and second, that the task is seen as a design problem, combining a set of necessary and desirable ingredients into a coherent, feasible, and acceptable proposal. This approach is quite commonly used in a partial kind of way, but to realize its full potential further principles need to be observed. It must maximize the use of the knowledge and skills of members of the design group, yet seek further advice wherever it is likely to be of benefit. It must strike a balance between the analytic and creative aspects of course design, thus avoiding the endorsement of existing practice at the expense of searching for new ideas. It must use its time efficiently by concentrating on the major problems, leaving matters that are easily delegated to be tidied up after the main strategy has been worked out.

My own resolution of these multiple requirements for good problem solving derives partly from research into problem-solving groups in industrial and other settings, and partly from practical experience. The archetypal five-stage model, from which groups will no doubt often deviate in practice, is as follows:

1. *Problem formulation* An initial exploration by the group of the parameters of the problem, and of necessary and desirable ingredients for the course. There will be agreement on many aspects but not all; and it is important not to press for consensus at this stage. Priority should be given to identifying and analysing critical problems, whose solution is necessary for the success of the design.
2. *Brainstorming* The group generates several 'images' of what a good course might be like, together with ideas about how some of the identified problems might be solved. Ideas may also be sought from outside the group. No evaluation of these images or ideas should be made at this stage.
3. *Creation of prototype designs* The group discusses the results of the brainstorming, trying to fit ideas together or expand on them, in order to arrive at two or three embryo designs. These are then mapped into the curriculum model depicted in Figure 2, and worked out in further detail to explore their potential. The group should neither separate at this stage nor get into too much detail, for issues of ownership could unduly affect the selection of prototypes in Stage 4.
4. *Selection of prototypes* This is done after the advantages and disadvantages of each prototype have been listed. Sometimes a new hybrid is developed at this stage which combines features from more than one prototype. One major concern should be that the chosen design incorporates solutions to the problems identified in Stage 1.
5. Further work is done on the chosen design, according to what is deemed to be appropriate, making full use of the resources of the group as a whole.

SOME FURTHER CONSIDERATIONS

Discussions about curriculum politics tend to treat schools as single units. But in practice there is considerable diversity of influence and opinion within each school and college; and curriculum designers need to pay at least as much attention to such institutional micro-politics as to external issues. Design groups working within schools and colleges have to decide how best to relate to these internal politics, how to cope with a variety of internal management styles, and how to handle any likely opposition to implementing their design. While it may seem logical to design a curriculum first and talk about implementing it afterwards, such an approach can easily lead to disaster. Without at least some consultation, and preferably a shared sense of ownership, rejection or token adoption of the new curriculum is likely. Hence the design process should not be totally separated from the process of negotiating implementation.

The personal characteristics of curriculum designers and their social interaction within the design group are seldom discussed but still of very considerable importance. Designers each bring their own sets of assumptions, derived from professional training and socialization, personal preferences, and years of experience in a variety of schools. They draw on a particular range of knowledge and skills; and they have personalities, habits, and working relationships which affect their contribution to the design process. Members of a design group will disagree not only about issues but also about the way in which the group approaches its task. Irrespective of their endorsement of particular curricular approaches, their behaviour will be affected by psychological factors: tolerance of uncertainty, a need for rapid progress very early on, willingness to take risks, concern for detail, rivalry within the group, etc. Whether through leadership or collaboration, a design group needs good internal management in order to realize its potential.

The external management of a design group can also be critical: first in briefing and recruitment; second through providing psychological support, resources, and advice; third through assisting in negotiations with various external groups. One factor militating against good design is too much pressure for early results, for this drives designers into routinized production of documents and resources to justify their existence, with little attention to quality, to appropriateness, or to the identification and solution of important curricular problems. This is not just a question of management style, it depends on the resources available to the design group, especially the time they are given for accomplishing their task. Thus it is important in briefing and resourcing a design group to make some assessment of the magnitude and difficulty of their task. Is it a routine job, or is some major innovation expected? Do they need help from a consultant? Do they need to make visits? Will they need to try out ideas in classrooms or to pilot pupil materials? With what other groups will they need to negotiate? Would there be a major advantage in giving the team a long uninterrupted period of working together, instead of relying on a series of short, snappy meetings? In design, as in many other activities, people often get what they pay for.

REFERENCES

1. Eraut, M. (1985) *Curriculum Development in Further Education*, University of Sussex Education Area Occasional Paper 11, University of Sussex, Falmer, Brighton: EDB.
2. Skilbeck, M. (1984) *School-Based Curriculum Development*, London: Harper & Row.

3. Joyce, B.J. and Weil, M. (1986) *Models of Teaching*, 3rd edn., New Jersey: Prentice Hall.
4. Reigeluth, M. (Ed.) (1983) *Instructional-Design Theories and Models*, Hillsdale, New Jersey: Lawrence Erlbaum Ass.
5. Posner, G. and Strike, K. (1976) 'A categorization scheme for principles of sequencing content', *Review of Educational Research*, 46, (4): 665–90.
6. Rowntree, D. (1982) *Educational Technology in Curriculum Development*, 2nd edn., London: Harper & Row.
7. Eraut, M. (1988) 'Specifying and using objectives', in M. Eraut (Ed.) *International Encyclopedia of Educational Technology*, Oxford: Pergamon Press.

5·3

THE CURRICULUM OF EARLY CHILDHOOD

MARY JANE DRUMMOND

The education of young children in this country today can be seen as the maturing offspring of a hallowed lineage, in which a philosophical tradition can be traced back through Rousseau (1712–1778) to Comenius (1592–1670), and a more practical one at least as far as the French pastor Jean Oberlin (1740–1826). In the small village schools he founded, there was no timetable and the children received no lessons; his methods were based on physical exercise, play, excursions, pictures, and stories. His work undoubtedly influenced early developments in Britain, particularly Robert Owen's New Lanark School, which opened in 1816. Owen's school was very different from the contemporary charity schools and dame schools, which were characterized by formal methods, large classes, and an emphasis on learning to read. In Owen's own words, the children at New Lanark were 'not to be annoyed with books', and singing, dancing, and outdoor play were important elements in the programme.

The work of Friedrich Froebel (1782–1852) continued and developed these themes. Froebel held that all young children are endowed with inner qualities that teachers can destroy through instruction and physical constraint; he rejected the conventions of orthodox German schooling, and created, literally, a garden for children, in which their abilities would flower. Key concepts in the Froebelian kindergarten are spontaneity, readiness, wholeness, and self-direction; play is seen as an educational necessity: in his own words – 'the highest level of child development; the spontaneous expression of thought and feeling.'[1]

Many features of the Froebel canon, especially the play principle, were assimilated into the work of Pauline Kergomard (1838–1925), who transformed late nineteenth century pre-school education in France by the establishment of the *écoles maternelles*. In these schools, children were not to be submitted to instruction: freedom, happiness, and individuality were more important goals than a few pages of the spelling book.

Meanwhile, another very different tradition was becoming established: sometimes referred to as the physiological approach, it was based on the work of the French doctors Itard and Seguin with severely retarded children. It came to its fullest expression in the work of Maria Montessori (1870–1952), who introduced highly structured apparatus for training the senses of young children. She too laid great stress on concepts of natural development, spontaneity, and the goodness of child nature; but her advocacy of perfect liberty for the young child was expressed in a system that was rejected by many, in later years, for its rigidity and strictness.

During these various European developments, education in Britain did not stand still. Robert Owen's nineteenth-century lead was followed in the early years of the twentieth by the nursery schools established by Margaret and Rachel McMillan, in Bradford and Deptford, London. These schools were established in the belief that the basis of an effective education system must be the health, cleanliness, and nourishment of its pupils. Children suffering from rickets and malnutrition were offered sanitary surroundings, fresh air, medical attention, and a carefully supervised diet.

The curriculum of the McMillan nurseries contained many elements we have already encountered: fresh air, free play, singing, and dancing. Embedded in this curriculum was the notion of rescue: the McMillans' version of early childhood education was designed for working-class children in the poorest areas of the city – the disadvantaged of society.

In 1933, the Hadow Report appeared: the official report of the consultative committee on Infant and Nursery Schools, published by the Board of Education. The early history of nursery education is sketched in the opening chapters, followed by a substantial account of the mental development of young children, which was written with the guidance of Susan Isaacs. She herself, through her accounts of her experimental school, the Malting House in Cambridge, would come to have a considerable influence on the further development of nursery education. But the most important chapter of the report is the authoritative exposition in Chapter 6: *The training and teaching of young children in infant and nursery schools*. Selective quotation, using phrases italicized in the original, gives us a clear picture of what should be done for three-, four- and five-year-olds in school:

> What is true of education at every period of child life is true most of all during the nursery period; its aim is not so much to implant the knowledge and the habits which civilised adults consider useful, as to aid and supplement the natural growth of the normal child. We may rightly regard the function of the nursery school or class as educational, but we must not regard it as didactic. The aim of the teacher will be primarily to assist the spontaneous unfolding of the child's natural powers.

555

> The curriculum is to be thought of in terms of activity and experience rather than of knowledge to be acquired and facts to be stored.

> What we desire to see is the acceptance of a different set of values from that which has been usual in the past; less weight on the imparting of an ordered body of knowledge and more on the development of the child's innate powers, less reliance on the artificial life of the classroom and more on the experience to be gained out of doors and the opportunities for experiment and discovery which close contact with the real world provides.[2]

The emphasis in Hadow on 'unfolding' and 'natural growth' may have been an important corrective to the direct instruction methods of the early elementary schools, but it precluded any sterner analysis of how young children learn.

More than thirty years later, following closely in the same tradition, the Plowden Report appeared. Parts of this report have come to be treated like Holy Writ, cited in and out of season, especially the famous statement that launches Chapter 2, 'At the heart of the educational process lies the child', and the summary at the end of Chapter 15:

> A school is not merely a teaching shop, it must transmit values and attitudes . . . The school sets out deliberately to devise the right environment for children, to allow them to be themselves and to develop in the way and at the pace appropriate to them . . . It lays special stress on individual discovery, on first-hand experience and on opportunities for creative work. It insists that knowledge does not fall into neatly separate compartments and that work and play are not opposite but complementary.[3]

The 'Plowden ethos', for many teachers, is a synonym for perfection, a monument to all their aspirations. And yet, as its critics have not hesitated to argue, the Plowden Report described a condition of excellence, and a set of principles and procedures, that probably existed in only a very small minority of schools – then or now. Furthermore, the justifications that Plowden offers for its recommendations have not escaped critical attention. Very shortly after its publication in 1967, the first dissenting voices were heard: Peters and others[4] argued that the Report was philosophically, sociologically, and psychologically inadequate. It must be galling for these authors, who hoped to open up debate and discussion about the relationship between theory and practice, between philosophy and actual classroom events, to realize that the questions they asked about Plowden have never become part of the general consciousness of practising teachers. By and large, for a substantial majority of teachers, the Plowden Report (or, rather, the few recommendations they remember from it) is still the official version of early childhood education.

For the child, Plowden stands for autonomy, individuality, discovery, creativity, and, following Piaget (who only merits a footnote in Hadow), active learning. For the teacher, the essentials are: starting where the child is, fostering individuality, and drawing on the child's own activities and interests. The

Plowden Report cannot be said to have broken new ground, but rather to have given a fresh endorsement to the long-established tradition of child-centredness. In addition, the old concept of deprivation and disadvantage was given a new lease of life by being incorporated into the creation of Educational Priority Areas, and the expensive experimental projects that were launched, with DES funding, to meet the needs of parents and children in these areas.

During the 1970s, the curriculum of early childhood education began to attract a good deal of critical investigation. In 1974, Barbara Tizard published a review of more than 50 current research projects. Her account is an interesting summary of early childhood research in action: an overview of what respectable academics thought we needed to know more about at the time. Her conclusion is remarkably sombre:

> In so far, then, as the expansion of early schooling is seen as a way of avoiding later school failure or of closing the social class gap in achievement, we already know it to be doomed to failure. It would perhaps be sensible for research workers to point this out very clearly to public authorities at an early stage.[5]

One of those she interviewed was Marianne Parry, who in the same year had published an unassuming account of a survey of current nursery practice. Unlike Tizard, Parry and Archer are unequivocally optimistic about the effects of pre-school education: 'The question is no longer whether children can profit from a quality pre-school programme but whether it will be provided.'[6]

Parry and Archer were particularly interested in the attention being paid to the spoken language of pre-school children, contrasting the use of structured programmes, such as the Peabody Language Development Kit, with a more unstructured approach, in which teachers tried to contribute to children's language development through increased attention to verbal communication in the classroom. This attention was more intense when teachers, using categories derived from the work of Bernstein,[7] judged their pupils to be using a 'restricted code' and to be suffering from linguistic deprivation. Parry and Archer pointed to the need for all teachers of young children to receive more guidance and help in this area of their work. In response, in 1973 the Schools Council funded the Communication Skills Project, directed by Joan Tough.

The theoretical basis of this project was very much a product of its time: taking for granted the notion of differential educational disadvantage, the Project drew on Tough's own research[8] to suggest that part of the problem might be ascribed to children's linguistic disadvantage in the school environment. The Project aimed to devise materials that would help teachers to describe young children's use of language, to establish the extent of their disadvantage, and then to use planned conversations or 'dialogue' to foster children's communication skills. Teachers were encouraged to make tape-recordings and observations of their own pupils, and to use these as the basis for small-group discussions.

In addition, the Communication Skills Project offered the possibility of a wider curriculum review. Tough[9] describes the early childhood curriculum in terms of five types of activity (investigational, representational, and receptional (listening) activities, play and 3Rs activities). For all its lack of philosophical grounding, teachers who adopted this classification as the basis for self-study were also committing themselves to a particular view of early childhood education, marked by an emphasis on first-hand experience and play, with relatively less attention being paid to the basic skills of reading, writing, and arithmetic.

The most striking weakness of the Communication Skills Project is that the analysis of children's language, which participating teachers undoubtedly learned to make, was firmly based on a model of disadvantage. Children were characterized as being, not incapable, as Tough was careful to emphasize, but 'indisposed' to use language in certain ways in school. The blame for this disposition was attributed to the disadvantaging language environment of the home: the unintentional effect was to encourage teachers to accept a parody of Bernstein's original elaborated/restricted code dichotomy, and to indulge in a kind of professional pessimism, in which, it seemed, schools could do little to alter the status quo. The belief in language-deprived children is proving to be extraordinarily difficult to eradicate: the vision of early-years education as the salvation of the inadequate and under-privileged of our society has not yet breathed its last.

Two other contemporary Schools Council-funded projects were organized on similar lines: *Early Mathematical Experiences* was directed by Geoffrey and Julia Matthews, and drew on teachers' observations of nursery school children in the compiling of a Teachers Guide. *The Structuring of Play in the Infant/First School*, directed by Kathleen Manning and Ann Sharp,[10] was aimed at teachers of children in the age-range five to eight. Teachers' observations, using detailed schedules prepared by the Project team, formed the backbone of a series of the workshop meetings. All three projects invited teachers to explore the curriculum they offered to young children: members of the workshops were given the opportunity to contribute to their own professional development, by framing questions to ask about their practice.

During the same decade, other publications implicitly encouraged teachers to look more closely at their classrooms and distinguish between what actually happened there, and what they proposed should happen. Sharp and Green's account[11] of child-centred methods in action in three infant classrooms of a primary school is an influential work of this kind. The authors tried to elicit, by interview and observation, the core concepts of the child-centred approach, and to study the way in which these ideas were expressed in action. They claim to have shown that some of the well-intentioned practices of self-defined liberal, progressive teachers contribute to a hierarchical, differentiated social order within the classroom and the school. However, for teachers without an interest in the sociological themes of the book, there are other important messages: at the heart of the authors' analysis is the discovery that a child-centred philosophy 'does not necessarily provide for the teachers clear explanations or legitimations which can bridge the gap between their substantive practice on the one hand and their educational aims on the other . . . the teacher when probed is unable to bridge the gap between her behaviour and the appropriate modes of explanation' (166–7). Key concepts such as readiness, stages of development, and children's needs, are, Sharp and Green argue, merely rhetorical devices used to represent a ritual of commitment to a weakly-constructed ideal: they are not used to express intricate meanings about how a child learns, how a teacher teaches, or how the two are related.

Further evidence of the gaps between what teachers believe, what they say, and what they do, is presented in King's study of three infant schools. Many teachers would question the readiness with which King seems to have swallowed the teachers' accounts of their work, and the literal interpretations he places on their spontaneous comments in the staffroom; but his work has raised awkward questions for early-childhood teachers. Like Sharp and Green, he detects a weakness in the central concept of child-centredness, which was used as common currency in all three schools; he goes on to argue that this weakness is not accessible to the teachers themselves, since their actions tend to confirm their ideas as realities. 'It is the definitions of the powerful that prevail,' writes King;[12] thus teachers' definitions (of innocence, individuality, and stages of development) shape their perceptions of classroom events. Infant teachers do not, according to King, perhaps cannot, use their first-hand experiences of teaching and learning to question or evaluate their belief systems.

Other recent research has focused more narrowly on actual classroom events, as seen by outsiders. Mary Willes[13] has investigated the process by which young children become socialized into the routines of school; routines, she argues, that may be at odds with the processes by which they have been learning in the first years of life. Ferreiro and Teberosky have independently developed this theme, and in their study of pre-writing and pre-reading behaviour in children both before and after starting school, conclude pessimistically that:

> School is directed toward passive children who know nothing, who must be taught. It is not directed toward active children who not only pose their own problems but spontaneously construct mechanisms for solving them, who reconstruct the object to appropriate it through the development of knowledge and

not through the exercise of skills. In short, school is not directed toward children as we know them from Piagetian psychology.[14]

Two important studies of children's language, one large-scale, directed by Gordon Wells,[15] and one much smaller, reported by Tizard and Hughes,[16] have dramatically challenged long-held assumptions about the young child's experiences of language at home and at school. By contrasting parent-child dialogue – frequently rich, sustained, complex, child-initiated, and centred on a child's topic – with teacher-child dialogue – which is far less frequent, shorter, less complex, more often teacher-initiated, and centred on a teacher's topic – these authors invite teachers to think again about the part their language plays in children's intellectual development. If spoken language between teachers and children is to play an important part in the early-years curriculum, then we are still a long way from defining or describing its effective use: but perhaps these two studies will give some impetus to teachers willing to examine and review their own practice, with a view to transforming it.

Members of Bruner's Oxford Pre-School Research Project have published a number of studies of children in a variety of pre-school settings: perhaps the most important of these is Sylva's study.[17] Sylva claims that the ethological method can be used to ask, and answer, educational questions: her study investigates the intellectual quality of children's involvement in nursery and playgroup activity. She concludes that the traditional unstructured play materials of the nursery (water, sand, dough), and untutored physical play do not challenge children to act at their intellectual best. The most demanding activities were art, constructional activities, and structured tasks, and Sylva notes that all these activities possess a definite goal structure. Further observations of the social context of activities showed that older children (four and a half to five and a half) achieve their highest levels of play when in the company of adults, whereas younger (three and a half to four and a half) children's play is enhanced when they are in child-child pairs.

It is unfortunate that many teachers have seen the work of Sylva and others in the Bruner group as having dangerous political implications for early-years provision. Suspicions that the results of these studies might be used to justify a reduction in nursery schools and classes, with a corresponding increase in play-group provision, may have prevented teachers from building on the promising themes for development that Sylva has identified.

Common methodological approaches can be discerned in all these recent enquiries, and there has been a common evaluative purpose to the work: researchers are seeking to establish the educational benefits of the early years of education. And yet, despite this common purpose, there is a remarkable absence of any encompassing philosophical or pedagogical framework within which to analyse the curriculum.

In the last few years, many LEAs have been responding to DES requirements by convening early-years curriculum groups with a brief to produce
guidelines for the education of young children. These have not yet been
extensively reviewed or collated, but there are discernible trends. Typically,
these early-years guidelines make some references to psychological principles
(the Piagetian inheritance, which is used to establish *how* children learn), and
there is an explicit commitment to the social, emotional, moral, and physical
development of children, as well as to their cognitive growth. But there is no
shared perception of how the curriculum itself, its content, and principles of
procedure, is to be represented. There is, unsurprisingly, substantial agreement
about overall aims, and there is a general consensus about the kinds of activities
that are to be provided: natural materials, construction materials, opportunities
for the expressive arts, and so on. The trappings of early-years education vary
little from establishment to establishment or from LEA to LEA: but sand,
water, clay, Lego, dressing-up clothes, and powder paint do not in themselves
constitute a curriculum, still less a workable curriculum model. Indeed Simon
suggests that primary education as a whole has been careering down a blind
alley since the early 1920s, when child-centred theories began to dominate
our thinking. He argues that the pedagogic romanticism of the Plowden Report
is to blame for our current confusion about the connection between teaching
and learning:

> ... by focusing on the individual child ('at the heart of the educational process
> lies the child'), and in developing the analysis from this point, the Plowden
> Committee created a situation from which it was impossible to derive an effective
> pedagogy (or effective pedagogical means). If each child is unique, and each
> requires a specific pedagogical approach appropriate to him or her and to no
> other, the construction of an all-embracing pedagogy, or general principles of
> teaching, becomes an impossibility. And indeed research has shown that primary
> school teachers who have taken the priority of individualisation to heart find it
> difficult to do more than ensure that each child is in fact engaged on the series
> of tasks which the teacher sets up for the child.[18]

Further indirect evidence of this intellectual hole at the centre of the early-
years universe can be found in the important review of Pre-School Education
(in its widest definition) based on the work of the Child Health and Education
Study.[19] The analysis of the curriculum offered in 17,000 pre-school institutions is based on four scales (labelled skills, language, finding out, and gross
motor), which record the availability of specified equipment and activities.
These scales were drawn up after a review of the literature on early-years
curriculum and with the assistance of nursery teachers involved in the project.
The early-years curriculum is here conceived strictly in terms of material
objects in the classroom: Wendy house, jigsaws, tricycles, and rabbits. Furthermore, in spite of the different origins and purposes of different types of pre-

school provision, Osborn and Milbank report that the cognitive gains ascribed to pre-school experience that they have detected in children at age ten are independent of the type of establishment attended (LEA nursery, private playgroup, or DHSS day nursery).

Meanwhile HMI are encouraging teachers to analyse curriculum in terms of a very much more abstract framework: *Curriculum Matters Two*[20] lists nine areas of experience: aesthetic and creative, human and social, linguistic and literary, mathematical, moral, physical, scientific, spiritual, technological. Audrey Curtis[21] reduces nine areas to six (self-awareness, cultural awareness, communication, motor and perceptual, analytical and problem-solving, aesthetic and creative) but there is little evidence to suggest that these, or any other polysyllabic terminologies, play much part in determining what actually happens in schools and classrooms.

It is in this cultural climate that the work of David Weikart and the High/Scope Foundation has created so much interest. Remarkable claims are made for the work of the Foundation: evidence, triumphantly reported by Schweinhart *et al.*[22] suggests that high quality pre-school programmes have an impressive long term effect on IQ and school achievement; and, more important, that one particular programme, the High/Scope Cognitively Oriented Curriculum, resulted in substantially lower rates of self-reported juvenile delinquency and associated problems (measured at the age of 15) than did two other pre-school programmes in the study.

There are certainly, at present, reasons for treating these claims with caution,[23] if not with downright scepticism, as Osborn and Milbank do, dismissing the very possibility that a pre-school programme could have such far-reaching effects.[24] But there is also considerable and justifiable interest in the structure and organization of the High/Scope Curriculum itself. Perhaps the most striking aspect of this curriculum is that its exponents offer a clear account of what, how, and why they teach young children in their care.[25] Hohmann acknowledges the profound influence of Piaget, and the programme's explicitly developmental structure is defined and justified by reference to his work. The process side of the curriculum is characterized by the expression 'active learning', and the content of the child's development is prescribed in a list of fifty key experiences, which are subdivided into four subsets: using language; representing experiences and ideas; developing logical reasoning; understanding time and space. Social and emotional development are acknowledged as important, but the programme 'deals with them through indirect means'. It is argued that the daily routine for each child participating in the programme – which is encapsulated in the rubric: Plan, Do, Review – is in itself sufficient to promote social and emotional growth. Hohmann presents this curriculum in a large, lavishly illustrated (and very expensive) volume, which includes diaries, planning schedules, and evaluations, and a summary of teaching methods. It remains to be seen whether growing professional interest and involvement in the High/Scope movement in this country will take the form of an uncritical acceptance of the Weikart gospel. Or perhaps early-years teachers, trained in the eclectic British tradition, will resist a programme that is so comprehensively and meticulously programmed, a programme in which children are encouraged to question everything except the structures of the programme itself.

Another recent development has been the increased interest, at all levels of education, in what is still sometimes called 'equal opportunities'. This umbrella term for issues of race, gender, and sometimes, class, is seen by some as an unacceptable euphemism which does not do enough to urge upon teachers their duty to provide anti-racist and anti-sexist education for all. In some parts of the country, these issues are seen as high priorities, and in others, particularly all-white rural areas, teachers have yet to be convinced that there is a need to investigate their attitudes to race and gender. In early-years education there has been a steady trickle of publications concerned with the effects on young children of early sex-stereotyping and other discriminatory practices, and some of these[26] offer evidence that increasing numbers of teachers are critically reviewing their practice in regard to these issues.

CONCLUSION

The honoured ancestors of early childhood education were driven by inner conviction and a sense of mission. Their beliefs were expressed categorically and their practices presented as self-evidently embodying those beliefs. Early-years teachers today are undoubtedly influenced by the great traditions of the past, but we have noted the difficulties they seem to have in defining and describing exactly what it is they have inherited. The reforming zeal of the pioneers led them to ask challenging questions about the beliefs and practices of others, rather than their own: this tendency seems to have been transmitted to their descendants.

During the last twenty years there has been a far-reaching critical review of the curriculum of early childhood by philosophers, sociologists, and psychologists, as well as by educationalists. But their questions and conclusions may have little constructive effect on what happens to children in classrooms if teachers are excluded, or exclude themselves, from the process of enquiry and reflection.

Thanks to the labours of others, teachers who are willing to examine the curriculum they offer to young children now have access to substantial (if not yet comprehensive) accounts of the processes of young children's learning, the contexts in which it takes place, and the long-term consequences of pre-school education. The challenge for teachers is to make these accounts their own; to use them to build a new and critical understanding of the connection between cherished philosophies and well-tried practices; and to forge a new synthesis between teaching and learning.

REFERENCES

1. Quoted in D. Deasey (1978) *Education Under Six*, London: Croom Helm, p.39.
2. Board of Education (1933) *The Official Report of the Consultative Committee on Infant and Nursery Schools*, London: HMSO, pp.117–23.
3. Central Advisory Council for Education (1967) *Children and their Primary Schools*, London: HMSO, pp.187–8.
4. Peters, R. S. (Ed.) (1969) *Perspectives on Plowden*, London: Routledge & Kegan Paul.
5. Tizard, B. (1975) *Early Childhood Education: A Review and Discussion of Current Research in Britain*, Slough: NFER, p.4.
6. Parry, M. and Archer, H. (1974) *Pre-School Education*, London: Macmillan, p.92.
7. Bernstein, B. (1971) *Class, Codes and Control*, London: Routledge & Kegan Paul.
8. Tough, J. (1977) *The Development of Meaning*, London: Allen & Unwin.
9. Tough, J. (1977) *Talking and Learning*, London: Ward Lock, pp.140–2.
10. Manning, K. and Sharp, A. (1977) *Structuring Play in the Early Years at School*, London: Ward Lock.
11. Sharp, R. and Green, A. (1975) *Education and Social Control*, London: Routledge & Kegan Paul.
12. King, R. (1978) *All Things Bright and Beautiful?*, London: Wiley, p.24.
13. Willes, M. (1983) *Children into Pupils*, London: Routledge & Kegan Paul.
14. Ferreiro, E. and Teberosky, A. (1982) *Literacy Before Schooling*, Portsmouth, NH: Heinemann, p.281.
15. Wells, G. (1986) *The Meaning Makers*, London: Hodder & Stoughton.
16. Tizard, B. and Hughes, M. (1984) *Young Children Learning*, London: Fontana.
17. Sylva, K., Roy, C., and Painter, M. (1980) *Childwatching at Playgroup and Nursery School*, London: Grant McIntyre.
18. Simon, B. (1985) *Does Education Matter?*, London: Lawrence & Wishart, p.98.
19. Osborn, A. F. and Milbank, J. (1987) *The Effects of Early Childhood Education*, Oxford: Clarendon Press.
20. DES (1985) *The Curriculum from 5 to 16: Curriculum Matters 2*, London: HMSO.
21. Curtis, A. (1986) *A Curriculum for the Pre-School Child*, Windsor: NFER-Nelson.
22. Schweinhart, L., Weikart, D. P., and Larner, M. B. (1986) 'Consequences of three pre-school curriculum models through age 15', *Early Childhood Research Quarterly*, 1 (1): 15–35.
23. Bereiter, C. (1986) 'Does direct instruction cause delinquency?', *Early Childhood Research Quarterly*, 1 (3): 289–92.
24. Osborn, A. F. and Milbank, J. op. cit.
25. Hohmann, M., Banet, B., and Weikart, D. P. (1979) *Young Children in Action*, Ypsilanti, Mich.: High/Scope Press.
26. Adams, S. (Ed.) (1986) *Primary Matters*, London: Inner London Education Authority.

5.4

THE AIMS AND CONTENT OF THE PRIMARY CURRICULUM

PATRICIA ASHTON

A STARTING POINT

When teachers are exhorted to do something, by politicians, or by other members of the education service, or by the public, there is an obvious implication that they are currently not doing that thing. The call, 'Back to the basics' signals that teachers have departed from them. Yet the conclusion by Galton et al.,[1] following their intensive ORACLE study of primary classrooms, that 'We find . . . that primary schools concentrate very heavily on basic number and language work. . . .' will have come as no surprise to most teachers.

So it is with the Secretary of State's statement in the Times Educational Supplement of January 1987, 'We cannot continue with a system under which teachers decide what to teach without reference to a clear nationally agreed set of objectives and without having to expose, and if necessary justify, their decisions to parents, employers and the public.' In fact, both requirements are already widely met by schools as a matter of course. There must be few schools without some documentation of their purposes and of the nature and shape of their curriculum. There must be even fewer where explicit account is not taken of the concerns of parents who, in themselves, reflect some cross-section of the public. Indeed, it is hard to imagine a discussion of the curriculum among teachers which would not include frequent references to the views of parents, to public opinion, to their LEA, and to other parts of the education service. Nevertheless, as these external demands become formalized into specific instructions, accompanied by indications of a nationally agreed set of objectives, potentially all teachers will be caught up in re-examinations and re-statements of their aims and curriculum. Virtue, however, can be made out of necessity. Existing statements of aims and current curriculum guidelines tend to enshrine good intentions detached from classroom practice. A major

565

consideration by school staffs could be used, not merely to rehearse previous arguments and to tidy up existing statements, but to reconsider the relationship of such frameworks of intention to the daily work of the school.

TAKING STOCK

There seem to be widely shared assumptions about what British primary schools are about and what goes on there. Former teacher and prolific writer on primary education, and now HMI, Colin Richards[2] has asserted that the curriculum has remained substantially unchanged for the last twenty years. Boyd,[3] a trainer of primary school teachers, claims that the curriculum is largely established and unlikely to undergo much change in the foreseeable future. Analysts of the primary curriculum observe its main educational heritage in the work of Rousseau and Dewey, and its psychological one in the work of Piaget which, together with the influences of Pestalozzi, Froebel, Montessori, and Isaacs on educational practice, and Bruner on learning theory, have cumulatively given rise to a distinctive child-centred ideology. Blenkin and Kelly[4] usefully summarize this as meaning the attempt to treat the child as a child (and not an inadequate adult), by emphasis on education through experience and learning by discovery, a view of knowledge as integrated – or, at least, not compartmentalized, by attending to developmental stages and by defining education and the curriculum in terms of processes. The Plowden Report,[5] of course, broadly encompassed this view and was a landmark in legitimizing this interpretation of the nature and purposes of primary education.

While, as some of these writers suggest, there may be a gap between the 'rhetoric and the reality' those familiar with primary schools seem to assume a broadly similar reality. On the whole, children seem to experience the same broad scope of curriculum areas within which language and mathematics are accorded the highest priority, and to be treated with the same concern for their individuality and their need to work at their own pace. Those themes are recurrent in any discussion with teachers.

Such a background of assumptions provides a sense of relative certainty about the direction and the overall content of primary work. Most teachers will have spent their entire careers within this ideological climate. There are relatively limited opportunities to see how those ideas are interpreted in other schools – sometimes, even in other classes. It is easy to take for granted a consensus of ideas and a similarity of practice far greater than may actually exist.

The Primary Survey[6] provided startling evidence of the wide variation between schools in the teaching of specific items within the curriculum areas of language, mathematics, aesthetic and physical education, social abilities and moral learning, history, geography, and science. HMI observed in over sixteen hundred classes and designated any item taught in more than 80 per cent of those classes as indicating a general priority among teachers. No item within history, geography, or science reached that level of commonness. Of a list more than twice as long, only 36 items were taught to more than 80 per cent of the classes observed, but fewer than a third of the classes experienced all of them. While this is only one piece of evidence, it is quite sufficient to disturb the assumption that primary schools are broadly similar in what they seek to achieve.

What of the nature of children's experience in primary schools? To what extent does it conform to Plowden's tenets of child-centredness, curriculum integration, and learning, developed through experiment and experience? In the ORACLE study, Galton et al.[7] carried out sustained observations in sixty junior classrooms in three LEAs. Summing up their findings, they return repeatedly to the mismatch between the teaching they observed and Plowden's prescripts. While much work was individualized, little of it was exploratory, engaging children in learning for themselves, prompted and guided by teachers. While children were frequently seated in groups, they were far more often instructed and managed than they were questioned and encouraged to think. Moreover, there is plenty of evidence from studies based on both questionnaires and observation, usefully summarized in Marriott,[8] that teachers can be very different in the nature of the learning experiences that they provide for children.

If practice is diverse, it is likely that so too are implicit aims. Working within an assumption of consensus, it may be that the meanings given to the language of primary philosophy and the interpretations of those meanings in practice, add up to 'a sheer complexity and diversity of practice which has scarcely been realized, let alone analysed' Marriott (op. cit.). The next step has to be a reexamination of aims.

THE PROBLEM WITH AIMS

Many primary schools have statements of their aims in one form or another; some are to be found heading the collected curriculum guidelines and others are included in information for parents. One primary head teacher recently initiated a reconsideration of aims in his school. The staff began by digging out (almost literally) existing statements. A variety of documents came to light; some teachers had one, some had several, and one or two had none. The oldest document had been written twenty years earlier. More important, although the staff had long earned the school a good reputation, none of them actually knew what its stated aims were. Their reaction to the head's invitation was to insist that if they were to spend time on aims, they had to be more useful than they had been in the past. This experience of aims will not be unique. Some teachers seem to find discussing aims interesting, take for granted that the usual statements reflect their beliefs and imbue their practice, and then set them aside to get on with teaching. Other teachers reject spending time on discussing aims at all as a fruitless and irrelevant exercise.

In a practical guidebook to planning the curriculum, Holt[9] has even wondered whether it is worth struggling to formulate aims at all but rather to spend the effort on working out the tasks that have to be done. Yet, as is compellingly argued by Barrow,[10] it is impossible to embark on an enterprise as complex and as important as education without a clear view of what education is and what broad purposes schooling should serve. The most prominent philosopher of primary education, Robert Dearden, argues that although 'it is the very nature of statements of aims to be general', they are needed to provide an 'overall orientation and direction'.[11] The everyday reality in many schools is probably that 'the overall orientation and direction' is assumed, rather than known, to exist. This state of affairs may come about largely because of the temptation to think of aims as finished with at the point at which they have been formulated. The solution lies in reconceiving aims and their use. They need to be viewed as active entities, the function of which is first, to be discussed, and second, to provide criteria for judging the worth of day-to-day classroom activity.

Many teachers will be familiar with the six aims first proposed by the DES and the Welsh Office in 'Education in Schools'[12] and subsequently repeated in 'A Framework for the School Curriculum',[13] 'The School Curriculum',[14] and 'The Curriculum 5–16'.[15] They thought that 'In general these aims command widespread support and they are reflected in the aims drawn up by many local education authorities (LEAs) and individual schools.' These aims are:

- to help pupils to develop lively, enquiring minds, the ability to question and argue rationally and to apply themselves to tasks, and physical skills;
- to help pupils to acquire knowledge and skills relevant to adult life and employment in a fast changing world;
- to help pupils to use language and number effectively;
- to instil respect for religious and moral values, and tolerance of other races, religions, and ways of life;
- to help pupils to understand the world in which they live, and the interdependence of individuals, groups, and nations;
- to help pupils to appreciate human achievements and aspirations.

More recently, the Select Committee on Achievement in Primary Schools[16] endorsed a set of aspects of achievement which had first been worked out by the Committee on the Curriculum and Organization of Secondary Schools.[17] Having reviewed an enormous collection of evidence furnished by large numbers of individuals and groups representing all those concerned with primary education, these are the areas with which the Committee thought primary schools should be concerning themselves. Though not expressed in the usual formula for aims, their function is the same.

'*Aspect 1*' academic attainment as measured by examinations of the traditional kind: it involves most of all the capacity to express oneself in a written form. It requires the capacity to retain propositional knowledge, to select from such knowledge appropriately in response to a specified request, and to do so quickly without reference to possible sources of information. The capacity to memorize and to organize material is particularly important.

'*Aspect 2*' the capacity to apply knowledge rather than knowledge itself; with the practical rather than the theoretical; with the oral rather than the written. Problem-solving and investigational skills are more important than the retention of knowledge.

'*Aspect 3*' is concerned with personal and social skills: the capacity to communicate with others in face-to-face relationships; the ability to co-operate with others in the interests of the group as well as the individual; initiative, self-reliance, and the ability to work alone without close supervision; and the skills of leadership.

'*Aspect 4*' involves motivation and commitment; the willingness to accept failure without destructive consequences; the readiness to persevere; the self-confidence to learn in spite of the difficulty of the task. This aspect may be seen both as a prerequisite to the other three aspects of achievement and as an achievement in its own right.

The first set of aims has been subjected to stringent criticism by White *et al.*[18] on the grounds of some lapses in logic, and the second set are not wholly free of the same charge. This is in part due, as White and his colleagues argue, to the lack of an overarching concept of the educated pupil. They continue, 'Most of those currently writing about the educated man depict him as someone who autonomously chooses his own path through life without overlooking his moral obligations to other people, and without allowing them to impose their own prescriptions on him, whether these concern personal ideals, moral values, religious beliefs or the organization of his working life.'

Some such fundamental view is vital as a reference point against which to test the value and the coherence of the more specific intentions which are contained in sets of aims like those illustrated above. If aims are then to be useful and to guide practice, they need, to use Holt's[19] attractive argument, to be 'tools not rules'. First, they need to be discussed and discussed again from time to time. This enables teachers both to clarify their personal views and to absorb ideas about aims into their daily way of thinking about what they do. Teaching is far too mentally demanding for ideas to remain fresh and alive if they have not been thought about and talked about for twenty years. Second, aims need to be used as criteria for judging the value of children's everyday experience in classrooms. From time to time, aims need to be taken out of the desk drawer and looked over. Is there evidence of the 'willingness to accept failure without destructive consequences', or 'the capacity to apply knowledge', or 'the capacity to communicate with others in face-to-face relationships'? Are these attributes developing in all children, some children, or none? Is some feature of the classroom not conducive to achieving a particular aim or is it perhaps unrealistic? This kind of reflection and debate may ensure that aims really do provide a sense of orientation and direction. Schwab[20] calls this process deliberation. He says 'Deliberation is complex and arduous. It treats both ends and means and must treat them as mutually determining one another. It must try to identify, with respect to both, what facts must be relevant. . . . It must generate alternative solutions. It must make every effort to trace the branching pathways of consequence which may flow from each alternative and affect desiderata. It must then weigh alternatives and their costs and consequences against one another, and choose, not the *right* alternative but the best one.'

FROM AIMS TO CURRICULUM

Through what set of learning experiences can a school's aims for children be pursued optimistically? In what way, first of all, is it helpful to think of the curriculum? Definitions abound in the literature which Lawton[21] argues can be placed on a continuum from the subjects on a timetable at one end to something akin to Kerr's[22] definition of 'all the learning which is planned and guided by the school, whether it is carried on in groups or individually, inside or outside the school' at the other. The word seems to be used familiarly by teachers in two senses. Curriculum seems to mean both the areas named in the curriculum guidelines, together with the list of objectives and content listed under each one, and all of that as it actually happens and is experienced by children. Thus teachers talk about 'the school curriculum' and 'the curriculum in my classroom'. Given that what actually happens depends in some measure upon what is written into the curriculum guidelines, then there is a good, though not exclusive, argument for beginning rethinking there. Oliver,[23] a primary headteacher, argues that teaching is first and foremost concerned with the transmission of knowledge. Such a statement is likely to attract greater support when it is remembered that this encompasses both propositional knowledge – knowing that – and procedural knowledge – knowing how. Since there are different ideas about the relative importance of these two, Oliver goes on to claim that 'Effective practice must therefore be founded on an adequate epistemology, or theory of knowledge.' The early decades of universal primary education were substantially founded on a rationalist epistemology. In this view, some kinds of knowledge have validity or truth which is universal because they derive from logical, coherent, rational relationships between concepts, and reflect universal values. In this view, such knowledge is separate from human experience and thus, true for all time. It follows inevitably that teachers of this persuasion can decide with certainty precisely what knowledge, skills, and attitudes children should acquire. Such knowledge, skills, and attitudes either inhere in the selected bodies of knowledge, or like language skills, they are necessary in order to acquire the knowledge. This exact prespecification is known as the objectives model of curriculum planning, and it is one which many teachers will have encountered in the course of their training. The idea of planning by objectives was first publicized in the USA by Tyler,[24] who was followed by influential writers such as Bloom,[25] with his *Taxonomy of Objectives*, and Mager,[26] on *Preparing Instructional Objectives*. It was argued that objectives must be behavioural, that is, they must specify exactly what the learner would know or be able to do. Specifications must be precise, unequivocal, and must make assessment obvious. The approach undoubtedly has its uses. It offers a reassuringly systematic way for teachers to sort out exactly what, given their overall aims, they should be teaching. It also provides clear indications of how successful are the pupils' learning and the teacher's teaching. Moreover, it helps in sorting out a sensible sequence for the teaching of skills and concepts, and many curriculum guidelines make use of an objectives approach to planning, particularly in language and mathematics, science, and environmental studies/project work.

The problem lies in deciding whether this approach matches teachers' view of knowledge. Do they subscribe to a rationalist epistemology? It is hard to listen in to any discussion of the curriculum amongst primary teachers and to suspect that the majority do. The general tenor of such discussions is the argument that process is more important than product, and that major emphasis should be given to 'learning how to learn'. This view is much more likely to stem from an empiricist view of knowledge. This sees knowledge as not fixed but constantly changing because it is the product of human enquiry and experience. The 'facts' change as experience accumulates and different modes of enquiry and different interpretations are brought to bear. A further version of this theory, known as pragmatist, suggests that knowledge is 'true' if it fits the facts and reflects 'what works'; inevitably such truth will change over time. This view of the nature of knowledge obviously gives rise to the belief that children should be helped, not primarily to acquire knowledge, but to learn how to acquire it. This best helps children not only to continue learning in the future but also to contribute to the development of new knowledge and understanding. Specific learning outcomes become, in this view, much more

unpredictable, and the emphasis on the activity of learning itself is characterized as a process curriculum.

The process model however, has two major variants, and this choice is
perhaps the most critical one facing teachers rethinking their curriculum.
One variant, supported perhaps most influentially by Stenhouse,[27] Hirst,[28] and
Dearden,[29] holds that an appreciation of various forms of knowledge is vital
to a concept of education as the development of understanding. Dearden
suggests that these are mathematics, science, history, ethics, and religion.
HMI, who strongly favour this view, extend the definition to 'areas of learning
and experience', and list aesthetic and creative, linguistic and literary, mathematical, moral, physical, scientific, spiritual, and technological. Each form of
knowledge, Stenhouse suggests, has a distinctive structure, its own concepts
and procedures for thinking and enquiry, and its own criteria by which the
validity of the knowledge is judged. These, in themselves, are problematic and
can change, and so the substance of the curriculum needs to be based on
principles for learning and enquiring in these various ways. Thus, for example,
learning to think mathematically overrides in importance acquiring specific
skills and concepts. Interestingly, school guidelines tend often to espouse the
supremacy of mathematical thinking in the aims section, but to proceed with
a catalogue of specific items appropriate to a much more rigid view of mathematical learning. The problem is that such 'knowing what it is to know'
(Oliver op. cit.)[30] across the whole spectrum of the primary curriculum is well-
nigh impossible for any individual teacher. The role of the curriculum leader
is vital in implementing this concept of a process curriculum.

The second variant of the model is that promoted by Blenkin and Kelly
(op. cit.)[31] for example. They suggest that, while forms of knowledge should
not be ignored, they should be 'second-order considerations'. The starting
point, they argue, should be the children's genuine activities, interests, or
enquiries. The teacher's role is then to diagnose their performances and to
widen and deepen their skills and understandings and sustain their interest in
a way which is logical from their point of view. Such enquiries will usually be
interdisciplinary. This, as indeed Blenkin and Kelly argue, is a genuinely child-
centred view of education. The difficulty is that education is concerned with
children, and managing such an approach with 25 or 30 is an inordinately
difficult task. Alexander[32] has said, for example, that classroom practice which
is superficially deemed to be 'open' and exploratory, in reality can provide
children with 'undemanding and stultifying topic work', where the choices
open to children are 'restricted and mundane'. Such a model, he suggests,
can be far more profoundly 'closed' than a subject-oriented one.

WHAT ABOUT THE BASIC SKILLS?

Even the most ardent advocates of a process curriculum agree that there are certain skills, and indeed some information, which parents and society in general have a right to expect children to acquire, and which can thus be prespecified as learning objectives. Downey and Kelly[33] point to four areas of skill; first, numeracy and literacy; second, specialist skills forming part of other curriculum activities; third, social skills; and fourth, critical thinking. It is convenient to list such skills, to consider the sub-skills which each involves, and to sort out a logical sequence in which it is helpful to acquire them. Indeed, curriculum guidelines often represent just such identification and planning. However, skills neither exist nor can be learned apart from their use. Just as Dearden (op. cit.), for example, argues that the skills which make up reading have no sense apart from their use in reading something, neither do those of a mathematical, scientific nature, or anything else. Thus identification of skills to be learned is only the first step. It has to be followed by considering through what educational activities children can be given opportunities to learn those skills. Following the Aims of Primary Education Project, (Ashton et al.)[34] many teachers did the exercise of looking again at every area of their curriculum to see where skills, and attitudes, which they aimed for, might be learned. Often, for example, 'language' was at risk of disappearing completely as a separate area, as teachers perceived the rich opportunities of teaching the skills of reading, writing, listening, and speaking through art, science, mathematics, and so on. Moreover, if skills can only be learned through content, questions need to be asked about the purposes that the content itself can fulfil. Teachers often seem to consider this a secondary, sometimes an incidental, sometimes even an unnecessary consideration. To agree that the prime concern is the process of learning how to enquire and to develop understanding does not need to mean that the content is unimportant. The question of what kind of knowledge is valuable is inescapable.

DOWN TO EARTH

When the curriculum plans are made, the information and skills specified, the learning process selected, and the approach to knowledge and understanding clarified, and all seen as a coherent and justifiable whole, the practical difficulties begin. There are two major ones. One is that curriculum plans are formulated as if their object was a single child, or perhaps a body of children behaving, thinking, responding, and learning as one. If account is taken of differences then it tends to be in regard to very broad notions of capability. The reality is that of twenty-five to thirty highly individual individuals, each one of whom makes, takes and demands something different from the theoreti-

573

cal notion the teacher has of the curriculum, whether he or she manifests that through talk, activities, or textbooks. The curriculum in action cannot be conceived to correspond in detail with the planned curriculum; the experiences, the difficulties, and the achievements diverge to a greater or lesser extent, and in different ways, from the concept. No planned curriculum is static; it involves the concept of progress both in time and according to a logic of the particular area. In practice, there are as many kinds and rates of progress as there are children. Add to this, the second difficulty that at least some of this differentiated response is unpredictable, depending upon mood, health, previous experience, and the talents and interests which may be evoked by the particular experience, and the conceived curriculum is out of shape, if not out of control. This can lead to a steady drift away from intentions in favour of solutions which are known to 'work'.

There needs to be a major shift away from the concept of a temporal sequence in which aims are identified first, then curriculum plans are worked out, and then, as the last stage, put into operation in the classroom. In this model, the stages tend to be very unequal, with classroom action constant, curriculum planning revisited occasionally, and aims rarely. Moreover, there is a tendency always to begin again at the beginning with both aims and curriculum plans, and not explicitly to modify them in the light of classroom action.

Within the classroom, teachers operate a cycle of action and reflection. They constantly, in every area of their work, note children's reactions, and modify what they had in mind to do next. This pattern obtains across the board from helping a child with a spelling to the course of an afternoon's art activity. What teachers do is modified by their perceptions of children's responses. This cycle needs to be enlarged to encompass their broader intentions and plans. Aims and curriculum plans need to be regarded as provisional, reflecting the best judgements that can be made at the time. Those aims and plans then need to be looked at in action – as they are reflected in the daily classroom lives of the children. Increasing numbers of teachers are now planning very brief but frequent spells of observation into their routines. They are also asking themselves the hard questions about the extent to which what they value is actually taking place. A few moments of looking at a child embarking on a new task in maths; a regular glance at a group intended to be co-operating on a piece of project work; a note of which children take part in a class discussion and what they say; a quick record of what questions children ask when they write a story; all reveal something of the nature and quality of the education the children are actually experiencing. These insights, particularly if all the staff are making similar, careful soundings, can be fed back into the curriculum discussions. Aims and plans can be refined, modified, and brought into closer, practical, explicit relationship with everyday classroom work. Through these means, teachers can expose and justify their decisions, not just to satisfy outsiders, but because so doing is central to the developing life of the school.

REFERENCES

1. Galton M., Simon, B., and Croll, P. (1980) *Inside the Primary Classroom*, London: Routledge & Kegan Paul.
2. Richards, C. (1983) 'Utopia deferred: curriculum issues for primary and middle school education' in M. Galton and B. Moon (Eds.) *Changing Schools: Changing Society*, London: Harper & Row.
3. Boyd, J. (1984) *Understanding the Primary Curriculum*, London: Hutchinson & Co.
4. Blenkin, G. M. and Kelly, A. V. (1981) *The Primary Curriculum*, London: Harper & Row.
5. Central Advisory Council for Education (England) (1967) *Children and their Primary Schools*, (Plowden Report), London: HMSO.
6. Department of Education and Science (1978) *Primary Education in England: a Survey by HM Inspectors of Schools*, London: HMSO.
7. op. cit.
8. Marriott, S. (1985) *Primary Education and Society*, Sussex: The Falmer Press.
9. Holt, M. (1983) *Curriculum Workshop: An Introduction to Whole Curriculum Planning*, London: Routledge & Kegan Paul.
10. Barrow, R. (1984) *Giving Teaching back to Teachers*, Sussex: Wheatsheaf Books Ltd.
11. Dearden, R. F. (1968) *The Philosophy of Primary Education: An Introduction*, London: Routledge & Kegan Paul.
12. Department of Education and Science and Welsh Office (1977) *Education in Schools*, London: HMSO.
13. Department of Education and Science (1980) *A Framework for the School Curriculum*, London: HMSO.
14. Department of Education and Science (1981) *The School Curriculum*, London: HMSO.
15. Department of Education and Science (1985) *The Curriculum from 5–16*, Curriculum Matters 2, London: HMSO.
16. House of Commons (1986) Third Report from the Education, Science and Arts Committee, *'Achievement in Primary Schools'*, London: HMSO.
17. Hargreaves, D. H. (1984) *Improving Secondary Schools*, Report of the Committee on the Curriculum and Organization of Secondary Schools, Inner London Education Authority.
18. White, J., Black, P., Ogborn, J., Crick, B., Porter, A., Hornsey A., Aspin, D., and Lawton, D. (1981) *No, Minister. A Critique of the DES Paper 'The School Curriculum'*, Bedford Way Papers 4, University of London Institute of Education.
19. op. cit.
20. Schwab, J. (1978) *Science, Curriculum and Liberal Education*, Selected essays edited by I. Westbury and N. Wilkof, University of Chicago Press.
21. Lawton, D. (1983) *Curriculum Studies and Educational Planning*, London: Hodder & Stoughton.
22. Kerr, J. F. (Ed.) (1968) *Changing the Curriculum*, London: University of London Press.
23. Oliver, D. (1982) 'The primary Curriculum: a proper basis for planning', in C. Richards (Ed.) *New Directions in Primary Education*, Sussex: The Falmer Press.
24. Tyler, R. (1949) *Basic Principles of Curriculum and Instruction*, Chicago: University of Chicago Press.
25. Bloom, B. S. (Ed.) (1954) *The Taxonomy of Objectives*, London: Longman.
26. Mager, R. F. (1962) *Preparing Instructional Objectives*, Palo Alto, California: Fearon.
27. Stenhouse, L. (1975) *An Introduction to Curriculum Research and Development*, London: Heinemann Educational Books.
28. Hirst, P. H. (1974) *Knowledge and the Curriculum*, London: Routledge & Kegan Paul.
29. Dearden, R. F. (1976) *Problems in Primary Education*, London: Routledge & Kegan Paul.
30. op. cit.
31. op. cit.
32. Alexander, R. (1984) *Primary Teaching*, London: Reinhart & Winston.

33. Downey, M. and Kelly, A. V. (1979) *Theory and Practice of Education: An Introduction*, London: Harper & Row.
34. Ashton, P., Kneen, P., and Davies, F. (1975) *Aims into Practice in the Primary School*, London: Hodder & Stoughton.

5·5

THE SECONDARY CURRICULUM 11–16: TOWARDS A COMMON CURRICULUM

KEITH McWILLIAMS

INTRODUCTION

The secondary curriculum is rather like a mirage which becomes increasingly more confused the closer one approaches it. It is possible to take a point of view extolling the virtues of the English and Welsh devolved system of education which has enabled independent development to flourish with the minimum of central government intervention; it is equally possible to emphasize the weaknesses of a fragmented pattern lacking shape and direction. Both polarizations contain grains of truth, but oversimplification makes any description of major influences upon the secondary curriculum highly speculative and controversial.

DEFINITION AND BACKGROUND

There are three interlocking aspects of the school curriculum: content, process, and context. Since the 1944 Education Act we have experienced three decades focusing upon context in which the structure of secondary education was the dominant factor. Initially the national priority was to establish the tripartite system of grammar, technical, and secondary modern schools. From the early 1960s it is possible to discern the move towards comprehensive re-organization, which was substantially accomplished between 1965 and 1975.

A powerful influence behind this reform was a desire to make a grammar school education available to all. The deep-rooted strands of grammar and secondary modern were to remain throughout the first three decades after the 1944 Act, and it is arguable that the introduction of CSE alongside GCE O level into comprehensive schools ensured that the emergence of a genuinely comprehensive curriculum became even more difficult. Thus despite the notable contribution of a few schools, the introduction of comprehensive education was largely confined to the provision of buildings with a common label, rather than the development of a comprehensive secondary curriculum.

During the 1970s there was a growing realization that changing the context of the secondary curriculum was a flawed innovation unless attention was given to content and process. Yet in 1972 the Secretary of State for Education and Science, Margaret Thatcher, issued a White Paper, 'Education: A Framework for Expansion', which still did not include the curriculum as a topic.

Less than five years later it was a labour Prime Minister, James Callaghan, who, at Ruskin College, initiated the so-called 'Great Debate' by questioning the ability of schools to reach acceptable standards and to provide the nation with a steady stream of quality leavers. The process and the content of the curriculum thereby became high profile issues for debate, and ensuing controversy, as the hitherto 'secret garden of the curriculum' was mercilessly unveiled and exposed to full public criticism. If a critical re-appraisal of the secondary curriculum had occurred ten years earlier debates might have been less negative. Undoubtedly the absence of an accepted rationale for a comprehensive secondary curriculum left most comprehensive schools vulnerable to the expressions of discontent, both informed and uninformed, that followed.

It is, therefore, within a hostile climate that the essential critical questions regarding the secondary curriculum have been postulated; it is a further irony that the discussion has occurred within a contracting system beset by a severe decline in pupil numbers, school closures and mergers, fewer teachers, financial stringency, rising unemployment, and a national concern about the long-term economic future of the country. Out of adversity has emerged a decade of intense thought, much paranoia, and some activity, leading inexorably towards a definition of a common or nationally agreed curriculum.

THE AWAKENING

As discussion about the curriculum assumed a higher profile it became evident that the traditional balance of power within the education service was changing. The key elements were twofold: first, central government was no longer prepared to concentrate primarily upon resource issues and very broad areas of policy. Successive Secretaries of State made it clear that they were concerned about the quality of all aspects of education, and that the curriculum was now a major element in that process. Second, local education authorities received a sharp reminder that they too had an obligation to consider the nature and content of the curriculum. These highly significant shifts not only began the movement towards accountability, and therefore altered the traditional practice of leaving matters concerning the curriculum to heads and teachers, but they also introduced the comparatively novel idea that it was necessary to consider the complete age range 5–16 when discussing the school curriculum.

Within secondary education there are two main historical strands of curriculum implementation. Largely derived from the selective grammar school tradition, there is a pattern of a core of subjects for all pupils 11–14, usually with a distinct break at about 14, followed by a selection of subjects mostly derived from the 11–14 menu. From the secondary modern tradition we can discern a curriculum based upon a narrower range of subjects available throughout with only very limited new elements introduced. The failure to develop a genuinely comprehensive secondary curriculum meant that the reorganized schools attempted to retain both traditions, and at the same time to extend pupils' opportunities by introducing increasingly complex option systems at 14 or earlier. It is a matter of conjecture whether or not this refinement produced a coherent curriculum for the 11–16-year-old pupils, particularly when by a variety of sometimes subtle and sometimes clumsy mechanisms the option choice system was used to differentiate between pupils.

Other factors affecting the secondary curriculum of the mid-1970s included the arrival of new topics unrelated to the traditional subjects. Schools were now expected to introduce careers education, health education, personal, social, and moral education, the latter within the context of the 'pastoral curriculum', linked to the introduction of elaborate pastoral care staffing structures as a concomitant to the idea of a comprehensive school. Thus the 1970s were largely a period of unplanned growth, and with an absence of an overall rationale it was possible for individual schools to take highly idiosyncratic decisions leading to a curriculum bursting at the seams through accretion. The secondary curriculum had become both overloaded and fragmented.

NATIONAL INITIATIVES

Since 1976, the secondary curriculum has thus become the object of intense national scrutiny. Following a series of regional conferences furthering the Great Debate, the Government issued a Green Paper, 'Education in Schools', in 1977.[1] Schools were reminded that changing demographic, social, and economic factors applied to them as well as everyone else, and there was a clear warning that 'the curriculum in many schools is not sufficiently matched to life in a modern industrial society'. Starkly emphasizing the dangers of an overloaded curriculum with excessively wide variations in provision, the Green Paper postulated that 'the time has come to try to establish generally accepted principles for the composition of the secondary curriculum for all pupils', and it made it quite clear that the preferred way of achieving this objective was by defining a 'core' or 'protected' element. The reference to the principle of protection should not be overlooked, and certainly suggests that initially the notion of a core curriculum was designed to identify and preserve essential elements only, leaving the remainder of the curriculum undefined and still subject to the vagaries of a free-range system in which the weaker subjects would struggle to survive. Nevertheless the notion of a 'core curriculum' remains a key aspect of any definition of a national curriculum.[2]

In 1977 HMI published a working paper, 'Curriculum 11–16'[3] in association with five LEAs, introducing the radical suggestion that the starting point for describing the curriculum should not be the conventional subjects, but that pupils were entitled to certain key 'areas of experience'.

The origins for this fresh approach can be found in a variety of sources, for example through the writings of Paul Hirst,[4] Denis Lawton,[5] Malcolm Skilbeck,[6] and Maurice Holt,[7] together with the significant Munn Report on secondary education in Scotland, also published in 1977, which outlined 'modes of activity' for all pupils. In 1979 HMI published 'Aspects of Secondary Education in England',[8] which reported the results of a survey undertaken from 1975–8, taking into account the effects of the raising of the school leaving age in 1973 and the achievement of a totally comprehensive system in most parts of the country. This survey revealed the full extent of the proliferation of elaborate option systems, indicated concern about the dangers of fragmentation, and suggested that option systems tended to restrict choice rather than the reverse, all of which could have serious implications for a pupil's choice of career and/or higher education routes.

'Curriculum 11–16' proposed that all pupils should be introduced to eight 'areas of experience': the aesthetic and creative, the ethical, the linguistic, the mathematical, the physical, the scientific, the social and political, and the spiritual, 'to be pursued to a depth appropriate to their ability by all pupils in secondary schools', perhaps as much as two thirds or three quarters of the total time available. In other words we are very close to a definition of a common curriculum for all pupils. Only slowly and with many difficulties did the schools involved begin to explore the practicalities of constructing a secondary curriculum based upon the HMI checklist.

At the same time as the notion of a common curriculum was being explored, LEAs, via Circular 14/77, had been reminded of their own curricular responsibilities, and were asked to describe their policies on the curriculum. The DES report on these responses, 'Local Authority Arrangements for the School Curriculum',[9] was published in 1979, and revealed the wide variety of approaches within the 104 English and Welsh LEAs, many of whom had found it necessary to devise procedures for gathering the requisite information from their schools. A number of areas of specific concern were highlighted – English, Mathematics, Modern Languages, Science, Religious Education, Preparation for Working Life, and the Welsh Language. The Secretaries of

State noted that the response to Circular 14/77 suggested 'that not all authorities have a clear view of the desirable structure of the school curriculum, especially its core elements. They believe they should seek to give a lead in the process of reaching a national consensus on a desirable framework for the curriculum and consider the development of such a framework a priority for the education service'. The Inspectorate were invited 'to formulate a view of a possible curriculum' with consultations on a draft policy document to take place during 1980.

Within a space of only two or three years secondary schools were taken from the era of near autonomy regarding the curriculum into a very open public debate at local and national levels. Whether the starting point was the 'areas of experience' approach or the more traditional subject titles embodied in the DES report on Circular 14/77 review, the inference was clear. From now onwards the school curriculum would be the subject of both LEA and national government attention.

Early in 1980 the Department of Education and Science and the Welsh Office published 'A Framework of the School Curriculum',[10] which told local authorities that they had a responsibility to formulate curricular policies and objectives which meet national policies and objectives, command local assent, and can be applied by each school to its own circumstances.

In the same year, HMI published a discussion document 'A View of the Curriculum'.[11] They emphasized the problem for secondary education in resolving the tension between common and individual needs, concluding that 'there are sufficient grounds for unease to suggest a need to re-examine the rationale and organizational structure of the prevailing curriculum in many secondary schools.'

HMI offered fourteen propositions for discussion covering areas such as the need for consensus on an appropriate range of knowledge and skills for all pupils, the need for cohesion between education up to 16 and after 16, coherence within the experience of individual pupils, a larger compulsory element in 14–16, with science education for all pupils to 16, and possibly modern languages, together with mathematics, social and political education, history, and personal and social development; a continuing need for differentiation and choice as well as room for new subjects.

In 1981 the Secretaries of State published 'The School Curriculum'.[12] Every local authority was expected to frame policies for the curriculum and 'plan the deployment of available resources to that end; and every school should analyse its aims, set these out in writing and regularly assess how far the curriculum within the school as a whole and for individual pupils measures up to these aims'. Secondary schools were asked to consider the need to plan their curriculum as a whole and not simply as a collection of separate subjects; the need to provide all pupils with a broadly common curriculum, designed to ensure balance and avoid subsequent restriction of choice, and the importance of preparing young people for adult life, and for work in a rapidly changing technological world.

Once again secondary schools were presented with a formidable list of topics to be included in the broad secondary curriculum. The introduction of issues such as micro-electronics, technology, and preparation for adult life, ensured that the problems of implementation remained daunting.

It was this problem of implementation that largely shaped the Schools Council Working Paper 70, 'The Practical Curriculum'.[13] The Council affirmed the need for a visible structure for the curriculum, and started from the pupil's right of access to different areas of human knowledge and experience. Such an approach was very close to that emerging from the HMI discussions on the 11–16 Curriculum where the concept 'entitlement curriculum' became a key component.

Further DES Circulars, 6/81 and 8/83, continued the by now familiar process of requiring LEAs to review their school curriculum policies and provision. Significantly, many local authority and school policy statements prepared between 1981 and 1986 rarely conflicted with the checklists described above, but it does not necessarily follow that there are common political, social, economic, and religious values and perspectives behind apparently broadly held statements of rationale. The curriculum can no longer, even if it ever could, be described solely as a list of subjects or solely in terms of areas of experience or elements of learning. The secondary curriculum must be perceived as a matrix in which many approaches and insights are relevant. Diversity and variety are as much an integral part of the secondary curriculum as are continuity and coherence.

In the eyes of many observers the process of moving towards agreement on curricular policies was given significant endorsement in January 1984 by the Secretary of State, Sir Keith Joseph, at the North of England Education Conference in Sheffield. He stated that 'the curriculum needs to accord more than it does now with four principles: breadth, relevance, differentiation and balance'. The White Paper 'Better Schools',[14] published just over a year later started from the Sheffield speech and devoted considerable space to arguing that there must be 'hard agreement about the objectives and content of the whole curriculum'.

The problem of an overloaded curriculum could be met by removing 'clutter', eliminating unnecessary repetition, and by improved planning and delivery. As far as the secondary curriculum was concerned, 'Better Schools' suggested that in the fourth and fifth years 80 to 85 per cent of the curriculum should consist of compulsory or constrained choices. Additionally, it indicated important topics for inclusion which were not normally defined as subjects: Economic

Awareness, Health and Sex Education, Careers Education, and Political Education.

'Better Schools' represented the watershed in the process leading to agreement upon a common curriculum. In seeking greater uniformity two modes of action were immediately identified and rapidly implemented. First, a series of DES policy statements was promised, starting with 'Science 5–16', which appeared only weeks after 'Better Schools' and enunciated a policy of 'Science for All' filling 20 per cent of the timetable in the fourth and fifth years. Notwithstanding the immense resource implications behind such a statement, the fact that it was issued in this form demonstrates that the debate has now proceeded well beyond a bland list of desirable aims. Similarly the draft policy statement on modern languages issued in 1986 urged LEAs 'to take steps to make a foreign language one of the compulsory elements of the 14 to 16 curriculum for those pupils who can benefit from it'. Second, HMI began to issue discussion documents in their 'Curriculum Matters' Series. By early 1987 eight had appeared, including 'The Curriculum 5–16',[15] which provided a synoptic view of developments, with a welcome emphasis upon the integrated nature of the school curriculum. The areas of experience first identified by HMI are discussed, with the addition of a ninth, 'technological'. The elements of learning, the characteristics of the curriculum, and assessment, are also dealt with in an approach 'which is designed to ensure a coherent, broad and balanced curriculum for all pupils irrespective of the size, type and location of the schools they attend.'

The ten years following the Ruskin speech have been concerned with analysis, enquiry, and proposals for action followed by policy statements. The direction was clear but the momentum insufficient to bring about the radical changes being proposed. However, in January 1987, in two major speeches at the North of England Conference, Rotherham, and to the Society of Education Officers, Kenneth Baker, Secretary of State for Education and Science, announced that he proposed to achieve 'a national curriculum which works through national criteria for each subject to be produced jointly by central government, LEAs, teachers, parents, and employers'. Mr Baker made it clear that 'we cannot continue with a system under which teachers decide what pupils should learn without reference to clear nationally agreed objectives'. In just over ten years we have moved from an assumed curriculum, via a debate about curricular aims and the notion of a core or common curriculum, to standing on the verge of a written national curriculum statement.

THE SECONDARY SCHOOL'S PERSPECTIVE

While it cannot be denied that the national debate has changed the secondary curriculum, from the perspective of the school, there are other influences for change that may have had a much more direct and immediate effect. Many of these are innovations which are in the process of implementation, and their ultimate significance for the secondary curriculum cannot yet be fully evaluated.

The General Certificate of Secondary Education (GCSE) and the Technical and Vocational Education Initiative (TVEI) are two particularly powerful influences which have emerged from separate government departments.

GCSE

One often-quoted convention is that the elaborate series of public examinations at 16+ and 18+ is the price paid for the considerable independence enjoyed by teachers in determining the nature and content of the secondary curriculum in England and Wales. Another is that unless innovations occur within the context of public examinations, the 11–16 curriculum is unlikely to change at all.

The belated reform of the 16+ examination system most certainly strengthens the claim made in the second statement, but the first may not hold if GCSE really does ensure that the key characteristic is curriculum-led assessment rather than the reverse.

The first examinations for the GCSE will be held in 1988, replacing the GCE O level and CSE with a single system of 16+ examining at long last consistent with the creation of secondary comprehensive education for all. For the first time there are nationally agreed general and subject-specific criteria used as a basis for monitoring all syllabuses. A cardinal feature of the general criteria is that candidates across the ability range should be given an opportunity 'to show what they know, understand and can do'. Syllabuses should be designed to 'help candidates to understand the subject in relation to other areas of study and its relevance to the candidate's own life'. GCSE will have an immediate influence upon the whole 11–16 curriculum.

TVEI

Introduced by the Manpower Services Commission (MSC) the first 14 TVEI projects began in September 1983. Although several of the DES and HMI documents discussed earlier include reference to preparation for the world of work and adult life generally, it has to be acknowledged that the secondary schools' performance in this area was distinctly patchy and uneven in quality. The swingeing criticisms made of schools by employers were still being voiced, and there were continuing expressions of dissatisfaction regarding secondary education's ability to balance the academic with the practical.

Some teachers see great danger in over-stressing the need to prepare pupils adequately for working life, fearing that it will encourage an instrumental view placing the liberal education tradition at risk. On the other hand there have been mounting criticisms of the narrow academic secondary curriculum.

TVEI endeavours to combine a general education with a strong technical and vocational element for groups of young people aged 14–18. From the small beginnings of 1983 all LEAs are now able to participate. There is an element of local determination, but all schemes must conform to MSC criteria, particularly maintaining a balance between the general and the vocational. All TVEI courses place emphasis upon initiative, motivation, enterprise, and problem-solving. Residential and work experience are integral components, and even at the 14–16 stage there are many examples of good practice involving partnership with further education colleges.

By stressing the notions of collaboration across school and FE, work experience, the negotiated curriculum, and progression, TVEI has made an impact, which has resulted in TVEI-type courses being made available to all LEAs from 1987. The effectiveness of the post-16 link with FE colleges remains to be evaluated, and it is still too early to chart the progress of pupils undertaking TVEI courses wishing to enter higher education.

MODULAR APPROACHES

At the time of writing, early 1987, it is debatable whether or not a third major influence upon the secondary curriculum should be included. Undoubtedly it is a topic of growing concern and interest to secondary schools, but it is too early to predict with any certainty the long-term significance of the innovation.

Modules are not in themselves a new concept. In the United States and Canada schools have worked semester-long courses and unit credits for many years. The Open University adopted a unit structure from its inception. Modules have been an integral feature of further education. The first reference to modules within the secondary curriculum occurs in the Munn Report. Eventually the Munn Committee decided not to implement the unit-credit system, but in 1983 the '16–18s in Scotland: an Action Plan' report endorsed a thoroughly modular approach, and it is this document that has had most influence upon pre-16 curriculum thinking in England and Wales.

A number of LEAs have advocated the development of modular approaches, including Coventry in its 1982 report 'Comprehensive Education for Life', and ILEA through the seminal influence of its 1984 report 'Improving Secondary Schools' (The Hargreaves Report). The impetus has been continued by other LEAs, such as Sheffield, Leicestershire, Somerset, and the Welsh LEAs, as well as individual schools.

Probably the most powerful influence for change in this respect is directly attributable to the development of TVEI. Most TVEI schemes have taken a modular approach, and their influence has spread rapidly to other areas of the curriculum.

In a review undertaken by the School Curriculum Development Committee it is evident that modules may be of varying length and be either free-standing or linked. They are typically of much shorter duration than conventional courses, i.e. 40 hours rather than a two-year course. Modules may be part of a traditional subject area or they may introduce new topics. They are an important mechanism for tackling cross-curricular issues, and they ensure that the positive virtues of the option system can survive. There is evidence that they can improve motivation and commitment by providing clear-cut and relatively short-term goals, although it is also apparent that assessment procedures are complex and there is a major requirement to offer counselling support to pupils and to monitor progression through a multiplicity of modules.[16]

The tyranny of the two-year course is challenged by the advent of modules into the secondary curriculum. Schools appear ready to take advantage of the opportunity provided by modular approaches despite the formidable organizational problems, and their willingness to engage in a fundamental review of curricular practices via consideration of modularization is one of the most positive elements of the contemporary scene.

TOWARDS A COMMON CURRICULUM

Looking at secondary schools in 1987 an optimist might describe them as volatile, exciting, and innovative institutions, buzzing with new ideas and innovative programmes, whereas a pessimist would focus upon their threatened status, confused perceptions of purpose, and the general uncertainty fostered by a belief that every aspect of the secondary curriculum is open to change. As before, the most likely answer lies somewhere in between such polarizations.

Agreement upon a national curriculum may provide a context in which the issues confronting the secondary curriculum can be addressed, but it would be unwise to overload that process with unreasonable demands.

Maurice Holt in his book 'Curriculum Workshop'[17] suggests a more direct and practical approach for schools. 'It may well be that in reshaping their curriculum schools would find it easier to secure a common platform of beliefs not by the laborious and unprofitable exercise of writing down aims, but by agreeing on tasks to be tackled.' What are some of these tasks?

1. To equip secondary schools to mediate national curricular policies through to local and individual needs, by agreeing a framework based upon mutual trust and confidence rather than suspicion and recrimination.
2. To understand and practise curriculum continuity, involving further

development between primary and secondary, and with similar attention to post-secondary education. There is growing evidence of the need for a coherent curriculum policy and a co-ordinated system of education and training 14–18; see the SHA documents 'A View from the Bridge' 1983, and 'Future Imperatives: A View of 14–18 and Beyond' 1987, and the NAHT document 'Action Plan: A Policy 14–18', 1987.

3. To produce a workable definition of 'relevance' and to apply it to the curriculum. But does this mean relevance in the eyes of adults – if so which adults – or does it refer to pupils? The danger of a mismatch is evident both in national statements and in school documents and practices.

4. To enable existing subject areas and syllabuses to develop content, concepts, skills, and attitudes equally and consistently, ensuring that the four characteristics of the curriculum are implemented throughout all areas of the curriculum 11–16.

5. To facilitate cross-curricular courses, both by cross-disciplinary courses, such as health and sex education, or careers and work experience, and by formulating effective mechanisms for introducing themes by permeation or diffusion, for example, economic awareness, equal opportunities, multicultural, special needs, and study skills. Permeation policies are attractive yet very hard to implement. They require an ability to relate the topic to the total curriculum-planning process of the individual school, as well as imposing considerable teacher training and support requirements.

6. To introduce curriculum-led assessment policies and practices. Earlier it has been suggested that GCSE is an important step in the right direction, but the discussions regarding TVEI, modularization, and pre-vocational education indicate that secondary schools need to have a liberal approach to assessment. Currently many schools are using various forms of records of achievement. The impact of the BTEC and City and Guilds general education courses and CPVE, will also encourage and challenge schools to review their assessment procedures.

7. To implement school self-appraisal in order to monitor and evaluate current provision and practice with a view to purposeful curriculum planning for the future.

The Education Reform Act (1988) provides for the adoption of core and foundation subjects with appropriate programmes of study, attainment targets, and assessment processes for all pupils of compulsory school age in maintained schools. So there is good reason to anticipate that after decades of indecision we are on the threshold of providing a coherent framework for the content, process, and context of the school curriculum as a whole.

REFERENCES

1. Department of Education and Science (1977) *Education in Schools*, London: HMSO.
2. Kirk, G. (1986) *The Core Curriculum*. Changing Perspectives in Education Series, London: Hodder & Stoughton.
3. HM Inspectors of Schools (1977) *Curriculum 11–16*, followed by (1981) *Curriculum 11–16: A Review of Progress*, and (1983) *Towards a Statement of Entitlement*, all London: HMSO.
4. Hirst, P. H. (1975) *Knowledge and the Curriculum*, London: Routledge & Kegan Paul.
5. Lawton, D. (1975) *Class, Culture and the Curriculum* and (1980) *The Politics of the School Curriculum*, both London: Routledge & Kegan Paul.
6. Skilbeck, M. (1982) *A Core Curriculum for the Common School*, London: University of London Institute of Education.
7. Holt, M. (1978) *The Common Curriculum*, London: Routledge & Kegan Paul, and (1983) *Curriculum Workshop*, London: Routledge & Kegan Paul.
8. HM Inspectors of Schools (1979) *Aspects of Secondary Education in England*, London: HMSO.
9. Department of Education and Science (1979) *Local Authority Arrangements for the School Curriculum*, London: HMSO.
10. Department of Education and Science (1980) *A Framework of the School Curriculum*, London: HMSO.
11. HM Inspectors of Schools (1980) HMI Series: *Matters for Discussion II. A View of the Curriculum*, London: HMSO.
12. Department of Education and Science (1981) *The School Curriculum*, London: HMSO.
13. Schools Council (1981) *Working Paper 70, The Practical Curriculum*, London: Methuen Educational.
14. Department of Education and Science (1985) *Better Schools*, London: HMSO.
15. HM Inspectors of Schools (1985) *Curriculum Matters 2. The Curriculum from 5 to 16*, London: HMSO.
16. Watkins, P. R. (1987) *Modular Approaches to the Secondary Curriculum*, London: Longman for the School Curriculum Development Committee.
17. op. cit.

5.6

THE EMERGING 14–19 CURRICULUM

JACK MANSELL

TRADITIONAL PATTERNS AND CONVENTIONS

14–16 Education

The most comprehensive and authoritative government statement on the secondary curriculum is probably *Better Schools*.[1] The extent to which it has been mediated to the practitioners and to the public at large is questionable, but *Better Schools* states the government belief that for most pupils the period of compulsory education should continue to culminate in assessment through public examinations (para 90). In this respect, the principle of an examination-based 14–16 secondary curriculum based on single subjects remains much as before. Through the 1988 Education Reform Act, the government has now imposed a national school curriculum, and the single-subject curriculum remains the dominant mode of teaching and learning.

16–19 Education

The traditional pattern of 16–19 education comprises two main streams: 'academic' and 'vocational'. The so called 'academic' stream consists of those who are repeating 16+ examinations, studying for A/S or A levels, or a combination of these. The 'vocational' stream consists of those who are studying for one or more vocationally specific qualification associated with examining bodies such as RSA, CGLI, B/TECH etc.

The 17+ debate

As it is non-compulsory, the 16–19 curriculum is thus more open to external pressures than the pre-16 curriculum, and it is not surprising therefore that many would claim that if there is an emerging new-style 14–19 curriculum, it

589

has its origins in post-16 developments. A classic confrontation took place in 1980, when the government accepted[3] as its 17+ curriculum philosophy the FEU 1979 (Mansell) report *A Basis for Choice* (ABC), in preference to the (Keohane) report espousing a collection of CEE (Certificate of Extended Education) subjects. *A Basis for Choice* was eventually translated into the Certificate for Pre-Vocational Education (CPVE). The 17+ debate still continues.

Apart from *A Basis for Choice*, the mid to late 1970s saw the development of two other programmes for young school leavers. They came from different ideologies, based as they were on the DES and MSC. The DES programme was the Unified Vocational Preparation (UVP) programme (1976). It was aimed at providing work-based education/training for young school leavers in 'dead-end' jobs. The MSC programme was also published in 1977 as *Young People and Work* (the Holland Report). This was concerned with bringing together a somewhat disparate array of *ad-hoc* arrangements for unemployed school leavers into a more coherent Youth Opportunities Programme (YOP).

These two initiatives show not only the differences in ideology that emanated from the top echelons of the education and training sectors, but also their respective time scales of working. UVP, although progressive in its curricular philosophy, was concerned to plug the gaps left in the day-release spectrum by the 1965/1973 Industrial Training Acts, and was by definition concerned with young people who were employed in 'dead-end' jobs with little or no formal training. YOP was responding to the emerging and more dramatic problem of unemployed school leavers. It concentrated on providing the confidence of work experience for young people in order to maintain or enhance their employability. *A Basis for Choice* drew on both of these ideologies and attempted to harmonize the tensions implicit in education and training by providing a full-time programme of general and vocational education, not primarily related to examinations.

Providing across the 16+ divide

The analysis above, with its distinction between compulsory and post-compulsory education, provides the basis for the remaining part of this chapter. The developments described form the seed-bed of any emerging 14–19 curriculum. Only one other development, the Technical and Vocational Initiative (TVEI), has deliberately attempted to bridge the 16+ divide, and its success in this respect will be commented on below. It is not within the scope of this chapter to comment on the organizational structures deemed necessary to provide 14–19 curricula. The 1986 government proposals to set up 20 city technology colleges, catering for 11–18 year-olds, do not at the time of writing seem likely to materialize as the major providers of 14–19 programmes. They could, however, create exemplars for bridging the many gaps that exist in this spectrum, and if they retain support, their effect could be catalytic.

Indeed, it is interesting to note that in August 1986 the DES followed up *Better Schools* with a draft circular,[4] *Providing for Quality*, aimed at providing a basis for rationalizing educational provision up to the age of 19. The circular notes that the 16–19-year-old population is falling from a 1983 peak of 2.4 million to a 1995 trough of 1.6 million, and it discusses criteria on which viable groups may be maintained. Nowhere is there a suggestion that the process of rationalizing provision should or could be used to achieve greater integration across the 14–19 curriculum. The persistent differentiation within the DES at the 16+ divide must be regarded as one of the major contributions to that divide.

CURRICULUM VALUES AND NEEDS

Adolescence

Whilst there is no lack of literature on the subject, many of the theoretical studies of adolescence stop at the end of compulsory schooling. Those dealing with post-school adolescence are usually more *ad hoc* and pragmatic. This discontinuity is often reflected in the training and vocabulary of school teachers and FE teachers: children versus youngsters, pastoral versus counselling, pupils versus students, etc. are small but significant examples of the differences. If we accept a working definition of adolescence as *the second decade of a young person's life*, then we inevitably include at least one and usually more transitions in that period: from lower to higher school, from school to FHE and/or to work or unemployment, through puberty and its associated rapid growth of physical, sexual, intellectual, and social awareness. These changes do not occur simultaneously, and teachers as well as parents are often deceived into linking together social, intellectual, and physical maturation, sometimes with disastrous results.

On top of this complex and uneven pattern of development, adults impose arbitrary boundaries: compulsory school-leaving age, cheap fares, the age of consent, technical adulthood. Consumer-oriented marketing pressures exploit most adolescent characteristics. And the education system adds its share of pressures, by devising qualifications that separate adolescents into a score or more categories: GCSE, A/S, A levels, prevocational, craft, technician, part-time, full-time, pass, fail, diplomas, certificates . . . and more recently employed and unemployed. There is no end to our divisiveness. In spite of this there do appear to be certain generic needs that require some degree of satisfaction.

Thomas,[5] for example, maintains that the road to maturity lies through the sound construction of five selves: physical, sexual, vocational, social, and philosophical; and that these are the basis of the goals of young people in westernized societies. He also suggests that these values of self would be more easily transmitted if self-education could be structured into the curriculum. Most of us would also accept that some conflict is inevitable during adolescence, but that self-assertion and the generation of self-confidence is essential to maturation.

Towards a common core

Many would maintain it follows from the above that there are strong grounds for a 14–19 curriculum core, based in part at least on the generic needs of adolescence. Such a curriculum would be concerned with maturation in the broadest possible sense, transition and change as a life-long phenomenon, and the generation of self-confidence. It is questionable how much our formal education and training systems provide this service for young people throughout the period of 14–19, but it remains a fundamental check-list of values to which perhaps we should return more often. The traditional characteristics of adolescence are often overlooked in our attempts to be responsive to the latest initiative.

A review, however, of the objectives of many of our 14–18 curricula, reveals that some common ground now exists. *Better Schools* (para 44) reiterates earlier documents and quotes school objectives such as helping pupils to:

> develop lively, enquiring minds . . . ;
> acquire understanding, knowledge and skills relevant to adult life . . . ;
> use language and number effectively . . . ;
> develop personal moral values;
> understand the world in which they live;
> appreciate human achievements and aspirations . . .

These objectives are compatible with many others, including those of TVEI which, whilst aimed more obviously at employment, is rapidly aligning itself with the *Better Schools* curriculum criteria.

The TVEI aims are similarly related to equipping students to enter the world of work, to appreciate the practical applications of their qualifications, and to develop personal qualities. The emphasis is on learning through doing. The curriculum is outlined in general terms: it should lead towards recognized vocational qualifications; it should not be restricted to one sex; it should contain computer literacy, science and technology, economic awareness, personal and social development; and have some relationship to local factors. Within this framework many local variations exist. In subject terms many programmes have adopted a core plus options approach. The core usually includes English, maths, science, humanities, and physical education. Careers guidance/counselling, work experience, IT, and some vocational studies may also be found in many 14–16 curricula.

In pursuance of a 14–19 core curriculum, the FEU in 1985 produced an outline 14–16 core within its document *Progressing to College*. Primarily intended to provide a basis for planning FE curricula for the 16–19 age group, the document makes a case for a 'compulsory' core to which young people would have an entitlement:

> The way it is provided, applied and made available should be a matter of negotiation and consultation between teachers, parents and pupils themselves. Although this appears radical, many core subjects such as mathematics, English, etc. are already agreed in this way. The only differences, . . . are that we are suggesting a core broader than a collection of single subjects.

In *Better Schools* it is suggested that some 80–85 per cent of each pupil's time is 'devoted to subjects which are compulsory or liable to constrained choices'. *Progressing to College* suggests that its core should occupy about 60 per cent of the time available; the core is outlined in the form of 15 aims, having the following headings:

1. *Adaptability*
2. *Role Transition*
3. *Physical Skills*
4. *Interpersonal Skills*
5. *Values*
6. *Communication/Numeracy*
7. *Problem Solving*
8. *Information Technology*
9. *Society*
10 *Learning Skills*
11. *Health Education*
12. *Creativity*
13. *Environment*
14. *Science/Technology*
15. *Coping*

With each heading was an associated aim. For example, in *Science/Technology*: 'To promote an understanding of the nature and discipline of science, and its relationships to technology via the processes of design and production.'

This core was jointly adopted by both the FEU and the School Curriculum Development Committee (SCDC) in its joint publication *Supporting TVEI* (1985). The 14–16 core is acknowledged to be similar in many respects to the 17+ CPVE core, on the basis that generic needs are being attended to. Unnecessary duplication is not intended but some reinforcement for mastery is considered desirable. Objectives common to both cores are expected to be treated in different contexts. A spiralling link is obviously intended to be the connection between the two cores.

The genesis of CPVE was *A Basis for Choice* (as described at the beginning of this chapter) and it is worth noting that the CPVE aims are to:

1. assist the transition from school to adulthood by *further* (my underlining) equipping young people with basic skills, experiences, attitudes, knowledge, and personal and social competences required for success in adult life including work;
2. provide individually relevant educational experience which encourages learning and achievement;
3. provide young people with recognition of their attainment through a qualification which embodies national standards;
4. provide opportunities for progression to continuing education, training and/or work.

These have some similarity with the *Better Schools* objectives summarized above, although a detailed analysis will show that the CPVE core aims contain the words *competence* and *progression*, which do not appear in the *Better Schools* objectives. These two words occur with increasing frequency as we cross the 16+ divide and tend towards more vocationalism.

The UVP scheme was unequivocally related to employment. It was for young people in jobs where no formal education/training would otherwise be received. Most of them in fact were in the service industries, particularly distributive. The aims of UVP were concerned with:

1. encouraging the continuation of learning, for personal satisfaction or otherwise;
2. developing maturity: independence of thought; an appreciation of social and moral values; rights, duties, and responsibilities;
3. acquiring occupational, social, and other skills needed in adult life;
4. understanding the demands of working life and employment;
5. giving access to guidance and counselling.

The two main principles of UVP were personal development and a greater understanding of their jobs. This scheme could have dramatically increased the participation rate in further education of employed school-leavers, but as implied earlier, it was out of time. Youth unemployment was increasing; 'time off' from work for continuing education (with minimal financial incentive) was not receiving increasing support from employers; the priorities were changing; and UVP was gradually subsumed into the Youth Training Scheme (YTS).

The current two-year YTS derives from the Youth Opportunities Programme (YOP), as mentioned previously. The YTS philosophy is to prepare young people for working life through a foundation of planned work experience and vocational education and training, which enables them to seek a relevant vocational qualification.[6] It is the mechanism by which the MSC implements Objective 2 of its 1981 New Training Initiative, whereby all young people under the age of 18 have the opportunity either of continuing in full-time education or of entering a period of planned work experience combined with work-related training and education. YTS outcomes require the trainee to acquire:

– competence in a job and/or range of occupational skills;
– competence in a range of core skills;
– ability to transfer skills and knowledge to real situations;
– personal effectiveness.

YTS is at the most instrumental end of the 14-19 spectrum of curricula. It is intended to provide foundation training; it is evolutionary; it is the only school-leavers' training programme which provides guaranteed income support. It is applauded by some as a progressive scheme giving training opportunities where none existed before; it is criticized by others as being not much more than a source of cheap labour. It is undoubtedly controversial, and although the word *education* is disappearing from its vocabulary, its sheer size of provision (approximately half of all school-leavers enter YTS) ensures that it cannot be ignored in any consideration of an emerging 14-19 curriculum.

Vocational qualifications

Alongside the curricula represented in *Better Schools*, TVEI, CPVE, YTS, etc. are arranged more vocationally specific schemes, most of which emanate from and are certified by the FE examining and validating bodies such as CGLI, BTEC, and RSA. Most of these bodies provide schemes for young people and adults wishing to pursue specific vocational qualifications. Many schools as well as colleges provide programmes of study leading to these qualifications, and many of these qualifications are part of TVEI programmes.

These FE examining and validating bodies are highly entrepreneurial, and between them they present to many a confusing array of vocational qualifications.[7] This confusion is compounded by the existence of some 250 professional bodies and some 120 industry training organizations – most of whom are involved in some aspect or other of vocational examining, accrediting, and/or training. Faced with this plethora of provision, a Review of Vocational Qualifications (RVQ) Working Group was set up by the DES and MSC, and its final report was issued in April 1986. The report, whilst acknowledging that the existing arrangements for vocational qualifications had advantages, such as dependable assessment procedures and responsiveness, confirmed that

595

it could find no clear, readily understandable pattern of provision. The RVQ report included two main recommendations:

1. vocational qualifications should be within a new framework to be called the National Vocational Qualification (NVQ);
2. an overarching New Council for Vocational Qualifications (NCVQ) should be set up with the task of developing this new coherent system of vocational qualifications in England, Wales and Northern Ireland.

The RVQ recommendations were generally accepted by the government in its July 1986 White Paper, *Working Together – Education and Training*.[8]

One of the RVQ recommendations was that assessments within YTS should be embraced within the new NVQ; it was less sure about the status of CPVE in the new framework. Another was that the NCVQ should discuss with the Schools Examination Council (now the Schools Examination and Assessment Council) the establishment of linkages between the new framework, GCSE, and A levels. From this, we may discern a government 16–19 curricular strategy whereby somehow or other the 'academic' and 'vocational' are to be linked within a new structure of vocational qualifications, with YTS occupying a pole position. There is less certainty with respect to the 14–16 curriculum, although the earlier paragraphs of the White Paper give some clues. 'The Government's policy (based on *Better Schools*) is that up to age 16 *all pupils* should be acquiring a *broad competence* in communication, numeracy, science and technology, design, foreign languages, and other subjects necessary in a successful modern society . . . Government policy for schools now emphasises *practical learning*: pupils of *all abilities* need to be taught to apply what they learn to what has to be done outside the classroom and in the real world of work . . . In the last two years of the compulsory period, the programme of *all pupils* should begin to have, for example through work experience, something of the flavour of what they will experience after 16 . . . Decisions at 16+ should not be irrevocable: bridges and ladders between the various routes to employment and to further and higher education will need to be built.'

Subsequent statements in the White Paper[8] make it clear that this competence-based practical approach to school curriculum is to be brought about by extending TVEI to all schools and colleges (although the recent Education Reform Act raises doubts about the status of TVEI in the national curriculum). Implemented by LEAs, but funded and administered by MSC in collaboration with the Education Departments, there remains little doubt as to the values and needs that, in 1987, are dominating the 14–19 curriculum, however that is defined.

CURRICULUM DESIGN

The target population

The quest for an emerging 14–19 curriculum must centre on those curricula that claim to be available for all young people, irrespective of ability, gender, and race. The quotations from the White Paper[8] make it clear that *all pupils* should have available to them a curriculum giving broad competence related to the world of work in a successful modern society. The rhetoric of CPVE, TVEI, and YTS also have in common this availability to all. Work experience, real or simulated, is also common, and the analysis of aims above indicates, albeit to different degrees, a common concern for maturation and the other generic needs of adolescence.

The consequences for curriculum design are also apparent. Some form of core curriculum is part of the vocabulary of *Better Schools, TVEI, CPVE* and *YTS*. They are obviously not identical, but various formulae exist to allow some harmonization, as exemplified earlier, although the proposed core of the new national curriculum is a very limited contribution to 14–19 thinking. With the core must come the availability of options in order to cater for a full range of ability, the wishes of individuals, and/or the preferences of employers. For both core and options, the values and needs discussed above have to be translated into 'content'. The FEU[9] interprets 'content' as *guidance, experience, skills, and knowledge*.

Towards a process-based curriculum

Some of the programmes discussed above carry out this translation of values into content more thoroughly than others. The YTS Illustrative Schemes define quite sharply the occupationally-related competences that trainees are expected to attain, although the status of core skills is not always clear – Managing Agents are not required to embrace all YTS core skills. The CPVE design is more rigorous. Core competences are described in some detail, and with vocational studies must occupy no less that 75 per cent of the course time. The core is expected to be used as:

1. a checklist against which previous achievements can be matched;
2. a checklist against which students' achievement on a course can be matched;
3. a resource from which objectives can be drawn to build into courses according to student need.

The CPVE design insists that 'each student must have the opportunity of relating to all core aims, in order to study, gain experience and optimise his/her competences according to individual need and potential'.

597

TVEI, *Better Schools*, and the national curriculum are weaker in their translation of values into content. Such translation is apparently restricted to a list of single subjects. There is, in paragraph 52 of *Better Schools*, an attempt to rectify this impression by claiming that the description of the curriculum in terms of subjects should not be misinterpreted. '... much curricular content is, for many purposes ... most conveniently described by reference to the body of knowledge and skills associated with a particular subject. Such a description implies no particular view of timetabling or of teaching approach. Nor does it deny that learning involves the mastery of processes as well as the acquisition of knowledge, skills and understanding.' Contrast this approach with the insistence of YTS that work experience, on-job training, off-job training, learning objectives, induction, participative learning, continuous assessment, guidance, and review, should all underpin the outcomes summarized earlier. Contrast it also with the 'learning by doing' rhetoric associated with TVEI.

YTS, and particularly CPVE, identify an increasing emphasis on processes in the design of 14–19 programmes. Notwithstanding the above almost negative acknowledgement in *Better Schools*, the work of Cockroft[10] and the Secondary Science Curriculum Review[11] do illustrate that subjects can and should stress process as well as product outcomes. Many of the GCSE grading criteria also reflect this emphasis.

Associated with this increasing emphasis on processes, skills, and competences is the general desire to inculcate transfer and transferability into curriculum. The ability to transfer skills and knowledge is specifically included in the YTS outcomes. It is explicitly referred to in each of the CPVE core headings. It remains a popular goal in both educational and training contexts, and including it in the design of programmes is a first necessary step and another example of the trend towards a process-based curriculum. The FEU has, however, pointed out elsewhere[12] that much remains to be done in this area.

A levels

At the time of writing, GCE A level syllabuses have been under review. The future role of A levels in any emerging 14–18 curriculum is therefore indeterminate. Although presently designed for a restricted range of high ability students, A levels dominate the sixth-form curriculum in terms of status and design. Much of the evidence to the (Higginson) Review Committee was in favour of reducing this dominance, but there is still no clear consensus of how this should be done. One persistent theme has been to suggest that A level syllabuses should be broken down into modules. This, it is claimed, may allow greater access to some A level-type study, alongside other broader-based study. It looks, however, as though A/S levels will, virtually by default, emerge as the only modification to the A level syllabus.

Modules, options and negotiation

The need for some degree of choice to exist in the 14–19 curriculum has already been referred to. Whether or not a core exists, the progression from broad-based to specific competence, as a young person moves from 14 to 19, is characteristic of many of our curricula; 'academic' or 'vocational'. It is not a universally accepted progression, and the over-specialization of our conventional sixth-form education is criticized as much as the occupational specificity of some of our so-called broad-based vocational programmes. Nevertheless, the concept of a 'balanced' programme, *somehow* becoming more specific, appears to be a characteristic of our educational/training culture. It is the task of curriculum design to translate this concept into practice. It usually means more options but less choice as the programme develops.

Modularization can be seen as a mechanism by which an appropriate degree of flexibility can be designed into the curriculum. Modules are usually defined as separate and self-standing parts of education or training programmes, designed as a series to lead to a qualification from which a programme may be constructed. They can be the building blocks of a curriculum, and in recent years the concept of modularization has been seized upon by some as a solution to the apparent inflexibility of the education/training system to cope with the diverse needs of employers and individual learners. Modules have the immediate attractiveness of 'pick and mix', whereby students (and employers) can choose any assortment of syllabuses to make up a complete programme. In practice they do not provide infinite flexibility, usually because of the demands of the programme as a whole – which should reflect values and needs such as those discussed earlier in this chapter. For example, in the context of a 14–19 curriculum, the imposition of a core will obviously restrict the range of modules that can be chosen. Many modules, especially those related to advanced programmes, also require prerequisite achievement for entry; for example to study mathematics at say, level three, achievement at a mathematics module level two (or equivalent) may be required.

It will be seen from the definition above that modules are not simply a collection of discrete single subjects such as GCSE or A levels. Modules are intended to serve the holistic aims of the programmes of which they are part. They often have a common format of presentation, and are expected to reflect a consistent system of assessment and teaching-learning strategies. They also, by definition, are expected to give progression within the programme and contribute to a larger qualification. Single subjects are much more independent and are not so amenable to holistic programme aims; this is not the basis of

599

their design. A typical example of an attempt to impose wider aims onto single subjects is the 1986 report of a Working Party on Criteria for Pre-vocational Courses Pre-16. The report recommended that all 14–16 pupils should have an opportunity to receive pre-vocational education, and it attempted to define both integrated-course and single-subject criteria. The FEU[13] and others were forced to conclude that the report was unable to resolve this ambiguity, because its remit rested on the concept in *Better Schools* that the characteristics and aims of pre-vocational education could be delivered by single subjects. The status of pre-vocational education is no clearer in the national curriculum.

Nevertheless, properly designed modules, with a supportive timetabling philosophy, or available within an open or distance-learning system, can liberate the learner from many of the constraints associated with formal programmes. The Open University uses modules; various institutions of higher education also offer modular degree courses; others – individually or collectively – offer post-experience (usually updating) modules for adults. The Technician Education Council (now B/TEC) offers a substantial number of programmes built around modules; and the National Council for Vocational Qualifications is moving towards the modularization of its new NVQ framework.

Nearer to the 14–19 curriculum, the CPVE programme combines a modular structure with a core philosophy, and an evaluation of how teachers dealt with the sometimes conflicting demands of core and vocational modules is contained in an FEU report.[14] The School Curriculum Development Committee (now the National Curriculum Council) has given guidance on modules to the schools: it points out that modules have been around for a long time, and quotes examples ranging from primary education to university courses. It described the modular approach as an alternative method of organizing the curriculum. Students are offered shorter-term goals. The flexibility of the system makes it possible to match learning programmes more closely to the needs of individual students.

Many SEC-based examination groups operate schemes termed modular. Such modules are usually smaller than GCSE subjects, and thus offer some element of choice within a GCSE subject. The guidance from such groups generally requires modules to specify a title, aims and objectives, content, teaching and learning strategies, and assessment methods. TVEI has proved to be an important catalyst in modular development in secondary schools. Initially, modules were a means of introducing MSC-preferred subjects (such as IT, business studies, design technology) into a conventional syllabus. There is now evidence to indicate that in some TVEI programmes, modules are used to cover other areas of the school curriculum. As already indicated, there has been some pressure to make GCE A levels modular. The extent to which this will ever be possible and effective will largely depend on how A levels relate to GCSE subjects in the way they are designed and assessed.

Arguably the most radical experiment in modularization is the Scottish 16–18 plan. Administered by SCOTVEC, it employs a modular system with apparently complete freedom being given as to choice of modules. However, there are some 'hidden' rules. For example, the choice of modules determined by a college often conforms to the subjects required under the old system, or to the existing schemes of external bodies such as CGLI. The structure of the module subjects imposes some horizontal and vertical rules on choice of modules. The modules are defined by time. The system is nevertheless flexible and permits cumulative credit; and more local 'independent' groupings may eventually appear.

Typical issues related to modules thus include their status, relative to any larger award; the amount of freedom allowed to 'pick and mix'; the extent to which their design is constrained; whether or not the 'content' has to include different domains of activity; and whether or not guidelines on their assessment are necessary. It follows from the above that different decisions on such issues would result in different definitions of modules.[15]

Whether the curriculum design employs modules, single subjects, and/or a core, the success of the design must depend on the quality of guidance and negotiation that supports the choice of options that are available. It should be axiomatic, in education at least, that choice should be accompanied by guidance. The extent to which programmes should be negotiated with individual learners and/or their parents is less unanimous. It could be argued that any curriculum, claiming to be responsive to individual needs, implies some negotiation. In many areas of education some negotiation is taken for granted, for example, in the choice of A levels, OU modules, B/TEC modules etc. In *Vocational Preparation*[16] the FEU argued that if programmes were to be related to the generic needs of adolescence, then as much negotiation as possible by young learners should be encouraged: '. . . part of the necessary process of self-fulfilment for the adolescent is the generation of self-confidence, mainly by the opportunity of making responsible choices'. The FEU went on to suggest that appropriate mechanisms to encourage negotiation included the construction of *personal programmes* (or agendas), of *contracts* between tutors and learners, and *profiling*. All of these have been used with success within the 14–18 curriculum and beyond. The claim to deal with an all-ability population makes some negotiation inevitable. Induction, guidance, contracts, and profiles (or records of achievement) are, for example, very much the vocabulary of YTS, notwithstanding the avoidance of the word negotiation.

Another characteristic of many 14–18 curricula is the use of more than one agency to provide the programme. With TVEI, CPVE, and YTS go work experience, on- and off-job training, and/or the pooling of resources via consortia. All require some negotiation between providers. It is at the curriculum design stage that a proper approach to negotiation begins.

SUMMARY

1. This chapter suggests that the 14–16 curriculum will probably continue to be based on prescribed single subjects. The 16–19 curriculum is 'voluntary'; spans a wide range of 'vocational' and 'academic' needs, and tends towards integrated courses or frameworks. Pre-vocational education is capable of providing some coherence across 14–18 curriculum, but its status, ideology, and curricular philosophy have yet to settle down.
2. The generic needs of adolescents in a changing adult world make a strong case for some form of interlocking cores in both 14–16 and 16–18 curricula. Some common ground already exists, but it appears fortuitous.
3. YTS, and the rationalization of vocational qualifications, are accelerating a drift towards vocationalism. The design of 14–18 curricula is thus having to pay increasing regard to competence-based practical curricula, with emphases on processes and skill. The position of A levels in this emerging scene is not yet clear.
4. Alongside the pressure for increased vocationalism, with its emphasis on competence, the 14–18 curriculum, in common with other curricula, is being subjected to suggestions of modularization. The final paragraphs of this chapter discuss how modularization can improve flexibility. But many issues require resolution, not least of which are those associated with curricular guidance, choice, and negotiation.
5. Although not specifically dealt with here, there is little doubt that the 14–19 curriculum is evolutionary, is provided by many agencies, and is associated with many innovations. However, there is as yet a lack of a unified concept of a 14–18 curriculum. This is reflected both in the support and the evaluation it receives. Perhaps the most disturbing aspect of this is that we have only a fragmented and often partisan view of how a unified 14–19 curriculum would affect the future of young people who were exposed to it.

REFERENCES

1. *Better Schools*, Cmnd 9469 HMSO March 1985.
2. *England and Wales Youth Cohort Study*, Preliminary results. Gill Courtney, Social and Community Planning Research, July 1986.
3. *Examinations 16–18*, DES October 1980.
4. *Providing for Quality: The Pattern of Organisation to Age 19*, DES August 1986.
5. Thomas, J. B. (1980) *The Self in Education*, NFER.
6. Final report of a working group set up by MSC under the chairmanship of Mr Peter Reay, MSC, June 1985.

7. See *CPVE: Confusion or Deception*, FEU, March 1985.
8. *Working Together – Education and Training*, Cmnd 9823 HMSO July 1986.
9. See *Relevance, Flexibility and Competence*, FEU, 1987.
10. *Mathematics Counts*, HMSO, 1982.
11. *Science Education 11–16*, SSCR, 1983.
12. *Assessment, Quality and Competence*, FEU, 1986.
13. Working Party on Criteria for Pre-Vocational Courses (The Stuart Johnson Group) – FEU Response, October 1986.
14. *CPVE in Action*, FEU 1985
15. This issue is examined in greater depth by the FEU report to NCVQ on *Modularisation and NVQ* (1987).
16. *Vocational Preparation*, FEU 1981.

5·7

IMPLEMENTING THE CURRICULUM

BOB MOON

On 4 October 1957 the Russian Sputnik circled the world. In the west there was astonishment and not a little dismay. In the USA a consensus formed around the need to reform the school curriculum. The first developments in Science and Mathematics were quickly followed by major projects across all areas of the curriculum and the early 1960s saw the spread of the curriculum movement to most Western countries. The impetus given by that first journey into space became part of curriculum folklore. In 1973, in a *Sunday Times* Colour Supplement (2 September) Brian Jackson reflected on more than a decade of development.

> It was, of course, the Russians who turned our maths classes into fun palaces. When Sputnik I circled Europe and America in 1957, its extraordinary wake smashed in one superior act the traditional mathematics which had dominated our schools unchallenged for a century. The maths that grandmother learnt was pretty hot at working out how many kippers at a penny-farthing each you might get for £5. But Greek geometry and Victorian mercantile conundrums clearly didn't lead to the stars. After Sputnik, the Americans set up the Madison Mathematics Project, the Canadians founded the Sherbrooke Mathematics Teaching Project, and Britain appointed an educational commission under Sir Geoffrey Crowther, which invented a new word – numeracy. Numeracy was what – after an average 3,276 hours learning maths in school – most of us did not possess. Five years after numeracy entered our vocabulary, the School Mathematics Project was floated, to be followed two years later by the Nuffield Mathematics Project for junior children, and several others.

In Britain the Nuffield Primary Mathematics Project was one of the first major attempts at subject-based curriculum reform. In that period no national organization existed to promote curriculum change, and a private foundation, the Nuffield Trust, sponsored projects across a range of subjects. The majority were linked to publishers either through the production of teacher guides, as in the case of Nuffield Primary Mathematics, or in the designing and writing of textbooks. The project approach to curriculum development represented, throughout the 1960s, a taken-for-granted organizational structure. It was the approach that the new national body, the Schools Council for England and Wales, adopted, and by the end of the decade nearly one hundred separate project teams had been established. One Professor of Education, writing in 1968 was to say,

> It is becoming manifest that the projects for curriculum renewal which have been introduced during the last five years by the Nuffield Foundation and the Schools Council are not passing phenomena but indicate what will become the accepted pattern for building new curriculum. (Kerr 1968:33–4)

Twenty years later the number of national curriculum development projects could be counted in single figures. A variety of economic and political factors contributed to this demise. The OPEC oil crisis of 1973 is commonly recognized as significant. Shipman for example suggests:

> It is becoming clear that the mid 1970s were a watershed in England. Any discussion of changes in the curriculum of schools has to be in the context of the switch from expansion to construction, and from confidence to doubt, that took place at that time. (Shipman 1981:21)

Equally, however, doubts were being expressed about the extent to which the projects were being taken up in schools. The fate of two projects, in primary mathematics and secondary integrated studies, are reported in studies by Moon (1986) and Shipman (1974). Project methodology became a dominant interest, and the literature on curriculum implementation was almost wholly concerned with alternative approaches and competing theoretical positions. This is most usefully summarized by Becher and Maclure (1978) in a chapter on subject-based developments. They suggest that the history of a subject-based development illustrates three basic approaches, each evolving as a reaction to the perceived limitations of its predecessor. Their analysis is based on the work of Havelock (1970, 1971) whose studies of innovation were frequently cited in the literature of that period.

The first project methodology recognized is the Research, Development, and Diffusion (RD and D) model. Earlier and parallel developments in, for example, the science of agriculture, had established clear ground rules for the application of these procedures. Behaviouristic psychology and the work of the early American curriculum theorists such as Ralph Tyler (1949) or Hilda Taba (1962) give added credibility to this approach. In practice, trying to establish aims and objectives for any part of the curriculum proved extremely difficult. Equally problematic was the task of devising appropriate teaching strategies and the diffusion of these aims and objectives to teachers in schools throughout the system. As Becher and Maclure suggest:

... the more specific the statement of curricular aims the more controversial it is likely to be. An extreme insistence on precisely defined behavioural objectives ('at the end of course, a pupil will be able to [a] enumerate the causes of the Peninsular War ...') in any case reduces the curriculum to a series of atomistic accomplishments which fail to add up to an organic and coherent whole. Yet a definition of aims which is general enough to be widely acceptable will give little practical guidance to anyone struggling to develop a new curriculum. To find a middle way between being comprehensive and vacuous and being specific and stultifying is far from easy. (Becher and Maclure 1978)

The second social-interaction strategy recognized the need to involve teachers in curriculum reform. The idea of the 'teacher-proof' package implicit in the RD and D style was seen as inadequate. The Nuffield Primary Mathematics project developers, for example, steadfastly opposed any idea of producing pupil texts. The emphasis was on teacher guides, and the dissemination work of the project was integral to the project strategy. The establishment of a network of teachers' centres to support Nuffield Primary Maths provided a model adopted by many local education authorities in subsequent years.

The third model, the problem-solving approach, represents a fusion of the first two models through accepting the need for central support but seeing this as fully rooted in practitioners' needs. Finding sufficient funding to support the full range of needs generated by schools raised, however, major questions of resources. An example quoted by Becher and Maclure is the Avon Resources for Learning Project, established in 1974. The production of materials and resources was matched by a participating approach to classroom methodology on the part of the central staff. This approach to curriculum development is explained by the first Director of the project, Philip Waterhouse (1983).

Fierce curriculum controversies ranged around competing methodologies. Most significant was the opposition mounted against the behaviourists' objectives-led approach. In England Lawrence Stenhouse was the leading advocate of an approach that laid greater stress on the active participation of the teacher in curriculum development. In 1975 he published *An Introduction to Curriculum Research and Development*, now reprinted many times, and argued strongly for bringing teachers into a research-oriented framework of curriculum analysis and reform. Stenhouse directed the Humanities Curriculum Project, which developed not only controversial materials but also controversial methods of using the materials in the classrooms. In 1970 he established, with the help of a number of former colleagues, the Centre for Applied Research in Education (CARE) at the University of East Anglia. In the subsequent decade the work of the Centre was to provide an influential role in the development of curriculum theory. One of Stenhouse's collaborators, Barry McDonald, saw Stenhouse as providing the promise of:

a future in which from a process of redefinition of the relationship between teachers, taught and knowledge ... teachers [would be transformed] into research-based master craftsmen of a new tradition.

This quotation is taken from the introduction to an edited collection of readings from the work of Lawrence Stenhouse, by Rudduck and Hopkins, which includes an abstract of a paper Stenhouse prepared shortly before his death. Again he marks out his opposition to curriculum prescription:

We cannot prove that this year's curriculum will serve appropriately for next year since contextual variables will change. Thus the view put forward here is a view supportive of critical pedagogy as a generally appropriate teaching style, rather than as a response to a non-recurrent innovative situation. (Rudduck and Hopkins: 70)

Stenhouse and others articulated a view of curriculum that took much more account of the total context in which implementation was to be carried out. This movement in the 1970s can be observed in a number of ways. Even some of the most determined advocates of curriculum building by objectives came to reappraise his position. Ralph Tyler's (1986) review of changing concepts of educational evaluation is indicative of a significant shift in opinion. In a passage that evokes the words of Lawrence Stenhouse he suggests that:

the recent rapid changes in modern societies have led to the increasing recognition that education cannot be conceived merely as a passing on to each new generation, the knowledge, attitudes and practices of the past. Most of the adults in modern societies have not encountered some of the situations and problems that their children are likely to meet when they are adults. Although some persons believe that they are able to predict the future in some detail and they recommend that children be taught the knowledge and skills which these Futurists believe will enable the adults of the next generation to handle these predicted events, the record of the past does not support this view. (Tyler 1986:15)

and he goes on to quote approvingly Kenneth Boulding, who in the 1982 presidential address for the Convention of the American Association for the Advancement of Science said:

One thing we know about the future. It will be full of surprises. Nearly 80 per cent of the specific predictions for 1980 made by Futurists in 1960 have proved erroneous. (Tyler 1986:15)

The 1970s, therefore, saw a burgeoning literature around the concept of school-based curriculum development. In many respects this mirrored Stenhouse's aversion to what he termed managerialism:

I mean by managerialism the idea that education can be improved by curriculum reform or innovation implemented in the school system by the influence or the power of the management hierarchy. (Stenhouse 1983)

A leading advocate of school-based development was Malcolm Skilbeck (1984) who, in a number of papers, developed the idea of 'situational analysis'. He saw this as an essential first stage prior to further processes such as goal formulation, programme building, monitoring, and evaluation. Learners are influenced by the cultural contact in which they reside, and teachers need to take account of this in formulating curriculum plans. The way these factors are interpreted is highly significant for the range of learning activities ultimately designed. Skilbeck saw a distinction, albeit not a rigid one, between internal and external factors.

1. External factors
    (a) Changes and trends in society which indicate tasks for schools.
    (b) Expectations and requirements of parents, employers.
    (c) Community assumptions and values including patterns of adult-child relations.
    (d) The changing nature of the subject disciplines.
    (e) The potential contribution of teacher support systems.
    (f) Actual and anticipated flow of resources into the school.

2. Internal factors
    (a) Pupils, their aptitudes, abilities, attitudes, values, and defined educational needs.
    (b) Teachers, their values, attitudes, skills, knowledge, experience, and special strengths and weaknesses.
    (c) School ethos and political structures, common assumptions and expectations, including traditions, power distribution etc.
    (d) Material resources, including plant, equipment, and learning materials.
    (e) Perceived and felt problems and shortcomings in existing curriculum.

Skilbeck was to provide a major input to the first full credit course in curriculum development by the Open University (1976) and the texts which include an extensive discussion of the situational analysis concept. The associated readers were extensively used in curriculum courses across the country.

Work by CARE added weight to the ideas developed by Skilbeck. The Ford Teaching Project provided evidence of how teachers and pupils can come to have very different perceptions of curriculum experience. Alongside this the mainstream of curriculum theory could be represented by the work of Dennis Lawton, who, in a number of publications, set out his ideas of curriculum as a selection from culture involving decision makers in political as well as cultural decisions. In Lawton's (1980) view consensus could be achieved if all the parties involved in the curriculum process could be linked in an accepted decision-making framework.

Such views were controversial. During the 1970s sociologists of education, beginning with the collection edited by M. F. D. Young, *Knowledge and Control* (1971), established a critique of the prevailing curriculum orthodoxy. A recent manifestation of this is the work of Whitty (1985) who focuses his attention specifically on the writings of Lawton and authors associated with CARE. He reviews the work of a number of authors who saw the apolitical model espoused by CARE as failing to have any significance in the public debate about education.

The main concerns, therefore, of curriculum study and theory in the 1960s and 1970s centred around three focuses for curriculum implementation. First the curriculum project and the variety of styles that came to characterize this approach. Second the role of the teacher, with Stenhouse's concept of teacher as researcher prominent in debate. And third the attempt to contextualize curriculum implementation as represented in Skilbeck's approach through situational analysis.

Outside mainstream academic debate, however, three further movements were providing the stimulus for curriculum questions. The first is represented by the small number of schools that carried through radical curriculum reforms in the later part of the 1960s and early 1970s. Newly-built comprehensive schools are most significantly represented in the literature (Moon 1983, Watts 1977). A number of these schools acquired media attention and sometimes notoriety. The ideological controversies, which often fuelled local political divisions, provide valuable case studies of the way implementing curriculum change must take account of a complex range of variables. There were a number of similar trends running through these reforms, most notably:

1. A questioning of the established authority relationship between teacher and student.
2. Changes in the traditional subject-based organization of the secondary school.
3. A commitment to community involvement in school life.
4. Avoidance of reliance on textbooks and attempts to define new approaches to resource-based learning.

The story of these schools represents, therefore, school-based experience of curriculum implementation. No substantive work has been done on the influence of these schools or others on prevailing ideas of the time. They were, however, much visited and well known in international circles. In the late 1980s a new generation of individual schools came to play a title role in the debate about alternative approaches to the curriculum. The literature is again biased towards reporting in the secondary sector. Many were associated with the Technical and Vocational Education Initiative (TVEI). The emphasis of the reform moves, however, from ideological to structural concerns. Examples are provided in the first full-length discussion of a modular curriculum by Watkins (1987).

The second influence is the increasing number of publications and reports emanating from central and local government. The most significant example, published in 1967, is the Plowden Report on primary education (HMSO 1967). This is seen as a landmark both for primary education and for the way the Committee functioned in preparing the report. Extensive appendices illustrate the wide-ranging enquiries, and both methodology and curriculum structure are extensively discussed. Para 58 for example suggests:

> The extent to which subject matter ought to be classified and the headings under which the classification is made will vary with the age of the children, with the demands made by the structure of the subject matter which is being studied, and with the circumstances of the school. Any practice which predetermines the pattern and imposes it upon all is to be condemned. Some teachers find it helpful in maintaining a balance in individual and class work to think in terms of broad areas of the curriculum such as language, science and mathematics, environmental study and the expressive arts. No pattern can be perfect since many subjects fall into one category or another according to the aspect which is being studied.

A few years afterwards the Bullock Report (HMSO 1975) on language used a similar approach. This report looked across the whole curriculum of both primary and secondary education. Again there was a concern with implementation.

> Not all in-service education is directly concerned with promoting innovation for curriculum change, but much of it has this intention. When the efforts have met with only modest success, as not infrequently happens, there has been a tendency to ascribe this to the school's natural resistance to the ideas the returning teacher brings with him. From this it has often been assumed that the remedy lies in an increase in the dose. However, it has rightly been argued that to rely exclusively upon formal courses is to misjudge the school as a social organism and underrate the part the teacher himself plays in initiating change. We believe that the individual school is a highly important focal point in in-service education, and that there should be an expansion in school-based approaches. For example, with the help of one or more members of the English advisory team as a catalyst, an entire primary school staff might study how the teaching of reading might be improved. This could result in several experimental measures and an agreed common policy arising from discussion among the teachers themselves. In addition, it might lead to identifying areas in which further outside help was needed. A staff that has played a part in deciding its own in-service education needs will be likely to receive and evaluate collectively the ideas that are brought back, not reject them unexamined. (para 24.5)

Plowden and Bullock predated the famous 1976 Ruskin College speech of Prime Minister Callaghan, seen as heralding a more interventionist stance by central government. In the 1980s the committee tradition is continued with the Cockcroft Report on Mathematics (HMSO 1986). A developing sense of the need for cross-curricular planning is reflected in para 485.

> because of the ways in which mathematics can be used as a means of communication, it can play an important role in the learning process in curricular areas which may seem to be far removed from mathematics, as well as in areas with which the links are more immediately apparent. The presentation of information by means of graphs, charts and tables, the use of time scales, the use of arrows to denote relationships are only a few examples. Teachers of other subjects, as well as mathematics teachers, need to be aware of the part which mathematics can play in presenting information with clarity and economy, and to encourage pupils to make use of mathematics for this purpose.

The follow-up to Cockcroft, however, represented a change from previous practice. Central government had taken powers to earmark in-service funds for specific purposes, and national programmes for mathematics INSET were established following the Cockcroft recommendations. These were locally administered, but submissions for funding were vetted and approved by central government.

In the late 1970s, and throughout the 1980s, both HMI and the Department of Education and Science produced a wide range of publications. The Primary and Secondary School surveys carried out by HMI (HMSO 1978 and 1979) provided early and much-discussed examples. HMI then went on to publish a series of general and subject specific reports beginning with a general overview (HMSO 1985).

The production of government and HMI reports with clear indications for curriculum reform was also matched by similar initiatives at the level of local education authorities. During the 1980s both local and central government were making increasing attempts to implement sometimes contradictory reforms in the school curriculum. At local level the two major reports on primary and secondary education produced by the Inner London Education Authority (1985 and 1984) provide examples of this more assertive approach. The report on secondary schools, for example, adopted a very direct approach.

> We turn now to the proposals which will, for most schools, take more time and resources to implement. We suggest that a relatively small number of schools (say 30) be designated phase 1 schools. In our view there should be at least two such schools in each division, and in the Authority as a whole the phase 1 schools should represent the full variety of schools: county and voluntary; large and small; single sex and co-educational; and certainly some schools with a high working class and/or ethnic minority intake. In our view it is essential that schools should volunteer for phase 1 status. The reason is quite simple. All schools can improve themselves, but improvement is more likely to occur where the schools want to do so and can build upon their previous experience and

achievements. We believe that there will be no shortage of volunteers for phase 1 status.

For each participating school in phase 1 there will be a period of negotiation between the governors, headteacher and staff with the inspectorate (both district and subject) concerning the content and process of implementation. We propose that all phase 1 schools develop units and unit credits in the fourth and fifth years (or third to fifth years), for we believe this to be the most central element in a programme designed to reduce underachievement and disaffection. Moreover it is the development which most closely accords with changes which are inevitable for all schools: the reform of the system of assessment for fourth and fifth year pupils. (ILEA 1984, Para 6.9–6.10)

Finally, the 1980s also saw the establishment of a third approach to influencing curriculum implementation. This again came from local government and is represented at its most influential by TVEI. This initiative, funded through the Manpower Services Commission, invited local contribution to bid for resources within the terms of implementation targets established centrally. Successful bidders were required to sign contracts, monitored by MSC, to ensure that the terms of this agreement were kept. The use of the law to guarantee implementation represents a significant new departure in the evolution of curriculum development in England and Wales. The first wave of projects, based on small groups of schools with each authority, later grew through an extension programme to cover all secondary schools and colleges of further education. Again the contractual method was used to provide funding.

Curriculum development plans and policies for implementation emanated, therefore, from a variety of sources. The ideas of Stenhouse and Skilbeck point to the school and the individual teacher as the major focus for change. The curriculum project, after the apparent disappointments of the 1970s, was resurrected in the 1980s, but in a much more systematic form, and with the use of legal contracts in an attempt to guarantee implementation and take-up. In a parallel move central government moved to detailed legislation on curriculum.

These wide-ranging approaches were reflected in equally divergent approaches in other countries. Towards the end of the third decade of curriculum development some workers attempted to synthesize the accumulated knowledge of the change and implementation process. The work of Michael Fullan (1982 and 1986), for example, provides theoretical evidence for some tentative general rules for curriculum reformers.

The individual teacher and those responsible for developing curriculum policy in schools have a rich source of literature to mine. Much of it, however, is slanted to those who have worked upon rather than within schools. Skilbeck's situational analysis comes closest to capturing the total range of variables that need consideration. His work, however, lacks the managerial perspective of

Fullan and the political analysis of, for example, Whitty. The interplay of personalities also provides an important perspective in the implementation of curriculum change. An interesting analysis of this, of relevance to but not wholly concerned with curriculum is the work by Ball (1987). Shipman's (1981) evaluation of the Schools Council integrated studies project referred to above covers similar territory, although the theoretical structure is less developed. Much of the literature now suggests that, however rational the planning process, curriculum implementation is inevitably an unpredictable affair. Plans need reformulation as the process unfolds. TVEI, for example, has been taken up on a voluntary basis by every authority, despite strong initial resistance from both teachers and many authorities. A more diffuse advocacy of 'paired reading' in primary schools has led to widespread take-up in schools across the country. A fourth decade of curriculum development will be characterized by increased control, often through legislation, of large areas of curriculum activity. Developing theories of change incorporating a record of individual and institutional ingenuity, reported most significantly in the work of Michael Fullan, provides a foundation from which new models of curriculum implementation are likely to emerge.

REFERENCES

Ball, S. (1987) *The Micro-Politics of the School. Towards a Theory of School Organization*, London: Methuen.

Becher, A. and Maclure, S. (1978) *The Politics of Curriculum Change*, London: Hutchinson.

Fullan, M. G. (1982) *The Meaning of Educational Change*, New York and London: Teachers College, University of Columbia.

(1986) 'Improvising the implementation of educational change', *School Organisation* 6 (3): 321–6.

Havelock, R. G. (1970) *Guide to Innovation in Education*, Ann Arbor: Centre for Research on the Utilisation of Scientific Knowledge, University of Michigan.

(1971) *Planning for Innovation*, Ann Arbor: Centre for Research on the Utilisation of Scientific Knowledge, University of Michigan.

HMSO (1967) *Children and their Primary Schools*.

(1975) *A Language for Life*.

(1978) *Primary Education in England*.

(1979) *Aspects of Secondary Education*.

(1985) *The Curriculum from 5–16*.

(1986) *Mathematics Counts*.

Improving Secondary Schools (1984) London: ILEA.

Improving Primary Schools (1985) London: ILEA.

Kerr, J. G. (1968) *Changing the Curriculum*, London: University of London Press.

Lawton, D. (1980) *The Politics of the School Curriculum*, London: Routledge & Kegan Paul.

Moon, B. (Ed.) (1983) *Comprehensive Schools: Challenge and Change*, London: NFER/Nelson.

Moon, B. (1986) *The 'New Maths' Curriculum Controversy: An International Story*, London: Falmer Press.

Open University (1976) *E203 Curriculum Design and Development*, Milton Keynes: Open University Press.

Rudduck, J. and Hopkins, D. *Research as a Basis for Teaching*, London: Heinemann.

Shipman, M. (1974) *Inside A Curriculum Project*. London: Methuen.

   (1981) *The School Curriculum in England 1970–1990*. (Compare Ball 1987 and ILEA 1985.)

Skilbeck, M. (1984) *School-based Curriculum Development*, London: Harper & Row.

Stenhouse, L. (1975) *An Introduction to Curriculum Research and Development*, London: Heinemann.

   (1983) 'The legacy of the curriculum development movement', in M. Galton and B. Moon (Eds.) (1983) *Changing Schools: Changing Curriculum*, London: Harper & Row.

Taba, M. (1962) *Fundamentals of Curriculum Development*, New York: Harcourt Brace.

Tyler, R. W. (1949) *Basic Principles of Curriculum and Instruction*, Chicago: University of Chicago Press.

   (1986) 'Changing concepts of educational evaluation', *International Journal of Educational Research*, 10 (1).

Waterhouse, P. S. (1983) *Managing the Learning Process*, London: McGraw Hill.

Watkins, P. (1987) *Modular Approaches to the Secondary Curriculum*, London: Longman.

Watts, J. (1977) *The Countesthorpe Experience*, London: George Allen & Unwin.

Whitty, G. (1985) *Sociology and School Knowledge: Curriculum Theory, Research and Politics*, London: Methuen.

Young. M. F. D. (1971) *Knowledge and Control: New Directions for the Sociology of Education*, London: Collier-Macmillan.

5.8

AGENCIES AND STRATEGIES FOR CURRICULUM CHANGE

MAURICE HOLT

A desire to bring about change in the intentions and practice of schooling is nothing new. Plato had firm ideas on the matter, to be followed much later by Rousseau, and in due course by nineteenth-century theorists like Herbart and Froebel – some of whom, and in particular Dewey, strongly influenced our own century.[1] Nor was this desire confined to individuals: the emergent nation states had political and social choices to make about their education systems, and the intentions of central government were often dominant, as in Prussia and Napoleonic France. The state as the directive agency was strongly characteristic of the continent of Europe: the Anglo-Saxon pattern in Britain and the United States was more relaxed, with the independent ('public') schools becoming the English exemplar for secondary education by social inclination rather than government fiat. Similarly, the equally distinctive notion of the American high school as a largely autonomous local provision emerged from a democratic concern with a common culture rooted in the life of a community.

What is assuredly new, and very much a modern phenomenon, is the view that the education system should be made to respond in a fluid and dynamic way to changes which arise outside it and which stem from political and economic rather than educational considerations. Again, we may note a contrast between European and Anglo-Saxon responses, but the tables have been turned. For whereas our European neighbours have generally confined reforms to small-scale enterprises dedicated to updating subject knowledge or learning styles (chairs in pedagogy are, for example, a commonplace in Europe, but rare elsewhere), British and North American developments have been conceived on a grander scale. The thrust towards organized, responsive planning has led to centrally-funded interventions such as the American 'new society' programmes of the late 1960s and early 1970s, the adoption by Canadian provincial governments of reform programmes such as the 1981 'consumer education' programme in British Columbia,[2] and the launch in 1983 in the UK of the Technical and Vocational Education Initiative, using the funds channelled through a non-accountable body (the Manpower Services Commission) to influence the education of 14–18-year-olds in schools and colleges.

It is important to locate curriculum change within these differing contexts, so as to extend our understanding of how forces for change emerge and how change might be justified. The market for curriculum journals, for example, is much stronger in Britain and North America, and in US-influenced countries like Israel, than in continental Europe. It is as if Europe, having established national education systems in the last century, is content to accord them durability backed by a careful regard for pedagogy; while countries linked (however loosely) to a British or American tradition (which would include Australia, another active force on the curriculum scene) find themselves insecure and uncertain, partly concerned to engage (with varying degrees of clarity) with long-neglected educational issues, and partly anxious to devise short-term expedients by which schools and colleges can supposedly respond to economic needs.

PRACTICAL AND MORAL ASPECTS OF CURRICULUM CHANGE

The aim, then, in many developed countries, is to form strategies for realigning whole systems of schooling or training to meet centrally-determined goals, and establish agencies for implementing these strategies. Generally, schools are viewed as organizations likely to respond to the same principles of management as business and commercial enterprises. It is supposed that once clear aims are set and detailed objectives agreed, schools will adopt the new schemes and, moreover, that their success can be determined by applying output measures to the system. This *logistic* model owes much to formal management theory, and to 'scientific' management in particular. Indeed, the model is often described as technocratic, bureaucratic, or managerial, or as the objectives or engineering model of curriculum change.

Despite its widespread adoption, the model suffers from two important deficiencies. First, change in the *practice* of education is very different from that in the *technique* of production. Carefully defined objectives may guarantee the success of a new manufacturing process; in schools, they must contend with the involvement of the learner and the state of mind of the teacher.[3] The more tightly such objectives are specified and enforced, the more likely that what ensues in the classroom is not education, but training. As W. H. Auden remarked: 'Of course behaviourism works: so does torture.' And while the outcomes of some educational processes may be specified in advance in general terms, these are essentially basic activities to do with low-level skill acquisition. Yet it is, ironically, higher-level capacities which governments seek to promote by central means, as the world becomes more complex and society more pluralist. The imperative, for example, that state secondary education should combine quality with equality – a commonplace of the 1980s – requires schools which transcend basic skills and offer all pupils access to a general culture of knowledge and understanding.

The second difficulty is that education is nothing if not a moral activity, undertaken for the good of students. Such activities require those undertaking them to make judgements of a particular kind, and they are judgements rooted in a particular context. Even if, for example, a science teacher is following a centrally-prescribed programme in a standardized classroom using nationally-distributed equipment, if he is to educate rather than indoctrinate he must judge what approach to adopt for a particular group of pupils, what questions are worth asking and pursuing and, indeed, what questions students should be encouraged to pose for themselves. This issue takes on particular importance in a democracy, where schooling must offer preparation for the tasks of citizenship. To see education as a matter of predetermined ends, to which the means are subordinate, and to suppose that individual institutions have no character other than as agencies for central directives, is to deny the personal, moral nature of what it is to be educated.

The view, therefore, that curriculum change can be brought about by central agencies and derived from ends framed outside institutional contexts may be appealing to bureaus but is unlikely to result in educational improvement. Not only does it ignore the difficulties of deciding what it is good for a student to do; it is likely to have only a superficial effect on practice.

CENTRAL INITIATIVES AND NATIONAL AGENCIES

Whatever force these reservations may have, there is something so innately rational about the appeal of the logistic model that bureaus find it almost impossible to resist. It represents a style of management which has been termed Apollonian, after the god of order:[4] it allows administrators to plan in advance, to control the action, and specify evaluative instruments of the kind that appeal to politicians. It also offers the aura of science and technology: the ends of the programme can be researched, and its delivery system framed managerially to make the best use of information technology. Planned educational change, therefore, generally boils down to expensive attempts to apply a logistic model to a culture to which its assumptions and methods are, on this argument, alien.

The notion of planned educational change first emerged in the US following the launch of the Russian Sputnik in 1957. This challenge to America's

617

technological ascendancy was to be met by equipping its schools with hardware and learning programmes that would give their ablest students a new cutting edge. The starting point was to determine what kind of mathematics and science represented advanced knowledge, and to find ways of translating this into school experience. High-powered academics formed teams to quarry the new knowledge, and there was talk of 'teacher-proof packages' which would ensure its assimilation by students in classrooms. The resulting materials placed a marked emphasis on abstraction and tended to have little sustained impact on school practice, despite the very large funds voted for these programmes, which were later characterized as the 'research, development and diffusion' (RDD) model of curriculum change.[5]

The effect of these innovations was soon felt in the UK. The Nuffield Foundation financed science schemes for new GCE O level courses, and oil companies backed another venture, the School Mathematics Project (SMP). But there was an important difference, most marked with the SMP: school teachers were involved from the beginning, and experimental work was valued as a way of developing abstract concepts informally and arriving at the general by way of the particular. By 1959 the Department of Education and Science (DES) had become interested, and proposed a 'task group' to see what professionals were up to in the 'secret garden' of the curriculum. But the teachers' organizations (enjoying the rare pleasure, in the post-war baby boom, of a sellers' market for education) successfully resisted this and eventually, in 1974, were given a dominant role in the Schools Council for Curriculum and Examinations, jointly funded by the DES and local education authorities (LEAs).

In due course the Schools Council took over some Nuffield curriculum projects and launched many more of its own. It soon became a stalking horse for right-wing politicians and was finally liquidated, after undergoing two constitutional upheavals, by the Conservative administration, in 1984. Its responsibilities were split between two separate bodies, each composed of persons nominated by the Secretary of State. The School Curriculum Development Committee (SCDC) was charged with the task of 'filling gaps' in curriculum provision, and given a tiny budget. The School Examinations Council (SEC), on the other hand, was given enhanced funding and status and soon emerged, with the responsibility for introducing the new General Certificate of Secondary Education (GCSE) at 16-plus, as the prime agency for examination-led curriculum change.

Detailed studies of the work of the Schools Council have been offered elsewhere.[6] Suffice it here to say that the RDD model dominated most of its projects, and its centralized bureaucracy made it a less flexible, less teacher-sensitive agency than the independent SMP. By the mid-1970s the 'top-down' RDD approach had been softened to facilitate better diffusion through teachers' centres, but few projects achieved the easy exchange between central innovator and peripheral user sought in the 'social-interaction' model, which gave prominence to the influence of group membership and informal contact on the adoption behaviour of users. By facilitating these interactions through local centres, it was hoped that innovations would take root in schools. In the Schools Council's last phase, from the late 1970s, funding was at last made available for school-based projects, marking a shift to a third approach to innovation – the 'problem-solving' model which focused on the school itself and took the function of the external agent to be primarily non-directive and consultative. However, the Council's infrastructure at the level of field and LEA support was never strong enough to render this final and welcome development really effective. Ironically, for a teacher-controlled organization, it had suffered permanent damage from the centralist steer given to it by its first administrators and the tight control exercised over its decisions for a long period by a caucus of teacher politicians. It lacked the capacity to evolve as an organic institution, and when the balance of power swung in the 1980s in favour of the DES and away from the teachers, its days were numbered.

While some of its most costly projects (like the Humanities Curriculum Project) have had little effect on practice, others (like the History 13–16 Project) have been influential beyond their subject domain: it is at least arguable that this project's emphasis on evidence and process rather than rhetorical content has had an effect on the development of criteria for the new GCSE at 16-plus. And much of the work carried out under the Schools Council's aegis in such areas as mixed-ability teaching has yet to be fully valued.

Growing political concern in the late 1970s with employment and training led to the establishment in 1977 by the DES of the Further Education Curriculum Review and Development Unit (FEU), and in 1983 (as the Further Education Unit) it was given a degree of financial independence. The further education sector was poorly represented on the Schools Council, and the FEU has been active in sponsoring a variety of projects and establishing a network of regional bases. It has taken an active part in promoting the jargon and practice of pre-vocational courses 14–18, and in comparison with the style of the Manpower Services Commission (MSC) has exerted a more liberal and less instrumental influence. But its approach to curriculum change is essentially that of Rational Curriculum Planning by Objectives and is wholly cognate with the RDD objectives-based models of the 1960s and 1970s.[7] Its adoption of the 'cascade' model in developing the new Certificate of Pre-Vocational Education for 17-year-olds, through which central prescriptions flow down to schools, is clear evidence of this.

COLLABORATIVE MODELS AND IN-SERVICE EDUCATION

Disappointment with top-down, descending models of change was identified in the US in the early 1970s. The Rand Study[8] of the impact of the federally-funded 'great society' programmes – which were broadly liberal and progressive in their intent – concluded that 'the problem of reform or change is more a function of people and organizations than of technology'. This was a substantial setback to the confident determinism of planned educational change: it seemed bizarre that a nation could put a man on the moon, but not change its schools. But just as these important evaluation results became available in the late 1970s, the social mood in the US had altered in a way which was to reinforce central initiatives and technological models of change. For the liberal inclinations towards social issues, widely evident in so many Western democracies in the 1960s, were everywhere giving ground to a harsher mood of self-reliance and retrenchment. By 1974 the US was gripped by the 'back to basics' movement, and the Labour government in the UK adopted in the late 1970s utilitarian policies which have been energetically developed by the subsequent Conservative administrations of the 1980s.

Given this political climate, it is not surprising that the failure of planned educational change was blamed not on the defects of the top-down model but on the schools. Clearly, schools could no longer be expected to achieve complete *fidelity* with central goals, but the doctrine of *mutual adaptation* would allow schools some local modification, while retaining the thrust of externally-derived programmes. This could perhaps be seen as a variant of the 'social-interaction' model, but with the emphasis on the capacity of schools to respond to change rather than to generate change for themselves. The putative progression to the school as its own 'problem-solving' agency was diverted and reinterpreted as the task of persuading the school to solve not its own problems but the problems of the bureaus.

Thus it became necessary to talk of 'the management of curriculum change', and to politicize and professionalize curriculum research and development.[9] This strategy requires a new *apparat* for transmitting central policies to institutions where education is practised, and a new relationship between government and academics. Thus a National Management Centre for schools was established in the UK at the University of Bristol in 1984, and American strategies devoted to promoting change through the concept of the school as an organization within a system, such as 'Organization Development' (OD),[10] are finding favour. Of particular importance is the suggestion that the failure of curriculum change strategies can be remedied by focusing on the *implementation* tasks facing the school. This device has the effect of treating the school as a deficit system: schools must learn how to implement change, not to originate it. The origins of this approach in the heavily centralized Canadian setting are significant,[11] and it is beginning to attract attention in the UK, where new funding arrangements for in-service education and training (INSET) were introduced by the DES in 1987, and mark a major shift towards central control.

The new INSET scheme achieves this in three ways. First, the route for channelling INSET funding to schools and teachers has been radically changed. Formerly, the costs of all but short INSET courses were met from a central pool to which both the DES and the LEAs contributed, and from which higher education providers could draw. This was in essence an input-led model which placed the prime responsibility for INSET provision on the higher education institutions, and fostered the growth of higher degree courses and reflective forms of professional development. Now, the central pool is abolished, and although the DES makes some funding available to higher education providers for longer courses, the bulk of DES INSET funding reaches schools directly via LEAs, through a bid system which is, in essence, output-led.

A second important change is that the available funding is to a considerable extent tied to particular topics, like management training and vocational courses, identified as priority concerns by the DES. And third, although the non-directed INSET requirements identified by LEAs are to be derived from a process of 'needs analysis' carried out in each authority's schools, they are still subject to DES approval. At first blush, it might appear that an analysis of needs could lead to a resurgence of 1960s-style school-based curriculum development (SBCD). But realism suggests that a more likely outcome is a form of SBCD in which the agenda is set by the priorities of bureaus, in the DES and in the LEA. The new scheme has led to an increase in the number of LEA advisers with an INSET remit, and it is likely that many schools will take their cue as to what constitutes a 'need' from the plethora of national prescriptions emerging from the DES and often reinforced (as will happen, in a descending model of control) by LEA proposals and requirements.

TOWARDS SCHOOL-FOCUSED DELIBERATION

The political reality, then, is that many countries are treading a similar path in a climate which favours central control of education and a contractual basis for schooling. But the practical reality is that past attempts to change school curricula this way have been notably unsuccessful. And there is the moral, as well as the empirical, argument: education is not reducible to a set of basic skills and competencies, but rather depends on the understanding that arises from the transactions between teacher and learner in the practice of a particular institution.

And while many countries are taking this centralized route, others are not.

In France and Scandinavia, where there is a tradition of central control, moves are afoot to allow more autonomy to schools, and in the US the 'excellence in education' and 'effective schools' movements have had the effect of consolidating state and school autonomy. It is, therefore, important to reinterpret SBCD in the light of these diverse trends, and forge an approach to curriculum change which is both educationally defensible and practically viable.[12]

This is not to propose that schools should be left to go their own individual way. On the contrary, no serious advocate of SBCD would want to suggest that the school separate itself from the purposes and concerns of central and local bureaus in national systems. But once it becomes merely an agent of these bureaus, it becomes a means rather than an end and ceases to be an educational institution, just as a teacher who is seen as a functionary rather than a professional ceases to be able to educate. These constraints are enjoined upon schools by the very nature of education as a political and moral activity, primarily to do with character and conduct rather than the inculcation of knowledge and skills. What the school seeks, in a healthy environment for change, is a symbiotic relationship with its bureaus that recognizes what each can do for the other. The prime task of bureaus is to fund, to support, to provide the security without which reflection is impossible, and to indicate from time to time those social and economic considerations which have a bearing on educational practice. Detailed policy making has no place in this, locally or nationally. The task for schools is to develop the capacity for identifying and solving curriculum problems, taking account of internal and external factors and the nature of the school's institutional life.

This is an altogether more elaborate and worthwhile task than 'needs analysis', and it presupposes a capacity for practical and moral judgement which cannot happen overnight or at the stroke of an administrator's pen. It must be nurtured over a period of time in an atmosphere of purposive tolerance. Given the 1987 INSET arrangements, there is now an opportunity for LEAs to work out new forms of relationship with schools and with their electorate. There are threats from central government to curtail their power: attempts by LEAs to mirror the centralism of government in the conduct of their own affairs and bureaucratize schools still further are not likely to win support from voters, particularly since recent Education Acts have substantially reinforced parental and community participation in the governing of schools.

Instead, an imaginative response by LEAs would invite a fundamental reconsideration of the role of the adviser or inspector, and fashion forms of administration which allowed a wide involvement in decision making at all levels. Cumbersome county-wide authorities need to be much more responsive to local circumstances; there is a need for elected bodies with a critical function, capable of examining the routine work of administration and drawing on professional experience to frame new policies. The school, and responsibility for making its practice as virtuous as possible, must lie at the centre of LEA concerns. A variety of support agencies for SBCD should be fostered, along with a curriculum development unit largely staffed by seconded teachers and working in conjunction with governors, practitioners and elected members to help schools establish a rationale for the whole curriculum and support its practice.

This is a starkly different vision from that currently associated with the prospect of a national curriculum, specified centrally as detailed objectives, locally assessed as measurable outcomes, and implemented as a managerial system of Prussian severity. Such a harsh and uncomprehending view of education sits ill with that of a participative democracy; in practice, we are likely to end up with a confusing prescriptive jumble that will only guarantee the worst of both worlds. To ensure strategies for curriculum change that will make real educational benefit possible, the chance must be seized to place the school at the centre and enhance the reflective professionalism of teachers. By thus fostering a tradition of deliberative inquiry, focused on the school, the twentieth-century dream of worthwhile mass education for all can become a reality.

NOTES

1. A useful survey is offered in P. Gordon and D. Lawton (1978) *Curriculum Change in the Nineteenth and Twentieth Centuries*, London: Hodder & Stoughton.
2. A helpful survey of the Canadian scene, and the way in which the concept of school 'implementation' assists state control, is given in D. Common 'The practice of curriculum fixing and the governance of Canada's public schools', *Curriculum Perspectives*, October 1986.
3. For a valuable analysis of threats to teacher professionalism from the pursuit of skills and utilitarian objectives, see R. Smith (1987) 'Teaching on stilts: a critique of classroom skills' in M. Holt (Ed.) *Skills and Vocationalism: The Easy Answer*, Milton Keynes: Open University Press.
4. For a full account see C. Handy (1979) *Gods of Management*, London: Pan Books.
5. This categorization of models of curriculum change will be found in R. Havelock (1969) *Planning for Innovation through Dissemination and Utilization of Knowledge*, University of Michigan.
6. See, for example, M. Skilbeck (1984) *School Based Curriculum Development*, London: Harper & Row.
7. There are few published accounts of the work of the FEU. A useful one is in P. Grosch (1987) 'The new sophists: the work and assumptions of the FEU', in M. Holt (Ed.) *Skills and Vocationalism: The Easy Answer*, Milton Keynes: Open University Press.
8. A summary of the Rand Study findings will be found in M. McLoughlin and D. Marsh (1978) 'Staff development and school change', *Teachers College Record*, September, 1978.
9. For a penetrating analysis of this trend, see H. Broudy (1981) 'The professionalization and politicization of the curriculum', *Journal of Curriculum Studies*, 13 (3).
10. Details are given in R. Schmuck, P. Runkel, J. Arends, and R. Arends (1977) *The 2nd Handbook of OD in Schools*, Oregon: Mayfield Publishing.
11. The concept of implementation is described in M. Fullan (1982) *The Meaning of Educational Change*, New York: Teachers College Press.
    The introduction of specific grants for favoured topics, marking an increase of central control, and the new form of INSET funding described here, are elaborated upon in Circular 6/86 (1986) of the Department of Education and Science.

12. These arguments are developed in M. Holt (1987) *Judgement, Planning and Educational Change*, London: Harper & Row.

5·9

CURRICULUM ANALYSIS
AND REVIEW

BRIAN WILCOX

Curriculum review can be discerned as a constant theme running through much of the unprecedented output of reports and other publications about the school curriculum which has so distinctively marked the educational debate of the last dozen or so years. The emphasis on review is, to a large extent, the consequence of more general concerns about the adequacy, relevance, and diversity of the contemporary school curriculum. These concerns have been given increasingly emphatic expression in recent years by successive governments. Curriculum review, however, tends to be a somewhat elusive process which, although frequently commended, lacks agreed definition and readily identifiable sources of guidance on how to carry it out.

This chapter seeks to clarify the notion of curriculum review by indicating how:

1. it is related to the analogous processes of evaluation, analysis, and planning;
2. it can be carried out at different levels of curriculum organization from the total curriculum of the school to individual aspects.

EVALUATION, REVIEW, ANALYSIS AND PLANNING

In recent years local education authorities (LEAs) have sought, as a result of promptings by the DES and HMI, to encourage their schools to adopt a more systematic approach to the appraisal of their activities by promoting schemes of *institutional self-evaluation*.

Two broad types of institutional self-evaluation can be distinguished – *authority-based institutional self-evaluation* and *responsibility-based institutional self-evaluation*.[1] The characteristics of the first type are that it tends to: involve senior staff; see the organization as a rational management system; be concerned with aims, objectives, and management structures; and be representative of a systems analysis tradition of evaluation. In contrast responsibility-based institutional self-evaluation is more likely to: involve staff at all status levels; be concerned with professional and curriculum development; see the organization in collegial terms; and draw on a process model of evaluation. This latter approach to self-evaluation has been strongly influenced by the seminal work of Stenhouse[2] – particularly his belief that educational improvement is best assured at the individual classroom level by teachers acting as researchers of their own practice.

By 1984 well over half the LEAs in England had instituted their own schemes or were supporting individual school initiatives.[3] These generally conform to the authority-based type of institutional self-evaluation rather than the responsibility-based type. In addition, many of the schemes are similar to each other and have clearly been influenced by the Inner London Education Authority progenitor *Keeping the School under Review*.[4] They are generally of the checklist type and consist of a large number of short questions covering the main aspects of a school's organization and activities. Amongst the latter some consideration is generally given to the curriculum. Although the treatment given to it is typically brief, superficial, and lacking an explicit rationale, it can be said to constitute at least a starting point for a review of the curriculum. Curriculum review then can be regarded as a specific aspect of the more general concept of institutional self-evaluation.

The distinction between the two forms of institutional self-evaluation should not be interpreted rigidly. A *rapprochement* between the two is clearly possible. Thus a school in which the senior staff keep the overall curriculum organization under review may very well create both the context and the climate for individual teachers to act as Stenhousian professionals in regularly appraising their own teaching. In fact it may be argued that if the latter activity is not simply to be an individual and private concern, then it needs to be shared with others so as to contribute to a collective understanding of the curriculum as a whole.

The term curriculum review suggests a process which involves a systematic scrutiny of the curriculum and its assessment against certain criteria. It is worth distinguishing curriculum review from curriculum evaluation. This is because there is a tendency in the literature to associate the latter with *innovations* involving specific aspects of the curriculum and the practice of professional evaluators. In contrast, curriculum review is seen as an integral part of the professional practice of teachers with respect to the *existing curriculum* in their schools.

In talking about curriculum review it is important to be clear also about what is meant by *curriculum*. There is a strong implication in the guidance of the DES in recent years that potentially it is the totality of curriculum provision which is to be reviewed, for example,

Every school should analyse its aims, set these out in writing and regularly assess how far the curriculum within the school *as a whole* and for individual pupils measures up to these aims.[5] (my emphasis)

Even if a review of *part* of the curriculum is undertaken, it is difficult to avoid at least a preliminary consideration of the *whole*. This is because few aspects of the curriculum exist as exclusively separate entities. This is particularly so in primary schools, and increasingly the case in secondary schools too. Thus an adequate review of the mathematics curriculum, for example, requires not only an examination of those activities formally timetabled as mathematics, but also those under other titles, such as science and technology, which may involve the use of mathematical knowledge and skills.

A total 'root and branch' review of the curriculum would be a complex and time-consuming task if properly carried out. It is probably unrealistic to expect schools to conduct such a comprehensive exercise other than once every few years. If, however, schools are to maintain an on-going scrutiny of the curriculum between such major events, it is necessary that they are able to generate relevant curriculum data for the purpose.

The latter is a very important point, for it reminds us that in the process of review it is not the curriculum itself which is directly encountered, but rather *representations* obtained by the analysis of curriculum documents and other information. The curriculum is not unambiguously 'out there' and ready for immediate inspection and review. The curriculum is what actually takes place between teachers and pupils – as individuals and groups – in classrooms, laboratories, and other locations over several years. It is impossible for that cumulative experience to be telescoped and directly apprehended by the curriculum reviewer. In other words curriculum review is inevitably based upon a prior process of *curriculum analysis*. In this process such things as timetables, syllabuses, schemes of work, and perhaps information collected specially for the purpose from teachers, pupils, and others are analysed to provide workable data for review. Analysis and review are in fact interrelated processes, since the kind of criteria on which a review will be based will in part determine the kind of information collected and analyses carried out.

Curriculum review – it should be noted – is not an end in itself. Its purpose is to identify weaknesses and deficiencies in the curriculum with a view to its improvement. It is an attempt to provide an explicit basis for the systematic planning of the curriculum. Ideally in a school the cycle of review–planning –review should be repeated regularly so that the development of the curriculum is a continuous process.

REVIEW OF THE OVERALL PATTERN OF CURRICULUM ORGANIZATION AND PROVISION

The curriculum of even a small school is a complex entity to comprehend in its entirety. In a secondary school both the scope of the curriculum and the fact that its delivery is very largely sub-contracted to specialist teachers makes it very difficult for any one individual to know in detail what the total curriculum actually is. The situation in primary schools is a little different, since the curriculum of a particular class of children is the responsibility generally of one teacher rather than many. However, a teacher in Infant 2 may only have the haziest notion of what her colleague is teaching to Junior 2. Furthermore, the freedom which primary teachers have generally had in recent years of developing the curriculum without regard to the demands of external examinations is greater than that enjoyed by most secondary teachers. As a result, the curriculum of a primary school is perhaps more likely to reflect the inclinations of individual teachers than is that of secondary schools. It is therefore generally the case that in most schools it is only the headteacher and senior staff who will have a developed understanding of the curriculum as a whole. This is to be regretted, since, if schools are to be truly corporate communities, then all staff should share a common understanding of what the school is offering to pupils.

The argument presented here is that any attempt at curriculum review needs to be firmly grounded within an explicit and agreed representation of the whole curriculum. Only when the main characteristics of a school's curriculum are clearly delineated can an assessment of its adequacy – either in part or whole – be properly undertaken. A methodology has been developed in the Sheffield LEA for summarizing economically a large amount of curriculum detail of a secondary school in terms of a set of standardized codes and conventions.[6] The system is a derivative of a more rudimentary one developed by Davies.[7] It allows a variety of different subjects, curricular activities, and organizational arrangements for teaching to be depicted succinctly. The system enables the curriculum of even the largest secondary school to be set out on a pupil-year basis on no more than two sheets of A4 paper. Because of the standardized format used, it is possible to compare not only the curriculum of different year and pupil groups *within* a school, but also the curriculum provision of *different* schools.

The system has been widely adopted by LEAs and extended further to deal with such innovations as modular courses. A modified version, due to Harrison,[8] is used as an important means for monitoring nationally the curriculum changes associated with the Technical Vocational and Education Initiative (TVEI). Although the notational system was developed specifically to deal with the curriculum of secondary schools, it can be modified to summarize adequately the generally more integrated and flexible provision of primary schools.[9]

In using this kind of curriculum analysis as the starting point for review a school may then wish to go on to consider the curriculum of a particular year group. Alternatively, a more comprehensive review might be attempted by starting with some such question as 'If the curriculum remains as it is for the next few years, what will a pupil have received by the end of his/her third year of fifth year?' This would mean aggregating the details of curriculum provision for year 1 with that for year 2, and so on.

The aggregated or cumulative curriculum experience is not however the same for all pupils – particularly in secondary schools. This is because different patterns of curriculum provision arise from such factors as the organization of the curriculum on the basis of pupil ability and the extent to which pupils are allowed to choose their curriculum. In other words curriculum review is invariably in practice the review of *curricula*.

The establishment of the pattern of curriculum provision – either aggregated over several year groups or specific to one – is an essential prerequisite for the process of review. A review becomes possible when the curriculum is assessed against some explicit criteria. What criteria might be used? The quotation given earlier[10] suggests that the DES identifies the *aims* of schools as an important set of criteria. It does seem at first blush eminently reasonable that schools should regularly assess how far the curriculum measures up to their aims. If schools are to be truly corporate communities then teachers and others associated with them should endorse a set of agreed aims as guides for individual and collective practice. Indeed most schools would be able to produce a statement of their aims. One cannot however, be overly sanguine about the efficacy of such statements. First, there is little evidence to suggest that teachers are guided by a set of generalized aims either when planning their programmes[11] or when actually teaching.[12] Second, aims are statements which in an abbreviated form encapsulate complex value issues. Their meaning and implications need to be explored in collective debate if they are to be actively assimilated and become a real guide for action. Few schools seem to have invested the time necessary for such a task, and probably even fewer have ensured that aims, once formulated and agreed, are regularly examined, reconsidered, and if necessary restated.

The reality is that the majority of schools are 'loosely coupled' systems of individual teachers, groups of teachers, departments, and the like, held together less by a set of core values – increasingly difficult to achieve in a pluralist society – than by a set of institutional and professional practices. Despite the difficulties, however, schools should continue to seek to ground their activities in a set of commonly agreed aims. It may be that one of the distinguishing features of the 'good' school, like that apparently of the 'good' company,[13] is the ability to make clear its values and ensure that they are known, understood, and felt throughout the organization.

With these provisos a review of the curriculum against school aims is both appropriate and indeed a potentially powerful means of fostering a sense of corporate endeavour. Although statements of aims abound, there is surprisingly little practical guidance available to teachers showing how they can be used in planning and reviewing the curriculum. Ashton's work however, provides a rare exception.[14] Ashton has identified, in conjunction with groups of teachers, 72 statements representing the aims of primary education. Although her main concern is to use these aims as a basis for *designing* the curriculum, they are equally applicable as a basis for review. A simple technique which she recommends involves the construction of a squared grid with the content areas of the curriculum (language, maths, etc.) set along the top and the aims listed down the side. Each aim is then considered in turn and ticked off against the content areas in which it is pursued. When completed the grid may be read vertically to see which aims contribute to which content areas. Reading the grid horizontally identifies in which curriculum areas a particular aim is being pursued. The overall task can be made more manageable by initially identifying from the 72 statements a smaller number (perhaps ten or so) which represent priority aims. Although Ashton is concerned with the aims of primary education her approach, of which the above is but one feature, is applicable also to secondary teachers wishing to review the curriculum against a set of aims appropriate to their sector.

Another approach to reviewing the curriculum, and one which has been particularly promoted by HMI in recent years, is in terms of the *areas of experience* which, it is argued, give coherence and balance to the overall curriculum. As initially formulated by HMI[15] the areas were: aesthetic and creative; ethical; linguistic; mathematical; physical; scientific; social and political; and spiritual. Wilcox and Eustace[16] have shown how, using the areas as a checklist, it is possible to provide a quantitative estimate of curriculum balance for a particular pupil-year group. In brief, this involves teachers of each subject area indicating the extent to which their subject contributes to the development of each of the eight areas of experience by allocating a maximum of ten points amongst them. The resulting data can then be combined with the number of periods per week (ppw) devoted to each subject to give a curriculum profile expressed in notional ppw of the various areas of experience. A similar quantification of curriculum balance has also been described in an exercise involving 9–13 middle schools.[17] The areas of experience checklist has also been more widely used in a major curriculum review exercise[18] which involved 41 secondary schools in five LEAs working jointly with a group of HMI and local advisers. The reaction of schools generally to the use of the checklist was varied.[19] Although it was found to have been 'a powerful analytical tool' some difficulties were encountered. Thus the vocabulary and degree of abstraction were considered to be difficult, and needed considerable time to talk through and absorb. It was also noted that the checklist could lead to artificial exercises in justification 'with subjects dredging deep to find some form of response under all eight headings'. These comments suggest that an essential prerequisite for the use of areas of experience, as with educational aims, is the investment of time to allow staff to explore meanings and arrive at agreed operational definitions. It is interesting to note therefore that a more recent formulation of the areas of experience[20] gives a detailed description of each with examples.

The HMI areas of experience is but one of several supra-subject curriculum models that can be used as an initial basis for curriculum review. Another which is worthy of serious consideration – not least because it is derived from a clearer theoretical basis than the HMI model – is that due to Lawton.[21] From a standpoint of cultural analysis Lawton argues that the curriculum should represent an adequate sampling of the following cultural subsystems: social; economic; communication; rationality; technology; morality; belief; and aesthetic.

REVIEW OF INDIVIDUAL ASPECTS OF THE CURRICULUM

The approach to curriculum analysis and review which has been outlined thus far has been at the most general level, i.e. the organization of the curriculum in terms of subjects or broader curriculum areas. Whilst it is possible at this level to get some appreciation of the adequacy of the overall curriculum in terms of breadth and balance, a deeper understanding is possible only by examining what lies beneath the individual curriculum labels. Studies have shown that in both the primary and secondary curriculum an intermediate level of analysis in terms of broad topics or themes may be sufficient to indicate the emphasis given within a particular curriculum area. Thus a review of the cross-curricular area of personal and social relationships was carried out in four secondary schools[22] using a topic checklist derived from a content analysis of relevant syllabuses and schemes of work. Individual teachers contributing to this area were able to estimate the amount of time which they gave to each of the topic items. These times were aggregated across contributing teachers and years groups, so as to give profiles of topic emphasis which indicated significant differences in coverage between the four (comparable) schools. A somewhat similar exercise using a health education checklist with primary school teachers successfully identified the main topics dealt with under this curriculum heading for pupils of various ages and the emphasis given to them.[23] Checklists of this kind can be derived for any curriculum area, but they are particularly useful for those which are not located within a single timetable slot, but are in fact dispersed across the curriculum in often quite complex ways.

Any curriculum area and the specific topics or themes which it subsumes may be analysed, in principle, into finer and finer detail, down to the level of individual elements of learning expressed in terms of knowledge, concepts, skills, and attitudes. The exercise if repeated for all year groups and for all curriculum areas would yield a comprehensive map of learning for the whole curriculum of a school. This would represent, even for a small school, a complex and time-consuming task. However, a school might carry through such detailed analysis on curriculum areas one at a time over a period of years.

Typically syllabuses and schemes of work have not been set out in terms of what is expected of the learner. The emphasis has generally been on things to be covered rather than on what the learner should be able to do or display. In the secondary sector, however, the new GCSE syllabuses at least have moved away from the traditional format by clearly showing the relationship between aims, national criteria, and objectives for individual subject areas. In general though – both in the primary and secondary sector – the analysis of a curriculum area will require not only close scrutiny of syllabuses and schemes of work but also of textbooks, teaching materials, and most important of all, the classroom practice of individual teachers.

Having identified an individual curriculum area and carried out an appropriate analysis, against what criteria might it be reviewed? One general set of criteria are those identified by HMI as *characteristics of the curriculum*[24], i.e. breadth, balance, relevance, differentiation, progression, and continuity. The meanings of these terms are not, however, self-evident. Like many used to describe the curriculum, they are themselves complex concepts which staff need time to explore if they are to invest them with similar meanings. Thus although it may seem very reasonable that the curriculum should be assessed in terms of its relevance, it is crucial to confront some prior questions such as, 'How is relevance to be defined?' And perhaps, more important, '*Who* determines what shall be deemed relevant?'

It may be useful at this stage to summarize the position reached so far. This has been to suggest that a whole curriculum review at the *organizational* level is a necessary preliminary to a more detailed examination of a specific part. This may lead to a further stage of analysis and review at the level of individual themes or topics. Further descent to deeper levels of analysis may only be feasible – given the likely availability of time – for specific curriculum areas. In such a case an identification of the elements of learning may be appropriate. A review of a curriculum area need not, however, stop there. Thus the staff of a department may wish to examine how their *intended* curriculum – whether expressed in themes or learning objectives – is developed in practice. They may, for example, wish to consider the variety of teaching/learning methods employed, the views and reactions of pupils, and whether the textbooks and other teaching materials used are consistent with the intended learning objectives. There may be a concern to identify the outcomes of the curriculum in terms of student achievement. The staff may also recognize that the delivery of the curriculum does not take place in a vacuum – that it may be facilitated or indeed inhibited by factors outside the classroom, and perhaps also their direct control. These might include a whole host of things from aspects of school policy and organization to constraints of the external examination system. Concerns such as these may require the collection of data through the use of such techniques as observation, interviews, questionnaire surveys, assessment, and testing.

It is not the purpose here to describe the complete panoply of techniques, for this has been done elsewhere,[25] but to make the point that the more such techniques are consciously and systematically used, the more a review shades into being an evaluation. How far an individual review exercise develops into a full-blown evaluation will crucially depend on the time and resources available. The application of specific evaluation techniques is usually a time-consuming business which may also require expertise which may not be available in the school. It is salutary to remember that for teachers review is always a subordinate task to their day-to-day ones of teaching, and running a school. Review, then, will seldom approximate to the rigour of a curriculum evaluation cast in the educational research tradition.

CURRICULUM REVIEW – THE ROLE OF 'INSIDERS' AND 'OUTSIDERS'

It should be apparent from what has been said about curriculum review that it is a complex process which involves more than one person – potentially the whole staff of a school. In organizing a curriculum review it is very easy to concentrate on the methods of obtaining appropriate data and to neglect the considerable social organization which is involved. This neglect is very apparent in the LEA institutional self-evaluation schemes referred to briefly at the beginning of this chapter. One scheme which has taken these concerns seriously is the *Guidelines for Review and Internal Development in Schools* (GRIDS) developed by the Schools Council. GRIDS exists in two forms – a secondary school handbook and a primary school handbook.[26] GRIDS sets out in clear terms the steps involved in carrying through a whole school review, although its concerns are wider than simply that of the curriculum. It is particularly sensitive to questions of consultation and the need to involve a wide cross-section of staff, and not to limit the exercise to the head and senior staff. The GRIDS materials are also noteworthy in that they operationalize the kind of 'progressive focusing' to review outlined here, i.e. an initial review of school-wide aspects is carried out and then priorities are agreed for specific review and development.

The GRIDS approach relies on 'insider' co-ordination of a review. However sometimes there may be advantages in co-ordination by an 'outsider' – someone with the expertise, and particularly the time, to collect relevant data, interpret them, and provide feedback to the staff from perhaps a more objective standpoint than may be possible with an insider. Appropriate outsiders might include LEA advisers, lecturers in education, and perhaps staff from other schools.

An interesting variant on the use of outsiders which shows promise is the IBIS (Inspectors Based in Schools) scheme developed by the Inner London Education Authority.[27] An IBIS team consists of inspectors with expertise across a range of specialisms who work for a time within a particular school. The team gathers data in a variety of ways, including observation and interviews, with the aim of producing a review of whole-school issues including, of course, the curriculum. The distinctive feature of the scheme is that the team stays on in the school after the review stage in order to implement, with the teachers, the agreed changes.

A curriculum review exercise should not be the exclusive concern of teachers and other educationalists. Much of the thrust of educational development in recent years has been concerned with opening up the 'secret garden' of the curriculum to others with a legitimate interest in it. These include parents, governors, pupils, and representatives of industry and commerce. The involvement of such groups in curriculum review can take place in two broad ways. On the one hand they can contribute relevant data to the review process. Thus there is considerable potential in incorporating the insights of parents and pupils concerning their experience of the curriculum in action. On the other hand they may also play an important part in the *organization* of a review, for example by involvement in relevant working groups and committees. That involvement may carry over into the subsequent action or development which is after all the prime reason for implementing a review.

CURRICULUM REVIEW IN THE FUTURE

In July 1987 the Government announced its intentions in a consultation document of introducing – with the backing of the law – a national curriculum with testing in key subject areas at prescribed pupil ages. One year later the requirements of a national curriculum had been enshrined as a key element in a new Education Act.[28] This can be seen as the final round in a struggle, waged over the years since the mid-1970s, concerned with wresting control of the curriculum away from both schools and LEAs.

The national curriculum is to consist of *core* subjects (mathematics, English, science), together with *foundation* subjects (history, geography, technology, music, art, physical education), and (for pupils 11–16 years), a modern language. The national curriculum will take up 70–80 per cent of the curriculum time in schools. Attainment targets will be set for all of the core subjects and most, if not all, of the foundations subjects, to establish what children should normally be expected to know, understand, and be able to do at seven, eleven, fourteen, and sixteen. The attainment targets are to be consistent with descriptions for each foundation subject of the content, knowledge, skills, and processes which pupils are to be taught. By December 1988, draft orders had already been proposed outlining attainment targets and programmes of study for two national curriculum subjects – mathematics and science.[29]

There are profound implications here for the process of curriculum review which the consultation document implicitly endorses within a broader notion of evaluation. A national curriculum will, dependent on the degree of detail in which it is formulated, reduce the freedom of schools and LEAs to determine what shall be taught. It will, however, provide a major set of criteria – an essential template – against which schools will be able to review what they do.

The emphasis which the consultation document gives to making information available about how pupils perform against attainment targets, as measured by test scores, introduces a potential *comparative* element into the review process. It is intended that comparison will be possible not only within a school but between schools in the same LEA and even between different LEAs.

There is also the implication that the process of evaluation which a national curriculum will facilitate will be a collective one. 'The governing body, head-teacher, and the teachers of every school will be better able to undertake the essential process of regular evaluation because they will be able to consider their school, taking account of its particular circumstances, against the local and national picture as a whole.'[30]

There are, of course, dangers here of review and evaluation generally relying exclusively on a limited number of quantitative indicators. There are, however, no short cuts to judging the effectiveness of complex entities like the curriculum. A whole range of information is necessary – and test results are but one – which require the mediation of professionals (teachers and others) if quality of provision is to be meaningfully assessed.

Whilst the detailed form which the national curriculum as a whole will take is not yet clear, there is not doubt that it brings the issue of curriculum review firmly on to the agenda of schools and LEAs.

REFERENCES

1. McCormick, R. and James, M. (1983) *Curriculum Evaluation in Schools*, London: Croom Helm, pp. 184–274.
2. Stenhouse, L. (1975) *An Introduction to Curriculum Research and Development*, London: Heinemann.
3. DES (1986) *Better Schools: Evaluation and Appraisal*. Report of the Birmingham Conference (14–15 November 1985), London: HMSO.
4. ILEA (1977) *Keeping the School under Review*, London: ILEA.
5. DES (1981a) *The School Curriculum*, London: HMSO.
6. Wilcox, B. and Eustace, P. J. (1980) *Tooling up for Curriculum Review*, Windsor: NFER.
7. Davies, T. I. (1969) *School Organisation*, Oxford: Pergamon Press.
8. Geoffrey Harrison, School of Design, Technology and Craft, Trent Polytechnic.
9. Wilcox and Eustace op. cit. p. 91.
10. DES (1981) op. cit.
11. Walker, R. (1975) 'Curriculum development in an art project', in W. A. Reid and D. F. Walker (Eds.) *Case Studies in Curriculum Change*, London: Routledge & Kegan Paul.
12. Lortie, D. (1975) *Schoolteacher: A Sociological Study*, University of Chicago Press.
13. Peters T. and Waterman R. H. (1982) *In Search of Excellence*, New York: Harper & Row pp. 279–91.
14. Ashton, P., Kneen, P., and Davies, F. (1975) *Aims into Practice in the Primary School*, London: University of London Press.
15. DES (1977) *Curriculum 11–16* (Working papers by HMI), London: HMSO.
16. Wilcox and Eustace op. cit. pp. 80–1.
17. Foster, A., Whitfield, R. C., and Coxhead, P. (1977) 'Assessing curriculum balance in middle schools', paper presented at the British Educational Research Association Conference, University of Nottingham, 7 September 1977.
18. DES (1981b) *Curriculum 11–16: A Review of Progress*. A Joint Study by HMI and Five LEAs, London: HMSO.
19. ibid pp. 59–60.
20. DES (1985) *The Curriculum from 5 to 16. Curriculum Matters 2*. An HMI Series, London: HMSO. The areas outlined here are increased to nine, and consist of aesthetic and creative; human and social; linguistic and literary; mathematical; moral; physical; scientific; spiritual and technological.
21. Lawton, D. (1983) *Curriculum Studies and Educational Planning*, London: Hodder & Stoughton.
22. Wilcox, B., Dunn, J., Lavercombe, S., and Burn, L. (1984) *The Preparation for Life Curriculum*, London: Croom Helm, pp. 36–49.
23. Wilcox, B. and Gillies, P. (1981) 'The curricular anatomy of primary school health education', *British Educational Research Journal*, 7 (1) 1981: 17–25.
24. DES (1985) op. cit. pp. 42–51.
25. McCormick and James op. cit. pp. 120–2.
26. McMahon, A., Bolam, R., Abbott, R., and Holly, P. (1984) *Guidelines for review and internal development in schools*. Secondary school handbook and primary school handbook, London: Longman.
27. Jenkins, V. (1987) 'School effectiveness and school change: the IBIS approach', paper presented at the British Educational Research Association Conference, Manchester Polytechnic, 4 September 1987.
28. *Education Reform Act 1988*, London: HMSO.
29. DES (1988) *National Curriculum Draft Orders for Mathematics and Science*, London: DES (Elizabeth House).
30. DES (1987) *The National Curriculum 5–16: A Consultation Document*, London: HMSO.

5.10

CURRICULUM EVALUATION: OLD AND NEW PARADIGMS

JON NIXON

This chapter reviews, in terms of a number of paradigm shifts, the changing context of ideas relating to curriculum evaluation over the last twenty years. These shifts, it is argued, have resulted in a new consensus regarding the purposes and procedures of evaluation – a consensus which is not without its own tensions and contradictions. The aim of this chapter is to illuminate some of the key concerns within the current theory and practice of curriculum evaluation by viewing them within a broad historical and contextual frame of reference.

THE NATURE AND PURPOSE OF CURRICULUM EVALUATION

Evaluation, as the term suggests, is inevitably concerned with human values: those espoused by individuals and groups in specific situations, and those implicit in the actual social practices to which these individuals and groups are committed. In the field of *curriculum* evaluation these situations are located within that arena of social practice referred to as 'schooling'. That arena, of course, includes a much broader range of institutions than just schools: tertiary colleges, institutions of higher education, HMI, and LEA advisory services, to name but a few, are also central to the task of curriculum evaluation. It is precisely because of the potential for mismatch between rhetoric and practice across, and within, these institutional boundaries that the role of evaluator is, in the context of the developing school curriculum, at once crucial and at the same time highly problematic.

The problem can be simply stated, though far from simply resolved: how can evaluators document impartially, analyse and – hopefully – make increas-

637

ingly refined and discriminating judgements regarding rhetorics and social practices that they are themselves inextricably caught up in?

Responses to this question can be seen somewhat crudely in terms of a continuum, with the 'measurement' of quantifiable data at one extreme and naturalistic 'description' of complex social settings at the other. Along the continuum, approaches can be distinguished in terms of the data drawn on, the data collection techniques employed, and the kinds of reporting that result.

The limitations of the notion of 'evaluation as measurement' are now well documented and widely accepted.[1] Such a conception presupposes the possibility of determining base lines and indexes, of isolating variables, and developing appropriate instruments; and each of these activities becomes highly problematic in situations where change is both rapid and varied. Given the many strategic interventions that are likely to be undertaken, base lines become blurred and variables shift between cases. Moreover, there may be serious differences of opinion between those involved regarding what constitutes change and how it should be 'measured'. These limitations, as Malcolm Parlett and David Hamilton have pointed out, suggest that applying this evaluation approach 'to the study of innovations is often a cumbersome and inadequate procedure'.[2]

Those approaches at the other end of the continuum which seek to provide naturalistic 'description' avoid many of these limitations. Indeed, their development has in many cases been prompted by a reaction against the reductionism of the more positivist 'evaluation as measurement' paradigm, together with a recognition of the need for alternative ways of seeing 'the complexities and richness of educational life'.[3] Such approaches raise their own problems, however; particularly when viewed in the context of school-focused curriculum innovation. For to describe changing social structures in such a way as to reflect their salient and idiosyncratic features is an immensely time-consuming task, both in terms of data collection and clearance. And time, for those who are caught up in the process of curriculum change, is always in short supply.

Viewed historically, the drift from 'measurement' to 'rich description' represents a fundamental paradigm shift, to which the style of evaluation that is now gaining dominance within educational circles can be seen as a significant response. That style owes something to the reconceptualization of research and evaluation as achieved within those approaches being located more towards the 'descriptive' end of the continuum. It is, however, a distinctive style, independent of this earlier orientation, and with its own characteristics and antecedents. What we are faced with is a real change in what is conceived of as the nature and purpose of curriculum evaluation.

The prime purpose of evaluation, as framed by the emergent paradigm, is to inform the immediate decisions of policy makers and practitioners. In this respect it differs significantly from those styles of evaluation at the 'descriptive' end of the continuum, the main aim of which was to aid reflection rather than action. Unlike those at the 'measurement' end, however, it fulfils its purpose by highlighting issues implicit in the process of curriculum development. It attempts, in other words, to be both user-focused (in terms of its orientation towards specific outcomes) and process-orientated (in terms of its focus on particular contexts). And the means by which it attempts this resolution is through its unfailing recourse to the notion of 'issues'.

Through common usage an 'issue' might be taken to denote a concern which is generally understood to be significant. (Though 'concern' here ranges across a broad semantic spectrum, everything, in fact, from a vague worry to a downright contradiction.) The term 'issue' also carries with it, however, the suggestion of emergence; an issue, in other words, is a problem-not-yet-defined, a question-about-to-be-framed. The prime function of curriculum evaluation as currently practised is to render explicit these as yet implicit probings, to track and frame them, to organize them into meaningful structures.

This, of course, places evaluators in an extremely *influential* (though not necessarily *powerful*) position. No longer primarily concerned with either the measurement of outcome or the chronicling of process, they are becoming the gatekeepers of educational thought. It is they who recognize and articulate the emergent press of opinion and practice; they, too, who scatter it into significant patterns. Given this degree of influence, the question, 'Whose interests do they serve?' is of paramount importance. In responding to that question we need to consider a further paradigm shift that has serious implications for the role of evaluation.

THE ROLE OF EVALUATION

In 1967 Michael Scriven[4] drew his now classic distinction between 'summative' and 'formative' evaluation. In retrospect that distinction can be seen to represent something of a watershed, though it is by no means as simple and straightforward as popular usage would sometimes seem to suggest. Primarily, it serves as a pointer to an emergent redefinition of the role of evaluation and the interests served by those who are involved in this process.

The distinction rests as much upon differing views of curriculum as upon conflicting notions of evaluation. Summative evaluation, as conceived by Scriven, is underpinned by the idea of a curriculum as a programme designed and implemented to meet certain pre-specified goals: the role of evaluation in this context was to assess the extent to which those goals had been achieved. Formative evaluation, on the other hand, arose as a response to a more general urge within curriculum studies to look critically at the kinds of educational goals being set, and at their function within curriculum development. Thus, in part, Scriven wanted to reclaim for evaluation the authority to question the value – or 'worthwhileness' – of these goals, rather than just to accept them as taken-for-granted yardsticks.

He wanted also, however, to draw attention to the *unintended* outcomes of curriculum programmes, and saw evaluation as having a key role to play in this respect; through, for example, a process of progressive focusing on emergent goals and changing emphases within the programme. Thus, while the notion of 'formative' evaluation implies regular though intermittent feedback, its stress initially was as much on the focus of the enquiry as on the styles and frequency of reporting.

The 'new wave' evaluators who followed Scriven were to a large extent exploring the implications of this stance. 'Illuminative',[5] 'holistic',[6] and 'responsive'[7] evaluation were three clearly articulated approaches which pushed forward the frontiers of thinking in this area. Though less judgemental and with a greater stress on audience, the advocates of these closely-related approaches shared with Scriven a common purpose. They saw the role of evaluation as being to problematize process: to question the assumptions which underpin the curriculum in action, rather than to view it as an unproblematic expression of its own stated aims. The paradigm shift – if it can be seen as such – was by way of a reasoned refusal to take at face value the rhetorics that justify and seek to explain curriculum practice.

An interesting parallel to this shift can be found in the field of literary criticism, where the notion of 'intentionalist fallacy' paved the way for a spate of theorizing whereby the text was no longer conceived as a direct expression of authorial intent, but as the product of a grid of socially constructed codes and conventions. The text, in other words, could no more be judged solely as a product of the author's meaning, than the curriculum could be judged solely in terms of the curriculum planners' stated objectives. The evaluator, like the critic, was obliged to recognize unintended meanings as well as acknowledge consciously implied intentions.

This reconceptualization of the evaluator's role is now being modified by a number of contextual factors, not least of which is the control of the school curriculum, increasingly centralized over the last ten years. This control is now exerted, in part, through 'categorical' funding programmes that specify priority areas, impose a strict system of accountability, and have government approval if not backing. The proposed 'national extension' to the MSC-funded TVEI serves as a useful example of the way in which 'categorical' funding programmes of this kind can influence both the pace and nature of curriculum change.

This shift in the power relation between those who fund the programme and those who deliver it has serious implications for the role of evaluation. Two basic 'kinds' of evaluation have begun to emerge within these programmes:

1. National or macro-evaluation, funded *directly* by the funding body and reporting in the first instance to that body.
2. Local or micro-evaluation, funded *indirectly* by the funding body through the project and reporting in the first instance to the project director.

Those involved in local evaluation, which has proliferated under the new dispensation, are likely to be acutely aware of the heavy accountability demands placed on the projects they are evaluating. There is a danger under these circumstances of evaluation losing its cutting edge and becoming, perhaps for very good reasons, increasingly instrumentalist in its thinking. The term 'formative' would thereby come to denote a process more akin to the fine tuning of a machine than to a close examination of the principles by which, and purposes for which, it operates. Evaluation, to draw on the jargon, would have gone 'cosy'.

These is also a danger that national evaluation will become little more than an instrument of accountability serving the interests of the funding body to which it reports. To make this point is not to cast doubt on the integrity of individual evaluators, but to highlight the tensions and contradictions inherent in the role of evaluation itself. Recourse to the notion of 'independence' fails to address the full complexity of the issue. Evaluators are inextricably entwined in the power relations that frame their object of study. They are not disinterested.

In turning to the third paradigm shift, we shall be examining a serious attempt to resolve some of these contradictions and tensions by switching the focus of attention from 'outsider' to 'participant' evaluation. As we shall see it is an attempt that trails in its wake its own set of problems and dilemmas.

TEACHERS AND EVALUATION

The argument so far has focused almost exclusively on the work and writings of professional, usually full-time evaluators. Throughout the late 1960s and 1970s, however, a number of projects began to define a stronger role for teachers in curriculum evaluation and development. These projects were funded in the main by the former Schools Council, but also to a lesser extent by the Nuffield and Ford Foundations and by a number of professional associations. Characterized by their large-scale structure and their emphasis on implementation through the development of teaching materials, several of them did nevertheless seek to involve teachers in the process of development, diffusion, and (later and to a lesser extent) classroom research.

Lawrence Stenhouse, drawing primarily on his experience of directing the Humanities Curriculum Project, typified this role as 'the teacher as researcher'. In a much-quoted passage, he defined its major characteristics as being '. . . a capacity for autonomous professional self-development through systematic self-study, through the study of the work of other teachers and through the testing of ideas by classroom research procedures'.[8] Although rarely alluded to by Stenhouse, there was a precedent for this reformulation in work carried out by Stephen Corey[9] and Abraham Shumsky[10] in America during the 1950s. John Elliott drew more explicitly on this earlier American tradition of 'action research', both in his direction of the Ford Teaching Project, and in his later establishment in 1977 of the Classroom Action Research Network. The latter, though not greatly influential, was significant in that it attempted to offer a framework whereby teachers involved in classroom research and evaluation could communicate across institutional and geographical boundaries. It sought, in other words, to establish a research community that was centred on the concerns of practising teachers. Action research as conceived by Elliott and others is essentially self-evaluative: a process of systematic enquiry by teachers into their own classroom practice. Indeed, teachers who have been involved in action research within their own classrooms have pointed to their own increased understanding and self-awareness as being one of its main areas of impact. The following comments, for example, made by practising teachers, stress the importance of action research as a means of prompting critical self-appraisal within the school:

> 'It has made me think twice about the things I say and do in the classroom . . . It enabled me to discover more about myself as a teacher.'
> 'Really taking control of and caring about the quality of what is going on in your classroom leads some teachers into seeing themselves as active initiators rather than child managers.'
> 'We found the activity of research to be both educative and humanising.'
> 'The department and school benefit by being formally told about the research and by the research being talked about and used as evidence in many different contexts, whether it be informally in the staffroom or in curriculum planning meetings.'[11]

In spite of the widespread recognition given to it, this shift towards teacher self-evaluation has failed to have the impact it might have had. Part of the reason for this is that teachers involved in such work have tended to look to national projects and networks for support rather than to their own institutions. Within their schools many of them have become increasingly isolated and are, therefore, unable to effect change across the broader organizational and curricular structures of the institutions in which they work.

This problem has been compounded by the hierarchical management structures of many schools and the lack of any forum within which reflective discussion might take place. The traditional stress on departmental territoriality and professional autonomy has made it extremely difficult for insights into specific instances of classroom practice to gain any critical purchase on the system as a whole. Teachers adopting an evaluative stance to their work in the manner envisaged by Stenhouse have been in the curious position of becoming increasingly marginalized, while at the same time being models of extended professionalism.

An important element in this equation is the increased accountability demands made on schools by LEAs and central government. In the face of these demands any attempt by particular teachers or groups of teachers to adopt a critical stance to their work is likely to be viewed defensively by those with responsibility for maintaining a specific system, be it a subject department, a school, or an LEA. Accountability, under such circumstances, acts as a strong magnetic field, within which the urge towards consensus constitutes a major force.

The protracted dispute of 1985–6 between the teacher unions, the LEAs, and central government has also taken its toll on in-school evaluation. In a climate of opinion where contractual obligations and responsibilities are being fiercely debated, there are understandable pressures on teachers to limit the range of their professional activities. The kinds of ongoing consultation and discussion which should permeate the process of in-school evaluation are likely to have a low priority in the embattled contexts that teachers have grown accustomed to.

At a more theoretical level teacher self-evaluation has borne the brunt of an influential methodological critique levelled at the use of empirical research within the social sciences. According to this critique such research lacks both theoretical and methodological rigour and thereby fails to gain any critical grasp on the macro-systems to which the specific instances being studied are taken to relate. Teacher self-evaluation, being case-bound and often weak on theoretical contextualization, is particularly prone to such criticisms.[12]

These points having been made, it should be stressed that the shift towards a more open and participant style of evaluation has perhaps been one of the most significant trends to have emerged over the last twenty years. If now the notion of 'the teacher as researcher' seems somewhat dated, it is because the political climate – under the influence of a central government which has assumed a mandate for a radical overhaul of the education system as a whole – has changed rapidly throughout the 1980s. As Rob Walker foresaw at the outset of the decade, the dominant trend has been the 'growing separation between the worlds of controllers and controlled throughout the education system'.[13]

The full impact of this separation, as far as curriculum evaluation is concerned, cannot as yet be gauged. The paradigm shifts reviewed in the previous pages do, however, provide us with some key reference points for locating new styles of evaluation emerging within the present context. There has, as I have tried to show, been a general movement from 'measurement' to 'description', from 'summative' to 'formative' reporting, and from 'outsider' to 'participant' evaluation. What will eventually emerge from these shifts is as yet uncertain. It is possible, however, by switching from an historical perspective to one which views evaluation in the present context, to define some of the characteristics of the emergent paradigm.

THE EMERGENT PARADIGM

The relation between evaluation and decision making has in theory always been close: evaluation aspires to inform those who have responsibility for making decisions within a specific arena of practice. Increasingly, that arena has been defined in terms of policy and structure. The emergent paradigm can be defined, in other words, in terms of the premium it places on policy making and decisions that affect the broad structures of schooling.

This, of course, lays it open to the criticism of being crudely instrumentalist. From this perspective the emergent paradigm is merely a tool of management, focusing on broad policy issues with a view to achieving ever increasing administrative efficiency.[14] Such criticisms are not entirely unfounded, but they do seem to me to oversimplify the complex role that curriculum evaluation fulfils within the contemporary educational scene. Unlike 'pure' research it aspires to be socially useful within specific domains; an aspect of that social usefulness, however, is the retention of critical distance. Evaluation is Janus-faced: its claims must be grounded in both truth criteria and utility value. There is little point in the evaluator forming decisions that are considered irrelevant or marginal.

This brings us to a further characteristic of the emergent paradigm: the authority it claims to define the agenda of issues that policy makers should be addressing. Evaluation is now less concerned with responding to prespecified problems than with discovering and articulating the problems that are pressing upon participants. Its judgements are concerned with defining a consensus regarding what is contentious: it maps divergencies of opinion and perception; it does not take upon itself the responsibility of resolving them. In short, evaluation aspires to be a major influence in shaping the *Zeitgeist*.

Such a role carries with it considerable responsibilities. In so far as it exerts an influence on the prevailing context of ideas, the new paradigm might well be seen as operating in the interests of ideologically imposed power. Its only rebuttal of these charges is its adherence to strict procedures regarding the negotiation and release of data based upon the principles of confidentiality and impartiality. The emergent paradigm does not claim 'objectivity'; it seeks, rather, to protect informants from the inevitably 'subjective' bias of its judgements through the negotiation of an agreed ethical code of conduct.

In what has since become a seminal paper, Helen Simons has defined negotiation as 'a two-way process' involving the evaluator in 'discussing with participants throughout the study whether or not they will allow their data to become public'.[15] This process is clearly time consuming, and time, as we have seen, is in short supply for evaluators committed to the rapid turnabout of data that the term 'formative' has come to imply. There is, therefore, some tension between the kinds of procedures advocated by Simons and the time scale within which evaluators are constrained to operate.

As always, evaluation relates to change through the agency of understanding: it can effect structural change only by changing perceptions. Increasingly, however, evaluation is characterized by the way in which the traditional *recipients* of evaluation themselves become *participants* in the process of evaluation. Within the emergent paradigm the evaluators relate to change through their own changing perceptions. This means that, potentially at least, teachers, headteachers, and advisers take upon themselves the task of evaluating their own practice.[16] This is an interesting extension of the notion of 'the teacher as researcher', whereby participants are involved in evaluating the curriculum *at their own level of responsibility.*

This extended notion of participant evaluation is, it should be noted, still very much in embryo, and is subject to the constant pull of the more traditional top-down model of curriculum evaluation. To be effective it would need a radical restructuring of roles and relationships, within both schools and LEA advisory services, so as to ensure a more democratic style of management in these institutions. Whether or not the existing hierarchical management structures have the capacity to respond to this need is still uncertain. What is certain, however, is that the notion of participant evaluation will become increasingly precious, if some such response is not forthcoming. The democratic and participative principles which underpin the notion of 'the teacher as researcher' demand a self-critical stance at every level of the management structure, together with much closer liaison among teachers, LEA staff, academic staff, and professional researchers in the development of a more 'open' and accessible educational research community.

The new paradigm is fundamentally concerned with issues of value. It renders highly problematic the notion of 'facts'. Matters of fact, it would claim, necessarily raise issues of value when they are used as a basis for policy making. We may, for example, establish as 'fact' the rate of pupil truancy within a particular school or LEA, or the rate of attendance at parent-teacher meetings within a particular area: but such statistics, to become a springboard for action, must address broader social and ethical questions. The new paradigm lays claim to these questions: their formulation, their implications, and their potential for effecting significant change at both the level of perception and of practice.

REFERENCES

1. Hamilton, D., Jenkins, D., King, C., Macdonald, B., and Parlett, M. (Eds.) (1977) *Beyond the Numbers Game: A Reader in Educational Evaluation*, London: Macmillan Education.
2. Parlett, M. and Hamilton, D. (1977) 'Evaluation as illumination: a new approach to the study of innovation', in D. Hamilton *et al.* op. cit. p.9.
3. Eisner, E. (1985) *The Art of Educational Evaluation*, London: Falmer Press, p.140.
4. Scriven, M. (1967) *The Methodology of Evaluation*. AERA Monograph Series on Curriculum Evaluation, No. 1, Chicago: Rand McNally, pp.39–83.
5. Parlett, M. and Hamilton, D. (1977) op. cit.
6. Macdonald, B. (1971) *The Evaluation of the Humanities Curriculum Project: A Holistic Approach.* Paper presented to the AERA Annual Meeting, New York, 1971.
7. Stake, R. (1972) *Responsive Evaluation.* (Mimeo). Urbana, Champaign: Centre for Instructional Research and Curriculum Evaluation, University of Illinois.
8. Stenhouse, L. (1975) *An Introduction to Curriculum Research and Development*, London: Heinemann, p.144.
9. Corey, S. (1953) *Action Research to Improve School Practice*, New York: Teachers' College, Columbia University.
10. Shumsky, A. (1956) 'Co-operation in action research: a rationale', *Journal of Educational Sociology* 30: 180–5; (1958) 'The personal significance of action research', *Journal of Teacher Education* 9: 152–5.
11. Nixon, J. (Ed.) (1981) *A Teacher's Guide to Action Research*, London: Grant McIntyre, pp. 51, 60, 94 and 120.
12. Hargreaves, A. (1985) 'The micro-macro problem in the sociology of education', in R. G. Burgess (Ed.) *Issues in Educational Research*, London: Falmer Press, pp. 21–47.
13. Walker, R. (1980) 'The conduct of educational case studies', in W. B. Dockrell and D. Hamilton (Eds.) *Rethinking Educational Research*, London: Hodder & Stoughton, p.51.
14. Becher, T. (1984) 'The political and organisational context of curriculum evaluation', in M. Skilbeck (Ed.) *Evaluating the Curriculum in the Eighties*, London: Hodder & Stoughton, pp. 100–9.
15. Simons, H. (1977) 'Building a social contract: negotiation and participation in condensed field research', in N. Norris (Ed.) *Safari: Theory in Practice* (Papers Two), Norwich: Centre for Applied Research in Education, University of East Anglia, Occasional Publications 4 p. 28.
16. Wilcox, B. (1986) 'Research communities, the White Paper chase and a new research ecumenism', *British Educational Research Journal* 12 (1): 3–13.

5.11

TOWARDS CURSSESSMENT: THE SYMBIOTIC RELATIONSHIP BETWEEN CURRICULUM AND ASSESSMENT

PATRICIA BROADFOOT

Measuring, classifying, appraising, and subsequent judging are endemic to any social situation. People size one another up and act in the light of the judgements they have made. When I meet someone for the first time, for example, I will attempt to identify clues that will allow me to judge whether or not they are likely to be friendly. The warmth of a smile, the twinkle in the eye, are signs I have learned to recognize as normally sound criteria for judging – that is, predicting – that certain kinds of behaviour are likely to follow if I myself give the right stimuli. It is through such a continuing process of appraisal and evaluation that we can categorize people and things and thus make sense of them. In so doing we also provide ourselves with the information we need to decide our own actions.

The assessment that goes on in schools and colleges is only a more or less formalized version of this process of appraising, judging, and classifying that goes on in every other aspect of social life. Teachers assess pupils' personal characteristics such as clothes, language, and personality in order to predict how they are likely to behave in class and thus how they may best be handled. Pupils assess teachers for the signs of bad temper, humour, warmth, or fear that they have learned are significant clues to the behaviour that will be tolerated in a particular lesson.

If assessment were confined to this inter-personal dimension, however, it would not be appropriate to link it to curriculum. Just as pedagogy is more than simply the interpersonal relations between teacher and taught, so assessment has become formalized in terms of particular criteria of success and particular ritualized practices and rewards. When the word assessment is mentioned, most people in education conjure up thoughts of exams, tests, and marks; of selection and rejection; the pleasure of success and the pain of failure. For pupils assessment is the arbiter; the hurdle that must be jumped; the judgement that must be endured if future rewards are desired. For teachers assessment is the key to control and motivation, the basis for quality control, and the chief source of professional satisfaction. Pupils' learning is identified by a series of number and letter codes in mark books, school reports, and examination certificates. Teachers use these same codes as both an *aide mémoire* for noting pupils' ability and a record of progress through the syllabus.

Assessment may therefore be defined as the making of a measurement and the subsequent interpretation or evaluation of that measurement in the light of particular criteria. Thus, for example, being measured as five and a half feet tall has little significance in itself until this result is set against some evaluative criterion such as the average height of the population as a whole. Being five and a half feet tall in a population of Pygmies would have very different implications from having that same height in contemporary Western Europe. Assessment, then, can never be an absolute; it always requires to be interpreted. It is the *judgements* that are made about people and their performance in the light of any particular measurements that are the key to the significance of assessment.

But powerful and pervasive as these ritualized judging procedures have become – so that it is almost literally impossible to imagine teaching and learning without them – they are not intrinsic to education, and indeed are a relatively recent innovation. Before 1772 when the Cambridge University examiner William Farish hit on the idea of awarding numerical scores to categorize different qualities of answer to each question in the MA Tripos,[1] education both here and elsewhere had proceeded quite satisfactorily without it. Since the dawn of civilization education had been taking place in a great variety of guises with no more need for assessment than the criterion of adequacy for the task in hand. What then happened to bring about such a momentous change in our approach to assessment? For an answer we must look at changes in the nature of the curriculum itself and in the social role of education.

There are in fact two main reasons for the rapid growth in popularity of explicit assessment procedures since the late eighteenth century, and both have to do with the formalization of education itself into set curricula and subjects. The first reason was the growth of the notion of progression *through* a body of knowledge, and associated with this, the idea of a particular body of knowledge being necessary for the pursuit of a particular calling. As the learned professions began to adopt the idea of a qualifying examination in the mid-nineteenth century, they helped to establish the idea that competence in relation to a defined curriculum could and should be measured and used as the criterion for deciding fitness to practise a particular professional skill. The second reason for the rapid growth in formal assessment procedures was the growing popularity of schooling itself, which began to create a need for some sort of rationing procedure amongst those with a similar level of performance. Assessment thus began to be used to rank scholars one with another, initially in terms of their performance, and subsequently in more global, predictive comparisons of those scholars' *capacity to perform* as notions of innate 'ability' and 'intelligence' began to develop. The idea of assessing innate 'ability' was greatly strengthened by the development of the study of individual differences in the late nineteenth and early twentieth centuries, and the associated growth of 'intelligence testing', which gave to such assessment the invaluable status of being apparently scientific and objective. Detailed accounts are available of this early history of both educational assessment in general[2] and intelligence testing[3] in particular.

Although space precludes more than a brief discussion of the historical roots of educational assessment, the account provided here is sufficient to underline the three themes which are central to the discussion that follows. These are:

1. that systematic assessment is both a cause and an effect of the formalization of the curriculum;
2. that the two functions for which educational assessment was originally instituted – the attestation of competence and the rationing of opportunity through competition, are still present today in the commonly-made distinction between *criterion-referenced assessment*, where performance is judged against a given criterion of success, and *norm-referenced assessment*, where candidates' performance is judged and subsequently ranked in relation to each other;
3. that the traditions of assessment with which education has come to be associated are essentially social in origin. They are thus not immutable, and indeed are changing at the present time, again in response to changes in the social context.

So far, I have argued that assessment is an integral feature of all social interaction and that educational assessment as we have come to know it, with its paraphernalia of marks, tests, and certificates, is simply a more formalized version of this endemic practice. I have suggested that it became formalized as education itself became more systematic and organized into subjects and classes and age-grades. From these early beginnings, it is now widely recognized as a dominating influence on the curriculum. And yet, most surprisingly, assessment as such has been the focus for very little sustained scholarly and professional questioning. Whilst its Siamese twin, curriculum, dominates bookshelves, professional training, and research and development work, the study of assessment has been confined largely to that of techniques. Some coverage of test theory and statistics has been a feature of many educational psychology courses. Extensive research has also gone into the creation of more and more sophisticated tests and examination procedures. But this psychometric tradition almost entirely ignores the relationship between curriculum and assessment; the role of assessment in the classroom as part of, not a bolt-on addition to, the process of teaching and learning itself.

Until recently most teachers knew little about assessment. Where they would struggle and plan in a detailed and sustained way to produce a coherent scheme of work, assessment typically has had an unproblematic part in this – perhaps as a homework to be marked or as a test to check comprehension and recall. In consequence, much of what teachers have tried to do for many of their pupils has been a failure. Because teaching has so often been regarded as synonymous with curriculum provision, teachers have been typically unaware of the vital part assessment can and will play in either reinforcing or negating that learning. Or, if aware, they have lacked the skills to harness assessment to their purposes.

On the intellectual side, assessment is essential for identifying a pupil's readiness to learn; for giving him or her formative feedback about strengths and weaknesses as learning progresses; for rewarding success; *and* for enabling the reasons for failure to be identified and constructively tackled. On the personal side, it is widely recognized that pupils have learned to need the spur of rewards in the form of marks to motivate them. But how much attention is given to the need to build that pupil's confidence and self-awareness; how much concern has typically been shown for reinforcing the pupil's self-image and self-respect, and thus the mutual respect between teacher and taught, which must be a feature of any non-coercive learning situation?

The neglect until recently of these aspects of assessment in virtually all mainstream educational thinking has been one of the principal causes of widespread disaffection and failure in our schools. Except for the successful few, pupils have tended to become disenchanted with education for the negative self-image which it constantly reinforces, and have sought to leave its embrace as quickly as possible. Our blindness to the importance of the entirely symbiotic relationship between curriculum and assessment has thus been the direct cause of massive and unnecessary educational failure.

As I have implied, however, we are now witnessing what promises to be a fundamental change in this respect. Major upheavals in the area of both policy and practice have been prompted by the combined effects of economic recession and the associated concern about supposedly falling standards, youth employment, and changing social attitudes. Practitioners, at one end of the spectrum, and politicians at the other, are united in their concern that education must be more relevant and useful to both the nation and the individual and, above all, that it must be more successful. For teachers this latter concern has been prompted by their daily awareness of large numbers of increasingly disillusioned young people; for politicians the concern has been the rather more utilitarian desire to get the maximum return on the money invested in education. In both cases, the solution has been perceived as lying in the area of assessment. The tides of concern about both relevance and failure have combined to establish assessment as a curriculum issue.

Many of the contributions to this section of the *Handbook* hark back to the mid-1970s and the watershed they represented for educational provision in England and Wales. When James Callaghan launched 'The Great Debate' on education with his 1976 Ruskin College speech, he was articulating a wide-spread concern that progressivism had been allowed to develop unchecked for too long; that the time had come to impose some limit on the almost complete autonomy hitherto enjoyed by schools. Teachers were to be called to account for the content and outcomes of education. Circular 14/77 required local authorities to identify the nature of curriculum provision in their area, and shortly after documents were issued by both central government[4] and HMI[5] to try to impose some homogeneity on the diversity of curriculum standards and practice that Circular 14/77 had revealed.

It was not long however before central government realized that exhortation would, on its own, have little impact. It became apparent that the two most effective means of bringing about change were, on the one hand, the life blood of finance and, on the other, the supporting skeleton of public examinations and certification. The power of the former may be illustrated by three highly visible examples. The first of these is the increasing use of selective central funds through the Educational Support Grant (ESG) to promote particular initiatives, such as the Lower Achieving Pupils Project (LAPP) and the Records of Achievement pilot schemes. The second is the explicit encouragement of curriculum change as through, for example, the Technical and Vocational Education Initiative (centrally funded through the Manpower Services Commission). In both these widely influential initiatives, central government has had a major impact through its control of resources. The third and most powerful example of all, is the institution of a national assessment programme at the ages of seven, eleven, fourteen, and sixteen for all children as part of the 1988 Education Reform Act.

But the use of resources in this way to ensure the implementation of curriculum policy has been closely and more or less deliberately complemented by initiatives in assessment. The Certificate of Pre-Vocational Education (CPVE) provides a good example of how changes in certification have been used in this respect. It combines a quite new curriculum thrust based on modules oriented towards vocational preparation, and an equally novel approach to assessment where certification is predominantly through a 'profile' of achieved objectives and skills.

Less explicit in curriculum terms, but embodying much of the same assessment philosophy, has been the more general government support for records of achievement and profiling. Such records are intended to broaden out certification in a way that recognizes the whole range of a pupil's achievements – personal, academic, and social – and in so doing, to enable all pupils, whatever their talents, to feel they have a chance of achieving something positive during their school years. In effect, records of achievement represent an attempt to enlarge the criteria of 'success' in education.

But, whilst this was an explicit intention of the government's 1984 policy commitment to the development of records of achievement for all pupils,[6] it was not the only one. In their policy statement the Secretaries of State for Education, and for Wales also, made it quite clear that they realized changes in certification could not, on their own, bring about the desired changes, rather that a new kind of certification would need to be supported by a new kind of curriculum approach.

These developments at policy level have not occurred in a vacuum, however. Rather, they reflect and reinforce a growing awareness among teachers of the potential for assessment to be a teaching tool. Whilst in the early stages of profile assessment many teachers recognized the need for the provision of a more comprehensive and positive testimony to a child's achievement in school than that provided by public examinations, they very rapidly became aware of the potential for such records to be the catalyst for a new approach to formative assessment within the curriculum itself. Thus increasingly, pupils are being encouraged to assess themselves in relation to clearly formulated curriculum objectives. They then share their assessment with that of the teachers during individualized 'review' sessions which provide an opportunity for progress to be recorded, difficulties and their causes to be identified, and resolutions agreed jointly about future learning targets. Teachers recognize that alongside the obvious benefits of the 'business' side of these meetings associated with pupils being encouraged to understand and to take joint responsibility for their own learning, are the less obvious but perhaps even more important social dimensions. For the first time pupils are being accorded the status of collaborators in both learning and assessment. What has hitherto been the sacred preserve of teachers, to decide the criteria of success, and then to judge how far these have been met in any given piece of work, is now being made democratic. More and more pupils are being encouraged to discuss what the criteria of success should be, and to negotiate, with the teacher, how far these criteria have been met in relation to a given objective. In many cases a joint report or record is the result of such a review, which can be used to give feedback to, and involve, parents. Such interim statements then build up into a final summative record of achievement which is a credential for use in the outside world.

Thus the large number of pilot schemes throughout England and Wales currently engaged in trying to develop workable procedures to meet these aims is in the van of a quite new way of thinking about assessment. First assessment is planned as an *integral part* of a scheme of work. Second, its power to motivate and reinforce, depress and disillusion, is explicitly recognized, leading to its identification as a key element in the provision of the sort of supportive, socio-emotional climate so essential to learning. This kind of development could, on its own, herald the end of the curriculum-assessment divide as we currently know it. It could well mean the redefinition of both concepts into a new one in which both were inextricable. Such a concept might, rather whimsically, be called 'curssessment'.

The combined commitment of both government and teachers has served to foster the growth of this new approach to assessment so that it has grown at a quite remarkable rate. Most schools are now providing CPVE and/or pre-vocational courses of a related kind for younger pupils, validated by Examination Boards such as the RSA (Royal Society of Arts) and the CGLI (City and Guilds of London Institute). Many schools have become caught up in 'profiling', either as an individual school, or as a member of a consortium of schools or one or more LEAs. A substantial number of these latter schemes are ambitious in scope and are designed to provide examination board accreditation for the resultant 'records of achievement'. The Oxford Certificate of Educational Achievement is perhaps the best known of these, and the Northern Partnership for Records of Achievement is probably the biggest, with some 36 participating LEAs. Still other schools have become involved through the profiling element of TVEI. And even if there are still many teachers, and even schools, whose thinking has as yet been little touched by the more radical of these developments, almost all are now having to grapple with the novel assessment demands of GCSE which, for the first time, requires all teachers to identify detailed performance criteria for each aspect of their subject, and to use these for regular in-course assessment.

The combined effect of all these initiatives can only be to change radically and for ever the way we think about curriculum. Course planning and syllabus design in terms of content is having to give way to the identification of skills and competencies to be pursued. The pressure to bring about such changes in the way the curriculum in secondary schools is delivered and assessed is now very strong. The widespread concern to motivate pupils hitherto unmotivated by traditional two-year examination syllabuses, combined with the steadily growing pressure to provide new vocationally-oriented learning programmes in schools, together represent a powerful force for change.

Clearly such developments pose major problems of time, skill, and resources. Most teachers have had very little in-service or pre-service training to equip them for this task, and little experience in integrating such heavy assessment demands into their teaching, so that they do not become an impossible burden. Much more development work is needed to find ways of making a reality of the 'curssessment' ideal – of integrating assessment so that it is actually *part* of the classroom teaching and learning process. Otherwise, the potentially substantial benefit of the more process-oriented approach to assessment is likely to be experienced in practice as a bureaucratic nightmare of assessment and recording. Existing experience in resource-based learning, pupil-initiated assessment, and various forms of diagnostic assessment,[7] show that it is possible to organize teaching in such a way that assessment is an integral part of it and not a 'bolt-on' addition.

The most obvious way of doing this is to ensure that curriculum and assessment procedures are planned as a package from the outset. One option in this respect is through the modularization of curriculum into shorter, discrete units of work. Many TVEI and GCSE courses are now being organized in this way, as well as more explicitly pre-vocational courses. Assessment objectives can be built into the module and the outcomes recorded descriptively in terms of these objectives. In Scotland, where the new National Certificate modular provision covers all non-advanced further education, we have perhaps the clearest example of such an approach. In theory at least students choose their own path through over 2,000 modules, their progression from one to the other determined by their successful achievement of the preceding one. The final credential is thus expressed in *curriculum* terms of modules studied rather than assessment terms of the relative success therein. Although there are once again many practical problems associated with such a radical curriculum plan – not least the availability of modules when required, and the ability of staff to implement the scheme in the ways intended – it does represent in principle an excellent example of 'curssessment', the almost total interdependence of curriculum and assessment. Developments in the ILEA provide another example of 'curssessment', where many schools are now involved with developing 'unit credits' and 'graded assessment' schemes, in subjects such as science and modern languages, as well as implementing more conventional GCSE courses, and are seeking to bring all these diverse initiatives together under the umbrella of the London Record of Achievement scheme, which will also embrace other kinds of achievement.

But even if teachers can resolve the practical challenges such initiatives will inevitably create, it is also quite possible that contradictions within current policy developments will serve to stultify, if not strangle, the 'curssessment' revolution. The new common system of examining at 16+, for example, despite its novel features, is still cast much more in the traditional mould, where assessment is clearly separate from curriculum. Paradoxically, it may have just the opposite effect from records of achievement in inhibiting grass-roots curriculum development through the imposition of national subject criteria.

Although the thinking behind GCSE, which emphasizes the identification of what pupils 'know, understand, and can do', reflects a very real movement towards a recognition of both the cognitive and affective impact on the curriculum of the way in which certification is carried out, the conception of what is still essentially a two-year, globally-graded examination, falls far short of the more radical assessment developments described above. Government, it seems, has woken up to the fact that the easiest way of controlling curriculum *content* is by controlling the criteria of certification. It has also realized that traditional certification methods limit the kinds of achievements that can be assessed, and thus inhibit the pursuit of other qualities and skills badly needed in the workplace.

So far lacking, however, has been the political will to put these two insights together; to depart in any major way from the security of past practice. Instead the desire to back both horses may well result in an uneasy and even inegalitarian compromise that offers the worst of both worlds. Thus, the situation that currently represents itself is one in which new ideas about more comprehensive, detailed, and positive assessment are being superimposed upon pedagogical approaches – and in some cases curriculum content – that remain as yet little changed. The result is an almost irreconcilable set of conflicting demands which for many teachers are posing acute practical and philosophical problems. To make time for the wide range of different assessments now required for GCSE: for peer assessment and self-assessment, record writing, and reviews, many teachers feel the curriculum itself is being sacrificed. If this is so it suggests the balance between curriculum and assessment has now been tipped towards the opposite and equally undesirable extreme where the integration of assessment into the curriculum without an equivalent change in the way that curriculum is delivered, results in even more assessment domination than before.

The notion that formal education should be charged with the responsibility of selecting and predicting for the purposes of rationing opportunity has for too long gone unchallenged. So great has been the concern to provide fair, objective assessment, which can identify individual talent in the minutest detail, the more important question of whether such a quest is legitimate has not even been posed. The result has been to confuse the vital curriculum role of assessment with its socially-imposed selection role. This is the distinction Goldstein[8] refers to as that between (learning-) 'connected' and (learning-) 'separated' assessment. The educationally legitimate – and indeed more or less unavoidable – aspects of assessment are those which are interactive; in which teacher and taught enter into various kinds of dialogue, the purpose of which is for *each* to recognize the other's vital role in successful learning. Where such an assessment dialogue is sustained, neither teacher nor pupil can unilaterally blame the other for lack of progress. Rare indeed is the pupil who cannot be won with genuine respect, openness, and understanding. Research evidence generally supports the view that pupils prefer teachers who can make them work and help them to feel successful.[9]

Yet, for the most of its history, mass education has been dominated by educationally 'separated', illegitimate assessment, assessment that has ranked pupils against each other, imposed very narrow definitions of success, and been blind to the wholesale antipathy towards education it has given many pupils. As I have suggested, however, this situation is now changing. For a variety of reasons these questions *are* now being asked, and a major struggle is currently being waged between 'separated' and 'connected' approaches to assessment. Whatever the outcome is, it is already certain that assessment will have a much closer connection with curriculum design as emphasis on subject content gives way to emphasis on generic skills.

A great deal of work still needs to be done, however, to make up for the gaps created by what has been historically a very blinkered research effort. Curriculum development needs to be informed by much more sophisticated techniques of 'learner-readiness' diagnosis. Such diagnostic tools as have been developed in the past have tended to concentrate on *ability* to learn, and have ignored the separate contribution of *willingness* to learn. Work on the more novel curricular approaches of primary schools reveals how difficult it is to provide pupils with the different activities that will stretch each just the right amount for maximum learning to take place.[10] Thus attempts to modularize the curriculum must ensure that they incorporate a sufficiently sophisticated assessment framework that some coherent learning progression can be plotted through the course content available. This will certainly require a good deal of effort to be put into refining and developing effective assessment procedures of the kind advocated by Raven[11] and others, which are currently in a most rudimentary form.

But, to the extent that such a shift in both curriculum and assessment emphasis can be achieved, despite the constraining effects of a national curriculum and national assessments, the results are likely to be a richer, more diverse, and more effective learning environment for pupils. In fact, the wheel will have turned full circle, so that learning situations resemble much more the fluid and holistic approach to education that prevailed before William Farish had his bright idea in 1779. Curriculum would be tailored as much by interest as by formal content; assessment would be very informal and based on demonstrated skills and personal qualities. Superficially this may appear a recipe for laxity and chaos. Whether this is so depends on the intrinsic motivating power of the need to acquire skills; the pleasure in pursuing interests; the reinforcement of a teacher's personal concern; and the encouraging effect of achievement itself. But of course, coercion is less risky.

REFERENCES

1. Hoskins, K. (1979) 'The examination, disciplinary powers and rational schooling', *History of Education*, 8 (2) pp. 135–46.
2. Broadfoot, P. (1979) *Assessment, Schools and Society*, London: Methuen. Mortimore, J. and Mortimore P. (1984) *Examinations: Helpful Servants or Dominating Master?*, Bedford Way Paper, London University Institute of Education. Roach, J. (1971) *Public Examinations in England 1850–1906*, Cambridge: Cambridge University Press.
3. Evans, B. and Thwaites, B. (1981) *IQ and Mental Testing: The History and the Controversy*, Basingstoke: Macmillan. Sutherland, G. (1977) 'The magic of measurement: mental testing in English Education 1900–1940', *Transactions of the Royal Historical Society*: 135–53.
4. HMI (1979) *Aspects of Secondary Education in England: A Survey by HM Inspectorate of Schools*, London: HMSO.
5. DES (1980) *A Framework for the School Curriculum*, London: HMSO.
6. DES (1984) *Records of Achievement: A Statement of Policy*, London: HMSO.
7. Black, H. and Broadfoot, P. (1982) *Keeping Track of Teaching: The Role of Assessment in the Modern Classroom*, London: Routledge & Kegan Paul.
8. Goldstein, H. (1986) *Psychometric Test Theory and Educational Assessment*, University of London Institute of Education.
9. Furlong, V. J. (1986) 'Interaction sets in the classroom,' in M. Hammersley and P. Woods (Eds.) *The Process of Schooling*, London: Routledge & Kegan Paul.
10. Bennett, N. and Desforges, C. (Eds.) (1985) *Recent Advances in Classroom Research*, Edinburgh: Scottish Academic Press.
11. Raven, J. (1981) *Competence in Modern Society*, London: H. K. Lewis. Biggs, J. and Collis, K. (1987) 'Towards a model of school-based curriculum development and assessment using the SOLO taxonomy', *Australian Journal of Education* (forthcoming).

C. THE LEARNING ENVIRONMENT

6. LEARNING AND TEACHING

6.0

INTRODUCTION: CHANGING CONCEPTIONS OF LEARNING AND TEACHING

NOEL ENTWISTLE

This section of the *Handbook* brings us into the classroom to consider the learning environment provided for students (using the term to cover all age ranges) and the way aspects of that environment influence the quality of the learning which takes place within it. Here our main concern is to examine recent research and development work designed to discover how learning takes place at different ages and in contrasting subject areas, and on that basis to suggest what changes might be necessary in teaching and in classroom management.

The section is divided into two parts. The first looks at learning and teaching in general at different stages of education and from different perspectives. This set of chapters is intended to provide concepts and ideas derived from the most recent research, which may help us to see how to improve both the efficiency and the quality of the education process. The second part takes a more practical path by considering the particular nature of learning in selected subject areas and looking at ways in which teaching can be made to facilitate learning in those areas.

CONTRASTING CONCEPTIONS OF LEARNING

As the individual authors have brought to their own topics differing theoretical perspectives, it would be misleading to suggest that any single consistent message will be found. Rather there are a series of threads running through the chapters, which reflect current views on learning in school and in higher education. There is an increasing recognition of the need to break away from a unitary theory of learning. Learning involves such a range and variety of activities, even within an academic setting, that it is essential to consider what processes are involved in each main category of activity with each age-group or within each subject area, and to consider how best to organize teaching at that level (see Neville Bennett's discussion in Chapter 6.5). From such analyses it should be possible to give more specific, and so more practical, guidance to teachers on how to improve the effectiveness of instruction.

Another element in several of the chapters involves a change in perspective. In the past, learning was generally considered from the point of view of the teacher or researcher. More recently there has been a growing emphasis on looking at learning from the perspective of the learners themselves.[1] This research has involved detailed observations of teachers and students, analyses of the work done by students in relation to the instructions given by the teacher, and interviews of the students which ask about the learning strategies adopted, and also seek explanations of why those strategies were used (as in the work described by Charles Desforges in Chapter 6.6).

Finally, several of the chapters are critical of the view of learning which was strongly emphasized by behaviourist psychologists, in which the learner was essentially a passive recipient of reinforcements which shaped future behaviour to match the requirements of the instructor. Teachers never accepted the behaviourist idea of the teacher as a 'manipulator of children's behaviour', but they did accept some of its associated principles – the formal definition of teaching objectives, the provision of tightly organized learning materials related to the objectives, and regular testing and feedback. This approach led to definite benefits in emphasizing a 'systems approach' to teaching, but some of its 'side-effects' have been unfortunate. It requires teachers to take total control of the learning of their students, and it also reduces the concept of knowledge to the ability to produce a series of correct answers.

Although many teachers have remained uncomfortable with aspects of the behaviourist model of learning, their own practices, and the pressures of formal assessment procedures, often seem to imply similar assumptions about the nature of knowledge. Learning, for many teachers and examiners, still involves presenting information which subsequently has to be reproduced accurately and essentially in the same form as it was presented. Emphasis on such reproductive learning implies a conception of knowledge as the accretion of discrete units of information. A 'good knowledge' of a subject area then becomes equated with the quantity of information which can be reproduced to order. But recent research in cognitive psychology suggests strongly that knowledge stored in that way is not easy to use for any purpose other than answering specific factual questions.[2] In real life, knowledge has to be put to use to solve problems or to deal with new situations, and for that purpose it is more important to stress the interrelationships between ideas, and between ideas and evidence. With that emphasis, knowledge is stored in ways which make it usable in a variety of ways in the future: it is building in the potentiality for *transfer*, which has always been one of the concerns of both psychologists and teachers. Along with this idea about how knowledge can best be stored comes the idea that it is essential in education to put more emphasis on *meaning*. And this is true, not just in the later stages of education, but right from the time when children first enter school. For example, knowing what it means to read and write seems to be essential in ensuring rapid progress in these skills (as Hazel Francis argues in Chapter 6.7).

CONCEPTUALIZATIONS AND COMMUNICATION

Students develop meaning in relation to bodies of knowledge, not by rote learning facts and procedures, but by building up effective and appropriate conceptualizations which help them to understand aspects of everyday experience. From this perspective, a sound grasp of a subject area depends on an active process of learning, which involves reflecting on linkages between new ideas and information, and on what is already known, both from previous academic study and from personal experience. Relating academic knowledge to the real world strengthens the bonds which hold ideas in an accessible form in the memory, and also encourages students actively to seek connections with relevant experience. But students will learn in this way only if teaching is designed specifically to encourage such ways of learning (according to the evidence presented by John Biggs in Chapter 6.2).

There is a problem, however, in asking students to make use of their own experience. Particularly in science, students bring into the classroom naive ideas about the world around them which can interfere with more effective conceptualizations. Science education has been making rapid strides in looking at the varieties of ways in which students misunderstand physical phenomena, and in helping teachers to use those misconceptions in building better forms of understanding (as Rosalind Driver explains in Chapter 6.11). The importance for modern society of ensuring that children develop a sound grasp of science and technology has led to major changes in emphasis in British education (which are described by David Layton in Chapter 6.12).

Running alongside the systems approach to teaching, and in ideological conflict with it, there has been an alternative view of the teaching-learning process, rooted not in cognitive psychology, but in humanistic ideas about the nature of learning.[3] From that perspective, learning depends on emotion, on the establishment of warm personal relationships, and on sharing knowledge without reliance on the authority structure implied by the systems approach. Carl Rogers[4] led an attack on the education establishment, which paralleled similar criticisms coming independently from educational innovators who advocated 'child-centred' methods of teaching. Following these ideas, many informal primary schools set out to create a warm and caring climate, and to teach in ways which would capitalize on children's interests and take account, on an individual basis, of their needs in relation to developmental stage. The progressive movement in primary education has had many successes in counteracting the excessive formalism of much schooling, but it has perhaps allowed children too much freedom to avoid the hard work, and the mastering of difficult and initially uncongenial curriculum areas, which can be seen as an essential part of learning and of preparation for everyday life. There is still room in education for encouraging a warm and trusting climate, for using the student's interests and experience outside school, and for treating feelings as a valuable resource within social education (as Alex Sharp argues in Chapter 6.10).

Experiential learning uses the interactions between individuals to explore feelings, but this can also be used to build up the skills of inter-personal communication which form an essential part of language education. Communicative competence is increasingly seen as an essential skill for students to acquire, and much recent development work has been carried out to provide suitable materials for teachers to use for this purpose (in ways which Carolyn Hutchinson reports in Chapter 6.9). Experiential learning also, by definition, asks the student to reflect on a variety of personal and social experiences. Of course, the range of experiences available to young people can be quite limited; education needs to encourage the anticipation of future situations. Here an appropriate choice of literature can be used to provide opportunities for a student to make imaginative projections into situations experienced by others (as William Gatherer argues in Chapter 6.8), and to consider alternative forms of actions and their consequences as part of a broad moral education.

APPROACHES TO LEARNING AND PERCEPTIONS OF TEACHING

The emphasis on meaning can also be considered in another way. What do the tasks set by teachers mean to the students? How do they interpret the requirements? Do they know what level of performance the teacher expects of them? What influence does that have on their learning strategies and on their actual level of performance? There is growing evidence that the students' perceptions of the teachers' expectations have profound, and still largely unrecognized, effects on how effectively a student will learn (see the review of research presented by Colin Rogers in Chapter 6.4). Teachers' expectations are generally communicated to students in indirect ways, by incidental comments, and through facial expressions or body language. But the message is still conveyed, all too clearly, when it leads to feelings of demoralization in the student. There are other indirect influences from what teachers reward or criticize about students' work, and by the form of the assessment procedures (see Chapters 6.1 and 6.6). Students can be led to believe that education requires no more than rote memorization, if that is what teachers and examiners seem to reward. The emphasis on the learning and examining of factual material pushes students into a mode of learning which few teachers would consciously accept as appropriate, but which many teachers currently repeatedly reinforce through their criteria for marking. And these indirect messages strongly influence students' approaches to learning.[5] They seem to determine to a large extent whether students even bother to look for meaning.

The approaches to learning discussed in the first two chapters, by Noel Entwistle and John Biggs, show how the processes students use in learning, both in higher education and at secondary level, reflect contrasting forms of motivation and differing intentions. It is also clear that the students' own expectations influence how they go about learning. The reasons students give for their own success or failure in learning are both a product of past experience and an anticipation of future performance. Students, and teachers, typically explain success or failure in terms of either 'ability' or 'effort'. Ability is thought to be relatively unchangeable, and so teachers urge pupils to 'try harder'. Yet if additional effort still leads to failure, students are led to see themselves as lacking the necessary ability and so doomed to continued failure.[6] A way out of this difficulty is to attribute failure to an inadequate strategy – that failure was caused by tackling the task in the wrong way.[7] A great deal of recent work has been carried out to indicate how learning strategies may be improved (as Lauren Resnick explains in Chapter 6.3).

The old idea of providing study skills workshops has proved ineffective. Instead students are being encouraged to take responsibility for their own learning by developing what has come to be called 'metacognitive awareness' or 'metalearning' (see Chapter 6.2). This can be done if teachers put much more emphasis on the process of learning, by modelling for the students their own ways of thinking and learning, and then encouraging them to follow more strategic approaches – asking themselves what the task involves, what relevant knowledge they have or could find, how they might get round difficulties, how well they have succeeded, and how they might do better next time.[8] Emphasizing process, rather than content, often proves difficult for teachers initially, but there is by now considerable evidence that teachers can make the change, and seem to enjoy teaching more once this more reflective approach is fully understood and adopted by the students.

The rationale underlying the choice of chapters within this section can be seen as an attempt to portray learning as an active process of making sense of the world around[10] by engaging with the subject matter in ways which develop both interest and a deeper level of understanding. Teachers can foster this process by recognizing how students conceptualize important aspects of their subject, and by encouraging strategies which empower the students to learn for themselves. It involves an important transfer of power from teacher to student, yet it is precisely the transfer that is essential to leave young people with the attitudes, skills, and competencies they require to make their way in the world.

REFERENCES

1. Entwistle, N. J. (1987) *Understanding Classroom Learning*, London: Hodder & Stoughton.
2. Biggs, J. B. (1987) *The Process of Learning*, (2nd edition), Sydney: Prentice-Hall.
3. Entwistle (1987) op. cit.
4. Rogers, C. R. (1969) *Freedom to Learn*, Colombus, Ohio: Merrill.
5. Entwistle (1987) op. cit.; Biggs (1987) op. cit.
6. Rogers (1969) op. cit.
7. Covington, M. (1983) 'Motivated cognitions', in S. G. Paris, G. M. Olson, and H. W. Stevenson (Eds.) *Learning and Motivation in the Classroom*, Hillsdale, N. J.: Lawrence Erlbaum.
8. Entwistle, N. J. (1988) 'Research on motivation to learn', *Proceedings of the Third Education Forum*, Edinburgh: Scottish Council for Research in Education.
9. Corno, L. (1986) 'Self-regulated learning and classroom teaching', paper presented at the annual meeting of the American Educational Research Association in San Francisco, April, 1986.
10. Marton, F. (1988) 'Describing and improving learning', in R. R. Schmeck (Ed.) *Learning Strategies and Learning Styles*, New York: Plenum Press.

Part I. General Aspects of Learning and Teaching

6.1

TEACHING AND THE QUALITY OF LEARNING IN HIGHER EDUCATION

NOEL ENTWISTLE

LEARNING AND INSTRUCTION

Attempts to improve teaching and learning in higher education have been hampered by the lack of any body of theory which could be used to provide a coherent framework. There has been a tendency to concentrate on improving *instruction* and this has led to stressing the importance of teaching skills. There has been little recognition that, particularly in higher education, there is by no means a simple relationship between teaching and learning. What students come to understand is only in part dependent on direct teaching, as they spend a great deal of their time in independent studying. In the past little was known about how students learn, and ideas about teaching and learning relied heavily on individual experience and findings from mainstream psychology.

More recently psychologists themselves have begun to recognize that general theories about human learning are of only limited value in explaining everyday learning. It is essential for the theories to have ecological validity, for them to apply specifically to the context in which they are to be used. It is only in the last decade that academic learning has become an acceptable target for research, but there is by now a coherent set of findings which could more effectively guide future thinking about teaching and learning in higher education. This chapter provides a summary of some of the major concepts and categories which have emerged from that research, and indicates how they can be integrated to suggest ways of improving, not just teaching, but more importantly, the quality of *learning* in higher education.

In the past, research on teaching and learning in higher education followed the idea that learning depended in a fairly simple way on the teaching provided and on the ability and motivation of the student. Thus the most effective teaching methods were investigated, and also the characteristics of the most successful students. It was possible to chart the purposes for which different types of teaching and learning resources would be most effective,[1] and also to identify which factors discriminated between successful students and those who dropped out.[2] But this research still assumed that teaching caused learning, and also that it would be possible to select students in advance with the required characteristics. More recent research has shown that teaching is only one factor influencing learning in higher education and, moreover, that reasonably accurate prediction of performance is possible only within higher education itself.[3]

It is possible to show how student characteristics influence subsequent learning, but this knowledge only takes us a short way in understanding how to influence the quality of learning. Students of high ability with high motivation and well-organized study methods will do well, on the whole, but we need to know how to improve the overall quality of student learning. To do this we need to know more about, first, the knowledge base that students have and the path their intellectual development follows in the 'college years'. Thereafter, we need to know more about how students learn and study.

CONCEPTUAL AND INTELLECTUAL DEVELOPMENT

Inadequate conceptualizations

In the past, good entry qualifications have often been taken as implying an equivalent level of understanding, but in practice students' conceptualizations are often found to be wholly inadequate for the higher level work to come. To build effectively on previous knowledge it is essential for the lecturer to know how extensive and firm the knowledge base is on entry. How many departments systematically test students' knowledge on entry to ensure that the first-year lectures are pitched at the right level? And even where such testing is carried out, the emphasis is likely to be on factual knowledge rather than on conceptual understanding. Yet at university level sound conceptual understanding is an essential prerequisite for subsequent learning.

When students' conceptualizations are systematically explored, the range of misconceptions unearthed surprises most lecturers. And yet it is on this variable and largely flimsy foundation that they are attempting to build subsequent understanding. Recent discussions about the problems created by variable and inadequate conceptualizations have led to suggestions about how best to deal with them (Svensson).[4] It seems that much more time and effort should be put into ensuring that the main concepts are taught systematically and thoroughly in first-year courses. Time spent at this stage is apparently justified through the more rapid and soundly-based understanding which develops subsequently.

Intellectual development

Many lecturers also seem to overestimate the level of intellectual development reached by students on leaving school. Even first-year lectures often seem to require a sophisticated appreciation of the nature and interpretation of evidence, which students in fact acquire only towards the end of degree courses, if at all. It is salutary to reflect on the findings of a research study which examined students' intellectual development in detail by individual interview.

Perry[5] interviewed a group of students every year over their four years in college, and came to the conclusion that they followed a similar developmental path. Students coming in as freshmen often expected their instructors to provide 'right' answers to everything. For them the world could readily be divided into 'right' and 'wrong' descriptions and explanations, as well as actions. These students were seen to be 'dualistic' in their thinking. Soon after entering higher education, however, they began to realize that their instructors rarely provided such clear-cut answers.

Perry found that students progressed gradually through various responses to this clash with their expectations. Initially they blamed the instructors for not knowing the 'right' answers. Then they began to believe that those answers were being deliberately withheld: it was part of the intellectual training to work out the 'right' answers for themselves. By now they were beginning to perceive that the process of learning was itself important, but they saw themselves as being forced to engage in an esoteric academic game with rules which required them to select evidence and analyse it within the conventions of their particular discipline. If they followed that pattern they found they got good grades, but the process was still not understood. It was not until much later on that they began to appreciate that most knowledge involved only relative truth, and that the conventions of the disciplines were necessary ways of dealing with the uncertainty of the real world. Only then did they themselves begin, consciously, to recognize relativism and to explore its implications.

Perry's interviews not only pointed up the problems most students have in understanding the philosophical bases underlying academic study, but also showed that intellectual development is by no means smooth and continuous. Students experience crises of confidence, and feel threatened, both by the dawning perception of pervasive relativism, and by their inability to make sense of the rules of an academic game which are rarely explained explicitly to them. What tutors may describe as laziness often proves to be no more than a phase during which students are making far-reaching adjustments to their knowledge structure and value systems, as a reaction to the invasive nature of the educational process they are going through in and out of class.

In the sciences, however, it seems unlikely that students will experience relativism with the same force. At undergraduate level at least, there are firmly accepted theories and fairly definite answers. Students still do, however, experience intellectual challenges which are likely to create uncertainty and to undermine confidence. The sciences demand of the students the capacity to cope with abstractions at a rapidly increasing level of complexity, and often to accept explanations of physical phenomena in mathematical formulations which have no immediately recognizable interface with the world of experimental measurements and observations. For science students, this experience of an unreal world of abstractions carries a challenge equivalent to that of relativism among humanities students. Added to that challenge there is a parallel, but in some sense opposite, requirement to master an extensive body of detailed factual material which imposes considerable strain on the memory. These competing demands create uncertainties among science students about what type of learning is really required of them, and guidance at this stage is essential.

Perry's work on intellectual development has recently had a marked impact in the USA.[6] In some colleges, for example, curricula have been reorganized to ensure that the intellectual demands being made of students in each year of the course are carefully matched to what can be expected of the majority of the students. Student counsellors have also been led to recognize students' reactions to the experience of relativism and encouraged to help students adjust to the sense of confusion which often follows. But there has also been a growing recognition of the need to consider the students' experiences of the overall academic context in which they learn and develop intellectually, and this has led to a series of related concepts describing *The Experience of Learning*[7] from the student's standpoint. This book contains summary research reports on the identification of most of the concepts described below.

Orientations and conceptions

Tutors often seem to expect students to have the same interest in *academic* goals as they have themselves. In fact, students vary markedly in their goals and purposes. To understand why students study in the ways that they do, it is essential first to understand those intentions. From extensive interviews with students, four distinct *educational orientations* have been identified (Taylor)[8] – academic, vocational, personal, and social – and the first three of these can be directed either intrinsically towards aspects of the course content or extrinsically towards the qualifications or satisfactions which are associated incidentally with that content. From these interviews, it was also found that students seem to hold to a form of a *study contract* with themselves. They know what they are aiming for, and their relative satisfaction is related more to their progress towards fulfilling their own contract than the formal course requirements. There is a danger, both in advising students about their progress and in designing courses, that students are assumed to be intent on becoming academics, which, of course, few are. Their purposes are idiosyncratic and varied.

Students' predominant educational orientations seem to affect strongly both the effort they put into studying and its quality. But how they study also depends on what they believe academic learning requires of them. Students have very different views about what learning means: there appears to be a hierarchy of *conceptions of learning* at increasing levels of sophistication (Marton & Saljo).[9] Learning, at its simplest, is seen as increasing knowledge, as memorizing, or as acquiring facts. In contrast, the more sophisticated learners see learning as requiring the abstraction of meaning or the interpretative understanding of reality. Students will go about their studying in very different ways if, on the one hand, they believe learning to involve memorization of dualistic information or, on the other, if they see it in the relativistic terms of abstraction of meaning or the development of personal understanding. And this is indeed what has been found.

Approaches to learning

In one influential study (Marton and Saljo),[10] students were asked to read an academic text and to be ready to answer questions afterwards. It was found that students differed in the level of understanding they displayed as a consequence of what was termed their *approach to learning*. Students adopted either a deep or a surface approach to their reading, and the concept has since been extended to describe how students tackle many other learning tasks in lectures, essay writing, and problem solving.[11]

The crucial difference lies in the contrasting *intentions* shown by students. A *deep approach* draws on a sophisticated conception of learning with an intention to reach a personal understanding of the material presented. To do this, the student has to interact critically with the content, relating it to previous knowledge and experience, as well as examining evidence and evaluating the logical steps by which conclusions have been reached. In contrast, a *surface approach* involves a simple conception of learning as memorization and an intention merely to satisfy task or course requirements, seen as external impositions largely remote from personal interests. The surface approach can still be active, but it relies on identifying the elements within the task most likely to be assessed, and then memorizing those details.

Of course, Marton's original categories were derived from the specific task of reading a non-technical article. In other circumstances, previous knowledge and skills play a substantial part in determining the level of understanding reached, but subsequent research has confirmed just how important the initial intention is (Laurillard, Ramsden).[12]

The influence of assessment on approach also has a crucial effect in everyday studying. The pervasive influence of assessment in everyday studying has necessitated the description of a *strategic approach* to learning with its own characteristic intention.[13] In this approach the student adopts deep and surface approaches in combinations designed to achieve the highest possible marks. The approach involves using well-organized study methods and careful time management, but above all there is an alertness to any cues given by tutors about what they are looking for in deciding grades or marks, or what questions they are going to set in the examinations. Students have separate focuses of attention – the content and the teacher's reward system. While lecturers expect the students to focus on the former, assessment demands shift attention to the latter (Laurillard).[14]

Factors influencing students' approaches to learning can be seen as originating in part in the students' own orientation to education, conception of learning, and contrasting forms of motivation (Entwistle and Marton,[15] Entwistle[16]), and in part from the student's perception of the educational context (Ramsden[17]). The effects of the context are particularly important as they indicate how teaching and assessment procedures might be modified so as to improve student learning – as we shall see later on.

Styles of learning

Another study found that even when students were required to learn in ways which would lead to understanding, they still showed distinct *preferences* in the *styles of learning* they adopted.[18] Some students adopted a *holist* style in which, right from the start, they tried to see the task in the widest possible perspective, establishing an overview which went well beyond the task itself. Their learning process involved the use of illustrations, examples, analogies, and anecdotes in building up an idiosyncratic form of understanding deeply rooted in personal experience and beliefs. Other students preferred a *serialist* style, in which they began with a narrow focus, concentrated on details and logical connections in a cautious manner, and looked at the broader context only towards the end of the topic. Extreme holists were impulsive, even cavalier, in their use of evidence, tending to generalize too readily and to jump to unjustified conclusions. Extreme serialists were often too cautious, failing to see important relationships or useful analogies, thus leaving their understanding impoverished.

This study also found that students matched with learning materials of their own style learned faster and more fully than students who were mismatched. Yet, as lecturers and textbooks adopt varying styles of presentation, there seems to be an advantage in everyday studying of being able to switch readily between styles, adopting what Pask describes as a *versatile* style. It may be possible to help students to become more versatile by deliberately adopting their weaker style in some tasks, but stylistic preferences are often strong, perhaps reflecting cerebral dominance of left (serialist) or right (holist) hemi-spheres of the brain, combined with firmly established personality character-istics of the individual. Strong stylistic preferences may be rather difficult to modify, implying that choice in both materials and methods of learning is important in allowing students to learn effectively.

There is evidence that there are systematic differences in preferred learning styles between students in contrasting academic disciplines.[19] Science students are more serialistic and arts students more holist, but to what extent students are socialized into the characteristic way of thinking of that discipline, and to what extent students of that learning style are attracted to the subject is not clear.

INSTITUTIONAL INFLUENCES ON LEARNING

Orientations, conceptions of learning, approaches, and styles, all describe aspects of how students relate to the courses they take. They can be seen as student characteristics, like ability or motivation, which help to explain aca-demic success and failure. But to view these concepts in this way implies that they are relatively fixed attributes of the student. It is probably true that students' stylistic preferences are well established and difficult to modify, but their orientations, conceptions, and approaches are strongly affected by the teaching and assessment they experience in higher education, and are thus descriptions only of a student's *current* goals and ways of thinking about studying. We have already seen that assessment influences approaches to learning, but what other aspects of the academic environment influence the quality of learning?

From both qualitative and quantitative studies, it has become clear that a *deep approach* is influenced most by students being given 'freedom in learning' (both in what to learn and how to learn it), and by experiencing 'good teaching'. Students see good teaching as involving pitching lectures at the right level, presenting material at a sensible pace within a clear structure, providing lively and striking explanations in an enthusiastic manner, and showing empathy with students' difficulties.[20] The importance of using real-life illustrations in explanations has been repeatedly stressed by students. Striking illustrations seem to help them to share the lecturer's enthusiasm and, in some instances, lead to immediate and lasting changes in the student's conceptions and ap-proaches to learning (Hodgson).[21]

A *surface approach* is attributable, in part, to assessment procedures which are perceived to require no more than detailed factual responses, but also to a heavy workload. It is also induced by lecturers who, often unconsciously, foster dependency through using learning materials which 'spoon-feed' pre-digested information, without requiring personal engagement in the learning process. The crucial influence of assessment procedures on the quality of learning has recently emerged clearly in a variety of subject areas, from medicine to teacher training (Newble and Clarke, Thomas).[22]

INFLUENCING THE QUALITY OF LEARNING

By focusing on students' experiences of academic learning we have seen that it is important to avoid a narrow emphasis on the effectiveness of teaching. A broader view which encompasses the whole learning environment is more likely to lead to improvements in higher education. The research indicates that we should try to match instruction to important characteristics of the learner, and also to pay as much attention to assessment procedures and learning resources as we do to teaching methods.

The research provides a language of concepts and categories through which to discuss more precisely teaching and learning in higher education. Through that language we should be able to explain to students how to become more effective learners. The research suggests that it is essential for students to become more aware of their own learning styles and strategies – to think out carefully what they are trying to achieve from their studying and to understand the implications of adopting deep or surface approaches to learning. At present students are only rarely given systematic preparation for higher education, and yet it requires a quite different way of studying than is used in school. We should surely not leave effective study strategies to evolve through trial and error when we are now in a position to provide coherent advice.

The concepts and categories described above have already been used to help students become more effective learners, both within a microcomputer simulation (Entwistle, Odor and Anderson)[23] and in workshops.[24] Conventional study skills courses have, however, been shown to be of limited value. The 'mechanics' of studying, such as speed reading, time management, or mnemonic devices, are important, but they can only be used effectively if brought under the control of the individual learner – and that rarely happens. Taught as separate skills, they push students towards adopting surface approaches more strategically (Marton and Ramsden).[25] Techniques of studying are better introduced within a framework which encourages students to reflect on how to set goals and priorities, how to interpret lecturers' requirements accurately, how to develop personal understanding, and how to monitor the effectiveness of their own learning. Even then workshops on 'learning to learn' lead to changes in students' study practices only if the advice is related directly to their own subject specialisms, and if the workshops encourage discussions between students about the strategies they are adopting in different circumstances.

Even if students do learn how to learn, there remains a crucial problem within the current higher education system. Through the teaching methods and the assessment procedures currently adopted, students detect an insistent, if implicit, message that reproductive learning is all that is required. Students' overriding concern is to fulfil assessment requirements and so, in most current courses, they will use any newly acquired awareness of study strategies to become more efficient surface learners. If we really do value critical thinking and deep levels of understanding, the way we teach and assess will have to carry a different message. Courses will have to be designed in ways which make understanding a core learning activity. There is still little experience of how this adaptation of research findings to the needs of an individual department should be carried out, and the following suggestions are thus necessarily speculative. They are, however, based on the report of one such attempt to remodel an undergraduate course (Eizenburg).[26]

It seems reasonable to suggest that each course should begin with a clear statement of its purposes, to allow students to apply their learning strategies to most effect. The course design should then take account of the current knowledge base and level of understanding the students show on entering the course. It was suggested earlier that existing knowledge and conceptualizations should be tested at the beginning of a course. Students should be given detailed feedback on their current knowledge to enable them to judge what they will have to do to make good progress on the course. From an analysis of the test results, lecturers will be in a better position to match teaching to previous knowledge, and also to devise remedial materials to overcome gaps in knowledge and common misunderstandings. As it is so important that key concepts and procedures are thoroughly understood, these should be repeatedly reinforced through a variety of concrete examples, and also by pointing out links with comparable ideas.

In the first year, in particular, it is essential to control both the speed and the volume of the material presented to students. Lecturers often have little feel for the total set of concepts and information students are being required to master, as they know in detail only about their own contributions. They also often seriously underestimate how long students have to spend on the assignments required of them. How many departments monitor the time students are spending on the work they are given? Many students find themselves overwhelmed by what they have to do in the first term – mastering a new way of studying, as well as substantial quantities of new material to understand. As a result a feeling of inadequacy sets in which may seriously affect their subsequent work. As we have seen, departments perceived by students as imposing a heavy workload also show a predominance of surface approaches to learning. While some disciplines do demand substantial factual learning, given the rate at which facts become outdated, it seems doubtful that the load currently imposed can be justified. Surely the emphasis needs to be on developing in students the skills involved in acquiring relevant and recent information and using it effectively, and this can be achieved by sampling the content domains more sparingly. It may also be more effective to present factual knowledge within a more meaningful, problem-based curriculum, which helps students to maintain a deep approach to learning (Newble and Clarke).[27] Besides being overdemanding, some lecturers also misjudge the intellectual level of incoming students, and so give inappropriately complex explanations. Few students will be able to cope with relativistic thinking until towards the end of their courses, and yet lecturers may be explaining topics in those terms right from the beginning.

As we have seen, the students themselves have a clear idea of what 'good teaching' involves, and such teaching helps students to adopt deep approaches to learning. They want lectures pitched at the right level, and information presented at a pace and within a structure which allows them to take good notes. They want clear and interesting explanations which help them to see the relevance of what they are being asked to learn. Varying the way information is presented, through the use of overheads, video or audio-taped material, buzz-groups, and so on, helps to maintain attention – and the typical length of a lecture session makes it very difficult for students to maintain concentration otherwise. We need to be clear what the function of lectures should be. Is it simply to present information? If so, is that still the most effective method of doing so in the age of the new information technology? If not, and if the function is rather to provide a mapping of the subject area and to demonstrate how to collect and interpret evidence, then the content and manner of presentation of the traditional lecture would have to be radically revised.

Besides providing appropriate forms of teaching, equivalent thought has to be given to the learning materials provided. Which books are to be recommended? What type of handouts are given out? Students will often learn as much, or more, from these materials than from the lectures, and if they emphasize factual detail rather than understanding, again students will put their effort into the accurate reproduction of factual material. Handouts are particularly influential, as they will be seen to reflect the lecturer's own priorities. Handouts can foster dependency, by purporting to provide all that is required to pass the examinations. Or, by including open-ended questions and stressing the provisional nature of knowledge, they can encourage students to challenge current theories, to consider alternative interpretations of data, and to think out issues for themselves.

Universities and colleges are increasingly conscious of their responsibility to employers and society at large. Most companies stress the importance of graduates being able to apply knowledge in a new situation, to communicate fluently, and to work effectively with others. These skills are, however, not directly encouraged in higher education at present. The emphasis is still on working independently in competition with others, except where group project work has been introduced. Collaborative learning is still often viewed as an attempt to subvert the assessment system. We are not only ignoring opportunities to develop important skills, but we are also failing to capitalize on a powerful way of improving students' understanding – through peer discussion. Testing out understanding against one's peers is less threatening than doing so against the critical superiority of a tutor. Yet we rarely provide systematic opportunities for students to discuss topics among themselves. There seems to be a concern that such sessions may multiply mistaken views, and yet without opportunities for discussion, misconceptions are widespread. Linking peer discussions with 'report back' sessions with tutors would seem to be an effective compromise in which misunderstandings can be checked.

Finally, the research findings have repeatedly shown the pervasive influence of assessment on the quality of student learning. We must reward what we value. Comments on assignments should make explicit what we value – clear thinking, appropriate use of evidence, logical analysis, and so on. If we pick up every factual error and fail to provide sufficiently detailed feedback on what else we require, students again drift towards surface approaches. Encouragement is also crucial. Academics are trained to be sharply critical of any inaccuracy, and become reluctant to praise anything but the outstandingly good. Few students are capable of such work, and so most students are fed on a diet of discouraging criticism. Self-confidence has to be built up by recognition being given to the *relatively* good, to the wholehearted but inadequate attempt, and to the interesting but inaccurate idea. Students have to see that thinking things out for oneself is at the heart of academic learning.

Examination questions and marking schemes should demand understanding; the simple listing of correct facts should not pay dividends. Of course, with large first-year classes there are considerable advantages in using easily marked questions, but even multiple-choice questions can be devised in ways which test understanding. In the end, however, it is likely to be through essay-type questions, or through problems which test the application of knowledge, that understanding can be fostered and most effectively judged. But there again the form of the question is important. It might be helpful to build up, in a range of subject areas, banks of questions and associated marking schemes which have been found to evoke, and to classify, different levels of understanding (Ramsden and Marton,[28] Biggs[29]).

The set of concepts and ideas emerging from this recent research on student learning ought to allow more soundly based teaching to emerge. For too long teaching in higher education has relied on outdated academic traditions uninformed by research evidence or systematic evaluation. Now a coherent set of concepts and ideas is emerging which could be reinterpreted within each academic discipline to provide guidelines for deciding how to improve the effectiveness of teaching, learning materials, and assessment. It is now possible to provide a heuristic model of the teaching-learning process to guide departments and institutions wanting to engage in a process of critical reflection on current practice (Entwistle).[30] And only by such a thoroughgoing reappraisal can the *whole learning milieu* within a particular department or institution be redesigned to ensure improvement in the quality of student learning.

REFERENCES

Note: references in the text to authors are intended to direct the reader to particular chapters in the edited books cited below.

1. Beard, R. and Hartley, J. (1984) *Teaching and Learning in Higher Education*, London: Methuen.
2. Entwistle, N. J. and Wilson, J. D. (1977) *Degrees of Excellence: The Academic Achievement Game*, London: Hodder & Stoughton.
3. Marton, F., Hounsell, D. J., and Entwistle, N. J. (1984) (Eds.) *The Experience of Learning*, Edinburgh: Scottish Academic Press.
4. Ramsden, P. (1988) (Ed.) *Improving Learning: New perspectives*, London: Kogan Page.
5. Perry, W. G. (1970) *Forms of Intellectual and Ethical Development in the College Years: A Scheme*, New York: Holt, Rinehart and Winston.
6. Parker, C. A. (1978) *Encouraging Development in College Students*, Minneapolis: University of Minnesota Press.
7. Marton *et al*. (1984) op. cit.
8. ibid.
9. ibid.
10. ibid.
11. ibid.
12. ibid.
13. Entwistle, N. J. and Ramsden, P. (1983) *Understanding Student Learning*, London: Croom Helm.
14. Marton *et al*. (1984) op. cit.
15. ibid.
16. Schmeck, R. R. (1988) (Ed.) *Learning Styles and Strategies*, New York: Plenum Press.
17. Marton *et al*. (1984) op. cit.
18. Pask, G. (1976) 'Learning styles and strategies', *British Journal of Educational Psychology*, 46:4–11.
19. Entwistle and Ramsden (1983) op. cit.
20. ibid.
21. Marton *et al*. (1984) op. cit.
22. Bowden, J. A. (1986) *Student Learning: Research into practice*, University of Melbourne, Centre for the Study of Higher Education.
23. Ramsden (1988) op. cit.
24. Biggs, J. B. (1987) *Student Approaches to Learning and Studying*, Melbourne: Australian Council for Educational Research.
25. Richardson, J. T. E., Eysenck, M. W. and Warren Piper, D. (Eds.) (1987) *Student Learning: Research in education and cognitive psychology*, London: SRHE/Open University Press.
26. Ramsden (1988) op. cit.; Bowden (1986) op. cit.
27. Bowden (1986) op. cit.
28. Ramsden (1988) op. cit.
29. Biggs (1987) op. cit.
30. Richardson *et al*. (1987) op cit.

6.2

TEACHING FOR DESIRED LEARNING OUTCOMES

JOHN BIGGS

LEARNING, TEACHING, OR BOTH?

The Russians have a word, *obuchenie*, which can mean 'learning', 'teaching', or both. That semantic usage implies a conception of learning and teaching that is often overlooked: it is that the processes of teaching and learning are complementary. Yet for perhaps the greater part of this century, neither teachers nor researchers saw things that way. Analyses of teachers' lesson plans revealed that they planned their lessons in terms of their own actions – what they themselves were going to do in the next forty minutes – not in terms of what the students were supposed to learn or do (Shavelson and Stern 1981). Assessment was likewise self-referential: students were assessed on how they compared with each other, not in terms of what it was they actually had, or had not, learned.

Research into teaching emphasized what teachers did, research into learning focused on what students did; neither research area much impinged on the other. Thus, while there has been a great deal of research into student learning this century, little has had much impact on teaching practice. In fact only in the last ten years has research focused significantly on relationships between teacher classroom behaviour and student achievement.

THE 3P MODEL

In this chapter, a model which stresses the interdependence of learning and teaching is introduced to show how to answer three questions of particular relevance for educators.

- What learning activities are likely to result in desirable outcomes?
- How can teachers engage those activities and not others?
- What learning outcomes do we in fact see as desirable?

681

The model draws attention to three stages, presage-process-product, hence 3P, in which *presage* refers to those factors which are established before the learning event takes place.

Presage

Presage factors set the scene for learning, and are of two kinds: those brought in by the student, and those brought in by the teacher.

Student characteristics

Among the many student characteristics that are likely to affect the learning process, and thence the outcome of learning, can be listed:

– general ability, such as is measured by IQ tests;
– special abilities and competencies;
– prior knowledge relating to the present topic or problem;
– interest in the particular topic or subject matter;
– age and experience;
– general conception of learning;
– usual approach to learning.

Most of these characteristics are self-explanatory. The last two are particularly important in determining learning processes and are discussed in more detail below.

Teaching factors

Some of the more important teaching factors that determine student learning activities are:

– curriculum content;
– course structure (for example core or elective);
– scheduled and expected time for learning;
– teaching methods;
– classroom climate;
– sources of stress (for example workload).

The effects of teaching on students' learning processes are the central issue here, and we return to this matter later.

Process

Process factors are those learning processes that teacher and student collectively set in train. They are based on three prototypical approaches to learning: surface, deep, and achieving. How each may relate to the particular set of processes involved during any given learning episode varies according to the nature of the task in question, the learner's predilections for any particular approach to learning, and not least on the context set up by the teacher.

The first reaction of students to a teaching demand is to set their own goals, and in light of those, to determine what they are going to do about it. They might passively accept the teacher's goals; they might modify them to suit their own purposes; they might reject the teacher's goals altogether. Having decided what to do, students then have to decide how to go about getting there. The processes then adopted will lead to some sort of outcome – and not necessarily that intended by the teacher.

Teaching, in the sense of *obuchenie*, leads to a variety of learning-related reactions on the part of the student and what the student does is actually more important in determining what is learned than what the teacher does (Shuell 1986: 429). The skill of the teacher is to see that those actions lead to desired outcomes. Rather like horses, students can easily be led to the trough of knowledge; the problem is to get them to drink.

Product

The product is the outcome of learning, which can be described and evaluated in various ways: *quantitatively*, or how much was learned; *qualitatively*, or how well it was learned; and *institutionally*, or what grades or public recognition it earns. Another important kind of outcome is whether the student feels that the learning experience was positive and fulfilling, or not. The question of how these aspects of the product may be characterized is addressed below, while the way these three stages inter-relate is shown in Figure 1.

Presage factors, both learning and teaching, affect the outcome via the process used. For example, IQ correlates positively with most measures of school learning because highly able students are more likely to use more sophisticated learning processes. Similarly, knowledge of the time available to complete the task greatly affects how students will decide to approach it.

DETERMINANTS OF PROCESS

All teaching decisions should therefore take into account the likely effects they might have on students' learning processes. Four determinants of process are considered below: the student's conception of learning, the student's typical approach to learning, the nature of the task, and the teaching context.

Figure 1 The 3P model of learning and teaching

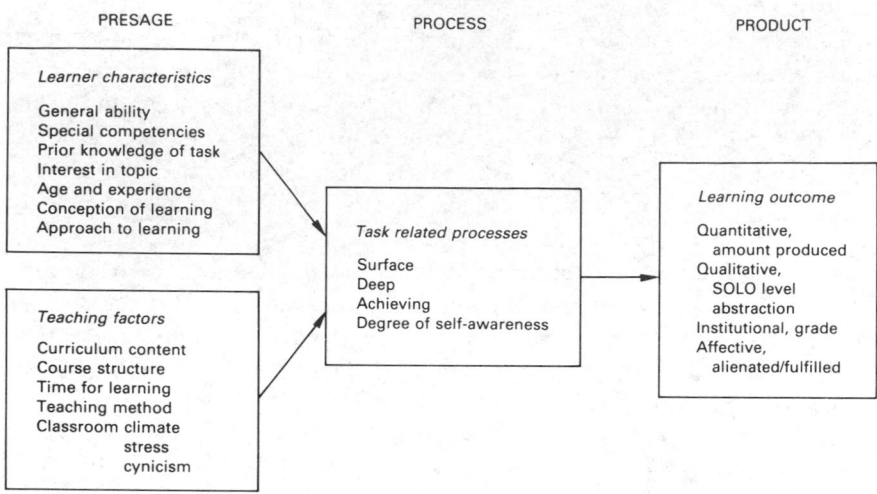

PRESAGE   PROCESS   PRODUCT

Learner characteristics

General ability
Special competencies
Prior knowledge of task
Interest in topic
Age and experience
Conception of learning
Approach to learning

Task related processes

Surface
Deep
Achieving
Degree of self-awareness

Learning outcome

Quantitative,
  amount produced
Qualitative,
  SOLO level
  abstraction
Institutional, grade
Affective,
  alienated/fulfilled

Teaching factors

Curriculum content
Course structure
Time for learning
Teaching method
Classroom climate
    stress
    cynicism

Conception of Learning

What do we mean when we say we 'learn' something? Both teachers and students enter the classroom with reasonably fixed ideas about the answer to that question. As we saw in the previous chapter, Marton and Saljo (1984) refer to five such conceptions of learning:

1. Learning means 'knowing more' in some vague way.
2. Learning means learning by heart.
3. Learning means acquiring various facts and skills, to be retained and used when necessary.
4. Learning means finding out what something really means.
5. Learning means using what is learned to construct a personal philosophy.

The first three conceptions offer a *quantitative* view of knowledge. When teaching in a secondary modern school some years ago, I came across a very typical example of this quantitative view in the form of a note, from an enthusiastic parent of a Form 2 boy, thanking me for setting some homework, and saying 'please continue to stuff the gen into him'. Learning, for this parent, was having a head stuffed full of facts. This is a common conception, heavily reinforced by TV quiz shows and games such as 'Trivial Pursuit'.

The last two conceptions reflect a *qualitative* view. This is seen in official statements of the aims of education referring to meaning, understanding, and the realization of potential; that by the end of schooling, for example, students should have some explicitly worked out view of society and of their role in it.

Knowing facts and how to do things are important only as a means for understanding the world, not as ends in themselves.

Still another conception of learning is *institutional*: the proof that learning has occurred is that a course had been passed, and the evidence of good learning is high marks. As with the quantitative conception, a means for realizing and encouraging learning – in this case the school – becomes identified with the purpose of learning.

The three conceptions of learning correspond to three basic approaches to learning, which again have been introduced in the previous chapter.

Approach to learning

An approach to learning is based on a *motive* or intention, which provides the general direction learning is to take, and a *strategy*, or set of strategies, that will pursue that general direction (Biggs 1987a). Whatever their interest in a particular task, students tend to have fairly stable motives towards their schoolwork, just as they have stable conceptions about what school learning might be. Accordingly, they tend to go about learning in a consistent way. This consistency of motive and strategy is what is meant by a student's 'approach' to learning.

The *surface approach* is based on extrinsic motivation: the student sees school learning as a means towards some other end, such as obtaining a better job, or just keeping out of trouble. Learning then becomes a balancing act between avoiding failure and not working too hard. The strategy appropriate to meeting that intention is to limit the target to essentials, reproducible through rote learning. A student who adopts a surface approach tends to:

- hold a quantitative conception of learning;
- see the task as a demand to be met;
- focus on the concrete and literal aspects of it, such as the actual words used rather than their meaning;
- see the components of the task as discrete, unrelated to each other or to other tasks;
- rely on memorization of these components;
- avoid personal meanings the task might have;
- worry about failing;
- be resentful of the time taken.

The *deep approach* is based on interest in the subject matter of the task. The strategy flowing from that is to maximize understanding so that curiosity is satisfied. A student adopting a deep approach tends to

- hold a qualitative conception of learning;

- see the task as interesting and personally involving;
- focus on underlying meaning rather than on literal aspects;
- integrate the task components, with each other and with other tasks;
- relate the task to what is already known, read widely, and discuss with others;
- theorize about the task, and form hypotheses about how it relates to other items of knowledge
- see the task as a possibility for enriching own experience;
- find learning emotionally satisfying.

The *achieving approach* is based on a particular form of extrinsic motive: the ego-enhancement that comes out of visibly achieving, and in particular through high grades. The related strategies refer to organizing time, working space, and syllabus coverage in the most efficient way (usually known as 'study skills'). A student adopting an achieving approach tends to:

- hold an institutional conception of learning;
- see high grades and marks as important, and be competitive about obtaining them;
- see it as important to meet formal requirements as to presentation, time of completion, interpreting the task, but otherwise be prepared to cut corners;
- see it as important to be self-disciplined, neat and systematic, and to plan ahead, allocating time to tasks in proportion of their 'importance';
- concentrate on 'what counts', avoiding interesting side tracks, which waste time;
- like highly structured and public learning contexts.

The surface and deep approaches are in some senses mutually exclusive. Focusing on the particular words used precludes simultaneously devoting attention to their meaning. An achieving approach, however, may be linked to either surface or deep. Surface-achievers, for instance, systematically rote learn selected detail to obtain high grades, while deep-achievers are organized and plan carefully in their search for meaning.

These approaches are general tendencies only. How a student behaves when facing a *particular* task depends on several other factors. We turn to this issue now.

The nature of the task

The learning processes used by students when handling any particular classroom task or assignment are a function of their perceptions of the task demands, the context in which they are placed, and what steps are necessary if the task is to be carried out effectively.

686

Some tasks, such as mechanical arithmetic, have little or no room for manoeuvre. Such tasks are called 'algorithmic': if the right steps are carried out in the right order, the correct outcome follows. In other tasks, the guidelines are not clear; there may be multiple routes towards solution, or different possible solutions. Such tasks require room for personal decision making, and the student needs to be 'strategic' in approaching the task.

The problem is that many classroom tasks can be treated either algorithmically or strategically. Take, for example, a task as basic as reading a passage for later testing (Marton and Saljo 1976). Some students operate with an algorithmic rule: 'Pick out the key words and phrases and learn them by heart.' Others use reading strategies that maximize comprehension: 'What point is the author trying to make? How can I test myself to see that I have understood correctly?' Similarly, an essay question can be treated either as an exercise in 'knowledge-telling', whereby the student simply lists details sufficient to impress the marker, or as an opportunity to reorganize the detail in order to make an original argument (Biggs 1987b).

The first option in each example represents a case of surface learning. The student selects discrete aspects of the task without reference to its overall structure, and retells them with minimal interpretation, focusing attention at no broader a unit of meaning than that contained in a sentence. In both reading and writing, the deep approach requires focus on the whole meaning or theme of the passage or essay question.

There are two issues here. There are, first, those sub-processes inherent in the task, the appropriate handling of which will lead to good performance; and second, those psychological factors that predispose the student to redefine the task into a reproductive chore, a search for meaning, or a public display of prowess. The interaction of these two issues determines what differentiates what learners actually do when handling a specific task.

Let us look, for example, at essay writing. This task can be divided into two main kinds of activity: parawriting activities, which do not directly involve making marks on paper, but which strongly affect the final outcome (such as planning, updating knowledge, composing general structure and content topics), and writing activities (such as transcribing, reviewing, revising, and editing). These activities can be directed at semantic or linguistic units of very low generality (such as punctuation, particular word choice, spelling) or high level (the main theme, the compatibility of two paragraphs with each other). Deep writers operate throughout the entire range of generality with most writing and parawriting activities. Surface writers operate at a level no higher than that corresponding to a sentence, and omit other activities, such as revision (as opposed to editing) (see Biggs 1987b for further details).

The factors that prompt students to take deep or surface options when handling a task are manifold. Some reside in their existing conception of learning and in their predilections arising therefrom. A student who has a quantitative view of learning, seeing it as a matter of covering enough facts to keep out of trouble, is clearly likely to operate with a surface approach in any particular situation.

A student's specific interest and existing competence in the topic or task is also likely to have an important effect on the approach adopted. Students who are really interested in a topic and feel sufficiently competent to interact with it in a meaningful way are likely to do so. If they are not interested, or feel that it demands too much of them, it is likely to be engaged on a surface basis, if at all.

Effects of teaching on approach

There is considerable evidence that the context the teacher sets up directly affects students' approaches to learning. First, the structures in the classroom, such as statements of objectives, assessment methods, and teaching methods themselves, formally and explicitly communicate expectations to the student. Second, the informal interactions between teacher and student set up a class-room climate that communicates a diffuse but powerful affective atmosphere, which produces a student reaction that in turn determines an approach to learning. If that reaction is one of anxiety, then surface learning follows; if of curiosity, then the deep search after meaning results; if the reaction is to perceive a competitive challenge, then the student will maximize the tokens of public achievement.

Two common reactions encourage surface learning: cynicism and anxiety. Both lead to short cuts during learning. Cynicism occurs when the teacher insists on *what students perceive* as trivia or make-work activities, game playing (pretending to students that an activity is important when it is not), or lack of commitment on the teacher's part (such as setting work and not collecting or marking it). Anxiety centres around three main sources: interpersonal (such as threatening or bullying on the part of the teacher), time pressures, and assessment. Assessment is particularly interesting because its effect is often not obvious. Teachers may believe that they design assessment methods to encourage and test deep approaches, but studies of their students often reveal the contrary:

> I hate to say it, but what you have got to do is to have a list of 'facts'; you write down the important points and memorise those, then you'll do all right in the test . . . if you can give a bit of factual information – so and so did that, and concluded that – for two sides of writing, then you'll get a good mark. (A psychology student, quoted in Ramsden 1984: 144)

Deep learning is by definition more personally involving for the student and therefore so much the harder to facilitate, relying as it does on student interest and prior knowledge of the particular task. Again, the 'hook' is affective: if the student's interest can be aroused then deep learning is likely to result. This is the point, of course, about inquiry methods of teaching, which either start with existing interests, or the student is presented with baffling demonstrations or paradoxes (see Suchman 1961). Other techniques rely on activities that require students to be self-insightful – or to use 'metacognitive' strategies – about their learning. Such, for example, would include:

– *think-aloud modelling*, where the teacher 'metacognizes' out loud to the class while performing a complex activity, such as composing an essay on an overhead, where all can see and hear the writer in action;
– *peer teaching*, where students have to be self-conscious of what they know, in order to reorganize it and teach someone else;
– *self-questioning*, or heuristic devices, whereby students give themselves systematic nudges during an activity;
– *group activities* of various kinds, including syndicate groups and process-discussion groups, where students learn about effective problem solving from others like themselves.

These and other techniques, and their role in encouraging deep learning, have been discussed in Biggs and Telfer (1987) and also in the previous chapter.

DETERMINANTS OF OUTCOME

It is now necessary to devote more attention to the question of outcome. How should outcomes be described and evaluated? What is the nature of the relationship between approach and outcome? What are desirable outcomes?

Characterizing outcomes of learning

The three ways of describing learning outcomes – quantitative, qualitative, and institutional – correspond to the quantitative, qualitative, and institutional conceptions of learning. Institutional evaluation is in practice overwhelmingly quantitative in that the number of sums correct, words spelled correctly, items correctly recalled, points made, and so forth, determine the final grade.

In essay writing, for example, it is often found that the mass of words tends to make the case rather than the quality of argument. In Form 5 Ancient History essays, Biggs (1987b) found that sheer length bore a closer relationship to the mark awarded than the level of abstraction and structure of the argument – and this was in a top stream where the students had been well prepared in writing history essays.

Part of the problem is that many teachers do not have adequate techniques for assessing quality, apart from subjective comments such as 'You really must develop your argument . . .' or 'You have missed the point, but a good try . . .' etc. In order to meet this problem, Biggs and Collis (1982) suggested a scheme they called the SOLO taxonomy, by means of which it is possible to classify a performance outcome in terms of the quality of learning revealed.

SOLO is an acronym for 'structure of the observed learning outcome', and it is based on the observation that in the progression from incompetence to competence in many learning tasks (including most school-based tasks), learning changes in two main ways: as learning progresses, the component elements of the task become structured in levels of increasing complexity, and the learner handles increasingly abstract aspects of the task.

Five levels of complexity are distinguished:

1. *Prestructural*   The task is engaged, but the learner is misled by an irrelevant aspect belonging to a previous and simpler mode of operating.
2. *Unistructural*   The learner picks up one or very few relevant aspects of the task.
3. *Multistructural*   The learner picks up more and more relevant features, but does not then integrate them.
4. *Relational*   The learner now integrates the parts so that the whole has a coherent structure and meaning.
5. *Extended abstract*   The learner generalizes the structure in 4 to take in new and more abstract features, representing a higher mode of operation.

Levels 2, 3, and 4 represent the level of abstraction which is the target of the lesson or learning episode. 5 overshoots, giving a higher level response than the teacher ought really to expect; 1 simply misses out altogether.

Within the target range there are two shifts. The first is from a unistructural to a multistructural level, which is a quantitative shift: from knowing a little to knowing a lot about the topic. The second shift is from multistructural to relational and is qualitative: all that knowledge is placed in a framework that gives it structure and enables it to be understood and applied. Another qualitative change comes later, when the student generalizes from that item to a new area, as happens in the shift from relational to extended abstract – but that is a later step. The 'natural' end point of a learning task is relational, where the student has 'got it all together'.

Precisely how this might apply to different subject areas, and how we characterize different levels of abstraction, are too complex to discuss in the space available here. (See Biggs and Collis, 1982, for further details.) The basic discrimination the classroom teacher has to make is between multistructural and relational: between knowing something about a topic, and understanding its meaning and being able to make use of it.

In mathematics, for example, the difference is between mastering the basic mathematical techniques and operations, such as the four rules, and knowing how to use them in order to fence a block of land, paint a house, or calculate one's tax. The latter requires a relational understanding, not a multistructural repertoire of rules. Similarly in history, knowing a lot of detail about a series of battles is one thing; being able to interpret those events and form a point of view about them is quite another.

Effects of approach on outcome

There is by now considerable evidence that a deep approach leads to superior performance, when judged either by structural complexity or by institutionally awarded grades (Biggs 1987a; Marton and Saljo 1984; Van Rossum and Schenck 1984; Watkins 1983). In one subgroup of lower ability students sitting the New South Wales equivalent of A levels, 52 aggregate marks (out of a total range of 400 marks) could be attributable to the use of a deep approach to study (which was assessed 15 month previous to the examination) (Biggs 1987a).

A surface approach usually relates negatively to institutional grades, but that needs careful interpretation, as a surface approach is effective for recalling unrelated detail (Biggs 1979). It thus depends on what the teacher values in awarding marks. A surface-achieving approach to writing history essays led to very long detail-rich essays that the marker rated highly. In one case study, the student in question had clearly read a lot, and gone to much trouble in preparing the work, perhaps temporarily obscuring the fact that she did not in fact answer the question set (Biggs 1987b).

The evidence is equally clear with respect to affective outcomes of learning. Students using a surface approach feel bored, alienated, or anxious about their learning, while students using a deep approach feel satisfied, challenged, or fulfilled.

What are desirable outcomes?

To conclude, we should consider what desirable outcomes might be. *Obuchenie* and the 3P model strongly imply that the teacher must be clear about what it is that he or she is trying to achieve, so that curriculum objectives are stated in terms compatible with these desired outcomes. Such objectives are not limited to behavioural ones, but refer to the level and quality of performance that indicates that a logical end-point in learning has been reached (Power 1986).

That end-point would in SOLO terms be the relational level of learning for important topics at the end of compulsory schooling, and the multistructural level for less important topics. In science, for example, it might be thought reasonable that the ordinary school leaver about to enter society should need only to 'know something about' acids and alkalis (a multistructural level), but to 'understand how' the human body works in concrete terms (a relational level). It then becomes a matter of selecting what topics should go into the syllabus and determining how one would know whether the appropriate level of knowledge or of understanding has been reached by a sufficient number of students to say that teaching – and learning – has been successful.

It is thus possible to determine topics and levels across the curriculum, using the structural complexity and level of abstraction of learning as the criteria. This problem, of determining standards in a way that applies across schools and subject areas, is one that has worried educators, parents, employers, and the community generally. The solution – and an increasingly unpopular one today – has been to peg standards to a common external examination. This is certainly one way of handling the problem, but it does create others. Most notably, external examinations are tremendous sources of stress and cynicism, which encourage surface learning by students, while teaching to the external syllabus with a view to maximizing marks strongly encourages a piecemeal packaging of the syllabus components, leading teacher and student alike towards a quantitative conception of learning. By using the internal logic of a topic to determine 'standards', the school is left free to develop its own curricula, and to assess student competence in that topic in terms of that internal logic, which in turn leaves the teacher free to structure the conditions likely to lead to deep learning and thence to the appropriate levels of complexity.

REFERENCES

Biggs, J. B. (1979) 'Individual differences in study processes and the quality of learning outcomes', *Higher Education*, 8: 381–94.

(1987a) *Student Approaches to Learning and Studying*, Hawthorn, Vic: Australian Council for Educational Research.

(1987b) 'Process and outcome in essay writing', *Research and Development in Higher Education*, 9: 114–25.

and Collis, K. (1982) *Evaluating the Quality of Learning: The SOLO Taxonomy*, New York: Academic Press.

and Telfer, R. (1987) *The Process of Learning* (2nd edn) Sydney: Prentice-Hall of Australia.

Marton, F. and Saljo, R. (1984 in F. Marton, D. Hounsell, and N. Entwistle (Eds.)) *The Experience of Learning*, Edinburgh: Scottish Academic Press.

Power, C. (1986) 'Criterion-based assessment, grading and reporting at year 12 level', *Australian Journal of Education*, 30: 266–84.

Ramsden, P. (1984) 'The context of learning' in Marton, Hounsell, and N. Entwistle.

Shavelson, R. and Stern, P. (1981) 'Research on teachers' pedagogical thoughts, judgments, decisions and behavior', *Review of Educational Research*, 51: 455–98.

Shuell, T. (1986) 'Cognitive conceptions of learning', *Review of Educational Research*, 56: 411–36.

Van Rossum, E. and Schenck, S. (1984) 'The relationship between learning conception, study strategy and learning outcome', *British Journal of Educational Psychology*, 54: 73–83.

Watkins, D. (1983) 'Depth of processing and the quality of learning outcomes', *Instructional Science*, 12: 49–58.

6.3

INSTRUCTION AND THE CULTIVATION OF THINKING

LAUREN RESNICK

In every country, although at somewhat different rates, education for masses of young people has been extended. Educators have come to treat secondary education of a much larger and more varied population as being their proper concern. The secondary schools have become in large part mass institutions, as the elementary schools had been. However, as we all now know, attending secondary school does not ensure that one will acquire the kinds of thinking skills cultivated in traditional élite institutions. Methods of instruction developed over centuries for selected populations of students left too much implicit and relied too heavily on the ingenuity and application of gifted teachers and students to be adequate for a mass educational system. The current educational challenge requires more explicit theories of thinking processes and of instruction in those processes, theories that can guide educators as they attempt to meet goals formulated in an élite educational system within a system intended for everyone.

COGNITIVE RESEARCH AND HIGHER-ORDER THINKING

Current cognitive research offers promise in providing such theories, for it is showing that some of the features of thinking traditionally associated with the high literacy tradition are in fact characteristic even of the most basic skills in the school curriculum when they are learned successfully. While it is difficult to define higher-order thinking exactly, it is not very difficult to recognize it when it occurs. Consider the following:

– Higher-order thinking is *non-algorithmic*. That is, the path of action is not fully specified in advance.

- Higher-order thinking tends to be *complex*. The total path is not 'visible' (mentally speaking) from any single vantage point.
- Higher-order thinking often yields *multiple solutions*, each with costs and benefits, rather than unique solutions.
- Higher-order thinking involves *nuanced judgement* and interpretation.
- Higher-order thinking involves the application of *multiple criteria*, which sometimes conflict with one another.
- Higher-order thinking often involves *uncertainty*. Not everything is known that bears on the task at hand.
- Higher-order thinking means *self-regulation* of the thinking process. We do not recognize higher-order thinking in an individual when someone else 'calls the plays' at every step.
- Higher-order thinking involves *imposing meaning*, finding structure in apparent disorder.

We need not look far to find evidence of this kind of higher-order thinking in current cognitive research. Consider what we are learning about reading and early mathematics, for example.

READING AS A HIGHER-ORDER SKILL

The process of reading, as it emerges in current psychological and artificial intelligence accounts, is one in which a reader uses a combination of what is written, what he or she already knows, and various general processes (for example making inferences, noting connections, checking, and organizing) to construct a plausible representation of what the author presumably had in mind. The mental representation constructed by the reader does not exactly match what the texts says – nor even try to, except under special circumstances. Instead it attempts to represent the situation the author had in mind or the argument the author hoped to build. The reader's representation omits details that do not seem central to the message. It also *adds* information that is needed to make the message coherent and sensible. Usually, these processes go on so automatically that skilled readers are quite unaware of them. Only when the flow of comprehension breaks down do competent readers become aware of their inferential and interpretive processes. Yet our models of skilled reading suggest that inferences are being drawn and interpretations being made throughout reading. Studies of eye movements during silent reading, of pause patterns as texts are read aloud, and of the disruptions in comprehension that can be caused by minor modifications at key points in the text, provide convincing evidence of inferential work in the reader's efforts to make sense of even quite simple texts.

This broad analysis of comprehension as a meaning-imposing process that depends on the reader's knowledge of text structure as well as linguistic, topical, and inferential knowledge, is common to all current cognitive theories of reading. There are important differences among theories with respect to specific aspects of these processes – their timing, the kinds of cues that set them in motion, the ways in which knowledge is organized – but there are no disagreements regarding the general characterization of comprehension. A point on which research still does not provide a clear answer is the extent to which meaning imposition proceeds *strategically* – that is, in a deliberate, self-conscious fashion – as opposed to automatically and unconsciously. Much evidence suggests that, for an individual who is skilled as a reader and not totally new to the topic of the text, most of the work of building a text representation goes on quite unconsciously, through processes of automatic activation. The process slows down, requires deliberate attention, and becomes accessible to conscious awareness under special conditions: when there is an anomaly in the text or some unusual linguistic construction; when the topical domain is so unfamiliar that the reader lacks necessary prior knowledge for interpretation; when a particularly complicated chain of reasoning is presented; or when the reader wants to study and remember the text rather than just read and understand it.

There is considerably more research needed to establish the kinds of teaching that are likely to produce general improvements in students' abilities to comprehend and interpret texts. It is striking, however, that the kinds of proposals emerging from cognitive research on reading comprehension are highly convergent with processes of textual exegesis and analysis – techniques that are common in high-level courses in literature, philosophy, and other disciplines in which multiple interpretations of texts are discussed as part of instruction. Cognitive theory, in other words, is suggesting that processes traditionally reserved for advanced students – that is, for a minority who had developed skill and taste for interpretive mental work – might be taught to all readers, including young children and, perhaps especially, those who learn with difficulty. These processes, cognitive researchers are saying, *are what we mean by reading skill.* Not to teach them is to ignore the most important aspects of reading. This convergence of cognitive research on reading with traditional high literacy competencies offers some promise that the goal of extending high literacy standards to the mass educational system can actually be achieved.

Meaning imposition in mathematics

Recent research on mathematics learning points to an apparent paradox. There is abundant evidence that young children – even before attending school – develop rather robust, although simple, mathematical concepts, and that they are able to apply these concepts in a variety of practical situations. Yet school mathematics is decidedly difficult to learn for many children. A close consideration of recent research on mathematical cognition suggests that in mathematics, as in reading, successful learners understand the task to be one of *imposing meaning*, that is, of doing interpretive work rather than routine manipulations. In mathematics, the problem of imposing meaning takes a special form: making sense of formal symbols and rules that are often taught as if they were arbitrary conventions rather than expressions of fundamental regularities and relationships among quantities and physical entities. Examination of research suggests that some of this difficulty could be avoided by teaching basic mathematical skills in a way that draws more strongly on children's intuitive knowledge and capabilities for meaning imposition.

Children's first and best developed mathematical competence is counting. Several investigations have shown that young children are able to use counting to solve informally a wide variety of arithmetic problems, including problems that they have difficulty with in school (Carraher *et al.* 1985). Furthermore, an examination of short-cut procedures invented by children suggests an implicit understanding of several basic arithmetic principles. For example, the *min* procedure is an addition strategy that involves setting a mental 'counter' at the larger of the two addends, regardless of whether it is the first or second, and then incrementing by the smaller. The child's use of such a procedure requires acknowledgment, at least implicitly, of the commutativity principle of addition. Several studies have shown that children, starting at about age seven, solve subtraction problems by either counting down from the larger number or counting up from the smaller number, whichever will require the fewest counts. This procedure reveals implicit knowledge of the complementarity of addition and subtraction. These examples and many others suggest that an intuitive understanding of many basic mathematical principles develops early and finds expression in various kinds of practical problem-solving tasks.

There is substantial evidence that children's difficulty in learning school mathematics derives in large part from their failure to recognize and apply the relations between formal rules taught in school and their own independently developed mathematical intuitions. Part of the evidence lies in close analysis of the kinds of errors that children typically make in the course of learning arithmetic. Errors in calculation derive, to an important degree, not from random or careless 'slips', but from systematically applying incorrect procedures. These incorrect rules, of course, are not taught. Like short-cut strategies, they are inventions by children, and by analyzing them we can understand what children are and are not attending to as they learn arithmetic.

The most carefully studied domain of arithmetic errors is subtraction. The kinds of errors (called 'bugs', from their similarity to computer programs with bugs in them) that children make have been carefully documented, and they serve as the basis for an artificial intelligence program (Brown and Van Lehn

1980) that invents the same subtraction bugs that children invent, but not the many other logically possible bugs that have not been observed in children. Because the program's performance largely matches that of children, we can use its processes and knowledge base as a theory of what children probably do and know what leads them to 'buggy' inventions. The strong suggestion is that children, like the program, solve arithmetic problems by manipulating symbols – while ignoring their meaning. The same conclusion can be reached from an analysis of the characteristic errors made by students learning decimal fractions and algebra.

It seems likely that a less routinized approach to mathematics could make for substantial improvements in learning. The evidence is limited, but it suggests that successful mathematics learners engage in more 'metacognitive' behaviours (for example, checking their own understanding of procedures, monitoring for consistency, trying to relate new material to prior knowledge) during mathematics learning, and they are less likely to practise symbol manipulation rules without reference to the meaning of the symbols (Resnick 1986). Strong mathematics learners also engage in more 'task analysis' (Dweck 1989) – i.e., figuring out alternative strategies for attacking problems and generating solvable sub-problems. These are sense-making activities generally viewed as characteristic of high levels of mathematics thinking and problem solving – and they are activities parallel to those that are well-documented for high levels of skill in reading. Thus, once again we see a convergence between the processes that are identified by cognitive research and those associated with traditional élite goals for education.

GENERAL REASONING AND HIGHER-ORDER THINKING

Mathematics and reading are not unique in the extent to which high-level performance depends upon processes of monitoring one's understanding, imposing meaning and structure, and raising questions about material that is presented. Much the same story can be told about every subject matter in the school curriculum, and indeed about all but the most routine job performances. Recent research in science problem solving, for example, shows that experts do not respond to problems as they are presented – writing equations for every relationship described and then using routine procedures for manipulating equations. Instead, they reinterpret the problems, recasting them in terms of general scientific principles until the solutions become almost self-evident. Expert writers treat the process of composing an essay as a complex task of shaping a communication that will appeal to and convince an intended audience rather than simply writing down everything they know on a topic. Skilled technicians repairing equipment do not just proceed through routine checklists, but instead construct 'mental models' of complex systems and use these to reason about observed breakdowns and potential repairs.

In all of these cases, certain kinds of higher-order thinking recur: elaborating and reconstructing the problem into a new form; looking for consistencies and inconsistencies in proposed solutions; pursuing implications of initial ideas and making modifications rather than seeking a quick solution and sticking with one's initial idea; reasoning by analogy to other, similar situations. These similarities, long noted in discussions of intelligence and problem solving lead naturally to the question of whether there might not be some general thinking skills that would produce improved ability to learn across many traditional curriculum areas. If such skills exist, and if we can find effective ways to teach them, then an important increase in educational efficiency can be imagined, for – it would seem – a relatively narrow instructional effort might produce wide learning results.

Processes that appear repeatedly in analyses of complex task performance play a kind of 'executive' or self-regulatory role in thinking. These are processes that people use to keep track of their own understanding, initiate review or rehearsal activities when needed, and deliberately organize their attention and other resources in order to learn something. All are activities that have been shown to be characteristic of effective learners, good readers and writers, and strong problem solvers. The same processes are relatively absent in younger or less intelligent individuals. These skills are sometimes called 'meta-cognitive skills' (Brown *et al.* 1983) since they operate on an individual's own cognitive processes. These have been suggested frequently as processes that could be taught and that would enhance learning and thinking in a wide range of specific situations. Many of the recently developed programs for teaching higher-order thinking focus on developing metacognitive skills or general problem-solving strategies. Some of these programs and their effects will be reviewed below. However, it is appropriate first to consider some of the historical evidence that argues for caution and scepticism about the possibilities for effectively teaching *general* thinking and reasoning skills.

First, cognitive research yields repeated demonstrations that specific knowledge plays a central role in reasoning, thinking, and learning of all kinds. General skills, such as analyzing the problem into simpler problems or checking to see whether one has captured the main idea of a passage, may be simply impossible to apply if one does not have a store of knowledge about similar problems – or know enough about the topic to be able to recognize its central ideas.

The second important reason to maintain some scepticism about the possibilities for directly teaching general skills for thinking and learning comes from a long history of research on transfer among school subject matters. It has been proposed for decades that certain school subject matters would 'discipline the mind' and therefore should be taught not so much for their own sake as for their value in facilitating other learning. Latin was defended for many years in these terms; mathematics and logic are often so defended today. Most recently, learning to program computers has been proposed as a way to develop general problem-solving and reasoning abilities, yet this view, that we can expect strong transfer from learning in one area to across-the-board improvements, has never been well-supported empirically.

Current programs for teaching higher-order skills

Recently, a variety of courses and programs claiming to teach reasoning and problem-solving abilities have emerged. These represent the newest wave of optimism concerning the teachability of general higher-order cognitive skills. While some programs focus on domain-specific knowledge and problem solving, most are aimed at enhancing general skills, or use a combination of both approaches. They thus offer a potential opportunity to update the empirical record concerning the effects of various kinds of instruction in thinking and reasoning skills.

General problem-solving skills   One group of programs aims to teach general problem-solving abilities that will be applicable in many different settings. Two organized programs of this kind are visible and useful examples of the general approach, the CoRT Thinking Program (de Bono 1985) and the Productive Thinking Program (Covington 1987). CoRT grows out of a tradition of training for executives and designers aimed at increasing fluency and creativity in practical problem solving. Lessons are as 'content-free' as possible – that is, they use familiar situations and very short presentations. The focus is on mastering a set of 'attention-directing' strategies that, when applied, lead one to consider multiple sides of an issue, evaluate consequences, select objectives, and weigh factors involved in a situation, and the like. The Productive Thinking Program was designed specifically for upper elementary school children. It teaches a variety of strategies for planning, managing, and monitoring one's own thinking that are similar in intent to those of the CoRT program. Covington's theory and program also emphasize motivation and self-concept – helping students to think of themselves as problem solvers and to resist being immobilized by fear of failing.

The Productive Thinking Program has been quite extensively evaluated over a number of years. There is evidence that students in the program become good at generating ideas and questions and show gains in the use of planning strategies in the kinds of problem situations on which training is given. However, we do not know if students actually apply these skills in practice. There has been far less attention given to evaluation of the CoRT program, other than observations of students during training and reports of teachers. Thus, judgements of the educational value of CoRT must depend upon the importance one attaches to the strategies directly taught and to ideational fluency as such. Despite many testimonials, we do not really know what kinds of effects these have on school learning or success in practical problem solving.

Reading and study strategies   Perhaps the largest set of training approaches and programs is directed at teaching strategies for reading and studying texts, several of which have been described in a recent symposium (Segal *et al.* 1985). These have been developed for virtually every educational level from the elementary school to the university. Different labels are used in various programs to describe a common set of strategies that include skimming, note-taking, using context to figure out words and meaning, self-testing to check one's understanding, and generating summaries as one reads. The strategies taught in these programs are all based on cognitive research in reading of the kind characterized earlier in this chapter; they are those that have been observed in expert readers and strong students but are often found to be lacking in weaker readers. Some include instruction to help students plan their time, manage study activities, control anxiety and mood, and apply deliberate learning strategies.

Strategy-training programs are among those with the best empirical data bases. Evaluation results reveal the complexities, both theoretical and practical, of all research efforts on teaching thinking. Paris and Jacobs (1984), for example, have shown that students' *awareness* of comprehension strategies increases with training. However, on standardized comprehension tests, which can be interpreted as measures of automatic comprehension processes, there is very little improvement. Thus there is a question about whether improvements in reading skill as such actually occurred. Weinstein and Dansereau (in Segal *et al.* 1985) have both reported positive effects using a general reading test. However, in both of these evaluations, it was difficult to establish optimal control groups. Furthermore, the effect of a total study skills program, rather than of a particular study strategy or teaching method, was under scrutiny. However, Dansereau has also conducted a number of separate studies of particular component strategies. This kind of mixture of global evaluation with detailed analyses of the effects of particular strategy-training components, pursued in a cumulative fashion, and extended so that long-term effects and transfer are evaluated, is precisely what will be needed to establish what elements of complex programs are important to their overall effects.

Some investigators have suggested that it might be more profitable to help readers – especially weak readers – develop skills of *self-monitoring* rather than to drill them on specific strategies for interpreting texts. The most striking and successful effort in this direction lies in the work of Palincsar and Brown

(1984) who developed a 'reciprocal teaching' method for middle school children who had extremely weak reading comprehension skills. This program uses social interaction to promote awareness of thinking processes. Students read short texts and then pose questions, summarize, ask for clarification, and make predictions about what will be said in a following section. Teachers may model these processes, and other group members comment on the quality of questions or summaries, and suggest improvements. Evaluation date suggest that this program is very effective in increasing comprehension, and self-monitoring skills learned in this way seem to generalize to other school topics.

In this study, learning occurred in a social setting in which tutor and child shared responsibility for interpreting a text, the tutor modelled certain interpretive processes which were then taken over by students, and there was some attention to building students' awareness of their own level of understanding.

Informal logic and critical thinking This approach to the teaching of higher-order skills emerges from a philosophical rather than the psychological tradition. Rooted in ancient traditions of rhetoric, the efforts focus on teaching general reasoning and argumentation skills. Most efforts to teach informal logic have been centred on university level courses. Organized 'programs' at this level are not common, but certain textbooks that are frequently used for informal logic courses provide a reasonable sense of the kinds of material included under the label. Texts contain passages for analysis, and often present techniques for displaying relationships among various segments of an argument. In addition to philosophers, there are a small number of people from other disciplines, such as English and history, linked to the informal logic movement.

The only fully developed and extensively assessed programme for pre-college students is Matthew Lipman's *Philosophy for Children*. The basic method of teaching in *Philosophy for Children* is extensive discussion organized around issues raised in the course of story-like texts. These texts pose traditional problems in philosophy – problems of meaning, truth, aesthetics, reality and imagination, ethics, and the like. The oldest and most widely used text, *Harry Stottlemeier's Discovery* is aimed at fifth and sixth grade students; there are texts for younger and older students as well. Several evaluations of *Philosophy for Children*, most conducted by evaluators not directly connected with development or implementation of the programme, provide evidence that the programme – when well implemented and given adequate time in the instructional calendar – is capable of producing rather general gains on tests such as reading comprehension and IQ scores (Lipman 1985). This programme, then, has been subjected more than most to evaluations on a transfer criterion, and has fared quite well.

IMPLICATIONS: CULTIVATING THE DISPOSITION TO HIGHER-ORDER THINKING

As the preceding review suggests, there are grounds for cautious optimism about the possibilities for realizing the goals of teaching reasoning and thinking on a broad scale in schools and other educational institutions. In the light of this, it is worth examining the various programmes that have shown some promising results to detect points of similarity that may suggest important basic mechanisms of instruction. Several such points of similarity might be mentioned, but I will limit my comments to one that has important implications for the future direction of research on learning and instruction. (Similar suggestions were made in the previous chapter, p.689.) This is the reliance in several programmes on a social setting and social interaction for much teaching and practice. While one can imagine individually worked exercises designed to improve aspects of thinking skill, very few programmes in fact propose much activity of this kind. Instead, students are encouraged to work at problems in pairs or small groups, or an instructor orchestrates special discussion and practice sessions. When investigators of different theoretical orientations and disciplinary backgrounds converge in this way on a common prescription, it is worth considering what roles social interaction may be playing.

One function of the social setting is, clearly, that it provides occasions for *modelling* effective thinking strategies. Thinkers with more skill (often the instructor, but sometimes more advanced fellow students) can demonstrate desirable ways of attacking problems, analysing texts, constructing arguments. This process opens to inspection mental activities that are normally hidden. Observing others, the student can become aware of mental processes that might otherwise remain entirely implicit. The research suggests, however, that modelling alone does not produce very powerful results. If all that students did was to watch more skilled thinkers perform, they would not substantially improve their own thinking.

There is, apparently, something about performing in social settings, as well as watching others perform, that seems to be important. One effect of thinking aloud in a social setting is that it becomes possible for others – peers or an instructor – to criticize and shape one's performance, something that cannot be done effectively if only the results, but not the process of thought, are visible. It also seems likely that the social setting can provide a kind of scaffolding for an individual learner's initially limited performance. Instead of practising small bits of thinking in isolation, so that the significance of each bit is not visible, a group solves a problem, or writes a composition, or analyses an argument, together. In this way, extreme novices can participate in actually solving the problem and can, if things go well, eventually take over all or most of the work themselves, with a developed appreciation of how individual elements in the process contribute to the whole. This theory is embodied explicitly in the 'reciprocal teaching' of Palincsar and Brown.

Yet another function of the social setting for practising thinking skills may be what many would call 'motivational'. Through encouragement to try new, more active approaches, and social support even for partially successful efforts, students may come to think of themselves as capable of engaging in independent thinking, of exercising control over their learning processes. The public setting also lends social status and validation to what can perhaps best be called the *disposition* to higher-order thinking. Engaging in higher-order thinking with others may teach students that they have the ability, the permission, and even the obligation, to engage in a kind of critical analysis that does not always accept problem formulations as presented, or that may challenge an accepted position.

There is good reason to believe that a central aspect of developing higher-order cognitive abilities in students is a matter of shaping this kind of disposition to critical thought. A common finding in research on strategy training is that, if the instruction is to work at all, it often works very quickly – in just a few 'lessons', or sometimes with little more than instructions to use some strategy. Indeed, one whole branch of research on higher-order skill development was, in a sense, launched by the observation that people who are induced to use a particular learning strategy will often do so on the immediate occasion, but will fail to apply the same strategy on subsequent occasions. Furthermore, it often requires little more than a suggestion that a strategy be used for it to be effectively applied. In other words, people have thinking abilities that they do not necessarily use.

This possibility puts the question of higher-order skill teaching in a new light. It suggests that the task for those who would raise the level of intellectual performance of children is not just to teach them new cognitive processes, but to get them to use those processes widely and deeply. The kinds of higher-order thinking discussed here require elaborating, adding complexity, and going beyond what is given to construct new formulations of issues. They also involve weighing multiple alternatives and, sometimes, accepting uncertainty. As such, higher-order thinking requires effort on the part of the individual, and may involve some social risk – of disagreeing with others perceived to be more powerful, of not arriving at the expected answers, above all of not always responding instantly. All of this points to the importance of the dispositional aspect of higher-order functioning. It stresses the potential role of educational institutions in cultivating *both* skills for thinking *and* the disposition to use them.

Considerable research has been done on a characteristic that can be broadly termed a 'sense of self-efficacy'. That is, the extent to which people believe that their actions can have a positive effect on what happens to them. This general characteristic has been studied under many labels – locus of control, internality-externality, origin-pawn, intrinsic versus extrinsic motivation. These terms all refer to differences in individuals' beliefs about the extent to which their actions can have an important effect on what happens to them. Extensive research on how people explain successes and failures has shown, broadly speaking, that individuals who attribute outcomes to effort are more likely to persist and try again – even after failure – while those who attribute outcomes to differences in ability are likely to give up in the face of failure. While this kind of attribution theory can tell us quite a bit about who will keep working on school tasks, and under what conditions, it too has focused largely on task persistence and not on the quality of thinking that is invoked.

Recent work by Dweck and her colleagues (Dweck, in press) takes an important step towards making the much needed links between quality of thinking and persistence. Dweck proposes that individuals differ fundamentally in their conceptions of intelligence, and that these conceptions mediate very different ways of attacking problems. A distinction is made between two competing conceptions of ability, or 'theories of intelligence' that children may hold. One, called the *entity* conception, treats ability as a global, stable quality. The second, called the *incremental* conception, treats ability as a repertoire of skills that can be expanded through efforts to learn. Entity conceptions orient children towards performing well, so that they can display their intelligence, and towards not revealing lack of ability by giving 'wrong' responses. Incremental conceptions orient children towards learning goals, seeking to acquire new knowledge or skill, to master and understand something new. Most relevant to the present argument, incremental conceptions of ability and associated learning goals lead children to analyse tasks and formulate strategies for overcoming difficulties. We can easily recognize these as close cousins of the kinds of higher-order thinking that have been discussed throughout this chapter. This work highlights the possibilities for an important convergence between efforts aimed at teaching particular kinds of higher-order cognitive skills and those aimed at cultivating dispositions to apply those skills.

On the basis of current findings, researchers have little ground for recommending to educators that courses in thinking skills be instituted – unless these are accompanied by efforts to embed such skills within the traditional school disciplines. Such discipline-embedding has the advantage of providing a knowledge environment in which to practise thinking skills; providing criteria from within a disciplinary tradition for what constitutes good thinking and reasoning; and ensuring that something worthwhile will have been taught and learned even if general transfer proves unattainable. Such efforts could transform the whole of the curriculum in fundamental ways. They would treat the development of higher-order skills as the paramount goal of all the schooling. Paradoxically, then, dropping the quest for general skills might, in the end, be the most powerful means of cultivating generally higher levels of cognitive functioning.

Another approach that can be recommended on the basis of current findings is to focus special efforts on those parts of the traditional curriculum that are inherently 'enabling' of further learning. Reading is of course a prime enabling skill. So is writing – at least if the focus is not entirely on issues of literary expression, but rather on the processes of argument construction and evaluation. Mathematics is another potential enabling discipline; in particular, mastering processes of 'mathematization' – i.e., the construction of formal representations and arguments – could be broadly empowering. Some would argue that the principles taught in informal logic courses, of the kind discussed very briefly in this chapter, are also generally enabling of productive thinking. Instruction in the principles of logic and rhetoric were assumed to be a valuable part of traditional élite education, but the role of explicit instruction in logic in promoting improved thinking remains virtually unexamined empirically. This is an arena in which cognitive scientists might well collaborate with philosophers in future research.

A final point concerns the role of social interaction in the cultivation of thinking. The idea that thought, and therefore the skills of thinking, are embedded in social experience, is an old one. Many investigators, however, have viewed social interaction mainly as an energizer and motivator of thinking, not as a process that shapes the form and content of thought itself. Vygotsky, Piaget, and some of their successors, have treated social interaction as a central aspect of the development of thinking. But this line of research has not until very recently attended in detail to the content and quality of thinking. Research that truly merges the social and the cognitive, rather than treating one as background for the other, promises to open truly new horizons for the study of learning and instruction.

REFERENCES

de Bono, E. (1985) 'The CoRT thinking programme', in Segal, Chipman and Glaser: 363–88.

Brown, A. L., Bransford, J. D., Ferrara, R. A., and Campione, J. C. (1983) 'Learning, remembering, and understanding', in J. H. Flavell and E. M. Markman (Eds.) *Cognitive Development* Vol. III of P. H. Mussen, (Ed.) *Handbook of Child Psychology*: 77–166, New York: Wiley.

Brown, J. S., and Van Lehn, K. (1980) 'Repair theory: A generative theory of "bugs" ', in T. P. Carpenter, J. M. Moser and T. A. Romberg (Eds.) *Addition and Subtraction: A Cognitive Perspective* (pp. 117–135), Hillsdale, NJ: Erlbaum.

Carraher, T. N., Carraher, D. W., and Schliemann, A. D. (1985) 'Mathematics in the streets and in schools', *British Journal of Developmental Psychology*, 3:21–29.

de Corte, E., Lodewijks, J. G. L. C., Parmentier, R., and Span, P. (Eds.) *Learning and Instruction*, Oxford: Pergamon Press.

Covington, M. V. (1987) 'Instruction in problem-solving planning', in S. L. Friedman, E. K. Scholnick, and R. R. Cocking (Eds.) *Blueprints for Thinking: The Role of Planning in Cognitive Development*, Cambridge: Cambridge University Press.

Dweck, C. S. (1989) 'Motivation', in R. Glaser and A. Lesgold (Eds.) *The Handbook of Psychology and Education* (Vol. 1), Hillsdale, NJ: Erlbaum.

Lipman, M. (1985) 'Thinking skills fostered by philosophy for children', in Segal, Chipman, and Glaser: 83–108.

Palincsar, A. S., and Brown, A. L. (1984) 'Reciprocal teaching of comprehension-fostering and comprehension monitoring activities', *Cognition and Instruction*, 1:117–75.

Paris, S. G., and Jacobs, J. E. (1984) 'The benefits of informed instruction for children's reading awareness and comprehension skills', *Child Development* 55(6): 2083–2093.

Perfetti, C. (1985) *Reading Ability*, New York: Oxford University Press.

Resnick, L. B. (1986) 'The development of mathematical intuition', in M. Perlmutter (Ed.) *Minnesota Symposium on Child Psychology* (Vol. 19), Hillsdale, NJ: Erlbaum.

Segal, J. W., Chipman, S. F., and Glaser, R. (Eds.) (1985) *Thinking and Learning Skills: Vol. 1. Relating Instruction to Research*, Hillsdale, NJ: Erlbaum.

NOTE

1. An extended version of this chapter appeared in De Corte, Lodewijks, Parmentier and Span. Reprinted by permission of Pergamon Press.

TEACHERS' EXPECTATIONS AND PUPILS' ACHIEVEMENTS

COLIN ROGERS

THE RESEARCH BACKGROUND

In 1968 the publication of Rosenthal and Jacobson's American Study, *Pygmalion in the Classroom*,[1] drew the attention of both educationalists and the popular press to the phenomenon that has come to be known as the teacher expectancy effect. Their study seemed to demonstrate that if teachers expected higher standards of work from some pupils than from others, then those former pupils would indeed do better over a school year. What made this study remarkable was that the results enabled the researchers to claim that, through their expectations, teachers had actually *caused* these differences, they had not merely predicted them.

In this study, primary school teachers, at the start of a school year, were presented with information regarding their pupils. This information led the teachers to believe that some of their pupils were likely to make particularly prominent gains during the school year ahead. In fact, the pupils thus identified as 'spurters' had been selected at random from each class. Any gains that were actually made, therefore, would be very unlikely to be the result of genuine extra potential, rather they would reflect the effects of a self-fulfilling prophecy. This experimental manipulation of the teachers' expectations by Rosenthal and Jacobson enabled them to rule out simple prediction as a possible explanation of any link established between what the teachers expected and what actually happened.

The results appeared to demonstrate that the expectations induced did indeed lead to higher levels of IQ in those children identified as spurters. In addition, at the end of the period of study, the teachers held generally more favourable attitudes towards the spurters than they did towards the other pupils. As the teachers could not remember by this stage which pupils had been identified as spurters and which had not, it seemed that they had genuinely developed a view of their class that had been determined by the bogus information that had been offered to them.

In this study the information that had been provided by outsiders had been favourable towards the pupils that it concerned. Under normal circumstances, Rosenthal and Jacobson assumed, teachers would form their own expectations concerning their pupils, and these could well be unfavourable. If the self-fulfilling prophecy could operate to increase pupil performance with favourable expectations, as Rosenthal and Jacobson's study suggested, then it could also operate to depress performance if the expectations were unfavourable. If we also assume that teachers may not always form their own expectations on the basis of totally reliable and valid information, then we have to face the possibility that some pupils will be handicapped from the outset by the biasing effects of unfavourable (and possibly unjustified) teacher expectations.

A further study carried out by Rist[2] at around the same time confirmed these fears. From an extended period of observation, Rist was able to investigate the ways in which a teacher's style of interaction with her pupils related to her early expectations for them. Rist's conclusion is a simple and in many respects a damning one. He took the view that children were effectively placed into different 'castes'. These placements followed from early teacher judgements that seemed to have more to do with the clues available as to the children's socio-economic status (dress, cleanliness, manners, etc.) than their actual attainment or academic promise. Rist's data indicated that, having judged that a child had little potential, the teacher would then proceed to give him or her much less attention, and thereby make it very difficult for the child to prove the teacher wrong. Children placed in the lower groups on the basis of this apparently flimsy evidence generally stayed there.

The Pygmalion study has been subjected to close scrutiny and careful criticism over the years.[3] These reviews indicate that different samples and context yield different results and that it is therefore important to exercise care in coming to any general conclusions. The teacher expectancy effect apparently does not operate in all classrooms, with all teachers, at all times. Nevertheless, there can now be little doubt that the effect can and does operate. Rosenthal himself has carried out a large-scale survey of research into the teacher expectancy effect,[4] and has concluded that since his own Pygmalion Study more than four hundred further studies have demonstrated the existence of the effect.

One individual study worthy of mention here was carried out by Crano and Mellon.[5] By using data gathered over a number of years, they were able to test in a fairly direct manner the claim that expectations *cause* performance differences rather than simply predict them. The method they adopted enabled them to use the expectations that teachers had formed for themselves, rather than artificially inducing them as Rosenthal and Jacobson had done. Crano and Mellon's results therefore have a greater likelihood of giving a valid picture of real classroom life. Their data show that expectations do have a clear causal influence on pupil performance, particularly when the expectations are based on the teacher's views of the social rather than the academic aspects of the pupil. That is, those pupils who are perceived as being well-behaved, friendly, and pleasant to work with are the ones likely to benefit from positive expectations. Those perceived in the opposite way are those most likely to suffer. Expectations relating to the actual academic ability of the pupil, while still important, were less likely to cause changes in pupil performance. In considering the processes likely to be involved in the teacher expectancy effect, this difference between the effects of social and academic expectations could well prove to be most important.

THE EXPECTANCY PROCESS

What now remains to be done is the task of making clear just what is the nature of the process by which expectations are formed, transmitted and then acted upon. Several models of this exist.[6] While these differ in detail they all share the same basic elements.

1. Expectations are formed from the information available to the teacher;
2. These expectations then lead to some systematic differences in teacher behaviour;
3. These differences are noted and responded to by the pupil, resulting in the pupil coming to match more closely the original expectation.

One characteristic of the research available to date is that it has centred on the teacher. The data available are therefore more complete with respect to stages 1 and 2, than with respect to stage 3. It is clear however, that each stage needs to operate in order for the effect to take place.

The formation of expectations

From an extensive review of studies, Dusek and Joseph[7] cautiously conclude that teachers' expectations do seem to be influenced by the attractiveness of the pupil, the pupil's classroom conduct, the school's cumulative records concerning the pupil, and the pupil's race and social class. Perhaps surprisingly, given the current concern with gender differences in educational performance, the gender of the pupil did not influence expectations, but there was some evidence to suggest a possible link between teacher expectation and the sex-role behaviour of the pupil. Similarly, there was evidence suggestive of a possible effect of the teacher's experience with an older sibling, and the stereotyped views that a teacher may hold in respect to a particular name. It is immediately apparent that not all of these types of information will have a necessary connection with actual pupil ability. Their effect comes through the impact that they have upon the way in which the teacher responds to the pupil concerned.

Dusek and Joseph's review serves to remind us that we still know relatively little about the sources of information that teachers actually do use in building up their expectations for individual pupils. In particular, it is clear that we need to know more about the ways in which the nature of the classroom conditions that the teacher works under has an effect upon the kind of expectations that are formed, and the degree to which these might persist over time. Rogers[8] has suggested that the less advantageous a teacher's conditions of work may be (in terms of support staff, class size, relationships between the school and the community and so forth) the more likely it is that relatively fixed expectations will be formed. The well-known work of Sharp and Green[9] serves to illustrate these points. Under difficult working conditions teachers will have less time to reflect upon the developing abilities of each individual in their classes and will therefore be more likely to hold on to judgements arising from early impressions formed on the above types of clear, but not necessarily accurate, types of information. Other reviewers, such as Blease[10] have suggested that we also need to look at the extent to which expectations are shared by several teachers in the same school. Expectations that are shared by many teachers are more likely to influence a pupil than those that are unique to an individual member of staff.

The consistent adoption of a developmental viewpoint is also necessary. The pieces of information that may play a critical role in determining early expectations (such as the attractiveness of a pupil) may be less important later in the school year. Information critical in the formation of expectations for young primary school children may not be relevant in the formation of expectations for young adults towards the end of their secondary schooling. Further detailed examinations of natural classrooms over extended periods are needed.

The transmission of expectations

A further review by Harris and Rosenthal[11] has examined evidence relevant to the second and third stages listed above. Harris and Rosenthal draw together conclusions relevant to the differences in teacher behaviour that follow from differences in expectation, and the degree to which these differences in behaviour in turn relate to pupil performance.

Teacher behaviour was shown by the Harris and Rosenthal analysis to vary in a number of respects. Further, these variations were associated with the teachers' prior expectations, and equally important, with the pupils' later per-formance levels. In particular, variations in expectation gave rise to differences in respect of: the amount of material that a teacher presented to a pupil (referred to as *Input* by Harris and Rosenthal); the degree of warmth and friendliness that is established in the relationship between the teacher and pupil (*Climate*); the degree to which the teacher will attempt to elicit responses from the pupil through questioning (*Output*) and the degree to which the teacher would supply the pupil with positive feedback through praise, accept-ance of pupil's ideas and so on (*Feedback*). In each case, the pupil for whom the higher expectations existed received the most favourable treatment.

Harris and Rosenthal have continued their analysis to demonstrate the degree to which each of these four areas of variation in teacher behaviour is associated with variations in levels of pupil performance. Such links are indeed found, particularly for those areas of teacher behaviour referred to as Climate, Input, and Output (in that order). This review of research, then, establishes some important links. It shows that if a teacher has varying expectations for the performance of his or her pupils then there are likely to be predictable variations in that teacher's behaviour towards those pupils. The chain appears to be completed by the further demonstration that these differences in teacher behaviour are also associated with levels of pupil performance.

The pupils' response

The final step in the chain, and the least adequately researched, concerns the nature of the pupil response. Whatever effects teacher expectancies might have upon pupils, they will not take place by directly influencing pupil ability. Rather the effects are likely to occur by promoting changes in pupil motivation and self-concept, which in turn enhance performance levels. Both self-concept and motivation have been extensively researched in general terms, but are only recently being subjected to detailed and systematic study within the context of the classroom.[12]

A promising line of investigation relates concern with motivational processes to the work of social psychologists in the field of attribution theory. Weiner[13] has argued that the causes people believe to be responsible for their own (and others') successes and failures will determine the way in which they sub-sequently behave. Those who believe that their failures are caused by variable and, ideally, controllable causes are more likely to make a positive response to the failure, in attempting to overcome it, than are those who believe that the same degree of failure is caused by stable or uncontrollable factors. For example, a failure attributed to lack of effort is more likely to be positively responded to than one attributed to lack of ability. Continued attributions for failure to lack of ability will progressively undermine the individual's confidence and feelings of self-worth until such time as they come to believe that success is unattainable.

CHANGING THE LEARNING ENVIRONMENT

A school environment that encourages the pupils within it to have confidence in their abilities, to increase effort, and to search for successful solutions when confronted with initial failure, will increasingly improve the motivation of those individuals. Recent research begins to show us how teacher behaviour can affect pupils' attributions.[14] Two general points emerge from this literature. While the social aspects of the classroom are important (the quality of the relationship between teacher and pupil, the type and amount of interaction encouraged between pupils), it is essential not to concentrate upon this at the expense of attention to the academic demands made on pupils. One of the major factors linking teacher expectation with pupil performance is the varying amount of work that teachers set for different pupils. A pupil who is only ever asked to do a little is unlikely to achieve any more. Second, it is clear that an unduly competitive classroom environment will have a deleterious effect upon those pupils towards the bottom end of the attainment range. Relatively high levels of competition have the effect of emphasizing the degree to which ability is seen to be the main cause of success and failure. Failure under such conditions is likely to be most damaging to the least able. Moves towards forms of assessment that play down the comparisons between pupils and highlight instead comparison between present and past performance by the same pupil are likely to help reduce teacher expectancy effects.

The attitudes of the teacher will often be critical here. A teacher who accepts that some pupils have low and fixed levels of attainment is most likely to produce damaging expectancy effects. It is possible that our own culture produces the view that ability is a major determinant of success and failure, particularly in respect to certain areas of the curriculum such as mathematics, and that those who lack these abilities will always lack them and will always fail. Positive approaches by teachers to the enhancement of motivation among their pupils require the abandonment of this view. Instead teachers should highlight the role played by effort and acquirable skills in the production of successful outcomes.

CONCLUSION

There is little point in simply telling teachers to avoid forming expectations. Expectations are an essential part of the process of conducting interactions with other people. What the practising teacher needs is an understanding of the kinds of working environments that will lead to positive and productive levels of motivation in pupils, coupled with an understanding of the degree to which teachers themselves can influence this. Positive intervention by the teacher aimed at encouraging an independent approach to learning and playing down the role of ability in producing success and failure will help to ensure that pupils develop some resistance to the relatively low expectations that some teachers are bound to have for some pupils. The child's early years in school are likely to be particularly important in this respect.

The processes involved in the expectancy effect are neither magical nor mysterious. They are, however, complex and subtle. Now that the effect and its significance are clearly established, it is necessary to pursue further the mechanisms by which it takes place in the classroom setting. The more precise understanding of the effects of teacher-pupil interaction that this will establish will have consequences that go far beyond the original concerns of *Pygmalion in the Classroom*.

REFERENCES

1. Rosenthal, R. and Jacobson, L. (1968) *Pygmalion in the Classroom*, New York: Holt, Rinehart and Winston.
2. Rist, R. G. (1970) 'Student social class and teacher expectation: the self-fulfilling prophecy in Ghetto education', *Harvard Educational Review*, 40:411–51
3. Dusek, J. B. (Ed.) (1985) *Teacher Expectancies*, London: Lawrence Erlbaum; Rogers, C. G. (1982) *A Social Psychology of Schooling*, London: Routledge & Kegan Paul; Blease, D. (1983) 'Teacher expectations and the self-fulfilling prophecy', *Educational Studies*, 9:123–30.
4. Harris, M. J. and Rosenthal, R. (1986) 'Four factors in the mediation of teacher expectancy effects', in R. S. Feldman (Ed.) *The Social Psychology of Education: Current Research and Theory*, London: Cambridge University Press.
5. Crano, W. D. and Mellon, D. M. (1978) 'Causal influence of teachers' expectations on children's academic performance: a cross-lagged panel analysis', *Journal of Educational Psychology*, 70:39–49.
6. Rogers (1982) op. cit.; Harris and Rosenthal (1986) op. cit.; Braun, C. (1976) 'Teacher expectation: socio-psychological dynamics', *Review of Educational Research*, 46: 185–213.
7. Dusek, J. and Joseph, G. (1983) 'The bases of teacher expectancies: a meta-analysis', *Journal of Educational Psychology*, 75:327–46.
8. Rogers (1982) op. cit.
9. Sharp, R. and Green, A. (1975) *Education and Social Control*, London: Routledge & Kegan Paul.
10. Blease (1983) op. cit.
11. Harris and Rosenthal (1986) op. cit.
12. Dusek (1985) op. cit.; Burns, R. (1982) *Self-concept: Development and Education*, London: Holt, Rinehart and Winston; Ames, R. E. and Ames, C. (Eds.) (1984, 1985) *Research on Motivation in Education (Volumes 1 and 2)*, London: Academic Press.
13. Ames and Ames (1984, 1985) op. cit.
14. ibid.; Bar-Tal, D. (1982) 'The effects of teachers' behaviour on pupils' attributions: a review', in C. Antaki and C. Brewin (Eds.) *Attributions and Psychological Change: Applications of Attributional Theories to Clinical and Educational Practice*, London: Academic Press; Deci, E. L. and Ryan, R. M. (1985) *Intrinsic Motivation and Self-Determination in Human Behaviour*, London: Plenum Press.

6.5

TEACHING AND LEARNING IN THE PRIMARY CLASSROOM

NEVILLE BENNETT

INTRODUCTION

The ways in which teaching and learning in primary classrooms have been conceived have changed radically over the last twenty years. Three distinct approaches are distinguishable, represented by studies on teaching styles, on opportunity to learn, and on classroom task processes. Each of these approaches is considered briefly in terms of their differing theoretical perspectives and the light they have thrown on teaching and learning.

TEACHING STYLES

Studies which attempted to relate classroom processes to pupil outcomes in the late 1960s had little to guide them theoretically. There was, at that time, a large literature on learning, but very few, crude, theories of teaching. As such researchers looked to prescriptive theory to guide their investigations. The most persuasive of these was that contained within the Plowden Report,[1] which posited a theory of teaching which distinguished between progressive and traditional teaching practices. The teacher activities and behaviours which differentiated these opposing styles included broad features of classroom and curriculum organization, such as the frequency and type of pupil groupings, the degree to which teaching was individualized, and the extent to which subject matter was integrated.

Early empirical studies were relatively crude, distinguishing only two types of teacher, but later studies provided more refined typologies. Bennett,[2] for example, identified twelve styles along a continuum from informal to formal teaching. Later Galton and his colleagues[3] distinguished six styles of teaching based on aspects of verbal interaction and classroom management. The most successful style was that labelled 'classroom enquirers' which placed emphasis on questioning, particularly relating to the tasks set, and involved more class teaching than any other style, so that much of the learning was teacher managed.

This finding supports the outcomes of most studies on teaching styles. These are, that formal or traditional teaching is related to slightly increased achievement gains in mathematics and language, but that there appear to be slight gains in motivation and attitudes from more informal styles.[4]

This approach to studying teaching and learning suffered from several drawbacks. The major problem was that since the styles were composed of several teacher behaviours and activities, it was impossible to ascertain the impact on learning of any individual teacher behaviours. Thus, for example, it was not possible to identify the behaviours within a formal, or a classroom enquirer style, which maximized achievement, or those within more informal styles, which sustained improved motivation. Second, the differences in outcomes between styles have, on average, tended to be slight. As such the approach lacked power in explicating the links between classroom processes and outcomes.

OPPORTUNITY TO LEARN

Dissatisfaction with the styles approach led to the search for alternative theoretical perspectives, a search which coalesced around the concept of opportunity to learn.[5] This perspective rejected the assumption underpinning the styles approach, that a direct relationship exists between teacher behaviours and pupil learning. Instead it was argued that all effects of teaching on learning are mediated by pupil activities. In particular, the amount of time the pupil spends actively engaged on a particular topic is seen as the most important determinant of achievement on that topic. The measurement of this time is generally referred to as time on task, pupil involvement, or engagement. In this approach the pupil is the central focus, with the teacher seen as the manager of the attention and time of pupils in relation to the educational ends of the classroom.

Research based on this approach has consistently linked pupil achievement to the quantity and pacing of instruction. Specifically the amount learned is related to opportunity to learn, measured, at its broadest, by the length of school day; by the time allowed for the study of different subjects in the curriculum; and by the amount of time pupils spend actively engaged on their tasks.[6]

These findings have, in the United States, been developed into a prescriptive model of direct instruction from which teachers are urged to run structured, orderly, teacher-directed classrooms, with clear academic focus, frequent

716

monitoring, and supervision, while maintaining a warm and encouraging climate. This model will not appeal to all teachers, but a very similar picture is portrayed by the most recent study of junior schools in Britain.[7]

CLASSROOM TASK PROCESSES

However, time, or involvement, while a necessary condition, is not a sufficient condition for learning. Exhortations to increase curriculum time, or to improve levels of pupil involvement, are of no avail if the quality of the curriculum tasks themselves is poor, not worthwhile, or not related to children's attainments. Consequently, contemporary thinking about teaching and learning has shifted the focus from time to the nature and quality of classroom tasks as they are worked under normal classroom conditions and constraints, i.e. to the interaction of teachers, pupils, and tasks in complex social settings.

This shift in focus is reflected in recent professional concerns about the appropriateness of tasks to children's attainments, which has centred on the concept of matching, i.e. the assignment to children of tasks which optimally sustain motivation, confidence, and progress in learning. Teachers must '. . . avoid the twin pitfalls of demanding too much and expecting too little'! It is a recommendation easier to state than achieve, as has been clearly demonstrated in a series of reports by Her Majesty's Inspectorate.

In a survey of over 500 primary schools in England, HMI concluded that teachers were underestimating the capabilities of their higher-attaining pupils, i.e., the top third of students in any class. In mathematics the provision of tasks that were too easy was evident in one half of the classrooms observed; and in geography, history, and science it was as high as two thirds.[8] In later reports their concern has broadened to include low-attaining children. In two recent surveys of schools catering for the age range eight to thirteen years, they argued that neither the more able nor the less able were given enough suitable activities in the majority of schools, and concluded that 'Overall, the content, level of demand and pace of work were most often directed toward children of average ability in the class. In many classes there was insufficient differentiation to cater for the full range of children's capabilities.'[9] However, the data on which these findings are based are, from a research perspective, unsatisfactory. HMI's observations of the match of tasks and children were unstructured, unstated, and undertaken without any clearly articulated view of learning or teaching.

Empirical research which has addressed this issue has been informed, at a theoretical level, by insights derived from cognitive psychology, and by theories of teaching which view classrooms as complex social settings. This theoretical background is considered briefly before the evidence available is summarized through the presentation of a model of classroom task processes.

The adoption of cognitive psychological principles has moved the focus on learning from a behaviourist to a constructivist perspective. The assumptions underpinning this perspective are that the tasks on which pupils work structure what information is selected from the environment and how it is processed. Learners, then, are not seen as passive recipients of sensory experience who can learn anything if provided with enough practice; rather they are seen as actively making use of cognitive strategies and previous knowledge to deal with cognitive limitations. In this conception, learners are active and interpretive, and learning is a covert, intellectual process providing the development and restructuring of existing conceptual schemes. As such, teaching effects learning through pupils' thought processes, i.e. teaching influences pupil thinking, pupil thinking mediates learning. Resnick, in an earlier chapter in this section, has utilized the same theoretical base to consider the development of higher-order thinking.

To monitor learning, an understanding of children's progressive performances on assigned tasks is required, and, to assess the impact of teaching on learning, it is necessary to ascertain the extent to which the intellectual demand in assigned work is matched to children's attainments. Further, since classroom learning takes place within a complex social environment, it is necessary to understand the impact of social processes on children's task performances.

Doyle[10] has produced the most elaborated model of classroom social processes. This views classrooms as complex social settings within which teachers and students are in a continuous process of adaptation to each other and the classroom environment. As Charles Desforges explains in some detail in the next chapter, students must learn what the teacher will reward, and the teacher must learn what the students will deliver. Mutual accommodation leads to co-operation between teacher and taught, and co-operation, in this theory, is the keystone to a classroom life acceptable to the participants. This perspective emphasizes the complex social interactions involved in classroom life, assigns a crucial role to the pupils in influencing the learning processes which teachers seek to manipulate, and places in central focus the role of assessment procedures. In this perspective, studying matching as it actually occurs in classrooms entails observing which tasks teachers assign, how and why they assign them, how and why pupils interpret and work on them, and how and why teachers respond to pupils' work.

A MODEL OF CLASSROOM TASK PROCESSES

Research undertaken from this perspective is still in its infancy. Nevertheless, the findings produced have been very fruitful in guiding attention to significant features of teacher and pupil behaviour, and to aspects of classroom organization, which have an impact on the quality of children's learning experiences. These findings can be summarized around the model of classroom task processes presented in Figure 1.

Figure 1

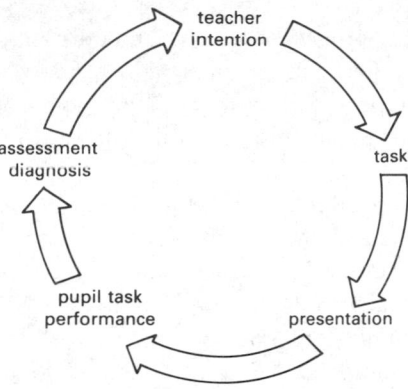

Models are, by definition, simplified versions of reality; their role is to highlight the major influential factors in an area or process. Figure I thus highlights the major elements in classroom task processes as delineated by recent research. It conceives classroom task processes as cyclic. It assumes that teachers plan the tasks they will present to pupils, or will allow their pupils to choose, on the basis of clear and specific intentions, such as 'Angela needs work reinforcing symbol-sound relationships', or 'John is now sufficiently competent in the basic computation of Area and this should now be extended to applied or practical problems.'

The tasks, once chosen, have to be presented to the child, group, or class in some way. The presentation of tasks can take many forms, the major criterion being that children are clear what it is they are supposed to do. The pupils will then work on their tasks, demonstrating through their performances their conceptions and understandings of them. When the work is completed it might be expected that the teacher would assess or diagnose the work in some way, and that the knowledge of the child's understandings gained would thereby inform the teacher's next intention.

This description is deceptively simple, however, since there is a possibility of a mismatch or an inappropriate link between every element of the model. These links are briefly considered below.

Intention and task

It has been argued that content, and the purposes for which it is taught, are at the very heart of teaching-learning processes. The focus of this model is on the purposes for which content is chosen, rather than on content *per se.* These purposes are defined in relation to the intellectual demand that content is designed to make on the learner, for example, to allow practice of previously encountered knowledge, to apply previously learned knowledge or skills in new contexts, and so on.

Despite the evident importance of content and purposes, their relationship, and their links with task selection and presentation, have rarely been studied, although case studies have indicated that teachers often adhere to laudable aims while maintaining classroom processes that do relatively little to promote them.

Recent studies have supported this by showing that the tasks teachers choose do not always match their intentions. In one study 600 tasks in maths and language were observed in top infant and bottom junior classes, and for each task observed the teachers were interviewed prior to the school day regarding their purposes and intentions for target children, their rationale, and the actual tasks chosen.[11] It was found that over 20 per cent of the tasks did not match the teachers' intentions.

Some of these mismatches could be identified by comparison of the stated intention with the content of the task. For example, one teacher gave a child an exercise designed to reinforce the relationship between the sound and the written symbol, whereas the task itself required the child to complete sentences containing missing words (i.e. there was no spoken component in the task). It was also fairly commonly found that teacher intentions to introduce new knowledge or skills to high attaining children in the class did not make the intended demand, since the pupils were already perfectly familiar with it. As such, a teacher intention for development actually turned out to be a task demanding consolidation through the practice of knowledge or skills already acquired.

Task and presentation

A task may be inappropriately presented or specified by the teacher. Inappropriate specification can occur through lack of clarity, inadequate explanation, a lack of necessary resource materials, or a mismatch between what the teacher demands and what is assessed. With respect to this latter issue, it has been argued that teachers' evaluative comments need to be matched to the purposes of the task. If teachers rely on assessment criteria ill-matched to the original intention, the pupils will learn to process at levels required by those criteria, as Charles Desforges describes in the next chapter.

Presentation may thus either aid or hinder pupil performance, and at worst the child may actually perform a different task to that intended by the teacher.

Task and pupil

Empirical studies of matching support the professional judgement of HMI. Among six- and seven-year-olds, it has been found that only 40 per cent of tasks are matched to children's attainments, and there is a very clear trend for the under-estimation of high attainers in the class and the over-estimation of low attainers. This pattern was identical in maths and language work[12] and has since been supported in a study of maths, language, topic work, and art and craft in junior schools.[13]

Teacher diagnosis

When children have completed their work it would be expected that teachers would assess or diagnose it. Assessment is here defined in terms of judgements of right and wrong, including ticking, crossing, and the provision of written comments. Diagnosis, on the other hand, is defined as teacher attempts to acquire a clearer view of pupils' understandings or misconceptions, by observation and careful questioning.

The evidence is that teachers assess, but do not diagnose. Teachers appear to spend much time at their desks marking work while pupils queue for attention. Because of this pressure, the time spent with each child is short, interactions are not extensive, and they tend to be at a low level.[14] Lack of diagnosis appears to be accompanied by teachers limiting their attention to the products of children's work, rather than focusing on the processes or strategies employed by children in arriving at that product. The quality of diagnosis is thereby diminished.

Lack of diagnosis does, of course, mean that teachers have insufficient knowledge of the children's understandings to enable optimal decisions to be made concerning the next task intention. It is clear from the evidence available so far that this, in part, explains the provision of inappropriate tasks to children. As Ausubel[15] argued many years ago 'the most important single factor influencing learning is what the learner already knows. Ascertain this and teach him accordingly.'

CONCLUSION

Research from each of these approaches has enhanced our understanding of teaching and learning in primary classrooms. The teaching-styles studies identified the strengths and weaknesses of general teaching approaches in relation to both cognitive and affective outcomes. The opportunity-to-learn studies provided more specific information on the impact on learning of various time allocations, such as time devoted to the various subjects in the curriculum, time spent on task; and in so doing highlighted hitherto neglected issues such as curriculum balance, and optimal ways of teaching children of differing levels of attainment.

Contemporary research on teaching-learning processes is focusing on the nature and quality of classroom tasks, the accuracy of diagnosis of children's understandings and misconceptions of concepts and content, and the quality of teacher explanations to this end. The centrality of these variables in effective teaching can be gauged from one of the conclusions of the House of Commons Select Committee Report which stated 'the skills of diagnosing learning success and difficulty, and selecting and presenting new tasks are the essence of teachers' profession and vital to children's progress'.[16]

This approach takes due account of the role of the pupil in mediating and structuring knowledge, and places even greater stress on teacher competence in subject matter, pedagogical, and curriculum knowledge. Such issues are important in primary schools, where teachers tend to be generalists, and where worries are currently being expressed about the proportion of teachers who have difficulty selecting and utilizing subject matter in some part of the curriculum.

Current work is addressing some of these issues. Studies are now underway on the characteristics of teacher knowledge which constitute cognitive skill in teaching in expert and novice teachers,[17] and on the manner in which teachers' knowledge of subject matter contributes to the planning and instructional activities of teaching.[18]

It has also become clear from the research to date that improvements in the management of tasks and their diagnosis need to be paralleled by improvements in classroom management. The perennial question of how teaching and learning can be individualized and appropriately differentiated to children's differing attainments in classes of some thirty children still remains. Attempts to confront this basic issue currently include parental participation in children's learning, and the utilization of co-operative grouping strategies. There is still much work to be done on innovations such as these, both on their short- and long-term effects, and on modes of implementation. They do, however, hold the promise of further improving teaching and learning in the primary classroom.

REFERENCES

1. Plowden Report (1987) *Children and their Primary Schools*, Report of the Central Advisory for Education (England), London: HMSO.
2. Bennett, S. N. (1976) *Teaching Styles and Pupil Progress*, London: Open Books.
3. Galton, M. and Simon, B. (Eds.) (1980) *Progress and Performance in the Primary Classrooms*, London: Routledge & Kegan Paul.
4. Giacona, R. M. and Hedges, L. V. (1983) 'Identifying features of effective open education,' *Review of Educational Research*, 52: 579–602.
5. Carroll, J. B. (1963) 'A model of school learning', *Teachers' College Record*, 64: 723–33;

Harnischfeger, A. and Wiley, D. E. (1976) 'Teaching-learning processes in the elementary school: a synoptic view', *Studies of Educational Processes* No. 9, University of Chicago.

6. Bennett, S. N. (1982) 'Time to teach: teaching-learning processes in primary schools', *Aspects of Education*, 27:52–70; Brophy, J. E. and Good, T. L. (1986) 'Teacher behaviour and student achievement', in M. C. Wittrock (Ed.) *Handbook of Research on Teaching*, New York: Macmillan.

7. Inner London Education Authority (1986) *Junior School Project*, London: ILEA Research and Statistics Branch.

8. Department of Education and Science (1978) *Primary Education in England* (Inspectorate Report), London: HMSO.

9. DES (1983) *9–13 Middle Schools: An Illustrative Survey* (Inspectorate Report), London: HMSO; DES (1985) *Education 8–12 in Combined and Middle Schools* (Inspectorate Report), London: HMSO.

10. Doyle, W. (1986) 'Classroom organization and management', in Wittrock, M. C. (Ed.) *Handbook of Research on Teaching*, New York: Macmillan; Doyle, W. (1979) 'Classroom tasks and students' abilities', in P. L. Peterson and H. J. Walberg (Eds.) *Research on Teaching*, Berkeley: McCutchan.

11. Bennett, S. N., Desforges, C. W., Cockburn, A., and Wilkinson, B. (1984) *The Quality of Pupil Learning Experiences*, London: Erlbaum.

12. ibid.

13. Bennett, S. N., Roth, E., and Dunne, R. (1987) 'Task processes in mixed and single age classes', *Education 3–13*, 15: 43–50.

14. ILEA (1986) op. cit.

15. Ausubel, A. (1968) *Educational Psychology: A Cognitive View*, New York: Holt, Rinehart and Winston.

16. House of Commons Education, Science, and Arts Committee (1986) *Achievement in Primary Schools*, London: HMSO.

17. Leinhardt, G. and Smith, D. A. (1985) 'Expertise in mathematics instruction: subject matter knowledge', *Journal of Educational Psychology*, 77: 247–71.

18. Shulman, L. S. (1986) 'Those who understand: knowledge growth in teaching', *Educational Researcher*, 15: 4–22.

6.6

UNDERSTANDING TASKS IN INFANT CLASSROOMS

CHARLES DESFORGES

THE INFANT CLASSROOM

The British infant school caters for classes of 30 children in the age range five to eight years, although recently large numbers of four-year-olds have been taken on roll. The philosophy or at least rhetoric of the infant school in Britain has been dominated for fifty years by child-centred theorists. The aspirations of this stage of schooling include enabling children to acquire a positive self-concept as a learner, to develop caring and sharing attitudes to others, to learn a corpus of basic knowledge and skills, especially in communication and mathematics, and, more broadly, to learn how to learn.

However, a considerable gap has been observed between the philosophy and the practice of teaching in the infant school.[1] Whilst the social relationships in these classrooms show a considerable degree of responsiveness to children's needs, in that friendly and informal relationships obtain between teachers and children, the academic work of the pupils is generally dominated by the teacher. A recent study[2] has shown that teachers exercise a considerable degree of choice in the precise contents of the curriculum, to the extent that there are wide variations, even within the same class, in the experiences met by the children. Whilst contents vary however, there seems to be a consistency of treatment.

Children are typically organized in groups which share resources for particular activities. Different groups may be working on different activities. At the level of organization and content there may be a large degree of variety and flexibility. At the level of teacher-pupil exchanges, however, a different picture emerges. These are generally dominated by the teacher. Teachers initiate, sustain, and terminate most activities. Discussions are teacher-orchestrated. There is a heavy emphasis on teacher-directed tasks demanding the routine practise of basic skills. Despite the abundance of practical materials, pencil-and-paper work is very salient, even with the youngest children. Tasks which

724

challenge children's problem-solving skills, or which stand to enhance children's intellectual autonomy, are rare.[3]

It is teachers' practices rather than their rhetoric which influence children. Whatever the teachers' intentions, children's learning is influenced only by the psychological processes which they engage in working on the tasks their teachers set them. Children, we might assume, will adopt those mental activities they consider appropriate to these tasks. If, as is generally assumed, children in these formative years are developing general approaches and attitudes to learning, as well as acquiring elements of knowledge and skill, it becomes important to understand what children make of their classroom experience. Specifically, a key question is, 'How do young children understand classroom tasks?'

UNDERSTANDING TASKS

There is very little evidence on how children process classroom experience, and in particular on how they learn large bodies of curriculum knowledge. Until very recently, major projects on primary schooling have concentrated either on the products of learning as measured by standardized tests,[4] or on teaching and learning as processes, but from a teacher perspective.[5] Children's experience has been taken to be self-evident.

The following analysis is based almost entirely on two small-scale but intensive studies.[6] It is in consequence rather tentative. Each study used a variety of techniques to establish the children's treatment of their tasks. These techniques included tailored testing both before and after the children worked on the tasks, on-task observations, and post-task interviews with the children. From these data it seems that young pupils take two major factors into account when processing classroom tasks. These factors are teachers' instructions and teachers' praise. The factors are hardly surprising, but they do not always, or perhaps even typically, operate in the way adults might assume.

TEACHERS' INSTRUCTIONS

Most of the maths and language tasks observed in the two studies were prefaced by detailed instructions from the teachers. They introduced the work, drew attention to key points, terms, and procedures, demonstrated routines, and then conducted a period of interaction in which desired routines were exercised. This was followed by a period of pupil activity which teachers closely monitored to ensure that desired practices were being used. The teachers' practices conformed closely to idealized models of direct instruction.[7]

It is hardly surprising that, at the level of performance at least, the children did exactly as they had been taught in 75 per cent of all cases. This was so even when the children already met more direct methods than those taught. In one case, for example, children had been taught that to add tens and units they were to make up the quantities using plastic blocks, add the units, and then add the tens. This they did even when, as the children announced and interviews confirmed, they could do these calculations in their heads. On the other hand, many children were able to carry out demonstrated routines even when they had no comprehension of the task. In one third of the cases observed, children reproduced their teachers' demonstrations but could not do the same calculations unaided twenty minutes later. It would seem that these children were engaging the capacities of recall from short-term memory rather than any higher levels of understanding. Children at both high and low levels of attainment, it is inferred, saw these tasks as necessitating the reproduction of teacher demonstrations. The tasks, it seems, had no more meaning than that for either group. All the children denied using maths outside the classroom. They also denied having seen anyone else doing anything like their classroom tasks. They could think of no reason for their doing this sort of thing except that it was their work. This denial of broader meaning contrasted sharply with the children's evident pleasure in their work. They took pleasure in getting on with their tasks and pushing ahead with the work cards. Their main business, it seemed, was to catch up with, or better yet to get ahead of, their friends. All the children knew exactly where their chief rivals were up to. The race was the thing. The reality of their own world was the self-imposed business of rushing through the maths scheme. This, rather conveniently for their purposes (or so it seemed), was well marked out in the form of pages, books, and stages. The marking of these was the most salient ink on the page.

The teachers did not urge this race. On the contrary, the children were told to work steadily or to do only a small number of problems each session. The children imposed the competition to complete work cards perhaps in the absence of any alternative meaning in the maths work as such.

In short, whilst the teachers' behaviour closely followed the principles of direct instruction, and the children's performances conformed to teacher demonstrations, few children were learning any mathematics. Most seemed to be learning mass production routines devoid of intellectual challenge.

TEACHERS' PRAISE

Teachers' praise seems to be a significant factor in directing children's thinking about their work. This is generally well recognized. However, detailed studies of children's interpretations of praise suggest that its effects are not necessarily those intended. In a recent study[8] several four-year-olds were observed working round a dough table. The teacher had asked them to make something they 'really liked'. She told the researchers that she wanted the pupils to 'exercise their imaginations'. Initially each child seemed intent on its own project. One made a ring and offered it to the teacher. She said, 'How lovely', and kept it on her finger. All the children immediately abandoned their own ideas, made dough rings, and rushed to present them to the teacher. It seems that the teacher's praise had acted as a very obvious signal as to what they ought to be doing.

More subtle effects of praise may be seen.[9] In one typical instance a teacher was observed conducting a session on creative writing. She told the researcher that she wanted the children to produce 'lively work'. To stimulate the children's imagination she activated a working model of a volcano. The children were extremely excited and a brisk discussion ensued. The teacher then asked the class to write her 'an exciting story about what it would be like to live near a volcano!' The children did no such thing. Instead they laboriously copied the date and title off the board, paying great attention to the quality of presentation. Their scripts were short and consisted mainly of descriptions of the demonstration. The children seemed pre-occupied with neatness. Despite the teacher's clearly expressed intention, it seemed that the children interpreted the task as a handwriting exercise.

To understand the children's response it is necessary to see it in the general context of writing lessons in the classroom. The teacher's behaviour in these lessons was to monitor the children closely as they wrote. She gave out copious quantities of praise for neat handwriting and drew attention – albeit in a kindly way – to script which should be 'tidied' or 'cleaned up'. Once the children started writing she made no reference to any properties of stories (such as 'excitement' or 'liveliness') other than neatness. It seems reasonable to assume that the children were indulging in those activities which they had learned would win them praise from their teacher. In both the above examples the praise distracted the children from their teachers' expressed main aims.

A similar influence within secondary schools seems to be the assessment system.[10] Praise is a very public element of the assessment system and pupils pay close attention to it because it shows clearly how to please the teacher.

A closer inspection of the above cases suggests why praise might operate in this way. Praise is always given for something tangible (a dough ring, neat handwriting). The children can literally see what is required and act to reproduce it. In contrast, the teachers' expressed aims ('lively writing', 'use of imagination') are abstract, and so more difficult to fulfil.

A further factor in explaining the salience of praise is that it permeates the whole lesson and is implicated not only in directing work, but also in establishing a warm and productive relationship between the teacher and the children. Praise is frequently given for the concrete products of work to sustain a child's confidence. However, it appears to be interpreted as a direct cue about what to do. In this way it actually distracts children from the use of the higher-order intellectual processes their teachers want them to engage.

THE CURRICULUM

Clear instructions and copious praise are considered to be important professional skills of teachers. Yet when misdirected, or misinterpreted, they manage, as we have seen, to reduce a potentially challenging task demanding higher-order skills to a concrete-level, reproductive experience. These effects, although generally seen, are not inevitable. They are certainly not an argument against the appropriate use of clear instructions and praise. They arise out of a particular way of managing a particular curriculum.

Work in the modern British infant school is increasingly structured by commercial schemes which take the form of carefully sequenced work books or cards. The cards take a great deal more than specific subject competence to complete them. They require, for example, competence in reading, general knowledge, the use of symbols, and the use of recording procedures. In recognition of these complexities teachers spend a great deal of time showing children how to do the cards.[11] Doing (i.e. completing) the cards becomes the chief objective for the children. There is, however, an alternative to this sort of task and its management. Consider, for example, the following incident.

A teacher felt that one of her seven-year-old pupils needed a lot more practical experience with the concept of weight. The boy, Ian, had resisted reworking some of the standard exercises. In consequence the teacher asked Ian to 'help Ben' who was a year younger than Ian and certainly needed practical experience with weight. Ian and Ben were given a beam balance and a deliberately familiar starter. 'Find heavier and lighter things and see how many small things weigh the same as the large blocks.'

Ian took the lead. He got out his work book and began to write down appropriate sentences, encouraging Ben to do likewise. Ian chose objects, operated the balance, and wrote out the answers. Ben watched. Ian sent Ben off to choose some shapes. Ben brought back a cube and a cylinder. He put them in the pans. The cube was heavier. Ian swapped the objects around. Ben looked very surprised at the new imbalance. He swapped the objects back and then back again. He continued to look puzzled. Ian wrote the result down. Ben put a pine cone in each pan and propped one up with his finger. Grinning he said, 'This one's gone heavier.' 'No – it's lighter,' said Ian. Ian wrote the result down. Ben looked puzzled and fiddled with the balance.

After further work, Ben began to make a balance by putting a long strip of wood across a block. He put some beads on the ends but nothing happened. Ian began to copy him, but used a smaller pivot block, albeit without success. Ben also tried a smaller pivot, and then announced he needed a longer piece of wood as a balance. Ian tried a cylinder as a pivot, but could not stop it rolling long enough to balance anything. Ben repeated the suggestion of using a longer beam. Ian began to build a longer beam by butt-ending two shorter beams and laying another short beam across the junction. He persevered with this device for about five minutes but it collapsed at each attempt.

In this example the children persistently concentrated and set themselves problems. There was no issue of reading the teacher's mind, following her instructions, or interpreting her praise. The work was sustained by the children's definition of the problem.

In contrasting the regular curriculum diet with this less common experience, we can see that the processes which define the real task have, in the latter case, been transferred to the children deliberately rather than accidentally. In consequence the children are involved in the type of learning the teacher intended. The quality of their experience is not being filtered through a series of social and managerial processes unrelated to the main aims of teaching and learning in the infant classroom.

However, it should be emphasized that teachers are not entirely free to choose between models of teaching and learning. They are under considerable pressure to cover an ever broadening curriculum, to obtain particular objectives in a specific time scale, and to deliver familiar products (such as a page of writing) to parents on a day-by-day basis. These pressures all sustain a teacher-directed, teacher-paced approach to classroom life, with the consequences indicated herein. Any efforts to change these predominant outcomes are going to involve much more than an appeal to teachers to change their classroom management techniques.

REFERENCES

1. Alexander. R. J. (1984) *Primary Teaching*, London: Holt.
2. Farquhar, C., Blatchford, P., Burke, J., Plewis, I., and Tizard, B. (1987) 'Curriculum diversity in London infant schools', *British Journal of Educational Psychology*, 57 (2): 151–65.
3. Bennett, S. N., Desforges, C. W., Cockburn, A. D., and Wilkinson, B. (1984) *The Quality of Pupil Learning Experience*, London: Lawrence Erlbaum Associates; Galton, M. (1987) 'Change and continuity in the primary school: the research evidence', *Oxford Review of Education, 13* (1): 81–94; Department of Education and Science (1978) *Primary Education in England*, London: HMSO.
4. Bennett, S. N. (1976) *Teaching Style and Pupil Progress*, London: Open Books; Galton, M. and Simon, B. (Eds.) (1980) *Progress and Performance in the Primary School*, London: Routledge & Kegan Paul.
5. Armstrong, M. (1980) *Closely Observed Children: The Diary of a Primary Classroom*, London: Chameleon; Rowland, S. (1984) *The Enquiring Classroom*, Lewes: Falmer Press.
6. Bennett *et al.* (1984) op. cit.; Desforges, C. W. and Cockburn, A. D. (1987) *Understanding The Maths Teacher*, Lewes: Falmer Press.
7. Rosenshine, B. and Stevens, R. (1986) 'Teaching functions', in M. C. Wittrock (Ed.) *Handbook of Research on Teaching*, New York: Macmillan.
8. Ward, G. and Rowe, J. (1985) 'Teachers' praise: some unwanted side effects', *Society for Extension of Educational Knowledge, 1:* 2–4.

9. Bennett *et al.* (1984) op. cit.
10. Doyle, W. (1983) 'Academic work', *Review of Educational Research*, *53*: 159–200.
11. Desforges and Cockburn (1987) op. cit.

Part II. Teaching and Learning within the Subject Areas

6.7

LEARNING TO READ AND WRITE

HAZEL FRANCIS

INTRODUCTION

'I did it my way.' This last line of a well-known song could be a postscript to becoming literate, but for teachers and psychologists looking for general principles of instruction and learning, the message is not easy. They are accustomed to viewing aspects of measured individual differences as a basis for categorization for educational or scientific ends, but not to looking to descriptions of individuals as agents with their own life histories and personal ways of doing things. Individuality is threatening, but recent developmental and ethnographic studies of individual children learning to read and write English in Britain and the USA suggest that useful general descriptions of development and principles for practice might be identified.

Both before and during their school years, children in literate societies are presented with opportunities for developing writing and reading within the practices of their neighbourhoods and homes. Numerous studies have described the ways they take them up, most stressing the 'wanting to know', and the interest and enthusiasm generated by those children whose success is most marked. Recent work has extended appreciation of the extent to which this development can be found in very different sub-cultures; it is not confined to the children of educated parents, or of the more socially or economically advantaged neighbourhoods.[1] What is more, research reports have stressed the way development is highly individual, and embedded in the personal and social significance and satisfaction of reading and writing, particularly in the home. Individuality under these conditions can be reconciled with three principles of the management of learning – tend the urge to learn, protect significance for the learner, and provide satisfying partnership in literacy.

LEARNING TO WRITE

There are distinct but connected developmental paths for reading and for writing, both with their roots in infancy, and both converging on a competent use of the written tongue. The interchangeability of the terms 'read' and 'understand' allows perception of the infant as a 'reader' of events, of smiles, of gestures, of drawings, and of speech. Equally the shared meanings of 'write' and 'express' point to the roots of authorship in facial expression, body movement, articulation, and making imprints on material surfaces. Observe the toddler with a crayon and paper, amazed and delighted to find that the act of making marks can be produced at will. And hear too, the interested parent or sibling encouraging such scribble and calling it writing. The analogy with the parental response to infant babbling is clear. The act is socially defined as significant in the context of developing forms of communication; and, having been thus defined, it will be the stem on which the significant use of conventional expression is grafted.

Children who have plenty of opportunity to scribble, with whatever materials are to hand, and whose scribbles are somehow given a seal of approval as writing, are enabled to practise to greater dexterity and to gain an embryonic understanding of authorship. They enact adult practices such as signing greetings cards, and writing letters and shopping lists. Slowly and surely they demonstrate an interest not only in the act of writing but also in the form it takes. For written English they show this in horizontal linearity and in spaced scribbles which look somewhat like words and show signs of alphabetic form. A critical accompaniment to this developing skill is the appreciation of a link between writing and speech. Imagine being able to watch adults writing, and to copy the action of writing, even naming it, but not knowing its linguistic communicative purpose, because no-one talked about it. Consider how different is the situation when remarks such as, 'What do you want to say to Grandma?' 'John says he's having a great time in Spain', are related to writing, transforming it into written speech. Imagine, too, being able to scribble and assert to someone else what you have written, but realizing that if you weren't there to say it, they wouldn't know what you wanted to say. Yet when a grown-up opens a letter from someone far away they know what is said. A non-arbitrary scribble! Once children have made this great discovery, one that all who become literate must make, however idiosyncratic the means, they set themselves, or are provoked into, a tremendous challenge – 'How do I write what I want to say?'

How some children have responded has been reported in various studies, where in spite of different personal histories there is discernible common ground. Exposure to print in the everyday world, and a strong interest in writing personal names and short messages, emphasize upper case letters at

733

the expense of lower case. Most children, in trying to write their own names, transform an undecipherable scribble into a recognizable upper case initial followed by a scribble, which in the course of time is further modified towards a correct spelling. At the same time they learn to move from left to right in their writing, and to develop an interest in letters.[2] Questions are directed to parents and others about how to write various words, and, in the course of conversations about writing, children learn names for letters. Thus they gradually learn the tools of the trade of alphabetic writing.

Simultaneously they learn that the world around them has ready-made writing for borrowing if it happens to be useful, as for example the name of the road in which they live; but much is not very useful since it is not what they want to write. What they want to express comes from their own thoughts and is mediated by their own speech. The fascinating ways in which they construct writing from the letter tools they have acquired are reported in works such as Charles Read's book *Children's creative spelling*.[3] Children transform the phonetic structure of their own articulation (dialect and all) into the letter names that seem best to fit the sounds, and thus produce strings of letters such as I.AM.WALANF.TO.RITEYOU.THES.LATRE. (I am well enough to write you this letter), with little of the conventional spelling or spacing expected by adult readers, and, according to Read, with more regard for phonetic form than for the more abstract phonemic structure of linguistic theory. One is reminded of the urge to communicate, the making do with partly developed tools, in the functional and playful use of articulation in the speech of infants.

Unfortunately, however, not only is their beginning writing somewhat difficult for others to read, they cannot always read it themselves! As they realize its importance, they begin to adopt conventional spacing, learning as they do to identify words as units. The transition from speech-based spelling to conventional spelling is particularly interesting, and can be illustrated with examples from past tense spellings. At first examples such as *worct* (worked), *laft* (laughed), and *drest* (dressed) are found alongside spellings such as *mad* (made), *sed* (said), *wantid* (wanted), *watid* (waited), *curld* (curled), and *livd* (lived). Gradually, however, *d* becomes a familiar ending and *ed* becomes more generally used. Indecision sometimes seems to lead to the abandonment of an ending, whilst over-generalization of a newly discovered regularity can produce spellings such as *lefed* (left), *slepted* (slept), and *maed* (made). Any seven-year-old child is capable of including 'creative' and conventional spellings in the same piece of writing. With more experience of writing and reading children gradually close the gap between their creative spellings and conventional wisdom. What is fascinating is that they do it as constructive learners developing their own knowledge over time.

Although major strides in mastering English spelling are generally made during the primary years of schooling, for many children substantial development continues into the secondary years; and all adults know they have unresolved weaknesses, and must have recourse to advice from others or from their dictionaries from time to time. The phenomenon of 'seeing if it looks right' is also a common strategy and a reminder that knowing how to spell implies a good visual memory, as well as the ability to encode from sound.

While learning to spell, children also learn to write for different purposes. Typically they imitate the practices of close adults but write for their own ends, 'signing' their names, listing the presents they would like for Christmas, and writing letters to relatives. They may also venture to write rhymes and stories, showing command of elementary narrative structure as they have heard it in adult conversations, from having stories read to them, and as they have used it in their own speech. Depending on practices in their homes, local communities, and schools, they may come to appreciate that the form and content of writing vary with authors' intended effects on readers, and then be well-placed not only to learn to write well, but also to appreciate richness and variety in reading.

LEARNING TO READ

Like writing, reading has its roots in early experience, but it may or may not be closely related to learning to write. Most notable in young children's direct experiences of reading are the generally informative signs embedded in their everyday environment, but much of their developing understanding of the practice of reading comes from involvement with the literacy-related activities of significant adults. Clearly, opportunities for observation and enquiry, and thus for learning, vary considerably, but so do those for instruction in the art of reading, whether at children's requests for information and help, or at parents' instigation. Books frequently figure as the medium, first through play of the 'What's that? That's a rabbit' kind of interaction, with parent and toddler sharing an open picture book, and also through parents' reading of stories. Thus before they can begin to read text themselves many children are helped to understand the nature and use of books for narrative, and to some extent for expository text. At some stage children begin to offer their own 'reading' – at first of a small number of words they have learned to identify in some manner, and then of familiar sentences, and even of whole sections of stories. Practices may develop of parents hearing children read, some of which have been shown to be particularly helpful for children's reading progress.[4]

Such reading is, however, very dependent on memory. It does not offer any obvious way for learning to read new text. For this reason some parents attempt to teach their children more specifically. Some start early, helping children to learn to say words and sentences shown to them on cards, and hoping to build such a large store in the memory as to form a good basis for attempting new reading. Some relate such materials to their children's speech and interests, others offer more arbitrary fare, or words which systematically draw attention to various letters of the alphabet. It would appear that parents have their own theories of teaching reading, some explicitly enough to write about them. These theories can also be found in formal school instruction in some form or other, but whereas the further step of trying to help children attack new words by some kind of coding from letter to sound is also widely used in schools, it seems to be relatively little used by parents before their children go to school. Thus children arrive at school with individual pools of knowledge of readily recognized words, some very small, some relatively large, and with the ability to enjoy joining in reading aloud with a fluent reader; but relatively few of them with developed strategies for independent new reading.

Research in the last decade has enabled the construction of a general picture of further development.[5] From inability to tackle a new word children begin to hazard well-founded estimates based on context, appearance, or both. At first they have recourse to words and phrases they have already met in their reading, surprisingly often producing a word which will fit sense at that point in a reading, and which shares the same initial letter as the word on the page. As reading improves, such intelligent errors show increasing similarity of spelling to that of the target word, as if a growing appreciation of the full spellings of words constrains the choices available from the reader's memory at the same time as memory becomes better stocked. In this context a correct reading on one occasion does not imply a firm knowledge of the full spelling of a word. Rather the nature of the child's knowledge of words seems to be partial, correct reading becoming increasingly probable over time.

During this development of the use of sense and visual memory, children's reading aloud begins to induce expectations of associating particular articulatory movements with particular letters, especially at the beginning of words where, in English, there happens to be a useful incidence of one-to-one correspondence between letter and sound. Whether or not children are aware of such learned associations, this is an important step in breaking out of the constraints of memory to the freedom of hazarding readings, prompted in part by what might sensibly be *said* in that particular context – a self-taught phonics. Such a strategy need not imply a full letter-sound analysis and synthesis, only one sufficient to provide a likely reading. How phonic strategies are of use in reading is a matter for debate, since children seem to vary in the extent to which they use them, whether self-taught or instructed, and in the extent to which they find them helpful or inhibiting. Whatever their strategies, children may make errors, and even 'learn' them if nothing points to correction, but in the long term further reading tends to increase the probability of correct rather than incorrect readings. Research has shown how children, in unaided oral reading, can learn to read new words simply through reading them in context in this probabilistic manner.[6] Finally, with greater sophistication, children learn how to pronounce frequently seen letter patterns as well as single letters, and to read new words through recognition of such patterns in known words.

This general picture of learning to read is like that of learning to write, in that intelligent error is integral to development. But, within a generally similar developmental pattern, children vary in their progress towards understanding and mastery, for learning to read and write depends so much on a combination of high motivation, analytical and constructive reasoning, general experience of literacy, and support from more or less expert guides.[7]

SCHOOLING AS INTERVENTION

It is in this context that schooling must be seen as an intervention, one made because without it, it is feared, literacy may not be learned, and also because much schooling demands reading and writing to more specific educational purposes than those of the home. Yet such intervention is fraught with hazard, most notably because schooling is effectively an additional sub-culture for children, because they stand at such different points on entering it, and follow such different literacy paths outside it, and because formal instruction may initially present learning literacy as a series of decoding and encoding strategies rather than a developing use of language. Notwithstanding these, the developmental story outlined above has been found to be robust across learning at home and school, though instructional practices may bias learners more towards some strategies than others. However, the hazards and opportunities of schooling are worth elaborating.

Schooling as a new cultural context presents children with the dual problem of discovering the significance of its practices and engaging with them in ways which both arouse and satisfy their curiosity. Teachers' time might be well spent in exploring children's understandings of literacy and of schooling, since children with most may be bored, and those with least have been found to make little sense of what is asked of them, and to be reduced to insecure rote learning.[8] Practices such as pattern copying, writing sentences from a limited array of reading scheme words or from some brief, hard-won suggestion from a child, and trying to 'decode' a word through letter-sound correspondences may seem to teachers to be evidently related to learning to read and write. To children they may be strange classroom rituals, far removed from writing letters and reading books, and done only to please their teachers.

Furthermore, if children use adults as models and as resources for literacy development, as the ethnographic literature suggests, then teachers carry a particular responsibility for demonstrating its utility, educational and otherwise, from the moment children enter school. Children need to see teachers as readers and writers, engaging in significant literacy practices. Why is story-time stressed as reading when 'taking the register' is not? Are children told often enough when teachers have obtained information from books or newspapers? How often do children see teachers writing, apart from on the blackboard or their work books? What do children understand of literacy in school? Understanding is needed if the urge to learn is to be protected.

In spite of, or because of, the very varied knowledge and insight shown by children entering school, it may be tempting to assume a zero initial state, and to provide a staged curriculum based on graded reading materials, or on the premiss that decoding strategies must be taught before children can begin to read. This does nothing, however, to eliminate differences in progress, makes no concession to qualitative differences of knowledge and strategy, and does little to build on strength or to support in weakness. For such reasons, individualized teaching may be adopted in the first year or so in school, with the expectation that children will thereafter be able to read and write well enough to manage the general curriculum of the later primary years. But literacy as a form of language development takes time; some children are late starters, and some are slow developers.[9] Teaching must accommodate this variation for longer than a year or two, in particular by showing toleration and respect for the constructive, intelligent errors made in learning to read and write. Accuracy is to be valued, but not at the expense of growth.

This leads to some comment on assessment. The variation in pattern and rate of literacy development suggests that any early identification of special educational needs on the grounds of 'poor' literacy performance could be misplaced. For example, an important distinction is currently being made between children who develop slowly over the years and those who 'start' slowly but then develop well.[10] Furthermore, the pressure to improve standards in language performance may lead to a focus on literacy in specified language lessons, aimed at reading test proficiency, rather than across the curriculum, where the wider range of interest and genre is likely to provide maximum opportunity for educated literacy. It would be a pity if pressure for national assessment of literacy performance were also to stress technical proficiency at the expense of development of understanding and expression, especially in the early years of primary schooling.

When instruction aims particularly at technical proficiency, often taking the form of general teaching of decoding strategies and spelling rules, it may not only inhibit the urge to learn, but may also cut across children's systematically developing knowledge, and interfere with their strategies of looking only for such information as they need for a particular problem. It also risks violating the principles of protecting significance and providing satisfying partnership for the learner. When, on the other hand, such proficiency is seen as the developmental outcome of reading and writing to various purposes, some of which truly require accuracy and precision, then significance is naturally entailed. Reading may be experienced as being prompted to act or feel or think, and writing may be seen to engage the attention and interest, and possibly the actions, of other persons. In such a context a well-stocked classroom library, catering for varied interests and competencies, can be much more useful than any reading scheme. With such materials and purposes teachers can become authoritatively, rather than arbitrarily, powerful partners in children's literacy, reading together with them, listening to them, and encouraging them in their own developing strategies.

In this respect it may be possible to learn from strategies adopted by parents. The recent enthusiasm for involving parents in hearing children read has developed in part from reports of the benefit of parents' spontaneous activity and in part from the reported success of some teacher-led schemes. An overview of various reports suggests that this is an area of practice worthy of more thorough investigation. Not only may some parental practices be worth extending, but teachers may also profit from insights into them, possibly refining and extending their own practices as a result. Since the value of hearing children read in the classroom has been questioned, this is a particularly important matter, especially if satisfying partnership in learning is to be provided in school.[11]

Both teachers and parents can also be good readers of children's writing, showing genuine interest in what they have to say, why they are saying it, what effect they hope to have, and how they can better achieve it. Parents provide a natural audience, but some may be virtually illiterate, and others may be less aware and tolerant of the 'creative' nature of children's writing than they are of efforts at reading. They may welcome guidance. Teachers are conscious of the problem of the management of error, and recent movements towards partnership in the 'editing' of children's work, rather than marking for mistakes, may, if sensitively conducted, achieve a nice balance between tolerance and correction. Sensitivity is enhanced if teachers have a sound knowledge of the nature of both written English and writing development.[12]

The more they engage in partnership with learners, the more teachers are confronted by individuality rather than variation within a class. Though they cannot work with individuals all of the time, they normally find great satisfaction in doing so some of the time. If by so doing they may tend and protect learning for the individual, and gain experience which enhances the quality of their teaching, then such a possibility requires evaluation of the practices concerned. That such evaluation is long overdue may in part be due to a preoccupation with the effects of teaching methods on standardized test scores, rather than with the effects of interventions in the developmental history of the individual.

REFERENCES

1. Schieffelin, B. B. and Gilmore, P. (Eds.) (1986) *The Acquisition of Literacy: Ethnographic Perspectives*, Norwood, New Jersey: Ablex Publishing Corporation.
2. Gibson, E. J. and Levin, H. (1975) *The Psychology of Reading*, Cambridge, Mass.: MIT Press.
3. Read, C. (1986) *Children's Creative Spelling*, London: Routledge & Kegan Paul.
4. Wolfendale, S. and Topping, K. (Eds.) (1985) *Parental Involvement in Children's Reading*, Beckenham: Croom Helm.
5. Marsh, G., Friedman, M., Welch, V., and Desberg, P. (1981) 'A cognitive-developmental theory of reading acquisition', in G. E. Mackinnon and T. E. Waller (Eds.) *Reading Research: Advances in Theory and Practice*, New York: Academic Press.
6. McNaughton, S. (1981) 'Becoming an independent reader: problem solving during oral reading', *New Zealand Journal of Educational Studies*, 16: 177–85.
7. Clark, M. M. (1985) *New Directions in the Study of Reading*, Lewes: Falmer Press.
8. Francis, H. (1982) *Learning to Read*, London: Allen & Unwin.
9. ibid.
10. Cox, T. (1987) 'Slow starters versus long-term backward readers', *British Journal of Educational Psychology*, 57: 73–86.
11. Francis, H. (1987) 'Hearing beginning readers read', *British Educational Research Journal*, 13 (3): 215–25.
12. Graves, D. (1984) *A Researcher Learns to Write*, Exeter, New Hampshire: Heinemann Educational.

6.8

THE TEACHING OF LITERATURE: PRINCIPLES AND PRACTICE

W. A. GATHERER

INTRODUCTION

Traditionally, English as a subject has appeared as an amalgam of disparate activities: reading, composition, and language work were the main components, and the different studies were carried on separately. The teaching of literature, similarly fragmented into lessons on poetry, prose, and drama, was often regarded as a purely academic pursuit, having little connection with the personal development of the pupil. This perception of 'English' as a portmanteau into which various pursuits can be squeezed persists in the separation of 'language' and 'literature' in state examination syllabuses. Literature is seen as an optional extra, or as an important but ancillary form of aesthetic education. In the modern curriculum, literature must be recognized as the central core of English. It is not only the teacher's principal source of language study; it is also, and most importantly, a discipline in its own right, the most effective means of training pupils' minds in clear thinking, forming independent judgements, and responding sensitively to the ideas and feelings of other people.

THE EMERGENCE OF MODERN 'ENGLISH'

What is meant by 'teaching literature' has changed profoundly in the century since English first appeared as a school subject. The ancient Classics had been a literary and linguistic study, and to begin with English literature was used as a substitute for pupils in elementary schools: a few staple texts were culled for lessons on vocabulary and figures of speech; passages were learned by rote; moral precepts were noted and reproduced. By the 1920s, however, English was perceived to contribute crucially to a liberal education. The Newbolt Report of 1921 on the teaching of English, and George Sampson's book, *English for the English*, published in the same year, saw English as a replacement for the Classics, but they also helped establish the subject as a major discipline, not only in schools but also at universities. Both took a strong Arnoldian line, seeing English literature as a great 'humanizing force', superseding religion as a source of spiritual influences to regenerate mankind and unify the social classes. To this end they promoted a new atmosphere in classrooms, stressing the importance of imaginative expression, personal development, and the study of literature for enjoyment. The progressive move-ment of the inter-war period encouraged the growth of self-expression as a function of English. It was during this period that there developed the two dominant conceptions of the functions and methodology of English which still persist: on the one hand it is viewed pragmatically as a vocational or instru-mental subject, its main objectives being the development of skills; on the other hand it is seen as sequential experience, a central aspect of the edu-cational process, its purposes being the development of a whole personality and the fostering of healthy judgement.

In pedagogical terms the 'new English' which emerged in the 1960s has a unitary identity in the curriculum, in contrast to the fragmentary character of old-fashioned English programmes. Varied classroom activities are brought into some theme or aspect of human experience selected as the focus of the class's work. Thematically related poems, short stories, plays, or novels are used as the basis of discussion, role-playing, or creative writing. Thus the literature enjoyed in the classroom is closely associated with relevant social or personal concerns of the pupils. Talk, drama, and creative writing are based on first-hand experience and aspects of real life. An experience of literature is intended to support and give meaning to these 'encounters' with life. Reading literature in the classroom aims partly at promoting a taste for private reading, but mainly to be a real personal experience for each pupil. Literature gives experience of life: as active spectators of that experience the pupils can study human values, and by so doing develop the ability to discriminate and absorb values for themselves.[1] In such uses of literature, teachers will concentrate on helping pupils to derive personal, life-enhancing experience from their study. 'Literary competence' – the skills of reading, understanding, interpreting, and so on – is not an end in itself, but a means towards aesthetic, cultural, and psychological benefits.[2]

LITERATURE AS MORAL TEACHING

Our perceptions of the uses of literature in schools reflect nearly all the facets of past debates on literature and criticism. A perennial topic has been the degree to which literature should be seen as pleasure-giving, recreative, to be enjoyed for itself, or how far it should be taken to educate, provide moral or religious instruction, or be used for the improvement of the self or society. Horace asserted in his *Ars poetica* that literature is both *dulce*, sweet, pleasure-giving, and *utile*, useful, instructive, and that the writer works *lectorem delectando pariterque monendo*, by delighting the reader and at the same time instructing him. This duality of function has been recognized through the centuries, with varying emphases.

To Matthew Arnold literature was the greatest of all teachers, and literary criticism was a mediator between 'the best that is known and thought in the world' and the young. Poetry charms and delights, but it is also profoundly educative, representing great human actions which appeal to our elementary feelings. As a 'criticism of life', literature is a repository of moral education. The Arnoldian doctrine was a major influence in the early decades of the twentieth century. Another powerful influence on the teaching of literature was F. R. Leavis. He and many brilliant school teachers whom he taught at Cambridge in the middle decades of this century were firm in their belief that the study of literature is conducive to moral understanding and spiritual refinement.[3] Leavis and his associates argued that literature and society are closely related, as are experience and culture; the intelligence trained in studying literature is truly educated.

That literature reveals 'truths' in the sense of publicly verifiable knowledge is questionable: the view of life which emerges from reading a work is as much the creation of the reader as of the writer; yet the notion is a precious one to many teachers, and is often adduced as a main function of literature study. Addison is said to have altered the social mores of his time, Dickens is credited with reforms of prisons, Harriet Beecher Stowe is called 'the little woman who made the great war'.[4] Literature can, of course, be used as social document; but we must be careful to note that the 'world' of a literary work is not the real word, but rather an invention, the product of language and literary conventions created by a writer whose view of reality is subjective, and a reader who brings an idiosyncratic set of preconceptions to the page. Modern critical theorists, indeed, claim that beneath the apparent meanings of a text there can be deep structures showing a very different meaning: in the 'unintended' use or absence of literary conventions writers may expose characteristics of society of which they themselves are oblivious.[5]

There can be little doubt that literature reveals the moral values, social attitudes, and economic conditions of the time in which it was produced, and for that reason it has unique educational value. It is doubtful, however, whether this could ever be a main starting point for the teaching of literature in schools. A work of literature is so complex an organization that the process of analysis is inevitably difficult and time-consuming, and in normal circumstances the sheer quantity of information the pupil would need in order to derive benefit would be unattainable. It is not the *results* of studying literature we must consider in order to justify its place in the curriculum: it is the studying process itself.

LITERATURE AS ART

The 'utilitarian' view was abjured by the Romantics, whose perception of literature as transcendental and autonomous was inimical to what Edgar Allan Poe called the 'didactic heresy'. From this viewpoint literature originates in a deep, instinctual human need for self-expression, and its appeal is essentially aesthetic: reading a poem is 'the contemplation of beauty'. The Victorian doctrine of 'art for the sake of art' and the more recent notion of '*poésie pure*' were not sterile from the educator's viewpoint: if literature was not of value regardless of its social or moral impact it would not survive. Teachers rightly accentuate the qualities of enjoyment and emotional response in their teaching of literature, and the development of aesthetic responses is an aim which English teachers share with colleagues concerned with the arts – drama, art, music, film and dance. A case can be made for locating English in the arts curriculum rather than the humanities: it may be seen as a 'literary-expressive discipline', with attention to the writer as 'art-maker' and to the pupil as apprentice artist learning from 'creative mimesis'.[6]

Since literature *is* an art it is essential that pupils should be taught to appreciate it. This means, in the first place, that they should become progressively more sensitive to the power and emotional impact of the language, and more aware of how it works to create effects. Creative responsiveness to the imaginative use of language, and the training of the critical intelligence, what Leavis called 'sensibility', are principal objects in a literature lesson. Another concern of the teacher is the development of 'taste', which is the ability to recognize quality in artistic objects. The impact of a literary work is often sufficient in itself to make it 'useful', in the sense of being a worthwhile thing to do, and at the same time satisfying and enjoyable: and a basic intention in teaching literature is to give pupils access to these satisfactions. This is accomplished by making suitable texts available, helping pupils to read them with understanding, and encouraging them to recognize and express their responses.

Training in literary appreciation need not be confined to older, more academic pupils. It can be given 'obliquely' in the form of various classroom experiences to younger or less able pupils: taped recordings, playlets, choral presentations, personal anthologies, wall charts, and many other devices can be used to make poems 'live'; role-playing, group discussions, making filmscripts, and many other activities can be designed to link a novel or play to the current interests and concerns of pupils.[7]

LITERATURE AS EXPERIENCE

Leavis taught that a study of literature gives access to the 'intimate operations of the mind' (by 'mind' he meant not just intellect but also feeling, purpose and imagination).[8] His disciples have extended his insights to construct a pedagogical theory of experiential growth which has won widespread acceptance: 'Literature', avers the official Bullock Report, 'brings the child into an encounter with language in its most complex and varied forms. Through these complexities are presented the thoughts, experiences, and feelings of people who exist outside and beyond the reader's awareness . . . It provides imaginative insight into what another person is feeling; it allows the contemplation of possible human experiences which the reader himself has not met.'[9]

The 'experience of life' derived from literature is, it must be remarked, the product of the reader's imagination much more than an intrinsic feature of the writing. It is in the active consideration of events, characterization, and statements that a relationship arises between the 'life' in the work and 'real life'. Whether the psychological activity relates to the detailed character portrayals in a Trollope novel, or the merely hinted-at persona in a lyric poem, the process involves speculation, identification, comparison, guesswork, and experimentation. Each reader constructs a unique interpretation for himself: and the ability to construct these interpretations will grow with practical critical experience. Hence the 'wisdom' or 'maturity' claimed as the product of reading literature comes from imaginative interaction with texts. Passive, unreflective reading may be pleasurable, but it will not much enrich one's experience of life. It is a central tenet for teachers of literature that pupils who learn to reflect, critically and imaginatively, on the human values and traits presented in literary characters, can learn to be reflective and judicious about the values they meet in their own lives. Thus it is claimed for literature study that it helps the pupil to grow as a morally educated person, able to identify with others so as to understand their beliefs and point of view, able to take account of other people's feelings, and to exercise these abilities in evolving moral principles and judgements.[10]

TEXTS AND TEACHING

An important aspect of literature teaching is the selection of texts, and this in turn depends on the teachers' conception of what literature is. The 'literature' shelves of most English departments in schools will hold a variety of types of book: works of poetry, prose fiction, expository prose, *belles lettres*, drama, and so on; nowadays they will also hold audiotapes, videotapes, computer software, and perhaps 'multi-media packages'. The etymology of the word *literature* does not exclude oral art from the corpus.

When it comes to selecting work for particular study as literature, however, it is not easy to be comprehensive in one's choice. Theoretically it is possible to define literature as any kind of writing which is highly valued, as do modern structuralists. The category of works we call 'literature' is not objective in the sense of being immutable. To some academic critics, anything can be literature. Teachers are unable to take this lofty position. Since the study of literature in schools must claim to provide real educational benefits if it is to retain its position in the curriculum, the literature studied must be such as to provide these benefits. And it is 'imaginative' literature which best meets this requirement. Pragmatically we must realize that there are many kinds of writing which, for different reasons and at different times, can be held to be literature: essays, biographies, letters, and so on. We must accept that works of popular literature can give many readers genuine emotional and imaginative experience. But, on the whole, teachers are wise to confine the main part of their attention to imaginative literature – poetry, drama, and fiction – which has been generally recognized to have genuine literary quality. Without that quality it would be difficult to use it for training pupils in literary competence.

Literary competence comprises a range of abilities which enable pupils to read (or witness) works of literary art with appreciation, taste, and discrimination. As we have seen, literature study can confer many different benefits. But they all depend crucially on the pupil's ability to read and interpret literature intelligently. Thus the teaching of literature must involve a concern for the objects of study as *literary works*, not documents about interpersonal relations. The basic work of the literature teacher *at all stages* is to train pupils in the activity which, in its academic form, is called literary criticism. This involves the study of the form, style, structure, texture, the 'unique verbal organization' of works of literature.[11] But it also involves the selection of suitable texts for particular pupils and for particular occasions; the creation of enjoyment and attention, without which the activity would be pointless; the joining together of textual appreciation and understanding with the meanings of the literature, interpreted in terms of the pupils' personal and educational interests. In brief, the teaching of literature aims at developing awareness of literary form and substance through the live engagement of pupils with relevant texts, and at the same time creating and exploiting educative interaction between the pupils' personal experience and the experience yielded by the literature.

APPROACHES TO TEACHING LITERATURE

Although the general principles underlying literature teaching are valid for all the developmental stages in the educational process, there will, of course, be different emphases and approaches appropriate to the age and capacity of the pupils. The appreciation of literature will not develop naturally: it must be taught, in the sense that the teacher must provide the most effective means of stimulating interest and promoting understanding. Learning to read literature with intelligence and sympathy is inevitably the result of prolonged experience and training.

At the earliest primary stage, the teacher's principal objective is to help pupils to develop a love of reading imaginative writing; all the activities of story telling, role-playing, creative writing, the re-creation of the experience through the expressive arts, all such teaching methods are employed to help make literature enjoyable and fulfilling. In a real sense they link the poems, rhymes, songs, and stories enjoyed in the classroom with all the other actual sources of pleasure open to children. But those activities do more: they mark the beginning of literary training. Children at this stage learn 'story grammar', the awareness of plot sequence and development; they learn how to interpret character by looking for clues and discussing their significance; they learn to attend to the language and interpret its meanings.

Throughout the primary and early secondary stages there should be a growing understanding of literature as artefact in its many forms. As literate reading develops, the pupils will become more skilled at probing the meaning of words and catching the subtler meanings intended by the writers in their imagery and in the formal structures they employ. By 'reading between the lines' they will be able to perceive meanings that (intended or not) contribute significantly to the impact of the writing. Books will become familiar, pleasure-giving objects, their contents open to discussion, criticism, and evaluation. Although 'practical criticism' may be too grandiose a term for most teachers at this stage, that is in effect what they are teaching.

There are of course a number of serious difficulties to be faced by teachers undertaking these tasks, especially in the middle and secondary stages. The first is that literature is primarily written texts, and must be read intelligently to be appreciated and understood; and many pupils fail to develop sufficient proficiency to be able to enjoy good literature. Teachers can overcome this obstacle to some extent by choosing simpler reading matter, or by supplementing the pupils' experience by using film and other audiovisual material. Essentially, however, it is a question of meeting pupils' actual needs by helping them to study material which is interesting, relevant, and accessible to them. Appreciation has to be worked for: well chosen, well presented imaginative writing will stimulate the effort required, provided always that the teacher is able to connect it with real-life interests and pleasures. Of course it is easy to offer such precepts. Against them lie perennial difficulties that cannot be easily dismissed: the reluctance of pupils whose cultural values are not readily catered for; the shortage of time and resources; the demands of an examination syllabus which may constrain the teacher's choices and approaches. It was ever thus; those difficulties are not peculiar to the teaching of literature.

They do, however, indicate the major requirements for effective literature teaching in the modern educational world. We must broaden our perception of 'literature' to include any imaginative experience which relies upon language for its impact, and the school stock must contain an ample variety of resources for this purpose. We must free literature teaching from the old restrictive bonds – the set lessons, the rigid rule-bound prescriptions, the prescribed text, the great-book theory – and allow it to provoke and release the energies of thought and imagination which all pupils possess. We must use literature, at all stages, as a prime source of vicarious experience, so that it forms an intrinsic part of the pupils' growing up. We must, perhaps above all else, devise a curriculum for literature teaching which gives the central place to training pupils to read it with understanding and responsive feeling, so that they get from it that growth of taste, judgement, and vitality of imagination which literature uniquely provides.

REFERENCES

1. Dixon, J. (1969) *Growth Through English*, Oxford: Oxford University Press.
2. Holbrook, D. (1979) *English for Meaning*, Windsor: National Foundation for Educational Research.
3. Inglis, F. (1969) *The Englishness of English Teaching*, London: Longman.
4. Warren, A. and Wellek, R. (1949) *Theory of Literature*, London: Jonathan Cape.
5. Gibson, R. (1986) *Critical Theory and Education*, London: Hodder & Stoughton.
6. Abbs, P. (1982) *English Within the Arts*, London: Hodder & Stoughton.
7. Fox, G. 'Twenty-four things to do with a book'; Fox, G. and Merrick, B. 'Thirty-six things to do with a poem', in A. Adams (Ed.) (1982) *New Directions in English Teaching*, Lewes: Falmer Press.
8. Leavis, F. R. (1944) *Education and the University*, London: Chatto & Windus. See also W. Walsh (1980) *F. R. Leavis*, London: Chatto & Windus.
9. Department of Education and Science (1975) *A Language for Life*, p. 125, London: HMSO.
10. Butler, C. (1977) 'Tragedy and moral education', in H. Schiff (Ed.) *Contemporary Approaches to English Studies*, London: Heinemann.
11. Rutherford, A. (1968) 'Literary criticism', in *The Teaching of Literature*, Bulletin No. 2 of the Central Committee on English, Scottish Education Department, Edinburgh: HMSO.

6.9

COMMUNICATIVE COMPETENCE IN LANGUAGE TEACHING

CAROLYN HUTCHINSON

WHAT IS COMMUNICATIVE COMPETENCE?

Probably the most important feature of communicative competence is that it is concerned with language *in context*. Up until relatively recently mastery of a language was thought of as knowing about the language system, its grammar, and phonology; with skill in its use as being the ability to manipulate the system in the 'correct' way. Language teaching was largely concerned with transmitting knowledge about how the system of either the native language or a second or subsequent language worked, through drills and exercises which exemplified acceptable ways of constructing phrases and sentences.

It was in the early 1970s that serious consideration was first given to the appropriateness of language to the context in which it was used. The notion of 'correctness' would now encompass not only aspects of grammar, but also the physical and linguistic circumstances in which language was produced or understood. The term 'communicative competence' thus came to include both grammatical competence and sociolinguistic competence.[1] It was suggested that fully competent users of language would be those who had control of the many uses to which language might be put, encompassing a wide range of functions for use in different contexts. Such individuals would be sensitive to what language was possible in terms of grammatical rules; but also to the appropriateness of language in relation to a particular context, and to its acceptability in terms of human and social behaviour and the culture of which it was a part.[2] Such sensitivity would involve taking into account, for example, our role in relation to the reader/listener, the degree of familiarity between us, and the nature of the transaction involved, which might have certain predetermined features, as for example in reading or writing a report, or in a game, or on the floor of the Stock Market.

In the case of a foreign language, our choices will also be influenced by the expectations of the native speakers with whom we wish to communicate, and their likely tolerance of errors and eccentric turns of phrase. All these features will affect the way in which we exercise choices about the options available to us. If we accept this view of language as a series of choices to be made in a social and behavioural context, then we must expect to take account of social factors in any systematic attempt to explain the nature of language, since there will be a constant interaction between patterns of behaviour and linguistic forms.[3]

More recently, the concept of communicative competence has been further elaborated by applied linguists.[4] It is seen as embodying the knowledge and forms required to participate in 'actual communication', which is what we can actually observe and describe. From this we can then infer competence, taking into account the fact that it will not represent a complete account of a person's competence, but only an indication of its potential, under conditions limited by constraints such as distractions, fatigue, and memory. Actual communication is seen as a purposeful form of social interaction which takes place in a context which will both constrain appropriacy and give clues to meaning. It will involve the listener/reader or the speaker/writer in a continuous process of evaluating and possibly negotiating meaning as further information becomes available, reducing by degrees the uncertainty which must necessarily be a part of the transmission of meaning from one individual to another. To understand, or to communicate effectively, the language user will need the knowledge and skills necessary to achieve competence in four areas which are interdependent.

In this framework, *grammatical competence* remains as an important component of communicative competence. The user of language will need knowledge of, and skill in using, the grammatical features and rules of the language in question, so that literal meaning can be understood and expressed. *Sociolinguistic competence* is concerned principally, as we would expect, with the notion of appropriacy, taking into account the status of the participants in the communication, and the norms and conventions of behaviour determined by the context. The meaning conveyed will need to consist of the proper functions, ideas, and attitudes in the context; and the form of the utterance will need to be appropriate in both its verbal and its non-verbal characteristics.

Originally considered as a part of sociolinguistic competence, *discourse competence* in this framework is separately distinguished as the combining of grammatical forms and meanings to understand or construct a cohesive and coherent whole in whatever type of text or genre is required. To understand or achieve a cohesive text, the user will need to be aware of the structural linking of utterances: coherence has to do with the relationship between meanings, so that the text shows continuity and progression, without contradictions and irrelevance. Clearly different types of text, spoken or written, will show

750

considerable variations in these respects: consider, for example, the differences between the text of an Act of Parliament and the way the same material is presented in a television news bulletin.

The final component of communicative competence in this framework is *strategic competence*, which enables the language user to enhance or recognize the effectiveness of various devices, such as for example metaphor and rhetorical devices in writing, or pitch, intonation, and modulation in spoken communication. Strategic competence will also allow the user to compensate for breakdowns in interactive communication which may occur as a result of the limiting conditions of actual communication: momentary lapses in memory or fluency, or shortcomings in any of the other areas of competence. This will apply particularly in a foreign language, where the user's options may be limited by a lack of knowledge of syntactic structures, or lack of experience of the culture.

While applied linguists have been concerned to explore the notion of communicative competence, psychologists have also been concerned to examine language as it is used for purposes other than that of communication. In particular, there has been concern with language as an 'instrument of thought'.[5] While communicative competence is seen to involve language as a way of expressing and representing concrete experiences, taking account of context, and recognizing the intentions of other people, *analytic competence* is concerned with the use of language which involves the prolonged operation of thought processes: adopting thinking and problem-solving strategies appropriate to sets of observations and interlinking propositions, rather than direct experience of objects and events. This is an internal language, which is potentially available to the individual as a means for going beyond immediate experience, and as a tool for innovation. It is suggested that analytic competence is best acquired through formal education, and is fostered in the context of the school, because schools decontextualize knowledge and demand the use of analytic competence as part of communicative competence. This would suggest that teaching in a way which encourages the development of communicative competence, both written and spoken, observed in situations which allow real communication, will not only improve the quality of the pupil's observable language resource, but also more indirectly alter the way in which the same individual thinks and perceives the world.

COMMUNICATIVE COMPETENCE IN THE SYLLABUS

Communicative competence as it is conceptualized here allows us to consider language not so much as a subject in its own right, but rather as an essential part of the study of any subject or discipline. The subject teacher will need to be concerned with the way in which the 'content' of the subject is given linguistic expression, and how language is used in the context of the subject area to carry out certain functions: to define, classify, generalize, make hypotheses, or draw conclusions, for example.

It has been suggested that the linguistic needs of groups of pupils for the purposes of a particular discipline should be determined with reference to several aspects of language use.[6] The first of these concerns the circumstances within which language will be used. We need to consider the various roles of the pupils in relation to the person or people who will read or listen to their language, or whose writing or talk they will need to understand: peer or superior, expert or novice, individual or part of a group. Whatever the roles, the emphasis will be on the pupils' ability to think themselves into the position of the other person or people involved in the exchange. We will also need to consider the physical contexts in which communication will occur, since this will affect the type and nature of the language. For example, the language appropriate to the academic seminar is different from that of the television studio or the shop floor. While the school classroom may be the actual setting for many of the language activities associated with a particular discipline, it may be that we would wish to simulate or arrange access to other settings which are considered relevant to pupils' present or future needs as active members of society. The topic of study will also be important as part of the context, since it will play an important role in determining the type of language which will be appropriate.

The second aspect for which a consideration of pupils' needs will be important is that of the uses to which language may be put; that is, the communicative functions which characterize a particular discipline or genre. Various suggestions have been made as to how functions can be broadly categorized. One useful framework, for example, contains seven broad categories: *modality*, for expressing degrees of certainty, necessity, or conviction; *moral discipline and evaluation*, for expressing approval and disapproval; *suasion*, for persuading, or suggesting, or urging a course of action; *argument*, for informing, or arguing, or asserting a point of view; *rational inquiry* or *exposition*, for exemplifying or defining, or expressing implications; *personal emotions*, for expressing pleasure, astonishment, shock, or annoyance; and *interpersonal relations*, for expressing degrees of formality or informality, and politeness.[7] We might add to the list a separate but overlapping category of *imaginative* functions, for using language in a creative way.[8] Once such functions as are relevant to a particular area of inquiry have been identified, it then becomes possible to identify particular language items, or 'exponents', associated with them, and with particular topics. These functions and their exponents form the basis of a 'semantic syllabus' which is tailored to the needs of pupils; for it can be seen that while a very wide range of functions may be possible in the context of a particular subject area, some will be more emphasized than others. Functions in the *moral discipline* and *suasion* categories may for example be of more relevance to subjects such as English or environmental studies than to physics or biology. Moreover, the exponents of functions within a category, for example the rational enquiry category, may be quite different from one discipline to another: the language associated with exemplification in a novel will be very different from the language of exemplification in the physical sciences.

A third aspect of importance in relation to pupils' needs will be that of language activities; is it appropriate to expect pupils to operate effectively in reading and listening to language receptively, and to produce language themselves in speaking, interacting, and writing, for all the identified functions and in all the relevant situations? It may well be that in some situations, and for some functions, the ability to understand and appreciate communicative meaning is more important than being able to produce it: for example, we may wish to encourage access to and appreciation of works of great literary merit, without necessarily expecting our pupils to be able to write like great novelists or poets. Similarly, where pupils are engaged in collaborating as a group to explore particular scientific or mathematical concepts, the language of interaction may be more appropriate than that of writing.

COMMUNICATIVE ACTIVITIES IN THE CLASSROOM

How are communicative activities different from any other legitimate teaching and learning activities in the classroom? Many of the activities which are part of good teaching practice will in fact fit into the communicative category: but it is helpful to consider systematically the close relationship between the concept of communicative competence and activities which will contribute towards its development.

Control of the grammatical and phonological systems of the language will be important if the pupil is to be allowed a real choice amongst the possible semantic options available for the expression of a particular function. The development of communicative competence will be concerned with the understanding or production of spoken or written text, rather than with knowledge of the subject concerned: this is an important distinction, since the emphasis is on transmitting information in an appropriate way, rather than on acquiring or understanding it. Communicative activities will thus tend to involve pupils in exploring and manipulating content which is familiar, or building upon what is already known, rather than the unfamiliar and/or conceptually complex, and will only be one of a number of types of activity in a teaching sequence.

In much the same way, understanding or producing text which is coherent or cohesive will involve pupils in dealing with and reflecting upon extended text, spoken or written. Short question-and-answer worksheets, or oral question-and-answer sessions between teacher and pupils may be valuable as a means of fostering knowledge and understanding; but they will not encourage consideration of the way functions characteristically operate, and in which positions in discourse in particular disciplines or genres, or how the language of oral communication may be different from that of written communication.

The concept of appropriacy as demonstrated in sociolinguistic competence would suggest that pupils must be given the opportunity to exercise choice and judgement in relation to a real purpose in using language to communicate. Particularly in interactive speech, but also in writing, 'communicative intent' will involve conveying information to someone who does not already have it, so that the participants can engage in a real attempt to reduce the discrepancy between their two different standpoints. This means that language activities will not involve 'the repetition of the known to the knowers', but rather the bridging of a real 'information gap'. There are many ways of providing opportunities for doing this: for example, giving different pupils access to different information and then requiring them to collaborate to carry out a particular task; and allowing pupils choice in what can be said, or an open-ended solution to a problem[9]. In the foreign language classroom, pupils can be encouraged to communicate to each other, and to the teacher, aspects of other school subjects, or personal interests, in which they are genuinely 'expert'. Such activities will inevitably involve the development of strategic competence, as pupils strive to overcome their own difficulties in getting their message across.

In designing communicative tasks, it is helpful to consider various permutations offered by considering classroom activities at three levels: at the first level there is the wealth of information, texts, and experiences which can be regarded as part of the source stimulus for any activity. This may be in spoken or written, pictorial or diagrammatic form, or simply a physical or emotional experience. Where material is verbal, the functions involved may be of any particular type, and will show a characteristic pattern in the way they are 'chained' into coherent text.

At the second level, this source stimulus may be 'filtered' through the perceptions of individuals, or pairs, or groups of pupils, or pupils with other adults or the teacher, in teaching and learning activities.

At the third level, actual communication about what has been learned occurs as an individual, or a pair, or a group participates in a purposeful communicative activity, based on their experiences, which will have its own contextual features and characteristics, and require rapid judgements about appropriate functions and their exponents. A careful sequencing of activities through these levels, with an eye to achieving a wide variation in text type and genre, and in context parameters, will help to ensure that a particular area of syllabus content is communicated in as many different ways as possible, given the limitations of the school environment. In this way, communicative activities can be seen as an integral part of the repertoire of teaching and learning strategies involved in the teaching of any school subject.

ASSESSING COMMUNICATIVE COMPETENCE

Regular assessment of communicative competence will be an essential part of its development, providing feedback to pupils about those aspects of their performance which relate to appropriacy of language in particular contexts. Assessment will necessarily be related to activities which take place at the third of the three levels described above, and will involve systematic observation of actual performance on tasks which are carefully defined and explicit in terms of purpose, context, and characteristics. Where receptive language is concerned, assessment is probably best done by observation of performance on a task which requires a detailed understanding of an extended text. Tasks involving information transfer or transformation, for example from one type of text to another, or from text to explanatory diagram, or summary of those parts of a spoken or written text relevant to a particular purpose, are examples of this type of activity. Where productive language is concerned, teachers will need to determine a criterion level for adequate performance on each task. This will need to take into account such characteristics as style and register; cohesion and coherence; and grammatical accuracy; and in the case of spoken language, aspects of interactive and non-verbal behaviour. Since particular features of the context will play a vital part in determining the appropriacy of these aspects of performance, the definition of what is an adequate performance will need also to take context features into account. For example, the language which is appropriate for one pupil to use to another in a group discussion where no teacher is present will differ markedly from the language which that same pupil might use when writing for or talking to an adult stranger. Each different task, in other words, will have its own task-specific features, which will need to be taken into account in the qualitative assessment of component skills.[10]

Provided that the purpose and context of any activity are made explicit to all the participants, there is no reason why pupils should not assess their own performance with reference to performance and task-specific descriptors for each communicative activity: and indeed, peer assessment in pairs or groups can in itself provide an admirable opportunity for a really purposeful communicative exchange.

REFERENCES

1. Campbell, R. and Wales, R. (1970) 'The study of language acquisition,' in J. Lyons (Ed.) *New Horizons in Linguistics*, Cambridge: Cambridge University Press.
2. Hymes, D. (1971) *On Communicative Competence*, Philadelphia: University of Pennsylvania Press.

3. Halliday, M. A. K. (1973) 'Towards a sociological semantics' in M. A. K. Halliday *Explorations in the Functions of Language*, London: Edward Arnold.
4. M. Canale (1983) 'From communicative competence to communicative language pedagogy', in J. C. Richards and R. W. Schmidt (Eds.) *Language and Communication*, London: Longman.
5. J. S. Bruner (1975) 'Language as an instrument of thought', in A. Davies (Ed.) *Problems in Language and Hearing*, London: Heinemann.
6. van Ek, J. A. and Alexander, L. G. (1980) *Threshold Level English*, Oxford: Pergamon Press.
7. Wilkins, D. A. (1973) 'The linguistic and situational content of a common core in a unit credit system', in D. A. Wilkins *Systems Development in Adult Language Learning*, Strasbourg: Council for Cultural Co-operation, Council of Europe.
8. M. Finnochiaro and C. J. Brumfit (1983) *The Functional-Notional Approach: From Theory to Practice*, New York: Oxford University Press.
9. van Ek and Alexander (1980) op. cit.
10. Hutchinson, C. J. and Pollitt, A. B. (1987) *The User's Guide to TELS Profile*, Basingstoke: Macmillan Education.

6.10

EXPERIENTIAL LEARNING AND SOCIAL EDUCATION

ALEX SHARP

EXPERIENTIAL LEARNING

The concept of experiential learning is a comparative newcomer in the world of educational terminology and, as with most new ideas, the reception has been mixed. This chapter considers how experiential learning applies to social education in the hope that this may provide readers with a basis from which they will be able to clarify further their own thinking on the subject.

As the concept is adopted more widely by educationalists, it is sometimes used where other, simpler terms would be more accurate. Experiential learning should be distinguished from such activities as practical exercises, projects, work experience, training, and the like. Although such applications do involve both experience and learning, the fundamental relationship remains an instrumental one. The experience is provided in order to promote learning for a particular purpose: it is a means to some largely pre-formulated end. Although there are learning situations where such an instrumental approach is appropriate, and may legitimately be termed experiential, the approach emphasized here represents an *inquiry* rather than a *means-end* model of the educational process, as we shall see.

SOCIAL EDUCATION

In understanding social education it is essential to recognize that the context of learning is itself a first-hand social reality. This is the paramount experiential factor in social education: that in a context where the *social* is the focus of learning, there are represented live social phenomena and processes. A social education which does not attend to such experiential actualities has lost touch with its most immediate and relevant concerns. There are, however, many instances of social education losing sight of this experiential principle. On one occasion, for example, a teacher was encouraging a group of adolescent pupils

757

to hold a discussion, and asked them to move from the ordinary classroom arrangement of parallel rows into a more circular setting. This meant that boys and girls found themselves in much closer proximity than usual, and they reacted in a somewhat embarrassed and boisterous manner. The teacher grew impatient with such 'immature behaviour', and abandoned the discussion altogether. One of the potential topics – proposed by the pupils themselves – had been relations with members of the opposite sex, and it is ironic that their actual behaviour, which so clearly illustrated their difficulties in this area, was not used as the opportunity for learning that it offered.

Sometimes an immediately present issue is seen as worthwhile but is deemed irrelevant because it is 'not on the syllabus', or because it would not be easy to demonstrate to others whether learning had been taking place:

> When teachers are searching for new ways of stimulating pupils into learning things that will really matter to them, they can be effectively hamstrung by premature demands for evidence that this learning is proving 'successful'. It may be that the exploration of what they and their pupils are experiencing together is more important than evaluation in the usual sense of the word.[1]

This quotation points to another feature of experiential learning – that it proceeds as an *exploration* (or *inquiry*) and that the teacher as well as the pupils learn from the experience. Experiential work thus requires teachers to relinquish their roles as didactic practitioners and instead to become both participants in and facilitators of a learning *process*.

THE PERSONAL AND THE LEARNING PROCESS

As an example of this inquiry method, take this chapter itself as a learning context. This chapter constitutes a kind of formal relationship between myself as writer and you the reader. Our relationship is inevitably impersonal and one-sided (initially in the writing, subsequently in the reading). As in most academic writing it is unlikely that writer and reader will meet in an actual social setting. Our relationship thus exists through, and is mediated by, the written word, and on the face of it this is quite a different situation from the live classroom setting. Yet there is perhaps a sense in which a chapter such as this typifies the codified, impersonal nature of much teaching and learning. For example, some teachers perform in a distant and didactic manner, and never seem to build up any personal rapport with their pupils or students. And even where teacher and students interact in the classroom, they may encounter each other through their respective institutional roles, and both may operate in a largely recipient attitude to what counts as knowledge (which usually stems from books or articles). What is missing is an *im-mediate* social engagement with the learning process – there is a lack of both a personal encounter between teacher and taught, and of their joint, actual involvement with the subject matter. When that subject matter is the social, this lack is not merely a shortfall in the educational experience, but a fundamental distortion of the educative enterprise.

A starting point for an experiential approach to social education thus involves establishing personal contacts in the classroom. Any learning context must accommodate the different perspectives and interests brought by those taking part. It cannot be assumed that each participant construes the situation – the aims, methods, vocabulary, rules of procedure, and so forth – in the same way. Some clarification, of at least the teacher's own position, is essential.

Returning to the present chapter, what does this imply? In approaching the task of writing, I had in mind an image of readers seeking to become better informed about 'experiential learning and social education'. I assumed that readers would expect definitions of the two terms, and perhaps a discussion of some methodological issues and practical applications. None of these is an unreasonable expectation, but I have chosen nevertheless to take a different approach in this chapter. My reason for this is that if I write the chapter along the lines suggested, I would be writing an article *about* experiential learning and social education and, somewhat paradoxically, this would be to demonstrate what experiential learning and social education are *not*. In fact, experiential learning and social education signal learning which is embedded in an actual, direct experience, and in which the social relations of the participants play a constituent and formative role. Obviously when learning is intended to take place by having someone write about (as here), or talk about (as in classroom teaching) a topic, the quality of a direct, social experience is likely to be missing. Instead, it will be replaced by an academic format, in which the topic stems from a planned curriculum, and the social roles become governed by a didactic pattern. It is of course impossible for me to transform this literary context into a direct social encounter, but in attending to the artificial, 'unexperiential' qualities of this article, we may be highlighting some of the problems faced in the live classroom setting.

One requirement of an experiential approach is, then, the explication of participants' aims and expectations. This is, on the whole, a cognitive activity involving the expressions of thoughts, assumptions, and other beliefs, but even more significantly it will involve *feelings*.[2] In experiential activities, appreciating and, when appropriate, articulating feelings is undoubtedly the most crucial aspect of the teaching-learning process. It requires skilled introspection on the educator's part to appreciate what part of a feeling state belongs to the experiential process occurring in the classroom, and what belongs elsewhere, and it requires skilled facilitation to establish, in an appropriate manner, those feelings which do belong within the experienced reality of the classroom.[3]

In the earlier example of a 'failed' classroom discussion, a variety of feeling

759

states is intimated. But what is the reality underlying the situation depicted as 'embarrassed', 'boisterous', 'impatient', 'immature'? Was the misbehaviour of the pupils an expression of their desire to discuss the subject, or an avoidance of doing so (bearing in mind the possibility that both motivations were operating)? Was their reaction a response to the prospective discussion, or to the change in their usual seating arrangements (had their feelings about such a change been explored)? Was the teacher's impatience a fear of losing control, an inability to give the pupils time to settle, an anxiety about the subject matter, a fear over wasting time, or an attempt to confront the pupils with a demand for more 'mature' behaviour? In arguing that a learning opportunity had been lost because certain awkward feeling states were not understood at the time, it is not suggested that there should have been some sort of emotional inquisition in the classroom, but rather that in the total experiential picture there are clues to the affective dynamics which are salient in any actual situation. The experiential educator is required to work with these dynamics simply because they are an actualization in the classroom of the biographical and institutional conditions which contribute to social life – the veritable subject matter of social education. It is by paying attention to these dynamics that certain ineffable or 'unknown' features of social life can be articulated and understood. And once an experience has been grasped in this way – experientially – there is then a foundation which can be built upon with conceptual work to elaborate and clarify the understanding.

The preceding paragraphs have been concerned with the need for direct, unmediated experiential work in the social education classroom, and yet through that 'third-party' description, the immediacy, the experiential quality of the writing, has vanished. This may seem a betrayal of experiential principles, but it is a dilemma constantly faced as the teacher is forced to move back and forwards between the current experience and reflections on past events, or other relevant, but less immediate, forms of knowledge.

RECAPITULATION

Let us now review the principles involved in the experiential learning process. *First*, subjectivity is involved, in particular the expression of personal feelings, so that the educational experience is an attempt to incorporate the authenticity of the whole person. The ability to understand and respect others is possible only on the basis of self-understanding and self-respect, and the social education classroom is a setting where the subjectivity of self and others can be explored. The teacher has a key role in modelling and encouraging self-expression, thereby helping pupils towards the possibility of representing the self more fully through words and actions.

Second, a social reality is paramount – the reality of the actual relationships of those taking part in the life of the classroom. How participants experience each other, the perceptions, feelings, and behaviours through which interaction occurs, and through which life experiences are constituted, operate in the real-life setting where they meet. Participants learn to notice how their own experiences are constituted, often by seeing their own behaviour 'mirrored' in others. There is an opportunity to pay attention to processes more usually taken for granted or submerged under the maelstrom of everyday interactions. The reality mirrored or exposed in this way is no longer unquestioningly accepted: subjective matters are placed in the space shared by others, and as a result personal fantasies or other distortions can no longer be easily sustained when confronted by other viewpoints. Experiential learning thus brings about insight into the nature of personal experience, and it does this by paying attention to actual experiences occurring in the learning context.

Third, effort is involved. It is not an easy matter to stay in contact with the live, experiential issues, and all too easily attention may drift to indirect, 'third-party', or other abstract issues. This may be because there are constraints which are allowed to superimpose upon the first-order experiential realities (such as the requirements of assessment). But it may also be because experiential learning is not always comfortable for participants, since questions are raised concerning matters taken for granted both personally and socially. An individual or a group may erect defences, often quite unconsciously, against the need to change in various ways. There must therefore be some willingness to struggle with uncomfortable issues: effort is required to remain focused on the 'here and now'.

Fourth, social responsibilities are involved. Experiential learning is not just to do with personal learning: it also concerns relating to others in the process of learning. This involves responsibilities for self and towards others. Self-awareness and self-expression represent only one side of social communication: self-other relationships, such as trusting, supporting, encouraging, or confronting, arise in the process of working with others. A crucial issue in this area is the manner in which the teacher handles responsibility and authority. Many teachers seem in practice to become hidebound by their formal status as a figure of authority, and pupils, or even older students, can also become restrictively involved in this pattern (for example, by being hostile or dependent). An inquiry approach to learning, which disrupts the more conventional hierarchic relationship between teacher and learner, offers a particular opportunity for learning about personal responsibility in the context of different role relationships.

Finally, a genuinely social education is involved, in the sense that the educative work in the classroom is inseparable from the wider social context. Perhaps it has become clear now why the title of this article is experiential learning *and* social education. Education which is experiential is essentially social.

Human social experience, which is the subject matter of social education however defined, presents itself for study in the learning context through the participants' actual relationships. And such a social education is also radical, since it involves a fundamental inquiry into the nature and conditions of social experience. This almost inevitably involves some disruption of personal and cultural frameworks, and resistance to change on either or both of these levels seems partly to underlie a hostility to experiential methods.

The highly organized – and increasingly centralized – character of formal education imposes further barriers to experiential approaches. Wherever learning is conceptualized in terms of pre-formulated aims and objectives, where curricula are defined by subject disciplines and content based, where teachers are in authority, where learning is assessed according to measured criteria, in short wherever education occurs in its conventional form, an experierential and social education will find it difficult if not impossible to become established.[4] The prevailing institutional climate is simply not conducive to the process and method of open inquiry. Formal education generates its own preoccupations – examples are the masses of information to be remembered, specialist terminologies to be mastered, books to be read, essays to be written, examinations to be taken – and it is hardly surprising therefore that alternate approaches to learning are squeezed out. There are then some educational contexts where experiential methods will be either impossible or impractical, but there are others where implementation should be attempted, even if the outcome is failure. This chapter is perhaps an example of the latter. In the end, this chapter must fail in its attempt to be experiential, simply because the context – a piece of academic writing – is inherently inimical to the experiential process. I have been trying to demonstrate in writing the nature of an experiential social education, but the written word cannot in fact convey the experiential process. If the reader has appreciated this message, then paradoxically the chapter may have succeeded after all. However it will now be understood that experiential learning is not book learning, and that real inquiry begins where this sentence ends.

REFERENCES

1. Richardson, E. (1975) *Authority and Organization in the Secondary School*, London: MacMillan Education, p. 47.
2. Salzberger-Wittenberg, I., Henry, G., and Osborne, E. (1983) *The Emotional Experience of Learning and Teaching*, London: Routledge & Kegan Paul.
3. Dreikurs, R., Grunwald, B. B., and Pepper, F. C. (1982) *Maintaining Sanity in the Classroom*, (2nd edn), New York: Harper & Row.
4. Claxton, G. (1985) 'Experiential learning and education', in N. Entwistle (Ed.) *New Directions in Educational Psychology: Learning and Teaching*, Lewes: Falmer Press, pp. 125–38.

6.11

THE TEACHING AND UNDERSTANDING OF CONCEPTS IN SCIENCE

ROSALIND DRIVER

ALTERNATIVE PERSPECTIVES

Traditionally the most important factor in the design of science teaching materials has been the structure of the knowledge to be taught. Domains of knowledge, such as the 'mole concept', 'genetics', or the 'concept of density' are analysed; component concepts and hierarchies of relationships are identified and used to design and structure teaching sequences.[1] This approach of task analysis has been shown to provide a useful basis for the teaching of skills. However, it has been found to be limited when applied to the teaching of any material which has a significant conceptual component.

A second tradition which has been influential in science teaching is that of Piaget's developmental model. This well-known model describes the stages through which children's thinking progresses in terms of their acquisition of general logical schemes or structures of thought. This model suggests that better understanding can be achieved if the logical demands of the science concepts to be taught are better matched to the stage of development of the learner.[2]

The extent to which the stage theory adequately describes the development of children's thinking has been a matter of some dispute. One of the significant criticisms of the model is the importance of the content and context of a task on subsequent reasoning. Research evidence indicates that human reasoning may be based more on implicit causal theories and models of situations than on formal logical argument.[3]

Recent studies of children's ideas in science have led to a view of conceptual learning which differs from both these previous perspectives. According to this emerging view, learners develop conceptual schemes or models of the world, which they use in responding to and making sense of new situations. Learners are thus seen as active architects of their own knowledge; furthermore learning outcomes depend not only on the instructional experiences provided, but also on the conceptual schemes of the learner.

CHILDREN'S CONCEPTIONS IN SCIENCE

A nine-year-old was listening to records in our house one day, and noticed that when he turned the record player off, it took a second or so for the sound from the speakers to die away. 'There must be miles and miles of wire in there,' he commented, 'for the electricity to go through for the sound to take that long to stop.' This youngster had not studied electricity in school, and yet he had constructed for himself notions about electricity, that it flows through wires, and that it flows very fast. It is now known that, before they are taught science in a formal way at school, children develop ideas about a wide range of physical and biological phenomena which they use to make sense of their daily experiences.[4]

One of the most thoroughly researched topics is that of intuitive mechanics. The main feature which characterizes the thinking of students, as well as adults, in this domain, is that 'motion implies force' (as opposed to the Newtonian view that 'a change in motion implies force'). Moving objects are seen to have an internal 'force' acting in the direction of motion. When an object, such as a ball or a supermarket trolley, is given a push to set it moving, the push is imparted to it. The moving object then has a force in it which, however, gets 'used up' as it slows down and eventually comes to rest. The converse situation 'no motion therefore no force' is also seen to hold. For an object in static equilibrium, such as a book at rest on a table, the downwards force due to the weight of the book may be acknowledged ('because if the table were not there the book would fall') but the table certainly is not considered as exerting a force on the book ('how can it – the table can't move!'). This direct association of force with motion has been identified even in the responses of university-level physics students to mechanics problems. Parallels have also been drawn with ideas such as 'impetus theory' in the history of science.

Investigations of children's ideas about matter and substance have shown that younger children tend to think of matter as 'continuous stuff'. Older children, however, in their attempts to explain processes such as the diffusion of liquids and gases, the dissolution of a solid in a liquid, or changes of state, begin to consider matter as being composed of discrete 'bits', which can be dispersed and brought together again. These 'bits' tend to be seen as having the characteristic properties of the substance itself (for example, they can expand on heating, melt, or burn) and do not therefore represent a scientific atomistic view.

When a substance burns, corrodes or dissolves, young children also believe that matter disappears. As they get older they may acknowledge that a substance continues to exist even if they cannot see it; however it may be considered to be weightless and not to occupy space.

In the domain of light and vision young children see light only as a source (an electric light bulb, the sun) or an effect (a bright patch on the wall). They do not consider light as existing in space or travelling out from the source. Children first construe light as travelling when they consider luminous objects. These are thought of as giving out light, but the light can only travel a certain distance before it loses its strength. Light is also considered to travel further at night when it is dark than in the daytime. The connection children make between light and sight is indirect, with notions of visual rays from the eye to an illuminated object being used to explain what is seen.

These are only a few exemplars of children's conceptions. Other domains which have been studied include energy, electric circuits, heat and temperature, the earth in space, the states of matter, air and air pressure, plant nutrition, inheritance, and the functioning of the human body.

FEATURES OF CHILDREN'S CONCEPTIONS

There is now a general consensus among science educators about a number of features of children's conceptions in science.

1. Children (and adults as well) do have conceptions about the natural world which develop independently of formal science teaching. It is likely that these conceptions have their origins in regularities in children's experiences with physical phenomena (in the playground, kitchen, bath, sandpit, etc.) and they may also be reinforced through everyday language use ('shut the door and keep the cold out'), as well as media images.
2. These naive conceptions are remarkably consistent across different populations, even different countries.
3. Although they may differ significantly from the scientific ideas taught in school, children's conceptions can usually be seen to be coherent within limited ranges of experience. For example the 'motion-implies-force' scheme works well within a world with friction.
4. The conceptions used to make predictions and explain natural phenomena do change in content and in character as children get older.[5] In general, children's conceptions move away from being egocentric (seeing action in the world as an extension of their behaviour), to attributing causal influences to physical systems outside themselves. Younger children's ideas tend to be dominated by perceptual features (sugar disappears when it dissolves), whereas older children construct entities such as 'unseen particles', 'rays of light travelling through space', which play a part in their conceptualizations.

Moreover, older children's conceptions tend to be more generalized, and account for a wider range of phenomena than those of younger children.

5. Children's conceptions have been found to be persistent and to continue to be used into adulthood despite formal instruction. It is this finding which has prompted science educators to look more carefully at the learning that goes on in science classrooms.

CONCEPTUAL UNDERSTANDING IN SCIENCE CLASSROOMS

Large-scale surveys of students' performances in science undertaken in various countries indicate the extent of the difference that can exist between the science that is taught and the level of understanding achieved by students. Furthermore, students' alternative conceptions have been found to persist through schooling, and have even been identified among undergraduate physics students. Such findings raise questions about what is happening in the course of learning programmes.

A number of studies have documented the conceptual understanding of children in classrooms as they follow a course of study. The picture that these studies paint is of learners actively engaged in bringing their prior knowledge to bear in constructing meanings. Thus students' prior conceptions are seen to influence the sense they make and the meanings they construct in science classes, whether from practical activities, text, or discourse.[6] The process of social construction of meanings has also been acknowledged.[7] What students learn in science classrooms is thus seen to depend not only on teaching materials and activities used, but on the conceptions that students bring to the situation. Since students ideas may differ from those being taught it means that the observations they make, the inferences they draw, what they understand from text, may differ from what was intended.

As a consequence of the research into students' prior conceptions, it has been recognized that promoting conceptual understandings of school science involves students in a process of *conceptual change* from prior conceptions towards school science ideas. This view is in contrast with the process of concept learning '*ab initio*', or the development of concepts in stages.

The process of conceptual change is one which takes place not just in students but in the history of science itself. Analyses of the conceptual change process both in students and in the history of science indicate that it is a slow and difficult process with many constraints acting to oppose change.

A number of conditions have been suggested as necessary for change to take place:[8] there needs to be dissatisfaction with existing conceptions in accounting for events, or in the way they fit with other aspects of current theory; a new conception needs to be available which is intelligible and which can be seen to account for events as experienced. Even if an alternative conception satisfies these conditions, it may not be sustained as part of the conceptual apparatus of scientists or students, unless it continues to be seen as useful both in interpreting the range of phenomena the previous conception addressed, and in opening up new ways of seeing things.

In addition it is recognized that other factors may influence whether or not a conceptual change is sustained. The conceptual ecology of the time may play an important role in determining whether a conception is in keeping with other metaphysical or ontological commitments held by scientists or students. An idea 'ahead of its time' may be overlooked or ridiculed, only to be adopted at a later date. The recognition that a conception may not fit with other prevalent beliefs can be a cause of some intellectual and emotional discomfort. Indeed, conceptual change may be potentially threatening to individuals; to change the way the world is construed, even what is accepted as reality itself, involves a process of risk-taking. This close association of affective and cognitive factors in learning has implications for instructional programmes. Students may need a supportive environment, in which an individual's ideas are valued, if new ways of thinking are to be explored, and conceptual change is to take place.

A number of studies have been conducted which attempt to work out the consequences of this view of learning for teaching, and to implement and evaluate conceptual change strategies in science classrooms.[9] There are some commonalities in the types of teaching strategies which have been proposed and implemented:

1. Opportunities are provided for students to make explicit their own conceptions about a particular topic area. Methods suggested for doing this in the classroom have included card-sort tasks, small-group discussions, drawing posters, brainstorming, and holding straw polls. Such activities enable students to clarify their own ideas in the process of sharing them with others. Such processes facilitate the clarification of concepts, and indicate to students that there may be a number of ways of interpreting the same situation.
2. Promoting conceptual conflict: strategies have been used which are designed to promote student dissatisfaction in their current conceptions. Teachers may demonstrate a discrepant event and ask students to consider alternative conceptions of the same event. The use of a discrepant event does not by itself generate an alternative conception. Indeed there is considerable evidence that students may avoid recognizing that the event conflicts at all with their current thinking. Students may select and fit observations to their existing conceptions, or they may claim that the discrepant event is a special case.
3. Consider and evaluate alternative conceptions: rather than using a conflict

strategy to promote conceptual change, some studies present students with an alternative view, and ask them to compare and contrast it with their current conceptions. Analogies play an important part in making new conceptions intelligible to students. In using analogies in teaching, it has been found important to ensure that they are ones which students understand, and that the correspondence between features in the situation and the analogy are made explicit. Students themselves also spontaneously attempt to understand something new by analogy with something with which they are familiar. In the following example, in which three 11-year-old boys were talking with a teacher about a simple circuit, we see a series of analogies being suggested and tried.

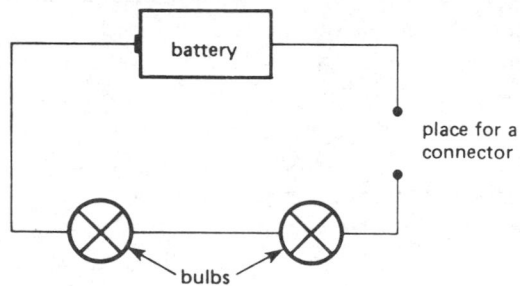

TEACHER: How am I going to get the bulb to light up?

PAPU AND PHILIP: By putting a connector in there, sir.

PAPU: Sir, sir, they will divide, sir.

TEACHER: What will divide?

PAPU: Sir, the electricity, one will go that way, sir, and one will go this way, sir. (Pointing to both ends of the battery) Sir, it will be very dim.

PHILIP: 'Cos there is only one battery.

TEACHER: Will they be as bright as each other, brighter or will one be brighter?

ALL: The same.

PHILIP: Sir, it's divided up the battery.

PAPU: Sir, equal parts of the battery, sir, are divided up into the bulbs, sir, and the other, sir.

This passage indicates that one of the boys at least has the idea that electricity comes out of each end of the battery to light each bulb. This idea causes some difficulty when it is suggested that they add a third bulb to the circuit.

PAPU: Sir, but sir, it would be even dimmer than dimmer.

PHILIP: I think it would be right dim 'cos there's only one battery, and it's got to charge all them up.

PAPU: Sir, it would have to split into thirds.

PAUL: It can't. Don't be silly. It can't split up into thirds because there are only two ways out.

PAPU: Sir, when you turn it on, sir, some of the electricity might go through the bulb, that bulb, sir, and into that bulb, sir.

This example illustrates a number of features of conceptual change; the initial model proposed – that current came out of both ends of the battery – seemed to account for the phenomenon initially. The discrepant event in terms of the introduction of a third bulb clearly promoted some conflict. A different model based on unidirectional flow was tentatively proposed – and checked to see if it gave a better account for the new situation.

4. Opportunities to use new conceptions in a range of situations: long-term accommodation or change in a person's conceptions are not likely to happen if new ideas are not seen as useful. Students need time to appreciate that a new conception can account for the things as well as their previous ideas – they need to re-interpret prior experiences. They may also need to use the conception in new situations to gain confidence in it.

5. Giving opportunities for students to become more aware of their own conceptions and how they change: students tend to think of learning in terms of 'taking in' ideas rather than restructuring the knowledge that they have. Various techniques have therefore been used in classrooms to encourage students to reflect on their own learning, including the use of concept maps, encouraging students to keep personal learning logs, giving opportunities for students to compare their understandings at the beginning and end of a sequence of work.

A number of experimental studies have been undertaken to evaluate the effectiveness of conceptual change strategies in classroom settings in a number of topic areas, and some positive results have been reported.

ON-GOING CONCERNS

Current developments in promoting conceptual understanding in science have drawn attention to the importance of considering learners' prior conceptions in the design of teaching programmes. They have also drawn attention to the fact that learning in science may involve radical change in a learner's conceptions, and this may take place over a long period of time.

Some progress has been made in understanding the parameters involved in promoting conceptual change. However, although some useful models have been proposed, and empirical results obtained, how the process itself can be described and promoted remains an open question, which is currently of interest to developmental psychologists and science educators.[10] Working through the implications for the science curriculum of such a view of learning presents an on-going programme for researchers, teachers and curriculum developers.

REFERENCES

1. Gagné, R. M. (1977) *The Conditions of Learning*, New York: Holt, Rinehart and Winston.
2. Shayer, M. and Adey, P. (1981) *Towards a Science of Science Teaching*, London: Heinemann.
3. Johnson-Laird, P. M. (1983) *Mental Models*, Cambridge: Cambridge University Press.
4. Driver, R., Guesne, E., and Tiberghien, A. (1985) *Children's Ideas in Science*, Milton Keynes: Open University Press.
5. Carey, S. (1985) *Conceptual Change in Childhood*, Cambridge Mass.: The MIT Press.
6. Driver, R. (1983) *The Pupil as Scientist?*, Milton Keynes: Open University Press.
7. Solomon, J. (1987) 'Social influences on the construction of pupils' understanding of science', *Studies in Science Education*, 14: 63–82.
8. Posner, G. J., Strike, K. A., Hewson, P. W., and Gertzog, W. A. (1982) 'Accommodation of a scientific conception: toward a theory of conceptual change', *Science Education*, 66, (2): 211–27.
9. Osborne, R. and Freyberg, P. (1985) *Learning in Science*, Auckland: Heinemann.
10. West, L. H. T. and Pines, A. L. (1985) *Cognitive Structure and Conceptual Change*, Orlando: Academic Press.

6.12

HELPING CHILDREN TO UNDERSTAND TECHNOLOGICAL CHANGE

DAVID LAYTON

INTRODUCTION

Technological change is not a new phenomenon. Its social and economic consequences have exercised scholars from classical antiquity onwards. Their analyses tend to emphasize the interactive nature of the relationship between technology and society, the former being neither an autonomous determinant of the latter, nor a mere response to social demands. All technologies have social origins, and both their manifestations and their impacts on society are mediated by social institutions.

Furthermore, we have no simple ways of measuring the rate and extent of technological change. Some commentators have argued, for example, that the social effects of modern technology, even computers, are unlikely to be as dramatic as those of the introduction of the factory system into eighteenth-century England. Even if such comparative propositions could be established uncontrovertibly, it would not follow that there was no need today to understand technological change. Amongst powerful reasons why this goal needs to be given a high priority on contemporary educational agendas are:

Technology is restructuring the workplace Advanced micro-electronics-based technology and new non-micro-electronic equipment and materials are reshaping dramatically the professional, scientific, and other skill requirements of industry. Indeed, the very concept of 'work' as a lifelong, paid, specific occupation is undergoing change.

Technology is invading the home Lifestyles are increasingly dependent on the availability of technological resources, not only for traditional domestic activities, but also now for the storing, accessing, and processing of many kinds of information.

Technology is transforming values Because it creates new opportunities for action, technological change confronts people with new options from which to choose. Previously unattainable, even unimagined, goals are brought into the realms of possibility, and costs associated with the achievement of other goals are reduced. In so far as values have their origin in individual and social patterns of choice behaviour, technological change is a potent agent for their transformation.

EDUCATIONAL RESPONSES TO TECHNOLOGICAL CHANGE

The profound and pervasive consequences of technological change constitute a major challenge to education. How can we best prepare children for life in a world of flux and uncertainty, in which many of the personal and social problems likely to confront them are without precedent, and in which their occupational opportunities are indeterminate?

Responses to such questions have been given at a variety of levels. In a previous chapter reference has been made to the importance, and present neglect in school curricula, of 'learning to learn' or metacognition.[1] The acquisition of generalizable skills and strategies such as identifying and solving problems, self-appraisal, and reflexivity, 'the secret algorithms of learning', would clearly help students in their attempts to cope with the consequences of rapid technological change.

However, current educational provision has been subjected to more comprehensive criticisms. In secondary education especially, dissatisfaction with the historic bias towards the learning, retention, and regurgitation of delocalized academic knowledge has provoked attempts to rehabilitate the practical and the vocational. The Education for Capability movement, launched in 1979 by the Royal Society of Arts, provides a good illustration. As its Manifesto declares:

> The great majority of learners . . . are destined for a productive life of practical action. They are going to do things, design things, make things, organize things, for the most part in co-operation with other people. They need to improve their *Competence*, by the practice of skills and the use of knowledge; to *Cope* better with their own lives and the problems that confront them and society; to develop their *Creative* abilities; and, above all, to *Co-operate* with other people.

A similar emphasis on more students being able to acquire occupationally useful qualifications, to take greater responsibility for their own lives and learning, to work effectively with others, to solve problems, and to take initiatives, characterizes the Technical and Vocational Education Initiative (TVEI).[2]

From 1987 the British Government established this as a national scheme available to young people aged 14–18 in all maintained schools and colleges, the supporting funds amounting to some £900 million over a ten-year period. Whereas few other countries have gone so far in their encouragement of the vocationalization of secondary education, many of the associated curriculum changes are prevalent elsewhere.

Bridges have been constructed from education into the worlds of industry and commerce, providing both students and teachers with diverse work experiences which, in some instances, are then used to nourish other aspects of the curriculum. In Finland, for example, carefully structured industrial visits, planned in collaboration with scientists in industry, are now a feature of secondary school science education. The incorporation of information technology, both as a subject of study, and as an instrument in the management and pedagogy of the school, is becoming widespread. Thus, manual and technical subjects in French secondary schools were replaced under the Law of December 1985 by a new programme of technology education, including informatics and electronics. The status of traditionally peripheral components of the secondary school curriculum is being elevated; an example is business studies, which is now attracting students of higher abilities than previously, and with them an increased allocation of resources, such as word processors and other modern office equipment. Personal and social education, similarly, has crystallized in some contexts as an identifiable curricular element. Its manifestations can often be interpreted as responses to messages from employers about their requirements for motivated, self-reliant young people, in possession of a range of communication and interpersonal skills. It is vocational, therefore, not in any narrow sense of being job specific, but by fostering personal qualities likely to be of general value irrespective of the kind of work involved.[3]

INTERPRETING EDUCATION RESPONSES TO TECHNOLOGICAL CHANGE

Unquestionably there is much evidence to support the contention that the prime aim of these curriculum changes is a better trained and more adaptable workforce, able to exploit the opportunities presented by new technologies. The institutional channels from which resources have flowed, and the accompanying rhetoric, frequently testify to concerns about the need for improved economic performance in a global struggle for survival. The opening words of the British government's White Paper announcing the extension of TVEI to all schools are typical. 'We live in a world of determined, educated, trained and strongly motivated competitors . . . For the nation . . . survival and success will depend on . . . maintaining an edge over all competition'.

The relationship between education and economic performance is far from simple, however, and this is especially the case with regard to education at school level. Several countries, including Japan, have achieved industrial success on the basis of a school curriculum which emphasizes high attainments by students in traditional, non-vocational subjects. It is by no means self-evident that curriculum innovations, such as those associated with TVEI, will on their own contribute significantly to economic pre-eminence. Their justification on economic grounds is at best partial.[4]

An alternative interpretation views TVEI and similar curricular initiatives from a social standpoint and yields two strands of argument. The first of these connects with Martin Wiener's thesis that Britain, though the first nation to industrialize, never allowed its educational system to come to terms with this. Instead, aristocratic, anti-industrial values have been propagated in schools.[5] Today, therefore, the problem is to elevate the social status of 'knowing how' as against 'knowing that'. Specifically, attitudes towards technology need to be changed to secure its acceptance as a third culture alongside 'arts' and 'sciences' in British society. More generally, practitioner knowledge, what Donald Schön terms 'competence in the indeterminate zones of practice', needs to be acknowledged as important alongside theoretical propositional knowledge. TVEI, with its emphasis on practical capability, can be seen as contributing to these ends.[6]

The second strand to the social argument focuses on the societal impacts of technology. It has been said that the scientist explores and explains what is, but the engineer creates what has never been. Furthermore, technological revolutions are irreversible; no technological change can be uninvented after it has taken place. We need to understand technology, therefore, not so much because we need to solve problems, invent, optimize, and realize solutions, but so that we can control it. As Hans Jonas has stated, 'The lengthened reach of our deeds moves responsibility into the centre of the ethical stage'. *Homo sapiens* might have opened Pandora's box to confront some of the deepest and most profound secrets of nature, but *homo faber* has incorporated himself as an object of technology. Technologies are not mere instrumentalities external to man; they represent interior transformations of consciousness, of the ways in which we see the world and respond to it. From this perspective, an understanding of technological change is necessary as a prophylactic against technological determinism.[7]

A third interpretation of the curriculum changes under review regards technology and, more generally, the competencies that distinguish skilful performance in the domains of practical action, as epistemologically distinct from technical rationality, the dominant epistemology of practice in professional fields such as engineering and medicine, and, to some extent, education. Technical rationality is posited upon a relationship between theory and practice, in which the former is a prior requirement whose application leads to successful problem solving in the latter.

The limitations of this epistemology have been well documented. Problems rarely come to practitioners ready made; they have to be constructed. Furthermore, the usual characteristics of their contexts – 'complexity, uncertainty, instability, uniqueness and value-conflict' – do not match the conditions appropriate to the application of technical rationality. Schön has coined the term 'professional artistry' to describe the kinds of competence which practitioners need in these situations.[8]

The existence of such practitioner knowledge-in-action has long been recognized, although its characteristics are not well explored. Michael Polanyi has written of the tacit knowledge which, for example, enables a psychiatrist to distinguish a true epileptic seizure from similar afflictions. Historians of technology, such as Eugene Ferguson, have emphasized the importance of the mind's eye and non-verbal thought in technological problem solving. The engineer James Nasmyth believed that knowledge of 'the nature and properties of materials must come in through the finger ends'. Clearly intelligent practice in fields such as these is not a simple derivative of scientific and other forms of propositional knowledge.

Viewed in this light, TVEI might be seen as an ambitious attempt to favour 'knowledge-in-action' in the curriculum of secondary schools, and to incorporate into English academic education something of the German *Technik*, with its concerns for optimal effectiveness. Furthermore, such practical capability must be promoted in all students, and not just in those labelled 'non-academic'.

Accepting the interpretation so far, there now arises the disturbing education problem of whether practitioner knowledge-in-action can be taught. Perhaps the school curriculum is as it is because we teach only that which has proved reducible to explicit skills and practices, and has been susceptible to analysis. Clearly practitioner knowledge can be learnt, but the traditions in which it is acquired have been ones of apprenticeship to a master practitioner, sharing and collaborating in the doing, and being subjected to the judgements and criteria immanent in the interactions over an extended period of time. The challenge, therefore, is whether we can incorporate this into a mass system of secondary education with only minimal additional resources.

Finally, from a range of other interpretations of educational responses to technological change, there is a Marxist analysis, which asserts that measures to achieve a more educated and better qualified workforce have little to do with the actual skills needed to perform efficiently all but the highest levels of industrial task. The true function of educational qualifications, it is asserted, is to provide a warrant for the existing hierarchical ordering of social relations in the workplace. At the same time, it is assumed, they also serve as a guarantee of the existence in individuals of personal traits such as reliability, compliance, and conscientiousness deemed necessary for the efficacy of labour in a capital-istic enterprise. As Roy Edgley has argued, 'more education' here means 'less insubordination'.[9]

A comment on this interpretation, as it applies to TVEI, is that, intentionally or not, the initiative contains within it at least the seeds of non-conformity. Its emphasis on the development of initiative, independence, problem-solving skills, and responsibility for one's own learning is, on the face of it, hardly compatible with the production of a docile, subservient labour force. Much depends on the extent to which the educational contexts for the exercise of these attainments are circumscribed. Will school technology be tamed, as David Noble has argued that modern technology in America has been, 'the most potent revolution in social production since the invention of agriculture' becoming a 'means to corporate ends, a vehicle of capitalist domination'?[10] Or can the conjunction of education and industry be liberating, as John Dewey hoped, school life becoming 'more active, more full of immediate meaning, more connected with out-of-school experience', and by implication more per-sonally empowering?[11] To these and other questions raised in this brief review of interpretations of education responses to technological change there are, if not definitive answers, at least suggestive insights derived from empirical evidence of the curriculum enacted in particular institutions.

THE TESTBED OF SCHOOL TECHNOLOGY

It could be argued that it is unfair to single out school technology as a testing-ground for interpretations of educational responses to technological change. It is a curriculum newcomer whose diverse manifestations suggest it still lacks a clear identity and purpose. However, its association with aims such as 'an appreciation and understanding of technological change and its effects on society', and its central place in schemes such as TVEI, make it a prime candidate. Figure 1 summarizes the more familiar versions encountered in secondary schools.

The increasing prevalence of technology in the curriculum might itself be seen as indicative that the educational status of practical capability has been enhanced. To match interpretations against empirical evidence, however, it is necessary to look beyond timetables into organizational settings, content, teach-ing styles, and forms of assessment.[12]

Considering organizational matters first, the epistemological argument that there is a distinctive technological area of learning and experience raises the issue of entitlement. To deny some children access to this area would be inequitable. If the epistemological claim is valid, technology must be for all.

In reality, few schools achieve this goal. Technology is frequently introduced as an optional study, rather than as a core component of the curriculum. With

Figure 1

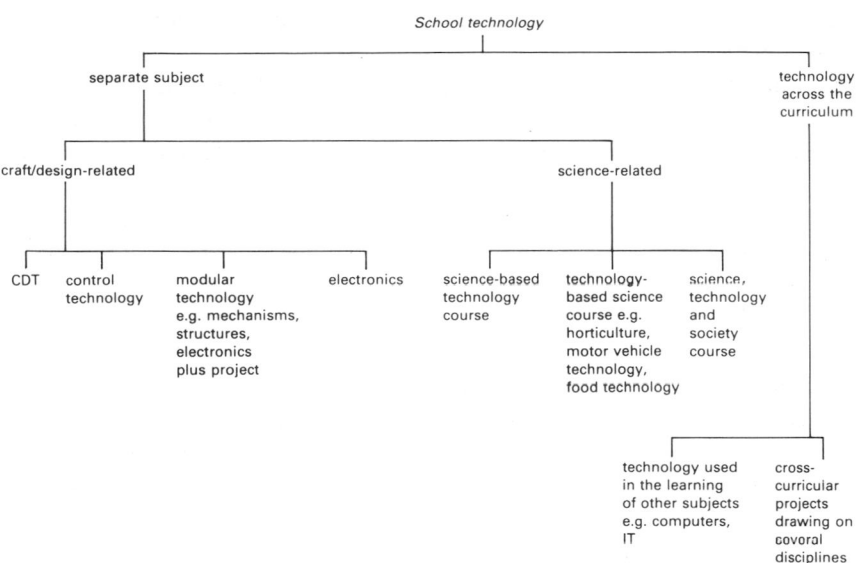

respect to both gender and intellectual ability students on technology courses are often unrepresentative of the population at large. Girls are in a minority, measures to remedy this state of affairs having so far proved ineffectual, whilst in an effort to recruit more able students some courses impose entry requirements including attainments in other subjects, notably physics. By default rather than intent such courses may reinforce existing stereotypes, if not occupational and other hierarchies.

The nature of technology courses – the type of knowledge in evidence, the processes in which students engage, and the values imbued – yields insights. On the knowledge dimension, technology is most frequently bonded to physics, through the incorporation of topics such as structures, mechanisms, electronics, energy, and pneumatics. This limits the contexts for technological problem solving, the interests of girls in particular being neglected. It also endorses a view of technology as *merely* applied sciences, and a relationship between theory and practice in which the former is a necessary prior resource for success in the latter. Manifestly, successful practice is not a stepchild of theory, as both the history of technology and observation of students engaged productively in technological problem solving testify. Many school technology projects are brought to satisfactory conclusions without systematic recourse to codified science.

In relation to values, the evidence is unequivocal. Although values inescapably enter the teaching of technology at many points, from identification of a problem to evaluation of an artefact, and although lip service is paid to 'Social, economic and environmental considerations', few technology courses appear as yet to treat these matters in a deliberate and comprehensive way. This is not to say that values are not communicated to students. By choice of project topic, and in other ways, a message is conveyed that technology is primarily concerned with meeting human needs. Critical exploration of the social processes by which such needs are expressed or diagnosed, and of the ways in which technology can create needs and reshape values, would seem essential to understanding and control of technological change. The implicit messages are unrealistic in other ways, not least in projecting an image of technological work as individualistic. The requirements for external assessment of project work are influential here, overriding what is acknowledged to be the case in industry and commerce, where technological activity is invariably co-operative.

Under the heading of pedagogy, a crucial issue is whether learners are assisted to acquire transferable knowledge and skills, and general problem-solving strategies.[13] Open-ended project work, in the choice of which the student's independence has been consulted, and which offers 'the satisfactions of the specific, the real and the here and now', would seem to hold out much promise. However, the necessary processes of student-teacher negotiation, the unpredictable demands on material resources, the usual lack of any policy for progression in project work throughout the school's curriculum, and the constraints of time and external assessment, all conspire to make difficult the realization of such project work. In some situations, the result is regression to an algorithmic 'design process', emphasizing systematic aspects of technological problem solving. This is as reflective of the complexity of the actual processes of invention as the so-called 'scientific method' is of the ways in which scientists generate new knowledge. It would also seem an inadequate preparation for the future 'adaptable worker', confident in his or her ability to face new occupational challenges by virtue of past successes in technological problem solving in a variety of real-life contexts.

Given that technology as an area of school learning and experience is very new, any conclusive judgement at this stage would be premature. Developments are taking place at a notable rate, for the most part, regrettably, without benefit of any established research base in the teaching and learning of technology. What can be said is that the present situation is one in which, in numerous ways, curriculum reality falls short of what is entailed by claims and intentions about the understanding of technological change.

REFERENCES

1. Nisbet, J. and Shucksmith, J. (1986) *Learning strategies*, London: Routledge & Kegan Paul.
2. Woolhouse, J. (1984) 'The Technical and Vocational Education Initiative', in D. Layton (Ed.) *The Alternative Road. The Rehabilitation of the Practical*, Leeds: Centre for Studies in Science and Mathematics Education, University of Leeds, pp. 133–47.

3. Barnes, D., Johnson, G., Jordan, S., Layton, D., Medway, P., and Yeomans, D. (1987) *The TVEI Curriculum 14–16. An Interim Report Based on Case Studies in Twelve Schools*, London: Manpower Services Commission.
4. Senker, P. (1986) 'The TVEI and economic performance in the United Kingdom: an initial assessment', *Journal of Educational Policy*, 1 (4): 293–303.
5. Wiener, M. (1981) *English Culture and the Decline of the Industrial Spirit, 1850–1980*, Cambridge: Cambridge University Press.
6. Schön, D. (1987) *Educating the Reflective Practitioner*, San Francisco: Jossey-Bass.
7. Jonas, H. (1983) *The Imperative of Responsibility. In Search of an Ethics for the Technological Age*, Chicago: University of Chicago Press.
8. Schön, D. (1983) *The Reflective Practitioner*, London: Temple Smith.
9. Edgley, R. (1977) 'Education for industry', *Educational Research*, 20: (1): 26–32.
10. Noble, D. F. (1979) *America by Design. Science, Technology and the Rise of Corporate Capitalism*, Oxford: Oxford University Press.
11. Wirth, A. G. (1980) *Education in the Technological Society: the Vocational-Liberal Studies Controversy in the Early Twentieth Century*, New York: University Press of America.
12. Barnes *et al.* (1987) op. cit.; Department of Education and Science (1985) *Technology and School Science. An HMI Inquiry*, London: HMSO; St. William's Foundation *Papers 1–18*, *Technology Education Project*, York: St. William's Foundation, 5 College Street, York YO1 2JF.
13. Annett, J. and Sparrow, J. (1985) 'Transfer of training: A review of research and practical implications', *Programmed Learning and Education Technology*, 22 (2): 115–24.

7. TECHNIQUES OF TEACHING AND ASSESSMENT

7.0

INTRODUCTION: TECHNIQUES OF TEACHING AND ASSESSMENT

GORDON KIRK

However teaching is regarded – as the liberation of talent, as an initiation into what is worthwhile, as the reproduction of the social order, or the means of maintaining economic productivity – it involves nurturing the human capacity to learn. The complex and expensive bureaucracy which the management of a public educational service appears to require has a central commitment: it exists to create contexts for the cultivation of skills, understandings, and dispositions. It is inevitable and appropriate, therefore, that this *Handbook* should provide for the consideration of teaching, for, in the public if not the professional mind, education is centrally and essentially concerned with teaching and learning.

As has already been made clear, this section and that immediately preceding it are intended to be complementary. Where Section 6 sought to offer an analysis of teaching, and its impact on learning, on the basis of classroom research and educational psychology, the present section illustrates how general theoretical principles can issue in different techniques of teaching and assessing.

The use of the term 'technique' should be interpreted to denote a distinctive strategy involving a combination of skills rather than a narrowly specific skill or aptitude. Teaching and assessing are complex enterprises which cannot be reduced to a routine set of practical manoeuvres. They are rooted in ideas, beliefs, and theories about what is worth learning, about how learning takes place, about the relevant characteristics of learners, and much else besides. However, in teaching and learning the ideas and theories need to be translatable into action of some kind. That is to say, ideas about teaching need to be sufficiently robust to be workable as ways of helping people to learn; and ideas about assessing need to be workable ways of measuring or describing accurately the achievements of learners. Over the years there has been a proliferation of suggestions about how teaching and assessing might best be conducted. Many of these have been tested in practice and developed to the point where they have become accepted, by no means universally, as having sufficient merit in certain contexts and for certain purposes to be worthy of inclusion in the repertoire of strategies that effective teachers have at their disposal. The present section seeks to offer a portrayal of a number of these, a portrayal that is illuminative rather than persuasive.

There are two clusters of chapters – nine on teaching and five on assessment. The nine teaching techniques portrayed show at least one common feature: they are all recognizable as alternatives to 'traditional' or 'didactic' teaching. Just as education is defined in the public mind as teaching and learning, so teaching is most commonly conceived as an adult imparting knowledge, explaining, or describing to a group of learners. That conception of the teacher as instructor, for all the criticisms it has received in the professional literature, has proved a remarkably sturdy survivor. Indeed, in many countries, even those that consider themselves to be educationally advanced, repeated surveys suggest that the commonest mode of teaching in the schools is the didactic – teachers teaching and pupils listening, or conveying the impression of listening.

Since that mode of teaching is so deeply entrenched in schools and is such a familiar feature of the educational landscape, this section concentrates on those teaching strategies which are thought to confer specific advantages over the traditional in the facilitation of learning. The superiority claimed for these alternative approaches is their learner-centredness: they seek to make learners more active agents in their own development of skills and understandings. A number of sub-themes relating to learner-centredness interweave the nine chapters on teaching strategies: the flexibility in timing and pacing in the learning milieu to take account of the characteristics of individual learners; the collaborative nature of learning; the interactive nature of learning – between teacher and learner, between learners themselves, and between learners and what is to be learned; the dependence on available resources of all kinds; and the creation of a supportive and challenging environment for learning.

Some accounts of learner-centredness in education sometimes reduce the teacher to the role of the impotent and passive spectator. The accounts of teaching provided in this section demonstrate, if such demonstration were required, that the teaching strategies described place the fullest demands on the skill and resourcefulness of the teacher.

It is a truism that assessment is integral to teaching on the grounds that teachers need constantly to check on the effectiveness of their teaching, to determine whether or not learning is taking place and, if necessary, what adjustments to teaching are necessary. Traditionally, formal school assessments have proved inefficient in this respect mainly because they offered global and therefore inadequate and uninformative descriptions of pupils' achievements, or because they were concerned to assess learners in relation to each other rather than in relation to certain standards of achievement. Contemporary developments in assessment seek to address these weaknesses, and the five chapters in this section consider the extent to which assessments can provide more accurate accounts of what pupils have learned, thus providing richer feedback to the teacher and offering pupils themselves – in their own interests and those of employers and others – a fuller description of their achievements. The role that teachers themselves might play in such work is considered in a concluding chapter.

Each of the strategies of teaching and assessment is analysed to make clear its underlying principles; to describe how it operates in practice; to identify potential operational problems and how these might be overcome; and, finally, to suggest criteria which might be used in its evaluation. Collectively, these various portrayals offer those involved in the discussion of the enrichment of teaching and learning a view of alternative possibilities.

TEACHING STYLES AND STRATEGIES IN THE OPEN-PLAN PRIMARY SCHOOL

DEREK SHARPLES

OPEN-PLAN PRIMARY SCHOOLS

Primary schools have traditionally been built as a series of separate rooms, each individually equipped and managed by a designated teacher. Open-plan schools provide a variety of teaching, recreation, and study spaces not based on separation or individuals; they encourage and provide for joint use of space and resources, for practical co-operation between teachers and for flexible grouping of children. 'Open-plan', therefore, applies as much to a sort of teaching as to a sort of accommodation.[1]

Some open-plan schools are simply large open spaces with flexible divisions provided only by furniture and low screens. Others have teaching spaces arranged with walls which have openings, or they have areas which can be opened or closed off with sliding screens. Most open-plan accommodation in this country is of the latter type. Teaching in open-plan areas might remain independent, but usually involves sharing resources and grouping children flexibly. The most common arrangement is for pairs of teachers and their pupils to share practical and teaching areas, but with a substantial degree of independence. In principle such arrangements provide for flexibility of grouping, instruction, and study, although practice is commonly at variance with this.

Open-plan schools were foreshadowed in the monitorial schools of the nineteenth century, which were justified by their economy and their authoritarian principles of instruction. Large open spaces were cheap, easy to manage, and made close supervision possible. Schools developed from this to the 'compartments' of the 1870s. At that time it was assumed that pupils could simply be grouped by age and sex. Individual teachers were increasingly better trained and capable, and so individual enclosed rooms for teaching were a logical development. Later school buildings were influenced by progressive theories, encouraging accommodation to provide for free and active movement by pupils and for a more fluid use of space than was encouraged in enclosed sitting areas dominated by a teacher. Post-war school building in the USA influenced open-plan school building here from the 1970s onward, and recent arguments have supported open-plan schools because of their accessibility to the community, their encouragement of democratic aims and practices, and their suitability for team teaching and co-operative curriculum development. It has been argued that open-plan schools make for efficient expenditure by providing maximum usable space, and they have developed in the UK during falling unit expenditure on schools. There must be some economic advantage in incorporating corridor and circulation space as a part of teaching accommodation.

The first English open-plan school, opened at Finmere, in Oxfordshire, in 1959, involved detailed discussions of teaching preferences and work patterns, of the practical organization of teacher's work, its variety and quality, and of the balance between individual and group activity. Open designs were thought to enhance teaching by opening out classrooms, providing different spaces and opportunities for movement and circulation, and incorporating storage for the increasing range of materials of teaching.[2] All this implies that teaching practices are to an extent affected by teaching accommodation – open planning does not of itself require new approaches, but it certainly makes traditional teaching more difficult.

Enthusiasts see in open-plan designs a commitment to education which is individualized and not conformist; which provides contrasting shapes and sizes of accommodation to appeal to children; where quiet and clean, noisy and dirty areas can be kept separate; where different set-ups can be arranged as appropriate for different curriculum activities; and where spaces can be adapted to individual teachers and pupils. There is a close relationship between the thinking behind open plan and the principles of teaching assumed within it, although that does not determine any particular approach to classroom teaching.[3]

PRINCIPLES AND STRATEGIES OF TEACHING

Thinking about teaching in open-plan schools involves recognizing the principles which the accommodation was designed for, and looking at the practical organization and methods used by the teachers working there.

Three organizational arrangements, or strategies, are commonly found in open-plan classrooms: team teaching, vertical grouping, and various patterns of integration of time and activity.[4] Vertical grouping is adopted as a way of focusing attention on the progress of each individual pupil and as a way of encouraging natural patterns of relationship rather than rigid 'institutional' grouping. Integration provides opportunity for individualized learning, and encourages a variety of work areas where the teacher can provide appropriate materials and resources for the different curriculum activities. Integrating time and breaking away from formal common lesson 'periods' allows teachers to provide for the variety of individual attention spans, interest patterns, and study preferences amongst children.

Co-operative and team teaching is common in open-plan schools. Sharing facilities is the simplest level of co-operation, but a key feature of most open-plan schools is the extent to which they encourage productive dialogue and planning between staff as they co-ordinate their aims, plan related pupil experiences, and arrange for the sharing of resources. This involves teachers sharing responsibility for planning, implementing, and evaluating, and means that they have to strike a balance between co-operative activity and the preservation and development of their own independence.[5]

Two further organizational features – discovery methods and individualized learning – are also common in open-plan schools. Teaching there commonly involves children in work on individually devised tasks, with the assumption that much of the initiative and motivation for learning arises from the pupil. This calls for a shift away from work in enclosed classrooms, from the assumption that the whole pupil groups should be involved in a common activity, from privacy of pupil groups and teachers, and from teaching approaches which rely heavily on instruction from the teacher. In practice the arrangements in open-plan schools range from open and experimental approaches to others which are indistinguishable from those used in traditional classrooms.

Compromise arrangements tend to emerge. For example, 'home' groups may be allocated to individual teachers for a 'core' curriculum, with more co-operative and resource-based teaching in the creative activities and humanities on the periphery. Compromise is also found in the tendency of teachers to claim their own space, using area markers and symbols, erecting screens to mark divisions, and arranging furniture to provide visual or physical boundaries of their individual influence. At their most radical open-plan schools encourage open and active learning, widen social awareness and involvement, and generate commitment to community involvement and relationship.

Whilst it is not possible to generalize, certain arrangements seem to be in accord with the ideals of the enthusiasts for open-plan schools. Such arrangements provide for pupil grouping across ages and abilities, and encourage creative and imaginative room arrangements with use of corridors, grounds, and community facilities. Pupils' work in these areas is active, and noisier than in traditional schools. There is a strong sense of community and mutual support, and childrens' playfulness and natural exuberance is incorporated in the learning approaches.

There are clear statements about the basic learnings required, with specific provision for these in time and place. Learning is guided by plentiful, structured resources enabling guided pupil choice within a flexible organization of work during the day. Teachers are involved in individual and group instruction rather than with whole classes, and they spend considerable time in co-operating and planning with colleagues. Evaluation is closely related to resources and individual progression, and there is little use of evaluation based on comparisons between pupils. There is good display, an openness to visitors, a readiness to change, and a lack of rigidity either in organization or in response.[6]

OPEN-PLAN TEACHING IN PRACTICE

The aims of teachers in open-plan schools do not appear to be different from those in traditional schools, but open-plan schools may attract those whose styles are 'progressive'. It is not easy to classify different teaching styles, but such features as teacher direction, pupil movement, frequency of testing, degrees of integration, levels of questioning and monitoring, direction of study, and the extent of pupil-teacher interaction are amongst the features which seem significant.[7] Open-plan schools might be seen to invite styles which involve much pupil movement, little testing, substantial integration, close monitoring of individuals, and flexible patterns of interaction. Teachers might be directing their pupils through their resources and enquiry methods, developing informal relationships among pupils and teachers, structuring materials and individual assignments, raising many open questions, and promoting a high quality of verbal interaction. (This is although much teacher time in open-plan schools is spent in consultation, and there might well be less interaction with individual pupils than in formal classrooms.) Teaching in open-plan schools assumes team work emphasizing co-operation and influence among colleagues, the management of common resources, arranging flexible groupings, sharing materials, pooling ideas, and exercising leadership in relation to specialist skills. Grouping across age and ability levels is claimed to foster thinking and communication, to develop interpersonal skills, and to benefit reticent pupils – who are less shy of risk there than in larger groups. Such grouping arrangements emphasize the social potential of collaborative approaches.

Time arrangements usually involve some integration, the most common approach being a 'split day' with a focus on skills and large-group work for part of the day and for project, group, or individual work for the other. This approach is perhaps only a weak response to the implications of open-plan schools, and richer varieties of integration involve many activities being pursued

788

at different difficulty levels at the same time, directed both by the teacher and through materials and resources. Integration of this sort, with wide varieties of activity and assignments managed by pupils and simultaneously monitored by the teacher, has a wide variety of interpretations and is encouraged by open-plan schools.

Some teachers have enthusiastically described their rapid change towards 'open' methods involving independence of pupil movement, open availability of materials and resources, rich variety of experiences, individualizing of study and time, and provision of a variety of concurrent individual activities; with teachers collaborating over their responsibilities for planning and managing learning.[8]

PROBLEMS AND SOLUTIONS IN TEACHING STRATEGIES

Problems often emerge between the preferences of teachers and the principles of open and co-operative learning built into the open-plan school. Conflict between principle and practice has been widely reported, and at its most severe leads to classrooms planned to be open but in which teaching is resistantly conventional. Resistance often emerges when accommodation takes no account of differences between teachers or allows for their personal expression. Shared areas in open-plan schools can become no man's lands rather than meeting grounds. Pupil movement can become constrained rather than encouraged, with pupils having their access to resources restricted by teachers who are anxious to manage pupil movement. These problems emerge from teachers' wish for privacy, from the high value they place on personal contact with pupils, and from their concern to direct and practically oversee pupils' work. When pupils do manage their own work they characteristically spend time off task, and they talk. This can be interpreted by teachers as non-work, and leads to heightened concern for them to control and manage the details of pupils' work. In this way the open-plan building can become its own enemy, because it can encourage and amplify the sorts of activities which will generate unease among the teachers working in it.[9]

Pressures for co-operation in teaching conflict with teachers' fondness for individualism. Co-operation calls for a radical departure from the private and individual world of the closed classroom. Teachers often think of many aspects of their work, such as reviewing pupils, planning teaching, designing materials, and so on, as a private activity, and so in open-plan schools they contrive private spaces. This is seen where teachers erect physical barriers to form private areas, and in some schools these barriers become permanent. It is not unusual to find an open-plan school structurally modified to produce conventional spaces in conflict with its original purposes.

More subtly, open-plan schools can be limited in their effect by teaching which does not encourage pupil initiative and freedom. Teacher control is sometimes exercised through such detailed organization and checking of materials and activities that 'open teaching' becomes no more than having children sitting in different spaces, rather than being free to learn responsibly through individual exploration.

Sudden changes to schools can, curiously, destroy the varied and different approaches which might go on within closed classrooms. Insensitive change can perversely lead to the introduction of common timetables, subject specialization, and forms of ability grouping where previously individual teachers had been more 'open' in approach within their individual classrooms. Some teachers have been particularly critical of movement and noise levels in open-plan schools, and have said that these lead to pupil distraction and failure in concentration. Others have suggested that discovery methods and individualized learning are not always easy in open spaces, and that pupils in open-plan schools often seek the quiet and avoidance of distraction which traditional classrooms could provide. Others have suggested that in open-plan schools teachers can be reduced to supervisors and resource managers, often involved in consulting with colleagues rather than being engaged with pupils.

One further problem of teaching strategy in open-plan schools is that those methods which are called for by the building arrangements are the very ones which recent studies have suggested might be less productive of skill achievement than class-instructional procedures. Some studies have certainly indicated higher levels of pupil skill achievements where teaching strategies involve reduced pupil movement, closer direction, frequent monitoring of learning programmes, and teacher oversight of pupil tasks.

SOLUTIONS

A very important problem then for open-plan schools is the conflict between the teaching practices which they are designed to encourage, and the preferences expressed by the teachers working within them. To resolve these difficulties teachers and planners need to clarify together the intentions behind open-plan designs, and to relate these to the preferences of the teachers and to their understanding of the nature of teaching. Open-plan schools demand a radical departure from the customarily accepted ideas that teachers are largely independent and autonomous in their work, and so the full adoption of 'open' teaching within them is rare. To be effective open-plan schools call for the appointment of teachers who are committed to their basic principles, and for staffing and advisory arrangements which will help and support them in developing open teaching. To be successful the teachers need good models and examples, and require support in developing resources for effective practice and management. Account has to be taken of the far-reaching demands which open-plan schools make on teacher co-operation, and all involved must be sensitive to the openness and visibility of practical teaching in such settings. Those involved must be prepared for some loss of privacy and of aspects of teacher autonomy.

This raises issues for teacher education both pre- and in-service. The teacher's task has to be thought out in open and co-operative settings, new roles have to be clarified, and new practical skills of management and co-operation mastered. A mutual respect for these new skills is demanded of teachers co-operating in teaching and managing pupil groups, ordering time and developing resources, monitoring pupil achievement and evaluating professional performance.

Such developments call for a gradual approach to new patterns of teaching for those unaccustomed to it, and for ample provision of materials and resources to enable the adequate development of individual methods. There needs also to be an openness to discussion of concerns amongst the staff involved, including the acceptance of common aims, the co-ordination of practice, and the open sharing of professional experience, including a frank preparedness to discuss problems of discipline, management, relationships, and personal insecurity. Such discussion is an integral part of the task of teaching, and sensitive management and leadership is essential. Each open-plan school has to find ways of preserving a measure of positive autonomy for each teacher, in ways which will preserve individual integrity whilst developing the purposes of the school as a whole. Teachers' anxieties concerning autonomy should be openly discussed, as should their positive development of the use of individual space. Encouraging individual teachers to give up 'ownership' of teaching space and rethinking the ways in which teachers can influence learning in the school are amongst the most difficult problems which must be resolved.

There are very few good case studies published which describe good practice and pupil achievement in open-plan schools, and more are urgently needed. Whilst there is a growing literature, much of it does not examine the principles in practice, or focus on the positive and productive aspects of open-plan schools as against the wide publicity of criticisms directed against them. Teachers in open-plan schools could usefully report on their experience and the ways in which their practice goes beyond that of traditional classrooms, displays a wider range of professional skills, and produces sound pupil achievement beyond performance in basic skill areas. Ideally this will help to redefine 'effective' schooling – a stimulating possibility in the current climate in which the focus is on more restricted areas of performance and skill achievement.

CRITERIA FOR EVALUATING SUCCESS

Open-plan schools might be evaluated in terms of pupil performance, teacher performance, and pupil-teacher interaction. Pupil performance will be of crucial concern in terms of basic skills and understandings, and in coverage of the centrally directed curriculum monitored through benchmarks. Open-plan principles suggest that many other aspects of pupils are important and ought to be monitored in any appraisal: these include pupil responsibility, concentration of time on task, initiative, and mutual co-operation. Evaluations must go beyond descriptions of teaching, examining the detail of professional development and co-operation which are encouraged by open planning. Evaluation should include consideration of the growth of shared understanding and responsibility amongst teachers, their openness to appraisal, and their personal perceptions of the effectiveness of open planning and its management. Effectiveness should be measured by the learning experiences of teachers as well as those of the pupils. The third focus of evaluation must be upon the quality of teacher-pupil interaction, given that open-plan schools provide for this in ways substantially different from traditional schools. The quality of interaction between pupils and with individuals, the level of questioning, and the degree of co-operation between teachers and pupils, particularly in their individual work, are all features to be reviewed.

Evaluations should be conducted at two levels. There is a need for a large-scale evaluation programme covering a wide range of schools and localities. Such an enquiry could give rise to a literature of good practice, guidelines for professional development and growth, models of effective materials, procedures for evaluation, and so on. There is also a need at school level for staff development and teaching review along the lines already discussed.

IMPLICATIONS

The introduction of open-plan schools is a striking instance of the difficulties which can arise from an ill-conceived innovation strategy. At the moment there is perhaps more to be learned from the problems encountered in the innovation process than from any particular educational practice which has been shown to come from open-plan schools themselves. They were introduced with much enthusiasm for their potential adaptability but without a parallel programme of development of personal flexibility and professional openness amongst staff. Teachers have had to work out for themselves an understanding of the implications of open-plan schooling, often without appropriate support, and particularly without adequate understanding of intentions or clarity of the procedures required. Teaching approaches in open-plan schools have often seemed threatening to teachers, and the absence of publications about good practice or the development of effective in-service training alongside sensitive appointment policies has commonly led to schools being inappropriately staffed or supported for the achievement of their intentions.

Open planning directs the educator's attention to the need for clarification and for the close analysis of the relationship between educational practice and the individual interests and understandings of all those who are involved. The interests, attitudes, and skills of teaching staff and the preferences and expectations of parents are clearly more important than the design of any particular teaching space, or of the introduction of any particular teaching methods. The intention of open-plan schools was to enhance learning opportunities through the provision of highly adaptable and sensitive accommodation. The extent to which this is unfulfilled in particular cases is a measure of the inadequate educational thinking and planning that accompanied the accommodation and resource provision. This should be a salutory observation in a context where educational decisions are increasingly being made on the grounds of resources and materials, and where educational practices are being instituted with less than full regard for their implications for the underlying educational understandings of the teachers who will be involved in them.

REFERENCES

1. Bennett, N. *et al.* (1980) *Open-plan Schools*, Slough: NFER.
2. Ministry of Education (1985) *Building bulletin 16. Junior schools*, London: HMSO.
3. Brogden, M. (1983) 'Open plan schools: rhetoric and reality', *School Organization*, 3 (1): 27–41.
4. Hatton, E. J. (1985) 'Team teaching in open plan classrooms: innovation or repression', *School Organization*, 5 (2): 203–9.
5. Pivnick, P. J. (1978) 'Open plan education in US Schools: the educators' view', *Aspects of Education*, 21: 64–74.
6. Meehan, W. (1986) 'The organization and management of an open-plan team teaching primary school', *School Organization*, 6 (2): 185–92.
7. Galton, M. *et al.* (1980) *Inside the Primary Classroom*, London: Routledge & Kegan Paul.
8. Meehan (1986) op. cit.
9. Giacquinta, J. B. and Kazlow, C. (1980) 'The growth and decline of public school innovations: a political study of the open classroom in the United States', *Journal of Curriculum Studies*, 12 (1): 61–73.

MIXED-ABILITY TEACHING IN THE SECONDARY SCHOOL

A. V. KELLY

Like many educational innovations, the introduction of mixed-ability teaching into secondary schools in the United Kingdom in the 1960s and 1970s represented a reaction against the system it was intended to replace – the practice of streaming pupils according to measurements of their academic ability. Research into this latter practice had begun to confirm the view that it was both socially divisive and productive of many inequalities which were regarded as unjustifiable. This research, and the thinking which had both prompted it and been reinforced by it, had already led to demands for the ending of selective forms of secondary education, demands which were acceded to when, in 1965, government circulars required all local education authorities in England and Wales as well as in Scotland to submit proposals for the reorganization of their secondary school provision along comprehensive lines. The introduction of mixed-ability classes into secondary schools was seen by many as a logical extension of that reorganization.

THE MAIN UNDERLYING PRINCIPLES OF THIS INNOVATION

The major factors which led to this innovation and which thus offer the best route to an understanding of its basic principles are to be found in reactions to the practice of streaming.

Streaming had been a natural concomitant of selective secondary education. The Hadow Report of 1926 had brought about the 'decapitation' of the all-age elementary schools, since, on its recommendation, there was established the notion of 'secondary education for all', with a clear division for every child at age 11+ between what was henceforth to be known as primary schooling and education in the new forms of secondary school – grammar schools, technical schools (although these were not common) and the new secondary modern schools.

This change of school for all pupils at the age of 11+ rendered obsolescent the system of grouping by standards which had been the accepted practice in the elementary schools. They could no longer move up from standard to standard when their level of academic attainment seemed to indicate that this was appropriate. At 11+ they all had to move up, or on, whatever their demonstrated levels of attainment or ability. It was suggested, therefore, that the best and most efficient form of class organization, for both primary and secondary schools, would be a system based on grouping by both age and ability. Each age cohort was to be divided into classes according to an assessment of each individual child's ability, and these classes were to flow through the schools like streams.

It should be noted that from the beginning streaming was intended as much to meet the needs of slow learners as to ensure 11+ 'passes' and public examination success for the high academic attainers. Indeed, almost every secondary school used it as a device for creating small 'remedial' classes, of a size to ensure greater attention to individual learning needs than was felt to be necessary for other pupils.

Criticisms of this approach began to be made, however, even before it was fully established. These were directed initially at the policy of selection at 11+ for different forms and levels of secondary education, but were soon extended to embrace also the practice of dividing children according to measured ability within both primary and secondary schools. Such criticism focused on four main issues, and it is from these that the basic principles of mixed-ability grouping can best be gleaned. These issues were: the validity of the testing procedures used to measure children's abilities, the many irrelevant factors which seemed to influence allocations, whether to class or to type of school, the resultant inequalities, and the social divisiveness of this system.

There is no doubt that the decision to implement selective secondary education and streaming within these selective schools was influenced by the confidence at that time being shown and asserted by psychologists both in the concept of intelligence they were using and their ability to measure its levels in schoolchildren. Once this confidence began to be eroded, therefore, it was inevitable that criticism should be directed at a system of schooling and school organization which was based on it. Thus a major principle in the establishment of mixed-ability classes was derived from the manifest inaccuracies of the devices used to produce the measurements of ability upon which selection and streaming were based, and the emergence of new concepts of intelligence and ability.

Associated with this was the growing evidence that the factors which were actually influencing the selection and allocation of pupils to secondary schools and to streamed classes were largely irrelevant to the task for which these schools and classes had been established, namely the proper education of pupils. Research by such people as Brian Jackson[1] and James Douglas[2] suggested that the placement of pupils in streams in the junior school was often linked rather more to factors such as the socio-economic status of the home, ethnic origins, prolonged absences from infant school due to childhood illnesses, and even to the month of the year in which a child had been born, than to academic ability, however defined.

A second underlying principle of mixed-ability grouping, therefore, was the conviction that justice required that educational decisions should be based on factors relevant to children's educational needs and capabilities.

Third, and consequently, there was a fundamental concern with the attainment of educational equality. For the practice of streaming was leading to many inequalities in educational provision, to a failure to achieve what the educational legislation at the end of the Second World War had described as 'education for all according to age, aptitude and ability'. In particular, evidence had emerged in the 1950s, especially through the research studies undertaken in connection with the Early Leaving Report[3] and the Crowther Report,[4] of a massive and disturbing wastage of talent from the education system, with many able children leaving at 15 with no qualifications whatever. This too was attributed to the inadequacies and inequalities of streaming.

Finally, it was claimed both that these forms of selection were socially divisive and that they led not only to inadequacies in the social education of all pupils but also to bad behaviour, disruptiveness, and alienation from the values of education and schooling for many. In short, they were seen as detrimental to the social health of schools. The work of David Hargreaves[5] and Colin Lacey[6] gave strong support to these arguments, indicating, as it did, that there emerged in the lower streams of the upper reaches of secondary schools 'delinquent sub-cultures' bound together by hostility to the school and disaffection from its values. A concern with social education was thus a further underlying principle of mixed-ability grouping.

The case against streaming, then, was a very strong one, and it began to persuade many that the time had come to abandon it in favour of mixed-ability grouping, in order to meet more effectively those principles which its advocates saw as fundamental educational concerns.

THE IMPLEMENTATION OF MIXED-ABILITY TEACHING

In view of this range of fundamental principles and of the consequent ambitions teachers and headteachers had when implementing mixed-ability groupings, it is not surprising that many different versions of it emerged in practice, as stress was placed on different aspects of its underlying philosophy. Some placed the emphasis on the social advantages they expected would be gained. Others were concerned at the possible effects that this innovation might have on academic attainment, especially of the brighter pupils, and on performance in public examinations, and thus they limited their mixed-ability groups to the early years of secondary schooling or to certain subjects only, mathematics, science, and modern languages being the subjects most usually excepted.

Inevitably, therefore, it was on this aspect of the effects of mixed-ability teaching that research concentrated, as attempts were made to discover what effects mixed-ability teaching seemed to have on academic attainment of a traditional kind, as defined especially by achievements in public examinations. The evidence of such research was remarkably inconclusive. For the most part, it seemed to suggest that, contrary to popular belief, streaming seemed to contribute little to academic success and, conversely, the introduction of mixed-ability teaching did little to reduce it. A study of a large comprehensive school at Banbury, for example, led to the claim that 'there was little direct evidence to suggest that high ability pupils were achieving markedly differently in the two systems. For low ability children there was a significant gain in the mixed-ability system compared with the streamed'.[7] Another study went further than this, after conducting a comparative analysis of CSE and GCE results, and recorded 'fewer bottom CSE grades from mixed ability pupils and more top O level grades for mixed ability pupils'.[8]

If the evidence of the effects of mixed-ability teaching on academic attainment was, or could be regarded as, largely inconclusive, no such uncertainty could be claimed for that of its effects on the social development of pupils and on the social health of the school. Indeed, this factor was pointed to as the major reason for a marked improvement in the self-image of the less able pupils, their consequent increased and enhanced response to the school and its curriculum, and a resultant upsurge in their levels of achievement. All the many case studies which emerged during the 1970s of mixed-ability teaching in secondary schools made positive assertions of its social effectiveness.[9] And these assertions were subsequently confirmed by more formal studies.

The picture, then, was one of major gains in the area, of social education and the social climate of the school, but of less certain effects on academic attainment. It was also clear that, in this latter area success depended to a large extent on a complete rethinking of curriculum and of methodology, and that those schools who held their own or even made gains in the academic sphere did so because they were prepared to direct a good deal of care, attention, and time to the major issues and problems which the implementation of mixed-ability teaching entailed. Several such issues emerged and were explored at many different levels.[10]

OPERATIONAL PROBLEMS

One set of problems derived from the overriding concern with the possible effects of mixed-ability groupings on academic achievement.

First, there was the concern with what it might mean for the less able pupil to be extracted from the relative security of the small 'remedial' class, possibly deprived of the individual care and attention such small classes had made possible, and plunged into the bustle of a full-sized mixed-ability class. Concern with 'the dull and the backward' had been a major factor in the introduction of streaming. Many, especially among the ranks of specialist 'remedial' teachers, felt that they would now be correspondingly disadvantaged. Other teachers too were concerned about how they could successfully attend to the needs of these slower learners in their mixed-ability classes. Much attention was thus directed at the problem of how to cater properly for the slow learner in this new system.

At the other end of the ability scale, similar concerns were being aired about the potential impact on the brighter children, especially those dubbed 'gifted'. Would they, indeed could they, be adequately stretched when no longer grouped together with their peers into 'A' stream classes, or even 'express streams'? Again, it was not only critics of the system who were asking this kind of question; it was also asked by the teachers who would be required to solve it. And again much attention was directed at this problem.

In particular, there was concern that such pupils might be inadequately prepared for the public examinations at 16+, that working in a mixed-ability class might make it difficult to ensure proper coverage of examination syllabuses, and especially that the new methods of teaching which these classes clearly demanded might be less effective than traditional, didactic methods in ensuring proper learning. Several different solutions were devised to solve this problem, and they reflect in an interesting way the conceptual confusion which was an important element in the development of mixed-ability teaching. Some schools simply abandoned their mixed-ability classes in the year, or sometimes two years, immediately prior to the public examination. They claimed – with some justification – that by that time the mixed-ability organization of the lower school would have done its work, both in creating greater social cohesion and in enabling some of the former 'B' stream children to improve their levels of academic achievement. Furthermore, it was felt that the 'options' system would ensure, at least to some extent, that grouping by ability at this stage would in practice be largely a matter of realistic self-selection rather than of streaming of a traditional kind with its consequent labelling effects. For the same reasons, other schools introduced 'setting' at this stage – and sometimes even earlier for certain subjects – a regrouping of pupils for the teaching of those subjects or in preparation for those examinations where it was felt that the mixed-ability class was unsuitable. Yet others, adopting a rather more extreme ideological stance, took the view that the examinations should follow the curriculum and its organization rather than directing it, and they thus either entered all their pupils doubly for both CSE and GCE examinations in the same subject to avoid early decisions to divide them by ability, or they negotiated joint syllabuses with examinations boards for both schemes, or new, cross-subject, inter-disciplinary syllabuses to match their new forms of curriculum, or individual forms of examination such as those made possible by the CSE 'Mode 3' regulations.

A second operational problem, which has already been touched on in this discussion of academic achievement, was that of developing new teaching techniques to meet these new forms of grouping. Clearly, whole-class teaching could not be the only approach to a class containing within itself a wide spread of abilities. Secondary teachers, therefore, found themselves having to learn new techniques – working much more with individual pupils, organizing the formation and the teaching of small groups, setting up project work and even, in some cases, exploring the advantages of team-teaching methods.

They also needed to learn about the use of appropriate resources other than basic textbooks. Workcards became the thing and 'death from a thousand workcards' became the danger. Like good primary teachers, however, they were driven to look for resources of all kinds matched to the interests and ability levels of their wide range of pupils. They also quickly discovered the need to store these properly for quick retrieval and, something perhaps quite new in secondary schools, the advantages of sharing such materials with their colleagues.

A further difficulty which faced many teachers in implementing this policy of mixed-ability grouping was the new teacher-pupil relationships which were the inevitable outcome of these new, less formal, ways of working. Old, traditional patterns of authority were eroded; reliance on 'positional' authority, on being *in* authority, was no longer possible. New authority patterns emerged; it became necessary to be *an* authority; 'expert' forms of authority were essential to success in the new context. Furthermore, even 'expert' authority was now to derive more from educational or professional expertise than from subject knowledge, the authority consequent on expertise in a subject study being of little value in a context where many pupils, for whatever reason, did not necessarily value that expertise or the knowledge on which it was based. This was another way in which the introduction of mixed-ability teaching can be seen to reflect not merely a methodological change but a fundamental shift in educational philosophy.

In all of these developments teachers needed a good deal of support, especially in the form of formal in-service training. They did not always receive it, but it is clear that, when they did, its effect was dramatic in improving the quality of their work.

OVERCOMING THE DIFFICULTIES

In the face of these problems of implementation, many schools very sensibly chose to institute these changes step by step, year by year, usually, but not always, beginning by introducing this form of grouping in the first year and letting it grow through the school. Some, whether this was their original intention or not, adopted modified versions of it. As we have seen, it could be, and often has been, confined to the first two or three years of secondary schooling, to the lower school. In many schools it was accompanied from the beginning by schemes for 'setting' pupils, grouping them by ability for certain subjects, perhaps only in certain years. A later modification was the introduction of 'broad-banding', the division of the intake from primary schools into three broad categories, based on ability as measured by whatever testing procedures are used at the age of transfer, with 'mixed-ability' groupings then being created within, but not between, the broad bands. These have been some of the devices by which many schools have endeavoured to overcome, or rather to obviate, some of the operational difficulties listed. They all represent a move away from purer forms of mixed-ability teaching, and, indeed, from purer forms of the equality principle which prompted its institution.

These modified forms are now the rule. Few secondary schools have streamed classes in the lower school, although many favour some kind of 'broad-banding'. Few do not have some kind of grouping by ability in the upper school, usually through a system of 'options'. In part, these modifications must be seen as a response to the difficulties of implementation we have just considered. They must also be viewed, however, in the changed political climate of the years since the mid 1970s, a climate whose main features are an increased emphasis on academic attainment, and on 'standards', defined in a highly traditional way and in largely academic terms, the introduction of notions of teacher accountability to sections of society whose view of education is framed in similar terms, an increased emphasis on vocationalism through such courses as those under the aegis of TVEI and CPVE, and a resultant return to forms, albeit perhaps new forms, of selectivity. This climate, created by current political policies and by the devices adopted to ensure that these policies are reflected in the realities of school curricula, has also led to significant reductions in the levels of professional autonomy open to teachers, and has thus had the effect of inhibiting further developments along the road we have been describing. They have thus not only reinforced the doubts listed earlier about the effect of mixed-ability teaching on academic attainment of a traditional kind, they have also discouraged teachers from attempting any approaches to teaching which would seem to be too different from what society, in the form of parents, governors, politicians, and industrialists, seems to want of them.

CRITERIA OF SUCCESS

How, then, does one judge the effectiveness of this approach? It is particularly difficult to answer this question since it begs the prior question of what the criteria of effectiveness might be. Indeed, lack of clarity over this has bedevilled the movement throughout. If we regard it as merely a methodological device, then the evidence would seem to suggest that, as such, it enhanced the social climate of most schools, and thus the social education of their pupils, while making very little difference to their academic achievements. Some would go further than this and claim positive academic gains, especially for pupils in the middle of the ability range.

If, on the other hand, one sees the approach as more than a methodology, as a development which reflected – for some at least – a deeper philosophical or ideological shift of view in education, even an attempt to rethink and redesign educational provision, and especially the school curriculum, in order to render these more effectively egalitarian and more conducive to universal education in the fullest sense, then one has to acknowledge that in this sense it has failed. For it has not led to many changes of this fundamental kind and, in the face of contrary pressures for the reassertion of traditional concepts of education, and even to approaches of an overtly instrumental, utilitarian, and economically motivated kind, it has given way and accepted modifications which have reduced it to a mere methodology.

Certainly, the mixed-ability approach has resulted in a move away from the most extreme forms of streaming, throughout most of the period of compulsory schooling, and thus to the disappearance of the worst disadvantages research has revealed as resulting from these forms. However, the vision of the educational potential of all pupils and of the desirability of releasing it, which characterized the attempts of many of the pioneers of this movement more than a decade ago, has given way to something rather more mundane. As in so many areas of education, a new philosophy has been viewed as, treated as, and thus has become, merely a methodological device for achieving old ends by new means. Mixed-ability teaching in the secondary school has settled, like so much of educational practice, into a compromise phase. Whether compromise is ever sound policy in educational planning is an open question.

REFERENCES

1. Jackson, B. (1964) *Streaming: An Education System in Miniature*, London: Routledge & Kegan Paul.
2. Douglas, J. W. B. (1964) *The Home and the School*, London: MacGibbon and Kee.
3. Central Advisory Council for Education (1954) *Early Leaving*, London: HMSO.
4. Central Advisory Council for Education (1959) *15 to 18* (The Crowther Report), London: HMSO.
5. Hargreaves, D. H. (1967) *Social Relations in a Secondary School*, London: Routledge & Kegan Paul; Hargreaves, D. H. (1972) *Interpersonal Relations in Education*, London: Routledge & Kegan Paul.
6. Lacey, C. (1970) *Hightown Grammar: The School as a Social System*, Manchester: Manchester University Press.
7. Newbold, D. (1977) *Ability Grouping – The Banbury Enquiry*, Slough: NFER.
8. Postlethwaite, K. and Denton, C. (1978) *Streams for the Future*, London: Pubansco.
9. Davies, R. P. (Ed.) (1975) *Mixed Ability Grouping*, London: Temple-Smith; Kelly, A. V. (Ed.) (1975) *Case Studies in Mixed Ability Teaching*, London: Harper & Row; Wragg, E. C. (Ed.) (1976) *Teaching Mixed Ability Groups*, Newton Abbot, London, North Pomfret, Vancouver: David and Charles.
10. Kelly, A. V. (1974) *Teaching Mixed Ability Classes*, London: Harper & Row; Kelly, A. V. (1978) *Mixed Ability Grouping: Theory and Practice*, London: Harper & Row.

7·3

LEARNING THROUGH DISCUSSION

HELEN COWIE AND JEAN RUDDUCK

THE NATURE OF DISCUSSION

The choice of discussion as a medium of learning may reflect a view of the nature of knowledge; or a set of ideas about the way in which understanding develops; or a view of the importance of fostering intellectual autonomy and social collaboration; or a set of political values about the basis of democracy in our society. In short, discussion-based learning may be justified in terms of intellectual, personal, social, or political purposes. But there is rarely, in practice, a coherent rationale; secondary school teachers may even opt for discussion-based learning because a new examination syllabus requires it. Nor is there, among practitioners, much evidence of a common conception of the distinguishing characteristics of discussion as a form of learning. Bridges[1] is helpful here. He asks what are the necessary and sufficient conditions for saying that people are engaged in the discussion of something, and he offers the following response: a) they are putting forward more than one point of view upon a subject; b) they are at least disposed to examine and to be responsive to the different points of view put forward; with c) the intention of developing their knowledge, understanding, and/or judgement on the matter under discussion. Abercrombie[2] takes a similar view, suggesting that members of a group will 'modify their attitudes or strategies as they see that there are as many alternatives on an issue as there are members of the group'. We would support this position, believing that the central feature of discussion is the opportunity to learn through the expression and exploration of diverse ideas and experiences in co-operative company. Discussion is different from debate, which has been described as the art of getting the best out of a dispute: it is not about winning an argument, but about using the diverse resources available in a group to deepen understanding, sharpen judgement, and extend knowledge.

In some discussions the construction of individual understandings is the main goal, and groups might, for example, be concerned with interpreting a poem or novel, or exploring the experience of bereavement. In a decision-making discussion group, however, whilst the exploration of diverse perspectives remains central to the process of learning, participants must at some point negotiate in order to arrive at a group consensus. Such a group might, for example, be concerned with interpreting the ambiguous evidence of an X-ray in order to make a diagnosis, or with considering the location and design of a community centre in a particular environment. What matters is that the organizers of discussion groups frame the task in ways that support the distinctive potential of learning through discussion.

Bridges also emphasizes the importance of a shared understanding of social and procedural rules. Both should, in his view, reflect such values as reasonableness, orderliness, truthfulness, freedom, equality, and respect for persons.

PROBLEMS OF DEVELOPING DISCUSSION-BASED LEARNING IN THE EDUCATION SYSTEM

... induction into the culture through education, if it is to prepare the young for life as lived, should also partake of the spirit of a forum, of negotiation, of the recreating of meaning. But this conclusion runs counter to traditions of pedagogy that derive from another time, another interpretation of culture, another conception of authority – one that looked at the process of education as a *transmission* of knowledge and values *by* those who knew *to* those who knew less and knew it less expertly.

Jerome Bruner (1986) *Actual Minds, Possible Worlds*, Cambridge, Massachusetts: Harvard University Press.

The problems, for pupils or students and for teachers or tutors, are largely the result of the intensity of their socialization into patterns of behaviour and perceptions of role that support didactic teaching. Traditionally, the aim of education was to instil in pupils the basic skills of literacy and numeracy, a grounding in science, geography, and history, and a sense of the values and morality of society. Teaching methods were expository, pupil-teacher ratios were high, and discipline strict. Talk was tightly controlled by the teacher. The use of the gallery lesson is an illustrative example. Large numbers of children were seated in a galleried classroom in such an arrangement that the teacher could observe them all at once. The content of the lesson was determined by the teacher in advance with the aim of providing material which was 'awakening, interesting, and stimulating' to all the children present: 'Don't forget that you have to work on the mass of minds, and not on a few or on one' was a common dictum. Children spoke only in response to the teacher. The 'catechetical method' was simple and systematic – tell and question, tell

804

and question. Concern was for the learning of a body of knowledge as defined and presented by an expert.

Despite support in principle for progressive methods in education, and despite the accessibility of various curriculum projects initiated in the 1970s, many of which endorsed the use of discussion, in practice the residual impact of the didactic tradition is still relatively strong. The problem in secondary schools, as many observers have suggested (but see Slavin[3] in particular), is that pupils for the most part work independently and are continually in competition with one another for grades, praise, and recognition. Classroom analysis studies have consistently shown that a very high percentage of classroom talk is still teacher talk, and that most questions asked by the teacher are closed questions, designed to test pupils' recall of factual material, and providing little opportunity for pupils to respond in thoughtful ways. Such teaching offers a view of the teacher as one who protects young people from the complexities of knowledge by holding out intellectual safety nets. Bridges observes that it is difficult to conduct discussion in a school or higher education setting if students are afraid to speak freely, if teachers and tutors do not think that students' opinions are worth attention, if students are rudely intolerant of opinions that they dislike, if students feel it improper to express a personal opinion, or if students are not amenable to the influence of reason, evidence, or argument. He adds, wryly, that in our education system 'the conjunction of all five of these conditions is not at all uncommon'. In our view he is somewhat over-pessimistic!

DISCUSSION-BASED LEARNING IN PRACTICE: STRATEGIES AND PROBLEMS

Higher education Concern to promote discussion-based learning in higher education gave rise in the 1970s to projects sponsored by the University Grants Committee and the Nuffield Foundation, and seminars on group work and discussion have become a regular feature of staff development programmes in higher education institutions. The lecture, however, retains its place as the most efficient and economical way of transmitting a common body of knowledge to a large number of students. Seminars (i.e. occasions for learning through discussion in small groups) are justified on various grounds. They are seen as an appropriate way of helping students grasp the structure of the controversies that lie at the heart of knowledge; as a means of helping students to define the individuality of their own minds; as a social anchor in the disturbing drift of large-scale institutional life; and as a way of helping students learn the discourse of their subject – that is to say, students should not just 'do physics' but should learn to talk about it as physicists do. Bligh[4] after surveying research evidence on different teaching approaches used in higher education, concludes that discussion methods are more effective than didactic methods for stimulating thought, for personal social adjustment, and for changing attitudes, and are no worse than the lecture for effectively transmitting information. The latter claim is undoubtedly the most contentious. Jaques[5] also makes strong claims for learning through discussion. He suggests that the aims of higher education are mostly, if not totally, achievable within well-organized discussion groups. The aims, as he lists them, are these: developing imaginative thinking; developing a critical and informed mind; developing an awareness of others' interests and needs; developing a sense of academic rigour; developing a social conscience; developing a willingness to share ideas; and developing an ability and sense of enjoyment in lifelong learning.

Without some confidence in dealing with different perspectives and different points of view, students will not be ready to exploit the distinctive potential of learning through discussion. But it is this capacity that students who come to higher education straight from school often seem to lack, as Entwistle,[6] quoting some American research, points out. He says that first-year higher education students have particular difficulty in moving from the stage of 'dualistic reasoning,' where they believe that there is always a right and a wrong answer to any question, to the stage of 'contextual dualistic reasoning' where they accept the partial validity of different interpretations. The problems of implementing discussion-based learning do not stem exclusively from the student's lack of appropriate experience. As in secondary education, they also stem from the tutor's lack of experience:

> Some lecturers come in and they just start, you know, like another lecture in the seminar.
> I suppose it would be best if the seminar leader spoke as little as possible. That would be ideal, but it just doesn't happen like that.
> One tends to find that the seminar leader will just say: 'Any questions? Right. Well I've got something for you to do'.
> 'We had one this term – he looked so nervous when he was taking us I thought he was going to die of fright'.
> (First-year students interviewed by Rudduck).[7]

Problems are also created by uncertainties about structuring discussion-based learning. The student seminar paper is a common structural device but it does not readily suit the logic of discussion. A poor seminar paper may put pressure on the tutor to conduct a salvage operation, possibly by moving into an instructional role, while a very good seminar paper may place the ideas beyond the reach of other student members of the group – unless they have covered the same group and can take up the issues. The most sustained attempt to work out an alternative structure for discussion-based learning is that of Collier,[8] who developed the 'syndicate' approach – which combines both small-group discussion and the economies of staffing that the lecture offers. A large class is broken down into small working units which meet regularly to work on a specified task with the support of given evidence. The questions that structure the learning task are open in the sense that solutions are not embedded in the resources for students to 'discover'. One or two tutors act as consultants to the small groups, meeting the whole class in a plenary session initially to outline the task, and finally to summarize the thinking and progress of the numerous small groups involved.

Secondary education   The debate about the place of discussion-based learning is currently greatest in relation to the secondary curriculum. Practice is immensely varied but can be roughly sorted into three broad approaches: the discussion of controversial issues; problem solving; and role play.

In the early 1970s, Stenhouse[9] set out to develop a strategy for handling *controversial issues* in the curriculum. He saw discussion as a fitting approach in that it supports the interplay of various perspectives and can permit individual members of a group to arrive at their own understandings in the light of evidence that has been critically examined within the group. In Stenhouse's strategy the teacher acts as a neutral chairperson, and in accepting this role, he or she expresses a procedural commitment not to endorse any single perspective on an issue by disclosing his or her own view. The teacher's authority is not therefore used to assert meaning but to foster the critical search for meaning. In the discussions the teacher acts as a model of an enquirer, as a listener, and as a respectful questioner. The main contributions to discussion made by successful chairpersons were identified as these:

1. asking questions or posing problems;
2. clarifying, or asking group members to clarify, what has been said;
3. summarizing the main trends in discussion;
4. keeping the discussion relevant and progressive;
5. helping the group to use and build on each other's ideas;
6. helping the group to decide on its priorities in discussion;
7. through careful questioning, helping the group towards a habit of reflection and self-criticism.

Aware that teachers would find it difficult to relinquish familiar patterns of classroom behaviour, Stenhouse offered the support of a strong self-monitoring framework. Teachers were encouraged to tape-record discussions and listen to them, bearing in mind questions such as these:

– To what extent, and why, do you interrupt pupils while they are speaking?
– What proportion of silences are interrupted by you?
– Are all the pupils in the discussion group treated with equal respect?
– Do you habitually rephrase and repeat pupils' contributions? If so, what is the effect of this?

- Is there any evidence of pupils looking to you for rewards rather than to the task?
- Do you generally ask questions to which you think you know the answer? If so, what is the effect of this?

The approach offered a clearly articulated code of practice for learning through discussion, but it seems to have been too formal and challenging to command widespread support among secondary teachers. While a teacher acting as chairperson can help pupils to adopt appropriate procedures and roles, he or she may also inhibit the development of talk, and in particular, of talk in a register that pupils can comfortably handle. Barnes and his colleagues explored the use of teacher-less groups which were designed to allow pupils freedom to construct their own meanings.

Working with twelve- to thirteen-year-olds, he set tasks which encouraged pupils to explore ideas tentatively, to confront uncertainties, to try out alternatives in an experimental way, and to deal with differences of opinion – things which have often been discouraged in traditional teacher-centred classrooms. He concluded, after analysing the tape-recorded discussions, that without a teacher present pupil talk is very different. Pupils are more ready to embark on an enquiry using language to test out the limits of knowledge and to re-shape it collaboratively, often drawing on personal experience as a way of making progress in understanding. Since the 1970s, small, teacher-less discussion groups have become more commonly used in relation to *problem solving* in the classroom, particularly, but not exclusively, in the secondary science curriculum. A group of science teachers developing work in biotechnology recently identified the following conditions for effective problem solving:

1. Pupils should feel that they 'own' the problem. Either they must have sufficient freedom to determine for themselves what it is they are investigating and how they should go about it, or the teacher must undertake preparatory work to ensure that they are engaged with the problem;
2. Principles of co-operative group work can define an appropriate structure for the pursuit of the problem-solving task and enable the development of skills of communication, listening, organizing, and decision-making;
3. Pupils should believe that there is some real uncertainty about the solution, and should not think that the teacher always knows the answer, and that different groups are merely competing to find out what is in the teacher's mind.

Role play as a technique for facilitating discussion has also become more widespread in recent years. One form which this can take is the assignment by the teacher of inter-connected roles to members of the discussion group. Roles may include: *presenter* of information on the topic of discussion; *observer* of other participants' responses and behaviour; *mediator* between different points of view; *facilitator* who ensures that all members of the group are taking part. By assigning such roles and carefully briefing group members in the parts which they are to play, teachers can create a structure which encourages all group members to work towards the achievement of group goals together. Roles simulating real-life situations may also be devised to extend pupils' ability to take a perspective which is not necessarily their own. Role-play exercises such as business games and simulations give participants the opportunity to enter into the experience of another person and to understand how that person thinks and feels. This use of role play in discussion groups enables pupils to express a point of view within the safety of the role, and can therefore have a liberating function in the development of discussion-based learning.

Barriers to the development of discussion-based learning that are commonly cited by teachers are the examination system – for its endorsement of conforming, recall-type responses; class size; and the inappropriateness of teaching spaces. But they also acknowledge their own lack of confidence and expertise, and in particular they refer to lingering anxieties about classroom control and about what counts as 'work':

> You know teachers have this kind of block about noise. If it's noisy you can't be doing work.
>
> I feel that maybe I'm not getting on with the work, you know . . . A bit relaxed you know or 'laid back' as they say, and there's not quite the grafting that we should be doing.
>
> I think that society tends to expect qualifications, and because society expects it, that's what the school gives, and because the school gives it, we have to conform, and because we have to conform, there's no discussion work.
> (From interviews with secondary school teachers conducted by the authors, 1987)

Problems commonly experienced by or exhibited by pupils in discussion include the following:

1. dependence on the teacher and reluctance to value the contribution of peers;
2. the habitual dominance of one or two pupils;
3. the breaking up of discussion groups into 'potentially combative' factions that 'argue' from a fixed perspective (these are sometimes gender related);
4. inequality in the acceptance of responsibility for the group's work;
5. the acceptance of an over easy consensus in the face of complex issues or problems;
6. the maintaining of roles defined by labels derived from other classroom activities – for example the pupil who is always laughed at, or ignored, or deferred to; this habit prevents pupils from taking each other's contributions at face value;

7. uncertainty as to whether discussion is 'real work' and can lead to 'proper learning'.

As new public examinations call for more discussion-based learning and collaborative group work, so one powerful set of constraints will diminish, and the legitimacy of discussion is likely to increase, but there will be a need for more definitive guidance on various aspects of discussion, including group size, group formation, and the contribution which discussion-based learning can make to anti-sexist and anti-racist goals in education. Assessment is a major concern, however. Teachers ask: 'Will pupils learn as much in discussion-based learning as in didactic approaches?' and 'Will pupils learn "academically", or is discussion mainly about personal and social development?' Criteria for judgement can relate to both the process of learning and to the products of learning. For instance, teachers may want to judge the success of discussion-based work in terms of such things as engagement, enthusiasm, participation levels, or enjoyment, comparing their pupils' response to discussion-based work with their response to more traditional teaching approaches. Where individual assessment is needed teachers face the challenge of unravelling and evaluating the contribution of each pupil in what is essentially a collaborative activity, and of balancing the quality against the quantity of contributions. They will also have to decide how to grade a pupil who clearly learns from discussion – but who learns by listening rather than by contributing. There is also the problem of knowing how to document the discussion, for research evidence suggests that the quality of interaction may be changed by the presence of a tape-recorder, a video camera or by an unfamiliar adult observer.

Primary education

The idea that learning is something you do sitting in a seat is a highly sophisticated notion and, to a young child, a very peculiar one.

So writes Britton[11] as he advocates the need for schools to build on the processes of learning which have begun at home during the pre-school years – in particular, the process of learning through talk. Informal child-child and child-adult dialogues may not be discussion but it can be argued that, broadly interpreted, they meet some of the criteria for discussion. Conversation, by its nature collaborative, aims at the establishment of shared meanings. The conversational skill of young children seems to have two aspects – learning about interpersonal relationships, and learning about ideas, and Wells[12] argues that the conversational mode seems to be the main way in which children learn during the pre-school years. By the 1960s, the extensive body of research into the relationship between child language and learning (see for example Piaget, Vygotsky, Chomsky, Bruner, Bernstein) was beginning to make an impact on educational practice. The Plowden Report (HMSO 1967) recognized the central role played by language in learning and, later, the Bullock Report (*A Language for Life* 1975) stressed the relationship of language to learning right across the curriculum and throughout pupils' years at school. Bullock recommended far greater use in schools of exploratory talk in group discussion as a means of enabling pupils to draw on their own linguistic resources when relating new knowledge to previous understanding. And Mallett and Newsome[13] document the importance of pupils' working and talking with one another:

> For the young child, such interaction through talk enables him to discover how other people tick, and provides him with a context in which he can reveal and present himself, and thus define and discover himself.

A similar perspective comes from Graves[14] investigating the power of dialogue in relation to writing processes in primary schools in America. He argues that:

> Children discover both new information and the personal satisfaction that goes with knowing something, when they hear the information from their own mouths. Best of all, there is the audience present to mirror the child's knowing.

Graves starts from the premiss that children have something important to say. Through the one-to-one dialogues between teacher and child, where the teacher is in the role of learner about the information which the writer wishes to impart, the young authors discover how to value what they know and how to express it in their own words. Thus, they learn to 'slow down and listen'.

Concern to foster dialogue in the primary classroom was a distinguishing feature of many curriculum projects taken up in the 1970s by schools in this country and abroad. *Man: a course of study*, a project used in Britain and in the USA, where it was developed, gives classroom discussions a central place; here is emphasis on dialogue within the community of learners. However, it is not easy to sustain such initiatives, and HMI pointed out in a survey of middle schools (1983) that 'not many opportunities are provided for extended discussion, for collaborative work in groups, or for the exercise of choice, responsibility and on initiative within the curriculum'. In the late 1980s, a concern to foster discussion-based learning has re-emerged at every level of the education system, and discussion deserves now to be given more systematic attention in courses of initial teacher training.

We end this review with primary education even though we recognize that the formal conditions of discussion are unlikely to be met in the verbal exchanges of younger children. We think it important, however, that 'talk', 'conversation' or 'dialogue' is recognized as an important means of helping young children articulate their own meanings, develop their sense of self, and begin to value learning as an interactive process. As such it is a foundation for more formal discussion-based learning in secondary and higher education.

REFERENCES

1. Bridges, D. (1979) *Education, Democracy and Discussion*, Windsor: NFER Publishing Company.
2. Abercrombie, M. L. J. (1971) *Aims and Techniques of Group Teaching* (2nd edn), Society for Research into Higher Education, Guildford. See also M. L. J. Abercrombie and P. M. Terry (1978) *Talking to Learn*, Guildford: Society for Research into Higher Education.
3. Slavin, R. (1978) *Learning to Co-operate: Co-operating to Learn*, New York: Plenum.
4. Bligh, D. A. (1972) *What's the Use of Lectures?* Harmondsworth: Penguin Books.
5. Jaques, D. (1984) *Learning in Groups*, Beckenham: Croom Helm.
6. Entwistle, N. (1981) *Styles of Teaching and Learning*, London: Wiley.
7. Rudduck, J. (1978) *Learning through Small Group Discussion*, Guildford: Society for Research into Higher Education.
8. Collier, K. G. (1983) *The Management of Peer Group Learning: Syndicate Methods in Higher Education*, Guildford: Society for Research into Higher Education.
9. Stenhouse, L. (1970) *The Humanities Project: an Introduction*, London: Heinemann Books; revised by J. Rudduck (1983), Norwich: University of East Anglia Press.
10. Barnes, D., Britton, J., and Rosen, H. (1969) *Language, the Learner and the School*, Harmondsworth: Penguin Books. See also D. Barnes and F. Todd (1977) *Communication and Learning in Small Groups*, London: Routledge & Kegan Paul.
11. Britton, J. (1970) *Language and Learning*, Harmondsworth: Penguin Books.
12. Wells, G. (1985) *Language Development in the Pre-school Years*, Cambridge: Cambridge University Press.
13. Mallett, M. and Newsome, B. (1977) *Talking, Writing and Learning 8–13*, London: Evans/Methuen Educational.
14. Graves, D. H. (1983) *Writing: Teachers and Children at Work*, London: Heinemann.

7·4

SYNDICATE METHODS

GERALD COLLIER

THE TECHNIQUE IN ACTION

The phrase 'syndicate methods' refers to a particular way of organizing teaching and learning in higher education, in which groups of four to eight students explore as small teams the various aspects of a problem or a topic set by the teaching staff, using appropriate sources, and drawing up a report of their findings. The use of the technique varies quite widely according to academic and institutional circumstances.

Size and composition of syndicates

There is considerable variation: at one end of the spectrum a class of 16 postgraduate students in a polytechnic has been divided into four syndicates of four (author's experience). At the other end a year-group of 64 undergraduates in a university has been divided into eight syndicates of eight.[1] Larger syndicates tend to establish some fairly formal structure, with a chairman and secretary; smaller groups are usually quite informal. In some cases the composition of the groups is determined by student choice, in others by random allocation, in yet others by teaching staff on the basis of such criteria as academic qualifications, sex, and age.

Assignments

There is again considerable variation, the subject area being a major factor. A first essential is that the assignments should have for the students the bite of reality. At one end of the spectrum an assignment may comprise a sequence of tasks revolving round an inherently controversial question having an immediate appeal. For example, student teachers studying the sociology of education may be asked a sequence of questions on the influence of social class background on children's academic attainments. At the other end of the range a medical students' syndicate may be presented with a clinical 'problem box' containing (say) a cassette of a doctor's interview with a patient, a set of slides, and a worksheet posing a series of questions. Equally, a task may involve a fieldwork exercise, a laboratory experiment, an analysis of given documents, and so on.

A second indispensable feature of an assignment is that a substantial range of suitable resources are made readily available to students, with detailed references. The members of a syndicate distribute among themselves the search of the various sources; the number of sources must be sufficient to ensure that a variety of evidence and views are fed into their debates. The sources are selected to provide material at a suitable academic level, with if possible a range of difficulty to cater for both the abler and the less able individuals.

A third essential feature is that an assignment should be so framed as to lead students into the exercise of both their critical and their constructive powers: promoting an examination of the evidence for a given view or a critique of a given concept, or drawing up a plan of action or a balanced judgement of a document.

Tutor's role

With a class of 16 students it is practicable for a tutor to design and run the course on his or her own and to circulate among the groups. In the case of the medical school the construction of the problem boxes is a massive undertaking, occupying lecturers from two or three disciplines, as well as technical staff, over a long period before the course is actually offered. Tutorial supervision is accordingly differently organized: one tutor is made available for each syndicate to advise on the organization of their work – in effect a 'process adviser'; tutors in the academic disciplines involved are accessible as 'resource persons'.

Process and product

Each syndicate works on the task presented: the intensive discussions within the syndicates are the heart of the technique. Each syndicate produces a report, which may be in any appropriate form. Written and oral reports are increasingly being replaced by multimedia presentations, on tape-slide or video. Some provision is made for a review of each assignment in plenary session: it is essential that students should emerge from it with a clear view of the basic concepts and evidence involved. If students are to sit a formal examination this needs to be designed, and known by students to be designed, to assess achievement in the full range of skills in which they are being trained.

UNDERLYING PRINCIPLES

Clarification of purposes

Teachers and students have a considerable range of different aims in their work and it is necessary to be clear as to how syndicate techniques are related to such aims. It is convenient to start from Bloom's celebrated *Taxonomy of Educational Objectives: Handbook I*,[2] using this as 'a relatively concise model for the analysis of educational outcomes in the cognitive area' (as the *Taxonomy* puts it). Under this formulation it is hoped that students will acquire:

1. A reasonable command of the basic facts, concepts, techniques, and authoritative views in the subjects studied.
2. A good understanding or comprehension of the subject discipline, in three respects: a grasp of its conceptual structure; a grasp of its characteristic ways of thinking; and some skills in applying the above in settings directly comparable to those in which they were learned.
3. A capacity for applying the learned material in entirely new settings; or in other words for solving problems of an entirely unfamiliar type using the material learned.
4. A capacity for analysing the structure of a given argument or other communication.
5. Some skill in expressing ideas or feelings in a variety of media.
6. Some skill in the exercise of inventive or creative talents.
7. Some skill in judiciously assessing the quality of given material.

Aims (1) and (2) may cover the whole of a customary didactic course. Aims 3–7, in technical terms known as 'process objectives', are sometimes grouped together under the heading of 'higher-order' skills or competences; objectives (4) and (7) may be referred to jointly as 'powers of critical judgement'. Over and above the first two purposes, (1) and (2), teachers who employ syndicate methods are usually heavily committed to the development of some at least of the higher-order skills.[3]

Depth of study

In higher education in this country 'depth' of study is continually emphasized by teachers and students alike.[4] The meanings attached to the word include an alertness of mind in the student, quick to see alternative explanations of an observation or to probe the assumptions underlying an idea. There is a search for a personal meaning for oneself in the material one is engaged with, accompanied by a recognition of the provisional nature of any 'knowledge'.

This emphasis on depth is paralleled in the work of Marton's team in Sweden.[5] Their investigations of undergraduates' approaches to academic study have yielded certain highly relevant findings.

First, these investigators uncovered a clear distinction between a 'deep approach' to the material studied and a 'surface approach'. A deep approach is characterized by a search for the inner core of the argument, for personal relevance or meaning in the material, and a questioning attitude to it. A surface approach tends to concentrate on memorizing facts or ideas.

It is not difficult to see the close connection between the qualities of mind indicated by 'depth' of study or a 'deep approach', and those of the higher-order skills listed above. For example, the search for the inner core of the argument in an article necessarily involves objectives (4) and (7) – the disen-tangling of the various segments of the article, and the assessing of their relative importance: which parts are crucial, which are entirely irrelevant, which are relevant but of minor importance, which compose the backbone of the argument.

Second, the Swedish workers showed that students usually expect examin-ation questions to test the array of facts that are acquired through a surface approach, and that this is often associated with a sense that there is a vast syllabus to be assimilated if examinations are to be passed, and accordingly a low level of interest and a high level of anxiety. The emphasis on a deep approach must not, however, be taken to imply a dismissal of a surface approach; the careful attention to detail and its commitment to memory are also for certain purposes necessary. What we need is to be clear as to what aims in fact govern our practice and what our priorities among them are to be.

Learning team work

Bloom's *Taxonomy Handbook I* is concerned with cognitive outcomes: it says nothing of such an aim as the training of students in the arts of collaboration with other people. This is a further aim that tends to receive emphasis from users of syndicate methods. A third underlying assumption, then, is the view that if students in a small group are given a task having an inherent interest for them and a suitable variety of source materials, a high degree of interaction is generated, and hence there is a high degree of personal involvement of the students in the work.

Practice in the higher order skills

Fourth, given a series of assignments that conform to the third requirement specified earlier under 'Assignments', the students will be led into practising the higher-order skills to which teachers and students both aspire.

Command of the basic material

Fifth, given an appropriate system for reporting, reviewing, and summarizing the findings of the syndicates after each assignment, students will emerge with a command of the basic knowledge and skills as indicated under objectives (1) and (2).

The tutor's role

Finally it is assumed that the role of the tutor is to generate active involvement of the students in their studies and active engagement in the practice of the skills listed under objectives (3) to (7), without neglecting the mastery of basic material indicated by aims (1) and (2).

PRACTICAL PROBLEMS IN IMPLEMENTATION

Size and composition of the syndicates

Self-selection has the advantage of bringing together individuals who are congenial in spirit and are likely therefore to develop some intimacy of rapport and mutual trust; hence – it is assumed – communication will be more sensitive and disagreement more acceptable and more fruitful. However, self-selection cannot be very dependable if it takes place as soon as the students arrive in the institution; and the less able students may be penalized if the most able and energetic choose one another to form rather high-powered groups. Again, students change and develop during a three-year course and firm friends may drift apart. Some adjustment of group membership may be advisable.

Assignments

The drafting of suitable assignments is a time-consuming business, as is also the searching out of appropriate resource material. Ease of access for students can also present problems: even to keep the material in a 'reserve room' in the library of a large institution can offer a serious disincentive. A judicious choice of paperbacks for purchase and a special arrangement for borrowing under a tutor's name may overcome the problem. In an institution where teaching is based primarily on independent study the problem is likely to be less serious. Photocopying of non-copyright material can be useful.

Some university teachers disapprove of an 'easy access' policy, which they regard as spoon feeding. But those who organize syndicate-based work have their eye on the target of the active use of multiple sources and the hammering out of views among peers: principles on which Newman had memorable things to say a century ago.

The tutor's role

In the case of the medical school mentioned earlier three groups of medical staff are involved. One group is the team that prepares the problem boxes. Second, there is the 'process adviser' tutor, whose role is to help a syndicate in organizing its researches and in overcoming the problem of group dynamics. Third, there are the 'resource persons', whose role is to provide advice on sources and references. In the latter two cases it is easy for the tutor to slip into the didactic role, and it has been found advisable to provide short training courses for the staff involved.[6]

In the case of the courses offered by individual tutors, particularly if they have designed a course on their own, they find themselves in an ambiguous position, having invested considerable effort and time in preparing the course, and then in some degree withdrawing from direct influence, and yet also returning to an overt influence in steering the consolidation of the students' learning after each assignment. As Owen has reported,[7] a tutor can in various ways exert an unfavourable influence on the interaction within the syndicates: he or she can act in collusion with a group to disguise real underlying differences of view among the members; she or he may revert to the dispensing of authoritative comments; or she or he may steer the discussion sternly towards the 'right' answers. Some form of collaboration at staff level is desirable in such circumstances, aided very possibly by a tape-recorder.

Another problem that can arise for tutors derives from their 'exposed' position in relation to their students: in a lecture/seminar course the material is closely controlled by the tutor; in a syndicate-based course students can dig out material from sources unfamiliar to the tutors or from first-hand experience unknown to them, and they need a more thorough and wide-ranging command of their subject to feel at ease.[8]

The students' angle: the influence of examinations

Students too need to learn how to use the method effectively. As Owen notes,[9] they may see the knowledge they are called on to acquire primarily as preparation for an examination testing memorized facts and received views.

They may see the tutor as setting the limits of acceptable knowledge, so that 'giving teachers what they want' takes precedence over genuine enquiry. The expectations built into students by school experience dominated by traditional examinations may be very difficult to overcome.[10] Much depends on the climate of relationships in the institution.[11]

A major implication of the above considerations is that serious attention needs to be paid to the assessment system within which the students are operating. There are two factors: the nature of the assessment, and the students' perception of the assessment. Academic staff appear to be often unaware how much they emphasize objectives (1) and (2) in practice while claiming to develop 'powers of critical judgement'. An academic department in Sweden was horrified to find the extent of the discrepancy between their declared aims and the actual emphasis of their examination papers. It is therefore essential that assessment techniques are used which do in fact test higher-order skills as well as command of the basic material: presenting questions (for example) that can only be answered by applying the learned material in entirely fresh situations (objective (3)), or by analysing the argument of a given text (objective (4)), and assessing the basic material by other means. Second, it is essential that students should be introduced in advance to the changed approach. The new types of questions need to be discussed and their significance for syndicate work explained, and the students given an opportunity for practising those skills in an examination setting.

CRITERIA FOR EVALUATION

There are two areas in particular where academic staff will be looking for indications of success or failure in the use of the method: the effectiveness of the syndicates in generating strong co-operative involvement in academic enquiry; and their effectiveness in developing the students' higher-order skills, over and above their acquiring a command of the basic material.

As regards involvement, a tutor may look for such indicators as evidence of: better attendance at timetabled sessions; a willingness to invest time and energy in the work; a stronger commitment among individual students to the homework required for their discussions; a stronger sense of mutual obligation among the members of a syndicate; an active search for information and wider than prescribed reading in the field studied. All these signs of personal involvement are on record.[12]

As regards the development of higher-order skills, a tutor may look at such indicators as evidence that students are showing a more critical approach to their reading; that they get a stronger sense of the personal meaningfulness of the material; that they appear to gain a fuller appreciation of the rich variety of opinion and experience in the consideration of any complex question and a keener awareness of the provisional nature of current knowledge in the topic studied, with a corresponding rejection of the search for 'right answers'.[13]

Well-grounded evidence is hard to come by. Examination scripts offer solid evidence as to how far students have developed higher-order skills; they also reveal how far students have emancipated themselves from the assumption that the questions were testing achievement under objectives (1) and (2). Video-recordings of syndicate discussions are expensive; audio recordings provide less material but can be useful.

GENERALIZABILITY

The above account describes the use of syndicate-based patterns of teaching in a few specific cases in universities and colleges. We have to ask how far they can be used at the higher education level in other subject areas, in other institutions, or in other societies; and at a less advanced academic level in schools or colleges of further education. These are considered in turn.

Subject area

It will be clear already that the material to be studied must lend itself to differences of view, to differences of interpretation of evidence, to differences of opinion on plans for action. The arts and social science subjects offer endless controversial material, but not so the physical and biological sciences. However, in biology it has been found possible to introduce the element of controversy by presenting students with specimens which require interpretation, for example X-ray photographs or plant anatomy slides.[14] In metallurgy it has proved practicable to base a large part of an undergraduate course on debatable questions: for each basic principle that is to be taught a problem has to be sought out or devised that can be handled by the use of that principle.[15] In medicine the creation of problem boxes has enabled the teaching staff to put a large part of the course into a controversial form. The physical sciences present the greatest difficulty, but distance-learning courses of the Open University type have shown that it is possible to design material that lends itself to debate in any subject.

Other institutions

We have already noted the dependence of a syndicate-based course on the prevailing climate of relationships and the ruling assessment system in an institution. Without a certain tolerance of variety and experiment in the institution it would probably be a hazardous undertaking to set up a syndicate-based course.

820

Other societies

A sympathetic climate, and a tolerance of variety and experiment, are unlikely to be found in a highly authoritarian society, and it would be difficult for a liberal-minded teacher to change the expectations of the students regarding the nature of the knowledge they were to assimilate. On the other hand, the extent of disruption of traditional practices and assumptions in many countries is such that there may well be pockets of opinion that would be favourable to a more collaborative form of learning.

Other levels of education

Primary schools have used small-group techniques for many years, though usually in a less systematic way than has been described here. The practice at the secondary level has been more individualistic and competitive, being geared to a traditional examination system. The gradual evolution of the public examination system in Britain in recent decades has probably made such an approach less difficult to introduce, but the weight of tradition at the university level exerts a powerful controlling force. Even when systematic 'self-study' is advocated, as by the Council for Educational Technology, and the teacher is recommended to provide tutorial guidance to groups of five pupils, the study itself is conceived in purely individual terms.

The Business and Technician Education Council encourages the use of small-group techniques in further education colleges, and the policy documents for the new Certificate of Pre-Vocational Education advocate a fairly extensive use of such methods. But the culture of the education system in this country at post-primary levels is heavily weighted towards an individualistic approach.

REFERENCES

1. Clarke, R. (1983) 'A new medical school in Australia', in G. Collier (Ed.) *The Management of Peer-Group Learning*, Guildford: Society for Research into Higher Education.
2. Bloom, B. S. (Ed.) (1956) *Taxonomy of Educational Objectives Handbook I*, New York: David McKay.
3. Collier (1983) op cit.
4. Group for Research and Innovation in Higher Education (1977) *Breadth and Depth*, London: Nuffield Foundation.
5. Entwistle, N. and Ramsden, P. (1983) *Understanding Student Learning*, London: Croom Helm.
6. Clarke (1983) op. cit.
7. Owen, G. (1983) 'The tutor's role', in Collier (1983) op. cit.
8. Glew, P. (1983) 'Kinesiology: academic aspects of physical education', in Collier (1983) op. cit.
9. Owen (1983) op. cit.
10. Entwistle and Ramsden (1983) op. cit.; Owen (1983) op. cit.; Rodger, I. (1983) 'The influence of examinations', in Collier (1983) op. cit.

11. Chambers, P. (1983) 'The six college project', in Collier (1983) op. cit.; Jaques, D. (1984) *Learning in Groups*, London: Croom Helm.
12. Collier (1983) op. cit.
13. ibid.
14. Miller, C. M. L. and Parlett, M. (1974) *Up to the Mark*, Guildford: Society for Research into Higher Education.
15. Abercrombie, M. L. J. (1979) *Aims and Techniques of Group Teaching*, (4th edn.), Guildford: Society for Research into Higher Education.
16. Boud, D. (Ed.) (1985) *Problem-based Learning in Education for the Professions*, Sydney: Higher Education Research and Development Society of Australasia.

7·5

SIMULATIONS, GAMES, AND ROLE-PLAY

MORRY VAN MENTS

INTRODUCTION – THE NEED FOR EXPERIENTIAL TECHNIQUES

Trends in recent years have highlighted the need for teaching methods other than the traditional 'chalk and talk'. There is an acknowledged need for students to learn how to use information and develop practical learning skills which will be useful to them in later life. The growth of electronic systems of data storage and retrieval has removed the need to retain vast amounts of factual material; it is more important to be able to manipulate this material into new frameworks. The community now expects education to be closely related to the practical world into which the student is sent.

From a conceptual point of view, it is desirable for students to internalize and personalize learning experiences so that they become firmly embedded into skills and behaviour. It is a question of closing the gap between thought and experience. As the saying goes:

I hear and I forget;
I see and I remember;
I do and I understand.

Ideally the rehearsal and experience which are needed should be acquired in real life; in practice this is often difficult or impossible. There may be too little time or not enough resources to try real applications of knowledge; it may be too dangerous or costly.

HISTORY

The use of games for teaching is not new; Plato advocated the use of play in teaching and learning. In war-gaming, which was introduced to train the Prussian army, the disposition of troops was represented on a model battlefield, and the opposing sides manoeuvred their forces under a strict and elaborate set of rules; more recently the Victorians used jigsaw puzzles to instil the elements of geography into children.

What is new is the extremely rapid growth since the early 1960s of gaming and simulation into all areas of teaching, starting in America, but coming into Britain and Europe in the 1970s. Children now play word games in primary school; young children learn the elements of economics by acting as lemonade or ice-cream sellers in computer-based simulations. Language, history, and geography lessons make use of role play and simulations to bring real life to the classroom. Teenagers learn social skills and interview techniques; teachers learn what it is like to be a slow learner or handicapped. Games are used to practise the skills needed to cope with diabetes, old age, and other aspects of life. And of course managers in industry play business games to improve their management skills. The techniques seem to have a universal application.

DEFINITIONS

The following definitions are the most widely accepted:

Simulation

A simulation is a working representation of reality; it may be an abstracted, simplified or accelerated model of the process. It allows students to explore systems where the real thing cannot be used for teaching purposes because it involves other people or is too expensive, complex, dangerous, fast, or slow. Simulations may be tightly or loosely structured but will always be dynamic, as opposed to a model, which is static.

Game

A game is played when one or more players compete or co-operate for pay-offs according to an agreed set of rules. It is designed so that success is achieved by the use of the materials to be learnt. The rules will usually include a scoring system and an indication of the objectives to be achieved. The competition may be against Nature, the player's previous best score, or other players. It is normally highly structured.

Simulation-game

A simulation-game combines the features of a game (competition, co-operation, rules, players) with those of simulation (incorporation of critical features of reality). It is particularly valuable where the real-life situation is competitive.

In practice, these terms are often used interchangeably, and only the context may indicate what the author had in mind. There is also a fuzzy area between these and case studies on the one hand, and experiential exercises on the other.

Role play

A role play involves students in undertaking tasks within the constraints of a particular role. These constraints will consist of the personal characteristics and expectations of the individual, the assumptions and expectations of others, and the boundaries to action placed by the organisational environment. The tasks will usually depend upon verbal communication.

One experienced games designer, Ken Jones,[1] disagrees with these definitions because, he says, they imply that what goes on during a simulation is in some sense not 'real'. As he points out, the feelings, actions, and emotions which develop during the running of a simulation may be every bit as real as they are in the situation from which the simulation is derived. Moreover, in a good simulation the participants are faced with real decisions and even real consequences.

A few examples may illustrate the types of activity covered by the above definitions. They have been chosen to emphasize the point that these techniques are of general application and not restricted to specific academic subjects such as science or geography.

Menu-maker

The players use cards on which are printed various dishes which might be included in a menu. They can exchange these for other cards in the same way that rummy is played. The aim is to produce a good menu, but the precise elements which go to make up a 'good' menu are not defined, and it is the discussion which follows which is the main instrument for learning.

Gorgeous gateaux

Four companies are in competition with one another selling gateaux. Every month they decide how many gateaux to produce and what price to charge. The orders they receive for that month depend on the prices quoted by the other companies. Each company works out its monthly profits and losses. The students learn about the effect of price on sales and profit; they also learn about profit and loss accounts.

Star power

A group of students trade for coloured counters. At the end of the first round they are divided into the more successful and less successful groups. Although it is possible to change groups it is relatively difficult. After a time the less successful groups become frustrated and tensions develop between groups which mirror the tensions in the world between the haves and the have-nots.

Greenham Gypsy site

A sub-committee of Greenham District Council meets to decide the Council's policy with regard to the location and planning of a site for Gypsies. You have a lot of information before you about the Gypsies and their needs, together with plans of the possible sites. After the simulation is over you will have a better understanding of the problems faced by one of the minority sub-cultures in our society, and also of the powers and responsibilities of local authorities.

BaFa BaFa

There are two groups who each develop their own method of communication and culture. Members of the groups visit each other as observers or visitors and try to interact. They quickly discover how important it is to try and understand the other culture in order to survive.

Countdown

You go shopping for a diabetic person. In the shop, on the shelves there are a lot of cards with coloured pictures representing different foodstuffs. When you have chosen the ones you want you go to the checkout where the organizer turns over the cards and totals the number of calories and carbohydrates you have in your shopping basket. You discover the problems of shopping and eating sensibly.

In-tray exercise

You have just taken up a new position and you arrive at your office with only an hour to spare before going on to a conference overseas. You have a pile of letters, memos, telephone messages and notes in the in-tray. You have to decide how to deal with them and which of your colleagues can help you. Time is pressing and someone has left a note to say that your secretary is ill and will not be in until tomorrow.

826

ADVANTAGES AND BENEFITS

A number of attempts have been made to assess the effectiveness of simulation and gaming in the classroom. An article by Barnett[2] gives a good account of the difficulties, together with a bibliography of some attempts. These attempts all founder on the basic problem of dealing with an extremely complex set of variables, none of which can effectively be held constant. The criteria of success are often subjective but are usually taken to be an increase in student activity and enquiries, long-term retention of material used within the exercise, and evidence of increased understanding of the issues involved. What follows in this and subsequent sections therefore can only be the collective practical wisdom of a number of experienced users of games and simulations.

The first thing that strikes anyone using these techniques is the high level of motivation and enjoyment they engender in participants. It is often difficult to stop the activity, and discussions about the outcome can continue for days or even weeks afterwards. This leads therefore to a high degree of retention of what has been learnt. Feedback of the effects of decisions and actions is usually clear and rapid, which produces reinforcement of appropriate behaviour.

Simulation techniques are most effective when dealing with complex situations involving several subject areas. They are particularly good at enabling the student to acquire an emotional, affective understanding which deepens the cognitive, intellectual grasp of the problem, an important element in the learning of social and communication skills.

Finally, the use of simulations and games alters the relationships between students and between students and teacher. The teacher is seen more as a facilitator for the exercise than as a source of knowledge. This change in relationships however leads to the first of the disadvantages.

DISADVANTAGES

To a teacher who is used to absolute control in the classroom and thinks it necessary to have total control over the learning that takes place, running a game or simulation can be a most disturbing experience. Once the exercise has started, the direction, pace, and process are no longer in the hands of the teacher. It is the participants who by their decisions and interactions consciously or unconsciously determine the way in which things go. The teacher can never be sure of how comprehensively the subject of the simulation will be covered, nor what other areas of concern may be revealed. This calls for very special skills and abilities on the part of both teacher and taught, and the success or failure of sessions will depend heavily on the quality of teacher and students. The discussion or debriefing which follows becomes an occasion for exploring everything that has become apparent during the running of the simulation, and an opportunity to draw out attitudes, experience, and knowledge from the students.

Simulations, games, and role-play activities have a voracious appetite for time and resources. It is usually necessary to have space available, with easily moved furniture. Complex exercises may need help from other members of staff. But the really scarce resource is time; time to prepare, time to run, and in particular time to debrief and discuss.

Finally, there is always the problem that simplifications can potentially mislead. Moreover, some of the assumptions and information contributed by other students may unthinkingly and perhaps subconsciously be incorporated into the learning which takes place.

CHOOSING OR DESIGNING GAMES AND SIMULATIONS

Buying an 'off-the-shelf' professionally produced game or simulation enables the teacher to take advantage of the skills of the experienced writer; this is particularly useful in the computer simulations in geography and science subjects. The best packages available are tried and tested and give clear instructions on how to proceed. It is possible to put them into use straight away with few problems and almost guaranteed results. The materials are attractively produced and conveniently packaged. On the other hand they are not tailored specifically for the needs of a particular teacher with a particular class. Most experienced teachers will at some stage want to design their own simulations or games; the following section concentrates therefore on the design aspects, but should be equally useful as the background to choosing.

The process of design is often portrayed as a linear one, beginning with a set of objectives and finishing with the piloting of the exercise and its modification into the final version. This is only a partial truth. In practice, the designer has a mixture of ideas about the material to be taught, the way in which her or his students learn, the available resources, and also an idea or two about existing games or simulations which approximate to her or his needs. There is a constant reappraisal of goals and how they are being approached, and the designer or user is best advised not to worry unduly if the final product varies from the original intent.

It is important when choosing or designing a game or simulation to ensure that the exercise embodies the material to be learnt, and yet can be played by those who have not yet mastered the material; it is equally important to ensure that students really have to use the material in order to play and cannot just, for example, refer to numbers at the corners of cards or on board spaces. The use of inappropriate scoring systems must be avoided; for example, designers often unconsciously reward speed whereas this is not always the characteristic the teacher wishes to emphasize.

Role play is perhaps the most widely used technique, especially in the development of social and managerial skills and the exploration of interpersonal and intragroup communication. It is a powerful tool for changing attitudes and creating empathetic understanding, but it can easily be misdirected and mis-used; these shortcomings can arouse emotional distress and tension in partici-pants, and be counterproductive. Unfortunately very few teachers indeed have ever had any formal training in the use of role play or allied techniques.

Most problems in the use of role play can be avoided if one or two simple principles are grasped.[3] In the first place, role play is not acting; nor is it allied to a theatrical performance. Role players are not being asked to mimic or imitate the characteristics of other persons. They are being asked to deal with a situation in which they accept the constraints of knowledge, skill, physical ability, status, power, and so on appropriate, for example, to the role of an elderly person, a police officer, a plumber, a disabled child, a football fan, or whatever.

There is a spectrum of types of role play ranging from those which enable the role player to practise well-defined skills to those which involve a deep exploration of a person's psychological make-up. The latter overlap with the therapeutic uses of role play and should be avoided in most school contexts.

The first step in writing a role play is to decide on the key roles and subsidiary roles. Having settled these, it is wise to build in spare roles to give flexibility of numbers. The next step is the detailed writing of role descriptions; the foundation for these is a list of key features such as physical attributes, age, sex, status, authority, knowledge, beliefs, and decisions to be made. Only those features essential to the role play need be built in. The circumstances should indicate to each role player what they are going to do, where, with whom, and for how long. Detail should be kept to a minimum as extra information can be introduced within the simulation if necessary. Role descrip-tions are normally written in the second person and in the appropriate language and style.

One danger in all simulations, but particularly those involving role play, is that of a hidden agenda. It is particularly noticeable in sexist or age-related stereotypes. To avoid this, it is wise to write the role description in terms of functions, powers, and constraints rather than physical attributes, leaving the age and sex of the player undefined.

USING GAMES AND SIMULATIONS

Preparation

Simulations can be used as an introduction, a central feature, an interlude, summing up, or revision. Many users or facilitators of games and simulation find it useful to use short warm-up games to start with, particularly with new groups of students.

It is necessary to provide complete documentation for the simulation. Care taken at this stage will be repaid in the smooth running of the exercise. Where possible a degree of verisimilitude is desirable by using headed paper or handwritten 'notes'. On the other hand it is equally desirable to produce written material in forms that are easy to handle, for example on cards or in bound booklets.

Before starting it may be necessary to brief observers. Trainers often feel that this briefing should be kept secret from the other participants. In most cases this is unnecessary. The points to be observed can be agreed between participants and observers; this leads to much more productive debriefing at the end.[4] It is also worth considering the organization of some preliminary interactions between role players so as to get them used to talking to one another.

Running the exercise

Once the exercise is under way it is wisest to allow events to take their course. The tutor should resist the temptation to throw in unexpected events to liven things up unless these are an integral part of the learning experience. If it is essential to influence what is happening, then this can often be done by feeding in material in the context of the game itself.

There are a few classic situations which teachers new to simulations dread although in practice they do not often occur.[5] The first is that of the role players drying up. Players will be put under less stress if they operate simultaneously in small groups rather than in a 'fishbowl' in front of others. Another technique is to give each player a support group to whom he or she can refer if in difficulties. Furthermore it can be beneficial to take time out from the enactment in order to discuss the point that has been reached and how to proceed. This technique of stopping for discussion can also be useful in the case of students not taking the exercise seriously. Their attitude will of course be influenced to a large degree by that of the tutor. It is important that teachers should themselves be committed and enthusiastic about the simulation. Players should be encouraged to react to the situation as a problem to be solved rather than as a platform for histrionics. In practice most simulations and games run very well. The students take them up eagerly and enthusiastically and are sorry when they come to an end. It is after the simulation has been played however that the most important phase is entered into: that of debriefing.

Debriefing

All too often after a game or simulation has been played the organizer and participants relax, agree it was interesting, have a short discussion, and go their ways. Unfortunately they do not realize that the debriefing phase is perhaps the most important part of the process, and the time to clarify issues, and ensure that students take something of value away with them. The most effective way of doing this is by organizing the debriefing in a series of stages.

The first step is to ask the main protagonists for their reactions to the exercise, and to follow this by comment from subsidiary players. The purpose here is to establish what happened, correct misunderstandings, bring out assumptions, and dissipate tensions and anxiety by allowing people to express their feelings. As far as possible the discussion should be conducted with the role players still partly in role, i.e. expressing the problems of the role rather than of the student. In this way one avoids hurting individuals by criticism. At this point the participants can be invited to step out of role, while the facilitator endeavours to analyse interactions, draw out conclusions, and establish sequences, causes, and effects. The use of experiential techniques must always be part of a complete programme or curriculum. It should be the aim at the final stage to extrapolate to the real world and integrate the exercise into the overall teaching strategy.

NEXT STEPS

Teachers who have never tried using simulations and games as part of their repertoire of teaching techniques will usually find that they are worth trying because of the high level of motivation and retention they produce. The techniques are not difficult but they require commitment and enthusiasm to make them work. Reading lists will help, but by far the best introduction to this work is to collaborate with an experienced practitioner, or attend workshops or conferences. An ounce of practical experience and observation is worth a pound of reading. And the experience is an enjoyable one.

REFERENCES

1. Jones, K. (1980) *Simulations: A Handbook for Teachers*, London: Kogan Page.
2. Barnett, T. (1984) 'Evaluation of simulation and gaming: A clarification', *Simulation/Games for Learning*, 14 (4) (Winter 1984): 164–75.

3. van Ments, M. (1983) *The Effective Use of Role-play: A Handbook for Teachers and Trainers,* London: Kogan Page.
4. Rackham, N. and Morgan, T. (1977) *Behaviour Analysis in Training,* London: McGraw Hill.
5. van Ments (1983) op. cit.

COMPUTER-ASSISTED LEARNING

JAMES KULIK and ROBERT BANGERT-DROWNS

The history of education is largely a story of gradual evolution, but education has also had its revolutions. The first use of writing as a teaching tool transformed education many centuries ago when it freed teachers from the constraints of the oral tradition. The invention of the printing press in the fifteenth century also had a revolutionary impact when it opened up vast new storehouses of knowledge to learners. Now, in the twentieth century, the invention of the computer may have equally profound effects. Like writing systems and the printing press, the computer gives teachers and learners new ways to organize, store, retrieve, and transform information. It seems likely therefore that it too will change the way individuals learn and perhaps even the way they think.

Although *computer-assisted learning* is a concept of almost unparalleled importance for education today, it is also a concept that is still developing and that is therefore difficult to bring into focus. Even the terminology of computer-assisted learning is in flux. Terms frequently used to describe this area or parts of it are *computer-assisted instruction, computer-based education, computer-managed instruction, computer-based learning, computer-augmented learning, computer-enriched instruction*, and many others. The term *computer-assisted learning* is used here as a generic term encompassing the full spectrum of computer applications in teaching.

In this chapter we first detail the major types of computer-assisted learning. We then suggest guidelines for teachers to use in evaluating materials for use in computer-assisted learning. We next describe the extent to which computers are now used in various instructional tasks. Finally, we examine results of evaluation studies on computer-assisted learning.

TYPES OF COMPUTER-ASSISTED LEARNING

Early taxonomies usually distinguished between four or five uses of the computer in instruction: drill and practice, tutorials, dialogues, computer-managed instruction, simulations. Recent taxonomies show that educators have a broader conception of the computer's role in teaching. Taylor,[1] for example, described three major uses: tutor, tool, and tutee.

Computer as tutor Computer tutors are characterized by the structure they impose on instruction. Computer tutoring features the nine instructional events as defined by *Gagné*.[2] Like thorough human tutors, computer tutors 1. gain the learner's attention; 2. stimulate the recall of prerequisite information; 3. state the objectives of the instruction; 4. present relevant stimuli; 5. provide guidance; 6. elicit student performance; 7. provide feedback; 8. assess student performance; and 9. ensure the retention and transfer of newly learned information. Computer tutors are most often used to teach specific facts, but some programs teach cognitive skills by modelling the processes that the students are expected to learn. These guided simulations present symbolic representations of real phenomena and direct students to manipulate elements of the representations.

Two common types of computer-assisted learning are actually incomplete forms of computer tutorials. Computer-managed instruction is primarily concerned with the third, fifth, and eighth instructional events (i.e. setting objectives, directing students to instructional resources, and monitoring student performance), but most of the actual instruction takes place without the computer. Similarly, drill-and-practice programs centre on the sixth and seventh instructional events, eliciting student performance and providing feedback. Drill-and-practice programs do not present new information to students.

The addition of *artificial intelligence* to computer-assisted learning promises to be the most important development in computer tutorials. Artificial intelligence is the use of computers to model human cognitive processes. Intelligent computer-assisted instruction programs model the mental processes of learners or of experts in the field. Such programs, for example, can gather information about a student's performance while the student is using a tutorial, test hypotheses about the kinds of mental processes the student is using to answer questions, and then determine instructional strategies on the basis of the learner's activities. Intelligent computer-assisted instruction can also contain large data bases and algorithms that enable the computer to solve problems, make predictions and reasonable guesses, and offer advice to students in a particular content area. If the students could access the intelligent tutor through natural language instead of special programming language, they could 'converse' with the computer as they would with a human expert.

Computer as tool Generally speaking, tools are devices that amplify, extend, or enhance human capacities for work. Computers were first created to serve as powerful calculators. Even now the most common applications of computers are as tools for payroll, inventory, and word processing. When computers are used as tools, we call them cognitive tools because they amplify, extend, or enhance human cognition.

As instructional devices, computer tools are very different from computer tutors. Cognitive tools are the most unstructured and nondirective instructional software. In fact, computer tools are not instructional in the conventional sense of instruction; they do not define specific instructional objectives; nor do they work to produce specific effects in learners. Yet they are instructionally significant in several ways.

Cognitive tools provide resources and opportunities for students to teach themselves. These resources will have different effects on the learning process. First, computer tools perform routine, effort-consuming tasks, such as statistical calculation or data base searches, so that a user's cognitive resources are freed for other higher level tasks.

Second, tools can be constructed to make certain cognitive processes explicit. For example, some word processors now have 'prewriting' and 'postwriting' utilities built in: brainstorming exercises, outliners, word counts, warning flags for ambiguous words, and so on. Users are not required to use these utilities, nor are they systematically taught about their importance to writing, but their presence in the tool makes these activities explicit and more likely to be internalized by the user.

Finally, tools may be designed to facilitate learning by including specific utilities for self-tutoring. Examples are data bases that allow students to create self-tests and check their answers against information in the data base, or word processors that can, on request, perform specific diagnostic evaluations of a document. Other tools could help students to set goals, build relationships between previous knowledge and new knowledge, and monitor their own progress. Thus students can be equipped with specific means to tutor themselves.

Computer as learner   A third type of computer-assisted learning is the use of the computer as a 'tutee'. Proponents of this approach argue that if students learn how to programme computers (i.e. 'teach' computers) to solve difficult problems, they will develop important analytical and problem-solving skills. Seymour Papert, the developer of the programming language *Logo*, is a well-known advocate of this position. In *Mind storms*,[3] his book on children's use of Logo, Papert suggested that programming in Logo could open up *microworlds* for children. In the simulated reality of these worlds, children would learn to manipulate objects, to apply themselves to long-range projects, and to construct new symbol systems.

Instruction that allows students to freely experiment with programming languages is one example of a larger class of instructional approaches called *exploratory environments*. Exploratory environments share some features of tools on the one hand and guided *simulations* on the other. Like simulations, exploratory environments are rule-based systems, and important skills may be gained from manipulating these systems. Like tools, exploratory environments provide resources and opportunities for students to teach themselves. Students are free to make undirected experiments with the many elements of the system.

SOFTWARE SELECTION AND EVALUATION

A computer is only as good as its software because users can interact with a computer only through software. Each piece of software defines a subset of the total population of a computer's possible operations and organizes that subset of operations to make the computer's capacities more easily accessible. Ultimately, the quality of instructional software can be judged only in the local context. The same software may be well suited for one school or classroom but not for another, depending on local resources, characteristics of students, qualifications of teachers, and other factors. However, several general comments can be made about software quality.

Definition of need   Computer-assisted learning must satisfy some instructional need if it is to be appropriately integrated into the curriculum. The more specifically the need can be defined, the more likely it is that appropriate software will be found. A sound definition of instructional purpose should at least characterize the instructional task to be accomplished and the students to be taught.

Some general comments can be made about matches between types of computer-assisted learning, instructional tasks, and student characteristics. Because of their structure, tutorials would be best used when the instructional task is the acquisition of specific factual information, especially when the students using the software do not have well-developed self-instructional skills, or when they have no previous experience with the instructional content. When students have sufficient skills to teach themselves, less structured programs, like exploratory environments and cognitive tools, are appropriate. For teaching specific intellectual skills and cognitive strategies, guided simulations are the software of choice because these kinds of software can provide participatory models for target cognitions.

Pilot-testing instructional software   There is no better way to evaluate the quality of software than by *pilot-testing*. Ideally, the software should be examined by the teachers and the students who are most likely to use it. Some indications of poor software are:

1. Inaccurate, incomplete, or unimportant content.
2. Treatment of computer screen as if it were a book page. Some software

simply displays screen images that are 'turned' like pages by pressing a key on the keyboard. If instruction can be done in so simple a manner, it can be done less expensively, and in some cases more effectively, by simply using a book.

3. Difficult interface. The interface includes those aspects of the computer and its software required for communication between the learner and the computer. Good interfaces can be used 'intuitively' with only minimal training or support from printed materials. Poorly designed interfaces will distract students from the learning process because of their complexity, their inefficiency, and their poor organization.

4. Inadequate attention to motivation. On the one hand, some instructional software can be too game-like. Too much use of special graphics and sound effects can distract students from instructional tasks. On the other hand, some programs can be quite bare and aesthetically unattractive. Good uses of colour, well-conceived graphics and animation to provoke users' imagination, and occasional challenges and surprises are good devices to motivate students.

In short, good instructional software will take advantage of the unique capacities of the computer. Computers can receive and present information in a variety of forms (text, graphs, sound, pictorial representations, etc.) and can allow users to manipulate the information in a variety of ways. Computers can allow quick access to large amounts of data. They can 'interact' with students, presenting stimuli that provoke responses, then providing feedback to the student's response. Effective use of instructional software will creatively employ at least some of these features.

CURRENT USES OF THE COMPUTER IN CLASSROOMS

How do teachers and students actually use computers in the schools? A series of surveys carried out by researchers at Johns Hopkins University in Baltimore, Maryland, provide a good picture of current uses of the computer.[4] The surveys were conducted in the United States, but they show trends in instructional computing that are likely to be important to all industrialized countries.

In the spring of 1985 school teachers reported that micro-computers were being used in schools for approximately equal amounts of time as tutorial devices, as tools, and as devices to be programmed. Across grade levels, about one third of student time on school computers was used in tutorial instruction, one third for programming, and one third for such tool uses of the computer as word processing and problem solving. However, patterns of use differed somewhat with grade level. In elementary school more than half of the computer use involved direct tutorial instruction, and only about 12 per cent of computer use was for programming. In contrast, high school students spent only 16 per cent of their computer time on computer tutorials, and spent half their time on computer programming.

Teachers surveyed by the Johns Hopkins researchers also indicated which types of computer uses they expected to increase and decrease in the future. At both elementary and secondary levels of education, teachers were coming to believe more and more that the best way to use computers in schools was as a tool to help students accomplish concrete tasks – tasks in writing, problem solving, data analysis, and perhaps tasks in other areas. Johns Hopkins researchers noted that researchers and developers were also giving increasing amounts of attention to the use of computers as a tool. It seems very likely therefore that tool uses of computers will grow in importance in schools in the immediate future.

It is important to note that in spite of great gains in the numbers of micro-computers in schools, they are far from accessible to all students in the United States. In 1980 the number of micro-computers in use in elementary and secondary schools in the United States was about 35,000; more than one million micro-computers were in use in 1985. Still, only about 30 per cent of elementary school children and about 20 per cent of all secondary school students were using micro-computers in school in 1985. The average computer user in elementary school spent about 35 minutes per week on the school computers, and the average secondary school user spent about 90 minutes per week. The Johns Hopkins researchers noted that 90 minutes per *day* could profitably be spent on computer-assisted learning in high schools. Very few schools, however, are able to provide that amount of computer access for their students.

EVALUATIONS OF COMPUTER-ASSISTED LEARNING

Educational researchers started to design *evaluation studies* of computer-assisted learning soon after its introduction. In a typical evaluation study, a researcher divided a group of students into an experimental and a control group. Members of the experimental group received part of their instruction with computer assistance, whereas members of the control group received their instruction by conventional teaching methods. At the end of the experiment, the researcher compared performance of experimental and control groups on a common measure. Such evaluation studies have been carried out often enough to give some indication of the value of the major types of computer uses in instruction.

Computer tutoring Extensive reviews on the effectiveness of computer tutoring have been carried out by our research group at the University of Michigan.

Our most recent reports covered a total of 181 studies of computer tutoring: 32 studies in elementary schools, 33 in high schools, 92 in universities and colleges, and 24 in adult education settings. Our approach has been to analyse statistically, or to *meta-analyse*, the accumulated results from these studies in order to reach overall conclusions.[5]

A few of our conclusions seem especially important to note. First, computer tutoring generally has positive effects on students' learning, as measured by achievement examinations. The average effect of computer tutoring in all 181 studies was to raise examination scores by 0.31 standard deviations. That means that computer tutoring raised average performance from the 50th to the 61st percentile.

Second, the size of effects from computer tutoring varies somewhat as a function of type of study. Published articles reported stronger effects than did unpublished dissertations and reports; studies without controls for teacher effects reported stronger results than did studies with controls; and shorter studies reported stronger results than did longer studies. The most important fact to note, however, is that studies of all types reported basically positive effects, even though effects are smaller in some studies than in others.

Third, computer tutoring has generally positive effects on student attitudes towards instruction and on student attitudes towards computers. Seven studies, for example, investigated attitudes towards instruction. The average effect of computer tutoring in these studies was to raise attitude scores by 0.28 standard deviations – a small but significant amount. In 17 studies that examined attitudes towards computers, the average effect of computer tutoring was again small but significant: 0.33 standard deviations. In 29 studies that examined attitudes towards subject matter, however, the average effect of computer tutorials was near zero.

Fourth, computer tutorials reduced the amount of time needed for instruction. The average reduction in instructional time in 28 investigations of this point was 32 per cent. It is clear therefore that computer tutoring can improve student learning and generate positive student attitudes while reducing the amount of time spent in instruction.

Computer Programming   Evaluators have also examined cognitive consequences of learning computer programming. The earliest evaluation studies were carried out by mathematics educators who believed that students who learned to programme the computer to solve algebra or calculus problems gained a deeper understanding of mathematics than did students who solved such problems without using a computer. Empirical studies of the content knowledge of students who wrote computer programs in mathematics classes have not provided support for this belief. Students who wrote programs to solve problems in algebra and calculus and students who solved problems by hand usually performed at about the same level on content examinations in mathematics.

Seymour Papert has suggested on a number of occasions that learning to programme in Logo should produce dramatic effects on children's thinking. Empirical studies have recently been carried out to investigate the validity of such claims. The studies have reported conflicting results, however. Some investigators have reported that learning Logo does not affect students' cognitive skills, whereas others have found some positive effects from experience with Logo. Given the contradictory findings, the need for more and better studies in this area is great.

Computer tools   Evaluators have given relatively little attention to the cognitive and attitudinal consequences of using the computer as a tool for accomplishing school tasks. This neglect is surprising because the use of computer tools is a controversial matter for parents, teachers, and students. Proponents of computer tools believe that their use in mathematics, writing, and other areas helps students to attend more to fundamental concepts in their school work. Opponents of computer tools believe that students learn their lessons less well when they can get computer help while working on them.

Similar controversies arose when electronic calculators first became available for use in mathematics teaching. Some argued that the calculators were 'toys' that had no real place in classrooms. Others argued that such devices helped students by focusing their attention on conceptual problems rather than on mere mechanical calculation. Evaluation studies were carried out on the question at the elementary, secondary, and college levels. The studies demonstrated that student learning often increased when students were allowed to use calculators in working problems in arithmetic or mathematics.

It seems likely that the use of the computer as a calculating device produces similarly positive effects on learners. More direct studies, however, are necessary to test this notion. Also needed are studies that evaluate other tool uses of computers by students. How is student writing affected when students use computers as *word processors*? Does use of computer-based spelling checkers affect spelling abilities? Does use of data banks affect students' reference skills? The variety of types of studies that are needed to evaluate computer tools is great because of the variety of computer tools now available for learners.

CONCLUSION

Computer-assisted learning has been shown to be an effective tool, but the research to date has mainly concentrated on tutorial uses of the computer. This is just one of the ways in which computers can be used instructionally. Over time, educators have realized that other instructional applications of computers are possible, and they have become more sophisticated in matching computer use with instructional tasks and student characteristics. Just as teachers are becoming more sophisticated computer users, the technology itself is becoming more sophisticated. The addition of such features as artificial intelligence, speech synthesis, and voice recognition will make the computer an even more powerful instrument for learning. Exactly what schools of the future will look like is impossible to tell, but it is inevitable that computers will ultimately revolutionize education.

REFERENCES

1. Taylor, R. P. (Ed.) (1980) *The Computer in the School: Tutor, Tool, Tutee*, New York: Teachers College, Columbia University.
2. Gagné, R. M. (1979) *Principles of Instructional Design* (2nd edn), New York: Holt, Rinehart & Winston.
3. Papert, S. (1980) *Mind Storms: Children, Computers, and Powerful Ideas*, New York: Basic Books.
4. Becker, H. J. (1986) *Instructional Uses of School Computers*, Baltimore, Maryland: Johns Hopkins University, Centre for Social Organization of Schools.
5. Kulik, J. A., and Kulik, C.-L. C. (in press) 'Review of recent research literature on computer-based instruction', *Comtemporary Educational Psychology*.

7·7

OPEN LEARNING[1]

GAYE MANWARING

WHAT IS OPEN LEARNING?

A sales assistant in a shop views a videotape describing a new product and then does a computer-marked test to check his knowledge. A nurse phones her tutor a hundred miles away to negotiate an assignment on patient care. An unemployed man works through a study pack on numeracy prior to a weekly tutorial in college. A secretary books time at a local centre to learn word processing on its machine using a self-teach package and help from a supervisor. A group of seven individuals planning to start their own businesses meets to discuss topics on accounts and income tax supported by resource material. Pupils in a classroom work individually on learning packages and other resources, guided and helped by the teacher.

These are all examples of open learning (OL). They are all related to the needs of individuals and they give some freedom to the learners. A general definition of OL is given in the *Open Learning Guides* edited by Roger Lewis.[2]

> 'Open Learning' is a term used to describe courses flexibly designed to meet individual requirements. It is often applied to provision which tries to remove barriers that prevent attendances at more traditional courses, but it also suggests a learner-centred philosophy. Open Learning courses may be offered in a learning centre of some kind or most of the activity may be carried out away from such a centre (e.g. at home). In nearly every case specially prepared or adapted materials are necessary.

Thus OL schemes are learner-centred rather than teacher-centred or institution-centred. Decisions that were taken by the teacher on content and objectives, and decisions controlled by the institution, such as starting date and time, may now be handed over to the learner. In OL there is a desire to increase access to training and education and to make it more available by removing or at least diminishing the barriers often found in conventional courses.[3] Some people believe it is the most effective form of learning and that in time it may become the major way of offering courses.

BARRIERS THAT OL MAY OVERCOME

Traditional education and training is usually organized for groups of learners and key decisions are taken for them. The learners opt into the course and to pre-set conditions. This may be highly suitable if the learners form a homogeneous group or if there can be no negotiation about the objectives and measurement of their achievement. For many other types of learners and types of courses, greater flexibility may be more effective, more efficient, and more appropriate. To achieve greater flexibility, some of the barriers must be removed. Different OL schemes seek to tackle different barriers.

Time and place of study

In conventional courses, classes are run at a set time and place. Many would-be learners, for example those in full-time employment, shift workers, or people confined to home, may find such arrangements inconvenient or impossible to meet. OL can make resources available at any time and the learning can be done at work, at home, at a community centre, or at any venue suitable to the learners.

OL can be used alongside conventional courses. Some schools find OL can resolve timetable clashes. A senior pupil can take both history and geography, one of them by OL packages with tutorial support from a teacher. In the majority of cases, such approaches have produced good exam results and responsible attitudes in the pupils.

Pace and sequence of study

People learn at different rates due to interest, previous knowledge, and ability levels. OL focuses on the needs of individuals and allows both self-pacing and a choice of sequence. An individual's specific retraining needs may lead him to select only certain parts of the syllabus.

Student numbers

Class size may be a controlling factor for traditional courses. Often a minimum enrolment figure must be achieved, and a large number would be beyond resources. OL allows resources to be spread over time and can cope with varying numbers. Small numbers wanting a course out of phase with normal enrolment date need not be disappointed.

Costs

When employers wish to train staff, the costs of travel, accommodation, lost production time and replacement workers usually exceed the course fees. Using OL, training can be brought to the workplace, adding immediate relevance and saving money.

Educational barriers

Conventional courses are planned for the learners; OL courses are planned with them. They negotiate the content, learning methods, and assessment. The skills of negotiating, self-motivation, and communication are a valuable spin-off in addition to the subject aims of the course.

Personal barriers

Some learners find personal commitments and preferences make traditional courses inappropriate. OL may be their only chance to gain a qualification, learn a skill, or find out more about a hobby. OL can provide personal development in a way that allows the clients to feel comfortable.

THE RANGE OF OL

The range of OL schemes includes learning by appointment, flexistudy, resource-based learning, supported self-study, distance learning, correspondence courses, study circles, directed private study and independent study contracts.

Some OL schemes are open to all, others have strict entry requirements. Some allow the learner to choose when and where to study but give no choice of content or sequence. Some have meetings at fixed times and places but allow negotiation of the objectives and methods of study. The dimensions of openness are illustrated in Figure 1, which shows a variety of issues. Any

Figure 1 Dimensions of openness

ISSUE FOR LEARNER	CLOSED	OPEN
Who?	qualified entrants ◄──►	anyone
Where?	study at one centre ◄──►	study at centre, home or work
Length?	fixed start and end ◄──►	flexible start and end times
Attendance?	prescribed times ◄──►	related to individual needs
Method?	set in advance ◄──►	negotiated by learner
Sequence?	A to Z inclusive ◄──►	variable related to needs
Assessment?	formal exams ◄──►	related to learners' objectives
Support?	timetabled ◄──►	on demand

scheme can be plotted on each axis to indicate its degree of openness and flexibility for each item.

The popularity of OL is growing. The greatest publicity has probably been given to major initiatives such as the Open University, the Open Tech Programme, and the Open College. Industry has also taken to OL and it is now used as part of the training for numerous firms such as Austin Rover, Britoil, B & Q, and Scottish Gas. Professional in-service training is moving to OL since staff do not need to be released, and OL is now being used for chiropodists, play leaders, bankers, firemen, teachers, and private investigators. The subjects available for study by OL are increasing and include zookeeping, hazardous cargoes, adult literacy, hairdressing, garage management, and quarrying.

ELEMENTS OF OL

Any course is a complex interacting system; an OL course is more intricate because of the flexibility and the learner control.[4] The elements of OL are summarized in Figure 2, which shows the learner in the centre and six main interacting areas.

There is no unique learning theory for OL and it does not need special treatment. John Bååth[5] considered OL against a number of teaching models and theories including those of Ausubel, Bruner, Gagné, and Rogers. He found all models to be applicable though different elements needed to be stressed.

Thus the learner will depend more on learning resources than in a traditional course; the role of the staff will be to write packages and to provide individual support rather than to lecture; communication and assessment will pose special problems.

Learning materials

Much of the input and content of OL courses usually comes via study materials. They are usually based on print but frequently include other media: video, audio, computer programs, slides, practical kits. The commonest features of OL materials are these:

    aims, goals, objectives, learning outcomes;
    structure: modular, signposting, summaries;
    interaction and feedback;
    friendly informal style;
    attractive presentation and layout.

Many OL packages now exist in a range of subject areas. They can be found in catalogues and databases such as MARIS-NET (Bank House, 1 St. Mary's Street, Ely, Cambs, CB7 4ER). If existing packages meet the criteria

Figure 2 Elements of an OL scheme

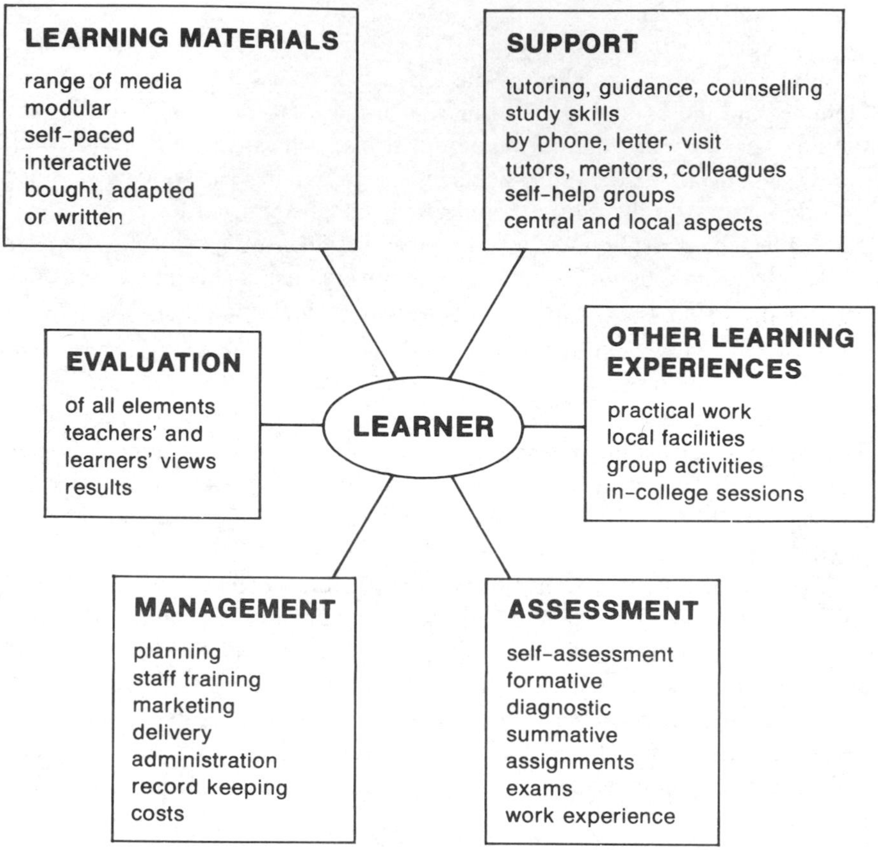

LEARNING MATERIALS	SUPPORT
range of media modular self-paced interactive bought, adapted or written	tutoring, guidance, counselling study skills by phone, letter, visit tutors, mentors, colleagues self-help groups central and local aspects

EVALUATION

of all elements
teachers' and
learners' views
results

LEARNER

OTHER LEARNING EXPERIENCES

practical work
local facilities
group activities
in-college sessions

MANAGEMENT

planning
staff training
marketing
delivery
administration
record keeping
costs

ASSESSMENT

self-assessment
formative
diagnostic
summative
assignments
exams
work experience

of the users, they can be bought and if necessary adapted. This is quicker and cheaper than expecting staff to create packages from scratch.

Student support system

OL is lonely. Schemes usually provide a comprehensive support system in addition to the learning packages, and this may include people, phone calls, meetings, newsletters, and access to facilities. One important aspect is tutor support for individual learners. The role of the tutor includes much more than advice on subject matter. It involves study skills, encouragement, guidance, interpretation of regulations, arranging equipment, etc. The needs of the learner often vary during a course; there may be problems with study skills at the start, loss of motivation in the middle, panic before the final exam. Links with other learners and other supporters such as line supervisor, friend, or neighbour can all help to monitor progress and give encouragement.

Other learning experiences

Not all OL takes place alone or via packages or with a tutor. Learners may be brought together for group activities such as discussion, lectures, team work, and role play. Getting groups of learners to share ideas and discuss problems is very valuable. Some courses include visits, practical work, carrying out investigations, or learning to operate a machine as essential course experience.

Assessment

Part of the philosophy of OL is to give greater responsibility to the learner, so most OL packages have frequent self-assessment items allowing learners to check their performance. Feedback is essential. Sometimes short questions are given with answers, or more open-ended activities are followed by detailed comments. Checklists and performance criteria linked to objectives are also useful.

Often the learners will ask their tutor for detailed comment on their work. Diagnostic assessment helps the learner and tutor to select the best route or choice of materials and to find out what remedial work is needed.

Some OL courses lead to standard external exams, others depend on tutor-marked assignments, projects, or observation of performance. If a learner sends in work for accreditation, the question of authenticity must be raised and some checking system developed.

Management

The management of an OL course is more complex than a traditional one because flexibility means the learners are at different points or on different routes.[6] The learners and the tutors are rarely all together in one place at one time and this creates communication problems. The planning stage involves deciding where flexibility is appropriate, organizing the production of materials and support systems, and probably training the staff in new skills. (SCOTTSU International located at the Dundee Campus of the Northern College of Education has training courses available by distance learning.)

Much of the mechanics of OL is concerned with the delivery system. This includes getting packages to the learner (by post, van, computer, resource centre, telephone, broadcast), providing support (letter, phone, visit, audiotape, electronic mail) and getting assignments and queries back from students.

Once a course is running it needs a good administrative secretary and an effective record-keeping system relating to learners (materials received, fees, assignments completed, rate of progress, problems) to tutors (comments on students' work, turn-round time), and to materials (stock control, updating).

Evaluation

Evaluation is essential in any course so that necessary changes can be made to improve it. OL is very public, and tangible learning packages can be scrutinized in detail. All aspects including course structure, allocation of staff time, administrative and support systems, costs, and marketing strategies need to be monitored. Staff, students, and employers all provide valuable evidence, and the whole range of techniques such as interviews, questionnaires, observation, and analysis of results is available.

PROBLEMS AND SOLUTIONS

Open learning is not intrinsically different from other methods of learning, but the emphasis on certain aspects and the resulting problems are special. They tend to be extreme versions of the types of problems found in traditional education, but solutions can be found.

Isolation

Open learners have all the problems and anxieties of other learners with additional ones. For many, it is a long time since they studied and they need help in time management, setting priorities, writing clearly, reading with a purpose, finding resources, recognizing when to ask a tutor for help. A large number of open learners have jobs and personal commitments and studying must be fitted into an already busy lifestyle. This needs a high level of motivation from the learner plus support from the others involved, whether workmates, family, or friends. For such busy people, OL may be the only possible way of making training a realistic possibility.

If class meetings are rare or non-existent, lack of peer contact can be demotivating. It may help to organize self-help groups so that learners can share ideas and compare frustrations. These groups can operate at a general level on the problems of OL, or can be related to a specific part of a particular course. It is of course difficult to find people at the same point in the course because individual rates of work and personal priorities vary. Encouraging learners to talk to anyone at all can help to overcome the feeling of loneliness. Providing an informal coffee room in an OL centre can be a real life-line for some students.

Phone calls, newsletters, even postcards can make learners feel less alone. Most tutors spend a lot of time building up a supportive relationship even if they rarely meet face-to-face. Tutors and students in some courses exchange photographs, personal details, and audiotapes, and became almost like pen pals.

Tutors suffer from loneliness too, especially in distance-learning courses where they may not work in the central institution offering the course. If a tutor does not hear from a student she or he does not know if the student is working well or is totally stumped. Instead of a pile of assignments all arriving to be marked at one time, they arrive over a period of months. This means that grading based on criteria rather than comparison between students is essential and OL courses tend towards criterion-referenced assessment. Just as self-help groups are important to open learners, they are useful to tutors too so that they can maintain standards, discuss issues, and keep up to date with course developments.

Motivation and self discipline

OL is not an easy option for any learner. Although it may have practical advantages it can be a hard slog and initial motivation can soon wane. Study can easily be edged over by other commitments. Even in an OL centre, self-pacing can become slower and slower. It helps if, before embarking on an OL course, a prospective student has realistic expectations of how much regular work is required and how easy it will be to get access to essential items such as a telephone or a computer. Learners should be encouraged to make regular reviews of progress and compare them with their immediate and long-term goals. Deadlines for the completion of modules or assignments may be set by the institution or negotiated with the learner. Deadlines can help to provide a target, but only if they are realistic. If a student is having a busy time at work or home, the OL will suffer first, and new deadlines will have to be set. Insisting that all learners work at a predetermined rate is unrealistic and counterproductive, and takes away some of their responsibility.

If a course takes a long time, the use of interim rewards can boost morale. Some courses give a credit for each topic as it is passed and these are accumulated to earn the final award. Another major way to maintain motivation and keep students working is to link the course to their job or promotion prospects. Relevance of examples and assignments is very important.

There are times when learners wish to drop out without completing their course. The reasons are variable and often complex and may relate to changed personal priorities. If a learner gets a new job, moves house, or has a change in family circumstances, the OL course may seem less necessary or less relevant. The part of the course already completed may have been very useful so dropouts should not be classed as failures. If students wish to withdraw from a course the tutor should help them examine their reasons. If the problems are temporary, an extension of time could be negotiated and the students could re-enter at a later date. If the problem is intractable or the students no longer want the course, the tutor's role is to ease the exit procedures leaving the students feeling comfortable with their decision.

Attitudes

OL requires a change in attitude by all involved. There is a shift in responsibility from the teacher to the learner. The teacher becomes less of an instructor and guardian of knowledge and moves towards being a guide and organizer of resources. The learners control some aspects of their learning and make decisions about what, where, and when to study. The OL approach is based on androgogy rather than pedagogy, and it accepts that individuals bring with them a vast amount of knowledge and experience that makes a positive contribution to learning. Equally learners can offer each other a great deal, and they need to learn to respect the views of learners as well as teachers. This change in role may need deliberate clarification.[7] Some courses issue a written contract between learners and institutions so that roles and responsibilities are clearly identified.

The attitude of the senior management of the institution must also change.[8] OL means fitting atypical starting times, new conditions of service, and unusual patterns of assessment into existing procedures designed to cope with traditional courses. There will be far-reaching implications.[9] There may be less use of classrooms, but higher phone and postal bills. Staff work loads may become caseloads rather than timetables. There will be contentious issues, such as who owns the copyright of OL materials, and who pays the phone bill when a tutor phones a student from home. If an institution wants to go into OL these topics will need to be discussed at length by staff, management, unions, local authorities, government departments, and validating bodies.

THE ADVANTAGES OF OL

The OL approach is very generalizable and can be applied to many situations: schools, colleges, on-the-job training, study at home. It can respond to the needs of learners, employers, and society. Its success is measured in part by the growth and development of OL in all spheres of education and training. OL reaches new clients and opens up new opportunities for providers.

A providing institution can measure the success of its OL schemes by asking key questions.

Do materials and support systems meet stated criteria?

Do the materials sell?

Do plenty of learners enrol on the courses?

Do learners come back for more?

Do the learners achieve success in exams, etc?

There are disadvantages with OL, but they can be overcome. If OL is given proper resources and a positive image it will succeed and could become a mainstream educational activity. It can be rewarding for staff, students, and institutions.

NOTES

1. I would like to thank Wyllie Fyfe for helpful comments on the manuscript.
2. Lewis, R. (Ed.) (1984–6) *Open Learning Guides* (a series of eight guides), London: Council for Educational Technology.
3. Daniel, J. S., Stroud, M. A., and Thompson, J. R. (Eds.) (1982) *Learning at a Distance: A World Perspective*, Edmonton: Athabasca University/ICCE; Holmberg, B. (1985) *Status and Trends of Distance Education* (2nd edn), Lund: Lector; Percival, F. and Ellington, H. (Eds.) (1981) 'Distance learning and evaluation', *Aspects of Educational Technology* XV, London: Kogan Page; Percival, F., Craig, D., and Buglass, D. (Eds.) (1987) 'Flexible learning systems', *Aspects of Educational Technology* XX, London: Kogan Page; Sewart, D., Keegan, D., and Holmberg, B. (Eds.) (1983) *Distance Education: International Perspectives*, London: Croom Helm; Scottish Education Department (1982) *Distance no Object: Examples of Open Learning in Scotland*, Edinburgh: HMSO.
4. Lewis, R., Faulkner, M., Mainwaring, G., and Paine, N. (1985) *Open Learning Toolkit*, Cambridge: National Extension College.
5. Bååth, J. A. (1979) *Correspondence Education in the Light of a Number of Contemporary Teaching Models*, Malmö: LiberHermods.
6. Birch, D. and Latcham, J. (1984) *Managing Open Learning*, Blagdon: Further Education Staff College; Further Education Unit (1986) *Implementing Open Learning in Local Authority Institutions*, FEU and the Open Tech Unit.
7. Boud, D. (Ed.) (1981) *Developing Student Autonomy in Learning*, London: Kogan Page.
8. Lewis, R. (1986) *The Schools Guide to Open Learning*, Cambridge: National Extension College (Scottish edition also available).
9. FEU (1986) op. cit.

7.8

CO-OPERATIVE
TEACHING

MARION BLYTHMAN AND DONNIE MACLEOD

Schools and in particular classrooms are extremely private places in that it is rare, in the normal course of events, to spend any significant periods of time either working alongside or observing other teachers at their work.[1]

BACKGROUND

Following on the problems created by the raising of the school leaving age in 1972, the assumptions underpinning the policies, provision, and practice for pupils with learning difficulties were coming under fire. The claims were that the impetus to provide 'remedial' education was humanitarian; the reality was that, as Sally Tomlinson said, it was a safety valve for the normal education system allowing it 'to function unimpeded by these troublesome deviants'.[2] The claim was that comprehensive schools were for all; the reality was that more and more pupils were being disconnected from ordinary class and segregated either in separate classes or through the pervasive system of withdrawal.

Many teachers, committed to the ideal of comprehensive education, were becoming uneasy and more conscious of the contradictions between the claims that were being made and the realities of their day-to-day practice. Questions were being asked: Was it appropriate or helpful to view learning difficulties from a pupil deficit perspective, i.e. the pupil is the 'problem', the response 'a remedy'? Was it acceptable, within the comprehensive system, that the remedial teacher should have the sole responsibility for the increasingly large numbers of pupils labelled 'remedial'? Was it acceptable, within the comprehensive system, to offer to large numbers of pupils a narrow restricted programme quite divorced from the mainstream curriculum? How could a system of segregation and withdrawal be justified, when, in effect, these same procedures made any return to the mainstream difficult if not impossible? Was there any mechanism by which class and subject teachers could get advice, support and help to meet the range of needs found in a mixed ability class?

Co-operative teaching is a new feature in Scottish schools, developed on a set of principles largely derived from the HMI Progress Report, 'The education of pupils with learning difficulties in primary and secondary schools in Scotland', published in 1978.[3] This radical report, which drew on the evidence of an extensive survey, reflected the emerging concerns, analysed the problems, and pinpointed many of the issues which were surfacing at different levels about policy and practice for pupils with learning difficulties.

The Report pointed out that the traditional definition of remedial education was far too limited since, as the survey confirmed, the range of learning difficulties was much wider than had hitherto been acknowledged and 'far more children suffered from learning difficulties than ever saw a remedial teacher'. The curriculum and how it is presented was seen as one of the main causes of learning difficulty. Therefore, the cure for many of these learning difficulties had to be in the design and presentation of the ordinary curriculum. It followed that the responsibility for dealing with these difficulties lay with all teachers in the school collectively and individually, and that any effective response to learning difficulties had to be planned on a whole-school basis.

If the main aim of co-operative teaching is to effect a match between the demands of the curriculum and the range of needs met in an ordinary class, then the main agents had to be the managers and deliverers of that curriculum – class and subject teachers. Underlying the practice of co-operative teaching is an optimistic view that 'pupil's learning can be enhanced given appropriate materials, organizations, expectations, self-image and social relationships.'[4] Finally co-operative teaching rests on the principle that 'the days of blaming the victim are gone . . .'[5] It therefore represents a clear move away from a child deficit model to one which sees learning as an active process for pupils and teachers alike.

WHAT IS CO-OPERATIVE TEACHING?

Co-operative teaching can take a number of forms, but it must be emphasized that it is not just about placing two teachers in a room with a class. Similarly, co-operative teaching is not team teaching, where two or more teachers from the same discipline share responsibility for a part of the curriculum, nor is it collaborative teaching, where each teacher is informed of what the other is doing but the work done by each may be distinct and separate. The new policies, which followed from the publication of the 1978 Progress Report, called for a redefinition of the respective roles and responsibilities of remedial and class teachers which would be both co-operative and complementary, and also recognized that class and subject teachers would require a new system of support if they were to bring about and sustain the kind of fundamental change that would enable them to meet the new demands. One form of support was co-operative teaching.

The earlier literature about co-operative teaching was concerned mainly with personal qualities and defined areas of responsibility, with the role of the learning support teacher restricted to pupils with learning difficulties, with the task of providing additional resources (mainly worksheets), or at worst simply providing another 'red pencil'. Predominantly, the work appears to have been, at that time, at the level of pupil supporter and resource provider.

It is now almost ten years since the new policies were accepted. It has become clear that co-operative teaching has developed and that at its best is 'a *joint enterprise* which expresses a *joint commitment* to the development of educational practices as forms of interaction which taken together form the fabric of social and educational relationships'.[6] Co-operative teaching provides the opportunity for two teachers with different backgrounds of training and experience to develop common understandings, shared meanings, and the will to explore teaching and learning within 'the habits, customs, precedents, traditions, control structures and bureaucratic routines' of schools and teachers in order to improve the quality of teaching and learning which goes on in their classrooms. It provides a sound basis for systematic reflection for individuals, groups, and schools which are trying to develop into self-reflective communities. Good co-operative teaching is more about 'praxis' than 'practice' in the sense that at best it involves educational and social values and 'has at its roots the commitment of the practitioner to wise and prudent action in a practical concrete historical situation'.[7]

To be effective co-operative teaching entails partnership, a joint enterprise involving what Aoki describes as 'communal venturing forth'.[8] It is now more evidently a partnership which expresses a commitment to the concept of shared responsibility and the will to take action designed to transform the mainstream system generally for the better and particularly for pupils with learning difficulties.

The strategies for developing the dynamic relationship which underpins good co-operative teaching include clarifying roles and establishing mutual acceptance, trust, and credibility. The teachers concerned have to engage in an 'open and unconstrained dialogue' which will help them 'to question assumptions and to move confidently to embrace alternative ways of working'.[9]

HOW DOES CO-OPERATIVE TEACHING OPERATE IN PRACTICE?

In practice the concern and attention of the co-operative partners in this enterprise will be constantly changing. Co-operative teaching is about *people*: it must centre around the range of pupil need and potential; the contributions, concerns, and commitment of the teachers and the contribution and involvement of parents, colleagues, and other professionals. Co-operative teaching is about *places*: the organization of schools and classrooms, meeting places, and support agencies. Co-operative teaching is about *procedures*, including methods of collecting and sharing information about pupils and how they learn. Co-operative teaching is about *politics* and must take account of internal and external political and ethical issues. The participants must be aware of and sensitive to the locus of power. And finally, co-operative teaching is about *protocol*: the system or organization and its ethos, culture, conventions, hierarchies, and constraints.

The focus is the curriculum and its delivery. If the work is to be genuinely co-operative and the response to the broad range of learning difficulties truly integrated, then the teachers will share in the debate about the appropriateness of the curriculum to the range of pupil need and ability. They will each bring their own particular perspective and expertise to a consideration of content (the aims and objectives, concepts, skills, progression, sequencing, etc); of methodology (the extent to which it matches the aims and objectives of the course and the development of the learners); of assessment (the purposes and techniques of diagnosing and responding to the range of individual need); of resources (the match between these, the range of individual need, and the intentions of the curriculum); of organization (pupil grouping, accessibility of resources); and of language (as it relates to text, instruction, discussion etc.).

In short, the people involved are engaged in the debate about, and the difficult process of, developing, monitoring, and evaluating curriculum differentiation. In this work it is often the processes which are more difficult to manage. These are essentially the processes of consultancy which are at the heart of effective co-operative teaching. These are strategies to which teachers can learn to become more sensitized and thus perhaps more skilled, and are not to be seen as solely dependent on those, perhaps unchanging, 'personal qualities' to which the earlier literature refers.

The teachers are involved in a range of processes including the negotiation of acceptance and the recognition of mutual credibility. They must actively pursue the development of an awareness of their colleagues at both a personal and professional level, becoming empathic. They must be consciously working towards developing an awareness of the factors which influence both the nature and extent of progress in terms of the relationship and the development of a differentiated curriculum: understanding the system in its widest sense. They must together become reflective: bringing to the surface those assumptions and understandings which have been implicit in action, criticizing these, restructuring them, and embodying them in future action. This is what Schon calls 'reflection in action' and is a part of what co-operative teaching enables teachers to do.[10]

To be effective teachers must continue to engage in that dialogue which will ensure that there is increasing clarification of the changing roles and relationships among the learners and teachers involved in this co-operative enterprise. They need to identify the basis on which negotiation takes place with regard to roles, relationships, and the development of appropriate curricula. Such a dialogue demands the development of effective communication skills – questioning, explaining, providing information, interpreting, and giving useful feedback – and the capacity for stimulating and supporting the motivation for change, and helping to extend the network of individuals, groups, and agencies which will support the change process.

No one partner in this enterprise is the 'hero innovator'; rather they are together exploring the range of alternatives and solutions and their implications. In this process they must take positive perspectives on conflict by recognizing that co-operative teaching is about managing change, and in that process conflict is not only inevitable but fundamental.[11] The implementation of change is supported through problem identification, description, discussion, demonstration, experimentation, and evaluation.

Both partners must, through their handling of these processes, demonstrate that they are working to ensure that the relationship remains genuinely co-operative. That is to say, no member of the partnership is being cast in the role of the 'expert' and so creating unhelpful dependency. 'The resolution . . . is not to choose between supplying content, and expertise, and facilitating; both kinds of help are needed and may be offered by the same person or by a combination of people. The ideal internal consultant would be able to provide both, being a good internal facilitator of the change process and being able to contribute and/or arrange for content assistance'.[12]

THE PROBLEMS AND ISSUES OF CO-OPERATIVE TEACHING

Discussions with teachers involved in co-operative teaching have consistently highlighted the fact that in this work there are always issues and problems which influence or indeed determine how the relationships and the processes are managed. There are issues of trust, loyalty, and mutual respect. The briefest disregard for these issues results in long-lasting impairment and perhaps even destruction of the co-operation. There are issues of ownership and professional self-esteem. As the contributions of the teachers and pupils are 'owned' and attributed, so the outcomes of this joint enterprise must have shared ownership. There are issues related to the institution, its organization and management, and the degree to which these are responsive to the needs of pupils with learning difficulties. There are issues of attitude, value, and belief. Failure to modify the nature and pace of the change to take account of the individual in respect of these will result in 'concomitant feelings of discomfort and anomie'.[13] This also relates closely to the issue of empathy. Where there is disregard for the perspective of the other, alienation and withdrawal will ensue. Each must work towards understanding the other from the other's frame of reference.

HOW GENERALIZABLE IS THIS APPROACH TO TEACHING AND LEARNING?

Almost ten years on, there has been no real questioning of the principles on which co-operative teaching is based and, indeed, co-operative teaching has become prevalent in Scottish schools despite the fact that it was a move away from the 'king of the castle' philosophy. The general impression is of a process beginning to change schools and classrooms in Scotland for the better in terms of the educational well-being of pupils with learning difficulties, recognizing that this may mean almost all pupils at some time or other in their school career. As one commentator has put it:

> As more teachers have experience of co-operative teaching the whole thing has, it seems, become less threatening, the idea that roles may be shared, swapped or even altered has become much more acceptable. More Learning Support specialists have been involved in such work and their confidence has increased as well.[14]

Co-operative teaching can be readily adopted, but for it to be successful there must be an acceptance of the philosophy that the aim of education is to enable all teachers to provide an appropriate education for *each* pupil as opposed to a general education for *all*; a commitment at education authority level in terms of resources, particularly for staff development, related to pupils with learning difficulties; a commitment at school level to facilitate a genuinely co-operative and collaborative way of working which will involve organization of time, resources, and staff development; a recognition that the contribution of learning support services to this process is unique and irreplaceable; and a recognition that none of the above will be effective unless the ordinary class and subject teachers are actively engaged in the whole process of providing an appropriate curriculum.

To sum up, from its tentative beginnings, surrounded as they were by feelings of apprehension and professional insecurity, co-operative teaching is clearly defining, developing, and shaping a new set of roles for class, subject, and learning support teachers. It is part of a process that has shifted the whole emphasis of work with pupils with learning difficulties from an approach which was both 'disconnected' and 'disconnecting' to one where the emphasis is on good teaching and learning strategies developed in co-operation and collaboration. Co-operative teaching is central to that process of transformation which will help the school, as a community, to begin to provide an appropriate education for each within the framework of a curriculum for all.

REFERENCES

1. Threadgold, M. W. (1985) 'Bridge the gap between teachers and researchers', in R. E. Burgess (Ed.) *Issues in Educational Research Qualitative Methods*, London: Falmer Press.
2. Barton, L. and Tomlinson, S. (1984) 'The politics of integration in England', in L. Barton and S. Tomlinson (Eds.) *Special Education and Social Interests*, London: Croom Helm: p.67.
3. Scottish Education Department (1978) *The Education of Pupils with Learning Difficulties in Primary and Secondary Schools in Scotland* (A Report of HMI), Edinburgh: HMSO.
4. McBride, G. (1986) Department policy statement, Craigbank Secondary School, Glasgow.
5. ibid.
6. Carr, W. and Kemmis, S. (1986) *Becoming Critical: Education, Knowledge and Action Research*, London: Falmer Press: p.204.
7. Carr and Kemmis (1986) op. cit. p.190.
8. Aoki, T. (1984) 'Towards a reconceptualization of curriculum implementation', in D. Hopkins and M. Wideen *Alternative Perspectives on School Improvement*, London: Falmer Press.
9. Mitchell, P. (1985) 'A Teacher's View of Educational Research' in M. Shipman (Ed.) *Educational Research: Principles, Policies and Practices*, London: Falmer Press: p.95.
10. Schon, D. A. (1983) *The Reflective Practitioner*, New York: Basic Books.
11. Fullan, M. (1982) *The Meaning of Educational Change*, Ontario: OISE Press.
12. Fullan (1982) op. cit. p.189.
13. Fraser, A. (1987) Co-operative teaching project, Moray House College of Education, Edinburgh.
14. Cole, D. (1986) Co-operative teaching project, Moray House College of Education, Edinburgh.

CO-OPERATIVE LEARNING

FRANK B. MURRAY

The term, *co-operative learning*, refers to a family of instructional practices in which the teacher gives various directions to groups of pupils about how to work together. Typically the class is divided into groups of four to six children usually of the same age, but differing in ability, ethnicity, and sex. The directions the teacher gives are designed, one way or another, to have the children work together as a team on some academic task. The children, of course, must learn to co-operate to follow the teacher's instructions, but co-operation itself, while a worthy curriculum objective, is not the principal objective in co-operative learning instruction. The claim of co-operative learning advocates, usually supported in field research, is that ordinary school learning is enhanced considerably when children, following one or another of the co-operative learning procedures, learn in groups rather than on their own or in competition with other pupils.

Schooling, largely for reasons of economics and efficiency, invariably takes place in class groups with the result that overall academic achievement is usually, but not always, superior when the groups are small – optimally about seven, but not above thirty – and when the members of the group are of different academic levels of prior achievement, with a disproportionate share of the academic benefits going to those of lower academic accomplishment. While traditional classroom instruction has always entailed a degree of co-operation and competition among pupils, co-operative learning practices require pupils to co-operate as a team as a necessary condition of acquiring academic information. This usually means that the instructional outcome results from the pupils' common effort, that the instructional goal is shared, and that each pupil's success depends upon and is linked with every other pupil's success and never their failure. Co-operative learning practices typically have pupils share materials, divide up the labour required to complete the assignment, assist the other members of the group, and receive rewards based upon the group's performance. Each variation in this pattern focuses on some salient aspect of a group working on a problem – teamwork, conflict resolution, and so on. Each variation, as well, stems from one of several theoretical views – some political and philosophical, and some about the nature of the pupil's development and mental functioning.

Basically the various kinds of co-operative instructions teachers give to their pupils come from four theoretical perspectives: social learning theory, Piagetian theory, Vygotskian theory, and the newer cognitive science research on experts and novices. Each of these perspectives is focused on one of the following basic characteristics of co-operative learning: *teamwork* (social learning theory); *conflict resolution* (Piagetian theory); *community collaboration* (Vygotsky); and *tutoring* (cognitive science).

SOCIAL LEARNING THEORY: TEAMWORK

Practices derived from the social learning tradition are the most widely used in the schools. They are based upon the common principle that the pupils will work hard on those tasks for which they secure a reward of some sort, and will fail to work on tasks that yield no reward or yield punishment. In co-operative learning instruction, the teacher employs the approval of other pupils and the expectations of the group, and relies heavily on the ability of the pupil to imitate the academic behaviour of others. These are the tools of the co-operative learning teacher.

When individuals work together towards a common goal, their mutual dependency often motivates them to work hard to help the group, and thereby themselves, to succeed. In addition they must often help the members of the group to do well, and they often come to like and value the other members of the group. The several co-operative learning practices are designed to provide incentives for the members of the group to participate in a group effort, because children will not spontaneously help their colleagues or work towards a common goal, for example. Thus it is critical that the teacher reward a pupil *only* when all members of the group succeed in learning the assignment or, in the case where the teacher assigned the pupils different parts of a complicated task, *only* on the basis of the group's overall achievement, and not according to the merit of any individual pupil's contribution to the group's effort. Also the teacher must ensure that the contributions of the weaker members of the group are genuinely important, so that the group's success cannot be attributable merely to the work of one or two pupils. If the teacher merely instructs the pupils to work together and to help each other, the academic gains are generally no greater than if the pupils had worked alone on the task.

The most thoroughly researched co-operative learning practices are these: Learning Together (Johnson and Johnson); Student Teams-Achievement Divisions or STAD Group Investigation (Sharan and Sharan); Team Assisted Individualization or TAI (Slavin, Leavey, and Madden); Teams-Games-Tournaments or TGT (DeVries and Slavin); and Jigsaw (Aronson) – all described and referenced in Slavin,[1] and in Stallings and Stipek.[2]

In a typical co-operative learning exercise the teacher might divide academic material into parts, and each member of the team would read and study one of the parts. Then the members of the different teams who had studied the same parts might meet to discuss and clarify their sections, after which they would return to their original group to teach and quiz their team-mates about their section; or they might enter into an academic game contest with their counterparts on the other teams to determine who performed best. Often each student takes an individual examination, with no help from the others, on the entire subject matter,and a score for the group is computed from the individual scores by a scheme that allows each member to contribute to the team's score in a significant way. For example, the team score might be based upon the amount of improvement in each member's grasp of the subject matter. The team with the highest group score is often rewarded with a certificate or some other attractive form of recognition. In some schemes the grade the student receives is the team score, and in others the grade follows the conventional practice and is based solely upon the pupil's own work.

Johnson and his colleagues[3] found 108 studies in which co-operation promoted higher academic achievement than independent work, six studies in which the reverse was true, and 42 in which no difference was found. Slavin,[4] in a review of selected research studies that had equivalent control groups and took place in real schools over a period of at least two weeks, found that the co-operative group achieved at higher levels than the control group in 22 of the 33 studies, with no difference being found in ten studies. Some co-operative schemes have been carefully researched; for example, Stallings and Stipek[5] evaluated TGT, in sample sizes ranging from 53 to 1,742, at both elementary and secondary levels, and in several subject matter domains. In these studies TGT was administered by classroom teachers with random assignment of teachers and pupils to the co-operative and control groups, and with both groups having the same curriculum materials and objectives. On four of the seven standardized achievement tests and eight of the nine classroom tests, the TGT group outscored the control group as well as showing positive effects for race relations, friendship, attitudes toward school, and self-esteem.

PIAGETIAN THEORY: CONFLICT RESOLUTION

Teachers working within the Piagetian tradition use co-operative learning lessons to accelerate the pupil's intellectual development by forcing one child systematically to confront another child who holds an opposing point of view about the answer to some school task. Basically, the teacher places two pupils who disagree about the answer to a problem in a group, called a dyad, and tells them to work together until they can agree or come to a common answer, at which time the lesson will conclude. Once the pupils agree, usually in about five minutes, the teacher tests the children alone and usually finds that the pupils who initially do poorly on the problem now, on their own, solve the problem in a way that is indistinguishable from the way a correct problem solver solved it in the first place. Murray,[6] has undertaken a review of this literature. In some instances teachers may also instruct the pupils in the dyad to simply imitate a correct problem solver, and on other occasions the teacher may instruct one child, in the presence of the other, to pretend to reason in a mature way. In other words the teacher places the pupil in some social situation where he or she is forced to take a viewpoint that conflicts with his or her own point of view. The practice of using dyads works best if the teacher ensures that one pupil understands the task, though some cognitive growth occurs when neither child knows the correct answer to the problem, but only when each initially offers an incorrect answer that contradicts the other's answer.

Overall, these social interaction or co-operative learning effects, documented consistently in some 30 studies, are limited to mental tasks that have strong relationships with age, but they do occur across a wide variety of such tasks and with groups of various sizes (two to five), grades (K-5) and ethnic and social diversity. These developmental tasks, nevertheless, are important parts of the school curriculum because they are about information that is necessarily true (for example, if A is older than B and B is older than C, then A is also older than C). These social interaction versions of co-operative learning, apart from being effective ways to promote cognitive growth, are also more effective for developmental tasks in the school curriculum than traditional instructional practices that are based upon direct teaching or conditioning.

VYGOTSKIAN THEORY: COMMUNITY COLLABORATION

Even though few educators are aware of it, the most compelling theoretical rationale for co-operative learning comes from the Russian psychologist, L. S. Vygotsky. He claimed that our distinctively human mental functions and accomplishments have their origins in our social relationships. Mental functioning in this view is the internalized and transformed version of the accomplishments of a group. The theory gives great weight to a group's common perspectives and solutions to problems as they are arrived at through debate, argument, negotiation, discussion, compromise, and dialectic. This collaboration by a community of learners is seen as indispensable for cognitive growth.

Its role is more than a mere facilitator of events; it is the means by which such growth occurs and a provision for it must be made in schooling.

Researchers and teachers often find that the dyad can solve a problem where individuals working on their own cannot solve it. There is a distance, called a *zone of proximal development* by Vygotsky, between what the pupil can do alone and what the child could achieve were the child to work under the guidance of teachers or in collaboration with more capable peers. Thus, teachers who wish to maximize what the child can accomplish will minimize the time the child works alone on school tasks.

Research in this tradition, reviewed by Forman and Cazden,[7] has not resulted so far in novel practices in the schools, but it has provided a demonstration of the growth in individual children's problem solving when the problems are approached collaboratively and when the teacher uses the other children in the class as an instructional resource.

COGNITIVE SCIENCE: TUTORING

The characteristics of ideal learning environments from the cognitive science perspective as described by Collins, Brown, and Newman[8] follow closely many features that are embedded in the common co-operative learning formats, all of which make provisions for modelling, coaching, and scaffolding, for example. However, some novel co-operative learning procedures, like *reciprocal teaching*, have been developed by cognitive scientists for classroom instruction.

Reciprocal Teaching, developed by Palincsar and Brown,[9] is a method of teaching reading in which the teacher and students take turns as teacher as follows: both read a passage to themselves, and the teacher demonstrates the process of formulating a question based upon the passage, summarizing the passage, clarifying it, and making predictions based on the information contained in it. When the pupil takes a turn as teacher, the teacher carefully coaches the pupil in these skills of comprehension, and offers prompts and criticism until none is needed by the pupil, at which time the teacher's role becomes more passive.

Both laboratory and classroom studies have demonstrated that the *Reciprocal Teaching* method is effective in significantly raising and maintaining the reading comprehension scores of poor readers.[10]

Basically the method is thought to be successful because the pupil gradually, but solidly, develops a new conceptual model for the skill and couples it with specific strategies that are used by expert readers. The co-operative learning features of these expert-novice teaching procedures lead the pupil to integrate the multiple roles that the successful problem solver inevitably masters. Thus, student writers are helped as writers when they read and criticize other pupils' work and when they have their own work read by others, and so on. By taking

863

turns in writing and reading they acquire a larger view of the writing task, a new conceptual model for it, a model closer to that possessed by the expert writer.

Tutoring, when it is viewed from the perspective of the benefits that accrue to the tutor, is also a form of co-operative learning, although it is difficult to know to what to attribute the benefits to the tutor – the tutoring act itself, the preparation for tutoring, or the kind of study the tutor engages in.[11]

CONCLUSION

In the end, the research literature will support the conclusion that teachers can increase their pupils' performance on academic tasks if they have their pupils work on the tasks in groups of two to seven under rules by which the pupils teach each other, coach each other, and succeed as a group, and if their teachers show them how to do and think about these things, and if they are rewarded, individually and as a group, for doing them. The various theories explain how the co-operative learning innovations produce their impressive results.

REFERENCES

1. Slavin, R. (1986) 'Small group methods', in M. Dunkin (Ed.) *The International Encyclopedia of Teaching and Teacher Education*, New York: Pergamon Press: pp.237–243.
2. Stalling, J. and Stipek, D. (1986) 'Research on early childhood and elementary school teaching programs', in M. Wittrock (Ed.) *Handbook of Research on Teaching* (3rd edn), New York: Macmillan Publishing Co: pp.727–53.
3. Johnson, D., Maruyama, G., Johnson, R., Nelson, D., and Skon, L. (1981) 'Effects of co-operative, competitive, and individualistic goal structures on achievement: A meta-analysis', *Psychological Bulletin*, 89: 47–62.
4. Slavin (1986) op. cit.
5. Stalling and Stipek (1986) op. cit.
6. Murray, F. (1986) 'Micro-Mainstreaming', in J. Meisel (Ed.) *The Consequences of Mainstreaming Handicapped Children*, Hillsdale, N.J.: Lawrence Erlbaum Associates: pp.43–54
7. Forman, E. and Cazden, C. (1985) 'Exploring Vygotskian perspectives in education: the cognitive value of peer interaction', in J. V. Wertsch (Ed.) *Culture, Communication and Cognition: Vygotskian Perspectives*, New York: Academic Press: pp.323–47.
8. Collins, A., Brown, J., and Newman, S. (1986) 'Cognitus apprenticeship: teaching the craft of reading, writing and mathematics', in L. Resnick (Ed.) *Cognition and Instruction: Issues and Agendas*, Hillsdale, N.J.: Lawrence Erlbaum Associates: pp.1–41.
9. Palincsar, A. and Brown, A. (1984) 'Reciprocal teaching of comprehension-fostering and monitoring activities', *Cognition and Instruction*, 1: 117–75.
10. Collins, Brown, and Newman (1986) op. cit.
11. Hufnagel, P. (1984) 'Effects of tutoring on tutors', unpublished doctoral dissertation, University of Delaware.

CRITERION-REFERENCED ASSESSMENT

SALLY BROWN

TRADITIONAL ASSESSMENT PRACTICE UNDER FIRE

There was a time when 'assessment' was equated with the production of marks or grades for students' end-of-term reports. Furthermore, 'real assessment' was the *external* examination which selected people for entry to courses or careers. The administrative convenience of being able to say that this young person had 'passed' the 11+, achieved enough marks to enter certificate classes, or obtained adequate grades for university entrance, was seductive. Employers, educators and the general public did not consider the *meaning* of grades, marks, or pass levels; these were part of the machinery in which almost everyone had implicit faith. An added advantage was that the assessments were not *absolute*. If, for example, too many pupils passed the 11+ or achieved the university requirements, the 'goal posts' of the pass level or entrance demands could be shifted. What mattered was how the performance of one individual compared with that of others.

Comfort was engendered by the knowledge that highly competent statisticians kept an eye on examination marks; ordinary mortals were in awe of the impressive, mystical talents of these experts. The aim was reliable systems indicating who had passed, how each candidate had performed relative to the others, and how a candidate's performance in one subject compared with his or her performance in another.

In the 1960s and 1970s it was suggested that assessment could have wider purposes than simply selection by overall grading, and this led to a critical examination of traditional practices. Many now looked to assessment to help the teacher or curriculum developer to make decisions. How, the remedial educationalists enquired, can assessment be designed to map out those things which pupils are failing to achieve? In what ways, others asked, can assessment indicate strengths and weaknesses of the curriculum? To what extent can reports on pupils' achievements facilitate judgements on whether their competencies match the entry requirements for a given course? There was a new emphasis which challenged the kind of information provided by the old measurement model.

This new approach was saying that assessing achievement does not, in itself, imply measurement. On the contrary, it implies that appraisal based on qualitative judgements responds to questions such as:

Does this pupil appreciate the mood of this poem?
Does she know how to set about writing this sort of computer programme?
Can she justify her conclusions?
Has he used that concept appropriately?
Can he think critically?
Does she appreciate the use of colour by the impressionists?
To what extent has he the skills for locating evidence in historical documents?

This is not to say there are no achievements that lend themselves to a measurement model. Competence in spelling or in multiplication, for example, may be translated into quantitative questions such as:

How many words on the prescribed list can be spelled correctly? What proportion of the items involving the multiplication of two-digit integers can she get right?

In certain subject areas, however, particularly the creative arts, some teachers have always been frustrated by the requirement that a mark or a grade be awarded. To rank pupils on, say, their essays or paintings, which may be quite different in kind, never was sensible. In 'real life' we constantly assess writing, dancing, painting, scientific activities, historical analysis, and competence in communication, without assigning numbers or grades; nor do we put them in rank order. It appears, therefore, that our preoccupation with easing the administrative problems of selection, led to educational assessment using a measurement model which contrasts starkly with the way we assess achievements in the wider world.

CRITERION-REFERENCED ASSESSMENT: DESCRIBING ACHIEVEMENT

In the early 1960s in North America, and rather later in the United Kingdom, the dissatisfactions with traditional methods of assessment led to a long, sometimes acrimonious, and often trivial debate. It centred on the relative value and the characteristics of *norm-referenced* assessment and *criterion-referenced* assessment.

Any assessment has to be referenced against something. A report such as 'Jane achieved 57' will elicit questions like '57 what?' or 'What did the others get?' or 'What did she get last time?'. To be helpful Jane's report must reference her performance against targets in the area assessed (i.e. *criterion-referencing* describing *what* she has achieved), the performance of others (i.e. *norm-referencing*) or her performance on some earlier occasion (i.e. *self-referencing*).

Fairly general definitions of these terms can be used. For example,

> *Norm-referenced* assessment provides marks or grades indicating how an individual's performance compares with that of others, but offers no information about what has been achieved.

Thus, a 'B for history' indicates that the performance is overall better than a C and worse than an A; but just what has been achieved in history is not revealed. In contrast,

> A *criterion-referenced* approach provides an evaluative description of what has been achieved by an individual without reference to the performance of others.

So, the argument for criterion-referencing goes, information from this kind of assessment would allow rational decisions to be made about

- what remedial attention (if any) is required by the individual;
- whether the individual has the skills or knowledge required for entry to a particular course or career;
- how effectively the teaching is achieving its objectives;
- whether standards are maintained by individuals or groups of pupils.

Furthermore, a criterion-referenced system claims to give recognition to those things the lowest achievers know or can do. A norm-referenced system simply identifies how badly their performance compares with those of others. Recognition of their achievements, it is suggested, motivates them to learn and improve their performance.

These arguments are manifest in the first recommendation of the Dunning Committee to the Scottish Education Department in 1977[1] that 'Assessment should make a positive contribution to the teaching and learning process for all pupils.' It follows that assessment should be integrated with teaching and learning and fulfil formative (i.e. while the learning is in progress) and diagnostic purposes. It should identify pupils' strengths and weaknesses, and the causes of failures, and help plan remedial action in response to the assessments.

The cosy notion of assessment as something between teacher and pupil, however, has to be extended. Other responsibilities to provide summative reports to pupils, parents, other teachers, employers or tertiary education, are accepted by examination boards, schools, and teachers. The adoption of criterion-referencing for these purposes introduces particular difficulties in design and implementation.

One form of summative report, relating to examinations, occupies a special area of the debate. Technical, and relatively unhelpful, definitions of terms have been used here. For example,

> A *norm-referenced* system scales performance on to a normal distribution. It conveys information about the performance of individuals in comparison with others, but contains no information about the substance or standards of performance.
>
> A *criterion-referenced* system provides information about whether candidates have performed to specified and predetermined levels in the subject.

In practice, the requirements of this norm-referenced definition have rarely been fulfilled. Where they have, the examinations either have been highly specialized or have demonstrated profound weaknesses. Unfortunately, this demanding definition allows systems which provide only comparative grades or marks, and no information about what has been achieved, to assert that they are not norm-referenced because they do not scale marks on to a normal distribution.

Similarly, the definition of criterion-referencing makes demands which can seldom be fulfilled. It implies that the knowledge and skills assessed be amenable to clear conceptualization as levels of increasing achievement. For example, Standard Grade in the Scottish Certificate of Education attempts to identify a specific number of levels of achievement. Knowledge, however, is not necessarily structured in that way. In the case of a performance such as high jumping, that number of levels may be readily (if arbitrarily) identified. The understanding of scientific theories, ability to ride a bicycle, appreciation of works of art, and application of the skills of historical analysis, however, cannot be similarly summarized as levels. To describe these achievements *adequately*, it may be necessary to use instead a 'mastery/non-mastery' distinction or a narrative account of the performance. If 'specific and predetermined levels' are requirements of a system, they will inevitably distort the valid reporting of pupils' performance.[2]

DOMAINS OF ACHIEVEMENT

The most fundamental question to be addressed is 'What is to count as achievement?' When assessment indicated only how a pupil had performed relative to others, the performance could be explained by alluding to the pupil's 'high' or 'low' level of ability. If reports now identify what has and has not been achieved, explanations will be expected to indicate *why* certain things have not been achieved when others have. Teachers will be expected, therefore, to give an account of the opportunities provided for pupils to develop the competences against which they are assessed.

'Achievement' will be different in different contexts and will include the knowledge, skills, or attitudes acquired. Knowledge may be substantive, emphasizing the outcomes of learning, or it may be experiential, emphasizing pupils' learning through reconstruction of their own experiences. Skills may be practical or intellectual, and attitudes strongly emotional or heavily cognitive.

The mapping of the area of achievement to be assessed constitutes a process of 'domain specification', describing and elaborating each domain of the achievement. The content and/or objectives and/or experiences, with which the teaching and learning are concerned in that domain, have to be identified. The structure of the subject matter could be used as the sole basis for domain specification. There are, however, many ways of structuring any given area of the curriculum, and it is important to consider also how teachers structure their teaching and how pupils most effectively learn. For example, if an assessment system in physical education is based on domains of *skills*, but physical education teachers continue to think about and structure their courses as *activities*, then the assessment is unlikely to provide a valid measure of achievements in those courses.

DOMAINS FOR FORMATIVE ASSESSMENT

When the purpose of assessment is formative or diagnostic, the domains of achievement will be small. At the extreme, each might relate to one specific objective, or even a single assessment item. Such domains would be 'homogeneous', and a pupil's performance on relevant assessment items would indicate a precise picture of what had been achieved.

In practice, such small and precise domains are used infrequently. Published 'diagnostic' tests usually relate to broader domains or include some progression of achievement. *Tour de France*[3] (a development sponsored by the Scottish Central Committee for Modern Languages and published in 1981), for example, includes a diagnostic speaking test in which the pupil is assessed on the 'basic message', and four error categories of grammar, pronunciation, social usage, and speed of response. Descriptions of these categories are available (domain specification) and the assessment identifies both the pupils' strengths and the aspects of their learning which require attention.

It is sometimes argued that formative tests map out strengths and weaknesses in domains of achievement but do not perform a diagnostic function.[4] Diagnosis has the additional requirement that domains and assessment procedures be capable of indicating the *causes* of pupils' failures. Domain specification for such diagnostic purposes in the classroom is not well developed, apart from attempts to include in domain descriptions the more common problems which pupils encounter in trying to learn. These common misunderstandings can then be built into distractors of multiple-choice assessment items.

Where domain specification builds on a research base, the diagnostic element may be more readily included. Fyfe and Mitchell,[5] for instance, carried out research on pupils' reading strategies and identified sources of difficulty in particular kinds of reading tasks. They then specified their domains in relation to what was to be achieved and to particular difficulties pupils might encounter. The assessments were designed, therefore, to indicate the progress of pupils' achievements, identify specific problems which individuals were encountering, and offer remedial help in areas of weakness.

For example, they considered a domain focusing on pupils' 'use of a dictionary'. They divided the domain into three sub-domains corresponding to the sub-tasks of 'searching', 'comprehending', and 'doing'. The difficulty of assessment items was then varied by manipulating the demands in the three sub-domains:

1. The 'search' element could
   - give the pupils the target word to look for
   or - ask them to select the target word
   or - require them to generate the target word.
2. The 'comprehend' element could involve
   - an uncluttered target entry in the dictionary
   or - a target entry with additional irrelevant information
   or - a target entry containing sub-entries
   or - a target word appearing in more than one entry.
3. The 'do' element could ask the pupil to
   - indicate only that the target has been found
   or - copy an entry
   or - select part of an entry and copy it
   or - select and manipulate information found in the entry.

By basing the domain specification on their research, Fyfe and Mitchell identify what is to be achieved, provide clear indication of the form assessment items can take, and offer a means of diagnosing particular causes of individuals' failure.

DOMAINS FOR SUMMATIVE ASSESSMENT

Where criterion referencing is used for summative reporting purposes, the problems of domain specification become more acute. The report may relate to a course of work lasting a term, a year, or longer. Performance on all of the small domains of achievement, used for formative assessment, could not be contained in a summative document – readers could not manage that much information. A succinct form for the information has to be found. Inevitably this results in some loss of meaning and detail of the assessment. There is a balance to be struck, therefore, between reducing the report to a manageable size and ensuring that better and more detailed information is provided.

The Scottish Certificate of Education, Standard Grade, has tackled this by using summary Grade Related Criteria (GRC) in each subject. Standard Grade assumes each subject comprises several elements (domains) and that a specific number of levels of achievement can be identified. The GRC were construed as 'broad indicators or descriptions of expected performance in key aspects of a given subject at different levels of award'.[6] The aspects (elements or domains) tend to be large. English, for example, is conceptualized as Writing and Speaking, Reading and Listening. 'Writing' is made up of smaller non-identical sub-domains such as conveying information, deploying ideas, arguing, evaluating, describing personal experiences, expressing feelings, and employing literary forms. The other three domains are, like Writing, non-homogeneous.

When a pupil is assessed against the summary GRC, his or her performance is mapped over the area included in the domain. It is unlikely, however, that the level of the performance will be the same for all the sub-domains. Nevertheless, an attempt has to be made to identify one specific level and to award an overall grade for that domain. Some system of aggregation, or trade-off for better and worse performances on the various sub-domains, has to be invoked. It is important to be aware, however, that such procedures lead to award of the same grade for very different patterns of performance.

The conceptualization of domains and sub-domains varies from subject to subject. Few GRC have had support from research investigations. In the domain of Practical Skills in science, however, a team at Jordanhill College of Education[7] developed detailed specifications and assessment procedures. They identified six sub-domains (observation, recording, measurement, manipulation, procedures, and following instructions) for the lower levels of award, and later increased this number for the higher levels. These sub-domains each encompass a set of specific, more or less homogeneous objectives. The objectives specify the sub-domains *and* indicate the appropriate assessment procedures. This provides a system giving information about achievement on sub-domains or in relation to the constituent objectives, but it still entails aggregation across different sub-domains for an assessment of performance on the Practical Skills domain.

This scheme assumes practical skills in science can be represented by a series of specific objectives. There is nothing sacred about this way of conceptualizing science, although many teachers agree it is helpful. In other subjects, the objectives model may be less acceptable. In foreign languages, for example, one approach to achievement in communicative competence identifies dimensions of grammatical competence, socio-linguistic competence, discourse competence, and strategic competence. The validity of this model is still to be established and teachers may need more experience in the communicative approaches before reaching agreement. If their teaching and their pupils' learning experiences are not structured according to these dimensions, however, then the validity of assessment based on the dimensions would be in doubt.

Since subjects have domains of achievement, it is implied that reports of achievement at Standard Grade will appear as a series of assessments or a profile. The number of elements in the profile will be the same as the number of domains. However, a second aggregation *across* different domains will be made to provide a single grade. The pressure for the familiar and administratively convenient single grade remains despite the fact that its retention undermines efforts to provide more and better information about achievement.

The National Certificate at 16+ in Scotland[8] has taken a different approach to the specification of domains. Curriculum modules, representing forty hours of work, are specified, together with learning outcomes. A mastery/non-mastery approach to assessment is used and the certificate awarded itemizes those modules (domains) on which the student has successfully achieved the learning outcomes. Information about *what* has been achieved is contained in the module descriptions. This avoids problems of specifying levels of performance, but inhibits differentiation among students' performances on the same module. Undoubtedly some achieve more than others, but this is recognized only by the completion of greater numbers of modules or of those modules accepted to be the most difficult.

CRITERION REFERENCING IN USE

The specification of domains is the most crucial process in criterion-referenced assessment. Very often it leads directly to the generation of assessment procedures. Sometimes it identifies areas where curriculum rhetoric has suggested pupils should be achieving, but there is no corresponding assessment. Always it aids understanding of the costs and benefits incurred when assessments are presented in particular ways or identified as specific levels of performance.

Because criterion-referenced assessment has an intimate relationship with teaching and learning, it may be most appropriately designed and implemented by those in classrooms. Its rise coincided with closer attention being paid to internal school assessments and less emphasis being put on external examinations. 'Validity' is seen as concerned with how the assessment procedures match those things pupils have the opportunity to learn. Traditional notions of reliability and validity, however, cannot be discarded; it is still necessary that assessments provide reliable accounts of those qualities which they claim to assess, and development of moderation procedures is needed where the responsibility for assessment rests with teachers.

While it may be necessary to generate new assessment procedures, many traditional test items will continue to be valuable. It seems the best way of providing an evaluative description of performance is to offer a profile.[9] But can such profiles fulfil the functions, demanded by employers and tertiary education, of selection and prediction of future success?

With regard to selection, a profile should put the reader in a better position to judge whether the individual has achieved those things being taken for granted in any future course or career to be undertaken. It will, however, require readers to examine their own assumptions about what they expect of potential entrants, and that is a demanding exercise.

Prediction of future performance is always dubious. There is no certainty that motivation and opportunity to achieve will remain constant over time. Traditional 'predictors' (the eleven plus, assessment at 14, O and H grades) have been, in fact, *barriers*. If, at 14, a pupil is 'predicted' not to be capable of achieving an O grade and is put into a non-certificate class, then the prediction becomes a self-fulfilling prophecy. In order to test whether H grade results are, indeed, good predictors of performance at university, then university entrance would have to be opened for a period of time to everyone, so that even those who failed to reach the entrance requirements could be admitted.

For the longer term, assessments probably have little predictive power. In the short term, criterion-referencing has a better chance than traditional measures. A criterion-referenced approach implies a scrutiny of *what* individuals will be expected to achieve. If they are expected to achieve 'Y' then logically it may be necessary that they have previously achieved 'X'. It may then be predicted, in the short term, that only those who have achieved X will be in a position to achieve Y.

In my view, any assessment should steer clear of prediction. What assessment can do is to report achievement at a specific time, and criterion-referenced reports are much more informative than traditional measures. But they are no more clairvoyant.

REFERENCES

1. Scottish Education Department (1977) *Assessment for All: Report of the Committee to Review Assessment in the Third and Fourth Years of Secondary Education in Scotland* ('Dunning Report'), Edinburgh: HMSO.
2. Drever, E. (1988) 'Criterion referencing and grade related criteria: The experience of standard grade,' in Brown, S. (Ed.) *Assessment – A Changing Practice*, Edinburgh: Scottish Academic Press.
3. Scottish Central Committee on Modern Languages (1981) *Tour de France*, London: Heinemann.

4. Simpson, M. (1988) 'The diagnostic assessment of pupil learning,' in Brown, S. (Ed.) *Assessment – A Changing Practice*, Edinburgh: Scottish Academic Press.
5. Fyfe, R. and Mitchell, E. (1985) *Reading Strategies and Their Assessment*, Windsor: NFER-Nelson.
6. Scottish Education Department (1982) *The Munn and Dunning Reports: Framework for Decision* (in mimeo).
7. Bryce, T., McCall, J., MacGregor, J., Robertson, I., and Weston, R. (1983) *Teachers' Guide in TAPS Assessment Pack*, London: Heinemann.
8. Black, H. (1988) 'The National Certificate', in Brown, S. (Ed.) *Assessment – A Changing Practice*, Edinburgh: Scottish Academic Press.
9. Brown, S. and Black, H. (1988) 'Profiles and records of achievement', in Brown, S. (Ed.) *Assessment – A Changing Practice*, Edinburgh: Scottish Academic Press.

DIAGNOSTIC ASSESSMENT THROUGH ITEM BANKING

ALISTAIR POLLITT

Teachers cannot teach without assessment. Indeed no skilled work of any kind can be carried out without frequent checking to ensure that the desired results are being achieved. Such assessment is often labelled 'diagnostic' to distinguish it from the more formal 'summative' testing in examinations. Item banks can provide a valuable resource for this kind of assessment, but if they are to be exploited successfully we must understand how an item bank measures attainment and how it provides a basis for interpreting the responses of students to tests drawn from its questions.

EDUCATIONAL TESTING IS A FORM OF MEASUREMENT

It is fashionable to disparage educational measurement, to argue that 'measurement' is incidental to the main concerns of teaching, or even the cause of most of its ills. Even when an evaluation is quite crude, however, as in judging whether a specific performance is acceptable, or which of two essays is better, it is still a simple form of measurement in that an underlying scale is imagined, with one end representing 'more' or 'better' than the other. Educational measurement is not concerned with measuring things for measurement's sake, but with providing better techniques for obtaining the measurements that teachers and others already want.

To understand the nature of assessment in education it helps to consider other familiar kinds of measurement, and temperature, in Centigrade or Fahrenheit, provides the best analogy. Temperature and ability are both qualitative properties of an object (or person) rather than measures of the amount of something present; formally, they are *intensive* properties where most measures are *extensive*.

How do we understand the significance of temperature measurements?

Certainly we do not explicitly choose to interpret a given temperature via *norm reference* (NR), or *criterion reference* (CR), or *domain reference*, even though some of our reactions might be describable in these terms. If the weather forecast predicts tomorrow's temperature as 20° Celsius we might evaluate it as 'not bad for April', where we are evaluating it against expectations of 'the seasonal average' (NR). We might consider a sugar temperature of 120° Celsius as 'still too cool' if we knew that 140 Celsius was required for making candy (CR). (I cannot think of any reasonable activity representing domain-referenced measurement of temperature unless it be making sure that the medium – air or sugar – is sufficiently well stirred!)

The important message of the analogy is that measurements are normally interpreted not against norms or criteria but against a background of *experience*. We are usually so quick to contextualize a measurement that we may be unaware that we are doing so. We know that tomorrow is April 1st, and that we are in Scotland, and these facts automatically select out of our network of experience those aspects that enable us to evaluate '20° Celsius' appropriately (assuming of course that we have managed to suppress any lingering Fahrenheit framework). The same applies any time that we measure people: their heights, weights, chest measurements, ages, or whatever are interpreted in the light of all our experience of people in general.

EXPERIENCE-REFERENCED MEASUREMENT

Why then do we behave differently in educational testing? Why concentrate on just one aspect at a time and ignore the wealth of experience available to us? The essential feature that is missing from most educational measurement is *constancy*. The Celsius scale is defined arbitrarily, though conveniently, and all measurements are expressed on that scale no matter what kind of thermometer was used to obtain them. All of our formal experience of temperature measurement, and a good deal of our informal experience of warmth and coldness, comes to be associated with that constant scale. In fact, experience gives meaning to the scale.

Think of phrases like 'a six-footer', a 'teenager' or 'the forty-hour week'. In each case the meaning of the phrase derives from our experience with the scales of measurement of height, age, or time in a given context. With experience a scale of measurement changes from being a complex idea to be understood, through being a tool to be used when required, to, eventually, becoming a part of how we see and think about the world itself, part of the 'language' through which we think.

In educational measurement this constancy is lacking. Each test we create defines a new scale unique to itself, and the scores that we observe are bound to that scale and that test only. We cannot transfer our experience of scores on one test to help us interpret scores on another: every time we must start again.

Norm Reference was one attempt both to overcome test-boundedness and to provide an interpretative framework, but it is too cumbersome and expensive for most purposes – imagine thermometer manufacturers' problems if they could not sell a new thermometer until it had been used to measure a 'representative sample of 3,000' afternoon temperatures! Item banking, on the other hand, provides a practicable way of achieving constancy of scale for all tests.

From a suitably large collection of *questions* catalogued in terms of *content* and *difficulty* an appropriate selection procedure generates a test which is *calibrated* to a standard scale before it is ever used. Just as the thermometer maker can use empirical knowledge of the properties of glass and mercury to pre-calibrate each instrument on to the common Celsius scale, so the tester can use empirical knowledge about the questions in the bank to pre-calibrate each test on to the commmon bank scale.[1]

THE BANK SCALE

An item bank contains a collection of questions all designed to assess one area of performance. The area may be as narrow as 'vocabulary' or as broad as 'language competence'; the tasks may be discrete-point single-mark items, cloze passages with ten to twenty marks each, or grade-related performance exercises. In any case, these questions can be sorted into order of difficulty from easiest to hardest. Any person who tackles some of these questions can be tagged on to the bank scale in terms of their performance. The important point is that people and questions appear on the same scale, measured in the same units. We see that ability and difficulty are two sides of the same phenomenon, each being defined and measured through the other. Wherever a person appears on the bank scale (and we expect people to rise over time) we would expect that person to do well on questions lower down the scale, especially on those that are much lower, but not on ones that are higher. This duality of ability-difficulty is crucial to diagnosis.

Whenever a simple picture is drawn from empirical data there are three aspects of it that need to be explained – the picture itself, its implications, and its limitations. In this case the 'simple picture' is the listing of all of the bank questions in difficulty order, and the issues are:

1. Why do the questions line up in this order?
2. What does this ordering of questions imply for teaching?
3. Why does this order sometimes break down?

These three questions relate in turn to construct validity, curriculum reference, and individual diagnosis.

Item banking and construct validity

The first aspect to be explained is the listing of the questions. Why this order? Why is this question harder than that question? Why can so many students manage that task easily when they cannot do this one? Discovering answers to these questions is one of the most important activities for educational research. If we can explain the order of difficulty then we can reasonably claim to understand the abilities we are measuring. Understanding the scale in this sense is a major part of establishing the *construct validity* of tests drawn from the bank.[2]

Traditional approaches to construct validity have been indirect, looking at the abilities of students as revealed by tests rather than directly at the tests themselves. The essence of item banking is that the questions *are* the scale. The construct 'Listening ability' is defined by the relative ordering of the questions in a listening bank; the factors or characteristics of test questions that determine their relative difficulties also determine just what it is that the test truly measures.[3]

Item banking and curriculum-referenced scales

This kind of construct validation is a research exercise that may demand the resources of trained researchers. With a large bank, however, there is another kind of investigation in which any teacher can take part. As more questions accumulate and are placed on the scale, so the specific features of particular questions tend to disappear, and clusters of questions that seem to assess much the same concept or process can be identified around a certain difficulty level. The scale acquires a new definition in terms of *curriculum*. The way in which an understanding of chemical equations grows, or mastery of algebra is achieved, can be seen in the way in which the nature of questions changes as learners move up the scale.[4]

An interpretation of a learner's status can – cautiously – be made by reference to this curriculum scale. A certain scale score should not be taken to imply that certain students can never, for example, 'infer emotion' when reading, nor that they can always 'complete a paraphrase'. It might, however, imply that a teacher may reasonably expect them to tackle exercises involving the easier processes on their own, but that they are likely to need help when those higher up the scale are involved. It is possible to alter the difficulty of a given question – and in particular to make it easier – by varying the amount of *support* provided for the student. Rather than interpreting the scale as indicating what students can and cannot do (as in traditional definitions of criterion reference) we may see it as separating those things they can do with little or no support – below their level – from those on which they will need

878

some or considerable support. Perhaps the main contribution of curriculum-referenced scales will be to encourage teachers to adjust the demands they make on individual students through varying support levels, rather than to adjust the curriculum through streaming or selection.

Item banking and individual diagnosis

There have been objections to the use of a simple model for item banking, with questions sorted on a single dimension called 'difficulty', as if this were sufficient for us to understand everything about how successful students would be with each question. It is argued that reality, and the concept of attainment in particular, is more complex than that, and that several components of people's abilities and of task demands must interact in unpredictable ways. In fact, the simplest item-banking model, the Rasch model, is remarkably successful in accounting for the patterns of students' responses to questions – but it does break down. The third aspect of the simple picture that needs explaining is this breakdown: why do students sometimes not behave as the simple model would predict?

With this question we come to true diagnostic assessment. Much of the assessment that is, or should be, carried out in teaching might be better described as *screening*, the systematic checking of students' learning to ensure that they have not failed to understand what they are taught, or *monitoring*, the routine checking of all of the evidence available to see that nothing is amiss. The item-banking model provides an ideal setting for these. At the heart of such monitoring is unexpectedness. A student's wrong answer to a question should not be considered remarkable merely because it is wrong; but it should be investigated if the question was easily answered by most people of about the same attainment level. We should take notice too if a relatively low scorer gets a relatively difficult question right, and should seek an explanation. Consider the following simple test of ten questions, sorted from easiest to hardest, and some children's scores on each question. Note that each child has five right answers.

	Q1	Q2	Q3	Q4	Q5	Q6	Q7	Q8	Q9	Q10
Ali	1	1	1	1	0	1	0	0	0	0
Ben	1	1	1	0	1	0	1	0	0	0
Cass	0	0	0	0	1	0	1	1	1	1
Dai	0	1	1	1	1	1	0	0	0	0
Ewan	1	1	1	1	0	0	0	0	0	1

Ali's and Ben's response patterns seem plausible; they both coped with most of the easy questions and failed on most of the hard ones. But Cass's is not; this pattern is so unexpected that we cannot consider that '5' represents a credible measurement of her ability. It looks as if, had we given her more difficult questions, she would have scored better! In fact Cass's pattern is never likely to occur, but Dai and Ewan show fairly common patterns. Would you consider '5' a credible measurement of either of them? Or would you credit them with '6' and '4'? We could, and ought to, monitor test responses routinely for anomalies like these. The credibility of each measurement we make should be considered as important as the reliability and validity of the test we use to make it.[5]

When a test is marked by machine it is of course easy to carry out such credibility checks, but there are several ways in which the power of the simple picture can be exploited when marking is not automated. Three examples will be described. In each case the Rasch model and a micro-computer will be used in order to make the diagnostic interpretation as convenient as possible.

Kidmap

If a test contains only right/wrong questions, then this procedure provides a clear visual analysis that students – and even quite young children – can complete for themselves. A computer can easily produce blank copies of Figure 1 – the *Kidmap*. In the centre is a representation of part of the bank's scale (Standard Score), from about 20 units to about 80. On the left side the numbers 2–29 represent the ability levels associated with raw scores on the test – these represent the vital *calibration* of test KP. On each side are the questions, Q1 to Q30, that constitute 'TEST KP', with each question appearing at the scale level corresponding to its difficulty.

After the test is corrected, each student is asked to complete a map, by circling right and wrong answers as shown. The RIGHT side gives a score – 22 in the example – which indicates an ability on the constant bank scale of about 62 units. Whether this is higher or lower than we would expect depends on our knowledge of Polly, or of children her age in general, or of the standards we demand on a given course.

The diagnostic value comes from considering the map in more detail. We would expect Polly not to make any mistakes on questions much below 62, and not to get right any much above 62. Is this what happened? There are certainly some surprising wrong answers – Q3, Q6, and Q11 – and one rather surprising right answer in Q30. Rather than merely note that Polly scored 22/30, the teacher should concentrate on these answers; the three wrong ones indicate misunderstandings or other weaknesses that Polly should be able easily to overcome, while the right one – if it is not just a lucky guess – may indicate a strength or interest worth exploiting.[6]

Figure 1 KIDMAP

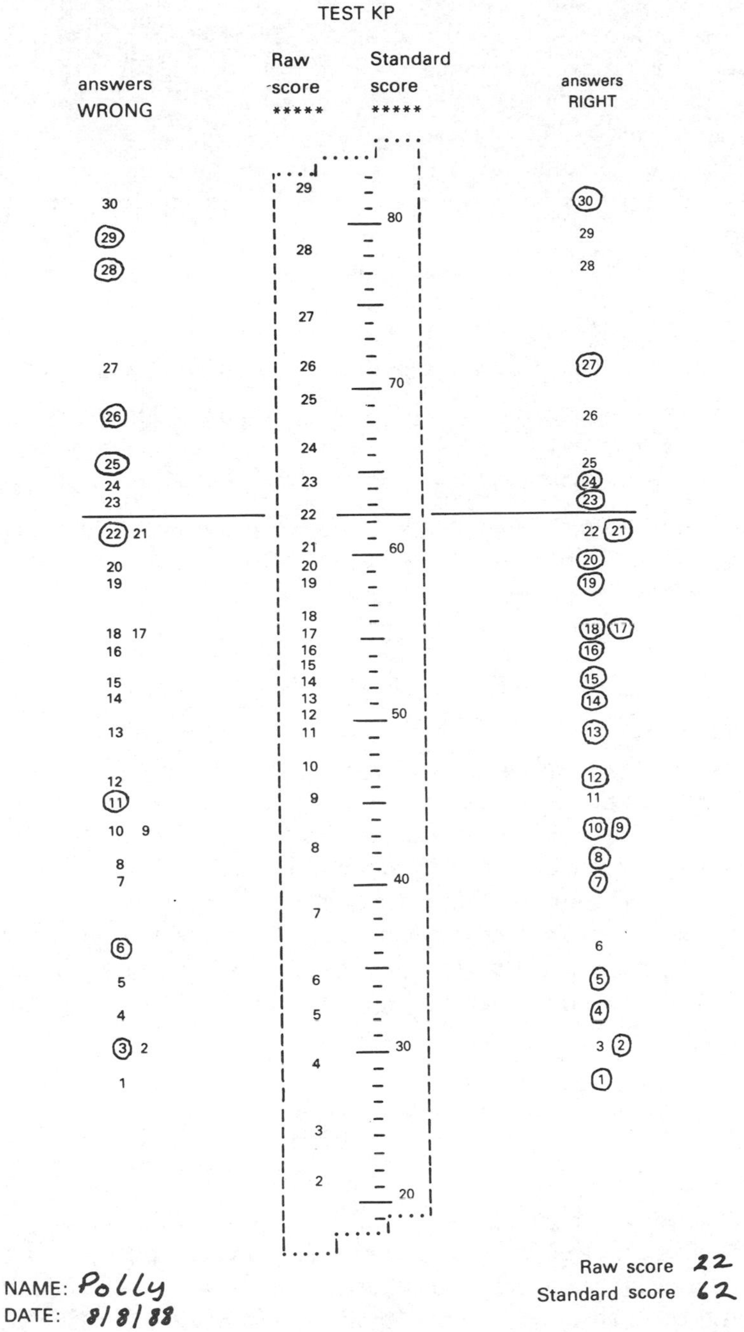

TEST KP

| answers WRONG | Raw -score ***** | Standard score ***** | answers RIGHT |

answers
WRONG
*****

Raw
-score
*****

Standard
score
*****

answers
RIGHT

30
29
28

27

26

25
24
23

22 21

20
19

18 17
16

15
14

13

12
11

10 9

8
7

6

5

4

3 2

1

29

28

27

26
25

24

23

22

21
20
19

18
17
16
15
14
13
12
11

10

9

8

7

6

5

4

3

2

80

70

60

50

40

30

20

30
29
28

27

26

25
24
23

22 21
20
19

18 17
16

15
14

13

12
11

10 9
8
7

6
5
4

3 2

1

NAME: *Polly*
DATE: *8/8/88*

Raw score **22**
Standard score **62**

881

Grademap

When the test questions are worth more than one mark each, a different visual presentation is necessary. Figure 2 shows a *Grademap* for a test consisting of 15 graded assessments in writing, obtained by marking each of five essays (on a 0–3 scale) on three components of writing ability. The expected score on each assessment is shown for each point on the scale; below the scale are raw score numbers indicating the calibration of the test on to the bank scale. Once again the map may be drawn quite easily by a micro-computer, or more laboriously by hand.

If we now draw a vertical line through a student's ability estimate the map indicates the score that student is most likely to get on each assessment. In the example, Polly scored 19/45, corresponding to a writing ability of 50 on the bank scale. Therefore we would expect a pattern of responses not very different from:

	211	111	111	221	111
Compare:	100	111	323	121	111

which was Polly's actual pattern. She wrote remarkably well on all components of essay 3, but rather poorly on essay 1. Can we, or Polly, explain her unexpected inconsistency?

Profiles

The Grademap is in fact a simple example of a standardized profile. In Figure 2 there are fifteen separate measurement scales, one for each assessment, all calibrated on to the constant bank scale. Suppose instead that a bank were used to generate three listening tests each designed to assess a different aspect of 'listening ability'. Each would provide a score for a student on that aspect only: how should the four scores be compared? The important principle is that the comparison *must* take into account the difficulties of the questions in each test. It is not reasonable to compare a student's abilities in different areas in terms of raw score (or percentages) as the *Profile* in Figure 3 shows.

Polly's scores were:

Listening for Information	15 / 21
Understanding Essential Ideas	9 / 15
Making Inferences	8 / 13
Total	33 / 50 (there was 1 extra mark)

The diagram shows the four scales calibrated to the common scale. Despite her score of 15/21, Polly in fact performed surprisingly poorly on the simple skill of listening for information. These questions were easy, and she ought to have scored about 20. Unless a profile is standardized in this sort of way

Figure 2 GRADEMAP: TELS Writing Sub-test

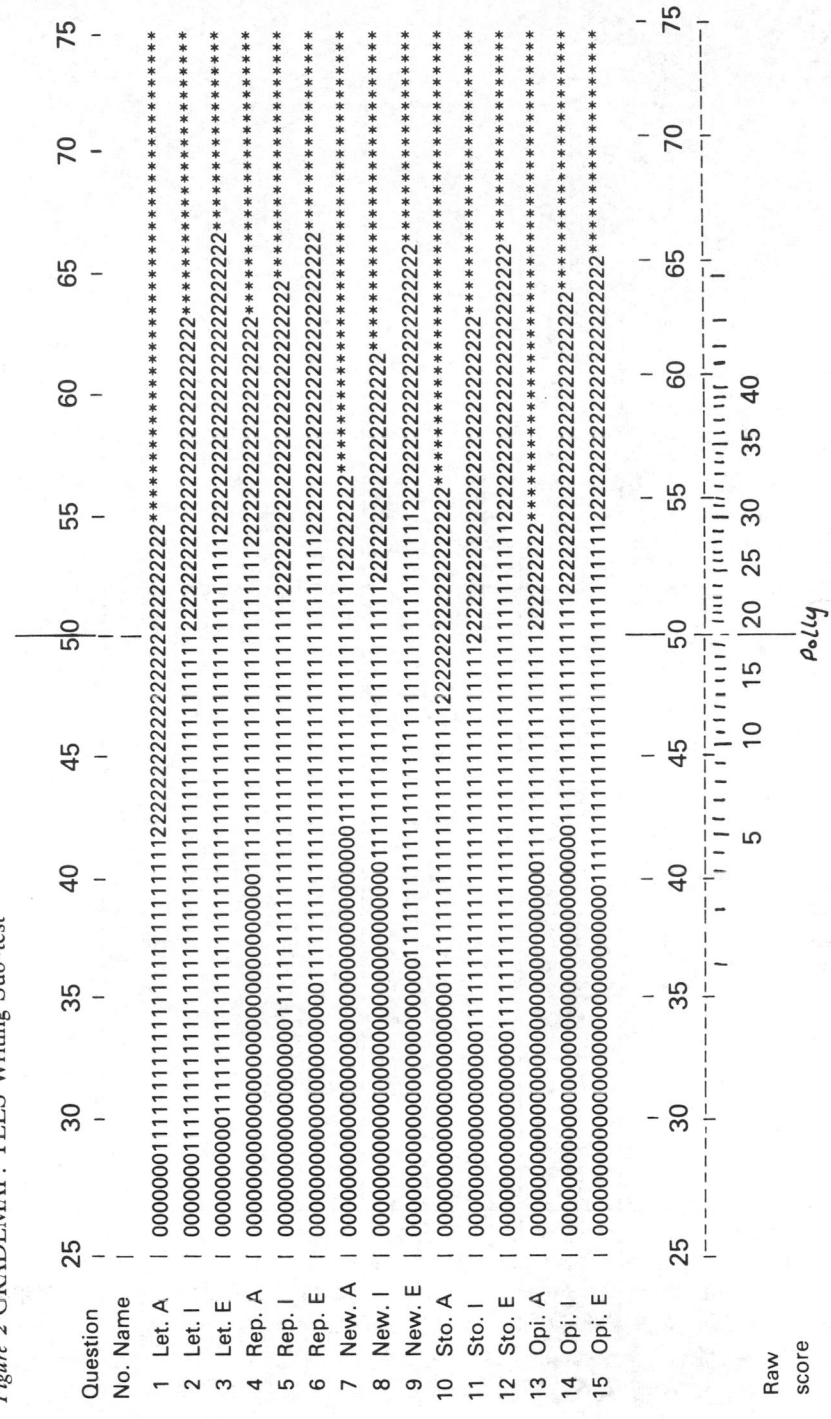

Figure 3 PROFILE: TELS Listening Sub-test

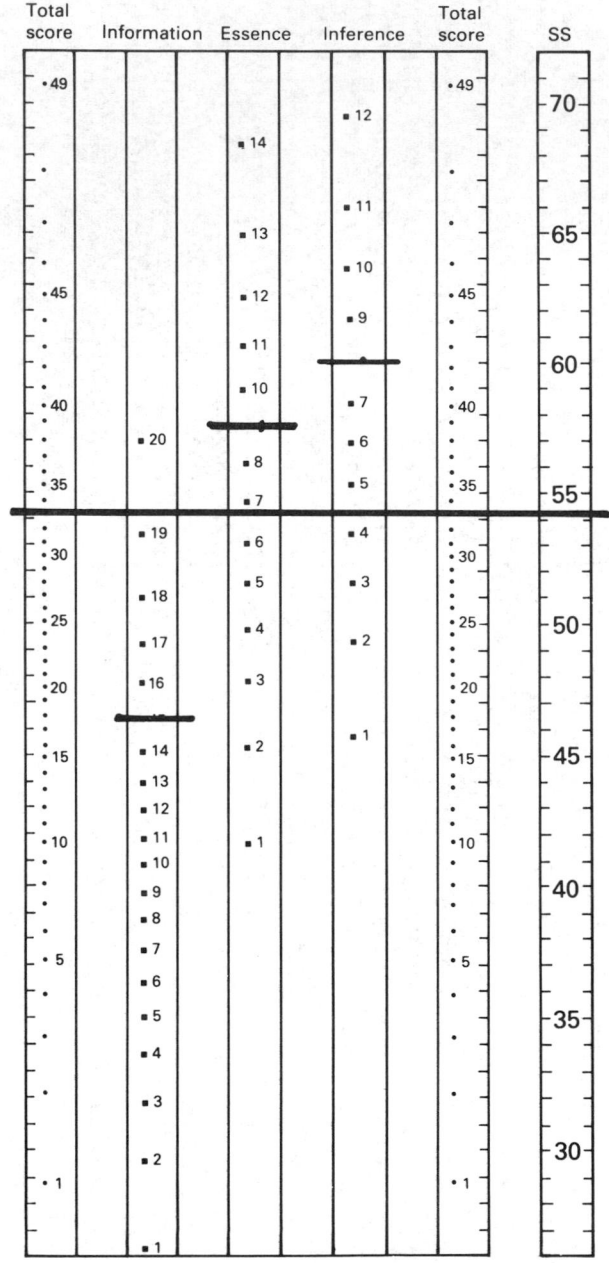

we are always in danger of being misled, and once again the item bank (with a simple micro-computer) provides a routine way of standardizing measurement scales.[8]

Since this is the same Polly whose writing ability was estimated to be 49 (see Figure 2) we can make a further interpretation. Overall, her listening performance – 54 – was better than her writing. The one very good essay she wrote, together with this evidence of good higher listening skills, suggests that she is capable of better writing than this, and that time could profitably be spent working on writing skills.

QUESTION CONTENT

These examples illustrate how item banking can help a teacher, or pupil, to extract the significant information from the rest of the detail. Such information might best be described as 'semi-diagnostic' since it can at best identify problems but not explain them. Just as with construct validation, so with true individual diagnosis we must study the content of the particular questions we are using.

In general it is the teacher who should look carefully at 'surprising' wrong questions, particularly since any error repeated by several students may indicate a teaching fault rather than a learning one. When item bank test results are processed by machine, however, it is easy to provide some further help. To illustrate, consider Test KP again from Figure 2. This was a maths test, drawn from a bank in which each item has associated with it a set of *Keywords* indicating its content and format. A simple program would generate for Polly the following report:

??   Q3   –   Word problem, weight, Kg, 3 decimal places
??   Q6   –   Place value, number line, decimal notation
?   Q11   –   Word problem, volume, litres, 3 decimal places

From this it would be clear to a primary teacher that Polly's problems were with the decimal number system.

If a student is being tested interactively at the terminal of a computer which contains the item bank, then there are almost limitless possibilities. The system could choose easier questions about decimal notation or the concept of place value for Polly, and continue down the difficulty scale until questions are reached that she can get right. If she is told the correct answers to the questions she may learn as she is tested; after a few easy examples the system could bring her gradually back up the bank scale, still on decimal questions, until she failed again. This pattern of supportive testing could continue as long as required – assuming that there are enough questions and that Polly can stand it – and the whole sequence of attempts could be recorded for the teacher if further action is needed.

CONCLUSION

Such schemes are still some way in the future. For the present there is much to be done if we are fully to exploit the simple picture of attainment provided by item banking with a constant scale. First we must understand the meaning of the simple scale. Then we must realize the significance of this in terms of the curriculum of teaching and learning. Finally we must learn how best to react when the simple picture does not fit for a particular student or class, in order to provide for each of them the best learning environment we can.

NOTES

1. For further discussion of calibrating item bank tests using the Rasch item response model, see B. D. Wright and M. H. Stone (1979) *Best Test Design*, Chicago: MESA Press.
2. For an extended discussion see A. J. Stenner, M. Smith, and D. S. Burdick (1983) 'Towards a theory of construct validity', *Journal of Educational Measurement*, 20: 305–17, and the next reference.
3. For an example of this approach in relation to English and French examinations at 16, see A. Pollitt and C. Hutchinson, 'The validity of reading comprehension tests: What makes questions difficult?' in D. Vincent, A. K. Pugh, and G. Brooks (1986) *Assessing Reading*, London: Macmillan.
4. This sort of interpretation – called 'content-referenced' – was developed for the Tests Of Reading Comprehension (TORCH), Australian Council for Educational Research, Hawthorn, Victoria, Australia (1987).
5. In B. D. Wright and G. N. Masters (1982) *Rating Scale Analysis*, Chicago: MESA Press, this concept is discussed as 'person misfit' and subsumed under the heading of Response Validity.
6. This technique is employed in A. Pollitt and L. Munro (1988) *The GTU Maths Bank*, London: Macmillan.
7. This example comes from the Writing sub-test of C. Hutchinson, A. Pollitt, and L. Munro (1987) *The English Language Skills Profile*, London: Macmillan.
8. This example is from the Listening sub-test of the same test as in the previous note.

ASSESSMENT OF PRACTICAL SKILLS

TOM BRYCE AND JIM McCALL

It is often said that you can tell what is valued in education by looking at what is assessed. Decades of convention would seem then to suggest that practical work was not worthy of formal assessment or, at the very least, not susceptible to those procedures reserved for 'knowledge and understanding'. Regrettably this is paradoxical, for the practical aspects of school work (whether in their own right or as a means to other ends) are indeed valued highly by teachers. The mismatch between practical instruction and non-practical assessment throughout the curriculum is in fact as uncomfortable as it is unnecessary, practical assessment only *seeming* to be unreliable and more difficult. Thankfully, there has been some redress in the balance with the emergence of manageable techniques for practical assessment and clearer conceptions of those skills and processes which are vital to education.

In this chapter we will consider the nature and range of skills and processes worthy of assessment, drawing our illustrations from science. Accepting that assessment should influence the learning of skills, a number of implications are drawn, concerning what may be usefully recorded and profiled for pupils. We then look at some of the techniques for practical assessment which are emerging as robust and practicable. Finally we refer to two of the controversial questions, namely the relationship between skills and the broader targets of education (the 'parts versus the whole'), and between skills and 'knowledge' itself.

THE NATURE OF SKILLS

We should start by recognizing that skills are assorted in character. Since some skills are basic whilst others are complex, they cannot all be learned independently or without regard for sequence. This has the implication that, if assessment is going to influence teaching in useful ways (which we consider to be essential), diagnostic checks must be made of any skills considered to be prerequisite to other, more complex, skills and processes. Any viable assessment system must therefore be 'step-up' in character, and not designed as a set of hurdles likely to create casualties. It might be instructive to consider these ideas in relation to practical activities in science.

Practical work in science serves a number of important purposes. First, it provides both a medium and a context in which learning can take place, giving pupils a feel for the ideas and phenomena which constitute science. Second, it ensures that pupils learn a range of useful practical skills and techniques. Third, it enables pupils to develop their skills of inference, in context, and to adopt the working habits of systematic investigation and experimentation. Any assessment associated with these purposes (particularly the second and third) must recognize the rich variety of skills and processes at work, as well as their interdependence. 'Basic' science skills (purpose two) include such varied skills as the ability to:

– identify potentially hazardous situations in school and everyday life (O1)
– arrange information in a tabulated form when given headings (R6)
– read the scales of laboratory and clinical thermometers and make appropriate measurements (Me3)
– use a test paper or test solution (P10)
– prepare a simple microscope slide (P17).

More complex 'process' skills include the ability to:

– use generalizations and observations to draw valid conclusions (In3)
– combine observations and given information to formulate hypotheses (In4)
– for a given practical problem, identify an appropriate procedure and select suitable apparatus (SP2).
(The categorizations in brackets refer to Figure 2.)

While pupils are engaged in practical science, diagnostic assessment checks of these skills must be made at times which suit the flow of instruction. Checking that a pupil can meet objectives P10 and P17 should follow laboratory instruction directed to these ends; equally, it should precede their use in any real piece of investigative work where pupils would resort to pH testing or microscope work. Likewise, inferential skills like In3 or In4 require careful teaching and testing before they can be put to good use during pupil experiments or fieldwork.

Inevitably the range and diversity of such skills is considerable, raising the question of whether any aggregation can be effected and reported meaningfully. In the case of science, it has been shown that skills can be categorized to create domains for purposes of assessment and reporting,[1] the proviso being that the particular techniques used for their assessment be fairly 'pure', and that any structured task used to assess particular skills must be designed to be free of skill demands other than those in question. Most basic practical science skills can be grouped into Observational (O), Recording (R), Measurement (Me), Manipulative (Ma), and Procedural (P) skills (where procedural refers to the use of techniques and apparatus), and Following instructions (F). Process skills in science include inference skills (In) and the ability to select procedures for particular problems (SP). A step-up model of science is then along the following lines (Figure 1):

Figure 1

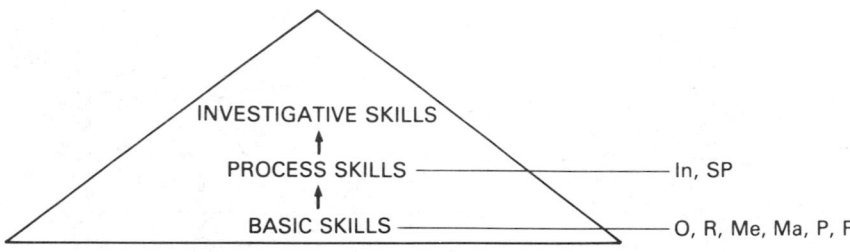

The eight skills used as examples are taken from the 61 practical skill objectives identified for Scottish Standard Grade Science (and grouped into the eight major areas described above) as shown in Figure 2.

Thus, while pupils acquire skills and progress steadily, their achievements can be recorded and profiled systematically. Such a profile provides a convenient summary of what has been achieved to date and shows what still remains unassessed or unattained. If grading is required, it can be obtained by matching grades to the achievement of a reasonably high proportion of the objectives in each of the various skill categories (each targeted appropriately). More important, the detailed records of the achievements of individual pupils should be kept in a form which pupils can appreciate and use themselves. Knowing that you were weak in say, particular measurement skills, and that the experimental work you are currently engaged in has improved these skills, simply begs that you be allowed to demonstrate your new competences and be credited accordingly.

It should also be clear that worthwhile assessment takes skills directly as they come in the curriculum, not artificially segmented into cognitive or psycho-motor components. It is futile to relegate practical skills to the 'psychomotor domain' in the conventional Bloomian sense.

TECHNIQUES FOR THEIR ASSESSMENT

Research[2] tells us that practical skills must be assessed practically. Both the nature of the task and the competence displayed change if a non-practical mode is adopted. Attempts to infer the existence of a skill through traditional

Figure 2

PRACTICAL SKILLS OBJECTIVES

STANDARD GRADE SCIENCE: Foundation and General levels

TAPS

The pupil should be able to:

OBSERVATIONAL SKILLS   LIST O

O1 identify coloured substances from their description or match them with reference colours.

O2 observe and describe changes in colour, in form and in level.

O3 match similar objects or representations of them and identify differences in detail.

O4 match an object with a variety of visual representations.

O5 classify objects from given information.

O6 identify potentially hazardous situations in school and everyday life.

O7 identify scientific artefacts or effects of technology in the landscape or in photographs.

O8 demonstrate careful listening.

RECORDING SKILLS   LIST R

R1 record simple information presented in a variety of formats

R2 make a brief spoken or written summary of presented information.

R3 label a diagram correctly

R4 draw simple shapes accurately.

R5 arrange information in a tabulated form when given headings.

R6 **generate appropriate headings and then order information.**

R7 complete a partially-drawn chart, graph or histogram.

R8 **construct a chart, graph or histogram when provided with ordered data and given axes and scales if required.**

R9 order simple data and draw a chart, graph or histogram.

FOLLOWING INSTRUCTIONS   LIST F

F1 set up apparatus or carry out a procedure after demonstration by the teacher.

F2 set up apparatus or carry out a procedure from spoken instructions.

F3 set up apparatus or carry out a procedure using a work card containing information in a mainly pictorial form.

F4 set up apparatus or carry out a procedure using a work card containing only verbal information.

MEASUREMENT SKILLS LIST Me

Me1 recognise or supply the correct units for common measurements.

Me2 read the scale of a metre stick or flexitape and make appropriate measurements.

Me3 read the scales of laboratory and clinical thermometers and make appropriate measurements

Me4 read the scale of a measuring cylinder or jug and make appropriate measurements.

Me5 read a variety of "upside down" linear scales and make appropriate measurements

Me6 read a variety of dial scales and make appropriate measurements and settings.

Me7 make rough estimates of relative weights, volumes and short time intervals.

Me8 use a grid to estimate areas.

MANIPULATIVE SKILLS LIST Ma

Ma1 demonstrate gross motor control in a variety of ways.

Ma2 demonstrate fine motor control in a variety of ways including:

  (a) making precise movements or adjustments.

  (b) completing a diagram or colouring to demonstrate control over area and shading.

  (c) cutting out a diagram keeping cuts within specified limits.

  (d) assembling cut out shapes and attaching them appropriately to a display sheet.

INFERENCE SKILLS   LIST In

In1 distinguish observations from inferences.

In2 make plausible generalisations from observations.

In3 use generalisations and observations to draw valid conclusions.

In4 combine observations and given information to formulate hypotheses.

In5 make deductions from hypotheses.

In6 use observations to confirm or refute existing hypotheses.

In7 modify hypotheses to accommodate new observations.

PROCEDURAL SKILLS   LIST P

P1 identify commonly used items of laboratory apparatus.

P2 select appropriate apparatus for a given task.

P3 adopt procedures which minimize specific laboratory hazards.

P4 transfer a solid or a liquid to a specified level in a container.

P5 use a measuring spoon or scoop to produce required volumes.

P6 use a dropper or syringe to transfer a liquid.

P7 combine small quantities of ingredients to match a given standard.

P8 dissolve a solid using an appropriate method.

P9 employ a suitable filtering technique.

P10 use a test paper or test solution.

P11 with safe working.

  (a) light a bunsen burner and adjust the flame as required.

  (b) heat a solid substance using an appropriate technique.

  (c) heat a liquid in a test-tube held in a suitable holder.

  (d) heat a beaker of water.

P12 use a Celsius laboratory thermometer and a clinical thermometer.

P13 use a magnifying lens.

P14 use a compound microscope.

P15 use a stopclock or stopwatch.

  (a) to make accurate measurements of time intervals.

  (b) to take readings at timed intervals.

P16 **set up a simple electrical circuit from a circuit diagram.**

P17 **prepare a simple microscope slide.**

P18 **use various field instruments (e.g. light meter, pH meter...).**

P19 **use various field techniques (e.g. quadrat, nets, ...).**

SELECTION OF PROCEDURES   LIST SP

SP1 **for any proposed laboratory experiment or practical investigation, anticipate hazards and adopt appropriate safety precautions and procedures.**

SP2 **for a given practical problem, identify an appropriate procedure(s) (e.g. observing, counting, measuring*, sampling, separating, dissolving, heating, using chemical indicators) and select suitable apparatus.**

SP3 **where measuring instruments are involved, choose the piece of apparatus or scale of suitable range and accuracy.**

SP4 **for a chosen procedure, choose suitable variables, collect relevant data and select an appropriate form for the presentation of results**

* e.g. length, weight, volume, temperature and time.

Performance criteria are contained in the item specifications.

paper-and-pencil approaches have had very limited success. Reviews of the literature stress that learners must be required to demonstrate their practical abilities and not simply be asked to describe them. Three practical modes are readily apparent in the case of science. First, checklists may be used, judging pupils' performances 'live' in the laboratory against a number of predetermined points or criteria. Second, structured or semi-structured tasks may be set, the process of instruction being temporarily stopped for the purposes of assessment.[3] Most frequently this means the pupil is given a short practical test item, or an 'item-set' (where that refers to a longer sequence of linked assessment tasks). Third, attempts have been made over the years to assess practical attainments on a more global basis, the pupil being assessed or rated on how well she or he has tackled an experiment or investigation.

Checklists work well if the skills in question are fairly well defined. Thus 'setting up a bunsen and using it to heat a liquid to boiling point' can be effectively assessed with a checklist of probably six to ten points (though even here, experienced teachers take some time to agree upon the checklist points which are worthwhile and can be practicably observed). More complex 'skills' cannot be usefully assessed using checklists, simply because the number of checklist points becomes too unwieldy. Anything approaching 'the experiment' falls into this category, and research indicates that teachers cannot assess reliably when, in effect, they are trying to operate several, often many, checklists simultaneously in the standard laboratory situation.

Structured tasks (practical test items) have much in their favour and most can be designed to have 'product' checks. One infers that the skill or process was carried out successfully from the conclusion reached/measurement taken/ answer given and written down for later checking. Thus practical test items for P10 and SP2 quoted above might, respectively, involve sets of prepared, labelled solutions and test papers (the pupil writing down pH values on a specially prepared answer sheet), and a mixture of chipped materials to be separated (the pupil being asked to record his or her choice from four suggested techniques – which he or she may separately try out on the constituent materials, though not on the problem mixture). Sequences of structured tasks have been devised to permit the assessment of a series of linked objectives, such as those higher skills which involve inference. Such 'item-sets' consist of linked steps each of which involves product checks.

One can therefore have practical assessment of basic and more complex process skills in a manageable, practicable form with the minimum of teacher involvement. The price, of course, is in lengthy preparation and set-up time, but most practitioners find this to be the only way to achieve worthwhile, interesting, and robust assessment in the laboratory. Test items can be arranged to form 'stations', pupils circulating through them on a timed basis (such as three minutes per station). Item-sets afford the assessment equivalent of resource-based learning. In both cases, arrangements can be formal (large circuits of stations at the end of a topic or term with the entire pupil group circulating through 'the practical exam') or informal (mini-circuits of a few items built in to a teaching sequence, checking achievement with individuals as the lessons ensue).

Either way, the use of structured tasks helps to minimize the subjectivity which occurs when teachers are asked to rate pupil performance on practical investigations. Rating the 'global performance' has been tried for decades with virtually no demonstrable evidence of validity or reliability. Not only that, the various proposals, which usually emanate from external examination boards, frequently offer little that is practicable to the teacher in the laboratory. However desirable it may be that pupils should be able to tackle 'whole experiments' or 'practical investigations', the direct assessment of these is still open to question. In the light of the available evidence about the lack of basic skills exhibited by many learners and of the known unreliability of holistic assessment approaches, valid and reliable forms of assessment for investigative work using semi-structured tasks are currently being trialled.[5]

THE PARTS VERSUS THE WHOLE?

Some have argued that practical test items or even item-sets have the disadvantage of fragmenting the whole and are the result of an atomistic approach to a complex practical situation. For the reasons given above these criticisms are in the main unjustified and, in our view, the many advantages of the process far outweigh the few disadvantages. Indeed it could be said that most of the criticism to date relates only to basic skill test items whose proponents do not argue them to be sufficient across the entire range of skills. Many practitioners have yet to become familiar with what can be achieved with the linked steps of an item-set. To take an example from science, an item-set such as *Plastics*[4] is based on the inference skills assessment strategy shown schematically in Figure 3.

The pupil is presented with a series of practical tasks and associated instructions together with written questions on what he or she observes and can infer from the findings obtained. All of the experimental work is based on simple, reliably obtainable test properties (in this case about the floating or sinking of plastic specimen samples). The pupil under test is invited to compare her or his reasoning with various suggestions on offer (such as those shown in Figure 4, which is concerned with step 3 (In3), 'the pupil's ability to use generalizations and observations to draw valid conclusions').

Item-sets like *Plastics* are designed to:

1. offer an appropriate context in which inference skills may be assessed (mirroring the experimental contexts in which they are taught);

Figure 3

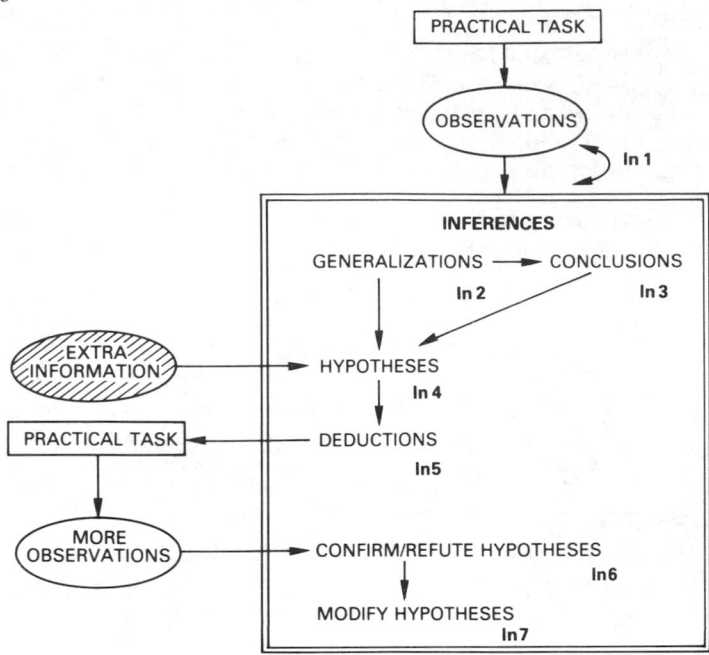

2. reduce the memory burdens on pupils, since they are not required to recall information for any of the steps involved; everything they need to know is supplied;

3. ensure that failure on particular steps does not impede progress through the subsequent steps in the series;

4. minimize the effects of inexperience in putting into words inferences which have been drawn;

5. ensure that genuine hypothesizing and concluding take place (as opposed to mere recall);

6. maximize motivation and pupil activity;

7. ask pupils to accept or reject inferential statements in accord with sound models of science and logic.

   Item-sets like *Plastics* present challenging situations to pupils and are far removed from anything that could be said to be 'atomistic' or fragmented aspects of science. On the contrary, pupils are assessed on their skills as thinking scientists; they are assessed as they act scientifically (or non-scientifically as the case may be), not on an ability to write about science.

Figure 4

These pupils did the same experiment and were asked 'What does the experiment tell you about the **green** sample?'
Which **two** pupils do you agree with?
Complete **part 3B** of your answer sheet.

The colourless tubing is PVC.
The yellow tubing is Polythene.

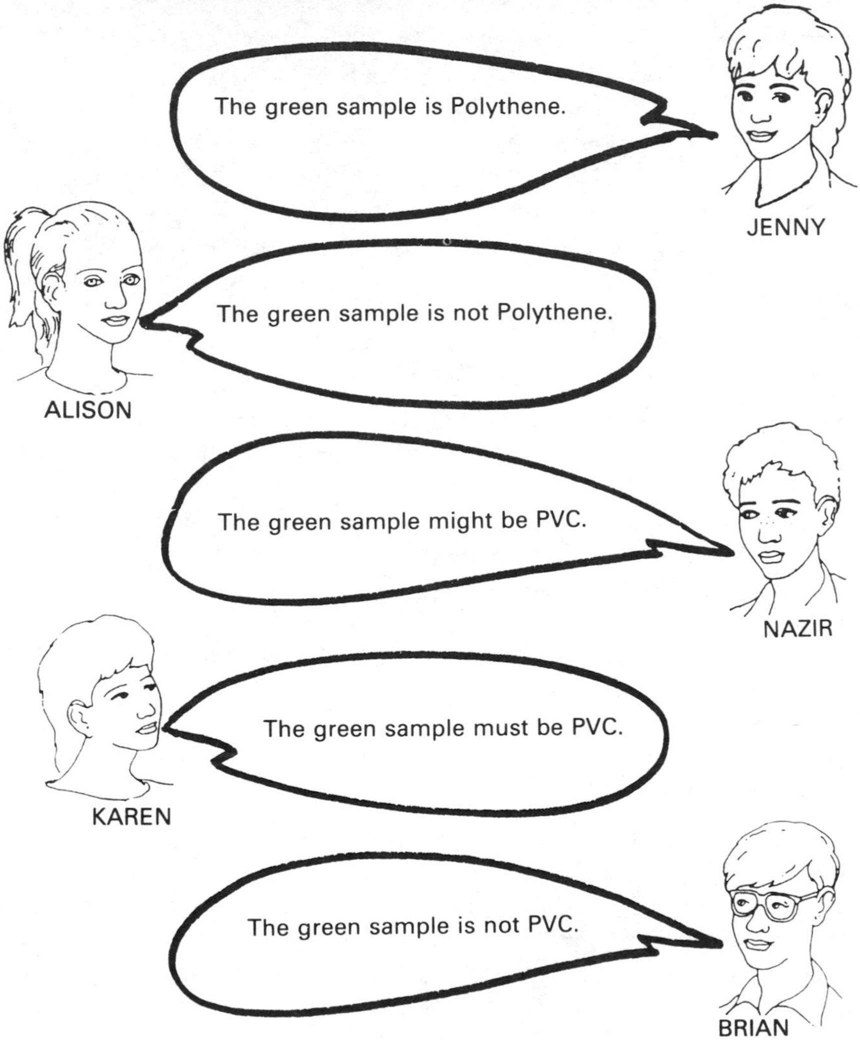

The green sample is Polythene.

JENNY

The green sample is not Polythene.

ALISON

The green sample might be PVC.

NAZIR

The green sample must be PVC.

KAREN

The green sample is not PVC.

BRIAN

SKILLS VERSUS KNOWLEDGE

Perhaps the most significant issue raised by such assessment techniques is the link between skills and knowledge. Skills of inference are clearly related to scientific understanding and the development of useful knowledge in the individual learner. It is certainly true that they go hand in hand, and it would be fruitless to suggest that skills of inference could be taught or assessed in some decontextualized way. It might be best to think of skills and knowledge like the two sides of the same coin. Surely it is impossible to have one without the other?

The conventional forms of written assessment which have dominated the curriculum would however suggest that, until recently, the coin has been double headed. There has undoubtedly been an over-emphasis on knowledge at the expense of process. Even where the intention has been to assess both 'knowledge and understanding', the expansion of content has been detrimental to understanding and meaningful learning experiences. In short, the backwash from non-practical assessment has led, in the classroom, to an over-concern with the 'coverage' of content. The record is unimpressive, for it is clear that many children have failed to master sufficient knowledge and understanding to equip them for life in the modern technological world. The balance would be redressed if knowledge and understanding were achieved through more not less practical 'hands-on' experiences and, contributing to this end, with more systematic and continuous forms of genuinely practical assessment.

REFERENCES

1. Bryce, T. G. K., McCall, J., MacGregor, J., Robertson, I. J., and Weston, R. A. J. (1984) *Techniques for the Assessment of Practical Skills in Foundation Science: Report of the Project: Phase 1, 1980–1983* (Jordanhill College of Education); Bryce, T. G. K., McCall, J., MacGregor, J., Robertson, I. J., and Weston, R. A. J. (1986) *Techniques for the Assessment of Practical Skills in Science: Report of the Project: Phase 2, 1983–1986* (Jordanhill College of Education).
2. DES/APU (1984) *Science in Schools: Ages 13 and 15, Research Report No. 3*, London: HMSO; Bryce, T. G. K. and Robertson I. J. (1985) 'What can they do? A review of practical assessment in science', *Studies in Science Education*, 12: 1–24; Robertson, I. J. (1987) 'Girls and boys and practical science', *International Journal of Science Education*, 9(5): 505-18 .
3. Bryce, T. G. K., McCall, J., MacGregor, J., Robertson, I. J., and Weston, R. A. J. (1983 and 1985) Teacher's Guide in *TAPS Assessment Pack*, London: Heinemann Educational Books; Bryce, T. G. K., McCall J., MacGregor, J., Robertson, I. J., and Weston, R. A. J. (1988) *TAPS 2 Assessment Pack: Techniques for Assessing Process Skills in Practical Science*, Oxford: Heinemann.
4. Bryce *et al.* (in press) op. cit.
5. Bryce *et al. TAPS 3 Research Project: The Assessment of Practical Investigations in Biology, Chemistry, Physics and Science, 1987–90* (Jordanhill College of Education).

7.13

ASSESSMENT OF ARTS ACTIVITIES

LESLIE HILLS

THE PURPOSE AND NATURE OF ASSESSMENT IN THE ARTS

When a child states that two and two make five, or writes that something is 'horribul' the appropriate response of the teacher is clear. Ways must be found to ensure that the child comes to understand that the rules of arithmetic decree that two and two make four, and that conventionally a 'horribul' thing is described on paper as 'horrible'. The case, however, when a child proudly, or more usually shyly, presents four red lines and a purple dot and describes the work as a fish, or characterizes a pattern of percussion as the sound of the sea, is different. A dialogue must be entered into, in which the teacher is as much the learner as the taught. This interaction lies at the heart of all the problems encountered when assessment of the arts in education is on the agenda. The teacher is interacting not merely with the material, the facts, the skills of the lesson, but with the pupil's developing consciousness, imagination, and perceptions. This is not the place to argue that the above could or should hold in other areas of education. What is certain is that it must hold in arts teaching, which is concerned with anything but mechanical reproduction.

Everyone is agreed that the arts in education are essential – the problem is that there is no consensus on what they are essential for. This is not surprising, for beliefs about the place and nature of the arts in education will vary with perceptions and beliefs about the nature of education. Since these have been, and continue to be, gloriously diverse, it is unlikely that there will ever be agreement on the nature of arts in education.

What has this to do with assessment? That depends on what you mean by assessment. In the last decade forests have been felled in the cause of teasing out the various meanings of measurement, assessment, and evaluation, and their relationship to certification. It is arguable whether any satisfactory conclusion has been reached about the nature and form of assessment in education.

896

What is certain is that no satisfactory conclusion has been reached about assessment in the arts.

Can this be because arts teachers do not know or are unable to articulate what happens when a pupil makes progress? That is unlikely to be the case. Rather, the apparent confusion stems from two fundamentals – that we know the arts are essential, but we do not agree on what for, and that teaching and learning in the arts are inextricably intertwined.

In the analytical world of the subject-centred curriculum, with its almost total emphasis on cognitive aspects, there is little room for the arts. The definition of subjects as having distinct bodies of knowledge and sets of concepts is inadequate for arts subjects. The justification that the arts are somehow 'good for' pupils often boils down in reality to a notion of therapy for the less able, not necessarily inappropriate unless therapy and education have conflicting aims. Another justification is that the arts minimize boredom and ennui. This is not an educational justification, but one which is often used. The most popular notion at the moment seems to be that of balance. The pupils' curriculum must be balanced, and the popular assumption is that this can be achieved by scrutinizing the subjects in the curriculum and organizing a diet of arts, science, number, language, physical activity, social education, and certain others, depending on the conceptual framework being used. This is a variation on the justification which relies on the arts being seen as an antidote to boredom, a leaven in the heavy mix of important subjects. Again this is not an educational justification for the arts. Moreover, the notion of curricular balance is suspect and will not bear examination. Assessment applied to any of the above purposes for the arts in education is not to be contemplated.

If, however, assessment is to be discussed, it is necessary to clarify the nature and purpose of the arts in education – what they are essential for. Any view of what the arts are for will inevitably be coloured by the value systems and attitudes which predispose one to the arts. This is not to say that my views are determined by crude preferences and innate dispositions. They are tempered by an attempt at the reasoned inspection of the views of others, and by experience, which includes most importantly the experience of feeling. They may not reflect the central concerns of those who deliberate on educational policy, but I think it is reasonable to say that they reflect the views of many working in arts education.

My view of the essential nature, indeed the primacy, of the arts rests on a belief that pupils must be provided with educational experiences designed to supply the knowledge and skills which will enable them to cope with information and make judgements in a complex and changing world. To do this they must have an education which is concerned with the affective and the aesthetic as well as with the cognitive. The arts contribute to this by their effect on consciousness and feeling. Education in the arts is concerned with personal awareness and imagination and with our cultural tradition. The arts in school education are also concerned with these. There is however a complicating factor. While the school teacher is in a position of responsibility, the means of evaluating pupils are not precisely established. It is therefore necessary that the teacher recognize the need to take responsibility, to make judgements. These judgements provide the focus for discussion about the purpose and nature of assessment in education in the arts.

It would seem obvious that if the teacher is supplying the pupils with knowledge and skills, these should be able to be assessed, and this is probably so. Moreover, it is, with practice, possible to assess progress in the pupil with regard to knowledge and skills. However, as was argued above, the knowledge and skills that go into the process of art-making are concerned with the affective and the aesthetic. Until we have – perish the thought – a method of calibrating emotion and feeling and beauty, we will not have an objective scale against which to measure the work of our pupils.

We have only to look at the discarded drafts of criteria devised to measure an entity described as 'expressive activity', by a committee charged with devising grade-related criteria, to know that we are very far from precise measurement with the language and concepts we have at our command. For example, in an honest and exhausting attempt to describe levels of achievement, a group of hand-picked and experienced practitioners arrived at the following:

Grade 6   With assistance, the candidate has demonstrated ability to utilize information from a given source and to use the medium to express ideas, thoughts, and feelings simply.

Grade 5   The candidate has demonstrated ability to utilize information from a given source and to use the medium to express ideas, thoughts, and feelings simply.

Grade 4   The candidate has demonstrated ability to select and utilize information from more than one source and to control the medium to express ideas, thoughts, and feelings with some imagination.

Grade 3   The candidate has demonstrated ability to select and develop from more than one source and to make moderately skilled use of the medium to express ideas, thoughts, and feelings with some imagination.

Grade 2   The candidate has demonstrated ability to select and develop information from a variety of relevant sources and to make skilled and sensitive use of the medium to express ideas, thoughts, and feelings imaginatively.

Grade 1   was not required. Presumably it was a bit better than grade 2!

The above demonstrates clearly the strain on language and concepts involved in trying to differentiate between levels of expression and imagination. How does one measure 'moderate skill', and what is 'sensitive' use of the medium? And is selecting and developing information from more than one source necessarily deserving of a higher grade than utilizing information from a given source? When the mind boggles to this extent one must suspect that it is not the mind that is at fault but possibly the activity.

COMMONALITY

Is it meaningful to posit a commonality of content, process, or purpose among art, drama, music, dance, literature, performance art, and composition?

Peter Abbs writes, 'Our concern is with the development of consciousness through expressive symbol making in the broad context of a collaborative community and an inherited culture.'[1] This is a useful definition of the business of arts teachers. The two aspects of arts education, so often placed in opposition, are in tandem. Expressive symbol making in the various arts media is fundamental to the purposes of arts education, and yet it cannot exist in isolation from the wider world of art and aesthetic experience. The full potential of the individual will be realized only if both are present. The developing of specific practical and conceptual skills, and the acquaintance with and appreciation of works of art go hand in hand. An attempt at art making at whatever level may be necessary for the full appreciation and enjoyment of a work of art. It will certainly enhance it. Inherited culture then is important for arts educators in their development of feeling and consciousness. Peter Abbs refers to a collaborative community of arts teachers. Ideally this community extends to all teachers in and out of institutions. In the context of schools, however, the point is an important one. If the arts are regarded as a number of subjects concerned with specific skills such as, for example, colour mixing and voice projection, and appreciation, then there is little commonality. If, however, they are about embodied meaning and expressive symbol making mediated through a variety of skills, arts teachers have much in common.

The nature of arts activities which follows logically from the above is a complex of practical making activities informed by a concern for the promotion of critical and evaluative faculties, and embedded in a concern for and an awareness of works of art in the past and present. There must be room for choice, for although there is commonality in the educational function and process of the arts, individual aptitudes and predilections will make some media more appropriate than others. Forcing a pupil who wants to make marks on paper to develop sensitivity by listening to sounds will develop nothing but a lasting distaste of music.

It is, then, reasonable to assume a commonality of purpose and problems in relation to assessment in the arts. Commonality will evidence itself in common language, and procedures in the assessment of making activities and a common critical vocabulary and a form of appreciative discourse. This has been much in evidence in recent years with the development of criteria-related assessment. The work of groups of practitioners entrusted with the task of defining basic elements of the arts subjects in order that criteria might be written for them has resulted in a remarkable measure of agreement. Assessment arrangements, however, for examinations in arts subjects rely to a great extent on the identification of performance levels in the two broad fields of critical activity and expressive activity or performance, and, as we have seen above, the identification of these performance levels is problematic to say the least.

THE EXPRESSIVE ARTS AND CERTIFICATION

The situation of the expressive arts in education is, as always, confused and paradoxical. On the one hand, in an age of economic recession and falling rolls, control is tightened, and the utility of education measured in terms of employment prospects by anxious parents and teachers. At the same time, however, there is currently a flowering of diversity and individuality in personal style. Employment opportunities in the arts and arts-related industries increase daily. Participation in arts activities of all kinds is everywhere widespread. Arguably the arts have never been as well taught as they now are, or by a body of people more committed to the importance of the arts in the process of education.

The main threat to arts education, at least in secondary schools, is the current preoccupation with certification of everything which is taught and experienced. Some arts teachers argue for the inclusion of the arts in the certification system on the grounds that only in this way will the arts be safeguarded and attract customers. This is perfectly understandable and may well be true.

National certification is concerned with the setting and maintaining of national standards and measurement according to these standards. Arts education is also concerned with standards, and measurements will be made daily. The standard of an individual pupil's work is of paramount importance. All pupils must be encouraged to attain the highest standard possible. The achievement of this entails the sympathetic evaluation of work by pupil and teacher together. Perhaps the most interesting example of this can be seen in the work being undertaken by teachers of dance as they prepare to enter the certification system. They have come to the devising of assessment criteria and procedures with fresh perspectives. In a study[2] into criterion-referenced assessment for modern dance the writers analyse teachers' aims and sort them into two broad categories. The first is concerned most with using dance to develop skills which will help the pupil in coping with everyday life, and the second with dance as performance art. However, it is clear that these areas overlap and are intertwined, and include within them a wide range of subsidiary aims which must be taken into account in devising assessment. The identification of criteria is therefore a complex task.

The authors of the study proceed to identify and specify criteria and develop them into pupil handouts, including checklists of activities and assessment decisions. From the assessment decisions profiles of pupil performance can be drawn up. Interestingly, the results of the study show that teachers want to proceed with the development of criterion-referenced assessment to give pupils accurate and meaningful statements about their experiences and achievements in their dance course, without comparison with others in the group. Other research now being undertaken in the field of dance points to marked differences in the evaluation criteria employed by pupils and teachers. Clearly, if the evaluative and critical faculty is one which we seek to educate, these differences must be explored. The nature of the work and the justification of arts in the curriculum discussed above imply that the only measurement which has any educational meaning is the progress achieved by the pupil. Arguably to compare progress is arrogant and possibly meaningless.

It is to be feared that demands for accountability and evidence of value for money will lead to assessment for certification which at best will be a cynical manipulation of subjective judgements and may be inimical to individual progress. The assessment and grading of personal expressive development is the logical outcome. If that turns out to be the case, schools will not be fit places for arts education.

ASSESSMENT IN THE CLASSROOM

We are left, then, with the problem of devising techniques to implement a collaborative form of assessment to be operated on work which contains at least a measure of the intensely personal, and involves subjective judgements. Teachers of the arts will gain little from the study of texts on assessment. Concepts such as those of mastery learning have little to offer. Mercifully such terms arc little heard in primary schools, and primary schools today have a great deal to offer those in search of possible modes of assessment in the arts. This has much to do with the primacy of pupil-centred learning and a concern for the individual which, however much it is desired and striven for, is not always possible in the later stages of schooling.

When an arts teacher sets about a lesson or a series of lessons, the aims and objectives will most often be couched in a description of process and of activities and media. At the end of the lesson or series of lessons it is possible to state that the process has been gone through, the activities undertaken, and the media experienced or used. This however is not an educational statement.

901

The educational statement in cognitive areas of experience is made when statements of understanding and mastery are made. In arts subjects the educational statement is more complex and can be concerned with the engagement of the pupil with the process, the quality of that engagement, and the nature of judgements. Discussion of these will involve the use of such concepts as imagination, confidence, intention, and sensitivity. We should not fear to use such concepts on the grounds that they are fuzzy. Many concepts are fuzzy and the arts do not have a monopoly. They are, however, not appropriate as constituents of a checklist, although there have been many examples of pupils being awarded grades and marks for imagination. Any educational assessment statement, then, of a pupil's achievement in a lesson will be discursive and intimately personal to that pupil. This is not the stuff of which report cards are made.

It is not the assessment statement which is crucial to the educational process, but the act of assessment itself. The teacher, in approaching the pupil or the pupil's work, will have in mind the qualities and skills with which the lesson is concerned. There is, however, no way in which the teacher can predict the effect of input in a creative arts situation, and therefore no way in which the outcome can be predicted. There is certainly no way it can be precisely quantified. It is not being implied that creative arts teaching is a matter of input and random output. This is where the experienced and professional judgement of the teacher is most crucial. Through discussion of the use of media, the introduction of new technique, suggestion, and questions as to intention, the teacher engages with the pupil in the arts activity. It is sensitive and relevant assessment and evaluation. There is an elegance of fit found nowhere else in the curriculum.

Assessment practice in the arts has been the subject of much debate and discussion of recent years mainly as a result of attempts at certification. There is as yet no corpus of techniques and procedures which are widely regarded as satisfactory. Perhaps there never will be. After all, the assessment of other areas of education with long assessment experience is still problematic. This should not be seen as reason for despair. Education must be dynamic and evolutionary to answer the needs of our customers, the pupils; and the assessment of arts education must also evolve.

This evolution depends on two factors; on the demands of assessment for certification and their associated literature and activities, and, crucially, on the developing expertise of the classroom teacher. Because of the nature of arts teaching and because of the developmental nature of arts assessment, the contribution of the classroom teacher is central. A concomitant of this must be that the teacher can nowhere find 'The Rules'. There are no 'Tips for Teachers' in this field, and probably never will be. There must however be a way of providing support to both tyro and experienced teachers. Where is that support to be found?

Given the argument above and the current climate with regards to assessment, it hardly seems necessary to state that neither psychometric nor normative approaches to assessment are appropriate. Nor do such instruments as the grid proposed by the Department of Education and Science's Assessment of Performance Unit's aesthetic development group, or the assessment arrangements for the Scottish Standard Grade, provide an answer. They can however be regarded as a staging point where the ground has been cleared for further development, and are as essential to the discourse as a discussion of the nature of the arts in education. More useful is the work of curricular bodies, such as the former subject committees of the Consultative Committee on the Curriculum in Scotland, and the Schools Curriculum Development Service's Arts in Schools Project in England and Wales. This work is firmly based in classroom experience. School-based research projects will also provide useful insights.

The process which will move instruments and techniques of assessment forward is the devising of such mundane articles as worksheets and checklists by informed teachers. There is no easy way out. And such worksheets and checklists will inevitably be open-ended and discursive if they are to be in any sense useful. Further, they may often involve collaboration with pupils and encourage self-assessment. They will be diverse and reflect local and individual preoccupations and strengths. That should not worry us, for an inevitable result of the analysis of the content and purpose of teaching must be a fuller and deeper understanding of the experience of arts education. I should also hope for a more comfortable and confident acceptance of the imponderable, the uncertain, and the diverse.

REFERENCES

1. Abbs, P. (1980) *English Within the Arts*, London: Hodder & Stoughton.
2. Criterion-Referenced Assessment for Modern Dance; Criterion-Referenced Assessment for Physical Education, Working Paper No. 4, Dunfermline College of Physical Education, March 1985.

SCHOOL-BASED ASSESSMENT

W. A. GATHERER

INTRODUCTION

Assessment is an integral feature of teaching, but there are many forms of assessment and various uses made of the results. At any stage assessment may be used to diagnose learning difficulties, to analyse and predict progress, to grade pupils within a class or year group in a school, to offer pupils a record of their achievements, or to select pupils for admission to a further stage of education. This discussion deals with assessment which yields a summative evaluation of pupils' achievements for purposes of certification or accreditation at the end of an educational stage.

The most common form of assessment for these purposes has traditionally been the external examination. This is still the most widespread means of arriving at exit levels of achievement in use in the world, and for secondary pupils it is likely to remain so in many countries. The most common alternative to external assessment is assessment conducted by teachers within their schools; however, external and internal assessment can be combined to produce summative evaluation of attainment.[1] Increasingly, public assessment authorities are delegating responsibility for summative assessment to schools: the actual degree of responsibility varies among the different systems, and varies also in different evolutionary phases of a developing system. Some systems accord almost total autonomy to schools; others accord very little. For various reasons which will be discussed there is now a growing movement towards autonomous school-based assessment, in which the schools are empowered to conduct all the assessment procedures leading to exit certification.

THE GROWTH OF TEACHER PARTICIPATION

In primary education there has been an increasing encouragement of professional autonomy for teachers throughout the twentieth century. But it was not until the availability of secondary schooling for all precluded the need for selection at the stage of primary-secondary transition that external assessment was discontinued. In more advanced school systems, such as in Canada, Australia, and New Zealand, external examinations for admission to secondary schools were discontinued in the 1930s and 1940s. Non-selective secondary schooling had been established in the USA and the Soviet Union long before the Second World War. In Britain teachers' internal assessments were beginning to replace the external attainment tests by the 1960s; and the establishment of comprehensive school systems virtually dispensed with the need for selective tests in primary schools.

In secondary education also the movement towards school autonomy in assessment was successful much earlier in Canada, Australia, and New Zealand. It was not until the 1960s that progress was achieved in Britain. The Norwood Committee's proposal in 1943 that all examining at 15+ should be left to schools was never seriously considered; but the new Certificate of Secondary Education (the CSE), introduced in 1963, gave strong encouragement to schools wishing to develop their own curricula and assessment schemes.

By the 1960s, however, there was a powerful movement among the more progressive educators in favour of school-based assessment, particularly for pupils leaving at the earliest statutory age. Experience from abroad, particularly the USA and some of the Commonwealth countries, showed that school-based assessment was compatible with a high level of public confidence and authority. The performance of secondary modern pupils in the GCE Ordinary Level examinations was sufficiently poor to reinforce the argument that the external examinations reflected university requirements rather than the desirable outcomes of a relevant modern education. Characteristically government responded not by abandoning external examinations for the ordinary school leavers, as had been done almost everywhere else in the developed world, but by instituting yet another set of examinations. Nevertheless the new Certificate of Secondary Education, introduced in 1963, encouraged schools themselves to assume greater responsibility for curriculum and assessment. Three modes of examination were allowed for the CSE: under Mode 1 the examination was set externally and based on a syllabus devised for the Regional Examination Board; under Mode 2 the examination was externally set but based on a syllabus devised by one or a group of schools; under Mode 3 the schools set and marked their own examinations, which were based on locally prepared syllabuses. Mode 3 represented a significant approach towards school-based assessment, but the schools' autonomy was strictly limited, as the Boards continued to moderate both syllabuses and assessments, and to award the certificates.

During the 1960s and 1970s the growing popularity of Mode 3 reflected the movement towards school autonomy. The percentage of subject entries under Mode 3 rose from about twelve per cent to over 26 per cent between 1969 and 1978. All 14 of the Regional Examination Boards were encouraging school-based assessment; a small number of schools even assumed responsibility for a measure of assessment in the more prestigious GCE. Unfortunately the trend was somewhat halted during the early 1980s.[2] The new General Certificate of Secondary Education, designed to replace the CSE and the GCE O Level by 1988, has several new features, such as the basing of all syllabuses and assessment and grading procedures on national criteria, the differentiation of assessments to meet the capabilities of a wide range of pupils, and the issuing of criteria-related grades; and there is a substantial element of coursework which will generally be assessed internally by teachers. Although all syllabuses will be scrutinized to ensure that they comply with the national criteria, all three of the 'CSE' Modes will be allowed. There can be little doubt that the GCSE examination system represents a decisive shift towards partial school-based assessment.

In Scotland, where the school system is separate from that of England and Wales, all terminal external examinations had been set, administered, and marked by the state inspectorate until the establishment of a national Examination Board in 1964. Although teachers were now predominant as examiners there was no move towards school-based assessment except in certain practical subjects such as music, home economics, and technical education. Two major reports were issued in 1977, one urging a more comprehensive curriculum for the 14- to 16-year-olds, and the other proposing a single certificate, with differential grading for all these pupils. The old Ordinary Grade of the Scottish Certificate of Education is to give way to an elaborate scheme of external examinations at three levels, Credit, General, and Foundation. By 1983 a three-level syllabus had been produced for all subjects; an element of coursework was included in many of these, and the internal assessment of proportions of the examination content was being piloted. The system acquired a number of technical innovations, such as grade-related criterial references, but it remained essentially centralist and conservative. A number of schools which had adopted the CSE Mode 3 from England now found themselves forced to move backwards. The new Standard Grade assessment scheme, however, represented a significant increase in the responsibility of schools in respect of assessment; unfortunately this was not accompanied by sufficient resources and staff training, and the new examinations were boycotted as part of a prolonged industrial dispute.

MODELS OF SCHOOL-BASED ASSESSMENT SCHEMES

The models of assessment which have developed in such systems as England and Wales, Scotland, Israel, and elsewhere are not school-based, however great the proportion of the actual marking may be done by teachers, in or out of their schools: these systems are centralist and externally controlled. School-based assessment schemes give the staff in schools the freedom to design courses, to collect their own data, and to decide on the balance to be struck as to different technical methods of assessment. In different systems the degree of autonomy accorded to schools will vary, and it is this which is the most distinctive feature of a scheme. In Britain school autonomy is nil. In the United States, it is virtually total.

In the USA, the school systems have grown historically as intensely localized organizations, and there has been no serious interest at either federal or State level in an imposed examination system. The high school diploma remains the standard academic target for the majority of pupils. Externally devised assessment is, certainly, abundant in the form of College Entrance examinations and a vast use of standardized tests of attainment. In recent times a number of States have made efforts to control the outcome of secondary schooling. Some stipulate that specific courses must be assessed for the high school diploma. The most typical situation is that some requirements are mandated by the State legislature and some by the local school board. Many States lay down performance standards as prerequisites for high school graduation; others merely require that instruction be provided on listed subjects or fields. The application of performance standards in the form of descriptors of competencies is now widespread: this allows a State to determine at least a general curricular core. Ultimately, however, the American high school retains its traditional freedom to identify the criteria and develop the mechanisms for the assessment of its graduating students.

In countries where a high percentage of pupils stay on beyond the minimum leaving age, as in the USA, Canada, and Australia, there is little emphasis on the certification of 15–16-year-olds, and less need to operate elaborate methods of comparing assessment standards for this age group. It is in countries where the staying-on rate is low, such as England and Wales and Scotland, that the summative assessment of the younger pupils assumes importance. In almost every country, however, there has been a greater willingness to relax formal assessment procedures for this age group. It is apparent that experimentation and innovation is less popular when it seriously affects the selection of candidates for higher education: in England and Wales, for example, the A level examinations remained virtually intact during twenty years of debate and change in the examining of the younger age group. Even in the more advanced systems in Canada, Australia, and New Zealand, university entrance or matriculation certificates are competed for by examination or some other formalized arrangement. The 'accrediting' or 'recommending' schemes whereby some pupils are awarded admission without sitting examinations are carefully supervised and moderated.

Nevertheless there are some interesting examples of school-based assessment for the older age group. In Victoria, Australia, courses for the Higher School Certificate are of two kinds: Group 1 courses are mainly assessed externally, though some components are assessed in schools; Group 2 courses are wholly school-based, though they must be approved by the Victoria Institute of Secondary Education.[3] A group of Victorian schools has developed an alternative certification scheme, the STC (the Schools Year Twelve and Tertiary Entrance Certificate), for which the courses are developed and assessed by the schools: the pupils are not graded, the certificate containing only verbal descriptions of the pupil's abilities, the work completed, and an indication of how well it was done for each subject.[4]

One of the most thoroughly developed systems of school-based assessment in the world is that of Queensland, Australia. Instituted in 1971, the Queensland ROSBA (Review of School Based Assessment) evinces many of the best features of a successful scheme. It was the result of several major reports which were intensively studied and debated by all interested bodies. The principles, procedures, and educational effects of a first model were reviewed after five years, and modifications were made to produce a new model which was more efficient and more acceptable to the profession and the public. From the beginning this was an assessment scheme designed in close association with curriculum development. There has been heavy investment in staff training. Strenuous and successful efforts were made to win the active support of the tertiary institutions in the state, and negotiations gained acceptance of the certificates by other Australian universities and colleges. The public, particularly parents and employers, are consulted regularly and kept informed about the system's rationale and procedures.

The Queensland system is run by a statutory Board of Secondary School Studies which is representative of the State, teachers' unions, tertiary staff, religious bodies, and industry. The Board issues Junior and Senior Certificates to pupils completing ten and twelve years of education. The system of accreditation involves teachers at every stage. As there are many independent schools in Queensland, the relationship between Board and school is a contractual one. A school may apply to offer courses of two kinds: Board Subjects, with syllabuses approved by the Board, and work programmes subject to its accreditation procedures; and Board Registered School Subjects, developed by individual schools, with work programmes conforming to guidelines provided by the Board. For each type of course the Board awards certificates recording the exit level of achievement in five categories: *very high, high, sound, limited*, and *very limited*. Standards are monitored and maintained by District Review Panels and State Review Panels, which are responsible for maintaining State-wide standards for both work programmes and assessment in their own subject.

By 1985 there were 35 State Review Panels comprising teachers, secondary and tertiary, who have applied for inclusion in a Register of Panelists and have been appointed by the Board.[5] It is still necessary to determine orders of merit for the candidates for admission to tertiary institutions in Queensland, and for this purpose Tertiary Entrance Scores summate the global achievements of pupils; these, combined with scholastic aptitude test scores and special subject assessments produced by the schools, determine a State rank order of Year 12 pupils.

Various methods of moderating school assessments are in use in different school-based assessment schemes. The most widespread is moderation by reference tests, which are used both to establish norms throughout the system, and internally to help teachers determine their own standards. Item banks are now widely accepted as a useful tool to help teachers compile their own tests. State or commercial testing services provide both item banks and scores from computer-assisted marking. Another common method is moderation by consortium, when teachers meet to study marked samples and discuss standards. A less common and less popular method is moderation by inspection, where full-time officers or seconded teachers visit schools to scrutinize samples of work.[6]

SOCIAL AND POLITICAL ISSUES

Assessments which lead to public credentials inevitably take on social importance. External examinations, conducted in accordance with overt rules and procedures, have earned a substantial measure of public trust. School-based assessment schemes, on the other hand, are open to certain fears and doubts. By far the most prevalent fear is variability in standards. Teachers may be able to discriminate quite efficiently among their own pupils, but they cannot reliably compare their own ratings with those of others in a larger system. As we have seen, there are satisfactory ways of ensuring that school assessments can be moderated and standardized, but these must be perfected and made explicit if a school-based assessment scheme is to gain the public confidence accorded to traditional systems.

Another doubt relating to school-based assessment is the ability of such schemes to maintain standards from year to year. That slippage can occur occasionally is evident from an experience such as that in Ontario in 1968, when, a year after the abolition of the external university entrance examination, the pass rate leapt from about 50 per cent to 69 per cent. It may have been the case, of course, that pass rates fixed on the basis of the external examinations had been too low; in any case there is insufficient evidence to suggest that school assessments will always tend to be over-generous. That teachers will be biased, either in favour of or against their pupils, is another widespread reservation. The very 'externality' of the external examiners seems to lend them greater impartiality. The external examinations are seen to be administered according to publicly reported rules, and their results arrived at in an atmosphere of confidentiality. In developing school-based assessment systems it is important that public respect be sought and won by providing ample information and explanation.

The recurrent cry that 'standards are falling' tends to act against public acceptance of school-based assessment. A state-controlled system of external examinations can respond swiftly to any such fear: standards can be forced up by making questions harder, pass marks higher, pass rates lower. The mechanisms available to a school-based system such as that of Queensland would allow such action by the authorities, but in any system dependent on teachers' in-school work it would be more difficult, and much more time-consuming, to influence results by decree.

Ultimately objections to school-based assessment would seem to be a product of educational conservatism. Traditional systems are seen to be 'safe', 'well-tried', 'reliable', while novel systems are thought to be 'trendy', 'sloppy', 'unreliable'. For some right-wing politicians it appears that school-based assessment gives teachers opportunities to promulgate subversive views. Some opponents make much of the likely increased cost of school-based assessment. It is true that the development of any new system will require additional investment, especially if school-based assessment is introduced as a supplement to external examinations. But the cost of a school-based assessment scheme cannot realistically be estimated until it has been designed, and until account has been taken, for example, of potential savings arising from reorganized arrangements.

It can be argued that school-based assessment tends to detract from schools' accountability to those who provide and manage them: the education authorities, the community, and society in general. The administrative apparatus of an externally controlled system is more readily subject to political control. The external examination itself can constitute a 'court of appeal' for pupils against their teachers' judgements. The results obtained by schools can be held to indicate their effectiveness. In contrast, schools' internal assessments may be thought to be more secretive and less amenable to public scrutiny. In fact a school-based assessment system can be just as easily observed and monitored. Provided that sufficient care has been taken, public accountability can even be much greater: parents can be kept informed continuously as to their children's progress; schools can be visited and their arrangements viewed in operation;

more detailed accounts can be given more frequently to the community. Since the curriculum and the assessment scheme are intimately related, the public can see more deeply into the processes whereby judgements are made. Finally, school-based assessment can involve individual pupils in assessing their own attainments, needs, interests, and capabilities, and thus can be held accountable to the person for whom the educational system primarily exists.

THE EDUCATIONAL CASE

On educational grounds, many educators deprecate the fact that external examinations dictate the curriculum from a distance, perpetuating practices which are inimical to the best features of modern pupil-centred education. External examinations are also limited in their technical efficiency. They tend not to assess oral proficiency or practical skills, or do so clumsily and partially; they neglect the important educational roles of growth, motivation, and experimentation. Worst of all, they produce judgements of pupils' ability on the basis of predesigned formulas from isolated, unnatural situations in which pupils are inhibited rather than encouraged to express themselves. Even the most modern external examinations are incapable of assessing the whole range of attributes now deemed to have educational significance.

School-based assessment can be designed to suit the specific needs and interests of particular pupils. Diagnostic and summative testing can be linked. Experiential learning gained in community service projects or aesthetic activities can be assessed. Personal qualities, academic abilities, practical skills can all be taken into account to produce a comprehensive, highly informative 'pupil profile' or 'record of achievement'.[7] Because the teachers are in control of both the curriculum and the means of assessment the relationship between learning and the measurement of achievement can be sensitive, responsive, and flexible.

For some teachers the external examination absolves them in part from their responsibility for their pupils' success or failure. It constitutes a target that teacher and pupils can tackle together; they can be allies against a common foe; the teacher can act as counsel rather than judge, mentor rather than arbiter. This is not a fruitful relationship, however: it compels both teacher and pupils to devalue the educational content of the curriculum, and it deprives pupils of the opportunity of engaging with their teachers in negotiating their own education. When the assessment is integral to the work of the school there can be a much more productive relationship. Assessment can then be a natural, even imperceptible, accompaniment to teaching. Pupils can more clearly understand why and how their understanding and skills are being measured. The pace of their learning can be controlled by their needs, rather than by the amount of content to be covered for an examination. Failure to master a learning task can be understood and acted upon much earlier.

The responsiveness of a school-based assessment system derives from its capacity to relate the curriculum to particular educational requirements. Any feature of the school's environment can be selected as a domain of learning and also as a focus for assessing pupils' attainments. Any change in the community can quickly be reflected in curricular change. Any change in a pupil's personal circumstances, such as prolonged absence, can be catered for. Most of these responses are, of course, possible within an externally controlled assessment system. It is argued in favour of school-based assessment that schools can respond to change more speedily and more sensitively.

The greater flexibility of school-based assessment lies in the wider range of assessment methods available. Testing can be more frequent and less conspicuous. Continuous assessment can be used more effectively. New modes of assessment can be used. Individual, group, and class assignments can be used. Work in class can be recorded with a range of attributes being described. Estimates of pupils' attainments can be obtained beyond the classroom: team teaching, community projects, work experience can all yield a wider range of judgements. Practical skills can be assessed by actual performance rather than in an artificial examination: for example, seamanship can be assessed while the pupil is actually sailing a boat.

It is sometimes alleged that school-based assessment contrasts with externally controlled assessment in being less 'systematic' or 'scientific'. This is not necessarily the case. Comprehensive structures of guidance are made available to teachers in such systems as those of Queensland or Ontario. The Ontario Assessment Instrument Pool, for example, consists of a variety of assessment instruments developed to meet the goals proposed for specific courses, comprising multiple choice, matching, and open-ended formats, applicable to oral and written tests, tasks, graphic display interpretation, and other mark-assigning situations.

School-based assessment is not necessarily a substitute for other means of summative evaluation. As we have seen, it may be developed as a component of an externally controlled system. It may be one of a variety of methods employed in an evaluation package, as in the USA. It may be simply an aspect of the day-to-day work of the classroom, as in most primary schools. More than anything else, it is an expression of teachers' professional concern for their pupils' progress in learning. It may well, in the future, develop as the only truly satisfactory method of monitoring learning in school.

NOTES

1. Macintosh, H. G. and Hale, D. E. (1976) *Assessment and the Secondary School Teacher*, London: Routledge & Kegan Paul.
2. Bowe, R. and Whitty, G. 'Teachers, boards and standards: The attack on school-based assessment in English public examinations at 15+', in Broadfoot, P. (Ed.) (1984) *Assessment, Schools and Society*, London: Methuen; *Selection, Certification and Control*, London: The Falmer Press.
3. Victoria Institute of Secondary Education (1984) *Handbook for 1985 Year 12 Curriculum and Assessment*, Melbourne: VISE.
4. Cole, P. (Ed.) (1984) *Curriculum Issues*, Melbourne: VISE.
5. Board of Secondary School Studies (1985) *Handbook of Procedures for Accreditation and Certification*, Brisbane. See also the Discussion Papers issued by the Board in January and April 1986.
6. Elley, W. B. and Livingstone, D. (1972) *External Examinations and Internal Assessments*, Wellington: New Zealand Council for Educational Research; also *Learning and Achieving*, Department of Education, Wellington, New Zealand, 1986; also D. A. Walker (1979) 'The standardisation of school assessments', in *Issues in Educational Assessment*, Scottish Education Department, Edinburgh: HMSO.
7. Burgess, T. and Adams, E. (1985) *Records of Achievement at 16*, London: NFER/Nelson.

D. INDIVIDUAL DEVELOPMENT

8. INDIVIDUAL DIFFERENCES AND DEVELOPMENT

8.0

INTRODUCTION: INDIVIDUAL DIFFERENCES AND DEVELOPMENT

MARGARET SUTHERLAND

When we are concentrating on the various ways of providing formal education, the curriculum, methods and assessment, or the place of education in different societies, it is sometimes easy to forget about the people who are at the receiving end. Yet in educating we are constantly reminded that individual children have distinct personalities and their own ways of behaving and learning. To educate effectively we need to give attention to these individual differences.

One of the main questions is where personality and other characteristics come from. Is the individual simply born to be like that or do the influences of parents, teachers and our neighbourhood environment decide what kind of people we are? There have been very many controversies as to whether most of the characteristics of the individual are due to heredity or are the result of experience, being produced by informal and formal learning. Some authorities state that highly important abilities and personal qualities are indeed decided by inborn factors, the result of genes inherited from the parents and more remote ancestors: others assert that abilities and personality depend on the environment provided from the earliest years onwards. Folklore gives great importance to heredity, seeing in children's behaviour resemblances to their parents or other relations, finding causes in 'bad blood' or 'good stock': it also expects boys and girls to be 'naturally' different in behaviour and personality. But various scientific arguments have given much greater weight to the effects of the environment – and pointed out that even within one family, the environment can be different for younger or older children, for boys or girls, according to parents' preferences and resources – and the child's interaction with them. Similarly, attention has been drawn to the effects that a good home environment can have on children's 'intelligence' as well as on their health – and health itself will affect the development of ability and personality. Deciding whether heredity or environment is more important is especially difficult, because for most children the parents (through whom various characteristics may be inherited) usually also provide the environment in which the child grows. So resemblance to one or other parent could be due either to inheriting that trait or to living in that parent's company. Definite conclusions have not yet been reached, though it seems probable that heredity and environment combine – in uncertain proportions – to produce the distinctive individual. But it is certainly important to think about the evidence available here.

Another important question is whether all children, in spite of individual differences, naturally go through the same stages of development. It has been recognized for a long time that children develop only gradually the ability to understand complex ideas and knowledge. In the eighteenth century Rousseau put forward the idea that children grow through distinctive stages of development: but it is only in comparatively recent times that methodical attempts have been made to discover what these stages are and if indeed all children go through them. We now have evidence of some such stages, not only in reasoning ability, but also in awareness of other people and in making moral judgements. So we can recognize that while individual children progress at different rates, there are common elements in individuals' development.

An important consideration here also has been to decide whether educators can affect the progress through the various stages or must simply wait for it to happen. Again, recent evidence suggests that educators can help progress to the next stage, and that some environments can speed up or retard this progress. It also indicates that we have to be careful in making sure we do understand children's thinking at any stage.

At the same time, recent scientific studies remind us of individual differences. They show personality characteristics which are not wholly due to learning experiences in a given environment. There are also differences in abilities, with some children performing much better than others in various school activities, in the arts, in athletics and sports, or socially. Educators have then to consider how best to adapt education to these differences in personality and abilities.

Among the abilities which have received most attention from educators and others is that of 'intelligence'. Here also we have different theories and definitions. It is useful, since the topic is so controversial, to reconsider how psychologists have thought about intelligence, since the end of the last century up to the present time; and how the much criticized tests of intelligence have been developed. It is useful also to note the findings of research on the social and health conditions which are likely to affect individuals' development and performance in this area.

In this section therefore we begin with a survey of thinking about intelligence and intelligence tests, and an outline of a new concept of 'intelligence'. We then have results of research indicating practical strategies in educating gifted children.

Moving to studies of children's development of thinking, we have a discussion of the abilities that children bring to the early years of schooling. To accompany this cognitive survey, we have an account of children's development of social awareness during these early years, followed by a parallel outline of their development of moral and religious thinking.

Yet individual differences do accompany these developments: so attention is next given to what seem to be innate differences in temperament, possibly bound up with physical characteristics, as well as to the differences in styles of thinking which combine cognitive and affective elements. It is interesting to note here how the teacher's own temperament and style of thought may interact favourably or less favourably with those of some children.

Combining interests in environment and heredity, we then have a chapter on the effects of both social and physical factors on children's ability and school performance. Similarly, a discussion of possible sex differences in personality and ability shows conflicting beliefs about inborn and acquired characteristics, revealing the effects which environment, social expectations and education may have here. Finally, since adolescence is a period of life when both physical and social changes may strongly affect the individual, the section concludes with a survey of the characteristics of this stage and of factors which may help adolescents.

There is much more that could be said on all these problems – all the authors would have liked to write at greater length. But it is hoped that these chapters will show the most important aspects and ideas. All the contributors would also have liked to suggest a great deal more reading on their special topic, but the references given should considerably help the reader who is anxious to know more about some of the areas discussed.

8.1

INTELLIGENCE AND INTELLIGENCE TESTS

DESMOND FURNEAUX

'Intelligence Tests' are designed to assess individual differences in cognitive development. They can rightly be classified as 'mental tests', because the operations they involve have to be specified in sufficient detail, and conducted in a standardized way; the rules governing the way in which their results are described (for example as a score or classification) have also to be explicit.

The work of the Frenchman Alfred Binet, and of the Englishman Charles Spearman, serves to illustrate important features of their evolution. Spearman had been an engineering officer in the British army, before retiring at the age of 34 to pursue a long-standing interest in psychology, working initially in several German universities. Binet had medical training and his interest in cognition developed out of an earlier commitment to abnormal psychology. The very different backgrounds of these two men profoundly influenced the nature of their researches.

EXAMINING THE DEVELOPING INTELLECT

From about 1887, Binet's studies of the higher mental functions involved the investigation not only of cognitive attributes such as memory, comprehension, and judgement, but also of non-cognitive qualities like suggestibility and persistence. Much of his work involved the schools of Paris, where he studied various methods of designing and using mental tests, and looked for reasonably objective methods for charting the development of the higher functions. Teachers established numerous 'criterion groups' for him, by picking out the pupils they judged to be the least and the most intelligent. Binet could then identify those tests which most clearly distinguished between the two levels. He undertook fundamental long-term studies of this own children, and his student, Th. Simon, tested subnormal children in the asylum of Vaucluse. In such ways, Binet gained an international reputation for his studies of intellectual development.

In 1904, at Binet's suggestion, the French Ministry of Public Instruction established a Commission to consider what measures should be taken for identifying and educating children who, perhaps because of mental defect, failed to profit from normal schooling. It recommended the provision of special schools, admission to which would be controlled by a medical and pedagogical examination which included a systematic psychological assessment. Binet undertook to design, with Simon's collaboration, what was then a novel form of assessment, based on mental testing instead of psychiatric examination. This was to be a 'scale' composed of 'a series of tests arranged in order of increasing difficulty'. Binet thought that 'intelligence' subsumed a variety of attributes, such as memory, comprehension, judgement, etc., and that his tests should therefore cover a broad spectrum of cognitive functions, as well as being easy to administer rapidly.

The first (1905) version of the Binet-Simon scale consisted of thirty tests. Illustrative of the ascending levels of function tapped are the following brief descriptions of selected tests, each numbered by its position in the scale.

9. Naming objects pointed to in a picture.
12. Picking out the heavier of two weights.
18. Drawing from memory two different designs shown simultaneously for ten seconds.
28. Giving the time that it would appear to be if the large and small hands of a clock were interchanged at various given times.
30. Giving distinctions between abstract terms, for example, liking and respecting a person; being bored and being sad.

For every test, Binet could define the standard of performance characteristic of average, retarded, and subnormal children assessed at ages of about three to eleven years, although the definition and selection of the relevant standardization samples did not of course satisfy modern requirements. A child would normally attempt all thirty tests and the diagnosis would then indicate by how many years his development was advanced or retarded, not only overall, but for each test separately, and whether in some (or all) ways he had to be classified in the subnormal category.

For a subsequent revision (1908) the number of tests and the age range covered were both increased, and, for each test, the lowest age at which children making normal progress at school could complete the task successfully was ascertained. This age was defined as the 'mental age' needed for success. The tests were then arranged in sets by mental age, which were administered in ascending order during testing. Performance was reported in terms of a mental-age score – this being the highest age level at which all the relevant tests had been performed satisfactorily. Curiously, Binet did not himself remark on the importance of the step he had taken in revising his scale in this way.

The original version provided a profile of performance over the variety of cognitive functions assessed. There was no 'score' for 'intelligence', although a judgement was made as to whether a child's performance was normal for her or his age. The revision took much greater account of Binet's view that, although intelligence was complex, it involved what he called 'a central organ' – some component or combination of qualities which was of crucial importance. The mental age score represented an attempt to specify the stage of development reached by this 'organ', as a numerical index. A further revision in 1911 improved the scale without changing its basic character.

W. Stern, a noted German psychologist, suggested in 1912 that a more useful index would specify the relationship between mental age (MA) and chronological age (CA), and from this suggestion the Intelligence Quotient (IQ) evolved, where $IQ = (MA/CA) \times 100$.

L. M. Terman, from Stanford university, published an American revision in 1916, and also, with M. Merrill, in 1937 and 1960. This latest version, still widely used, incorporates every improvement in content, standardization, and calibration available when it was produced, but it still employs many of Binet's original tests, and uses the basic principles of measurement that he introduced.

MAPPING THE STRUCTURE OF INTELLECT

Spearman's work involved data analysis at a much more sophisticated level than did Binet's. His objective was to determine whether the complex activities of intellect might be classified, for purposes of description and measurement, in some comparatively simple way. His method was to study the relationships between different kinds of cognitive test, the degree of relationship between any two tests being measured by the extent to which they both placed people in the same rank order. The 'correlation coefficient' developed by Galton and Pearson was used to provide an objective numerical index of such similarity. Comparing every test in a set with every other generates a set of such coefficients, which can then be arranged systematically into a Table of Correlations for purposes of analysis.

In 1904, Spearman described a method of 'Factor-Analysis' for facilitating the interpretation of a Table of Correlations. Using this, he concluded that his data supported his 'two-factor theory'. This was that only two kinds of independent descriptive categories, or 'factors', were needed for categorizing individual differences in cognitive task performance. One kind, the 'general factor' ('g'), covered some function active in every test performance. The other covered functions specific to each individual task. A 'central organ of intellect' could thus be postulated, but only tests involving mainly 'g' could contribute usefully to its description.

Subsequent British research showed that Spearman's conclusions were partly justified. However, they implied that within groups of people having the same level of 'g', tests would not intercorrelate at all, and this proved to be untrue. In such groups, tests which all involve verbal, numerical, or similar abstract coding operations fundamental to academic learning, do intercorrelate. So do tests which all involve the ability to visualize, manipulate, or analyse images in visual space. Since virtually all tests examined fell into one of these two subsets, the factors their interrelatedness defined were called 'major group-factors' – the 'verbal-educational' (v:ed) factor on the one hand, and the 'spatial-mechanical' (k:m), on the other. Similarly, after removing the joint effects of 'g' and the major group-factors, the persistence of further remaining correlations generated a fairly large number of minor group-factors. Each of these turned out to involve a subset of tests assessing the same intellectual operations – numerical in one case, verbal in another, and so on. The development of this theoretical model, involving a hierarchy of independent factors, owed much to ideas worked out by Cyril Burt and Philip Vernon.

In the United States, however, L. L. Thurstone developed an improved form of factor-analysis, and by 1938 had identified seven independent 'primary mental abilities' (PMA) – verbal meaning, numerical ability, spatial ability, perceptual speed, rote memory, inductive reasoning, and verbal fluency. He found no reason to postulate any general factor.

The controversy about 'g' was resolved when it was realized that Thurstone had tested mainly groups of students, within which the range of intelligence represented was too small for a 'g' factor to be easily demonstrated. In the general population, most of the supposedly independent PMA factors proved to be intercorrelated. They were thus measuring in part something common to all, which Spearman would have identified as 'g', and insofar as they were independent of 'g', they defined a factor structure at a level intermediate between the major and minor group-factors of the Burt/Vernon model.

INTELLIGENCE-TESTING TOOLS

The kind of research described has led to the development of a multiplicity of 'intelligence tests'. By no means all of these derive directly from the Binet, Spearman, or Thurstone approaches, but the majority of procedures can be regarded as variants of these. They divide into a relatively small number of overlapping categories.

In the United Kingdom, Binet scales are still widely used, and numerous studies have shown that what they measure relates closely to 'g'. Spearman-type 'g' tests are also widely used, each consisting of a set of 'items' (i.e. questions, problems, designs, etc.) so chosen as to assess almost entirely 'g' when considered together. From some of these, scores for v:ed and k:m can also be derived. Any desired combination of 'g' with selected major and/or minor group-factors can be assessed by appropriate design, and such tests are used for many specialized purposes.

In the United States, there is greater emphasis on assessment that ignores 'g' in favour of Thurstone's PMA tests, or other similar procedures. A 'g' score can easily be computed as a weighted average from such tests, however. Particular combinations of PMA scores are useful for specialized purposes.

Any test may be designed as either an age-scale or a point-scale. An age-scale reports the chronological age at which a 'normal' person would just reach the level of attainment achieved. A point-scale simply gives a mark, for comparing with marks achieved by other people.

Almost any intelligence test is likely to be designated an 'IQ Test', but strictly speaking, this nomenclature is justified only for an age scale. For most people, moreover, mental age stops increasing before they reach a chronological age of about nineteen. An IQ of one hundred at age twenty would thus drop to only fifty at age forty, and would decline through every level of imbecility thereafter. This difficulty could be avoided by reporting mental age rather than IQ, but few mature adults would relish being told that they had a mental age of (say) sixteen, although this would actually mean that they were above average. The difficulty is overcome by assigning a so-called 'deviation IQ'. This is a sort of age-corrected IQ, based on how much above or below average the person has scored in some suitable point-scale test. A 'real' IQ, based on a comparison of mental and chronological ages, is known as a classical IQ.

'Group tests' are designed for simultaneous administration to groups as large as can effectively be supervised. The salient features of responses must therefore be easily recorded for marking. 'Paper-and-pencil' tests, for example, require either written responses or the use of answer sheets in multiple-choice format. The latter may be suitable for scoring by 'mark-sensing' techniques involving optical or electronic scanning. 'Individual tests' such as Binet scales, are evaluated in terms of features of response which are too complex, difficult, or expensive to record adequately, or which might be influenced undesirably in a group context. They have therefore to be administered to just one person at a time. Practitioners may need a much higher level of training for individual than for group tests.

'Performance tests' assess the integrated activity of perceptual and manipulative skills – for example, in the Porteus Maze the subject is required to trace a path through a printed maze, and in Formboard tests he or she is required to fit variously shaped blocks (such as circles, squares, and crosses) into matching depressions in a board. The average mark for a varied set of performance tests can be expressed as a 'performance IQ', although the capacity that this is concerned with resembles the major group-factor k:m more closely than Spearman's 'g', which latter capacity may be referred to as the 'verbal IQ' to avoid confusion. Some tests, such as those devised for children and adults by D. Wechsler, yield both performance and verbal IQs, and the difference between these may be taken to indicate whether a person is more suited to matters requiring 'practical intelligence' rather than 'abstract (academic) intelligence'.

All tests assume a certain background of knowledge and experience on the part of the individual tested, and are therefore to some degree 'culture-bound'. Those designed to be as universal as possible may be designated as 'culture-free', but the term 'culture-fair' is more common. Some writers reserve 'culture-free' for tests little influenced by even major cross-cultural differences, such as those distinguishing (for example) Scandinavians from Southern Chinese; they then describe as culture-fair tests which are relatively insensitive to differences of education, home background, etc., as between different sub-groups (e.g. social classes) within a culture. An example of a test shown to be substantially culture-fair within a range of western cultures is J. C. Raven's 'Progressive Matrices'. This avoids the problems associated with verbal material, and consists of sixty abstract designs from each of which a part has been removed. A set of six inserts goes with each design, only one of which completes it correctly.

A distinction can be made between 'speed tests' and 'power tests', i.e. between tests designed to be administered with and without a time limit. Early work on this question was poorly designed, and it was wrongly concluded that speed and power were virtually identical. Research by W. D. Furneaux has however shown that measuring mental speed is more difficult than has been assumed, and that if properly accomplished, it does provide information complementary to that from a power test.

WHAT DO INTELLIGENCE-TESTS MEASURE?

The names given to Thurstone-type factors, such as verbal-reasoning ability, etc., serve adequately to define the intellectual operations they are concerned with. One way of defining 'g' would therefore be as that quality common to all those factors. As they correlate closely with 'g' tests, Binet scales could be said to address the same quality. But just what sort of entity or process is involved?

Binet used tests as little dependent as possible on formal instruction at school, but one of his criteria for inclusion was that a test should discriminate effectively between normal and retarded pupils. His scales must thus be regarded as measures of some kind of scholastic aptitude, and there is indeed ample evidence that they can diagnose the capacity for high levels of scholastic attainment even in children who, because of poor home background, absence, and the like, have not previously demonstrated it. However, to say that 'g' is scholastic aptitude is simply to associate two undefined abilities.

At one time or another Binet singled out such qualities as judgement, adaptability, and will, as having a crucial role in the definition of his 'central organ of intellect', but he eventually decided that it was distinct from such qualities, that its development was difficult or impossible to influence directly, and that his scales did not address it directly. His position was thus similar to that of Stern, who in 1914 asserted that tests reached, not the innate intellectual endowment, but that endowment in conjunction with other influences acting up to the moment of testing. Similarly, in 1949 D. O. Hebb distinguished between 'intelligence A', defined as basic neural capacity which could probably not be measured directly, and 'intelligence B', resulting from the interaction of intelligence A and experience, which could be measured by tests. A somewhat similar distinction was made by Cattell in 1963.

If such formulations imply that intelligence is an entity, rather than the name of an examination mark, this does no more than recognize that it is an entity that is postulated. For example, the operations of intellect may reflect outputs generated by neural mechanisms, and specifying their structure and physiology would then provide a description of the postulated 'organ'.

An organ may be described as a set of integrated functions, before its structure is discerned, and cognition is in fact studied increasingly in process terms, and models of intellect based on information-processing ideas. Eysenck, moreover, has reported correlations between IQ and processes discernible from the study of electroencephalograph records (i.e. recordings of electrical pulses in the brain). Spearman himself favoured a process perspective, and his 'neogenetic laws' attempt to describe the psychological processes through which novel mental content is generated. In these he stresses the central role, in determining 'g', of the ability to discern and invent relationships. Thorndike's definition of intelligence as the capacity to bring ideas into association is not dissimilar. Vernon and others suggest that 'g' involves the capacity to acquire, break up, and recombine habits, percepts, concepts, and schemata.

What is needed to legitimize intelligence test scores, however, is not the identification of some capacity that they uniquely address, but the demonstration that, since they correlate usefully with performance in a variety of 'real-life' situations, they can legitimately be used for predicting such performances, and thus for purposes such as diagnosis and selection.

Lewis Terman, of Stanford university, started reporting in 1925 on a study of the development of over fifteen hundred children, aged about eleven, with measured IQs of 140 and over, a score equalled by less than one per cent of children in general. The majority were followed up for some forty years. Compared with average children, they proved to be healthier, better adjusted, more highly educated, more highly achieving, and more socially active. Taken at their face value, such results suggest that IQ tests do have potential as predictors. There have however been comparatively few studies that have examined such correlations with the degree of sophistication required to achieve definitive conclusions. The most adequately researched studies have been of the relationships between IQ and performance in learning situations, such as at all levels of education, officer training in the army, and pilot training in the Air Force. In all these the predictive power of the tests seems to have been adequately demonstrated.

When interpreting correlational studies, a major difficulty is that the underlying relationships may not be with IQ at all, but with some other variable related to IQ. School attainment and IQ are correlated, as are social class and IQ. Does social class determine both IQ and school attainment, or does IQ determine both social class and attainment? If such studies are repeated in samples in which everyone belongs to much the same social class, a (rather smaller) correlation between IQ and attainment still appears: but it is not always possible to control for the influence of variables in this way.

The early designers of tests expected that scores would be influenced by environmental factors, including education, but the users of tests usually found that the IQ measured in late infancy changed little in later years. It is now known that tests applied before the age of about five years give little valid indication of the fully developed IQ. As would be expected, beyond this point successive annual measurements give a closer and closer approximation to the terminal value, and really substantial changes are rare after the age of about ten.

This relative constancy, however, is observed under normal conditions of life, when it might be expected that environmental conditions capable of influencing development would remain fairly constant. Can IQ be substantially affected by environmental factors? Although the USA study 'Operation Headstart' produced only disappointing and apparently temporary results, the Milwaukee programme achieved an apparently stable enhancement of about 20 IQ points in children whose mothers had an IQ below 75, if those mothers accepted an extremely intrusive level of intervention in their child-rearing practices. This study does therefore seem to have demonstrated unequivocally that environmental manipulation, albeit of a most comprehensive (and expensive) kind, can be effective.

This brief exposition has had to be highly selective, and many important researchers, and many important topics, have been omitted. Further reading is essential for anyone whose interest extends beyond the sketch-plan presented here. A well organized and very readable overview, with an excellent bibliography, is available in *Human Intelligence, its Nature and Assessment*, by H. J. Butcher (Methuen). *Human Intelligence, Perspectives and Prospects*, by R. Kail and J. W. Pellegrino (Freeman & Co) can also be strongly recommended, in spite of some lacunae in the coverage of European research – it is particularly good when dealing with process-models for intellectual activities, and it too has a useful bibliography. *The Role of Testing in Schools* by Ray Sumner (NFER-Nelson) gives useful information for the teacher who has to decide what procedures to use.

8.2

THE THEORY OF MULTIPLE INTELLIGENCES[1]

HOWARD GARDNER

CONTRASTING POINTS OF VIEW

Two 11-year-old children are taking a test of 'intelligence'. They sit at their desks labouring over the meanings of different words, the interpretation of graphs, and the solutions to arithmetic problems. They record their answers by filling in small circles on a single piece of paper. Later these completed answer sheets are scored objectively: the number of right answers is converted into a standardized score that compares the individual child with a population of children of similar age.

The teachers of these children review the different scores. They notice that one of the children has performed at a superior level; on all sections of the test, she answered more questions correctly than did her peers. In fact, her score is similar to that of children three to four years older. The other child's performance is 'average' – his scores reflect those of other children his age.

A subtle change in expectations surrounds the review of these test scores. Teachers begin to expect the first child to do quite well during her formal schooling, whereas the second should have only moderate success. Indeed these predictions come true. In other words, the test taken by the 11-year-olds serves as a reliable predictor of their later performance in school.

How does this happen? One explanation involves our free use of the word 'intelligence': the child with the greater 'intelligence' has the ability to solve problems, to find the answers to specific questions, and to learn new material quickly and efficiently. These skills in turn play a central role in school success. In this view, 'intelligence' is a singular faculty that is brought to bear in any problem-solving situation. Since schooling deals largely with solving problems of various sorts, predicting this capacity in young children predicts their future success in school.

'Intelligence', from this point of view, is a general ability that is found in varying degrees in all individuals. It is the key to success in solving problems. This ability can be measured reliably with standardized pencil-and-paper tests that, in turn, predict future success in school.[2]

What happens after school is completed? Consider the two individuals in the example. Looking further down the road, we find that the 'average' student has become a highly successful mechanical engineer who has risen to a position of prominence in both the professional community of engineers as well as in civic groups in his community. His success is no fluke – he is considered by all to be a talented individual. The 'superior' student, on the other hand, has had little success in her chosen career as a writer; after repeated rejections by publishers, she has taken up a middle management position in a bank. While certainly not a 'failure' she is considered by her peers to be quite 'ordinary' in her adult accomplishments. So what happened?

This fabricated example is based on the facts of intelligence testing. IQ tests predict school performance with considerable accuracy, but they are only an indifferent predictor of performance in a profession after formal schooling.[3] Furthermore, even as IQ tests measure only logical or logical-linguistic capacities, in this society we are nearly 'brain-washed' to restrict the notion of intelligence to the capacities used in solving logical and linguistic problems.

To introduce an alternative point of view, undertake the following *Gedanken* experiment. Suspend the usual judgement of what constitutes intelligence and let your thoughts run freely over the capabilities of humans – perhaps those that would be picked out by the proverbial Martian visitor. In this exercise, you are drawn to the brilliant chess player, the world-class violinist, and the champion athlete; such outstanding performers deserve special consideration. Under this experiment, a quite different view of *intelligence* emerges. Are the chess player, violinist, and athlete 'intelligent' in these pursuits? If they are, then why do our tests of 'intelligence' fail to identify them? If they are not 'intelligent', what allows them to achieve such astounding feats? In general, why does the contemporary construct 'intelligence' fail to explain large areas of human endeavour?

In this chapter we approach these problems through the theory of Multiple Intelligences (MI). As the name indicates, we believe that human cognitive competence is better described in terms of a set of abilities, talents, or mental skills, which we call 'Intelligences'. All normal individuals possess each of these skills to some extent; individuals differ in the degree of skill and in the nature of their combination. We believe this theory of intelligence may be more humane and more veridical than alternative views of intelligence and that it more adequately reflects the data of human 'intelligent' behaviour. Such a theory has important educational implications, including ones for curriculum development.

WHAT CONSTITUTES AN INTELLIGENCE?

The question of the optimal definition of 'intelligence' looms large in our inquiry. Indeed, it is at the level of this definition that the theory of Multiple Intelligences diverges from more traditional points of view. In a more traditional view, intelligence is defined operationally as the ability to answer items on tests of intelligence. The inference from the test scores to some underlying ability is supported by statistical techniques that compare responses of subjects at different ages; the apparent correlation of these test scores across ages and across different tests corroborates the notion that the general faculty of intelligence, 'g', does not change much with age or with training or experience. It is an inborn attribute or faculty of the individual.[4]

Multiple Intelligences theory, on the other hand, pluralizes the traditional concept. An intelligence entails the ability to solve problems or fashion products that are of consequence in a particular cultural setting. The problem-solving skill allows one to approach a situation in which a goal is to be obtained and to locate the appropriate route to that goal. The creation of a *cultural* product is crucial to such functions as capturing and transmitting knowledge or expressing one's views or feelings. The problems to be solved range from creating an end to a story to anticipating a mating move in chess to repairing a quilt. Products range from scientific theories to musical compositions to successful political campaigns.

MI theory is framed in light of the biological origins of each problem-solving skill. Only those skills that are universal to the human species are treated. Even so, the biological proclivity to participate in a particular form of problem solving must also be coupled with the cultural nurturing of that domain. For example, language, a universal skill, may manifest itself particularly as writing in one culture, as oratory in another culture, and as the secret language of anagrams in a third.

Given the desire of selecting intelligences that are rooted in biology, and which are valued in one or more cultural settings, how does one actually identify an 'intelligence'? In coming up with our list, we consulted evidence from several different sources; knowledge about normal development and development in gifted individuals; information about the breakdown of cognitive skills under conditions of brain damage; studies of exceptional populations, including prodigies, *idiots savants*, and autistic children; data about the evolution of cognition over the millenia; cross-cultural accounts of cognition; psychometric studies, including examinations of correlations among tests; and psychological training studies, particularly measures of transfer and generalization across tasks. Only those candidate intelligences that satisfied all or a majority of the criteria were selected as bona fide intelligences.

In addition to satisfying these criteria, each intelligence must have an identifiable core operation or set of operations. As a neutrally based computational system, each intelligence is activated or 'triggered' by certain kinds of internally or externally presented information.

An intelligence must also be susceptible to encoding in a symbol system – a culturally contrived system of meaning, which captures and conveys important forms of information. Language, picturing, and mathematics are but three nearly worldwide symbol systems that are necessary for human survival and productivity. The relationship of a candidate intelligence to a human symbol system is no accident. In fact, the existence of a core computational capacity anticipates the existence of a symbol system which exploits that capacity. While it may be possible for an intelligence to proceed without an accompanying symbol system, a primary characteristic of human intelligence may well be its gravitation toward such an embodiment.

THE MULTIPLE INTELLIGENCES

Note: This section summarizes descriptions and contains quotations from Gardner's book *Frames of Mind*.[5]

This analysis of a wider and more disparate set of data about human intellectual abilities suggests a minimum of seven distinct intelligences; logical-mathematical, linguistic, spatial, bodily-kinaesthetic, musical, interpersonal, and intrapersonal. A brief description of each of these intelligences is now presented.

Logical-mathematical intelligence

This intelligence can be understood as the ability, described in Piaget's theory of intellectual development, which involves the formal operation of symbols according to accepted rules of logic and mathematics. It is this intelligence that has been almost exclusively measured in 'intelligence tests'. Although it has been given pre-eminence in Western societies, there is no reason to believe that it is more fundamental than the other intelligences. There is more than one form of logic and each intelligence has an equally valid logic of its own.

Linguistic intelligence

There is strong neurological evidence for citing the existence of a separate linguistic intelligence. People with brain damage to a specific location in the left hemisphere have grave difficulty in forming grammatical utterances, although other thought processes are apparently unaffected. The linguistic intelligence makes use of rhetoric, for persuasion, allows us to develop semantic storage of information, and also to explain events, including its own operations.

933

It differs from logical-mathematical intelligence in having a strong auditory/oral component and in not being tied to the world of physical objects.

Spatial intelligence

This intelligence enables us to recognize faces, to find our way around a site, and to notice fine details. All these capacities are affected by damage to parts of the right hemisphere of the brain. Spatial intelligence is perhaps seen at its most developed among certain islanders who are able to navigate long distances by the stars.

> Central to spatial intelligence are the capacities to perceive the visual world accurately, to perform transformations and modifications upon one's initial perceptions, and to be able to re-create aspects of one's visual experience, even in the absence of relevant physical stimuli. (Gardner 1983:173)

Bodily-kinaesthetic intelligence

This intelligence describes the abilities to use the body or parts of the body to solve problems or to produce worthwhile products or displays. It involves at its core the capacities to control bodily motions and to handle objects skilfully. In different forms and combinations it is exemplified by skilled dancers, athletes, surgeons, and instrumentalists. Again it is possible to identify these skills with a specific area of the brain, in this case the motor cortex.

Musical intelligence

It is possible that language and music evolved together as a single auditory-oral intelligence, but in the present day they appear to be separate, with many examples of people with high musical, but low linguistic, intelligences. Musical intelligence involves the capacities for imitation of vocal targets, for sensitivity to relative as well as absolute pitch, and for appreciating various kinds of musical transformations.

Interpersonal intelligence

> The core capacity here is *the ability to notice and make distinctions among other individuals* and, in particular, among their moods, temperaments, motivations, and intentions ... Interpersonal knowledge permits a skilled adult to read the intentions and desires – even when these have been hidden – of many other individuals and, potentially, to act upon this knowledge – for example, by influencing a group of disparate individuals to behave along desired lines. We see highly developed forms of interpersonal intelligence in political and religious leaders ... in skilled parents and teachers, and in individuals enrolled in the

934

helping professions, be they therapists, counsellors, or shamans. (Gardner 1983:240)

Intrapersonal intelligence

The core capacity at work here is *access to one's own feeling life* – one's range of affects or emotions: the capacity instantly to effect discriminations among these feelings and, eventually, to label them, to enmesh them in symbolic codes, to draw upon them as a means of understanding and guiding one's behaviour ... One finds this form of intelligence in a novelist (like Proust) who can write introspectively about feelings, in the patient (or therapist) who comes to attain a deep knowledge of his own feeling life, in the wise elder who draws upon his own wealth of inner experiences in order to advise members of his community. (Gardner 1983:239–40)

Of these seven intelligences, spatial, logical-mathematical, and bodily-kin-aesthetic are all 'object related': they depend on relationships with the external physical world. Language and music are, in contrast, 'object-free'.

Finally, the personal forms of intelligence reflect a set of powerful and competing constraints: the existence of one's own person; the existence of other persons; the culture's presentations and interpretations of selves. There will be universal features of any sense of person or self, but also considerable cultural nuances, reflecting a host of historical and individuating factors. (Gardner 1983:278)

THE UNIQUE CONTRIBUTIONS OF THE THEORY

As human beings, we all have a repertoire of skills for solving different kinds of problems. Our investigation has begun, therefore, with a consideration of these problems, the contexts they are found in, and the culturally significant products that are the outcome. We have not approached 'intelligence' as a reified human faculty that is brought to bear in literally any problem setting; rather, we have begun with the problems that humans *solve* and worked back to the 'intelligences' that must be responsible.

Evidence from brain research, human development, evolution, and cross-cultural comparisons was brought to bear in our search for the relevant human intelligences: a candidate was included only if reasonable evidence to support its membership was found across these diverse fields. Again, this tack differs from the traditional one: since no candidate faculty is *necessarily* an intelligence, we could choose on a motivated basis. In the traditional approach to 'intelligence', there is no opportunity for this type of empirical decision.

We have also determined that these multiple human faculties, the intelligences, are to a significant extent *independent*. For example, research with brain-damaged adults repeatedly demonstrates that particular faculties can be

935

lost while others are spared. This independence of intelligences implies that a particularly high level of ability in one intelligence, say mathematics, does not require a similarly high level in another intelligence, like language or music. This independence of intelligences contrasts sharply with traditional measures of IQ that find high correlations among test scores. We speculate that the usual correlations among subtests of IQ tests come about because all of these tasks in fact measure the ability to respond rapidly to items of a logical-mathematical or linguistic sort; we believe that these correlations would be substantially reduced if one were to survey in a contextually appropriate way the full range of human problem-solving skills.

Until now, we have supported the fiction that adult roles depend largely on the flowering of a single intelligence. In fact, however, nearly every cultural role of any degree of sophistication requires a combination of intelligences. Thus, even an apparently straightforward role like playing the violin transcends a reliance on simple musical intelligence. To become a successful violinist requires bodily-kinaesthetic dexterity, and the interpersonal skills of relating to an audience and, in a different way, choosing a manager; quite possibly it involves an intrapersonal intelligence as well. Dance requires skills in bodily-kinesthetic, musical, interpersonal, and spatial intelligences in varying degrees. Politics requires an interpersonal skill, a linguistic facility, and perhaps some logical aptitude. Inasmuch as nearly every cultural role requires several intelligences, it becomes important to consider individuals as a collection of aptitudes rather than as having a singular problem-solving faculty that can be measured directly through pencil-and-paper tests. Even given a relatively small number of such intelligences, the diversity of human ability is created through the differences in these profiles. In fact, it may well be that the 'total is greater than the sum of the parts'. An individual may not be particularly gifted in any intelligence; and yet, because of a particular combination or blend of skills, he or she may be able to fill some niche uniquely well. Thus it is of paramount importance to assess the particular combination of skills which may earmark an individual for a certain vocational or avocational niche.[6]

COPING WITH THE PLURALITY OF INTELLIGENCES

Under the Multiple Intelligences theory, an intelligence can serve both as the *content* of instruction and the *means* or medium for communicating that content. This state of affairs has important ramifications for instruction. For example, suppose that a child is learning some mathematical principle but is not skilled in logical-mathematical intelligence. That child will probably experience some difficulty during the learning process. The reason for the difficulty is straightforward: the mathematical principle to be learned (the content) exists only in the logical-mathematical world and it ought to be communicated through mathematics (the medium). That is, the mathematical principle cannot be translated *entirely* into words (which is a linguistic medium) or spatial models (a spatial medium). At some point in the learning process, the mathematics of the principle must 'speak for itself'. In our present case, it is at just this level that the learner experiences difficulty – the learner (who is not especially 'mathematical') and the problem (which is very much 'mathematical') are not in accord. Mathematics, as a *medium*, has failed.

Although this situation is a necessary conundrum in light of the Multiple Intelligences theory, we can propose various solutions. In the present example, the teacher must attempt to find an alternative route to the mathematical content – a metaphor in another medium. Language is perhaps the most obvious alternative, but spatial modelling and even a bodily-kinaesthetic metaphor may prove appropriate in some cases. In this way, the student is given a *secondary* route to the solution to the problem, perhaps through the medium of an intelligence that is relatively strong for that individual.

Two features of this hypothetical scenario must be stressed. First, in such cases, the secondary route – the language, spatial model, or whatever – is at best a metaphor or translation. It is not mathematics itself. And at some point, the learner must translate back into the domain of mathematics. Without this translation, what is learned tends to remain at a relatively superficial level; cookbook-style mathematical performance results from following instructions (linguistic translation) without understanding why (mathematics re-translation).

Second, the alternative route is not guaranteed. There is no *necessary* reason why a problem in one domain *must be translatable* into a metaphorical problem in another domain. Successful teachers find these translations with relative frequency; but as learning becomes more complex, the likelihood of a successful translation diminishes.

While Multiple Intelligences theory is consistent with much empirical evidence, it has not been subjected to strong experimental tests within psychology. Within the area of education, the applications of the theory are even more tentative and speculative. Our hunches will have to be revised many times in the light of actual classroom experience. Still there are important reasons for considering the theory of Multiple Intelligences and its implications for education. First of all, it is clear that many talents, if not intelligences, are overlooked nowadays; individuals with these talents are the chief casualties of the single-minded, single-funnelled approach to the mind. There are many unfilled or poorly filled niches in our society and it would be opportune to guide individuals with the right set of abilities to these billets. Finally, our world is beset with problems; to have any chance of solving them, we must make the very best use of the intelligences we possess. Perhaps recognizing the plurality of intelligences and the manifold ways in which human individuals may exhibit them is an important first step.

NOTES

1. This chapter is based on extracts from an article by J. H. Walters and H. Gardner (1984) published by and reprinted with the permission of the Association for Supervision and Curriculum Development, and on summaries from *Frames of Mind* by Howard Gardner (1983) published by Basic Books (New York).

2. Cooley, W. W. and Lohnes, P. R. (1976) *Evaluation Research in Education*, New York: Irvington Publications Inc.

3. Jencks, C. (1972) *Inequality: A Reassessment of the Effect of Family and Schooling in America*, New York: Basic Books.

4. Eysenck, H. J. (1983) 'The nature of intelligence', in M. P. Friedman, J. P. Das, and N. O'Connor (Eds.) *Intelligence and Learning*, New York: Plenum Press.

5. Gardner, H. (1983) op. cit.

6. Walters, J. M. and Gardner, G. (1985) 'The theory of multiple intelligences: Some issues and answers', in R. Sternberg and R. Wagner (Eds.) *Practical Intelligence: Origins of Competence in the Everyday World*, Cambridge: University Press.

8.3

EDUCATING GIFTED CHILDREN

JOAN FREEMAN

Though the study of exceptionally high ability, or giftedness, is primarily concerned with a minority of children, it includes all aspects of child development and educational expertise, and must therefore be seen in the context of all children. However, to merit special attention for the highly able it must be (and is) assumed that they are somehow different from other children, that the differences are worthy of concern and investigation, and that some action can be taken on their behalf.

The idea that the highly able can make sturdy growth with minimal help is fading. Even if we were merely to use that crude educational ruler, the normal curve of the distribution of intelligence, a high proportion of children in the top five per cent of the ability range are unlikely to be having their educational needs met. On the assumption that it is the right of all children to fulfil their potential, so far as circumstances allow, teachers often find themselves wondering just what they should do for and with their very brightest pupils.

ATTITUDES TO GIFTEDNESS

The acceptance of some children as very much better at some things than others is affected by social and political outlooks. Consequently, at different times and in different parts of the world, there is great variation in recognition and educational provision for them. In Britain attitudes to the gifted encompass both fear of élitism, implying special privilege, and alternatively the wish to help children who are seen as a national asset.

In practice, the term gifted is always used in comparison with others, to indicate outstanding abilities. But even in the same area of activity, children are called gifted at different levels of achievement, depending on who they are being compared with. Labelling a child as gifted will affect his or her self-concept, and also the attitudes and behaviour of others.

FINDING THE GIFTED

Gifted children do not rise like cream to the top. Talents and gifts are unlikely to develop to anything like their full potential without both the psychological and the physical means of developing them. This implies that resources for the development of any special ability are themselves somehow part of the giftedness. Indeed, some American States, realizing the unfairness of nationally designed tests for culturally deprived children, have devised special tests for them. Children who would have scored only average or below on a nationally standardized measure can now be selected as in the top few per cent of their cultural group, and offered special education. However, any comparison between different tests of ability, which incorporate such variables as local dialect or diet, is clearly impossible.

Tests, though, are not in favour with everyone. The somewhat unreliable paper-and-pencil creativity test, for example, has largely been replaced by evidence of progress from a child's daily work, which is more meaningful to him or her. There is considerable evidence to suggest that when children are identified as gifted by intelligence tests in both Britain and the United States (in spite of the wide spectrum of IQ cut-off points), less than half of them had been recognized as such by their teachers. Teachers are good at spotting performance gifts, such as in the arts and sport, which are then helped along by experts. And teachers do identify able secondary children effectively in their own subject areas, as measured by O level results (Denton and Postlethwaite 1985).

It is the potential for achievement which we should be after – not easy when the child is doing his or her clever best to conform to the group norms. Hence, in the same way as poor hearing may not be recognized and coped with, giftedness may also lie fallow, unchallenged and neglected.

In the last decade, there has been a fundamental shift of psychological perspective on children's abilities, such as the appreciation of what a child could do, rather than what he or she can do. Were this information to be acted upon, it would greatly increase the proportion of children we now see as highly able, or gifted.

DEVELOPMENTAL CHARACTERISTICS OF GIFTED CHILDREN

Though children who merit the adjective 'gifted' are in a minority numerically, this does not imply that, apart from their recognized abilities, they are different from other children. One of the ways in which teachers are helped to identify their gifted pupils is by a check-list of their supposed characteristics. These check-lists should be treated with caution. They often start out short, but as gifted children are seen to have wider and wider characteristics, they become so long and comprehensive that they would fit most children. The authors then star the most important characteristics, and so it goes.

As yet, no links have been shown in any research between exceptionally high ability and disturbed behaviour. Such links are based on subjective impressions of children who have come to be noticed because of problems, and then recognized as gifted.

In Britain, 210 children aged from five to fourteen, with IQ scores ranging from 100 to 170, were studied in their homes and schools (Freeman 1985a and 1985b). When the children in the intellectual top one per cent of the population were compared with those of more moderate abilities for social behaviour, there was no difference. The only real differences between them was their abilities. Such matters as quality of sleep, temper tantrums, or over-activity, were significantly related to other disturbing matters in the children's lives, which could have affected any children adversely. Ten years later, the follow-up study (81 per cent of the original sample) has shown that the development of the (by then) young people's gifts continued to be dependent on whatever provision they had received, both physical and psychological (Freeman 1988).

Some myths

Physical superiority Though children with high IQs are likely to be physically better developed than those with lower scores, this correlation is usually due to the better physical and intellectual nurturing which middle-class children are more likely to enjoy (Tanner 1978; Davie *et al.* 1972). The gifted are, however, more frequently first-borns and only children.

Friendships Gifted children mingle as freely as any other children at school. But at home they may have fewer friends because of the nature of their out-of-school activities, such as musical instrument practice.

Boredom On the evidence available, it is not possible to say whether gifted children are more or less bored than their class-mates in a normal classroom.

Emotional development Gifted children, however measured, seem to be as emotionally stable, though as affected by life circumstances, as other children. However, the gifted child is more vulnerable in certain respects, such as adverse reactions to 'put-downs' from other people, because of being exceptional.

Personality Characteristics, such as ambition or curiosity (especially asking questions), are aspects of culture rather than abilities, though the gifted are likely to be more intense about them.

Some guidelines

There are however, some aspects of children's behaviour, taken in the contexts of their lives, which point to the possibility of exceptionally high ability.

Mental development　A child can accept educational provision only at his or her personal level of ability and outlook. Television, for example, is merely passive entertainment to one, but a source of exciting ideas to another. The brighter the child, the more he or she will be able to absorb (and consider) what is offered at home and at school.

The environmental factors which count most are
- the experience of educational activities
- material provision (you can't become Yehudi Menuhin without a violin).

Concentration　The ability to concentrate, and to derive great benefit from it, is a notable feature of a fine intellect. It shows itself from an early age, and does not seem to be dependent on environmental circumstances.

Memory　From a very early age, gifted children appear to have exceptionally good memories which they keep through life. Sometimes, though, such children can appear as 'know-alls', perhaps having to live up to their reputation as clever.

Verbal development　Highly able children are often verbally precocious in the symbolic skills of talking, reading, and writing. This can be apparent from just a few months old. But paradoxically, the late development of these skills, especially handwriting, is not a sign that children are not gifted.

Leisure activities　The gifted can have a great number of leisure activities, which they often approach in a dynamic manner. They sometimes take their interests to an extreme degree, then drop them for another when they feel satisfied. The gifted, however, do not make collections of things more than other children, and they are more discriminating than other children in their television viewing.

Feeling different　Gifted children often feel themselves to be different from others, and recognize that the difference is due to their exceptional ability. They can be very sensitive, both for themselves and others.

Barriers to gifted development

There are two major, pervasive influences which can cripple the development of gifted level ability. The first is social class, which even in the late 1980s can prevent working-class youth from reaching their natural level. The second is gender, which slots boys and girls into areas of the curriculum which are not necessarily the most appropriate for their abilities. Added to those are the problems of minority cultures, physical handicaps, and emotional mal-adjustment.

However, the overriding problem for the under-achieving gifted is quite simply the lack of provision for them to learn at their own level, usually in circumstances where their potential has not been identified (Whitmore 1985).

THE GIFTED CHILD IN SCHOOL

It is arguable that if educational provision were to meet the needs of each child, then there would be no reason for special concern for any exceptional group. Yet how is education to be provided appropriately when their capacities are unknown? In his experimental teaching with previously unrecognized primary school gifted children, Callow (1982) found that before they had been identified and given special teaching, the children had been on their way to developing poor work habits and poor academic results.

Rutter and his associates concluded on the basis of both new research data and the re-examination of published statistics that schools did indeed have considerable impact. After adjusting for intake characteristics: 'children at the most successful secondary school got four times as many exam passes on average as children at the least successful school' (Rutter 1983). Hence, it is not ability alone which accounts for achievement.

It is understandable that most schools try to encourage their gifted pupils' examination-passing potential. At some schools, however, too much academic emphasis can unbalance the curriculum, because the more aesthetic subjects are given low status. It can also affect the pupils, who take their examination prowess as the source of their self-esteem. This is not good for their relation-ships, and it can diminish the sparkle and excitement of discovery in learning, which is so vital to creative endeavour.

Whatever psychological freedom to learn has been given to the child at home, the teacher is in the position to improve on it with an open, questioning style of teaching. This means that the teacher gives only enough information and direction to help the child start thinking about the subject, and inspires him or her to ask the questions beyond the work-sheet, the textbook, and the 'correct' answer; to try out his or her ingenuity. Problems are a diagnostic measure for the very bright – their intelligence will show up in their answers. A teacher who is ready to listen and guide, rather than dictate, provides a safe haven in which the gifted may try out their creative and intellectual wings.

One problem of teaching the intellectually gifted is that their thinking is often at a more advanced stage and quality than its practical presentation. For example, when they first learn to write, their thoughts may run ahead of their pencils, so that the content of their written work is relatively superficial and incomplete. This is confusing for teachers, since the children usually talk with considerable fluency. Such children will derive more excitement and take their ideas further by discussing them, than by associating them with the tiresome business of always having to write them down. Some teachers have said that this problem is largely overcome by teaching the children to type, though perhaps even this has now been superseded by word-processing for the lucky ones.

EDUCATION FOR THE GIFTED IN PRACTICE

To put any form of education for the gifted into operation, it is essential to know how the children differ in their educational needs from other children. It is also important to be able to help them without access to expensive resources. In brief – whatever their talents, those who are exceptionally good at learning will do it faster and in greater depth and breadth than other children (Wallace 1983). But this simple statement brings about a host of problems.

They learn faster

When a child has the ability to grasp a concept quickly, it means that he or she will need minimum, if any, practice to retain what he or she has learned, and consequently little if any revision. As all classrooms are to some extent mixed-ability, this throws the timing of lessons and problem-posing/solving strategies into disarray. Additionally, the gifted pupil may not only need an accelerated pace, but may quite naturally skip over sequences in the learning, which the other children will have to master before they can move on. A gifted child may know the answer before the teacher has finished the question.

This problem of pace is particularly noticeable in the teaching of the mathematically able, though there is considerable disagreement as to whether to accelerate young mathematicians or offer them a change of subject, such as art, which may be more beneficial than simply more of the same – a tendency which one could describe as 'overteaching' the gifted in the area of their gift.

The ability to grasp ideas and reach conclusions more quickly can mean in practice that gifted pupils may complete a work-sheet so rapidly that they may do it several times to keep themselves occupied in the classroom – a boring, soul-destroying sampling of school life – it is not only teachers who can complain of too much paper-work. Pace is also a big problem in the use of language, especially in reading; the very young gifted child seems to absorb the written word almost on impact, without the need to practise, and often before the age of five. Starting school, they speed through conventional reading schemes, absorbing complex ideas and word patterns, so that a reading diet

944

more advanced in both content and skill is required. This is particularly notable in primary school project work, when gifted children will need to seek reference from adult level source-books, having soon exhausted those considered suitable for their age.

Greater depth and breadth

To extend the 'core-curriculum' for the gifted, one can take a subject in greater depth or breadth, either poring over the same problem in finer and finer detail, or relating it to other subjects outside the basics. Children who are exceptionally good learners need both.

There are far-reaching consequences of educating gifted children appropriately: it will inevitably increase the intellectual gap between them and their age peers. This growing disparity can be handled most easily in a class where every member is aware that he or she is valued. Gifted children often have a natural desire for detail, to get to know all there is about a subject, so that the teacher may have to press for the greater educational benefits of a broader perspective. It is also important to see that as children move from one teacher to another, this extension of the curriculum is continued; therefore, careful notes should be made (as they should be for all children) to see that the gifted child is not provided with a stimulating education one year, only to be told to conform the next.

Specific Skills

Thinking Historically, most teaching has been concerned with conveying a body of knowledge, rather than attempting to develop independent thinking. The highly able can greatly benefit by exercises which involve the creative processing of information. The skills of communicating what they have found are as important as the discoveries themselves, and need practising.

Gifted children could, for example, learn how to obtain information and put it into a form in which it may later be retrieved in different ways. At its simplest this might be to file it under different headings. This requires their full understanding of the material so as to relate it to categories, as well as the higher-level thinking skills to synthesize from and follow it through to novel ideas. Problem-solving skills should be included in teaching in many subject areas, so that the pupils are obliged to think things through for themselves.

The gifted who find the mechanical part of reading easy may sometimes miss out on the cognitive and linguistic aspects of meaning and expression. A clear sign is turgid writing, lagging behind their reading and speaking standards. Are the books, to which the child has access, bromides rather than stimulants, information-givers rather than sources of ideas? Exercises in different types of writing, such as reports, stories, and advertising all help, with some non-intrusive guidance on spelling and grammar.

Independent learning All children find it easier to take their learning from the teacher, rather than find it for themselves. Yet the gifted are particularly able, and often keen to be involved in the design and to take some responsibility, for their own education. They might, for example, be invited to plan their timetables, encouraging organizational skills, with some freedom to choose their own activities as part of it. It develops their own values, interests, and special abilities.

EXTRA-CURRICULAR ACTIVITIES

Every neighbourhood, no matter how culturally deprived, has its share of interesting things for pupils to see and do, and interesting people to meet. Numerous activities and ways of participating in the community for clever children are given in Freeman (1983).

Many schools run clubs and societies for children's interests, which, because they are for specialists, often reach a very high standard, presenting a challenge to the very bright. Pupils can start such activities themselves, with help from teachers or parents, and several schools could combine their efforts. Such groups often find that they can have access to different kinds of institutions which welcome keen pupils, such as radar stations, computer laboratories, farms, etc.

These societies not only provide the gifted with the opportunity to learn more about their particular interest, but to mix with others who think and react as they do. That facility, so much taken for granted by most people, of being able to share their reality with someone of their own age, is a vital help to strengthening the gifteds' sense of self. The Branches of the National Association for Gifted Children (1, South Audley Street, London W1Y 5DQ) run Explorer Groups at weekends, and holidays.

Teachers

Adequate training, good in-service support, and posts of special responsibility help teachers recognize and encourage the special talents of all their pupils. Local authorities and teacher training establishments are showing growing interest in the highly able, and the provision of special advisory teachers, inspectors, and courses for teachers of the gifted is spreading. Teachers of the highly able need good communication skills and a willingness to become involved with their pupils, and they do also have to be competent.

REFERENCES

Callow, R. (1982) 'The Southport Inquiry and after', in D. H. W. Grubb (Ed.) *The Gifted Child at School*, Oxford: Oxford Society for Applied Studies in Education.

Davie, C. E., Hutt, S. J., Vincent, E., and Mason, M. (1983) *The Young Child at Home*, Windsor: NFER-Nelson.

Denton, C. and Postlethwaite, K. (1985) *Able Children: Identifying them in the Classroom*, Windsor: NFER-Nelson.

Freeman, J. (1983) *Clever Children: A Parents' Guide*, London: Hamlyn Paperbacks.

(1985a) 'A pedagogy for the gifted', in Joan Freeman (Ed.) *The Psychology of Gifted Children*, Chichester: Wiley.

(1985b) 'Emotional aspects of giftedness', in Joan Freeman (Ed.) *The Psychology of Gifted Children*, Chichester: Wiley.

(1988) *Bright youth . . . Bright Future?*, London: Penguin Books.

Rutter, M. (1983) 'School effects on pupil progress: research findings and policy implications', *Child Development*, 54: 1–29.

Tanner, J. M. (1978) *Foetus Into Man*, London: Open Books.

Wallace, B. (1983) *Teaching the Very Able Child*, London: Ward Lock Educational Ltd.

Whitmore, J. R. (1985) 'New challenges to common identification processes', in J. Freeman (Ed.) *The Psychology of Gifted Children*, Chichester: Wiley.

8.4

DEVELOPMENT IN HOME AND SCHOOL ENVIRONMENTS

ROBERT GRIEVE

INTRODUCTION

One view of the development of children in home and school environments stresses the *discontinuities* between development at home and development in school. Another more recent view stresses that there are important *continuities* between such developments, and that learning in school can be made easier for the young child if these continuities are recognized and built upon. These two views can be considered in turn.

The development of children in home and school environments has been viewed as a discontinuous process. At home, care-givers first nurture the relatively helpless infant, who is later encouraged to walk, to talk, to play, and to begin to interact with others in a civilized fashion. Early development has been considered a time of trial and error; it is essentially carefree; and learning is typically informal. However, when the child reaches the age of four, five, six, or seven years (depending on the country the child is in), a major change occurs. To develop further, the child goes to school. Though there are still periods of play (for example at 'playtime', or in periods of sports and recreation), these are occasional, the bulk of the child's time at school being given over to formal learning – to the acquisition of the 'three Rs', in order to become literate and numerate; and to the development of religious/moral/social/cultural precepts, in order to appreciate self and society. Compared to development at home, development at school is a much more serious business, for new social skills and new skills in reading, writing, and number must be acquired if the child is to succeed in a society which is literate and numerate. Thus the skills to be acquired in the formal school environment have been seen as discontinuous with the carefree informal learning that takes place in the home environment before the child goes to school.

In recent years, however, this view of discontinuity in development at home and school has been challenged by an alternative view which stresses that there are important continuities between developments that occur at home and in school. While recognizing that the social experience of school entrants is limited, and that most children do not yet read, write, or manipulate number, the alternative view emphasizes that school entrants have already developed skills that are directly relevant to their further elaboration in the school environment. Thus the development of abilities in the 'three Rs' in school, for example, does not consist of development that is entirely new. Rather, such development builds on what the child brings to the school environment from previous learning and development in the home environment.

Later in the chapter these continuities between home and school will be illustrated. We will also consider some of the adverse effects that can arise if continuities are not encouraged. But first, to understand why continuities between development at home and school have recently come to be emphasized, we need briefly to survey some recent findings on the needs and abilities of infants and young children.

YOUNG CHILDREN'S NEEDS AND ABILITIES

The needs of young children are many and varied. Most obviously, they require physical care, comfort, and protection, both for their physical well-being and the adequate development of motor abilities. Also required, for adequate social and emotional development, are love, kindness, and emotional warmth, provided in stable social relationships which engender a sense of security. Just as importantly, though perhaps less obviously, children also need adequate stimulation, so that their perceptual, intellectual, and linguistic capacities are realized.

The past two decades have seen a significant increase in the amount of scientific research conducted on the abilities of infants and young children. This research has resulted in some important revisions being made as to how we perceive the nature of young children's skills and capacities.

During the first year of life, infants exhibit an impressive array of motor, perceptual, intellectual, and social skills (Bower 1979). From birth, the infant can imitate the facial gestures of an adult. Tongue protrusion, mouth opening, and eyebrow raising can be reciprocated. What this means is that if you stick your tongue out at a new born baby, the baby can imitate and stick his or her tongue out at you! Infants do not simply imitate, though. Shortly after birth, the infant can quickly learn to complete relatively complex patterns of movement. Young babies can learn to turn their heads in sequences (for example, twice to the left, once to the right) to obtain rewards such as seeing a flashing light or hearing a buzzer sound. Infants also soon exhibit knowledge of their

949

mothers, and by a few months of age, they appreciate that a mother is a unique individual. Before then, if multiple images of the mother are projected in front of the infant, they exhibit little concern. However when they have learned that the mother is unique, multiple images of the mother can now result in their showing distress. Infants also exhibit knowledge of the properties of physical objects in the environment – their solidity, constancy of size, trajectories of movement, size-weight relationships, etc. The infant's motor behaviour – the ways in which he or she grasps at objects – is adapted according to this knowledge of the objects' physical properties.

Towards the end of their first year of life, infants increasingly contribute to social interactions with adults, and begin to acquire knowledge of how to play social roles, as well as how actions and words are synchronized in interaction and dialogue (Bruner 1974).

During the second year of life, the child's major achievements are the acquisition of the abilities to walk and to talk. The child's acquisition of language, between the ages of about one and three years, is widely recognized to be a quite remarkable achievement (Brown 1973). In addition to learning the meanings of words (semantics), the child also acquires a complex system of rules related to how words are combined to form phrases and sentences (syntax). Also acquired is knowledge of how language is used in different circumstances and contexts (pragmatics). By the age of four years, children also begin to provide evidence that they are becoming aware of some aspects of the nature and functions of the language system they are acquiring (Pratt and Grieve 1980).

Regarding social development, recent studies have found that children of pre-school age are adept at practising and maintaining social roles, particularly in fantasy play (Garvey 1977). They also acquire a variety of skills in interacting with other children and making friends (Rubin 1980). Generally, young children are more autonomous with respect to social learning than has often been acknowledged. Important aspects of their social knowledge are obtained not from adults, but from other children.

With respect to intellectual development, recent investigators have drawn attention to the considerable range of intellectual skills possessed by children of pre-school age. For example, by four years of age, children can think and reason in consistent and non-egocentric ways in certain contexts; they can classify and compare in an adequate manner given the right circumstances; they possess some knowledge of the properties of number; they have some knowledge of the nature of measurement; and so on (Donaldson, Grieve, and Pratt 1983).

These findings and observations should not be taken to suggest that young children are without limitations. Young children obviously exhibit various limitations in knowledge that usually gradually decrease as they progress through primary and secondary schooling. However, the trend apparent in recent research, which recognizes young children's abilities rather than stressing their deficiencies – an emphasis on what they can do rather than on what they cannot do – has led to a reappraisal of the nature of young children's abilities (Donaldson 1978; Donaldson *et al.* 1983).

THE NATURE OF YOUNG CHILDREN'S ABILITIES

In the previous section, when commenting on recent research on intellectual development, it was noted that children can reason in consistent and non-egocentric ways *in certain contexts*; and they can classify and compare adequately *given the right circumstances*. What are these contexts, and what makes circumstances 'right' for adequate intellectual functioning in young children? Here we can look at some recent research on young children's intellectual skills in more detail, for it is important to understand why children function adequately in some contexts but not in others.

In a classic series of studies on young children's ability to measure, Piaget (Piaget *et al.* 1960) described how young children failed to measure adequately when asked to build a tower of blocks on a table, equal in height to a tower of (differently sized) blocks on the floor. Since the towers were on different levels, the child could not solve the problem by making the heights of the towers coincide. And since the blocks were of different sizes, the problem could not be solved by counting the blocks in one tower and making the other tower have the same number. The only way to solve the problem is to use an intermediate measure (such as a stick), which is equal to the height of one tower, and then to ensure that the other tower is the same height as the stick. The logic is quite straightforward: if height tower 1 = length of stick, and if length of stick = height tower 2, then height tower 1 = height tower 2. The sort of logical inference the child must make is called a *transitive inference*, and it is fundamental to systems of measurement and systems of number. However, Piaget found that children of pre-school age were poor at completing the towers of blocks task, for he considered that they did not yet possess the ability to make the sort of transitive inference required to solve the task successfully.

However this conclusion has recently been questioned by some research by Harris and Singleton (1978). In their task, four-year-olds were shown two strips of cardboard on tables at opposite sides of a room. Let us call one the red strip and the other the blue strip. The two strips differed in length by a small amount, and the child's task was to find out which strip was the longer. Since the two strips differed in length by a small amount, the child could not solve the problem simply by looking between the two strips. Rather, to solve the problem they needed to use a third cardboard strip, which was provided, equal in length to one of the two original strips. Now they could solve the problem as follows. They could take the third strip to one of the tables at one side of the room and compare it with say the red strip on that table. Suppose the red strip is the same length as the third strip. They could then take the third strip to the opposite table, and compare it with the blue strip. If the blue strip is longer than the third strip, the child knows that the blue is longer than the red (red = third, third shorter than blue, therefore blue longer than red). If the blue strip had been shorter than the third strip, then the child would know that the red is longer than the blue (red = third, third longer than blue, therefore red longer than blue). What the children are doing in this measuring task is, of course, making transitive inferences. Why do they do so successfully in this measuring task, but fail to do so in Piaget's tower of blocks task? Before we try to answer that question, we can consider two other examples of when young children fail to show an ability in one context that they do show in another.

The first involves young children's perspective-taking ability, which has been tested in what is known as Piaget's three mountains problem. Here young children are seated at a table which displays a model of three mountains of different sizes and colours so that the three are readily distinguishable – for example there could be a large white mountain, a medium-sized brown one, and a small grey one. Photographs taken from various vantage points round the display are then shown, and the children are asked to select the photograph that shows what they can see from where they are seated. Children can do this successfully. The task is as follows: the child is told to imagine that another child was seated opposite them, or to one side, and asked what photographs show what that child would see. Pre-school-aged children are not successful in this task, for they tend to select the photograph which shows what they can see from their own perspective rather than photographs showing the perspectives from other positions. This led to the view that young children are *egocentric*, and unable to adopt perspectives other than the one they themselves now have.

However this view has been challenged by some recent work of Hughes (described in Donaldson 1978). He presented children with a hide-and-seek game of the sort illustrated in Figure 1, where a small boy (doll) is being chased by a policeman (doll). The boy finds some walls, which intersect at right angles as shown in the figure. From the child's point of view the boy doll is hidden from view when placed in quadrants A and B. This is the egocentric response. The problem given to the child is this: if the policeman stands where shown in Figure 1(a), he is able to see into quadrants B and D. Where can the boy hide? The non-egocentric response is to nominate A and C, and this is what the great majority of three and four year old children do. The task can be further complicated by introducing a second policeman as in Figure 1(b). Now quadrants A, B, and D can be seen into by the two policemen.

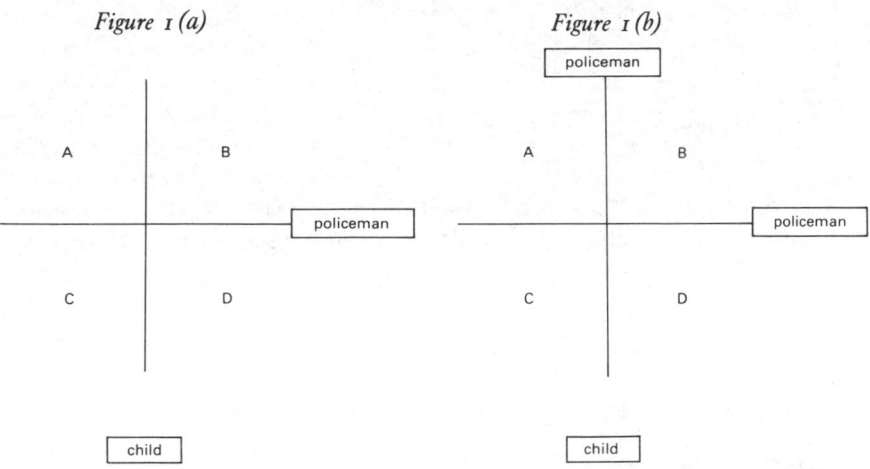

Figure 1 (a)

Figure 1 (b)

Can young children work out that the only quadrant the boy can now hide in is C? Again, most of them can, indicating not only that they can adopt a perspective other than their own, but also that they can adopt two perspectives other than their own, and integrate these in giving a non-egocentric response to the problem. Again we have an example of intellectual ability – non-egocentric perspective-taking – evident in one context, hide-and-seek, but absent in another, the three mountains problem.

Our third example also comes from work by Hughes (1983), this time on some studies of young children's understanding of number. Consider the following interviews with three different children aged three to four years. In the first, the child expresses his disgruntlement at the adult who assumes knowledge the child does not in fact possess.

ADULT: What's three and one more? How many is three and one more.
CHILD: Three and what? One what? Letter – I mean number? (We have earlier been playing a game with magnetic numbers and the child is presumably referring to them here.)
ADULT: How many is three and one more?
CHILD: One more what?
ADULT: Just one more, you know?
CHILD: I don't know (disgruntled).

In the second interview, the child can add two and one, and one and one, provided they refer to bricks, but she cannot complete the same addition when there is no such reference:

ADULT: How many is two and one?
CHILD: (long pause: no response)
ADULT: Well, how many bricks is two bricks and one brick?
CHILD: Three.

953

ADULT: OK ... so how many's two and one?
CHILD: (pause) Four? (hesitantly)
ADULT: How many is one brick and one more brick?
CHILD: Two bricks.
ADULT: So how many is one and one?
CHILD: One, maybe.

In the third interview, the child can add two and one if they refer to lollipops, elephants, or giraffes, but he cannot do so when there is no such reference:

ADULT: How many is two and one more?
CHILD: Four.
ADULT: Well, how many is two lollipops and one more?
CHILD: Three.
ADULT: How many is two elephants and one more?
CHILD: Three.
ADULT: How many is two giraffes and one more?
CHILD: Three.
ADULT: So how many is two and one more?
CHILD: (looks adult straight in the eye) Six.

Thus young children can succeed at arithmetic additions in some contexts, but fail to complete the identical additions in other contexts. As with the previous illustrations, we see young children's intellectual success in some contexts, and their intellectual failure in other contexts, even though to an adult the mental abilities required across the two sets of contexts appear virtually the same.

To explain such surprising results, Donaldson (1978) has made a distinction between what she calls 'embedded' and 'disembedded' thought.

Embedded thought involves intellectual functioning in contexts which, as Donaldson puts it, 'make human sense' to the young child. That is, the motives and intentions of the participants in the interaction are clear, and the child can understand what is required in the task at hand. The thought required of the child is *embedded* within his or her realm of understanding, and what is required can be readily appreciated. Young children often succeed in tasks which require this type of thought – for example, finding out which one of two cardboard strips is longer; playing a simulated game of hide-and-seek; adding two objects (bricks, lollipops, giraffes, elephants) to another of the same; and so on.

By contrast, *disembedded* thought is required in contexts which may not readily make human sense to the child, and here the young child often experiences difficulties, as in Piagetian tasks such as the towers of blocks and three mountains tasks, and in Hughes's arithmetic addition task where the child has to add 'two and one'. 'One more what?', the child asks. 'Just one more, you know?' As the child says, 'I *don't* know', nor does he – the point of the task and the meaning of the questions is not clear to him, for the context is disembedded and beyond the realm of the child's comprehension.

Utilizing this distinction between embedded and disembedded thought, we can begin to gain a better understanding of the nature of young children's mental abilities. Young children at pre-school age tend to think and reason well when their abilities are gauged in embedded contexts where they can readily appreciate the point of the task and what is required of them. However when their abilities are gauged in disembedded contexts, which to them make no or little 'human sense', they often fail to think and reason adequately. In such disembedded contexts, they fail to deploy mental abilities which we can see being deployed in embedded contexts. Thus an important aspect of the intellectual functioning of young children involves not the presence *versus* absence of mental abilities, but rather their ability to deploy thought in certain embedded contexts, and their inability to deploy thought in other, disembedded contexts. This view holds considerable interest for the debate on continuities *versus* discontinuities in development between home and school environments.

CONTINUITIES AND DISCONTINUITIES IN DEVELOPMENT BETWEEN HOME AND SCHOOL ENVIRONMENTS

If we adopt the view just presented, then the child's development in the school environment is seen as being different from the acquisition of totally new skills. Young children do, indeed, develop various skills in school. With regard to intellectual functioning, for example, the child must acquire the ability for disembedded thought. In the formal learning of school, it is no longer enough to be able to think and reason in contexts which make immediate human sense. The child has to learn how to think and reason in any context, embedded or disembedded. This is closely allied to the acquisition of skills such as the ability to read. Before school, the child has mostly been dealing with language in an embedded way. What is said by participants in social interaction in which the child participates often makes immediate sense. But in reading, apart from the technical skills involved in learning to decode the written representation of language, the child has to deal with language in a way that is quite different from his or her previous experience of language. Now the written language is divorced from the contexts of on-going interaction. It may not be immediately clear to the child who it was that produced the piece of written text that the child is trying to read. The events that the text describes can be remote from the child's experience, as can the people that the text refers to. And in understanding this type of (written) language, there are no helpful cues, such as previous knowledge of the people and events involved, or non-verbal information that accompanies verbal interaction in spoken dialogue, or other non-

955

linguistic contextual information that is often available when spoken language is used. Instead, in reading, the child encounters language that is shorn of all the non-verbal and non-linguistic supports that typically accompany spoken language. Thus in learning to read, the child must acquire facility in dealing with language that is often highly disembedded. The same is true of learning to produce written language, and of learning to manipulate number systems such as in arithmetic. The whole point about arithmetic addition, for example, is that two and one makes three – not that two giraffes and one giraffe make three giraffes, or that two bricks and one brick make three bricks. The fact is that two – of anything, and one – of anything, make three – of anything. The system derives its power from the fact that it is disembedded, and not tied to any particular context.

In this sense, then, there is an important discontinuity in the child's development. If the child is to succeed in our system of formal education, the ability to deploy disembedded thought and other intellectual skills required for mastery of the 'three Rs', is essential.

However there is also a need to stress that the skills involved in disembedded thought and in literacy and numeracy are not entirely new, for they develop in children who in fact bring to the school environment an amount of relevant knowledge and skills in deploying thought in embedded contexts. The development that occurs in school therefore extends and builds on developments that have taken place at home before the child enters formal schooling. Those who emphasize the continuities in development suggest that greater recognition needs to be given to this, and an approach to early learning in school adopted whereby skills already possessed by school entrants are first engaged. An example of this can be found in an approach to learning to read pioneered by Clay (1972) in New Zealand.

As Clay points out, children possess considerable facility with spoken language when they arrive at school. They are used to stories being either read or recounted to them by their parents, and so have experience of language in unified sequences. Though they cannot yet read, they are not wholly unfamiliar with print and written language. Children have experience of road signs, shop names, shopping lists, brand names of favourite foods, and perhaps simple written language shown on television. They see adults reading books, newspapers, or magazines, and reading and writing letters. They are often able to recognize their own name when written, and may be able to print their own first name. Clay suggests that such knowledge in school entrants can be utilized, initially in simple ways – for example, in the notion that the child's picture or drawing can be given a written caption to describe it. Pictures and captions that tell a story can next be built up into brief caption books which convey a message. Progress can then be made to simple written sentences, again, involving the notion that the written language conveys a message. Clay's point is that children are well used to such concepts with regard to spoken language, and in introducing young children to reading, it is useful to capitalize upon such concepts, but now with regard to written language. The more general point is that if formal learning in school can be introduced in ways which allow the child to bring to bear knowledge which he or she already possesses from informal learning at home, then the transition that the child must negotiate between home and school environments can be made easier for the child to master.

ENHANCING DEVELOPMENT BETWEEN HOME AND SCHOOL ENVIRONMENTS

So far, we have paid considerable attention to intellectual development and to literacy and numeracy. This is understandable, for these developments are crucial to children's success in education. If children do not succeed in these domains, their educational success is not only impeded, but they may also experience such feelings of inadequacy as to lose an appreciation of self-worth. Their psychological well-being may therefore be adversely affected, for feelings of self-worth and educational attainments can be intimately related.

However, important as the child's mastery of literacy and numeracy is in our society, in this concluding section we can look at certain aspects of the wider context in which children's development takes place.

Relative success or failure in school is not just the responsibility of individual children. Parents, schools, and the wider community also have important roles to play if children's development in school is to be enhanced. To appreciate this, it is instructive to consider the problems that children can encounter when support from parents and the wider community is not forthcoming.

Regrettably, such problems are readily evident in parts of so-called 'third world' countries which have no long tradition of formal education such as westernized countries have, and which are beset with a range of problems, particularly poverty. A striking example of such problems is that in parts of India and other Asian countries, 40 per cent of children drop out of formal education *after only one year of primary schooling*. Drop-out rates can thus be high, as can repetition rates where children have to repeat a year of schooling. The proportion of children who progress to the next year of schooling can be correspondingly low, as can the numbers of children who ever complete primary schooling, far less secondary education. The social, economic, and personal costs of such lack of achievement in school – to societies, parents, and children – are unbearably high, and reasons why children fail to realize their potential in school need to be identified (Grieve 1985).

Relevant factors include the *lack of preparation* for schooling. Children may not be adequately prepared for school in that their intellectual and social

957

background at home may not be conducive to the school experience, which involves a degree of social formality. Children may also be ill-prepared for what happens in school, in the sense that their curiosity has not been engaged and encouraged during the pre-school years – they may not know that curiosity, and satisfying curiosity, is enjoyable, and that school learning can help to satisfy curiosity in intelligent and rewarding ways. Their expectations of school may therefore be missing, awry, or quite unrealistic. Renwick (1978) provides an anecdote of the child who, after all of *three days* at primary school, complained: 'I can't read, I can't write, and I can't even do up my shoelaces!' Children may have quite unrealistic expectations of instantaneous success at school.

Parents may also be unprepared for their children's going to school through not having had the experience of education themselves. In parts of India, particular problems are encountered with children who are referred to as 'first generation learners'. Such children are the first generation in their community to go to school, and previous generations including their parents, grandparents, and other adults in the community have had no formal education. They are therefore often ignorant of what schooling involves, and find it difficult if not impossible to help their children succeed in school through the provision of *appropriate parental support*. If parents have not themselves been educated, then their knowledge of schooling will be absent; their knowledge of how to interact with teachers will be missing; and their expectations of what progress their children can be expected to make may often be lacking or unrealistic. In fact uneducated parents *can* help their children before and during schooling, despite their own lack of education, but they require considerable support and advice from the school and its teachers.

Another factor has already been referred to, that of poverty or economic pressure. Parents who are under *economic stress* may feel obliged to pressure their children against participation in school. The short-term attractiveness of having children help in the fields, homes, or workshops, may seem to outweigh the benefits of education, which often become apparent only in the longer term.

Cultural *attitudes* are also important. Communities which have no tradition of formal education in their cultural history may find it difficult to generate positive attitudes towards primary school education. Traditional (non-formal) education imparts skills for living, and the point of acquiring formal skills – such as the 'three Rs', which are often not fully deployed except in the longer term – may be difficult to understand. However, if positive attitudes are missing – or if community attitudes discriminate against achievement, for example with respect to girls, or with respect to certain religious, social, tribal, or caste groups – then children's progress in education is unlikely to be fully realized.

Lack of adequate development and achievement in school can also result from the *inadequacies in school* that children encounter, including poorly trained teachers, poor instructional methods, the lack of appropriate curricula, or the lack of adequate advisory teaching and support services. The quality of educational programmes therefore needs to be ensured.

Educational *administration* also needs to be of good quality. If the administration of educational services fails to ensure the availability of well trained teaching staff, the availability of appropriate educational materials, and the provision of relevant support services and advisory staff, the achievement of children in primary education cannot be expected. Making such provisions is not easy, especially for groups beset by poverty, for groups disadvantaged by geographical remoteness or isolation, and for groups with no tradition of formal education for young children, particularly girls. Nevertheless, it is to such difficult cases that educational administrators and policy makers need to devote attention if children's development at school is to be achieved.

In countries in Asia and the Pacific which are encountering significant problems in trying to educate young children, United Nations educational agencies such as UNESCO and UNICEF are involved in projects aimed to enhance children's chances of success at school. Particular attention is being paid to the effective preparation of children for school; to the provision of effective educational methods and materials and the appropriate training of teachers; to the effective involvement of parents and the community in young children's education; to ensuring that educational administration and supervision are conducive to children's educational success; and to ensuring that children's health and nutritional status is conducive to optimal school attendance and learning in school.

While such projects are being introduced to Asian and Pacific countries which do not have a long tradition of formal education, their emphases are by no means irrelevant for westernized countries, which *do* have a history of formal education. Children whose development in school proceeds well and who enjoy educational success are those who encounter good educational programmes, who are expected to succeed in school, and who receive good parental support. If children are to be helped to negotiate the transition between home and school environments successfully, then we need to ensure that their preparation for school, their educational programmes and teaching, and their parental and community support, are made both appropriate and effective.

REFERENCES

Bower, T. G. R. (1979) *Human Development*, San Francisco: Freeman.
Brown, R. (1973) *A First Language*, Cambridge, Mass.: Harvard University Press.

Bruner, J. S. (1974) 'From communication to language: a psychological perspective', *Cognition*, 3: 255–87.

Clay, M. M. (1972) *The Early Detection of Reading Difficulties*, Auckland: Heinemann.

Donaldson, M. (1978) *Children's Minds*, Glasgow: Collins (Fontana).

Donaldson, M., Grieve, R., and Pratt, C. J. (1983) *Early Childhood Development and Education*, Oxford: Blackwell.

Garvey, C. (1977) *Play*, Glasgow: Collins (Fontana).

Grieve, R. (1985) 'Raising the achievement level of children in primary education', *Occasional Paper No 14*, Bangkok: UNESCO Regional Office.

Harris, P. L. and Singleton, W. M. (1978) 'The child's understanding of measurement', in R. Glaser and S. Fokkema (Eds.) *Cognition and Instruction*, Proceedings of the NATO Conference.

Hughes, M. (1983) 'What is difficult about learning arithmetic?' in Donaldson *et al.*: 204–21.

Piaget, J., Inhelder, B., and Szeminska, A. (1960) *The Child's Conception of Geometry*, London: Routledge & Kegan Paul.

Pratt, C. J. and Grieve, R. (Eds.) (1980) 'Language awareness in children', *Education Research and Perspectives*, 7: 1–112.

Renwick, M. (1978) *Going to school. A Guide for Parents*, Wellington: New Zealand Council for Educational Research.

Rubin, Z. (1980) *Children's Friendships*, Glasgow: Collins (Fontana).

8.5

THE DEVELOPMENT OF SOCIAL COGNITION

NICOLA YUILL

INTRODUCTION

Consider a child on her first day at school: she enters a new, unpredictable social world. What sort of person is the teacher? What will her new fellow pupils be like? How can she make friends? What sorts of rules are there? What happens if someone breaks a rule? How are the other children feeling on their first day? What are they thinking about her? The way that children come to make sense of issues such as these is the main concern of research in social cognitive development. This is an area of research that has emerged as an important part of developmental psychology in the past 15 or 20 years.[1] It concerns the child's developing ability to understand and explain properties of the social world: characteristics of individuals – their motives, dispositions, beliefs and feelings – of relationships between individuals – friendship and conflict – and of social systems – social norms, moral rules, and obedience to authority.

The explicit agenda facing the child beginning school is to learn about the physical world, and this is typically investigated under the heading of 'cognitive development'. However, there is an increasing interest in the child's under-standing of the social world. If we know how the child thinks about other people, then we can have a better understanding of the child's own social behaviour. This chapter describes the developing awareness of such skills in children of school age. It is divided into four sections. The first short section gives a brief introduction to the background and theoretical issues involved. The next section covers research on children's perceptions of others – social perception and attribution. The following section is concerned with the under-standing of relationships and social systems, and the final section brings us back to current theoretical issues.

BACKGROUND

Piaget's work on children's thinking laid the foundations of modern cognitive developmental psychology when it became widely known in the 1950s. His research dealt primarily with the child's understanding of the physical world: understanding of causality, number, space, and so on. In this research, the child was depicted as a miniature scientist who constructed the world actively, through increasingly complex mental frameworks, or schemata. This contrasted with the view of the early behaviourists, who depicted children as passive receivers of stimuli. From the early 1970s, developmental psychologists sought to apply Piagetian theory to the child's construction of the social world. This coincided with a growing interest on the part of social psychologists in social cognition, and, primarily, the issue of how people took in information about other people and how they processed this information to make judgements about others. Broadly, the developmental research can be characterized as having two predominant interests: one is to set out how children's abilities to describe and explain the behaviour of others differ from adults' skills, and the other is to develop a 'stage' theory, along the lines of Piaget's, to account for social cognition.

For both these aims, Piaget's construct of egocentrism (see Chapter 8.4, by R. Grieve) assumed considerable importance. Egocentrism refers to the young child's apparent failure to appreciate that people can have different points of view, and children's resulting tendency to take their own perspective as representing reality. Piaget provided examples of this tendency in visual perspective-taking tasks, for example the 'three mountains' task (see Chapter 8.4), and his work has been extended to explain changes in children's ability to take the role of another person. Although recent work has suggested that young children are not as egocentric as Piaget claimed, and that role-taking skills begin to be evident from at least the age of four, egocentrism and role-taking remain useful constructs around which to organize the research.

The main assumption underlying most work in social cognition is that children's cognitive skills can be used to explain their social competence. Factors such as egocentrism are seen as playing a *causal* role, or are *mediating factors* in children's social behaviour. If children are egocentric, then they will be unable to understand the internal mental states of other children, or to see another person's point of view. For example, a young girl choosing a present for her mother might select something that she would like herself, because she fails to take into account the ways in which the recipient's tastes and interests differ from her own. More recently, social cognitive research has posed a different question: can social experience play a causal role in children's cognitive development? For example, Piaget himself suggested that children's understanding of the rules of games developed through social interaction with peers. A new trend is therefore to look for *bidirectional effects*: how does cognitive development influence social competence, and in turn, how does social experience advance thinking skills? This review of research concentrates mainly on the cognitive factors underlying social understanding.

SOCIAL PERCEPTION: WHAT ARE OTHER PEOPLE LIKE?

When children enter school, they are faced with a sudden increase in the number of unfamiliar people they interact with, and correspondingly, new demands on their abilities to form impressions and predict the behaviour of others. Social psychologists suggest that we predict behaviour by making inferences about the psychological states of others – their dispositions, intentions, motives, thoughts, and feelings. What sorts of inferences do children make about others?

Dispositions

One way of investigating children's understanding of psychological states is to ask them to describe people they know. A study of 320 seven to sixteen-year-olds[2] showed that at the age of about seven to eight, children tend to describe their peers in terms of external, observable aspects, such as name, age, sex, appearance, habits, and possessions. Older children use descriptions that require inferences about mental make-up, such as personality characteristics, values, and motives. Such descriptions require generalizations about behaviour patterns, and hypotheses about the internal, psychological causes of behaviour. For example, describing someone as 'kind' is based on several observations of behaviour, and for each one, an inference that the act was prompted by a generous motive rather than by self-interest. Furthermore, older children make more qualifications in what they say. Young children use strong evaluative terms in their descriptions: people are either good or bad. Children over seven to eight years are more likely to mention both good and bad points in a single person, and to qualify their judgements. The progression with age from 'surface' to relatively 'deep' characteristics has been shown in many studies, and marks an important change in how children choose to express their perceptions of others. This does not mean that younger children cannot use certain sorts of descriptions. Although at five children seem unable to make generalizations about others' dispositions, seven-year-olds can, but do not do so spontaneously, unlike older children. It seems that there is a stage at which children are not oriented towards drawing inferences about dispositions, even though they are capable of doing so.[3] It is therefore important to bear in mind that children's spontaneous descriptions demonstrate not purely their abilities, but also their interests and motivations.

There are also changes in children's explanations of specific actions. These changes have been studied by showing children filmed sequences of behaviour, and asking them to describe and explain what they have seen. Children move from describing observable events and obvious emotions, at the age of about six, to increasingly complex and differentiated accounts that explain actions in terms of subjective psychological states such as motives and intentions.

This work in 'person perception' often relies on children's spontaneous verbal descriptions of people they know and events they have seen. The strength of this approach is that children can bring all their experience to bear on the task of describing and accounting for the actions of familiar people. However, these descriptive methods also rely on children's abilities to reflect on their experiences with others and to express those reflections coherently. Can children understand the basic principle that people's overt behaviour can be explained in terms of internal psychological states such as intentions and motives?

Intentions and motives

Everyday observation suggests that even very young children can see the difference between intended and accidental actions, particularly when excusing a misdemeanour by claiming that it was 'not on purpose'. Such claims do not prove that children understand the distinction: they may have learnt the words merely as a formula for avoiding punishment, just as children first seem to learn 'please' and 'thank you' as part of a social routine, without knowing their meanings. However, there is experimental evidence that children from the age of three can distinguish reliably between actions that they intended, and various non-intentional behaviours such as mistakes and reflex actions. They are also able to discriminate the intended results of actions from unintended side-effects. Of course, this does not mean that children will always judge intentionality correctly in practice. Young children seem biased towards judging accidental actions as intended. Such over-attribution of intentionality could lead children to judge accidental mishaps more harshly. Furthermore, individual children will differ in the way they respond to such mishaps. For example, when asked to judge a story where one character bumps into another, aggressive children are more likely than non-aggressive ones to assume that the action was intended. Thus, biases in attributing the causes of social behaviour can be linked to individual differences in personality.

Given that a behaviour is intended, we are then usually interested in working out why the actor behaved in that way. For example, if one child hits another on purpose, was it because he just didn't like the victim, or was he trying to take a toy that the victim had (instrumental aggression), was he provoked, or was he venting his anger with the teacher on to a less powerful victim (displaced aggression)? As this list shows, motives seem to vary in complexity. The limited work done on this topic seems to support the idea that young children can understand motives that are related to the immediate situation, such as instrumental aggression, but they only later understand the more complex, remote causal chains involved in motives such as displaced aggression. One particularly interesting issue is children's understanding of 'ulterior motives', in view of the many attempts in the mass media to persuade and influence consumers. Research indicates[4] that children under seven do not generally realize that the purpose of television commercials is to sell goods, but that they can be trained to adopt a more reflective and critical attitude. Interestingly, children who watched educational programmes showed better understanding of techniques used in presenting television, and in visual perspective-taking skills, compared to children who did not watch such programmes.

Beliefs

One of the most basic assumptions that we make about people's behaviour is that they plan their actions on the basis of their beliefs about the world. Usually, this assumption works well, because people's beliefs generally coincide with reality, but problems arise when people act on beliefs that are false. In such cases, we can only understand why people acted as they did by distinguishing between what is really the case, and what the person thought was the case. If young children are egocentric, then they should be unable to see that another person acts on what they think, rather than what the child knows to be true. Recent research shows that children below the age of four do seem to assume that other people act on the basis of reality, rather than on their false beliefs about reality. For example, children are told a story about two characters who see a bar of chocolate put into a cupboard. Then one character leaves, and the chocolate is placed in a different cupboard. The character who left then returns, and the subject is asked where this character will look for the chocolate. We know the character will look where they mistakenly *think* the chocolate is, rather than where it *really* is. But children around four tend to say that the character will look in the true location, despite being absent when the chocolate was moved. Older children, however, respond correctly, showing an appreciation that people act on the basis of their beliefs about the world, rather than on how the world really is.

Emotions

Understanding how others feel has been used as a further 'test case' of the extent of children's egocentrism. If children do not distinguish different viewpoints, then they would not be able to infer emotions in others. Early work showed that even three- to four-year-olds could predict the emotions of story characters in particular situations: a child at the dentist will feel afraid, one at a birthday party will be happy. Although this demonstrates children's appropriate use of terms such as 'happy', 'sad', 'frightened', and so on, critics argued that children did not have to view the situations from a *different* perspective from their own; they could just imagine how they themselves would feel in such a situation. For this reason, new tests were developed[5] in which children had to infer the emotions and thoughts of a character who had a different perspective on the situation. For example, one such story concerns a girl who sees her father off on a plane, and is then sad when she receives a present of a toy aeroplane, through the post. Children are asked to explain the story both from their own point of view, and from the perspective of the postman, who is understandably puzzled that the girl seems sad to receive a present, because he does not know about the girl's father leaving. In tasks such as this, only from about the age of seven can children give appropriate explanations of the postman's perspective.

The work just described concerns children's understanding of emotions from a cognitive viewpoint, as part of the child's knowledge about internal psychological states. However, understanding another's feelings involves not just a cognitive appreciation of what those feelings are, and how they affect behaviour, but also an empathic understanding, in the sense that the other's feelings are shared or sympathized with. Most parents and teachers will be able to think of incidents in which young children become distressed by the sufferings of others, and attempt to console their peers. But it is difficult to distinguish between 'contagion' of emotions – when one child cries, others start crying too – with a more mature response to others' feelings that involves some cognitive appreciation of the emotions involved. Work on empathy is beyond the scope of this review, but it is worth remembering that children's behaviour can be influenced not just by their cognitive appreciation of another person's perspective, but also by their emotions and motivations.

Combining information

We have already seen that children have some grasp of basic psychological characteristics of intention and belief by the time they are five, and can use dispositions from the age of about seven. However, this understanding does not guarantee that children will be able to reason correctly in explaining the causes of particular behaviour. The *process* of how we explain such causes is the province of attribution theory, which provides a useful adjunct to analyses of the *content* of children's descriptions. Attribution theory draws a distinction between explanations of action in terms of persons and situations. For example, if one child hits another, is this because of something about the *situation* (for example the other child hit first) or because of the child's *disposition* (for example he is aggressive by nature)? The attribution a child makes can affect future actions – for example, retaliating, crying, or going to tell the teacher. In general, young children tend to explain actions in situational terms, and only later use dispositions, as we have already seen.

Attribution is generally not as simple as just identifying a single cause. Often, there are several pieces of information available, that the perceiver must integrate. Attribution theorists have described ways in which adults typically combine different possible causes, and these patterns of integrating information, or causal schemas, have also been studied in young children. One way of explaining someone's behaviour is to discount one potential cause in favour of another. For example, a boy might be playing with a particular toy either because he likes the toy (internal cause) or because his teacher rewards him when he plays with that toy (external cause). For adults and children over about seven to nine years, if the boy was given an external incentive, then the internal cause, liking the toy, can be disregarded or discounted. A child who plays with a toy without reward probably likes the toy better than one who is rewarded for playing with it. However, younger children seem not to discount one cause, but to add the two causes together: they say that the rewarded child likes the toy better. It has been suggested that these children see rewards as bonuses, rather than as bribes. This supports the work described above, suggesting that young children do not understand ulterior motives. Despite these surprising attributions, young children seem to behave rather differently when their own actions are involved. When children are rewarded for activities that are intrinsically enjoyable, such as artwork, they later show less of a tendency to engage in that sort of work than do children who have not been rewarded. This is presumably because children have an extrinsic reason for engaging in art – the reward – and so they can rule out the possibility that they are doing it because they enjoy it – an intrinsic motivation. There seems to be a difference, then, between how children behave, and how they explain the behaviour of others. The attributions that children make about their own motives can have an important influence on their future behaviour. Psychologists[6] have argued that children are more likely to develop intrinsic motivation for their work if they see their activities as emerging from their own choice, rather than from coercion by an outsider.

One area in which children's explanations of their own behaviour are particularly important for their future behaviour is that of achievement. Given two children who score the same mark on a spelling test, one who tried hard and one who did not, older children and adults see that the less industrious child must be better at spelling: the more ability you have, the less effort you need to expend. Children under about seven, however, add effort and ability: the child who tried harder has better spelling ability. These children's use of additive rules rather than compensatory reasoning is influenced by factors in their social experience. While they do not correctly infer ability from effort, as in the example, they can infer effort from ability: someone who is good at spelling doesn't have to try. This might be because children are exhorted to 'try harder to get better'. They therefore know about the rule linking increased effort with greater future ability, but not about the inference that those with greater ability do not have to try so hard. The explanations that children give, or are presented with by others, for their own performance, can have important implications for their self-esteem and future behaviour. For example, two children may fail a test. One child tells herself, 'Well, I wasn't really trying': she can therefore be more confident that next time, if she tries harder, she will pass the test. The other child, however, sees failure as showing her lack of ability. Such attributions can become self-fulfilling prophecies: ability is seen as a relatively stable and enduring trait, and the second child may feel there is not much she can do about increasing her ability.

Communicating with others

Understanding episodes such as the ones described above depends on a whole network of concepts that we use to explain behaviour: intentions, motivations, and beliefs. We all have an implicit 'theory of mind' to do this, making assumptions that people have intentions, that these intentions cause their behaviour, and that people try to fulfil their intentions on the basis of their beliefs about the world. Records of children's speech show that even from their second year of life, children are using 'mental verbs' such as 'know', 'remember', and 'think'. However, experimental evidence shows that children's understanding of such words develops over several years. Misunderstandings can arise when children use the behaviour that they can see to guide them in their comprehension of mental processes. For example, four-year-olds asked to search for a hidden object will say that they remembered where it was if they are successful, and forgot if they fail, even though they did not know where the object had been hidden in the first place. It is only from the ages of five to seven that children understand that they are just guessing in such circumstances.

Children's use of a word is therefore not a reliable indication that they understand it in the same way as an adult would. A good example of this is shown in children's understanding of the beliefs of others, and in particular, of deception. Young children will argue that any untrue statement is a lie, even to the extent of calling themselves liars when they discover that they have unknowingly said something false, or when they change their minds. As we have seen, children become able to reason about others' beliefs from about four years of age. Taking into account other people's knowledge is important for the child's ability to communicate adequately with others. For example, if a boy tells his teacher that he wants 'the book', the message is ambiguous unless it is clear from the context which book he means. Research on communication skills shows that children under about seven, despite their skill in adapting their language to listeners of different ages and abilities, do not explicitly recognize when a message they hear or produce is ambiguous,[7] although they may hesitate and show uncertainty. Telling children explicitly, 'I don't know what you mean' in response to an ambiguous message seems to help them to understand the distinction between what they meant and what they said.

RELATIONSHIPS AND SOCIAL SYSTEMS

The research described above deals with children's understanding of the characteristics of individuals. However, there has been a move, both in social and developmental psychology, away from individual characteristics to more truly social factors that involve the relationships between people. Relationships between people are influenced not only by the characteristics of each individual, but also by the sorts of roles that people occupy, the social norms or standards that are socially agreed, social institutions such as friendship, and the rules, both explicit and implicit, that govern social behaviour.

Selman[8] has developed a theory of 'social perspective-taking' that covers a wide range of social relationships. Each level of perspective-taking describes what the child understands about the psychological make-up of others, and about relationships between people. For example, Selman uses his theory to describe how children change in their accounts of what a friend is: a momentary playmate (Level 0: egocentric, three to six years), someone who helps or benefits you (Level 1: subjective, five to nine years), someone with whom there is co-operation when circumstances are favourable (Level 2: reciprocal, seven to twelve years), an intimate companion engaging in mutual sharing (Level 3: mutual, ten to fifteen years) and finally, a relationship in which two people are interdependent, but autonomous (Level 4: societal-symbolic, twelve years to adulthood). Other work using different theoretical backgrounds has generally supported the idea of a change in ideas about friendship from a one-sided to a mutual relationship.

Selman has applied his theoretical framework to children's understanding of authority, as well as using it more generally as a description of children's social cognition. Selman points out that the ages given for each stage are approximate, and concern children's ability to reflect on and state explicitly their reasoning about hypothetical dilemmas. This is an important point, particularly in view of recent work, showing that children's social cognitive abilities are more advanced than was previously thought. However, whether or not

Selman's model is accurate in this respect, it provides a much-needed theoretical framework for the work in this area.

We can see from children's spontaneous behaviour that they respond differently to different social 'categories' of person well before school age: mother is often the main source of security, father might be expected to be a good play companion, adults in general are sources of authority, boys and girls are played with in different ways, and so on. However, we cannot be sure from this behavioural evidence that children have a 'concept of role' as complex as that of an adult. Observations of children's doll play have shown that even the youngest pre-schoolers have expectations about the sorts of behaviour appropriate to a familiar role such as 'doctor', and by four to five years, they can act out complementary roles such as the interaction of 'doctor' and 'patient' dolls. Only at about six do children seem to grasp that a single person could occupy two roles, such as doctor and father. Even then, children do not necessarily see that the person can be both doctor and father at the same time.

An issue of considerable interest to those who are responsible for controlling or disciplining children concerns the understanding of social rules, and children's moral understanding. The child is faced with several different kinds of injunctions: those that relate specifically to conventions at home or school – go to bed at 7.30, put up your hand if you want to say something – those that are considered 'prudent behaviour' in both – don't go out in the rain without a coat – and those that are universal moral rules – don't hit other children. Although there is some debate amongst psychologists studying moral development about how to classify different rules, it is clear that five to six-year-old children do make distinctions between different types of rule. Thus, children react sharply when their peers violate rules about accepted conventions, and moral rules, but, unlike adults, tend to overlook breaches of regulations. Young children also understand that moral rules are unchangeable, whereas conventions can be altered by mutual consent, and may differ from one social group to another.[9]

Understanding of rules is particularly significant in the field of social cognition, because it is one of the few 'social' topics investigated by Piaget. It is also the one place where Piaget assigned a crucial role to social influences on cognitive development. He studied children's rules by watching and talking to children playing marbles.[10] He found that children under seven tended to take an absolute view of rules – they are invented by some high authority and cannot be changed – whereas older children see that rules are socially constructed, and can be altered by mutual agreement. From such observations, Piaget developed the idea that interaction with peers was important for development, because it enables children to come into contact with conflicting opinions. He contrasts this with interactions with adults, which are more one-sided: the adult has all the authority, power, and experience, and the child has little opportunity for conflict among equals. Through conflict with peers, children come to realize that there are different points of view, and that rules derive their authority from the fact that everyone agrees to abide by them.

FUTURE DIRECTIONS

Recently there has been a growing convergence of interests between researchers in social cognition and those looking at social development and personality. Although social cognition was always founded on the assumption that cognition mediated behaviour, there is a growing dissatisfaction with the idea that children's performance in experiments and interviews can be used in isolation to predict their behaviour. This dissatisfaction is fuelled by the failure to find consistent relationships between what children say in interviews and how they actually behave. Of course, the cognition-behaviour relationship is not a simple one, for several reasons. First, in 'real life', social behaviour depends not just on children's thinking about others, but also their motivation. A good example of this is a study of children's helping behaviour.[11] We might predict that children who were better at taking the role of the other would be more ready to help others in need. But there was no straightforward relationship: the tendency to help was also mediated by how assertive children were. So for assertive children, the better they were at role-taking, the more helpful they were in reality. But for unassertive children, role-taking skill was irrelevant: if children are unwilling to take the initiative, then it does not matter that they can see another child's need for help, because they will not act on their perception of that need. Second, role-taking skill does not automatically coincide with good intent: such skills are just as useful for a confidence trickster as they are for a philanthropist. Finally, social psychologists have suggested that much of our behaviour is relatively 'mindless': rather than thinking out the other person's perspective carefully, we rely on generalizations and 'scripts' – knowledge of stereotyped situations.

Despite these cautions, social cognition plays an important part in understanding children's social behaviour. Now that psychologists are more aware of the complexities of the cognition-behaviour relationships, it is possible to consider the boundaries within which cognitive skills are applied in social behaviour, and how their use is affected by motivation, emotion, and 'cognitive short-cuts'. The area of social cognitive development is now going through an interesting transition period. After the 'cognitively-biased' work of the late 1970s, researchers are now considering the more 'social' influences, and the ways in which children's social experiences influence the development of social cognitive skills.

One of the most exciting prospects in social cognitive research lies in its application to improving the social skills of children who, for one reason or another, do not get on with their peers.[12] The initial approach was to assume that such children could be taught the social skills used by well-adjusted children. Researchers emphasized that flexibility is the key to social adjustment: children who can think of many ways of solving an interpersonal problem, such as obtaining a toy from another child, tend to be more socially successful than those who have a more limited repertoire of strategies, and children can be instructed so as to expand their repertoire of social skills. Such work concentrates on children's ability to reflect on their social behaviour, the underlying assumption being that poor social adjustment is due to a lack of reflective social cognitive skills. Other approaches have stressed the potentially beneficial effects of altering children's social environment, such as giving socially isolated children play experience with younger children. Because of the increasing convergence of work in cognitive and social development, and the adoption of observational methods in addition to traditional experimental methods, researchers are becoming more aware of the importance of considering motivational factors, and of the individual differences between children. For example, as we saw above, unassertive children are not necessarily deficient in their social cognitive knowledge: they just have trouble putting this knowledge into practice. On the other hand, children who are rejected by their peers seem less able to think flexibly about different ways of achieving interpersonal goals: their problem may be due more to their lack of social cognitive skills than to any lack of assertiveness. More effective ways of helping socially maladjusted children may be developed by considering how social cognitive skills interact with motivation and the social environment to produce each person's style of social behaviour.

REFERENCES

1. Shantz, C. U. (1983) 'Social cognition', in J. H. Flavell and E. M. Markman (Eds.) *Cognitive Development*, Vol. 3 of P. H. Mussen (Ed.) *Handbook of Child Psychology*, (4th edn), New York, Wiley: 495–555.
2. Livesley, W. J. and Bromley, D. B. (1973) *Person Perception in Childhood and Adolescence*, London: Wiley.
3. Rogers, C. (1978) 'The child's perception of other people', in H. McGurk (Ed.) *Issues in Childhood Social Development*, London: Methuen, 107–29.
4. Greenfield, P. M. (1984) *Mind and Media: The Effects of Television, Computers and Video Games*, London: Fontana.
5. Chandler, M. (1976) 'Social cognition: a selective review of current research', in W. F. Overton and J. Gallagher (Eds.), *Knowledge and Development*, Vol. 1, New York: Plenum: 93–147.
6. Lepper, M. R. (1983) 'Social control processes, attributions of motivation and the internalization of social values', in E. Higgins, D. Ruble and W. Hartup (Eds.), *Social Cognition and Social Development: A Sociocultural Perspective*, Cambridge: Cambridge University Press: 294–330.
7. Robinson, E. J. and Robinson, W. P. (1983) 'Ways of reacting to communication failure in relation to the development of the child's understanding about verbal communication', in M.

Donaldson, R. Grieve, and C. Pratt (Eds.) *Early Childhood Development and Education: Readings in Psychology*, Oxford: Blackwell: 83–103.
8. Selman, R. (1980) *The Growth of Interpersonal Understanding: Developmental and Clinical Analyses*, New York: Academic Press.
9. Shweder, R. A., Turiel, E., and Much, N. C. (1981) 'The moral intuitions of the child', in J. Flavell and L. Ross (Eds.) *Social Cognition: Frontiers and Possible Futures*, Cambridge: Cambridge University Press: 288–305.
10. Piaget, J. (1965) *The Moral Judgement of the Child*, London: Kegan Paul.
11. Barrett, D. E. and Yarrow, M. R. (1977) 'Prosocial behaviour, social inferential ability and assertiveness in children', *Child Development*, 48:475–81.
12. Rubin, K. and Ross, H. (Eds.) (1982) *Peer Relations and Social Skills in Childhood*, New York: Springer-Verlag.

8.6

THE DEVELOPMENT OF MORAL AND RELIGIOUS IDEAS AND BEHAVIOUR

ROGER STRAUGHAN

We all, whether aged seven or seventy, represent at this moment in our lives the results of our prior 'development'. Individual human beings are in a constant state of change, various aspects of which have already been discussed in this section; such changes are normally called 'development', in ordinary language usage at least, when we *approve* of them in some way.

Two of the most fundamental ways in which individuals change or develop are in their view of the world and of their actions within it. Show a picture of a starving refugee child to a baby and to a fifteen-year-old. Both will 'see' the same picture in that their optical nerves receive the same stimuli, but there the similarity of the experiences ends. The baby may well react to the colours and shapes of the picture, but the teenager will normally be able to *interpret* the pictorial data *as* a starving refugee child by applying the *concepts* of hunger, homelessness, deprivation, need, etc. to the situation as portrayed. These concepts in turn carry with them emotional and motivational overtones which may lead the teenager to think that something ought to be *done* about the situation – even that he or she should do something about it, perhaps. We develop, then, in the way that we both conceptualize our experiences to interpret the world and use these conceptualizations to motivate us and provide us with reasons for acting in a particular way.

THE NATURE OF MORALITY AND RELIGION

Morality and religion feature prominently in both of these aspects of development. First, they each possess their own sets of distinctive concepts which we can use as templates to fit on to our 'raw' experiences and so produce particular kinds of interpretation; and second, these interpretations often contain implicit prescriptions in favour of certain actions and against others.

Let us take an example from both the moral and religious areas to illustrate these features:

1. A child sees a friend enter a garden and take some apples off a tree. This 'raw' experience can become a moral situation if appropriate moral concepts are applied to it. So if the garden belongs to a stranger who has not invited the child to pick apples, the concepts of ownership, property, permission, trespassing, and stealing could be used to interpret the situation. Such concepts are not merely descriptive; they also convey values and norms – for example trespassing is entering an area where one has no *right* to be, and stealing is the *wrongful* taking of another's property. To conceptualize the incident in such moral terms, therefore, is to acknowledge these evaluative, prescriptive overtones, which suggest that there are moral reasons for not trespassing or stealing in normal circumstances. This does not of course mean that the child will necessarily *act* upon those reasons by persuading the friend to return the apples.

2. A child regularly witnesses his parents thanking and seeking help from an invisible being they call 'God'. This experience needs religious concepts to be applied to it if it is to be interpreted and explained. The parents' behaviour then comes to be understood as 'prayer' or 'worship', concepts whose meaning is linked to that of other religious concepts ('God', 'grace', 'sin', 'salvation', etc.). Religious concepts too are not just descriptive: 'Worship', for example, is what is *due* to God, and 'sin' is a *wrongful* state of affairs involving separation from God. So to conceptualize experiences in religious terms is to open oneself to the possible influence of another set of considerations and reasons in deciding what to do and not to do.

But are morality and religion distinct and separable areas of development? If so, what exactly are these areas, what are their dimensions and limits? What does it mean to 'be moral' or to 'be religious'?

These are difficult and complex questions about which volumes have been written and disagreement has been common. Two problems of particular concern to us here will serve to illustrate some of the difficulties:

1. Should morality and religion be defined in terms of particular ways of thinking, reasoning, judging, and deciding, or in terms of particular beliefs, principles, values, and behaviour? This distinction is usually described as being one between *form* and *content*. On the one hand, some have argued that morality is characterized by its form, which is reflected in the way in which moral judgements are made and moral conclusions reached (for example by appealing to general, universal principles which are then applied impartially and impersonally to justify specific actions). On the other hand, others have felt that morality is essentially concerned with the content of particular principles and values (for example the pursuit of justice or the consideration of other people's interests). A similar distinction can be drawn in the case of religion between

the form of religious thought and practices and the content of particular religious beliefs and observances.

2. Should morality and religion be defined in terms of judgements and beliefs or of actions and behaviour? Could people count as being moral or morally developed, for example, on the basis of being mature in their moral judgements, logical in drawing moral conclusions, or adept at considering moral dilemmas – even if they were very bad at translating their moral judgements and decisions into action? Or alternatively could people be said to be moral or morally developed if they appeared to be paragons of virtue in all they did, but never took the trouble to reflect upon the reasons and justifications for their actions? Similarly, should people be called religious if they are conversant with religious ways of thinking and reasoning, or if they regularly participate in religious practices?

Shortage of space forbids a lengthy discussion of these two problems, which have nevertheless to be addressed in any investigation of moral and religious development. All that we can do here is to short-cut arbitrarily the problems by suggesting that in each case a balance of both elements is probably required. On this view, morality and religion will have both a distinctive form and a distinctive content and will refer to both judgements and actions. This implies that development in each area will have to span a wide spectrum and that a distorted picture will result if one element is overemphasized at the expense of the other. A good example of an attempt to do justice to form, content, judgement, and action within morality would be John Wilson's well-known analysis of the 'morally educated person'.[1]

But what of the *relationship* between morality and religion? If these two areas are closely connected or interdependent, then development within them will presumably reflect this connection; if they are discrete and independent of each other, then there seems little justification for considering moral and religious development under the same heading. Controversy again rages over this issue, and again all that can be offered here is a provisional short-cut resolution of this complex question.

On the one hand, morality and religion certainly seem independent of each other in so far as each has its own distinctive language, concepts, and procedures; 'sinful' is not, for example, the equivalent of 'morally wrong';[2] on the other hand, religion and morality are both essentially concerned with how people ought to behave. Our moral treatment of others is largely determined by what we believe is good and ultimately beneficial for them, and that in turn will depend upon our view of the nature of human beings – for example are they my 'brothers' and 'sisters', sharing the same Father, or just a random collection of atoms and molecules? It seems, then, that morality and religion are in certain respects independent of each other, but in other respects are closely interlocked. If this is true, the relationship between moral and religious *development* is likely to follow a similar complex pattern.

DEVELOPMENT IN MORALITY AND RELIGION

So far we have been struggling to get to grips with the terms 'moral' and 'religious', without paying much attention to the notion of 'development'. But what exactly is thought to be 'developing' in these areas of our experience? From what and into what is this development taking place? The importance of conceptual development was mentioned earlier, but we have also seen that there are more dimensions to morality and religion than just the conceptual one.

The very idea that children (and adults) do 'develop' in terms of morality and religion probably runs counter to the common-sense assumptions of many people. Many parents and even teachers hold a relatively uncomplicated view of how children become moral and/or religious: children learn what is right and wrong by being told firmly and unambiguously what *is* right and wrong, and by having this instruction clearly reinforced by various forms of reward and punishment, thereby coming to conform to a moral and/or religious code and to acquire the appropriate virtues.

This common-sense view is inadequate on several counts:

1. Learning to conform to a particular code cannot be the sum total of morality or religion, for this is to over-emphasize behaviour at the expense of judgement and reasoning. No behaviour can in itself count as moral or religious, without reference being made to the conceptions and motives underlying it.
2. The value and importance of obedience in morality and religion is overestimated. It may often be the mark of a moral or religious person *not* to do as he or she is told, for the dictates of an authority can never conclusively define what is morally or religiously 'right' and 'wrong'.[3]
3. There is a considerable amount of evidence that children do not learn and progress in these areas primarily through the medium of direct instruction, and that 'development' is indeed the most apposite word to describe the process. This evidence will now be briefly reviewed by referring selectively to the work of a few representative key figures: this survey is of course merely illustrative and by no means comprehensive.

Jean Piaget was one of the first researchers to probe the notion of 'moral development' in depth, and his studies, though frequently criticized and challenged, have been highly influential. From a series of interviews with Swiss children he constructed a complex theory of moral development which interlinked with his more general theory of intellectual development.[4]

Piaget identified two distinct types of morality, which he labelled 'heteronomy' and 'autonomy'. At the heteronomous stage young children were found to regard rules of various kinds as absolute, sacrosanct, and inviolable ('It's right because the rule says so.'). Their moral judgements at this stage were similarly inflexible, determining the rightness or wrongness of an action in terms of its physical consequences and disregarding the motives and intentions of the agent ('It's worse to drop a pile of plates accidentally than to smash one deliberately.'). As children learned to co-operate more with their peers and to gain greater understanding of other viewpoints, they developed towards the autonomous stage. Here rules were freely chosen and internalized when the reasoning behind them was appreciated; moral judgements were made in the light of situational circumstances and extenuating factors were allowed for ('He's too young to know better.').

This developmental sequence is not, however, according to Piaget a clear-cut, all-or-nothing affair. Not everyone reaches the higher stage, and children do not always operate exclusively at the level of either one stage or the other: nor can precise ages be allotted to the stages.

More recently the American psychologist, Lawrence Kohlberg, and his associates have tried to refine Piaget's stages, and over a period of more than 20 years have built up an extensive corpus of theoretical and practical work.[5] As a result of cross-cultural and longitudinal studies, based on interviews using hypothetical moral dilemmas (for example should a penniless husband steal a drug to save his dying wife?), Kohlberg claimed to have distinguished six stages of moral reasoning, extending from childhood well into adulthood – though he later came to doubt whether the sixth stage is ever achieved in practice.

Elaborate descriptions of all aspects of these stages are offered, but perhaps the clearest way of illustrating them is in terms of the kind of reasons given at each stage for doing what is judged to be right. Examples would be:

Stage 1 wanting to avoid punishment
Stage 2 wanting to satisfy one's own needs
Stage 3 wanting to gain the good opinion of others
Stage 4 wanting to uphold the authority of social institutions
Stage 5 wanting to uphold the contractual obligation of respecting the rights of others
Stage 6 wanting to uphold a personal commitment to universal, self-chosen moral principles.

Like Piaget, Kohlberg argued that there is an invariant sequence in which everyone must pass through the stages, but that one does not always reason consistently at the level characteristic of the particular stage one has reached; many adults do not proceed beyond Stages 3 and 4. Other important claims by Kohlberg of particular educational significance within the context of this article include:

1. that development through the stages can be accelerated not by direct instruction, which is ineffective, but by exposing the subject to argument and discussion which exhibits elements of reasoning from the stage which is one higher than his or her present level.
2. that the higher one proceeds up through the stages, the more likely one is to *act* upon one's moral judgements.

The work of both Piaget and Kohlberg has generated considerable controversy, and certainly should not be accepted as established fact. Nevertheless it does illustrate how some flesh might be put on the bones of the concept of 'moral development' and also underlines the centrality of the form/content and the judgement/action issues. Their work has given impetus to what is usually referred to as the 'cognitive-developmental' approach to moral development, and has strongly influenced other important research, which cannot be summarized here.

A cognitive-developmental approach can also be adopted towards religion as well as morality, though the work in this area is less extensive and well-known. Goldman, for example, drew upon Piaget's general theory of intellectual development to suggest a sequence as follows: from 'pre-religious' thinking at about five to seven years, where religious understanding is at a fairy-tale level and concepts of God are crudely anthropomorphic; to 'sub-religious' thinking at about seven to eleven, where a more logical understanding is evident, though at a concrete and materialistic level; to 'personal religious' thinking from eleven onwards, where a more abstract, spiritual level of understanding involving non-literal interpretations becomes possible.[6]

Just as Piaget's work influenced Goldman's, so more recently Kohlberg's studies have suggested a possible parallel account of religious development. Fowler, for instance, has described six stages of 'faith development', extending from a minimum age of four at Stage 1 (intuitive-projective faith) to a minimum of forty at Stage 6 (universalizing faith).[7] A less abstract account is offered by Oser, which closely follows Kohlberg's stages and is worked out in terms of children's conceptions of God; thus, at Stage 1 He is seen as a physically powerful figure; at Stage 2 as one who grants benefits on a *quid pro quo* basis; at Stage 3 as a personal friend or caring shepherd; at Stage 4 as a law-giver; and at Stage 5 as an 'energizer' who supports autonomous moral action.[8] Such a sequence raises interesting questions about the relationship between moral and religious stages of development.

The cognitive-developmental approach which has been exemplified here is by no means the only possible one, but it has been picked out for special attention because it demonstrates a clear sense in which 'development' can be claimed to take place in morality and religion. Learning theory approaches, by contrast, are more applicable to morality than religion, and focus largely upon the shaping and modification of behaviour by rewards and punishments or by imitation of other people.[9] Appropriate behaviour is thus 'reinforced', and inappropriate behaviour 'extinguished', but such terminology does nothing to solve the problem of content. Who is to decide what is morally appropriate and inappropriate? Is it justifiable to seek to inculcate specific patterns of behaviour in children in ways which some would claim come close to conditioning? Although such approaches may perhaps be justified in terms of social control, it seems doubtful whether they have much to do with *moral development* as such, if they attempt to identify morality with limited items of behaviour, and fail to look beyond that behaviour to the conceptions, beliefs, feelings, and intentions which form an essential part of 'being moral' – and indeed of 'being religious'.

It is difficult, if not impossible, therefore, to speak of moral or religious development purely in terms of behaviour, and while there is an obvious danger that the cognitive-developmental approach may err in the opposite direction by over-emphasizing judgemental factors at the expense of behavioural ones, that approach seems at present to offer the most illuminating picture of how individuals develop in the areas of morality and religion.

REFERENCES

1. Wilson, J. (1973) *The Assessment of Morality*, Slough: NFER. See also (1971) *Education in Religion and the Emotions*, London: Heinemann.
2. Hirst, P. H. (1974) *Moral Education in a Secular Society*, London: University of London Press.
3. Straughan, R. (1982) *Can we Teach Children to be Good?*, London: Allen & Unwin.
4. Piaget, J. (1932) *The Moral Judgement of the Child*, London: Routledge & Kegan Paul.
5. Kohlberg, L. (1981 and 1984) *Essays on Moral Development*, Volumes One and Two, San Francisco: Harper & Row.
6. Goldman, R. (1964) *Religious Thinking from Childhood to Adolescence*, London: Routledge & Kegan Paul.
7. Fowler, J. (1976) 'Stages in faith: the structural developmental approach', in T. Hennessey (Ed.) *Values and Moral Development*, New York: Paulist Press.
8. Oser, F. (1980) 'Stages of religious judgment', in J. Fowler and A. Vergote (Eds.) *Toward Moral and Religious Maturity*, Morristown, New Jersey: Silver-Burdett.
9. Eysenck, H. J. (1964) *Crime and Personality*, London: Routledge & Kegan Paul; Bandura, A. and Walters, R. H. (1963) *Social Learning and Personality Development*, New York: Holt, Rinehart & Winston; Skinner, B. F.(1962) *Walden II*, New York: Macmillan.

PERSONALITY AND COGNITIVE STYLE

DAVID FONTANA

With a vast subject like personality, there are a number of different approaches. In the space of one short chapter we can do no more than select and discuss one or two of these. But central to them all is the idea that the term personality covers the *affective* side of the individual's psychological life as opposed to the *cognitive*. Affective refers to emotions and feelings, the process by which we actually experience ourselves, while cognitive refers to mental abilities, the process by which we categorize and make sense of the world. The affective side of life includes in addition to emotions and feelings such things as attitudes, opinions, and moods, while the cognitive side includes intelligence, creativity, and problem solving in general.

Obviously the two sides are closely linked at a number of points. For example our emotions influence the way in which we use our intelligence, and our intelligence influences the way in which we deal with our emotions. And as we shall see shortly, what psychologists call *cognitive style* is a habitual mode of responding which contains both cognitive and affective elements. But the scores individuals obtain on tests of personality show little correlation with the scores they obtain on cognitive tests (for example the fact that individuals score high on a particular personality trait tells us little or nothing about their level of intelligence), which allows psychologists to suggest that the affective and cognitive sides of our being are relatively distinct from each other.

HEREDITY AND ENVIRONMENT

From an educational point of view, the most important issue in personality is the extent to which, as a component of psychological life, it influences and is in turn influenced by learning. We know that cognitive abilities and human learning are intimately linked, but is the same true of personality? And if so, what is the nature of the link? Does a student's personality affect the way in which he or she approaches learning tasks, and do the tasks influence his or her personality? Behind the question lies another more fundamental one, namely, is the personality inherited or acquired? If inherited, its development lies outside the influence of education. If acquired, the development potentially lies very much within it.

Research into the relative effect of nature/nurture upon personality suggests strongly that we inherit what psychologists call *temperament*, the raw material of our personality. Investigations by Thomas, Chess, and Birch (1970) and more recently by Thomas and Chess (1977) indicate that differences in temperament are apparent in small babies from their early weeks of life (long before nurture has had much chance to influence things), that these differences are sufficiently marked to allow babies to be placed into distinct categories, and that membership of these categories remains markedly constant through childhood and into adolescence. Further, these temperamental differences play a significant part in the way children react to parental styles and to life experiences generally. Thus children placed for instance in the so-called *easy* category (characterized by regularity, adaptability, tolerance, and a cheerful positive approach) appear less reliant for satisfactory personality development upon specific aspects of parental behaviour or early school experiences, while children placed in the so-called *difficult* category (characterized by irregularity, low adaptability and tolerance levels, and a general crankiness and negativity of mood) are crucially dependent upon consistent, encouraging, and above all, patient handling.

Another approach to the nature/nurture issue is that of Eysenck. By examining the evidence for twin studies, which reveals that identical twins are more alike on personality test scores than fraternal twins, Eysenck suggests that some 70 per cent of the measurable personality differences between people may be due to inherited factors, and only 30 per cent to environment. He even suggests precise psychological mechanisms to account for this. The degree of anxiety with which we habitually approach life for example may be determined by the speed of arousal of the autonomic nervous system. Some people are born with a system that easily arouses the sweating, palpitations, and so on associated with fear, while others have a system which is much less readily prompted into action. Thus an external event which produces a fear response in one person may elicit no reaction from another. In the face of frequent experiences of fear the first individual will be much more likely to develop an anxious personality than will the second.

From the educational perspective, this evidence for a strong inheritance factor in personality means that teachers should be concerned less with effecting radical changes in child personality than with ensuring that educational experiences are designed to accommodate individual differences. A child with a 'difficult' or with a 'nervous' temperament may require more in the way of patience and support from a teacher than may a child with an 'easy' or with a 'stable' temperament. This applies particularly to the matter of teacher-child relationships, but it also applies to the way in which learning materials are presented. One child may do badly with any material that prompts anxiety (such as tests and examinations, public performances, competitive exercises), while another may find it no more than an interesting challenge. Further, teachers whose temperaments differ markedly from those of the children they teach often find it hard to understand what children are actually experiencing. This is perhaps particularly true of the highly stable teacher who cannot appreciate just how anxiety-provoking his or her general approach may be to certain members of the class, or who has no patience with what he or she sees as their over-emotional reactions.

OTHER PERSONALITY TRAITS AND THEIR INFLUENCE ON EDUCATION

A quality like anxiety (or neuroticism as it is more technically called) is described as a personality *trait*, that is as a relatively enduring characteristic. There are numerous other personality traits recognized by psychologists, but many of them are simply expressions of comprehensive underlying factors or source traits. Thus low self-confidence, fear of authority, and a range of other timid responses may for example all stem from the source trait of anxiety.

The psychologists most associated with investigations into personality traits are H. J. Eysenck in the UK and R. B. Cattell in the United States. In addition to a trait of anxiety, Eysenck's most recent personality test (the EPQ, 1975) measures extroversion and psychoticism. Scores on these traits are arranged along bi-polar dimensions. Thus we have three dimensions of, respectively, neuroticism-stability, extroversion-introversion, and high psychoticism-low psychoticism. Cattell's tests, on the other hand (most recently Cattell and Kline 1977), measure up to 16 traits or factors such as sociable-reserved, stability-instability, exuberance-sobriety, and sensitivity-toughness, though Cattell accepts that some of these dimensions intercorrelate and may be related to underlying source traits similar to those of Eysenck.

A number of studies have attempted to show a relationship between Eysenck's or Cattell's tests and educational attainment, but results have been disappointing and variable. There is, for example, some link between extroversion and success at primary school level, and some link between neuroticism and certain kinds of success and failure in higher education, but the correlations are small and somewhat localized. This doesn't mean, however, that the dimensions isolated by Eysenck and by Cattell have little relevance for education. It means simply that the relationship between them and academic success and failure is highly complex and difficult to measure by current research methodology. The teacher's own personality, for example, enters crucially into the equation. Thus extroverted children may perhaps do significantly better than introverted children in the primary school, provided their teacher is also extroverted. And neurotic children may get by quite happily provided their teacher is sensitive to their problems.

Teaching materials and teaching methods will also come into it. Arts subjects could be more suitable for introverts and science subjects for extroverts maybe, though a lot will depend upon the particular approach of the teachers or lecturers concerned, and the kind of study habits they demand from their students. A further variable is student age. In most people there is a tendency to become more introverted as they grow through childhood, which may mean that children who show up as successful extroverts in the primary school may have developed into successful introverts by the time they are in secondary school or higher education (Anthony 1973). Yet another variable is ability levels, since less able children may make increased demands upon teacher time and patience.

Something of the complexity of classroom interactions at the various levels associated with learning has been shown over the years by the work of Bennett and his colleagues (most recently 1984), and we are bound to conclude that a more refined methodology is needed before we can identify the part played by dimensions such as those of Eysenck and Cattell in academic success.

TEACHER PERSONALITY

The same difficulties attend any investigation into teacher personality. Though on the common sense level there is no doubt that good teachers have certain identifiable features of personality in common, attempts to identify these by the use of standardized tests of personality have proved relatively unsuccessful. On the face of it, one might suppose that the good teacher is outgoing (and therefore extroverted) and well-balanced (and therefore stable), but the evidence doesn't strongly support this (see Fontana 1986). Once again, other variables (in this case the subject being taught, job satisfaction, the behaviour of the children, length of classroom experience) all conspire to confuse the issue. An extroverted teacher may be more successful than an introverted teacher in one teaching context but not in others. Even high neuroticism scores do not preclude a teacher from making an outstanding success of the profession, just as low neuroticism scores do not guarantee it.

Research into teacher personality looks more promising, however, when instead of using standardized tests we ask *students* to carry out assessments on their teachers. So far work of this kind has been conducted primarily in higher education, but results suggest that two composite dimensions labelled respectively *achievement orientation* (made up of traits such as dominance, ambition, leadership, intelligence, and endurance) and *interpersonal orientation* (comprising such things as supportiveness, non-authoritarianism, non-defensiveness, and objectivity) account together for the main personality characteristics associated by students with successful teaching (Rushton and Murray 1985). It would be harder to carry out research of this kind at school level, but even young children hold remarkably definite and articulate views on their teachers, and my prediction would be that if warmth and friendliness (identified back in 1960 by Ryans as of particular importance at primary level, and linked to the interpersonal orientation dimension mentioned above) were added the picture would be remarkably consistent across most teaching situations.

Another area in which research into teacher personality looks promising is teacher stress. Teaching is a stressful profession, and it is clearly relevant to know what personality characteristics render a teacher best suited to cope with this stress. Perhaps against expectations, the stress-prone teacher does not necessarily appear to be the nervous person or the person low in self-confidence. Instead he or she seems to be the individual who is over-dedicated to work and takes things too seriously. These qualities are frequently associated with a hard-driving, determined state of mind, impatient of opposition and frustrated by failures (in other words the Type A personality identified by medical research as associated with susceptibility to coronary heart disease). Though we have at present no way of confirming it, many of these characteristics would appear to be learnt responses to challenge, rather than the inborn temperamental dispositions referred to earlier in this chapter. As such they should, in theory, be susceptible to re-education through stress management courses and workshops.

THE STATE-BASED APPROACH

Due to the generally ambivalent findings of research into links between personality traits and educational performance, some psychologists suggest it would be more profitable to adopt a state-based approach. That is, to abandon our concern with relatively fixed characteristics and concentrate instead upon fluctuating aspects of personality (personality *states*), many of which appear to be due to learning rather than inheritance and thus to be more susceptible to modification in the face of educational influence (and therefore of particular practical relevance to teachers).

One state-based approach is that of Bloom (1983). Without putting forward a specific theory of personality, Bloom suggests that we should look at each task in turn, and ask ourselves what affective state individuals should ideally be in if they are to maximize their chances of tackling it successfully. Such an affective state (*affective entry behaviour*) should then be encouraged by the teacher.

Some learning tasks (for example examination preparation, factual learning, accurate reporting) demand purposive, goal-directed entry behaviours, with the goal seen as all important, while others (for example creative pursuits, sport, classroom debates) demand less structured ones, with the activity itself seen as what really matters. Children need help in identifying which set of behaviours is appropriate for each task, and in consciously producing these behaviours. Apter (1982) suggests that the individual who is rigidly locked into one affective state (taking everything seriously or taking nothing seriously), and unable to switch voluntarily to another, has personality problems. And as with children so with teachers. The rigidly serious-minded, purposeful teacher is unlikely to succeed in educational tasks which demand inspiration and sponta-neity, while a consistently non-serious teacher is unlikely to do well in tasks of a purposive nature.

Another state-based approach to personality is that of Kelly. Relatively unconcerned with theory building, Kelly's main aim was to develop ways of exploring an individual's current affective states, that is, the way he feels about (and for that matter thinks about) the world. Kelly's device for doing this (see for example Bannister and Fransella 1980), called the *repertory grid*, allows the researcher to make a detailed examination of an individual's life space at a given moment in time. Thus for example we can use a grid to explore how children presently feel about any or all of their school subjects, or about their teachers, or about their friends, or about their life goals. Once we understand their current state, we can devise ways of helping them change negative aspects of it, and can use further grids over a period of time to monitor if and how this change is taking place.

Recent work by Thomas and Harri-Augstein (1985) shows how grid-based computer programmes can be used to help children to explore their own states, and to assess the consequences of any self-mediated change in these states. Similar programmes can be used to help children to hold 'conversations', through the computer, with significant others in their lives, both persons exploring together their feelings about each other and the possibilities for effecting positive improvements in these feelings. As the approach pioneered by Thomas and Harri-Augstein can be used in other areas of learning besides personality, it represents a particularly valuable development.

SELF-ESTEEM

One of the most productive uses to which the repertory grid can be put is in the exploration of the individual's levels of *self-esteem*. The importance of self-esteem in personality development and in academic success is fully explored elsewhere (Fontana 1986), and space allows only the main points to be summa-rized here. Individuals high on self-esteem (which has nothing, incidentally, to do with that crude, defensive posture known as conceit) are more realistic in their appraisal of self and others, less wounded by and more able to profit from criticism, less anxious for approval, more ready to participate, more inclined to aim high, more consistently successful, and less daunted by failure than individuals whose self-esteem is low.

Due to its apparent persistence within the individual's life, self-esteem could be regarded as a personality trait rather than a state, but the evidence suggests (see the last two references) that self-esteem is primarily a learnt response, and that with appropriate re-education it can be positively modified in a way rarely possible with traits such as those of Eysenck and of Cattell. Such modification can be brought about through the use of grids, in the manner just described, but much would also seem to depend at school level upon the relationship between teacher and child. Extrapolating from research in parent-child relationships, it would seem that the teacher most likely to enhance self-esteem is the one who is fair, consistent, friendly, democratic, and interested in the children. Crucially, he or she is also the teacher who relies on encouragement rather than censure, on praise rather than on blame, and on protecting children from the damaging effects of either unexpected or repeated failure. The teacher, in short, who offers every child success at his or her own level, and also has the gift of making every child feel a valued, significant, and respected member of the class.

The importance of the teacher in helping a child generate self-esteem stems from the fact that our picture of ourselves develops primarily from the way in which others behave towards us. Rogers (1961), who has done much to focus attention upon the role of self-esteem in the genesis of the healthy personality, insists that this behaviour should reflect positive and unconditional regard. Such regard does not imply the absence of clear standards and expectations. Quite the contrary. Consistently applied, these standards and expectations help children towards a realistic appraisal of the world and of their own place within it. What it does imply is that the adult prizes and values the child as a unique human being, with his or her own unique potential and with his or her own right to realize that potential.

At a practical level, positive regard for a child means that the adult gives assurance by word and deed that he or she is acceptable as a person. The adult's concern for the child is not something provisional, to be withdrawn abruptly each time the child proves to be 'unworthy'. This means for example that the adult avoids labelling the child in a negative and rejecting way. Attention is drawn to behaviour rather than to the child: 'That was a silly thing to do' rather than 'You are a silly boy'; 'That isn't true' rather than 'You are an untruthful girl'. Additionally, the adult accepts the child's emotions, rather than turning them into a source of shame and guilt. Certainly children can't be allowed to vent negative emotions on others, but they need the assurance that these emotions are part of being human, and have to be recognized and understood if they are to be sensibly handled and integrated into a mature and responsible personality.

But self-esteem is not just about individuals' attitudes to themselves. For with self-esteem comes the ability to esteem others. Low self-esteem leads either to the unrealistic feeling that others are always superior to oneself, or to the constant need to denigrate others as a way towards boosting one's own depressed sense of worth. The more closely one studies the role of self-esteem in the development of the healthy personality, the more one understands the observation from clinical psychology that the prime cause of psychological problems is the inability to value and accept oneself.

COGNITIVE STYLE

I mentioned earlier that affective factors and cognitive factors are linked to each other in a number of ways. We can see this for example in self-esteem. Children who feel good emotionally about themselves also have good positive thoughts about themselves and vice versa. They accept themselves as people, can take a clear and objective view of their own emotions and of their relationships with others, and have a good degree of self-insight and self-understanding. At each of these points, affective and cognitive factors interact critically together.

But we can also see the links between the two aspects of psychological life in *cognitive style*. Cognitive style relates to the way in which we usually approach experiences, whether they be affective or cognitive, social or academic, internal or external. So important does cognitive style appear to be that there have been suggestions that it may be the most useful way of looking at human abilities. This is not something we can pursue, since the concern in this chapter is with affective rather than ability factors, but a word of caution is perhaps appropriate. More perhaps than any other similar area in psychology, cognitive style research is badly in need of new initiatives. In spite of the promise such research appeared to offer in the 1960s and early 1970s, the amount of hard data available to us is as yet rather limited, and whereas some parts are conflicting, others are merely repetitive.

One way of understanding what is meant by cognitive style is to look at intelligence. Since intelligence appears to involve a convergent pattern of thinking, there is a sense in which it is an example of cognitive style. Similarly we could say that creativity, which appears to involve divergent thinking, is another. We could go further and say that whether we tend to approach experiences convergently or divergently will influence not only our cognitive life but also our affective life, and that in consequence both convergent and divergent thinking are linked to personality as well as to mental processes.

The best known approaches to cognitive style, and the only ones for which we have space, are those of Bruner (Bruner, Goodnow, and Austin 1956), Witkin (1966) and Kagan (1966). To take these in turn, Bruner had identified a style dimension which he calls *focusing-scanning*. When approaching problems, focusers characteristically delay hypothesis making until they have enough evidence, while scanners characteristically form a hypothesis on slimmer evidence and have no option but to begin afresh if subsequently they are shown to be wrong. The relevance of this at school level is considerable. For example, scanners may be at a marked disadvantage in oral work, since they cannot go back and check earlier clues in the event of errors. On the other hand focusers may be at a disadvantage in situations where they have to make a decision on incomplete evidence, since they may find themselves unable in such circumstances to reach conclusions. And as with incompatibilities between teacher and pupils in other areas of personality, it may be that a teacher who focuses may have little understanding of children who scan, while a teacher who scans may fail to understand focusers.

Witkin's approach is of similar potential importance to the classroom. Identifying a dimension called *field dependence-field independence* (sometimes called *global-articulated*), Witkin has drawn attention to the fact that some individuals seem less, and others more, able to separate a given variable from its context. Field-dependent individuals are more at the mercy of their surroundings than field-independent people, and are less autonomous and less perceptive. They are less likely to remember detail than field-independent people, and less able to separate feelings from thoughts. Also they do less well generally on analytical academic tasks, though equally well on verbal. On the other hand, they may be more sensitive to other people and to experiences, and less likely to withdraw socially.

Kagan's dimension, *reflectivity-impulsivity*, takes yet another aspect of cognitive style. Characteristically, the reflective person has a *slow conceptual tempo* and thus tackles learning tasks by categorizing the information and generating solutions in a methodical, thoughtful way. He or she has a strong desire to get things right, even if this means lengthy deliberation and suffering the impatience of others. By contrast, the impulsive person adopts a *fast conceptual tempo*, firing out several answers either in the hope that one of them may be right or that feedback from the teacher will provide the necessary clues. As with both Bruner's and Witkin's dimensions, an understanding by the teacher of the tendency in a child towards reflectivity or impulsivity is a valuable contribution to effective education. The impulsive child is likely to be impulsive in all behaviour, not just in the approach to problem solving, while the reflective child is likely to be reflective. A teacher who constantly seeks to repress the one or to hurry the other is unlikely to get satisfactory learning responses or to help children understand and accept themselves.

With all three dimensions of cognitive style (as with the personality traits of

989

Eysenck and Cattell), some individuals will not be located at either of the extreme ends. Nevertheless many children will show a marked tendency in one or other direction, and the research initiatives which I earlier identified as necessary could well seek to determine the extent to which a child's position on a dimension can be modified by appropriate teaching. Obviously it would be better if an individual could reverse along a cognitive style dimension in response to the particular needs of the situation. There could be temperamental factors which limit the freedom to do so, but if there are we need to know the nature of these limits. Perhaps above all we need to know more about the ways in which dimensions of cognitive style relate to each other, thus helping us produce a more integrated picture of how affective and cognitive factors influence each other.

CONCLUSION

School learning involves two distinct though interrelated areas, which I have elsewhere called *knowing* and *being* (Fontana 1987). Knowing refers to those facts and skills which children require if they are to build up an effective body of knowledge about the world, while being refers to how children actually experience their lives. To help children learn in both areas requires a sound understanding of child personality, and of the way in which it interacts with what schools have to offer. Through an examination of personality traits and states, of cognitive style, of the vital area of self-esteem, and of the related area of teacher personality, this chapter has attempted to isolate issues essential to this understanding. Definitions of the 'good' teacher abound, but central to most of them is that the teacher must be sensitive to the real nature of childhood, and to the complex and subtle ways in which early experiences help determine the pattern and quality of later life. By virtue of such awareness, the study of personality must rank high on any teacher's list of priorities.

REFERENCES

Anthony, W. S. (1973) 'The development of extraversion, of ability, and of the relation between them', *British Journal of Educational Psychology*, 43 (3):223–7.

Apter, M. J. (1982) *The Experience of Motivation*, London: Academic Press.

Bannister, D. and Fransella, F. (1982) *Enquiring Man*, Harmondsworth: Penguin Books.

Bennett, N., Desforges, C., Cockburn, A., and Wilkinson, B. (1984) *The Quality of Pupil Learning Experiences*, London: Lawrence Erlbaum.

Bloom, B. S. (1983) *Human Characteristics and School Learning*, New York: McGraw Hill.

Bruner, J., Goodnow, J., and Austin, G. (1956) *A Study of Thinking*, New York: Wiley.

Cattell, R. B. and Kline, P. (1977) *The Scientific Analysis of Personality and Motivation*, New York: Springer.

Eysenck, H. J. (1975) *The Eysenck Personality Questionnaire*, Slough, Bucks: NFER.

Fontana, D. (1986) *Teaching and Personality*, Oxford: Blackwell.

(1987) 'Knowing about being', *Changes* 5 (2):342–7.

Kagan, J. (1966) 'Developmental studies in reflection and analysis', in A. Kidd and J. Rivoire (Eds.) *Perceptual Development in Children*, London: University of London Press.

Rogers, C. R. (1961) *On Becoming a Person*, Boston, Mass.: Houghton Mifflin.

Rushton, J. P. and Murray, A. G. (1985) 'On the assessment of teaching effectiveness in British universities', *Bulletin of the British Psychological Society*, November.

Thomas, A., and Chess, S. (1977) *Temperament and Development*, New York: Brunner/Mazel.

Thomas, A., Chess, S., and Birch, H. (1970) 'The origin of personality', *Scientific American*, August.

Thomas, L., and Harri-Augstein, S. (1985) *Self-Organized Learning*, London: Routledge & Kegan Paul.

Witkin, H. A. (1966) 'Psychological differentiation and forms of pathology, *Journal of Abstract Psychology*, 70:317–36.

8.8

BIOLOGICAL AND SOCIAL ASPECTS OF DEVELOPMENT

C. G. N. MASCIE-TAYLOR

A child does badly at school. There are a multitude of possible causes – for instance he or she comes from a broken home; he or she is from a large family living in overcrowded conditions; the parents aren't interested; he or she is a member of an ethnic minority. Some of these reasons are questionable, others more reasonable. Most workers in this field would argue that poor performance involves a whole complex of factors which broadly fall into biological and social categories.

GENETIC ASPECTS

It is well documented that children from working-class families are academically less successful than those from middle-class families. Is this because they are naturally less intelligent? Even to pose such a question will seem repugnant or insulting to many people – but it would be wrong to pretend that no one has taken such a possibility seriously. The British psychologist H. J. Eysenck wrote 'All the evidence to date suggests the strong and indeed overwhelming importance of genetic factors in producing the great variety of intellectual differences which we observe in our culture . . .'[1]

A common assumption is that an IQ score reflects a child's potential in the sense that it measures a fixed, innate ability. It is true that IQ scores are relatively stable; a child's IQ at the age of six or seven will predict quite well the IQ at 16 or 17. But large changes are quite common. It is also possible that inheritance plays some part in determining IQ. That is to say, it seems probable that some of the differences in IQ observed in the population of a country are caused by genetic differences between its members. How important genetic factors may be is contentious. Jensen, an American psychologist, and Eysenck claimed that no less than 80 per cent of the variation in IQ is genetically caused. How do they come up with such a figure, and can they be so quantitatively precise?

The proportion of the total variation in any characteristic that can be attributed to genetic differences between members of a population is termed the 'heritability' of the characteristic. Heritability can, in principle, be calculated for any characteristic than can be measured, whether it be height, weight, colour of hair or of skin, musical ability, or IQ. However, it is not easy to measure the heritability of a character in humans. Indeed the concept derives from animal and plant genetics where it is possible to organize specific matings and to experiment at will. With humans such experimentation is of course not possible and most heritability estimates derive from examining differences between twins.

Twins are of two basic types, either developing from one single fertilized egg which then divides to produce two foetuses, or from two separately fertilized eggs which develop separately. The two types are called identical (or monozygotic) and non-identical (fraternal or dizygotic) twins respectively. An identical twin pair have identical genes, and consequently any differences between them should be the result of environmental differences, whereas a non-identical twin pair will be different because they have different genetic make-ups as well as environments.

Geneticists compare identical and non-identical twins. For characters with a high heritability, i.e. where genes are important, identical twins should be very similar and non-identical twins less similar. This is what we tend to find for IQ. However there are a number of reasons why we should treat such a result with caution. Twins are rare. On average they occur once in about 80 births. They show on average a reduced gestational period, reduced birth weight, increased levels of birth disorders, and perform less well than average on IQ tests (usually by about five IQ points). Thus we are basing the results on a very atypical segment of society. Even if we accept the heritability estimate then two points should be stressed. First, heritability is a statistic applicable only to a particular population at a particular time. Second, high heritability does not mean that the characteristic in question is genetically fixed and therefore unamenable to environmental influence. The heritability of height, for example, is generally taken to be very high, of the order of 0.90, in most modern populations. But changes in the diet of a particular population can still produce large increases in average height; that of the Japanese, for example, has increased by over five cm. since 1945.

The most reasonable conclusion is that there are far too many problems inherent in all the data to justify a precise, quantitative statement of the heritability of IQ. The figure put forward by Jensen and Eysenck of 80 per cent has not been substantiated by estimates based on more recent and better data, which have given estimates of the order of 50 per cent; the safest claim is that probably somewhere between one quarter and three quarters of the variation seen in IQ in most communities within a Western society is due to genetic differences between members of these societies.[2]

OTHER BIOLOGICAL ASPECTS

A number of studies have dealt with the relationship between low birth weight and subsequent intellectual development. In general low birth weight is associated with lowered IQ score. However the results should be treated with some caution since low birth weight is an ambiguous variable: it includes both children born prematurely and children who are born at, or near, term but who are born small for gestational age.

Smoking during pregnancy has been shown to be associated with lowered birth weight and with increased risk or perinatal mortality. Children born to mothers who smoked during pregnancy are shorter by about one centimetre at age 11, three months behind other children in general intelligence, and four months behind in reading at this age. If this association is causal then the ill effects should be preventable.[3]

Sex differences also occur. It has frequently been suggested that girls are better on tasks involving verbal skills and boys on tasks involving visuo-spatial concepts. Sex differences in cognitive style have been said to be related to different patterns of lateralization of function. Reading difficulties have also been associated with unusual patterns of eye-hand dominance, and left-handers in general have been suggested to be of lower overall ability. The proportion of left-handed children has also been found to be higher in the educationally subnormal.

Numerous studies have shown a consistent association between a child's height and IQ, taller children scoring, on average, higher on IQ tests. The causes of this association remain unclear. However it is likely that genetic factors, damage during development in the womb, and poor nutrition after birth may all play a part.

SOCIAL CORRELATES

Little enough is known about the environmental factors that affect IQ in any population – let alone those that might be responsible for differences between classes or ethnic groups within that population. It is known, for example, that differences in IQ are correlated with differences in social class or socio-economic status, but many psychologists have argued that these may partly reflect genetic rather than environmental differences between the classes.

Demographic variables such as family size, and other related factors such as birth order, also correlate with IQ.[4] Although the majority of studies have found that first-born, on average, have higher IQs than later born offspring, this is not always the case. Some of the inconsistency in results stems from the fact that birth order is associated with family size and both intercorrelate with social class.

A large number of studies have shown that children from larger families tend to have reading and mathematics attainments which are inferior to those of children from smaller families. For instance, one survey showed that an only child was on average 26 months ahead in reading age and 12 months ahead in mathematics age when compared to a child with three or more brothers and sisters. The fact that the association between family size and attainment is strongest with verbal skills has led some workers to suggest that at least part of the explanation lies in the child's linguistic environment at home during the pre-school years.

Although one cannot give direct evidence of a causal relationship between family size and performance on IQ and other attainment tests there are two plausible explanations: the poorer performance of children in large families is due to the necessity of the family's resources being shared more thinly. Alternatively, family size is related to parental attitudes and it is the latter which are affecting progress. On balance, the evidence tends to support the 'shared resources' explanation.

Furthermore there is evidence that children who are socially disadvantaged – coming from overcrowded homes where there is financial hardship – tend to do less well on IQ and attainment tests. All these variables correlate with test scores, but they are also highly intercorrelated. Given their high interrelatedness, it is difficult to be precise on the importance of any specific variable.

Recent research based on a large random sample of British children examined the relationship between IQ score and 29 variables, including maternal history of smoking, mean parental age and age difference, social class, tenure, whether the child was receiving free school meals, crowding status, shared amenities including bedroom and bed, financial status, and the number of school and family moves in the past four years.[5] Each variable when considered in isolation showed a significant association with IQ test scores, but the magnitude of an association dropped considerably when the interrelatedness with other variables was taken into account. Thus although the majority of these effects are almost certainly environmental in origin, it is uncertain just how they are produced and what is their relative importance.

Finally the influence of nutrition on intelligence has been the subject of increasing attention in recent years. Much of this research has centred on the possibility that malnutrition during the prenatal or early postnatal period may lead to structural damage to the brain and as a result lead to inadequate intellectual development. However the evidence for the influence of nutrition on intelligence test scores is indirect and confused. Much of the evidence derives from animal studies with questionable relevance to humans, or from third world countries whose people are living under extreme nutritional deprivation. In summary, there is little evidence at present that suggests that nutritional factors account for any appreciable amount of the variation in intelligence test scores in a representative sample from a developed country.

DIFFERENCES BETWEEN ETHNIC GROUPS; SOCIAL OR BIOLOGICAL CAUSES?

Children from ethnic minorities do not always do as well at school in Britain as do indigenous children though some do as well or better. Might this be because they are naturally less intelligent?[6] More specifically, for example, is there any evidence that the average IQ of West Indian children in Britain is lower than that of Whites?

In the USA there has been substantial evidence available for 50 years or more that Blacks on average obtain significantly lower scores than Whites on standard IQ tests.[7] The difference is usually said to average about 15 points, although it varies considerably from study to study. But this tells us little or nothing about the standing of West Indian children in Britain; there have been, not surprisingly, far fewer studies comparing the IQ scores of West Indians and Whites in the UK, and they go back for no more than ten to fifteen years.

There can be little doubt that on average West Indian children in Britain obtain significantly lower scores on a variety of IQ tests than do White children. The overall difference is not as large as the 15–point difference said to hold between American Blacks and Whites, and it is considerably smaller than this when the West Indian child has been resident in Britain for any length of time. This is not entirely surprising, for there is evidence that Blacks from the West Indies are more successful than other Blacks in the USA. It is important not to generalize too readily from the American case. Nevertheless there is still a difference of about five to twelve points on a variety of tests between West Indian and other children, even among children born in Britain.

Much of this difference in IQ scores between West Indian and indigenous children appears to be related to differences between them in their social environments – factors such as parental occupation, income, size of family, degree of overcrowding, and neighbourhood. All of these factors are related to IQ among Whites, and when they are taken into account, the difference between West Indian and indigenous children is sharply reduced, to somewhere between one and seven points.

These findings tend to argue against those who would seek to provide a predominantly genetic explanation of ethnic differences in IQ, but they equally imply that such differences are not due to a special set of factors unique to the West Indian experience. Although discrimination against West Indian families in Britain may have an important indirect effect on their children's IQ scores by ensuring that they live in impoverished circumstances, there is less reason to believe that such discrimination, whether by society as a whole or by teachers and IQ testers in particular, has any direct effect on the West Indian child's performance.

The evidence is not compelling, but on balance it does seem to point one way rather than others; ethnic differences in IQ scores are probably largely caused by the same factors as are responsible for differences in IQ within the White population as a whole. If, therefore, we wish to raise the IQ scores of children from one particular segment or ethnic minority in our society we might make a start by improving the social and economic circumstances of their families.

Finally it seems worth stressing that the possibility that such a programme might have beneficial effects on IQ scores is surely not the best reason for wishing to improve the conditions in which a substantial minority of the community is forced to live. There are many things in life substantially more important than IQ. Even in a narrow educational context, no one should be particularly interested in IQ scores. Educationalists should be concerned rather with how well children do at school, how adequately they master certain basic skills, and, if need be, with their examination results – since these results will affect their future chances in life in a multitude of ways. They should ask, for example, why, on average, West Indian children do not read as well as White children, and rather than wondering whether this is due to a difference in IQ, they would be better advised to tackle the problem directly – by relying on those factors, such as parental involvement, actually shown to be capable of affecting a child's ability to read.

REFERENCES

1. Eysenck, H. J. (1971) *Race, Intelligence and Education*, London: Temple Smith.
2. Scarr, S. and Carter-Saltzman, L. (1982) 'Genetics of IQ', in R. J. Sternberg (Ed.) *Handbook of Human Intelligence*, New York: Cambridge University Press.
3. Vernon, P. E. (1969) *Intelligence and Cultural Environment*, London: Methuen.
4. Rutter, M. and Madge, N. (1976) *Cycles of Disadvantage*, London: Heinemann.
5. Mascie-Taylor, C. G. N. (1985) 'Biosocial correlates of IQ', in C. J. Turner and R. Chester (Eds.) *The Biology of Intelligence*, Driffield: Nafferton Books.
6. Loehlin, J. C., Lindzey, G., and Spuhler, J. N. (1975) *Race Differences in Intelligence*, San Francisco: Freeman.
7. Shuey, A. M. (1966) *The Testing of Negro Intelligence*, New York: Social Sciences Press.

8.9

EDUCATION AND GENDER DIFFERENCES

MARGARET SUTHERLAND

Should education be different for boys and girls? In some societies, being male or female decides largely what kind of life the individual leads: so education is expected to prepare girls to be womanly and boys to be manly. It must prepare them to do the kind of work thought suitable for their sex, and develop in them differing behaviours and emotions. Other societies do not make such an effort to differentiate: they accept that females and males can do the same kind of work, have much the same attitudes, and behave in similar ways. All the same, it is rare to find a society which makes no distinction at all between males and females so far as work and behaviour are concerned. Equal opportunities legislation in many countries has aimed at reducing differences in employment and other aspects of life, but considerable differences remain in most societies, especially in people's beliefs about 'natural' differences between females and males. For some individuals, one of the most frustrating experiences in life is to encounter the determination of society or other individuals to make people conform to male or female roles. In a society which has strong beliefs about sex differences, those who deliberately do not conform, or find it impossibly difficult to conform, may be left with feelings of uncertainty about their own identity or worth.

But is different education for girls and boys in fact necessary because differences are inborn? There are obvious physical differences between females and males: there is difference of function since women bear children and can suckle them. There are other differences in physiology: different hormones, in different concentrations, circulate in the blood; women have the recurrent changes of menstruation. In addition there are physical differences in strength, skeleton structure, and stamina. So are there also inborn differences in personality and ability? But before considering such possible differences, we have to realize that even some of the physical differences are not absolute. There is overlap between the two groups, for example, some women are taller or have greater strength than some men; in some situations they have greater stamina.

There are differences within groups too: women differ from other women in such respects, and men differ from other men. So it would be unwise to assume that simply by knowing if people are male or female we know how physically strong or resistant they are, and must provide different education accordingly. Is it the same for other abilities and characteristics?

ARE THERE IMPORTANT INNATE SEX DIFFERENCES IN ABILITIES, ATTITUDES, EMOTIONS?

At various times people have believed the following differences are based on inborn characteristics:

1. women are less intelligent than men; women are also less capable (because of general physical frailty and, especially, menstruation) of study at high intellectual levels;
2. men are good at mathematics and physical sciences, women at languages and verbal performance;
3. men are more aggressive and more self-confident than women;
4. men are less interested in people and less loving and attentive towards babies and young children.

In deciding which differences may be innate we have the complication that from the earliest moments of their existence individuals are influenced by people around them. Babies respond to the way people treat them. Parents may expect different characteristics in males and females and, as some researchers have found, speak differently to their sons and daughters and handle them or play with them differently: parents often give different toys to boys and girls. So some children will find that adult – and also peer-group – approval depends on behaving in what is considered the 'right' way for their sex, even if they would not 'naturally' behave like this or choose certain toys and activities. Thus it is almost impossible to know, even when children are very young, exactly which characteristics are inborn and which have been produced by learning from experience.

But let us look at differences which have been claimed as innate.

1. Objective intelligence testing does not support the belief that females are less intelligent. Admittedly, much depends on the construction of the tests: some questions may be better answered by boys or by girls – and such questions would often be discarded from the final version of a test for this reason. Different scales may have to be used for boys and girls; for example, about the age of eleven girls tend to do better on some verbal reasoning tests, so when such tests were used for secondary school selection, two different sets of norms were sometimes used. On the other hand, boys may do better on

some kinds of intelligence tests which include spatial ability. (The difficulty is that what tests define as intelligence is not always the same – and not what the ordinary person thinks of as intelligence. The chapters on Multiple Intelligences and on Intelligence and Intelligence Tests discuss these matters more fully.) Males more often score extremely high (or extremely low) on some intelligence tests. But the weight of the evidence is that there is no innate sex difference affecting the immense majority of people: one sex is not more intelligent than the other. As for the supposed inability of women or girls to cope with serious study, this has been disproved by experience; even the alleged handicap of menstruation has not prevented girls from achieving, on average, as well as boys, if not better, in secondary school work; women's success in higher education also disproves this assumption.

2.   What about other abilities? Maccoby and Jacklin carried out a comprehensive survey of results reported from researches on different abilities and attitudes. Their conclusions were that very few sex differences have been established. The areas where real differences may exist are those of spatial ability and verbal ability. It has been argued that these differences depend on different rates of development of the cerebral cortex in early childhood, its more rapid development in females being associated with greater verbal development, while slower development in males produces better spatial ability. But these early physical developments are difficult to measure and have not been conclusively shown to be related to either ability. It has alternatively been suggested that differences in some forms of spatial ability can be traced to the kind of play experiences enjoyed by boys, who are given toys – constructive building sets, for example – which encourage spatial perception. Some experimental work seems to indicate that encouraging girls to play with similar materials does lessen apparent sex differences. Yet it has also been pointed out that as differentiation in spatial ability – or in performances apparently requiring it – becomes more evident in adolescence, this might indicate a physiologically based effect, associated with other physical changes at this age, rather than learning by experience. Similarly, the fact that girls often show superior verbal ability to boys about age eleven, while boys later overtake them or at least equal them in verbal achievement, has been attributed to the earlier maturing of girls in adolescence, that is, to an objective, physical difference. But again the effects of education and social expectations are difficult to disentangle from physiological development.

These controversial differences have been associated with objectively observed differences in achievement in some school subjects. International research in many countries has indicated male superiority in maths and most branches of the physical sciences, and female superiority in language, reading, and comprehension. But there are other factors affecting these differences, for example, the kind of school teaching received, options in the curriculum, popular attitudes towards subjects, vocational prospects. Moreover, although there may be differences between boys' and girls' *average* achievement within a country, there is always considerable overlap; and if we compare the perform- ance of girls in one country with that of boys in another country, the girls' average score in science may be higher than that of the boys; similarly the average performance of boys in a language test in one country may be better than that of girls in that test in another country. If there are innate differences in ability here, they are not absolute; the level of achievement for either sex does not reach a 'ceiling' predetermined by sex – in another country, people of the same sex may do better, and again there are considerable differences within a sex group.

In thinking about such differences, we have to notice also that children learn a lot from other children. The peer-group has distinct views as to what constitutes appropriate behaviour; so boys and girls who choose studies or activities considered appropriate to the other sex in a given culture are likely to experience mockery or criticism. Similarly for social behaviour: the peer- group has definite norms of behaviour which are usually differentiated for girls and boys. The chauvinistic attitudes of kindergarten or junior school boys can be particularly forceful in some societies and some neighbourhoods.

3. Are there innate differences in self-confidence and aggression? In spite of their often superior performance in school work, girls in the United Kingdom, Australia, and North America have been found to be less confident than boys about their ability to succeed in future studies. This difference is evident in their general 'academic self-image' as well as in their estimates of their future performance in such subjects as arithmetic, maths, and physical sciences. The difference is the more remarkable because some writers have argued that boys have a difficult time in the early school years when they are taught mainly by women whose standards of neatness and care they may find rather too demand- ing (but why should there be a difference in standards?). On this basis, one would expect boys to be less self-confident about their ability: but they are not. Some researchers have therefore suggested that although boys are more often criticized by teachers than girls, these criticisms tend to focus on boys' behaviour rather than on their ability to do the work, while criticisms of girls may imply a weakness in ability. Hence boys can remain confident about their ability while girls lose confidence (despite better school marks). Such observations of differences in criticism are possibly more often from American than British sources: some British studies of classroom situations have sug- gested that teachers' comments do not differentiate on a sex basis, and obvi- ously it is very much a matter of the individual class and teacher. Reasons for

girls' generally lower self-confidence remain unclear, though there seems no good argument for assuming it innate.

We still also have the problem of knowing why boys' behaviour more often demands critical comment from teachers. And why do they remain confident – on average though not in all individual cases – in spite of more frequent reprimands for bad behaviour? It is here suggested that social conditioning encourages boys to express themselves more freely, with less consideration for others, as well as to engage in more exploratory behaviour, more risk-taking and more aggression than is expected of girls. If boys are encouraged in such behaviours out of school, adaptation to the more ordered life of the classroom may well be more difficult for them than for girls. Possibly too, girls' training, from early years, to behave in a more orderly way, may explain to some extent the frequent finding that girls' attitudes to school during adolescence tend to be more favourable than those of boys.

But are differences in aggression innate? Again, some writers have argued that different sex hormones may produce more aggressive behaviour in males. Here we have to be careful how aggression is defined. There is, for instance, the question whether we pay attention to verbal aggression or focus on physical aggression, and whether physical contacts, 'rough-and-tumble' play, are to be interpreted as aggression. Certainly, figures for violent crime throughout the world show that males are more aggressive – and though this might be related to physical strength, such violence does not always depend on strength. Some research evidence does show greater aggressiveness, in the physical sense, among young boys. But children learn at early ages which expressions of anger are socially permitted – including facial expressions – so it is again impossible to be sure how much is innate and how much is the result of learning through social training.

Aggression and self-confidence can be evident in more general attitudes to life. The relative lack of confidence girls show about their academic ability has been found in their views on other situations. Studies have been made of whether individuals see themselves as largely responsible for what happens to them or whether they attribute events to forces outside themselves – to luck or to other people's actions, for example. Some have found that females are more likely to think the 'locus of control' is outside them, that is, that they are at the mercy of external forces and not able to decide the outcomes of various situations by their own hard work or ability; males seem more likely to think they can control situations by their own efforts. There has not yet been enough testing of this view in different societies to decide whether such differences exist generally and reliably: in Japan, for instance, males may attribute success *both* to luck and hard work. It is tempting to associate such differences in confidence, if they are reliably established, with greater physical strength in males or with females' involuntary subjection to the recurrent changes of menstruation – or of childbearing. But it is also very easy to see how these different feelings could be produced by the amount of personal freedom a society gives to males and females to decide their own actions – whether, for example, women have to follow stricter standards of dress and behaviour in public than males, and are less free to go where they will.

A related difference has been found, in Britain and North America, in tests of anxiety. Girls and women tend to have higher anxiety levels than boys and men. It is of course possible that females feel less inhibited by social conventions about expressing anxiety. But it is remarkable that, given the higher levels of approval of their behaviour in primary school and their often superior performance, girls should be more anxious than boys. One explanation offered is that girls attach more importance to adult approval while boys rely on peer-group approval; the latter is said to be easier to achieve. But why should there be a difference in preferring adult or peer-group approval? Is it innate or do many societies keep girls more closely under adult supervision and so make them more accustomed to adult supervision? Certainly we need much more intercultural research in order to discover whether such differences are found widely, and if so, whether they do depend on social conditioning. Here we would have to take into account the possible effects of being given responsibility and freedom to make choices. Graduated exercise of these, as the individual grows older, may well contribute to developing greater confidence, even if some choices can have discouraging results.

4. It has commonly been believed that males are less interested than females in people, especially in babies and young children. Evidence about empathy, the ability to understand or enter into the feelings of others, is at times conflicting: some authorities claim no differences exist, others suggest a slight superiority for females. (It may depend on how empathy is measured.) But it has also been found that empathy for, and interest in, young children may be associated with having responsibility for looking after young children. Since most societies give this responsibility to females, empathy may thus be developed more strongly in girls than in boys. Observation of the changes in men's patterns of behaviour in many societies today certainly shows many men enjoying a lively and practical interest in babies and young children. This would suggest that differences here owe much, if not everything, to social training.

The discussion of allegedly innate sex differences keeps bringing us back to the obvious effects which can result from different treatment of males and females in society. There is little firm evidence for significant inborn differences in abilities and emotions. Repeatedly too, research work shows the very extensive overlap between the sexes when such characteristics are measured; it also reveals that differences among members of one sex group may be considerably greater than differences between the average of each sex group. Common experience shows us that while some babies behave 'like a real little boy' – or girl – a great many others do not: they may differ strongly in temperament from other members of the family who are of the same sex. Hence, education does not have to be governed by supposedly innate differences in abilities and emotions between males and females. (Education indeed may be thought of in any case as an attempt to *improve* what is given.) It has to consider the characteristics of individuals, not to assume these characteristics simply from gender.

But research on possible sex differences has also the advantage of making us aware of the effects of different treatment of boys and girls, in school or at home, and the effects on the individual's development and happiness which environment and education may have. Efforts are now being made (see Chapter 1.9 by Sandra Acker) to make educators (parents included) aware of the dangers of some sex-role differentiations which stereotype individuals and thwart individual development. Yet efforts to give an unbiased education may encounter difficulties since many adults (teachers and parents) have a self-concept in which being clearly male or female is important: they have comfortably adjusted to the expected way of life. They have been assured, sometimes on religious authority, that the characteristics and behaviours of males and females are, and should be, different. Naturally, they feel uneasy and threatened if such differentiation is challenged. For other people, different characteristics – their professional skills, their leisure or sporting activities, their work group – have been more salient in deciding their self-concept, and they are happy to accept that education should concentrate on characteristics other than being female or male. Strategies of change must take these facts into account – and avoid imposing new stereotypes in place of the old.

ADDITIONAL READING

Department of Education and Science (1985) *Statistics of Education, CSE and GCE*, London: HMSO.
Kelly, A. (1978) *Girls and Science*, Stockholm: Almqvist and Wiksell International.
Linn, M. C. and Petersen, A. C. (1985) 'Emergence and character of sex differences in spatial ability: a meta-analysis', *Child Development*, 56 (6): 1479–98.
Maccoby, E. E. and Jacklin, C. N. (1975) *The Psychology of Sex Differences*, Stanford, L. A.: Stanford University Press.
(1980) 'Sex differences in aggression: a rejoinder and reprise', *Child Development*, 51 (4): 964–80.
Sutherland, M. B. (1981) *Sex Bias in Education*, Oxford: Blackwell.
'Anxiety, aspirations and the curriculum' in M. Marland (Ed.) (1983) *Sex Differentiation and Schooling*, London: Heinemann.

8.10

ADOLESCENT NEEDS AND PRIORITIES IN MODERN SOCIETY

LEO B. HENDRY

INTRODUCTION: SOCIAL CHANGES

It has become a cliché to talk about the speed and rapidity of social and technological change in modern times but these changes have implications for us all, particularly for young people growing up in ever shifting social settings.

There are now greater public concerns about personal and community health, for example, the current AIDS epidemic and ecological pollution. There are also increases in stress-related illnesses and increases in drinking and drug taking. Yet running alongside these stress-related patterns are trends towards greater longevity and more active healthy lifestyles of senior citizens. There are ever higher divorce rates and changes in family living patterns, including many more single-parent units. There has been a clear emergence of feminism, and some moves towards sex role equalities, with a higher percentage of women in the labour market (though not absolute equality in the domestic sphere). Migration and settlement of large numbers of British West Indians and Asians and the presence of a sizeable migrant work force from the European community have focused attention on the extent of cultural diversity.

SOCIAL CHANGE AND ADOLESCENT DEVELOPMENT

In this context of change what are the central issues in the adolescent's life? From the physical and physiological changes which herald the teenage years, the adolescent has various personal and social tasks to achieve in modern society.

Some of these psycho-social tasks in the transition towards adulthood are:

1. developing a self identity in the light of biological and bodily changes;

2. developing a gender identity;
3. gaining a degree of independence from parents;
4. accepting or rejecting family values;
5. shaping up to an occupational (or unemployed) role;
6. developing and extending friendships, particularly with the opposite sex.

These six developments are encapsulated in the notion that the chief task of adolescence is identity formation. Erikson (1968) believed that the search for identity becomes especially acute during adolescence as a result of rapid changes in the biological, social, and psychological aspects of the individual, and because of the necessity for occupational decisions to be made, ideals to be accepted or rejected, and sexual and friendship choices to be determined.

Further, he considered that society creates a 'psychosocial moratorium' in adolescence which provides the individual with the opportunity to experiment freely. When this is combined with a vulnerability of personality it can create possible crises in the individual's development. For a relatively small number – and then usually at only one period during their teenage years – adolescence can be a time of disturbance, disruption, or inner stress. Is it possible, then, to equate the apparently easy adaptation of the majority of teenagers with the periods of stress and disruption characteristically attributed to adolescence?

A 'focal' theory of adolescence relating to self-image, parental relationships, peer relationships, friendships, and larger group situations has been outlined by Coleman (1979). Basing his theory on his empirical data he showed that these relationships changed as a function of age, and that concern about different issues reached a peak at different stages in the adolescent process. In general, anxiety over heterosexual relationships declines from a peak around 13 years, fears of rejection from peers is highly important around 15 years, while conflict with parents climbs steadily in importance from 13 to 15 years, and then tails off.

Clearly the patterns overlap, different issues come into focus at different times, but simply because an issue is not important at a particular age this does not mean that it may not be critical for some teenagers. Such a theory may provide an explanation of the amount of disruption implicit in adolescence on the one hand, and the relatively successful adaptation of most adolescents on the other. The majority of teenagers cope by dealing with one issue at a time. Adaptation covers a number of years, attempting to solve one issue, then the next. Thus, any stresses resulting from the need to adapt to new modes of behaviour are rarely concentrated all at one time. Those who, for whatever reason, do have more than one issue to cope with at one time are most likely to have problems of adjustment.

Focal theory allows the development of young people to be seen as a unified concept – not a series of bursts, but a continuous process in which ultimate balance is required and sought, even within the myriad possibilities to be found because of individual differences.

Lewin (1970) has argued that the adolescent passing through childhood to adulthood is in a 'marginal' position and is entering a 'cognitively unstructured region'. Their sense of competence and ultimately their self-concept and future personal identity depend on how well expectations are accepted and processed into their personal lifestyle. If these behaviour patterns fit the requirements of roles encountered at school, at work, in heterosexual relationships, and in community life generally, then the outcome is satisfactory. Alternatively, if adolescents fail to gain structure in their personal identity, diffusion, confusion, and conflict may result. This is particularly relevant for various adolescent sub-cultures who resolve these conflicts, confusions, and contradictions by celebrating their own rituals and lifestyles. For example, some adolescents are willing acolytes of the ceremonies of school rituals, while others choose to celebrate their own rituals within 'pop' culture, which may be part of an overall pattern of school rejection.

Many young people today appear to accept adult models in their social environment and develop lifestyles commensurate with the values of their subcultural backgrounds and upbringing. But since children may be reared in a social milieu which is quite different from that of their parents' generation, individuals have to carry with them into society their own particular family lifestyle 'tailored' to present social requirements.

The importance of the family in establishing children's general lifestyles, attitudes to, and success in the education system, and their involvement in leisure activities, has been clearly demonstrated. Yet a number of influences and forces in modern society may have led to changes in the family's potential to help young people in their transition towards adulthood. Some of these variations in family living patterns – for instance the growth of one-parent families – may create a situation where there may be less parental interest. In such settings the adolescent is more likely to turn to peers for help and advice. The individual adolescent will conform to social pressures – either from parents or teachers or peers – but the direction of this conforming behaviour will vary depending on the individual's own psychological resources, social background, and the particular social context of issues to be faced.

All these uncertainties and social shifts suggest the need for the individual adolescent to be aware of his or her own orientations to the social context and be aware of alternative social choices and strategies. There is a need to be both stable and flexible. The key elements in the adolescent's progress towards adulthood in modern society may be seen in terms of both absorption and adaptation.

ADOLESCENT LEISURE

Leisure activities may be chosen for their personal meaning and for social expression at various age levels, and these choices will, in turn, be coloured by influences such as the family, peers, the educational systems, the media, leisure promotion industries, and changes in the general social context such as massive unemployment.

Three of the main factors influencing leisure pursuits are age, sex, and social class. When these are associated with the shifting focus of social relationships postulated by Coleman, a framework can be offered for a changing pattern of leisure in the teenage years. This leisure focus generally shifts from adult organized clubs and activities, through casual leisure pursuits, to commercially organized leisure, and these transitions may occur roughly at the ages when main relationship issues – sex, peers, parents – come into focus.

In this general leisure pattern, for instance, the earlier physical and psychological maturity of girls underpins their relatively earlier transition towards a focus on peers and casual leisure pursuits, and then towards more exclusive courting couples and commercial leisure provision. It may also be linked to a more rapid move to social sophistication, if not maturity, and to what has been called their perceived 'career' as girlfriends and wives, though it should be noted that the proportion of teenage brides has dropped considerably (in 1974, one in three single women married under 20 years of age; by 1984 the figure had dropped to one in six).

Is change gradual? Are there identifiable 'triggers' in terms of altered perceptions or social factors that shift individuals to new ventures and activities?

Socio-cultural factors would seem to predominate over physical and psychological factors at the juncture between childhood and adolescence. If we look at the pre-adolescent period, we find that as children emerge from the middle years of childhood they are engaged in play patterns that are basically traditional, conformist, and possibly strongly influenced by family patterns, but that these are slowly eroded by a more adult concept of leisure and recreation. In particular, Hendry and Percy (1981) found that by the upper stages of the primary school social pressures and the influence of the media were pushing boys and girls into much more gender-specific roles in terms of their leisure activities, reading interests, and their television-viewing preferences. With these social triggers, young people move towards organized adult-run leisure activities as a context for slowly acquainting themselves with the opposite sex, after a childhood where single sex groupings are the norm. Such activities include clubs run at school, youth clubs, church groups, and so on.

Conversely, the process which triggers the transition from organized activities towards casual activities a few years later is one where physical and physiological factors may be to the forefront. For girls in particular, the relatively rapid changes in body shape and size, and the onset of menstruation, may well explain the loss of interest in physical activity and organized games at this stage. The physiological and psychological changes experienced by all adolescents, however, require them to reappraise their self-images, and at this stage it is important for these self-images to be reinforced by peers; Weinstein (1973) suggested that peer-group relationships offer multiple opportunities for witnessing the social strategies of others, seeing how far these are effective, and learning self-presentation.

This may result in strong sex differences in leisure pursuits – many girls, for instance, may seem at first to skip this stage of casual peer-orientated activities, except in sharing fashion or social strategies with one or two close friends within 'the culture of the bedroom' as Frith (1978) has described it. This is also the period within which there is the widest variation of leisure activities oriented towards particular peer groups. In particular, working-class teenagers, in an 'escape' from adult influences, often have strong attachments to gangs or groups clearly designated by their allegiance to fashion or music trends.

Schools' attempts to promote leisure and sport activities at this stage often create attitudes and perceptions about leisure pursuits which persist into later adolescence. An emphasis in schools on organization and structure in leisure may run counter to the perceived needs of young people, and may hasten the flight into alternative youth sub-cultures.

The factors which lead to an involvement with commercial leisure are more socio-psychological than somatic in character and have to do with the growing adolescent's desire to be seen as playing an adult role. Pubs, clubs, discos, commercial leisure facilities, and even foreign travel, all feature in the leisure activities of young people at this stage.

Clearly, participation in these sorts of activities is influenced by occupational status and sub-cultures, peer-group membership, and whether or not by this stage 'courting' pairs have been formed. Hence, again the broad influencing factors are mainly socio-cultural values, available cash and employment opportunities, family commitments, and the effects of the broad leisure interests developed in the previous stages.

ADOLESCENTS AND UNEMPLOYMENT

Jahoda's (1979) analysis of the functions of employment in an individual's life can be presented as follows:

1. it provides a structure for time;
2. it allows regular shared experiences outside the family;
3. it links the individual to goals outside him/herself;

4. it defines aspects of personal status and identity; and
5. it enforces activity.

So employment – and unemployment – have a multi-faceted impact on the life of any individual, involving such diverse matters as self-esteem and income, lifestyle and leisure pursuits. This may be particularly important in adolescence.

In October, 1984, Youthaid estimated that half the under 18s and one in four under 25s in the UK were out of work. According to the World Health Organization these figures are comparable with many European countries and with North America. (Only Germany, Sweden, and Japan can boast lower percentages for youth unemployment.) Over half a million under-25-year-olds had been unemployed for more than six months, and there were over a quarter of a million unemployed young people aged 18 and over who had *never* had a full-time job since leaving school. On the other hand, it has been suggested that with the introduction of the extended (two-year) Youth Training Scheme in the UK no one under the age of 18 years need be unemployed! Of course, YTS may be perceived by young people as being a 'gang plank to the dole' as much as a 'permanent bridge to work'.

Kelvin (1981) has suggested that unemployment is becoming an acceptable aspect of young people's self-perceptions and self-identity as more and more adolescents fail to find a niche in the job market when they leave school. Nevertheless, unemployment creates a structureless, confused time state for some adolescents within which leisure, with all its concomitant social opportunities, vanishes. The major impact of unemployment on adolescents may be its ultimate effect on socialization and the transition from adolescence to adulthood.

Bloxham (1984) has made a plea for the development of lifeskills within the vocational structure of Youth Training Schemes which would help young people to cope with unemployment if they cannot find work at the end of the course. Yet there is little research evidence to suggest that the experience of YTS has helped prepare adolescents for a return to a 'leisured' existence on the dole. Further, there is a crucial unresolved conflict in that YTS encourages a vocational perception among trainees, yet it leaves them without the sure identity of being a young worker, and confers no promise that this status will even be achieved in their future lives.

It may be no coincidence that the rise in youth unemployment rates has corresponded with a growing national concern about vocational education. It is when this new vocationalism is viewed from within the context of high and rising youth unemployment that the full complexity of the situation for young people can be seen. Like adults, unemployed teenagers curtail their leisure activities. If they continue to visit pubs and cafés they spend less. They are less likely to reduce their frequency of activity than their expenditure. When they 'go out' they usually remain close to their homes. Local discos replace city-centre nightspots. Even travelling costs are prohibitive.

For many adults, employment is an important element in their social networks. However, unemployed young people appear better able than adults to protect their leisure. Their peer groups are more resilient. Out-of-work youths spend more, not less, time with peers than when in employment. This is not to say that anyone actually enjoys unemployment. The research evidence is clear: young people resent the restrictions of unemployment; compared with teenagers in jobs, the young unemployed worry more about their dress and appearance. They are more prone to loneliness, anxiety, and self-doubt. According to one enquiry, the long-term young unemployed are also more likely to have contemplated suicide.

Unemployed young people do not abandon conventional aspirations. They usually believe that unemployment is temporary, and they desire employment in secure jobs, earning the wages to enable them to go out with cash in their pockets and enjoy conventional leisure. This is reinforced because parents, if they retain any influence over their adolescents, discourage adaptation and reconciliation to joblessness. Yet today's young people who do not regard their current employment as life-long, and who are equipping themselves to cope with economic, technological, and occupational turbulence, are probably better attuned to their futures. Nowadays, young people who are learning to live with change and flux in temporary relationships, may have stronger claims to maturity than those seeking occupations in which to remain for life, and settling into hopefully life-long relations.

Several clear responses to the situation now surrounding young people can be distinguished:

1. Increasing numbers of adolescents are taking on low-paid, often temporary and part-time jobs for economic survival and some independence while earning the qualifications that eventually unlock more attractive opportunities.
2. Other young people are opting for sub-employment. They drop out from education but refuse to commit themselves psychologically to low-status jobs. They work for a bit in order to earn 'vacational' breaks. Neither employment nor unemployment are considered tolerable for long unbroken periods.
3. Some young people are building medium-term careers from recently introduced projects, courses, and training schemes. The stated aim of such projects is usually to assist the unemployed towards conventional jobs. However, individuals sometimes move from scheme to scheme and achieve upward mobility in the process, eventually obtaining instructor, supervisor,

or management positions. Unemployment projects have become an important economic sector, sometimes the sole growth sector in high unemployment areas.

4. Soon after completing compulsory education other young people are deciding that the most secure and rewarding careers on offer are as welfare claimants, especially when supplemented by unofficial earnings. In the longer term, however, the claimant role invariably leads into a poverty trap – an unattractive lifetime condition for the individuals directly involved, and expensive for their wider societies.

5. In some countries, the trend towards staying on in full-time education instead of facing a choice between unemployment and low-status jobs has been particularly strong among females and among some ethnic groups. More are delaying their entry into the labour market, earning higher qualifications, and then obtaining 'good jobs'.

6. There are also trends towards pre-marital cohabitational relationships, and towards the formation of temporary households by groups of young adults who may not be sexually related.

7. For women without the prospect of rewarding occupational careers, marriage and parenthood have provided traditional alternatives. In high unemployment girls' first reactions often include more strenuous efforts to 'get a man'. Unemployment does not undermine but rather reinforces traditional feminine aspirations. Unfortunately, it also undermines the traditional male role as breadwinner. For girls 'respectable' escapes to economic security and adult status may still be available with older men. However, some young women in high unemployment areas are deciding that the claimant role is more accessible. They know that the quickest route to independent accommodation is to 'get pregnant'. Single parenthood and welfare may be no greater economic disaster than dependence on a low-paid or unemployed male, especially when supplemented by casual earnings and gifts from boyfriends.

Earlier it was explained how some young people can find the teenage years stressful while the majority cope well. Sources of stress, like identity crisis or role development, rarely occur at the same time; usually they can be dealt with separately and cause the adolescent little or no distress. Similarly, the unemployed adolescent will usually undergo a mixture of positive and negative experiences. It is only when a number of negative factors impinge on the individual concurrently, and cumulatively, to create a focal issue, that unemployment becomes an ordeal like other adolescent crises. By interpreting the effects of a variety of aspects which combine to create positive or negative feelings an understanding of particular individual reactions to youth unemployment is possible.

ADOLESCENTS AND SOCIAL ISSUES

Yet whether at school, working, or unemployed there are a number of other social issues facing young people today – some of which they share with their parents' generation, some which have emerged as elements of our ever-changing society.

Lord Scanlan has suggested that youth unemployment, with associated despair and desperation, are parts of a social background that breeds crime against property; violence on the streets and soccer terraces, against women and ethnic minorities; and alcoholism and drug-abuse when frustrated and depressed boys may 'act out' their problems on the street, whereas girls may be more likely to 'bottle up' their problems and display more evidence of psychological disturbance and stress. Thus one cannot discount the possibility that crime and delinquency in our society are in some measure the cost of certain kinds of social development. As a reaction against the growing institutionalization of daily life in society – mass education, mass entertainment, mass unemployment – some adolescents turn to delinquent patterns of behaviour in search of personal identity. These are the teenagers who 'live for kicks'. It has also been argued that the predominant ethic of our society is acquisitiveness and desire for success. These values are transmitted to the population by the mass media, but unfortunately not everyone can be rich or successful.

Several writers have, therefore, pointed out that the values underlying juvenile delinquency may be far less deviant than is commonly assumed. Delinquency is part of some adolescents' leisure existence, and may also be associated with non-conformist and anti-authority attitudes.

With a backcloth of economic recession – unemployment, political and social class divisions – where young working-class people are a particularly vulnerable group, football's professionalization has caused the creation of spectacular theatre, and the mass media's reaction to football support has been to 'sensationalize'. The social controls of such groups of supporters are clearly and radically different from those that are predominant in society – the values encouraged are norms of aggressive masculinity.

Associated with this, working-class boys are often placed in the contradictory situation of attracting attention and having to deal with any resultant challenge. Various fashion styles are worn to attract attention, but 'battle scars' and other insignia are presented to indicate masculine aggression and dominance. These 'warring' symbols within working-class territories have implications for race relations. Pride in the local territory can become a misguided expression of conservation, with the protection of the neighbourhood flaring into prejudice and racism. It can even manifest itself in the defence of its 'turf' by violence around the local soccer stadium.

Delinquency is not solely a working-class phenomenon. Nevertheless, the vicious circle of slum dwelling, poor job opportunities, few leisure facilities, boredom, and relations with the police creates a social environment which breeds 'trouble'.

It has also been suggested in recent times that girls involved in delinquent sub-cultures may be in rebellion against their traditional sex roles. This has important implications for present and future society. Smith (1978) found that court records revealed that female delinquency was in no way restricted to sexual misconduct, but also included the usual delinquent acts of boys of similar age. In Smith's study, girls reacted to being labelled as 'sluts' or as 'common' or 'loose' by behaving aggressively rather than by accepting the label of promiscuity. They developed self-images as tomboys – tough, dominant, and willing to join in fights on equal terms with boys.

Pop culture can consist of dancing, records, teenage magazines, fashion and aspects of the mass media and cinema, and involvement in aspects of pop culture seems central to the leisure lives of many teenagers. In adolescence most young people experiment and explore within the framework of pop culture. An important point to be made is that venues such as dance halls, discotheques, or pop concerts allow young people to experiment with various roles in association with their peers (rather than with adults), and to experience behaviour patterns and stimulants more usually approved for adults. Within pop culture the adolescent can achieve transitory loss of self by moving into diffuse groups or crowds of peers in which there is a high degree of anonymity, general adherence to dress patterns and hair styles, and a wide range of permissible behaviour. In such settings alcohol and other drugs also enable the adolescent to use emblems of adult power, and allow evasion of self by reducing or altering consciousness.

It is interesting to note the apparent ritualization of trends in adolescent 'pop' culture, where the influence of 'pop' heroes can sometimes lead to imitative styles in behaviour and fashion. In this way the links among teenage magazines, pop music, and programme preferences in television may be close. Adolescent girls have more magazines to choose from than boys, and most of these journals appear to reinforce stereotypical sex roles. Boys' magazines stress sports and hobbies and 'cartoon' violence, while girls' papers and comics deal with romance, fashion, and pop.

The use of drugs, alcohol, and smoking is on the increase in the adolescent population. Our society relies upon legal drugs of various kinds to help individuals in their day-to-day living to withstand strains, stresses, and anxieties with equanimity. Modern medicine has made drugs highly legitimate, as something to be taken casually and not only during moments of pain or of acute and certified stress. From this viewpoint, adolescents, far from being in revolt against an older generation, seem to acknowledge how influential the older generation are as behavioural models.

If psychological problems related to sex identification, dependency needs, control of aggression, early social or emotional deprivation, or lack of interpersonal relationships, do predate drug usage, then drugs can be seen as a help with personal problems – a pseudo-coping strategy. To these personal problems can be added drug-taking for curiosity; for kicks, for fun; for giving individuals greater insights and perceptual variations; or as a retreat from reality. But we can add to this picture by suggesting that drug-taking is also a socio-cultural phenomenon related to attitudes within society, sub-cultural values, and adolescents' orientations to life generally. An achievement-based society valuing success through education, jobs, and wealth creates frustrations for the failures and for the rejected, and adolescents may be highly sensitive to these nuances. Thus differing values and meanings are involved in the 'interaction' between individuals and the drugs they take.

The importance of sexual behaviour, drinking, and drug-taking may be that they link to other adolescent leisure pursuits involving peers, and influenced by peers; yet paradoxically reflect attempts to act like adults. The gap between physical and social maturity may be widening in our highly complex society. Thus a tremendous strain may be put on adolescents in developing stable sexual patterns. Sex-role identity is very important during adolescence. Yet societal changes do not occur evenly, so that adolescents may be caught in possible paradoxes of male-female differences and chastity-sexuality dilemmas. Cultural influences can be a powerful determinant of these paradoxes for adolescents. Society places value on adolescents' physical development, and in turn they judge themselves in relation to these responses – feeling rejected or of low value if they do not conform to social ideals. In certain settings peer pressure may create a conflict between what the individual adolescent thinks is right in sexual behaviour and what many of his or her friends are doing. Because peers play such an important role in the leisure lives of most adolescents, social acceptance is likely to be an urgent concern for most young people. An increasing concern about 'body image', a refusal to 'grow up', 'a rejection of femininity', or a reaction to criticism or ridicule by embarking on a diet can set a young person on the pathway to anorexia nervosa (i.e. the 'slimmers' disease').

Such findings raise important questions about the source of sexual information and sex education for adolescents. Thornburg (1975) showed that from eleven different 'target figures and sources' American adolescents estimated that they obtained about 40 per cent of all their information concerning sexual behaviour from peers, another 40 per cent from school literature, and only about 15 per cent was believed to come from parents. In Britain it is reported that a large number of both boys and girls obtained information from friends, with both parents and teachers coming very low in the list. But interestingly, more than half the boys and girls questioned mentioned a school teacher as the preferred source of information on sexual matters.

Another social issue is that more and more concern is being shown by both 'experts' and the media about life-span health and fitness. Yet despite the greater promotion of approaches to healthy living (i.e. diet, exercise, anti-smoking, moderate drinking, drug avoidance) young people appear to be very susceptible to media advertising which makes smoking and drinking seem attractive 'adult' forms of behaviour.

The relatively inactive lifestyle of Britain's youth has also been commented on, and some research has shown that British adolescents are as fat and unfit as their American counterparts. The imperatives here are the elimination of physical and mental conditions that militate against the individual maintaining a reasonably healthy lifestyle, and the promotion of conditions and regimens of living that put agency in the hands of the individual.

CONCLUDING REMARKS

In bringing together adolescents' needs and priorities within the context of social change, perhaps we should recognize that the ways in which young people understand and perceive themselves, their own agency and personality, and their various social situations, have a powerful effect on their subsequent reactions to various life events. It is the interplay of internal forces (i.e. physiological and emotional) and external forces (for example peers) which contributes to the success or failure of progress towards adulthood.

The essential dilemma for the individual adolescent in wishing to be fully integrated and accepted in society is between 'playing appropriate roles' and 'selfhood'. On the one hand it is important to be able to play appropriate roles in a variety of social settings and to follow the prescribed rules for these situations. On the other hand, it is equally important to be able to maintain elements of individuality. The denial of self can lead to depersonalization. Relative freedom for the individual from 'rule-regulated' behaviour is to be achieved through variations of role and rule structures, and through alternative social and physical contexts, to provide appropriate levels of variety and opportunity. Here the role of 'education for leisure' may be significant, in that alternative forms of self-presentation and style can be tried out without dire consequences.

In the process of socialization, the various adults (for example, parents, teachers, youth leaders) and other adolescents with whom young people will interact are important as role models. But equally important are selfhood, perceived competence, and identity for the individual adolescent, together with the need to make sense of his or her social world and his or her place in it (i.e. meanings ascribed to situations and to one's own and others' behaviour). The individual adolescent should learn as a key priority to be an 'active agent' in shaping and determining his or her own social development in the process of transition from childhood to adulthood in modern society.

REFERENCES

Bloxham, S. (1984) 'Social behaviour and the young unemployed', in R. Fiddy (Ed.) *Young People's Work: Policy and Provision for the Young Unemployed*, London: Falmer.

Coleman, J. C. (1979) *The School Years: Current Views on the Adolescent Process*, London: Methuen.

Damstrup, V. (1985) *Review of Literature on the Effects of Youth Unemployment*, Copenhagen: World Health Organization.

Erikson, E. H. (1968) *Identity, Youth and Crisis*, New York: Norton.

Frith, S. (1978) *The Sociology of Rock*, London: Constable.

Hendry, L. B. and Percy, A. (1981) 'Pre-adolescents' television styles and leisure', unpublished memorandum, University of Aberdeen. Cited in L. B. Hendry (1983) *Growing Up and Going Out*, Aberdeen University Press.

Jahoda, M. (1979) 'The impact of unemployment in the 1930s and 1970s'. *Bulletin of the British Psychological Society*, 32: 309–14.

Kelvin, P. (1981) 'Work as a source to identity: the implications of unemployment', *British Journal of Guidance and Counselling* 9 (1): 2–11.

Lewin, K. (1970) 'Field theory and experiment in social psychology', in R. Muuss (Ed.) *Adolescent Behaviour and Society*, New York: Random House.

Smith, L. S. (1978) 'Sexist assumptions and female delinquency', in C. Smart and B. Smart (Eds.) *Women, Sexuality and Social Control*, London: Routledge & Kegan Paul.

Thornburg, H. D. (1975) 'Adolescent sources of initial sex information', in R. E. Grinder (Ed.) *Studies in Adolescence*, London: Collier-McMillan.

Weinstein, E. A. (1973) 'The development of inter-personal competence', in D. A. Goslin (Ed.) *Handbook of Socialisation Theory and Research*, New York: Rand McNally.

9. SPECIAL EDUCATIONAL NEEDS

9.0

INTRODUCTION: SPECIAL EDUCATIONAL NEEDS

PHILLIP WILLIAMS

Special education used to maintain a somewhat uneasy relationship with the rest of the educational world. For many years, for reasons which this section mentions, special education was seen as separate education, education in the separate campus of the special school. Since special schools were unknown territory, never visited by the great majority of teachers and administrators, it was assumed that education there was somehow different. Exactly how it was different was never really explained, and while these educational areas remained remote, the rest of the educational world remained ignorant.

During the last decade or so, the special education frontier has been disappearing. All educators have gradually realized that special education is education first and special second. To modify very slightly a well-known quotation from the Warnock report,[1] 'the purpose of education for all children is the same, the goals are the same, it is only the help needed that is different'. And at a time when educators recognize that most children benefit from individually planned educational help, why separate some in segregated institutions for this purpose?

All education starts with assessment, and special education is no exception. But until recently, special education often also finished with assessment, an assessment that usually allocated a child to a diagnostic category. This is called by the three authors of the first chapter in this section the 'defect model' of assessment. For the great majority of children with special needs, as they point out, this is a useless activity. What is required is a statement of the kind of educational help needed, giving indications of new teaching plans and management strategies which can be put into practice, later to be evaluated in turn. This 'intervention assessment', founded on a partnership between interested parties, is the basis of the current approach to assessment in special education, formalized in England and Wales in the circulars governing the interpretation of the 1981 Education Act.

This Act extended formal assessment procedures to children below the age of two. This illustrates the importance attached to offering special education to very young children, and the second chapter in the section outlines the kinds of provision available to pre-school children with special needs. Here Geoff Lindsay emphasizes the importance of organizing and planning the curriculum and resources of nursery schools and classes so that an effective education for young children with special needs can be provided.

Until children enter the main school system – at five years of age in the UK – integration is hardly an issue. Children with special needs live in their families and enjoy similar experiences to those of their brothers, sisters, and friends. Their pre-school education is nearly always gained in the nursery schools and classes that other children attend: Geoff Lindsay's chapter makes no mention of segregated education at this stage. But a change occurs when children reach compulsory school age, for now education for children with special needs can be either integrated or segregated: there is a choice. In the third chapter in this section, David Mitchell examines the challenges posed by the move towards integration, a move which, as his chapter demonstrates, is being made in many different countries. Starting from the theme that 'Special education is the responsibility of every teacher in every school', he outlines the policies and practices that help to ensure the success of integrated education, from teaching strategies in the classroom to community attitudes. One of his key areas is the curriculum.

It is no coincidence that the curriculum chapter which follows has been placed in the centre of this section, for the changes that are taking place in special education can be summarized as a move from an assessment-led activity to a curriculum-led activity; the curriculum is now pivotal. Seamus Hegarty takes as his point of departure the belief that the curriculum in special education has to be seen in the context of the main curriculum; distinctive, yes, but different, no. Since the educational aims for all children are the same, the curricular targets should be similar. Of course there will need to be modifications to the detail of the content, but as he points out, good educators make variations to cater for the needs of different children anyway: the variations for children with special needs may be greater in degree, but they are not different in kind. The latter part of his chapter gives examples of how these principles apply to the curriculum, taking illustrations from children whose special educational needs arise from a variety of physical, sensory, or psychological difficulties.

At this point the section moves to consider the special needs of these pupils in more detail. Categorizing pupils by medical condition has been one of the reasons for the separation of special education from the rest of the educational world. We used to think of blind pupils as blind first and pupils second. But now they are pupils first and foremost, for the disappearance of categories following the 1981 Education Act in England and Wales – and the Education

(Scotland) Act, 1981 – has focused attention on educational need rather than medical condition. These educational needs fall into three main groups, those which characterize children with physical and sensory handicaps, those which characterize children with learning difficulties, and those which characterize children with emotional and behavioural difficulties, though it must be emphasized that there is variation within each grouping and overlap between: there is no escaping the importance of planning programmes for individuals.

In the last three chapters in this section Elizabeth Chapman, Phillip Williams, and Maurice Chazan focus on the policies and practices that are being introduced in these areas. While the different treatments are interesting, the similarities are fascinating. For each of the three chapters ends with a section stressing the importance of teacher education for their particular field. This raises a point of substance for this section as a whole. To cover the ideas and practices of special education within the constraints of seven short chapters requires careful selection. Some topics, such as special education in higher and further education, have had to be denied their due treatment. Others, such as the increasing importance of parental links in the new framework of special education, have not been accorded a chapter of their own, but permeate each one. Teacher education is a good example of an issue of central importance in special education, which has no separate treatment in its own right, but which has nevertheless been addressed in nearly every chapter. This is no accident. Great changes have taken place in the ideas underpinning special education. Teacher education is essential for these ideas to take root and so sustain and encourage the developments which the contributors to this section outline.

As this section goes to press the changes required by the 1988 Education Act (the Education Reform Act) are being planned. In particular, the introduction of national assessment requirements and a national curriculum will have some implications for the education of children with special needs. Practitioners in this area hope that the effects of these changes on the spirit in which special educational needs are currently being met, and which this section reflects, will not be substantial. But it will not be possible to appreciate these effects properly until the changes have been introduced and have been in operation for some time.

REFERENCE

1. Department of Education and Science (1978) *Special Educational Needs* (The Warnock Report), London: HMSO.

9.1

CHANGES IN ASSESSMENT

REA REASON, PETER FARRELL, AND PETER MITTLER

INTRODUCTION

This chapter describes the current ethos underlying assessment of special educational needs and provides an outline of the historical context of recent developments, including the influence of the 1981 Education Act. The final part of the chapter discusses some key issues in assessment. Although it is relevant to the full range of special needs and to all age groups, the emphasis is on those children whose needs can be met in mainstream schools. The focus of the chapter is on children with learning difficulties. Readers interested in other aspects, such as emotional and behavioural difficulties, will find later chapters in this section very relevant. Similarly, we cannot here cover more specialist areas of assessment, and recommend the reader to additional publications (for example Hogg and Raynes for the area of mental handicap[1]).

THE CONCEPT OF ASSESSMENT

In the early 1970s 'special education' in Britain usually referred to some two per cent of children educated in segregated schools or classes designated to cater for particular disabilities categorized in the 1944 Education Act. Since then educational thinking and practices, reflected in the 1981 Education Act, have resulted in a marked shift away from that very narrow focus. Now the term 'special educational need' applies to a large proportion of children, estimated as one in five, who may at some time in their school careers have educational difficulties which require additional help from their teachers. Consequently the purpose and methods of assessment have become much more closely related to the planning of intervention in all schools, rather than to the categorization of children's difficulties.

But the concept of assessment is not restricted to children with special educational needs. All children are assessed in all kinds of ways throughout their school careers. Parents may assess whether their children are ready to learn to ride a bicycle or to go to the library with a friend. Teachers will assess to what extent the child has mastered concepts such as the passage of time or units of measurement. Secondary teachers can help pupils assess for themselves what formal examinations are best suited to their interests and aptitudes.

Assessment in the context of special education is no different from these kinds of judgements. It can be useful and constructive if it leads to realistic forecasts and plans of instruction, and harmful if it only labels the child as unintelligent, lazy, or disruptive. So assessment of special needs does not differ in kind from other assessment. It only requires more detail and, in the case of children with marked difficulties, a systematic approach to the collection of information which ensures that all relevant professionals, parents, and the children themselves have been consulted.

Furthermore, problems do not always lie in the child. There is now a growing awareness of the ways in which schools as organizations can cause or exacerbate special needs in their pupils. This is in strong contrast to the 'defect' model of assessment which assumes that the problem, whether it is a learning or behavioural difficulty, or an impairment of some kind, lies largely within the child. It then becomes the task of the school to pinpoint the nature of the 'defect' and to help the child to overcome or compensate for it. The alternative environmental model, while not denying that children have specific or general difficulties, additionally seeks to examine the school setting. Explanations may lie within the organization and consist, for example, of curricular demands which are only partially comprehended by many of the pupils. The language of instruction may be such that pupils fail to understand what they are expected to do particularly if worksheets and textbooks require a level of readability beyond many pupils. Similarly, disruptive behaviour may be the function of management styles within the school or the control strategies adopted by individual teachers in the classroom. These examples highlight the importance of assessing the learning environment as well as the child.

So the concept of special educational need is relative and depends to a large extent on the particular context. Given adequate resources, it can be assumed that teacher competence in assessment and planning for a wide range of pupils will result in fewer children requiring additional or segregated provision. These considerations form the basis for the concept of integration, i.e. for ensuring that every effort is made to meet children's special needs within ordinary schools. Consequently, those local authorities supporting integrated provision will emphasize staff development and additional resources in mainstream schools rather than assessment for the purpose of transfer to special schools.

Assessment cannot be isolated from the context of intervention, i.e. the results of the assessment must be relevant to management strategies and teaching plans which, in turn, may lead to further assessment. Indeed, the phrase 'assessment by intervention' has been used to reinforce the relationship between the two terms. But although assessment at its best is a continuous process, there are formal occasions, such as school examinations, which assume great importance. In the case of children with special educational needs, the involvement of professionals other than teachers, for example speech therapists, doctors, or psychologists, can give the assessment that formal nature which places undue emphasis on one-off observations and the mystique associated with them. If these people are regarded as having power to act on the basis of their assessments, their role may be exaggerated, resulting in the denigration of the skills of others. These issues will be elaborated later in this chapter; the point to be made here is that assessment is not the prerogative of any one group of practitioners. Most of all it should involve a partnership between parents, teachers, pupils, and other professionals.

We have now outlined the current ethos underlying assessment of special educational needs: the much wider focus, the environmental model of assessment, the principles of integration, the close link between assessment and intervention, and the central role played by parents, teachers, and the pupils themselves. Next we shall consider the historical context which has led to these developments.

A HISTORICAL PERSPECTIVE

For children with special educational needs clinic-based assessments were prevalent in the 1960s. Typically they involved school doctors, psychiatrists, and, to a lesser extent, educational psychologists. Schools might be asked for reports but would rarely receive copies in return. The confidential nature of the information obtained by the clinic was emphasized. Assessment tended to be completed in one session, with a heavy reliance on normative testing, i.e. on comparing the child's level of ability with that of the 'average child' of his or her age. According to Tyson,[2] full-scale intelligence tests, resulting in IQ scores, were almost always administered, and 'projective' tests of personality were also popular. As far as schooling was concerned, the main emphasis was on the 'defect' model, on diagnosing within child variables and not the context of learning. The purpose was to determine whether the child required transfer to a special school, and what category of special school would be most suitable. There were schools for the 'delicate', the 'educationally subnormal', the 'emotionally disturbed', and for children with physical or sensory impairments. Remedial programmes were rarely planned, and the professionals did not think that they had a role in planning or implementing detailed strategies for intervention.

It should be emphasized that the restricted function of assessment was at least partly caused by the shortage of staff, particularly remedial teachers and psychologists. The early 1970s saw a rapid expansion in the number of psychologists and a shift of focus from clinic to school. Remedial services also expanded and children were withdrawn from the classroom, individually or in small groups, for additional help with reading and writing.

Educational psychologists began to rely less on global IQ scores and to refer to subtests of the Wechsler Intelligence Scales, the Illinois Test of Psycholinguistic Abilities, or to the Frostig Test of Visual Perception. Results were related to educational programmes designed to 'strengthen' the cognitive or perceptual deficits assumed to underpin the particular subtests. For example, pupils considered to have poor auditory memory were given exercises consisting of the recital of sequences of numbers, and it was suggested that weakness in visual memory could be improved with practice in recollecting the order of sequences of abstract symbols.

Although the weight of research evidence has since shown that attempts to train up these assumed areas of deficit do not directly affect educational progress,[3] the programmes seemed to herald at the time an important shift towards linking assessment with intervention. During this phase several authors, for example Wedell,[4] devised procedural flow diagrams of assessment which incorporated these developments but placed much more emphasis on a framework of 'hypothesis testing' through systematic questions related to intervention.

The late 1970s saw growing dissatisfaction with models of assessments based on analysing the results of tests such as the ones mentioned above. It was argued that these hypothetical constructs did not relate to instructional programmes of use in the classroom, and only focused on 'deficits' within the child. Furthermore the tests were only available to psychologists, thus accentuating the mystique which had separated assessment from intervention. An approach was needed which could be shared by teachers, parents, and psychologists, and which related directly to educational progress.

Work originating in the USA has been adapted to British circumstances and is currently very much in vogue.[5] Curriculum-based assessment, the generic term for these approaches, focuses on pupil performance in specific curriculum areas. Educational difficulties are not seen only as problems within the child, but are related to instructional conditions. In other words, if children are not learning a particular task, then we may not have taught them the earlier skills they should have mastered before being ready to tackle that task.

These kinds of assessments assume that the curriculum can be drawn up as a hierarchy of target skills/knowledge to be mastered. At the top of the hierarchy is the basic subject area (such as mathematics) which has targets (for example, number bonds, estimating, money, volume). Each of these targets is broken down into teaching aims (such as addition and subtraction with numbers less than 20) and these are further divided into pupil objectives which state what pupils have to do to demonstrate that they have mastered the teaching objective. For children with learning difficulties the pupil objectives are divided into sequences of even smaller steps until a level of practice is reached at which the children can succeed.

With the curriculum specified as a series of objectives, assessment takes the form of determining, for a particular subject area, what exactly the pupil can do in order to decide what he or she can learn next. It assumes that a standard of mastery can be set, and involves the design of criterion-referenced tests which state how many times the task has to be performed accurately and fluently to show that the pupil has acquired the skill in question.

We now have an 'assess, teach, assess again' approach, as illustrated by the phrase 'assessment by intervention' mentioned earlier on in this chapter. The approach can be made relevant and comprehensible to all those involved, including the pupils themselves and their parents. It has resulted in the proliferation of in-service training 'packages' for teachers, such as the Special Needs Action Programme,[6] and culminated in the mammoth Data-Pac[7] collection of intervention-related assessment materials which, unfortunately, bring us full-circle back to some of the mystique of assessment, as the materials are rather unwieldy, not necessarily related to the school's own curriculum, and initially only available to psychological services. But Data-Pac was a response to the lack of objectives-based curriculum planning in the schools themselves; its authors would be the first to express a preference for school-focused programmes.

Although the positive thinking underpinning curriculum-based assessment has brought significant advances to all areas of special education, whether in mainstream or segregated schools, the apparent simplicity of the assessment masks many obstacles, not least the pitfalls of narrowing teaching methods and the curriculum to that which can be directly assessed. This clearly has important implications for all areas of assessment, not least the attainment targets at ages seven, 11, 14 and 16 in the national curriculum. We shall return to these issues in the final part of this chapter.

Many of the developments in the last twenty years are reflected in journal articles and books. But we know much less about the assessment practices adopted by schools and professionals in reality as compared with the examples of good practice and the recommendations made in the literature. Some preliminary surveys of assessment methods used by educational psychologists suggest a continued focus on within-child variables and psychometric methods such as the British Ability Scales.[8] While considerable variations in practice are likely, depending on the emphasis of the organizations and the individuals involved, approaches advocated in the literature may not necessarily be apparent in everyday application.

THE INFLUENCE OF THE 1981 ACT

The current British legislative basis for the assessment of children with special educational needs is embodied in the 1981 Education Act which became Law in 1983. The purpose of the Act was to:

- abolish categories of handicap in special education and replace them with the concept of special educational needs;
- define more precisely the responsibilities of schools to identify and provide for those of their pupils who may have special educational needs;
- provide a framework for multi-disciplinary assessment of children with special educational needs;
- promote a genuine partnership with parents.

As full summaries of the 1981 Education Act and the resultant administrative procedures are provided elsewhere for example by the Advisory Centre for Education[9] we shall here only mention the main features of the Act. These can be considered under two headings: first, within-school practices and procedures and, second, the formal assessments undertaken by a multi-disciplinary team.

Within-school practices and procedures

The 1981 Education Act lays down, under Section 2, a duty on the Governors of all schools to nominate a 'responsible person' to manage the within-school identification, assessment, and monitoring procedures, and report on these to the school's governing body and the LEA. In practice, this responsible person has usually been the Headteacher who has the following managerial responsibilities:

1. *The identification of pupils within the school who may have special educational needs:*
   DES Circular 1/83, to be amended in 1989 to include the national curriculum, recommends that the identification and assessment of pupils should be a continuous process concerned with the whole child as well as with the child's performance in specific subject areas. The identification of needs should be carried out within the context of the school's own curriculum. There is consequently a close link between identification, assessment, the planning and modification of the curriculum, and the forecasting and recording of progress for individual pupils.
2. *Ensuring that the provision made by the school is meeting the pupil's needs:*
   The effectiveness of the education offered by the school must be carefully monitored. If individual educational difficulties persist, advice from other support agencies should be sought following parental consent.

3. *Parent and pupil involvement:*

If teachers have any concerns about individual pupils, parents should be involved. They must be aware of the assessments and the provision made by the school and be informed regularly of the progress made by their child. DES Circular 1/83 also mentions that the views of the pupils themselves should be taken into account. The importance of the views of the pupils themselves will indeed be stressed in the revised Circular to be issued in 1989.

Formal assessment

If it is considered that a pupil has special educational needs which cannot be met in the ordinary school without significant additional resources, a process of formal assessment must be initiated under Section 5 of the Education Act. Most local authorities advise their schools that such assessments should take place only after the informal procedures outlined under the first heading have been followed and found insufficient. Parents have a right to request formal assessment.

Formal assessment under Section 5 is lengthy and multi-disciplinary. The local authority collates written advice from parents, the school, any specialist teachers who have been working with the child during the period of informal assessment, the educational psychologist, the medical officer, and other relevant professionals such as social workers, speech therapists, or physiotherapists. Parents have a right to be present at all assessments and should receive copies of all the reports on their children.

The local authority then decides, on the basis of these reports, whether the child requires a Statement of Special Educational Needs. In this case a Statement is issued which outlines the pupil's needs and the provision which the authority intends to make in meeting these needs. The Statement is a legal contract between the authority and the child's parents. The parents may appeal against any part of the Statement. Most local authorities provide information booklets for parents which outline the assessment procedures and parental rights. But these tend to vary in clarity and comprehensiveness.[10]

Statements are reviewed annually to ensure that the child's needs are being met and formal re-assessments take place during the year before the child's 14th birthday. These re-assessments usually follow the same procedure as outlined under Section 5 for the initial formal assessment.

The legal framework of assessments, statements, and reviews has largely been of benefit to children with special educational needs. It has resulted in the standardization of procedures across local education authorities, the involvement of parents and their access to all reports, and the requirement to monitor the progress of every child with special needs.

But there are some serious problems about the implementation of the 1981 Act. Although formal assessment under Section 5 was intended for a small minority of children, administrative responses to the Act appear to have focused on the setting up of these expensive and time-consuming procedures for a larger number of children in order to access additional resources. Meanwhile Section 2 of the Act has received less attention, so that the school-based assessment and intervention strategies, outlined under the first heading above, have not always been implemented. Consequently the balance of assessment has remained within a complex legal process, and has not shifted to preventative approaches based on adequate facilities for those children whose special needs can be met through staff development and well-resourced mainstream schools.

Secondly, the bureaucratic nature of the formal assessment, involving local authority personnel in seemingly endless copying and distribution of forms, has delayed the completion of the assessment to the extent that some children have waited for additional special provision for at least one year.[11] This is clearly contrary to the sound delivery of services for the children.

A third weakness in the implementation of the Act has to do with the different ways in which local education authorities have responded to its implications regarding integration. A few have made concerted efforts to educate children with Statements in mainstream schools, whereas others have continued with segregated provision. This means that the assessment of children's special educational needs will result in different kinds of provision according to the ethos and resources available in the authority in which they reside. The report in 1987 of the House of Commons Enquiry contains most recent critiques, comments, and recommendations about the implementation of the 1981 Education Act.[12]

ISSUES IN ASSESSMENT

Despite significant developments in the assessment of special educational needs, incorporated in principle in the 1981 Act, several issues continue to be debated. Some of these are considered below.

Is assessment of intelligence obsolete?

On the basis of the historical overview provided earlier the simple answer to this question should be 'yes'. Assessment of intelligence reinforces the 'defect' model with its sole focus on within child variables. Attention is deflected from instructional conditions and the more constructive approaches of curriculum-based assessment. Moreover, it is not at all clear what tests of intelligence really measure. But some authors, for example Herstein,[13] consider that these criticisms are poorly founded in socio-political ideology, and do not acknowledge the potential relevance of the concept of intelligence and its assessment.

The judgement of individuals in terms of their intelligence is deeply embedded in our culture. Children are labelled 'not very bright' or 'quite able', and poor educational performance is explained in terms of low intelligence, as if the latter was the cause of the former. Consequently research evidence about the relationship between intelligence tests and achievement must be considered. Although there is an extensive literature showing positive correlations ranging from 0.4 to 0.7 between IQ and achievement, these results relate to large samples and not to the predictive value for the individual. In any case achievement influences test results; for example, verbal measures of intelligence are likely to rise as reading attainments improve. Indeed in the 1960s Morris[14] suggested that the measure of Reading Quotient was the best predictor of Intelligence Quotient!

If both measures of attainment and intelligence improve as a result of good education, it is particularly dangerous to regard IQs as fixed entities within the child and invariable predictors of later achievement. Only if children's scores on intelligence tests fall at the extremes of the normal distribution curve can one make tentative predictions about academic achievement. But even at these extremes prediction may be unreliable. There may be valuable and complex tasks which a child with low scores on intelligence tests can perform better than a child who has been labelled 'bright'. Consequently intelligence tests must be interpreted with much caution. It may indeed be much better to avoid such tests if results are likely to be misinterpreted.

Cognitive profiles and curriculum-based assessment

There is continued interest in the development and application of cognitive profiles, which can contribute to strategies of intervention becoming better matched to the particular profile of the individual child. Indeed the British Ability Scales were designed primarily to help psychologists and teachers use cognitive profiles to plan effective programmes for children with learning difficulties. But although current research results may be of potential value to practitioners, these approaches will remain of theoretical interest only until there is a demonstrated link between subtest profiles and methods of teaching which have an effect on academic achievement.[15]

As described in the historical overview, curriculum-based assessment has gained in popularity over the last ten years. Although conceptually simple, this approach has also been the source of conflicting opinion. A major problem is the assumption that every curriculum area can be subdivided into a hierarchy of measurable objectives and, indeed, curriculum-based assessment has been charged with limiting teaching to that which can be measured, rather than that which is educationally worthwhile. Although this is a misunderstanding of the purpose of the assessment, which does not aim to specify teaching methods, and is certainly not intended to limit the curriculum, there is increasing recognition that assessment cannot be divorced from methods of teaching; even simple skills are not necessarily learnt in distinct sequentially ordered steps. For example, early number concepts can be listed as hierarchical targets, but these targets may then disregard the less structured linguistic interactions essential to the child's development of conceptual understanding. Similarly the area of literacy has become the focus of considerable controversy regarding the relevance of an approach which analyses the process into subskills. While there is currently an emphasis on psycholinguistic methods, the suggestion that assessment should pinpoint the child's level in acquiring, say, phonic skills, will not be acceptable in isolation from a more holistic approach.

Theoretical viewpoints about learning clearly affect the curriculum-related assessment offered to the child. Furthermore, these kinds of assessments may not be sensitive to individual differences, because they have been tailored more to fit pre-conceived programmes than to investigate the child's own strategies of learning. We need more sophisticated assessment based on a clearer understanding of the various different ways in which children learn complex skills such as reading (see for example Reason and Boote[16]). To incorporate these ideas, curriculum-based assessment will have to take account of individual strengths and weaknesses, so that the best of both the 'defect' and the environmental models are encompassed in the assessment.

Who benefits from assessment?

At first glance this question might appear facile, as the parents and professionals involved in the assessment surely have the children's interests at heart. But the legislative framework of the 1981 Education Act only ensures that parents and relevant professionals are consulted. There is but passing mention in Circular 1/83, to be amended in 1989, of the desirability of taking into account the views of the pupils themselves. So currently children do not have a formal say in their own assessment, and may indeed feel that the focus of assessment ignores the real issues such as the inadequacy of those who care for them or attempt to educate them.

The limitations of the 'defect' model of assessment have already been stressed. But it is not easy to shift the emphasis of assessment to an environmental model which may challenge the competence of those involved in helping the child. In order to avoid conflict, it is easier to attribute failings by the school and by others to difficulties within the child. Current practices are then exonerated because educational intervention cannot be blamed for within-child shortcomings. In such cases it is not unreasonable to argue that institutional needs are being assessed and met in the guise of helping the child, particularly if the child then transfers to segregated provision which does not necessarily meet his or her needs.

Increasingly schools are prepared to face this dilemma. The current interest in curriculum-based assessment, teacher accountability, and school management has led to a more open and self-critical approach to children's difficulties, and a genuine desire by teachers to develop their own skills and approaches for meeting the special educational needs of the pupils in their care. This change of focus in assessment has been endorsed by the national curriculum through programmes of study and attainment targets which permit modifications but do not exclude pupils with special educational needs.

CONCLUSION

We have now outlined the ethos and legislative underpinnings of the assessment of special educational needs in England and Wales. It should be emphasized, however, that parallel developments have taken place in many other countries, in particular the USA, where the Education of All Handicapped Children Act of 1975 ('P.L. 94–142') has made curriculum-based assessment mandatory through the design of individual educational programmes. Furthermore, countries such as Norway and Denmark are well ahead of us in ensuring that the views of the pupils themselves are consulted, and in making assessment in the context of integrated education a well-established way of life.

This chapter has set the scene for many of the themes which will be elaborated in later contributions. We have considered the wider focus of assessment, the links between assessment and intervention within the whole-school context, and the central role played by parents, teachers, and the pupils themselves. As these issues are relevant to the full age range of children, the next chapter describes their application in ensuring that the special educational needs of the pre-school child are being met.

REFERENCES

1. Hogg, J. and Raynes, N. (Eds.) (1987) *Which Assessment? A Guide to Tests, Batteries and Checklists in Mental Handicap*, London: Croom Helm.
2. Tyson, M. (1970) 'The design of remedial programmes', in P. Mittler (Ed.) *The Psychological Assessment of Mental and Physical Handicap*, London: Methuen.
3. Ysseldyke, J. E. (1987) 'Do tests help in teaching?' *Journal of the Association of Child Psychology and Psychiatry*, 28 (1): 21–5; Wagner, R. K. and Sternberg, R. J. (1984) 'Alternative conceptions of intelligence and their implications for education,' *Review of Educational Research*, 54 (2): 179–223.
4. Wedell, K. (1970) 'Diagnosing learning difficulties: a sequential strategy', *Journal of Learning Disabilities*, 3 (6):23–9.
5. Ainscow, M. and Tweddle, D. A. (1984) *Early Learning Skills Analysis*, Chichester: Wiley; Solity, J. and Bull, S. (1987) *Special Needs: Bridging the Curriculum Gap*, Milton Keynes: Open University Press.

6. Ainscow, M. and Muncey, J. (1981) *Special Needs Action Programme (SNAP)*, Swansea: Drake Education Associates.
7. Akerman, T., Cooper, P., Faupel, A., Gillett, D., Kenwood, P., Leadbetter, P., Mason, E., Matthews, C., Mawer, P., Tweddle, D., Williams, H., and Winteringham, D. P. (1984) *The Data Pac Users Guide*, Birmingham University.
8. Farrell, P., and Smith, N. (1982) 'A survey of methods educational psychologists use to assess children with learning difficulties', *The British Psychological Society: Occasional Papers of the Division of Educational and Child Psychology*, 6 (2): 31–42; Farrell, P., Dunning, A., and Foley, J. (in preparation) *Innovations in Psychological Assessment?*
9. Advisory Centre of Education (1983) *The 1981 Education Act.*
10. Rogers, R. (1986) *Caught in the Act*, London: C.S.I.E. Spastics Society.
11. Policy and Provision for Special Needs (1987) Newsletter number 5, University of London Institute of Education.
12. House of Commons (1987) *The 1981 Education Act: Report of a Select Committee Enquiry*, London: HMSO.
13. Herstein, J. (1983) 'IQ encounters with the press', *New Scientist*, April, 230–2.
14. Morris, J. M. (1966) *Standards and Progress in Reading*, London: NFER Newnes Educational Publishing Company.
15. Elliott, C. D. (1982) *British Ability Scales: Introductory Manual*, Windsor: NFER-Nelson; Elliott, C. D. and Tyler, S. (1987) 'Learning disabilities and intelligence test results: a principal components analysis of the British Ability Scales', *British Journal of Psychology*, 78: 325–33.
16. Reason, R. and Boote, R. (1986) *Learning Difficulties in Reading and Writing*, Windsor: NFER-Nelson.

PRE-SCHOOL CHILDREN WITH SPECIAL NEEDS

GEOFF LINDSAY

Two boys, Jason and Nicky, attend a nursery class attached to a first school. Each is about four years old and has been attending school for a matter of weeks. After a phasing-in period of visits and short stays accompanied by a parent, they are both now attending five mornings a week. The nursery is lively and exciting with a good array of equipment. There are two teachers and two nursery nurses for the forty children in the nursery during the morning session.

Both boys have quickly taken to the large apparatus available inside the nursery and in the playground. Jason has also discovered the jigsaws, large Lego, and other constructional toys. He has also started to play in the home corner with other children, although he doesn't have any particular friends. Jason is chatty and enjoys talking with the other children as he plays, and with the staff. He is also confident enough to join in short conversations with other children.

Nicky appears much less confident. Apart from his enthusiasm on the larger apparatus, especially the slide, he often wanders during free play. It is noticeable that he never starts a conversation with another child, and rarely replies when others talk to him. He avoids the small construction toys and jigsaws, and the home corner. He will paint, producing pictures of single colours covering most of a sheet. He does not like to join a member of staff for a story. Closer observation suggests that he has very little spoken language and that his speech is severely impaired.

These two boys, although different, are not untypical of children to be found in a nursery. Although they differ they have similar needs. What are those needs and how can they be provided for?

CHILDREN'S NEEDS

Some people's idea of a nursery education is of a space where children are led in and allowed a free experience of whatever is provided. In this extreme view of child-centred education adults provide materials, implements, and space, but little guidance. The cynic sees this as resulting in paint flowing under the doors, large numbers of unrecognizable models made from egg boxes, and little obvious learning. The contrary view sees a nursery as a modified first school, with a particular emphasis on early acquisition of basic attainments, and ordered behaviour. This would be characterized by neat pieces of paper with a few words written on, a 'reading book' for every child, and a relative lack of movement.

These two views are extreme. In practice probably all nurseries fall somewhere in between. But they do represent the ends of a continuum of debate on the appropriate methods and approaches suitable for nursery provision. The purpose of nurseries and other pre-school facilities has been the subject of much controversy. The issue of the early education of children with special educational needs can only be considered within the context of this general debate.

Consider Nicky and Jason, and what this suggests about the needs of children of pre-school age (about three to five years), concentrating on the area of language. These years are a time when language development is rapid. There has been much research on this age group, which has revealed how vocabulary and structures develop from infancy until the children are of school age (about five years old). Furthermore children will be developing an interactional style, being able to converse, discuss, argue, describe, generate ideas and evaluate their actions. They will also develop and express the views of others, including teachers and parents!

Jason is progressing well along this developmental path, Nicky is not. Nicky's development of spoken language is at about a two-year-old level – he uses single words and the occasional two-word phrase. Also, his speech is impaired, so that what he does say may not be understood.

Yet both children have a need to develop language, although they are at different stages. Are the same methods suitable for each child? Is it that Jason needs only the opportunity to be with others to develop his language, while Nicky requires very specific and structured teaching, possibly from a speech therapist?

INTERVENTION

How should Nicky and others with special needs be helped? We must consider this question within the context of the effectiveness of early childhood education in general, still a controversial area. There have been many studies which have reported upon the effects of pre-school programmes, but there are problems of adequate research design, and of generalizing from studies of experimental endeavours to normal educational provision. However, when the developmental gains of children attending pre-school provision are measured against those of non-attenders, the weight of evidence increasingly indicates that pre-school provision can be effective. For a report of a large-scale study in the United Kingdom and a review of this area, see Osborn and Milbank.[1]

But what of children with special needs? The research problems faced by those investigating this area are even more formidable. However, Guralnick and Bennett[2] have presented an interesting account of a variety of attempts, mainly American, to develop early intervention programmes for children with special needs. The general conclusion again is encouraging. There is evidence of the benefits of pre-school programmes in general, but we can be less confident in distinguishing a 'best buy'. This is not surprising, given the differences between the types of disabilities of the children and the range of programmes designed to meet the children's needs.

What can we conclude? At the lowest level it is clear that pre-school intervention can be beneficial for all children, and that the common themes running through successful schemes are that they should be *sustained* and have *structure*, although this does not imply that the programme should be *formal*.

The structured approach incorporates assessment, record keeping, and planning (see below) but does not limit the nature of the experiences enjoyed by the child. This distinction can be shown in Figure 1.

Figure 1

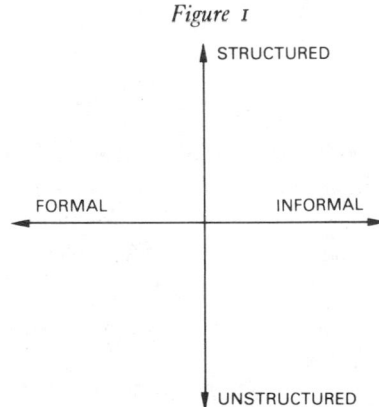

A structured approach will make use of high levels of planning and frequent monitoring of progress. There will be specific objectives set for the child (such as learning certain colours) but room for other objectives to arise naturally from the child's play. The formal approach is characterized by very specific detailing of tasks, with set tasks being presented to the child in standardized ways. The teacher makes use of routines and contrived situations, not those arising naturally in the nursery, often based upon published programmes of language development, for example.

In practice, of course, there is not a simple dichotomy between formal and informal approaches. We can perhaps consider this more usefully as a continuum. At one end is the child-centred or experiential approach, while at the other is that of the behavioural programme where the child's activities, and those of the teacher, may be specified in great detail. This dimension, therefore, is concerned more with the strategies of delivering the programme rather than the content.

In recent years we have seen a growth in formal, highly structured programmes for pre-school children with special needs. A useful review of those concerned with language development can be found in Harris.[3] More recently, however, there has been a shift away from the formal, teacher-directed end of the continuum, as professionals have attempted to modify the programmes to fit in more easily to the natural happenings of the child's experience. This reflects three factors. First, the practicalities of organizing such specific and formal presentation of programmes within nursery settings. Second, the concern of researchers who are more cognitive than behavioural in orientation about the extent of generalization of such experiences, particularly with respect to the meaningfulness of what is learned. Third, 'culture clash' between the more rigid programme and the early childhood philosophy widespread in nursery and infant schools in this country. As a result, attempts are now being made to use structured approaches, but in a more flexible way, and as part of the natural experience of the day.

PORTAGE

The Portage Scheme is one example of a structured approach for children with special needs. Originating as a home teaching approach, Portage has now been developed for use in a variety of ways, including nurseries. There are specific objectives for the child to attain in several areas (for example, expressive language). Teaching sessions are designed with specific tasks and materials to meet these objectives. There is also a detailed monitoring and assessment aspect.

Experience has led to various modifications, and workers will now be wary of too rigid an adherence to the Portage Scheme in its entirety. Some objectives may be redundant or of little use for most children. None the less, Portage has been found to be useful with many children, particularly those with moderate and severe learning difficulties.

Other schemes, for example the Derbyshire Language Scheme, are similar in certain aspects, and also based upon a structured approach. The work with children with severe and profound learning difficulties using the EDY approach (Education for the Developmentally Young) is another example.

All these schemes are highly structured, but users are able to increase their flexibility and reduce their rigid adherence to scripts and specific sessions during the day. We must continue to evaluate the implementation of such schemes, and the modifications to allow more flexible use, in order to judge the optimal approach.

PARENTAL INVOLVEMENT

One of the transformations in education, particularly at the primary stage, has been the increase in the involvement of parents. Nurseries would claim, with much justification, that they have always involved parents. But what is the truth behind the rhetoric? Some recent studies, such as Lunt and Sheppard,[4] have shown the clear benefits of parental involvement, but others, such as Tizard and Hughes,[5] have challenged such assumptions.

One strand of parental involvement is parental rights, particularly linked to women's rights. Thus one argument for nursery provision is not the benefit to the child, but the desire of parents for such provision. Currently provision of all forms of child care varies greatly across local authorities. In 1986 the percentage of three- and four-year-old children attending maintained schools (i.e. nurseries, nursery classes, and rising five classes) varied from 12 per cent in Kent to 79 per cent in Walsall. One political party, Labour, made the provision of nursery places for all who want them an election plank for 1987.

As suggested above, there is now a general weight of evidence supporting the benefits of pre-school education for children with special needs. As with studies of the wider pre-school population, the evidence tends to support the involvement of parents as an important element of this success. However, much more research is necessary to determine the mechanisms whereby parental involvement is effective.

The evidence from Portage programmes is that parents generally have a great enthusiasm for the approach, willingly engage in it, welcome the support of the visiting Portage worker, and see clear benefits for their child.[6] Parents are involved not only as clients but also as co-workers, indeed they are the front-line workers supported by the professionals. This is a major change in the parent-professional relationship, which goes beyond rhetoric to a true partnership.

This approach is easier when home visiting is the method. Once parents need to visit institutions, other problems occur. They are no longer on home territory, and may be faced with several professionals. Their worker, for example a teacher, can only consider the child in a context of a group of children. Despite being very welcoming and truly open, nurseries can underestimate the problems of access. Beyond the psychological barriers, there are logistic problems for the parents of children with special needs. Often the child will need to travel to a nursery, and there may be other children in the family to have looked after or take along. A study of children attending three integrated nurseries serving the city of Sheffield showed that the nurseries' openness was not enough if the parents had difficulties in access.[7]

The 'partnership' approach has much to commend it. To an extent it is enshrined in the 1981 Education Act. Parents can request a formal assessment under this Act, as a means of procuring provision to meet their child's needs, even from the child's infancy. This in itself adds legitimation to pre-school education for children with special needs.

Parents also have the right to contribute their own advice on the child's needs, and must see all the advice of professionals, which they can challenge. However, whether this legislation leads to partnership or better informed confrontation will still rest on the sensitivity of professionals and the appropriate provision being made by LEAs.

Furthermore, a more critical look is now being taken at the types of parental involvement schemes. Doubts are now being expressed about asking parents to carry out direct teaching, as with Portage. Rather, it is suggested, the main focus should be on helping the development of warm, reciprocal, and supportive parent-child relationships, as the focus on direct teaching runs counter to the establishment of adaptive child-parent relationships.[2]

The task now is to determine the optimal process of parent-professional involvement. There is a rights issue, i.e. access to provision, but also one of best practice to help the child. The research to date is only just beginning to allow us to unpack the different elements.

ASSESSMENT AND RECORD KEEPING IN THE PRE-SCHOOL

Some children will have their developmental problems identified very early on, perhaps at birth or even before. There are also now many screening procedures available which are designed to pick out children with a variety of problems. Screening procedures, however, are of variable quality and validity.[8] While screening for phenylketonuria, for example, is simple, highly accurate, and covers most new-born babies, other screening procedures during the pre-school years are much less satisfactory. They suffer from lower accuracy, and do not achieve the same coverage of the population.

Screening, when it does occur, must be followed by a more detailed assessment. This will usually be conducted by one or more highly trained professionals, take longer, be more thorough, and should lead to action. A number of children will have received a detailed assessment before entry into nursery, and much may be known about their conditions. They are likely to be the more seriously impaired, although there are still many children with major problems who are not identified early.

What are the implications for nursery staff? It is important to recognize first of all that even the diagnosis of a specific condition gives no automatic indication of what the education system should offer. There will be a range of profiles of abilities and disabilities even among children with the same condition. Second, the nature of the diagnosis will be variable. In some cases a specific disorder will be identified. In most cases, however, what will be found will be a developmental pattern that deviates from the normal in one or more ways. For the majority of children, in fact, a diagnosis is not a realistic or helpful expectation.

This leads to the main implication, which is true for all pre-school children. There must be a system of continuous monitoring of their development with specific assessments at particular times built into the system as necessary. Thus, rather than have a system comprising only discrete assessments, the child's assessment should be over a period of time (for example six to twelve months) and often involve several professionals, and indeed the parents.

For most aspects of development the most sensible way of approaching this is by linking assessment with intervention as mentioned in Chapter 9.1. For example, Nicky, our child with a language problem, may have an initial assessment by a speech therapist to judge a baseline for intervention. The therapist, involving teachers and parents, will introduce a programme, and Nicky's progress through this will be monitored. This becomes part of a dynamic assessment system, enabling rate of change as well as absolute change to be examined.

For such a system to work efficiently there must be close collaboration between the professionals and the parents. Furthermore, it is necessary to have a thorough and detailed record-keeping system, linked to the learning programme. Many nurseries have found the Portage Scheme a good model on which to base this, and some nurseries have computerized their schemes.

The development of such record-keeping schemes requires much careful consideration. Ideally it should be possible to graft them onto any existing scheme, especially in a mainstream nursery. They must not be too complex or cumbersome, or they will not be completed. Also, they should not require a series of formal assessment sessions to complete. As mentioned above, a structured approach can still be informal, and it is important to draw information from the child's normal, natural behaviour. Some specific formal assessments may be helpful at times, particularly by other professionals, but these also must be integrated into this general record-keeping system.

PROVISION

The range of pre-school provision is far from coherent. The voluntary and state sectors have organized different schemes, and even within a local authority system there may be facilities provided by social services (for example day nurseries) and the education department (for example nursery schools). This chaotic and largely unplanned array of services has been the subject of much criticism, and some local authorities have made attempts to integrate services.

One of the most extensive attempts has been the Mosborough Pre-Five Project in Sheffield. Here an integrated service for pre-fives has been instituted in the Mosborough township, a new development in south Sheffield. Childminders and nurseries have been integrated into one service. The nurseries themselves have both education and social service staff, and have flexible extended days and an extended year. Recent studies have suggested the scheme is successfully meeting its objectives and is popular with its clients.

Pre-school provision in general, therefore, is becoming, gradually, more integrated. At the same time there is probably a tendency to integrate more children with special needs into this provision, rather than segregate them into special school nurseries. This is part of a general move towards integration, and is based upon views of children's rights and what will best help their development[9] (see Chapter 9.3). The exact nature and size of this shift is not yet apparent, as many LEAs are in the process of such a change, its planning, and its implementation. Furthermore, health authorities in many areas are arranging for profoundly intellectually impaired children, previously segregated into hospitals, to be placed in the education system, with no more admissions into hospitals for children with severe learning difficulties. Consequently there is a more complex process of integration occurring, with a general shift of children into less restrictive and segregated environments. For some children this new environment will be a special school nursery, while for others it will be a mainstream nursery. There are also nurseries which have been resourced to allow for the integration of a small group of children with special needs into a mainstream nursery.

Thus provision is undergoing a change, with the impetus for development coming from several directions. Integration is probably increasing, at least at the level of where the children are placed, but are the children functionally more integrated, and do they benefit? Work in the United States[10] and in this country[7] provides some positive answers to both questions, but we must consider such conclusions tentative at present.

However, what is apparent now is that integration should not be seen simply as a rights issue. In order to work well, it must be organized. The needs of the child must be examined carefully, along with those of the parents. Not all nurseries will benefit all children. The ecology, for example, including the degree of 'open plan' may be a factor – some children function much better in small groups in limited, 'safe' space. Although an ideal placement is unlikely, attempts must be made to match child and facility, but bearing in mind considerations such as nature, support available, distance, etc.

EDUCATION AND TRAINING

There are two main issues here. First, individual professionals have a need to learn both new methods of intervention and how they can be adapted. New teaching programmes are appearing such year, some aimed at improving general development, while others aim at narrower targets, such as improving language development. The evidence does not support one clear 'best buy'. What is needed, therefore, is training in not only what appear to be soundly developed schemes, but also in critical and thoughtful appraisals of the schemes and their implementation. We should be helping practitioners to develop their use of published schemes, but in a careful and critically evaluated manner. Moreover, training should be available to a wider range of workers than in the past – nursery nurses, for example, are an important resource, yet rarely receive further training once qualified.

Second, there is a need to develop joint training initiatives, both between different professionals, and between professionals and parents. The Department of Health and Social Security has carried out pilot studies of such schemes. One simple, yet very important, finding from the Sheffield initiative already mentioned was the lack of awareness of participants even of the numbers of their colleagues in other professional groups in the locality. Beyond this, of course, is the need to develop an understanding of what each can do and, more important, how service delivery from all the professionals can be optimized.

This must also include parents. As I have suggested above, the most effective way of parents and professionals collaborating is still to be determined. There is no doubt it will vary from person to person. We should be training ourselves to work collaboratively but, as with the programmes, we must also build in flexibility and critical evaluation.

CONCLUSION

Children with special needs in the pre-school age range must still be considered with respect to the needs of all children. This chapter argues for an approach which grows out of the regular provision for children at this age – the resources, curriculum, and record keeping.

In some ways this is at variance with recent developments in special education. Over the past ten to twenty years or more there has been a focus on special education being different in kind not degree. Teachers in mainstream used to believe that they could not provide what a child needed, but that special school teachers could. The revelation in the Warnock Report[11] that only a quarter of those teachers in England and Wales had extra qualifications surprised many. The findings of recent research and the development of professional practice has suggested that the appropriate experiences and arrangements for children with special needs are very similar to those of their peers.

What distinguishes the provision for pre-school children with special needs is a greater appreciation of and attention to detail. The balance is tilted towards more active intervention by adults, with more specific learning objectives for the children, and less reliance on leaving the child to develop as a result of his or her own self-guidance. Play requires more structure, social encounters need planning, and parental involvement must be arranged more specifically. Parents should be true partners, not clients, or 'experts'. The emphasis should be on determining the appropriate aims and objectives for the child, in conjunction with parents, arranging suitable programmes of intervention, usually involving several professionals and parents, and monitoring the child's development closely.

REFERENCES

1. Osborn, H. and Milbank, J. (1987) *The Effects of Early Education*, Oxford: Clarendon Press.
2. Guralnick, M. and Bennett, F. (1987) *The Effectiveness of Early Intervention for At-Risk and Handicapped Children*, London: Academic Press.
3. Harris, J. (1984) 'Early language intervention programmes: an update', *Association for Child Psychology and Psychiatry Newsletter*, 6 (2): 2–20.
4. Lunt, I. and Sheppard, J. (1986) *Participating Parents*, Leicester: British Psychological Society.
5. Tizard, B. and Hughes, M. (1984) *Young Children Learning*, London: Fontana.
6. Daly, B., Addington, J., Kerfoot, S., and Sigston, A. (Eds.) (1985) *Portage: The Importance of Parents*, Windsor: NFER-Nelson.
7. Lindsay, G. and Desforges, M. (1986) 'Integrated nurseries for children with special educational needs', *British Journal of Special Education*, 13: 63–6.
8. Lindsay, G. (Ed.) (1984) *Screening for Children with Special Needs*, London: Croom Helm.
9. Lindsay, G. (Ed.) (1985) *Integration: Practice, Possibilities and Pitfalls*, Leicester: British Psychological Society.
10. Guralnick, M. (1976) 'The value of integrating handicapped and non-handicapped pre-school children', *American Journal of Orthopsychiatry*, 46: 236–43.

11. Department of Education and Science (1978) *Special Educational Needs* (The Warnock Report), London: HMSO.

9.3

INTEGRATED EDUCATION

DAVID MITCHELL

No longer is it seen as appropriate for children with special educational needs to be educated in segregated settings. No longer are such children taught exclusively by special educators. Special education is now the responsibility of every teacher in every school. The past decade or so has seen children with special educational needs being moved out of segregated special schools into special classes or units within regular schools, and out of special classes into regular classes. This process of integration, or mainstreaming, is not only changing the character of special education, but it is also posing one of the most dramatic challenges facing education in general as the twentieth century draws to a close.

Within the Western world, at least, this trend towards integrating children with special educational needs into regular education settings reflects two main factors. First, it is argued that both disabled and non-disabled children can obtain benefits from closer association with each other. Second, it is now generally accepted in most countries that disabled children have a right to be educated alongside their non-disabled peers.

This chapter is divided into two main sections. In the first of these, various issues concerning integration will be analysed. After consideration of the concept, a case will be developed for the adoption of the notion of 'integrated education'. Forms of integrated education will then be discussed, and the relevant sections of the Education Act (1981) will be summarized. The second section will present a series of propositions regarding ways in which integrated education can be facilitated. The underlying theme of this section is that integrated education should be seen in systems terms, depending for its success not only on what goes on in classrooms and schools, but also on the level of commitment from the broad educational system, and from society as a whole.

ISSUES IN INTEGRATION

The concept of integration

The concept of integration takes various forms and rests on a range of assumptions. At the broadest level, it may be defined as the process of educating children with special educational needs in settings where they have the maximum association, consistent with their interests, with other children.[1] In some countries, for example, the USA, Canada, and Australia, a distinction is made between the terms integration and mainstreaming. The former term usually refers to the broad practice of locating children with special educational needs in regular schools, while the latter refers to such children spending a substantial proportion of their time (at least 50 per cent) in regular classes, and receiving specialist assistance either in that setting or through being withdrawn. In the United Kingdom, however, the term integration is normally used to refer to both practices. That approach will also be followed in this chapter, with mainstreaming being used only where a writer makes specific reference to it.

The above definition gives consideration to two important and inter-related elements of integration: its *process* ('maximum association with other children') and its *outcome* ('their interests'). Strong arguments to justify integration can be built around both of these elements. From a process perspective, it can be argued that in societies which accept the principles of democracy and social justice, children with special educational needs have a fundamental right to participate in their communities and to be educated alongside other children.[2] This right is in accord with the notion of 'normalization', first articulated in Scandinavia in the 1960s, in which there is recognition of disabled persons' rights to participate in society and to live under conditions as similar as possible to those of other citizens.[3] It also reflects the civil rights movement in the USA, in which principles that were developed to enhance the status of people from disadvantaged backgrounds were extended to people with handicaps. This eventually culminated in PL 94–142, the Education for All Handicapped Children Act 1975, which has had a major impact on special education in most developed countries.

From an outcome perspective, the focus shifts from moral to empirical issues. Now the question becomes one of evaluating how well integration contributes to outcomes which are in the best interests of children with special educational needs. Hence, the proponents of integration argue that it leads to improved academic and social performances in such children. Unfortunately, however, the research provides only equivocal support for this assumption, most studies indicating that there are few differences in the academic or social performances of children placed in regular and special classes.[4] Much of this research is marred, however, by methodological problems. For example, the bulk of it has been carried out with mildly handicapped children, many models of integration have not been researched, and matched groups of children have rarely been studied. Much of the research, too, may be time-based and culture-specific.

Ultimately, of course, the concern for all those involved in educating young children with special educational needs must be to ensure their fullest development as individuals and as members of the society in which they live. Future research should focus on the extent to which integration, in the form outlined in this chapter, contributes to this goal in a specific educational and societal context.

Integrated education

In order to give expression to both the process and the outcome elements of integration, the term *integrated education* will generally be used in the remainder of this chapter. Such a term carries with it two major implications. First, it suggests that educators should see the placement of children with special educational needs in regular schools as being but one component of an appropriate educational programme. Many other adaptations are necessary if such children are to receive an education which is in their interests (see below for a discussion of this theme). Second, the term has the connotation that the distinctions at present made between special and general education should eventually disappear. Integrated education carries with it the obligation of all schools to accept their responsibility for providing an appropriate education for all children.

In the event of the outcomes of integrated education being negative, however, what should be the response of educators? Should it give way to a new wave of segregated education? Such a reaction would mean compromising the moral right of children with special educational needs to have access to integration. The other alternative is to accept the Swedish approach to handicap. During the past decade or so, Sweden has increasingly adopted the view that handicap is not a characteristic of a person with an impairment, but is, instead, the relation between the impairment and the environment of the person.[5] This approach has also been skilfully argued by Sarason and Doris,[6] who have described handicap as a 'social invention'. As such, it reflects the transactions that take place between an individual, a social context, and the culturally determined values that characterize that context at any particular time. More specifically, in a school setting the labelling of a child as handicapped is often less reflective of qualities possessed by the child than it is of the interactions between the child, the personality of the teacher, his or her teaching strategies, the curriculum, and the ethos of the school. This notion finds support in the evidence that some schools successfully meet the needs of children who would at others be labelled as handicapped or maladjusted.[7] This 'transactional' approach suggests that when an outcome of integrated education on a child with special educational needs is negative, the responsibility is on the educators to modify handicapping environments and not to 'blame' the child.

Thus, it is argued that integrated education is not only a moral right to which children with special educational needs can legitimately lay claim, but also that the primary onus is on educators to work within those parameters to achieve the best possible educational outcomes for such children. This is neither more nor less than the obligation educators have towards children not deemed to have special needs.

As educators adapt their organization, attitudes, and methods to children with special educational needs, they are also faced with the tasks of weighing up the relative merits of competing rights. Three moral dilemmas are of particular importance.[8] First, there is the question of whether the right of a child with special needs to be educated alongside her or his peers should take precedence over the right of the latter to receive an education 'unimpeded' by children who may call upon a disproportionate amount of teacher time or who may slow down the pace of instruction. Second, teachers are faced with an even more personal moral dilemma: should they accept students with special educational needs into their regular classes when they consider there are insufficient human or material resources to provide effectively for them? This question becomes even more acute when it is recognized that without adequate resources the opportunities afforded such children by being placed in regular educational settings may be reduced, even negated. A third moral dilemma is posed by two competing principles: the right to integrated education and the right to exercise choice. Thus, if children with special educational needs and/or their parents prefer their education to take place in segregated settings, should this be permitted? For example, persuasive arguments have been put forward for exercising caution in mainstreaming deaf children into regular education. Thus, it is pointed out that because of their separate language (signing) and distinct social networks, deaf people should be viewed more as an ethnic group with a distinct culture than as a handicap group. As such, it is argued deaf children should be given the opportunity to preserve their group identity and to have access to role models of successful deaf persons.[9] The challenge to educators is to develop an approach to integrated education for deaf children which is based on a multicultural rather than an assimilation model. If this is accepted, the next question becomes whether other categories of children with special educational needs should be given similar opportunities to develop or maintain their own identity and culture. If so, how can these opportunities be provided in integrated educational settings?

Forms of integrated education

Integrated education includes within its ambit a range of provisions. The Warnock Committee,[10] for example, distinguished between three levels of integration: locational, social, and functional. In locational integration, the minimum requirement is that children with special educational needs are physically present in the same buildings or campus as other children for at least some of their education. Social integration refers to both groups of children having significant opportunities to interact with each other in regular classes, on either a part-time or full-time basis. Functional integration includes opportunities for students with special educational needs not only to engage in social interaction with their age-mates, but also for them to be taught skills and content from an appropriately modified form of the normal curriculum.

Within the third of these arrangements, functional integration, two main models of integrated education may be identified, with several variants in each.[11] First, provisions may be made for children with special educational needs within regular classes, with support services being provided for them and/or their classroom teachers in the classroom. This may take the form either of a) resource personnel working directly with the children (for example providing specialized help for individual children for particular lessons, interpreters for deaf children, or orientation and mobility assistants for blind children), or of b) resource personnel advising the classroom teacher in a consultancy role (for example dealing with curriculum adaptations or the physical arrangements of the classroom). Second, children with special educational needs may be placed in regular classes for varying periods of time, and withdrawn for individual or group work offered by a teacher or other specialist personnel in a resource room or special class within or outside the regular school. This withdrawal may be either a) on an 'as necessary' basis (for example when a learning-disabled child has difficulty with a particular concept or skill), or b) regularly scheduled for certain subjects or therapies (for example physiotherapy, speech therapy, work experience).

The Education Act (1981)

In England and Wales, the Education Act (1981), which came into force in April 1983, gives partial expression to the philosophy of integrated education as outlined earlier in this chapter. Of particular relevance to this theme, the Act imposes three principal duties on educators.[12] First, it provides that where a local education authority arranges special educational provision for a child this must be provided in an ordinary school. This is a conditional rather than an absolute right, however, as it is subject to a) the views of the child's parents; b) required special education being provided; c) the provision of efficient education for other children; and d) the efficient use of resources. The latter two caveats make this Act considerably weaker than PL 94–142, the corresponding American legislation. Second, the Act provides that, so far as is reasonably practicable, teachers should ensure that children with special educational needs should be assisted to engage in the activities of the school together with other children. Third, it is the duty of the school governors to ensure that children with special educational needs have special education provisions made for them, and that their needs are made known to all those likely to teach them.

FACILITATING INTEGRATED EDUCATION

While integrated education is now widely recognized as being a good idea that can be made to work, in most countries where it is accepted in principle there are wide variations in its practice. These variations reflect a complex amalgam of factors, including community attitudes, political forces, judicial processes, parent advocacy, administrative leadership, resource allocation, and teachers' attitudes and skills. What follows is an attempt to crystallize the essential components for the successful integrated education of children with special educational needs. The focus will be on mainstreaming such children into regular schools. For the purposes of clarity and brevity, criteria will be expressed in the form of propositions. Space limitations preclude acknowledging the sources of all of the criteria, but in general they have been developed from the writer's observations of integrated education in several countries, and from sources such as those indicated in the references.

The overriding assumption is that the success of integrated education depends upon it being viewed as part of a system which extends from the classroom to the broader society. Accordingly, the criteria are arranged in the following order: teaching strategies and classroom management, curriculum, school policy and management, teacher education, policies of the broad education system, and community attitudes towards persons with disabilities.

Teaching strategies and classroom management

To facilitate integrated education, teachers in classrooms in which children with special educational needs are placed exhibit behaviour such as the following:

1. They act as appropriate role models for other children's attitudes and behaviours towards children with special educational needs.
2. They set a tone towards such children which is likely to enhance their self confidence.

3. They organize and evaluate their teaching in such a way that the individual learning needs of all children in the class are taken into account. For example, they ensure that texts are written at the appropriate level of readability, and that they give consideration to the needs of many children for practical, experiential approaches to learning.

4. The physical environment of the classroom is organized to accommodate to children with special educational needs. This includes such matters as ensuring appropriate seating arrangements for children with hearing difficulties, appropriate lighting for visually impaired children, and adequate physical access and furniture for physically disabled children.[13]

5. Appropriate adaptations are made for children with special educational needs to take tests and examinations. For example, a visually impaired student may require large print, or more time to complete a test, and a child with cerebral palsy may require oral testing, or a computer-assisted approach. A greater emphasis is placed on criterion-referenced tests.

6. The teachers enter into collegial relationships with special education consultants and support staff, and effectively use ancillary class time.

The curriculum

The curriculum of the school has the following features:

1. It is accessible to all children (see Chapter 9.4) and, as such, reflects the diverse and common desires, aspirations, interests, and backgrounds of all pupils.[14] (Conversely, special educational needs are created when a curriculum is not accessible to all children.[15]) This criterion appears to be met in Sweden, where a curriculum for comprehensive compulsory schools (Lgr 80) has been in force since 1983.

2. It includes a concern for assisting children with special educational needs to develop social skills, including an ability to engage in and respond to socially appropriate non-verbal behaviour. Teachers also take steps to reduce or eliminate disruptive behaviour in such children.

3. There is a concern for assisting non-disabled children to develop strategies for working with children with special educational needs in integrated educational settings. To this end, co-operative learning[16] and 'buddy' systems may be employed.

4. It includes a significant concern for assisting children with special educational needs to participate in community life and to make the transition to post-secondary-school years. This criterion is met in Madison, Wisconsin, where, for example, a large number of community job sites are used to teach severely handicapped students practical vocational skills, and the school district employs transition specialists to help place severely handi-

capped school leavers in regular jobs – all from the base of regular schools.[17] In Sweden, too, there is an effective transition programme, with the compulsory school curriculum giving prominence to working life orientation and to work experience. Job opportunities are provided for unemployed 18–20-year-olds (18–25 in the case of mentally handicapped people) in supervised 'youth teams'.[18]

School policy and management

The success of integrated education is, to a large extent, contingent upon school policies and management practices such as the following:

1. The school has an explicit philosophy of valuing and accommodating to differences in children, and it accepts that children with special educational needs have the right to lead as normal an existence as possible in their local communities. It is vital that the school principal (headteacher) actively supports and articulates this philosophy.

2. The school communicates its policies towards children with special educational needs to parents, children, and staff. For example, it has an effective procedure for inducting new staff members into their responsibilities towards such children.

3. The school regularly reviews the effects on children with special educational needs of policies and practices in all areas of its work. In particular, it takes account of the impact on these children of decisions made in such areas as school organization, curriculum, and the allocation of space, time, and personnel resources.

4. The school has a senior person on its staff, a designated teacher, whose major responsibility is for the welfare and educational progress of children with special educational needs. In Victoria, Australia, for example, a 1984 report on integration in education recommended the appointment of 'integration teachers' to all schools with 350 or more students. These teachers were expected to develop, implement, and evaluate teaching programmes in collaboration with regular teachers, and to co-ordinate 'integration aides' and other support staff.[19]

5. Parents are closely involved in all major decisions regarding their children's integrated education, and are given opportunities to pursue partnership relationships with school staff in designing and implementing teaching programmes for their children. In this consultative process, due consideration is given to ethnic and cultural differences.

6. There is an effective system of liaison between the school and the other schools or agencies from which it draws its students, as well as with those schools and agencies to which its students progress. An example of such

a programme is in Banbury, Oxfordshire, where secondary schools, their 'feeder' primary schools, and resource personnel, such as educational psychologists, developed a co-ordinated system of identifying and teaching children with special educational needs.[20]

7. The school has a comprehensive method for identifying children with special educational needs as early as possible, with a view to providing them with appropriate integrated education. In implementing this policy, precautions are taken to minimize the stigmatizing effects of labelling.

8. The administration of the school adjusts the size of classes in which children with special educational needs are placed, and ensures that such children are distributed around several classrooms within the school.

9. The principal areas of the school are fully accessible to physically disabled persons (parents and staff, as well as children). This means, for example, that there is an adequate provision of ramps, adapted toilets, and guide rails.

10. The allocation of duties and the lines of communication among the various staff who work with children with special educational needs are clearly specified. Normally, this means that regular classroom teachers carry the primary responsibility for the integrated education of these children, a principle that can cause initial problems to special educators as they relinquish their responsibility for children who are being returned to the mainstream. (Where children with special educational needs are being *retained* in the mainstream, this division of responsibility is less problematic.)

Teacher education

To prepare teachers to work effectively in integrated education, in-service education and pre-service education prepares all teachers for this aspect of their professional responsibilities. It seeks to achieve this by such means as the following:

1. Courses give consideration to the rights of disabled persons to normalization, in particular to integrated education.

2. They provide students with a broad knowledge of the psychological, social, and physical characteristics of children with special educational needs whom they are likely to encounter in integrated education.

3. They provide students with information on the range and function of community support services and resources.

4. Teaching practices in integrated educational settings are arranged.

5. Students are prepared for working co-operatively with other professionals on the school staff and from outside agencies.

6. All curriculum and pedagogy courses include consideration of children with special educational needs.
7. There is a concern for planning and implementing individual teaching programmes.

One of the most comprehensive national systems for training teachers to work in special education is that of Norway.[21] There, a high proportion of pre-school and primary school teachers include a substantial study of special education in their pre-service preparation – either by including a six-month period of their three-year course studying in this area, or by completing an additional one year course.

The education system

For integrated education to stand a chance of being successfully implemented on a large scale, two broad conditions at the 'education system' level are met:

1. The broad education system has an explicit and unambiguous commitment to providing integrated education. As noted earlier, in the United Kingdom the Education Act 1981 provides only qualified support for integration. This is in contrast with the United States, where PL 94–142 requires that any federally-funded special education programme for handicapped children must be delivered in the most normal or 'least restrictive environment', to the greatest extent possible in the company of their non-handicapped peers. In Italy, Law 118 of 1971 requires that all compulsory schooling for handicapped children must be provided in the ordinary classes of state schools, while Denmark has subscribed to a similar principle since 1969.
2. The education system's commitment to integrated education is reflected in its provision of adequate resources for its policy to be implemented. These resources are sufficient to enable the services outlined above to be provided on an adequate basis. In particular, there is funding to cover physical adaptations to schools, specialist equipment, ancillary aides, access to specialist support services, teacher education, and the provision of information on children with special educational needs. With respect to the last point, the province of Alberta in Canada has set up 'education response centres' which include among their functions a clearing-house role in which information on special education can be accessed by telephone, electronic mail, or direct use of reference centres.

The community

The wider community accepts the rights of persons with disabilities to participate fully in its affairs and it expresses this in its legislation. Thus, the Canadian Charter of Rights and Freedoms includes the following clause on equality rights, which came into effect in 1985: 'Every individual is equal before and under the law . . . without discrimination based on race, national or ethnic origin, colour, religion, sex, age or mental or physical disability'. Principles such as these open the way for non-discriminatory access to appropriate educational, employment, and leisure opportunities, and access to appropriately adapted generic support services.

CONCLUSION

Integrated education involves educating children with special educational needs in settings where they have the maximum association, consistent with their needs, with other children. For it to succeed in these terms, integrated education must go beyond the mere placement of such children alongside their non-disabled peers. Rather, it must be seen as an approach which has quite profound effects on the way in which educational systems are organized and administered, and on the way in which classroom teachers and special educators design curricula and teach children. Integrated education must be seen, too, as existing within a broad social and political framework; the principles that underpin it do not stop at the school gate. Ultimately, it reflects what should be a societal concern for opening rather than closing doors on persons with disabilities. Integrated education is a moral imperative for those who respect the right of those with special needs to lead as normal a life as possible. To deny this right is to create handicap.

REFERENCES

1. Mitchell, J. W. and Mitchell, D. R. (1987) 'Integration/mainstreaming', in D. R. Mitchell and N. N. Singh (Eds.) *Exceptional Children in New Zealand*, Palmerston North: The Dunmore Press.
2. Booth, T. (1983) 'Integrating special education', in T. Booth and P. Potts (Eds.) *Integrating Special Education*, Oxford: Basil Blackwell.
3. Nirje, B. (1969) 'The normalisation principle and its human management implications', in R. Kugel and W. Wolfensberger (Eds.) *Changing Patterns in Residential Services for the Mentally Retarded*, Washington: President's Committee on Mental Retardation.
4. Gottlieb, J., Aller, M., and Gottlieb, B. W. (1983) 'Mainstreaming mentally retarded children', in J. L. Matson and J. A. Mulick (Eds.) *Handbook of Mental Retardation*, New York: Pergamon.
5. Government of Sweden (1986) 'The education of the handicapped adolescent: Swedish national report', Paper 86.15, CERI, OECD.
6. Sarason, S. B. and Doris, J. (1979) *Educational Handicap, Public Policy and Social History*, New York: The Free Press.
7. Galloway, D. (1985) *Schools, Pupils and Special Educational Needs*, London: Croom Helm.

8. Mitchell and Mitchell, op. cit.
9. Booth, op. cit.; Rodda, M., Grove, C., and Finch, B. M. (1986) 'Mainstreaming and the education of deaf students', *The Alberta Journal of Educational Research*, *32*: 140–153.
10. Department of Education and Science (1978) *Special Educational Needs* (The Warnock Report), London: HMSO.
11. Fish, J. (1985) *Special Education: The Way Ahead*, Milton Keynes: Open University Press.
12. Cox, B. (1987) *The Law of Special Educational Needs*, London: Croom Helm.
13. Hodgson, A., Clunies-Ross, L., and Hegarty, S. (1984) *Learning Together: Teaching Pupils With Special Educational Needs in the Ordinary School*, Windsor: NFER-Nelson.
14. Booth, op. cit.; Booth, T., Potts, P., and Swann, W. (1987) *Preventing Difficulties in Learning: Curricula for All*, Oxford: Basil Blackwell.
15. Government of Sweden, op. cit.
16. Johnson, R., Johnson, D. W., De Weerdt, N., Lyons, V., and Zaidman, B. (1983) 'Integrating severely adaptively handicapped seventh grade students into constructive relationships with nonhandicapped peers in science class', *American Journal of Mental Deficiency*, *87*: 611–18.
17. Taylor, S. J. (1982) 'Madison Metropolitan Public Schools – a model integrated program for children with severe disabilities', Syracuse University: Special Education Resource Center.
18. Government of Sweden, op. cit.
19. Victorian Government (1984) *Integration in Victorian Education*, Melbourne: Victorian Government.
20. Gulliford, R. (1986) 'The education of the handicapped adolescent: Integration and training of teachers', Paper 84.02, CERI, OECD.
21. ibid.

THE CURRICULUM IN SPECIAL EDUCATION

SEAMUS HEGARTY

The curriculum in special education has to be seen in relation to the normal curriculum – whatever form that may take at a particular point in time. Pupils with special needs are not totally different from their peers, and neither is the education that should be offered to them. Special education has too long been bedevilled by isolation from the mainstream of schooling. Even though as far back as 1929 the Wood Committee urged a view of the special school as no more than 'a helpful variation of the ordinary school', the prevailing ethos has been one of separate development: once pupils enter a special school they seldom return to ordinary schools, and the work they engage in there often has little connection with the work being done in neighbouring ordinary schools.

This separation between the two sectors is reflected in many indicators – resourcing, staff career patterns, community links. It is particularly evident in respect of the curriculum. Curriculum development in special schools has tended to proceed quite separately from curriculum development in ordinary schools, and until recently many special schools have not been touched by the mainstream curriculum debates.

The Education Act 1981, which is the major legislative statement in England and Wales relating to special education, is quite clear that there should be links between the two sectors. It does not speak of special education but rather of 'special educational provision', which it defines as 'educational provision which is additional to, or otherwise different from, the educational provision made generally for children in schools maintained by the local education authority concerned'. In other words, the curriculum in special education – along with all other aspects of educational provision – has to be seen in the context of the mainstream curriculum, and not as something quite separate.

The purpose of this chapter is to set out some basic ideas regarding the curriculum – what it encompasses in general terms and how the curriculum in special education is distinctive – and outline some of the implications for practice. In particular, it examines the ways in which curriculum content and teaching approaches have to be modified in respect of pupils with special educational needs. Finally, it considers the impact of the new information technologies, since they have major potential for contributing to the curriculum in special education.

DEFINING THE CURRICULUM

The curriculum is concerned with all aspects of a school's life and work. It is not confined to school subjects or to what is taught in a literal sense. Schools tend to specify their curriculum in terms of the range of subjects on offer – mathematics, history, Spanish, and so on – or in terms of an alternative breakdown into areas such as language development, numeracy, motor development, and independence skills. This is understandable since it offers a convenient starting point for examining the learning experiences provided by the school.

It is only a starting point however. Teaching and learning take place within a context of purpose and intention. The same academic content or activity may serve different purposes, and simply describing the content of a lesson does not necessarily specify the learning that takes place within it. For instance, pupils may engage in discussion in order to practise skills of oral communication, to promote self-confidence, to develop social skills of turn-taking, listening, and interrupting appropriately, or to deepen understanding of the matter under discussion. We need to know which objective, or set of objectives, is in mind before we can say what the learning experience is.

It is necessary also to know how the teaching is conducted. Teachers can teach in different ways, drawing on a wide variety of teaching methods and resources. Again, the particular selection made determines critically the nature of the learning experience. Finally, the whole process takes place within a context of assessment and evaluation – assessment of the learning achieved by individual pupils, and evaluation of the teaching programme as a whole.

This leads to a definition of the curriculum as a *process whereby pupils are assisted toward desired learning*. This entails four interrelated components:

– aims and objectives
– content or learning activities
– teaching methods and resources
– assessment and evaluation.

Too often the curriculum is seen primarily in terms of content, with the result that the formal syllabus is given undue importance. If the aims and objectives are not clearly in view, it is very difficult to provide a rationale for a teaching programme, or to match teaching method and subject matter in a coherent way. Rational curriculum planning has to encompass all four components in an integrated way.

Figure 1 The curriculum in context

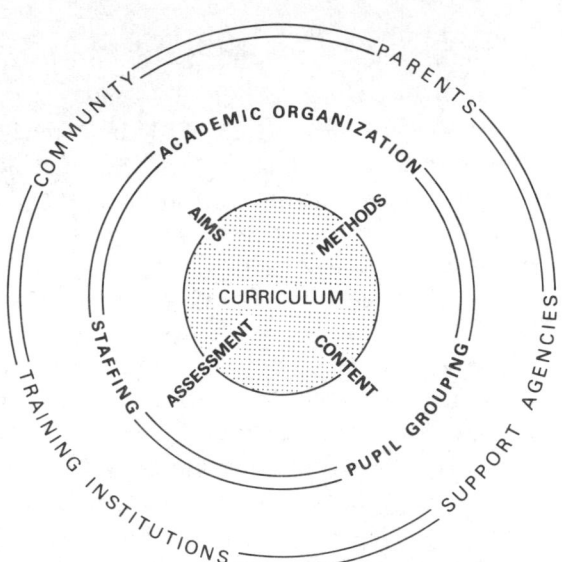

The curriculum must be located within even broader contexts, however. Figure 1 outlines some of the factors that impinge on it both within the school and outside it. A key context is provided by the academic organization of the school – pupil grouping, structure of the school day, timetable – since this provides the essential framework within which the curriculum is delivered in practice. The curriculum is implemented by the school staff, so one has to take account of the number and type of staff, their professional competence, and the way in which they are deployed.

From outside the school there are numerous factors that bear on the school curriculum, both directly and through their influence on school-level factors. These include teacher training institutions and the other agencies responsible for securing teachers' professional development through initial and in-service training. Local authority support services have a major responsibility for both direct and indirect curriculum support. While parents are often afforded a negligible role in either developing or implementing the curriculum, they can make a significant contribution to both aspects, particularly in the case of pupils with special needs.

WHY IS THE CURRICULUM IN SPECIAL EDUCATION DIFFERENT?

One of the widely quoted lines from the Warnock Report[1] is its assertion that 'the purpose of education for all children is the same ... but the help that individual children need in progressing towards [the goals] will be different' (1.4). This is true of all pupils, whether they have special needs, exceptional talents or whatever. Indeed, the document produced by Her Majesty's Inspectorate on the curriculum from five to sixteen,[2] which offers a comprehensive curriculum framework addressed to all schools, takes its statement of the aims of education from the same paragraph of the Warnock Report:

> to enlarge a child's knowledge, experience and imaginative understanding, and thus his awareness of moral values and capacity for enjoyment; and secondly, to enable him to enter the world after formal education is over as an active participant in society and a responsible contributor to it, capable of achieving as much independence as possible.

The significance of this is that it implies a single curriculum framework for all pupils and holds out the promise of locating curricular provision for pupils who have special needs within this common framework.

Where then do curricular differences come from? Why is there a curriculum in special education conceived of as something separate from the mainstream curriculum? The reason for these differences can be set out in terms of the elements of the curriculum given above. Such an account will also begin to specify the nature of the differences.

First, the aims of education may be the same for all pupils, but the objectives by which they are translated into actual teaching and learning can and do vary. The aim of enlarging a child's knowledge must be achieved in terms of the child's existing knowledge and experience, interests, capacity to retain information and gain new insights, and other factors relating to that child. All of this necessitates a set of teaching objectives specific to the child.

Where pupils with special needs are concerned, the tendency has been to assume too large a degree of common needs, leading to curricula shaped around particular handicapping conditions. There is now a greater recognition of the individual needs of children, and these needs tend to be assessed in more specific detail, with the result that many pupils are likely to be following individualized educational programmes. There are still clusters of objectives held in common – many pupils, especially those described as having moderate learning difficulties, have a common need for more extensive work on the basics of reading than their age peers; pupils with hearing impairment need specific instruction in language and auditory training; pupils with severe learning difficulties need to follow detailed programmes in areas such as self-care and communication.

Second, the content of educational programmes and the learning activities that children engage in must reflect the objectives laid down for them. If a particular set of objectives is established for a given pupil, an appropriate selection of learning activities must be made. This can lead in practice to programmes which are very different from each other.

A Department of Education and Science document on the curriculum in special schools[3] proposes three broad approaches to the curriculum, distinguished in large measure by content differences. The three approaches are labelled: mainstream plus support; modified; and developmental. The emphasis in the first approach is on giving access to the mainstream curriculum, but content differences are envisaged especially in subjects which have a practical element; some pupils too will progress more slowly than peers, so that material must be presented at a slower rate. Pupils following a modified curriculum would not be expected to cover the full extent of the secondary curriculum – probably no foreign language, science as a combined general subject rather than as three separate subjects, and strong emphasis on personal and social development and on subjects such as home economics. A developmental curriculum, intended for pupils with severe learning difficulties, would be based on the acquisition of communication, self-help, mobility and social skills, very basic literacy and numeracy, and an understanding of the world about them. Variation in curriculum content can of course be described in other ways, and an alternative model is described below.

A third source of curricular variation is the different teaching methods and resources that teachers consider necessary to achieve particular objectives with given pupils. Teachers may need to modify the approaches they use with other pupils and, occasionally, draw on techniques which are either specific to special education or used primarily within it. Likewise, textbooks, worksheets, and other resources may have to be modified, and some quite specialized resources may be necessary. This too is discussed in more detail below.

A further source of differentiation comes from organizational factors. The global setting – special school, unit, ordinary school – within which the curriculum is delivered affects it in various ways. For example, a special school may allow for teaching to be planned around individuals' special needs in a comprehensive way, whereas an ordinary school may provide broader curriculum opportunities and readier access to 'normal' activities. Likewise, within a given setting, organizational factors such as the timetable and the way in which pupils are grouped for teaching purposes are important determinants of the learning activities that take place.

MODIFICATION OF CURRICULUM CONTENT

The content of the curriculum on offer to pupils with special needs varies widely. The DES three-part model has been referred to already. A study conducted at the National Foundation for Educational Research on efforts to modify the curriculum in mainstream settings provides a more detailed account of the range of variation in practice.[4] This is described in terms of a continuum running parallel to those used in describing schools' organizational patterns. (The latter go from full participation in an ordinary school at one end to segregation in a special school at the other.) With a notional mainstream curriculum followed by the main pupil body at one end, and a totally separate curriculum for pupils with severe and complex needs at the other, this continuum is described in terms of five points:

1. mainstream curriculum
2. mainstream curriculum with some modification
3. mainstream curriculum with significant modification
4. special curriculum with additions
5. special curriculum

1. Mainstream curriculum
Pupils do the same work in the same teaching groups as their peers. In the study this usually concerned pupils who were either physically handicapped or visually impaired. Efforts might be made, by modifying the teaching approach, to enhance access to the content, but the content itself was not changed.

2. Mainstream curriculum with some modification
Some pupils with sensory impairment followed essentially the same curriculum as their peers apart from modifications related directly to their impairment. Thus some visually impaired pupils learned typing or braille, physically handicapped pupils developed skills which compensated for specific motor deficiencies, and hearing impaired pupils engaged in extra work on language. These alternative activities sometimes necessitated omitting an area of the mainstream curriculum; hearing impaired pupils, for instance, were frequently obliged to drop foreign languages.

3. Mainstream curriculum with significant modification
This was usually for pupils with moderate learning difficulties, or those with severe hearing losses, and involved a unit base or a significant amount of withdrawal from mainstream lessons. The most common pattern was to supplement mainstream English and mathematics lessons with additional work on a withdrawal basis or, alternatively, to provide language and number work on an entirely separate basis. Depending on how much supplementary time was involved, some other subjects were dropped or given less time and attention.

4. *Special curriculum with additions*
5. *Special curriculum*

These were fundamentally different from the others in that they were detached from the mainstream curriculum. Where the others sought to make as much of the mainstream curriculum available as possible, while taking account of individual needs and capacities, these took pupils' special needs as their starting point, and regarded the mainstream as a secondary consideration, if indeed they took account of it at all. The pupils in question were those with severe and complex learning difficulties. They tended to be on individual programmes, with a heavy concentration on basic work in language and number, instruction in social and motor co-ordination skills and, where appropriate, speech therapy and physiotherapy.

MODIFYING TEACHING

Whatever the curriculum content, pupils with special needs require extra help in gaining access to it. By definition indeed, they are pupils for whom the educational facilities generally available are not adequate. This calls for modifications to the teaching approaches and classroom resources in common use. They may also require approaches and resources not used with other pupils.

An essential prerequisite in all cases is adequate assessment (see Chapter 9.1). Teaching pupils with special needs requires careful planning and a close match between teaching approach and learning need. The scattergun approach, whereby teaching is directed at some presumed average range of ability, will not suffice and has to be replaced by a precisely targeted approach. Assessment is the key to this. Pupils' programmes of work must be drawn up on the basis of comprehensive, detailed information on individuals' strengths and weaknesses, the nature and likely effect of any handicapping conditions, and any other factors likely to bear on their educational progress. Medical and psychological perspectives should be taken into account, but the central concern has to be educational. Assessment must be curriculum-led: the information collected is for the purpose of shaping pupils' learning activities in the most productive ways. Care must be taken to ensure that all relevant information is obtained, and that whatever information is collected is used to promote pupil learning.

The most straightforward case, in principle at least, is teaching pupils with physical or sensory impairments who fall within the normal range of ability. The emphasis is on access and finding appropriate modes of communication. The teacher has to present classwork in ways that are accessible to pupils whatever their limitations; the pupils in turn must be able to record their work and, if necessary, present set work in a form that is accessible to the teacher. Practical work in science, for example, may need to be modified so that pupils with limited hand movement or control can do experiments. Tactile maps can be used in geography lessons with blind pupils, as can solid objects in mathematics. Teaching academically able pupils who are visually impaired is in fact a considerable challenge to teachers who make extensive use of visual stimuli, whether they be blackboard, overhead transparency, or audiovisual materials. As well as making greater use of concrete objects and providing tactile/kinaesthetic experiences, teachers may need to use language with greater care, and take account of the fact that the pupils have reduced, or no, access to a major source of perceptual input.

Pupils have the reverse problem as it were. They must be able to take notes, organize their work, and present it for assessment and feedback. There are various possibilities, depending on a pupil's impairments and the resources available – braille, tape-recording, adapted keyboards. Teaching and classroom organization may need to be modified to ensure that any such forms of alternative communication fit into lessons unobtrusively; special arrangements may be necessary too in order to mark pupils' work.

While presenting material in alternative ways is important, teaching these pupils is more than a matter of providing access to 'normal' curriculum content. Pupils' cognitive development may have been affected by their sensory limitations. There is in any case likely to be some interaction between perceptual input and the cognitive activity to which it gives rise. Thus, spatial problems as in geometry or design may pose particular difficulty for pupils with impaired vision. Teachers should be aware of these factors and know when they need to seek expert advice.

Pupils with sensory impairments illustrate one, relatively clearcut, form of modification to teaching that may be required. However difficult in practice the modifications may be, these pupils are a special case in terms of modifying teaching approach. We need to turn to pupils with learning difficulties to see the full range of modifications that are necessary. A general account would encompass the whole process of classroom teaching and would need to cover: the way in which the classroom is organized; lesson preparation; presenting material to the class; interacting with pupils to facilitate learning; monitoring progress; and using other workers in the classroom. It is only possible here to give a brief account of the issues.

Classroom organization in the sense of physical layout has to do with the seating and grouping of pupils and, in the case of some pupils, with acoustics and lighting. The teacher has to manage the physical space available in accordance with the teaching approach(es) in use – small-group work, team teaching, use of flexible groupings, and so on. When pupils with special needs are integrated into a mainstream setting, a balance must be struck between their need for individual attention and their need to be physically part of the class. Where wheelchair users are concerned, mobility is a primary consideration –

for the wheelchair users themselves and for other pupils – and careful use of space may be necessary, especially in small classrooms. In the case of pupils with sensory impairments, there are various accommodation requirements – induction loops, enhanced lighting, and so on – that must be seen to, whether the classroom is in an ordinary or a special school.

In principle, lesson preparation is no different for teaching pupils with special needs than for other pupils. The teacher has to plan the lesson activities in accordance with the lesson objectives and the pupils' knowledge and cognitive development, and assemble the necessary materials. In practice, it is far more demanding, since it has to be done with precision, taking account of any assessment information available, and attempting to translate it into curricular terms. It is likely that materials may have to be adapted into tailor-made programmes for individual pupils. Thus, teachers may need to establish the key concepts which have to be covered before a pupil can tackle a given topic, and devise ways of working through those concepts with the pupil.

Presenting lesson material has already been discussed with reference to pupils who have physical or sensory impairments. The more general problem with pupils who have learning difficulties is how to break down material into steps geared to pupils' cognitive grasp, and ensure adequate repetition based on feedback from pupils. This is a particular difficulty in mixed ability classes where the amount of repetition and simplification of instruction necessary for one or two pupils may be counterproductive for the rest. As well as being able to pitch material at the appropriate level, teachers in this situation must be able to operate at several different levels and switch between them in the course of a lesson.

Teacher interaction with pupils to facilitate learning is at the core of the teaching process – and is a major challenge to teachers of pupils with special needs. It entails asking questions, eliciting pupil response, promoting discussion, and generally engaging in verbal interaction. One characteristic that many pupils with special needs have in common is a limited command of language. Teachers have therefore to find ways of achieving the necessary verbal interaction within a restricted linguistic repertoire. Their own speech must relate to the pupils' level of language development, and they have to find a balance between pupils' existing language and any technical terms or formal discourse judged necessary. Questions may need careful phrasing to ensure that pupils go beyond monosyllabic answers, and special steps may have to be taken to promote discussion. All of this must of course relate to the detailed assessment of individual pupils' curricular needs.

Monitoring pupils' progress should be an integral part of teaching as far as all pupils are concerned. It takes on particular import in the case of pupils with special needs, since their pedagogical requirements are so demanding. Individual programmes may be worked out in fine detail, but their successful implementation is critically dependent upon regularly updated information on how the programme is working. Decisions on whether to continue with the programme, modify it, re-present parts of it, or abandon it totally, must be taken in the light of feedback from practice. Teaching pupils with special needs can be described as developing and testing a succession of hypotheses, each hypothesis depending on the outcome of the preceding one; the information produced by monitoring performance is the intelligence that drives this process and ensures that pupils make progress in a coherent way.

Class teachers' efforts can be supplemented by the judicious use of additional help in the classroom. This is relatively more common in special schools, but ordinary schools are increasingly aware of the benefits of having a second adult in classes containing pupils with special needs. The second adult may be a classroom assistant, another teacher, or a parent or other voluntary worker. Classroom assistants can perform a wide range of functions – providing physical care, implementing physiotherapy exercises, helping pupils in practical work, and generally giving them a degree of individual attention that would not otherwise be possible. The use of a second teacher in a class is not common, but it does allow a high level of expert attention, and makes it possible for pupils with complex learning difficulties to be supported in a very flexible way. Whatever form of additional help is provided, it is essential that this extra resource fit into an overall plan, and that it be managed as a coherent part of the classroom activities and not as an adjunct to it or, even worse, a contrary focus within it.

There is a considerable body of literature covering these topics, and only a brief discussion has been appropriate here. The reader is referred in particular to the new series for teachers published by Cassell. When complete this will comprise a library of 20 texts on the practicalities of teaching pupils with a wide variety of special needs in ordinary school settings. (Many of them are just as relevant to teachers in special schools.) The first books published[5] include an overview volume, special needs in the primary school, special needs in the secondary school, teaching science to secondary school pupils with learning difficulties, and teaching children with speech and language difficulties. Other books already published or in preparation cover humanities teaching for children with special needs in secondary schools, fostering mathematical and scientific thinking in primary schools, teaching pupils described as 'disruptive', and visual handicaps in the classroom. Another source of useful information is the periodical *British Journal of Special Education*, published quarterly by the National Council for Special Education. This contains accounts of practice, information on curriculum materials and applications, and a wealth of practical advice and ideas for teachers.

NEW TECHNOLOGIES

The use of technology in education is growing. Pupils with special needs stand to benefit in major ways from this, even though many developments have been slower to reach fruition than early enthusiasm would have allowed. Three principal areas of benefit can be discerned: mobility; communication; and teaching/learning activities. In addition, teachers gain from an enhanced capacity to manage the curriculum.

Mobility may be peripheral to the curriculum, but limitations on mobility frequently result in curricular limitations. By the same token, advances in mobility aids and environmental control can be the means of opening up areas of the curriculum hitherto closed to pupils with physical or visual impairments. Advances in communication technology improve access to the curriculum for pupils with physical or sensory impairments: they make it possible for them to attend mainstream lessons, and they facilitate note-taking, personal record keeping, and drafting written work. They also make it easier for pupils to interact with peers.

The core concern of curriculum delivery is the teaching and learning that go on in the classroom. Developments in this area are more significant in the long run, although less dramatic, than advances in mobility or communication. There is a wide, and growing, range of computer software available to schools, some of it subject specific, some of it geared to particular developmental stages. Hope[6] offers a good overview of current initiatives with respect to pupils with moderate learning difficulties, describing both software and implementation. The text is divided into sections covering: improving self-esteem and motivation; general language skills; reading, writing, and spelling; number skills; problem-solving strategies; and interpersonal skills. Software appropriate to the different areas is outlined, but the book's key contribution is its account of practical classroom experiences in using programs. It describes particular pupils' learning difficulties and discusses their response to programs in terms of their self-esteem as learners and their progress in acquiring knowledge and skills.

Teaching pupils with special needs can present major problems of curriculum management. The teacher may have every pupil in a class on a different program, each consisting of a large number of closely related steps. Devising individual programs in the first instance and monitoring pupils' progress through them entail a good deal of clerical effort which detracts from teaching time. Richards[7] describes a curriculum management program which simplifies the work and has the potential to contribute in a major way to curriculum design and management.

While the use of such programs is still at an early stage in Britain, there has been rather more development in the United States, partly because of the pressure of legislation which calls for individualized educational programmes (IEPs) and requires teachers to have a method of evaluating student progress towards the objectives laid down. Behrmann[8] defines 'computer managed instruction' as the systematic control of instruction by the computer, encompassing testing, diagnosis, prescription of learning, and record keeping. He describes two major applications: generating IEPs; and analysing student performance data. Programs to generate IEPs are based on curriculum data banks from which teachers make individual selections on the basis of their diagnosis of pupils' needs. Analysis programs are based on pupil performance data and enable teachers to monitor pupils' progress on a regular, even daily, basis and to modify individual programmes in the light of that information. It is clear that computer-managed instruction is a powerful tool in both the development and the management of individual learning programmes and has the potential to make a major contribution to the curriculum in special education.

REFERENCES

1. Department of Education and Science (1978) *Special Educational Needs* (Warnock Report), London: HMSO.
2. Department of Education and Science (1985) *The Curriculum from Five to Sixteen: Curriculum Matters 2*, London: HMSO.
3. Department of Education and Science (1984) *The Organisation and Content of the Curriculum: Special Schools*, London: DES.
4. Hodgson, A., Clunies-Ross, L., and Hegarty, S. (1984) *Learning Together: Teaching Pupils with Special Educational Needs in the Ordinary School*, Windsor: NFER-Nelson.
5. Hegarty, S. (1987) *Meeting Special Needs in Ordinary Schools*, London: Cassell; Wolfendale, S. (1987) *Primary Schools and Special Needs: Policy, Planning and Provision*, London: Cassell; Sayer, J. (1987) *Secondary Schools for All?: Strategies for Special Needs*, London: Cassell; Reid, D. J. and Hodson, D. (1987) *Science for All: Teaching Science in the Secondary School*, London: Cassell; Webster, A. and McConnell, C. (1987) *Children with Speech and Language Difficulties*, London: Cassell.
6. Hope, M. (Ed.) (1986) *The Magic of the Micro: A Resource for Children with Learning Difficulties*, London: Council for Educational Technology.
7. Richards, C. (1986) 'Can micros change the curriculum?' in Hope (6).
8. Behrmann, M. (1985) *Handbook of Microcomputers in Special Education*, Windsor: NFER-Nelson.

9.5

CHILDREN WITH PHYSICAL AND SENSORY IMPAIRMENTS

ELIZABETH K. CHAPMAN

Pupils whose special educational needs derive from the presence of physical and sensory impairments are at present educated in a range of settings, such placements being influenced not only by their individual requirements but also by local resources and priorities. Which pupils are being referred to in these terms? The process of decategorization stresses the individual needs of children, and moves away from medically orientated groupings, but the terminology has always been gross. Physically disabled children, for example, may have orthopaedic conditions affecting mobility, cerebral conditions affecting both movement and speech, or chronic disabling illnesses; deaf and hearing-impaired children have long been differentiated, but their functioning may be further diversified by early experiences of a communicating background, age at onset of the condition, and ability to use a hearing aid; the term 'visually handicapped' is now frequently used to refer to the whole continuum of possible sight levels from total congenital blindness to useful but defective vision. Nevertheless there remain some approaches to environmental and educational factors that are shown by such pupils, and an understanding of these forms an invaluable background against which the specific needs of individual children can more easily be both understood and met. In this context the somewhat generalized terms of 'physical' or 'sensory' handicap, the effect of 'physical' or 'sensory' impairment, are used as signposts to help to clarify the paths through the complexities of terminology, not as labels to categorize particular children.

Increasingly, as pupils with complex handicaps reach school age, special schools for specific handicaps change their roles and there are some closures, while mainstream schools accept more disabled pupils and a diverse pattern of educational placements emerges. A pupil may attend a special school on a residential or day basis; pupils may have a split placement which includes some mainstream school attendance; pupils may attend unit provision within an ordinary school or be in an integrated placement.

From this complex picture it is possible to draw out some examples of organization, of environmental and curriculum planning, and even of detailed adaptations to equipment, that have implications for good practice in meeting the needs of pupils whose physical or sensory handicap is a factor in their educational needs.

ORGANIZATION AND HUMAN RESOURCES

The extent to which a pupil spends part of each day at school in a special class or unit to learn specific skills such as braille, or to undertake intensive work on language, or anticipatory or follow-up work, will vary both in terms of individual need and of the organizational policy of the school. The unit or support teacher may also work in the ordinary classroom clarifying aspects of a lesson that involves concepts or processes which may afford difficulty for a pupil with a sight or hearing defect. The unit or support teacher may also work in the ordinary class or subject room. The pupil may be supported by a peripatetic teacher/adviser who will also provide adapted educational materials, advise on the pupils' special needs, and provide special programs, for instance in language development or in the enhancement of residual vision. Some teachers, particularly at the secondary level, may be unfamiliar with working in the classroom with other adults, and when support teaching is given a clarification of roles is needed. It will be the class or subject teacher who is responsible for the content and direction of the lesson; the support teacher will clarify concepts when necessary, explain or demonstrate procedures, and possibly suggest alternative presentations or activities when those offered to other pupils are inapplicable. Clunies-Ross[1] describes a specialist teacher of the deaf resolving communication problems in the ordinary classroom, ensuring that set tasks are understood, and using a variety of techniques including pointing to text being read aloud by other children. Forward planning is essential, involving both regular and support or specialist teachers. Regular meetings are usually scheduled, so that lesson content is available in advance for tactile or enlarged diagrams, or brailled notes can be made, and introductory and follow-up work given to the relevant pupils. Individual work in such areas as training to use low-vision aids, or closed circuit television effectively, developing literacy through braille, or concentrating on language development and speech, may also be necessary.

A classroom assistant can be an invaluable intermediary and facilitator; for instance, under the teacher's direction, making specialized materials such as enlarged diagrams, and helping with practical activities. Ancillary helpers may be deployed to meet transport bringing disabled pupils to school, deal with wheelchairs and hoists, and assist with toiletting, and with feeding and dressing for younger pupils. These are also teaching activities in some cases, and self-management rather than dependence needs to be considered as an aim and implemented consistently throughout the support team. Physiotherapy and speech therapy will be essential to some pupils, making a considerable difference to their mobility and potential for communication. Therapists are also part of the educational team, in that they can contribute information and suggested activities relevant to classroom practice for individual pupils. Co-ordinating the different contributions of advisory services and support teaching, therapy, and ancillary services presents a considerable and necessary challenge within the school.

There may be fresh challenges too, if the aspirations of 'conductive' education are increasingly realized. This intensive program aims to teach physically disabled children to master small repeated movements which, it is hoped, culminate in increased ability to walk, sit upright, and communicate. It is carried out by specially trained 'conductors' who need to work with the child on a continual and individual basis.

In some larger schools, a designated teacher is appointed to be responsible for disseminating information and co-ordinating support for pupils with special needs. Adapting timetables to include withdrawal and therapy sessions and co-ordinating specialist input requires good managerial skill and positive interaction with colleagues. Regular staff meetings which include discussion of progress as well as conveying information about individual pupils who require special teaching or support can help to promote a consistent approach towards individual pupils.

Successful examples of integrated provision for pupils with physical or sensory handicap tend to reflect personal enthusiasm for this on the part of the headteacher and a staffing situation in which specialist and support teachers are themselves integrated into the social and educational ethos of the school.

Peer group assistance to disabled and visually and hearing-impaired pupils has in many instances also been encouraged as a natural and normal interaction from the time of the first acceptance of such pupils into a mainstream school. Acting as a sighted guide to a blind pupil, checking the lesson notes of a hearing impaired classmate, or giving a hand in a practical activity to a physically handicapped friend constitutes a normal friendly action. Too much help can sometimes be offered at first, and a balance between friendship and dependence needs to be developed. Friendships will tend to arise from shared interests and enthusiasms.

THE PLACE OF TECHNICAL RESOURCES AND EQUIPMENT

Whilst human resources are a first line of educational and social support for pupils with physical and sensory disabilities, advances in educational technology are being shown to have considerable potential for such pupils. Communication channels can be opened up, and concentration and attention span frequently appear to be increased as pupils learn to master and enjoy using this equipment. Both advice and information on the use of micro-electronics for handicapped pupils were located in the four regional Special Education Micro-electronic Centres; advice and lists of software programs developed in their own region are now available through local education authority advisers.

There are some interesting examples of micro-electronics used to facilitate communication when this is a difficulty. A device which undoubtedly helps communication is the *Vincent workstation*. The transcription of braille into print has always been a time-consuming process, but the use of the BBC micro-computer, a speech synthesizer, print-out, monitor, and adapted brailler can with the appropriate program be used to transcribe braille into print immediately, making the blind pupil's work instantly accessible, and being used for the transcription of examination papers, texts, and notes. This has been found to be invaluable in both unit and special school situations.

There are examples of adaptations in the control of input for individual pupils. Although the QWERTY keyboard can be used by many pupils with hearing or sight defects, physical handicap which affects hand control or manipulation may necessitate the use of an extended keyboard, and the use of a light pen or 'mouse' which can link with a cursor on the display screen. Adaptations have been devised by Aids for Communication in Education, basing the nature of the input on consistent movement which can be used as a link to the equipment. The *Headstart workstation*, used with an appropriate program, has a control attached to the head of a pupil unable to use hand control.[2] A sensitive 'touchscreen' can be used by pupils with physical handicap or low levels of vision; the size of letters displayed on a monitor and the colour contrast used can be altered to suit individual pupils with defective vision in some of the software programs developed at the Research Centre for the Education of the Visually Handicapped at Birmingham University.

This Centre has also developed visual enhancement activities through software programs based on the 'Look and Think' approach.[3] Firminger (op. cit.) describes the successful use of micro-technology as a breakthrough into curriculum areas that have in the past been unavailable to some disabled pupils. She instances the simulation of scientific experiments and practical work as well as the graphic requirements of students unable to draw as being potential contributions by micro-technology. The use of micros can begin in the primary school, usually at the age of eight, when language development and perceptual training programs can be especially valuable for children with hearing or sight difficulties. Of particular relevance to physically handicapped pupils are the programs contributing to personal independence and environmental control; spatial concepts for example can be explored by programs including the 'floor turtle'.

There is, however, considerable agreement that the use of micro-electronics, although of great value, is not a panacea; it needs to be viewed in terms of its place within the taught curriculum, with the evaluation of programs and the increased in-service training of teachers being essential elements in continuing developments. Not all the equipment useful in facilitating communication and enhancing learning opportunities is micro-electronic. As well as word processors, electric typewriters are invaluable for some visually handicapped pupils, and with the POSSUM foot control they are useful for pupils with little or no hand control. Closed circuit television monitors are a reading aid, and can also be used to magnify processes such as drawing letter shapes. These can be shown in standard or intaglio presentation for pupils with different visual disabilities. Aids which are designed to help pupils with visual or auditory impairment to make maximum use of residual sight or hearing can make an appreciable difference to level of functioning in the classroom. Hand- or spectacle-mounted low-vision aids custom-made for individual use may incorporate optical correction, clarifying and enlarging an image, or in the case of tunnel vision reducing it. But the effective use of such aids needs to be taught, and they can have disadvantages that need to be overcome, in that their unusual appearance may cause them to be rejected by some pupils.

Cayton,[4] in describing the use of hearing aids, emphasizes that these devices are not a curriculum substitute, but must be used effectively within it. Thus it is important for the teacher to present auditory material clearly. Personal hearing aids and educational hearing or communication aids may be used, but these do not totally compensate for hearing loss, and thus may produce distortions and amplify background noise. Aids incorporating a radio receiver necessitate the teacher wearing a small radio microphone. Non-specialist teachers need to be aware of the limitations of hearing aids and some of the difficulties involved for users.

IMPLICATIONS

The view that education should be led by the curriculum has some significant implications for those with handicaps, since the curriculum in the mainstream school is designed in broad terms for able-bodied, fully hearing, and fully sighted pupils. The individualization of programs can do much to give pupils the opportunity for learning in their own way, but these become more difficult to offer when work hardens into curriculum areas at the middle school and secondary stages. There are some challenging questions which must be faced when the special needs of pupils with physical or sensory handicap are considered in terms of curriculum design. How can maximum curriculum access be ensured for the individual pupil? How can special curriculum areas specific to the needs of individual or small groups of handicapped pupils be included in the school day? How can balance in the curriculum be maintained in the face of these demands?

Physical access rather than curriculum content is likely to be the major constraint for pupils with physical handicap, unless there are other significant handicaps or developmental delay. Adapted equipment, transport to and within the school campus, appropriate environmental conditions, and ancillary helps can be tailored to meet the access needs of individual pupils, but still be within the realms of the attainable. But the teacher's understanding of the effort and fatigue involved in some curriculum areas is vital; the process as well as the result needs to be seen as valuable. The volume of work expected from some physically handicapped pupils may need to be carefully considered, but content and comprehension remain crucial. Some curriculum areas may not be possible to undertake because of physical factors, but wherever possible activities in the same curriculum area may be substituted, as in the case of physically handicapped pupils going swimming instead of working in the gym. There are limits to the real possibilities of providing curriculum alternatives, but ingenuity and flexibility on the part of teachers increases viable choices.

Curriculum access for hearing impaired or visually impaired pupils can be enhanced by:

1. the presentation of learning materials with maximum visual and auditory clarity;
2. the use of carefully prepared material in the pupil's main channel of communication (for example tactile diagrams, tape-recorded work);
3. the use of specialized equipment for communicating information (for example micro-electronics, closed circuit television, radio microphone);
4. the provision of support teaching, including introductory, explanatory, and follow-up work.

Pupils with defective sight or hearing will need some specialized and additional curriculum input. Braille, mobility, and self-help skills are among the most evident for the blind pupil, but visual enhancement programs and training in listening skills will be necessary for some visually handicapped pupils with residual vision. Deaf pupils require intensive work in communication skills, and the hearing-impaired will need auditory training, language, and speech work. These special areas are usually effectively taught in the special school setting, and warrant curriculum priority in any setting. They are aspects of the curriculum that may be taught on a withdrawal basis in the ordinary school, but the more they can be incorporated into activities and practice across the curriculum areas the better.

The curriculum may be eroded because of the necessity for therapy sessions, and pupils may need a longer time to complete tasks if they have physical auditory or visual disabilities. There is no easy or universal answer to these pressures on the curriculum, and often a pragmatic solution may need to be sought. For example, a secondary school with integrated blind pupils held a lunchtime braille club which included pupils, parents, and teachers. French was dropped by the blind pupils in order to have necessary time for other work.[5] Physically handicapped pupils in another integrated situation took three instead of five curriculum options but perfected typewriting skills. An approach which gives room for the individual pupil's priorities is desirable, but attention to the balance of the curriculum is equally so. In terms of considering what constitutes core curriculum some special skills such as braille or speech development may well be considered as 'core' since they are the key for access to other curriculum areas. Curriculum areas which have sometimes been considered as expendable in the face of other priorities are physical education, art, and music, but all pupils have a need for creative and expressive activities, and can participate in them in their own way.

THE SCHOOL ENVIRONMENT

Although headteachers and staff usually inherit the buildings in which they work and have little or no say in their design, they can have an influence on the way that rooms are used, maintained, and equipped that is particularly significant for pupils with physical or sensory handicap. Buildings themselves dictate a level of suitability in environmental terms to the different needs of pupils. Open-plan schools, now less popular, offer few problems for wheelchair users, but may have high levels of background noise unhelpful to the hearing-impaired, and variable lighting levels presenting difficulties for the visually handicapped. Ramps and lifts are obvious needs for some physically handicapped pupils, but such pupils also need plenty of room to move about within the classroom. Floor space can be cleared by arranging furniture in double rows or blocks; workstations or special desks can isolate pupils physically from their classmates unless seating is well arranged. Pupils with defective sight or hearing are in particular need of a clear uninterrupted view of the teacher, since lipreading, facial expression, and gesture all convey and extend meaning. Blackboard and demonstration work also needs to be clearly seen, and seating arrangements can be decided with the special individual requirements of these sensory disabilities in mind. When pupils choose their own places they will often take up a position that suits them in the room, but this can be checked. Lighting should come from behind the pupil onto desk work and on to the teacher's face or demonstration work. Blinds are useful to control window glare which may be dazzling for pupils with photophobic visual conditions, but some pupils may need individual task lighting, especially when using low-vision aids. Relevant literature gives detailed environmental recommendations.[6] There is an unseen auditory environment particularly important to hearing-impaired pupils; background noise including reverberation from hard surfaces can be reduced by the acoustic treatment of the classroom. Environmental awareness is desirable in terms of all pupils, but essential to facilitate the integration of those with physical or sensory handicaps.

Some pupils may need to have attention given to the furniture they use. The inability to reach or see material at a distance means that materials must be used in a contained situation, or in the case of papers, secured by tape to the working surface. The size of furniture in relation to that of the pupil dictates whether there will be postural fatigue, and the height and angle of working materials can be adjusted for physically and visually handicapped pupils by the provision of reading stands and slant boards.

The ethos of the school is an unrecorded and unquantified aspect of the environment that is nevertheless crucial in terms of the suitability for accepting pupils with physical or sensory handicap. The encouragement of co-operative learning, availability of counselling, and acceptance of pupils who need to move about, communicate, or work in unusual ways are prerequisites for successful integration.

IMPLICATIONS FOR TEACHER TRAINING

Although special education elements in initial teacher training should help teachers to be better prepared and more confident in teaching pupils with special needs, there is clearly already a considerable need for continuing in-service training in this context.

There are examples of in-service training offered by local education authorities, specializing in physical or sensory handicaps. The Special Needs Action Programme (SNAP) training material from Coventry, compiled by specialist advisers in the authority, includes text and video presentation. Designated teachers or advisers are arranging school-based in-service courses which may include unit staff, and which take up the specific concerns of teachers who have or are about to receive handicapped pupils in their classes. Voluntary organizations, such as Royal National Institute for the Blind, Royal National Institute for the Deaf, and the Spastics Society, mount courses which relate to particular developmental stages or curriculum areas; for instance pre-school children or adolescents with visual handicap, or the provision of self-help skills. But in-service training needs to be more extensive, more co-ordinated, and more universally available if pupils with physical or sensory handicaps are to have expert understanding of their needs. The White Paper 'Better Schools'[7] propounds the new role of Grant-Related In-service Training which looks to the provision of more one-term courses, a closer link between theoretical and practical aspects of training, and greater flexibility in the way in which courses are offered. However, the aim of spreading expertise more widely among educational practitioners by means of increased and diversified training opportunities requires a careful consideration of course content and its relevance to the real situation of teaching pupils with physical and sensory handicaps. Meeting the immediate needs of adapting educational materials or managing specialized curriculum areas necessary for such pupils will need to be complemented by increasing the awareness of teachers with regard to vital but less evident issues. The significance of interpersonal relationships, the potential problems of reduced communication and mobility, and of delayed or fragmented concept development also need to be well understood so that habilitating attitudes and strategies can be developed. In-service training can help teachers to master skills which include devising and implementing individual educational programs that take cognisance of the difficulties which may arise from physical or sensory handicaps, but which are not substantially disability-orientated. Longer courses with in-depth theoretical aspects as well as practical content remain essential for training experts in the peripatetic and advisory services.

REFERENCES

1. Clunies-Ross, L. (1984) 'Supporting the classroom teacher', *Special Education: Forward Trends*, 11 (3): 11–13.
2. Firminger, J. (1987) 'Microtechnology and students with disabilities: the Hereward Project', in T. Booth and W. Swann (Eds.) *Including Pupils with Disabilities*, Milton Keynes: Open University Press.
3. Tobin, M. J. and Chapman, E. K. (1979) *Look and Think: Teacher's Handbook*, London: Schools Council in association with the RNIB.
4. Cayton, H. (1987) 'The place of hearing aid technology in the education of deaf children', in Booth and Swann.
5. Hughes, D. (1984) 'The role of a visual handicap department in an integrated secondary school', *British Journal of Visual Impairment*, 11 (1): 8–11.
6. Chapman, E. K. and Stone, J. (1987) *The Visually Handicapped Child in Your Classroom*, London: Cassell.
7. Department of Education and Science (1985) *Better Schools*, London: HMSO.

FURTHER READING

Fullwood, D. and Cronin, P. (1986) *Facing the Crowd*, Melbourne: Royal Victorian Institute for the Blind.
Madge, N. and Fassam, M. (1982) *Ask the Children*, London: Batsford Academic and Educational.

Newson, E. and Hipgrave, T. (1982) *Getting Through to Your Handicapped Child*, Cambridge: Cambridge University Press.

Varma, V. P. (Ed.) (1973) *Stresses in Children*, London: University of London Press.

9.6

CHILDREN WITH
LEARNING DIFFICULTIES

PHILLIP WILLIAMS

BACKGROUND

Probably the most significant event in drawing attention to children's learning difficulties was the establishment of a system of compulsory education. In the later decades of the nineteenth century, in most developed countries, schools and teachers met for the first time with the full range of reluctant learners, a meeting which focused attention on learning difficulties. Whether the education system's demands for literacy and numeracy caused these difficulties or revealed them is a matter for philosophical debate. What cannot be debated is that the solutions proposed by the various committees set up to deal with the question were based mainly on the principle of segregation, i.e. setting up separate schools and classes for the reluctant learners.

There was at least one very good reason for this. In most countries, an unusual human condition was dealt with by doctors, who diagnosed children with marked learning difficulties as 'mentally defective', by analogy with the physically defective. Doctors believed in the value of isolating patients, a procedure which was applied to children with learning difficulties, just as it had been to sufferers from physical and mental illnesses. Moreover, teachers, whose task became easier with the departure of the hard to teach, were generally not opposed to this, and the number of special schools and classes grew slowly but steadily.

The situation changed radically in the years following the Second World War, when the 1944 Education Act was being implemented. This Act, and the official regulations and publications which followed it, retained the idea of learning difficulties as a diagnostic category, but adopted a much more liberal attitude to their existence. Thus it was suggested that the post-war educational system should work on the assumption that all children whose attainments were 20 per cent or more below the average for their age group, children who were called educationally subnormal, should receive special education. It is worth remarking that the estimate of prevalence that the Ministry of Education provided was ten per cent of the school population. Even more interestingly, if the prevalence estimates for all ten defined categories of handicap are totalled, the full proportion of pupils in need of special education reaches 14–17 per cent, a remarkably similar figure to the prevalence figure of one child in six suggested by the Warnock report over thirty years later.[1]

While the Ministry of Education could be given full marks for prescience, it did less well otherwise. In the optimistic atmosphere of the late 1940s, to aim to meet the learning difficulties of ten per cent of a young and growing school population was a bold enterprise, though very much in harmony with the liberal spirit of post-war reconstruction. We can applaud the intention, but we must castigate the impracticability. For the target was set at a time when resources were unbelievably limited: to illustrate, courses of training for teachers of 'backward' children were just starting: there was just one HMI at the Ministry with responsibility for the whole of special education in England and Wales: there was not one educational psychologist per LEA. What were the 'special methods' that the Ministry's publications advocated, and who would institute them?

It can be argued that this approach set back the cause of special education for children with learning difficulties for decades. Faced with the impossibility of meeting the intentions of the Act, authorities fell back on the old system of a small number of segregated places, rationed at first by the use of a simple criterion that doctors, who were in better supply, could use, namely the test of intelligence. Many years passed before the human and physical resources were available in sufficient quantity to challenge the existing order, to substitute educational assessment and teaching for medical diagnosis and an undefined treatment, and if not to be within striking distance of a minimal supply of trained staff, at least to be able to see that goal on a distant horizon.

THE CURRENT SITUATION

During the decades following the Second World War, concern over the policy of segregation grew. Movement was accomplished when children whose learning difficulties were so acute that they had been excluded from the education system altogether were, in 1971, brought into the system under the slogan 'no child is ineducable'. By 1978, when the Warnock Committee reported, the climate had changed still further, both in relation to the segregation issue and also in relation to other mounting concerns. Some of the Committee's many recommendations were given force with the 1981 Education Act. That Act, with its emphasis on integration, on the identification of special *educational* needs, rather than a medical categorization or defect model, and on the rights and responsibilities of parents, applies to all children with special needs, as other chapters in this section indicate. Whether the recommendations and the Act which followed them are both robust and flexible enough to meet the changed circumstances of the latter years of this century is a question which lies outside the scope of this chapter. But the Act defines the conditions under which special education currently operates,[2] and its application to meeting needs which arise from learning difficulties follows.

The meaning of learning difficulties

Although categorization of children has been abolished, it is found helpful to group special needs (not children) into three broad groups, those which arise from physical and sensory handicaps, those which arise from emotional and behavioural difficulties, and those learning difficulties which arise for other reasons. This broad division has been followed in this section of the *Handbook*, and it is with the third of these groupings that this chapter is concerned.

The definition of special needs that the 1981 Act set out includes all difficulties with the curriculum, not just the more serious. Thus the work of the remedial teaching service, usually providing extra help in reading or mathematics for children who otherwise make reasonable progress, is now clearly seen as an example of meeting special educational needs arising through a learning difficulty. In this example the learning difficulty may be specific to one area of the curriculum, such as reading, rather than a general learning difficulty. This use of the term learning difficulty means that children who are sometimes described as dyslexic can be brought under the learning difficulties umbrella, thus helping to avoid some of the sterile controversy that has accompanied the use of the term.

Note that the term specific learning difficulty, which can apply to any curriculum area, is different from specific learning disability (SLD), as used in the USA and elsewhere; SLD is defined by the American legislation as a group of ill-defined symptoms essentially characterized by difficulties with language. So while it includes dyslexia, it also includes diagnostic categories such as minimal brain damage and hyperactivity. In short the American term is based on a diagnostic model, the British term on a curriculum model. The curriculum occupies a commanding position in the model of special education shaped by the UK legislation. This position is central for all special needs, but for learning difficulties it is crucial.

LEARNING DIFFICULTIES AND THE CURRICULUM

The Department of Education and Science describes three types of curriculum for meeting the needs of children with learning difficulties (see Hegarty p. 1062). The first of these, a mainstream-with-support curriculum, is intended to meet the needs of children whose learning difficulties are mild. These are children who can follow the curriculum as organized in most schools, given some assistance beyond that normally available. Thus children who can manage their lessons with the help of occasional remedial teaching, or with the help of a particular piece of equipment, would be following a mainstream-with-support curriculum.

The second, or modified curriculum, is intended for children whose learning difficulties are moderate. The ordinary curriculum may well be a target, but the rate at which these children can master it may well be slower and for this reason it may need modification. Thus, to give two examples from the secondary school, it may be wiser to drop a modern language in favour of more intensive work on skills of expression in the native language; the science curriculum may need to be modified so as to be less theoretical and more directly useful. How changes such as these are accomplished will depend upon the attitudes and resources of the individual school, and entails careful planning on the part of the school staff. Unfortunately this has not always been in evidence, for surveys carried out in Scotland as well as England and Wales have suggested that many schools were not providing successful curricular experiences for children with moderate learning difficulties.

The third type of curriculum is designed for children whose learning difficulties are severe, and is termed a developmental curriculum. Here, the departure from the usual school experience becomes sharper and more pronounced. Children whose learning difficulties are severe need to learn and relearn many of those everyday skills which most children acquire before starting school or in their early school-days. Social skills, such as communication, personal skills, such as dressing and washing, are examples of elements which receive much greater emphasis in a developmental curriculum, and usually at a time when most children would already have acquired them.[3]

Great changes have occurred in the methods of educating children with learning difficulties, whatever the curriculum they follow. These changes are broadly of two kinds; on the one hand, there are changes in methods of teaching the curriculum, following research and development, and on the other, there are changes in methods of organizing and delivering the curriculum, following movements in social attitudes and values. The next two sections examine these changes and the reasons for them.

CHANGES IN TEACHING METHODS

Probably the greatest contributions to advances in teaching methods for children with learning difficulties have come from advances in psychology, and behavioural psychology in particular. Interestingly enough, the greatest developmental psychologist of the century, Piaget, has had a substantially smaller influence, although his account of the development of thinking skills has had some application to educating children with severe learning difficulties.

Other approaches, some based on the work of less well-known individuals, some derived *ad hoc* from the teaching situation, have also been developed.

The behaviourist tradition

Two important principles of behavioural psychology underpin many advances in educational practice, namely reinforcement and structure. The view that reinforcement, i.e. rewarding a response, is central to learning that response, characterizes many classroom programmes. Reinforcement may take the form of praise from the teacher, or a star or a sweet for good work, or any one of a large number of possibilities. It is because one kind of reward may be reinforcing for one child but not for another that the opportunity of personal choice of reward through the use of a system of tokens was introduced. This system, which in full flower leads to a class or even a school being run as a 'token economy', is not dissimilar to the gift token system designed by petrol companies to encourage motorists to learn the habit of stopping again at that company's chain of stations.

Like reinforcement, structure is an old educational principle. Like reinforcement, the behavioural psychologists have developed and extended it and applied it rigorously to teaching children with learning difficulties. The argument, in essence, is that learning becomes difficult when the teaching has no clear aim and the difficulty steps are too great. Hence, as well as many other procedures, behavioural teaching involves defining the teaching aims and objectives clearly and analysing carefully the steps needed to reach them. Programmed learning was an early example of these techniques which was used to good effect with children with learning difficulties. More recently, *mastery learning* principles have been advocated.

One of the more popular behaviourally-based teaching methods is Direct Instruction, founded on work arising from the North American *Headstart program*, but increasingly used in the UK. DISTAR, or Direct Instructional System for Teaching And Remediation, is a set of programmes for teaching basic skills, derived from it. Like other behavioural methods, Direct Instruction has been criticized for its apparent rigidity; prescribed lesson plans and heavy use of drill exercises do not suit all teachers. Nevertheless it has its champions, and some results with children with learning difficulties are encouraging.[4]

It is sometimes argued that the behavioural approach is more effective for teaching lower-level motor skills, for example those involved in dressing and feeding, than for teaching higher-level intellectual skills, for example those involved in language use. Nevertheless programmes for developing language, based on behavioural principles, have been developed, and the DISTAR materials contain an example.

OTHER DEVELOPMENTS

Language is in fact an area providing good examples of teaching approaches which are in contradistinction to those based on behavioural psychology. Teacher groups involved with the Swansea Project identified seven key language skills and designed a set of games and exercises, based on their own classroom experience, to develop these skills in young disadvantaged children. An example of many more recent programmes is the Derbyshire Language Scheme, intended to improve language skills in young children with learning difficulties whose language development is below a four-and-a-half year level. The scheme emphasizes the use of play and adult-child interaction. The activities suggested are linked to assessments of the child's expressive and receptive language.[5]

Instrumental Enrichment is another approach designed for use with children with learning difficulties, but not restricted to improving language skills. The point of departure of its originator, Feuerstein, is his dissatisfaction with the intelligence test as an aid to teaching. He believes that intelligence tests measure what children have learnt, not how they learn. He therefore designed a method of assessing how well a child might learn, the Learning Potential Assessment Device. This led him to believe that many children with learning difficulties function at a low level because they have never learnt how to learn. So he developed a set of teaching exercises, the Instrumental Enrichment programme, aimed at remedying this. Essentially the programme requires the child to complete a series of intellectual exercises, such as identifying patterns, classifying concepts, etc., on materials different from those usually used in school. Discussion with the teacher is intended to modify the child's thinking skills and improve his or her performance in more conventional educational activities.[6]

As several of the contributions to this section of the *Handbook* stress, parents are playing an increasingly important part in the education of children with special needs. This applies not only to collaboration in the assessment process, but also to collaboration in teaching itself. This is not only good for the children's progress, but also helps many parents by harnessing their own wishes to play a significant part in the education of their own child, particularly when he or she needs extra help. One example of this is the Portage Scheme, which is aimed at the early education of pre-school children with special needs. This scheme is in effect a systematic programme of home teaching, using parents as teachers. The teaching activities for a week or so are planned in advance, usually with the aid of an experienced teacher. They are then carried out by the parent. The scheme involves regular monitoring of the child's progress and has been welcomed by parent groups.[7]

Another development which, in the interests of the child, involves capitalizing on parents' skills and motivation, is the paired reading technique. The advantage of pairing a child who has a reading difficulty with a fluent reader is well known. This scheme was developed to use a parent as the fluent reader, hence Parent Assisted Instruction in Reading. The parent has to follow a specified procedure, so that the child is encouraged rather than discouraged. Some remarkable gains in reading performance have been demonstrated using this technique, but it has to be remembered that evaluations of remedial reading have traditionally shown substantial gains initially, gains which gradually diminish when the programme is withdrawn, and we shall need to suspend judgement until the results of several long-term follow-up studies are available.[8]

DELIVERING SPECIAL EDUCATION

Probably the biggest changes ushered in by the 1981 Act have resulted from the emphasis it placed on integration, or educating children with special needs in the ordinary school. Although the number of children with special needs being educated in special schools and units has not yet fallen substantially, and indeed there is evidence that for the first few years of the decade the numbers have risen slightly, nevertheless the ordinary school has seen a sea-change in the way that it deals with the needs of children on roll. The issues underlying this change are discussed in Chapter 9.3; the intention here is to examine the way in which it has affected the delivery of special education to children with learning difficulties. These include both those children who might, a few years ago, have received a segregated education, and also those children who would then, as now, have been on the roll of the ordinary school, though perhaps dealt with very differently then.

Of the three curriculum types that were mentioned on pp. 1082–3, the developmental curriculum is the most difficult to offer in the ordinary school. At the pre-school and infant level, given adequate support from, for example, classroom assistants, it may be possible, but as children grow older and the ordinary curriculum changes, so it becomes increasingly difficult to offer a developmental curriculum within the usual school organization. So most children with severe learning difficulties have special schools or units as their educational base. Base is the key word here, for a base is a point to which one returns for sustenance. And recent surveys of practice in special schools for children with severe learning difficulties show that in many of them pupils spend some time each week in a nearby ordinary school, that pupils from the ordinary school may spend some time in activities in the special school, and that in many cases staff members are timetabled to spend time in each other's schools.

These last points are important. They underline the view that integration is a valuable and important experience for all pupils, not solely those with special needs – and for teachers, too. This is one of the benefits of the arrangements just described. Where these developing arrangements will lead is uncertain, for the arrangement *per se* is only a gesture: as with so many educational procedures, it is not what is done but the way that it is done that is vital. What is clear is that at present, in the UK, even for children who need the most distinct curriculum of all, there is definite evidence of a movement towards a greater association with mainstream education.

For children who need a modified or mainstream-with-support curriculum there is evidence of more substantial movement. In the past, these children, if not actually in special schools, were usually to be found either in special classes in the ordinary school, taught by a special teacher, or in the ordinary classes, but receiving extra help through a system of withdrawal to small groups for part of the time. These small groups provided intensive remedial teaching, usually in reading or number.

Both these systems had drawbacks. In both cases the children were seen as different from their peers, and labelled accordingly. They were taught by teachers who were members of special or remedial departments, who had few links with the rest of the school, and who were sometimes regarded as of low status. For example, the head of the remedial department was rarely a member of the school senior management team and his or her recommendations for curriculum changes were rarely implemented.

Lately this structure has changed. What is the point of legislating for educating all children with special needs in the ordinary school, if they are effectively segregated when they get there? An acceptable answer to this argument has been found by changing the structure of special education in the ordinary school. In its full form, the most widely practised method involves dismantling the remedial department and abolishing special and withdrawal classes. All children are taught in the ordinary class. The remedial and special teachers are then available to work alongside their colleagues in normal lessons, supporting in any appropriate way those children who find difficulties with the lesson. This change in function from remedial to support teaching has not been accomplished painlessly, and at secondary level problems over relationships between subject specialists and support teachers, shortage of time for planning team teaching, etc. are some of the disadvantages of this scheme.[9] But these can be minimized given good will. Moreover, a complete change in school organization is not always made, and in many schools support teaching replaces part only of the old system of special groups.

In some schools the change to support teaching is seen as part of a movement which has been called the 'whole-school approach'. This is a phrase which means many different things to different people. But in essence it implies that the whole school recognizes its responsibility for meeting the special needs of its pupils, and does not feel that it has discharged its duty by leaving this to members of a special or remedial department. This will entail all staff having some say in the planning of the curriculum for all children, that subject specialists and special educators agree to work side by side, and that all those resources on which a school can draw for support – including the community outside the school – are available to all.[10]

This change in the philosophy of the school and in the roles of its members has significant implications for teacher education.

TEACHER EDUCATION

Where every teacher is involved in the education of children with special needs, every teacher must be prepared for a new role. This was the reason for the priority accorded to teacher education in the Warnock Report and the reason why so many commentators saw teacher education as the keystone of the Warnock recommendations.

There is little evidence of the extent to which institutions of initial training have responded to the Warnock view that every course of initial training should include an element of a week or its equivalent devoted to meeting special educational needs in the ordinary school, a week which would inevitably place a substantial emphasis on learning difficulties. The likelihood is that the great majority of institutions will have responded well to the challenge, for under the new arrangements for approving courses of initial training this would be one of the elements expected.

Training in special needs for the teaching force already in post is a much more formidable task, rendered even more challenging by its extension to teachers in further education and in the pre-school. Here, much of the initiative has come from local education authorities, who have realized the magnitude of the task of making training arrangements for every teacher on roll, and so have often followed the more manageable policy of aiming in-service courses at an identified key person in each school, usually the designated teacher. The key persons are then expected to spread the message of the course when they return to their own schools.

An example of this is the Special Needs Action Package, or SNAP, designed by the Coventry Authority. This is a structured approach to supporting children with special needs in the ordinary school, aiming to help teachers identify needs, develop curricula, and make best use of support services. It provides handbooks for the use of school-based co-ordinators, who are expected to use these to develop courses for their own colleagues.[11]

An example of an in-service arrangement targeted particularly on the needs of children with learning difficulties is the Education of the Developmentally Young – or EDY – project. This project, which has been based at the University of Manchester, aims to teach behavioural principles to key personnel in the education of children with severe learning difficulties. It is a national rather than a local scheme, and those educational psychologists and special education advisers who complete the course are expected to return to their own authorities and run workshops in which they can pass on the skills they have learnt.[12]

This last example illustrates a third kind of training, namely a specialized training for teachers who have a specific responsibility for special educational needs. For teachers wishing to specialize in working with children with learning difficulties, much of this training is gained through following a one-year course of advanced education, usually leading to a Master's Degree in special education. These programmes have depended heavily on the national arrangements for grants to local education authorities whose teachers follow these courses, arrangements which are currently the subject of debate.

CONCLUSIONS

Meeting the intentions of the 1981 Education Act, both in letter and in spirit, presents a formidable set of challenges. For children with learning difficulties, the greatest challenge is offered to the ordinary school. Here, changing practices is a necessary but not a sufficient condition for success; for the Act to be implemented satisfactorily, attitudes must change as well as practices. Now, as ever, it is the education of the teaching force and of others concerned with the well-being of children with learning difficulties which is the key to change.

REFERENCES

1. Department of Education and Science (1978) *Special Educational Needs* (The Warnock Report), London: HMSO.
2. Adams, F. (Ed.) (1986) *Special Education*, London: Councils and Education Press.
3. Brennan, W. (1985) *Curriculum for Special Needs*, Milton Keynes: Open University Press; Gulliford, R. (1985) *Teaching Children With Learning Difficulties*, Windsor: NFER-NELSON.
4. Solity, J. and Bull, S. (1987) *Special Needs: Bridging the Curriculum Gap*, Milton Keynes: Open University Press (especially Chapter 3); Ainscow, M. and Tweddle, D.A. (1979) *Preventing Classroom Failure: an Objectives Approach*, London: Wiley.
5. Webster, A. and McConnell, C. (1987) *Children with Speech and Language Difficulties*, London: Cassell (especially Chapter 4).
6. Feuerstein, R. (1980) *Instrumental Enrichment*, Baltimore: University Park Press.
7. Cameron, R. (Ed.) (1986) *Portage: Preschoolers, Parents and Professionals*, Windsor: NFER-NELSON.
8. Topping, K. and McKnight, G. (1984) 'Paired reading – and parent power', *Special Education: Forward Trends*, 11 (3): 12–13.
9. Ferguson, N. and Adams, M. (1982) 'Assessing the advantages of team teaching in remedial education: the remedial teacher's role', *Remedial Education*, 17 (1): 24–30.
10. Sayer, J. (1987) *Secondary Schools for All? Strategies for Special Needs*, London: Cassell.

11. Ainscow, M., and Muncey, J. (1981) *Special Needs Action Programme* (SNAP), Swansea: Drake Educational Associates.
12. McBrien, J. (1981) 'Introducing the E.D.Y. Project', *Special Education: Forward Trends*, 8 (2): 29–30.

9.7

CHILDREN WITH EMOTIONAL AND BEHAVIOURAL DIFFICULTIES

MAURICE CHAZAN

INTRODUCTION

Pupils presenting emotional and behavioural difficulties (EBD pupils, in the past usually referred to as 'maladjusted' children) cause a great deal of concern and often stress to teachers at all stages of the educational system. In recent years, much attention has focused on disruptive behaviour in class, such as abusiveness, defiance, aggression, and bullying, but the needs of children who are inhibited, withdrawn or timid have not been altogether overlooked.

In general, surveys have shown that the prevalence of emotional and behaviour problems in schools is surprisingly high, ranging up to about 30 per cent of pupils, though estimates are varied and affected by a number of factors. These include the criteria adopted for regarding a particular pattern of behaviour as maladaptive; the location and ethos of individual schools; the assessment techniques used; the perceptions of raters; and the sex and age distribution of the samples involved. Boys tend to show far more behaviour problems than girls, at least of an over-reactive kind, and a higher prevalence of E/B difficulties is usually found in areas which may be termed 'socially disadvantaged' than in other areas. For example, a study carried out by Rutter *et al.* estimated that ten-year-olds in Inner London showed nearly twice as many E/B problems as did pupils of the same age in the Isle of Wight.[1] The Swann Report discusses the question of the prevalence of behaviour problems in some ethnic-minority groups.[2]

EBD pupils cover the whole spectrum of intellectual ability and scholastic attainment and have a very wide range of educational needs. For example, studies have established an association between behaviour problems and reading difficulties,[3] and children with marked physical or sensory handicap may be particularly susceptible to emotional disturbance. However, many EBD children will be making satisfactory or even good progress in school. It is, therefore, difficult to discuss the education of these children in general terms, and it is hardly surprising that opinions diverge on the most appropriate ways of meeting their needs. Nevertheless, a well-planned educational programme is important for EBD children, and there has been a marked tendency to move away from the treatment of problem behaviour in a predominantly clinical context to a focus on the role of schools in both prevention and management.

The main aim of ordinary as well as special schools has been seen as facilitating learning in the case of EBD pupils rather than as providing them with a special curriculum, unless these pupils require special education for other reasons. While some EBD children may benefit from a reduction of pressure on them in relation to their academic progress, most will profit from the sense of achievement which comes from successfully completing school-based tasks. It should not be assumed that an EBD child is unwilling or unable to participate in normal learning activities, and the value of remedial education for those pupils who are underfunctioning needs to be fully recognized.

This chapter will consider two major and somewhat conflicting trends in the education of EBD children (used here to include adolescents) since the publication in 1955 of the Underwood Report, which was concerned with the education of maladjusted children in England and Wales:[4]

1. the increasing emphasis on the role of mainstream schools and class teachers in coping with problem behaviour; and
2. the growth of specific educational provision for EBD children, to some extent separate from mainstream education.

The advantages and disadvantages of the different forms of special provision will be outlined, and the evaluation of this provision and the question of teacher training will also be briefly discussed. The chapter will be concerned mainly with policies and practice in England and Wales, though some reference will be made to developments elsewhere, particularly to ideas emanating from the USA which have influenced work in Britain.

THE ROLE OF MAINSTREAM SCHOOLS IN THE PREVENTION AND MANAGEMENT OF E/B PROBLEMS

Although specific educational provision for EBD children, particularly those at the secondary school stage, has continued to expand over the past thirty years or so (see below), most pupils presenting behaviour problems remain in their normal class in the ordinary school. This is partly because transfer of pupils from their usual environment to a special class, unit or school is generally considered as a last resort, and partly because special provision in most local authorities has been inadequate to meet all the demands made on it. The trend to integrate children with special educational needs into the mainstream system as far as practicable is a further factor inhibiting the removal of children presenting problems from their normal schools.

This trend was reinforced by the Warnock Report on Special Educational Needs and the ensuing Education Act of 1981,[5] although legislative pressures are still much weaker in Britain than in the USA, where all children with special needs must be educated in the least restrictive environment. Further a number of sociologists, psychologists, and others have argued powerfully that special education for so-called 'maladjusted' children cannot be regarded as a well-intentioned response to individual problems, but can be understood only in the context of political and economic constraints on family life, educational policy, and professional theories and practices.

According to this standpoint, special units and schools are designed to control those pupils who challenge the disciplinary structures of mainstream schools, and encourage the view that the solution to problems lies in changing the individual rather than the schools and the teachers.[6]

Here ideas and practices will be discussed in relation to a) making the management structure of the schools more conducive to the efficient handling of E/B problems; b) the skills and strategies needed by teachers if they are to cope appropriately and effectively with the behaviour problems which they face in the classroom; and c) the kinds of internal and external support required by teachers in dealing with these problems.

Improving the management structure of schools

Research studies have suggested that, although standards of pupil behaviour are related to classroom management and teachers' styles of discipline, the practices and philosophies of individual schools have an effect on children's behaviour as well as on their attainments. The values and expectations of schools, the relationships fostered within them, and the models they present are all likely to influence the development of their pupils' attitudes and how children behave. Even if it is the school ethos or climate rather than its formal organization which is important in this respect, the way in which a school is governed and managed will have some effect on pupil behaviour.

Increasing attention is now being given to improving the management structure of schools, which need to devote much thought to considering how they can help in the prevention and treatment of E/B problems. In particular, schools need to be organized in such a way that they

1. encourage a positive, sympathetic, and tolerant attitude on the part of the school staff as a whole towards pupils presenting E/B difficulties;

2. do not over-emphasize differences between pupils, for example in ability or social background;
3. facilitate the prompt identification of pupils 'at risk' because of E/B problems, but without the negative consequences that often follow labelling and stereotyping;
4. ensure that each child has a curriculum appropriate to his or her needs, providing remedial education where necessary;
5. make support readily available to the classroom teacher through the senior staff;
6. provide an effective pastoral care service;
7. forge close links with parents, the school psychological service, and other agencies concerned with the welfare of children and families; and
8. increase the opportunities for staff to undertake specific in-service training.

In order to achieve the ends outlined above, schools need to undergo a process of self-examination, in an effort to strengthen positive practices and to discover gaps and deficiencies. Such self-examination is not likely to be easy, especially if a school has been accustomed to functioning under autocratic leadership, however benevolent; but it is essential if the school is to create a climate in which, for example, disruptive behaviour is rare and in which teachers can deal with E/B problems effectively and with minimum stress. Self-examination is basically an internal matter, but schools may find the participation of advisory staff and the school psychological service helpful to them in some of their discussions.

Classroom strategies

The way in which a teacher manages a class, the extent to which the individual pupil's needs are met within a lesson, and the relationships between teacher and pupils will all be important factors in determining whether behaviour difficulties arise in class and how pupils who present problems are handled. However, even in the best-managed classrooms, there may be pupils who will call for special attention, especially those who are unable to persevere with the tasks set them, who disrupt the work of others, or who are so inhibited that they take little part in group activities. Some pupils, for instance those prone to being restless and distractible, are likely to benefit from careful grading and structuring of material, through which they may experience at least some degree of success. Some may need remedial teaching, individually or in small groups. Some may require, perhaps in addition to remedial assistance in the basic subjects, a specific programme designed to modify their behaviour. The planning and application of such a programme may involve considerable time and thought on the part of the classroom teacher, but a variety of classroom-based strategies are available to help in coping with behaviour problems.[7]

The strategies selected by a teacher in any case of behaviour difficulties will vary according to individual circumstances and preferences, as well as in the light of the support available, for example, from other teachers or educational psychologists. In the main, the following approaches, which can be discussed only very briefly here, have been shown to be worth considering:

1. *Play techniques* Play techniques are especially appropriate in the case of children of nursery and first school age, when learning through play forms a substantial part of their daily activities. Through well-planned play, mainly in pairs or small groups, teachers may help young children to improve their social skills and to relate more effectively to others. Withdrawn or shy children, for example, may gradually be encouraged to participate more actively in group play, while aggressive or hyperactive children may be assisted in adopting a more constructive role in various play situations that demand co-operation. The use of play approaches to modify behaviour demands imaginative participation in children's play on the part of the teacher.[8]

With older children, it is perhaps more difficult to use play techniques as a natural part of classroom activities, but the gymnasium or sports field may provide opportunities for teachers to help children to acquire skills in co-operating with others, which they may lack. Additionally, play situations may be devised in the classroom to facilitate the acquisition of knowledge about appropriate social behaviour and to give scope for practising such behaviour.

2. *Behaviour modification strategies* Behaviour modification strategies in the classroom, which have been more widely used in the USA than in Britain, aim to encourage teachers to adopt an experimental approach to EBD children and to offer a positive and practical programme of help. These strategies require that the problem be assessed in precise terms before an intervention plan is drawn up with clearly defined objectives. A full behaviour modification programme will usually involve a working partnership between a teacher and an educational psychologist, but many behavioural principles can be incorporated into teachers' natural interactions with their pupils. The emphasis in behaviour approaches is on immediate reinforcement of desired behaviour, making a positive response to those actions which merit approval but which are often ignored, and the developing of appropriate behaviour to replace that which is disruptive or otherwise inappropriate.

3. *Problem-solving and social skills training* Schools at all levels should regard the teaching and enhancement of social skills as an essential part of the curriculum for all pupils, and accept some responsibility for helping those children who have failed to learn to interact with others in an age-appropriate

manner. In recent years, some promising approaches have been developed to improving both cognitive problem-solving and behavioural skills in children.

Spivack et al.[9] have suggested a variety of strategies which encourage children to think up their own ideas of how to behave in specific situations; to consider alternative courses of action for themselves; and to have regard for possible outcomes of behaviour rather than act impulsively and without consideration of consequences. Other approaches to social skills training have emphasized the behavioural rather than the cognitive aspects, aiming, for example, to increase eye contact, improve conversation skills, or encourage assertiveness. The practice of both cognitive and behavioural social skills training has involved the use of many different techniques, including modelling, role-play, simulation exercises, video feedback, stories, cartoons, puppets, and discussion.

4. *Self-monitoring techniques* Encouraging pupils to monitor and evaluate their own behaviour is a relatively simple but potentially effective approach to E/B difficulties in the classroom.[10] Self-monitoring, inasmuch as it emphasizes a pupil's existing strengths rather than teaching new skills, is usually best used in conjunction with other forms of intervention. It has the advantage of not making undue demands on the teacher's time, while giving the pupil some responsibility for improving behaviour. It is useful for the pupil to keep a daily record of progress in a specially devised booklet, and for a record of this kind to be used as a basis for discussion between pupil and teacher.

5. *Counselling* Class teachers have to consider carefully to what extent they themselves should become involved with individual pupils in discussions of a personal nature. It is all too easy to become more and more enmeshed with personal and family problems which are outside the province of the class teacher. Much will depend on the existence and quality of a pastoral care network within the school, as well as on the age of the child and the circumstances of the case. It will usually be desirable, at least with older children and adolescents, for the teacher to discuss openly with the pupil concerned the aims and objectives of any intervention proposed, rather than impose a programme upon a pupil. Some practitioners like to enter into a contract with pupils which sets out precisely what the commitments of all the parties are.

Most schools communicate with parents in cases of the more serious E/B problems, but only infrequently does a class teacher have the opportunity to have direct contact with the parents of an EBD pupil. However, a constructive meeting with parents is likely to add to the information which a teacher needs in order to plan intervention. In talking to parents, teachers need to have a clear idea about the kind of information they want, to establish rapport conducive to a relaxed discussion, and to keep to factual matters until parents are receptive to discussing more sensitive aspects of the problem, if indeed it is thought desirable to probe more deeply. In the past, not enough attention has been given to the nature of the interaction between teachers and parents, and it is desirable that workshops be set up for training teachers in ways of communicating with parents.

Support for teachers

Mention has been made above on the need for teachers to have easy access to senior colleagues, on whom they can call for support in dealing with EBD children without feeling that they themselves will be unfairly blamed for the problems which have arisen. Many teachers prefer to seek support from within the school rather than have recourse to the external agencies which exist to help them. Some LEAs have developed a peripatetic teacher support service which provides additional help for classroom teachers in coping with special educational needs.[11] In the USA much use is made of resource rooms or units in schools, which offer appropriate support to both pupils and teachers.

The LEA school psychological service is well equipped to help with E/B difficulties, but it is often the case that teachers do not feel that the kind of help available is what they really need, i.e. highly practical in their own classroom situation. The aims and expectations of teachers and educational psychologists may be quite different, and so it is important that these should be openly discussed with a view to improving working relationships. In some cases, particularly where the E/B problem is related to family difficulties, advice from Social Service Departments may be required.

A large-scale project in England, comparing and evaluating different forms of intervention in primary and secondary schools found that a) direct treatment of children, especially through behaviour-shaping techniques and group therapy, was more effective than indirect methods (for example, parent counselling and teacher consultation) and b) relatively brief therapeutic programmes were surprisingly effective.[12] The findings of the project were complex, but they suggest that too much may be expected from the 'consultation' model becoming increasingly popular with professionals working in the support agencies, who have been stressing the importance of working with teachers rather than directly with children.

SPECIFIC EDUCATIONAL PROVISION FOR EBD PUPILS

EBD pupils who are considered, after assessment, to be in need of some form of special educational provision may be recommended for placement in a special class, unit, or school which caters specifically for pupils with behaviour problems. Such a recommendation may be put in the form of a 'statement' under the 1981 Education Act. Some highly disruptive pupils may be suspended or expelled from school; some children, while presenting E/B problems, may, because of the extent or nature of their learning difficulties, be placed in classes or schools catering mainly for pupils with moderate or severe learning difficulties; and, in rare cases, a child may need care and treatment in a hospital. Here, the discussion will be confined to a consideration of special classes, units and schools established specifically for children presenting E/B difficulties.

Special classes and units

In spite of increasingly vocal opposition to segregating children in any way from their normal school environment, the number of special classes and units set up for EBD pupils has continued to expand over recent years, although in the USA this type of provision has been increasingly replaced by other provision within mainstream schools. Information on the functioning of these classes and units has been provided by a variety of studies.[13] A 'class' is usually set up within an ordinary school, serving one or more schools, while a 'unit' is normally separately administered apart from any school, and caters for a whole area. More off-site units have been established in England and Wales than classes within schools; both classes and units cater predominantly for secondary school pupils, mainly those causing disruption or failing to attend school for some reason. Typically, a class or unit caters for about ten to sixteen pupils, not necessarily all attending on a full-time basis, who tend to stay for varying lengths of time; the staff-pupil ratio is in the region of one to six or eight. A high proportion of pupils admitted need remedial teaching, usually but not always available. Approaches to the curriculum vary considerably, the main focus being on social training and the development of personal relationships. In general, the teaching has been found to be fairly formal and the content of the curriculum necessarily restricted because of the small number of staff involved; space and equipment are also often limited.

Mixed views have been reported on the question of benefits gained by schools and pupils making use of special classes and units. In a study of provision in the Inner London Education Authority, pupils were generally positive about their experiences, though some had a negative initial reaction; schools, too, felt that their pupils were, on the whole, benefiting from attendance at special classes and units, even if a number of headteachers expressed reservations about the effectiveness of these special centres.[14]

In general, those in favour of special classes and units for EBD pupils have put forward the following arguments:

1. they offer relief to the staff of ordinary classes, who may be under considerable strain because of a pupil's behaviour;
2. they provide immediate help for pupils in difficulty;

3. placement is usually of a temporary nature, with the pupil often continuing part-time in the mainstream school;
4. they enable pupils to receive more individual and more relaxed attention than is possible in their usual class;
5. they may prevent suspension, expulsion, or removal to a special school some distance away; and
6. they encourage a focus on treatment in an educational rather than a clinical context.

The chief disadvantages of these classes and units are seen to be as follows:

1. children once placed in special provision (particularly in units outside school) may be permanently labelled in a negative way (such as 'disruptive') and find it difficult to return to mainstream schools;
2. removing the child from his or her normal setting tends to put the blame on the individual rather than on the system;
3. special centres serve to distract attention away from the consideration of what extra resources are needed by ordinary schools and classes, as well as from a reappraisal of the curriculum;
4. the restricted curriculum of special classes and units may cause disruption to the child's education;
5. special centres easily become a 'dumping-ground' for pupils whom teachers do not want in their class; and
6. there is little evidence of permanent benefits accruing from a period in a special class or unit.

It is generally acknowledged that if special classes or units are established, they need to have clear aims and functions, understood by staff and pupils in ordinary schools; to maintain close links with the mainstream system and support services; to have well-trained staff with suitable personal qualities; to give careful thought to the mechanisms for referral as well as to each pupil's eventual return to full-time mainstream education; and to be involved in a continuous evaluation of their work.

Special schools for pupils with emotional and behavioural problems

Parallel with the growth of special classes and units, special school provision for pupils with E/B problems has also increased considerably in England and Wales over the last twenty-five years or so. This has been particularly the case with day-school provision in England. Between 1955 and 1983, the number of day schools there grew from three to 89, while the number of residential schools in England and Wales grew from 32 to 131 (including 20 schools not maintained by a local authority).[15] Relatively few studies of special schools for

EBD pupils have been carried out, and much of our information about them comes from Wilson and Evans's Schools Council Project on the Education of Disturbed Pupils in England and Wales.[16]

Day schools It is somewhat surprising that so many local education authorities in England have favoured the expansion of day-school provision for pupils with E/B difficulties. It is true that day schools, with a larger staff than most special units, are able to offer a more varied curriculum to their pupils, and that their availability may mean that some severely disturbed pupils need not be educated away from home. However, a school needs at least 50 pupils to be viable, and questions may be raised about the desirability of educating such a large number of EBD children together, when alternative day provision can be made in smaller groups.

Residential schools Residential schools for EBD children tend to cater for about 30 to 50 pupils, mainly for boys in the age range nine or ten to sixteen years. Although these are intended as short-stay placements, many pupils stay for over four years. Some schools are purpose-built, others are housed in adapted country mansions.

In spite of the current opposition to segregated education, and the isolation of many residential schools from the mainstream systems, these schools should have little difficulty in making out a case for their continued existence. A high proportion of disturbed pupils have adverse home backgrounds or live in families which need some respite, and it is often a matter of urgency that an EBD child should be placed away from home for a period. Some pupils are totally unable to cope with conditions at home or at school, and need at least a temporary period in a setting providing calm and stability, where education, daily living and therapy can be integrated. However, the best use is not always made of the limited number of residential places available. Children should not be placed in boarding schools unless they need special schooling as well as a change of home environment, nor should such schools be used as permanent homes. Rather, an important aim of these residential schools should be to return pupils to their normal environment as soon as possible.

It is recognized that the family should receive support while the pupil is at school. There would also be much agreement with the view that, while locating a school in a large country house may have advantages in regard to space and provide opportunities for vigorous outdoor activities, it is usually preferable to keep pupils within or close to their own communities rather than educate them in a highly artificial environment. Indeed, many residential schools now regularly send most of their pupils home for the weekend. Any temporary upset caused by this is usually felt to be outweighed by the benefits to be gained from pupils keeping in close touch with their families.

Curricular considerations   Laslett has stressed the great difficulties faced by special schools for EBD pupils in planning their curricula.[17] They need to cater for children who have come to them with a variety of problems, and who have a wide range of abilities and attainments. They may also have to plan for pupils of both primary and secondary age. Most schools will focus on personal skills and relationships; social education; and the increase of self-awareness, self-confidence, and the ability to co-operate with others. They will aim to encourage individual interests and to emphasize learning through play, drama, art and craft, music, and physical education, while providing remedial teaching to fill gaps in basic attainments.

In the past, some schools for EBD pupils (especially independent schools) have been greatly influenced by particular philosophies, for example those based on psychodynamic principles. In the USA many of those working with disturbed children have been attracted to behaviourist ideas. However, special schools for EBD pupils in Britain tend to work along highly pragmatic lines, choosing an eclectic approach rather than an attachment to a specific school of thought. Indeed, Wilson and Evans found that in these schools psychotherapy or behaviour therapy was little used, perhaps because of the lack of specialist staff. Their survey of 114 special schools (day and boarding) in England and Wales showed that the six 'treatments' most used in these schools were:

1. fostering caring attitudes in adult-child relationships;
2. improving self-image through success;
3. remedial teaching in the basic skills;
4. creative work in the arts;
5. providing opportunities for shared activity with other children; and
6. individual counselling and discussion.

TEACHER TRAINING

The key to successful work with EBD children must be the enhancement of teachers' skills in the management of their classes and in coping with behaviour problems as they arise. Research in the USA has shown that teachers in mainstream schools are lacking in their knowledge and use of effective management skills.[18] In England and Wales, too, very few teachers in ordinary schools have received any training in the management of behaviour problems as part of their initial professional course. The situation is changing, as teacher training courses in Britain are now paying more attention to children with special educational needs. Even so, the time which can be devoted to considering behaviour problems must be very limited at the initial stage, when, in any case, trainees have insufficient normal teaching experience to enable them to profit fully from courses concerned with special education.

It will, therefore, be mainly through in-service training that teachers will be enabled to increase their skills in dealing with children presenting E/B problems. Up till now, in-service training opportunities have been sparse, and they need to be greatly increased if available knowledge and practical techniques are to be transmitted to teachers. In-service training is urgently called for, not only in the case of ordinary class teachers, but to enhance the expertise of teachers working in special classes, units, and schools for EBD pupils. The majority of these teachers have not received any specific training for their work, and attendance at in-service courses serves not only to increase skills but also to relieve the feeling of professional isolation often felt by those working in special education.

CONCLUSION

Much attention has been given over the past two or three decades to the education of children with emotional and behavioural problems. Although opinion is still sharply divided on the desirability of the establishment of segregated educational provision to cater for some of these children, it is generally acknowledged that most of them will continue to be the responsibility of mainstream school and ordinary class teachers. There is now available, as well as many practical ideas, a considerable amount of resource material aimed at helping teachers in the management of behaviour problems, but little of this material seems to have become a part of the repertoire of teachers.

Much further work has to be done on the evaluation of practices, procedures, and programmes relating to EBD pupils, but the outstanding current need would seem to be to increase opportunities for all teachers to enhance their skills in dealing with the wide variety of emotional and behavioural difficulties which they will face.

REFERENCES

1. Rutter, M., Cox, A., Tupling, C., Berger, M., and Yule, W. (1975) 'Attainment and adjustment in two geographical areas. 1. The prevalence of psychiatric disorder', *British Journal of Psychiatry*, 126: 493–509.
2. Department of Education and Science (1985) *Education for All* (The Swann Report), London: HMSO.
3. Chazan, M. (1985) 'Behavioural aspects of educational difficulties', in D. D. Duane and C. K. Leong (Eds.) *Understanding Learning Disabilities: International and Multidisciplinary Views*, New York: Plenum Press.
4. Ministry of Education (1955) *Report of the Committee on Maladjusted Children* (The Underwood Report), London: HMSO.
5. Department of Education and Science (1978) *Special Educational Needs* (The Warnock Report), London: HMSO; Department of Education and Science (1981) *Education Act 1981 – Special Educational Needs*, London: HMSO.

6. Coulby, D. and Harper, T. (1985) *Preventing Classroom Disruption: Policy, Practice and Evaluation in Urban Schools*, London: Croom Helm.
7. See, for example, M. Chazan, A. F. Laing, J. Jones, G. Harper, and J. Bolton (1983) *Helping Young Children with Behaviour Difficulties*, London: Croom Helm; and E. V. S. Westmacott and R. J. Cameron (1981) *Behaviour Can Change*, Basingstoke: Globe Education.
8. Chazan *et al.*, op. cit. pp. 92–128.
9. Spivack, G., Platt, J. and Shure, M. B. (1978) *The Problem-Solving Approach to Adjustment*, San Francisco: Jossey-Bass.
10. McNamara, E. and Heard, C. (1976) 'Self-control through self-recording', *Special Education: Forward Trends*, 3 (2): 21–3.
11. Coulby and Harper, op. cit.
12. Kolvin, I., Garside, R. F., Nicol, A. R., MacMillan, A., Wolstenholme, E., and Leitch, I. M. (1981) *Help Starts Here*, London: Tavistock Publications.
13. See, for example, H.M.I. (1978) *Behavioural Units*, London: HMSO; K. J. Topping (1983) *Educational Systems for Disruptive Adolescents*, London: Croom Helm; and M. Wilson and M. Evans (1980) *Education of Disturbed Pupils*, London: Schools Council/Methuen Educational.
14. Mortimore, P., Davies, J., Varlaam, A., and West, A. (1983) *Behaviour Problems in Schools*, London: Croom Helm.
15. Department of Education and Science (1984) *Statistics of Education: Schools 1983*, Crown Copyright.
16. Wilson and Evans, op. cit.
17. Laslett, R. (1977) *Educating Maladjusted Children*, London: Crosby Lockwood Staples.
18. Jones, V. F. (1986) *Classroom Management in the United States: Trends and Critical Issues*, Chichester: John Wiley.

INDEX OF NAMES

INDEX OF SUBJECTS